The Renaissance New Testament

Randolph O. Yeager

VOLUME SEVEN

Mark 10:2–14:21
Luke 16:1–22:23
John 11:1–13:30

PELICAN PUBLISHING COMPANY
GRETNA 1981

Library of Congress Cataloging in Publication Data

Yeager, Randolph O.
The Renaissance New Testament.

Volumes 1-4 originally published in 1976-1978 by Renaissance Press, Bowling Green, Ky.
1. Bible. N.T. – Concordances, Greek. 2. Greek language, Biblical. I. Title.
BS2302.Y4 1981 225.4'8'0321 79-28652
ISBN: 0-88289-457-9 (v. 7)

Manufactured in the United States of America

Published by Pelican Publishing Company, Inc.
1101 Monroe Street, Gretna, Louisiana 70053

Introduction

Soon after the appearance of the first volume of *The Renaissance New Testament*, a highly respected friend called to offer congratulations and a very valuable bit of advice. I was being approached by proponents of various theological points of view who wanted my help is proving that this or that heresy was demonstrably false on the basis of this or that isolated verse of scripture. My friend advised that I should avoid getting involved in such skirmishes. My task, rather, he said, was to produce a work that would help every Bible student to conduct his own research of the entire message of the Word of God, both mircoscopically and telescopically.

The microscopic study pays due regard to diction, grammar and syntax. What is the basic meaning of the word which the Holy Spirit allowed the writer to use at this point? In what sense is this basic meaning applied in this particular context? Has the passage been studied in the light of what von Ranke called *zeitgeist* - "the spirit of the times." Who wrote the passage? Where, why and under what local and contemporary circumstances? Whom, if anyone was he quoting? That is the study of diction.

How does the word, once we have solved the problems of diction and *zeitgeist* relate to the other words in the phrase and clause? This is the grammatical question. If it is a noun, pronoun, adjective, participle or the article is it singular or plural, masculine, feminine or neuter? In what case does it appear? If it is a participle, since a participle is a verbal adjective what is its tense? Is it adjectival or adverbial? If the former, is it ascriptive or restrictive? If the latter is it telic, temporal, causal, conditional, concessive, instrumental, modal, complementary or circumstantial? Or is it used like an imperative? If it is an infiitive, since an infinitive is a verbal noun, does its noun or verbal use predominate? If it is more a substantive than a verb is it the subject or the object of a finite verb. If the object, is it direct or indirect? Or perhaps it is instrumental, in apposition or a modifier?

Introduction

A major contribution to our understanding of any Greek sentence is that of the preposition. This is especially true in the κοινή. The classical Greek writers did not have any except ἐν. They used them like adverbs. In the story of the development of the preposition from Homer down to New Testament times, it is well to remember the advice of Giles when he says, "Between adverbs and prepositions no distinct line can be drawn." (Giles, *A Short Manual of Comparative Philology, 2d. ed.,341, as cited in Robertson, Grammar*, 554). Written originally in composition with verbs they were later written separately and joined to a substantive in some case. The beginner often falls into the error of concentrating his attention upon the preposition, not upon the case with which it appears. Thus we learn in first year Greek class that ἐκ means "out of" and ἀπό means "away from" while περί means "around/about" and παρά means "beside/parallel to." But "It is the *case* which indicates the meaning of the *preposition*, and not the preposition which gives the meaning to the case." (Farrar, *Greek Syntax*, 94, as cited in *Ibid.*).

A.T.Robertson in his *A New Short Grammar of the Greek Testament* lists six guidelines which we must use when we are interpreting a prepositional phrase: We must know (1) the meaning of the case, (2) the meaning of the preposition, (3) the historical evolution of the case from Homer down, (4) the history of the preposition, (5) the context in which the passage occurs and (6) the meaning of other words involved in the context. (Robertson, *Short Grammar*, 249).

Verbs present a different problem. They are written both singular and plural, in the first, second or third persons, they come in present, imperfect, future, aorist, perfect and pluperfect tenses. They are either in the active, middle or passive voices and they have either indicative, imperative, subjunctive or optative modes. Once we encounter them, therefore, we must know five things about them: person, number, tense, voice and mode, just as we must know about a noun, pronoun, article, adjective or participle its case, number and gender.

Syntax relates the phrases, clauses and sentences to the context, and approaches the division between the microscopic and the telescopic study of the Word of God. Diction and grammar are analytical. Syntax is comprehensive. Diction and grammar examine the Word of God in its isolated, microscopic components. Syntax is holistic.

The holistic approach involves more than a look at all of the material in a particular paragraph, or on the page or in the chapter immediately before us. It involves us in the entire body of truth which the Holy Spirit conveys in the Word of God. Since no scripture is of its own isolated interpretation (2 Peter 1:20) no thorough exegete will build a doctrine upon a single proof text. We say this, not because we fear that the Holy Spirit has lied to us in any text, but rather, because the truth that He always tells us in every text will be found to be consistent with other truths which He has revealed to us in other texts. The Holy Spirit is God and He has motivated the Biblical writers in both the Old and New Testaments to give us a beautifully consistent *gestalt* - a heavenly inspired jigsaw puzzle which it is our task, our joy and our delight to put together. And as the *gestalt* forms and approaches closure under our hermeneutical touch, we see connections which had previously been hidden to us. New insights into the total meaning of God's message in His Word give us the thrill, in a much more sublime sense, that we experienced as children when we happened upon the spot where our parents had hidden another gaily colored Easter egg.

What the Word of God clearly teaches in one verse will never be contradicted in another. There are no inconsistencies to embarrass us once we know our diction, grammar, syntax and the manner in which the Holy Spirit has chosen to teach us. But we must be certain that we know what is clearly taught in any particular passage. Which leads us to the only safe rule to follow. It is this: no verse teaches *anything* until we have allowed all the other verses which are in any way pertinent to the point, to shine their light upon it. This does not mean that we must cross reference every verse in the Bible to bring it into contact with every other verse. Job 16:1 says, "Then Job answered and said, . . . " It is not probable that there is any light there to shed upon John 3:16. But while I am dealing with extreme and silly illustrations of the point the practice of basing a doctrine upon an isolated scripture opens the door for the Biblical support of all manner of heretical views. Let the reader imagine any wild concept of which he is capable in the moment of his greatest insanity and the chances are good that some one will take the proof text method of interpretation and support it with the Bible. Isolated texts out of context will prove anything. The preacher who put together Matthew 27:5, Luke 10:37 and John 13:27 on Sunday morning might have precipitated mass suicide if his congregation had taken him seriously. If you think that extreme please recall that something like that occurred in Guiana, Venezuela recently.

If we fail to study the Greek New Testament "in the light of historical research" as Dr.A.T.Robertson named his grammar, and if we employ anything less than a holistic approach, the New Testament becomes a document that teaches everything. And a document that teaches everything teaches nothing.

So I have tried to follow the advice of my friend and avoid the street corner brawls that generally develop when one attempts to convince a heretic that he is wrong about the isolated verse of scripture upon which he is currently depending. If you saw off the limb where he is sitting, he will find another and misinterpret that. Since there are many verses in which he can take false refuge, the piece meal approach will take so much time that before you are through with the discussion the Lord Jesus will come back and really convince him that he is wrong.

The Lord has called many splendid Christian witnesses to a ministry among the cultists. There are missionaries to the Jehovah's Witnesses, the Mormons, the Moonies, the Seventh Day Adventists and to the various Oriential cults. They are doing yeoman duty in the work to which the Lord has called them. Meanwhile every Christian is surrounded by heresies of every sort. The Greek New Testament contains the antidote for them all. It is the purpose of *The*

Renaissance New Testament to enable every Christian, who has at least a minimal capacity to handle the English language, to open his New Testament at random and find at his fingertips, wherever he may choose to begin his study, every tool that he needs, in terms of diction, grammar, syntax to derive from the verse before him the concept which the Holy Spirit intends to convey. He also finds there the numerical guide to every word in the verse to which he can refer to get the holistic approach. As this method is followed with diligence, soon the New Testament becomes a beautifully, because supernaturally organized body of truth in the brilliant light of which no heresy can live for a moment. If the cultists who have rejected the "Light of the World" and are therefore stumbling about in the darkness will study the Bible in this manner, instead of searching its pages for one more verse which they can twist until it seems to them to support what they have already determined to believe, they will soon find that the Holy Spirit has just one purpose in the New Testament. Jesus outlined it to the disciples in John 16:13: "Howbeit when he, the Spirit of truth, is come, he will guide you into all truth: for he shall not speak of himself; but whatsoever he shall hear, that shall he speak: and he will shew you things to come. He shall glorify me: for he shall receive of mine, and shall shew it unto you. All things that the Father hath are mine: therefore, said I, that he shall take of mine, and shall shew it unto you."

The Greek New Testament settles every controversy that has ever arisen between conflicting parties within the church. None of us have all of the answers. No one can find the time in this life to plumb it to its glorious depths. But the fact that we do not know it all does not mean that we do not know it *at all.* Few people become millionaires but the fact that they do not own a million dollars does not mean that they are paupers, nor does it detract from the thrill which they get when they earn another honest dollar. There is no thrill for the Christian like that of gaining another new and therefore, for them, fresh insight into the message about Christ which the Holy Spirit has given us.

The church is often torn in disagreement about matters of faith and practice. Some of the controversies might well be left for their solution until we all meet around the glory illuminated throne of God. Their solution may not be worth the candle. When a church splits over insignificant matters, she might well have spent her time digging more deeply into her New Testament to come to a greater appreciation of and love for the Lord Jesus Christ. None of us know Him as well as we all should like to know Him. So some questions do not deserve our time and effort. Should we serve wine or grape joice at the Lord's table? Should women wear a hat at church? Should she be allowed to speak? Should she wear skirts only or may she also wear slacks? Does a piano, an organ or any other musical instrument beside the human voice box belong in a worship service? If not a piano, does a tuning fork insult the Lord? Scholarly exegesis of the Greek New Testament, viewed with *zeitgeist*, in the light of historical research will answer all of these questions to the satisfaction of all sincere Christians who would rather know the truth than experience the thrill of carrying on a raucous argument. But these questions are not in the same category at all with questions about the person and work of Christ, the efficacy of His death, the reality of His resurrection, the person and work of the Holy Spirit and the biblical view of the world and the interpretation of history which the Bible dictates.

The greatest advice that Paul gave to Timothy and through him to every preacher and Bible teacher was "Preach the Word." He did not tell the young preacher to preach *about* the Word. Nor did he tell him to praise it, defend it, argue about or with it or to deny it. He did tell him to preach it. And how can a preacher preach it if he does not know what it says? And how can he know what it says until he has spent his life prayerfully and intently gazing into its depths?

Let us imagine that we are on a visit to the zoo, standing before the cage of a huge and ferocious Bengal tiger. He is pacing back and forth behind the bars, emitting vociferous and blood curdling roars in response to the taunts and jibes, the sticks and stones of a gang of boys. The beast has been neglected by his keeper. Without food and water he has developed a voracious appetite and a maddening thirst. Now suppose we decide to liberate him and defend him from his tormentors? Once he is set free do we need to defend him or is he capable of defending himself? All we need do is to let him out.

The apostle Paul wrote from a Roman prison that he was suffering, as if he were an evil doer, but he added that "the word of God is not bound." Unfortunately in what may be the closing days of a corrupt age which is fast approaching judgment, it is the Word of God that is bound, while the preachers are running free. The Word of God, "living and operative and sharper than a twoedged sword" that bifurcates with psychiatric precision between glands and nerves, between emotions and thoughts and cannot be deceived about the thoughts and intentions of our hearts, and which, if liberated would be much more effective in disposing of the enemies of Christ than that Bengal tiger, is in fact bound. Let us let the tiger out, even if it means putting the preachers in jail.

So, in keeping with the advice of my friend, while I shall continue to accept preaching and teaching appointments at the Bible conferences where the saints are struggling with this or that specific bit of false teaching, and I shall continue to try to answer my mail which comes from all directions for my help with this or that false view, I intend always to concentrate on the task of teaching all who ask for my help to study the Greek New Testament for themselves and learn to appreciate it from the holistic, rather than from the textual point of view. Textual exegesis is the means; holism is the end.

The Renaissance New Testament

Two Parables on Stewardship

(Luke 16:1-31)

Luke 16:1 - "And he said also unto his disciples, There was a certain man, which had a steward; and the same was accused unto him that he had wasted his goods."

Ἔλεγεν δὲ καὶ πρὸς μαθητάς, Ἄνθρωπός τις ἦν πλούσιος ὃς εἶχεν οἰκονόμον, καὶ οὗτος διεβλήθη αὐτῷ ὡς διασκορπίζων τὰ ὑπάρχοντα αὐτοῦ.

Ἔλεγεν (3d.per.sing.imp.act.ind.of λέγω, inceptive) 66.
δὲ (continuative conjunction) 11.
καὶ (adjunctive conjunction) 14.
πρὸς (preposition with the accusative of extent, after a verb of speaking) 197.
τοὺς (acc.pl.masc.of the article in agreement with μαθητάς) 9.
Ἄνθρωπός (nom.sing.masc.of ἄνθρωπος, subject of εἶχεν) 341.
τις (nom.sing.masc.of τις, indefinite pronoun, in agreement with ἄνθρωπος) 486.
ἦν (3d.per.sing.imp.ind.of εἰμί, progressive description) 86.
πλούσιος (nom.sing.masc.of πλούσιος, predicate adjective) 1306.
ὃς (nom.sing.masc.of ὅς, subject of εἶχεν) 65.
εἶχεν (3d.per.sing.imp.act.ind.of ἔχω, progressive description) 82.
οἰκονόμον (acc.sing.masc.of οἰκονόμος, direct object of εἶχεν) 2488.
καὶ (continuative conjunction) 14.
οὗτος (nom.sing.masc.of οὗτος, anaphoric, subject of διεβλήθη) 93.

#2559 διεβλήθη (3d.per.sing.aor.pass.ind.of διαβάλλω, culminative).

accuse - Luke 16:1.

Meaning: A combination of διά (#118) and βάλλω (#299). *Cf.* also διάβολος (#331). Hence to cast through; to attack thoroughly; to accuse; to file a complaint against. With reference to the dishonesty and inefficiency of a steward - Luke 16:1.

αὐτῷ (dat.sing.masc.of αὐτός, indirect object of διεβλήθη) 16.

ὡς (particle with the circumstantial participle) 128.

διασκορπίζων (pres.act.part.nom.sing.masc.of διασκορπίζω, adverbial, circumstantial) 1538.

τὰ (acc.pl.neut.of the article in agreement with ὑπάρχοντα) 9.

ὑπάρχοντα (pres.act.part.acc.pl.neut.of ὑπάρχω, substantival, direct object of διασκορπίζων) 1303.

αὐτοῦ (gen.sing.masc.of αὐτός, possession) 16.

Translation - "And again He began to speak to the disciples: 'There was a certain rich man who had a business manager, and he was accused as one who was squandering his property.'"

Comment: The parables of chapter 15 were spoken to a large company, including the critical Scribes and Pharisees. Jesus now directs the following remarks to His disciples, whether to the Twelve only, or to a larger group, of whom, by this late date, Jesus had many, is not clear. Note the indefinite pronoun τις. Jesus is not speaking of any specific person. He is described as rich (πλούσιος) and as having employed a business manager to superintend his enterprises. The definite relative pronoun ὅς is attracted to its antecedent ἄνθρωπος. His manager had been in his employ for some time as the imperfect εἶχεν indicates. *Cf.*#2488 for a study of stewardship in Christ.

The manager was the object of an allegation brought before his employer. He was represented as one who, by inefficiency and prodigality, was squandering the assets of the estate. The substance of the allegation is set forth in ὡς διασκορπίζων τὰ ὑπάρχοντα αὐτοῦ. The participle διασκορπίζων serves as a substantive - "as a waster of his property." Robertson says, "The ancient Greek had quite a list of adverbs (particles) that were used with the circumstantial participle on occasion to make clearer the relation of the participle to the principal verb of substantive. . . These particles do not change the real force of the participle. They merely sharpen the outline. . . The participle with ὡς may be causal, temporal, conditional, manner, etc. Then again ὡς may be used to express the notion of the speaker or writer as well as one who is reported. In truth, ὡς implies nothing in itself on that point. The context alone must determine it." (Goodwin, *Moods and Tenses*, 343, as cited in Robertson, *Grammar*, 1139-1140 *et passim.*). In our passage the accusation is given as represented by the accuser. The context implies that the charge is false. Pilate used ὡς in Luke 23:14 to show that he did not believe the charge of the Sanhedrin against Jesus. *Cf.* also Acts 23:15,20; 27:30.

Fruitful sermon material is available here in the careful study of all of the key words, *viz.*#'s 1303, 1306, 2488 and 1538. Objective exegesis, however, interprets these words in this context only. A business manager is alleged to be dishonest and/or inefficient. This passage is not talking about the riches of Christ or of any other, but about the material wealth of a rich man. The key to the passage is in verse 13. The rich man who dismissed the dishonest manager is not God, but the wicked, commercial world system, which is unfriendly to the Christian and will endeavor to impoverish him. In this world, mammon, even the mammon of unrighteousness, which sinners serve, if necessary for the Christian believer. We must have some money and some degree of economic security if we are to be Christ's witnesses in an unfriendly world. Therefore the Christian, represented in the story as the dismissed business manager, can expect discrimination against himself from the world system. He must make some arrangement with mammon, not because he wants to serve it, but in order that *he can make it serve him.* This will become clearer as we exegete our way through the parable.

Verse 2 - "And he called him and said unto him, How is it that I hear this of thee? Give an account of thy stewardship; for thou mayest be no longer steward."

καὶ φωνήσας αὐτὸν εἶπεν αὐτῷ, Τί *τοῦτο ἀκούω περὶ σοῦ; ἀπόδος τὸν λόγον τῆς οἰκονομίας σου, οὐ γὰρ δύνῃ ἔτι οἰκονομεῖν.*

καὶ (inferential conjunction) 14.
φωνήσας (aor.act.part.nom.sing.masc.of *φωνέω*, adverbial, temporal) 1338.
αὐτὸν (acc.sing.masc.of *αὐτός*, direct object of *φωνήσας*) 16.
εἶπεν (3d.per.sing.aor.act.ind.of *εἶπον*, constative) 155.
αὐτῷ (dat.sing.masc.of *αὐτός*, indirect object of *εἶπεν*) 16.
Tί (nom.sing.neut.of *τίς*, interrogative pronoun, predicate nominative) 281.
τοῦτο (nom.sing.neut.of *οὗτος*, subject of *ἐστίν*, understood) 93.
ἀκούω (1st.per.sing.pres.act.ind.of *ἀκούω*, iterative) 148.
περὶ (preposition with the genitive of reference) 173.
σοῦ (gen.sing.masc.of *σύ*, reference) 104.
ἀπόδος (2d.per.sing.aor.act.impv.of *ἀποδίδωμι*, command) 495.
τὸν (acc.sing.masc.of the article in agreement with *λόγον*) 9.
λόγον (acc.sing.masc.of *λόγος*, direct object of *ἀπόδος*) 510.
τῆς (gen.sing.fem.of the article in agreement with *οἰκονομίας*) 9.

#2560 *οἰκονομίας* (gen.sing.fem.of *οἰκονομία*, reference).

dispensation - 1 Cor.9:17; Eph.1:10; 3:2; Col.1:25.
stewardship - Luke 16:2,3,4.
fellowship - Eph.3:9.
edifying - 1 Tim.1:4.

Meaning: A combination of *οἰκία* (#186) and *νόμος* (#464). Hence, the principle that governs, regulates, dictates and conducts the affairs of a household. The function of a business manager; the area of responsibility of the *major domo.* With reference to the financial affairs of a business enterprise - Luke 16:2,3,4. In a spiritual sense, the obligation of a preacher to preach the Word of God to men. Paul's charge from God to preach to the Corinthians - 1 Cor.9:17; to the Ephesians where we have *οἰκονομίαν τῆς χάριτος τοῦ θεοῦ τῆς δοθείσης μοι εἰς ὑμάς,* - "the stewardship of the grace of God, given to me, for you" *i.e.* the divine charge laid upon one to dispense the means of divine grace, *i.e.* the gospel, to you - Eph.3:2,9. To the Colossians - *οἰκονομίαν τοῦ θεοῦ τὴν δοθεῖσαν μοι εἰς ὑμᾶς πληρωσαῖ τὸν λόγον τοῦ θεοῦ* - "a stewardship of God, given to me for you to fulfill the word of God" - Col.1:25. In Eph.1:10, in a slightly different sense - *οἰκονομίαν τοῦ πληρώματος τῶν καιρῶν* - "in the general management of God's affairs across the many dispensations until all time is passed and God's eternal purpose is fulfilled." In 1 Tim.1:4, followed by a genitive of description - *θεοῦ*.

σου (gen.sing.masc.of *σύ*, possession) 104.
οὐ (summary negative conjunction with the indicative) 130.
γὰρ (causal conjunction) 105.
δύνῃ (2d.per.sing.pres.ind.(contr.for *δύνασαι*) of *δύναμαι*, aoristic) 289.
ἔτι (temporal adverb) 448.

#2561 *οἰκονομεῖν* (pres.act.inf.of *οἰκονομέω*, epexegetical).

be steward - Luke 16:2.

Meaning: Cf.#2560. To exercise the office of a business manager - Luke 16:2.

Translation - "Therefore having called him he said to him, 'What is this I am hearing about you? Submit your accounts for an audit, because you are no longer permitted to be manager.' "

Comment: *καὶ* is inferential. It was the accusation of verse 2 that prompted the action of verse 3. The question Τί . . . *σοῦ* is rhetorical. The owner did not wish to be informed. The manager was given no opportunity to refute the charge. The owner's mind was already made up. He ordered a final audit of the manager's books and told him that he was dismissed. There is no evidence that the manager was guilty as charged. The audit had not yet been demanded and submitted. The dismissal was arbitrary. This was manifestly unfair. So the world system, in the lap of Satan and dominated by his philosophy is equally unfair to the child of God, as it condemns him without a hearing. The Christian has an Advocate but He practises in a heavenly court of justice (1 John 2:1). His imperial dignity does not permit Him to ask for admittance to practise in a court of this world. Thus the Christian need not expect to be defended against unfounded charges of wrong doing. The point so far is the basic unfriendly, arbitrary unfairness of the world, represented in the parable by the rich man, toward the Christian, represented by the business manager. Having as yet committed nothing worthy of judgment, he is placed in an embarrassing financial position. He is out of work - without a means of support.

Verse 3 - "Then the steward said within himself, What shall I do? for my lord taketh away from me the stewardship: I cannot dig; to beg I am ashamed."

εἶπεν δὲ ἐν ἑαυτῷ ὁ οἰκονόμος, Τί ποιήσω, ὅτι ὁ κύριός μου ἀφαιρεῖται τὴν οἰκονομίαν ἀπ' ἐμοῦ; σκάπτειν οὐκ ἰσχύω, ἐπαιτεῖν αἰσχύνομαι.

εἶπεν (3d.per.sing.aor.act.ind.of *εἶπον*, constative) 155.
δὲ (continuative conjunction) 11.
ἐν (preposition with the locative, adverbial) 80.
ἑαυτῷ (instru.sing.masc.of *ἑαυτός*, adverbial) 288.

ὁ (nom.sing.masc.of the article in agreement with οἰκονόμος) 9.
οἰκονόμος (nom.sing.masc.of οἰκονόμος, subject of εἶπεν) 2488.
Τί (acc.sing.neut.of τίς, object of ποιήσω, direct question) 281.
ποιήσω (1st.per.sing.fut.act.ind.of ποιέω, deliberative) 127.
ὅτι (conjunction introducing a subordinate causal clause) 211.
ὁ (nom.sing.masc.of the article in agreement with κύριός) 9.
κύριός (nom.sing.masc.of κύριος, subject of ἀφαιρεῖται) 97.
μου (gen.sing.masc.of ἐγώ, relationship) 123.
ἀφαιρεῖται (3d.per.sing.pres.mid.ind.of ἀφαιρέω, static) 1594.
τὴν (acc.sing.fem.of the article in agreement with οἰκονομίαν) 9.
οἰκονομίαν (acc.sing.fem.of οἰκονομία, direct object of ἀφαιρεῖται) 2560.
ἀπ' (preposition with the ablative of separation) 70.
ἐμοῦ (abl.sing.masc.of ἐγώ, separation) 123.
σκάπτειν (pres.act.inf.of σκάπτω, complementary) 2141.
οὐκ (summary negative conjunction with the indicative) 130.
ἰσχύω (1st.per.sing.pres.act.ind.of ἰσχύω, aoristic) 447.

#2562 ἐπαιτεῖν (pres.act.inf.of ἐπαιτέω, complementary).

beg - Luke 16:3; 18:35.

Meaning: A combination of ἐπί (#47) and αἰτέω (#537). Hence, to ask for more; to ask repeatedly; to beg; to plead. For money - Luke 16:3; as a substantival participle in Luke 18:35.

#2563 αἰσχύνομαι (1st.per.pres.pass.ind.of αἰσχύνομαι, aoristic).

be ashamed - Luke 16:3; 2 Cor.10:8; Phil.1:20; 1 Pet.4:16; 1 John 2:28.

Meaning: To be filled with shame. In the passive only in the New Testament. With a complementary infinitive - Luke 16:3. To be ashamed to boast of one's authority - 2 Cor.10:8. With reference to the offense of the cross because of a chain in a Roman prison - Phil.1:20. Of the offense of the cross generally - 1 Pet.4:16. With reference to one's own record of Christian service at the judgment seat of Christ - 1 John 2:28.

Translation - "And the manager said to himself, 'What am I to do since my lord is taking away the stewardship from me? I am not able to dig; I am ashamed to beg."

Comment: The manager did not say this aloud. He was doing some quick thinking. Note the deliberative future in Τί ποιήσω. Why should he be worried? The ὅτι clause is causal. He has lost his lucrative position and his financial security. Not that he was guilty of fraud or malfeasance. Such charges were never substantiated with evidence. The question of innocence or guilt is not germane to the point. The fact is that he is out of a job and faced with the problem of finding another means of support. He begins to consider possible solutions and immediately rules out farming and begging. He lacks the physical strength to farm. A man who has held a responsible position in management is ashamed to beg. But he must make some arrangement so that when he leaves his present position and has no salary, his needs will be provided. He arrives at a solution in

Verse 4 - "I am resolved what to do that, when I am put out of the stewardship, they may receive me into their houses."

ἔγνων τί ποιήσω, ἵνα ὅταν μετασταθῶ ἐκ τῆς οἰκονομίας δέξωνταί με εἰς τοὺς οἴκους ἑαυτῶν.

ἔγνων (1st.per.sing.2d.aor.act.ind.of *γινώσκω*, culminative) 131.
τί (acc.sing.neut.of *τίς*, direct object of *ἔγνων*, indirect question) 281.
ποιήσω (1st.per.sing.fut.act.ind.of *ποιέω*, predictive) 127.
ἵνα (conjunction introducing a final clause with the subjunctive) 114.
ὅταν (temporal conjunction in an indefinite temporal clause) 436.

#2564 *μετασταθῶ* (1st.per.sing.aor.pass.subj.of *μεθίστημι*, indefinite temporal clause).

remove - Acts 13:22.
put out of - Luke 16:4.
remove - 1 Cor.13:2.
translate - Col.1:13.
turn away - Acts 19:26.

Meaning: A combination of *μετά* (#50) and *ἵστημι* (#180). To remove; to change one's status or position; to change one's allegiance. To remove in a physical sense. Saul was removed from the throne to make room for David - Acts 13:22. With reference to the dismissal of the business manager - Luke 16:4; to move a mountain from its place - 1 Cor.13:2. To be converted spiritually from the power of darkness into the kingdom of God's Son - Col.1:13; Acts 19:26.

ἐκ (preposition with the ablative of separation) 19.
τῆς (abl.sing.fem.of the article in agreement with *οἰκονομίας*) 9.
οἰκονομίας (abl.sing.fem.of *οἰκονομία*, separation) 2560.
δέξωνταί (3d.per.pl.1st.aor.act.subj.of *δέχομαι*, final clause) 867.
με (acc.sing.masc.of *ἐγώ*, direct object of *δέξωνταί*) 123.
εἰς (preposition with the accusative of extent) 140.
τοὺς (acc.pl.masc.of the article in agreement with *οἴκους*) 9.
οἴκους (acc.pl.masc.of *οἶκος*, extent) 784.
ἑαυτῶν (gen.pl.masc.of *ἑαυτός*, possession) 288.

Translation - "I know what I will do, so that when I have been dismissed from the stewardship they will receive me into their own homes."

Comment: *ἔγνων* - a culminative aorist indicates that the man had come to a definite conclusion. The doubt of the deliberative future in verse 3 is gone. He has hit upon a plan. *ἵνα* is joined in the purpose clause to *δέξωνταί*, while *ὅταν* in the indefinite temporal clause is joined to *μετασταθῶ*. "In order that when he is forced to leave his position (the indefinite temporal clause), the people will receive him into their own homes" (the purpose clause). He is not sure of the precise time when his position will be terminated; hence the indefinite temporal clause, but he has made plans to insure an income after he is dismissed.

Up to this point he has done nothing to merit his dismissal. But he has been fired and he faces an insecure financial future. Since he has been fired for graft, of which he is innocent, he decides that a little graft and the benefits which will accrue to him from it is something to which he is entitled. So he plans to settle his lord's accounts in full but with only a partial payment to his lord. Then his books will be short, thus confirming the employer's opinion of him and justifying the decision which he has already made. Thus he will have put his lord's debtors under obligation to himself for future board and room.

Jesus is not putting His stamp of approval upon sharp and unethical business practises. He is only using a parable to make a point which comes out later.

Verse 5 - "So he called everyone of his lord's debtors unto him, and said unto the first, How much owest thou unto my lord?"

καὶ προσκαλεσάμενος ἕνα ἕκαστον τῶν χρεοφειλετῶν τοῦ κυρίου ἑαυτοῦ ἔλεγεν τῷ πρώτῳ, Πόσον *ὀφείλεις τῷ κυρίῳ μου;*

καὶ (inferential conjunction) 14.
προσκαλεσάμενος (aor.mid.part.nom.sing.masc.of *προσκαλέω*, adverbial, temporal) 842.
ἕνα (acc.sing.masc.of *εἷς*, direct object of *προσκαλεσάμενος*) 469.
ἕκαστον (acc.sing.masc.of *ἕκαστος*, in agreement with *ἕνα*) 1217.
τῶν (gen.pl.masc.of the article in agreement with *χρεοφειλετῶν*) 9.
χρεοφειλετῶν (gen.pl.masc.of *χρεωφειλέτης*, partitive genitive) 2169.
τοῦ (gen.sing.masc.of the article in agreement with *κυρίου*) 9.
κυρίου (gen.sing.masc.of *κύριος*, relationship) 97.
ἑαυτοῦ (gen.sing.masc.of *ἑαυτός*, possession) 288.
ἔλεγεν (3d.per.sing.imp.act.ind.of *λέγω*, inceptive) 66.
τῷ (dat.sing.masc.of the article in agreement with *πρώτῳ*) 9.
πρώτῳ (dat.sing.masc.of *πρῶτος*, indirect object of *ἔλεγεν*) 487.
Πόσον (acc.sing.neut.of *πόσος*, direct object of *ὀφείλεις*) 603.
ὀφείλεις (2d.per.sing.pres.act.ind.of *ὀφείλω*, aoristic) 1277.
τῷ (dat.sing.masc.of the article in agreement with *κυρίῳ*) 9.
κυρίῳ (dat.sing.masc.of *κύριος*, personal advantage) 97.
μου (gen.sing.masc.of *ἐγώ*, relationship) 123.

Translation - "So when he had called in each one of the debtors of his master, he began by asking the first, 'How much do you owe to my master?' "

Comment: The aorist participle *προσκαλεσάμενος* indicates that he called in all of the debtors before he began to negotiate with the first. The inceptive imperfect in *ἔλεγεν* - "he *began* to speak . . . " would seem to indicate his negotiations with each of the group. Whether each negotiation was held in the presence of the entire group is not clear. His treatment of the first set the pattern for his treatment of all of the others, although the settlements of only the first two are recorded.

Verse 6 - "And he said, An hundred measures of oil. And he said unto him, Take thy bill, and sit down quickly, and write fifty."

ὁ δὲ εἶπεν,Ἑκατὸν βάτους ἐλαίου. ὁ δὲ εἶπεν αὐτῷ, Δέξαι σου τὰ γράμματα καὶ καθίσας ταχέως γράφον πεντήκοντα.

ὁ (nom.sing.masc.of the article, subject of εἶπεν) 9.
δὲ (continuative conjunction) 11.
εἶπεν (3d.per.sing.aor.act.ind.of εἶπον, constative) 155.
Ἑκατὸν (acc.sing.masc.of ἑκατός, in agreement with βάτους) 1035.

#2565 βάτους (acc.pl.masc.of βάτος, direct object of ὀφείλω, understood).

a measure - Luke 16:6.

Meaning: a Jewish liquid measure of a capacity of 8 or 9 gallons. In the parable of the steward - Luke 16:6.

ἐλαίου (gen.sing.neut.of ἔλαιον, description) 1530.
ὁ (nom.sing.masc.of the article, subject of εἶπεν) 9.
δὲ (adversative conjunction) 11.
εἶπεν (3d.per.sing.aor.act.ind.of εἶπον, constative) 155.
αὐτῷ (dat.sing.masc.of αὐτός, indirect object of εἶπεν) 16.
Δέξαι (2d.per.sing.1st.aor.impv.of δέχομαι, command) 867.
σου (gen.sing.masc.of σύ, possession) 104.
τὰ (acc.pl.neut.of the article in agreement with γράμματα) 9.
γράμματα (acc.pl.neut.of γράμμα, direct object of δέξαι) 2100.
καὶ (adjunctive conjunction joining verbs) 14.
καθίσας (aor.act.part.nom.sing.masc.of καθίζω, adverbial, temporal) 420.
ταχέως (adverbial) 2531.
γράφον (2d.per.sing.aor.act.impv.of γράφω, command) 156.
πεντήκοντα (acc.pl.masc.of πεντήκοντα, direct object of γράφον) 2172.

Translation - "And he said, 'Eight hundred gallons of oil.' But he said to him, 'Take your receipts, sit right down and write four hundred gallons.' "

Comment: The second δὲ is adversative, as the debtor did not expect to settle the account at a fifty percent discount. We have taken the adverb ταχέως as joined to καθίσας, not to the imperative γράφον. The steward is being very hospitable - "You owe him 800 gallons, *but* (adversative δὲ) sit right down and rewrite your note for 400 gallons." Thus the account is settled. The steward, acting for the master, wrote off a debt of 800 gallons of oil for 400 gallons. The debtor, armed with the receipt marked "Paid in full" is free from the obligation to pay the other half. But in the process he has acquired a moral obligation to the steward, who will soon be unemployed. The master is robbed of half his claim against the debtor, which is the basis for his action in dismissing the steward in the first place, despite the fact that the original accusation was not supported by evidence. In modern parlance the manager was saying, "If I have the name, I may as well play the game."

The Christian, robbed unjustly of his place in the commercial world because he is a Christian, should work within the world system to make certain that his financial security is assured, despite discrimination. Keep in mind that the lord in the parable represents the unsaved world system which is prejudiced against Christianity and unable to treat it fairly. The manager is the Christian. His action in this verse cannot be defended on ethical grounds, but that is not Jesus' point in the parable. Though he maneuvered dishonestly, the manager used the world system, which had just deprived him of a job, albeit unjustly, to make his own future secure. A practical application of this parable would lead the child of God to own a home, get out of debt, stay out of debt, carry an adequate insurance program and save enough money to provide for a minimal standard of decent living for himself and his family until he dies and goes to heaven. This we must do within the world system, though, of course, we should not emulate this steward's unethical action.

Verse 7 - "Then said he to another, And how much owest thou? And he said, An hundred measures of wheat. And he said unto him, Take thy bill and write fourscore."

ἔπειτα ἑτέρῳ εἶπεν, Σὺ δὲ πόσον ὀφείλεις; ὁ δὲ εἶπεν,Ἑκατὸν κόρους σίτου. λέγει αὐτῷ, Δέξαι σου τὰ γράμματα καὶ γράφον ὀγδοήκοντα.

#2566 *ἔπειτα* (temporal adverb).

afterward - 1 Cor.15:23,46.
afterwards - Gal.1:21.
after that - 1 Cor.12:28; 15:6,7; Heb.7:2.
then - Luke 16:7; John 11:7; Gal.1:18; 2:1; 1 Thess.4:17; Heb.7:27; James 3:17; 4:14.

Meaning: A combination of *ἐπί* (#47) and *εἶτα* (#2185). A temporal adverb - thereupon, thereafter, then, afterwards. (1) Chronologically - Luke 16:7; Gal.1:21; James 4:14; John 11:7 with *μετὰ τοῦτο*; Gal.1:18, with *μετὰ ἔτη τρία*; Gal.2:1 with *διὰ δεκατεσσάρων*. (2). When used in enumerating items, both chronologically and in ordinal sequence - with *πρῶτον* - 1 Cor.15:46; 1 Thess.4:17; Heb.7:2; James 3:17; with *πρότερον* - Heb.7:27; with *ἀπαρχὴ* - 1 Cor.15:23; with *εἶτα* - 1 Cor.15:5,6,7. (3). In ordinal sequence only, with *τρίτον*. . *ἔπειτα*. . . *ἔπειτα* - 1 Cor.12:28,28.

ἑτέρῳ (dat.sing.masc.of *ἕτερος*, indirect object of *εἶπεν*) 605.
εἶπεν (3d.per.sing.aor.act.ind.of *εἶπον*, constative) 155.
Σὺ (voc.sing.masc.of *σύ*, address) 104.
δὲ (continuative conjunction) 11.
πόσον (acc.sing.neut.of *πόσος*, direct object of *ὀφείλεις*) 603.
ὀφείλεις (2d.per.sing.pres.act.ind.of *ὀφείλω*, aoristic) 1277.
ὁ (nom.sing.masc.of the article, subject of *εἶπεν*) 9.

δὲ (continuative conjunction) 11.
εἶπεν (3d.per.sing.aor.act.ind.of εἶπον, constative) 155.
Ἑκατὸν (acc.sing.masc.of ἑκατός, in agreement with κόρους) 1035.

#2567 κόρους (acc.pl.masc.of κόρος, direct object of ὀφείλω, understood).

measure - Luke 16:7.

Meaning: corus or *cor*. The largest Hebrew dry measure. Equal to ten Attic *medimni* (μέδιμνος). "ὁ δὲ κόρος δύναται μεδίμνους ἀττικοὺς δέκα, "But the cor contains ten Attic *Medimni* (about 120 gallons)," (Josephus, *Antt.*, xv. 9.2., as cited in Meyer, *Commentary on the New Testament, Gospel of Mark and Luke*, 465).

σίτου (gen.sing.masc.of σῖτος, description) 311.
λέγει (3d.per.sing.pres.act.ind.of λέγω, historical) 66.
αὐτῷ (dat.sing.masc.of αὐτός, indirect object of λέγει) 16.
Δέξαι (2d.per.sing.aor.impv.of δέχομαι, command) 867.
σου (gen.sing.masc.of σύ, possession) 104.
τὰ (acc.pl.neut.of the article in agreement with γράμματα) 9.
γράμματα (acc.pl.neut.of γράμμα, direct object of δέξαι) 2100.
καὶ (adjunctive conjunction joining verbs) 14.
γράφον (2d.per.sing.aor.act.impv.of γράφω, command) 156.
ὀγδοήκοντα (acc.sing.neut.of ὀγδοήκοντα, direct object of γράφον) 1911.

Translation - "Then to another he said, 'You - and how much do you owe?' And he said, 'Twelve hundred bushels of wheat.' He said to him, 'Take your receipt and write nine hundred, sixty bushels.' "

Comment: We cannot be sure about the exact amount of wheat. Goodspeed has fifteen hundred bushels as the debt and twelve hundred as the amount to be paid. The amount is not important in the story. This second debtor was allowed to settle at a twenty percent discount. The implication is that the steward made similar arrangements with all of his master's debtors, thus ingratiating himself for future favors with all those who had been favored by him.

The reaction of the master, who has been robbed by the steward, because he himself dismissed his steward on what was an unproved accusation, is recorded in

Verse 8 - "And the lord commended the unjust steward, because he had done wisely: for the children of this world are in their generation wiser than the children of light."

καὶ ἐπῄνεσεν ὁ κύριος τὸν οἰκονόμον τῆς ἀδικίας ὅτι φρονίμως ἐποίησεν. ὅτι οἱ υἱοὶ τοῦ αἰῶνος τούτου φρονιμώτεροι ὑπὲρ τοὺς υἱοὺς τοῦ φωτὸς εἰς τὴν γενεὰν τὴν ἑαυτῶν εἰσιν.

καὶ (adversative conjunction) 14.

#2568 ἐπῄνεσεν (3d.per.sing.aor.act.ind.of ἐπαινέω, constative).

commend - Luke 16:8.
laud - Romans 15:11.
praise - 1 Cor.11:2,17,22,22.

Meaning: A combination of ἐπί (#47) and αἰνέω (#1881). Hence, a heightened form of αἰνέω - to heap praise upon; to approve heartily. With reference to the lord's praise of the unjust business manager - Luke 16:8. In Romans 15:11 it is the Greek word for the Hebrew in Psalm 117:1 - "extol," "laud," "heap praise upon." Paul's praise of the Corinthian saints - 1 Cor.11:2,17,22,22.

ὁ (nom.sing.masc.of the article in agreement with κύριος) 9.
κύριος (nom.sing.masc.of κύριος, subject of ἐπῄνεσεν) 97.
τὸν (acc.sing.masc.of the article in agreement with οἰκονόμον) 9.
οἰκονόμον (acc.sing.masc.of οἰκονόμος, direct object of ἐπῄνεσεν) 2488.
τῆς (gen.sing.fem.of the article in agreement with ἀδικίας) 9.
ἀδικίας (gen.sing.fem.of ἀδικία, description) 2367.
ὅτι (conjunction introducing a subordinate causal clause) 211.

#2569 φρονίμως (adverbial).

wisely - Luke 16:8.

Meaning: Cf. φρόνημα (#3931), φρονέω (#1212), φρόνησις (#1801), φρόνιμος (#693) and φροντίζω (#4902). Hence, an adverb - wisely; with prudence, wisdom, careful thought. With reference to the action of the business manager of Luke 16:8.

ἐποίησεν (3d.per.sing.aor.act.ind.of ποιέω, constative) 127.
ὅτι (conjunction introducing a subordinate causal clause) 211.
οἱ (nom.pl.masc.of the article in agreement with υἱοὶ) 9.
υἱοὶ (nom.pl.masc.of υἱός, subject of εἰσιν) 5.
τοῦ (gen.sing.masc.of the article in agreement with αἰῶνος) 9.
αἰῶνος (gen.sing.masc.of αἰών, description) 1002.
τούτου (gen.sing.masc.of οὗτος, in agreement with αἰῶνος) 93.
φρονιμώτεροι (nom.pl.masc.of φρονιμώτερος, predicate comparative adjective) 693.
ὑπὲρ (preposition with the comparative and followed by the accusative) 545.
τοὺς (acc.pl.masc.of the article in agreement with υἱοὺς) 9.
υἱοὺς (acc.pl.masc.of υἱός, comparison) 5.
τοῦ (gen.sing.neut.of the article in agreement with φωτὸς) 9.
φωτὸς (gen.sing.neut.of φῶς, description) 379.
εἰς (preposition with the accusative, static use) 140.
τὴν (acc.sing.fem.of the article in agreement with γενεὰν) 9.
γενεὰν (acc.sing.fem.of γενεά, static use) 922.
τὴν (acc.sing.fem.of the article in agreement with γενεὰν) 9.
ἑαυτῶν (gen.pl.masc.of ἑαυτός, description) 288.
εἰσιν (3d.per.pl.pres.ind.of εἰμί, aoristic) 86.

Translation - "But the lord praised the steward of unrighteousness because he acted with prudence. For the sons of this age are wiser in dealing with their own contemporaries than the sons of light."

Comment: #2568 indicates that the word means "high praise." The lord, somewhat ruefully perhaps, yet honestly gave high praise to his dismissed manager, because by the standards of the world of mammon, the manager's action was thoughtful, logical and wise. He was *ὁ οἰκονόμος τῆς ἀδικίας* - an efficient manager with reference to the manner in which unrighteous people play the game. He was a con artist who put a great many people under obligation to him. He could cash this obligation in the future when he needed it. To be sure this meant a financial loss to the master, but he had to admit that it was smart. After all he had asked for it by firing the manager in the first place. "The sons of this age" obviously refers to the unsaved people who march to the beat of Satan's drum. In contrast the "sons of light" are God's children who are out of step with the world and thus often victimized by it. As a result their efficiency in Christian service is impaired. This is what the teaching of the parable seeks to avoid. Christians live in an unfriendly world. They should be aware of this. Jesus pointed this out to His disciples many times - Mt.10:22; 24:9; Mk.13:13; Lk.6:22,27; 21:17; John 15:18,19; 17:14; 1 John 3:13. Christians should not expect accolades and kudos from the unsaved "sons of this age." Nor should we hope for rich financial rewards. On the contrary we should not be surprized when unfair discrimination robs us of our just deserts. Our Lord did not deserve a cross, but that is what He got from the world.

A correct understanding of the Christian's relationship to the world will not result in paranoia, nor should it leave in us a residue of bitterness. *Au contraire* it should be a cause for rejoicing. (Mt.5:11,12; 1 Pet.4:12-14). But though the enlightened child of God will reap a harvest of joy from his interactions with the world, he may also suffer acute financial embarrassment. The joy of knowing that we are suffering for Jesus' sake and thus identifying with Him in the offense of His cross, does not pay the bills. Thus we are to be as astute in reference to the devil's world as the devil's children are. This is what the steward in the parable did. Unjustly accused and charged with a crime which he did not commit, he did what he thought he had to do in order to survive. The children of God are busy in the world witnessing for our Lord. We should make the world pay the bills. We should make the world provide whatever financial security we need in order not to be hampered in our ministry for Christ. This need not be done unethically. If fact it dare not be done unethically. There is never any justification for the child of God to behave on any lower than an honorable level.

Christians who miss the point of this parable are naive and often hindered unduly from fulfilling their divinely appointed destinies because, while being as harmless as doves as they ought to be, they failed to be as wise as serpents. This is our Lord's advice in

Verse 9 - "And I say unto you, Make to yourselves friends of the mammon of unrighteousness; that when ye fail, they may receive you into everlasting habitations."

Καὶ ἐγὼ ὑμῖν λέγω, ἑαυτοῖς ποιήσατε φίλους ἐκ τοῦ μαμωνᾶ τῆς ἀδικίας, ἵνα ὅταν ἐκλίπῃ δέξωνται ὑμᾶς εἰς τὰς αἰωνίους σκηνάς.

Καὶ (inferential conjunction) 14.
ἐγὼ (nom.sing.masc.of *ἐγώ*, subject of *λέγω*, emphatic) 123.
ὑμῖν (dat.pl.masc.of *σύ*, indirect object of *λέγω*) 104.
λέγω (1st.per.sing.pres.act.ind.of *λέγω*, aoristic) 66.
ἑαυτοῖς (dat.pl.masc.of *ἑαυτός*, personal advantage) 288.
ποιήσατε (2d.per.pl.aor.act.impv.of *ποιέω*, command) 127.
φίλους (acc.pl.masc.of *φίλος*, direct object of *ποιήσατε*) 932.
ἐκ (preposition with the ablative of source) 19.
τοῦ (abl.sing.masc.of the article in agreement with *μαμωνᾶ*) 9.
μαμωνᾶ (abl.sing.masc.of *μαμμωνᾶς*, source) 608.
τῆς (gen.sing.fem.of the article in agreement with *ἀδικίας*) 9.
ἀδικίας (gen.sing.fem.of *ἀδικία*, description) 2367.
ἵνα (conjunction introducing a final clause) 114.
ὅταν (conjunction introducing an indefinite temporal clause) 436.

#2570 *ἐκλίπῃ* (3d.per.sing.2d.aor.act.subj.of *ἐκλείπω*, indefinite temporal clause).

fail - Luke 16:9; 22:32; Heb.1:12.
darken - Luke 23:45.

Meaning: A combination of *ἐκ* (#19) and *λείπω* (#2636). Hence, to lack; to fail; to be in short supply. With reference to the failure of the world system, *ὁ μαμμωνᾶς τῆς ἀδικίας*, to live up to its obligations - Luke 16:9; With reference to Peter's faith - Luke 22:32. God's years shall not fail, *i.e.* God is eternal - Heb.1:12. With reference to the failure of the sun - Luke 23:45.

δέξωνται (3d.per.pl.aor.subj.of *δέχομαι*, purpose clause) 867.
ὑμᾶς (acc.pl.masc.of *σύ*, direct object of *δέξωνται*) 104.
εἰς (preposition with the accusative of extent) 140.
τὰς (acc.pl.fem.of the article in agreement with *σκηνάς*) 9.
αἰωνίους (acc.pl.fem.of *αἰώνιος*, in agreement with *σκηνάς*) 1255.
σκηνάς (acc.pl.fem.of *σκηνή*, extent) 1224.

Translation - "Therefore I am telling you, 'Make for yourselves friends out of the mammon of unrighteousness, in order that, when it fails, they may receive you into permanent living quarters."

Comment: *ἐκ τοῦ μαμωνᾶ τῆς ἀδικίας* is an ablative of source, not agency. The interpretation that we are to use money to make friends is wrong. We make friends with the money, not by means of it. Why? In order that when it fails . . When what fails? The mammon of unrighteousness. When the world system lets the Christian down, as the master imposed upon his manager, the friends you made may give you their hospitality. The approval of our Lord here is not upon the fact that the manager was a rascal, but that he was shrewd enough to make the world around him serve him when he needed it.

Verse 10 - "He that is faithful in that which is least is faithful also in much; and he that is unjust in the least is unjust also in much."

ὁ πιστὸς ἐν ελαχίστῳ καὶ ἐν πολλῷ πιστός ἐστιν, καὶ ὁ ἐν ἐλαχίστῳ ἄδικος καὶ ἐν πολλῷ ἄδικος ἐστιν.

ὁ (nom.sing.masc.of the article in agreement with *πιστὸς*) 9.
πιστὸς (nom.sing.masc.of *πιστός*, subject of *ἐστιν*) 1522.
ἐν (preposition with the locative of sphere) 80.
ἐλαχίστῳ (loc.sing.masc.of *ἐλάχιστος*, sphere) 159.
καὶ (adjunctive conjunction joining substantives) 14.
ἐν (preposition with the locative of sphere) 80.
πολλῷ (loc.sing.masc.of *πολύς*, sphere) 228.
πιστός (nom.sing.masc.of *πιστός*, predicate adjective) 1522.
ἐστιν (3d.per.sing.pres.ind.of *εἰμί*, customary) 86.
καὶ (continuative conjunction) 14.
ὁ (nom.sing.masc.of the article in agreement with *ἄδικος*) 9.
ἐν (preposition with the locative of sphere) 80.
ἐλαχίστῳ (loc.sing.masc.of *ἐλάχιστος*, sphere) 159.
ἄδικος (nom.sing.masc.of *ἄδικος*, subject of *ἐστιν*) 549.
καὶ (adjunctive conjunction joining substantives) 14.
ἐν (preposition with the locative of sphere) 80.
πολλῷ (loc.sing.masc.of *πολύς*, sphere) 228.
ἄδικος (nom.sing.masc.of *ἄκικος*, predicate adjective) 549.
ἐστιν (3d.per.sing.pres.ind.of *εἰμί*, customary) 86.

Translation - "The one who can be trusted in a small matter can also be trusted with much, and the one who cannot be trusted in a small matter cannot be trusted with much."

Comment: Earthly matters are temporal and relatively insignificant. They are not worth the Christian's time and effort. The great sphere of Christian activity is the heavenly, eternal realm or spiritual values. One who is a good manager in earthly things will also prove to be an efficient steward of the manifold grace of God - and *vice versa.* The cheat in the world of business will cut the corners in his service for God. The Christian should be diligent and honest in both realms. This verse supports Weber's Protestant Ethic concept.

Verse 11 - "If therefore ye have not been faithful in the unrighteous mammon, who will commit to your trust the true riches?"

εἰ οὖν ἐν τῷ ἀδίκῳ μαμωνᾷ πιστοὶ οὐκ ἐγένεσθε, τὸ ἀληθινὸν τίς ὑμῖν πιστεύσει;

εἰ (particle introducing a first-class condition) 337.
οὖν (inferential conjunction) 68.
ἐν (preposition with the locative of sphere) 80.
τῷ (loc.sing.masc.of the article in agreement with *ἀδίκῳ*) 9.
ἀδίκῳ (loc.sing.masc.of *ἄδικος*, in agreement with *μαμωνᾷ*) 549.

μαμωνᾷ (loc.sing.masc.of μαμμωνᾶς, sphere) 608.
πιστοὶ (nom.pl.masc.of πιστός, predicate adjective) 1522.
οὐκ (summary negative conjunction with the indicative) 130.
ἐγένεσθε (2d.per.pl.aor.ind.of γίνομαι, first-class condition) 113.
τὸ (acc.sing.neut.of the article in agreement with ἀληθινὸν) 9.
ἀληθινὸν (acc.sing.neut.of ἀληθινός, direct object of πιστεύσει) 1696.
τίς (nom.sing.masc.of τίς, interrogative pronoun, subject of πιστεύσει) 281.
ὑμῖν (dat.pl.masc.of σύ, indirect object of πιστεύσει) 104.
πιστεύσει (3d.per.sing.fut.act.ind.of πιστεύω, deliberative, indirect question) 734.

Translation - "If then you have not been trustworthy in the business world, who will trust you with the true riches?"

Comment: A first-class condition in which the premise in the protasis is assumed to be true. The apodosis is in the form of indirect question with the deliberative future. God's business, of infinitely greater importance than that of the world demands the prudent management which is demonstrated by the successful business man. Preachers, missionaries and other full-time Christian workers need special skills in handling their personal finances since the demands made by society upon their budgets are greater than the average and their salaries, generally, are below the average. The business community generally looks upon preachers as bad credit risks without asking why this should be so. It is a situation that is not likely to change for the better. The child of God must carry his cross and do his best not to disgrace the cause of Christ by living beyond his income.

Verse 12 - "And if ye have not been faithful in that which is another man's, who shall give you that which is your own?"

καὶ εἰ ἐν τῷ ἀλλοτρίῳ πιστοὶ οὐκ ἐγένεσθε, τὸ ὑμέτερον τίς δώσει ὑμῖν;

καὶ (continuative conjunction) 14.
εἰ (particle introducing a first-class condition) 337.
ἐν (preposition with the locative of sphere) 80.
τῷ (loc.sing.masc.of the article in agreement with ἀλλοτρίῳ) 9.
ἀλλοτρίῳ (loc.sing.masc.of ἀλλότριος, sphere) 1244.
πιστοὶ (nom.pl.masc.of πιστός, predicate adjective) 1522.
οὐκ (summary negative conjunction with the indicative) 130.
ἐγένεσθε (2d.per.pl.aor.ind.of γίνομαι, first-class condition) 113.
τὸ (acc.sing.neut.of the article in agreement with ἡμέτερον) 9.

#2571 ἡμέτερον (acc.sing.neut.of ἡμέτερος, direct object of δώσει).

our - Acts 2:11; 26:5; Rom.15:4; 2 Tim.4:15; 1 John 1:3.
ours - Titus 3:14; 1 John 2:2.
your own - Luke 16:12.

Meaning: The possessive pronoun. First person plural - our, ours. Mistranslated in the KJV in Luke 16:12 as "*your* own."

τίς (nom.sing.masc.of τίς, interrogative pronoun, rhetorical question) 281.
δώσει (3d.per.sing.fut.act.ind.of δίδωμι, deliberative) 362.
ὑμῖν (dat.pl.masc.of σύ, indirect object of δώσει) 104.

Translation - "And since you were not trustworthy in the interests of others, who will give to you our own?"

Comment: When this passage was first encountered in the organization of *The Renaissance New Testament*, I was following the Westcott / Hort text, which has ἡμέτερον in the text and ὑμέτερον in the margin. Since this was the first occurrence of ἡμέτερος in the New Testament I gave the concordance analysis and assigned the appropriate number. Since then the editorial committee of the United Bible Societies has opted for ὑμέτερον, with a B degree of certitude, since most of the major manuscripts (p75, Sinaiticus, A D K P W X Δ Θ Ψ) and many minuscules read it. Metzger explains: "The reading ἡμέτερον (B L *al*) has the appearance of being a later theological refinement ("belonging to the Father and the Son"), expressing the divine origin of the true riches (ver. 11) — as is also expressed by the Marcionite reading ἐμόν. It may be, however, that, owing to the constant scribal confusion between υ and η (in later Greek the two vowels came to be pronounced alike), copyists who wrote ἡμέτερον intended ὑμέτερον — for in the context the correct antithesis to "another's" is "yours." (Metzger, *A Textual Commentary on the Greek New Testament,* 165). Rather than confuse my reader with the numbering system of my work, I have opted for ἡμέτερον and enter this *caveat.* ὑμέτερος is analyzed at #2127.

The first-class condition assumes that the one addressed was not trustworthy in his management of the property of others and the rhetorical question implies that he would not be trusted with the jurisdiction over "ours." #2571 is the lst.person plural possessive pronoun - "ours" not "yours." By "ours" Jesus means those things having to do with the spiritual realm as contrasted with ἀλλοτρίῳ, *i.e.* the realm of the world system of the mammon of injustice.

The thrust of the entire passage is that a good manager, in whatever realm of activity he may engage, is thoughtful, wise, prudent and sagacious and thus efficient. Efficiency will be rewarded and praised, whether such efficiency was involved in good ethics or bad. Since the Christian is in the world,though not of it, and subject, so far as his earthly life is concerned, to its rules, he must somehow survive in order to live for Christ. Our Lord does not want dead heros. He wants "living sacrifices" (Rom.12:2). Thus there is a need for the Christian steward to play the game by the world's rules and make the world provide for him at least a minimal subsistence and security, so that he can live out his destiny according to the will of God and "finish (his) course" (2 Tim.4:6,7). Thus Paul made tents for a living in the pagan commercial world, although his priority was the ministry of the gospel of Christ. We may be sure that he made good tents which were worth all that he charged for them. One need not be an unjust business manager in order to be efficient. Our Lord is looking for efficient administrators who understand cost/benefit analysis to conduct for Him the greatest business in the universe - the display and sale ("without money and without price") of "the unsearchable riches of Christ" (Eph.3:8). *Cf.*also Rom.2:4; 9:23; 11:12; Eph.1:18; 2:7; Phil.4:19; Col.1:27; Rev.5:12; Heb.11:26.

A tract published some years ago entitled *Packing Pork to Pay Expenses* was written by a Christian meat packer who, when asked about his business, replied, "Serving the Lord is my business and I pack pork to pay expenses." As an efficient steward he packed pork in keeping with the highest standards of quality control. He was an honest pork packer who gave to his employer an honest day's work for an honest pay. We will forgive him for packing a product which was blacklisted by Leviticus 11:7, since all the Gentiles and many unorthodox Jews enjoyed his product, despite the fact that it was not kosher.

The context is complete with

Verse 13 - "No servant can serve two masters: for either he will hate the one, and love the other; or else he will hold to the one, and despise the other. Ye cannot serve God and mammon."

Οὐδεὶς οἰκέτης δύναται δυσὶ κυρίοις δουλεύειν, ἢ γὰρ τὸν ἕνα μισήσει καὶ τὸν ἕτερον ἀγαπήσει, ἢ ἑνὸς ἀνθέξεται καὶ τοῦ ἑτέρου καταφρονήσει. οὐ δύνασθε θεῷ δούλεύειν καὶ μαμωνᾷ.

Οὐδεὶς (nom.sing.masc.of οὐδείς, in agreement with οἰκέτης) 446.

#2572 οἰκέτης (nom.sing.masc.of οἰκέτης, subject of δύναται).

household servant - Acts 10:7.
servant - Luke 16:13; Rom.14:4; 1 Pet.2:18.

Meaning: Cf. οἰκέω (#3926). A house servant. One who sustains a closer relationship with the family he serves than ὁ δοῦλος (#725). In the household of Cornelius - Acts 10:7. Generally in Romans 14:4; 1 Pet.2:18. Parabolically in Luke 16:13.

δύναται (3d.per.sing.pres.ind.of δύναμαι, static) 289.
δυσὶ (dat.pl.masc.of δύο, in agreement with κυρίοις) 385.
κυρίοις (dat.pl.masc.of κύριος, personal advantage) 97.
δουλεύειν (pres.act.inf.of δουλεύω, complementary) 604.
ἢ (disjunctive particle) 465.
γὰρ (inferential conjunction) 105.
τὸν (acc.sing.masc.of the article in agreement with ἕνα) 9.
ἕνα (acc.sing.masc.of εἷς, direct object of μισήσει) 469.
μισήσει (3d.per.sing.fut.act.ind.of μισέω, predictive) 542.
καὶ (adjunctive conjunction joining verbs) 14.
τὸν (acc.sing.masc.of the article in agreement with ἕτερον) 9.
ἕτερον (acc.sing.masc.of ἕτερος, direct object of ἀγαπήσει) 605.
ἀγαπήσει (3d.per.sing.fut.act.ind.of ἀγαπάω, predictive) 540.

ἢ (disjunctive particle) 465.
ἑνὸς (gen.sing.masc.of εἷς, description with a verb of touching) 469.
ἀνθέξεται (3d.per.sing.fut.mid.ind.of ἀντέχομαι, predictive) 606.
καὶ (adjunctive conjunction joining verbs) 14.
τοῦ (gen.sing.masc.of the article in agreement with ἑτέρου) 9.
ἑτέρου (gen.sing.masc.of ἕτερος, description with a verb of emotion) 605.
καταφρονήσει (3d.per.sing.fut.act.ind.of καταφρονέω, predictive) 607.
οὐ (summary negative conjunction with the indicative) 130.
δύνασθε (2d.per.pl.pres.mid.ind.of δύναμαι, static) 289.
θεῷ (dat.sing.masc.of θεός, personal advantage) 124.
δουλεύειν (pres.act.inf.of δουλεύω, complementary) 604.
καὶ (adjunctive conjunction joining nouns) 14.
μαμωνᾷ (dat.sing.masc.of μαμωνᾶς, personal advantage) 608.

Translation - "No servant is able to serve two masters. Therefore either he will hate the one and the other he will love, or to the one he will give loyal support and the other he will hold in contempt. You cannot serve God and money."

Comment: *Cf.*#2572. ὁ οἰκέτης is not a menial slave in a socially degrading sense, but rather a domestic or house servant who has good social relations with the family whom he serves and in whose house he lives. Hence the relationship here is not one of hostility, overt or covert, *vis a vis* cordial affection. The degree of devotion is more or less. He cannot serve two masters with the same degree of zeal, devotion and diligence. μισέω and ἀγαπάω here (#'s 542, 540) are used in a less intense sense - "have respect for" as opposed to "have somewhat less respect for." Loving one and loving the other less results in serving one with the utmost loyalty and looking with some disdain upon the other. The one is worthy of every effort to serve and the other is somewhat less deserving of the servant's sacrificial service. Note the basic meaning of #'s 606 and 607. - "To sustain an intimate and loyal relationship" in the former case and "to view with less regard" in the latter.

The entire passage (vss.1-13) reveals that the Christian is not a hermit, but an active participant in the affairs of this age which, in the economy of God, is marked for ultimate judgment and destruction. Yet he works within its system for the economic purpose of making a living, so that he can carry on the service for Christ, his true Master. The ascetic who withdraws from this world, lest in his participation in it, he becomes contaminated by it, is a moral coward who is running away from a fight. The soldier of the cross of Christ is no coward. The true ascetic must resign from the human race and leave the planet (1 Cor.5:10). But if he does this he cannot maintain his witness for Christ. The Christian witness is in this world, though not of it, and he must learn to get along in it. This means that he owes some loyalty to his worldy associates so long as he can discharge his obligation without compromising his loyalty to Christ. Loyalty to Christ does not require us to withdraw totally from society, any more than the discharging of our obligations to society requires us to compromise our commitment to our Lord. A Christian university professor can serve his institution even though the goals of a state university are not necessarily the goals of the Holy Spirit in this age of grace. But they are honorable. Hence, though the professor views his classroom lecture, his research and publishing in his academic field as a necessary part of his service to the world system, he views his service to Christ as more important. If he had to choose between the two there would be no hesitation in spurning the university chair in favor of Christ's work, however financially devastating the choice might prove to be. But if he is a wise steward, who has made friends with mammon, for reasons of expediency, he will make mammon serve him in earthly things, such as grocery bills, shelter, and social and economic security, so that he in turn can serve Christ. Since a Christian cannot serve both God and money and must support one with total loyalty and view the other with some contempt, he will play it smart and make mammon support him so that he can serve God. This is the policy of burning one's candle in the service of Christ and blowing the smoke in the devil's face. He need not cheat mammon as the steward in the parable did. He can give the world its "money's worth" in value received. He can render to mammon his full due in exchange for his salary, without lessening his service for Christ. As a matter of fact, if he were bankrupt and hungry because he severed connections with the world he would be less able to serve God. The logical Gnostic is an anchorite. The Syrian desert was peopled with these fanatics in the fourth and fifth centuries. One of them, Simeon Stylites (390?-459) thought himself so holy that he lived for thirty years atop a pillar sixty feet high. "Its circumference at the top was little more than three feet; a railing kept the saint from falling to the ground in his sleep. . . He bound himself to the pillar by a rope; the rope became embedded in his flesh, which putrefied around it, stank, and teemed with worms." (Will Durant, *The Age of Faith*, 60). If he had read 1 Cor.5:10 he might have descended from his lofty perch, even at the expense of a little contamination from the world, and been a more effective witness for Christ.

This principle applies to any steward of Christ, who is making an honest living in any field - banking, auto repair, marketing, athletics, medicine, law, etc. Martin Luther understood this and developed his concept of "The Calling" by which he taught that every Christian has been assigned to specific good works (Eph.2:10) which he is expected to perform for the Lord, and that these designated good works are component parts of the operation of a well ordered society. Thus all work is ennobling and all workers are dignified. Let us then serve God in whatever capacity He has assigned to us and thus we serve society in a constructive manner. And by "packing pork" we "pay the expenses" incurred while we are serving the Lord.

The covetous Pharisees got the point, and, of course, they disagreed as we see in

Verse 14 - "And the Pharisees also, who were covetous, heard all these things: and they derided him."

Ἤκουον δὲ ταῦτα πάντα οἱ Φαρισαῖοι φιλάργυροι ὑπάρχοντες, καὶ ἐξεμυκτήριζον αὐτόν.

Ἤκουον (3d.per.pl.imp.act.ind.of *ἀκούω*, progressive duration) 148.

δὲ (explanatory conjunction) 11.
ταῦτα (acc.pl.neut.of οὗτος, direct object of ἤκουον) 93.
πάντα (acc.pl.neut.of πᾶς, in agreement with ταῦτα) 67.
οἱ (nom.pl.masc.of the article in agreement with Φαρισαῖοι) 9.
Φαρισαῖοι (nom.pl.masc.of φαρισαῖος, subject of ἤκουον) 276.

#2573 φιλάργυροι (nom.pl.masc.of φιλάργυρος, predicate adjective).

covetous - Luke 16:14; 2 Tim.3:2.

Meaning: A combination of φίλος (#932) and ἄργυρος (#860). *Cf.* also ἀργύριον (#1535). Hence, in love with money. Covetous. Avaricious. Of the Pharisees in Luke 16:13; end-time apostates - 2 Tim.3:2.

ὑπαρχοντες (pres.act.part.nom.pl.masc.of ὑπάρχω, adverbial, causal) 1303.
καὶ (continuative conjunction) 14.

#2574 ἐξεμυκτήριζον (3d.per.pl.imp.act.ind.of ἐκμυκτηρίζω, inceptive).

deride - Luke 16:14; 23:35.

Meaning: A combination of ἐκ (#19) and μυκτηρίζω (#4455), from μυκτήρ - "nose." Hence, to turn up the nose; to scoff, sneer, deride. Make fun of in a hateful manner. With reference to the Pharisees' attitude toward Christ's teaching - Luke 16:14. Of the ridicule heaped upon Jesus at the cross - Luke 23:35.

αὐτόν (acc.sing.masc.of αὐτός, direct object of ἐξεμυκτήριζον) 16.

Translation - "Now the Pharisees had been listening to all this and, because they were avaricious they began to turn up their nose at Him."

Comment: The Pharisees had been listening to Jesus' parable of the first 13 verses, even though it was directed to His disciples (Luke 16:1). They listened carefully (imperfect tense in ἤκουον). They are characterized by Luke as "lovers of money" - avaricious, greedy, covetous - φιλάργυροι ὑπάρχοντες. The participle is causal. Jesus had taught in the parable that the steward had made provision for himself for the future, but only to the extent that he was assured of a minimal standard of living. To one in love with money this teaching was, of course, totally unacceptable. Thus the Pharisees began to ridicule Jesus (inceptive imperfect in ἐξεμυκτήριζον). *Cf.*#2574 for this colorful word. It indicates an attitude of contempt, born of a false sense of superiority. How natural it is for the unregenerate mind to view with amused contempt that which it does not have sufficient spiritual and intellectual perception to understand. This is typical of the close-minded, prejudicial, egotistical bigot.

The parable teaches a basic dualism in the universe. Good and evil coexist as objective entities. Light and darkness are in diametric opposition. God is in the universe; so is mammon. They cannot both receive worship. One must yield its service to the other. So the child of God is taught to dominate mammon for his

own uses so that he, in turn, can submit efficiently to the domination of God. Mammon serves the Christian; the Christian serves God. The reverse order will not be permitted. It is scant wonder that the Pharisees scoffed at Him! Jesus had an incisive analysis in

Verse 15 - "And he said unto them, Ye are they which justify yourselves before men; but God knoweth your hearts; for that which is highly esteemed among men is abomination in the sight of God."

καὶ εἶπεν αὐτοῖς,Ὑμεῖς ἐστε οἱ δικαιοῦντες ἑαυτοὺς ἐνώπιον τῶν ἀνθρώπων, ὁ δὲ θεὸς γινώσκει τὰς καρδίας ὑμῶν. ὅτι τὸ ἐν ἀνθρώποις ὑψηλὸν βδέλυγμα ἐνώπιον τοῦ θεοῦ.

καὶ (continuative conjunction) 14.
εἶπεν (3d.per.sing.aor.act.ind.of εἶπον, constative) 155.
αὐτοῖς (dat.pl.masc.of αὐτός, indirect object of εἶπεν) 16.
Ὑμεῖς (nom.pl.masc.of σύ, subject of ἐστε, emphatic) 104.
ἐστε (2d.per.pl.pres.ind.of εἰμί, aoristic) 86.
οἱ (nom.pl.masc.of the article in agreement with δικαιούντες) 9.
δικαιοῦντες (pres.act.part.nom.pl.masc.of δικαιόω, substantival, predicate nominative) 933.
ἑαυτοὺς (acc.pl.masc.of ἑαυτός, direct object of δικαιοῦντες) 288.
ἐνώπιον (improper preposition with the genitive) 1798.
τῶν (gen.pl.masc.of the article in agreement with ἀνθρώπων) 9.
ἀνθρώπων (gen.pl.masc.of ἄνθρωπος, place description) 341.
ὁ (nom.sing.masc.of the article in agreement with θεὸς) 9.
δὲ (adversative conjunction) 11.
θεὸς (nom.sing.masc.of θεός, subject of γινώσκει) 124.
γινώσκει (3d.per.sing.pres.act.ind.of γινώσκω, static) 131.
τὰς (acc.pl.fem.of the article in agreement with καρδίας) 9.
καρδίας (acc.pl.fem.of καρδία, direct object of γινώσκει) 432.
ὑμῶν (gen.pl.masc.of σύ, possession) 104.
ὅτι (conjunction introducing a causal clause) 211.
τὸ (nom.sing.neut.of the article in agreement with ὑψηλὸν) 9.
ἐν (preposition with the locative of sphere) 80.
ἀνθρώποις (loc.pl.masc.of ἄνθρωπος, sphere) 341.
ὑψηλὸν (nom.sing.neut.of ὑψηλός, subject of ἐστιν understood) 358.
βδέλυγμα (nom.sing.neut.of βδέλυγμα, predicate nominative) 1492.
ἐνώπιον (improper preposition with the genitive) 1798.
τοῦ (gen.sing.masc.of the article in agreement with θεοῦ) 9.
θεοῦ (gen.sing.masc.of θεός, place description) 124.

Translation - "And He said to them, 'You are always justifying yourselves before men, but God knows your hearts. For what is considered impressive in the human sphere is contemptible before God.' "

Comment: The Pharisees were greatly concerned about public relations. Modern Pharisees hire agents who devise means to improve their public image.

Madison Avenue can be very effective whether it is selling soap or politicians. But Madison Avenue does not work for nothing. Its services cost a great deal of money. That is why the Pharisees were avaricious. When one does not possess the qualities that make for greatness he buys advertizing, if he can afford it. Whether or not the money is well spent depends upon whom one is trying to impress. The conjunction δὲ is adversative. It makes no difference how we attempt to justify ourselves before society the cruel fact is that God knows our hearts. He sees beyond the television screen and listens to a different melody from that of the singing commercial. Jesus follows this chilling thought with another causal clause and says that what looks impressive when judged by the standards of the human sphere is detestable in the sight of God. God sees the glittering, highly touted exterior, but He also sees the rotten interior. What men consider laudable is at best worthy of scant attention to God and at worst revolting to Him. The higher in the scale of man's esteem we stand, the more repulsive we are to God. *Cf.*#1492 and run the references. Every person or thing in the New Testament considered abominable to God will be or is now worshipped by man. The popularity seeker has his values completely in reverse, unless, of course, he is an atheist. The man who is certain that God does not exist, and therefore that His opinion is not important, since He has no opinion, should seek assiduously, as did the Pharisees, to seduce the public to believe that he is as great as he thinks he is. But God is, and He rewards them who forget mammon and his slaves and diligently seek His approbation alone. The values of the world of mammon are exactly opposite to God's values. One of the best dressed men? One of the ten most popular men of the year? Widest read? Most sought after? Most admired? Sports figure? Movie star? Show business celebrity? A good press? Vote getter? - An abomination before God!!!

Verse 16 - "The law and the prophets were until John; since that time the kingdom of God is preached, and every man presseth into it."

Ὁ νόμος καὶ οἱ προφῆται μέχρι Ἰωάννου, ἀπὸ τότε ἡ βασιλεία τοῦ θεοῦ εὐαγγελίζεται καὶ πᾶς εἰς αὐτὴν βιάζεται.

Ὁ (nom.sing.masc.of the article in agreement with *νόμος*) 9.
νόμος (nom.sing.masc.of *νόμος*, subject of the verb understood) 464.
καὶ (adjunctive conjunction joining nouns) 14.
οἱ (nom.pl.masc.of the article in agreement with *προφῆται*) 9.
προφῆται (nom.pl.masc.of *προφήτης*, subject of *ἦσαν* understood) 119.
μέχρι (adverbial preposition with the genitive of time description) 948.
Ἰωάννου (gen.sing.masc.of *Ἰωάνης*, time description) 247.
ἀπὸ (preposition with the ablative of time separation) 70.
τότε (temporal adverb) 166.
ἡ (nom.sing.fem.of the article in agreement with *βασιλεία*) 9.
βασιλεία (nom.sing.fem.of *βασιλεία*, subject of *εὐαγγελίζεται*) 253.
τοῦ (gen.sing.masc.of the article in agreement with *θεοῦ*) 9.
θεοῦ (gen.sing.masc.of *θεός*, description) 124.
εὐαγγελίζεται (3d.per.sing.pres.pass.ind.of *εὐαγγελίζω*, iterative) 909.
καὶ (continuative conjunction) 14.

πᾶς (nom.sing.masc.of πᾶς, subject of βιάζεται) 67.
εἰς (preposition with the accusative of extent) 140.
αὐτὴν (acc.sing.fem.of αὐτός, extent) 16.
βιάζεται (3d.per.sing.pres.mid.ind.of βιάζομαι, progressive) 918.

Translation - "The law and the prophets (were preached) until John; since then the Kingdom of God is being preached and everyone is forcing his way into it."

Comment: *Cf.* comment on Mt.11:12,13. Jesus is accusing the covetous Pharisees, whom He attacked in verse 15, of trying to exploit the popularity of the Kingdom of God movement and to turn it to their own selfish account. Before the appearance of John the Baptist the message was contained in the law of Moses and the writings of the Old Testament Prophets, the ethical message of which finds fulfillment in Jesus Christ (Mt.5:17). The Pharisees made a great boast of their interpretation of and obedience to the law and the prophets. When John the Baptist came he castigated the Jewish Establishment and demanded their repentance and confession of sin as prerequisite to his baptism. He also foretold the divine judgment upon Israel as a nation (Mt.3:1-12). Thus John was in line morally with the law and the prophets, just as official Israel was out of line.

Since John's day Jesus and His movement had continued the preach the same ethical message. The continuity is complete. God spoke through Moses's legal code and the messages of the prophets. He then spoke through John and now He was speaking through Jesus.

In every age the religious hypocrites have tried to use their profession of orthodoxy as a means to their avaricious ends. They murdered the prophets and then honored them with ornate sepulchers. They obeyed the law in their interpretation of its letter and ignored its spirit. They came to receive John's baptism openly confessing their sins, but their insincerity was apparent to the Baptist who denounced them openly as a generation of snakes. *Cf.*#275 as contrasted with #688. Later they consented to his beheading. Now they are trying to draw Jesus into their circle of influence to use Him for their own selfish purposes. This is an attempt to dilute the standards of Divine holiness with man's situation ethics philosophy. The relative ethics of expediency which appeared often in the Old Testament age and revealed itself again during John's ministry was still working to compromise Jesus' ministry. It is still at work to compromise the message of His church in the late twentieth century.

However, Jesus informs them that all such pressing attempts to participate in the Kingdom of God at the expense of its moral standards is destined to fail. Any unfortunate unregenerate would be glad to have the glory and the beauty, the pomp and the circumstance of the Kingdom of God, if he could have it without the exasperating restrictions upon the free exercise of his overwhelming urge to ignore its morals.

Verse 17 - "And it is easier for heaven and earth to pass, than one tittle of the law to fail."

Εὐκοπώτερον δέ ἐστιν τὸν οὐρανὸν καὶ τὴν γῆν παρελθεῖν ἢ τοῦ νόμου μίαν κεραίαν πεσεῖν.

Εὐκοπώτερον (acc.sing.neut.comparative of *εὐκοπώτερος*, predicate adjective) 783.
δὲ (adversative conjunction) 11.
ἐστιν (3d.per.sing.pres.ind.of *εἰμί*, static) 86.
τὸν (acc.sing.masc.of the article in agreement with *οὐρανὸν*) 9.
οὐρανὸν (acc.sing.masc.of *οὐρανός*, general reference) 254.
καὶ (adjunctive conjunction joining nouns) 14.
τὴν (acc.sing.fem.of the article in agreement with *γῆν*) 9.
γῆν (acc.sing.fem.of *γῆ*, general reference) 157.
παρελθεῖν (aor.inf.of *παρέρχομαι*, complementary) 467.
ἢ (disjunctive particle) 465.
τοῦ (gen.sing.masc.of the article in agreement with *νόμου*) 9.
νόμου (gen.sing.masc.of *νόμος*, description) 464.
μίαν (acc.sing.fem.of *εἷς*, in agreement with *κεραίαν*) 469.
κεραίαν (acc.sing.fem.of *κεραία*, general reference) 470.
πεσεῖν (aor.act.inf.of *πίπτω*, complementary) 187.

Translation - "But it is easier for the heaven and the earth to pass away than for one dotting of an i in the law to lack fulfillment."

Comment: *τὸν οὐρανὸν καὶ τὴν γῆν* and *μίαν κεραίαν* are accusatives of general reference in conjunction with the infinitives *παρελθεῖν* and *πεσεῖν*. Which is more likely because easier? The former or the latter? Heaven and earth will pass away before one tiny diacritical punctuation mark of God's holy law is denied fulfillment. Thus the moral and spiritual realm is declared to be superior to that of the physical, social, economic and political. It was the lesser realm in which the Pharisees were interested. The heavens above our heads and the earth beneath our feet, as solid and enduring as they seem to be to the materialist, have less viability than God's holy law. Thus the very existence of the material universe depends upon the holy sanctity of God's law. His law, set forth by Moses, proclaimed by the prophets, preached by John the Baptist and expounded by Jesus is the moral law for all of God's dealings with sinful men of all ages. The Kingdom of God is committed with all of its power to the law's observance. Only by conformity to this moral law can man, made in God's image, be free and happy. The Pharisees who tried to prostitute it by forcing their way into God's kingdom on their own sinful terms have always failed and will continue to fail.

Jesus now illustrates the sanctity of the law by citing one regulation, the terms of which cannot be modified by human sociology or humanly conceived legal decrees. He could have cited the law against stealing, murder, lying or any other, since all of God's laws will be enforced to the letter. He chose to cite the law dealing with illicit sex in

Verse 18 - "Whosoever putteth away his wife and marrieth another, committeth adultery: and whosoever marrieth her that is put away from her husband committeth adultery."

Πᾶς ὁ ἀπολύων τὴν γυναῖκα αὐτοῦ καὶ γαμῶν ἑτέραν μοιχεύει, καὶ ὁ ἀπολελυμένην ἀπὸ ἀνδρὸς γαμῶν μοιχεύει.

Πᾶς (nom.sing.masc.of πᾶς, in agreement with ἀπολύων) 67.
ὁ (nom.sing.masc.of the article in agreement with ἀπολύων) 9.
ἀπολύων (pres.act.part.nom.sing.masc.of ἀπολύω, substantival, subject of μοιχεύει) 92.
τὴν (acc.sing.fem.of the article in agreement with γυναῖκα) 9.
γυναῖκα (acc.sing.fem.of γυνή, direct object of ἀπολύων) 103.
αὐτοῦ (gen.sing.masc.of αὐτός, relationship) 16.
καὶ (adjunctive conjunction joining participles) 14.
γαμῶν (pres.act.part.nom.sing.masc.of γαμέω, substantival, subject of μοιχεύει) 512.
ἑτέραν (acc.sing.fem.of ἕτερος, direct object of γαμῶν) 605.
μοιχεύει (3d.per.sing.pres.act.ind.of μοιχεύω, static) 498.
καὶ (continuative conjunction) 14.
ὁ (nom.sing.masc.of the article in agreement with γαμῶν) 9.
ἀπολελυμένην (perf.pass.part.acc.sing.fem.of ἀπολύω, substantival, direct object of γαμῶν) 92.
ἀπὸ (preposition with the ablative of separation) 70.
ἀνδρὸς (abl.sing.masc.of ἀνήρ, separation) 63.
γαμῶν (pres.act.part.nom.sing.masc.of γαμέω, substantival, subject of μοιχεύει) 512.
μοιχεύει (3d.per.sing.pres.act.ind.of μοιχεύω, static) 498.

Translation - "Every man who divorces his wife and marries another commits adultery; and the man who marries her who has been divorced from her husband is committing adultery."

Comment: *Cf.* comment on Mt.19:9 and Mk.10:11,12. Note that Matthew's account includes the extenuation μὴ ἐπὶ πορνείᾳ. Neither Mark nor Luke include the phrase, though there is nothing to suggest that such a case would not constitute an exception to the rule. Our Lord's point in Luke, following upon the teaching that God's moral law in the universe is inviolate in every dispensation, and that Pharisaic political tactics to crash the party and bring into the Kingdom of God their own shabby ethical standards would not be permitted, is that God meant exactly what He said and that the unequivocal statements of His law are not subject to the casuistry of human rationalization. He now tells a story designed to round out the teaching about the unjust business manager.

There we learned that a wise Christian steward provides for his social security while he is in the world of mammon, thus making mammon serve him and not the reverse. This policy permits a minimally decent standard of living. But the true Christian steward of the gospel of the grace of God should seek for no more than that (Mt.6:19). It is easy for a covetous Christian to push the parable of the unjust steward to the point of justifying affluence. If so, the story of the rich man and Lazarus provides a necessary corrective.

The Rich Man and Lazarus

(Luke 16:19-31)

Luke 16:19 - "There was a certain rich man which was clothed in purple and fine linen, and fared sumptuously every day."

Ἄνθρωπος δέ τις ἦν πλούσιος, καὶ ἐνεδιδύσκετο πορφύραν καὶ βύσσον εὐφραινόμενος καθ' ἡμέραν λαμπρῶς.

Ἄνθρωπος (nom.sing.masc.of ἄνθρωπος, subject of ἦν) 341.
δέ (explanatory conjunction) 11.
τις (nom.sing.masc.of τις, indefinite pronoun, in agreement with ἄνθρωπος) 486.
ἦν (3d.per.sing.imp.ind.of εἰμί, progressive description) 86.
πλούσιος (nom.sing.masc.of πλούσιος, predicate adjective) 1306.
καὶ (inferential conjunction) 14.

#2575 ἐνεδιδύσκετο (3d.per.sing.imp.mid.ind.of ἐνδιδύσκω, direct, customary).

be clothed in - Luke 16:19; Mark 15:17.

Meaning: Cf. ἐνδύω (#613). To clothe; in the middle voice, to clothe oneself. With reference to the rich man - Luke 16:19. To put clothing upon another - of Jesus at His trial - Mark 15:17.

#2576 πορφύραν (acc.sing.fem.of πορφύρα, accusative of the thing with the middle voice).

purple - Mark 15:17,20; Luke 16:19; Rev.17:4; 18:12.

Meaning: The purple fish - a species of shell fish or mussel. Never in this sense in the New Testament. A fabric dyed purple. The robe of mock royalty which Jesus wore at His trial - Mk.15:17,20. The clothing of the rich man - Lk.16:19; The attire of the Babylon whore - Rev.17:4. One of the articles of merchandise in Babylon - Rev.18:12.

καὶ (adjunctive conjunction joining nouns) 14.

#2577 βύσσον (acc.sing.fem.of βύσσος, accusative of the thing with the middle voice).

fine linen - Luke 16:19.

Meaning: A species of Egyptian flax or the linen made from it; very costly, delicate and soft. Comes in white or yellow. The garment of the rich man - Luke 16:19.

εὐφραινόμενος (pres.mid.part.nom.sing.masc.of *εὐφραίνω*, adverbial, complementary) 2479.
καθ' (preposition with the accusative, distribution) 98.
ἡμέραν (acc.sing.fem.of *ἡμέρα*, distribution) 135.

#2578 *λαμπρῶς* (adverbial).

sumptuously - Luke 16:19.

Meaning: splendidly; with magnificance. With reference to the affluent life style of the rich man in Luke 16:19.

Translation - "Now a certain man was rich; therefore he always clothed himself in purple and fine linen and made merry luxuriantly day by day."

Comment: The indefinite pronoun *τις* does not identify the man beyond indicating that he was a historic person. He had enjoyed wealth for a long period of time (imperfect tense in *ἦν*). He always dressed himself richly (customary imperfect, direct middle in *ἐνεκιδύσκετο*). Note the accusative of the thing following the middle voice in *πορφύραν καὶ βύσσον*. Luke is employing the ancient classical Greek which made great use of the accusative without a preposition to help out the case idea. They did this because they had no other case but the accusative and in earliest Greek there were no prepositions - only adverbs. Thus the adverbial use of the accusative. The rich purple color of his robe and the soft white or yellow linen of his tunic indicated his great wealth as well as his good taste. Purple harmonizes both with white and yellow. The linen was imported from Egypt. His life was a constant round of parties, banquets and fetes of festive merrymaking. These social events occurred every day. *Cf.*#98 for *καθ' ἡμέραν* in other passages. The affairs were sumptous. No expense was spared. Thus Jesus introduces one extreme of the socio-economic order - a very rich and a very comfortable man. The opposite extreme is introduced in verses 20 and 21.

Verse 20 - "And there was a certain beggar named Lazarus, which was laid at his gate, full of sores."

πτωχὸς δέ τις ὀνόματι Λάζαρος ἐβέβλητο πρὸς τὸν πυλῶνα αὐτοῦ εἱλκωμένος.

πτωχὸς (nom.sing.masc.of *πτωχός*, subject of *ἐβέβλητο*) 423.
δέ (continuative conjunction) 11.
τις (nom.sing.masc.of *τις*, indefinite pronoun, in agreement with *πτωχὸς*) 486.
ὀνόματι (dat.sing.neut.of *ὄνομα*, reference) 108.

#2579 *Λάζαρος* (nom.sing.masc.of *Λάζαρος*, appellation).

Lazarus - Luke 16:20,23,24,25.

Meaning: Lazarus. The poor man of Luke 16:20,23,24,25.

ἐβέβλητο (3d.per.sing.pluperfect pass.ind.of *βάλλω*, consummative) 299.
πρὸς (preposition with the accusative of extent) 197.
τὸν (acc.sing.masc.of the article in agreement with *πυλῶνα*) 9.
πυλῶνα (acc.sing.masc.of *πυλών*, extent) 1610.
αὐτοῦ (gen.sing.masc.of *αὐτός*, possession) 16.

#2580 *εἱλκωμένος* (perf.pass.part.nom.sing.masc.of *ἑλκόω*, consummative).

be full of sores - Luke 16:20.

Meaning: To make sore. Cause to ulcerate. In the passive, to be afflicted with sores. With reference to Lazarus - Luke 16:20.

Translation - "And a certain poor man named Lazarus had been laid near his doorway covered with sores."

Comment: For *ὀνόματι* in the dative in an identical usage *cf.* Mt.27:32; Lk.5:27; 10:38. The locative, instrumental and dative cases, which share the same case endings must be interpreted with the help of prepositions, if any, which may be adjoined and in the light of the context. The meaning here seems to be - "a certain poor man - with reference to his name - it is Lazarus." Personal advantage, one of the concepts which the dative conveys, is farfetched. We could construe it as an instrumental of means by supplying some other words - "who was known by means of his name, Lazarus." In any event the meaning is clear. The man's name was Lazarus. He is not to be confused with Jesus' friend in Bethany (#2596).

His body covered with sores (the perfect passive participle in *εἱλκωμένος*), Lazarus had been thrown at the gate of the rich man (pluperfect passive in *ἐβεβλητο*). The passive voice in these two words is significant. Beggars are seldom active - often acted upon in ways that they are powerless to prevent. He had been "thrown near the gate" at some time in the remote past, perhaps by someone who thought that the gate of a rich man was a propitious place for a beggar. He had remained there since that time. His body was covered with sores, possibly caused by malnutrition and the debilitation which made him subject to infection. Thus we have the picture of a man who was in a continuous state of misery and degradation. Always poor; always lying at the gate; unable to move; always tortured with the ulcers which had beset him in the past; always hungry; forsaken and ignored by all except the dogs.

The beggar's continuing misery is the counterpart of the rich man's continuing affluence. He was always clothed luxuriously and fed and entertained in a manner that speaks of the conspicuous consumption of fabulous wealth.

The point of the passage is contrast between the two men, both in this life and in eternity. One had laid up treasures on earth and ignored his need for heavenly treasures. The other had probably in early life neglected to make friends with the mammon of unrighteousness. Better financial management in his youth could possibly have prevented his squalor in later life. The description continues in

Verse 21 - "And desiring to be fed with the crumbs which fell from the rich man's table: moreover the dogs came and licked his sores."

καὶ ἐπιθυμῶν χορτασθῆναι ἀπὸ τῶν πιπτόντων ἀπὸ τῆς τραπέζης τοῦ πλουσίου. ἀλλὰ καὶ οἱ κύνες ἐρχόμενοι ἐπέλειχον τὰ ἕλκη αὐτοῦ.

καὶ (adjunctive conjunction joining participles) 14.
ἐπιθυμῶν (pres.act.part.nom.sing.masc.of ἐπιθυμέω, adverbial, complementary) 500.
χορτασθῆναι (aor.pass.inf.of χορτάζω, completes ἐπιθυμῶν) 428.
ἀπὸ (preposition with the ablative of source) 70.
τῶν (abl.pl.masc.of the article in agreement with πιπτόντων) 9.
πιπτόντων (pres.act.part.abl.pl.masc.of πίπτω, substantival, source) 187.
ἀπὸ (preposition with the ablative of separation) 70.
τῆς (abl.sing.fem.of the article in agreement with τραπέζης) 9.
τραπέζης (abl.sing.fem.of τράπεζα, separation) 1176.
τοῦ (gen.sing.masc.of the article in agreement with πλουσίου) 9.
πλουσίου (gen.sing.masc.of πλούσιος, possession) 1306.
ἀλλὰ (alternative conjunction) 342.
καὶ (ascensive conjunction) 14.
οἱ (nom.pl.masc.of the article in agreement with κύνες) 9.
κύνες (nom.pl.masc.of κύων, subject of ἐπέλειχον) 651.
ἐρχόμενοι (pres.part.nom.pl.masc.of ἔρχομαι, adverbial, temporal) 146.

#2581 **ἐπέλειχον** (3d.per.pl.imp.act.ind.of ἐπιλείχω, inceptive).

lick - Luke 16:21.

Meaning: A combination of ἐπί (#47) and λείχω - "to lick." Hence to lick or lap with the tongue upon - the ulcers of Lazarus - Luke 16:21. *Cf.* Micah 7:17, LXX, for λείχω - in that case "to lick the dust."

τὰ (acc.pl.neut.of the article in agreement with ἕλκη) 9.

#2582 **ἕλκη** (acc.pl.neut.of ἕλκος, direct object of ἐπέλειχον).

sore - Luke 16:21; Rev.16:2,11.

Meaning: A suppurated wound, discharging pus; hence, an open sore; an ulcer. With reference to Lazarus' sores - Luke 16:21. Of the sores that will fall upon the unsaved under the judgment of the first vial - Rev.16:2,11.

αὐτοῦ (gen.sing.masc.of αὐτός, possession) 16.

Translation - "And craving to be filled with the morsels which were falling from the table of the rich man, but even the dogs as they approached began to lick his sores."

Comment: ἐπιθυμῶν, the present participle and εἱλκωμένος, the perfect passive participle of verse 20 are joined to the main verb ἐβέβλητο. They serve to complement the picture as the beggar is thrown down at the rich man's door. He was covered with sores and very hungry. *Cf.*#500 and note that ἐπί is added for purposes of intensity. Always suffering from the running sores and always craving the food that was being thrown from the table of the man who refused to help him. The ablative phrase ἀπὸ τῶν πιπτόντων is followed immediately by another ablative phrase ἀπὸ τῆς τραπέζης. The first is source; the second is separation. Note the substantival participle πιπτόντων - The beggar would have been happy to eat whatever might fall from the table.

But (alternative ἀλλὰ) his craving for food, however intense, was not to be satisfied. On the contrary, as if to add insult to injury, an added indignity was perpetrated upon this miserable man. Even (ascensive καὶ) the dogs, as they approached (temporal adverb in ἐρχόμενοι, indicating simultaneous action) began (inceptive imperfect in ἐπέλειχον) to lick his sores. This attention, no doubt intended as a gesture of friendship, provided a constant irritant as the beggar, perhaps too weak to resist, lay and suffered. Note that one of God's judgments upon the unsaved during the tribulation period will be the same open sores - Rev.16:2, 11.

Thus the contrast between saints and sinners, before and after death is in the making. The rich man has everything that money can buy and none of the ills that plague the beggar, who is alone, but for the dogs, hungry, sick and penniless. But this is only a short-run situation. God's eternal long-run situation is about to present a totally opposite picture. To pass from the one to the other is only a little matter of the deaths of both the comfortable rich man and the miserable beggar. Jesus tells us of these transitions in

Verse 22 - "And it came to pass that the beggar died, and was carried by the angels into Abraham's bosom: the rich man also died and was buried."

ἐγένετο δὲ ἀποθανεῖν τὸν πτωχὸν καὶ ἀπενεχθῆναι αὐτὸν ὑπὸ τῶν ἀγγέλων εἰς τὸν κόλπον Ἀβραάμ. ἀπέθανεν δὲ καὶ ὁ πλούσιος καὶ ἐτάφη.

ἐγένετο (3d.per.sing.aor.ind.of γίνομαι, constative) 113.
δὲ (adversative conjunction) 11.
ἀποθανεῖν (2d.aor.inf.of ἀποθνήσκω, noun use, subject of ἐγένετο) 774.
τὸν (acc.sing.masc.of the article in agreement with πτωχὸν) 9.
πτωχὸν (acc.sing.masc.of πτωχός, general reference) 423.
καὶ (adjunctive conjunction joining infinitives) 14.

#2583 ἀπενεχθῆναι (aor.pass.inf.of ἀποφέρω, noun use, subject of ἐγένετο).

bring - 1 Cor.16:3; Acts 19:12.
carry - Luke 16:22.
carry away - Mark 15:1; Rev.17:3; 21:10.

Meaning: A combination of ἀπό (#70) and φέρω (#683). Hence, to carry away; to carry from one place to another. With reference to the delivery of a money gift from Corinth to Jerusalem - 1 Cor.16:3. Jesus was escorted to Pilate - Mk.15:1. An angel transported John to a desert to reveal Babylon - Rev.17:3; and to a high mountain - Rev.21:10. With reference to the delivery of Lazarus into "Abraham's bosom - Luke 16:22. Handkerchiefs were carried from Paul to the sick - Acts 19:12.

αὐτὸν (acc.sing.masc.of αὐτός, general reference) 16.
ὑπὸ (preposition with the albative of agent) 117.
τῶν (abl.pl.masc.of the article in agreement with ἀγγέλων) 9.
ἀγέλλων (abl.pl.masc.of ἄγγελος, agent) 96.
εἰς (preposition with the accusative of extent) 140.
τὸν (acc.sing.masc.of the article in agreement with κόλπον) 9.
κόλπον (acc.sing.masc.of κόλπος, extent) 1702.
'Αβραάμ (gen.sing.masc.of 'Αβραάμ, possession) 7.
ἀπέθανεν (3d.per.sing.aor.act.ind.of ἀποθνήσκω, constative) 774.
δὲ (continuative conjunction) 11.
καὶ (adjunctive conjunction joining nouns) 14.
ὁ (nom.sing.masc.of the article in agreement with πλούσιος) 9.
πλούσιος (nom.sing.masc.of πλούσιος, subject of απέθανεν and ἐτάφη) 1306.
καὶ (adjunctive conjunction joining verbs) 14.
ἐτάφη (3d.per.sing.2d.aor.pass.ind.of θάπτω, constative) 748.

Translation - "But the poor man died and was carried by the angels into the bosom of Abraham, and the rich man also died and was buried."

Comment: δὲ is adversative. The state of affairs described in verses 19-21, unequal and unjust as it was, could not continue indefinitely. Death has a way of levelling matters. Note Luke's classic Greek use of the infinitives ἀποθανεῖν and ἀπενεχθῆναι as nouns, subjects of the verb ἐγένετο. The death and burial of the poor man occurred. Once again we must warn the beginning Greek student not to explain the accusative case in τὸν πτωχὸν and αὐτὸν by saying that they are *subjects* of the infinitives. Since the infinitive is not a finite verb it cannot have a subject. The accusative case is explained as the accusative of general reference. The English student must learn to look at it from the Greek point of view. The infinitive is both a noun and a verb - hence a verbal noun. In each context one of the two uses predominates, although the subordinate use in that context is not totally absent.

"Carried away εἰς τὸν κόλπον 'Αβραάμ - "into the bosom of Abraham" is a Jew's way of saying what an American Indian would say about "the happy hunting ground" where all good Indians are alleged to go. Angels are ministering spirits, charged with the responsibility of caring for the saints (Heb.1:14). Guardian angels make periodic reports to Heaven in our behalf (Mt.18:10) and they will be involved with us in the rapture of the saints (Mt.24:31; Ps.91:11,12). Lazarus' guardian angels were watching for his homecoming. When he died they carried him down to Paradise. There is little to say about the death of the rich man, except that he was buried. It sounds final, except that the next four Greek words are καὶ ἐν τῷ ᾅδῃ!

Verse 23 - "And in hell, he lift up his eyes, being in torments, and seeth Abraham afar off, and Lazarus in his bosom."

καὶ ἐν τῷ ᾅδῃ ἐπάρας τοὺς ὀφθαλμοὺς αὐτοῦ, ὑπάρχων ἐν βασάνοις, ὁρᾷ Ἀβραὰμ ἀπὸ μακρόθεν καὶ Λάζαρον ἐν τοῖς κόλποις αὐτοῦ.

καὶ (continuative conjunction) 14.
ἐν (preposition with the locative of place where) 80.
τῷ (loc.sing.masc.of the article in agreement with *ᾅδῃ*) 9.
ᾅδῃ (loc.sing.masc.of *ᾅδης*, place where) 947.
ἐπάρας (1st.aor.act.part.nom.sing.masc.of *ἐπαίρω*, adverbial, temporal) 1227.
τοὺς (acc.pl.masc.of the article in agreement with *ὀφθαλμοὺς*) 9
ὀφθαλμοὺς (acc.pl.masc.of *ὀφθαλμός*, direct object of *ἐπάρας*) 501.
αὐτοῦ (gen.sing.masc.of *αὐτός*, possession) 16.
ὑπάρχων (pres.act.part.nom.sing.masc.of *ὑπάρχω*, adverbial, causal) 1303.
ἐν (preposition with the instrumental, means) 80.
βασάνοις (instru.pl.masc.of *βάσανος*, means) 413.
ὁρᾷ (3d.per.sing.pres.act.ind.of *ὁράω*, constative) 144.
Ἀβραὰμ (acc.sing.masc.of *Ἀβραάμ*, direct object of *ὁρᾷ*) 7.
ἀπὸ (preposition with the ablative of space separation) 70.
μακρόθεν (an adverb of place) 1600.
καὶ (adjunctive conjunction joining nouns) 14.
Λάζαρον (acc.sing.masc.of *Λάζαρος*, direct object of *ὁρᾷ*) 2579.
ἐν (preposition with the locative of place where) 80.
τοῖς (loc.pl.masc.of the article in agreement with *κόλποις*) 9.
κόλποις (loc.pl.masc.of *κόλπος*, place where) 1702.
αὐτοῦ (gen.sing.masc.of *αὐτός*, possession) 16.

Translation - "And in Hades he rolled his eyes upward, because he was in torments and he saw Abraham far away and Lazarus close beside."

Comment: Verse 22 closes with the rich man in his grave, but that is not the end of the story. The action shifts downward to Hades and Paradise "in the heart of the earth" (Eph.4:9; Mt.12:40). *Cf.*#947. *ᾅδης* was the abiding place of the souls of the dead before the resurrection of Jesus Christ. Acts 2:27,31 declare that Jesus' soul at His death upon the cross went to Hades, but that He did not remain there. To the saved thief at Calvary Jesus said that they both would go that very day to Paradise. Therefore Paradise and Hades were one and the same place *before* the resurrection of Jesus. For Paul declares that he was caught up to the Third Heaven (2 Cor.12:2), and follows in 2 Cor.12:4 with a repetition of the statement, except that he calls the place Paradise. We conclude that *after* the resurrection, Paradise was up, identical with the Third Heaven, where Christ sits at the right hand of God (Heb.1:3). *Cf.*2 Cor.12:2 with 2 Cor.12:4. Yet Jesus and the saved thief went *down* to Paradise on the evening of the crucifixion day. *Cf.* Mt.12:40. They stayed for three days and nights. The place is also called Sheol in the Old Testament (Ps.16:10; Acts 2:27). Thus what the Hebrew calls Sheol the Greek calls Hades. Jesus and the saved thief went there.

But clearly there are two divisions of Hades/Sheol, separated by a great gulf, making traffic back and forth impossible. Yet the gulf between them is not so wide as to prevent sight and sound from crossing.

Hades/Sheol is the hot side; the side of torment; the abode of the unrighteous dead to this day. Paradise/Sheol is the comfortable side, where Lazarus went and where Jesus and the saved thief spent the three days between the crucifixion and the resurrection. After the resurrection of Christ Paul said that Paradise was *up* - in the heaven of heavens. Obviously Paradise was moved from Sheol, which is down, in the heart of the earth, and which, before the resurrection was the abiding place of the souls of both saved and unsaved dead, to the third heavens, which is the throne of God, where Christ is now seated at the Father's right hand (Ps.110:1). This move occurred at the resurrection of Jesus Christ (Eph.4:8-10). The hot side of the gulf, designated Hades, is still down there and will serve its infernal purpose until the end of the Millenium. As a result of the Great White Throne Judgment the victims in Hades will be transferred to Hell (γέεννα, #483, *The Renaissance New Testament*, I, 381. Inadvertently the number was omitted from the text). Γέεννα, translated "Hell" is called "the lake of fire" in Rev.20:14.

The rich man went to Hades. So did Lazarus, Jesus and the saved thief on the cross, because the term, synonymous with the Hebrew "Sheol" is the general term denoting the place of abode for souls, whose bodies have died and are buried in earthly tombs. But it is possible to be in Hades, Sheol and not be in Paradise, Sheol, just as a man in Pittsburg, Pennsylvania is not in Philadelphia, Pennsylvania. Yet both men are in Pennsylvania. In this analogy Sheol answers to the state of Pennsylvania and Pittsburg and Philadelphia answer to the two areas within the state. We shall not try to determine which of the two cities is which. Perhaps the mayors of the two cities can settle that!

What sort of a place is Hades and what sort was Paradise, which is here called "Abraham's bosom." The former is a place of torment and the latter a place of comfort. Yet these terms cannot mean physical comfort and/or torture, because the physical bodies of both the rich man and Lazarus were in earthly tombs on the surface of the earth, not at its "heart." Though anatomical terms are used, such as ὀφθαλμός (#501), κόλπος (#1702), δάκτυλος (#1434) and γλῶσσα (#1846), the language is figurative in order to make the point in the story. Actually the eyes, bosoms, fingers and tongues of both rich man and Lazarus were buried along with their bodies (σῶμα #507). The saints of all of the ages who have died have no physical bodies at this time; nor will they have until the coming of Christ at the end of this age (1 Cor.15:51-58; 1 Thess.4:13-18). The unsaved will have no physical bodies until the resurrection of the lost at the end of the millenium (Rev.20:12,13). Yet without bodies, there is perception and torture on the Hades side of the gulf and comfort on the Paradise side. Before the resurrection of Christ the general area, which included both sides was called Sheol , but it was divided into Hades and Paradise.

This material will be referred to again when other passages that touch upon it are in view.

Verse 24 - "And he cried and said, Father Abraham, have mercy on me, and send Lazarus, that he may dip the tip of his finger in water, and cool my tongue; for I am tormented in this flame."

καὶ αὐτὸς φωνήσας εἶπεν, Πάτερ Ἀβραάμ, ἐλέησόν με καὶ πέμψον Λάζαρον ἵνα βάψῃ τὸ ἄκρον τοῦ δακτύλου αὐτοῦ ὕδατος καὶ καταψύξῃ τὴν γλῶσσάν μου, ὅτι ὀδυνῶμαι ἐν τῇ φλογὶ ταύτῃ.

καὶ (inferential conjunction) 14.
αὐτὸς (nom.sing.masc.of *αὐτός*, subject of *εἶπεν*, emphatic) 16.
φωνήσας (aor.act.part.nom.sing.masc.of *φωνέω*, adverbial, temporal) 1338.

εἶπεν (3d.per.sing.aor.act.ind.of *εἶπον*, constative) 155.
Πάτερ (voc.sing.masc.of *πατήρ*, address) 238.
Ἀβραάμ (voc.sing.masc.of Ἀβραάμ, address) 7.
ἐλέησόν (2d.per.sing.aor.act.impv.of *ἐλεέω*, entreaty) 430.
με (acc.sing.masc.of *ἐγώ*, direct object of *ἐλέησόν*) 123.
καὶ (adjunctive conjunction joining verbs) 14.
πέμψον (2d.per.sing.aor.act.impv.of *πέμπω*, entreaty) 169.
Λάζαρον (acc.sing.masc.of Λάζαρος, direct object of *πέμψον*) 2579.
ἵνα (conjunction introducing a final clause with the subjunctive) 114.

#2584 *βάψῃ* (3d.per.sing.aor.act.subj.of *βάπτω*, purpose).

dip - Luke 16:24; John 13:26; Rev.19:13.

Meaning: Cf. βάπτισμα (#278), *βαπτισμός* (#2298), *βαπτιστής* (#248) and *βαπτίζω* (#273). The root of all of these words is *βαπ*, which means to dip, dip in, immerse, submerge, sink beneath, overwhelm, in such manner that the object is totally covered. Lazarus was asked to immerse the tip of his finger in water - Luke 16:24. Jesus dipped (immersed) the sop into the sauce and gave it to Judas (John 13:26). Jesus' garments will be red, as those dipped or dyed red in blood (Rev.19;13). The idea of sprinkling (*ῥαντίζω* - #2297) cannot be made to fit any of these concepts. It was not suggested that Lazarus hold up the tip of his finger and sprinkle water upon it with the other hand. Jesus did not sprinkle sauce on a piece of bread. Jesus' garments will not have been sprinkled with blood until saturated.

τὸ (acc.sing.neut.of the article in agreement with *ἄκρον*) 9.
ἄκρον (acc.sing.neut.of *ἄκρον*, direct object of *βάψῃ*) 1509.
τοῦ (gen.sing.masc.of the article in agreement with *δακτύλου*) 9.
δακτύλου (gen.sing.masc.of *δάκτυλος*, description) 1434.
αὐτοῦ (gen.sing.masc.of *αὐτός*, possession) 16.
ὕδατος (gen.sing.neut.of *ὕδωρ*, place) 301.
καὶ (adjunctive conjunction joining verbs) 14.

#2585 *καταψύξῃ* (3d.per.sing.aor.act.subj.of *καταψύχω*, purpose).

cool - Luke 16:24.

Meaning: A combination of *κατά* (#98) and *ψύχω* (#1489); hence, to cool down; to reduce the heat. With reference to the rich man's tongue - Luke 16:24.

τὴν (acc.sing.fem.of the article in agreement with *γλῶσσαν*) 9.

γλῶσσαν (acc.sing.fem.of γλῶσσα, direct object of καταφύξῃ) 1846.
μου (gen.sing.masc.of ἐγώ, possession) 123.
ὅτι (conjunction introducing a subordinate causal clause) 211.
ὀδυνῶμαι (1st.per.sing.pres.pass.ind.of ὀδυνάω, progressive) 1920.
ἐν (preposition with the instrumental of means) 80.
τῇ (instru.sing.fem.of the article in agreement with φλογὶ) 9.

#2586 φλογὶ (instru.sing.fem.of φλόξ, means).

flame - Luke 16:24; Acts 7:30; Heb.1:7; Rev.1:14; 2:18; 19:12.
flaming - 2 Thess.1:8.

Meaning: Cf. φλέγω - "to burn" (does not occur in the New Testament). Flame - absolutely in Luke 16:24. With πύρ in Acts 7:30; Heb.1:7; Rev.1:14; 2:18; 19:12; 2 Thess.1:8. The fire of Hades - Luke 16:24. The Shekinah fire of the burning bush - Acts 7:30. Metaphorically, of angels - Heb.1:7; figuratively in Rev.1:14; 2:18; 19:12. Literally of the fire of judgment at the Second Coming of Christ - 2 Thess.1:8. *Cf.*#298.

ταύτῃ (instru.sing.fem.of οὗτος, in agreement with φλογὶ) 93.

Translation - "And he cried out and said, 'Father Abraham, have mercy on me and send Lazarus, in order that he may dip the tip of his finger in water and cool my tongue, because I am being tortured by this flame.' "

Comment: Note αὐτὸς here in emphasis, since otherwise it is not needed, as it is implicit in εἶπεν. The aorist participle φωνήσας indicates action prior to that of εἶπεν, which probably indicates that the rich man called out to gain attention of those beyond the gulf, before he made his request. Otherwise the action of the participle and of the main verb εἶπεν is simultaneous. There are a few places where the context demands simultaneity of action between the main verb and the aorist participle.

The rich man addressed Abraham as "Father" which proves that for all of his bohemian life style on earth he was orthodox enough. A barren correctitude in doctrine is no guarantee of salvation nor of the transformed life which is supposed to adorn the doctrine when it is held in sincerity, as a survey of the average Sunday morning church congregation will attest. If Abraham had been the rich man's father in a spiritual as well as in a genetic sense, he would have cared for his unfortunate brother at the gate. It is convenient to have Abraham, or some other saint, to call on when one is tormented by the fires of hades, although people like the rich man are destined to discover that "Father Abraham's" help is not available under such circumstances.

Two imperatives of entreaty are followed by a double purpose clause and a ὅτι clause of cause. He wants pity from Abraham and an order to Lazarus that he dip his finger in water and cool his tongue, because he is tormented. The genitive of place description in ὕδατος is interesting. "Here ὕδατος emphasizes the *kind* of material which the speaker clearly has in mind." (Robertson, *Grammar*, 495).

It is worth noting that ἐν and the instrumental τῇ φλογὶ ταύτῃ means "by means of this flame." A flame can be uncomfortable by virtue of its proximity. The tortured need not be *in* the flame - only near enough to feel its heat. Fire fighters know this very well indeed. However, the language here is figurative, since nothing corporeal was present in ᾅδης - only that which was psychic. The point of the story is that the rich man spent his life on earth being covetous (Luke 16:14) and instead of making friends of the mammon of unrighteousness in a legitimate and constructive way, he became a slave to it and was thus unable to serve God (vs.13). Thus, since he had all of his comfort upon earth, while Lazarus was suffering, he now suffers in eternity, while Lazarus is comforted. There is therefore a moral reason why Abraham cannot grant the rich man's request. Abraham explains to him in

Verse 25 - "But Abraham said, Son, remember that thou in thy lifetime received thy good things and likewise Lazarus evil things: but now he is comforted, and thou art tormented."

εἶπεν δὲ Ἀβραάμ, Τέκνον, μνήσθητι ὅτι ἀπέλαβες τὰ ἀγαθά σου ἐν τῇ ζωῇ σου, καὶ Λάζαρος ὁμοίως τὰ κακά. νύν δὲ ὧδε παρακαλεῖται σὺ δὲ ὀδυνᾶσαι.

εἶπεν (3d.per.sing.aor.act.ind.of εἶπον, constative) 155.
δὲ (adversative conjunction) 11.
Ἀβραάμ (nom.sing.masc.of Ἀβραάμ, subject of εἶπεν) 7.
Τέκνον (voc.sing.masc.of τέκνον, address) 229.
μνήσθητι (2d.per.sing.1st.aor.act.impv.of μιμνήσκω, command) 485.
ὅτι (conjunction introducing an object clause in indirect discourse) 211.
ἀπέλαβες (2d.per.sing.aor.act.ind.of ἀπολαμβάνω, constative) 2131.
τὰ (acc.pl.neut.of the article in agreement with ἀγαθά) 9.
ἀγαθά (acc.pl.neut.of ἀγαθός, direct object of ἀπέλαβες) 547.
σου (gen.sing.masc.of σύ, possession) 104.
ἐν (preposition with the locative of time point) 80.
τῇ (loc.sing.fem.of the article in agreement with ζωῇ) 9.
ζωῇ (loc.sing.fem.of ζωή, time point) 668.
σου (gen.sing.masc.of σύ, possession) 104.
καὶ (continuative conjunction) 14.
Λάζαρος (nom.sing.masc.of Λάζαρος, subject of ἀπέλαβες understood) 2579.
ὁμοίως (adverbial) 1425.
τὰ (acc.pl.neut.of the article in agreement with κακά) 9.
κακά (acc.pl.neut.of κακός, direct object of ἀπέλαβες) 1388.
νῦν (temporal adverb) 1497.
δὲ (adversative conjunction) 11.
ὧδε (an adverb of place) 766.
παρακαλεῖται (3d.per.sing.pres.pass.ind.of παρακαλέω, progressive) 230.
σὺ (nom.sing.masc.of σύ, subject of ὀδυνᾶσαι, emphatic) 104.
δὲ (adversative conjunction) 11.
ὀδυνᾶσαι (2d.per.sing.pres.pass.ind.of ὀδυνάω, progressive) 1920.

Translation - "But Abraham said, 'Son, keep in mind that you received your good things during your lifetime and Lazarus the misfortunes in his. But here and now he is receiving comfort, but you are being tortured.' "

Comment: It is the *ὧδε καὶ νῦν* - "the here and now" that counts, not the fleeting span of time of one's life on earth.

Abraham will not, because indeed he cannot grant the rich man's request. As justification for his refusal he reminds the rich man of something.The *ὅτι* clause introduces the indirect discourse in the object clause. During the same time upon earth that the rich man was enjoying all of his luxurious lifestyle, Lazarus was enduring all of his misfortunes. The adversative *δὲ* indicates that the situation is reversed. Here (*παράδεισος* for Lazarus and *ᾅδης* for the rich man) and now (the eternal state for both of them) he is always comforted as he never was on earth and you are always tortured as you never were on earth. Which was the wiser? Comfort in the shortrun temporal; anguish in the longrun eternal. Tempory anguish and eternal comfort or temporary comfort and everlasting anguish? The rich man had a temporal point of view; Lazarus had an eternal point of view. The rich man's virtue was that he had made a friend of mammon; his mistake was that he had become a slave of mammon. Lazarus' virtue was that he refused to be enslaved by mammon; his mistake was that he failed to make friends with it to the extent that he could make it serve him while he spent his time serving God. It is not God's will for Christians to be miserable beggars like Lazarus. It is also against His will that they should be as fabulously affluent as the rich man, unless they are willing to spend most of it in charity to the less fortunate. Hence, in the two parables, we have a warning against the two extreme attitudes toward money.

There was also a physical reason why the rich man's request was denied, as explained in

Verse 26 - "And beside all this between us and you there is a great gulf fixed; so that they which pass from hence to you cannot; neither can they pass to us, that would come from thence."

καὶ ἐν πᾶσι τούτοις μεταξὺ ἡμῶν καὶ ὑμῶν χάσμα μέγα ἐστήρικται, ὅπως οἱ θέλοντες διαβῆναι ἔνθεν πρὸς ὑμᾶς μὴ δύνωνται, μηδὲ ἐκεῖθεν πρὸς ἡμᾶς διαπερῶσιν.

καὶ (emphatic conjunction) 14.
ἐν (preposition with the instrumental of association) 80.
πᾶσι (instru.pl.neut.of *πᾶς*, in agreement with *τούτοις*) 67.
τούτοις (instru.pl.neut.of *οὗτος*, association) 93.
μεταξὺ (improper preposition with the ablative of separation) 1262.
ἡμῶν (abl.pl.masc.of *ἐγώ*, separation) 123.
καὶ (adjunctive conjunction joining pronouns) 14.
ὑμῶν (abl.pl.masc.of *σύ*, separation) 104.

#2587 *χάσμα* (nom.sing.neut.of *χάσμα*, subject of *ἐστήρικται*).

gulf - Luke 16:26.

*Meaning: Cf.*χάσχω- "to yawn; gape." Hence, a gaping opening. A chasm; gulf - between Paradise and Hades - Luke 16:26.

μέγα (nom.sing.neut.of μέγας, in agreement with χάσμα) 184.
ἐστήρικται (3d.per.sing.perf.pass.ind.of στηρίζω, consummative) 2359.
ὅπως (conjunction introducing a purpose clause) 177.
οἱ (nom.pl.masc.of the article in agreement with θέλοντες) 9.
θέλοντες (pres.act.part.nom.pl.masc.of θέλω, substantival, subject of δύνωνται) 88.

#2588 διαβῆναι (aor.act.inf.of διαβαίνω, complementary).

come over - Acts 16:9.
pass - Luke 16:26; Heb.11:29.

Meaning: A combination of διά (#118) and βαίνω - "to go." Hence, to pass through; to cross over. Through the Red Sea - Heb.11:29; to go to Macedonia - Acts 16:9; to pass from Hades to Paradise - Luke 16:26.

ἔνθεν (for ἐντεῦθεν, adverbial) 1236.
πρὸς (preposition with the accusative of extent) 197.
ὑμᾶς (acc.pl.masc.of σύ, extent) 104.
μὴ (qualfied negative conjunction with the subjunctive) 87.
δύνωνται (3d.per.sing.pres.subj.of δύναμαι, purpose) 289.
μηδὲ (continuative disjunctive) 612.
ἐκεῖθεν (adverbial) 396.
πρὸς (preposition with the accusative of extent) 197.
ἡμᾶς (acc.pl.masc.of ἐγώ, extent) 123.
διαπερῶσιν (3d.per.pl.pres.subj.of διαπεράω, purpose) 777.

Translation - "In fact, in addition to all these factors, between us and you a great chasm stands, permanently fixed, in order that those who wish to cross over there to you are not able, nor can they cross from there to us."

Comment: καὶ can be taken here as emphatic. The antecedent of τούτοις is the material of verse 25. Abraham had given the moral reasons why the rich man could not expect relief. ἐν πᾶσι τούτοις is an interesting idiom - "in association with (addition to; besides all this) - where "all these things" means the material of verse 25, there is a great chasm . . . κ.τ.λ. He points to the topographical reason. Even if it were in keeping with moral rectitude for me to grant your request, which it is not, it is physically impossible to comply. Lazarus' comfort and your torment is necessarily the fact of the case, not only from the moral point of view, but also from the physical point of view. μεταξὺ with the ablative of separation. The perfect tense in ἐστήρικται is consummative. The gulf was permanently established in a completed action in the past, as a result of which the present situation will exist forever. *Cf.*#2359 for the other uses of στηρίζω. There is much good material here on Christian steadfastness. ὅπως here with the subjunctive in a purpose clause. οἱ θέλοντες is substantival. "Those wishing . . . cannot."

Everyone in Hades, no doubt, would be happy to cross over into Paradise, though it is not likely that Lazarus was anxious to change places with the rich man. The time to think about that is in this life when we are asked to choose between purple, fine linen and sumptuous feasts on the one hand and hunger, running sores and dogs on the other. After death it is too late. This the rich man recognizes in verse 27. This passage denies the possibility, taught by some that souls after death can be released from purgatory by the meritorious performances of those still upon earth.

Verse 27 - "Then he said, I pray thee therefore, Father, that thou wouldst send him to my father's house:"

εἶπεν δέ, Ἐρωτῶ σε οὖν, πάτερ, ἵνα πέμψῃς αὐτὸν εἰς τὸν οἶκον τοῦ πατρός μου,

εἶπεν (3d.per.sing.aor.act.ind.of εἶπον, constative) 155.
δέ (inferential conjunction) 11.
Ἐρωτῶ (1st.per.sing.pres.act.ind.of ἐρωτάω, aoristic) 1172.
σε (acc.sing.masc.of σύ, direct object of ἐρωτῶ) 104.
οὖν (inferential conjunction) 68.
πάτερ (voc.sing.masc.of πατήρ, address) 238.
ἵνα (conjunction introducing a purpose clause) 114.
πέμψῃς (2d.per.sing.aor.act.subj.of πέμπω, purpose) 169.
αὐτὸν (acc.sing.masc.of αὐτός, direct object of πέμψῃς) 16.
εἰς (preposition with the accusative of extent) 140.
τὸν (acc.sing.masc.of the article in agreement with οἶκον) 9.
οἶκον (acc.sing.masc.of οἶκος, extent) 784.
τοῦ (gen.sing.masc.of the article in agreement with πατρός) 9.
πατρός (gen.sing.masc.of πατήρ, possession) 238.
μου (gen.sing.masc.of ἐγώ, relationship) 123.

Translation - "So he said, 'I beg you therefore, Father, that you will send him to my father's house,' "

Comment: ἐρωτῶ (#1172) - a strong word for making a request - beg, plead, entreat. οὖν is inferential - "since you cannot send Lazarus to help me bear this agony, my second request is that my family be warned." It appears that if Lazarus had gone across the gulf to alleviate the rich man's miseries, he would have been content to let his family go to Hades also! He had put himself first during his entire life. This habit, once formed, is difficult to break. In Hades he is still thinking of himself first and of his brothers second. There is a psychological principle at work here. The "self" which we create on earth by our reaction to our sociological environment is the "self" we carry over into the next life. Always selfish in life, the rich man's first thought in Hades was for his own relief from pain. That being denied, he now thinks of his brothers back on earth. But that is a secondary consideration! Learned attitudes and the responses which they produce are enduring even over into eternity.

Some commentators have remarked that here is a man in Hades with a spiritual concern for the salvation of his unsaved brothers back on earth. Hence he suggests a missionary enterprise. Could this man be all bad and hence worthy of damnation? (*Expositors' Greek Testament*, I, 590). *Au contraire* he is thoroughly bad and totally worthy of the treatment which he received. The idea of sending Lazarus to preach to his brothers came only after his request for his own relief was denied. A sprinkling system in Hades would make a godless society comfortable, and, after all, that is all that the selfish sinner wants. In such a case he would have said, "Let my brothers join me here. It is not too bad. Some one turn on the air conditioning!"

Verse 28 - "For I have five brethren; that he may testify unto them, lest they also come to this place of torment."

ἔχω γὰρ πέντε ἀδελφούς, ὅπως διαμαρτύρηται αὐτοῖς, ἵνα μὴ καὶ αὐτοὶ ἔλθωσιν εἰς τὸν τόπον τοῦτον τῆς βασάνου.

ἔχω (1st.per.sing.pres.act.ind.of *ἔχω*, aoristic) 82.
γὰρ (causal conjunction) 105.
πέντε (numeral) 1119.
ἀδελφούς (acc.pl.masc.of *ἀδελφός*, direct object of *ἔχω*) 15.
ὅπως (conjunction with the subjunctive, purpose) 177.

#2589 *διαμαρτύρηται* (3d.per.sing.pres.dep.subj.of *διαμαρτύρομαι*, purpose).

charge - 1 Tim.5:21; 2 Tim.2:14; 4:1.
testify - Luke 16:28; Acts 2:40; 8:25; 10:42; 18:5; 20:21,24; 23:11; 28;23; 1 Thess.4:6; Heb.2:6.
witness - Acts 20:23.

Meaning: A combination of *διά* (#118) and *μαρτυρέω* (#1471). Hence, to witness, testify, affirm, tell or say with thoroughness and earnestness; to speak with intense conviction. It is a stronger word than *μαρτυρέω*, *λέγω* or *λαλέω*, all of which mean to bear witness, though without necessary conviction or emphasis. With reference to Paul or the other Apostles and early Christians in all places except Luke 16:28 (Lazarus) and Acts 20:23 (Holy Spirit). Joined with *ἵνα* and the subjunctive - 1 Tim.5:21; Lk.16:28 (with *μὴ*); by the infinitive, 2 Tim.2:14 (with *μὴ*); Acts 18:5. With the imperative - 2 Tim.4:1. With *παρακαλέω* and the imperative - Acts 2:40. Absolutely, with *λαλέω* - Acts 8:25; absolutely in Acts 23:11; with *κηρύσσω* and *ὅτι* and an objective clause - Acts 10:42; with the participle *λέγον* and followed by *ὅτι* and an object clause - Acts 20:23. Followed by the accusative and a direct object - Acts 20:21,24; 28:23; by *λέγω* and direct discourse - Heb.2:6; with *προεῖπον* - 1 Thess.4:6.

αὐτοῖς (dat.pl.masc.of *αὐτός*, indirect object of *διαμαρτύρηται*) 16.
ἵνα (conjunction with the subjunctive, negative purpose) 114.
μὴ (qualified negative conjunction in a negative purpose clause) 87.
καὶ (adjunctive conjunction joining substantives) 14.

αὐτοὶ (nom.pl.masc.of αὐτός, subject of ἔλθωσιν) 16.
ἔλθωσιν (3d.per.pl.aor.subj.of ἔρχομαι, negative purpose) 146.
εἰς (preposition with the accusative of extent) 140.
τὸν (acc.sing.masc.of the article in agreement with τόπον) 9.
τόπον (acc.sing.masc.of τόπος, extent) 1019.
τοῦτον (acc.sing.masc.of οὗτος, in agreement with τόπον) 93.
τῆς (gen.sing.masc.of the article in agreement with βασάνου) 9.
βασάνου (gen.sing.masc.of βάσανος, description) 413.

Translation - "Because I have five brothers, in order that he may earnestly witness to them, lest they also come to this place of torment."

Comment: γὰρ is causal. The clause ἔχω γὰρ πέντε ἀδ ελφούς is parenthetical. The sentence, without the parenthesis is "... in order that you may send him to my father's house... in order that he may witness to them ... κ.τ.λ." #2589 - any word that carries the idea of earnest, passionate discourse will do. Why should Lazarus plead so earnestly? Another negative purpose clause with ἵνα μὴ and the subjunctive in ἔλθωσιν - "lest they also (adjunctive καὶ) should come. . . "

Taken by itself, the request to send Lazarus sounds commendable and indeed it would be, had the rich man requested it first without his previous request for relief from his own torture. A true missionary spirit is driven only by the tragedy of the condemnation of the lost. Abraham's suggestion in verse 29 leads the rich man to a statement that reveals that he knew nothing about the theology of "effectual call" and hence nothing about evangelistic and missionary methods in verse 30. After which Abraham seeks to educate him in verse 31.

Verse 29 - "Abraham saith unto him, They have Moses and the prophets; let them hear them."

λέγει δὲ Ἀβραάμ, Ἔχουσι Μωϋσέα καὶ τοὺς προφήτας, ἀκουσάτωσαν αὐτῶν.

λέγει (3d.per.sing.pres.act.ind.of λέγω, historical) 66.
δὲ (adversative conjunction) 11.
Ἀβραάμ (nom.sing.masc.of Ἀβραάμ, subject of λέγει) 7.
Ἔχουσι (3d.per.pl.pres.act.ind.of ἔχω, aoristic) 82.
Μωϋσέα (acc.sing.masc.of Μωϋσῆς, direct object of ἔχουσι) 715.
καὶ (adjunctive conjunction joining nouns) 14.
τοὺς (acc.pl.masc.of the article in agreement with προφήτας) 9.
προφήτας (acc.pl.masc.of προφήτης, direct object of ἔχουσι) 119.
ἀκουσάτωσαν (3d.per.pl.aor.act.impv.of ἀκούω, command) 148.
αὐτῶν (gen.pl.masc.of αὐτός, description, after a verb of hearing) 16.

Translation - "But Abraham said, 'They have Moses and the Prophets. Let them hear them.' "

Comment: δὲ is adversative. Abraham is not going to grant the request. On the contrary he is going to argue that Lazarus' return to earth, even if it were possible, would be fruitless. The rich man's brother had what Moses and the Prophets wrote. It was read and expounded every week in the synagogue, just as it had been when the rich man was still alive. Abraham then suggested that the five brothers pay attention to what had been written. The genitive αὐτῶν after the verb of hearing means "let them hear them *and no one else.*"

It requires faith and childlike humility to hear, believe and obey God's law and prophetic messages. One must assume, to begin, that they are true and that they came from God. But God is not visible! Is there a God? Did Moses really speak for God? And the prophets? Why should one believe that they had God's true message? The world is full of prophets and law givers. All claim a monopoly on the truth and all consign the others to the eternal burnings fit only for heretics. The unsaved man regards himself as a sophisticated, tough minded, skeptical person - thoroughly pragmatic. He takes nothing on faith. That is naive. He demands proof - proof that he can see, hear, smell, touch and taste. He demands reality in terms of sense perception. He is determined to base his life pattern upon what he can observe and measure. That is the scientific method - the approach of all mature epistemologists.

The rich man in Hades knew that that was the attitude of his five brothers. It had been his own attitude when he was upon earth. He was prepared to argue that soul winning must be done by presenting startling, sensational, pragmatic, observable and measurable evidence. This he believed because he knew nothing of the call of the Holy Spirit of God exercising convicting power, to bring the proud human will and intellect to the humility of a trusting child. That these were his views is clear from what he said in

Verse 30 - "And he said, Nay, father Abraham; but if one went unto them from the dead, they will repent."

ὁ δὲ εἶπεν, Οὐχί, πάτερ Ἀβραάμ, ἀλλ' ἐάν τις ἀπὸ νεκρῶν πορευθῇ πρὸς αὐτοὺς μετανοήσουσιν.

ὁ (nom.sing.masc.of the article, subject of εἶπεν) 9.
δὲ (adversative conjunction) 11.
εἶπεν (3d.per.sing.aor.act.ind.of εἶπον, constative) 155.
Οὐχί (negative exclamation) 130.
πάτερ (voc.sing.masc.of πατήρ, address) 238.
Ἀβραάμ (voc.sing.masc.of Ἀβραάμ, address) 7.
ἀλλ' (alternative conjunction) 342.
ἐάν (conditional particle in a third-class condition) 363.
τις (nom.sing.masc.of τις, indefinite pronoun, subject of πορευθῇ) 486.
ἀπὸ (preposition with the ablative of source) 70.
νεκρῶν (abl.pl.masc.of νεκρός, source) 749.
πορευθῇ (3d.per.sing.aor.subj.of πορεύομαι, third-class condition) 170.
πρὸς (preposition with the accusative of extent) 197.
αὐτοὺς (acc.pl.masc.of αὐτός, extent) 16.
μετανοήσουσιν (3d.per.pl.fut.act.ind.of μετανοέω, predictive) 251.

Translation - "But he said, 'No, father Abraham, but if someone from the dead goes to them, they will repent."

Comment: δὲ is adversative as the rich man tries to make his pragmatic point. He disagrees with Abraham's suggestion that the messages of Moses and the Prophets are enough inducement for repentance. He has an alternative suggestion. ἀλλά is the strong alternative conjunction. Evidently the rich man felt strongly that his pragmatic approach to evangelism was far better than the simple proclamation of God's word and a challenge to men to lay their intellects on the altar and believe like little children. He had no doubt about the result if Lazarus would go back to earth and preach to them. The predictive future in the apodosis of the third-class condition, μετανοήσουσιν, is full of his assurance. His doubt was expressed in the protatis ἐάν τις ἀπὸ τῶν νεκρῶν πορευθῇ - "if someone will go" (he was not sure that Lazarus would) "they will repent" (he was certain of that). It was his conviction that the reappearnce of Lazarus upon the earth would be an event so startlingly pragmatic that its evidence that life beyond the grave was a reality, that his sophisticated, tough minded brothers, empiricists that they were, just as he had been, would be forced to change their thinking.

He was asking that an appeal be made to the intellect. What he did not understand is that such an appeal compromises the claims of the Gospel of Christ. If the gospel story must depend for its validity upon its ability to appear reasonable to the depraved and darkened intellects of fallen men, then it stands in wisdom of sinful men rather than in the power of God. Review our comments on Luke 11:14-52. The rich man in Hades was making the same mistake that the Pharisees made in Luke 11:14. Jesus did not accede to it then; nor does Abraham accede to it now.

This passage will correct, if we will allow it to do so, the fallacious view, currently popular, that successful evangelism must be sensational. Indeed genuine evangelism is sensational, but the difference is that the sensation comes from the Holy Spirit, not from the evangelist and his public relations expert and his property man. Many who call themselves evangelists go to the west coast to borrow from Hollywood and to the east to borrow from Madison Avenue. Human, fleshly psychological measures are taken. Cowboy evangelists, converted movie stars, Olympian athletes, regenerated bums (are not we all?!), born again scamps, former convicts, prostitutes, dope peddlers and atheists. This fare is not as good as Lazarus from the dead, but it is as close as they can come. One converted cowboy, turned evangelist, wore chaps, broad hat, holster and six-gun in the pulpit. Prominent newspaper chains lay claim to the successes of some preachers because they "made him" by giving him unlimited newspaper coverage. Nothing succeeds like success. A name on a marquee will draw the crowds better than the Holy Spirit's response to mighty prevailing prayer.

Some evangelists are not necessarily to be condemned for this since they did not seek it and perhaps would give much to rid their ministry of it. But if sensationalism is the true method of evangelism, all modern sensationalists are second-rate when compared to the rich man in Hades. He wanted to send a man back to the earth from the portals of Paradise. One can see the headlines now, "LAZARUS RETURNS FROM ABRAHAM'S BOSOM." Let him put up a tent. Let him buy newspaper space and national television time. Let the camera crews come - NBC, CBS, ABC. He is certain to be invited to appear on the Johnny Carson Show. Here is evidence that there is life beyond the grave. Hear his testimony: "I was a beggar. I was poor. I was hungry. The dogs licked my sores. The rich man would give me nothing — not even the scraps! We both died. I went to Abraham's Bosom. He went to Hades. It was hot over there. His tongue was hanging out. My sores were healed. Repent. Repent! Repent!!" Here is sensational evangelism at its garish best. "Let us try it," said the rich man. Abraham's response was δὲ in

Verse 31 - "And he said unto him, If they hear not Moses and the prophets,neither will they be persuaded, though one rose from the dead."

εἶπεν δὲ αὐτῷ, Εἰ Μωϋσέως καὶ τῶν προφητῶν οὐκ ἀκούουσιν, οὐδ' ἐάν τις ἐκ νεκρῶν ἀναστῇ πεισθήσονται.

εἶπεν (3d.per.sing.aor.act.ind.of εἶπον, constative) 155.
δὲ (adversative conjunction) 11.
αὐτῷ (dat.sing.masc.of αὐτός, indirect object of εἶπεν) 16.
Εἰ (conditional particle in a first-class condition) 337.
Μωϋσέως (gen.sing.masc.of Μωϋσῆς, description after a verb of hearing) 715.
καὶ (adjunctive conjunction joining nouns) 14.
τῶν (gen.pl.masc.of the article in agreement with προφητῶν) 9.
προφητῶν (gen.pl.masc.of προφήτης, description, after a verb of hearing) 119.
οὐκ (summary negative conjunction with the indicative) 130.
ἀκούουσιν (3d.per.pl.pres.act.ind.of ἀκούω, aoristic, first-class condition) 148.
οὐδ' (disjunctive particle) 452.
ἐάν (conditional particle in a third-class condition) 363.
τις (nom.sing.masc.of τις, indefinite pronoun, subject of ἀναστῇ) 486.
ἐκ (preposition with the ablative of source) 19.
νεκρῶν (abl.pl.masc.of νεκρός, source) 749.
ἀναστῇ (3d.per.sing.aor.act.subj.of ἀνίστημι, third-class condition) 789.
πεισθήσονται (3d.per.pl.fut.pass.ind.of πείθω, predictive) 1629.

Translation - "But he said to him, 'Since they are not listening to Moses and the Prophets, they will not be convinced even if someone arose from the dead.' "

Comment: This δὲ is the final adversative of the story. It indictes how wrong the rich man was. We have a first-class condition in the protasis, with a third-class protasis contained in the apodosis. It was apparent that the rich man's brothers were not listening to either Moses or the Prophets. The result was therefore certain - "they will not be persuaded." Not under any circumstances. Not even "if someone arose from the dead." Neither Moses nor the Prophets accompanied their message with sensational evidences of their truth. They only stated their propositions and the audience is challenged to believe and dared to disbelieve.

Not all who hear Moses and the Prophets reject them. The audience is divided betweem those to whom the message smells like life and those to whom it smells like death (2 Cor.2:14-17). Unwillingness to obey the Word of God is not an evidence of blind intellect alone, but, what is more to the point, of the stubborn rebellion against God of the human will. When a sinner's will is opposed to God, he is not helped toward repentance and faith by having his intellect bombarded by evidence, however convincing it is, when viewed by the open mind. A closed mind, deeply afflicted by the blind prejudice of the unregenerate will, only rationalizes away whatever evidence is presented. This is why Jesus never yielded to the suggestion that He perform miracles to prove that He was God. "A wicked and adulterous generation seeks after a sign." The attempt to convince the unregenerate mind has no effect upon the decision of the unregenerate will, because the intellect of man is as depraved as are his emotional nature and his will, Thomas Aquinas and Arminius to the contrary notwithstanding.

Concerning Offenses, Forgiveness and Faith

(Luke 17:1-10)

Luke 17:1 - "Then said he unto his disciples, It is impossible but that offenses will come: but woe unto him, through whom they come."

Εἶπεν δὲ πρὸς τοὺς μαθητὰς αὐτοῦ, Ἀνένδεκτόν ἐστιν τοῦ τὰ σκάνδαλα μὴ ἐλθεῖν, πλὴν οὐαὶ δι' οὗ ἔρχεται.

Εἶπεν (3d.per.sing.aor.act.ind.of *εἶπον*, constative) 155.
δὲ (continuative conjunction) 11.
πρὸς (preposition with the accusative of extent, after a verb of speaking) 197.
τοὺς (acc.pl.masc.of the article in agreement with *μαθητὰς*) 9.
μαθητὰς (acc.pl.masc.of *μαθητής*, extent after a verb of speaking) 421.
αὐτοῦ (gen.sing.masc.of *αὐτός*, relationship) 16.

#2590 *ἀνένδεκτόν* (acc.sing.neut.of *ἀνένδεκτος*, predicate adjective).

impossible - Luke 17:1.

Meaning: *ἀ* privative plus *ἔνδεκτος* from *ἐνδέχομαι* (#2516). Hence, impossible; inadmissible, improper. As a predicate adjective with a genitive articular infinitive as the subject in Luke 17:1.

ἐστιν (3d.per.sing.pres.ind.of *εἰμί*, static) 86.
τοῦ (gen.sing.neut.of the article, description) 9.
τὰ (acc.pl.neut.of the article in agreement with *σκάνδαλα*) 9.
σκάνδαλα (acc.pl.neut.of *σκάνδαλον*, general reference) 1082.
μὴ (qualified negative conjunction with the infinitive) 87.
ἐλθεῖν (aor.inf.of *ἔρχομαι*, subject of *ἐστιν*) 146.
πλὴν (adversative conjunction) 944.
οὐαὶ (exclamation) 936.
δι' (preposition with the genitive, agent) 118.

οὗ (gen.sing.masc.of ὅς, agency) 65.
ἔρχεται (3d.per.sing.pres.ind.of ἔρχομαι, static) 146.

Translation - "And He said to His disciples, 'It is inevitable that impediments will occur, but woe (to him) through whom they come.'"

Comment: We have here τοῦ ἐλθεῖν, the articular infinitive in the genitive as the subject of the verb ἐστιν. "The origin of this nominative or subject is probably due to its use with impersonal expressions. Moulton (*Prolegomena*, 210) illustrates it by the Latin *humanum est errare*, where the force of the locative form *errare* may be seen by translating: 'There is something human in erring.' This may have been the original idiom, but it has gone beyond that to mean: 'Erring is human.' English students often forget that 'erring' is here infinitive, not participle, both in sense and history. It is a step further in the N.T. to see τοῦ and the inf.used as subject nominative. *Cf.* Lu.17:1; Ac.10:25; 1 Cor.16:4." (Robertson, *Grammar*, 1059). Literally we read "It is impossible that stumbling blocks will *not* come." Therefore, "It is inevitable that they will come."

The road which the true Christian disciple must follow is beset with difficulties (Mt.7:13,14). This is true because of human depravity. Even Christians are still in the flesh and, unfortunately, too often subject to it. Thus, whether we are aware of it or not, we offend each other. *Cf.*#1082 for a study on offenses. *Cf.* our comment on Mt.18:7.

Perfect love in the believer is the effective antidote against offense (1 John 2:10). Paul warned the Roman church against offenders (Rom.14:13; 16:17). The preaching of the cross is offensive to the unsaved (Gal.5:11; 1 Cor.1:23). Those who speak against the cross, as even Peter did are offensive to God (Mt.16:23). Eventually, at His second coming, our Lord will eliminate offenses (Mt.13:41).

After describing the judgment upon him who is the agent of the offense, with a particular reference perhaps to Judas Iscariot and to apostate teachers, Jesus made the application to offenders within the body of Christ. Thus the passage becomes a guide to Christian behavior *vis a vis* our Christian brothers who are offensive.

Verse 2 - "It were better for him that a millstone were hanged about his neck, and he cast into the sea, than that he should offend one of these little ones."

λυσιτελεῖ αὐτῷ εἰ λίθος μυλικὸς περίκειται περὶ τὸν τράχηλον αὐτοῦ καὶ ἔρριπται εἰς τὴν θάλασσαν ἢ ἵνα σκανδαλίσῃ τῶν μικρῶν τούτων ἕνα.

#2591 λυσιτελεῖ (3d.per.sing.pres.ind.of λυσιτελέω, static).

be better - Luke 17:2.

Meaning: A combination of λύω (#471) and τέλη (from τέλος ((#881))). Hence, properly, to pay taxes; to return a profit; hence, to be advantageous; to be better. Followed by the dative of personal interest - Luke 17:2.

αὐτῷ (dat.sing.masc.of αὐτός, personal advantage) 16.
εἰ (conditional particle in a first-class condition) 337.
λίθος (nom.sing.masc.of λίθος, subject of περίκειται) 290.

#2592 μυλικὸς (nom.sing.masc.of μυλικός, in agreement with λίθος).

of a mill - Luke 17:2.

Meaning: A combination of μύλη - "mill" and μύλος (#1250). Of a mill. Pertaining to a mill where grain is ground into flour - Luke 17:2.

περίκειται (3d.per.sing.pres.pass.ind.of περίκειμαι, first-class condition) 2351.
περὶ (preposition with the accusative of extent) 173.
τὸν (acc.sing.masc.of the article in agreement with τράχηλον) 9.
τράχηλον (acc.sing.masc.of τράχηλος, extent) 1252.
αὐτοῦ (gen.sing.masc.of αὐτός, possession) 16.
καὶ (adjunctive conjunction joining conditional clauses) 14.
ἔρριπται (3d.per.sing.perf.pass.ind.of ῥίπτω, consummative, first-class condition) 837.
εἰς (preposition with the accusative of extent) 140.
τὴν (acc.sing.fem.of the article in agreement with θάλασσαν) 9.
θάλασσαν (acc.sing.fem.of θάλασσα, extent) 374.
ἢ (disjunctive particle) 465.
ἵνα (conjunction introducing a subject clause) 114.
σκανδαλίσῃ (3d.per.sing.aor.act.subj.of σκανδαλίζω, sub-final) 503.
τῶν (gen.pl.masc.of the article in agreement with μικρῶν) 9.
μικρῶν (gen.pl.masc.of μικρός, partitive genitive) 901.
τούτων (gen.pl.masc.of οὗτος, in agreement with μικρῶν) 93.
ἕνα (acc.sing.masc.of εἷς, direct object of σκανδαλίσῃ) 469.

Translation - "It would be better for him if a millstone were tied about his neck and he were thrown into the sea, than that he offend one of these little ones."

Comment: *Cf.* comment on Mt.18:6; Mk.9:42. *Cf.*#837. Luke uses the same word as Matthew did to describe Judas' action with the betrayal money. Judas, of course, is in view as one of the chief offenders. Now Jesus applies this teaching about offending one another to Christian believers in

Verse 3- "Take heed to yourselves; if thy brother trespass against thee, rebuke him: and if he repent, forgive him."

προσέχετε ἑαυτοῖς. ἐὰν ἁμάρτῃ ὁ ἀδελφός σου ἐπιτίμησον αὐτῷ, καὶ ἐὰν μετανοήσῃ ἄφες αὐτῷ.

προσέχετε (2d.per.pl.pres.act.impv.of προσέχω, command) 555.
ἑαυτοῖς (dat.pl.masc.of ἑαυτός, reference) 288.
ἐὰν (conditional particle introducing a third-class condition) 363.
ἁμάρτῃ (3d.per.sing.aor.act.subj.of ἁμαρτάνω, third-class condition) 1260.

ὁ (nom.sing.masc.of the article in agreement with ἀδελφός) 9.
ἀδελφός (nom.sing.masc.of ἀδελφός, subject of ἁμάρτῃ) 15.
σου (gen.sing.masc.of σύ, relationship) 104.
ἐπιτίμησον (2d.per.sing.aor.act.impv.of ἐπιτιμάω, command) 757.
αὐτῷ (dat.sing.masc.of αὐτός, indirect object of ἐπιτίμησον) 16.
καὶ (adversative conjunction) 14.
ἐὰν (conditional particle introducing a third-class condition) 363.
μετανοήσῃ (3d.per.sing.aor.act.subj.of μετανοέω, third-class condition) 251.
ἄφες (2d.per.sing.aor.act.impv.of ἀφίημι, command) 319.
αὐτῷ (dat.sing.masc.of αὐτός, personal advantage) 16.

Translation - "Discipline yourselves. If your brother sins rebuke him, but if he repents, forgive him."

Comment: When offenses occur there is a loss of reward to the offender and the efficiency of the one offended is reduced. The Christian should therefore pay the closest attention, not only to his own conduct, as it relates to his own spiritual development, but also as it relates to the development of other saints in the fellowship. Watch (guard, discipline) yourselves. Note that our Lord's command applies first to ourselves. A great many Christians never watch themselves because they are too busy watching other people. We are to make every effort to answer our own prayer after we pray, "Lead us not into temptation and deliver us from the evil one."

If another Christian commits an offense, we are to take it up with him. A quick rebuke, if offered in the spirit of Gal.6:1, will result in fewer offenses. Social control is here declared to be a factor in upholding high moral standards within the group. If he repents as a result of your discussion, changes his mind, adjusts his attitude and asks for forgiveness, with appropriate restitution, insofar as he is able to pay it, if restitution is required, forgive him (Mt.6:14,15). *Cf.* comment on Mt.18:15-17; Gal.6:1. Peter, according to Mt.18:21, at this point asked Jesus how many times a Christian is expected to forgive a brother who makes a career out of offending. The answer is in Mt.18:22 and in

Verse 4 - "And if he trespass against thee seven times in a day, and seven times in a day turn again to thee, saying, I repent, thou shalt forgive him."

καὶ ἐὰν ἑπτάκις τῆς ἡμέρας ἁμαρτήσῃ εἰς σὲ καὶ ἑπτάκις ἐπιστρέψῃ πρὸς σὲ λέγων, Μετανοῶ, ἀφήσεις αὐτῷ.

καὶ (continuative conjunction) 14.
ἐὰν (conditional particle introducing a third-class condition) 363.
ἑπτάκις (numeral) 1269.
τῆς (gen.sing.fem.of the article in agreement with ἡμέρας) 9.
ἡμέρας (gen.sing.fem.of ἡμέρα, time description) 135.
ἁμαρτήσῃ (3d.per.sing.aor.act.subj.of ἁμαρτάνω,third-class condition) 1260.
εἰς (preposition with the accusative, like a dative of personal disadvantage) 140.

σὲ (acc.sing.masc.of σύ, like a dative of personal disadvantage) 104.
καὶ (adjunctive conjunction joining verbs) 14.
ἑπτάκις (numeral) 1269.
ἐπιστρέψῃ (3d.per.sing.aor.act.subj.of ἐπιστρέφω, third-class condition) 866.
πρὸς (preposition with the accusative of extent) 197.
σὲ (acc.sing.masc.of σύ, extent) 104.
λέγων (pres.act.part.nom.sing.masc.of λέγω, adverbial, complementary) 66.
Μετανοῶ (1st.per.sing.pres.act.ind.of μετανοέω, aoristic) 251.
ἀφήσεις (2d.per.sing.fut.act.ind.of ἀφίημι, imperative) 319.
αὐτῷ (dat.sing.masc.of αὐτός, personal advantage) 16.

Translation - "And if he sins against you seven times a day, and seven times he turns to you saying, 'I repent,' forgive him."

Comment: *Cf.* comment on Mt.18:22. This Christian brother is nothing if not consistent. Repeated offenses, however many, if followed by repeated apologies are to be met by repeated acts of forgiveness. The reason that this must be so is obvious. The opposite to forgiveness is judgment. We must either forgive or judge. And we dare not judge lest we ourselves be judged on the same basis. No one is qualified to judge except the One Who died for our sins. *Cf.* John 5:22; Mt.7:12; Rev.5:1-10.

If it be objected that a literal compliance with this directive on the part of a Christian would result in his exploitation by unscrupulous "brothers" who would offend and repent, offend and repent, offend and repent, - - it must be replied that such a rationalization does not change the plain teaching of our Lord. Even if such an obedient Christian should be reduced to Lazarus' status as a beggar, he would look forward to the compensating comfort and reward in eternity. It is also well to remember that there is a limit beyond which the child of God cannot go in his rebellion against the body of Christ without the intervention of the "Head over all things to the church" (Eph.1:22), Who may, if it pleases Him step in with disciplinary measures. The offended Christian, though often sinned against should leave the judgment up to the only One Who is qualified to administer it.

Verse 5 - "And the disciples said unto the Lord, Increase our faith."

Καὶ εἶπαν οἱ ἀπόστολοι τῷ κυρίῳ, Πρόσθες ἡμῖν πίστιν.

Καὶ (continuative conjunction) 14.
εἶπαν (3d.per.pl.aor.act.ind.of εἶπον, constative) 155.
οἱ (nom.pl.masc.of the article in agreement with ἀπόστολοι) 9.
ἀπόστολοι (nom.pl.masc.of ἀπόστολος, subject of εἶπαν) 844.
τῷ (dat.sing.masc.of the article in agreement with κυρίῳ) 9.
κυρίῳ (dat.sing.masc.of κύριος, indirect object of εἶπαν) 97.
Πρόσθες (2d.per.sing.2d.aor.act.impv.of προστίθημι, entreaty) 621.
ἡμῖν (dat.pl.masc.of ἐγώ, personal advantage) 123.
πίστιν (acc.sing.fem.of πίστις, direct object of πρόσθες) 728.

Translation - "And the apostles said to the Lord, 'Give us more faith.' "

Comment: *Cf.*#621. Place faith at our disposal. Place faith near us. Make faith available. Since the Apostles had some faith, the translation, "Increase faith for us" is not wrong, but it is not what the text says. To be quite informal we might translate, "Bring on the faith," in the spirit of one who enjoys some small quantity of something and is asking for more.

Verse 6 - "And the Lord said, If ye have faith as a grain of mustard seed, ye might say unto this sycamine tree, Be thou plucked up by the root, and be thou planted in the sea, and it should obey you."

εἶπεν δὲ ὁ κύριος, Εἰ ἔχετε πίστιν ὡς κόκκον σινάπεως, ἐλέγετε ἂν τῇ συκαμίνῳ (ταύτῃ), Ἐκριζώθητι καὶ φυτεύθητι ἐν τῇ θαλάσσῃ, καὶ ὑπήκουσεν ἂν ὑμῖν.

εἶπεν (3d.per.sing.aor.act.ind.of *εἶπον*, constative) 155.
δὲ (continuative conjunction) 11.
ὁ (nom.sing.masc.of the article in agreement with *κύριος*) 9.
κύριος (nom.sing.masc.of *κύριος*, subject of *εἶπεν*) 97.
Εἰ (conditional particle introducing a first-class condition) 337.
ἔχετε (2d.per.pl.pres.act.ind.of *ἔχω*, first-class condition) 82.
πίστιν (acc.sing.fem.of *πίστις*, direct object of *ἔχετε*) 728.
ὡς (particle introducing a comparative clause) 128.
κόκκον (acc.sing.masc.of *κόκκος*, general reference) 1067.
σινάπεως (gen.sing.neut.of *σίναπι*, description) 1068.
ἐλέγετε (2d.per.pl.imp.act.ind.of *λέγω*, mixed condition) 66.
ἂν (contingent particle in the apodosis of a mixed condition) 205.
τῇ (dat.sing.sfem.of the article in agreement with *συκαμίνῳ*) 9.

#2593 *συκαμίνῳ* (dat.sing.fem.of *συκάμινος*, indirect object of *ἐλέγετε*).

sycamine tree - Luke 17:6.

Meaning: a tree having the form and foliage of a mulberry tree, but with fruit resembling a fig. A sycamine tree - Luke 17:6.

(*ταύτῃ*) (dat.sing.fem.of *οὗτος*, in agreement with *συκαμίνῳ*) 93.
Ἐκριζώθητι (2d.per.sing.aor.pass.impv.of *ἐκριζόω*, command) 1062.
καὶ (adjunctive conjunction joining verbs) 14.
φυτεύθητι (2d.per.sing.aor.pass.impv.of *φυτεύω*, command) 1154.
ἐν (preposition with the locative of place where) 80.
τῇ (loc.sing.fem.of the article in agreement with *θαλάσσῃ*) 9.
θαλάσσῃ (loc.sing.fem.of *θάλασσα*, place where) 374.
καὶ (continuative conjunction) 14.
ὑπήκουσεν (3d.per.sing.aor.act.ind.of *ὑπακούω*, mixed condition) 760.
ἂν (contingent particle in a mixed condition) 205.
ὑμῖν (dat.pl.masc.of *σύ*, personal advantage) 104.

Translation - "And the Lord said, 'If you have faith as big as a mustard seed, you might have said to this mulberry tree, 'Be uprooted and planted in the sea,' and it would have obeyed you.' "

Comment: We have a mixed condition. The protasis has εἰ ἔχετε πίστιν - a first-class condition. The premise is assumed to be true. Surely the apostles had that much faith, although the comparative clause with ὡς indicates that their faith was not impressive. But in the apodosis we have the imperfect indicative with ἂν in the first verb (ἐλέγετε ἂν) and the aorist with ἂν in the second (ὑπήκουσεν). Mixed conditions often occur in the New Testament. Robertson comments: "The human mind does not always work in stereotyped forms, however excellent they are. Grammatical construction is merely the expression of the mental conception. Freedom must be acknowledged without any apology. I say these somewhat commonplace things because of the bill of "exceptions" which meet us in so many grammars at this point. It would have been a miracle if the four classes of conditions were never "mixed," that is, if the protasis did not belong to one class, while the apodosis fell in another. . . Thus in Lu. 17:6, εἰ ἔχετε, ἐλέγετε ἂν, we have a protasis of the first class (determined as fulfilled) and the apodosis of the second (determined as unfulfilled)." (Robertson, *Grammar*, 1022). Since Jesus was willing to grant that the Apostles had some faith, albeit not to an impressive degree, He tells them what they *might have done* if they had exercised their faith. The secondary tenses with ἂν in the apodosis indicate that the Apostles did not in fact command the trees to be plucked up by the roots and transplanted in the sea. Nor did the trees obey such a command, since it was never given. Christians ought not to pray for an increase in faith until they have exercised what faith they already have. The Apostles did not realize how powerful faith is, or they might have exercised it more. They were delighted once that "even the demons (were) subject unto (them)" (Luke 10:17), but it had never occurred to them that they might even transplant a forest. Jesus makes His point with hyperbole. He exaggerates the size of their faith and at the other extreme the greatness of the miracle which it would accomplish. If faith, no larger than a mustard seed could accomplish the miracle which He describes, why had they not used it more? It is a dramatic statement of the superiority of faith, with its powerful connection with the sovereign God of miracles, over the realms of reason and experience. Even so small an amount of faith can perform the miracle which Jesus suggests. How much faith does it take for the Christian who suffers offenses seven times a day to forgive the offender seven times a day? Why should he not be able to submit to these repeated acts of injustice and wait patiently for the time when in eternity all injustices will be rectified? Why should the Christian indulge in self-pity, and thus reduce his own efficiency in the service for the King, because he has been repeatedly imposed upon by his erring brother? Is that not our role as servants of God? This is the thought of verses 7-10.

Verse 7 - "But which of you, having a servant plowing or feeding cattle, will say to him by and by, when he is come from the field, Go and sit down to meat?"

Τίς δὲ ἐξ ὑμῶν δοῦλον ἔχων ἀροτριῶντα ἢ ποιμαίνοντα, ὃς εἰσελθόντι ἐκ τοῦ ἀγροῦ ἐρεῖ αὐτῷ, Εὐθέως παρελθὼν ἀνάπεσε,

Τίς (nom.sing.masc.of *τίς*, interrogative pronoun, subject of *ἐρεῖ*) 281.
δὲ (explanatory conjunction) 11.
ἐξ (preposition with the partitive genitive) 19.
ὑμῶν (gen.pl.masc.of *σύ*, partitive genitive) 104.
δοῦλον (acc.sing.masc.of *δοῦλος*, direct object of *ἔχων*) 725.
ἔχων (pres.act.part.nom.sing.masc.of *ἔχω*, adverbial, complementary) 82.

#2594 *ἀροτριῶντα* (pres.act.part.acc.sing.masc.of *ἀροτριάω*, adverbial, complementary).

plow - Luke 17:7; 1 Cor.9:10,10.

Meaning: Cf.ἄροτρον (#2362).To plow. Parabolically in Luke 17:7; in Paul's teaching in 1 Cor.9:10,10.

ἢ (disjunctive particle) 465.
ποιμαίνοντα (pres.act.part.acc.sing.masc.of *ποιμαίνω*, adverbial, complementary) 164.
ὃς (nom.sing.masc.of *ὅς*, relative pronoun, nominative absolute) 65.
εἰσελθόντι (2d.aor.part.dat.sing.masc.of *εἰσέρχομαι*, adverbial, temporal) 234.
ἐκ (preposition with the ablative of separation) 19.
τοῦ (abl.sing.masc.of the article in agreement with *ἀγροῦ*) 9.
ἀγροῦ (abl.sing.masc.of *ἀγρός*, separation) 626.
ἐρεῖ (3d.per.sing.fut.act.ind.of *εἶπον*, deliberative) 155.
αὐτῷ (dat.sing.masc.of *αὐτός*, indirect object of *ἐρεῖ*) 16.
Εὐθέως (adverbial) 392.
παρελθὼν (aor.part.nom.sing.masc.of *παρέρχομαι*, adverbial, temporal) 467.
ἀνάπεσε (2d.per.sing.aor.act.impv.of *ἀναπίπτω*, command) 1184.

Translation - "Now which of you who has a servant plowing or keeping sheep, who, when he comes in from the field, will say to him, 'Come at once and sit down at the table.' "

Comment: Τίς, the interrogative pronoun, with the partitive genitive *ἐξ ὑμῶν*. "Which one of you disciples . . . . ?" The complementary participle *ἔχων* explains the situation. Jesus is speaking of one who has a servant who is working in the field - the participles suggest what he might have been doing - "plowing or grazing livestock." Will he say to this slave when he comes in from the field, "Quickly, go ahead and eat"? Literally, "Pass by and sit down at the table." An unlikely story, Jesus thinks. No one with a servant under those circumstances is going to allow his slave to eat first, while the master waits. On the contrary in

Verse 8 - "And will not rather say unto him, Make ready wherewith I may sup, and gird thyself, and serve me, till I have eaten and drunken; and afterward thou shalt eat and drink?"

ἀλλ' οὐχὶ ἐρεῖ αὐτῷ, Ἑτοίμασον τί δειπνήσω, καὶ περιζωσάμενος διακόνει μοι ἕως φάγω καὶ πίω, καὶ μετὰ ταῦτα φάγεσαι καί πίεσαι σύ.

ἀλλ' (alternative conjunction) 342.
οὐχὶ (summary negative conjunction with the indicative in rhetorical question) 130.
ἐρεῖ (3d.per.sing.fut.act.ind.of εἶπον, rhetorical question) 155.
αὐτῷ (dat.sing.masc.of αὐτός, indirect object of ἐρεῖ) 16.
Ἑτοίμασον (2d.per.sing.aor.act.impv.of ἑτοιμάζω, command) 257.
τί (acc.sing.neut.of τίς, relative pronoun in indirect question) 281.

#2595 δειπνήσω (1st.per.sing.fut.act.ind.of δειπνέω, deliberative future in indirect question).

sup - Luke 17:8; 1 Cor.11:25; Rev.3:20.
supper - Luke 22:20.

Meaning: To eat food. In an articular infinitive with μετὰ and the accusative, - "after eating" - 1 Cor.11:25; Luke 22:20. Parabolically in Luke 17:8; metaphorically in Rev.3:20 - "I will share with him and he with me all spiritual blessings."

καὶ (adjunctive conjunction joining verbs) 14.
περιζωσάμενος (aor.mid.part.nom.sing.masc.of περιζώννυμι, adverbial, temporal) 2486.
διακόνει (2d.per.sing.pres.act.impv.of διακονέω, command) 367.
μοι (dat.sing.masc.of ἐγώ, personal advantage) 123.
ἕως (conjunction in an indefinite temporal clause) 71.
φάγω (1st.per.sing.aor.act.subj.of ἐσθίω, indefinite temporal clause) 610.
καὶ (adjunctive conjunction joining verbs) 14.
πίω (1st.per.sing.aor.act.subj.of πίνω, indefinite temporal clause) 611.
καὶ (continuative conjunction) 14.
μετὰ (preposition with the accusative of time extent) 50.
ταῦτα (acc.pl.neut.of οὗτος, time extent) 93.
φάγεσαι (2d.per.sing.fut.act.ind.of ἐσθίω, predictive) 610.
καὶ (adjunctive conjunction joining verbs) 14.
πίεσαι (2d.per.sing.fut.act.ind.of πίνω, predictive) 611.
σύ (nom.sing.masc.of σύ, subject of φάγεσαι and πίεσαι) 104.

Translation - "Rather will he not say to him, 'Prepare what I will eat, and get dressed and wait on me while I eat and drink, and after that you yourself may eat and drink."

Comment: ἀλλ' is the alternative conjunction. The question is whether the procedure described in verse 7 or that in verse 8 was followed. Did the servant eat first or (alternative ἀλλα') did he serve his master first and eat later? Note that the servant was not permitted to serve his master until he had bathed and dressed properly for the occasion. He was forbidden to serve in the clothing which he wore in the field as a plowman. Furthermore he was to serve his master throughout the entire meal. ἕως with the two subjunctives in φάγω and πίω indicates an indefinite time period.

The good servant serves. The master is the one who is to be served. The good servant takes the subordinate position. He permits himself to be exploited, if necessary. He suffers in silence and forgives as often as his forgiveness is sought. A good servant does not expect to be treated like a lord. Does the good servant expect to be congratulated and thanked because of all of this? Jesus thinks not in verse 9 and closes the context in verse 10 by admonishing the apostles to be good servants.

Verse 9 - "Doth he thank that servant because he did the things that were commanded him? I trow not."

μὴ ἔχει χάριν τῷ δούλῳ ὅτι ἐποίησεν τὰ διαταχθέντα;

μὴ (qualified negative conjunction in a rhetorical question expecting a negative reply) 87.

ἔχει (3d.per.sing.pres.act.ind.of *ἔχω*, static) 82.

χάριν (acc.sing.fem.of *χάρις*, direct object of *ἔχει*) 1700.

τῷ (dat.sing.masc.of the article in agreement with *δούλῳ*) 9.

δούλῳ (dat.sing.masc.of *δοῦλος*, personal advantage) 725.

ὅτι (conjunction introducing a subordinate causal clause) 211.

ἐποίησεν (3d.per.sing.aor.act.ind.of *ποιέω*, constative) 127.

τὰ (acc.pl.neut.of the article in agreement with *διαταχθέντα*) 9.

διαταχθέντα (aor.pass.part.acc.pl.neut.of *διατάσσω*, substantival, direct object of *ἐποίησεν*) 904.

Translation - "He does not thank the servant because he did the things which were ordered, does he?"

Comment: "There is no adequate reason which could account for the omission of *αὐτῷ* or *οὐ δοκῶ*, if either had been present originally; whereas the retort *οὐ δοκῶ* has the appearance of being a marginal comment that found its way into the Western text, and more than one scribe would have been likely to attach *αὐτῷ* to *τὰ διαταχθέντα*, which seems to cry out for such a complement." (Metzger, *Textual Commentary*, 166). *οὐ δοκῶ* adds nothing to the text in any case, since the rhetorical question clearly expects a negative reply. Do we expect a master to thank a servant because he was obedient? Of course not. Jesus has set the scene, told the story and raised an obviously negative rhetorical question. Now He makes the application in

Verse 10 - "So likewise ye, when ye shall have done all those things which are commanded you, say, We are unprofitable servants: we have done that which

was our duty to do."

οὕτως καὶ ὑμεῖς, ὅταν ποιήσητε πάντα τὰ διαταχθέντα ὑμῖν, λέγετε ὅτι Δοῦλοι ἀχρεῖοί ἐσμεν. ὃ ὠφείλομεν ποιῆσαι πεποιήκαμεν.

οὕτως (demonstrative adverb) 74.
καὶ (adjunctive conjunction, joining substantives) 14.
ὑμεῖς (nom.pl.masc.of σύ, subject of λέγετε) 104.
ὅταν (conjunction introducing an indefinite temporal clause) 436.
ποιήσητε (2d.per.pl.aor.act.subj.of ποιέω, indefinite temporal clause) 127.
πάντα (acc.pl.neut.of πᾶς, in agreement with διαταχθέντα) 67.
τὰ (acc.pl.neut.of the article in agreement with διαταχθέντα) 9.
διαταχθέντα (aor.pass.part.acc.pl.neut.of διατάσσω, substantival, direct object of ποιήσητε) 904.
ὑμῖν (dat.pl.masc.of σύ, indirect object of διαταχθέντα) 104.
λέγετε (2d.per.pl.pres.act.ind.of λέγω, customary) 66.
ὅτι (recitative) 211.
Δοῦλοι (nom.pl.masc.of δοῦλος, predicate nominative) 725.
ἀχρεῖοι (nom.pl.masc.of ἀχρεῖος, in agreement with δοῦλοι) 1544.
ἐσμεν (1st.per.pl.pres.ind.of εἰμί, aoristic) 86.
ὃ (acc.sing.neut.of ὅς, direct object of πεποιήκαμεν) 65.
ὠφείλομεν (1st.per.pl.imp.act.ind.of ὀφείλω, progressive duration) 1277.
ποιῆσαι (aor.act.inf.of ποιέω, complementary) 127.
πεποιήκαμεν (1st.per.pl.perf.act.ind.of ποιέω, consummative) 127.

Translation - "In the same way also you, when you have done all that was commanded you, say, 'We are poor servants. We have been doing that which we were under obligation to do.' "

Comment: οὕτως tells us that the truth in the parable just finished is to be applied in some spiritual way to what follows.

When a Christian lives in obedience to all of the ethical ideals that Christ has set before His disciples, he will be forced to admit that the Christian life is not designed to enrich one in the wealth of this world. Our Lord has presented us with quite a long list of duties. It calls for complete crucifixion of self. We are to forgive our trespassing brother as often as he asks to be forgiven, even though forgiveness costs us the opportunity cost which, under the law of Moses, could be collected - an eye for an eye, a tooth for a tooth, dollar for dollar. Any Christian who obeys that order will find that he is a failure, when judged by the standards of the unsaved world. "We are poor servants, indeed." Not *poor* in the sense of inefficient or inept, but financially poor. *Cf.*#1544 for ἀχρεῖος. The man in Mt.25:30 was ἀχρεῖος because he missed the opportunity to invest his lord's talent in the money market. The good Christian does all of that which it has been his duty to do. He has done it consistently and completely (perfect tense in πεποιήκαμεν). It was always our duty to do it (imperfect tense in ὠφείλομεν). What was always our duty to do, we have always done. As a result, we are poor in this world's goods. But rewards are coming, as they came for Lazarus. In the meantime should Christ congratulate us for superior service as Christian disciples? No more than the man in the story praised his slave for serving his master first, while he took second place. That is what is normally expected of a servant.

This passage, coming after the two parables of chapter 16 and the teaching on the inevitable offenses which Christians must learn to absorb (Luke 17:1-4), followed by the teaching on the need for great faith (Luke 17:5-6), will serve to warn the obedient Christian disciple not to expect high words of praise and also not to feel sorry for himself. Sometimes, when we forget to seek the fellowship of our Lord in prayer and become depressed we imagine that we are carrying more than our share of the load as we endure ". . . the slings and arrows of outrageous fortune," but we must remember that we were clearly warned by our Lord that the world that hated Him will not be friendly to us if we identify with Him.

This passage will also serve to teach us that though we may make friends with mammon so that we may serve the Lord, we shall never command a great quantity of mammon. Therefore we should look forward to "Abraham's bosom" and we should stop crying. "Our light affliction, which is but for a moment, worketh for us a far more exceeding and eternal weight of glory, while we look not at the things which are seen, but at the things which are not seen: for the things which are seen are temporal; but the things which are not seen are eternal" (2 Cor.4:17-18).

We return now to John's gospel and the story of another Lazarus.

Jesus Raises Lazarus From the Dead

(John 11:1-44)

John 11:1 - "Now a certain man was sick named Lazarus, of Bethany, the town of Mary and her sister Martha."

Ἦν δέ τις ἀσθενῶν, Λάζαρος ἀπὸ Βηθανίας, ἐκ τῆς κώμης Μαρίας καὶ Μάρθας τῆς ἀδελφῆς αὐτῆς.

Ἦν (3d.per.sing.imp.ind.of *εἰμί*, progressive duration) 86.

δέ (explanatory conjunction) 11.

τις (nom.sing.masc.of the indefinite pronoun *τις*, in agreement with *ἀσθενῶν*) 486.

ἀσθενῶν (pres.part.nom.sing.masc.of *ἀσθενέω*, substantival, subject of *ἦν*) 857.

#2596 *Λάζαρος* (nom.sing.masc.of *Λάζαρος*, appellation).

Lazarus - John 11:1,2,5,11,14,43; 12:1,2,9,10,17.

Meaning: Lazarus of Bethany. Brother of Mary and Martha, whom Jesus raised from the dead - John 11:1,2,5,11,14,43; 12:1,2,9,10,17. Not to be confused with #2579).

ἀπὸ (preposition with the ablative of source) 70.

Βηθανίας (abl.sing.fem.of Βηθανία, source) 1363.
ἐκ (preposition with the ablative of source) 19.
τῆς (abl.sing.fem.of the article in agreement with κώμης) 9.
κώμης (abl.sing.fem.of κώμη, source) 834.
Μαρίας (gen.sing.fem.of Μαρία, description) 2439.
καὶ (adjunctive conjunction joining nouns) 14.
Μάρθας (gen.sing.fem.of Μάρθα, description) 2436.
τῆς (gen.sing.fem.of the article in agreement with ἀδελφῆς) 9.
ἀδελφῆς (gen.sing.fem.of ἀδελφή, apposition) 1025.
αὐτῆς (gen.sing.fem.of αὐτός, relationship) 16.

Translation - "Now there was a certain sick man, Lazarus, from Bethany, of the village of Mary and Martha, her sister."

Comment: δέ is explanatory. Lazarus had been sick for some time as the imperfect periphrastic ἦν . . . ἀσθενῶν indicates. Bethany is about two miles from Jerusalem, to the southeast, just beyond the Mount of Olives. The place was a village where he lived with Mary and Martha, his sisters. John, writing in the l0th decade to a Greek audience in Ephesus, was aware that they were not familiar with things Jewish and he includes explanatory material which would be unnecessary if he were writing exclusively for a Jewish audience.

Verse 2 - "It was that Mary which anointed the Lord with ointment, and wiped his feet with her hair, whose brother Lazarus was sick."

ἦν δὲ Μαριὰμ ἡ ἀλείψασα τὸν κύριον μύρῳ καὶ ἐκμάξασα τοὺς πόδας αὐτου ταῖς θριξὶν αὐτῆς, ἧς ὁ ἀδελφὸς Λάζαρος ἠσθένει.

ἦν (3d.per.sing.imp.ind.of εἰμί, progressive description) 86.
δὲ (explanatory conjunction) 11.
Μαριὰμ (nom.sing.fem.of Μαριάμ, subject of ἦν) 2439.
ἡ (nom.sing.fem.of the article in agreement with ἀλείψασα) 9.
ἀλείψασα (aor.act.part.nom.sing.fem.of ἀλείφω, substantival, apposition) 589.
τὸν (acc.sing.masc.of the article in agreement with κύριον) 9.
κύριον (acc.sing.masc.of κύριος, direct object of ἀλείψασα) 97.
μύρῳ (instru.sing.neut.of μύρον,means) 1562.
καὶ (adjunctive conjunction, joining participles) 14.
ἐκμάξασα (aor.act.part.nom.sing.fem.of ἐκμάσσω, substantival, apposition) 2167.
τοὺς (acc.pl.masc.of the article in agreement with πόδας) 9.
πόδας (acc.pl.masc.of πούς, direct object of ἐκμάξασα) 353.
αὐτοῦ (gen.sing.masc.of αὐτός, possession) 16.
ταῖς (instru.pl.fem.of the article in agreement with θριξὶν) 9.
θριξὶν (instru.pl.fem.of θρίξ, means) 261.
αὐτῆς (gen.sing.fem.of αὐτός, possession) 16.
ἧς (gen.sing.fem.of ὅς, relative pronoun, relationship) 65.

ὁ (nom.sing.masc.of the article in agreement with ἀδελφὸς) 9.
ἀδελφὸς (nom.sing.masc.of ἀδελφός, subject of ἠσθένει) 15.
Λάζαρος (nom.sing.masc.of Λάζαρος, apposition) 2596.
ἠσθένει (3d.per.sing.imp.act.ind.of ἀσθενέω, progressive description) 857.

Translation - "Now Mary was the one who anointed the Lord with ointment and wiped His feet with her hair, whose brother, Lazarus, was sick."

Comment: The main verb is ἠσθένει, joined to the definite relative pronoun ἧς, which has Μαριὰμ as its antecedent. Μαριὰμ is identified by apposition by the two aorist participles ἀλείψασα and ἐκμάξασα. Mary, whose brother, Lazarus, was sick is the same one who anointed and wiped Jesus' feet. This event took place at a dinner party in Bethany, six days before the Passover and Jesus' death, as recorded in John 12:1-8. This is probably the same event as that recorded in Mt.26:6-13 and Mk.14:3-9. It is *not* the same event recorded in Lk.7:36-50. Mary of Bethany, the sister of Lazarus, is not the converted prostitute of Luke's account. That event took place at least twenty-one months prior to the event of John 12:1-8; Mt.26:6-13 and Mk.14:3-9.

Verse 3 - "Therefore his sisters sent unto him, saying, Lord, behold, he whom thou lovest is sick."

ἀπέστειλαν οὖν αἱ ἀδελφαὶ πρὸς αὐτὸν λέγουσαι, Κύριε, ἴδε ὃν φιλεῖς ἀσθενεῖ.

ἀπέστειλαν (3d.per.pl.aor.act.ind.of ἀποστέλλω, constative) 215.
οὖν (inferential conjunction) 68.
αἱ (nom.pl.fem.of the article in agreement with ἀδελφαὶ) 9.
ἀδελφαὶ (nom.pl.fem.of ἀδελφή, subject of ἀπέστειλαν) 1025.
πρὸς (preposition with the accusative of extent) 197.
αὐτὸν (acc.sing.masc.of αὐτός, extent) 16.
λέγουσαι (pres.act.part.nom.pl.fem.of λέγω, adverbial, complementary) 66.
Κύριε (voc.sing.masc.of κύριος, address) 97.
ἴδε (2d.per.sing.aor.act.impv.of ὁράω, entreaty) 144.
ὃν (acc.sing.masc.of ὅς, relative pronoun, direct object of φιλεῖς) 65.
φιλεῖς (2d.per.sing.pres.act.ind.of φιλέω, aoristic) 566.
ἀσθενεῖ (3d.per.sing.pres.act.ind.of ἀσθενέω, aoristic) 857.

Translation - "Therefore his sisters sent to him, saying, Lord, Look! The one whom you love is sick.' "

Comment: Mary and Martha knew Whom to call in an emergency. Mary was deeply devoted to Jesus. She expressed her love for Him a little later at the dinner party (John 12:1-8). It was natural that when Lazarus' condition became critical they should send for Jesus. Note the form of the message. There was not a word about themselves - only a reference to Lazarus and his illness and a comment about the close friendship between Jesus and their brother. They knew that Jesus loved them too, but they did not seek to exploit the fact. Now we have an interesting parenthesis containing much valuable teaching, in verses 4-17.

Verse 4 - "When Jesus heard that he said, This sickness is not unto death, but for the glory of God, that the Son of God might be glorified thereby."

ἀκούσας δὲ ὁ Ἰησοῦς εἶπεν, Αὕτη ἡ ἀσθένεια οὐκ ἔστιν πρὸς θάνατον ἀλλ' ὑπὲρ τῆς δόξης τοῦ θεοῦ, ἵνα δοξασθῇ ὁ υἱὸς τοῦ θεοῦ δι' αὐτῆς.

ἀκούσας (aor.act.part.nom.sing.masc.of ἀκούω, adverbial, temporal) 148.
δὲ (explanatory conjunction) 11.
ὁ (nom.sing.masc.of the article in agreement with Ἰησοῦς) 9.
Ἰησοῦς (nom.sing.masc.of Ἰησοῦς, subject of εἶπεν) 3.
εἶπεν (3d.per.sing.aor.act.ind.of εἶπον, constative) 155.
Αὕτη (nom.sing.fem.of οὗτος, in agreement with ἀσθένεια) 93.
ἡ (nom.sing.fem.of the article in agreement with ἀσθένεια) 9.
ἀσθένεια (nom.sing.fem.of ἀσθένεια, subject of ἔστιν) 740.
οὐκ (summary negative conjunction with the indicative) 130.
ἔστιν (3d.per.sing.pres.ind.of εἰμί, aoristic) 86.
πρὸς (preposition with the accusative, purpose) 197.
θάνατον (acc.sing.masc.of θάνατος, purpose) 381.
ἀλλ' (alternative conjunction) 342.
ὑπὲρ (preposition with the ablative, "for the sake of. . . ") 545.
τῆς (abl.sing.fem.of the article in agreement with δόξης) 9.
δόξης (abl.sing.fem.of δόξα, "for the sake of") 361.
τοῦ (gen.sing.masc.of the article in agreement with θεοῦ) 9.
θεοῦ (gen.sing.masc.of θεός, possession) 124.
ἵνα (conjunction introducing a subfinal clause) 114.
δοξασθῇ (3d.per.sing.aor.pass.subj.of δοξάζω, purpose/result) 461.
ὁ (nom.sing.masc.of the article in agreement with υἱὸς) 9.
υἱὸς (nom.sing.masc.of υἱός, subject of δοξασθῇ) 5.
τοῦ (gen.sing.masc.of the article in agreement with θεοῦ) 9.
θεοῦ (gen.sing.masc.of θεός, relationship) 124.
δι' (preposition with the genitive, means) 118.
αὐτῆς (gen.sing.fem.of αὐτός, means) 16.

Translation - "Now when He heard it Jesus said, 'This sickness will not result in death, but it is for the glory of God, in order (and with the result) that the Son of God will be glorified by means of it.' "

Comment: One would normally expect when Jesus heard of Lazarus' illness that He would hasten to his bedside. On the contrary He calmly announced what we have in this verse. Note πρὸς with the accusative of purpose and ὑπὲρ with the ablative - "in behalf (or for the sake) of" and διά with the genitive of means. Yet Jesus knew that Lazarus would die. In fact, He deliberately postponed His return to Bethany until his friend was dead. But death was not the ultimate purpose for the sickness. The glory of God and the glorification of the Son of God were to be both the purpose and the result of this episode. Thus the ἵνα clause is subfinal. Is not this the original purpose and final result of all that God does in human history? (Eph.2:7).

Verse 5 - "Now Jesus loved Martha and her sister, and Lazarus."

ἠγάπα δὲ ὁ Ἰησοῦς τὴν Μάρθαν καὶ τὴν ἀδελφὴν αὐτῆς καὶ τὸν Λάζαρον.

ἠγάπα (3d.per.sing.imp.act.ind.of ἀγαπάω, progressive duration 540.
δὲ (explanatory conjunction) 11.
ὁ (nom.sing.masc.of the article in agreement with Ἰησοῦς) 9.
Ἰησοῦς (nom.sing.masc.of Ἰησοῦς, subject of ἠγάπα) 3.
τὴν (acc.sing.fem.of the article in agreement with Μάρθαν) 9.
Μάρθαν (acc.sing.fem.of Μάρθα, direct object of ἠγάπα) 2436.
καὶ (adjunctive conjunction joining nouns) 14.
τὴν (acc.sing.fem.of the article in agreement with ἀδελφὴν) 9.
ἀδελφὴν (acc.sing.fem.of ἀδελφή, direct object of ἠγάπα) 1025.
αὐτῆς (gen.sing.fem.of αὐτός, relationship) 16.
καὶ (adjunctive conjunction joining nouns) 14.
τὸν (acc.sing.masc.of the article in agreement with Λάζαρον) 9.
Λάζαρον (acc.sing.masc.of Λάζαρος, direct object of ἠγάπα) 2596.

Translation - "Now Jesus always loved Martha and her sister and Lazarus."

Comment: We note John's use of δὲ in the explantory sense in vss.1, 2, 4 and 5. The continuing steadfast love of Jesus for His friends is indicated by the imperfect tense in ἠγάπα. Since other scriptures teach that Jesus loves all the world this special mention would seem to indicate a special devotion and fondness in a human sense, which Jesus felt for Martha, Mary and Lazarus. The Mormon suggestion that this love involved sex is an exceptionally hellish invention. It illustrates how heretics, who ignore the Bible when it denies what they wish to believe, read into the Bible what they want it to teach.

The supposed distinction between ἀγαπάω and φιλέω will not endure the light of investigation. *Cf.*#'s 540 and 566. Instances abound to show each word in the "wrong" sense for those who have imagined a difference between them.

Verse 6 - "When he had heard therefore that he was sick, he abode two days still in the same place where he was."

ὡς οὖν ἤκουσεν ὅτι ἀσθενεῖ, τότε μὲν ἔμεινεν ἐν ᾧ ἦν τόπῳ δύο ἡμέρας.

ὡς (conjunction introducing a definite temporal clause) 128.
οὖν (inferential conjunction) 68.
ἤκουσεν (3d.per.sing.aor.act.ind.of ἀκούω, constative, definite temporal clause) 148.
ὅτι (conjunction introducing an object clause in indirect discourse) 211.
ἀσθενεῖ (3d.per.sing.pres.act.ind.of ἀσθενέω, indirect discourse) 857.
τότε (temporal adverb) 166.
μὲν (particle of affirmation) 300.
ἔμεινεν (3d.per.sing.aor.act.ind.of μένω, constative) 864.

ἐν (preposition with the locative of place where) 80.
ᾧ (loc.sing.masc.of ὅς, relative pronoun, place where) 65.
ἦν (3d.per.sing.imp.ind.of εἰμί, description) 86.
τόπῳ (loc.sing.masc.of τόπος, place where) 1019.
δύο (numeral) 385.
ἡμέρας (acc.pl.fem.of ἡμέρα, time extent) 135.

Translation - "When therefore He heard that he was sick, he then stayed in the place where in fact he had been for two days."

Comment: What a paradox! Jesus loved Lazarus and his sisters. Therefore when He heard that Lazarus was sick He deliberately delayed his departure to Bethany, despite the fact that He had the message from the sisters, urging Him to come at once. Only would the Incarnate Son of God, Who is supreme even over death, have done this. On the surface it looks like a callous disregard for the feelings of those He loved so much. Poor and helpless mortals that we are, powerless to arrest the hand of death, either upon us or upon our loved ones, we would have hastened to Lazarus' bedside to bid a final farewell to him and to comfort his bereaved sisters. Not Jesus. He deliberately stayed on for two more days. Let him die! How could the Son of Man be glorified any more than He already had been, if He had hastened back to Bethany to prevent Lazarus' death? He had healed hundreds of sick people. Nobody ever died in the living presence of Jesus. If Jesus had gone back to Bethany forthwith, Lazarus would have recovered. No. The divine policy was to stay away until he died. That gives opportunity for what happened. It is important for all Christians to remember that even the death of a loved one glorifies the Son of God. (Ps.116:15).

Jesus' command of this situation and the ultimate disposition of the matter can be explained only in terms of His essential deity. In fact He did not need the message from the girls that Lazarus was sick. He was already aware of the fact. He also knew that his condition was worsening and He knew when he died. He knew how far He was from Bethany and the time required to go there. He planned the trip so as to arrive at the tomb four days *too late.* Why? Because He also knew what He was going to do about it when He arrived. AndHe announced to the disciples that Lazarus' illness was all a part of the divine plan of the ages, for the purpose of glorifying God and bringing honor to Himself. The result, of course was consistent with the purpose, - a fact which is always the case when the Sovereign God is directing the course of events.

Verse 7 - "Then after that, saith he to His disciples, Let us go into Judea again."

ἔπειτα μετὰ τοῦτο λέγει τοῖς μαθηταῖς,Ἄγωμεν εἰς τὴν Ἰουδαίαν πάλιν.

ἔπειτα (temporal adverb) 2566.
μετὰ (preposition with the accusative of time extent) 50.
τοῦτο (acc.sing.neut.of οὗτος, time extent) 93.
λέγει (3d.per.sing.pres.act.ind.of λέγω, historical) 66.
τοῖς (dat.pl.masc.of the article in agreement with μαθηταῖς) 9.

μαθηταῖς (dat.pl.masc.of μαθητής, indirect object of λέγει) 421.
Ἄγωμεν (1st.per.pl.pres.act.subj.of ἄγω, hortatory) 876.
εἰς (preposition with the accusative of extent) 140.
τὴν (acc.sing.fem.of the article in agreement with Ἰουδαίαν) 9.
Ἰουδαίαν (acc.sing.fem.of Ἰουδαία, extent) 134.
πάλιν (adverbial) 355.

Translation - "Then, after this, He said to the disciples, 'Let us go into Judea again."

Comment: *μετὰ τοῦτο, i.e.* after the two days of deliberate delay in Perea had elapsed. Jesus knew that Lazarus had now died. It was time to go to Bethany. Note the hortatory subjunctive in *Ἄγωμεν. Cf.*#876 for other examples.

Jesus is now less than three months away from Calvary. Bethany is less than two miles from the Mount of Olives and the garden where He will sweat drops of blood. Lazarus lies dead almost within the shadow of Golgotha. Yet Jesus goes to Bethany. He must demonstrate His own superiority over death, before He yields voluntarily to the hideous,hellish thing upon the cross. It is as though He was saying, "I will stage a demonstration within the shadow of the court of Annas and Caiphas, that they are dealing with One Who is greater than death. Let us go to Judea."

The disciples, despite the advantages of His teaching and constant companionship, still did not understand, as is clear from their objection in

Verse 8 - "His disciples say unto him, Master, the Jews of late sought to stone thee; and goest thou thither again?"

λέγουσιν αὐτῷ οἱ μαθηταί, Ῥαββί, νῦν ἐζήτουν σε λιθάσαι οἱ Ἰουδαῖοι, καὶ πάλιν ὑπάγεις ἐκεῖ;

λέγουσιν (3d.per.pl.pres.act.ind.of λέγω, historical) 66.
αὐτῷ (dat.sing.masc.of αὐτός, indirect object of λέγουσιν) 16.
οἱ (nom.pl.masc.of the article in agreement with μαθηταί) 9.
μαθηταί (nom.pl.masc.of μαθητής, subject of λέγουσιν) 421.
Ῥαββί (voc.sing.masc.of Ῥαββί, address) 1443.
νῦν (adverbial) 1497.
ἐζήτουν (3d.per.pl.imp.act.ind.of ζητέω, progressive duration) 207.
σε (acc.sing.masc.of σύ, direct object of λιθάσαι) 104.
λιθάσαι (aor.act.inf.of λιθάζω, complementary) 2377.
οἱ (nom.pl.masc.of the article in agreement with Ἰουδαῖοι) 9.
Ἰουδαῖοι (nom.pl.masc.of Ἰουδαῖος, subject of ἐζήτουν) 143.
καὶ (adversative conjunction) 14.
πάλιν (adverbial) 355.
ὑπάγεις (2d.per.sing.pres.act.ind.of ὑπάγω, futuristic) 364.
ἐκεῖ (adverb of place) 204.

Translation - "The disciples said to Him, 'Rabbi, the Jews have recently been trying to stone you, and yet are you going back there again?"

Comment: νῦν adjoined to the imperfect of ἐζήτουν means "in the immediate past." Note the continuous efforts of the Jews to stone Jesus, reflected in the continuous action of the imperfect tense. καὶ is adversative if we look at it from the standpoint of the disciples. Contrary to human judgment, which dictated that Judea was off limits to Jesus, if He expected to remain alive, Jesus had just announced that they would return. Their question indicates their surprize. "You are going to Judea knowing that you may be going to your death?" They still failed to understand that our Lord had an hour of destiny to meet - a rendezvous with Calvary, despite Jesus' plain teaching, *e.g.* in John 10:14-18.

Verse 9 - "Jesus answered, Are there not twelve hours in the day? If any man walk in the day, he stumbleth not, because he seeth the light of this world."

ἀπεκρίθη Ἰησοῦς, Οὐχὶ δώδεκα ὧραί εἰσιν τῆς ἡμέρας; ἐάν τις περιπατῇ ἐν τῇ ἡμέρᾳ, οὐ προσκόπτει, ὅτι τὸ φῶς τοῦ κόσμου τούτου βλέπει.

ἀπεκρίθη (3d.per.sing.aor.ind.of ἀποκρίνομαι, constative) 318.
Ἰησοῦς (nom.sing.masc.of Ἰησοῦς, subject of ἀπεκρίθη) 3.
Οὐχὶ (summary negative conjunction with the indicative in a rhetorical question expecting an affirmative reply) 130.
δώδεκα (numeral) 820.
ὧραί (nom.pl.fem.of ὥρα, subject of εἰσιν) 735.
εἰσιν (3d.per.pl.pres.ind.of εἰμί, static) 86.
τῆς (gen.sing.fem.of the article in agreement with ἡμέρας) 9.
ἡμέρας (gen.sing.fem.of ἡμέρα, description) 135.
ἐάν (conditional particle introducing a third-class condition) 363.
τις (nom.sing.masc.of τις, indefinite pronoun, subject of περιπατῇ) 486.
περιπατῇ (3d.per.sing.pres.act.subj.of περιπατέω, third-class condition) 384.
ἐν (preposition with the locative of time point) 80.
τῇ (loc.sing.fem.of the article in agreement with ἡμέρᾳ) 9.
ἡμέρᾳ (loc.sing.fem.of ἡμέρα, time point) 135.
οὐ (summary negative conjunction with the indicative) 130.
προσκόπτει (3d.per.sing.pres.act.ind.of προσκόπτω, customary) 352.
ὅτι (conjunction introducing a subordinate causal clause) 211.
τὸ (acc.sing.neut.of the article in agreement with φῶς) 9.
φῶς (acc.sing.neut.of φῶς, direct object of βλέπει) 379.
τοῦ (gen.sing.masc.of the article in agreement with κόσμου) 9.
κόσμου (gen.sing.masc.of κόσμος, description) 360.
τούτου (gen.sing.masc.of οὗτος, in agreement with κόσμου) 93.
βλέπει (3d.per.sing.pres.act.ind.of βλέπω, progressive) 499.

Translation - "Jesus answered, 'There are twelve hours in the day, are there not? If anyone walks around in the day, he never stumbles, because he always sees the light of this world."

Comment: Οὐχὶ . . . τῆς ἡμέρας is a rhetorical question that expects an affirmative reply. The genitive in τῆς ἡμέρας indicates distinction of time rather than time point (locative) or time extent (accusative). There are twelve hours which we call day as distinct from the period we call night. The third-class condition lays down a principle. Those who walk about in the day are not going to stumble. The ὅτι clause tells us why? *Cf.*#'s 352 and 699 for a distinction between the two words, especially as they are used in Mt.7.

Jesus' statement is rather obvious. The opposite proposition is set forth in verse 10, but with a change in the causal clause.

Verse 10 - "But if a man walk in the night, he stumbleth, because there is no light in him."

ἐὰν δέ τις περιπατῇ ἐν τῇ νυκτί, προσκόπτει, ὅτι τὸ φῶς οὐκ ἔστιν ἐν αὐτῷ.

ἐὰν (conditional particle introducing a third-class condition) 363.
δέ (adversative conjunction) 11.
τις (nom.sing.masc.of τις, indefinite pronoun, subject of περιπατῇ) 486.
περιπατῇ (3d.per.sing.pres.act.subj.of περιπατέω, third-class condition) 384.
ἐν (preposition with the locative of time point) 80.
τῇ (loc.sing.fem.of the article in agreement with νυκτί) 9.
νυκτί (loc.sing.fem.of νύξ, time point) 209.
προσκόπτει (3d.per.sing.pres.act.ind.of προσκόπτω, customary) 352.
ὅτι (conjunction introducing a subordinate causal clause) 211.
τὸ (nom.sing.neut.of the article in agreement with φῶς) 9.
φῶς (nom.sing.neut.of φῶς, subject of ἔστιν) 379.
οὐκ (summary negative conjunction with the indicative) 130.
ἔστιν (3d.per.sing.pres.ind.of εἰμί, static) 86.
ἐν (preposition with the locative of place where) 80.
αὐτῷ (loc.sing.masc.of αὐτός, place where) 16.

Translation - "But if anyone walks in the night he always stumbles because the light is not in him."

Comment: Anyone should be able to walk about in the daytime because he has the benefit of the sunlight, so that he can see where he is going and thus avoid stumbling. But (adversative δέ) if a man walks in the night (loc.of time in τῇ νυκτί) when the sun is not shining he will stumble because he is not carrying his own light with him. Thus τὸ φῶς here means spiritual and intellectual light, since it obviously does not mean sunlight as in verse 9. The application is clear. It was night - the darkest in human history. The Jews, presumably the most enlightened race of men on earth were plotting to murder the incarnate Son of God, the sovereign Lord of Creation. The disciples had just stumbled. Their remark of verse 8 showed a complete lack of grasp of God's eternal plan of redemption, despite Jesus' oft repeated teaching. Why? Because the light of God's illumination was not in them. Thus in verses 9 and 10 we have our Lord's sharp rebuke to twelve Galileans who seemed never to think God's thoughts after Him.

Verse 11 - "These things said he; and after that he saith unto them, Our friend

Lazarus sleepeth, but I go, that I may awake him out of sleep."

ταῦτα εἶπεν, καὶ μετὰ τοῦτο λέγει αὐτοῖς, Λάζαρος ὁ φίλος ἡμῶν κεκοίμνται, ἀλλὰ πορεύομαι ἵνα ἐξυπνίσω αὐτόν.

ταῦτα (acc.pl.neut.of οὗτος, direct object of εἶπεν) 93.
εἶπεν (3d.per.sing.aor.act.ind.of εἶπον, constative) 155.
καὶ (continuative conjunction) 14.
μετὰ (preposition with the accusative of time extent) 50.
τοῦτο (acc.sing.neut.of οὗτος, time extent) 93.
λέγει (3d.per.sing.pres.act.ind.of λέγω, historical) 66.
αὐτοῖς (dat.pl.masc.of αὐτός, indirect object of λέγει) 16.
Λάζαρος (nom.sing.masc.of Λάζαρος, subject of κεκοίμηται) 2596.
ὁ (nom.sing.masc.of the article in agreement with φίλος) 9.
φίλος (nom.sing.masc.of φίλος, apposition) 932.
ἡμῶν (gen.pl.masc.of ἐγώ, relationship) 123.
κεκοίμηται (3d.per.sing.perf.pass.ind.of κοιμάω, consummative) 1664.
ἀλλὰ (adversative conjunction) 342.
πορεύομαι (1st.per.sing.pres.ind.of πορεύομαι, futuristic) 170.
ἵνα (conjunction with the subjunctive in a subfinal clause) 114.

#2597 ἐξυπνίσω (1st.per.sing.1st.aor.act.subj.of ἐξυπνίζω, purpose/result).

awake out of sleep - John 11:11.

Meaning: A combination of ἐκ (#19) and ὕπνος (#126). Hence, to awaken. With referernce to the raising of Lazarus from the dead - John 11:11.

αὐτόν (acc.sing.masc.of αὐτός, direct object of ἐξυπνίσω) 16.

Translation - "He said these things and a little later He said to them, 'Lazarus, our friend has fallen asleep, but I will go in order to awaken him.' "

Comment: ταῦτα refers to Jesus' comments in verses 9 and 10. Then Jesus added - "Lazarus has been put to sleep" - note the perfect passive in κεκοίμηται. ὁ φίλος ἡμῶν is in apposition with Λάζαρος. But Jesus intended to change that. The strong adversative ἀλλὰ represents His resolve. πορεύομαι is a futuristic present - "I am going. . . " Why? The ἵνα clause is both purpose and result, since our Lord is speaking. Lazaros is going to awaken, for this is the purpose of Jesus' visit as well as its result.

We could not expect the disciples to understand this language of equivocation. Their response in quite logical in

Verse 12 - "Then said his disciples, Lord, if he sleep he shall do well."

εἶπαν οὖν οἱ μαθηταὶ αὐτῷ, Κύριε, εἰ κεκοίμηται σωθήσεται.

εἶπαν (3d.per.pl.aor.act.ind.of εἶπον, constative) 155.
οὖν (inferential conjunction) 68.
οἱ (nom.pl.masc.of the article in agreement with μαθηταὶ) 9.

μαθηταὶ (nom.pl.masc.of μαθητής, subject of εἶπαν) 421.
αὐτῷ (dat.sing.masc.of αὐτός, indirect object of εἶπαν) 16.
Κύριε (voc.sing.masc.of κύριος, address) 97.
εἰ (conditional particle in a first-class condition) 337.
κεκοίμηται (3d.per.sing.perf.pass.ind.of κοιμάω, first-class condition) 1664.
σωθήσεται (3d.per.sing.fut.pass.ind.of σώζω, predictive) 109.

Translation - "Then the disciples said to Him, 'Lord, since he has been put to sleep he will recover.' "

Comment: οὖν is inferential, as the disciples respond to Jesus' statement of verse 11. The first-class condition indicates that the disciples assume that since Lazaros is sleeping, he is on the road to recovery. The implication is that since **the patient will recover there is no further need for Jesus to make the trip back to Judea. John clears up the difficulty in**

Verse 13 - "Howbeit Jesus spoke of his death: but they thought that he had spoken of taking of rest in sleep."

εἰρήκει δὲ ὁ Ἰησοῦς περὶ τοῦ θανάτου αὐτοῦ. ἐκεῖνοι δὲ ἔδοξαν ὅτι περὶ τῆς κοιμήσεως τοῦ ὕπνου λέγει.

εἰρήκει (3d.per.sing.pluperfect act.ind.of ἐρρήθην, consummative) 116.
δὲ (adversative conjunction) 11.
ὁ (nom.sing.masc.of the article in agreement with Ἰησοῦς) 9.
Ἰησοῦς (nom.sing.masc.of Ἰησοῦς, subject of εἰρήκει) 3.
περὶ (preposition with the genitive of reference) 173.
τοῦ (gen.sing.masc.of the article in agreement with θανάτου) 9.
θανάτου (gen.sing.masc.of θάνατος, reference) 381.
αὐτοῦ (gen.sing.masc.of αὐτός, possession) 16.
ἐκεῖνοι (nom.pl.masc.of ἐκεῖνος, subject of ἔδοξαν) 246.
δὲ (adversative conjunction) 11.
ἔδοξαν (3d.per.pl.aor.act.ind.of δοκέω, constative) 287.
ὅτι (conjunction introducing an object clause in indirect discourse) 211.
περὶ (preposition with the genitive of reference) 173.
τῆς (gen.sing.fem.of the article in agreement with κοιμήσεως) 9.

#2598 κοιμήσεως (gen.sing.fem.of κοίμησις, reference).

taking of rest - John 11:13.

*Meaning: Cf.*κοιμάω (#1664). Hence reposing; taking rest. With reference to Lazarus - followed by τοῦ ὕπνου - John 11:13.

τοῦ (gen.sing.masc.of the article in agreement with ὕπνου) 9.
ὕπνου (gen.sing.masc.of ὕπνος, definition) 126.
λέγει (3d.per.sing.pres.act.ind.of λέγω, historical) 66.

Translation - "But Jesus had spoken about his death, but they thought that it was with reference to sleep that He spoke."

Comment: John cleared up the confusion in the minds of his audience in verse 13. Now in verse 14 Jesus explains to the disciples what He meant.

Verse 14 - "Then said Jesus unto them plainly, Lazarus is dead."

τότε οὖν εἶπεν ὁ Ἰησοῦς παρρησίᾳ, Λάζαρος ἀπέθανεν.

τότε (continuative conjunction) 166.
οὖν (inferential conjunction) 68.
εἶπεν (3d.per.sing.aor.act.ind.of *εἶπον*, constative) 155.
αὐτοῖς (dat.pl.masc.of *αὐτός*, indirect object of *εἶπεν*) 16.
ὁ (nom.sing.masc.of the article in agreement with *Ἰησοῦς*) 9.
Ἰησοῦς (nom.sing.masc.of *Ἰησοῦς*, subject of *εἶπεν*) 3.
παρρησίᾳ (instru.sing.fem.of *παρρησία*, manner) 2319.
Λάζαρος (nom.sing.masc.of *Λάζαρος*, subject of *ἀπέθανεν*) 2596.
ἀπέθανεν (3d.per.sing.aor.act.ind.of *ἀποθνήσκω*, culminative) 774.

Translation - "So then Jesus said to them plainly, 'Lazarus is dead.' "

Comment: *οὖν* is inferential since the disciples were confused and needed an explanation in unequivocal terms. There seems to be an air of finality in the statement of Jesus - *Λάζαρος ἀπέθανεν* - but Jesus continued in

Verse 15 - "And I am glad for your sakes that I was not there to the intent ye may believe; nevertheless, let us go unto him."

καὶ χαίρω δι' ὑμᾶς, ἵνα πιστεύσητε, ὅτι οὐκ ἤμην ἐκεῖ. ἀλλὰ ἄγωμεν πρὸς αὐτόν.

καὶ (continuative conjunction) 14.
χαίρω, (1st.per.sing.pres.act.ind.of *χαίρω*, aoristic) 182.
δι' (preposition with the accusative, cause) 118.
ὑμᾶς (acc.pl.masc.of *σύ*, cause) 104.
ἵνα (conjunction with the subjunctive in a purpose clause) 114.
πιστεύσητε (2d.per.pl.aor.act.subj.of *πιστεύω*, purpose) 734.
ὅτι (conjunction introducing an object clause) 211.
οὐκ (summary negative conjunction with the indicative) 130.
ἤμην (1st.per.sing.imp.ind.of *εἰμί*, progressive description) 86.
ἐκεῖ (local adverb) 204.
ἀλλὰ (adversative conjunction) 342.
ἄγωμεν (1st.per.pl.pres.act.subj.of *ἄγω*, hortatory) 876.
πρὸς (preposition with the accusative of extent) 197.
αὐτόν (acc.sing.masc.of *αυτος*, extent) 16.

Translation - "And because of you I am glad that I was not there - in order that you may come to believe. But let us to go him."

Comment: If we had only the last two words of verse 14 and the first two of verse 15 we should be shocked - *Λάζαρος ἀπέθανεν, καὶ χαίρω* - "Lazarus is dead, and I am glad. . . !" Imagine our Lord saying that! But He follows χαίρω with δι' ὑμᾶς - "I am glad because of you (for your sakes, as far as you are concerned)" Why? Because only in the death of Lazarus and what Jesus is about to do can the disciples, who are all too soon to be trusted with His word and work in the world, be made to believe that Jesus is truly sovereign, incarnate deity. ἵνα πιστεύητε - "in order that you may believe." The purpose is so important that it is emphasized ahead of the object clause, introduced by ὅτι and joined to χαίρω. "I am glad that I was not there." Why? "For your sakes." Why? "In order that you may begin to believe." (ingressive aorist subjunctive in πιστεύσητε). Then comes His suggestion, "But let us go to him."

If Jesus had been present in Bethany when the crisis developed, Lazarus would not have died and the disciples would only have recorded another one of hundreds of healings, which they had seen in the past two and one half years. They needed something more dramatic.

Thomas, still confused, attempted to say something heroic, and succeeded only in saying something incredibly stupid. That is often the result when we feel compelled to say something despite the fact that we have nothing to say. Wisdom dictates that on such occasions we remain silent.

Verse 16 - "Then said Thomas, which is called Didymus, unto his fellowdisciples, Let us also go, that we may die with him."

εἶπεν οὖν Θωμᾶς ὁ λεγόμενος Δίδυμος τοῖς συμμαθηταῖς, Ἄγωμεν καὶ ἡμεῖς ἵνα ἀποθάνωμεν μετ' αὐτοῦ.

εἶπεν (3d.per.sing.aor.act.ind.of εἶπον, constative) 155.
οὖν (continuative conjunction) 68.
Θωμᾶς (nom.sing.masc.of Θωμᾶς, subject of εἶπεν) 847.
ὁ (nom.sing.masc.of the article in agreement with λεγόμενος) 9.
λεγόμενος (pres.pass.part.nom.sing.masc.of λέγω, substantival, apposition) 66.

#2599 Δίδυμος (nom.sing.masc.of δίδυμος, appellation).

Didymus- John 11:16; 20:24; 21:2.

Meaning: twofold; double. *Cf.* τρίδυμος and τετρόδυμος - threefold and fourfold - triplets, quadruplets. Hence δίδυμος means "twins." The nickname of Θωμᾶς, ὁ ἀπόστολος - John 11:16; 20:24; 21:2.

τοῖς (dat.pl.masc.of the article in agreement with συμμαθηταῖς) 9.

#2600 συμμαθηταῖς (dat.pl.masc.of συμμαθητής, indirect object of εἶπεν).

fellowdisciple - John 11:16.

Meaning: A combination of σύν (#1542) and μαθητής (#421). Hence, a fellowdisciple - John 11:16. (Phrynichus says that σύν is not prefixed to πολίτης, δημότης, φολέτης and the like, but only to those nouns which denote an association which is *προσκαίρος i.e.* temporary, as *συνέφηβος, συνθιασώτης, συμπότης*. The Latin also observes the same distinction and says, *commilito mens*, but not *concivis*, but civis meus. (Thayer, 596).

Ἄγωμεν (1st.per.pl.pres.act.subj.of ἄγω, hortatory) 876.
καὶ (adjunctive conjunction joining substantives) 14.
ἡμεῖς (nom.pl.masc.of ἐγω, subject of ἀποθάνωμεν) 123.
ἵνα (conjunction introducing a purpose clause) 114.
ἀποθάνωμεν (1st.per.pl.aor.act.subj.of ἀποθνήσκω, purpose) 774.
μετ' (preposition with the genitive, accompaniment) 50.
αὐτοῦ (gen.sing.masc.of αὐτός, accompaniment) 16.

Translation - "Then Thomas, the one nicknamed Twin, said to his fellowdisciples, 'Let us also go in order that we may die with Him.' "

Comment: οὖν here is possibly only continuative, although the inferential idea is not absent. Thomas, the Twin, who combined doubt and love in the same personality, certain that the movement that Jesus had begun would end in liquidation, was nevertheless sufficiently devoted to Jesus to wish to die with him rather than to face the future without Him. He still had not come to believe that Jesus' death was God's plan and that Jesus' resurrection would follow on the third day. So he made a heroic suggestion to the other disciples. A hortatory subjunctive in Ἄγωμεν, followed by a ἵνα clause of purpose in the subjunctive in ἀποθάνωμεν - "Let us also go in order that we may die with Him." One wonders why, if Thomas was so eager to die with Jesus, he ran when Jesus was arrested?! (Mark 14:50). Apparently he made a quick decision that discretion was the better part of valor.

Verse 17 - "Then when Jesus came, he found that he had lain in the grave four days already."

Ἐλθὼν οὖν ὁ Ἰησοῦς εὗρεν αὐτὸν τέσσαρας ἤδη ἡμέρας ἔχοντα ἐν τῷ μνημείῳ.

Ἐλθὼν (aor.part.nom.sing.masc.of ἔρχοαμι, adverbial, temporal) 146.
οὖν (continuative conjunction) 68.
ὁ (nom.sing.masc.of the article in agreement with Ἰησοῦς) 9.
Ἰησοῦς (nom.sing.masc.of Ἰησοῦς) 3.
εὗρεν (3d.per.sing.aor.act.ind.of εὑρίσκω, constative) 79.
αὐτὸν (acc.sing.masc.of αὐτός, direct object of εὗρεν) 16.
τέσσαρας (acc.pl.fem.of τέσσαρες, in agreement with ἡμέρας) 1508.
ἤδη (an adverb of time extent) 291.
ἡμέρας (acc.pl.fem.of ἡμέρα, time extent) 135.
ἔχοντα (pres.act.part.acc.sing.masc.of ἔχω, adverbial, circumstantial) 82.
ἐν (preposition with the locative of place where) 80.
τῷ (loc.sing.neut.of the article in agreement with μνημείῳ) 9.
μνημείῳ (loc.sing.neut.of μνημεῖον, place where) 763.

Translation - "Then when Jesus arrived, He found that Lazarus had been in the grave four days already."

Comment: Literally we should read " . . . found him already having four days in the grave," as we often say, "I have ten years on this job." Lazarus had put in four days time lying in the grave. ἔχοντα the participle agrees in case and number with αὐτὸν, which is accusative by virtue of being the direct object of εὗρεν. John could have followed εὗρεν with an object clause introduced by ὅτι. His thirty years in Ephesus had given him a more facile use of the Greek idiom.

This late arrival, four days after the burial of Lazarus was, of course, our Lord's deliberate design. *Cf.* John 5:5 for a similar use of the participle ἔχων, joined with an accusative of time extent and a prepositional phrase in explanation.

Verse 18 - "Now Bethany was nigh unto Jerusalem, about fifteen furlongs off."

ἦν δὲ ἡ Βηθανία ἐγγὺς τῶν Ἱεροσολύμων ὡς ἀπὸ σταδίων δεκαπέντε.

ἦν (3d.per.sing.imp.ind.of εἰμί, progressive description) 86.
δὲ (explanatory conjunction) 11.
ἡ (nom.sing.fem.of the article in agreement with Βηθανία) 9.
Βηθανία (nom.sing.fem.of Βηθανία, subject of ἦν) 1363.
ἐγγὺς (nom.sing.masc.of ἐγγύς, predicate adjective) 1512.
τῶν (abl.pl.masc.of the article in agreement with Ἱεροσολύμων) 9.
Ἱεροσολύμων (abl.pl.masc.of Ἱεροσολύμων, separation) 141.
ὡς (particle introducing a comparative clause) 128.
ἀπὸ (preposition with the ablative of separation) 70.
σταδίων (abl.pl.masc.of στάδιος, separation) 1127.

#2601 δεκαπέντε (numeral).

fifteen - John 11:18; Acts 27:28; Gal.1:18.

Meaning: A combination of δέκα (#1330) and πέντε (#1119). The earlier form was πεντεκαίδεκα - "five and ten." In later Greek δεκαπέντε - with reference to distance, with σταδίωμ - John 11:18; with ὀργυιὰς - Acts 27:28; with reference to time, with ἡμέρας - Gal.1:18.

Translation - "Now Bethany was near Jerusalem - about two miles away."

Comment: Jesus was almost within the shadow of the court that would try Him and within reach of the police and the Roman governor who would yield to the pressure of the Jewish mob, as a result of the demand of which, He was to be crucified. The main reason why John told us the proximity of Bethany to Jerusalem was to tell of the Jerusalem Jews who came out to visit Mary and Martha. Thus the story of the miracle of the resurrection of Lazarus reached the gossip mongers and therefore came to the attention of Annas and Caiphas and precipitated the course of events that culminated in Jesus' arrest and death.

Verse 19 - "And many of the Jews came to Martha and Mary, to comfort them concerning their brother."

πολλοὶ δὲ ἐκ τῶν Ἰουδαίων ἐληλύθεισαν πρὸς τὴν Μάρθαν καὶ Μαριὰμ ἵνα παραμυθήσωνται αὐτὰς περὶ τοῦ ἀδελφοῦ.

πολλοὶ (nom.pl.masc.of πολύς, subject of ἐληλύθεισαν) 228.
δὲ (continuative conjunction) 11.
ἐκ (preposition with the partitive genitive) 19.
τῶν (gen.pl.masc.of the article in agreement with Ἰουδαίων) 9.
Ἰουδαίων (gen.pl.masc.of Ἰουδαῖος, partitive) 143.
ἐληλύθεισαν (3d.per.pl.pluperfect act.ind.of ἔρχομαι, consummmative) 146.
πρὸς (preposition with the accusative of extent) 197.
τὴν (acc.sing.fem.of the article in agreement with Μάρθαν) 9.
Μάρθαν (acc.sing.fem.of Μάρθα, extent) 2436.
καὶ (adjunctive conjunction joining nouns) 14.
Μαριάμ (acc.sing.fem.of Μαρίας,extent) 2439.
ἵνα (conjunction introducing a purpose clause) 114.

#2602 παραμυθήσωνται (3d.per.pl.aor.mid.subj.of παραμυθέομαι, indirect).

comfort - John 11:19,31; 1 Thess.2:12; 5:14.

Meaning: A combination of παρά (#154) and μυθέομαι - "to talk to, relate explain, tell, converse or identify with." Hence to talk along with. The adjuncts reveal the content of the conversation, *e.g.* comfort and consolation in John 11:19,31; exhortation in 1 Thess.2:12. Psychiatric counselling in 1 Thess.5:14.

αὐτὰς (acc.pl.fem.of αὐτός, direct object of παραμυθήσωνται) 16.
περὶ (preposition with the genitive of reference) 173.
τοῦ (gen.sing.masc.of the article in agreement with ἀδελφοῦ) 9.
ἀδελφοῦ (gen.sing.masc.of ἀδελφός, reference) 15.

Translation - "And many of the Jews had come to Martha and Mary to comfort them concerning their brother."

Comment: Verse 18 with its information that Jerusalem was not far away, a little less than two miles from Bethany, explains how it was possible for many of the Jews who lived in Jerusalem to make the short trip - perhaps a thirty minutes walk, to the home of Martha and Mary. We need this information to understand fully the material in John 12:9-11. The purpose clause tells us why they came. It was to console the sisters in their grief. Did they also ask them about their connections with Jesus? In the absence of textual evidence we must assume that the motives of the Jews were pure. It was perhaps inevitable that they would tell the story of Lazarus' resurrection when they returned to Jerusalem.

Verse 20 - "Then Martha, as soon as she heard that Jesus was coming, went and met him: but Mary sat still in the house."

ἡ οὖν Μάρθα ὡς ἤκουσεν ὅτι Ἰησοῦς ἔρχεται ὑπήντησεν αὐτῷ. Μαριὰμ δὲ ἐν τῷ οἴκῳ ἐκαθέζετο.

ἡ (nom.sing.fem.of the article in agreement with Μάρθα) 9.
οὖν (inferential conjunction) 68.
Μάρθα (nom.sing.fem.of Μάρθα, subject of ὑπήντησεν) 2436.
ὡς (particle introducing a definite temporal clause) 128.
ἤκουσεν (3d.per.sing.aor.act.ind.of ἀκούω, constative) 148.
ὅτι (conjunction introducing an object clause in indirect discourse) 211.
Ἰησοῦς (nom.sing.masc.of Ἰησοῦς, subject of ἔρχεται) 3.
ἔρχεται (3d.per.sing.pres.ind.of ἔρχομαι, indirect discourse) 146.
ὑπήντησεν (3d.per.sing.aor.act.ind.of ὑπαντάω, constative) 762.
αὐτῷ (dat.sing.masc.of αὐτός, personal interest) 16.
Μαριὰμ (nom.sing.fem.of Μαριάμ, subject of ἐκαθέζετο) 2439.
δὲ (adversative conjunction) 11.
ἐν (preposition with the locative of place where) 80.
τῷ (loc.sing.masc.of the article in agreement with οἴκῳ) 9.
οἴκῳ (loc.sing.masc.of οἶκος, place where) 784.
ἐκαθέζετο (3d.per.sing.imp.mid.ind.of καθέζομαι, progressive description) 1599.

Translation - "Therefore when Martha heard that Jesus had come she went to meet Him, but Mary remained seated in the house."

Comment: Martha went out to meet Jesus when she heard that He was coming. The temporal clause is definite (*ὡς ἤκουσεν*). It is followed by the object clause in indirect discourse. In such constructions, the tense of the verb is the same as in direct discourse. The word was, "Jesus is coming" - Ἰησοῦς ἔρχεται. Martha, having heard it left the house to meet Him. That is why we have taken οὖν as inferential. If she had not heard the report she would not have gone out. That He was near enough to the house to see is obvious. Hence we have translated, "had come" although "is coming" would be more literal.

Her guests, the Jews from Jerusalem, were there talking with Martha and Mary about Lazarus. Jesus had not yet arrived at the threshold of the door, though He was close enough to be seen. Normal courtesy would dictate that Martha, the hostess, would not forsake her guests who had walked two miles to offer their sympathy. But when Martha heard that Jesus was coming, she forgot her manners. Whether she excused herself or not we do not know. The text says that she went out to meet Jesus. *Cf.*#762.

But (adversative δὲ) Mary remained seated in the house. Thus we have the stage set for the conversation between Jesus and Martha in verses 21-27. This conversation took place outside the village. Martha had run some distance to meet Jesus (vs.30).

Verse 21 - "Then said Martha unto Jesus, Lord, if thou hadst been here, my brother had not died."

εἶπεν οὖν ἡ Μάρθα πρὸς τὸν Ἰησοῦν, Κύριε, εἰ εἰ ἦς ὧδε οὐκ ἂν ἀπέθανεν ὁ ἀδελφός μου.

εἶπεν (3d.per.sing.aor.act.ind.of *εἶπον*, constative) 155.
οὖν (continuative conjunction) 68.
ἡ (nom.sing.fem.of the article in agreement with Μάρθα) 9.
Μάρθα (nom.sing.fem.of Μάρθα, subject of *εἶπεν*) 2436.
πρὸς (preposition with the accusative of extent, after a verb of speaking) 197.
τὸν (acc.sing.masc.of the article in agreement with Ἰησοῦν) 9.
Ἰησοῦν (acc.sing.masc.of Ἰησοῦς, extent, after a verb of speaking) 3.
Κύριε (voc.sing.masc.of *κύριος*, address) 97.
εἰ (conditional particle in a second-class condition, contrary to fact) 337.
ἦς (2d.per.sing.imp.ind.of *εἰμί*, second-class condition) 86.
ὧδε (adverb of place) 766.
οὐκ (summary negative conjunction with the indicative) 130.
ἂν (contingent particle in a second-class condition) 205.
ἀπέθανεν (3d.per.sing.aor.act.ind.of *ἀποθνήσκω*, second-class condition) 774.
ὁ (nom.sing.masc.of the article in agreement with *ἀδελφός*) 9.
ἀδελφός (nom.sing.masc.of *ἀδελφός*, subject of *ἀπέθανεν*) 15.
μου (gen.sing.masc.of *ἐγώ*, relationship) 123.

Translation - "Then Martha said to Jesus, 'Lord, if you had been here my brother would not have died.' "

Comment: *οὖν* here is transitional. The rule for second-class (contrary to fact) conditional clauses is that those which deal with past time (relative to the time of the speaker/writer) have the aorist or pluperfect in both protasis and apodosis. *Cf.* Mt.11:21; Mk.13:20. But here we have the imperfect (*ἦς*) in the protasis and the aorist in the apodosis. Martha's statement refers of course to an event in her past. Her brother had been buried for four days. The statements in both her protasis and apodosis were contrary to fact. "Lord, if you had been here (He was not) my brother would not have died (he did)." Note that she emphasized the fact of the death ahead of the fact that Lazarus was her brother, because it was the tragedy of his death that concerned her, something that might have been avoided had Jesus been present. Martha was not certain that Jesus could or would have saved him. This is clear from *ἂν* in the apodosis, although she implied in verse 22 that He could if He had chosen to do so. There was no doubt in her mind that Jesus had the ability to heal, however critical the illness might be. She may have had some doubts about whether or not He would choose to do so. No one ever died in the living presence of Jesus unless He willed that it should be so. The thief on the cross remained alive until after Jesus died. Martha was not rebuking Jesus because He was not present to prevent the death of her brother. She was only lamenting the fact (Meyer, *John*, 344).

Verse 22 - "But I know that even now, whatsoever thou wilt ask of God, God will give it thee."

(*ἀλλὰ*) *καὶ νῦν οἶδα ὅτι ἂν αἰτήσῃ τὸν θεὸν δώσει σοι ὁ θεός.*

(ἀλλά) (adversative conjunction) 342.
καὶ (ascensive conjunction) 14.
νῦν (temporal adverb) 1497.
οἶδα (1st.per.sing.2d.perf.from obsolete εἴδω, with a sense of the present) 144.
ὅτι (conjunction introducing an object clause) 211.
ὅσα (acc.pl.neut.of ὅσος, impersonal, direct object of αἰτήσῃ) 660.
ἂν (contingent particle) 205.
αἰτήσῃ (2d.per.sing.aor.act.subj.of αἰτέω, in an indefinite relative clause) 537.
τὸν (acc.sing.masc.of the article in agreement with θεὸν) 9.
θεὸν (acc.sing.masc.of θεός, direct object of αἰτήσῃ) 124.
δώσει (3d.per.sing.pres.act.ind.of δίδωμι, predictive) 362.
σοι (dat.sing.masc.of σύ, indirect object of δώσει) 104.
ὁ (nom.sing.masc.of the article in agreement with θεός) 9.
θεός (nom.sing.masc.of θεός, subject of δώσει) 124.

Translation - "But even now I am convinced that whatever you may ask God, He will give to you."

Comment: καὶ is ascensive. Whatever doubts Martha may have entertained about Jesus' intentions, she believes that "even now" (καὶ νῦν), though her brother is dead, Jesus' relation with the Father is such that God will grant whatever Jesus might ask. There was no doubt in her mind that Jesus could have prevented the death, had He been in Bethany. But the Lord was there now and help was still available. The indefinite relative clause with the subjunctive leaves the area of possibility limitless. Whatever He might ask - who could tell what it might be? But there was no doubt that if Jesus asked for it, God would do it. Martha was not sure what Jesus would ask, or, indeed if He would ask anything. She was very sure that His prayer would be answered.

She may have been told what Jesus said when her messenger reported to Him in Perea that Lazarus was sick (vs.4). The text does not tell us that the messenger returned to Bethany, or that, if he did, he told Martha what Jesus said. Did Jesus mean that Lazarus would not die or that, if he died, he would be raised from the dead? Obviously Jesus did not mean the former, since Lazarus did, in fact, die. Then Jesus meant the latter. But when would the resurrection take place? Martha knew that it would occur at the last day, if not before. Therefore, the question comes down to this: will Jesus raise Lazarus from the dead before the resurrection of all of the saints? (1 Cor.15:51; 1 Thess.4:13-18, *et al.*). Martha has delicately hinted at the idea that He might, and Jesus teased her a little with the equivocal comment in

Verse 23 - "Jesus saith unto her, Thy brother shall rise again."

λέγει αὐτῇ ὁ Ἰησοῦς, Ἀναστήσεται ὁ ἀδελφός σου.

λέγει (3d.per.sing.pres.act.ind.of λέγω, historical) 66.

αὐτῇ (dat.sing.fem.of αὐτός, indirect object of λέγει) 16.
ὁ (nom.sing.masc.of the article in agreement with Ἰησοῦς) 9.
Ἰησοῦς (nom.sing.masc.of Ἰησοῦς, subject of λέγει) 3.
Ἀναστήσεται (3d.per.sing.fut.pass.ind.of ἀνίστημι, predictive) 789.
ὁ (nom.sing.masc.of the article in agreement with ἀδελφός) 9.
ἀδελφός (nom.sing.masc.of ἀδελφός, subject of ἀναστήσεται) 15.
σου (gen.sing.fem.of σύ, relationship) 104.

Translation - "Jesus said to her, 'Your brother will be resurrected.' "

Comment: Note that ἀναστήσεται is passive. The dead are never active in their own resurrection from the dead (Except in the case of Jesus - John 10:18). Therefore neither active nor middle voice can occur with ἀνίστημι, where it is used to mean resurrection from the dead. Lazarus did not rise; he was resurrected. *Cf.*#789 for the long list of references which refer to the resurrection of dead bodies. The scriptures clearly teach that both Jesus rose from the dead in the same body in which He suffered, and that He will raise from the dead the bodies of the saved at the end of this age, and of the unsaved, a thousand years later. The Scriptures nowhere teach the immortality of the soul or spirit of man apart from the immortality of the body. Jesus' pedagogical method, so often used elsewhere, is here being applied to Martha. He speaks truth, but He uses words capable of other interpretations and then, slowly and surely leads the student to apply *His* meaning to *His* words instead of the student's meaning to His words. This does not mean that Jesus employed equivocation with an intent to mislead. But equivocation creates doubt in the mind of the student, and a doubting student is a learning student. Examples of our Lord's method of teaching are: the temple of His body (John 2); birth (John 3); water (John 4); healing (John 5); bread (John 6) and here resurrection. Physical? Of course, for if there is no resurrection of the physical body, there is no resurrection at all, since the soul and the spirit of man does not die. Thus only that which dies can be resurrected. Is the resurrection to be today or later? This was the question in Martha's mind, and thus Jesus toyed with her. She tried to play the game with Him by putting upon His words the only interpretation that she knew about in

Verse 24 - "Martha saith unto him, I know that he shall rise again in the resurrection at the last day."

λέγει αὐτῷ ἡ Μάρθα, Οἶδα ὅτι ἀναστήσεται ἐν τῇ ἀναστάσει ἐν τῇ ἐσχάτῃ ἡμέρᾳ.

λέγει (3d.per.sing.pres.act.ind.of λέγω, historical) 66.
αὐτῷ (dat.sing.masc.of αὐτός, indirect object of λέγει) 16.
ἡ (nom.sing.fem.of the article in agreement with Μάρθα) 9.
Μάρθα (nom.sing.fem.of Μάρθα, subject of λέγει) 2436.
Οἶδα (1st.per.sing.2d.perf. from the obsolete εἴδω, with a sense the present) 144.
ὅτι (conjunction introducing an object clause in indirect discourse) 211.

ἀναστήσεται (3d.per.sing.fut.pass.ind.of ἀνίστημι, predictive) 789.
ἐν (preposition with the locative of time point) 80.
τῇ (loc.sing.fem.of the article, in agreement with ἀναστάσει) 9.
ἀναστάσει (loc.sing.fem.of ἀνάστασις, time point) 1423.
ἐν (preposition with the locative of time point) 80.
τῇ (loc.sing.fem.of the article in agreement with ἡμέρᾳ) 9.
ἐσχάτῃ (loc.sing.fem.of ἔσχατος, in agreement with ἡμέρᾳ) 496.
ἡμέρᾳ (loc.sing.fem.of ἡμέρα, time point) 135.

Translation - "Martha said to Him, 'I am convinced that he will be raised at the resurrection on the last day.' "

Comment: Οἶδα, the perfect tense, indicates a present condition as the result of a past action. She had learned earlier about the resurrection and she was now convinced that it would take place. Note the two locative time phrases ἐν τῇ ἀναστάσει ἐν τῇ ἐσχάτῃ ἡμέρᾳ - "at the time of the resurrection" which would take place "on the last day." *Cf.*#1423 for all of the uses of this word, with particular attention to those which refer to physical resurrection of the human body, whether with reference to Jesus, saints or sinners, and whether at the resurrection on the last day or in some special miracle (*e.g.* Heb.11:35a).

Martha had the usual understanding of Jewish eschatology. All Jews expected to be raised from the dead on the last day of general judgment. Distinctions, now made on the basis of a fuller revelation, not available to Martha, between the last day of the age of grace, or of the tribulation period (for those who believe these two are distinct), or of the millenium, were not made by her. She simply looked forward to some day when all faithful Jews would be rescued from their graves. Was this what Jesus meant in verse 23? Or did He mean that her brother would be raised on that very day?

Still in pursuit of His pegagogical method, Jesus contined to speak in what to Martha *at that time* were words of obscure meaning.

Verse 25 - "Jesus said unto her, I am the resurrection and the life: he that believeth in me, though he were dead, yet shall he live."

εἶπεν αὐτῇ ὁ Ἰησοῦς, Ἐγώ εἰμι ἡ ἀνάστασις καὶ ἡ ζωή. ὁ πιστεύων εἰς ἐμὲ κἂν ἀποθάνῃ ζήσεται.

εἶπεν (3d.per.sing.aor.act.ind.of εἶπον, constative) 155.
αὐτῇ (dat.sing.fem.of αὐτός, indirect object of εἶπεν) 16.
ὁ (nom.sing.masc.of the article in agreement with Ἰησοῦς) 9.
Ἰησοῦς (nom.sing.masc.of Ἰησοῦς, subject of εἶπεν) 3.
Ἐγώ (nom.sing.masc.of ἐγώ, subject of εἰμι) 123.
εἰμι (1st.per.sing.pres.ind.of εἰμί, aoristic) 86.
ἡ (nom.sing.fem.of the article in agreement with ἀνάστασις) 9.
ἀνάστασις (nom.sing.fem.of ἀνάστασις, predicate nominative) 1423.
καὶ (adjunctive conjunction joining nouns) 14.
ἡ (nom.sing.fem.of the article in agreement with ζωή) 9.

ζωή (nom.sing.fem.of ζωή, predicate nominative) 668.

ὁ (nom.sing.masc.of the article in agreement with πιστεύων) 9.

πιστεύων (pres.act.part.nom.sing.masc.of πιστεύω, substantival, subject of ζήσεται) 734.

εἰς (preposition with the accusative, cause) 140.

ἐμὲ (acc.sing.masc.of ἐγώ, cause) 123.

κἂν (conditional particle) 1370.

ἀποθάνῃ (3d.per.sing.aor.act.subj.of ἀποθνήσκω, third-class condition) 774.

ζήσεται (3d.per.sing.fut.pass.ind.of ζάω, predictive) 340.

Translation - "Jesus said to her, 'I am the resurrection and the life. The one who believes on me, even though he die, he shall be made alive.' "

Comment: Another ἐγώ εἰμι for our Lord. *Cf.* John 8:58 and comment *en loc. Cf.* also John 8:12. *Cf.*#668 for references on ζωή, with observation of the fact that overwhelmingly it means spiritual life, in contrast to βίος (#2202), which never means spiritual life. Acts 3:15 says that Jesus is ὁ ἀρχηγὸς τῆς ζωῆς. Study ἀρχηγός (#3013) in Acts 3:15; 5:31; Heb.2:10; 12:2. Since Jesus is ὁ ἀρχηγὸς τῆς ζωῆς, He certainly is also ἡ ἀνάστασις. Only one who originated and delivered ζωήν to man could restore it to him if he had lost it. Christ, of course is also the creator of βίος, since He is the creator of everything (John 1:3; Col.1;16). Biologists have long since rejected the ancient myth of spontaneous generation, by which the ancients were accustomed to explain the origin of life. It was Louis Pasteur, with his experimental attempts to purify milk, who proved that abiogenesis (spontaneous generation) is fallacious. That life now exists, whether we think of it as biological or spiritual, is evidence that it has always existed. John, in speaking of the Eternal Λόγος said, "in Him was life and the life was the light of men" (John 1:4). It is impossible to deny the creation account of Genesis and postulate any of the naturalistic views of the origin of the universe without accepting the old exploded view of spontaneous generation. If the earth was once a flaming mass of gas, pulled off from the sun by the gravitational attraction of a passing star, which later cooled to become the planet where life first appeared, it is logical to demand to know where the first life came from . Only the Christian who accepts the biblical account of creation has an answer to this question. He, in Whom life has always been, stood before Martha outside the little village of Bethany and declared, "I am the resurrection and the life."

Having declared Himself to be, not only the restorer of life, but life itself, Jesus was in a position to set forth the third-class condition which follows. The subject ὁ πιστεύων εἰς ἐμὲ is emphasized ahead of κἂν, because Jesus was stressing Martha's need to believe upon Him at that critical time. There is an element of contingency in κἂν. The protasis does not dogmatize that the believer will die.But *if he dies*, there is no doubt that he will live again. This is declared by the predictive future in the apodosis. "Even if the one who believes on me die" (as Lazarus did) "he shall live."

But Jesus has not yet said specifically when the new life will come. In the future, to be sure, but was it to be on that very day? It was this question that especially interested Martha. The view that ζήσεται refers to the life of the spirit and soul, and that Jesus is not promising eternal life to the body, is wrong since ἀποθάνῃ refers only to the death of the body; hence ζήσεται can refer only to the death of the body which the protasis mentions as having died. If there is no resurrection of the body, there is no resurrection at all since only the body is subject to death in the physical sense. Those who deny the resurrection of the body have no alternative but to charge John with false witness in the verses which follow. The rest of Jesus' statement, begun in verse 25, is finished in

Verse 26 - "And whosoever liveth and believeth in me shall never die. Believest thou this?"

καὶ πᾶς ὁ ζῶν καὶ πιστεύων εἰς ἐμὲ οὐ μὴ ἀποθάνῃ εἰς τὸν αῳῶνα. πιστεύεις τοῦτο;

καὶ (continuative conjunction) 14.
πᾶς (nom.sing.masc.of πᾶς, in agreement with ζῶν) 67.
ὁ (nom.sing.masc.of the article in agreement with ζῶν) 9.
ζῶν (pres.act.part.nom.sing.masc.of ζάω, substantival, subject of ἀποθάνῃ) 340.
καὶ (adjunctive conjunction joining participles) 14.
πιστεύων (pres.act.part.nom.sing.masc.of πιστεύω, substantival, subject of ἀποθάνῃ) 734.
εἰς (preposition with the accusative, cause) 140.
ἐμὲ (acc.sing.masc.of ἐγώ, cause) 123.
οὐ (summary negative conjunction with μή, emphatic negation) 130.
μὴ (qualified negative conjunction with οὐ and the subjunctive, emphatic negation) 87.
ἀποθάνῃ (3d.per.sing.aor.act.subj.of ἀποθνήσκω, emphatic negation) 774.
εἰς (preposition with the accusative of time extent) 140.
τὸν (acc.sing.masc.of the article in agreement with αἰῶνα) 9.
αἰῶνα (acc.sing.masc.of αἰών, time extent) 1002.
πιστεύεις (2d.per.sing.pres.act.ind.of πιστεύω, direct question) 734.
τοῦτο (acc.sing.neut.of οὗτος, direct object of πιστεύεις) 93.

Translation - "And all those who live and believe in me shall never die in the eternal ages. Do you believe this?"

Comment: We could take καὶ as emphatic. Jesus' statement of verse 25 is strong. "Even if the believer dies he will live again." "*In fact*" (emphatic καὶ) "all who live and believe in me shall never die." Thus our Lord piled up the assurances. Notice the two participial substantives, double subjects of the verb. The one who lives, physically and, during the course of his physical life commits himself to Christ, shall never die! The statement would not be true without the qualifying phrase εἰς τὸν αἰῶνα. Lazarus was a dead example of one who had been living and who, during his lifetime believed on Jesus. Yet he died. Most Christians, who are saved because of their faithful commitment to Christ during their lives, have since died. Only a tiny percentage of the total number of the elect are alive today.

Jesus did not say that they would not die in the physical sense, in time. They will never die, physically or spiritually *in eternity* - εἰς τὸν αἰῶνα. After the resurrection of the bodies of the saints, at the end of this age, these bodies will never die in eternity. There is no promise of immunity from physical death for anyone, saints or sinners, until we get into eternity. The eternal ages will be endless time of separation from God for the lost. For the saints eternity will be endless time of fellowship with God in bodies that never again will suffer from sickness and death. This is why Jesus must be the resurrection, if He is to be the life. Our Lord was not physical life to a corpse like Lazarus, not at least until after He had become his resurrection. After He had called Lazarus from the tomb He became for him life εἰς τὸν αἰῶνα.

Lazarus had lived and while he lived he believed on Christ, and thus he fulfilled the conditions of verse 25. And then he died. "Yet shall he live." So it happened before the day had passed, as we shall see. But did Jesus promise that, once resurrected, Lazarus would never die again? No, He did not. He promised that when Lazarus (and all of the other saints) had moved into eternity, he would never die again. There is no death for the believer in eternity.

The scriptures close the record on Lazarus after John 12:11, but there is no reason to suppose that he did not die again, nor to deny that his body is not now lying in some forgotten grave awaiting the resurrection of 1 Cor.15:51 and 1 Thess.13-14. After that he will never die again. We must respect the divine reticencies. If the Holy Spirit had wanted us to know precisely about these matters, He could and would have told us. Lazarus was not the only one resurrected from the dead. The young man of Nain (Lk.7:11-17), the daughter of Jairus (Mt.9:18-26), Dorcas, the Joppa disciple (Acts 9:36-43), the son of the Shunammite woman (2 Kings 4:18-37) and the saints who arose from the grave when our Lord died (Mt.27:52-53) - these are all cases in point. And the scriptures are silent about what happened to them after that.

In view of the ultimate victory over death, which is coming to every believer in eternity, there is really no reason to be unduly upset over physical death in time. Normal grief because of the death of a loved one is to be expected, but unrelenting sorrow, unmixed with Christian hope and comfort is not becoming to one who professes to have faith in Christ.

Martha gave up trying to figure out what Jesus meant by what He said, or what, if anything, He was going to do about Lazarus. All that she could think to say was in terms of a general assertion of her faith in His person and work, as we see in

Verse 27 - "She saith unto him, Yea, Lord: I believe that thou art the Christ, the Son of God, which should come into the world."

λέγει αὐτῷ, Ναί, κύριε. ἐγὼ πεπίστευκα ὅτι σὺ εἶ ὁ Χριστὸς ὁ υἱὸς τοῦ θεοῦ ὁ εἰς τὸν κόσμον ἐρχόμενος.

λέγει (3d.per.sing.pres.act.ind.of λέγω, historical) 66.
αὐτῷ (dat.sing.masc.of αὐτός, indirect object of λέγει) 16.
Ναί (affirmation) 524.
κύριε (voc.sing.masc.of κύριος, address) 97.
ἐγὼ (nom.sing.masc.of ἐγώ, subject of πεπίστευκα, emphatic) 123.
πεπίστευκα (1st.per.sing.perf.act.ind.of πιστεύω, consummative) 734.

ὅτι (conjunction introducing an object clause in indirect discourse) 211.
σὺ (nom.sing.masc.of *σύ*, subject of *εἶ*, emphatic) 104.
εἶ (2d.per.sing.pres.ind.of *εἰμί*, static) 86.
ὁ (nom.sing.masc.of the article in agreement with *Χριστὸς*) 9.
Χριστὸς (nom.sing.masc.of *Χριστός*, predicate nominative) 4.
ὁ (nom.sing.masc.of the article in agreement with *υἱὸς*) 9.
υἱὸς (nom.sing.masc.of *υἱός*, apposition) 5.
τοῦ (gen.sing.masc.of the article in agreement with *θεοῦ*) 9.
θεοῦ (gen.sing.masc.of *θεός*, relationship) 124.
ὁ (nom.sing.masc.of the article in agreement with *ἐρχόμενος*) 9.
εἰς (preposition with the accusative of extent) 140.
τὸν (acc.sing.masc.of the article in agreement with *κόσμον*) 9.
κόσμον (acc.sing.masc.of *κόσμος*, extent) 360.
ἐρχόμενος (pres.mid.part.nom.sing.masc.of *ἔρχομαι*, substantival, apposition) 146.

Translation - "She said to him, 'Yes, Lord. I have believed (and I now believe) that you *are the Messiah, the Son of God, the One coming into the world.' "*

Comment: Note *ἐγὼ* in emphasis before *πεπίστευκα* and *σὺ* before *εἶ*. Both these pronouns are emphasized, since, otherwise they are not needed, as they are implicit in their respective verbs. Martha used the perfect tense in *πεπίστευκα*. "In the past I came to believe, and, as a result, I am now convinced that . . . *κ.τ.λ.*" She was committed to the position. The Messiah is also the Son of God and the One Who was to come into the world - *ὁ υἱὸς* and *ὁ ἐρχόμενος* in apposition with *Χριστὸς*.

Martha did not choose to elaborate further. Perhaps she was afraid to sound presumptuous. "You are the Lord Christ - Son of God - Incarnate Deity. Of this I am convinced. What you plan to do for us in our sorrow I do not know. Whatever you do or choose not to do will be the best for us." This expresses the degree of resignation that comes from perfect faith in Christ. Whether Martha was thinking all of this we do not know. The converstion is finished. It is time to call for Mary.

Jesus Weeps

(John 11:28-37)

John 11:28 - "And when she had so said, she went her way, and called Mary, her sister secretly, saying, The Master is come, and calleth for thee."

Καὶ ταῦτα εἰποῦσα ἀπῆλθεν καὶ ἐφώνησεν Μαριὰμ τὴν ἀδελφὴν αὐτῆς λάθρᾳ εἰποῦσα, Ὁ διδάσκαλος πάρεστιν καὶ φωνεῖ σε.

Καὶ (continuative conjunction) 14.
ταῦτα (acc.pl.neut.of *οὗτος*, direct object of *εἰποῦσα*) 93.

εἰποῦσα (aor.act.part.nom.sing.fem.of εἶπον, adverbial, temporal) 155.
ἀπῆλθεν (3d.per.sing.aor.act.ind.of ἀπέρχομαι, constative) 239.
καὶ (adjunctive conjunction joining verbs) 14.
ἐφώνησεν (3d.per.sing.aor.act.ind.of φωνέω, constative) 1338.
Μαριὰμ (acc.sing.fem.of Μαρίας, direct object of ἐφώνησεν) 2439.
τὴν (acc.sing.fem.of the article in agreement with ἀδελφὴν) 9.
ἀδελφὴν (acc.sing.fem.of ἀδελφή, apposition) 1025.
αὐτῆς (gen.sing.fem.of αὐτός, relationship) 16.
λάθρᾳ (adverbial) 91.
εἰποῦσα (aor.act.part.nom.sing.fem.of εἶπον, adverbial, complementary) 155.
'Ο (nom.sing.masc.of the article in agreement with διδάσκαλος) 9.
διδάσκαλος (nom.sing.masc.of διδάσκαλος, subject of πάρεστιν and φωνεῖ) 742.
πάρεστιν (3d.per.sing.pres.ind.of πάρειμι, aoristic) 1592.
καὶ (adjunctive conjunction joining verbs) 14.
φωνεῖ (3d.per.sing.pres.act.ind.of φωνέω, progressive present) 1338.
σε (acc.sing.fem.of σύ, direct object of φωνεῖ) 104.

Translation - "And having said these things she went away and called Mary, her sister and whispered to her, 'The Teacher is here and He is calling you.' "

Comment: Martha finished her statement of faith. She did not understand much of what Jesus said, but she believed in Him and she said so. Now she left Him and returned to the village and whispered to her sister. Perhaps she did not wish to excite the Jewish guests with the information that Jesus had come and was waiting outside the village limits. At this point Jesus was both Διδάσκαλος and Κύριος to Martha, but the former function, at the moment, seemed predominate to her. She probably meant to say to Mary, "Go out and meet the Teacher. He will explain it to you, even if you do not understand it."

Verse 29 - "As soon as she heard that, she arose quickly, and came unto him."

ἐκείνη δὲ ὡς ἤκουσεν ἠγέρθη ταχὺ καὶ ἤρχετο πρὸς αὐτόν.

ἐκείνη (nom.sing.fem.of ἐκεῖνος, subject of ἤκουσεν, ἠγέρθη and ἤρχετο) 246.
δὲ (continuative conjunction) 11.
ὡς (particle introducing a definite temporal clause) 128.
ἤκουσεν (3d.per.sing.aor.act.ind.of ἀκούω, definite temporal clause) 148.
ἠγέρθη (3d.per.sing.1st.aor.pass.ind.of ἐγείρω) 125.
ταχὺ (adverbial) 491.
καὶ (adjunctive conjunction joining verbs) 14.
ἤρχετο (3d.per.sing.imp.mid.ind.of ἔρχομαι, inceptive) 146.
πρὸς (preposition with the accusative of extent) 197.
αὐτόν (acc.sing.masc.of αὐτός, extent) 16.

Translation - "And when she heard she sprang up quickly and started toward Him."

Comment: ὡς introduces the definite temporal clause. When she heard Martha's whispered message, Mary "was raised up quickly." The verb ἠγέρθη is passive. The news that Jesus was there so electrified the girl that it was as if she had been picked up from the floor bodily. Edersheim says, "Mary was probably sitting in the chamber of mourning, with its upset chairs and couches and other melancholy tokens of mourning, as was the custom, surrounded by many who had come to comfort her." (*The Life and Times of Jesus*, II, 322). Since the chairs were upset, she was probably seated on the floor. Picked up by her elation that Jesus had arrived and her great desire to see Him, she speedily ran to His side. Jesus was still outside the village at the spot where Martha met Him, as we learn in

Verse 30 - "Now Jesus was not yet come into the town, but was in that place where Martha met Him."

οὔπω δὲ ἐληλύθει ὁ Ἰησοῦς εἰς τὴν κώμην, ἀλλ' ἦν ἔτι ἐν τῷ τόπῳ ὅπου ὑπήντησεν αὐτῷ ἡ Μάρθα.

οὔπω (adverbial) 1198.
δὲ (explanatory conjunction) 11.
ἐληλύθει (3d.per.sing.pluperfect ind.of ἔρχομαι, consummative) 146.
ὁ (nom.sing.masc.of the article in agreement with Ἰησοῦς) 9.
Ἰησοῦς (nom.sing.masc.of Ἰησοῦς, subject of ἐληλύθει) 3.
εἰς (preposition with the accusative of extent) 140.
τὴν (acc.sing.fem.of the article in agreement with κώμην) 9.
κώμην (acc.sing.fem.of κώμη, extent) 834.
ἀλλ' (alternative conjunction) 342.
ἦν (3d.per.sing.imp.ind.of εἰμί, progressive description) 86.
ἔτι (adverb of time) 448.
ἐν (preposition with the locative of place where) 80.
τῷ (loc.sing.masc.of the article in agreement with τόπῳ) 9.
τόπῳ (loc.sing.masc.of τόπος, place where) 1019.
ὅπου (particle introducing a definite local clause) 592.
ὑπήντησεν (3d.per.sing.aor.act.ind.of ὑπαντάω, constative) 762.
αὐτῷ (dat.sing.masc.of αὐτός, personal interest) 16.
ἡ (nom.sing.fem.of the article in agreement with Μάρθα) 9.
Μάρθα (nom.sing.fem.of Μάρθα, subject of ὑπήντησεν) 2436.

Translation - "Now Jesus had not yet come into the village, but was still in the place where Martha had met Him."

Comment: We might reasonably expect that, while Martha was going back to Bethany with her message for Mary, Jesus would procede toward the village to meet Mary. On the contrary now we learn that Jesus had not yet (οὔπω) come into the village (pluperfect tense in ἐληλύθει). The alternative ἀλλ' follows. Instead He was still at the spot where Martha had met Him. Thus Jesus and Mary were permitted to talk alone, beyond the hearing of the Jerusalem Jews, whose motives for being there were perhaps not wholly pure. The Jews were not far behind Mary, however (vss.31-33). We assume that those disciples who were with Jesus in Perea when He first received the sisters' message were still with Him.

Verse 31 - "The Jews then which were with her in the house and comforted her, when they saw Mary, that she rose up hastily and went out, followed her, saying, She goeth unto the grave to weep there."

οἱ οὖν Ἰουδαῖοι οἱ ὄντες μετ' αὐτῆς ἐν τῇ οἰκίᾳ καὶ παραμυθούμενοι αὐτήν, ἰδόντες τὴν Μαριὰμ ὅτι ταχέως ἀνέστη καὶ ἐξῆλθεν, ἠκολούθησαν αὐτῇ, δόξαντες ὅτι ὑπάγει εἰς τὸ μνημεῖον ἵνα κλαύσῃ ἐκεῖ.

οἱ (nom.pl.masc.of the article in agreement with Ἰουδαῖοι) 9.
οὖν (inferential conjunction) 68.
Ἰουδαῖοι (nom.pl.masc.of Ἰουδαῖος, subject of *ἠκολούθησαν*) 143.
οἱ (nom.pl.masc.of the article in agreement with *ὄντες*) 9.
ὄντες (pres.part.nom.pl.masc.of *εἰμί*, substantival, apposition) 86.
μετ' (preposition with the genitive of accompaniment) 50.
αὐτῆς (gen.sing.fem.of *αὐτός*, accompaniment) 16.
ἐν (preposition with the locative of place where) 80.
τῇ (loc.sing.fem.of the article in agreement with *οἰκίᾳ*) 9.
οἰκίᾳ (loc.sing.fem.of *οἰκία*, place where) 186.
καὶ (adjunctive conjunction joining participles) 14.
παραμυθούμενοι (pres.mid.part.nom.pl.masc.of *παραμυθέομαι*, substantival, apposition) 2602.
αὐτήν (acc.sing.fem.of *αὐτός*, direct object of *παραμυθούμενοι*) 16.
ἰδόντες (aor.act.part.nom.pl.masc.of *ὁράω*, adverbial, temporal) 144.
τὴν (acc.sing.fem.of the article in agreement with Μαριὰμ) 9.
Μαριὰμ (acc.sing.fem.of *Μαρίας*, direct object of *ἰδόντες*) 2439.
ὅτι (conjunction introducing an object clause in indirect discourse) 211.
ταχέως (adverbial) 2531.
ἀνέστη (3d.per.sing.aor.act.ind.of *ἀνίστημι*, constative) 789.
καὶ (adjunctive conjunction joining verbs) 14.
ἐξῆλθεν (3d.per.sing.aor.ind.of *ἐξέρχομαι*, constative) 161.
ἠκολούθησαν (3d.per.pl.aor.act.ind.of *ἀκολουθέω*, ingressive) 394.
αὐτῇ (instru.sing.fem.of *αὐτός*, association) 16.
δόξαντες (aor.act.part.nom.pl.masc.of *δοκέω*, adverbial, causal) 287.
ὅτι (conjunction introducing an object clause in indirect discourse) 211.
ὑπάγει (3d.per.sing.pres.act.ind.of *ὑπάγω*, aoristic) 364.
εἰς (preposition with the accusative of extent) 140.
τὸ (acc.sing.neut.of the article in agreement with *μνημεῖον*) 9.
μνημεῖον (acc.sing.neut.of *μνημεῖον*, extent) 763.
ἵνα (conjunction introducing a purpose clause with the subjunctive) 114.
κλαύσῃ (3d.per.sing.aor.act.subj.of *κλαίω*, purpose) 225.
ἐκεῖ (adverbial) 204.

Translation - "Therefore when the Jews who were with her in the house and were comforting her saw that Mary arose quickly and went out, they began to follow her, because they supposed that she was going to the grave to weep there."

Comment: It was Mary's abrupt departure from the house that caused the Jews' reaction which is here described. The participial constructions with which the verse abounds explain who the Jews were, what they were doing there, when they began to follow Mary and why. It is worth noting that when the Holy Spirit first described Mary's reaction to Martha's message, that He used the passive form ἠγέρθη (vs.29). *Cf.* our comment. Now in verse 31, describing what the Jews thought they saw, He uses the active form ἀνέστη. How were the Jews to know that the news that Jesus had arrived would "give the lift" to Mary, so that she was lifted up from her seated position on the floor? To their insensitive perception she appeared simply to rise by her own power.

Why did the Jews begin (ingressive aorist in ἠκολούθησαν) to follow Mary? The causal participle δόξαντες tells us that they thought that she was going to the grave to weep there.

This is one of John's most interesting verses from a grammatical standpoint. It is excellent Greek. The image which this verse gives to the Jerusalem Jews is not flattering. It was the custom for Jews to impose themselves into the homes and upon the attentions of the bereaved. *Cf.* Edersheim, II, *en loc.*. It is pretty revolting. They had been around the house for four days now. It is likely that Mary and Martha were getting tired of them and their endless speeches, oft repeated, extolling the virtues of the departed Lazarus. Their sonorous quotations from the scriptures must have fallen upon the ears of the sisters like "sounding brass and clanging cymbals." Of course the Jews were in no position to appreciate the love which Mary, Martha and Lazarus had for Jesus. They probably did not know that the sisters had sent the message to Jesus before Lazarus died (vs.3). Nor did they know that Jesus had arrived and was waiting outside the village limits. They could not have known what Martha whispered to her sister (vs.28), nor why Mary left the house so abruptly (vs.29). But they had to go along and almost intruded into what Mary, of course, should have liked to have been a quiet conversation with her beloved Lord. Those who are unregenerate and insensitive to spiritual values are often boorish, albeit unintentionally. We should not expect swine to demonstrate the cultured characteristics that are the hallmark of polite society (Mt.7:6).

Verse 32 - "Then when Mary was come where Jesus was, and saw him, she fell down at his feet, saying unto him, Lord, if thou hadst been here, my brother had not died."

ἡ οὖν Μαριὰμ ὡς ἦλθεν ὅπου ἦν Ἰησοῦς ἰδοῦσα αὐτὸν ἔπεσεν αὐτοῦ πρὸς τοὺς πόδας, λέγουσα αὐτῷ, Κύριε, εἰ ἦς ὧδε οὐκ ἄν μου ἀπέθανεν ὁ ἀδελφός.

ἡ (nom.sing.fem.of the article in agreement with Μαριὰμ) 9.
οὖν (continuative conjunction) 68.
Μαριὰμ (nom.sing.fem.of Μαρίας, subject of ἦλθεν and ἔπεσεν) 2439.
ὡς (particle introducing a definite temporal clause) 128.

ἦλθεν (3d.per.sing.aor.ind.of ἔρχομαι, constative, definite temporal clause) 146.

ὅπου (particle introducing a definite local clause) 592.

ἦν (3d.per.sing.imp.ind.of εἰμί, progressive description) 86.

Ἰησοῦς (nom.sing.masc.of Ἰησοῦς, subject of ἦν) 3.

ἰδοῦσα (aor.act.part.nom.sing.fem.of ὁράω, adverbial, temporal) 144.

αὐτὸν (acc.sing.masc.of αὐτός, direct object of ἰδοῦσα) 16.

ἔπεσεν (3d.per.sing.aor.act.ind.of πίπτω, constative) 187

αὐτοῦ (gen.sing.masc.of αὐτός, possession) 16.

πρὸς (preposition with the accusative of extent, place where) 197.

τοὺς (acc.pl.masc.of the article in agreement with πόδας) 9.

πόδας (acc.pl.masc.of πούς, extent) 353.

λέγουσα (pres.act.part.nom.sing.fem.of λέγω, adverbial, complementary) 66.

αὐτῷ (dat.sing.masc.of αὐτός, indirect object of λέγουσα) 16.

Κύριε (voc.sing.masc.of κύριος, address) 97.

εἰ (conditional particle introducing a second-class condition) 337.

ἦς (2d.per.sing.imp.ind.of εἰμί, second-class condition) 86.

ὧδε (adverb of place) 766.

οὐκ (summary negative conjunction with the indicative) 130.

ἄν (contingency particle in a second-class condition) 205.

μου (gen.sing.fem.of ἐγώ, relationship) 123.

ἀπέθανεν (3d.per.sing.aor.act.ind.of ἀποθνήσκω, second-class condition) 774.

ὁ (nom.sing.masc.of the article in agreement with ἀδελφός) 9.

ἀδελφός (nom.sing.masc.of ἀδελφός, subject of ἀπέθανεν) 15.

Translation - "Then when Mary came where Jesus was and saw Him, she fell at His feet, saying to Him, 'Lord, if you had been here, my brother would not have died.'"

Comment: Here we have πρὸς and the accusative of extent in a construction that resembles a locative of place. She fell toward (accusative of extent) and therefore near to (πρός) or at His feet. Note that ἀπέθανεν is emphasized ahead of the subject and that μου is emphasized even above the verb. The first emphasis therefore is "He is *my* brother." The second is "He is *dead*." Compare it with Martha's similar utterance in verse 21. Apparently the girls had made similar observations before and after Lazarus died. *Cf.* our comments on the second-class, contrary to fact condition in verse 21.

Verse 33 - "When Jesus therefore saw her weeping, and the Jews also weeping, which came with her, he groaned in the spirit, and was troubled."

Ἰησοῦς οὖν ὡς εἶδεν αὐτὴν κλαίουσαν καὶ τοὺς συνελθόντας αὐτῇ Ἰουδαίους κλαίοντας, ἐνεβριμήσατο τῷ πνεύματι καὶ ἐτάραξεν ἑαυτόν,

Ἰησοῦς (nom.sing.masc.of Ἰησοῦς, subject of ἐνεβριμήσατο and ἐτάραξεν) 3.

οὖν (inferential conjunction) 68.

ὡς (particle introducing a definite temporal clause) 128.
εἶδεν (3d.per.sing.aor.act.ind.of ὁράω, constative) 144.
αὐτὴν (acc.sing.fem.of αὐτός, direct object of εἶδεν) 16.
κλαίουσαν (pres.act.part.acc.sing.fem.of κλαίω, adverbial, complementary) 225.
καὶ (adjunctive conjunction joining substantives) 14.
τοὺς (acc.pl.masc.of the article in agreement with συνελθόντας) 9.
συνελθόντας (aor.part.acc.pl.masc.of συνέρχομαι, adjectival, in agreement with Ἰουδαίους) 78.
αὐτῇ (instru.sing.fem.of αὐτός, association) 16.
Ἰουδαίους (acc.pl.masc.of Ἰουδαῖος, direct object of εἶδεν) 143.
κλαίοντας (pres.act.part.acc.pl.masc.of κλαίω, adverbial, complementary) 225.
ἐνεβριμήσατο (3d.per.sing.aor.mid.ind.of ἐμβριμάομαι, ingressive) 831.
τῷ (loc.sing.neut.of the article in agreement with πνεύματι) 9.
πνεύματι (loc.sing.neut.of πνεῦμα, sphere) 83.
καὶ (adjunctive conjunction joining verbs) 14.
ἐτάραξεν (3d.per.sing.aor.act.ind.of ταράσσω, ingressive) 149.
ἑαυτόν (acc.sing.masc.of ἑαυτός, direct object of ἐτάραξεν) 288.

Translation - "Therefore when Jesus saw her weeping and the Jews who came with her weeping, He was seized with impatience and became agitated."

Comment: *Cf.*#831 for the meaning of this interesting word. The other New Testament passages where it occurs indicate disapproval, perhaps accompanied by sharp retort. Classical Greek writers used it of the snorting of a horse impatient for the race or the battle. "Jesus snorted with impatience." Followed by a locative of sphere, τῷ πνεύματι, indicates that it is an intellectual storm with which our Lord was seized as He saw the evidence of what death could do to His friends. He was impatient or restive in the sphere of His spirit, or His intellect. Hence, perhaps "disgust" is a part of it. Angry because His bitter and implacable enemy, death, had laid its grisly hands upon His dear friend, Lazarus, and had broken the hearts of Mary and Martha. He was also disgusted with the hypocrisy of the Jews who were weeping, not from any deeply felt sense of loss, but because society demanded such histrionics.

Jesus was impatient for for His hour to come, when he would, once for all, deal with him who had the power of death and impose the sentence of His supreme court of universal justice (Heb.2:14,15). The highly trained athlete who wants very much to win, and who is psychologically "up" for the game, knows Jesus' mood on this occasion. A sports announcer once described a left jab delivered by a prize fighter by saying that ". . . he put his heart into that punch!" Jesus had His heart in this contest with death. He would now prove beyond all doubt that He was bigger than death, and that He would, on resurrection day, do for all of the saints what He was now about to do for Lazarus. Anyone who can raise a dead man who had been dead and buried for four days, can lay down His own life on a cross and take it again on the third day (John 10:16-18).

Spinoza, the great Dutch pantheist, once said that if he could believe the Lazarus story, he would abandon his entire philosophical system and become a Christian. Similarly, if I could not believe the Lazarus story, I would be forced to abandon the entire system called Christianity. Jesus was angry at sin and death, sorry for Mary and Martha, disgusted with the Jews, impatient for Calvary and eager to approach the tomb and rob it of its victim. John adds *καὶ ἐτάραξεν ἑαυτόν* - "He troubled Himself." *Cf.*#149, with special attention to John 12:27, where He was thinking of the agonies of the cross, and to John 13:21 where He predicted that Judas would betray Him. Thus we see the other side of Jesus' nature - the human side. *ἐνεβριμήσατο τῷ πνεύματι* - reveals God, angry at sin, disgusted with hypocrites, sorry for victimized people, impatient with delay and eager for the showdown fight at the cross. But also *ἐτάραξεν ἑαυτόν* - Man, shrinking from the pain and disgrace of arrest, a mock trial, the indignities of the mob, the agony of the crucifixion.

Verse 34 - "And said, Where have ye laid him? They said unto him, Lord, come and see."

καὶ εἶπεν, Ποῦ *τεθείκατε αὐτόν; λέγουσιν αὐτῷ,* Κύριε, *ἔρχου καὶ ἴδε.*

καὶ (continuative conjunction) 14.
εἶπεν (3d.per.sing.aor.act.ind.of *εἶπον*, constative) 155.
Ποῦ (interrogative adverb of place, in direct question) 142.
τεθείκατε (2d.per.pl.perf.act.ind.of *τίθημι*, direct question) 455.
αὐτόν (acc.sing.masc.of *αὐτός*, direct object of *τεθείκατε*) 16.
λέγουσιν (3d.per.pl.pres.act.ind.of *λέγω*, historical) 66.
αὐτῷ (dat.sing.masc.of *αὐτός*, indirect object of *λέγουσιν*) 16.
Κύριε (voc.sing.masc.of *κύριος*, address) 97.
ἔρχου (2d.per.sing.pres.impv.of *ἔρχομαι*, entreaty) 146.
καὶ (adjunctive conjunction joining verbs) 14.
ἴδε (2d.per.sing.aor.act.impv.of *ὁράω*, entreaty) 144.

Translation - "And He said, 'Where have you laid him?' They said to Him, 'Lord, come and see.' "

Comment: Ποῦ in a direct question. *Cf.*#142 for other examples. #455 has the list where *τίθημι* is used elsewhere with reference to burial. It was natural for the man Christ Jesus to ask where the tomb was located. It was unnecessary for the incarnate Son of God to ask. His humanity is very much in view in

Verse 35 - "Jesus wept."

ἐδάκρυσεν ὁ Ἰησοῦς.

#2603 *ἐδάκρυσεν* (3d.per.sing.aor.act.ind.of *δακρύω*, ingressive).

weep - John 11:35.

Meaning: to shed tears; to weep silently - John 11:35; Acts 20:19,31. Synonyms:

δακρύω (#2603), to shed tears silently; *κλαίω* (#225), to weep audibly; to weep like a child; *ὀδύρομαι* (not in the N.T.), to give verbal expression to grief; to lamenet; *θρνέω* (#928), to give formal expression to grief; to sing a dirge; *ἀλαλάζω* (#2241), *ὀλολύζω* (#5151), *στενάζω* (#2310), to express grief by inarticulate or semi-articulate sounds; to groan. *δακρύω* - with reference to Jesus - John 11:35; Paul - Acts 20:19,31.

ὁ (nom.sing.masc.of the article in agreement with Ἰησοῦς) 9.
Ἰησοῦς (nom.sing.masc.of Ἰησοῦς, subject of *ἐδάκρυσεν*) 3.

Translation - "Jesus burst into tears."

Comment: The aorist is inceptive, inchoative or ingressive, indicating incipient grief, though not expressed audibly as would be the case if it were *ἔκλαυσεν* as in Lk.19:41. Our Lord was suddenly shaken by a paroxysm of silent grief as His body shook with sobs and silent tears coursed down His cheeks. There was no outcry. It was dignified, controlled and yet uncontrollable human sorrow.

Verse 36 - "Then said the Jews, behold how He loved him."

ἔλεγον οὖν οἱ Ἰουδαῖοι, Ἴδε πῶς ἐφίλει αὐτόν.

ἔλεγον (3d.per.pl.imp.act.ind.of *λέγω*, inceptive) 66.
οὖν (continuative conjunction) 68.
οἱ (nom.pl.masc.of the article in agreement with Ἰουδαῖοι) 9.
Ἰουδαῖοι (nom.pl.masc.of Ἰουδαῖος, subject of *ἔλεγον*) 143.
Ἴδε (2d.per.sing.aor.act.impv.of *ὁράω*, exclamation) 144.
πῶς (exclamatory adverb) 627.
ἐφίλει (3d.per.sing.imp.act.ind.of *φιλέω*, progressive description) 566.
αὐτόν (acc.sing.masc.of *αὐτός*, direct object of *ἐφίλει*) 16.

Translation - "Then the Jews began to say, 'See how much He has always loved him.' "

Comment: Jesus' grief, though silent, was visible and it motivated the comment of the Jews. Any attempt to distinguish between *φιλέω* (#566) and *ἀγαπάω* (#540) will not endure the light of scholarly research. Jesus loved Lazarus both divinely and humanly and He could not hold back the tears when he died, even though He knew that in a moment He was going to call Lazarus from the tomb. The Jews' remark, though not intentionally so, was self incriminating. At least they were perceptive enough to recognize the difference between the grief that expresses true love, which they saw in Jesus' face, and the professional caterwaulling in which they had been engaging for four days.

Verse 37 - "And some of them said, Could not this man which opened the eyes of the blind, have caused that even this man should not have died?"

τινὲς δὲ ἐξ αὐτῶν εἶπαν, Οὐκ ἐδύνατο οὗτος ὁ ἀνοίξας τοὺς ὀφθαλμοὺς τοῦ τυφλοῦ ποιῆσαι ἵνα καὶ οὗτος μὴ ἀποθάνῃ;

τινὲς (nom.pl.masc.of τις, indefinite pronoun, subject of εἶπαν) 486.
δὲ (continuative conjunction) 11.
ἐξ (preposition with the genitive, partitive) 19.
αὐτῶν (gen.pl.masc.of αὐτός, partitive) 16.
εἶπαν (3d.per.pl.aor.act.ind.of εἶπον, constative) 155.
Οὐκ (summary negative conjunction in rhetorical question expecting an affirmative reply) 130.
ἐδύνατο (3d.per.sing.imp.ind.of δύναμαι, progressive description) 289.
οὗτος (nom.sing.masc.of ουτος, in agreement with ἀνοίξας, deictic) 93.
ὁ (nom.sing.masc.of the article in agreement with ἀνοίξας) 9.
ἀνοίξας (aor.act.part.nom.sing.masc.of ἀνοίγω, substantival, subject of ἐδύνατο) 188.
τοὺς (acc.pl.masc.of the article in agreement with ὀφθαλμοὺς) 9.
ὀφθαλμοὺς (acc.pl.masc.of ὀφθαλμός, direct object of ἀνοίξας) 501.
τοῦ (gen.sing.masc.of the article in agreement with τυφλοῦ) 9.
τυφλοῦ (gen.sing.masc.of τυφλός, possession) 830.
ποιῆσαι (aor.act.inf.of ποιέω, complementary) 127.
ἵνα (conjunction with the subjunctive in a negative result clause) 114.
καὶ (ascensive conjunction) 14.
οὗτος (nom.sing.masc.of οὗτος, subject of ἀποθάνῃ) 93.
μὴ (qualified negative conjunction with the subjunctive in a result clause) 87.
ἀποθάνῃ (3d.per.sing.aor.act.subj.of ἀποθνήσκω, result clause) 774.

Translation - "And some of them said, 'Was this man who opened the eyes of the blind not able to prevent this man from dying?' "

Comment: Only the Christian who is yielded to the will of God and filled with the Holy Spirit, has the finely tuned spiritual and intellectual sensibility to know when speech is appropriate and when, on the other hand, silence would become him. All others, even backslidden Christians, not to mention the unsaved, particularly if they are nursing a prejudice against Jesus, are, in the nature of the case, so insecure and hence intellectually and emotionally off balance, as to speak at the wrong time and hence, since they should have remained silent, to say something stupid and heartless. Not all of the Jews who were present spoke, but some of them did - *τινὲς . . . ἐξ αὐτῶν εἶπαν*. They must have annoyed Jesus with their inane, vapid and vacuous, if not deliberately malicious remark, because they were damning Him with faint praise. To ask whether the incarnate Son of God, who was about to rescue a dead man from corruption, could not have prevented his death, since He had already demonstrated His ability to open the eyes of a blind man, is like asking whether a gold medal winner at the Olympics could beat a beginner?

They were not suggesting that Lazarus' illness was a case too difficult for Jesus. They did imply that the man who had opened the eyes of a blind man could have prevented Lazarus' death if only He had come to Bethany sooner. Their remark can be interpreted as a criticism of Jesus for not having hastened to Bethany before Lazarus died. None of them, of course, understood that Jesus had deliberately tarried in Perea until He knew that Lazarus was dead, and had told His disciples that He would raise him from the dead (vs.11). They were totally unprepared to consider the possibility that Lazarus could be restored to life. This is the difference between them and Martha, whose remark in verse 22 seems to hint that she knew that Jesus could *if He wished* bring her brother back to life.

That the remark of verse 37 annoyed Jesus is clear in

Verse 38 - "Jesus therefore again groaning in himself, cometh to the grave. It was a cave, and a stone lay upon it."

Ἰησοῦς οὖν πάλιν ἐμβριμώμενος ἐν ἑαυτῷ ἔρχεται εἰς τὸ μνημεῖον. ἦν δὲ σπήλαιον, καὶ λίθος ἐπέκειτο ἐπ' αὐτῷ.

Ἰησοῦς (nom.sing.masc.of Ἰησοῦς, subject of ἔρχεται) 3.
οὖν (continuative conjunction) 68.
πάλιν (adverbial) 355.
ἐμβριμώμενος (pres.mid.part.nom.sing.masc.of ἐμβριμάομαι, adverbial, temporal) 831.
ἐν (preposition with the locative of place where) 80.
ἑαυτῷ (loc.sing.masc.of ἑαυτός, place where) 288.
ἔρχεται (3d.per.sing.pres.ind.of ἔρχομαι, historical) 146.
εἰς (preposition with the accusative of extent) 140.
τὸ (acc.sing.neut.of the article in agreement with μνημεῖον) 9.
μνημεῖον (acc.sing.neut.of μνημεῖον, extent) 763.
ἦν (3d.per.sing.imp.ind.of εἰμί, progressive description) 86.
δὲ (explanatory conjunction) 11.
σπήλαιον (nom.sing.neut.of σπήλαιον, predicate nominative) 1358.
καὶ (continuative conjunction) 14.
λίθος (nom.sing.masc.of λίθος, subject of ἐπέκειτο) 290.
ἐπ' (preposition with the locative of place where) 47.
αὐτῷ (loc.sing.masc.of αὐτός, place where) 16.

Translation - "Jesus then, as He repressed a groan, came to the tomb. Now it was a cave, and a stone had been laid upon it."

Comment: The remark of verse 37 contributed to Jesus' emotional reaction. Again He "snorted" in disgust, though He internalized it. The participle ἐμβριμώμενος is present tense. As He was walking to the tomb He was struggling to conceal the impatience which He felt as He approached the moment for His greatest miracle.

John now finds it necessary to describe the physical circumstances of the situation. Thus δὲ is explanatory and καὶ is continuative. A stone had been laid upon the entrance of the cave and had been in place since the burial. Note the repetition of ἐπί in ἐπέκειτο ἐπ' αὐτῷ, as if to convey the idea of extra pressure upon the tomb. The barrier could be removed, but only with some effort. Thus the corpse was protected from predators, animal and human.

Verse 39 - "Jesus said, Take ye away the stone. Martha, the sister of him that was dead, saith unto Him, Lord, by this time he stinketh: for he hath been dead four days."

λέγει ὁ Ἰησοῦς, Ἄρατε τὸν λίθον. λέγει αὐτῷ ἡ ἀδελφὴ τοῦ τετελευτηκότος Μάρθα, Κύριε, ἤδη ὄζει, τεταρταῖος γάρ ἐστιν.

λέγει (3d.per.sing.pres.act.ind.of *λέγω*, historical) 66.
ὁ (nom.sing.masc.of the article in agreement with *Ἰησοῦς*) 9.
Ἰησοῦς (nom.sing.masc.of *Ἰησοῦς*, subject of *λέγει*) 3.
Ἄρατε (2d.per.pl.aor.act.impv.of *αἴρω*, command) 350.
τὸν (acc.sing.masc.of the article in agreement with *λίθον*) 9.
λίθον (acc.sing.masc.of *λίθος*, direct object of *ἄρατε*) 290.
λέγει (3d.per.sing.pres.act.ind.of *λέγω*, historical) 66.
αὐτῷ (dat.sing.masc.of *αὐτός*, indirect object of *λέγει*) 16.
ἡ (nom.sing.fem.of the article in agreement with *ἀδελφή*)) 9.
ἀδελφὴ (nom.sing.fem.of *ἀδελφή*, subject of *λέγει*) 1025.
τοῦ (gen.sing.masc.of the article in agreement with *τετελευτηκότος*) 9.
τετελευτηκότος (perf.part.gen.sing.masc.of *τελευτάω*, relationship) 231.
Μάρθα (nom.sing.fem.of *Μάρθα*, apposition) 2436.
Κύριε (voc.sing.masc.of *κύριος*, address) 97.
ἤδη (temporal adverb) 291.

#2604 *ὄζει* (3d.per.sing.pres.act.ind.of *ὄζω*, progressive).

stink - John 11:39.

Meaning: To emit an odor, either pleasing or displeasing, depending upon the context. With reference to the decomposing body of Lazarus - John 11:39. *Cf.* LXX, Exodus 8:14.

#2605 *τεταρταῖος* (ordinal numeral).

dead four days - John 11:39.

Meaning: an ordinal number. Fourth. In John 11:39, *τεταρταῖος γάρ ἐστιν* - "It is the fourth day."

γάρ (causal conjunction) 105.
ἐστιν (3d.per.sing.pres.ind.of *εἰμί*, aoristic) 86.

Translation - "Jesus said, 'Lift up the stone.' Martha, the sister of the dead man, said to Him, 'Lord, by this time he has begun to decompose, because it is the fourth day.' "

Comment: Note that the imperative *Ἄρατε* is plural, which is logical since the stone was too heavy for a single person to lift. The verb also indicates that the stone had to be "lifted up," in order to be taken away, - a hint about the physical arrangement of the tomb in relation to the stone cover.

Jesus' order was peremptory. It is the sharp, crisp command of a military officer who knows exactly what he is going to do and will brook no nonesense. Martha now indicates that she does not believe in her Lord much more than do the other Jews. There is no way to translate *ὄζει* literally without using the offensive word. Literally it means "to emit an odor" without designating good or bad. Montgomery says, "he is offensive." Goodspeed has, "he is decaying." Martha was objecting on the grounds that the dead body of her brother had decomposed to a considerable degree after four days in the hot climate of the area in late spring. Her remark is helpful is disproving the skeptic's view that the entire story was based upon a hoax, promoted by Lazarus and his sisters to promote Jesus. Martha was as surprized as the others when Jesus raised her brother from the dead. A practical joker does not stink except in an accommodated sense! Martha's statement, as ill advised as the statement by the Jews in verse 37, draws Jesus' sharp rebuke in

Verse 40 — "Jesus saith unto her, Said I not unto thee that, if thou wouldst believe, thou shouldst see the glory of God?"

λέγει αὐτῇ ὁ Ἰησοῦς, Οὐκ εἶπόν σοι ὅτι ἐὰν πιστεύσῃς ὄψῃ τὴν δόξαν τοῦ θεοῦ;

λέγει (3d.per.sing.pres.act.ind.of *λέγω*, historical) 66.
αὐτῇ (dat.sing.fem.of *αὐτος*, indirect object of *λέγει*) 16.
ὁ (nom.sing.masc.of the article in agreement with *Ἰησοῦς*) 9.
Ἰησοῦς (nom.sing.masc.of *Ἰησοῦς*, subject of *λέγει*) 3.
Οὐκ (summary negative conjunction in rhetorical question expecting an affirmative reply) 130.
εἶπόν (1st.per.sing.aor.act.ind.of *εἶπον*, constative) 155.
σοι (dat.sing.fem.of *σύ*, indirect object of *εἶπόν*) 104.
ὅτι (conjunction introducing an object clause) 211.
ἐὰν (conditional particle in a third-class condition) 363.
πιστεύσῃς (2d.per.sing.aor.act.subj.of *πιστεύω*, third-class condition) 734.
ὄψῃ (2d.per.sing.fut.act.ind.of *ὁράω*, predictive) 144.
τὴν (acc.sing.fem.of the article in agreement with *δόξαν*) 9.
δόξαν (acc.sing.fem.of *δόξα*, direct object of *ὄψῃ*) 361.
τοῦ (gen.sing.masc.of the article in agreement with *θεοῦ*) 9.
θεοῦ (gen.sing.masc.of *θεός*, description) 124.

Translation - "Jesus said to her, 'I said to you, did I not, that if you would believe, you would see the glory of God?' "

Comment: It is a rhetorical question expecting Martha to agree. The third-class condition offers no certainty that Martha would in fact rise to the occasion and believe, but in the event that she did, there is no doubt about the conclusion in the result clause. "If you believe (which you may or may not be able to do) you will see the glory of God (and there is no doubt whatever about that") *Cf.*#361 for other uses of *δόξα* in this sense. Jesus did not tell Martha when she would see the glory of God if she believed in Him. The evidence of His glory, Jesus was soon to provide.

Verse 41 - "Then they took away the stone from the place where the dead was laid. And Jesus lifted up his eyes and said, Father, I thank thee that thou hast heard me."

ἦραν οὖν τὸν λίθον. ὁ δὲ Ἰησοῦς ἦρεν τοὺς ὀφθαλμοὺς ἄνω καὶ εἶπεν, Πάτερ, εὐχαριστῶ σοι ὅτι ἤκουσάς μου.

ἦραν (3d.per.pl.aor.act.ind.of *αἴρω*, constative) 350.
οὖν (inferential conjunction) 68.
τὸν (acc.sing.masc.of the article in agreement with *λίθον*) 9.
λίθον (acc.sing.masc.of *λίθος*, direct object of *ἦραν*) 290.
ὁ (nom.sing.masc.of the article in agreement with *Ἰησοῦς*) 9.
δὲ (continuative conjunction) 11.
Ἰησοῦς (nom.sing.masc.of *Ἰησοῦς*, subject of *ἦρεν*) 3.
ἦρεν (3d.per.sing.aor.act.ind.of *αἴρω*, constative) 350.
τοὺς (acc.pl.masc.of the article in agreement with *ὀφθαλμοὺς*) 9.
ὀφθαλμοὺς (acc.pl.masc.of *ὀφθαλμός*, direct object of *ἦρεν*) 501.
ἄνω (adverbial) 1973.
καὶ (adjunctive conjunction joining verbs) 14.
εἶπεν (3d.per.sing.aor.act.ind.of *εἶπον*, constative) 155.
Πάτερ (voc.sing.masc.of *πατήρ*, address) 238.
εὐχαριστῶ (1st.per.sing.pres.act.ind.of *εὐχαριστέω*, aoristic) 1185.
σοι (dat.sing.masc.of *σύ*, indirect object of *εὐχαριστῶ*) 104.
ὅτι (conjunction introducing an object clause in indirect discourse) 211.
ἤκουσάς (2d.per.sing.aor.act.ind.of *ἀκούω*, culminative) 148.
μου (gen.sing.masc.of *ἐγώ*, description after a verb of hearing) 123.

Translation - "Therefore they took down the stone. And Jesus lifted His eyes heavenward and said, 'Father, I thank you that you have heard me.' "

Comment: *οὖν* is inferential. The look on Jesus' face, the tone of His voice and what He said to Martha was enough to move someone to obedience, despite the fact that the command seemed to them to be contrary to good reason. Jesus' statement of verse 42 is an explanation to the Father of our Lord's reason for praying aloud in the presence of the people. He certainly had no need to pray aloud to the Father in order to communicate with Him.

Verse 42 - "And I knew that thou hearest me always; but because of the people which stand by, I said it, that they may believe that thou hast sent me."

ἐγὼ δὲ ᾔδειν ὅτι πάντοτέ μου ἀκούεις, ἀλλὰ διὰ τὸν ὄχλον τὸν περιεστῶτα εἶπον, ἵνα πιστεύσωσιν ὅτι σύ με ἀπέστειλας.

ἐγὼ (nom.sing.masc.of *ἐγώ*, subject of *ᾔδειν*, emphatic) 123.
δὲ (explanatory conjunction) 11.
ᾔδειν (1st.per.sing.pluperfect ind.of *ὁράω*, consummative) 144.

ὅτι (conjunction introducing an object clause in indirect discourse) 211.
πάντοτέ (adverbial) 1567.
μου (gen.sing.masc.of ἐγώ, description after a verb of hearing) 123.
ἀκούεις (2d.per.sing.pres.act.ind.of ἀκούω, progressive) 148.
ἀλλὰ (adversative conjunction) 342.
διὰ (preposition with the accusative, cause) 118.
τὸν (acc.sing.masc.of the article in agreement with ὄχλον) 9.
ὄχλον (acc.sing.masc.of ὄχλος, cause) 418.
τὸν (acc.sing.masc.of the article in agreement with περιεστῶτα) 9.

#2606 περιεστῶτα (perf.act.part.acc.sing.masc.of περιΐστημι,in agreement with ὄχλον).

stand by - John 11:42.
stand round about - Acts 25:7.
avoid - Titus 3:9.
shun - 2 Tim.2:16.

Meaning: A combination of περί (#173) and ἵστημι (#180). Hence, to stand around. Properly in John 11:42; Acts 25:7. In the middle voice, to maneuver oneself around, that is, to shun or avoid - with reference to useless controversy - Titus 3:9; 2 Tim.2:16.

εἶπον (1st.per.sing.aor.act.ind.of εἶπον, constative) 155.
ἵνα (conjunction introducing a purpose clause) 114.
πιστεύσωσιν (3d.per.pl.1st.aor.act.subj.of πιστεύω, purpose) 734.
ὅτι (conjunction introducing an object clause) 211.
σύ (nom.sing.masc.of σύ, subject of ἀπέστειλας, emphatic) 104.
με (acc.sing.masc.of ἐγώ, direct object of ἀπέστειλας) 123.
ἀπέστειλας (2d.per.sing.aor.act.ind.of ἀποστέλλω, culminative) 215.

Translation - "Now I have always known that you listen to me, but because of the people who have been standing around I have said it, in order that they may believe that I am here as your messenger."

Comment: δὲ is explanatory. ἐγὼ is emphasized, since otherwise it is unnecessary because it is implicit in the verb ᾔδειν. It is as though Jesus is hastening to explain that His thanks to the Father for hearing Him (vs.41) did not in any way imply that Jesus doubted that the Father listened to Him always. On the contrary "I have always known (and I know now) that . . . κ.τ.λ." (pluperfect tense in ᾔδειν). Jesus' statement to the Father also rescues Him from any charge that He was being histrionic. A ham actor on such an occasion would be certain to make a great production out of His conversation with God, just before raising a dead man from the tomb. What had Jesus always known? The object clause with ὅτι tells us. Note the genitive μου after ἀκούεις - "you always hear me and nobody else." Jesus explains why He did thank the Father audibly. The διὰ phrase is causal. It was on account of the crowd that had been standing around (perfect tense in the participle περιεστῶτα), and were still present. The purpose clause with ἵνα and the subjunctive in πιστεύσωσιν tells us why Jesus wanted the people to hear - "in order that they might believe that I am here as your messenger." I have translated like this because ἀπέστειλας is a culminative aorist. "You sent me, and as a result, here I am in the capacity as your messenger." Note the emphasis in σύ in the last clause.

Jesus was maneuvering the situation in such a way that when Lazarus came out of that tomb, the people would be forced to agree that the only rational explanation for it was that the Father had sent Jesus Christ, His Son into the world. The super miracle that provides authentication for every claim that Jesus ever made for Himself was about to take place.

Verse 43 - "And when he thus had spoken, he cried with a loud voice, Lazarus, come forth."

καὶ ταῦτα εἰπὼν φωνῇ μεγάλῃ ἐκραύγασεν, Λάζαρε, δεῦρο ἔξω.

καὶ (continuative conjunction) 14.
ταῦτα (acc.pl.neut.of οὗτος, direct object of εἰπὼν) 93.
εἰπὼν (aor.act.part.nom.sing.masc.of εἶπον, adverbial, temporal) 155.
φωνῇ (instru.sing.fem.of φωνή, means) 222.
μεγάλῃ (instru.sing.fem.of μέγας, in agreement with φωνῇ) 184.
ἐκραύγασεν (3d.per.sing.aor.act.ind.of κραυγάζω, constative) 984.
Λάζαρε (voc.sing.masc.of Λάζαρος, address) 2596.
δεῦρο (adverbial interjection with the imperative) 1304.
ἔξω (adverbial) 449.

Translation - "And when He had said these things, with a loud voice He shouted, 'Lazarus, come out of there!' "

Comment: *Cf.*#984 for other uses of κραυγάζω. It was a mighty shout with all of the authority of heaven, earth and hell back of it. This was a great moment for Jesus - His personal preview for what He will do for all of the sleeping saints when He comes again. Note that on that glorious occasion He will shout again (1 Thess.4:16).

Note that He prefaced His mighty command δεῦρο ἔξω with the vocative, Λάζαρε. One often thinks that if our Lord had not told the dead which one He wanted that day, there would have been a general resurrection!

It is unfortunate that Spinoza could not believe this story. What a great Christian he would have been.

Verse 44 - "And he that was dead came forth, bound hand and foot with graveclothes: and his face was bound about with a napkin. Jesus saith unto them, Loose him, and let him go."

ἐξῆλθεν ὁ τεθνηκὼς δεδεμένος τοὺς πόδας καὶ τὰς χεῖρας κειρίαις, καὶ ἡ ὄψις αὐτοῦ σουδαρίῳ περιεδέδετο. λέγει αὐτοῖς ὁ Ἰησοῦς, Λύσατε αὐτὸν καὶ ἄφετε αὐτὸν ὑπάγειν.

ἐξῆλθεν (3d.per.sing.aor.ind.of *ἐξέρχομαι*, constative) 161.
ὁ (nom.sing.masc.of the article in agreement with *τεθνηκὼς*) 9.
τεθνηκὼς (perf.part.nom.sing.masc.of *θνήσκω*, substantival, subject of *ἐξῆλθεν*) 232.
δεδεμένος (perf.pass.part.nom.sing.masc.of *δέω*, adverbial, circumstantial) 998.
τοὺς (acc.pl.masc.of the article in agreement with *πόδας*) 9.
πόδας (acc.pl.masc.of *πούς*, accusative of the thing with the passive voice) 353.
καὶ (continuative conjunction) 14.
τὰς (acc.pl.fem.of the article in agreement with *χεῖρας*) 9.
χεῖρας (acc.pl.fem.of *χείρ*, accusative of the thing with the passive voice) 308.

#2607 *κειρίαις* (instru.pl.fem.of *κειρίαι*, means).

grave clothes - John 11:44.

Meaning: a band of cloth used as swathing bands for preparing a corpse for burial - John 11:44.

καὶ (adjunctive conjunction joining participial constructions) 14.
ἡ (nom.sing.fem.of the article in agreement with *ὄψις*) 9.
ὄψις (nom.sing.fem.of *ὄψις*, subject of *περιεδέδετο*) 2370.
αὐτοῦ (gen.sing.masc.of *αὐτός*, possession) 16.

#2608 *σουδαρίῳ* (instru.sing.neut.of *σουδάριον*, means).

handkerchief - Acts 19:12.
napkin - Luke 19:20; John 11:44; 20:7.

Meaning: A handkerchief, or a cloth for wrapping about the face of the dead - Lazarus - John 11:44; Jesus - John 20:7. With reference to the cloth used in healing - Acts 19;12. In the parable of the pounds - Luke 19:20.

#2609 *περιεδέδετο* (3d.per.sing.perf.pass.ind.of *περιδέω*, intensive).

bind about - John 11:44.

Meaning: A combination of *περί* (#173) and *δέω* (#998). Hence, to bind round about. To wrap or wind about. With reference to the cloth wrapped around the dead face of Lazarus - John 11:44.
λέγει (3d.per.sing.pres.act.ind.of *λέγω*, historical) 66.
αὐτοῖς (dat.pl.masc.of *αὐτός*, indirect object of *λέγει*) 16.
ὁ (nom.sing.masc.of the article in agreement with *Ἰησοῦς*) 9.
Ἰησοῦς (nom.sing.masc.of *Ἰησοῦς*, subject of *λέγει*) 3.
Λύσατε (2d.per.pl.aor.act.impv.of *λύω*, command) 471.
αὐτὸν (acc.sing.masc.of *αὐτός*, direct object of *Λύσατε*) 16.
καὶ (adjunctive conjunction joining verbs) 14.
ἄφετε (2d.per.pl.aor.act.impv.of *ἀφίημι*, command) 319.
αὐτὸν (acc.sing.masc.of *αὐτός*, direct object of *ἄφετε*) 16.

ὑπάγειν (pres.act.inf.of ὑπάγω, complementary) 365.

Translation - "The dead one came out with his feet and hands still bound with wrappings and his face was still bound around with a cloth. Jesus said to them, 'Untie him and let him go.' "

Comment: The perfect participles τεθνηκὼς and δεδεμένος and the perfect indicative περιεδέδετο normally speak of a present condition as the result of a past completed action. In the case of δεδεμένος and περιεδέδετο the rule applies. Lazarus, buried four days before with hands, feet and face prepared for burial was still encumbered with the grave clothing when he came from the tomb. But the participle τεθνηκὼς, is an exception to the rule. He had been dead, but he was now alive. His present condition (alive) did not result from his past death, but from his current resurrection. A similar situation is found in Mk.5:15, where we have θεωροῦσιν τὸν δαιμονιζόμενον καθήμενον ἱματισμένον καὶ σωφρονοῦντα, τὸν ἐσχηκότα τὸν λεγιῶνα, καὶ ἐφοβήθησαν. This is a most instructive passage. The historical present and the aorist indicative here occur side by side. The attributive and the predicate participles appear side by side. The present and the perfect participles come together. Of the two perfect participles, one, ἱματισμένον, is still true (punctiliar and linear) and describes the man's present state; the other, τὸν ἐσχηκότα, is no longer true, and describes the state of the man before Jesus cast out the demon, which casting-out is itself in the past. This participle is therefore a sort of past perfect. Cf.also John 8:31. Another striking example is Jo.11:44, ἐξῆλθεν ὁ τεθνηκὼς δεδεμένος. Here δεδεμένος is still true, though τεθνηκώς is not. Lazarus had been dead, but is not now. We see the same situation in 1 Cor.2:7, τὴν ἀποκεκρυμμένην. The wisdom of God is no longer hidden. The point is still clearer in Rom.16:25f., μυστηρίου χρόνοις αἰωνίοις σεσιγημένου φανερωθέντος δὲ νῦν, where the long silence is now expressly said to be broken." (Robertson, *Grammar*, 1117).

One can imagine the scope and variety of the emotional reactions in the crowd as this miracle occurred. Lingering unbelief, then amazement, and, for Mary and Martha, great joy. It was for some of the Jews the moment of truth, when they came to believe upon Him. For others it suggested a fast trip back to Jerusalem to report the event to the authorities. These last never considered their own moral obligation to face up to the facts and accept Christ. Truly, those who will not hear Moses and the Prophets, will not believe, though one rise from the dead (Lk.16:31).

Jesus Withdraws to Ephraim

(Mt.26:1-5; Mk.14:1-2; Lk.22:1-2; John 11:45-54)

John 11:45 - "Then many of the Jews which came to Mary and had seen the things which Jesus did, believed on him."

Πολλοὶ οὖν ἐκ τῶν Ἰουδαίων, οἱ ἐλθόντες πρὸς τὴν Μαριὰμ καὶ θεασάμενοι *ἃ ἐποίησεν, ἐπίστευσαν εἰς αὐτόν.*

Πολλοὶ (nom.pl.masc.of *πολύς*, subject of *ἐπίστευσαν*) 228.
οὖν (inferential conjunction) 68.
ἐκ (preposition with the partitive genitive) 19.
τῶν (gen.pl.masc.of the article in agreement with Ἰουδαίων) 9.
Ἰουδαίων (gen.pl.masc.of Ἰουδαῖος, partitive genitive) 143.
οἱ (nom.pl.masc.of the article in agreement with *ἐλθόντες*) 9.
ἐλθόντες (aor.part.nom.pl.masc.of *ἔρχομαι*, apposition) 146.
πρὸς (preposition with the accusative of extent) 197.
τὴν (acc.sing.fem.of the article in agreement with Μαριὰμ) 9.
Μαριὰμ (acc.sing.fem.of Μαρίας, extent) 2439.
καὶ (adjunctive conjunction joining participles) 14.
θεασάμενοι (aor.mid.part.nom.pl.masc.of *θεάομαι*, substantival, apposition) 556.
ἃ (acc.pl.neut.of *ὅς*, relative pronoun, direct object of *θεασάμενοι*) 65.
ἐποίησεν (3d.per.sing.aor.act.ind.of *ποιέω*, constative) 127.
ἐπίστευσαν (3d.per.pl.aor.act.ind.of *πιστεύω*, ingressive) 734.
εἰς (preposition with the accusative, cause) 140.
αὐτόν (acc.sing.masc.of *αὐτός*, cause) 16.

Translation - "Many of the Jews, therefore, who came to Mary and saw the things which He did, believed upon Him."

Comment: *οὖν* is inferential. The miracle at the tomb of Lazarus convinced some of the Jews. *Cf.* Lk.16:31. These Jews who now made their commitments to Jesus Christ were already sincere hearers of and believers in Moses and the Prophets. When we react humbly to the light of the revelation which God has given, it is His obligation to give us more light. These Jews were receptive to new light. Conversely, one who will not hear Moses and the Prophets deserves no further evidence to aid his faith. He would not believe though Lazarus (either the Lazarus of Bethany or the Lazarus of Luke 16) rose from the dead. So why should we present evidence to a wicked and adulterous generation? Such people only twist the evidence into another false rationalization to support their prejudices. One sees this every day if he is acquainted with the behavioral sciences. Modern unbelievers are no different from those who must have been startled when they saw Lazarus, bound hand and foot, emerge from the grave. Yet they went back to Jerusalem to play the story into the hands of Jesus' enemies.

That light which is rejected because of the moral obligation involved in its acceptance, results in judgment is clear from Romans 1:18-32, upon which *cf.* our comment.

Verse 46 - "But some of them went their ways to the Pharisees, and told them what things Jesus had done."

τινὲς δὲ ἐξ αὐτῶν ἀπῆλθον πρὸς τοὺς Φαρισαίους καὶ εἶπαν αὐτοῖς ἃ ἐποίησεν Ἰησοῦς.

τινὲς (nom.pl.masc.of τίς, indefinite pronoun, subject of ἀπῆλθον and εἶπαν) 486.
δὲ (adversative conjunction) 11.
ἐξ (preposition with the partitive genitive) 19.
αὐτῶν (gen.pl.masc.of αὐτός, partitive) 16.
ἀπῆλθον (3d.per.pl.aor.act.ind.of ἀπέρχομαι, constative) 239.
πρὸς (preposition with the accusative of extent) 197.
τοὺς (acc.pl.masc.of the article in agreement with Φαρισαίους) 9.
Φαρισαίους (acc.pl.masc.of Φαρισαῖος, extent) 276.
καὶ (adjunctive conjunction joining verbs) 14.
εἶπαν (3d.per.pl.aor.act.ind.of εἶπον, constative) 155.
αὐτοῖς (dat.pl.masc.of αὐτός, indirect object of εἶπαν) 16.
ἃ (acc.pl.neut.of ὅς, direct object of εἶπαν) 65.
ἐποίησεν (3d.per.sing.aor.act.ind.of ποιέω, constative) 127.
Ἰησοῦς (nom.sing.masc.of Ἰησοῦς, subject of ἐποίησεν) 3.

Translation - "But some of them went away to the Pharisees and told them the things that Jesus did."

Comment: δὲ is adversative. Many of the Jews believed and remained to worship, *but* (adversative δὲ) some of them took an adverse attitude. It is heartening to note the difference between πολλοὶ who believed and τινὲς who did not.

Jesus and His works and message will divide any audience (2 Cor.2:14-17; John 6:63-71).

The reaction of the Pharisees to the report of the Jews who came rushing back from Bethany, precipitated in human history what had its incipient development in Israel in the days of John the Baptist, but that had its original impetus in the redemptive plan of the eternal God. The raising of Lazarus brought to a head the movement of the Jewish Establishment against Jesus and started in motion a chain of events that brought Him to the cross.

Verse 47 - "Then gathered the chief priests and the Pharisees a council, and said, What do we? for this man doeth many miracles."

συνήγαγον οὖν οἱ ἀρχιερεῖς καὶ οἱ Φαρισαῖοι συνέδριον, καὶ ἔλεγον, Τί ποιοῦμεν, ὅτι οὗτος ὁ ἄνθρωπος πολλὰ ποιεῖ σημεῖα;

συνήγαγον (3d.per.pl.aor.act.ind.of συνάγω, constative) 150.
οὖν (inferential conjunction) 68.
οἱ (nom.pl.masc.of the article in agreement with ἀρχιερεῖς) 9.
ἀρχιερεῖς (nom.pl.masc.of ἀρχιερεύς, subject of συνήγαγον and ἔλεγον) 151.
οἱ (nom.pl.masc.of the article in agreement with Φαρισαῖοι) 9.
Φαρισαῖοι (nom.pl.masc.of Φαρισαῖος, subject of συνήγαγον and ἔλεγον) 276.

συνέδριον (acc.sing.neut.of *συνέδριον*, direct object of *συνήγαγον*) 481.
καὶ (adjunctive conjunction joining verbs) 14.
ἔλεγον (3d.per.pl.imp.act.ind.of *λέγω*, inceptive) 66.
Tί (acc.sing.neut.of *τίς*, interrogative pronoun, direct object of *ποιοῦμεν*) 281.
ποιοῦμεν (1st.per.pl.pres.act.ind.of *ποιέω*, deliberative) 127.
ὅτι (conjunction introducing a subordinate causal clause) 211.
οὗτος (nom.sing.masc.of *οὗτος*, in agreement with *ἄνθρωπος*, contemptuous use) 93.
ὁ (nom.sing.masc.of the article in agreement with *ἄνθρωπος*) 9.
ἄνθρωπος (nom.sing.masc.of *ἄνθρωπος*, subject of *ποιεῖ*) 341.
πολλὰ (acc.pl.neut.of *πολύς*, in agreement with *σημεῖα*) 228.
ποιεῖ (3d.per.sing.pres.act.ind.of *ποιέω*, progressive) 127.
σημεία (acc.pl.neut.of *σημεῖον*, direct object of *ποιεῖ*) 1005.

Translation - "Therefore the chief priests and the Pharisees called a council, and they began to say, 'What are we doing? Because this man is performing many miracles.' "

Comment: It is not necessary to suppose that *συνέδριον* means the entire official roster of the San Hedrin. *Cf.*#481. This meeting was probably a hastily called affair of all who could be reached for an *ad hoc* conference to discuss policy. They were upset by the report of the Jews from Bethany. There is no indication that they did not believe the report, despite the unusual nature of the episode. Something had to be done to stop this man Jesus, because His ministry, both teaching and works, was certain to gain for Him a following of dangerous proportions to the entrenched interests of the Jewish Establishment.

The present tense in *ποιοῦμεν* in a deliberative question, something that we would normally find in a deliberative future, is interesting. "Rhetorical deliberative questions may be put by the presend indicative, but it is rather a rhetorical way of putting a negation than a question of doubt."(Robertson, *Grammar*, 880). What Robertson means is that the same idea can be put by saying, "We are not doing anything!" "The implication of the question in Jo.11:47 is that nothing was being done. In Mt.12:34, *πῶς δύνασθε ἀγαθὰ λαλεῖν*; a durative deliberative question is expressed by means of *δύνασθε* and the pres.inf. Cf. a similar construction with *δεῖ* in Ac.16:30." (*Ibid.*). "The inquiry of Caiaphas is rather indignant protest against the inactivity of the Sanhedrin than a puzzled quandary as to what they should do. The indicative suits exactly his purpose. He charges them with doing nothing and knowing nothing and makes a definite proposal himself." (*Ibid.*,924).

Having vented their respective spleens at the beginning of their meeting, the Establishmentarians got down to the material essence of what was bothering them in

Verse 48 - "If we let him thus alone, all men will believe on Him: and the Romans shall come and take away both our place and nation."

ἐὰν ἀφῶμεν αὐτὸν οὕτως, πάντες πιστεύσουσιν εἰς αὐτόν, καὶ ἐλεύσονται οἱ

Ῥωμαῖοι καὶ ἀροῦσιν ἡμῶν καὶ τὸν τόπον καὶ τὸ ἔθνος.

ἐὰν (conditional particle in a third-class condition) 363.
ἀφῶμεν (1st.per.pl.aor.act.subj.of *ἀφίημι*, third-class condition) 319.
αὐτὸν (acc.sing.masc.of *αὐτός*, direct object of *ἀφῶμεν*) 16.
οὕτως (demonstrative adverb) 74.
πάντες (nom.pl.masc.of *πᾶς*, subject of *πιστεύσουσιν*) 67.
πιστεύσουσιν (3d.per.pl.fut.act.ind.of *πιστεύω*, predictive) 734.
εἰς (preposition with the accusative, cause) 140.
αὐτόν (acc.sing.masc.of *αὐτός*, cause) 16.
καὶ (continuative conjunction) 14.
ἐλεύσονται (3d.per.pl.fut.act.ind.of *ἔρχομαι*, predictive) 146.
οἱ (nom.pl.masc.of the article in agreement with *Ῥωμαῖοι*) 9.

#2610 *Ῥωμαῖοι* (nom.pl.masc.of *Ῥωμαῖος*, subject of *ἐλεύσονται* and *ἀροῦσιν*).

Roman - John 11:48; Acts 16:21,37,38; 22:25,26,27,29; 23:27; 25:16; 28:17.

Meaning: A Roman. With reference to the political power that held jurisdiction over Palestine - John 11:48; Acts 25:16; 28:17. A citizen of Rome - Acts 16:21,37,38; 22:25,26,27,29; 23:27.

καὶ (adjunctive conjunction joining verbs) 14.
ἀροῦσιν (3d.per.pl.fut.act.ind.of *αἴρω*, predictive) 350.
ἡμῶν (gen.pl.masc.of *ἐγώ*, possession) 123.
καὶ (adjunctive conjunction joining nouns) 14.
τὸν (acc.sing.masc.of the article in agreement with *τόπον*) 9.
τόπον (acc.sing.masc.of *τόπος*, direct object of *ἀροῦσιν*) 1019.
καὶ (adjunctive conjunction joining nouns) 14.
τὸ (acc.sing.neut.of the article in agreement with *ἔθνος*) 9.
ἔθνος (acc.sing.neut.of *ἔθνος*, direct object of *ἀροῦσιν*) 376.

Translation - "If we leave Him alone like this, everybody will believe on Him, and the Romans will come and take away both our place and the nation."

Comment: A third-class condition occupies the entire verse. The apodosis has two predictive futures - "The Romans will come and they will take away our place and the nation." The Sanhedrin had no intention of leaving Jesus alone. They were only speculating about what the results would be if they did. How wrong they were! Walking in the dark (John 11:10) they were stumbling. They looked upon everything with the double eye and were filled with so great darkness (Mt.6:22,23; Lk.11:34,35). The wisdom of men is nonesense to God (1 Cor.1:18-20).

Their first mistake was in predicting any future historical development that might be contingent upon their action or lack of action, as though the sovereign God was bound in His eternal purpose by the decisions of small time politicians. But City Hall has always had an exaggerated conception of its own importance, with seldom a thought as to exactly how insignificant it is, relative to the total universal picture.

The second mistake the Sanhedrin made was their statement that all men would believe upon Jesus if they allowed Him to continue in His ministry. This is manifestly untrue. Did they mean that they also would believe upon Him? And, if not, that everyone except them would? In so, were they implying that they alone were sufficiently erudite so as not to be persuaded by one whom they obviously thought to be a demagogue? Or did they admit that He was the Messiah, and, if so, were they saying that they were the only ones who would reject Him?

The truth is that not all men will believe upon Jesus regardless of what the Jewish Establishment did. It was already evident that Jesus had not been universally accepted. The Light of the World showed up and confounded the darkness of sin (John 1:5; 3:19; 8:12). Thus He brought a sword, not peace (Mt.10:34). The divided household which He predicted (Lk.12:53) dictates that not all men will believe on Christ.

But it can be argued that we are pushing *πάντες* too far, and that they did not mean "all" but "most" men. If they meant that, Jesus, if they did not stop Him, would be accepted by most of the people in Israel and His claim to Messiahship would be authenticated, not only by God, as it already abundantly had been, but also by the people. Thus the triumphal entry, with the crowds shouting "Hosanna to the Son of David" would be an event to be celebrated from Dan to Beersheba. Thus if the Sanhedrin was correct in saying that Jesus would be enthroned by the people as Messiah, unless they moved to prevent it, then when He was enthroned as Israel's Sovereign King He would deal with Rome in His own sovereign way. In this event Rome would be subjugated to Messiah's hegemony like all of the other Gentile nations (Isa.2:3-4; 11:1-16; Micah 4:1-5). This is a far cry from what the Jerusalem politicians were predicting, with their jeremiad that the Romans would come and take away the national foundation of Messiah's chosen people. Or had the Sanhedrin by this time sunk so low that they had abandoned the Messianic hope and were now convinced that the Imperial power of the Eternal City on the Tiber was here to stay and would brook no interference, not even from Messiah? If so Annas and Caiaphas would find fellowship (if one can call it that!) with the Reformed Rabbis of modern times.

The Sanhedrin went astray again with their implication that if they crucified Him, they would, by that event, stop His ministry. They feared that He would win all of the Jews in Palestine to His side. The truth is that it was only *because of* the crucifixion of the Son of God that He drew "all men unto Him" (John 12:32,33). They tried to murder Him, albeit in a manner that their public relations people could describe to the populace as "legal" and "orthodox" and in keeping with "the law of Moses." Since they did not have jurisdiction in their inferior courts over capital crimes, they incited the Jewish mob to force Pilate's hand. Thus a squad of drunken Roman soldiers "lifted Him up" on a cross, and the glorious result is that He is now, two thousand years later, still drawing to Himself "men of every kindred, tribe, tongue, people and nation" (Rev.5:9). He had "other sheep" which He must bring that there might be "one fold and one shepherd" but this could be done only if He submitted to the cross (John 10:10-18). So, if Caiaphas and his hatchetmen wished to prevent Jesus from being the Eternal Magnet of Holiness, Love, Grace, Truth and Peace, Who was about to draw unto Himself the elect of every nation, they should have moved heaven and earth, if possible, to keep Him off the cross. They should have preached what Modernists do today - that the crucifixion of a good man is a tragedy, to be forestalled at whatever cost, however prohibitive. It is gloriously ironic that in trying to prevent our Lord from being universally accepted, Annas and Caiaphas precipitated the chain of events that ultimately fulfilled the very prophecy, the fulfillment of which they were determined to prevent. Satan and his unfortunate brood characteristically make such consummate fools of themselves!

It was not Caiaphas' day. When one walks in the darkness he stumbles (John 11:9,10). This blind bigot, for all of his disgust with his colleagues for their failure to act, and with his own brilliant suggestions about what to do, could do nothing but stumble. He said that in order to prevent Rome from destroying both their own lucrative positions and the national existence of Israel, they would find it necessary to murder Jesus. So it developed that, at His trial before Pilate, the Jewish mob cried out, "Let his blood be upon us and on our children." One must be afflicted with incipient insanity to ask God in heaven to visit His righteous judgment upon those who had the blood of the Son of God upon their hands. They even prayed that the wrath of heaven might be poured out upon their unborn children. They asked for the very thing that Caiaphas was trying to avoid. God heard their request and the answer was not long in coming. In A.D.70 Titus, the son of the Emperor Vespasian, who nine years later himself was elevated to the Imperial throne, came to Jerusalem with an army and, as if in fulfillment of the prophecy of Caiaphas, he abolished the high paying political positions of the Sanhedrin, and literally took away "(their) place and nation." The sack of Jerusalem was so complete that not one stone of the Solomonic temple was left upon another (Mt.24:2), and, having destroyed the city, he crucified upon a long row of Roman crosses around the burning city, the very men who had asked Heaven to retaliate for the shedding of the blood of Christ. On that day Israel, as a nation in the political sense, disappeared from the map, not again to be restored until 1948.

Finally, let us notice the crass selfishness of these wicked men. Note that they put the emphasis upon *ἡμῶν τὸν τόπον* ahead of *καὶ τὸ ἔθνος*. We generally speak first about what is dearest to our hearts. The City Hall politicians in Jerusalem were most concerned that so many Jews would believe upon Jesus that they would come to recognize what hypocrites their Jewish leaders were and that the people, enlightened and enraged by Jesus' slashing attacks (Mt.23:1-39) would "take away their place." Of course they could not admit that the revolt would come from within, as the common people, bent on readjusting the social and economic balance, carried off a *coup d' etat*, and sent them packing, so they accused the Romans in advance. It was not conceivable to a Pharisee or a High Priest that their Jewish subjects could become so aroused by their hypocritical showmanship and political and religious skulduggery that they would attack the temple and its court in force.

Caiaphas tried to summarize all that they were thinking in verses 49 and 50.

Verse 49 - "And one of them, named Caiaphas, being the high priest that same year, said unto them, Ye know nothing at all."

εἷς δέ τις ἐξ αὐτῶν Καϊάφας, *ἀρχιερεὺς ὢν τοῦ ἐνιαυτοῦ ἐκείνου, εἶπεν αὐτοῖς, Ὑμεῖς οὐκ οἴδατε οὐδέν,*

εἷς (nom.sing.masc.of *εἷς*, subject of *εἶπεν*) 469.
δέ (adversative conjunction) 11.
τις (nom.sing.masc.of *τις*, indefinite pronoun, in agreement with *εἷς*) 486.
ἐξ (preposition with the partitive genitive) 19.
αὐτῶν (gen.pl.masc.of *αὐτός*, partitive) 16.
Καϊάφας (nom.sing.masc.of Καϊάφας, apposition) 1555.
ἀρχιερεὺς (nom.sing.masc.of *ἀρχιερεύς*, predicate nominative) 151.
ὢν (pres.part.nom.sing.masc.of *εἰμί*, adverbial, causal) 86.
τοῦ (gen.sing.masc.of the article in agreement with *ἐνιαυτοῦ*) 9.
ἐνιαυτοῦ (gen.sing.masc.of *ἐνιαυτός*, time description) 2025.
ἐκείνου (gen.sing.masc.of *ἐκεῖνος*, in agreement with *ἐνιαυτοῦ*) 246.
εἶπεν (3d.per.sing.aor.act.ind.of *εἶπον*, constative) 155.
αὐτοῖς (dat.pl.masc.of *αὐτός*, indirect object of *εἶπεν*) 16.
Ὑμεῖς (nom.pl.masc.of *σύ*, subject of *οἴδατε*) 104.
οὐκ (summary negative conjunction with the indicative) 130.
οἴδατε (2d.per.pl.pres.act.ind.of *ὁράω*, aoristic) 144.
οὐδέν (acc.sing.neut.of *οὐδείς*, direct object of *οἴδατε*) 446.

Translation - "But one of them, Caiaphas, because he was High Priest for that year, said to them, 'You know nothing about it.' "

Comment: A typical comment from a High Priest. It sounds like a denominational Secretary or a Bishop. *δὲ* is adversative. Caiaphas had been listening to the palaver and his role, of course, was to appear to know more about every subject that might come before them than they. He appeared to disagree with what they had been saying, and yet his suggestion which follows was in line with their thought. But it carried more authority if it came from the mouth of the High Priest. In *τοῦ ἐνιαυτοῦ ἐκεῖνου* - the genitive of time description, we have an example of the precision of the Greek idiom. The locative would convey the notion of a point in time and the accusative the extent of time. John means to convey neither of these ideas, and the language has the capability of describing the time period involved.

Caiaphas' blunt analysis was that his colleagues did not know one single thing (!) which is extreme. According to him they did not even know what town they were in. Thus His Highness revealed that he was emotionally off balance. "How great is that darkness!" (Mt.6:23).

Now the High Priest offers his analysis, and in his blind prejudice he opened his mouth and God put divine wisdom into it, no thanks to Caiaphas. Thus God makes "the wrath of man (to) praise (Him)" (Ps.76:10). Caiaphas was in the High Priest post from A.D. 18 to 36, when he was deposed by Vitellius (*Expositors' Greek Testament*, en loc). The *Expositors' Greek Testament* is entirely too conciliatory to the Jews who came to Bethany to attend Lazarus' wake. It attacks the view that, in some cases, the weeping was hypocritical and that this hypocrisy was a partial reason for Jesus' emotion as described in verses 33 and 38. They try to show that all of the Jews who witnessed the resurrection believed upon Jesus and that Jesus did not hear the remark of verse 37. To the contrary note again that *οὖν* of verse 38 can be taken either as continuative or inferential. It is possible to say that *οἱ ἐλθόντες πρὸς . . . ὃ ἐποίησεν* is in apposition to *πολλοὶ* and that *τινὲς δὲ ἐξ αὐτῶν* refers to *τῶν Ἰουδαίων*, not to *πολλοί*. Thus, of all of the Jews, many, *viz.* those who followed Mary to the tomb and witnessed the resurrection, believed on Jesus, while certain others of the total number of Jews, who did not follow Mary to the tomb, nor see the miracle, went away and reported it to the Sanhedrin. Thus the Jews who did not follow Mary can be defended on the basis of the text. But, even though they may not have witnessed the resurrection of Lazarus, they certainly knew about it and reported it to the Sanhedrin as a well documented and attested miracle. Either view is possible exegetically, but the overall picture favors the notion that Jesus had some enemies in Mary's house and at the tomb, some of whom were saved, while some were not.

Verse 50 - "Nor consider that it is expedient for us that one man should die for the people, and that the whole nation perish not."

οὐδὲ λογίζεσθε ὅτι συμφέρει ὑμῖν ἵνα εἷς ἄνθρωπος ἀποθάνῃ ὑπὲρ τοῦ λαοῦ καὶ μὴ ὅλον τὸ ἔθνος ἀπόληται.

οὐδὲ (disjunctive particle) 452.

#2611 *λογίζεσθε* (2d.per.pl.pres.mid.ind.of *λογίζομαι*, aoristic).

account - Heb.11:19; Rom.8:36; Gal.3:6.
account of - 1 Cor.4:1.
conclude - Rom.3:28.
consider - John 11:50.
count - Rom.2:26; 4:3,5; 9:8; Phil.3:13.
esteem - Rom.14:14.
impute - Rom.4:6,8,11,22,23,24; 2 Cor.5:19; Jam.2:23.
lay to one's charge - 2 Tim.4:16.
reckon - Luke 22:37; Rom.4:4,9,10; 6:11; 8:18.
suppose - 2 Cor.11:5; 1 Pet.5:12.
think - Rom.2:3; 1 Cor.13:5,11; 2 Cor.3:5; 10:2,7,11; 12:6; Phil.4:8.
be despised - Acts 19:27.
think of - 2 Cor.10:2.

Meaning: (I). To think about something and reach a rational conclusion (a) fol.by *ὅτι* and an object clause - Heb.11:19; John 11:50; Rom.8:18; 2:3. (b) fol.by an infinitive like an object clause - Rom.3:28. (c) fol. by ἑαυτούς and the infinitive - Rom.6:11. (d) followed by an infinitive - 2 Cor.11:5. (e) absolutely - 1 Pet.5:12. (f). accusative with direct object - 1 Cor.13:5; Phil.4:8. (g) followed by ὡς νήπιος 1 Cor.13:11. (II). To think and conclude that someone or something is in a certain category. (a) followed by ὡς - Rom.8:36; 1 Cor.4:1; 2 Cor.3:5 (with τι); 2 Cor.10:2b. (b) followed by εἰς and the accusative - Rom.9:8; Acts 19:27. (c) followed by ἑαυτόν and the infinitive - Phil.3:13. (d) followed by the infinitive - Rom.14:14. (e) joined to μετὰ ἀνόμων - Lk.22:37. (f) followed by ἐφ' ἑαυτοῦ and the accusative of direct object - 2 Cor.10:7. (g) followed by the accusative of direct object and ὅτι and an object clause - 2 Cor.10:11. (h) followed by ὑπὲρ με - 2 Cor.12:6. (III). In an accounting sense; to impute; to enter upon the books as an asset or liability - (a) followed by αὐτῷ as indirect object - Gal.3:6; Rom.4:3,11,23; 2 Tim.4:16. (b) followed by εἰς and the accusative - Rom.2:26; 4:5,8. (c) followed by αὐτῷ and indirect object and εἰς with the accusative - Rom.4:22; 2 Cor.5:19; Jam.2:23. (d) followed by οἷς or ᾧ as indirect object - Rom.4:6,24. (e) followed by κατά and the accusative - Rom.4:4. (f) followed by Ἀβραάμ as indirect object and εἰς with the accusative - Rom.4:9. (g) absolutely - Rom.4:10. (IV). Thought that results in a definite policy - a plan - 2 Cor.10:2a.

ὅτι (conjunction with an object clause in indirect discourse) 211.
συμφέρει (3d.per.sing.pres.act.ind.of συμφέρω, static) 505.
ὑμῖν (dat.pl.masc.of σύ, personal advantage) 104.
ἵνα (conjunction introducing a consecutive clause) 114.
εἷς (nom.sing.masc.of εἷς, in agreement with ἄνθρωπος) 469.
ἄνθρωπος (nom.sing.masc.of ἄνθρωπος, subject of ἀποθάνῃ) 341.
ἀποθάνῃ (3d.per.sing.aor.act.subj.of ἀποθνήσκω, result) 774.
ὑπὲρ (preposition with the ablative, substitution) 545.
τοῦ (abl.sing.masc.of the article in agreement with λαοῦ) 9.
λαοῦ (abl.sing.masc.of λαός, substitution) 110.
καὶ (adjunctive conjunction joining result clauses) 14.
μὴ (qualified negative conjunction with the subjunctive in a result clause) 87.
ὅλον (nom.sing.neut.of ὅλος, in agreement with ἔθνος) 112.
τὸ (nom.sing.neut.of the article in agreement with ἔθνος) 9.
ἔθνος (nom.sing.neut.of ἔθνος, subject of ἀπόληται) 376.
ἀπόληται (3d.per.sing.aor.mid.subj.of ἀπόλλυμι, result clause) 208.

Translation - "Nor are you considering that it is to your advantage that one man should die for the people and not that the entire nation should perish."

Comment: οὐδὲ is joined to οὐκ in the last clause of verse 49. The οὐκ . . . οὐδέ sequence means "neither . . nor." "You neither know anything nor are you thinking about the problem sufficiently to conclude that . . κ.τ.λ." The ὅτι clause gives us the conclusion to which Caiaphas has come. *Cf.*#505 for its exact meaning. - "it is to your advantage." Goodspeed has, "it is to your interest. . . " The ἵνα clause is result. The sense of the passage is that if the two results are realized - *viz.*, that one man die for the people and that the entire nation not perish, it will be better for them. *Cf.*#545 for ὑπέρ, with the ablative in a substitutionary sense. Thus Caiaphas inadvertently gave expression to the central fact of the cross. Of course he meant that if the Sanhedrin dispose of Jesus, by murder, judicious or otherwise, the movement built around Him would collapse and the nation, for centuries serving as slaves under the heel of the Romans, could continue in the *status quo*. If Jesus dies, the nation continues; if He continues to live the nation will be destroyed - *i.e.* He will eventually be placed upon a Jewish throne by the people and the Romans will move in with sufficient force to stop it. The worst that could happen would be only that Israel would continue in slavery to Rome, perhaps with stricter regulations, such as the abolition of the temple worship, which would abolish the lucrative position of Caiaphas. Israel was already under political slavery to Rome, to say nothing of the greater bondage of sin, of which she seemed to be oblivious.

The idea that if Jesus became the Messiah, He would overthrow Rome and bring the entire world under His control, while completely consistent with Jewish expectations, as derived from both Moses and the prophets, was rejected by the Sanhedrin, since they did not believe that Jesus was, in fact, the Messiah, but only a usurper. This, in spite of the fact that He had just raised Lazarus from the dead.

There is, of course, the deeper spiritual meaning in the words which Caiaphas uttered, although he had no intention of preaching the gospel of substitution. It was indeed necessary for and beneficial to the Jewish people that Christ should die instead of them, to pay the sin debt which they owed to God and were unable to pay for themselves. If He did not the entire nation, indeed, the entire human race, would perish in hell. Christ's death will not save the entire nation. That is to say that a Jew is not going to be saved because he is a Jew, but some Jews were destined to be saved by His sacrifice at Calvary. All of the earliest converts in the church in Jerusalem were Jews.

Also from the national point of view the seed of Abraham will not perish, the amillenialists to the contrary notwithstanding. Messiah will seal a representative number of them - twelve thousand out of every tribe, one hundred, forty four thousand in all, to serve as His chosen nation when He returns at His second coming (Rev.7:1-8). These young people will populate the land which God gave to Abraham, during the millenium, under the reign of perfect righteousness and world peace, and rule the world in a period of constructive human development such as has never been seen in all of the history of the race.

Caiaphas meant nothing like this. He only meant that Jesus had to die in order that Israel could stagger on under the yoke of her Roman slavery, and that he could continue to draw his salary. The Apostle John introduces the deeper meaning that can be derived from Caiaphas' words in verses 51 and 52.

Verse 51 - "And this spake he not of himself: but being high priest that year, he prophesied that Jesus should die for that nation."

τοῦτο δὲ ἀφ' ἑαυτοῦ οὐκ εἶπεν, ἀλλὰ ἀρχιερεὺς ὢν τοῦ ἐνιαυτοῦ ἐκείνου ἐπροφήτευσεν ὅτι ἔμελλεν Ἰησοῦς ἀποθνῄσκειν ὑπὲρ τοῦ ἔθνους.

τοῦτο (acc.sing.neut.of *οὗτος*, direct object of *εἶπεν*) 93.
δὲ (adversative conjunction) 11.

ἀφ' (preposition with the ablative of source) 70.
ἑαυτοῦ (abl.sing.masc.of ἑαυτός, source) 288.
οὐκ (summary negative conjunction with the indicative) 130.
εἶπεν (3d.per.sing.aor.act.ind.of εἶπον constative) 155.
ἀλλὰ (alternative conjunction) 342.
ἀρχιερεὺς (nom.sing.masc.of ἀρχιερεύς, predicate nominative) 151.
ὢν (pres.part.nom.sing.masc.of εἰμί, adverbial, causal) 86.
τοῦ (gen.sing.masc.of the article in agreement with ἐνιαυτοῦ) 9.
ἐνιαυτοῦ (gen.sing.masc.of ἐνιαυτός, time description) 2025.
ἐκείνου (gen.sing.masc.of ἐκεῖνος, in agreement with ἐνιαυτοῦ) 246.
ἐπροφήτευσεν (3d.per.sing.aor.act.ind.of προφητεύω, constative) 685.
ὅτι (conjunction introducing an object clause) 211.
ἔμελλεν (3d.per.sing.imp.act.ind.of μέλλω, inceptive) 206.
Ἰησοῦς (nom.sing.masc.of Ἰησοῦς, subject of ἔμελλεν) 3.
ἀποθνήσκειν (pres.act.inf.of ἀποθνήσκω, complementary) 774.
ὑπὲρ (preposition with the ablative, substitution) 545.
τοῦ (abl.sing.neut.of the article in agreement with ἔθνους) 9.
ἔθνους (abl.sing.neut.of ἔθνος, substitution) 376.

Translation - "Now he said this, not from himself, but, because he was High Priest that year, he predicted that Jesus was going to die for the nation."

Comment: John is saying that Caiaphas is not to be given credit for his statement of verse 50, as though it originated in his own intellect, but rather (alternative ἀλλὰ), since he was the High Priest that year (causal adverbial participle in ὢν), he was inspired to speak prophetically in a way that was fulfilled in a higher and deeper sense than he realized. It is also possible to interpret ἀφ' ἑαυτοῦ as meaning that he was speaking, not unofficially as a private citizen, but in his official capacity as High Priest.

His prediction was that, for reasons of political expediency, the Sanhedrin should move to sacrifice Jesus and thus prove the unquestioned loyalty of Israel to Rome. This they could do by accusing Jesus of having a Messianic complex with designs upon the political hegemony of the Emperor. The person and work of our Lord was so attractive - His charisma was so compelling and His miracles so astounding that it would be easy to show to Pilate that if He were not stopped, He would indeed lead a popular revolution among the people and march on Rome to liberate Israel from the Caesars. Thus Jesus' death would save Israel from Rome's wrath, not from God's wrath. If this be the interpretation, then it appears that Caiaphas had apostatized to the point that he had forgotten God in his zeal to placate Caesar. The meanderings of the degenerate mind of this "whited sepulcher" had gone far enough. The Apostle John, speaking from the vantage point of a fuller revelation, and sixty years later, explains the real purpose of Jesus' death in verse 52.

Verse 52 - "And not for the nation only, but also he should gather together in one the childrenof God that were scattered abroad."

καὶ οὐχ ὑπὲρ τοῦ ἔθνους μόνον ἀλλ' ἵνα καὶ τὰ τέκνα τοῦ θεοῦ τὰ διεσκορπισμένα συναγάγῃ εἰς ἕν.

καὶ (continuative conjunction) 14.
οὐχ (summary negative conjunction with the indicative) 130.
ὑπὲρ (preposition with the ablative, substitution) 545.
τοῦ (abl.sing.neut.of the article in agreement with *ἔθνους*) 9.
ἔθνους (abl.sing.neut.of *ἔθνος*, substitution) 376.
μόνον (acc.sing.neut.of *μόνος*, adverbial) 339.
ἀλλ' (alternative conjunction) 342.
ἵνα (conjunction introducing a purpose clause) 114.
τὰ (acc.pl.neut.of the article in agreement with *τέκνα*) 9.
τέκνα (acc.pl.neut.of *τέκνον*, direct object of *συναγάγῃ*) 229.
τοῦ (gen.sing.masc.of the article in agreement with *θεοῦ*) 9.
θεοῦ (gen.sing.masc.of *θεός*, relationship) 124.
τὰ (acc.pl.neut.of the article in agreement with *διεσκορπισμένα*) 9.
διεσκορπισμένα (perf.pass.part.acc.pl.neut.of *διασκορπίζω*, adjectival, in agreement with *τέκνα*) 1538.
συναγάγῃ (3d.per.sing.aor.act.subj.of *συνάγω*, purpose) 150.
εἰς (preposition with the accusative, adverbial) 140.
ἕν (numeral, adverbial) 469.

Translation - "But not for the nation only; rather so that He might bring together into one the children of God who are scattered throughout the earth."

Comment: *καὶ* is adversative. John is trying to refute the idea that Jesus, the Jewish Messiah died only for those who are genetically Jewish. "Not for the nation only; rather (alternative *ἀλλ'*) in order that . . . *κ.τ.λ.*" The *ἵνα* clause of purpose completes the sentence. The participle *διεσκορπισμένα* is an adjective, modifying *τὰ τέκνα τοῦ θεοῦ*. They have been scattered throughout the earth and as John wrote they were still scattered, as indeed they still are in the closing days of the 20th century. They are scattered geographically, culturally, religiously, philosophically, politically. They are children of God (*τὰ τέκνα τοῦ θεοῦ*) in the only manner that counts - they are chosen in Christ before the foundation of the world. He will gather them together into one fellowship. For this He was to pray in John 17:21. It was this that He predicted in John 10:16.

This idea of a universal Saviour, not merely a local or national Jewish Messiah, was perfectly clear in the tenth decade when John wrote. It was not so clear to the disciples at the time of His death, despite the fact that Jesus had made it clear many times (John 10:16; 17;20,21; Lk.13:29). *Cf.*Mt.24:31 where *ἐπισυνάγω* (#1476) is used. Through His vicarious death, something far beyond what Caiaphas had in mind, Jesus is gathering together Jews and Gentiles alike, "elect according to the foreknowledge of God" (1 Pet.1:2; Eph.1:4,5) into His body. This is the work of the worldwide missionary enterprise, being conducted by the Holy Spirit through the church. The angels will gather us together in a physical sense when we get our resurrected and raptured bodies at the last day (Mt.24:31).

Verse 53 - "Then from that day forth they took counsel together for to put him to death."

ἀπ' ἐκείνης οὖν τῆς ἡμέρας ἐβουλεύσαντο ἵνα ἀποκτείνωσιν αὐτόν.

ἀπ' (preposition with the ablative of time separation) 70.
ἐκείνης (abl.sing.fem.of ἐκεῖνος, in agreement with ἡμέρας) 246.
οὖν (inferential conjunction) 68.
τῆς (abl.sing.fem.of the article in agreement with ἡμέρας) 9.
ἡμέρας (abl.sing.fem.of ἡμέρα, time separation) 135.
ἐβουλεύσαντο (3d.per.pl.aor.mid.ind.of βουλεύομαι, ingressive) 90.
ἵνα (conjunction introducing a purpose clause) 114.
ἀποκτείνωσιν (3d.per.pl.pres.act.subj.of ἀποκτείνω, purpose) 889.
αὐτόν (acc.sing.masc.of αὐτός, direct object of ἀποκτείνωσιν) 16.

Translation - "Therefore, from that day, they began to develop a plan to kill Him."

Comment: The resurrection of Lazarus thus precipitated a series of events that culminated in the death of the Son of God. The Jews who had witnessed the miracle in Bethany reported it to the Jerusalem officials who immediately called the Sanhedrin into session. Out of the discussion came the decision that Jesus had to be silenced. From that time on they planned, plotted and counselled together about ways and means. *Cf.*#90 for the meaning of βουλεύομαι. The Sanhedrin was composed of politicians. Politicians are always sensitive to public opinion. There was no doubt that Jesus was popular with a large segment of the population. How could they arrest and murder Him without creating a riot among the people? Jesus' hour, the eternally predetermined moment when Messiah would be cut off (Dan.9:26) was drawing near, but it was yet a few days in the future. Jesus, of course knew of the Sanhedrin's plans and withdrew into Ephraim for a few days.

Verse 54 - "Jesus therefore walked no more openly among the Jews, but went thence unto a country near to the wilderness, into a city called Ephraim, and there continued with His disciples."

Ὁ οὖν Ἰησοῦς οὐκέτι παρρησίᾳ περιεπάτει ἐν τοῖς Ἰουδαίοις, ἀλλὰ ἀπῆλθεν ἐκεῖθεν εἰς τὴν χώραν ἐγγὺς τῆς ἐρήμου, εἰς Ἐφραὶμ λεγομένην πόλιν, κἀκεῖ διέτριβεν μετὰ τῶν μαθητῶν.

Ὁ (nom.sing.masc.of the article in agreement with Ἰησοῦς) 9.
οὖν (inferential conjunction) 68.
Ἰησοῦς (nom.sing.masc.of Ἰησοῦς, subject of περιεπάτει, ἀπῆλθεν and διέτριβεν) 3.
οὐκέτι (adverb of denial) 1289.

παρρησίᾳ (instru.sing.fem.of παῤῥησία, means) 2319.

περιεπάτει (3d.per.sing.imp.act.ind of περιπατέω, progressive description) 384.

ἐν (preposition with the locative, with a plural noun) 80

τοῖς (loc.pl.masc.of the article in agreement with Ἰουδαίοις) 9.

Ἰουδαίοις (loc.pl.masc.of Ἰουδαῖος, place where) 143.

ἀλλὰ (alternative conjunction) 342.

ἀπῆλθεν (3d.per.sing.aor.ind.of ἀπέρχομαι, constative) 239.

ἐκεῖθεν (adverbial) 396.

εἰς (preposition with the accusative of extent) 140.

τὴν (acc.sing.fem.of the article in agreement with χώραν) 9.

χώραν (acc.sing.fem.of χώρα, extent) 201.

ἐγγὺς (adverbial) 1512.

τῆς (gen.sing.fem.of the article in agreement with ἐρήμου) 9.

ἐρήμου (gen.sing.fem.of ἔρημος, description, after ἐγγὺς) 250.

εἰς (preposition with the accusative of extent) 140.

#2612 Ἐφραὶμ (acc.sing.masc.of Ἐφραίμ, indeclin., extent).

Ephraim - John 11:54.

Meaning: "a city situated, acc. to Eusebius eight, acc.to Jerome, twenty miles from Jerusalem; acc. to Josephus, not far from Bethel; conjectured by Robinson, Ewald, *et al* dissenting, to be the same as the village now called *et-Taiyibeh*, a short day's journey N.E. of Jerusalem." (Thayer, *Lexicon*, 265). Jesus visited there a short time before His death - John 11:54.

λεγομένην (pres.pass.part.acc.sing.fem.of λέγω, adjectival, restrictive, in agreement with Ἐφραὶμ) 66.

πόλιν (acc.sing.fem.of πόλις, extent) 243.

κἀκεῖ (adverb of place) 204.

διέτριβεν (3d.per.sing.2d.aor.act.ind.of διατρίβω, constative) 1991.

μετὰ (preposition with the genitive, accompaniment) 50.

τῶν (gen.pl.masc.of the article in agreement with μαθητῶν) 9.

μαθητῶν (gen.pl.masc.of μαθητής, accompaniment) 421.

Translation - "Therefore Jesus no longer walked openly among the Jews, but He left the vicinity and went into the area near the desert, to a city called Ephraim, and there he stayed with the disciples."

Comment: The fact that the Sandedrin was now actively plotting to kill Jesus resulted in His decision to stay out of sight. οὖν therefore is inferential. Rather (alternative ἀλλὰ) He went away to a region near the desert and stopped at a city named Ephraim, about twenty miles northeast of Jerusalem.

Here is another example of the sovereign God of creation and history, incarnate in human flesh, Who knew every detail of the divine game plan, and went about maneuvering history with the result that prophecy and its fulfillment coincides. Had He gone into Jerusalem sooner, incidents would have occurred

which would not have served the divine purpose. Sometimes we serve God better by restraint than by aggressive action.

The Last Journey to Jerusalem by way of Samaria and Galilee

The Healing of Ten Lepers

(Luke 17:11-19)

Luke 17:11 - "And it came to pass, as he went to Jerusalem, that he passed through the midst of Samaria and Galilee."

Καὶ ἐγένετο ἐν τῷ πορεύεσθαι εἰς Ἰερουσαλὴμ καὶ αὐτὸς διήρχετο διὰ μέσον Σαμαρείας καὶ Γαλιλαίας.

Καὶ (continuative conjunction) 14.
ἐγένετο (3d.per.sing.aor.ind.of γίνομαι, constative) 113.
ἐν (preposition with the locative of time point) 80.
τῷ (loc.sing.neut.of the article, time point, in an articular infinitive) 9.
πορεύεσθαι (pres.part.of πορεύομαι, articular infinitive, locative of time point) 170.
εἰς (preposition with the accusative of extent) 140.
Ἰερουσαλὴμ (acc.sing.masc.of Ἰερουσαλύμα, extent) 141.
καὶ (continuative conjunction) 14.
αὐτὸς (nom.sing.masc.of αὐτός, subject of διήρχετο, emphatic) 16.
διήρχετο (3d.per.sing.imp.ind.of διέρχομαι, progressive description) 1017.
διὰ (preposition with the accusative, physically through) 118.
μέσον (acc.sing.neut.of μέσος, extent) 873.
Σαμαρίας (gen.sing.fem.of Σαμαρεία, description) 1998.
καὶ (adjunctive conjunction joining nouns) 14.
Γαλιλαίας (gen.sing.fem.of Γαλιλαία, description) 241.

Translation - "And it happened that on His way to Jerusalem he passed through the midst of Samaria and Galilee."

Comment: The articular infinitive with ἐν is in the locative case indicating time point. Literally we translate "during the time that (while/when) He was going to Jerusalem . . . κ.τ.λ." Enroute to Jerusalem He passed through Samaria and Galilee. If Jerome was correct in saying that Ephraim is twenty miles northeast of Jerusalem, it is obvious that we do not have all of the story. This need not concern us since John 21:25 tells us that we do not have the entire record of all that Jesus did and where He went. John 11:54 tells us that Jesus had spent some time with His disciples in Ephraim. A straight line from Ephraism to Jerusalem does not lead through Samaria and Galilee, but lies wholly within the confines of Judea. Thus, either Jesus left Ephraim and went north to Galilee, in ministry the record of which is not recorded, after which point we pick up the story in Luke 17:11, or Luke 17:11 means that He left Ephraim and made a circuitous route to

Jerusalem - north to Galilee and then south through the middle of Galilee and Samaria, to Jerusalem. The point is not essential to the story that follows in

Verse 12 - "And as he entered into a certain village, there met him ten men that were lepers, which stood afar off."

καὶ εἰσερχομένου αὐτοῦ εἴς τινα κώμην ἀπήντησαν (αὐτῷ) δέκα λεπροὶ ἄνδρες, οἳ ἔστησαν πόρρωθεν.

καὶ (continuative conjunction) 14.
εἰσερχομένου (pres.part.gen.sing.masc.of *εἰσέρχομαι*, genitive absolute) 234.
αὐτοῦ (gen.sing.masc.of *αὐτός*, genitive absolute) 16.
εἴς (preposition with the accusative of extent) 140.
τινα (acc.sing.fem.of *τις*, indefinite pronoun, in agreement with *κώμην*) 486.
κώμην (acc.sing.fem.of *κώμη*, extent) 834.

#2613 *ἀπήντησαν* (3d.per.pl.aor.act.ind.of *ἀπαντάω*, constative).

meet - Mk.14:13; Lk.17:12.

Meaning: - A combination of *ἀπό* (#70) and *ἀντάω* - "to meet face to face." Hence, to meet but at some distance. The lepers met Jesus but stood *πόρρωθεν* - Lk.17:12. With reference to the man carrying the pitcher of water - Mk.14:13. *Cf.ὑπαντάω* (#762).

δέκα (numeral) 1330.
λεπροὶ (nom.pl.masc.of *λεπρός*, in agreement with *ἄνδρες*) 708.
ἄνδρες (nom.pl.masc.of *ἀνήρ*, subject of *ἀπήντησαν*) 63.
οἳ (nom.pl.masc.of *ὅς*, relative pronoun, subject of *ἀνέστησαν*) 65.
ἀνέστησαν (3d.per.pl.aor.act.ind.of *ἀνίστημι*, constative) 789.

#2614 *πόρρωθεν* (adverb).

afar off - Luke 17:12; Heb.11:13.

Meaning: Cf.πόῤῥω (#1147) - from afar; afar off. With reference to the lepers who met Jesus - Luke 17:12, in the sense of physical distance. In a chronological sense - "in the future" - Heb.11:13.

Translation - "And as He was entering a certain village, there met Him at a distance ten leprous men, who stood at some distance away."

Comment: *εἰσερχομένου αὐτοῦ* is a genitive absolute in the present tense, indicating simultaneous action with that of the main verb *ἀπήντησαν*. Luke is careful to choose a verb that says that the ten lepers met Jesus, but avoids saying that the meeting took place at close range. Not e *λεπροὶ* - a noun, but used here like an adjective to define *ἄνδρες*. The definite relative clause supports the basic meaning of *ἀπήντησαν*. The meeting took place - *i.e.* they saw each other, but in keeping with the custom, the lepers did not come too close. As Jesus approached, while He was yet some distance away, they spoke to Him, in

Verse 13 - "And they lifted up their voices, and said, Jesus, Master, have mercy on us."

καὶ αὐτοὶ ἦραν φωνὴν λέγοντες, Ἰησοῦ ἐπιστάτα, ἐλέησον ἡμᾶς.

καὶ (continuative conjunction) 14.
αὐτοὶ (nom.pl.masc.of *αὐτός*, subject of *ἦραν*) 16.
ἦραν (3d.per.pl.aor.act.ind.of *αἴρω*,constative) 350.
φωνὴν (acc.sing.fem.of *φωνή*, direct object of *ἦραν*) 222.
λέγοντες (pres.act.part.nom.pl.masc.of *λέγω*, adverbial, modal) 66.
Ἰησοῦ (voc.sing.masc.of *Ἰησοῦς*, address) 3.
ἐπιστάτα (voc.sing.masc.of *ἐπιστάτης*, address) 2047.
ἐλέησον (2d.per.sing.aor.act.impv.of *ἐλεέω*, entreaty) 430.
ἡμᾶς (acc.pl.masc.of *ἐγώ*, direct object of *ἐλέησον*) 123.

Translation - "And they called out, saying, 'Jesus, Master, have mercy on us.' "

Comment: *αὐτοὶ* here in a personal sense, as subject of *ἦραν*. Note the singular in *φωνὴν* with the plural subject *αὐτοὶ* and the plural verb *ἦραν*. We might translate, "They called out as with a single voice, saying, 'Jesus, . . . *κ.τ.λ.*' " It was quite to be expected that these unfortunate men, cursed with a terminal disease, would immediately rise and cry out for help when they saw Jesus approaching.

Verse 14 - "And when he saw them, he said unto them, Go show yourselves unto the priests. And it came to pass, that, as they went, they were cleansed."

καὶ ἰδὼν εἶπεν αὐτοῖς, Πορευθέντες ἐπιδείξατε ἑαυτοὺς τοῖς ἱερεῦσιν. καὶ ἐγένετο ἐν τῷ ὑπάγειν αὐτοὺς ἐκαθαρίσθησαν.

καὶ (continuative conjunction) 14.
ἰδὼν (aor.act.part.nom.sing.masc.of *ὁράω*, adverbial, temporal) 144.
εἶπεν (3d.per.sing.aor.act.ind.of *εἶπον*, constative) 155.
αὐτοῖς (dat.pl.masc.of *αὐτός*, indirect object of *εἶπεν*) 16.
Πορευθέντες (aor.mid.part.nom.pl.masc.of *πορεύομαι*, adverbial, temporal) 170.
ἐπιδείξατε (2d.per.pl.aor.act.impv.of *ἐπιδείκνυμι*, command) 1189.
ἑαυτοὺς (acc.pl.masc.of *ἑαυτός*, direct object of *ἐπιδείξατε*) 288.
τοῖς (dat.pl.masc.of the article in agreement with *ἱερεῦσιν*) 9.
ἱερεῦσιν (dat.pl.masc.of *ἱερεύς*, personal interest) 714.
καὶ (continuative conjunction) 14.
ἐγένετο (3d.per.sing.aor.ind.of *γίνομαι*, constative) 113.
ἐν (preposition with the locative of time point) 80.
τῷ (loc.sing.neut.of the article, articular infinitive, time point) 9.
ὑπάγειν (pres.act.inf.of *ὑπάγω*, loc.sing.neut., time point) 364.
αὐτοὺς (acc.pl.masc.of *αὐτός*, general reference) 16.
ἐκαθαρίσθησαν (3d.per.pl.aor.pass.ind.of *καθαρίζω*, constative) 709.

Translation - "And when He saw them He said to them, 'Go and show yourselves to the priests.' And while they were on their way they were cleansed."

Comment: This instruction was in conformity to the Mosaic law (Lev.13,14). Jesus always fulfilled the law of Moses (Mt.5:17). He had given it to Moses as a written code that fulfilled all of the divine demands for holiness, and during His incarnation He fulfilled it to the letter. The ten lepers obeyed by faith. Normally a leper would not go to his priest until he was healed. Jesus did not heal them first and then tell them to visit the priest. This would have required no faith on their part. It was while they were enroute to their priests that the miracle of cleansing occurred. This is the meaning of the articular infinitive in the locative case - *ἐν τῷ ὑπάγειν αὐτοὺς ἐκαθαρίσθησαν.*

The story recalls the man with the paralyzed hand who found that it was healed only after he had obeyed Jesus' order to "stretch it forth." Healing results from faith; and faith is active and obedient.

Verse 15 - "And one of them, when he saw that he was healed, turned back, and with a loud voice glorified God."

εἷς δὲ ἐξ αὐτῶν, ἰδὼν ὅτι ἰάθη, ὑπέστρεψεν μετὰ φωνῆς μεγάλης δοξάζων τὸν θεόν,

εἷς (nom.sing.masc.of εἷς, subject of ὑπέστρεψεν) 469.
δὲ (continuative conjunction) 11.
ἐξ (preposition with the partitive genitive) 19.
αὐτῶν (gen.pl.masc.of αὐτός, partitive genitive) 16.
ἰδὼν (aor.act.part.nom.sing.masc.of ὁράω, adverbial, temporal) 144.
ὅτι (conjunction introducing an object clause) 211.
ἰάθη (3d.per.sing.aor.pass.ind.of ἰάομαι, constative) 721.
ὑπέστρεψεν (3d.per.sing.aor.act.ind.of ὑποστρέφω, ingressive) 1838.
μετὰ (preposition with the genitive of time description, simultaneous action) 50.
φωνῆς (gen.sing.fem.of φωνή, simultaneous action) 222.
μεγάλης (gen.sing.fem.of μέγας, in agreement with φωνῆς) 184.
δοξάζων (pres.act.part.nom.sing.masc.of δοξάζω, adverbial, complementary) 461.
τὸν (acc.sing.masc.of the article in agreement with θεόν) 9.
θεόν (acc.sing.masc.of θεός, direct object of δοξάζων) 124.

Translation - "And one of them, when he saw that he was healed, started back, with a loud voice glorifying God."

Comment: Ten lepers, obedient to Jesus' order although as yet they had no evidence that they were healed, complied with His directive. As faith became obedient and active they were healed. Nine of them never returned. One did. The verb ὑπέστρεψεν is an ingressive aorist. He "started back" shouting out his praises to God as he hastened back to Jesus. Verse 16 describes his behavior after he got back to Jesus. It also gives us the point in the story that makes it significant.

Verse 16 - "And fell down on his face at his feet, giving him thanks: and he was a Samaritan."

καὶ ἔπεσεν ἐπὶ πρόσωπον παρὰ τοὺς πόδας αὐτοῦ εὐχαριστῶν αὐτῷ. καὶ αὐτὸς ἦν Σαμαρίτης.

καὶ (adjunctive conjunction joining verbs) 14.
ἔπεσεν (3d.per.sing.aor.act.ind.of *πίπτω*, constative) 187.
ἐπὶ (preposition with the accusative, metaphorical place) 47.
πρόσωπον (acc.sing.neut.of *πρόσωπον*, metaphorical place, adverbial) 588.
παρὰ (preposition with the accusative, extent, place where) 154.
τοὺς (acc.pl.masc.of the article in agreement with *πόδας*) 9.
πόδας (acc.pl.masc.of *πούς*, extent, place where) 353.
αὐτοῦ (gen.sing.masc.of *αὐτός*, possession) 16.
εὐχαριστῶν (pres.act.part.nom.sing.masc.of *εὐχαριστέω*, adverbial, complementary) 1185.
αὐτῷ (dat.sing.masc.of *αὐτός*, personal advantage) 16.
καὶ (emphatic conjunction) 14.
αὐτὸς (nom.sing.masc.of *αὐτός*, subject of *ἦν*) 16.
ἦν (3d.per.sing.imp.ind.of *εἰμί*, progressive description) 86.
Σαμαρίτης (nom.sing.masc.of *Σαμαρίτης*, predicate nominative) 856.

Translation - "And he fell upon his face at His feet as he thanked Him. As a matter of fact he was a Samaritan."

Comment: The two prepositional phrases *ἐπὶ πρόσωπον* and *παρὰ τοὺς πόδας αὐτοῦ* are used liked adverbs to describe the man's action as he prostrated himself before Jesus - face downward beside/at (*παρὰ*) His feet. This picture of a former leper, now miraculously healed, on his face in the dust at the feet of the Son of God, Who healed him, is emotionally intensified by one more interesting fact - - the man was a Samaritan - a half-breed Jew, whose claim to a genetic connection with Abraham had been corrupted in part by Gentile blood. This is why I have taken *καὶ* in the last clause as emphatic.

The other nine men, apparently Jewish, were nowhere in sight.

Verse 17 - "And Jesus answering said, Were there not ten cleansed? but where are the nine?"

ἀποκριθεὶς δὲ ὁ Ἰησοῦς εἶπεν, Οὐχὶ οἱ δέκα ἐκαθαρίσθησαν; οἱ δὲ ἐννέα ποῦ;

ἀποκριθεὶς (aor.part.nom.sing.masc.of *ἀποκρίνομαι*, adverbial, modal) 318.
δὲ (continuative conjunction) 11.
ὁ (nom.sing.masc.of the article in agreement with *Ἰησοῦς*) 9.
Ἰησοῦς (nom.sing.masc.of *Ἰησοῦς*, subject of *εἶπεν*) 3.
Οὐχὶ (summary negative conjunction in rhetorical question, expecting an affirmative reply) 130.

οἱ (nom.pl.masc.of the article in agreement with δέκα) 9.
δέκα (numeral, subject of ἐκαθαρίσθησαν) 1330.
ἐκαθαρίσθησαν (3d.per.pl.aor.pass.ind.of καθαρίζω, culminative) 709.
οἱ (nom.pl.masc.of the article in agreement with ἐννέα) 9.
δὲ (adversative conjunction) 11.
ἐννέα (numeral, subject of εἰσίν, understood) 1259.
ποῦ (interrogatory adverb of place) 142.

Translation - "And Jesus replied by saying, 'There were ten men cleansed were there not? But the nine - where are they?' "

Comment: The second δὲ is more decidedly adversative than the first. One would reasonably expect that all of the lepers would return to thank Jesus as did the Samaritan. But such was not the case. Jesus asks His rhetorical question in mock surprize. It expects an affirmative answer. Yes, there were ten lepers cleansed. Ten lepers cleansed. One returns to say, "Thank you." The nine? Where are they?

Verse 18 - "There are not found that returned to give glory to God, save this stranger."

οὐχ εὑρέθησαν ὑποστρέψαντες δοῦναι δόξαν τῷ θεῷ, εἰ μὴ ὁ ἀλλογενὴς οὗτος;

οὐχ (summary negative conjunction with the indicative) 130.
εὑρέθησαν (3d.per.pl.aor.pass.ind.of εὑρίσκω, culminative) 79.
ὑποστρέψαντες (aor.act.part.nom.pl.masc.of ὑποστρέφω, adverbial, circumstantial) 1838.
δοῦναι (aor.act.inf.of δίδωμι, purpose) 362
δόξαν (acc.sing.fem.of δόξα, direct object of δοῦναι) 361.
τῷ (dat.sing.masc.of the article in agreement with θεῷ) 9.
θεῷ (dat.sing.masc.of θεός, indirect object of δοῦναι) 124.
εἰ (conditional particle in an elliptical condition) 337.
μὴ (qualified negative conjunction, with εἰ in an elliptical condition) 87.
ὁ (nom.sing.masc.of the article in agreement with ἀλλογενὴς) 9.

#2615 ἀλλογενὴς (nom.sing.masc.of ἀλλογενής, subject of the verb understood).

stranger - Luke 17:18.

Meaning: A combination of ἄλλος (#198) and γενός (#1090). Hence, one born of another genetic origin. An alien. With reference to the Samaritan leper who returned to thank Jesus - Luke 17:18. *Cf.* LXX, Gen.17:27; Ex.12:43, *et al.*

οὗτος (nom.sing.masc.of οὗτος, in agreement with ἀλλογενὴς, deictic) 93.

Translation - "Were none of them found coming back to give glory to God except this foreigner?"

Comment: Another rhetorical question with the expectation of a reply in agreement. Only the foreigner was grateful enough for his cleansing to return and give thanks. The condition is elliptical. The complete conditional sentence would be, "If the foreigner did not return to give thanks, no one did." The thrust of the passage seems to be that, at this late date in Jesus' ministry, only a few days before they murder Him, Israel is interested only in what He could do for them, not in worshipping Him or even being grateful to Him for His favors. It is the mark of a nation grown hopelessly apostate. These nine Jewish lepers should have had a greater interest in the spiritual benefits that Jesus could give them than in the physical blessing of rescue from leprosy. Both individually and as citizens of the nation Israel, they needed to be saved. Apparently as they went on their way, rejoicing in health restored, they forgot their moral responsibility to accept the commitment of discipleship. Thus Israel refuses the invitation to the dinner party, while an outsider comes into the Lord's banquet (Lk.14:16-24). The Samaritan leper was not only healed of his dread disease, but also saved from a worse fate in

Verse 19 - "And He said unto him, Arise, go thy way; thy faith hath made thee whole!"

καὶ εἶπεν αὐτῷ, Ἀναστὰς πορεύου, ἡ πίστις σου σέσωκέν σε.

καὶ (continuative conjunction) 14.
εἶπεν (3d.per.sing.aor.act.ind.of εἶπον, constative) 155.
αὐτῷ (dat.sing.masc.of αὐτός, indirect object of εἶπεν) 16.
Ἀναστὰς (aor.act.part.nom.sing.masc.of ἀνίστημι, adverbial, temporal) 789.
πορεύου (2d.per.sing.pres.mid.impv.of πορεύομαι, command) 170.
ἡ (nom.sing.fem.of the article in agreement with πίστις) 9.
πίστις (nom.sing.fem.of πίστις, subject of σέσωκέν) 728.
σου (gen.sing.masc.of σύ, possession) 104.
σέσωκέν (3d.per.sing.perf.act.ind.of σώζω, consummative) 109.
σε (acc.sing.masc.of σύ, direct object of σέσωκέν) 104.

Translation - "And He said to him, 'Get up and go away. Your faith has saved you.' "

Comment: The adverbial participle ἀναστὰς is temporal, with action indicated prior to the action of the imperative πορεύου. The man was lying on the ground at Jesus' feet. Thus the command, "Get up and go." Then the simple statement, "Your faith has saved you." In what sense? All the lepers were healed physically. One saw in Jesus, Who healed him, the incarnate Son of God, the Messiah of Israel. As a Samaritan he could not expect to share in the glories of the Messianic kingdom on the same basis as could the Jews. Jesus was the hope for Israel's future glory as a nation. What he could and did share in Jesus' ministry was the salvation of his own soul. As far as we know the other nine enjoyed good health for the remainder of their natural lives. We cannot know whether they ever trusted Christ as their personal saviour. The Samaritan also was free from leprosy, but he had been given a far more important freedom. He was free from the condemnation of sin.

Discourse on the Coming of the Kingdom

(Luke 17:20-37)

Luke 17:20 - "And when He was demanded of the Pharisees, when the kingdom of God should come, he answered them and said, The kingdom of God cometh not with observation."

Ἐπερωτηθεὶς δὲ ὑπὸ τῶν Φαρισαίων πότε ἔρχεται ἡ βασιλεία τοῦ θεοῦ ἀπεκρίθη αὐτοῖς καὶ εἶπεν, Οὐκ ἔρχεται ἡ βασιλεία τοῦ θεοῦ μετὰ παρατηρήσεως,

Ἐπερωτηθεὶς (aor.pass.part.nom.sing.masc.of ἐπερωτάω, adverbial, temporal) 973.
δὲ (explanatory conjunction) 11.
ὑπὸ (preposition with the ablative of agent) 117.
τῶν (abl.pl.masc.of the article in agreement with Φαρισαίων) 9.
Φαρισαίων (abl.pl.masc.of Φαρισαῖος, agency) 276.
πότε (interrogative adverb) 1233.
ἔρχεται (3d.per.sing.pres.ind.of ἔρχομαι, deliberative) 146.
ἡ (nom.sing.fem.of the article in agreement with βασιλεία) 9.
τοῦ (gen.sing.masc.of the article in agreement with θεοῦ) 9.
θεοῦ (gen.sing.masc.of θεούς, description) 124.
ἀπεκρίθη (3d.per.sing.aor.ind.of ἀποκρίνομαι, constative) 318.
αὐτοῖς (dat.pl.masc.of αὐτός, indirect object of ἀποκρίθη) 16.
καὶ (adjunctive conjunction joining verbs) 14.
εἶπεν (3d.per.sing.aor.act.ind.of εἶπον, constative) 155.
Οὐκ (summary negative conjunction with the indicative) 130.
ἔρχεται (3d.per.sing.pres.ind.of ἔρχομαι, static) 146.
ἡ (nom.sing.fem.of the article in agreement with βασιλεία) 9.
τοῦ (gen.sing.masc.of the article in agreement with θεοῦ) 9.
θεοῦ (gen.sing.masc.of θεός, description) 124.
μετὰ (preposition with the genitive, accompaniment) 50.

#2616 παρατηρήσεως (gen.sing.fem.of παρατήρησις, accompaniment).

observation - Luke 17:20.

Meaning: *Cf.* παρατηρέω (#2104). A combination of παρά (#154) and τηρέω (#1297). Hence, to place alongside for the purpose of observation. The method by which two things are observed, side by side, to determine if the presence of the one proves the presence of the other. To observe in comparison. Observation by comparison. With reference to the signs which are alleged to be indicative of the approach of the Kingdom of God - Luke 17:20.

Translation - "Now when He was grilled by the Pharisees about when the kingdom of God would come He said to them, 'The kingdom of God does not come by observation.' "

Comment: *ἐπερωτάω* (#973) is a stronger word than *ἐρωτάω* (#1172). The Pharisees were being aggressive, possibly to the point of hostility, with this question. Their attitude seems to have been, "Very well, you are a miracle worker. You say that you are the Son of God and the Messiah of Israel. You have even raised a dead man from the grave. Now when are you going to produce the Kingdom of God? When are you going to redeem Israel from political bondage? When are you going to produce on a grand and comprehensive scale what you are doing on a piecemeal basis?" "Demand" is a good word, but it requires an object which is not in the text. They demanded an answer from Him. #973 means "to ask" but "to ask with spirit" - "to ask firmly/insistently/definitely/even defiantly." Note the deliberate present tense in *ἔρχεται*, although the question here is not rhetorical. *Cf.* our discussion of Tί *ποιοῦμεν* in John 11:47.

Our Lord replied, not directly, but by pointing out that the Kingdom of God is not something that can be predicted on the basis of human events. The Kingdom of God will come, but not in any way that permits the one who expects it to predict upon the basis of his observation of the so-called "signs of the times." It is most important, even crucial, to note that verses 20 and 21 contain Jesus' answer to the unsaved Pharisees, while what follows in vss.22-37 is His answer to His disciples, which is quite a different story. To the unsaved there are no outward signs that He will recognize. That day will come upon the unsaved as a complete surprize, regardless of the signs of the times (1 Thess.5:1-3). But the Christian believer will not be surprized (1 Thess.5:4,5). To the Pharisees, He is saying, "Do not look for signs. Look for the King." Because an evil and adulterous generation seeks a sign (Mt.12:39; Lk.11:29).

Verse 21 - "Neither shall they say, Lo, here! or lo, there! for, behold, the kingdom of God is within you."

οὐδὲ ἐροῦσιν, Ἰδοὺ ὧδε, ἤ, Ἐκεῖ. ἰδοὺ γὰρ ἡ βασιλεία τοῦ θεοῦ ἐντὸς ὑμῶν ἐστιν.

οὐδὲ (disjunctive particle) 452.
ἐροῦσιν (3d.per.pl.fut.act.ind.of *εἶπον*, predictive) 155.
Ἰδοὺ (exclamation) 95.
ὧδε (local adverb) 766.
ἤ (disjunctive) 465.
Ἐκεῖ (local adverb) 204.
ἰδοὺ (exclamation) 95.
γὰρ (causal conjunction) 105.
ἡ (nom.sing.fem.of the article in agreement with *βασιλεία*) 9.
βασιλεία (nom.sing.fem.of *βασιλεία*, subject of *ἐστιν*) 253.
τοῦ (gen.sing.masc.of the article in agreement with *θεοῦ*) 9.
θεοῦ (gen.sing.masc.of *θεός*, description) 124.

ἐντὸς (an adverb of place) 1460.
ὑμῶν (gen.pl.masc.of σύ, place description) 104.
ἐστιν (3d.per.sing.pres.ind.of εἰμί, aoristic) 86.

Translation - "They shall neither say, 'Look! Here!!' nor 'There!!'. Because, Look! The kingdom of God is in your midst."

Comment: The οὐδὲ . . . ἤ sequence means "neither . . . nor." The Kingdom of God will be announced neither by signs to be observed nor by proclamations to be heard. The Pharisees were told not to look for signs nor to listen for announcements. There would be those who would cry out, "Look here" or "Look there." But informed citizens of the Kingdom of God will know better than to be seduced by false claims. Why? The γὰρ clause is causal. "Because I order you to look now! (ἰδού is 2d.per.sing.aor.act.impv.of ὁράω). The Kingdom of God *is* (present tense in ἐστιν) in the midst of all of you (plural in ὑμῶν).

If Jesus had meant that the Kingdom of God is the divine spark of human goodness within every man (a view supported by the AV, ASV, except in the margin, and Goodspeed, with their translation, "within you") the text would have read ἐντός σου - (singular) - "within each of you as individuals." But it is ἐντὸς ὑμῶν - "within you as a group." There they stood. There also stood Jesus. He is the Kingdom of God, since He is God's King. He was standing within the circle of people many of whom were the Pharisees who had asked the question of verse 20. Jesus was saying, "Behold, here I am. See me! I am the Kingdom of God." Moffatt, Montgomery and the American Revised Standard Version support our translation with "in your midst" or "within the midst of you." If a man cannot see in Jesus Christ, the Kingdom of God, he will not be able to recognize the kingdom when it comes regardless of what fantastic signs and portents point to it or blatant announcements that precede it. In fact, those who do not recognize Jesus Christ as the only one who is able to establish the Kingdom of God on earth, will receive Antichrist when he comes (John 5:43; Rev.13:11-18).

But believers, who love and trust Jesus Christ as God's Son and their Saviour, still would like to know of any evidences in human history that will telegraph to us the approach of His personal return to earth. It is to this question that Jesus devotes the rest of the chapter. Since this instruction is only for regenerated ears, it is spoken quite properly to His disciples.

Further to refute the view ἐντὸς ὑμῶν ἐστιν means "in the hearts of the Pharisees" we point out that at that time they were plotting to kill Him.

Verse 22 - "And he said unto the disciples, The days will come, when ye shall desire to see one of the days of the Son of Man, and ye shall not see it."

Εἶπεν δὲ πρὸς τοὺς μαθητάς,Ἐλεύσονται ἡμέραι ὅτε ἐπιθυμήσετε μίαν τῶν ἡμέρων τοῦ υἱοῦ τοῦ ἀνθρώπου ἰδεῖν καὶ οὐκ ὄψεσθε.

Εἶπεν (3d.per.sing.aor.act.ind.of εἶπον, constative) 155.

δὲ (continuative conjunction) 11.
πρὸς (preposition with the accusative of extent after a verb of speaking) 197.
τοὺς (acc.pl.masc.of the article in agreement with μαθητάς) 9.
μαθητάς (acc.pl.masc.of μαθητής, extent, after a verb of speaking) 421.
Ἐλεύσονται (3d.per.pl.fut.ind.of ἔρχομαι, predictive) 146.
ἡμέραι (nom.pl.fem.of ἡμέρα, subject of ἐλεύσονται) 135.
ὅτε (conjunction introducing a definite temporal clause) 703.
ἐπιθυμήσετε (2d.per.pl.fut.act.ind.of ἐπιθυμέω, predictive) 500.
μίαν (acc.sing.fem.of εἷς, in agreement with ἡμέραν) 469.
τῶν (gen.pl.fem.of the article in agreement with ἡμερῶν) 9.
ἡμερῶν (gen.pl.fem.of ἡμέρα, partitive genitive) 135.
τοῦ (gen.sing.masc.of the article in agreement with υἱοῦ) 9.
υἱοῦ (gen.sing.masc.of υἱός, description) 5.
τοῦ (gen.sing.masc.of the article in agreement with ἀνθρώπου) 9.
ἀνθρώπου (gen.sing.masc.of ἄνθρωπος, description) 341.
ἰδεῖν (aor.act.inf.of ὁράω, complementary) 144.
καὶ (adversative conjunction) 14.
οὐκ (summary negative conjunction with the indicative) 130.
ὄψεσθε (2d.per.pl.fut.ind.of ὁράω, predictive) 144.

Translation - "And He said to the disciples, 'There will be days when you will long to see one of the days of the Son of Man, but you will not see.' "

Comment: The Pharisees, whose motive in asking Jesus the question of verse 20 was not pure were told nothing about the course of human history before the Second Coming of the King. They were only told that He was the King. But Jesus then told the disciples something more. They already knew that the Kingdom of God was present with them in the person of Jesus. Now they are to learn a little about what to expect before He comes again to establish the Kingdom of God upon earth.

First he tells the disciples that the days would come (Ἐλεύσονται ἡμέραι) when Christians will become dissatisfied and unhappy with "man's day") 1 Cor.4:3) and when we will look forward with great longing for even a single day (if nothing more could be had) of the Son of Man. How true our Lord's prediction was. How many Christians have often sighed, "If we could only see for one day how the world will be when our Lord comes again!" This we greatly desire. Note the intensity of the desire in ἐπιθυμέω, #500).

From man's unregenerate point of view his "day" began when he crucified Christ (1 Cor.4:3). But God called that day night (John 9:4). "Day" is the time when Christ was permitted to perform the works of the Father Who sent Him, such as the healing of the blind man (John 9:1-41). The night, when He was crucified came, when all of man's works are for nothing. (John 6:63). Only the Holy Spirit can work during the night of man's supremacy, a time which man calls his "day" (1 Cor.4:3). The only work that is ultimately constructive that has been done since the crucifixion of Christ is that of the Holy Spirit in calling out the elect (John 16:7-11) and in leading them after they are saved to do the will of

God. Man's day, since Calvary, is the time when the world is being dominated and its affairs conducted by the antigod, antichrist, antirevelation point of view. Laws and the court procedures that enforce them, institutions, principalities and powers, customs, standards of ethics, matters relating to commerce, business, the humanities and arts, will eventually all be brought under the control of Satan and his incarnate administrator, the Man of Sin. Eternal good has been done in the world only as the Holy Spirit has worked through Christian believers in keeping with the Word of God. It pleases God in this age to remain outside the sphere of human activity. Man made it clear to God at Golgotha that he did not want "this man to reign over us." He "(had) no king but Caesar." What should be done with God's Son? "Crucify Him!" Why? What evil has He done? "Crucify Him!!" God said, "Very well. You want to run the world without me or my Son? So be it. Run it. Assume control of all of its institutions. Be responsible for the social, economic and political impacts of all that you do. Assume the blame for all of the tragedies of history. Run the world during a period that your own historians will call the Dark Ages. Conduct in it an industrial revolution. Overpopulate it. Pollute its air and the water of its rivers. Exhaust its natural resources and solve the problems that will arise from its energy shortages. Wage your wars across its continents and upon its broad ocean expanses. Sink your ships and blow up your cities. Fill its prisons with the criminals that you created and its mental institutions with the psychopaths that you have driven to distraction. I intend to have only one function in your world for the next two thousand years. My Holy Spirit will work only through Christian believers and the Bible which He will inspire some of them to write and a few others properly to exegete and preach. He will direct a worldwide missionary enterprise and He will call out from the Gentiles a people for my name. After sinners are saved by my grace, they may try to introduce Biblical ethics into world affairs. But sinners cannot take the credit for that. The flesh profits nothing. The world may seek to do many "good things" but without love, it is nothing (1 Cor.13:1-3). The world of man's day, never sympathetic to Christ or to His followers (John 15:18,19), will get worse and worse (2 Tim.3:13). They will become increasingly sophisticated, as they measure themselves by their own standards, but they will never come to a knowledge of the truth (2 Tim.3:7). As a matter of fact, unregenerate man will create such havoc upon earth in his "day" that my believer's will "earnestly desire to see just one of the days of the Son of Man" of which there will be an unlimited number after His second coming."

This distinction between "man's day" and "the days of the Son of Man" is fundamental to an understanding of this passage. But, despite our great desire to do so, we shall not be permitted to see even one of God's days, until the Second Coming of His Son. Therefore Jesus is about to show His disciples, not the unsaved Pharisees, how they can read the signs of the times that herald the dawning of Christ's day. *Cf.*#135 for this distinction between God's day and man's day.

The above exposition answers conclusively the atheistic argument that God is responsible for human tragedy upon earth. On the contrary God has had nothing to do with human history since Calvary, except as it relates to the effectual call by the Holy Spirit of the elect and the activities which He directs in the lives of the individual members of the united body of Christ. The rest of it, including a great deal of misdirected activity, popularly known as "church work" is the work of man. World society in the late 20th century is chaotic only because man crucified the Light of the World. Mankind has been stumbling around in the dark since the dark day that the Son of God died on a cross (Lk.23:44). Since the light that is in man is darkness, how great is the darkness! (Mt.6:23).

Verse 23 - "And they shall say to you, See here; or, see there: go not after them, nor follow them."

καὶ ἐροῦσιν ὑμῖν, Ἰδοὺ ἐκεῖ (ἤ,) Ἰδοὺν ὧδε. μὴ ἀπέλθητε μηδὲ διώξητε.

καὶ (continuative conjunction) 14.
ἐροῦσιν (3d.per.pl.fut.act.ind.of *εἶπον*, predictive) 155.
ὑμῖν (dat.pl.masc.of *σύ*, indirect object of *ἐροῦσιν*) 104.
Ἰδοὺ (exclamation) 95.
ἐκεῖ (adverb of place) 204.
(*ἤ*,) (disjunctive) 465.
Ἰδοὺ (exclamation) 95.
ὧδε (adverb of place) 766.
μὴ (qualified negative conjunction with the subjunctive, prohibition) 87.
ἀπέλθητε (2d.per.pl.aor.subj.of *ἀπέρχομαι*, prohibition) 239.
μηδὲ (negative continuative particle) 612.
διώξητε (2d.per.pl.aor.act.subj.of *διώκω*, prohibition) 434.

Translation - "And they will say to you, 'Look! There!!' or 'Look! Here!!' Do not go away nor follow them.' "

Comment: The frustrated Christian, weary in well doing, may become so eager to see his Lord, that in a moment of weakness he may be victimized by the false prophets who will be pointing here and there and heralding a new day. We have had many panaceas for the world's ills. "This is the solution." "Try this." "Listen to him." These Pollyannas are not speaking of Christ, as the crucified, risen, glorified and returning Lord, but of someone or something who/which is certain to bring in God's day by means of man's wisdom. Democracy, education, birth control, civil rights, sex education, fluoridation, slum clearance, progressive income tax policy, women's liberation, zero population, etc.etc. The list is endless. Man is determined to prove that he can run affairs on this planet without the help of God or His Christ. We once had Father Divine. We recently had Jim Jones. We still have Reverend Moon. AntiChrist himself, Satan incarnate, will be the last to appear and all of the unsaved on earth will say, *Ἰδοὺ ἐκεῖ*. But the true disciple of our Lord will not be deceived. *μὴ ἀπέλθητε μηδὲ διώξητε*. *Cf.*#434. Here only in this sense. We are not to believe the world. In their attempt to bring in an artificial "day of God" they will become frenetic. Why will not the Christian be deceived? Because of what we learn in

Verse 24 - "For as the lightning, that lighteneth out of the one part under heaven, shineth unto the other part under heaven; so shall also the Son of Man be in his day."

ὥσπερ γὰρ ἡ ἀστραπὴ ἀστράπτουσα ἐκ τῆς ὑπὸ τὸν οὐρανὸν εἰς τὴν ὑπ' οὐρανὸν λάμπει, οὕτως ἔσται ὁ υἱὸς τοῦ ἀνθρώπου (ἐν τῇ ἡμέρᾳ αὐτοῦ).

ὥσπερ (intensive particle introducing a comparative clause) 560.
γὰρ (causal conjunction) 105.
ἡ (nom.sing.fem.of the article in agreement with *ἀστραπὴ*) 9.
ἀστραπὴ (nom.sing.fem.of *ἀστραπή*, subject of *λάμπει*) 1502.

#2617 *ἀστράπτουσα* (pres.act.part.nom.sing.fem.of *ἀστράπτω*, adjectival, ascriptive).

lighten - Luke 17:24.
shine - Luke 24:4.

Meaning: Cf.ἀστήρ (#145). To lighten; to shine. Of the illuminating effect of the lightning (#1502) as it flashes across the sky - Luke 17:24. In the description of the dress of the two angels at the empty tomb of Jesus - Luke 24:4.

ἐκ (preposition with the ablative of source) 19.
τῆς (abl.sing.fem.of the article in agreement with *μερίδος* understood, ellipsis) 9.
ὑπό (preposition with the accusative, under) 117.
τὸν (acc.sing.masc.of the article in agreement with *οὐρανὸν*) 9.
οὐρανὸν (acc.sing.masc.of *οὐρανός*, extent) 254.
εἰς (preposition with the accusative of extent) 140.
τὴν (acc.sing.fem.of the article in agreement with *μερίδος*, ellipsis) 9.
ὑπ' (preposition with the accusative of extent, under) 117.
οὐρανὸν (acc.sing.masc.of *οὐρανός*, extent) 254.
λάμπει (3d.per.sing.pres.act.ind.of *λάμπω*, customary) 458.
οὕτως (demonstrative adverb) 74.
ἔσται (3d.per.sing.fut.ind.of *εἰμί*, predictive) 86.
ὁ (nom.sing.masc.of the article in agreement with *υἱὸς*) 9.
υἱὸς (nom.sing.masc.of *υἱός*, subject of *ἔσται*) 5.
τοῦ (gen.sing.masc.of the article in agreement with *ἀνθρώπου*) 9.
ἀνθρώπου (gen.sing.masc.of *ἄνθρωπος*, relationship) 341.
(*ἐν* (preposition with the locative of time point) 80.
τῇ (loc.sing.fem.of the article in agreement with *ἡμέρᾳ*) 9.
ἡμέρᾳ (loc.sing.fem.of *ἡμέρα*, time point) 135.
αὐτοῦ (gen.sing.masc.of *αὐτός*, possession) 16.

Translation - "Because precisely as the lightning shines from one part under heaven unto the other part, so shall the Son of Man be in His day."

Comment: *γὰρ* is causal, as Jesus explains why the informed Christian will not be deceived by those who point to localized events as the fulfillment of the promise of the Second Coming. Quite the contrary. Jesus employs a familiar sight for the analogy. The lightning, streaking, spreading and fingering its electrical way here and there shines from one horizon to the other. In this same way (note the intensive ὥσπερ) the Son of Man will be seen by everyone when He comes. The margin adds ἐν τῇ ἡμέρᾳ αὐτοῦ - "on His day" *i.e.* the day when He returns to earth. The point is the universality of the sight. When the lightning flashes its brilliant pattern all over the sky, it is not necessary to ask someone to come here or there in order to see it. Everyone sees it from his own vantage point. So when Jesus comes He will be seen by all on earth, without the necessity of looking here or there. "Behold He cometh with clouds, and every eye shall see Him" (Rev.1:7).

When Messiah came the first time He had a forerunner who announced His coming. After John the Baptist was certain of the identity of the Messiah, he then pointed Him out and introduced Him to Israel. When Messiah comes again He will need neither a forerunner nor an introduction. One need not introduce the lightning in a thunderstorm.

Lest the disciples think that the glorious second coming of Messiah was to be the next event on the divine schedule and that Jesus was soon to manifest Himself as the King of King and Lord of Lords, He reminds them of something of which He had told them before. Before Messiah can come in His universal glory, He must suffer and die. This is the message of

Verse 25 - "But first must he suffer many things, and be rejected of this generation."

πρῶτον δὲ δεῖ αὐτὸν πολλὰ παθεῖν καὶ ἀποδοκιμασθῆναι ἀπὸ τῆς γενεᾶς ταύτης.

πρῶτον (acc.sing.neut.of πρῶτος, adverbial) 487.
δὲ (adversative conjunction) 11.
δεῖ (3d.per.sing.pres.impersonal) 1207.
αὐτὸν (acc.sing.masc.of αὐτός, general reference) 16.
πολλὰ (acc.pl.neut.of πολύς, direct object of παθεῖν) 228.
παθεῖν (2d.aor.inf.of πάσχω, completes δεῖ) 1208.
καὶ (adjunctive conjunction joining infinitives) 14.
ἀποδοκιμασθῆναι (aor.pass.inf.of ἀποδοκιμάζω, completes δεῖ) 1390.
ἀπὸ (preposition with the ablative of agent) 70.
τῆς (abl.sing.fem.of the article in agreement with γενεᾶς) 9.
γενεᾶς (abl.sing.fem.of γενεά, agent) 922.
ταύτης (abl.sing.fem.of οὗτος, in agreement with γενεᾶς) 93.

Translation - "But first He must suffer many things and be rejected by this generation."

Comment: The picture in verse 24 is glorious and thrilling. In verse 25 it is a picture of suffering and death. Hence δὲ is adversative. Before Jesus comes in power and great glory He must suffer. δεῖ (#1207), in the sense that the necessity that rested upon Him to die grew out of the eternal plan of redemption. γενεᾶς ταύτης means the generation of Jews who were living in the first century, not the Jewish race as a whole. The word for the genetic class known as Jews and used in the sense in which we say the Americans, Irish, English, etc. is γένος (#1090). *Cf.*#1390 for ἀποδοκιμάζω in relation to Christ, *e.g.* 1 Pet.2:4,7; Mt.21:42; Mk.12:10; Lk.20:17; Mk.8:31; Lk.9:22; 17:25. Official Israel looked Him over, assessed what He could do and who He was, raised the question as to whether, if they accepted Him, He would fit compatibly into their program, decided that He would not, and rejected Him. The builders did not want that sort of stone in their building (1 Pet.2:7). He certainly did not fit into the establishment they were building. The rock which they rejected will fall upon them and grind them to powder while He becomes the Chief Cornerstone of God's eternal building, a house, not made with hands, fitly framed together and made solid by that which every joint supplies (Mt.21:44; Eph.2:20-22; 4:16). Any society that rejects the Son of God gives itself over to materialism and falls under the sentence of divine judgment. This principle is illustrated in the historic examples which are described in verses 26 - 29.

Verse 26 - "And as it was in the days of Noah, so shall it be also in the days of the Son of Man."

καὶ καθὼς ἐγένετο ἐν ταῖς ἡμέραις Νῶε, οὕτως ἔσται καὶ ἐν ταῖς ἡμέραις τοῦ υἱοῦ τοῦ ἀνθρώπου.

καὶ (continuative conjunction) 14.
καθὼς (adverb introducing a comparative clause) 1348.
ἐγένετο (3d.per.sing.aor.act.ind.of γίνομαι, constative) 113.
ἐν (preposition with the locative of time point) 80.
ταῖς (loc.pl.fem.of the article in agreement with ἡμέραις) 9.
ἡμέραις (loc.pl.fem.of ἡμέρα, time point) 135.
Νῶε (gen.sing.masc.of Νῶε, description) 1514.
οὕτως (demonstrative adverb) 74.
καὶ (adjunctive conjuncion joining prepositional phrases) 14.
ἐν (preposition with the locative of time point) 80.
ταῖς (loc.pl.fem.of the article in agreement with ἡμέραις) 9.
ἡμέραις (loc.pl.fem.of ἡμέρα, time point) 135.
τοῦ (gen.sing.masc.of the article in agreement with υἱοῦ) 9.
υἱοῦ (gen.sing.masc.of υἱός, description) 5.
τοῦ (gen.sing.masc.of the article in agreement with ἀνθρώπου) 9.
ἀνθρώπου (gen.sing.masc.of ἄνθρωπος, relationship) 341.

Translation - "And just as it was in the days of Noah, so shall it be also in the days of the Son of Man."

Comment: The connection between verse 25, which points out that Jesus' contemporaries would reject and crucify Him and the allusion to the antediluvians in verse 26 is clear. Noah's contemporaries rejected him also. Called of God in a time of impending divine judgment and directed to provide a way of escape for all who would listen to his warning, Noah appeared naive and foolish for 120 years while he occupied himself building an ark, on the assumption that a universal flood would destroy all who did not seek its shelter. He built obediently and preached faithfully. His contemporaries rejected him. The antediluvians were pragmatists. They regarded faith in divine revelation as the function of intellectual children. The wise and prudent (Mt.11:25) checked the weather records and announced that the fulfillment of Noah's prediction was supported by only the slightest degree of probability - so slight in fact that it could safely be ignored. Rejecting faith in God's revelation, they devoted themselves wholly to materialistic activities. They lived existentially - for the moment. One of them may have written a book entitled "God is Dead." Jesus here declares that another wave of cynical and hypersophisticated disregard for or amused contempt toward the revelation of God, would engulf human society in the days, during which the Son of Man would again personally intervene in human history to establish the Kingdom of God.

Note *καθὼς . . . οὕτως καὶ* in the "just as . . . even so also" sequence.

The activities of Noah's detractors, his activities and God's activities are all described in

Verse 27 - "They did eat, they drank, they married wives, they were given in marriage, until the day that Noah entered into the ark, and the flood came, and destroyed them all."

ἤσθιον, ἔπινον, ἐγάμουν, ἐγαμίζοντο, ἄχρι ἧς ἡμέρας εἰσῆλθεν Νῶε *εἰς τὴν κιβωτόν, καὶ ἦλθεν ὁ κατακλυσμὸς καὶ ἀπώλεσεν πάντας.*

ἤσθιον (3d.per.pl.imp.act.ind.of *ἐσθίω*, progressive description) 610.
ἔπινον (3d.per.pl.imp.act.ind.of *πίνω*, progressive description) 611.
ἐγάμουν (3d.per.pl.imp.act.ind.of *γαμέω*, progressive description) 512.
ἐγαμίζοντο (3d.per.pl.imp.pass.ind.of *γαμίζω*, progressive description) 1426.
ἄχρι (preposition introducing a relative clause in the genitive) 1517.
ἧς (gen.sing.fem.of *ὅς*, time description) 65.
ἡμέρας (gen.sing.fem.of *ἡμέρα*, time description) 135.
εἰσῆλθεν (3d.per.sing.aor.ind.of *εἰσέρχομαι*, constative) 234.
εἰς (preposition with the accusative of extent) 140.
τὴν (acc.sing.fem.of the article in agreement with *κιβωτόν*) 9.
κιβωτόν (acc.sing.fem.of *κιβωτός*, extent) 1518.
καὶ (adversative conjunction) 14.
ἦλθεν (3d.per.sing.aor.ind.of *ἔρχομαι*, constative) 146.
ὁ (nom.sing.masc.of the article in agreement with *κατακλυσμὸς*) 9.
κατακλυσμὸς (nom.sing.masc.of *κατακλυσμός*, subject of *ἦλθεν* and *ἀπώλεσεν*) 1515.
καὶ (adjunctive conjunction joining verbs) 14.
ἀπώλεσεν (3d.per.sing.aor.act.ind.of *ἀπόλλυμι*, constative) 208.
πάντας (acc.pl.masc.of *πᾶς*, direct object of *ἀπώλεσεν*) 67.

Translation - "They were always eating; always drinking; they were marrying and being given in marriage, until the day on which Noah entered into the ark;

but the flood came and destroyed them all."

Comment: Note the activities of the antediluvians. A constant round of eating, drinking and marriage. The verbs, all in the imperfect tense, denote continuous action. There is no sin involved in any of these activities if they are accompanied by faith in God and faithful service to Him. Here we have an expression of extreme materialism by a civilization that had rejected God and Noah, their warning about coming judgment and their offer of a safe passage through the flood inside the ark. These things were greeted only with scorn and derision - another banquet, another drink, another round of sex. This continued ἄχρι ἧς ἡμέρας . . . κιβωτὸν - "until the day on which Noah entered the ark." There was no cessation in their sinful activity (Gen.6:5); no sign that they paused to reflect whether or not Noah could be right.

Note Noah's activities. He knew that God's judgment would come in his lifetime. He was ordered to build an ark (Gen.6:7,8; Heb.11:7; 1 Pet.3:18-22). During this period of 120 years, Noah knew only that he would live to see the flood; that he and those who entered with him into the ark would be saved; that all others would be lost. During this period he did not know the precise day when the flood would come. But during the last seven days of that 120 year period, Noah did know precisely when the flood would come (Gen.7:4). During that last week Noah was a datesetter. "Seven days from today; six days hence; five, four, three, two - - - tomorrow - - today is the day. Come into the ark." This was Noah's message. Where was Noah during those last seven days? He was outside the ark (Gen.7:11-13). Note Gen.7:13 - the 17th day of the second month of Noah's 600th year. On that day the flood came (vs.11). The rain continued for forty days and forty nights (vs.12). That last day Noah entered the ark (vs.13). On that day his contemporaries ate their last meal, had their last drink and went to their last wedding. To them the cataclysm was a great surprize, despite that they had been told about it for 120 years. To Noah it was no surprize at all. He had been told 120 years before that he would live to see it, and he had been told seven days before that it would happen on that day on which it did, in fact, take place.

Keep in mind that the subject of Jesus' remarks is evidence that the Kingdom of God is at hand (Lk.17:20-27). He had refused to give any information to the unsaved Pharisees, but He is informing His disciples (vss.22-27). Endtime Christians can observe the sociological evidences that antediluvian permissivism is rampant in the world. All of the signs are right. As this is written (July 8,1980) we do not have God's revelation that Christ will come back to earth in our lifetime. Perhaps we are not the generation who will live to see the rapture. But that endtime generation, whoever they may be and whenever they may live, will know, as Noah did, when the Lord is coming.

In 1 Thess.5:1-6 Paul distinguishes between the saved and the unsaved and how the coming of the Lord relates to each. 1 Thess.5:3 speaks of the unsaved. It is they who will say, "Peace and safety" and it is upon them that sudden destruction will come. The unsaved will not escape. But note the fourth verse: "But ye, brethren, are not in darkness, that that day should overtake you as a thief." The Lord will come "as a thief" to the unsaved, not to the children of God. Thus the view that the rapture of the church can occur at any time, previously unannounced and that the Christians will be surprized when He comes is wrong. Even the best Christian does not think about the rapture with his eyes glued to the heavens continuously.

In speaking about His coming in A.D.33, our Lord, employing the present tense, said, "But of that day and hour knoweth no man, no, not the angels of heaven, but my Father only." (Mt.24:36). He did not say that no man would ever know.

Note finally God's activities. The flood came and destroyed them all, except Noah and his family (1 Pet.3:18-20). *Cf.* also 2 Pet.2:5 with comment, *en loc.*.

To those materialists who could not recognize the Kingdom of God, incarnate in Jesus Christ, as He stood before them (Lk.17:21) no other sign will be given. They are to be left to their eating, drinking and sex. But to the disciples who will be longing for just "one day of the Son of Man" because they are so disgusted with the world and its folly (Lk.17:22) He has given clues as to when we can expect deliverance. The final generation of endtime Christians, who have not been deceived by pretribulation rapture, the popular delusion that swept through Fundamentalist ranks since the days of the Plymouth Brethren, will, like Noah, not be children of darkness. Luke does not tell us in this passage what event God will use to indicate that His prophetic clock is running again and that the last countdown has begun. Matthew 24:15, which is parallel to Luke 21:20-24 provides us with the answer. Those who teach that Christians should not be looking for events, but for the rapture, are likely not to be able to recognize the events that telegraph the end of the endtime, when they come. If the Rider on the White Horse (Rev.6:1-2) came today, he would be ignored by those who are convinced that nothing prophetic can happen on earth until *after* the Church is translated out of the world. Perhaps their prejudice, now so concretely set, will be dispelled in that day. If they are truly regenerate, indeed they will come to understand. 1 Thess.5:4 applies to all of the saints, even to those who are unduly influenced by the Schofield footnotes.

We get another illustration in

Verse 28 - "Likewise also as it was in the days of Lot; they did eat, they drank, they bought, they sold, they planted, their builded."

ὁμοίως καθὼς ἐγένετο ἐν ταῖς ἡμέραις Λώτ. ἤσθιον, ἔπινον, ἠγόραζον, ἐπώλουν, ἐφύτευον, ᾠκοδόμουν.

ὁμοίως (adverbial) 1425.
καθὼς (adverbial) 1348.
ἐγένετο (3d.per.sing.aor.ind.of *γίνομαι*, constative) 113.
ἐν (preposition with the locative of time point) 80.
ταῖς (loc.pl.fem.of the article in agreement with *ἡμέραις*) 9.
ἡμέραις (loc.pl.fem.of *ἡμέρα*, time point) 135.

#2618 *Λώτ* (gen.sing.masc.of *Λώτ*, description).

Lot - Luke 17:28,29,32; 2 Pet.2:7.

Meaning: Lot - a veil, a covering. Lot, the son of Haran, the nephew of Abraham - Luke 17:28,29,32; 2 Pet.2:7.

ἤσθιον (3d.per.pl.imp.act.ind.of ἐσθίω, progressive description) 610.
ἔπινον (3d.per.pl.imp.act.ind.of πίνω, progressive description) 611.
ἠγόραζον (3d.per.pl.imp.act.ind.of ἀγοράζω, progressive description) 1085.
ἐπώλουν (3d.per.pl.imp.act.ind.of πωλέω, progressive description) 892.
ἐφύτευον (3d.per.pl.imp.act.ind.of φυτεύω, progressive description) 1154.
ᾠκοδόμουν (3d.per.pl.imp.act.ind.of οἰκοδομέω, progressive description) 694.

Translation - "So also was it in the days of Lot. They were always eating and drinking; they were buying and selling; they were planting; they were building."

Comment: The people of Sodom, like the antediluvians, were always busy eating, drinking, buying, selling, planting and building. There is no mention of sex here, but the commercial activities are listed. Sodom, an urban culture, had all of the vices of Noah's day, complicated by a more highly developed commercial and agricultural system. The verbs are all in the imperfect tense denoting the frenzy of continuous activity. Economic growth (ᾠκοδόμουν), and commerce (ἠγόραζον and ἐπώλουν) bring with them the social ills that are certain to develop among the unregenerate. Overpopulation, crowding, slums, vice, disease, pollution, crime and violence, with the added aberration - homesexuality (Gen.19:4-11). Paul alludes to this along with a catalogue of other vices, the natural result of the materialism that rules out faith in a personal God (Rom.1:21-32, with particular attention to verses 26,27). There was too much democracy in Sodom (2 Pet.2:7), at least for a godly man. *Laissez faire* permissiveness, such as the bill of rights grants to Americans in a democracy, becomes repulsive to the Christian who, like Lot, is vexed with what he sees, hears and could read if he chose to.

Yet, since this is man's day, not God's, and because democracy, with all of its faults, is better than the dictatorship of some wicked man, the Christian is under the obligation of patriotism to support the bill of rights, even though it permits pornography, free speech in however bad taste and the vapid and vacuous drivel that originates on Madison Avenue. Many Christians apparently fail to realize that not since Calvary has there ever been a "Christian country" founded on "Christian principles." The United States is not a Christian country. It is a free country, in the sense that it is committed to democratic principles.

No democratic country is viable without good morals and good morals are not forthcoming except through the Holy Spirit's activities in the Christian. Therefore, unless democracies are also Christian, and therefore moral, their permissiveness results in social, economic, political and national collapse. Sodom banished God and His authority and every man did what he pleased. This is democracy. So indeed did Noah's civilization. So indeed has America to a great extent. The flood destroyed the antediluvians. The firestorm destroyed Sodom. The Second Coming of Christ will end democracy and replace it with the divine authority of Plato's Philosopher-King, the Lord Jesus Christ.

Verse 29 - "But the same day that Lot went out of Sodom it rained fire and brimstone from heaven, and destroyed them all."

ᾗ δὲ ἡμέρᾳ ἐξῆλθεν Λὼτ ἀπὸ Σοδόμων, ἔβρεξεν πῦρ καὶ θεῖον ἀπ' οὐρανοῦ καὶ ἀπώλεσεν πάντας.

ᾗ (loc.sing.fem.of ὅς, time point) 65.
δὲ (adversative conjunction) 11.
ἡμέρᾳ (loc.sing.fem.of ἡμέρα, time point) 135.
ἐξῆλθεν (3d.per.sing.aor.ind.of ἐξέρχομαι, constative) 161.
Λὼτ (nom.sing.masc.of Λώτ, subject of ἐξῆλθεν) 2618.
ἀπὸ (preposition with the ablative of separation) 70.
Σοδόμων (abl.sing.of Σοδόμων, separation) 871.
ἔβρεξεν (3d.per.sing.aor.act.ind.of βρέχω, ingressive) 548.
πῦρ (nom.sing.neut.of πῦρ, subject of ἔβρεξεν) 298.
καὶ (adjunctive conjunction joining nouns) 14.

#2619 θεῖον (nom.sing.neut.of θεῖον, subject of ἔβρεξεν).

brimstone - Luke 17:29; Rev.9:17,18; 14:10; 19:20; 20:10; 21:8.

Meaning: *Cf.*θεῖος (#3422). θεῖον is the neuter form. Brimstone, which, according to Thayer, has the power to purify and ward off contagion. With reference to the divine judgment which fell on Sodom - Luke 17:29. Of apocalyptic judgments - Rev.9:17,18. Of Gehenna - "hell fire" and brimstone - Rev.14:10; 19:20; 20:10; 21:8. Always joined to πῦρ in the New Testament.

ἀπ' (preposition with the ablative of source) 70.
οὐρανοῦ (abl.sing.masc.of οὐρανός, source) 254.
καὶ (adjunctive conjunction joining verbs) 14.
ἀπώλεσεν (3d.per.sing.aor.act.ind.of ἀπόλλυμι, constative) 208.
πάντας (acc.pl.masc.of πᾶς, direct object of ἀπώλεσεν) 67.

Translation - "But on the day on which Lot left Sodom, fire and brimstone rained from heaven and destroyed them all."

Comment: The Sodomites carried on a continuous program of bustling activity but God had other plans. His judgment waited only until Lot left town. Just as the flood came on the day that Noah entered the ark, so the fire fell from heaven on the day that Lot left. God always cares for His own before He visits judgment upon the lost. Whether it is a flood (2 Pet.2:5) or a firestorm (2 Pet.2:6), God's judgment comes at the eariest possible moment after His chosen ones are delivered (2 Pet.2:7).

The story of Lot and Sodom has introduced the urban society with its economic growth, a factor missing in the Noah story. There is also the element of homosexuality. A third element is Lot's characteristic fulfillment of Jesus' remark in verse 22 about the saints, heartsick and disgusted with the world about them, longing for "one day" on which the Kingdom of God could rule the world.

Righteous Lot felt this longing (2 Pet.2:7) just as the saints long for Christ's return at the end of this age. The destruction of Sodom and the antediluvians, after Noah and his family and Lot had been taken out, was total.

Verse 30 - "Even thus shall it be in the day when the Son of Man is revealed."

κατὰ τὰ αὐτὰ ἔσται ᾗ ἡμέρᾳ ὁ υἱὸς τοῦ ἀνθρώπου ἀποκαλύπτεται.

κατὰ (preposition with the accusative, standard rule) 98.
τὰ (acc.pl.neut.of the article in agreement with αὐτὰ) 9.
αὐτὰ (acc.pl.neut.of αὐτός, standard rule) 16.
ἔσται (3d.per.sing.fut.ind.of εἰμί, predictive) 86.
ᾗ (loc.sing.fem.of ὅς, time point) 65.
ἡμέρᾳ (loc.sing.fem.of ἡμέρα, time point) 135.
ὁ (nom.sing.masc.of the article in agreement with υἱὸς) 9.
υἱὸς (nom.sing.masc.of υἱός, subject of ἀποκαλύπτεται) 5.
τοῦ (gen.sing.masc.of the article in agreement with ἀνθρώπου) 9.
ἀνθρώπου (gen.sing.masc.of ἄνθρωπος, relationship) 341.
ἀποκαλύπτεται (3d.per.sing.pres.pass.ind.of ἀποκαλύπτω, futuristic) 886.

Translation - "This is how it is going to be on the day on which the Son of Man is revealed."

Comment: κατὰ τὰ αὐτὰ refers to the antecedent material in verses 26-29. The Noah story and the Lot story are said to be typical of events which will transpire immediately preceding and simultaneous with the second coming of Christ, when He comes to establish the Kingdom of God upon earth.

In each case there was a materialistic, utterly corrupt society, which had rejected the revelation of God's Word. In each case society had descended to such depths of internal self-contradiction that there was no remedy but judgment. So shall it be again. In each case, however, God had His small elect group, totally out of step with their sinful peers, who were themselves totally out of step with God. Noah and Lot longed for a restoration of the Kingdom of God. In each case they had it revealed to them that judgment was imminent, and in each case they were removed from the scene of the judgment of God *on the same day* that judgment fell upon the ungodly. So shall it be again. (1 Thess.5:1-5). If the church is raptured five minutes after you read this, millions of God's saints would be as surprized as the unsaved antediluvians were about the rainstorm and the Sodomites were about the firestorm. There is an alternative conclusion to which we can come, but it is doubtful that many will wish to accept it: perhaps the vast majority of church members in the 20th century church are unregenerate. There is scant doubt that many people are involved in *churchianity* who know nothing of *Christianity*, but even the most devout Christian believer does not spend every waking moment looking into the sky and listening for the shout. But if our Lord tells the endtime church, as He told Noah and Lot, precisely when He is coming, then every saint will be watching, while every sinner, those within and those without the institutional church, will be scoffing. One cannot imagine Noah or any of his family spending the appointed day in any other way than in entering into the ark and listening for the thunder in the sky. Nor was Lot without concern for the events on the fateful day! Nor will the endtime saints be.

Verse 31 is parallel to Mt.24:17,18, which are a part of Matthew's context which begins in Mt.24:15. It is clear from Mt.24:15-31 that the events of verse 15 come in the middle of Daniel's 70th week, and that the events described in Mt.24:15-31 stretch across the last half of the week - a period of three and one-half years, forty-two months or twelve hundred, sixty days. Mt.24:29,30 is clearly a description of the Second Coming and verse 31 is a picture of the rapture of the church. Luke 17:31-37 fit into the Matthew parallel at verse 17. Note the parallel between Luke 17:37 and Matthew 24:28. Thus we must interpret the words *ἐν ἐκείνῃ τῇ ἡμέρᾳ* (Lk.17:31) as meaning the day when the Abomination of Desolation, spoken of by Daniel the prophet, stands in the holy place in Jerusalem. This is a mid-week event. *ἐν ἐκείνῃ τῇ ἡμέρᾳ* (Lk.17:31) does not mean the day of the second coming, but rather a day three and one-half years before. Jesus, in Luke is not attempting to give a detailed, chronologically structured schedule of events. *Cf.* comment on Mt.24:15-31. Study the Matthew passage carefully. It is clear that in Luke 17:31, Jesus is returning chronologically from the end of the tribulation week where we stood in verse 30, to the middle of it in verse 31, immediately after AntiChrist reveals himself in his true murderous colors as described in Mt.24:15,16.

Verse 31 - "In that day he which shall be upon the housetop, and his stuff in the house, let him not come down to take it away; and he that is in the field, let him likewise not return back."

ἐν ἐκείνῃ τῇ ἡμέρᾳ ὅς ἔσται ἐπὶ τοῦ δώματος καὶ τὰ σκεύη αὐτοῦ ἐν τῇ οἰκίᾳ, μὴ καταβάτω ἆραι αὐτά, καὶ ὁ ἐν ἀγρῷ ὁμοίως μὴ ἐπιστρεφάτω εἰς τὰ ὀπίσω.

ἐν (preposition with the locative of time point) 80.
ἐκείνῃ (loc.sing.fem.of *ἐκεῖνος*, in agreement with *ἡμέρᾳ*) 246.
τῇ (loc.sing.fem.of the article in agreement with *ἡμέρᾳ*) 9.
ἡμέρᾳ (loc.sing.fem.of *ἡμέρα*, time point) 135.
ὅς (nom.sing.masc.of *ὅς*, relative pronoun, subject of *ἔσται*) 65.
ἔσται (3d.per.sing.fut.ind.of *εἰμί*, deliberative) 86.
ἐπὶ (preposition with the genitive of place description) 47.
τοῦ (gen.sing.neut.of the article in agreement with *δώματος*) 9.
δώματος (gen.sing.neut.of *δῶμα*, place description) 888.
καὶ (adversative conjunction) 14.
τὰ (nom.pl.neut.of the article in agreement with *σκεύη*) 9.
σκεύη (nom.pl.neut.of *σκεῦος*, subject of *ἔσται* understood) 997.
αὐτοῦ (gen.sing.masc.of *αὐτός*, possession) 16.
ἐν (preposition with the locative of place where) 80.
τῇ (loc.sing.fem.of the article in agreement with *οἰκίᾳ*) 9.
οἰκίᾳ (loc.sing.fem.of *οἰκία*, place where) 186.
μὴ (qualified negative conjunction with the imperative in a prohibition) 87.
καταβάτω (3d.per.sing.aor.act.impv.of *καταβαίνω*, prohibition) 324.

ἆραι (1st.aor.act.inf.of αἴρω, purpose) 350.
αὐτά (acc.pl.neut.of αὐτός, direct object of ἆραι) 16.
καὶ (continuative conjunction) 14.
ὁ (nom.sing.masc.of the article, subject of ἐπιστρεψάτω) 9.
ἐν (preposition with the locative of place where) 80.
ἀγρῷ (loc.sing.masc.of ἀγρός, place where) 626.
ὁμοίως (adverbial) 1425.
μὴ (qualified negative conjunction with the imperative in a prohibition) 87.
ἐπιστρεψάτω (3d.per.sing.aor.act.impv.of ἐπιστρέφω, prohibition) 866.
εἰς (preposition with the accusative of extent) 140.
τὰ (acc.pl.neut.of the article, extent) 9.
ὀπίσω (adverb of place) 302.

Translation - "On that day whoever may be upon the roof of his house, but his goods are in the house, must not go down to carry them out, and the one who is in the field likewise must not turn back."

Comment: This admonition belongs immediately after Mt.24:15,16 *q.v.* It is therefore parallel to Mt.24:17,18 and Mk.13:15,16, comment upon which passages should be reviewed. Mark 13:16 explains that Luke's phrase εἰς τὰ ὀπίσω refers to τὸ ἱμάτιον αὐτοῦ. The farmer in the field had worn an extra jacket for protection from the early morning chill. As the sun arose, he became too warm and shed his coat and left it hanging on a post at one end of the furrow. Now Jesus warns him to forget his coat and to flee posthaste from the persecuting police of the Man of Sin, who will have revealed himself in his true antichristian character and will be bent upon making war with the saints (Rev.6:8-11; 13:7).

Verse 32 - "Remember Lot's wife."

μνημονεύετε τῆς γυναικὸς Λώτ.

μνημονεύετε (2d.per.pl.pres.act.impv.of μνημονεύω, command) 1199.
τῆς (gen.sing.fem.of the article in agreement with γυναικὸς) 9.
γυναικὸς (gen.sing.fem.of γυνή, description) 103.
Λώτ (gen.sing.(indeclin.) of Λώτ, relationship) 2618.

Translation - "Always remember Lot's wife."

Comment: So as not to fall into her error. She was a child of God, as is clear from the fact that God could not punish the city until she left with her husband. But, though she was a child of God, she had allowed the wicked city to attract her. She had orders to flee with her husband with specific instructions not to look back at the city which would be in the process of being destroyed. She disobeyed. She looked back and was overwhelmed in the judgment of the city. She became a pillar of salt (Gen.19:26).

The thrust of the passage is that, though the Christian will be in the world until the very last day - the day of its destruction, yet he is not of it. He should not concern himself when it is destroyed. He should not reveal the slightest interest in it, not even the idle curiosity of wanting to see it burn. When the saints are caught up (1 Thess.4:13-18) we shall be so delighted to "meet the Lord in the air" that the destruction that will be going on upon the earth will not interest us.

Verse 33 - "Whosoever shall seek to save his life shall lose it; and whosoever shall lose his life shall preserve it."

ὅς ἐὰν ζητήσῃ τὴν ψυχὴν αὐτοῦ περιποιήσασθαι ἀπολέσει αὐτήν, ὅς δ' ἂν ἀπολέσῃ ζῳογονήσει αὐτήν.

ὅς (nom.sing.masc.of ὅς, indefinite relative pronoun, subject of ζητήσῃ) 65.
ἐὰν (conditional particle in an indefinite relative clause, more probable condition) 363.
ζητήσῃ (3d.per.sing.aor.act.subj.of ζητέω, indefinite relative clause, more probable condition) 207.
τὴν (acc.sing.fem.of the article in agreement with ψυχὴν) 9.
ψυχὴν (acc.sing.fem.of ψυχή, direct object of περιποιήσασθαι) 233.
αὐτοῦ (gen.sing.masc.of αὐτός, possession) 16.

#2620 περιποιήσασθαι (aor.mid.inf.of περιποιέω, completes ζητήσῃ).

save - Luke 17:33.
purchase - Acts 20:28; 1 Tim.3:13.

Meaning: A combination of περί (#173) and ποιέω (#127). Hence, to maneuver around. To avoid evil consequences by negotiation or purchase, or to achieve some goal by maneuver. To manipulate events in order to achieve some goal, positively or negatively. To save one's life by compromise with the enemy - Luke 17:33. To gain an honorable position as a deacon - 1 Tim.3:13. To secure redemption from sin for His church - Acts 20:28.

ἀπολέσει (3d.per.sing.fut.act.ind.of ἀπόλλυμι, predictive) 208.
αὐτήν (acc.sing.fem.of αὐτός, direct object of ἀπολέσει) 16.
ὅς (nom.sing.masc.of ὅς, indefinite relative clause, more probable condition, subject of ἀπολέσει) 65.
δ' (adversative conjunction) 11.
ἂν (conditional particle in a more probable condition, with the future indicative) 205.
ἀπολέσει (3d.per.sing.fut.act.ind.of ἀπόλλυμι, more probable condition) 208.

#2621 ζῳογονήσει (3d.per.sing.fut.act.ind.of ζῳογονέω, predictive).

preserve - Luke 17:33.
live - Acts 7:19.
quicken - 1 Tim.6:13.

Meaning: - A combination of ζωός and γένω - to bring forth alive, or to give life, in classical Greek. In the New Testament, to preserve life. To save one's life from martyrdom - Luke 17:33; to spare the life of an infant - Acts 7:19; to make alive - 1 Tim.6:13.

αὐτήν (acc.sing.fem.of αὐτός, direct object of ζῳογονήσει) 16.

Translation - "Whoever shall try to negotiate for his life will lose it, but whoever loses his life will preserve it."

Comment: We have a contingent or indefinite idea here in the context. Jesus is not speaking specifically of anyone, but of him, whoever he might be who would seek to negotiate with the forces of the Antichrist, in order to escape martyrdom. In such a construction the indefinite relative pronoun is used with the subjunctive and ἐάν. Mantey (*Manual*, 273) calls this a More Probable Condition. In the second clause we have the relative pronoun with ἂν and the future indicative in a definite condition. Jesus is not speaking of actual cases but of probable ones, although He is more definite in the second clause than in the first.

If someone should try to negotiate with Antichrist and offer to compromise in order to escape death, he will find such an attempt doomed to failure. The Abomination of Desolation (Mt.24:15) will be utterly implacable in his war against the saints. No compromise will be made. On the other hand, whoever loses his life will preserve it eternally. There will be a great many endtime Christians who will pay the supreme price rather than deny the Lord. (Rev.6:9-11). With only three and one-half years, or less, remaining in the Times of the Gentiles (Rom.11:25) before the Second Coming and the rapture of the saints, whether one lives to the end or suffers martyrdom at the hands of the Antichrist, will be of scant eternal consequence. All that the Beast can do is kill the body (Mt.10:28).

Jesus has just spoken of the preservation of the Christian life. It is fitting then that He should now mention the events connected with the first resurrection and the rapture in verses 34 and 35.

Verse 34 - "I tell you, in that night, there shall be two men in one bed: the one shall be taken, and the other shall be left."

λέγω ὑμῖν, ταύτῃ τῇ νυκτὶ ἔσονται δύο ἐπὶ κλίνης μιᾶς, ὁ εἷς παραλημφθήσεται καὶ ὁ ἕτερος ἀφεθήσεται.

λέγω (1st.per.sing.pres.act.ind.of λέγω, aoristic) 66.
ὑμῖν (dat.pl.masc.of σύ, indirect object of λέγω) 104.
ταύτῃ (loc.sing.fem.of οὗτος, in agreement with νυκτὶ) 93.
τῇ (loc.sing.fem.of the article in agreement with νυκτὶ) 9.
νυκτὶ (loc.sing.fem.of νύξ, time point) 209.
ἔσονται (3d.per.pl.fut.ind.of εἰμί, predictive) 86.
δύο (nom.sing.masc.of δύο, subject of ἔσονται) 385.
ἐπὶ (preposition with the genitive of place description) 47.
κλίνης (gen.sing.fem.of κλίνη, place description) 779.

μιᾶς (gen.sing.fem.of εἷς, in agreement with κλίνης) 469.

παραλημφθήσεται (3d.per.sing.fut.pass.ind.of παραλαμβάνω, predictive) 102.

καὶ (continuative conjunction) 14.

ὁ (nom.sing.masc.of the article in agreement with ἕτερος) 9.

ἕτερος (nom.sing.masc.of ἕτερος, subject of ἀφεθήσεται) 605.

ἀφεθήσεται (3d.per.sing.fut.pass.ind.of ἀφίημι, predictive) 319.

Translation - "I am telling you that on that night there will be two men on the same pallet; the one will be taken away and the other will be left."

Comment: A nighttime scene is described here, and we have a daytime scene in verse 35. Since the coming of the Lord is to be a universal event (vss.24,37) it will be night on one side of the planet and day on the other side. Two men upon one pallet. It is interesting that Jesus should use ἐπὶ and the genitive with κλίνης (#779) - "upon a pallet" rather than ἐν with the locative - "*in* a bed," because κλίνη is not a bed in the modern sense - something one can get into. It is rather a piece of bedding, suitable for spreading upon the floor - a pallet. The point is important when we consider that in Mk.7:4 κλινῶν are adjoined with βαπτισμούς (though the entire passage is not found in the best manuscripts, and even in some of those which include it, καὶ κλινῶν is omitted). Nevertheless pedobaptists have urged that it is impossible to immerse a "bed." Hence, that Mark 7:4 supports the view that βάπτω and related words can mean "to sprinkle." If we agree that the passage is spurious, the result of a copyist's error, or an unwarranted addition not supported by the best manuscript authority, and read κλίνων as an adjunct of βαπτισμοὺς, it does not support sprinkling as a mode of "baptism" since it is not only readily possible but frequently the case that a pallet is immersed in water in the process of washing. *Cf.*#779 and examine all of the references. You will note that in Rev.2:22 John wrote εἰς κλίνην - "into a bed" (!), but the Revelation is full of grammatical errors. John did not know his Greek when he wrote the Revelation as he did in the tenth decade when he wrote the Gospel and the Epistles. The grammatical errors in the Revelation provide evidence that divine inspiration does not overpower the writer to the point that he is not himself. Just as Mary's human characteristics (except sin) were genetically transferred to Jesus, her son, so the Holy Spirit's cooperation with a human author does not prevent the author's human characteristics from coming through into the manuscript. Indeed εἰς κλίνην could, even in classical Greek circles, be rendered "*unto* a bed."

The night in question is the night when the Son of Man returns to earth. The fact that two people shall be found on the last day upon a pallet, the one a Christian and the other unsaved, proves that Antichrist's war upon the saints shall not have liquidated all of them. Nor must we believe that the issue of Christ versus Antichrist shall have divided saints from sinners socially in all cases. Here are two sleeping upon the same pallet. One shall be taken. *Cf.*#102 and note Mt.24:40,41, the parallels to Lk.17:34,35 and John 14:3 where παραλαμβάνω is used for the rapture (1 Thess.4:13-18; 1 Cor.15:51). Verse 35 gives a daytime picture of the same event.

Verse 35 - "Two women shall be grinding together; the one shall be taken, and the other left."

ἔσονται δύο ἀλήθουσαι ἐπὶ τὸ αὐτό, ἡ μία παραλημφθήσεται ἡ δὲ ἑτέρα ἀφεθήσεται.

ἔσονται (3d.per.pl.fut.ind.of *εἰμί*, future periphrastic) 86.
δύο (nom.pl.fem.of *δύο*, subject of *ἔσονται*) 385.
ἀλήθουσαι (pres.act.part.nom.pl.fem.of *ἀλήθω*, future periphrastic) 1519.
ἐπὶ (preposition with the accusative of place) 47.
τὸ (acc.sing.neut.of the article in agreement with *αὐτό*) 9.
αὐτό (acc.sing.neut.of *αὐτός*, place description) 16.
ἡ (nom.sing.fem.of the article in agreement with *μία*) 9.
μία (nom.sing.fem.of *εἷς*, subject of *παραλημφθήσεται*) 469.
παραλημφθήσεται (3d.per.sing.fut.pass.ind.of *παραλαμβάνω*, predictive) 102.
ἡ (nom.sing.fem.of the article in agreement with *ἑτέρα*) 9.
δὲ (adversative conjunction) 11.
ἑτέρα (nom.sing.fem.of *ἕτερος*, subject of *ἀφεθήσεται*) 605.
ἀφεθήσεται (3d.per.sing.fut.pass.ind.of *ἀφίημι*, predictive) 319.

Translation - "There will be two women grinding together; the one will be taken, but the other will be left."

Comment: *ἐπὶ τὸ αὐτό* - "upon the same thing." Engaged in the same task of grinding. A cooperative effort. *Cf.*Mt.24:41 where *ἐν τῷ μύλῳ* is added. This is a daytime scene, on the other side of the planet from the one described in verse 34.

ἔσονται . . . ἀλήθουσαι is a future periphrastic construction - the future participle with some form of the verb *εἰμί*. It is decidedly durative. "The very failure of the future to express durative action clearly led to the use of the present participle with *ἔσομαι*." (Janneris, *A Historical Greek Grammar*, 444, as cited in Robertson, *Grammar*, 889).

Verse 36 is not found in the best manuscripts. It is however found in the parallel passage in Mt.24:40.

Verse 37 - "And they answered and said unto him, Where, Lord? And he said unto them, Wheresoever the body is, thither will the eagles be gathered together."

καὶ ἀποκριθέντες λέγουσιν αὐτῷ, Ποῦ, κύριε; ὁ δὲ εἶπεν αὐτοῖς, Ὅπου τὸ σῶμα, ἐκεῖ καὶ οἱ ἀετοὶ ἐπισυναχθήσονται.

καὶ (continuative conjunction) 14.
ἀποκριθέντες (aor.part.nom.pl.masc.of *ἀποκρίνομαι*, adverbial, modal) 318.
λέγουσιν (3d.per.pl.pres.act.ind.of *λέγω*, historical) 66.
αὐτῷ (dat.sing.masc.of *αὐτός*, indirect object of *λέγουσιν*) 16.

Ποῦ (interrogative adverb of place, in direct question) 142.
κύριε (voc.sing.masc.of κύριος, address) 97.
ὁ (nom.sing.masc.of the article, subject of εἶπεν) 9.
δὲ (inferential conjunction) 11.
εἶπεν (3d.per.sing.aor.act.ind.of εἶπον, constative) 155.
αὐτοῖς (dat.pl.masc.of αὐτός, indirect object of εἶπεν) 16.
Ὅπου (adverb introducing a local clause) 592.
τὸ (nom.sing.neut.of the article in agreement with σῶμα) 9.
σῶμα (nom.sing.neut.of σῶμα, subject of ἔστιν understood) 507.
ἐκεῖ (adverb of place) 204.
καὶ (adjunctive conjunction joining nouns) 14.
οἱ (nom.pl.masc.of the article in agreement with ἀετοὶ) 9.
ἀετοὶ (nom.pl.masc.of ἀετός, subject of ἐπισυναχθήσονται) 1503.
ἐπισυναχθήσονται (3d.per.pl.fut.pass.ind.of ἐπισυνάγω, predictive) 1476.

Translation - "And they responded by saying to Him, 'Where, Lord?' Therefore He said to them, 'Where the body is, there also the vultures will be gathered together.' "

Comment: *Cf.* comment on Mt.24:28. Wherever there is an unsaved person, there the vultures will flock to feast upon his rotting carcass. He will have fallen victim to the wrath of God which will be poured out upon the earth on that day. Mt.24:31 tells us also that wherever there is a child of God on that great day, the angels will go to gather them together in the clouds of glory with the Son of Man. Here is another statement of the universality of His coming.

Two Parables on Prayer

The Parable of the Widow and the Judge

(Luke 18:1-14)

Luke 18:1 - "And he spake a parable unto them to this end, that men ought always to pray, and not to faint."

Ἔλεγεν δὲ παραβολὴν αὐτοῖς πρὸς τὸ δεῖν πάντοτε προσεύχεσθαι αὐτοὺς καὶ μὴ ἐγκακεῖν.

Ἔλεγεν (3d.per.sing.imp.act.ind.of λέγω, inceptive) 66.
δὲ (continuative conjunction) 11.
παραβολὴν (acc.sing.fem.of παραβολή, direct object of ἔλεγεν) 1027.
αὐτοῖς (dat.pl.masc.of αὐτός, indirect object of ἔλεγεν) 16.
πρὸς (preposition with the accusative of general reference) 197.
τὸ (acc.sing.neut.of the article in agreement with δεῖν) 9.
δεῖν (infinitive of δεῖ, noun use, general reference) 1207.
πάντοτε (adverbial) 1567.
προσεύχεσθαι (pres.mid.inf.of προσεύχομαι, general reference) 544.

αὐτοὺς (acc.pl.masc.of αὐτός, general reference) 16.
καὶ (adversative conjunction) 14.
μὴ (qualifed negative conjunction with the infinitive) 87.

#2622 ἐνκακεῖν (pres.inf.of ἐγκακέω, general reference).

be not weary - 2 Thess.3:13; Gal.6:9.
faint - Lk.18:1; 2 Cor.4:1,16; 2 Thess.3:13; Eph.3:13.

Meaning: To grow weary; to become discouraged and dispirited. Paul admonished the Ephesians against it - Eph.3:13; in the midst of Christian service - 2 Thess.3:13; Gal.6:9; 2 Cor.4:1,16; to become discouraged when prayers seem unanswered - Luke 18:1.

Translation - "And He began to show them a parable to the effect that they ought always to prayer and not to become discouraged."

Comment: πρὸς τὸ δεῖν is not a purpose construction. We have three infinitives, δεῖν, προσεύχεσθαι and ἐγκακεῖν. The latter two are dependent upon δεῖν. They accusatives of general reference while δεῖν is in the accusative after πρὸς. It is not that He gave the disciples the parable in order that they would always pray and not faint (the final use), but that He gave the parable, with reference to their need not to faint, but to pray always. πάντοτε here, not in the continuous sense, *i.e.* without interruption, but in the *continual* sense (consistently, though with brief intermittent periods devoted to other activity). Christians are not to pray all of the time, to the exclusion of all else. But they are to pray often, with no extended periods of prayerlessness. This is what the following parable is about.

Verse 2 - "Saying, There was in a city a judge, which feared not God, neither regarded man:"

λέγων, Κριτής τις ἦν ἔν τινι πόλει τὸν θεὸν μὴ φοβούμενος καὶ ἄνθρωπον μὴ ἐντρεπόμενος.

λέγων (pres.act.part.nom.sing.masc.of λέγω, recitative) 66.
Κριτής (nom.sing.masc.of κριτής, subject of ἦν) 492.
τις (nom.sing.masc.of τις, the indefinite pronoun, in agreement with κριτής) 486.
ἦν (3d.per.sing.imp.ind.of εἰμί, imperfect periphrastic) 86.
ἔν (preposition with the locative of place where) 80.
τινι (loc.sing.fem.of τις, the indefinite pronoun, in agreement with πόλει) 486.
πόλει (loc.sing.fem.of πόλις, place where) 243.
τὸν (acc.sing.masc.of the article in agreement with θεὸν) 9.
θεὸν (acc.sing.masc.of θεός, direct object of φοβούμενος) 124.
μὴ (qualified negative conjunction with the participle) 87.
φοβούμενος (pres.mid.part.nom.sing.masc.of φοβέομαι, imperfect periphrastic) 101.

καὶ (adjunctive conjunction joining participles) 14.
ἄνθρωπον (acc.sing.masc.of *ἄνθρωπος*, direct object of *ἐντρεπόμενος*) 341.
μὴ (qualified negative conjunction with the participle) 87.
ἐντρεπόμενος (pres.mid.part.nom.sing.masc.of *ἐντρέπω*, imperfect periphrastic) 1385.

Translation - "Saying, 'There was some judge in a certain city, who neither feared God nor was he ever influenced by men.' "

Comment: The double imperfect periphrastic with *ἦν* and the two present participles describe the total objectivity of the judge. Never had he allowed either His attitude toward God or the opinion which the public might have of him to influence the decisions which he handed down from the bench. This need not mean that when he was off the bench he had no reverence for God nor regard for human rights. It only means that he had a consistent record of handing down decisions only in conformity with the facts of the case and the proper interpretation of the law. If he had never feared God, either on or off the bench, then it follows that he would never have had respect for the rights of mankind, but that is not the point of the parable. The judge's objectivity is established to forestall any conclusion that his ultimate acquiescence in the woman's persistent request was because he felt sorry for her, nor because she had a good case. His decision was made on an altogether different basis.

Verse 3 - "And there was a widow in that city; and she came unto him, saying, Avenge me of mine adversary."

χήρα δὲ ἦν ἐν τῇ πόλει ἐκείνῃ καὶ ἤρχετο πρὸς αὐτὸν λέγουσα, Ἐκδίκησόν με ἀπὸ τοῦ ἀντιδίκου μου.

χήρα (nom.sing.fem.of *χήρα*, subject of *ἦν*) 1910.
δὲ (explanatory conjunction) 11.
ἦν (3d.per.sing.imp.ind.of *εἰμί*, progressive duration) 86.
ἐν (preposition with the locative of place where) 80.
τῇ (loc.sing.fem.of the article in agreement with *πόλει*) 9.
πόλει (loc.sing.fem.of *πόλις*, place where) 243.
ἐκείνῃ (loc.sing.fem.of *ἐκεῖνος*, in agreement with *πόλει*) 246.
καὶ (continuative conjunction) 14.
ἤρχετο (3d.per.sing.imp.ind.of *ἔρχομαι*, progressive duration) 146.
πρὸς (preposition with the accusative of extent) 197.
αὐτὸν (acc.sing.masc.of *αὐτός*, extent) 16.
λέγουσα (pres.act.part.nom.sing.fem.of *λέγω*, adverbial, complementary) 66.

#2623 *ἐκδίκησόν* (2d.per.sing.aor.act.impv.of *ἐκδικέω*, entreaty).

avenge - Luke 18:3,5; Rom.12:19; Rev.6:10; 19:2.
revenge - 2 Cor.10:6.

*Meaning: Cf.*ἔκδικος (#4035), ἐκδίκησις (#2625). To decree as a judge in a court of law that injustice shall be rectified. To rule for the plaintiff in a civil suit - Luke 18:3,5. To even a score; to get even - Rom.12:19. To adjust differences in a church - 2 Cor.10:6; to wreak vengeance upon murderers - God's judgment - Rev.6:10; 19:2.

με (acc.sing.fem.of ἐγώ, general reference) 123.
ἀπὸ (preposition with the ablative, source) 70.
τοῦ (abl.sing.masc.of the article in agreement with ἀντιδίκου) 9.
ἀντιδίκου (abl.sing.masc.of ἀντίδικος, source) 490.
μου (gen.sing.fem.of ἐγώ, relationship) 123.

Translation - "Now there was a widow in that city and she was always coming to him, saying, 'Award compensation for me from my adversary.' "

Comment: δὲ is explanatory. Having introduced the judge, famous for his objectivity, Jesus now introduces the other member of the cast. She was an importunate widow who refused to take "no" for an answer. The plaintiff in a civil suit seeking to be awarded damages from her adversary who, as she alleged, had imposed some wrong upon her, she came to court again and again. This is clear from the imperfect tense in ἤρχετο. She did not come one time only. She came again and again. She asked the court to find in her favor and to hand down a court order for the defendant to pay her what she thought was due. *Cf.*#490 for other uses of ἀντίδικος.

Apparently the judge was not impressed with the soundness of the widow's case, as we see in

Verse 4 - "And he would not for a while: but afterward he said within himself, Though I fear not God, nor regard man,"

καὶ οὐκ ἤθελεν ἐπὶ χρόνον, μετὰ δὲ ταῦτα εἶπεν ἐν ἑαυτῷ, Εἰ καὶ τὸν θεὸν οὐ φοβοῦμαι οὐδὲ ἄνθρωπον ἐντρέπομαι,

καὶ (adversative conjunction) 14.
οὐκ (summary negative conjunction with the indicative) 130.
ἤθελεν (3d.per.sing.imp.act.ind.of θέλω, progressive description) 88.
ἐπὶ (preposition with the accusative of time extent) 47.
χρόνον (acc.sing.masc.of χρόνος, time extent) 168.
μετὰ (preposition with the accusative of time extent) 50.
ταῦτα (acc.pl.neut.of οὗτος, time extent) 93.
δὲ (adversative conjunction) 11.
εἶπεν (3d.per.sing.aor.act.ind.of εἶπον, constative) 155.
ἐν (preposition with the locative with the reflexive pronoun) 80.
ἑαυτῷ (loc.sing.masc.of ἑαυοτός, place where, adverbial) 288.
Εἰ (conditional particle in a first-class condition, like a concessive clause) 337.
καὶ (emphatic conjunction) 14.
τὸν (acc.sing.masc.of the article in agreement with θεὸν) 9.
θεὸν (acc.sing.masc.of θεός, direct object of φοβοῦμαι) 124.

οὐ (summary negative conjunction with the indicative) 130.
φοβοῦμαι (1st.per.sing.pres.mid.ind.of *φοβέομαι*, customary) 101.
οὐδὲ (disjunctive particle) 452.
ἄνθρωπον (acc.sing.masc.of *ἄνθρωπος*, direct object of *ἐντρέπομαι*) 341.
ἐντρέπομαι (1st.per.sing.pres.mid.ind.of *ἐντρέπω*, customary) 1385.

Translation - "But he was not willing for a while; however later he said to himself, 'Though in fact I do not fear God, nor have consideration for man . . .' "

Comment: *καὶ* is adversative. The judge did not agree with the widow. *ἐπὶ χρόνον* - in a time extent construction with the accusative. *δὲ* is also adversative as the judge, after thinking it over, changed his mind. *ταῦτα* refers to the oft repeated appearances of the widow in his court. Eἰ *καὶ* is common. It can be considered as introduction to a concessive clause, although ". . . (t)hese are really just conditional clauses with the addition of *καί*. . . . Here the protasis is treated as a matter of indifference. If there is a conflict, it makes no real difficulty. There is sometimes a tone of contempt in *εἰ καί*. The matter is belittled. There is often some particle in the conclusion in this construction as in Lu.18:4, *εἰ καὶ τὸν θεὸν οὐ φοβοῦμαι οὐδὲ ἄνθρωπον ἐντρέπομαι, διά γε τὸ παρέχειν, κτλ.*" (Robertson, *Grammar*, 1026).

Note the customary present tenses in the protasis. It was the judge's consistent policy neither to fear God nor have regard for man. Logic would dictate that, in keeping with his usual policy, he should send the widow away with orders not again to appear in his court. The judge concedes this, but passes it off as a conflict in his policy which he can afford to disregard. Objectivity, for which he was famous would dictate that the woman's case was not worthy of his consideration. Jesus is screening out all explanations for the judge's decision, except the one offered in the apodosis in verse 5. Thus our Lord makes His point that God rewards importunity in prayer, in verses 6-8.

Verse 5 - "Yet because this widow troubleth me, I will avenge her, lest by her continual coming she weary me."

διά γε τὸ παρέχειν μοι κόπον τὴν χήραν ταύτην ἐκδικήσω αὐτήν, ἵνα μὴ εἰς τέλος ἐρχομένη ὑπωπιάζῃ με.

διά (preposition with the accusative of cause) 118.
γε (intensive particle) 2449.
τὸ (acc.sing.neut.of the article in agreement with *παρέχειν*) 9.
παρέχειν (pres.act.inf.of *παρέχω*, noun use, accusative of cause, with *διὰ*) 1566.
μοι (dat.sing.masc.of *ἐγώ*, indirect object of *παρέχειν*) 123.
κόπον (acc.sing.masc.of *κόπος*, direct object of *παρέχειν*) 1565.
τὴν (acc.sing.fem.of the article in agreement with *χήραν*) 9.
χήραν (acc.sing.fem.of *χήρα*, general reference) 1910.
ταύτην (acc.sing.fem.of *οὗτος*, in agreement with *χήραν*, contemptuous use) 93.
ἐκδικήσω (1st.per.sing.fut.act.ind.of *ἐκδικέω*,predictive) 2623.

αὐτήν (acc.sing.fem.of αὐτός, direct object of ἐκδικήσω) 16.
ἵνα (conjunction introducing a negative result clause) 114.
μή (qualified negative conjunction with the subjunctive in a negative result clause) 87.
εἰς (preposition with the accusative, time extent) 140.
τέλος (acc.sing.neut.of τέλος, time extent) 881.
ἐρχομένη (pres.part.of ἔρχομαι, adverbial, instrumental) 146.

#2624 ὑπωπιάζῃ (3d.per.sing.pres.act.subj.of ὑποπιάζω, negative result).

keep under - 1 Cor.9:27.
weary - Luke 18:5.

Meaning: A combination of ὑπό (#117) and πιάζω (#2371). Hence, to suppress; hold down; keep under control. Liddell & Scott say that the word results from ὑπό and ὤψ - "eye." Hence, to strike the face below the eye; to inflict a black eye. To treat severely. Paul's determination to discipline his flesh in the battle for Christian victory - 1 Cor.9:27. With reference to the judge's fear that the woman, by her constant coming would annoy him. It is not probable that the judge feared that the widow would literally hit him under the eye - Luke 18:5.

με (acc.sing.masc.of ἐγώ, direct object of ὑπωπιάζῃ) 123.

Translation - "Yet because this widow is always causing me annoyance, I will rule in her favor, lest that by her continual coming here she will finally wear me out."

Comment: γε intensifies the fact that the woman was always coming into the judge's court with her trouble. Note the infinitive τὸ παρέχειν, in the accusative case with διά is a causal sense. Literally, "because of the fact that this widow is always bringing trouble to me." The trouble that she was causing outweighed the other minor consideration that, if order to solve his problem, the judge would be acting contrary to his usual policy. Note the contemptuous use of ταύτην. The negative result clause with ἵνα μή and the subjunctive, has the instrumental adverbial participle ἐρχομένη. It was by means of her constant coming to court that she was wearing the judge's patience thin. *Cf.*#'s 1565 and 1566 for παρέχω followed by κόπον - "presenting with difficulty" or "causing trouble."

The judge made his decision - ἐκδικήσω αὐτήν - "I will rule in her favor." The women's adversary was going to be served with a court order to give the woman what she wanted. Why? Not because the judge thought that it was right or because he had any regard for the woman, but because of the consequences to himself if he did not. What consequences? The negative result clause tells us. The judge did not wish to be annoyed further. He was afraid that her constant appearance would consume the court's time and obstruct the processing of his crowded docket. *Cf.*#2624. That the judge did not fear that the woman would attack him physically is evident fromthe means she used to "suppress him."

The heart of the teaching in the parable is that victorious prayer is such because when we pray we refuse to take "no" for an answer.

Verse 6 - "And the Lord said, Hear what the unjust judge saith."

Εἶπεν δὲ ὁ κύριος, Ἀκούσατε τί ὁ κριτὴς τῆς ἀδικίας λέγει.

Εἶπεν (3d.per.sing.aor.act.ind.of εἶπον, constative) 155.
δὲ (continuative conjunction) 11.
ὁ (nom.sing.masc.of the article in agreement with κύριος) 9.
κύριος (nom.sing. masc.of κύριος, subject of εἶπεν) 97.
Ἀκούσατε (2d.per.pl.aor.act.impv.of ἀκούω, command) 148.
τί (acc.sing.neut.of τίς, interrogative pronoun, direct object of ἀκούσατε) 281
ὁ (nom.sing.masc.of the article in agreement with κριτὴς) 9.
κριτὴς (nom.sing.masc.of κριτής, subject of λέγει) 492.
τῆς (gen.sing.fem.of the article in agreement with ἀδικίας) 9.
ἀδικίας (gen.sing.fem.of ἀδικία, description) 2367.
λέγει (3d.per.sing.pres.act.ind.of λέγω, historical) 66.

Translation - "And the Lord said, 'Hear what the judge of unrighteousness said.' "

Comment: τῆς ἀδικίας, because it has the article is a genitive of description - "the judge of unrighteousness." Without the article the genitive would modify the noun to read "the dishonest judge." *Cf.*#2367 for other uses of ἀδικία. Jesus calls the attention of the disciples to the comment of the judge because the point in the parable is in his statement of verses 4 and 5. He was a judge of unrighteousness because he decided to hand down a decision which was contrary to his opinion as a judge, but which would relieve him of a burden that he was no longer willing to bear. A dishonest judge, though unmoved by the lack of probity in the case before him, will yield to importunity if it is to his own personal advantage to do so.

Verse 7 - "And shall not God avenge his own elect, which cry day and night unto him, though he bear long with them?"

ὁ δὲ θεὸς οὐ μὴ ποιήσῃ τὴν ἐκδίκησιν τῶν ἐκλεκτῶν αὐτοῦ τῶν βοώντων αὐτῷ ἡμέρας καὶ νυκτός, καὶ μακροθυμεῖ ἐπ' αὐτοῖς;

ὁ (nom.sing.masc.of the article in agreement with θεὸς) 9.
δὲ (continuative conjunction) 11.
θεὸς (nom.sing.masc.of θεός, subject of ποιήσῃ) 124.
οὐ (summary negative conjunction with μὴ in a rhetorical question) 130.
μὴ (qualified negative conjunction with οὐ and the subjunctive in a rhetorical question, which expects an affirmative reply) 87.
ποιήσῃ (3d.per.sing.aor.act.subj.of ποιέω, rhetorical question) 127.
τὴν (acc.sing.fem.of the article in agreement with ἐκδίκησιν) 9.

#2625 ἐκδίκησιν (acc.sing.fem.of ἐκδίκησις, direct object of ποιήσῃ).

punishment - 1 Pet.2:14.

revenge - 2 Cor.7:11.
vengeance - Luke 18:7,8; 21:22; Rom.12:19; 2 Thess.1:8; Heb.10:30.
avenge - Acts 7:24.

*Meaning: Cf.*ἐκδικέω (#2623). Vengeance, justly administered to rectify wrong doing. By public officials - 1 Pet.2:14. By private individuals - 1 Cor.7:11; Acts 7:24. By God - Luke 18:7,8; 21:22; Rom.12:19; Heb.10:30; 2 Thess.1:8.

τῶν (gen.pl.masc.of the article in agreement with ἐκλεκτῶν) 9.
ἐκλεκτῶν (gen.pl.masc.of ἐκλεκτός, description) 1412.
αὐτοῦ (gen.sing.masc.of αὐτός, possession) 16.
τῶν (gen.pl.masc.of the article in agreement with βοώντων) 9.
βοώντων (pres.act.part.gen.pl.masc.of βοάω, adjectival, restrictive) 256.
αὐτῷ (dat.sing.masc.of αὐτός, indirect object of βοώντων) 16.
ἡμέρας (gen.sing.fem.of ἡμέρα, time description) 135.
καὶ (adjunctive conjunction joining nouns) 14.
νυκτός (gen.sing.fem.of νύξ, time description) 209.
καὶ (concessive conjunction) 14.
μακροθυμεῖ (3d.per.sing.pres.ind.of μακροθυμέω, progressive) 1274.
ἐπ' (preposition with the instrumental of cause) 47.
αὐτοῖς (instru.pl.masc.of αὐτός, cause) 16.

Translation - "And shall not God settle the account of His elect, who are crying to Him by day and by night, even though they try His patience?"

Comment: The rhetorical question expects an affirmative reply. Certainly God, the righteous judge, is going to effect a settlement/square accounts/visit vengeance - any of these expressions can serve to translate ποιήσῃ τὴν ἐκδίκησιν. There must be a fair settlement at the expense of an adversary who has perpetrated an injustice. In whose favor? God's elect ones, who have suffered at the hands of unsaved men in the world (Lk.17:33; Mt.5:10-12, *et al.*) These elect saints, persecuted and killed, are defined by the adjectival participle τῶν βοώντων αὐτῷ. They are demanding vindication. They continue to cry out to Him during the day and in the night. The genitive of description in ἡμέρας καὶ νυκτός defines the time, rather than measures its extent - as the accusative would do. The saints cry out to God as the widow did unto the judge, until God is tired of it - μακροθυμεῖ ἐπ' αὐτοῖς - "being patient because of them." We have a picture of this in Rev.6:9-11, where the Christians, killed by the Man of Sin as he appears in the middle of the tribulation period, cry out to God for His vengeance upon their killers. They are impatient. "How long, O Lord. . . ?" And God is a little impatient with them, as He tells them that they must wait a little longer. Thus the similarities in the parable with the situation in real life. A plaintiff,the widow, and the Christian martyr, unjustly treated, demanding that vengeance be carried out on a just basis and insistently repeating the demand until the judge finds their repeated demands for action something only to be patiently endured.

Now the contrasts between the parable and its historic application. The judge in the parable was unjust. He feared neither God nor those who appeared in his court. What he did was done strictly to satisfy his own selfish desires. But Christ is God, the Judge of all the earth (John 5:22) Who always does right (Gen.18:25). He fears, loves and associates with God. He is God. He not only regards those who have suffered in His name and for His cause, but He also is "angry with the wicked every day" (Ps.7:11). His saints are His elect ones (John 15:16). He chose them. If the unjust judge in the parable made the adjustment, how much more will the Eternal Judge of all the earth? There have been many aggrieved plaintiffs in the court of heaven. There will be many more before the "day of the Son of Man." The blood of righteous Abel cries out to God for vengeance against Cain (Mt.23:35). The Old Testament prophets and preachers have yet to be vindicated for the indignities and cruelties perpetrated upon them (Mt.23:34). Zacharias, the son of Barachias, slain between the temple and the altar (Mt.23:35) awaits his day of vindication. Jerusalem is going to be made to pay when her house is made desolate on pay day (Mt.23:37,38). Thus it has been with many saints (Heb.11:36-38). And there have been more - Paul, Peter, indeed, if tradition can be trusted, all of the Apostles except John, not to mention the early Christian martyrs and John and Betty Stam and the Three Freds in recent years. In the great tribulation there will be some whose flight to the mountains will not be fast enough (Rev.6:9-11). Shall Christ the Judge sit idly by, at the right hand of God, forever, and do less than the unjust judge in the parable? The answer in in

Verse 8 - "I tell you that He will avenge them speedily. Nevertheless when the Son of Man cometh, shall he find faith on the earth?"

λέγω ὑμίν ὅτι ποιήσει τὴν ἐκδίκησιν αὐτῶν ἐν τάχει. πλὴν ὁ υἱὸς τοῦ ἀνθρώπου ἐλθὼν ἆρα εὑρήσει τὴν πίστιν ἐπὶ τῆς γῆς;

λέγω (1st.per.sing.pres.act.ind.of *λέγω*, aoristic) 66.
ὑμίν (dat.pl.masc.of *σύ*, indirect object of *λέγω*) 104.
ὅτι (conjunction introducing an object clause in indirect discourse) 211.
ποιήσει (3d.per.sing.fut.act.ind.of *ποιέω*, predictive) 127.
τὴν (acc.sing.fem.of the article in agreement with *ἐκδίκησιν*) 9.
ἐκδίκησιν (acc.sing.fem.of *ἐκδίκησις*, direct object of *ποιήσει*) 2625.
αὐτῶν (gen.pl.masc.of *αὐτός*, description) 16.

ἐν (preposition with the instrumental of manner) 80.

#2626 *τάχει* (instru.sing.neut.of *τάχος*, manner).

quickly - Acts 12:7; 22:18.
shortly - Acts 25:4; Rom.16:20; Rev.1:1; 22:6.
speedily - Luke 18:8.

Meaning: Qucikness, speed. *ἐν τάχει* - speedily. Not at present but in the near future. Soon. It would not be used if the suggested action were already in progress. With *ἐν* in Acts 12:7; 22:18; 25:4; Rev.1:1; 22:6; Rom.16:20. With reference to the Second Coming - Rom.16:20; Lk.18:8. In Rev.1:1 and 22:6 in in reference to the Revelation which would transport John out of lst century Patmos into the heavens to view endtime events. *Cf.* comment on Rev.1:1; 22:6.

πλὴν (adversative conjunction) 944.
ὁ (nom.sing.masc.of the article in agreement with υἱὸς) 9.
υἱὸς (nom.sing.masc.of υἱός,subject of εὑρήσει) 5.
τοῦ (gen.sing.masc.of the article in agreement with ἀνθρώπου) 9.
ἀνθρώπου (gen.sing.masc.of ἄνθρωπος, relationship) 341.
ἐλθὼν (aor.part.nom.sing.masc.of ἔρχομαι, adverbial, temporal) 146.

#2627 ἆρα (interrogative particle).

(not translated) - Luke 18:8; Acts 8:30.

Meaning: Cf.#995, which is an illative particle. ἆρα is an interrogative particle, marking an inferential question to which a negative answer is expected.

εὑρήσει (3d.per.sing.fut.act.ind.of εὑρίσκω, deliberative) 79.
τὴν (acc.sing.fem.of the article in agreement with πίστιν) 9.
πίστιν (acc.sing.fem.of πίστις, direct object of εὑρήσει) 728.
ἐπὶ (preposition with the genitive of place description) 47.
τῆς (gen.sing.fem.of the article in agreement with γῆς) 9.
γῆς (gen.sing.fem.of γῆ, place description) 157.

Translation - "I am telling you that He will vindicate them without delay. Nevertheless when the Son of Man arrives, will He indeed find the faith upon the earth?"

Comment: Note the phrase ἐν τάχει - "with speed" or "soon." It holds the key to our understanding of the Book of Revelation. "Not now but soon." Not in this dispensation of God's dealings with man but in the next. Note again the clause ποιήσει τὴν ἐκδίκησιν as in verse 7. "Bring about/effect/achieve a vindication." Goodspeed translates, ". . . he will make haste to provide it."

When we compare the time still remaining before our Lord Jesus returns "in flaming fire, taking vengeance upon on them that know not God, and that obey not the gospel of our Lord Jesus Christ" (2 Thess.1:8), with eternity, the avenging wrath of the Son of Man upon the murderers of the saints, waits only a short time, even if, as in Abel's case, it should be six thousand years or more. The eternal God looks upon the passage of thousands of years of human history as a trifle. Hence His judgment will come ἐν τάχει. The question is whether there will be any of the saints surviving the wrath of the world, when He comes? We know from 1 Thess.4:16 that there will be.

The Parable of the Pharisee and the Tax Collector

(Luke 18:9-14)

Luke 18:9 - "And he spake this parable unto certain which trusted in themselves that they were righteous and despised others."

Εἶπεν δὲ καὶ πρός τινας τοὺς πεποιθότας ἐφ' ἑαυτοῖς ὅτι εἰσὶν δίκαιοι καὶ ἐξουθενοῦντας τοὺς λοιποὺς τὴν παραβολὴν ταύτην.

Εἶπεν (3d.per.sing.aor.act.ind.of εἶπον, constative) 155.
δὲ (continuative conjunction) 11.
καὶ (adjunctive conjunction joining verbs) 14.
πρός (preposition with the accusative of extent, after a verb of speaking) 197.
τινας (acc.pl.masc.of τις, in agreement with πεποιθότας) 486.
τοὺς (acc.pl.masc.of the article in agreement with πεποιθότας) 9.
πεποιθότας (perf.act.part.acc.pl.masc.of πείθω, substantival, extent after a verb of speaking) 1629.
ἐφ' (preposition with the dative of reference) 47.
ἑαυτοῖς (dat.pl.masc.of ἑαυτός, reference) 288.
ὅτι (conjunction introducing an object clause in indirect discourse) 211.
εἰσὶν (3d.per.pl.pres.ind.of εἰμί, static) 86.
δίκαιοι (nom.pl.masc.of δίκαιος, predicate adjective) 85.
καὶ (adjunctive conjunction joining participles) 14.

#2628 ἐξουθενοῦντας (pres.act.part.acc.pl.masc.of ἐξουθενέω, substantival, extent after a verb of speaking).

despise - Luke 18:9; Rom.14:3; 1 Cor.1:28; 16:11; Gal.4:14; 1 Thess.5:20.
set at naught - Luke 23:11; Acts 4:11; Rom.14:10.
be least esteemed - 1 Cor.6:4.
contemptible - 2 Cor.10:10.

Meaning: To despise; reject as worthless; look down upon - Luke 18:9; Rom.14:3,10, because of supposed spiritual superiority. To disdain along social and economic lines - 1 Cor.1:28. Because of age - 1 Cor.16:11. Because of bodily affliction - Gal.4:14. Because of intellectual prowess - 2 Cor.10;10; 1 Thess.5:20. Because of prestige - 1 Cor.6:4,10. With reference to Herod's attitude toward Jesus - Luke 23:11; of the Jews' attitude toward Jesus - Acts 4:11.

τοὺς (acc.pl.masc.of the article in agreement with λοιποὺς) 9.
λοιποὺς (acc.pl.masc.of λοιπός, direct object of ἐξουθενοῦντας) 1402.
τὴν (acc.sing.fem.of the article in agreement with παραβολὴν) 9.
παραβολὴν (acc.sing.fem.of παραβολή, direct object of εἶπεν) 1027.
ταύτην (acc.sing.fem.of οὗτος, in agreement with παραβολὴν) 93.

Translation - "And He also spoke to those who had always trusted in themselves that they were righteous and looked down upon the others, this parable."

Comment: καὶ is adjunctive since it joins the verb Εἶπεν of verse 9 with Ἔλεγεν of verse 1. The people to whom the parable is given are emphasized ahead of the parable itself. They are described by two substantival participles - τοὺς πεποιθότας and ἐξουθενοῦντας. They were those who trusted in themselves and took a superior attitude toward the rest of mankind. The ground for their faith in themselves is set forth in the ὅτι clause and indirect discourse. They considered themselves righteous. They had always held this opinion of themselves, as the perfect tense in *πεποιθότας* indicates. Having come to that conclusion at some time in the past, they had believed it ever since. It was natural, therefore that they should despise the rest of the human family as having failed to attain to their lofty standard of righteousness. That they always looked down upon the others is clear from the present tense in *ἐξουθενοῦντας*. So we have two durative attitudes, set forth by the perfect participle in the first case and the present participle in the last. This attitude was typically Pharisaical. It is religious bigotry at its revolting worst. The parable begins in

Verse 10 - "Two men went up into the temple to pray; the one a Pharisee, and the other a publican."

Ἄνθρωποι δύο ἀνέβησαν εἰς τὸ ἱερὸν προσεύξασθαι, ὁ εἷς Φαρισαῖος καὶ ὁ ἕτερος τελώνης.

Ἄνθρωποι (nom.pl.masc.of *ἄνθρωπος*, subject of *ἀνέβησαν*) 341.
δύο (numeral) 385.
ἀνέβησαν (3d.per.pl.aor.act.ind.of *ἀναβαίνω*, constative) 323.
εἰς (preposition with the accusative of extent) 140.
τὸ (acc.sing.neut.of the article in agreement with *ἱερὸν*) 9.
ἱερὸν (acc.sing.neut.of *ἱερόν*, extent) 346.
προσεύξασθαι (aor.mid.inf.of *προσεύχομαι*, purpose) 544.
ὁ (nom.sing.masc.of the article in agreement with *εἷς*) 9.
εἷς (nom.sing.masc.of *εἷς*, subject of *ἦν* understood) 469.
Φαρισαῖος (nom.sing.masc.of *Φαρισαῖος*, predicate nominative) 276.
καὶ (continuative conjunction) 14.
ὁ (nom.sing.masc.of the article in agreement with *ἕτερος*) 9.
ἕτερος (nom.sing.masc.of *ἕτερος*, subject of *ἦν* understood) 605.
τελώνης (nom.sing.masc.of *τελώνης*, predicate nominative) 550.

Translation - "Two men went up into the temple to pray: the one was a Pharisee and the other was a revenue officer."

Comment: Thus our Lord sets the stage for the parable. The reader should bow his head in reverence. The Pharisee is about to pray!

Verse 11 - "The Pharisee stood and prayed thus with himself, God, I thank thee, that I am not as other men are, extortioners, unjust, adulterers, or even as this publican."

ὁ Φαρισαῖος σταθεὶς πρὸς ἑαυτὸν ταῦτα προσηύχετο, Ὁ θεός, εὐχαριστῶ σοι ὅτι οὐκ εἰμὶ ὥσπερ οἱ λοιποὶ τῶν ἀνθρώπων, ἅρπαγες, ἄδικοι, μοιχοί, ἢ καὶ ὡς οὗτος ὁ τελώνης.

ὁ (nom.sing.masc.of the article in agreement with *Φαρισαῖος*) 9.
Φαρισαῖος (nom.sing.masc.of *φαρισαῖος*, subject of *προσηύχετο*) 276.
σταθεὶς (aor.pass.part.nom.sing.masc.of *ἵστημι*, adverbial, temporal) 180.
ταῦτα (acc.pl.neut.of *οὗτος*, direct object of *προσηύχετο*) 93.

προσηύχετο (3d.per.sing.imp.mid.ind.of *προσεύχομαι*, inceptive) 544.
Ὁ (nom.sing.masc.of the article in agreement with *θεός*) 9.
θεός (nom.sing.masc.of *θεός*, exclamation) 124.
εὐχαριστῶ (1st.per.sing.pres.act.ind.of *εὐχαριστέω*, aoristic) 1185.
σοι (dat.sing.masc.of *σύ*, indirect object of *εὐχαριστῶ*) 104.
ὅτι (conjunction introducing an object clause in indirect discourse) 211.
οὐκ (summary negative conjunction with the indicative) 130.
εἰμὶ (1st.per.sing.pres.ind.of *εἰμί*, static) 86.
ὥσπερ (intensive particle introducing a comparative clause) 560.
οἱ (nom.pl.masc.of the article in agreement with *λοιποὶ*) 9.
λοιποὶ (nom.pl.masc.of *λοιπός*, subject of *εἰσίν*,understood) 1402.
τῶν (gen.pl.masc.of the article in agreement with *ἀνθρώπων*) 9.
ἀνθρώπων (gen.pl.masc.of *ἄνθρωπος*, description) 341.
ἅρπαγες (nom.pl.masc.of *ἅρπαξ*, predicate nominative) 674.
ἄδικοι (nom.pl.masc.of *ἄδικος*, predicate adjective) 549.

#2629 *μοιχοί* (nom.pl.masc.of *μοιχός*, predicate nominative).

adulterer - Luke 18:11; 1 Cor.6:9; Heb.13:4; James 4:4.

Meaning: adulterer. One who is unfaithful to a marriage vow. Figuratively, any Christian who by undue friendship with the world becomes unfaithful to God - James 4:4. In the physical sense in Luke 18:11; 1 Cor.6:9; Heb.13:4.

ἤ (disjunctive particle) 465.
καὶ (emphatic conjunction) 14.
ὡς (comparative particle) 128.
οὗτος (nom.sing.masc.of *οὗτος*, in agreement with *τελώνης*, contemptuous use) 93.
ὁ (nom.sing.masc.of the article in agreement with *τελώνης*) 9.
τελώνης (nom.sing.masc.of *τελώνης*, subject of *ἐστίν*, understood) 550.

Translation - "The Pharisee stood up and began to pray as follows to himself: 'O God! I thank you that I am not like the rest of mankind - extortioners, dishonest, adulterers or especially like **this** revenue official.' "

Comment: The first thing the Pharisee did was to stand up. Thus he made a Hollywood production out of his prayer. If he had not stood the people in the temple would have had difficulty hearing. When one is not praying to God it is important that one be heard on earth! Contrast *μακρόθεν ἑστὼς* in verse 13. He also stood in order that he might be seen (Mt.6:5). He prayed *πρὸς ἑαυτόν* - "near unto himself." *Cf.*#197 for other examples of *πρός* meaning an intimate spiritual fellowship. Intimacy is the thought, but with whom? Note our discussion of *πρὸς τὸν θεόν* in John 1:1 (*The Renaissance New Testament*, 4, 4) and compare with Jesus' description of the intimacy of His relationship with the Father in John 17:21.

The Pharisee was not praying at all. He was communing *with himself.* He was as close to himself as it is possible to get. He had enjoyed this close relationship with himself for years. Apparently it was the only relationship that he did enjoy, since οἱ λοιποὶ τῶν ἀνθρώπων excludes the rest of the human race.

Jesus said that the Pharisee "*began* to pray." The verb προσηύχετο is an inceptive imperfect. The emphasis is upon the beginning of an exercise that might go on interminably. That he was not praying to God is clear from the fact that Jesus did not use the vocative of address in Ὁ θεός. It is an exclamation, indicating some emotion, although the revenue officer used the same form in verse 13, although with a different emotion. The Pharisee did, of course say εὐχαριστῶ σοι - "I thank you." Since he was praying aloud, hoping to be heard by all who stood around, it would have been improper to depart from the standard formulation. What he really meant was, "O God! I thank myself that I am not . . . κ.τ.λ." The ὅτι clause in indirect discourse continues the "prayer." It was not enough to congratulate himself that he was better generally than the rest of the human family. The article with ἀνθρώπων indicates that he meant the quantitative whole of the human race. This clown thought that he was the best there was! He went on to specify. He was not an extortioner, nor a swindler nor an adulterer. To be even more specific he was not like the publican, whom he accused by implication of being all of those things. Calling attention to himself, for the purpose of glorification, he also called the public's attention to the publican for his embarrassment and degradation.

Some Pharisees indeed were ἅρπαγες, ἄδικοι καὶ μοιχοί. Whether this Pharisee was or not, the text does not say. His sin was his lack of humility. It is good to be free of the sins which he listed. Perhaps the greatest sin of all is to be proud of the fact. There is abundant evidence that the Pharisee delighted in reflecting upon his spotless record of probity.

Having defined his perfection in a negative sense, by pointing out to God what he was not, he proceded to tell God in a positive way what he did as evidence to what he was.

Verse 12 - "I fast twice in the week, I give tithes of all that I possess."

νηστεύω δὶς τοῦ σαββάτου, ἀποδεκατῶ πάντα ὅσα κτῶμαι.

νηστεύω (1st.per.sing.pres.act.ind.of νηστεύω, customary) 332.

#2630 δὶς (adverbial).

again - Phil.4:16; 1 Thess.2:18.
twice - Mk.14:30,72; Lk.18:12; Jude 12.

Meaning: An adverb. Twice. With καὶ ἅπαξ καὶ δὶς - Phil.4:16; 1 Thess.2:18. The second time - Mk.14:30,72; Lk.18:12; Jude 12 (in a figurative sense - "doubly dead.").

τοῦ (gen.sing.neut.of the article in agreement with σαββάτου) 9.
σαββάτου (gen.sing.neut.of σάββατον, time description) 962.
ἀποδεκατῶ (1st.per.sing.pres.act.ind.of ἀποδεκατόω, customary) 1448.
πάντα (acc.pl.neut.of πᾶς, in agreement with ὅσα) 67.

ὅσα (acc.pl.neut.of ὅσος, direct object of κτῶμαι) 660.
κτῶμαι (1st.per.sing.pres.ind.contraction of κτάομαι, customary) 859.

Translation - "I fast regularly twice a week. I always give back ten percent of all of that which I get."

Comment: Even an uninspired economist can see the fallacy in the Pharisee's argument. The real question to ask is, "What is the *average* caloric intake daily?" It would be interesting to know how much he ate the days before and after fast days. It would also be interesting to know how much he weighed. There are many weight watchers in our affluent and obese society who also fast twice in the week. Some fast seven days a week, but they do not stand up at church and boast about it. They might announce the results to their friends, but if so, it would be for social, not religious reasons.

Nor can the tither lay claim to spiritual excellence unless his tithing reduces the ninety percent of disposable income below the level of noticeable diminishing marginal utility. There is no sacrifice involved for the rich man who tithes (Mk.12:41-44). The real question here is not how much the Pharisee gave but how much he had left for himself after he gave ten percent. This is the point that is missed by many preachers who make a fetish out of preaching the tithe. Such preaching receives enthusiastic support from the wealthy members of the congregation, who are glad to have the poor people in the church, who normally comprise the majority of the membership, shoulder the burden of the church budget. For the poor this is a great sacrifice, whereas the rich escape sacrifice by also giving by the same rule. A proportional tax is much more burdensome on the poor than on the rich. Anyone would find it easier to give ten percent of a million dollars, which leaves nine hundred thousand of discretionary money, than to give ten percent of one hundred dollars, leaving only ninety dollars for his own use. Anyone would rather give ten percent of a lot than ten percent of a little.

Our analysis of the tithe was not available to the Pharisee in our Lord's parable, since the concept of diminishing marginal utility was not clearly understood until the days of Alfred Marshall and the Neoclassical economists of the late 19th century.

We turn now to the publican and his prayer in

Verse 13 - "And the publican, standing afar off, would not lift up so much as his eyes unto heaven, but smote upon his breast, saying, God, be merciful to me a sinner."

ὁ δὲ τελώνης μακρόθεν ἑστὼς οὐκ ἤθελεν οὐδὲ τοὺς ὀφθαλμοὺς ἐπᾶραι εἰς τὸν οὐρανόν, ἀλλ' ἔτυπτεν τὸ στῆθος αὐτοῦ λέγων, Ὁ θεός, ἱλάσθητί μοι τῷ ἁμαρτωλῷ.

ὁ (nom.sing.masc.of the article in agreement with τελώνης) 9.
δὲ (adversative conjunction) 11.
τελώνης (nom.sing.masc.of τελώνης, subject of ἤθελεν and ἔτυπτεν) 550.

μακρόθεν (adverbial) 1600.
ἑστὼς (perf.act.part.nom.sing.masc.of ἵστημι, adverbial, temporal) 180.
οὐκ (summary negative conjunction with the indicative) 130.
ἤθελεν (3d.per.sing.imp.act.ind.of θέλω, progressive description) 88.
οὐδὲ (disjunctive particle) 452.
τοὺς (acc.pl.masc.of the article in agreement with ὀφθαλμοὺς) 9.
ὀφθαλμοὺς (acc.pl.masc.of ὀφθαλμός, direct object of ἐπᾶραι) 501.
ἐπᾶραι (aor.act.inf.of ἐπαίρω, complementary) 1227.
εἰς (preposition with the accusative of extent) 140.
τὸν (acc.sing.masc.of the article in agreement with οὐρανόν) 9.
οὐρανόν (acc.sing.masc.of οὐρανός, extent) 254.
ἀλλ' (alternative conjunction) 342.
ἔτυπτεν (3d.per.sing.imp.act.ind.of τύπτω, inceptive) 1526.
τὸ (acc.sing.neut.of the article in agreement with στῆθος) 9.

#2631 στῆθος (acc.sing.neut.of στῆθος, direct object of ἔτυπτεν).

breast - Luke 18:13; 23:48; John 13:25; 21:20; Rev.15:6.

Meaning: Cf. ἵστημι (#180); that which stands out; is prominent anatomically; the breast, bosom. In an expression denoting grief - Luke 18:13; 23:48, with τύπτω. In John 13:25; 21:20, of the position of John, lying near Jesus' breast. With reference to the angels - Rev.15:6.

αὐτοῦ (gen.sing.masc.of αὐτός, possession) 16.
λέγων (pres.act.part.nom.sing.masc.of λέγω, recitative) 66.
'Ο (nom.sing.masc.of the article in agreement with θεός) 9.
θεός (nom.sing.masc.of θεός, exclamation) 124.

#2632 ἱλάσθητί (2d.per.sing.aor.pass.impv.of ἱλάσκομαι, entreaty).

make reconciliation - Heb.2:17.
be merciful - Luke 18:13.

Meaning: Cf. ἱλασμός (#5289), ἱλαστήριον (#3873) and ἵλεως (#1211). Hence, to be gracious; gentle. *From* ἵλαος, which does not occur in the New Testament. In the New Testament, in the passive, to be propitiated; to be reconciled; to be put into a position where grace can justly be given rather than punishment justly exacted. LXX in Ex.32:14; 2 Maccab.3:33. Ps.78 (79): 9; 24 (25):11. In the publican's prayer - Luke 18:13. With reference to the work of the High Priest - Heb.2:17.

μοι (dat.sing.masc.of ἐγώ, personal advantage) 123.
τῷ (dat.sing.masc.of the article in agreement with ἁμαρτωλῷ) 9.
ἁμαρτωλῷ (dat.sing.masc.of ἁμαρτωλός, apposition) 791.

Translation - "But when the revenue official had taken his place far away, he was unwilling to lift his eyes to heaven, but began to beat upon his breast saying, 'O God be reconciled unto me the sinner.' "

Comment: δὲ is adversative. The attitude and behavior of the tax collector is diametrically opposite to that of the Pharisee. He took his place at a distance from the temple. He was so embarrassed about his lost condition as a sinner that he was unwilling even to look up to heaven. The inceptive imperfect in ἔτυπτεν indicates that he began and continued to beat his breast as he prayed. While the Pharisee was giving public recognition to the failings of the publican, he made no effort to defend himself nor did he attempt to refute the accusation. On the contrary he admitted it. How idle it is for us to defend ourselves before God when we know that the accusation is the truth. As if God does not know the truth! His prayer begins as did that of the Pharisee, not with a vocative of address (θεέ) but with an exclamation (O θεός) - in his case an expression of his grief and shame. The Pharisee used the same expression to give vent to his contempt for the rest of the human race who were not fortunate enough to be as good as he.

The essence of the publican's prayer can be understood only as we see the significance of the word ἱλάσθητί which he used. - "Be propitiated unto me." *Cf.*#2632. "Be unto me as you are able when you look upon the mercy seat." *Cf.*ἱλασμός (#5289). The mercy seat was the place where the blood of the sacrificial Paschal lamb was sprinkled. The revenue official was asking for the forgiveness for his sins and salvation and he was basing his plea upon the blood of God's Lamb (John 1:29). The Pharisee was filing his claim for salvation, not upon any divine provision for him, but upon his own merit, positively, in terms of fasting and tithing, and negatively, in terms of the comparison with others.

How often has the Pharisee's religious philosophy been echoed by the untaught! One often hears, "My mother (father, brother, Mr.Jones, Mrs. Smith *et al*) was a good woman. If she did not go to heaven, there isn't any use for me to try!" As though salvation is something that God measures out to people on the basis of how well they did in life in comparison to others. God is not a teacher who is giving the human race a test which He expects to grade on the curve. If He were, no one could ever know that he was saved. There must have been someone in the world who was better than the Pharisee.

The Pharisee and the revenue official who had sold his soul to Rome - totally opposite characters, with totally opposite philosophies, resulting in totally opposite behavior, brings totally opposite results, as we hear our Lord's conclusion of the matter in

Verse 14 - "I tell you, this man went down to his house justified rather than the other; for everyone that exalteth himself shall be abased; and he that humbleth himself shall be exalted."

λέγω ὑμῖν, κατέβη οὗτος δεδικαιωμένος εἰς τὸν οἶκον αὐτοῦ παρ' ἐκεῖνον. ὅτι πᾶς ὁ ὑψῶν ἑαυτὸν ταπεινωθήσεται, ὁ δὲ ταπεινῶν ἑαυτὸν ὑψωθήσεται.

λέγω (1st.per.sing.pres.act.ind.of λέγω, aoristic) 66.
ὑμῖν (dat.pl.masc.of σύ, indirect object of λέγω) 104.
κατέβη (3d.per.sing.aor.act.ind.of καταβαίνω, constative) 324.
οὗτος (nom.sing.masc.of οὗτος, subject of κατέβη, deictic) 93.

δεδικαιωμένος (perf.pass.part.nom.sing.masc.of δικαιόω, adverbial, circumstantial) 933.

εἰς (preposition with the accusative of extent) 140.

τὸν (acc.sing.masc.of the article in agreement with οἶκον) 9.

οἶκον (acc.sing.masc.of οἶκος, extent) 784.

αὐτοῦ (gen.sing.masc.of αὐτός, possession) 16.

παρ' (preposition with the accustive of comparison) 154.

ἐκεῖνον (acc.sing.masc.of ἐκεῖνος, comparison) 246.

ὅτι (conjunction introducing a subordinate causal clause) 211.

πᾶς (nom.sing.masc.of πᾶς, in agreement with ὑψῶν) 67.

ὁ (nom.sing.masc.of the article in agreement with ὑψῶν) 9.

ὑψῶν (pres.act.part.nom.sing.masc.of ὑψόω, substantival, subject of ταπεινωθήσεται) 946.

ἑαυτὸν (acc.sing.masc.of ἑαυτός, direct object of ὑψῶν) 288.

ταπεινωθήσεται (3d.per.sing.fut.pass.ind.of ταπεινόω, predictive) 1248.

ὁ (nom.sing.masc.of the article in agreement with ταπεινῶν) 9.

δὲ (adversative conjunction) 11.

ταπεινῶν (pres.act.part.nom.sing.masc.of ταπεινόω, substantival, subject of ὑψωθήσεται) 1248.

ἑαυτὸν (acc.sing.masc.of ἑαυτός, direct object of ταπεινῶν) 288.

ὑψωθήσεται (3d.per.sing.fut.pass.ind.of ὑψόω, predictive) 946.

Translation - "I am telling you, this man went down to his house justified, rather than that one. Because everyone who exalts himself will be brought low, but the one who humbles himself will be exalted."

Comment: Here is a different application, based upon the same spiritual principle of the parable of Luke 14:7-11. Note the deictic uses of οὗτος and ἐκεῖνον - "this man - that man." The perfect passive participle δεδικαιωμένος is circumstantial. When was the publican made righteous? Clearly when he prayed outside the temple area and asked God for mercy on the basis of the blood of the Lamb of God. Having been made righteous (a completed action in the past) he went home enjoying the permanent condition of being justified (a present condition as a result of a past action). When the publican prayed he was saved (vs.13) *Cf.* Rom.10:13; Rom.5:1. For how long a period of time? The perfect tense is decidedly durative. The publican will always be justified. παρ' ἐκεῖνον - an accusative use with παρά indicating comparison.

The causal clause sets forth the basic spiritual principle by which God conducts affairs in His moral universe. *Cf.* comment on Lk.14:11. All men are sinners (Rom.3:23). Humanly contrived distinctions seem apparent on earth when examined superficially, but in God's sight all men, be they Pharisees or revenue officials, blend together into one sad, wicked, sinful mass of depraved homogeneity. The Pharisee did not understand this and he assumed that heaven's court weighed matters on the Pharisaic scale. The publican was so intent upon beating his breast that he was not listening to the Pharisee nor thinking of him. He was comparing himself only to God and he did not like what he saw. He was honest enough to tell God about it, even though he was certain that the Lord already knew all about it. The Pharisee was unwise enough to compare himself with the publican. He liked what he saw and he was blind enough to think that God was as blind as he. So he boasted about it to God. This was exceedingly unwise (2 Cor.10:12). It was a costly error. He will pay for it in hell forever.

(3). In Perea Teaching Concerning Divorce

(Matthew 19:1-12; Mark 10:2-12)

Mark 10:2 - "And the Pharisees came to him and asked him, Is it lawful for a man to put away his wife? tempting Him."

καὶ (προσελθόντες Φαρισαῖοι) ἐπηρώτων αὐτὸν εἰ ἔξεστιν ἀνδρὶ γυναῖκα ἀπολῦσαι, πειράζοντες αὐτόν.

καὶ (continuative conjunction) 14.
(*προσελθόντες* (aor.part.nom.pl.masc.of *προσέρχομαι*, adverbial, temporal) 336.
Φαρισαῖοι (nom.pl.masc.of *Φαρισαῖος*, subject of *ἐπηρώτων*) 276.
ἐπηρώτων (3d.per.pl.imp.act.ind.of *ἐπερωτάω*, inceptive) 973.
αὐτὸν (acc.sing.masc.of *αὐτός*, direct object of *ἐπηρώτων*) 16.
εἰ (conditional particle with the indicative in indirect question, ellipsis) 337.
ἔξεστιν (3d.per.sing.pres.ind.of *ἔξεστιν*, indirect question) 966.
ἀνδρὶ (dat.sing.masc.of *ἀνήρ*, reference) 63.
γυναῖκα (acc.sing.fem.of *γυνή*, direct object of *ἀπολῦσαι*) 103.
ἀπολῦσαι (aor.act.inf.of *ἀπολύω*, completes *ἔξεστιν*) 92.
πειράζοντες (pres.act.part.nom.pl.masc.of *πειράζω*, adverbial, telic) 330.
αὐτόν (acc.sing.masc.of *αὐτός*, direct object of *πειράζοντες*) 16.

Translation - "And the Pharisees came and in order to cross examine Him they began to ask Him if it was lawful for a man to divorce his wife."

Comment: Here is another typical attempt by the Pharisees to engage Jesus in controversy, which they hoped would become so heated that they could force Him off balance and cause Him, in an unguarded moment, to make an unwise and inconsistent statement that they could use against Him. But Jesus, never unduly emotional, was never off balance. There were no unguarded moments nor unwise or inconsistent statements. "The use of *εἰ* in a question is elliptical. It is really a condition with the conclusion not expressed or it is an indirect question. . . In Mk.10:2 (parallel to Mt.19:3) the question is indirect. The idiom, though singular, has "attained to all the rights of a direct interrogative" (Winer-Thayer, *A Grammar of the Idiom of the New Testament*, 509, as cited in Robertson, *Grammar*, 916) by this time. The idiom may be illustrated by the Latin *an* which in later writers was used in direct questions." (*Ibid.,* 916). The telic participle *πειράζοντες* reveals their motive for badgering Jesus.

Verse 3 - "And He answered and said unto them, What did Moses command you?"

ὁ δὲ ἀποκριθεὶς εἶπεν αὐτοῖς, Τί ὑμῖν ἐνετείλατο Μωϋσῆς;

ὁ (nom.sing.masc.of the article, subject of *εἶπεν*) 9.
δὲ (continuative conjunction) 11.
ἀποκριθεὶς (aor.part.nom.sing.masc.of *ἀποκρίνομαι*, adverbial, modal) 318.
εἶπεν (3d.per.sing.aor.act.ind.of *εἶπον*, constative) 155.
αὐτοῖς (dat.pl.masc.of *αὐτός*, indirect object of *εἶπεν*) 16.
Τί (acc.sing.neut.of *τίς*, interrogative pronoun,direct object of *ἐνετείλατο*) 281.
ὑμῖν (dat.pl.masc.of *σύ*, indirect object of *ἐνετείλατο*) 104.
ἐνετείλατο (3d.per.sing.aor.ind.of *ἐντέλλομαι*, direct question) 349.
Μωϋσῆς (nom.sing.masc.of *Μωϋσῆς*, subject of *ἐνετείλατο*) 715.

Translation - "And in reply He said to them, 'What did Moses command you?'"

Comment: Direct question. Jesus used a similar approach in Luke 10:26. Jesus did not ask what Moses *allowed* (Deut.24), but what he commanded in the ideal state. The Pharisees thought that He meant the commandment of concession (Deut.24:1*ff*), not the ideal state (Gen.2:24,25). *Cf.* comment on Mt.19:3,4.

Verse 4 - "And they said, Moses suffered to write a bill of divorcement, and to put her away."

οἱ δὲ εἶπαν, Ἐπέτρεψεν Μωϋσῆς βιβλίον ἀποστασίου γράψαι καὶ ἀπολῦσαι.

οἱ (nom.pl.masc.of the article, subject of *εἶπαν*) 9.
δὲ (continuative conjunction) 11.
εἶπαν (3d.per.pl.aor.act.ind.of *εἶπον*, constative) 155.
Ἐπέτρεψεν (3d.per.sing.aor.act.ind.of *ἐπιτρέπω*, constative) 747.
Μωϋσῆς (nom.sing.masc.of *Μωϋσῆς*, subject of *ἐπέτρεψεν*) 715.
βιβλίον (acc.sing.neut.of *βιβλίον*, direct object of *γράψαι*) 1292.
ἀποστασίου (gen.sing.neut.of *ἀποστάσιον*, description) 508.
γράψαι (aor.act.inf.of *γράφω*, completes *ἐπέτρεψεν*) 156.
καὶ (adjunctive conjunction joining infinitives) 14.
ἀπολῦσαι (aor.act.inf.of *ἀπολύω*, completes *ἐπέτρεψεν*) 92.

Translation - "And they said, 'Moses permitted (us) to write a divorce decree and to set (her) free.'"

Comment: This is a reference to Deut.24:1*ff*. Note the difference between *ἐντέλλομαι* (#349) in verse 3 and *ἐπιτρέπω* (#747) in verse 4. Jesus asked them what Moses commanded, and they answered in terms of what Moses permitted. Thus they indicated their choice for the minimum rather than the maximum requirement in the ideal situation as set forth in Gen.1:27; 2:18-25. Jesus analyzes them in these terms in

Verse 5 - "And Jesus answered and said unto them, For the hardness of your heart, he wrote you this precept."

ὁ δὲ Ἰησοῦς εἶπεν αὐτοῖς, Πρὸς τὴν σκληροκαρδίαν ὑμῶν ἔγραφεν ὑμῖν τὴν ἐντολὴν ταύτην.

ὁ (nom.sing.masc.of the article in agreement with Ἰησοῦς) 9.
δὲ (adversative conjunction) 11.
Ἰησοῦς (nom.sing.masc.of Ἰησοῦς, subject of εἶπεν) 3.
αὐτοῖς (dat.pl.masc.of αὐτός, indirect object of εἶπεν) 16.
Πρὸς (preposition with the accusative, general reference) 197.
τὴν (acc.sing.fem.of the article in agreement with σκληροκαρδίαν) 9.
σκληροκαρδίαν (acc.sing.fem.of σκληροκαρδία, general reference) 1293.
ὑμῶν (gen.pl.masc.of σύ, possession) 104.
ἔγραφεν (3d.per.sing.aor.act.ind.of γράφω, constative) 156.
ὑμῖν (dat.pl.masc.of σύ, indirect object of ἔγραφεν) 104.
τὴν (acc.sing.fem.of the article in agreement with ἐντολὴν) 9.
ἐντολὴν (acc.sing.fem.of ἐντολή, direct object of ἔγραφεν) 472.
ταύτην (acc.sing.fem.of οὗτος, in agreement with ἐντολὴν) 93.

Translation - "But Jesus said to them, 'It was with reference to the hardness of your heart that he wrote this commandment for you.' "

Comment: δὲ is adversative, as Jesus is about to disagree with the construction that the Pharisees were putting upon Deut.24. They thought of it as the perfect will of God, without asking why such a precept should be laid down. Jesus has a somewhat different and less flattering explanation. Πρὸς here with the accusative of general reference. It can be thought of as a causal construction, though πρός with the accusative is seldom used for cause. It was because the heart of man is perverse that Moses added this rule. Human beings know little of forgiveness, either in precept or in practice. If we found it easier to forgive the concession of Deut.24 would never have been given. It was God's concession to what He foresaw to be the selfrighteous, unforgiving, intolerant, bigoted attitude toward the immoral woman (Deut.24:1-4). The idea that a woman who had lost her virginity before her wedding night could repent and receive God's forgiveness and therefore that her husband should also forgive her, since God had, would never occur to a Pharisee. Therefore since their selfrighteous hearts were so hard, Moses, realizing that it was not to be expected that a man would forgive and forget a wrong such as that, had lowered the standard.

But the law of Deut.24:1-4 does not suggest that if a man obeyed it and divorced his unfaithful wife, he was thereby demonstrated to be spiritually mature, because he took advantage of the letter of the law, however much he may have violated its spirit. Rather, if the Pharisee, standing on his rights, invoked the law of Deut.24, he revealed that he was so spiritually immature that he could not forgive the woman whom he had professed to love.

The woman, however, is not punished. She may be remarried. Note also that the same law forbids the first husband ever to marry her again, after he has once divorced her. The implication is that, having divorced her once, to demonstrate the hardness of an unforgiving heart, he might wish to take her again to satisfy an unrelenting and voracious lust. It is generally true that the self-righteous Pharisee who is first and loudest in condemnation of a harlot's sins, is among the first to succomb to the temptation of her charms.

As usual the Pharisees, who started the argument (vs.2) were bested in the encounter.

Verse 6 - "But from the beginning of the creation God made them male and female."

ἀπὸ δὲ ἀρχῆς κτίσεως ἄρσεν καὶ θῆλυ ἐποίησεν αὐτούς.

ἀπὸ (preposition with the ablative of time separation) 70.
δὲ (adversative conjunction) 11.
ἀρχῆς (abl.sing.fem.of ἀρχή, time separation) 1285.

#2633 κτίσεως (gen.sing.fem.of κτίσις, description).

creation - Rom.1:20; Rev.3:14; Mark 10:6; 13:19; 2 Pet.3:14; Mark 16:15.
creature - Rom.1:25; Heb.4:13; Rom.8:39; Gal.6:15; 2 Cor.5:17; Col.1:15,23; Rom.8:19,20,21,22; 2 Cor.5:17.
building - Heb.9:11.
ordinance - 1 Pet.2:13.

Meaning: The creation of the heaven and the earth and everything in them - Rom.1:20; Mk.10:6; 13:19; 2 Pet.3:4; that which is created - human - Mk.16:15; Col.1:23; non-human - Rom.1:25; 8:19,20,21,22; where both human and non-human creatures are in view - Heb.4:13; Rom.8:39. With reference to the new nature of the regenerate believer - Gal.6:15; 2 Cor.5:17; Col.1:15. With reference to Christ, who is called ἡ ἀρχὴ τῆς κτίσεως τοῦ θεοῦ in Rev.3:14. Of the construction activity of a human carpenter - Heb.9:11. With reference to a law or legal ordinance, a legislative enactment or an executive order, coming from a human source - 1 Pet.2:13.

ἄρσεν (acc.sing.masc.of ἄρσεν, general reference) 1286.
καὶ (adjunctive conjunction joining nouns) 14.
θῆλυ (acc.sing.neut.of θῆλυς, general reference) 1287.
ἐποίησεν (3d.per.sing.aor.act.ind.of ποιέω, culminative) 127.
αὐτούς (acc.pl.masc.of αὐτός, direct object of ἐποίησεν) 16.

Translation - "But from the first act of creation He made them male and female."

Comment: Adversative δὲ. Though the hardness of the unforgiving heart makes necessary a concession in Moses' law, in order to protect the poor woman, who, for all of her past failures, has nevertheless repented and been forgiven, yet (adversative δὲ) that is not God's original ideal plan. He made only one male and one female in the first act of human creation. Adam and Eve, in God's ideal Eden were faithful to each other by virtue of the fact that there was no one else. And their union in the Garden of Eden is the pattern for all future marital unions.

This is the conclusion of the next three verses. *Cf.* comment on Mt.19:4.

Verse 7 - "For this cause shall a man leave his father and mother, and cleave to his wife;"

ἕνεκεν τούτου καταλείψει ἄνθρωπος τὸν πατέρα αὐτοῦ καὶ τὴν μητέρα (καὶ προσκολληθήσεται πρὸς τὴν γυναῖκα αὐτοῦ),

ἕνεκεν (improper preposition with the genitive) 435.
τούτου (gen.sing.neut.of οὗτος, description of cause) 93.
καταλείψει (3d.per.sing.fut.act.ind.of καταλείπω, imperative future) 369.
ἄνθρωπος (nom.sing.masc.of ἄνθρωπος, subject of καταλείψει) 341.
τὸν (acc.sing.masc.of the article in agreement with πατέρα) 9.
αὐτοῦ (gen.sing.masc.of αὐτός, relationship) 16.
καὶ (adjunctive conjunction joining nouns) 14.
τὴν (acc.sing.fem.of the article in agreement with μητέρα) 9.
μητέρα (acc.sing.fem.of μήτηρ, direct object of καταλείψει) 76.
(καὶ (adjunctive conjunction joining verbs) 14.

#2633A προσκολληθήσεται (3d.per.sing.fut.pass.ind.of προσκολλάομαι, imperative).

cleave to - Mark 10:7.
be joined unto - Eph.5:31.
join one's self to - Acts 5:36.

Meaning: A combination of πρός (#197) and κολλάομαι (#1288), where πρός intensifies the relationship resulting from the merge. With reference to the marriage relationship in Mark 10:7 and Eph.5:31, although Mt.19:5, the parallel passage to Mark 10:7 has κολλάομαι (#1288). With reference to a military alliance in Acts 5:36.

πρὸς (preposition with the accusative of extent, metaphorical) 197.
τὴν (acc.sing.fem.of the article in agreement with γυναῖκα) 9.
γυναῖκα (acc.sing.fem.of γυνή, extent, metaphorical) 103.
αὐτοῦ) (gen.sing.masc.of αὐτός, relationship) 16.

Translation - "This is why a man must leave his father and mother and cling to his wife."

Comment: The final clause καὶ προσκολληθήσεται πρὸς τὴν γυναῖκα αὐτοῦ is not supported in the W/H text. When this passage was first researched and written up I was following W/H. Thus the verb προσκολληθήσεται was omitted from the numerical order of words. It is here included with the number #2633A assigned. The United Bible Societies' Committee has accepted it in Acts 5:36 and Eph.5:31 without question. The Committee has however included it in Mark 10:7, but with considerable reservation. Metzger explains:

"Have the words καὶ προσκολληθήσεται πρὸς τὴν γυναῖκα (or τῇ γυναικὶ) αὐτοῦ been added in most copies in order to assimilate the quotation to the fuller form of text found in Mt.19:5 (and Gn 2.24), or were they inadvertently omitted in transcription (the eye of the scribe passing from καί to καί)? In order to represent the very close balance of probabilities, a majority of the Committee decided to include the clause in the text (where it seems to be necessary for the sense, otherwise οἱ δύο in ver. 8 could be taken to refer to the father and the mother!), but to enclose it within square brackets. As between πρὸς τὴν γυναῖκα and τῇ γυναῖκι, the former was preferred because it reproduces more exactly the quotation from Genesis, and because the dative construction is obviously a stylistic correction." (Metzger, *A Textual Commentary on the Greek New Testament*, 104,105).

ἕνεκεν τούτου means much the same as διὰ τοῦτον. It is a causal construction. τούτου refers to the fact of verse 6, *viz.* that in the original creation there was one man and one woman only. Jesus uses this fact to say that monogamy, with fidelity of each mate to the other, was God's original intention. Eph.5:31 cites this fact and relates it to the spiritual relationship that exists between Christ and His church. *Cf.* comment *en loc.* Jesus' statement continues in

Verse 8 - "And they twain shall be one flesh: so then they are no more twain, but one flesh."

καὶ ἔσονται οἱ δύο εἰς σάρκα μίαν, ὥστε οὐκέτι εἰσὶν δύο ἀλλὰ μία σάρξ.

καὶ (continuative conjunction) 14.
ἔσονται (3d.per.pl.fut.ind.of εἰμί, predictive) 86.
οἱ (nom.pl.masc.of the article in agreement with δύο) 9.
δύο (nom.sing.masc.of δύο, subject of ἔσονται) 385.
εἰς (preposition with the accusative of extent) 140.
σάρκα (acc.sing.fem.of σάρξ, extent) 1202.
μίαν (acc.sing.fem.of εἷς, in agreement with σάρκα) 469.
ὥστε (conjunction introducing a result clause with the indicative) 752.
οὐκέτι (temporal adverb of denial) 1289.
εἰσὶν (3d.per.pl.pres.ind.of εἰμί, result) 86.
δύο (numeral, with σάρξ) 385.
ἀλλὰ (alternative conjunction) 342.
μία (nom.sing.fem.of εἷς, in agreement with σάρξ) 469.
σάρξ (nom.sing.fem.of σάρξ, predicate nominative) 1202.

Translation - "And the two will become one flesh, with the result that they are no longer two but one."

Comment: The use of εἰς in the predicate can also be seen in Acts 8:23. *Cf.*#140 for other uses. εἰς with the accusative indicating equivalence is found also in Acts 7:23; 13:22. Jesus is saying here that the marriage relationship works a mystical miracle. God made one man and one woman. Neither were fulfilled without the other. Their mutual interdependence is the greatest - greater than that which exists between a man and his parents. This is why he is willing to leave his father and mother. He is searching for the complete fulfillment to be found only in his wife. He and she then become the equivalent of one body of flesh. The result (ὥστε) is that from henceforth (οὐκέτι) they are no longer two people but one. Paul (Eph.5:31) calls this fact a great mystery, and is analogous to the relationship between Christ and His body, the Church. Whatever it means in its fullness, it is at least clear that on the basis of this fact, Christ lays down His command in verse 9.

ὥστε with the indicative expresses actual result, while with the infinitive it expresses only "conceived or intended result." Actual result "may also be expressed by the infinitive with ὥστε (Mt.8:24; 12:22; Lk.5:7). (Mantey, *Manual*, 286).

Verse 9 - "What therefore God hath joined together, let not man put asunder."

ὃ οὖν ὁ θεὸς συνέζευξεν ἄνθρωπος μὴ χωριζέτω.

ὃ (acc.sing.neut.of ὅς, direct object of χωριζέτω) 65.
οὖν (inferential conjunction) 68.
ὁ (nom.sing.masc.of the article in agreement with θεὸς) 9.
θεὸς (nom.sing.masc.of θεός, subject of συνέζευξεν) 124.
συνέζευξεν (3d.per.sing.aor.act.ind.of συζεύγνυμι, culminative) 1290.
ἄνθρωπος (nom.sing.masc.of ἄνθρωπος, subject of χωριζέτω) 341.
μὴ (qualified negative conjunction with the imperative) 87.
χωριζέτω (3d.per.sing.pres.act.impv.of χωρίζω, prohibition) 1291.

Translation - "Therefore let no man separate that which God has yoked together."

Comment: οὖν is inferential and rests for its validity upon what Jesus has said in verses 5-8. The prohibition in the imperative is stern. For man to try to separate that which God has joined together is to say that God made a mistake. Marriages that are "made in heaven" should not be broken on earth. When a marriage is broken, if we assume that it was made in heaven, we must conclude that someone on earth thought that his opinion on the matter was better than God's. *Cf.* 2 Cor.6:14, where we have a definite rule. God never marries a Christian to an unbeliever. Such "marriages" which are not true unions in the biblical sense, but only sociological arrangements to live together, are not necessarily protected by the ban of verse 9, although Paul suggests in 1 Cor.7:12-14 that even the marriage of a Christian to an unbeliever need not be broken is there is reasonable compatability between the partners. In verse 9 our Lord commands that couples that have been yoked together by God shall not be separated.

Are other separations permitted in the cases in which a Christian is married to an unbeliever? Note Paul's discussion of this in 1 Cor.7:10,11,15,15 where χορίζω (#1291) occurs. The case under discussion in 1 Cor.7 may have been one in which both parties were unsaved at the time of the marriage, after which one of them became a Christian. Certainly, marriage vows taken by two children of God, with the divine permission, are inviolate. Divorce between two Christians is tragic. *Cf.* our comments on Mt.19:3-12.

Verse 10 - "And in the house his disciples asked him again of the same matter."

Καὶ εἰς τὴν οἰκίαν πάλιν οἱ μαθηταὶ περὶ τούτου ἐπηρώτων αὐτόν.

Καὶ (continuative conjunction) 14.
εἰς (preposition with the accusative, static use, like a locative of place where) 140.

τὴν (acc.sing.fem.of the article in agreement with οἰκίαν) 9.
οἰκίαν (acc.sing.fem.of οἰκία, static use, like a locative, place where) 186.
πάλιν (adverbial) 355.
οἱ (nom.pl.masc.of the article in agreement with μαθηταὶ) 9.
μαθηταὶ (nom.pl.masc.of μαθητής, subject of ἐπηρώτων) 421.
περὶ (preposition with the genitive of reference) 173.
τούτου (gen.sing.neut.of οὗτος, reference) 93.
ἐπηρώτων (3d.per.pl.imp.act.ind.of ἐπερωτάω, inceptive) 973.
αὐτόν (acc.sing.masc.of αὐτός, direct object of ἐπηρώτων) 16.

Translation - "And in the house the disciples began to ask Him about this again."

Comment: We have the original static use of εἰς with the accusative like ἐν with the locative of place where. There are several instances of this use of εἰς which persisted in Greek from Homeric days. *Cf.*#140. περὶ τούτου, the genitive of reference with περί (#173) is regular, but with ἐπερωτάω (#973) we have here the only instance. Note the inceptive imperfect in the verb. The disciples waited until they had some privacy in the house, and then, their own interest in the subject having been aroused by Jesus' comments to the Pharisees, they began to ask Him more about it.

Verse 11 - "And he saith unto them, Whosoever shall put away his wife, and marry another, committeth adultery against her."

καὶ λέγει αὐτοῖς, Ὃς ἂν ἀπολύσῃ τὴν γυναῖκα αὐτοῦ καὶ γαμήσῃ ἄλλην μοιχᾶται ἐπ' αὐτήν,

καὶ (continuative conjunction) 14.
λέγει (3d.per.sing.pres.act.ind.of λέγω, historical) 66.
αὐτοῖς (dat.pl.masc.of αὐτός, indirect object of λέγει) 16.
Ὃς (nom.sing.masc.of ὅς, indefinite relative clause, with the subjunctive, more probable condition) 65.
ἂν (contingent particle in an indefinite relative clause) 205.
ἀπολύσῃ (3d.per.sing.aor.act.subj.of ἀπολύω, indefinite relative clause, more probable condition) 92.
τὴν (acc.sing.fem.of the article in agreement with γυναῖκα) 9.
γυναῖκα (acc.sing.fem.of γυνή, direct object of ἀπολύσῃ) 103.
αὐτοῦ (gen.sing.masc.of αὐτός, relationship) 16.
καὶ (adjunctive conjunction joining verbs) 14.
γαμήσῃ (3d.per.sing.aor.act.subj.of γαμέω, indefinite relative clause, more probable condition) 512.
ἄλλην (acc.sing.fem.of ἄλλος, direct object of γαμήσῃ) 198.
μοιχᾶται (3d.per.sing.pres.act.ind.of μοιχάω, static) 513.
ἐπ' (preposition with the accusative, to express hostility) 47.
αὐτήν (acc.sing.fem.of αὐτός, hostility) 16.

Translation - "And He said to them, 'Whoever divorces his wife and marries another is committing adultery against her.' "

Comment: *Cf.* comment on Mt.19:9. Luke does not mention the extenuating clause παρεκτὸς λόγου πορνείας. A full discussion is found in our comment on Mt.19:3-12. God's best plan - His original pattern, as established in creation in Eden, is His one man, always for His one woman, even if this marital permanence requires that one party be generous enough to forgive the other party who may be guilty of adultery. The Deut.24:1-3 regulation is a concession based upon the realistic acceptance of the fact that such an attitude of forgiveness on the part of the innocent spouse is entremely rare.

Verse 12 - "And if a woman shall put away her husband, and be married to another, she committeth adultery."

καὶ ἐὰν αὐτὴ ἀπολύσασα τὸν ἄνδρα αὐτῆς γαμήσῃ ἄλλον μοιχᾶται.

καὶ (continuative conjunction) 14.
ἐὰν (conditional particle in a third-class condition) 363.
αὐτὴ (nom.sing.fem.of αὐτός, subject of γαμήσῃ and μοιχᾶται) 16.
ἀπολύσασα (aor.act.part.nom.sing.fem.of ἀπολύω, adverbial, temporal) 92.
τὸν (acc.sing.masc.of the article in agreement with ἄνδρα) 9.
ἄνδρα (acc.sing.masc.of ἀνήρ, direct object of ἀπολύσασα) 63.
αὐτῆς (gen.sing.fem.of αὐτός, relationship) 16.
γαμήσῃ (3d.per.sing.aor.act.subj.of γαμέω, third-class condition) 512.
ἄλλον (acc.sing.masc.of ἄλλος, direct object of γαμήσῃ) 198.
μοιχᾶται (3d.per.sing.pres.act.ind.of μοιχάω, static) 513.

Translation - "Moreover, if, after she has divorced her husband, she marries another, she commits adultery."

Comment: The same proposition is stated in verse 11 in the form of an indefinite relative clause, while in verse 12 we have a third-class condition. *Cf.* comment on Mt.19:3-12.

Christ and Little Children

(Matthew 19:13-15; Mark 10:13-16; Luke 18:15-17)

Mark 10:13 - "And they brought young children to him, that he should touch them: and his disciples rebuked those that brought them."

Καὶ προσέφερον αὐτῷ παιδία ἵνα αὐτῶν ἅψηται, οἱ δὲ μαθηταὶ ἐπετίμησαν αὐτοῖς.

Καὶ (continuative conjunction) 14.
προσέφερον (3d.per.pl.imp.act.ind.of προσφέρω, inceptive) 190.
αὐτῷ (loc.sing.masc.of αὐτός, after πρός in composition and a verb of rest) 16.
παιδία (acc.pl.neut.of παιδίον, direct object of προσέφερον) 174.
ἵνα (conjunction introducing a purpose clause) 114.

αὐτῶν (gen.pl.masc.of αὐτός, description) 16.
ἅψηται (3d.per.sing.aor.mid.subj.of ἅπτω, purpose) 711.
οἱ (nom.pl.masc.of the article in agreement with μαθηταὶ) 9.
δὲ (adversative conjunction) 11.
μαθηταὶ (nom.pl.masc.of μαθητής, subject of ἐπετίμησαν) 421.
ἐπετίμησαν (3d.per.pl.aor.act.ind.of ἐπιτιμάω, ingressive) 757.
αὐτοῖς (loc.pl.masc.of αὐτός, after ἐπί in composition and a verb of emotion) 16.

Translation - "And they began to bring to Him little children in order that He might touch them, but the disciples started to rebuke them."

Comment: Note the inceptive action in the imperfect προσέφερον and the ingressive action in the aorist ἐπετίνησαν. As the parents and friends of the little children began to bring them to Jesus,the disciples were just as quick to rebuke them for it. Note the purpose clause with ἵνα and the subjunctive in ἅψηται. δὲ of course is adversative as the disciples object to the action. They probably thought that the practice was an unwise use of Jesus' time and energy. The action of the disciples is another example of their crass insensitivity to true spiritual values. We cannot judge them too harshly because they had not yet received the Holy Spirit (John 20:22) nor been filled by Him (Acts 2:4). Their action reminds us of Luke 9:49. *Cf.*comment on Mt.19:13 and Luke 18:15.

Verse 14 - "But when Jesus saw it, he was much displeased, and said unto them, Suffer the little children to come unto me, and forbid them not: for of such is the kingdom of God."

ἰδὼν δὲ ὁ Ἰησοῦς ἠγανάκτησεν καὶ εἶπεν αὐτοῖς,Ἄφετε τὰ παιδία ἔρχεσθαι πρός με, μὴ κωλύετε αὐτά, τῶν γὰρ τοιούτων ἐστὶν ἡ βασιλεία τοῦ θεοῦ.

ἰδὼν (aor.act.part.nom.sing.masc.of ὁράω, adverbial, temporal/causal) 144.
δὲ (adversative conjunction) 11.
ὁ (nom.sing.masc.of the article in agreement with Ἰησοῦς) 9.
Ἰησοῦς (nom.sing.masc.of Ἰησοῦς, subject of ἠγανάκτησεν and εἶπεν) 3.
ἠγανάκτησεν (3d.per.sing.aor.act.ind.of ἀγανακτέω, ingressive) 1331.
καὶ (inferential conjunction) 14.
εἶπεν (3d.per.sing.aor.act.ind.of εἶπον, constative) 155.
αὐτοῖς (dat.pl.masc.of αὐτός, indirect object of εἶπεν) 16.
Ἄφετε (2d.per.pl.aor.act.impv.of ἀφίημι, command) 319.
τὰ (acc.pl.neut.of the article in agreement with παιδία) 9.
παιδία (acc.pl.neut.of παιδίον, general reference) 174.
ἔρχεσθαι (pres.mid.inf.of ἔρχομαι, completes ἄφετε) 146.
πρός (preposition with the accusative of extent) 197.
με (acc.sing.masc.of ἐγώ, extent) 123.
μὴ (qualified negative conjunction with the imperative, in a prohibition) 87.
κωλύετε (2d.per.pl.pres.act.impv.of κωλύω, prohibition) 1296.
αὐτά (acc.pl.neut.of αὐτός, direct object of κωλύετε) 16.

τῶν (abl.pl.neut.of the article in agreement with τοιούτων) 9.
γὰρ (causal conjunction) 105.
τοιούτων (abl.pl.neut.of τοιοῦτος, source) 785.
ἐστὶν (3d.per.sing.pres.ind.of εἰμί, static) 86.
ἡ (nom.sing.fem.of the article in agreement with βασιλεία) 9.
βασιλεία (nom.sing.fem.of βασιλεία, subject of ἐστὶν) 253.
τοῦ (gen.sing.masc.of the article in agreement with θεοῦ) 9.
θεοῦ (gen.sing.masc.of θεός, description) 124.

Translation - "But when (because) Jesus saw it He was seized with indignation and He said to them, 'Let the little children come to me. Stop forbidding them. Because it is of people like this that the kingdom of God is composed.' "

Comment: *Cf.* comment on Mt.19:14 and Lk.18:16. The object of the verb Ἄφετε is the infinitive ἔρχεσθαι in its noun use in the accusative case. τὰ παιδία ἔρχεσθαι πρός με is a syntactical unit. It is the object of the verb. Hence παιδία is not the object of ἄφετε, but rather an accusative of general reference, as a part of the infinitive construction. Jesus said, "Step aside and let what is going on continue." What was going on? The little children were coming to Jesus. The English student must seek to look at it like a Greek.

When Jesus said that the kingdom of God would be composed of people like the little children, He was speaking, of course of their attitude - one of humility. Keep in mind the παιδίον means a little child who is seven years old or less. It is the same thought as that found in Mt.18:1-3 and Mt.11:25.

Verse 15 - "Verily I say unto you, Whosoever shall not receive the kingdom of God as a little child, he shall not enter therein."

ἀμὴν λέγω ὑμῖν, ὃς ἂν μὴ δέξηται τὴν βασιλείαν τοῦ θεοῦ ὡς παιδίον, οὐ μὴ εἰσέλθῃ εἰς αὐτήν.

ἀμὴν (explicative) 466.
λέγω (1st.per.sing.pres.act.ind.of λέγω, aoristic) 66.
ὑμῖν (dat.pl.masc.of σύ, indirect object of λέγω) 104.
ὃς (nom.sing.masc.of the relative pronoun ὅς, subject of δέξηται, in an indefinite relative clause, more probable condition) 65.
ἂν (contingent particle, in an indefinite relative clause, more probable condition) 205.
μὴ (qualified negative conjunction with the subjunctive) 87.
δέξηται (3d.per.sing.aor.mid.subj.of δέχομαι, indefinite relative clause, more probable condition) 867.
τὴν (acc.sing.fem.of the article in agreement with βασιλείαν) 9.
βασιλείαν (acc.sing.fem.of βασιλεία, direct object of δέξηται) 253.
τοῦ (gen.sing.masc.of the article in agreement with θεοῦ) 9.
θεοῦ (gen.sing.masc.of θεός, description) 124.
ὡς (adverb introducing a comparative phrase) 128.
παιδίον (nom.sing.neut.of παιδίον, subject of δέχεται, understood) 174.
οὐ (summary negative conjunction with μὴ and the subjunctive) 130.

μὴ (qualified negative conjunction with οὐ and the subjunctive, emphatic negation) 87.
εἰσέλθῃ (3d.per.sing.aor.mid.subj.of εἰσέρχομαι, emphatic negation) 234.
εἰς (preposition with the accusative of extent) 140.
αὐτήν (acc.sing.fem.of αὐτός, extent) 16.

Translation - "Truly, I am telling you that he who does not receive the Kingdom of God as a little child, shall never enter it."

Comment: In ὃς ἂν μὴ δέξηται τὴν βασιλείαν τοῦ θεοῦ we have an indefinite relative clause, like a conditional clause. If ὅτι had been added we would also have indirect discourse. Jesus is not making any specific prediction as to who will or will not receive the Kingdom of God humbly, like a little child, but He is very emphatic in the apodosis. Whoever does not will never enter the Kingdom at all. In οὐ μὴ εἰσέλθῃ, we have emphatic negation.

The natural man (ψυχικός #4112) does not receive the things of the Spirit (1 Cor.2:14) because he thinks himself so sophisticated, with his assumed intellectual superiority, that Christian theology appears to him to be foolish. He feels that he must first think about it, despite the fact that Jesus told Nicodemus not to think about it (John 3:7), because if it is not scientifically valid or philosophically coherent he cannot accept it, despite the fact that neither the philosophical mind nor the scientific spirit is the route to faith (1 Cor.2:9,10,11). The "adult" mind is skeptical about the truth of God's revelation and thus he disdains it (2 Thess.2:10) and becomes so gullible that he falls victim to the deceit of Antichrist. Reception of the Word and the salvation that it brings requires meekness (James 1:21) that cannot be generated in the unregenerated heart. The repentance which is associated with humility is the gift of the Holy Spirit (Acts 11:18). The meek will inherit the earth (Mt.5:5), but only little children and adults who can be as humble as little children have the required meekness. Of such a type as this (Mk.10:14) comes the participants of the Kingdom of God. This is a paradox but it is God's way. Jesus expressed delight that the deepest theological truths are, in the plan of God, hidden from the intellectual giants and revealed only to babes (Mt.11:25). *Cf.* our comment on Mt.18:3,4. Review the material in Luke 11:14-52.

At the risk of being unduly repetitious we insist that we only compromise the claims of our ascended Lord when we seek to "prove" to the unsaved mind, by appeals to his intellect, that he should accept Jesus as Lord. Those who think their way to the foot of the cross do not kneel there like little children. They are more apt to stand there and boast about the fact that they have come to accept the claims of Christ, but only after giving them their closest scrutiny. Any philosophy that the unregenerate mind can review and approve as true is demonstrated by that fact alone to be on a plane no higher than the plane on which the unsaved thinker moves. Such philosophy cannot be the revealed truth of God. God's revelation stands on a higher plane than Euclidean geometry, Cartesian trigonometry and Newtonian or nuclear physics. To think with Einstein is to be proud of one's acumen. To accept Christ calls for humility. It is the child-like humility that saves. Hell will be full of people who "understood" the gospel but were too proud to accept it. Let evangelists who spend their time "explaining" theology take careful note.

Verse 16 - "And he took them up in his arms, put his hands upon them, and blessed them."

καὶ ἐναγκαλισάμενος αὐτὰ κατευλόγει τιθεὶς τὰς χεῖρας ἐπ' αὐτά.

καὶ (continuative conjunction) 14.
ἐναγκαλισάμενος (aor.mid.part.nom.sing.masc.of ἐναγκαλίζομαι, adverbial, temporal) 2350.
αὐτὰ (acc.pl.neut.of αὐτός, direct object of ἐναγκαλισάμενος) 16.

#2634 κατευλόγει (3d.per.sing.imp.act.ind.of κατευλογέω, inceptive).

bless - Mark 10:16.

Meaning: A combination of κατά (#98) and εὐλογέω (#1120). Hence, to call down blessings upon someone. With reference to Jesus and the children - Mark 10:16.

τιθεὶς (pres.act.part.nom.sing.masc.of τίθημι, adverbial, temporal) 455.
τὰς (acc.pl.fem.of the article in agreement with χεῖρας) 9.
χεῖρας (acc.pl.fem.of χείρ, direct object of τιθεὶς) 308.
ἐπ' (preposition with the accusative of place) 47.
αὐτά (acc.pl.neut.of αὐτός, place) 16.

Translation - "And He took them into His arms and laid His hands upon them and blessed them."

Comment: Jesus and the children had a real love fest. What a relief it must have been to our Lord to be free,for a moment from the boorish Pharisees. This picture reveals in a small way the love which Jesus felt for the little children. It is shared by all true Christians. It is impossible to imagine or describe the delight of the children as they crowded about Him, looked into His face, held His hands and listened with wide-eyed rapture to what He had to say. *Cf.* comment on Mt.19:13-15 and Luke 18;15-17 which follows.

Luke 18:15 - "And they brought unto him also infants, that he would touch them: but when his disciples saw it, they rebuked them."

Προσέφερον δὲ αὐτῷ καὶ τὰ βρέφη ἵνα αὐτῶν ἅπτηται, ἰδόντες δὲ οἱ μαθηταὶ ἐπετίμων αὐτοῖς.

Προσέφερον (3d.per.pl.imp.act.ind.of προσφέρω, inceptive) 190.
δὲ (continuative conjunction) 11.
αὐτῷ (loc.sing.masc.of αὐτός, after πρός in composition with a verb of rest) 16.

καὶ (adjunctive conjunction) 14.
τὰ (acc.pl.neut.of the article in agreement with *βρέφη*) 9.
βρέφη (acc.pl.neut.of *βρέφος*, direct object of *προσέφερον*) 1821.
ἵνα (conjunction introducing a purpose clause) 114.
αὐτῶν (gen.pl.masc.of *αὐτός*, description) 16.
ἅπτηται (3d.per.sing.pres.mid.subj.of *ἅπτω*, purpose) 711.
ἰδόντες (aor.act.part.nom.pl.masc.of *ὁράω*, adverbial, temporal/causal) 144.
δὲ (adversative conjunction) 11.
οἱ (nom.pl.masc.of the article in agreement with *μαθηταὶ*) 9.
μαθηταὶ (nom.pl.masc.of *μαθητής*, subject of *ἐπετίμων*) 421.
ἐπετίμων (3d.per.pl.imp.act.ind.of *ἐπιτιμάω*, inceptive) 757.
αὐτοῖς (loc.pl.masc.of *αὐτός*, after *ἐπί* in composition, with a verb of emotion) 16.

Translation - "And they began to bring to Him the babies in order that He might touch them. But when (because) the disciples saw it they began to rebuke them."

Comment: *Cf.* comment on Mt.19:13 and Mk.10:13. Note that Mark and Luke uses the imperfect *προσέφερον* while Matthew uses the aorist *προσηνέχθησαν*. Luke says that babies were brought (*τὰ βρέφη*) instead of little children (*παιδία*). Matthew and Mark use the aorist *ἐπετίμησαν* while Luke has the imperfect *ἐπετίμων*. These "differences" of course are not difficult to reconcile. A baby (*βρέφος*) is also a small child (*παιδίον*). The aorist can be taken in its ingressive sense (with the emphasis upon the beginning of the action) in which case it is no different from the inceptive imperfect. Mark and Luke telescope Matthew's *τὰς χεῖρας ἐπιθῇ αὐτοῖς καὶ προσεύξηται* to *αὐτῶν ἅψηται* for Mark and *ἅπτηται* for Luke. Verbal inspiration means that the Holy Spirit allowed the writers to use their own words, subject only to the limitation that He did not permit them to use words which were objectionable to Him. Inspired words need not be exact words in the dictation sense. Inspired words are those words which clearly convey to the reader the *total* thought which the Holy Spirit wished to convey. In cases where too much freedom for the writers would result in the wrong impression being conveyed to the exegete who understands the nuances of the *κοινή* Greek and views it in *zeitgeist*, then the Holy Spirit would dictate the precise formulation for the writer, in terms of diction, grammar and syntax. Thus we speak of divine, inerrant, plenary inspiration. The total message comes through with clarity and precision. In the battle over the Bible, those who argue for a dictation theory of inspiration are certain to lose, because they are contending for a position that simply does not fit the facts.

There is no question that some people brought their children, ranging in age from babes in arms to little boys and girls up to seven years, to Jesus for His blessing, and that when (and because) the disciples saw what was happening they began to offer arguments that such should not be done. That is all that the passage intends to convey. Any honest exegete can derive this sense from the passages, whether he reads what was written by Matthew, Mark or Luke.

This philosophy of inspiration applies in all cases where the synoptic writers used varying diction, grammar and syntax to convey their message. If the intended exegetical thrust of the passage were ever in doubt, due to synoptic differences in style, then we should be compelled to doubt that the New Testament is an unerring guide to the truth which the Holy Spirit wishes to convey. But the supposed contradictions exist only in the minds of those who do not know their Greek and/or those who have forgotten Peter's warning that no scripture is of its own interpretation (2 Pet.1:20). As we read the Greek properly and allow every scripture to crossfertilize every other scripture the Word of God comes through with clarity and precision.

Verse 16 - "But Jesus called them unto Him, and said, Suffer little children to come unto me, and forbid them not: for of such is the kingdom of God."

ὁ δὲ Ἰησοῦς προσεκαλέσατο αὐτὰ λέγων, Ἄφετε τὰ παιδία ἔρχεσθαι πρός με καὶ μὴ κωλύετε αὐτά, τῶν γὰρ τοιούτων ἐστὶν ἡ βασιλεία τοῦ θεοῦ.

ὁ (nom.sing.masc.of the article in agreement with Ἰησοῦς) 9.
δὲ (adversative conjunction) 11.
Ἰησοῦς (nom.sing.masc.of Ἰησοῦς, subject of προσεκαλέσατο) 3.
προσεκαλέσατο (3d.per.sing.aor.mid.ind.of προσκαλέω, constative) 842.
αὐτὰ (acc.pl.neut.of αὐτός, direct object of προσεκαλέσατο) 16.
λέγων (pres.act.part.nom.sing.masc.of λέγω, adverbial, temporal) 66.
Ἄφετε (2d.per.pl.aor.act.impv.of ἀφίημι, command) 319.
τὰ (acc.pl.neut.of the article in agreement with παιδία) 9.
παιδία (acc.pl.neut.of παιδίον, general reference) 174.
ἔρχεσθαι (pres.mid.inf.of ἔρχομαι, noun use, accusative case, direct object of ἄφετε) 146.
πρός (preposition with the accusative of extent) 197/
με (acc.sing.masc.of ἐγώ extent) 123.
καὶ (adjunctive conjunction joining verbs) 14.
μὴ (qualified negative conjunction with the imperative) 87.
κωλύετε (2d.per.pl.pres.act.impv.of κωλύω, prohibition) 1296.
αὐτά (acc.pl.neut.of αὐτός, direct object of κωλύετε) 16.
τῶν (abl.pl.neut.of the article in agreement with τοιούτων) 9.
γὰρ (causal conjunction) 105.
τοιούτων (abl.pl.neut.of τοιοῦτος, source) 785.
ἐστὶν (3d.per.sing.pres.ind.of εἰμί, static) 86.
ἡ (nom.sing.fem.of the article in agreement with βασιλεία) 9.
βασιλεία (nom.sing.fem.of βασιλεία, subject of ἐστὶν) 253.
τοῦ (gen.sing.masc.of the article in agreement with θεοῦ) 9.
θεοῦ (gen.sing.masc.of θεός, description) 124.

Translation - "But Jesus called them to Him as He said, 'Allow the little children to come to me, and do not forbid them, because the kingdom of God is made up of such as these."

Comment: *Cf.* comment on Mt.19:14 and Mk.10:14.

Verse 17 - "Verily I say unto you, Whosoever shall not receive the kingdom of

God as a little child shall in no wise enter therein."

ἀμὴν λέγω ὑμῖν, ὃς ἂν μὴ δέξηται τὴν βασιλείαν τοῦ θεοῦ ὡς παιδίον, οὐ μὴ εἰσέλθῃ εἰς αὐτήν.

ἀμὴν (explicative) 466.
λέγω (1st.per.sing.pres.act.ind.of *λέγω*, aoristic) 66.
ὑμῖν (dat.pl.masc.of *σύ*, indirect object of *λέγω*) 104.
ὃς (nom.sing.masc.of *ὅς*, subject of *δέξηται*, in a relative clause, more probable condition) 65.
ἂν (contingent particle in a relative clause, more probable condition) 205.
μὴ (qualified negative conjunction with the subjunctive) 87.
δέξηται (3d.per.sing.aor.mid.subj.of *δέχομαι*, relative clause, more probable condition) 867.
τὴν (acc.sing.fem.of the article in agreement with *βασιλείαν*) 9.
βασιλείαν (acc.sing.fem.of *βασιλεία*, direct object of *δέξηται*) 253.
τοῦ (gen.sing.masc.of the article in agreement with *θεοῦ*) 9.
θεοῦ (gen.sing.masc.of *θεός*, description) 124.
ὡς (comparative adverb) 128.
παιδίον (nom.sing.neut.of *παιδίον*, subject of *δέχεται*, understood) 174.
οὐ (summary negative conjunction with *μὴ*, emphatic negation) 130.
μὴ (qualified negative conjunction with *οὐ* and the subjunctive, emphatic negation) 87.
εἰσέλθῃ (3d.per.sing.aor.mid.subj.of *εἰσέρχομαι*, emphatic negation) 234.

εἰς (preposition with the accusative of extent) 140.
αὐτήν (acc.sing.fem.of *αὐτός*, extent) 16.

Translation - "Truly, I am telling you, Whoever does not receive the Kingdom of God as a little child does, will never enter it."

Comment: *Cf.* comment on Mt.18:3; Mk.10:17.

The Rich Young Ruler and Teaching on Riches

(Matthew 19:16 - 20:16; Mark 10:17-31; Luke 18:18-30)

Luke 18:18 - "And a certain ruler asked him, saying, Good Master, what shall I do to inherit eternal life?"

Καὶ ἐπηρώτησέν τις αὐτὸν ἄρχων λέγων, Διδάσκαλε ἀγαθέ, τί ποιήσας ζωὴν αἰώνιον κληρονομήσω;

Καὶ (continuative conjunction) 14.
ἐπηρώτησέν (3d.per.sing.aor.act.ind.of *ἐπερωτάω*, constative) 973.
τις (nom.sing.masc.of tiw, indefinite relative pronoun, in agreement with *ἄρχων*) 486.
αὐτὸν (acc.sing.masc.of *αὐτός*, direct object of *ἐπηρώτησέν*) 16.

ἄρχων (nom.sing.masc.of ἄρχων, subject of ἐπηρώτησέν) 816.
λέγων (pres.act.part.nom.sing.masc.of λέγω, adverbial, modal) 66.
Διδάσκαλε (voc.sing.masc.of διδάσκαλος, address) 742.
ἀγαθέ (voc.sing.masc.of ἀγαθός, in agreement with διδάσκαλε) 547.
τί (acc.sing.neut.of τῖς, interrogative pronoun, direct object of ποιήσας) 281.
ποιήσας (aor.act.part.nom.sing.masc.of ποιέω, adverbial, causal) 127.
ζωὴν (acc.sing.fem.of ζωή, direct object of κληρονομήσω) 668.
αἰώνιον (acc.sing.fem.of αἰώνιος, in agreement with ζωὴν) 1255.
κληρονομήσω (1st.per.sing.fut.act.ind.of κληρονομέω, deliberative future) 426.

Translation - "And some ruler asked Him, saying, 'Good Teacher, what do I have to do to inherit eternal life?'"

Comment: *Cf.* comment on Mt.19:16 and Mk.10:17. The indefinite pronoun, adjoined to ἄρχων indicates that the identity of the man is not important. His question, literally translated is, "Because I have done what, will I inherit eternal life?" Thus he reveals that he supposes that eternal life is something to be gained in exchange for the accomplishment of something good. He little realized until Jesus had answered his question that he needed a revision of his system of values.

In Acts 16:30 the Philippian jailor, a Gentile, asked τί με δεῖ ποιεῖν ἵνα σωθῶ, but he was frightened by an earthquake and was less interested in what good he had done in the past than what remained for him to do in the future. The self-righteous ruler in our story had his mind on a past record of what he considered to be an acceptable observance of the Mosaic code. In modern parlance we say, "What do you have to do to . . . κ.τ.λ.?" or "What else do I have to do? Have I not done enough?" It is the statement of one who is satisfied with his past performance and confident of his ability to continue to behave properly. Acts 16:30 is the frantic question of a sinner who is deeply convinced that he is lost and who has no idea what he can do about it.

Jesus delayed His answer to the man's question by asking him another in

Verse 19 - "And Jesus said unto him, Why callest thou me good? None is good, save one, that is God."

εἶπεν δὲ αὐτῷ ὁ Ἰησοῦς, Τί με λέγεις ἀγαθόν; οὐδεὶς ἀγαθὸς εἰ μὴ εἷς ὁ θεός.

εἶπεν (3d.per.sing.aor.act.ind.of εἶπον, constative) 166.
δὲ (adversative conjunction) 11.
αὐτῷ (dat.sing.masc.of αὐτός, indirect object of εἶπεν) 16.
ὁ (nom.sing.masc.of the article in agreement with Ἰησοῦς) 9.
Ἰησοῦς (nom.sing.masc.of Ἰησοῦς, subject of εἶπεν) 3.
Τί (acc.sing.neut.of τίς, interoggative pronoun, with διά understood) 281.
με (acc.sing.masc.of ἐγώ, direct object of λέγεις) 123.
λέγεις (2d.per.sing.pres.act.ind.of λέγω, direct question) 66.
ἀγαθόν (acc.sing.masc.of ἀγαθός, predicate adjective, to agree with με) 547.
οὐδεὶς (nom.sing.masc.of οὐδείς, subject of ἐστίν, understood) 446.

ἀγαθὸς (nom.sing.masc.of ἀγαθός, predicate adjective, in agreement with οὐδεὶς) 547.
εἰ (conditional particle in an elliptical first-class condition) 337.
μὴ (qualified negative conjunction in a first-class condition) 87.
εἷς (nom.sing.masc.of εἷς, predicate nominative) 469.
ὁ (nom.sing.masc.of the article in agreement with θεός) 9.
θεός (nom.sing.masc.of θεός, subject of ἐστιν understood) 124.

Translation - "But Jesus said to him, 'Why are you calling me good? Not one is good unless he is God."

Comment: *Cf.* comment on Mt.19:17 and Mk.10:18. δὲ is adversative as Jesus prepares to unmask the man with a subtle argument. The ruler had seemed to imply: "You are a good teacher. I also am good." He addressed a good teacher and implied that he wanted to be a good student. What did he need to do that he had not already done? Thus he damned Jesus with faint praise. If he had called Jesus the Son of God, it would have been incumbent upon him to accept Him as his Messiah. Unwilling to credit Jesus with deity, he is willing at least to put Jesus on the same level with himself.

Our Lord decided to ask him for a definition of terms. Why call Jesus good, unless he had a perverted conception of goodness. How can one call any man good? If the man is good is he not also God? So, if the man really believed that Jesus was good he should have called Him God. If Jesus is not God then He is only a man like the rich young ruler. And if that is true He is not good. So why did the man call Him good? In order that he also could call himself good. Thus Jesus was saying, "Either worship me as God if you really think that I am good, or keep your compliments to yourself, since they are obviously insincere."

The elliptical conditional sentence means, "If God is not the One who is good, then nobody is good."

Having made this point, Jesus then proceded to suggest that the man could answer his own question in

Verse 20 - "Thou knowest the commandments; Do not commit adultery, Do not kill, Do not steal, Do not bear false witness, Honour thy father and thy mother."

τὰς ἐντολὰς οἶδας, Μὴ μοιχεύσῃς, Μὴ φονεύσῃς, Μὴ κλέψῃς, Μὴ ψευδομαρτυρήσῃς, Τίμα τὸν πατέρα σου καὶ τὴν μητέρα.

τὰς (acc.pl.fem.of the article in agreement with ἐντολὰς) 9.
ἐντολὰς (acc.pl.fem.of ἐντολή, direct object of οἶδας) 472.
οἶδας (2d.per.sing.pres.ind.of ὁράω, aoristic) 144.
Μὴ (qualified negative conjunction with the subjunctive in a prohibition) 87.
μοιχεύσῃς (2d.per.sing.aor.act.subj.of μοιχεύω, prohibition) 498.
Μὴ (qualified negative conjunction with the subjunctive in a prohibition) 87.
φονεύσῃς (2d.per.sing.aor.act.subj.of φονεύω, prohibition) 476.
Μὴ (qualified negative conjunction with the subjunctive in a prohibition) 87.
κλέψῃς (2d.per.sing.aor.act.subj.of κλέπτω, prohibition) 597.

Μὴ (qualified negative conjunction with the subjunctive in a prohibition) 87.
ψευδομαρτυρήσης (2d.per.sing.aor.act.subj.of ψευδομαρτυρέω, prohibition) 1299.
Τίμα (2d.per.sing.pres.act.impv.of τιμάω, command) 1142.
τὸν (acc.sing.masc.of the article in agreement with πατέρα) 9.
πατέρα (acc.sing.masc.of πατήρ, direct object of τίμα) 238.
σου (gen.sing.masc.of σύ, relationship) 104.
καὶ (adjunctive conjunction joining nouns) 14.
τὴν (acc.sing.fem.of the article in agreement with μητέρα) 9.
μητέρα (acc.sing.fem.of μήτηρ, direct object of τίμα) 76.

Translation - "You know the commandments: never commit adultery, never kill, never steal, never bear false witness, always honor your father and mother."

Comment: The prohibitions are expressed with μή and the aorist subjunctive and the positive commandment with the present imperative. Note that Mt.19:18 uses οὐ and the future indicative. Robertson says, "It seems clear that originally both in Sanskrit and Greek prohibition was expressed only by the subjunctive. Hence the growth of the imperative never finally displaced it. In particular the aorist subjunctive (a late form anyhow). . . The aorist subjunctive is of course punctiliar and the present imperative linear. Inasmuch as the prohibition is future, the aorist subjunctive would naturally be ingressive." (Robertson, *Grammar,* 851). Hence our translation - "Never commit adultery (do not kill once, do not begin to steal, do not tell the first lie) . . . " all of which translations render the ingressive action, while the present imperative says, "Go on honoring (always honor) your father and mother."

The rich ruler conducted a quick inventory of his life and felt confident that he was in a strong position as he boasted in

Verse 21 - "And he said, All these have I kept from my youth up."

ὁ δὲ εἶπεν, Ταῦτα πάντα ἐφύλαξα ἐκ νεότητος.

ὁ (nom.sing.masc.of the article subject of εἶπεν) 9.
δὲ (continuative conjunction) 11.
εἶπεν (3d.per.sing.aor.act.ind.of εἶπον, constative) 155.
Ταῦτα (acc.pl.neut.of οὗτος, direct object of ἐφύλαξα) 93.
πάντα (acc.pl.neut.of πᾶς, in agreement with ταῦτα) 67.
ἐφύλαξα (1st.per.sing.aor.act.ind.of φυλάσσω, culminative) 1301.
ἐκ (preposition with the ablative of time separation) 19.

#2635 νεότητος (abl.sing.fem.of νεότης, time separation).

youth - Mk.10:20; Lk.18:21; Acts 26:4; 1 Tim.4:12.

Meaning: Cf. νεόφυτος (#4736), νέος (#809), νεοσσός (#1892), νεωτερικός (#4831) and νεώτερος (#2543). Hence, youth. The early chronological period of life. With ἐκ and the ablative of time separation - Mk.10:20; Lk.18:21; Acts 26:4.

In a genitive of description in 1 Tim.4:12, *i.e.* "Let no man view the inexperience of your youth with contempt."

Translation - "And he said, 'All these commandments I have observed since I was a child.' "

Comment: *Cf.* comment on Mt.19:20; Mk.10:20. Apparently the man was telling the truth insofar as he understood it. Mark 10:21 says that Jesus loved him. Matthew adds that he went on to ask, τί ἔτι ὑστερῶ - "What yet do I lack?" Here is a sincere young man who has tried hard and succeeded in keeping the fifth, sixth, seventh, eighth and ninth commandments. Note that he did not say that he had kept the tenth, or the first four, though perhaps he thought that he had kept them all except the tenth. Review again our comments on Mt.19:18.

Verse 22 - "Now when Jesus heard these things, he said unto him, Yet lackest thou one thing: sell all that thou hast, and distribute unto the poor, and thou shalt have treasure in heaven: and come, follow me."

ἀκούσας δὲ ὁ Ἰησοῦς εἶπεν αὐτῷ Ἔτι ἕν σοι λείπει. πάντα ὅσα ἔχεις πώλησον καὶ διάδος πτωχοῖς, καὶ ἕξεις θησαυρὸν ἐν (τοῖς) οὐρανοῖς, καὶ δεῦρο ἀκολούθει μοι.

ἀκούσας (aor.act.part.nom.sing.masc.of ἀκούω, adverbial, temporal/causal) 148.
δὲ (continuative conjunction) 11.
ὁ (nom.sing.masc.of the article in agreement with Ἰησοῦς) 9.
Ἰησοῦς (nom.sing.masc.of Ἰησοῦς, subject of εἶπεν) 3.
εἶπεν (3d.per.sing.aor.act.ind.of εἶπον, constative) 155.
αὐτῷ (dat.sing.masc.of αὐτός, indirect object of εἶπεν) 16.
Ἔτι (adverbial) 448.
ἕν (nom.sing.neut.of εἷς, subject of λείπει) 469.
σοι (dat.sing.masc.of σύ, personal interest) 104.

#2636 λείπει (3d.per.sing.pres.act.ind.of λείπω, aoristic).

be wanting - Titus 1:5; 3:13.
be destitute - James 2:15.
lack - Luke 18:22; James 1:5.
want - James 1:4.

Meaning: To lack; to be without; fail to have. To be in a state of being unfinished - Titus 1:5; to be imperfectly equipped as a Christian in terms of spiritual qualities - James 1:4; to lack wisdom - James 1:5; to lack food - James 2:15; generally, to lack money, food, etc., - Titus 3:13. To have failed to keep all of the law of God - Luke 18:22.

πάντα (acc.pl.neut.of πᾶς, direct object of πώλησον) 67.
ὅσα (acc.pl.neut.of ὅσος, direct object of ἔχεις) 660.
ἔχεις (2d.per.pl.pres.act.ind.of ἔχω, aoristic) 82.

πώλησον (2d.per.sing.aor.act.impv.of *πωλέω*, command) 892.
καὶ (adjunctive conjunction joining verbs) 14.
διάδος (2d.per.sing.2d.aor.act.impv.of *διαδίδωμι*, command) 2279.
πτωχοῖς (dat.pl.masc.of *πτωχός*, indirect object of *διάδος*) 423.
καὶ (continuative conjunction) 14.
ἕξεις (2d.per.sing.fut.act.ind.of *ἔχω*, predictive) 82.
θησαυρὸν (acc.sing.masc.of *θησαυρός*, direct object of *ἕξεις*) 189.
ἐν (preposition with the locative of place where) 80.
(*τοῖς*) (loc.pl.masc.of the article in agreement with *οὐρανοῖς*) 9.
οὐρανοῖς (loc.pl.masc.of *οὐρανός*,place where) 254.
καὶ (continuative conjunction) 14.
δεῦρο (adverbial interjection with the imperative) 1304.
ἀκολούθει (2d.per.sing.pres.act.impv.of *ἀκολουθέω*, command) 394.
μοι (dat.sing.masc.of *ἐγώ*, personal advantage) 123.

Translation - "And when Jesus heard it He said to him, 'You still lack one thing: sell everything that you have and distribute the money among the poor, and you will have treasure in the heavens, and come back and always follow me.' "

Comment: Jesus reacted favorably to the man's statement when He noted its sincerity and honesty. He loved him (Mk.10:21). Note that Jesus did not challenge the statement of his record. He was not an adulterer, killer, thief or liar and he had always taken care of his parents. But he transgressed the tenth commandment. Like the Pharisee in Luke 16:14 he was covetous. Here is a sin of the mind and heart, not one of the body or the tongue.

Saul of Tarsus had the same experience. It was only when the law of God said, "Thou shalt not covet" that he realized that he was guilty of all of the other commandments (Rom.7:7-11).

There is a sure cure for covetousness. "Sell all that you have and spread the money around among the poor." *Cf.*#2279. This calls for such a thorough distribution that each poor man will have a little and the rich man will have nothing left for himself. Thus the former rich man takes his place among the poor and thus he learns by experience to identify with them. That is where Jesus and the disciples stood (vs.28). This was Jesus' experience on the cross, when He sensed the total loneliness of being forsaken by God (Mt.27:46). Though He was rich, for our sakes He became poor in order that, through His poverty, we might be rich (2 Cor.8:9). This kind of sacrifice brings great reward - not upon the earth, but in the heavens. Now that the man is as poor as everyone else he should always follow Jesus (present imperative in *ἀκολούθει*).

Note here Jesus' emphasis, not upon the theological gospel of the first four commandments (which, of course is important), but upon the social gospel of commandments five through nine, which are the fruit in society of which the first four are the root in heaven. The man got Jesus' point. His reaction indicates that he clearly understood it.

Verse 23 - "And when he heard this, he was very sorrowful: for he was very rich."

ὁ δὲ ἀκούσας ταῦτα περίλυπος ἐγενήθη, ἦν γὰρ πλούσιος σφόδρα.

ὁ (nom.sing.masc.of the article, subject of *ἐγενήθη*) 9.
δὲ (adversative conjunction) 11.
ἀκούσας (aor.act.part.nom.sing.masc.of *ἀκούω*, adverbial, temporal/causal) 148.
ταῦτα (acc.pl.neut.of *οὗτος*, direct object of *ἀκούσας*) 93.
περίλυπος (nom.sing.masc.of *περίλυπος*, predicate adjective) 1586.
ἐγενήθη (3d.per.sing.aor.ind.of *γίνομαι*, ingressive) 113.
ἦν (3d.per.sing.imp.ind.of *εἰμί*, progressive description) 86.
γὰρ (causal conjunction) 105.
πλούσιος (nom.sing.masc.of *πλούσιος*, predicate adjective) 1306.
σφόδρα (adverbial, modifying *πλούσιος*) 185.

Translation - "But when (because) he heard these things he became grief stricken, because he was very rich."

Comment: The impact of Jesus' statement upon the rich man was devastating. Note the ingressive aorist in *ἐγενήθη*. *Cf.*#1586. He was surrounded (overcome) with sorrow. The causal clause with *γὰρ* tells us why. The admonition to a pauper to sell all that he possessed and divide the money with other poor people would mean little. But this man was very rich. *Cf.* Mt.19;22; Mk.10:22.

Verse 24 - "And when Jesus saw that he was very sorrowful, he said, How hardly shall they that have riches enter into the kingdom of God."

Ἰδὼν δὲ αὐτὸν ὁ Ἰησοῦς (περίλυπον γενόμενον) εἶπεν, Πῶς δυσκόλως οἱ τὰ χρήματα ἔχοντες εἰς τὴν βασιλείαν τοῦ θεοῦ εἰσπορεύονται.

Ἰδὼν (aor.act.part.nom.sing.masc.of *ὁράω*, adverbial, temporal) 144.
δὲ (continuative conjunction) 11.
αὐτὸν (acc.sing.masc.of *αὐτός*, direct object of *Ἰδὼν*) 16.
ὁ (nom.sing.masc.of the article in agreement with *Ἰησοῦς*) 9.
Ἰησοῦς (nom.sing.masc.of *Ἰησοῦς*, subject of *εἶπεν*) 3.
(*περίλυπον* (acc.sing.masc.of *περίλυπος*,predicate adjective) 1586.
γενόμενον (2d.aor.part.acc.sing.masc.of *γίνομαι*, adverbial, circumstantial) 113.
εἶπεν (3d.per.sing.aor.act.ind.of *εἶπον*, constative) 155.
Πῶς (exclamatory conjunction) 627.
δυσκόλως (adverbial) 1307.
οἱ (nom.pl.masc.of the article in agreement with *ἔχοντες*) 9.
τὰ (acc.pl.neut.of the article in agreement with *χρήματα*) 9.

#2637 *χρήματα* (acc.pl.neut.of *χρῆμα*, direct object of *ἔχοντες*).

money - Acts 4:37; 8:18,20; 24:26.
riches - Mark 10:23; Luke 18:24.

Meaning: Cf.χράω (#2447). Hence, anything useful. In the New Testament anything useful in economic monetary exchange. Money - the price of a farm - Acts 4:37; the sorcerer's bribe - Acts 8:18,20; Felix's bribe - Acts 24:26; the rich man's wealth - Mk.10:23; Lk.18:24.

ἔχοντες (pres.act.part.nom.pl.masc.of *ἔχω*, substantival, subject of *εἰσπορεύονται*) 82.
εἰς (preposition with the accusative of extent) 140.
τὴν (acc.sing.fem.of the article in agreement with *βασιλείαν*) 9.
βασιλείαν (acc.sing.fem.of *βασιλεία*, extent) 253.
τοῦ (gen.sing.masc.of the article in agreement with *θεοῦ*) 9.
θεοῦ (gen.sing.masc.of *θεός*, description) 124.
εἰσπορεύονται (3d.per.pl.pres.mid.ind.of *εἰσπορεύομαι*, static) 1161.

Translation - "And when Jesus saw that he had become sad, He said, 'With what difficulty do those who have money enter into the Kingdom of God!' "

Comment: Jesus' reaction to the great sorrow of the rich man motivated His comment. *Cf.*#2637. Jesus, of course, referred to those who have so much money that it becomes for them a means to an end. He did not mean to teach that a pauper would experience difficulty in deciding for Christ, to the same extent as would one who had great wealth. The word should really be "wealth" or "capital accumulation", since in modern economics wealth is not necessarily synonymous with money. But the word is *χρῆμα*, which in New Testament usage means "money."

The materialist views everything in the short run. The idea that there is a life of great blessing beyond this temporal existence is grasped only by those who are naive enough to accept the revelation of the Word of God. Since this is a world of creature comforts which are to be had in an exchange market of non-zero prices, and, since the unsaved man is not certain whether there is or is not a Kingdom of God in eternity, he finds it difficult to surrender the wealth which brings creature comforts now on a certain basis, for the promise of eternal life in glory, which, at best, is offered on an uncertain basis. This philosophy, of course, is from the point of view of the unsaved man who sees no certitude in the promises of God. A pauper finds it easier to follow Christ, since he has nothing of material value to distribute anyway before he takes up his cross. He has nothing to lose in this world and everything to gain in the next. The rich man is certain to lose that which he knows is his to enjoy and he is uncertain as to whether or not there will be an eternal gain. The choice for the pauper is between this world, in which he has nothing anyway, and wealth in the next, if indeed there is another world, and if, in fact, he is fortunate to enter into it.

Verse 25 - "For it is easier for a camel to go through a needle's eye, than for a rich man to enter into the kingdom of God."

εὐκοπώτερον γάρ ἐστιν κάμηλον διὰ τρήματος βελόνης διελθεῖν ἢ πλούσιον εἰς τὴν βασιλείαν τοῦ θεοῦ εἰσελθεῖν.

εὐκοπώτερον (acc.sing.neut.of *εὐκοπώτερος*, predicate adjective) 783.
γάρ (inferential conjunction) 105.

ἐστιν (3d.per.sing.pres.ind.of εἰμί, static) 86.
κάμηλον (acc.sing.masc.of κάμηλος, general reference) 262.
διὰ (preposition with the genitive, physically through) 118.
τρήματος (gen.sing.neut.of τρῆμα, place description) 1308.

#2638 βελόνης (gen.sing.fem.of βελόνη, description).

needle - Luke 18:25.

*Meaning: Cf.*βέλος (#4536). "This medical term for the needle used in surgical operations (see Hobart, *Medical Language of St. Luke,* p.61) is substituted by Luke for ῥαφίς in Lk.18:25, but does not occur elsewhere in Bibl.Grk. See for its more general use the magic papyrus P Lond 121442 (iii/A.D.) (I.p.98) χαλκῷ βελόνῃ ἀκεφάλῳ. MGR βελόνι. (Moulton & Milligan, *The Vocabulary of the Greek Testament*, 108).

διελθεῖν (2d.aor.infinitive of διέρχομαι, noun use, subject of ἐστιν) 1017.
ἤ (disjunctive particle) 465.
πλούσιον (acc.sing.masc.of πλούσιος, general reference) 1306.
εἰς (preposition with the accusative of extent) 140.
τὴν (acc.sing.fem.of the article in agreement with βασιλείαν) 9.
βασιλείαν (acc.sing.fem.of βασιλεία, extent) 253.
τοῦ (gen.sing.masc.of the article in agreement with θεοῦ) 9.
θεοῦ (gen.sing.masc.of θεός, description) 124.
εἰσελθεῖν (aor.infinitive of εἰσέρχομαι, noun use, subject of ἐστιν understood) 234.

Translation - "Because a camel's passage through the eye of a needle is easier than a rich man's entrance into the Kingdom of God."

Comment: We have translated in order to show the precise syntactical structure of the verse. The subject of ἐστιν is the infinitive διελθεῖν, in its noun use, with κάμηλον adjoined to it as an accusative of general reference. The predicate adjective is εὐκοπώτερον, accusative also in agreement with κάμηλον. Similarly the rest of the sentence, following ἤ has the infinitive εἰσελθεῖν used in the same way as the subject of ἐστιν understood, with πλούσιον, the accusative of general reference. English students, when I was a school boy were taught that an infinitive could have a subject and that its subject was in the objective case. Greek students know better. Since the infinitive is not a finite verb (why do we call it an *infinitive?*) it cannot be limited by a subject. It is a verbal noun and when its noun use is paramount, as in this passage, it is the subject of some verb, in this case ἐστιν. Its adjuncts are in the accusative case because of general reference.

The extreme example of verse 25 indicates how difficult it is, indeed humanly impossible, for a rich man to be saved. There has been much idle speculation about whether Jesus intended us to take this illustration literally. Some have supposed that κάμηλος is a copyist's error for κάμιλος, a cable. Others have supposed that "the needle's eye" refers to the gate of an Oriental house, through which a camel could pass if he were stripped of his load and made to creep through on all fours. All such attempts to explain away clear Greek are puerile, since Jesus says in verse 27 that such is impossible for man. The thrust of the passage is that salvation is impossible for man to attain. Only God can do that which is humanly impossible. So, to distort the passage to mean something humanly difficult but not impossible is the destroy the point of the entire passage. It is manifestly impossible for a literal camel, not a cable or a rope, but a dromedary to pass through the perforation of a needle. This is an example of Oriental hyperbole. Yet Jesus says that even that is easier than for a rich man to enter into the kingdom of God. In other words that also is impossible, but only when the attempt is made by the rich man without the limitless resources of the grace of God.

Verse 26 - "And they that heard it said, Who then can be saved?"

εἶπαν δὲ οἱ ἀκούσαντες, Καὶ *τίς δύναται σωθῆναι;*

εἶπαν (3d.per.pl.aor.act.ind.of *εἶπον*, constative) 155.
δὲ (continuative conjunction) 11.
οἱ (nom.pl.masc.of the article in agreement with *ἀκούσαντες*) 9.
ἀκούσαντες (aor.act.part.nom.pl.masc.of *ἀκούω*, substantival, subject of *εἶπαν*) 148.
Καὶ (inferential conjunction) 14.
τίς (nom.sing.masc.of *τίς*, interrogative pronoun, subject of *δύναται*, direct question) 281.
δύναται (3d.per.sing.pres.ind.of *δύναμαι*, static) 289.
σωθῆναι (aor.pass.inf.of *σώζω*, completes *δύναται*) 109.

Translation - "And those who heard said, 'Who then can be saved?' "

Comment: In commenting upon verse 24 we took the liberty to interpret Χ*ρήματα* as "much money" or "wealth" in the layman's sense, because Jesus was talking about the rich ruler who indeed was very wealthy. But it is important to note that the adjective "much" (*πολύς* #228) is not present and that Jesus said, "It is difficult for the one who has money (in any amount) to enter the Kingdom of God." His listeners interpreted His statement in this literal sense by asking, "Who, then can be saved?" For everyone has *some* money.

Money tends to make our lot in the temporal world endurable, while surrendering it in favor of Christ calls for the kind of faith which the natural man cannot produce from his own resources. It is the principle of Luke 16;13 again. The Christian holds cash so that it can serve him. The unbeliever holds money so that he can serve it. To shift one's allegiance away from this material world and the money which is an indispensable part of it, to the spiritual and eternal realm, where gold is used only as paving material (Rev.21:21), is an impossible achievement for an unregenerate man. The pauper, with scarcely a cent, yet longs for the day when he can command millions in this world. To say, in truth, "I care not a whit for gold, except as it is able to give to me a minimal subsistence in this world, which is all I want, since my citizenship is in heaven (Phil.3:20), where I have a building, a house not made with hands, eternal in the heavens (2 Cor.5:1)" is possible only for one who is the recipient of the manifold grace of the sovereign God. This is the thought of

Verse 27 - "And he said, The things which are impossible with men are possible with God."

ὁ δὲ εἶπεν, Τὰ ἀδύνατα παρὰ ἀνθρώποις δυνατὰ παρὰ τῷ θεῷ ἐστιν.

ὁ (nom.sing.masc.of the article, subject of εἶπεν) 9.
δὲ (continuative conjunction) 11.
εἶπεν (3d.per.sing.aor.act.ind.of εἶπον, constative) 155.
Τὰ (nom.pl.neut.of the article in agreement with ἀδύνατα) 9.
ἀδύνατα (nom.pl.neut.of ἀδύνατος, subject of ἐστιν) 1310.
παρὰ (preposition with the locative of sphere) 154.
ἀνθρώποις (loc.pl.masc.of ἄνθρωπος, sphere) 341.
δυνατὰ (nom.pl.neut.of δυνατός, predicate adjective) 1311.
παρὰ (preposition with the locative of sphere) 154.
τῷ (loc.sing.masc.of the article in agreement with θεῷ) 9.
θεῷ (loc.sing.masc.of θεός, sphere) 124.
ἐστιν (3d.per.sing.pres.ind.of εἰμί, static) 86.

Translation - "And He said, 'Things impossible in the human sphere are possible for God.' "

Comment: Not much comment is necessary. Salvation is impossible to attain by any man, be he rich or poor. It requires repentance - a change of mind. There must be a shift in our values away from the earthly, temporal and material things to the heavenly, eternal and spiritual things. It also requires faith - a cordial commitment to unseen reality. Both these achievements are beyond man's ability. Neither rich man nor pauper can enter the Kingdom of God without the effectual call of the Holy Spirit (1 Cor.12:3). To say that the rich may have more inducement to decide for the world rather than for Christ, is not to say that the poor, because they are poor, need less of God's grace in order to be saved.

The two types - those, rich and poor, who repent and cast their lot with Christ, and those, rich and poor, who reject the gospel and place their hopes in this world, are represented by those who stood by Jesus and heard Him speak when the Greeks came to see Him. When God the Father spoke from heaven, "I have glorified it and I will glorify it again," some said that an angel spoke to Him. Others said that it thundered! (John 12:27-29).

Verse 28 - "Then Peter said, Lo, we have left all, and followed thee."

Εἶπεν δὲ ὁ Πέτρος, Ἰδοὺ ἡμεῖς ἀφέντες τὰ ἴδια ἠκολουθήσαμέν σοι.

Εἶπεν (3d.per.sing.aor.act.ind.of εἶπον, constative) 155.
δὲ (continuative conjunction) 11.
ὁ (nom.sing.masc.of the article in agreement with Πέτρος) 9.
Πέτρος (nom.sing.masc.of Πέτρος, subject of εἶπεν) 387.
Ἰδοὺ (exclamation) 95.

ἡμεῖς (nom.pl.masc.of ἐγώ, subject of ἠκολουθήσαμέν) 123.
ἀφέντες (aor.act.part.nom.pl.masc.of ἀφίημι, adverbial, temporal) 319
τὰ (acc.pl.neut.of the article in agreement with ἴδια) 9.
ἴδια (acc.pl.neut.of ἴδιος, direct object of ἀφέντες) 778.
ἠκολουθήσαμέν (1st.per.pl.aor.act.ind.of ἀκολουθέω, culminative) 394.
σοι (dat.sing.masc.of σύ, personal advantage) 104.

Translation - "And Peter said, 'Look! We walked away from all our property and we have followed you.' "

Comment: τὰ ἴδια means all of their possessions, including home, capital equipment - in Peter's case, boats, fishing nets, - everything. Peter's statement elicits Jesus' promise in verses 29-30.

Verse 29 - "And he said unto them, Verily I say unto you, There is no man that hath left home, or parents, or brethren, or wife, or children, for the kingdom of God's sake . . . "

ὁ δὲ εἶπεν αὐτοῖς, Ἀμὴν λέγω ὑμῖν ὅτι οὐδείς ἐστιν ὃς ἀφῆκεν οἰκίαν ἢ γυναῖκα ἢ ἀδελφοὺς ἢ γονεῖς ἢ τέκνα ἕνεκεν τῆς βασιλείας τοῦ θεοῦ,

ὁ (nom.sing.masc.of the article, subject of εἶπεν) 9.
δὲ (inferential conjunction) 11.
εἶπεν (3d.per.sing.aor.act.ind.of εἶπον, constative) 155.
αὐτοῖς (dat.pl.masc.of αὐτός, indirect object of εἶπεν) 16.
Ἀμὴν (explicative) 466.
λέγω (1st.per.sing.pres.act.ind.of λέγω, aoristic) 66.
ὑμῖν (dat.pl.masc.of σύ indirect object of λέγω) 104.
ὅτι (conjunction introducing an object clause in indirect discourse) 211.
οὐδείς (nom.sing.masc.of οὐδείς, subject of ἐστιν) 446.
ἐστιν (3d.per.sing.pres.ind.of εἰμί, static) 86.
ὃς (nom.sing.masc.of ὅς, relative pronoun, subject of ἀφῆκεν) 65.
ἀφῆκεν (3d.per.sing.aor.act.ind.of ἀφίημι, culminative) 319.
οἰκίαν (acc.sing.fem.of οἰκία, direct object of ἀφῆκεν) 186.
ἢ (disjunctive particle) 465.
γυναῖκα (acc.sing.fem.of γυνή, direct object of ἀφῆκεν) 103.
ἢ (disjunctive particle) 465.
ἀδελφοὺς (acc.pl.masc.of ἀδελφός, direct object of ἀφῆκεν) 15.
ἢ (disjunctive particle) 465.
γονεῖς (acc.pl.masc.of γονεύς, direct object of ἀφῆκεν) 878.
ἢ (disjunctive particle) 465.
τέκνα (acc.pl.neut.of τέκνον, direct object of ἀφῆκεν) 229.
ἕνεκεν (improper preposition with the genitive, "for the sake of") 435.
τῆς (gen.sing.fem.of the article in agreement with βασιλείας) 9.
βασιλείας (gen.sing.fem.of βασιλεία, "for the sake of") 253.
τοῦ (gen.sing.masc.of the article in agreement with θεοῦ) 9.
θεοῦ (gen.sing.masc.of θεός, description) 124.

Translation - "And He said to them, 'Truly I am telling you that there is no man who has left house or wife or brothers or parents or children for the sake of the Kingdom of God. . . "

Comment: ὅτι introduces the object clause in indirect discourse. *οὐδείς ἐστιν* - "there is not one person . . . " The definite relative clause with ὅς describes the person of whom Jesus is speaking - "who has left . . . everything dear to him . . . ἕνεκεν - for the sake of the Kingdom of God." This is in response to Peter's statement of verse 28 that certainly if anyone had made the sacrifice of turning their backs upon material things, for the sake of salvation, the disciples had. The disciples needed the assurance at this point that Jesus is in the process of giving. The next verse also with the definite relative pronominal clause completes the thought.

Verse 30 - " . . . who shall not receive manifold more in this present time, and in the world to come, life everlasting."

ὅς οὐχὶ μὴ ἀπολάβῃ πολλαπλασίονα ἐν τῷ καιρῷ τούτῳ καὶ ἐν τῷ αἰῶνι τῷ ἐρχομένῳ ζωὴν αἰώνιον.

ὅς (nom.sing.masc.of ὅς, relative pronoun, subject of ἀπολάβῃ) 65.
οὐχὶ (summary negative conjunction with μὴ and the subjunctive, emphatic negation) 130.
μὴ (qualified negative conjunction with οὐχὶ and the subjunctive, emphatic negation) 87.
ἀπολάβῃ (3d.per.sing.aor.act.subj.of ἀπολαμβάνω, emphatic negation) 2131.
πολλαπλασίονα (acc.sing.neut.of πολλαπλασίων, direct object of ἀπολάβῃ) 1314.
ἐν (preposition with the locative of time point) 80.
τῷ (loc.sing.masc.of the article in agreement with καιρῷ) 9.
καιρῷ (loc.sing.masc.of καιρός, time point) 767.
τούτῳ (loc.sing.masc.of οὗτος, in agreement with καιρῷ) 93.
καὶ (adjunctive conjunction joining prepositional phrases) 80.
ἐν (preposition with the locative of time point) 80.
τῷ (loc.sing.masc.of the article in agreement with αἰῶνι) 9.
αἰῶνι (loc.sing.masc.of αἰών, time point) 1002.
τῷ (loc.sing.masc.of the article in agreement with ἐρχομένῳ) 9.
ἐρχομένῳ (pres.part.loc.sing.masc.of ἔρχομαι, adjectival, restrictive, in agreement with αἰῶνι) 146.
ζωὴν (acc.sing.fem.of ζωή, direct object of ἀπολάβῃ) 668.
αἰώνιον (acc.sing.fem.of αἰώνιος, in agreement with ζωὴν) 1255.

Translation - " . . . who will not get back many times more in this time and in the coming age, life everlasting."

Comment: Note the emphatic negation in οὐχὶ μὴ ἀπολάβῃ. "There is not one who has forsaken all . . . κ.τ.λ. who shall not certainly receive. . . κ.τ.λ."

πολλαπλασίονα is not to be taken here in terms of material wealth in all cases, though it has pleased the Lord to allow some Christians to prosper more financially after they made a complete surrender than before. But some Christians do not find the victorious life in Christ financially rewarding. Yet the promise in our verse is that all those who leave all to follow Christ will receive a far greater return on their investment for Him in terms of psychic utility. Spiritual blessings - the fruits of the Spirit (Gal.5:22,23) far outweigh financial and social assets surrendered for Christ. It is impossible to put a monetary price upon the confident joy and peace that we are abiding in Him, just as He is abiding in us and in the Father. In this state of absolute surrender to His will we know that He will care for us as He does the birds of the air and the lilies of the field and that for us Romans 8:28 is literally true. Knowing this the totally surrendered Christian learns how to cash the promise that "All things work together for good to them that love God, to them who are the called ones according to His purpose." Of course in the coming age, eternal ife awaits the Christian disciple. No Christian in his moment of fondest expectation can begin to anticipate how great our lives in the Kingdom will be. We can only read Romans 8:18 and 2 Corinthians 4:17,18 and rejoice.

We now look at Mark's parallel account in Mark 10:17-31.

Mark 10:17 - "And when he was gone forth into the way, there came one running, and kneeled to him, and asked him, Good Master, what shall I do that I may inherit eternal life?"

Καὶ ἐκπορευομένου αὐτοῦ εἰς ὁδὸν προσδραμὼν εἷς καὶ γονυπετήσας αὐτὸν ἐπηρώτα αὐτόν, Διδάσκαλε ἀγαθέ, τί ποιήσω ἵνα ζωὴν αἰώνιον κληρονομήσω;

Καὶ (continuative conjunction) 14.

ἐκπορευομένου (pres.mid.part.gen.sing.masc.of ἐκπορεύομαι, genitive absolute) 270.

αὐτοῦ (gen.sing.masc.of αὐτός, genitive absolute) 16.

εἰς (preposition with the accusative of extent) 140.

ὁδὸν (acc.sing.neut.of ὁδός, extent) 199.

προσδραμὼν (2d.aor.act.part.nom.sing.masc.of προστρέχω, adverbial, temporal) 2333.

εἷς (nom.sing.masc.of εἷς, subject of ἐπηρώτα) 469.

καὶ (adjunctive conjunction joining participles) 14.

γονυπετήσας (aor.act.part.nom.sing.masc.of γονυπετέω, adverbial, temporal) 1229.

αὐτὸν (acc.sing.masc.of αὐτός, direct object of γονυπετήσας) 16.

ἐπηρώτα (3d.per.sing.imp.act.ind.of ἐπερωτάω, inceptive) 973.

αὐτόν (acc.sing.masc.of αὐτός, direct object of ἐπηρώτα) 16.

Διδάσκαλε (voc.sing.masc.of διδάσκαλος, address) 742.

ἀγαθέ (voc.sing.masc.of ἀγαθός, in agreement with διδάσκαλε) 547.

τί (acc.sing.neut.of τίς, interrogative pronoun, direct object of ποιήσω) 281.

ποιήσω (1st.per.sing.fut.act.ind.of ποιέω, deliberative) 127.

ἵνα (conjunction introducing a sub/final clause) 114.
ζωὴν (acc.sing.fem.of ζωή, direct object of κληρονομήσω) 668.
αἰώνιον (acc.sing.fem.of αἰώνιος, in agreement with ζωὴν) 1255.
κληρονομήσω (1st.per.sing.aor.act.subj.of κληρονομέω, purpose/result) 426.

Translation - "And as He went out into the road a man came running and knelt before Him and asked Him, 'Good Teacher, what must I do in order that I can inherit eternal life?' "

Comment: *Cf.* comment on Luke 18:18 and Mt.19:16. Mark adds the facts that the man came running and knelt before Jesus before he asked the question. Note the genitive absolute in the present tense in the first clause. The grammatical and syntactical differences between the accounts only accentuate the personal differences in the styles of the writers. All methods used are equally good Greek and they all say essentially the same thing.

Verse 18 - "And Jesus said unto him, Why callest thou me good? There is none good but one, that is God."

ὁ δὲ Ἰησοῦς εἶπεν αὐτῷ, Τί με λέγεις ἀγαθόν; οὐδεὶς ἀγαθὸς εἰ μὴ εἷς ὁ θεός.

ὁ (nom.sing.masc.of the article in agreement with Ἰησοῦς) 9.
δὲ (adversative conjunction) 11.
Ἰησοῦς (nom.sing.masc.of Ἰησοῦς, subject of εἶπεν) 3.
εἶπεν (3d.per.sing.aor.act.ind.of εἶπον, constative) 155.
αὐτῷ (dat.sing.masc.of αὐτός, indirect object of εἶπεν) 16.
Τί (acc.sing.neut.of τίς, the interrogative pronoun, cause) 281.
με (acc.sing.masc.of ἐγώ, direct object of λέγεις) 123.
λέγεις (2d.per.sing.pres.act.ind.of λέγω, aoristic, direct question) 66.
ἀγαθόν (acc.sing.masc.of ἀγαθός, predicate adjective) 547.
οὐδεὶς (nom.sing.masc.of οὐδείς, subject of ἐστιν, understood) 446.
ἀγαθὸς (nom.sing.masc.of ἀγαθός, predicate adjective) 547.
εἰ (conditional particle in a first-class conditional elliptical clause) 337.
μὴ (qualifed negative conjunction in a first-class conditional ellipitcal clause) 87.
εἷς (nom.sing.masc.of εἷς, subject of the verb understood) 469.
ὁ (nom.sing.masc.of the article in agreement with θεός) 9.
θεός (nom.sing.masc.of θεός, apposition) 124.

Translation - "But Jesus said to him, 'Why are you calling me good? No one is good, except one - God."

Comment: *Cf.* comment on Mt.19;17 and Lk.18:19.

Verse 19 - "Thou knowest the commandments, Do not commit adultery, do not kill, Do not steal, Do not bear false witness, Defraud not; Honour thy father and mother."

τὰς ἐντολὰς οἶδας. Μὴ φονεύσῃς, Μὴ μοιχεύσῃς, Μὴ κλέψῃς, Μὴ ψευδομαρτυρήσῃς, Μὴ ἀποστερήσῃς, Τίμα τὸν πατέρα σου καὶ τὴν ματέρα.

τὰς (acc.pl.fem.of the article in agreement with *ἐντολὰς*) 9.
ἐντολὰς (acc.pl.fem.of *ἐντολή*, direct object of *οἶδας*) 472.
οἶδας (2d.per.sing.pres.act.ind.of *ὁράω*, aoristic) 144.
Μὴ (qualified negative conjunction with the subjunctive in a prohibition) 87.
φονεύσῃς (2d.per.sing.aor.act.subj.of *φονεύω*, prohibition) 476.
Μὴ (qualified negative conjunction with the subjunctive in a prohibition) 87.
μοιχεύσῃς (2d.per.sing.aor.act.subj.of *μοιχεύω*, prohibition) 498.
Μὴ (qualified negative conjunction with the subjunctive in a prohibition) 87.
κλέψῃς (2d.per.sing.aor.act.subj.of *κλέπτω*, prohibition) 597.
Μὴ (qualified negative conjunction with the subjunctive in a prohibition) 87.
ψευδομαρτυρήσῃς (2d.per.sing.aor.act.subj.of *ψευδομαρτυρέω*, prohibition) 1299.
Μὴ (qualified negative conjunction with the subjunctive in a prohibition) 87.

#2639 ***ἀποστερήσῃς*** **(2d.per.sing.aor.act.subj.of** ***ἀποστερέω*****, prohibition).**

defraud - Mk.10:19; 1 Cor.6:7,8; 7:5.
keep back by fraud - James.5:4.
destitute - 1 Tim.6:5.

Meaning: To defraud; to withhold that which rightfully belongs to another; to cheat. Absolutely in Mark 10:19; to perpetrate financial injustice in matters that are subject to litigation - 1 Cor.6:8; in the middle voice, to submit to such fraud; to be defrauded - 1 Cor.6:7; to refuse sex in the marital relationship - 1 Cor.7:5; to withhold wages earned by workers - James 5:4; to be cheated intellectually, *i.e.* to be deprived of teaching - 1 Tim.6:5.

Τίμα (2d.per.sing.pres.act.impv.of *τιμάω*, command) 1142.
τὸν (acc.sing.masc.of the article in agreement with *πατέρα*) 9.
πατέρα (acc.sing.masc.of *πατήρ*, direct object of *τίμα*) 238.
σου (gen.sing.masc.of *σύ*, relationship) 104.
καὶ (adjunctive conjunction joining nouns) 14.
τὴν (acc.sing.fem.of the article in agreement with *μητέρα*) 9.
μητέρα (acc.sing.fem.of *μήτηρ*, direct object of *τίμα*) 76.

Translation - "You know the commandments: Never kill, never commit adultery, never steal, never bear false witness, never defraud. Always honor your father and mother."

Comment: *Cf.* comment on Mt.19:18 and Luke 18:20. Note that Mark adds the prohibition against fraud. The prohibitions are in the aorist tense. They are bans against future action and are thus ingressive. The Ten Commandments forbid that we should commit any of the deeds mentioned even once. Hence, "Never (Do not begin to; Do not even once) . . . kill, commit adultery, steal, lie, defraud." But the positive command *Τίμα* is in the present tense. "Always (continue to; make a practice of) honor your father and mother."

The man is prepared to report that he has a clear record in all the categories which Jesus mentioned. Since we are told that he was rich, and since he was not guilty of fraud, it is clear that he was a good business man, unless of course he inherited his wealth.

Verse 20 - "And he answered and said unto him, Master, all these have I observed from my youth."

ὁ δὲ ἔφη αὐτῷ, Διδάσκαλε, ταῦτα πάντα ἐφυλαξάμην ἐκ νεότητός μου.

ὁ (nom.sing.masc.of the article, subject of *ἔφη*) 9.
δὲ (continuative conjunction) 11.
ἔφη (3d.per.sing.aor.act.ind.of *φημί*, constative) 354.
αὐτῷ (dat.sing.masc.of *αὐτός*, indirect object of *ἔφη*) 16.
Διδάσκαλε (voc.sing.masc.of *διδάσκαλος*, address) 742.
ταῦτα (acc.pl.neut.of *οὗτος*, direct object of *ἐφυλαξάμην*) 93.
πάντα (acc.pl.neut.of *πᾶς*, in agreement with *ταῦτα*) 67.
ἐφυλαξάμην (1st.per.sing.aor.mid.ind.of *φυλάσσω*, culminative) 1301.
ἐκ (preposition with the ablative of time separation) 19.
νεότητός (abl.sing.masc.of *νεότης*, time separation) 2635.
μου (gen.sing.masc.of *ἐγώ*, possession) 123.

Translation - "And he said to Him, 'Teacher, all these things I have kept since my youth."

Comment: *Cf.* comment on Mt.19:20 and Luke 18:21. Note that Matthew and Luke use the active *ἐφύλαξα* while Mark uses the middle voice *ἐφυλαξάμην*. "I have submitted myself to the discipline of all these commandments since my youth."

Verse 21 - "Then Jesus beholding him loved him, and said unto him, One thing thou lackest: go thy way, sell whatsoever thou hast, and give to the poor, and thou shalt have treasure in heaven: and come, take up the cross, and follow me."

ὁ δὲ Ἰησοῦς ἐμβλέψας αὐτῷ ἠγάπησεν αὐτὸν καὶ εἶπεν αὐτῷ, Ἕν σε ὑστερεῖ, ὕπαγε ὅσα ἔχεις πώλησον καὶ δὸς (τοῖς) πτωχοῖς, καὶ ἕξεις θησαυρὸν ἐν οὐρανῷ, καὶ δεῦρο ἀκολούθει μοι.

ὁ (nom.sing.masc.of the article in agreement with *Ἰησοῦς*) 9.
δὲ (continuative conjunction) 11.
Ἰησοῦς (nom.sing.masc.of *Ἰησοῦς*, subject of *ἠγάπησεν* and *εἶπεν*) 3.
ἐμβλέψας (aor.act.part.nom.sing.masc.of *ἐμβλέπω*, adverbial, complementary) 614.
αὐτῷ (dat.sing.masc.of *αὐτός*, personal advantage) 16.
ἠγάπησεν (3d.per.sing.aor.act.ind.of *ἀγαπάω*, ingressive) 540.
αὐτὸν (acc.sing.masc.of *αὐτός*, direct object of *ἠγάπησεν*) 16.
καὶ (adjunctive conjunction joining verbs) 14.
εἶπεν (3d.per.sing.aor.act.ind.of *εἶπον*, constative) 155.
αὐτῷ (dat.sing.masc.of *αὐτός*, indirect object of *εἶπεν*) 16.
Ἕν (acc.sing.neut.of *εἷς*, direct object of *ὑστερεῖ*) 469.
σε (acc.sing.masc.of *σύ*, general reference, double accusative after *ὑστερεῖ*) 104.

ὑστερεῖ (3d.per.sing.pres.act.ind.of ὑστερέω, static) 1302.
ὕπαγε (2d.per.sing.pres.act.impv.of ὑπάγω, command) 364.
ὅσα (acc.pl.neut.of ὅσος, direct object of πώλησον) 660.
ἔχεις (2d.per.sing.pres.act.ind.of ἔχω, aoristic) 82.
πώλησον (2d.per.sing.aor.act.impv.of πωλέω, command) 892.
καὶ (adjunctive conjunction joining verbs) 14.
δὸς (2d.per.sing. 2d. aor.act.impv.of δίδωμι, command) 362.
(τοῖς) (dat.pl.masc.of the article in agreement with πτωχοῖς) 9.
πτωχοῖς (dat.pl.masc.of πτωχός, indirect object of δὸς) 423.
καὶ (continuative conjunction) 14.
ἕξεις (2d.per.sing.fut.act.ind.of ἔχω, predictive) 82.
θησαυρὸν (acc.sing.masc.of θησαυρός, direct object of ἕξεις) 189.
ἐν (preposition with the locative of place where) 80.
οὐρανῷ (loc.sing.masc.of οὐρανός, place where) 254.
καὶ (continuative conjunction) 14.
δεῦρο (adverbial interjection with the imperative) 1304.
ἀκολούθει (2d.per.sing.pres.act.impv.of ἀκολουθέω, command) 394.
μοι (dat.sing.masc.of ἐγώ, personal advantage) 123.

Translation - "And Jesus looked at him and fell in love with him and said to him, 'One thing you lack. Go away, sell whatever you have and give to the poor, and you will have treasure in heaven, and come back and follow me.' "

Comment: *Cf.* comment on Mt.19;21 and Lk.18:22. Mark alone records ἠγάπησεν αὐτὸν. Note the ingressive aorist. Note Mark's double accusative in ἕν σε ὑστερεῖ as opposed to Luke's ἕν σοι λείπει, a dative of personal disadvantage. Since ὕπαγε - "go away" is here we can translate δεῦρο as "come back." - "go away . . . sell. . . give away . . . come back . . . follow. . . " Note the linear action in the present tense in ἀκολούθει μοι, - "*always follow me.*" Note also that Luke uses διαδίδωμι (#2279) while Mark and Matthew use δός (#362).

Verse 22 - "And he was sad at that saying, and went away grieved: for he had great possessions."

ὁ δὲ στυγνάσας ἐπὶ τῷ λόγῳ ἀπῆλθεν λυπούμενος, ἦν γὰρ ἔχων κτήματα πολλά.

ὁ (nom.sing.masc.of the article, subject of ἀπῆλθεν) 9.
δὲ (adversative conjunction) 11.
στυγνάσας (aor.act.part.nom.sing.masc.of στυγνάζω, adverbial, modal) 1194.
ἐπὶ (preposition with the instrumental of cause) 47.
τῷ (instru.sing.masc.of the article in agreement with λόγῳ) 9.
λόγῳ (instru.sing.masc.of λόγος, cause) 510.
ἀπῆλθεν (3d.per.sing.aor.ind.of ἀπέρχομαι, constative) 239.
λυπούμενος (pres.pass.part.nom.sing.masc.of λυπέω, adverbial, circumstantial) 1113.
ἦν (3d.per.sing.imp.ind.of εἰμί, imperfect periphrastic) 86.

γὰρ (causal conjunction) 105.
ἔχων (pres.act.part.nom.sing.masc.of ἔχω, imperfect periphrastic) 82.
κτήματα (acc.pl.neut.of κτῆμα, direct object of ἔχων) 1305.
πολλά (acc.pl.neut.of πολύς, in agreement with κτήματα) 228.

Translation - "But with a sad expression he went away, grieved because of the saying, because he owned much property."

Comment: *Cf.* comment on Mt.19:22 and Lk.18:23. Mark adds στυγνάσας ἐπὶ τῷ λόγῳ - "his face having clouded because of the saying." The first adverbial participle is modal; the second is circumstantial.

Verse 23 - "And Jesus looked round about, and saith unto his disciples, How hardly shall they that have riches enter into the kingdom of God!"

Καὶ περιβλεψάμενος ὁ Ἰησοῦς λέγει τοῖς μαθηταῖς αὐτοῦ, Πῶς δυσκόλως οἱ τὰ χρήματα ἔχοντες εἰς τὴν βασιλείαν τοῦ θεοῦ εἰσελεύσονται.

Καὶ (continuative conjunction) 14.
περιβλεψάμενος (aor.mid.part.nom.sing.masc.of περιβλέπω, adverbial, temporal) 2107.
ὁ (nom.sing.masc.of the article in agreement with Ἰησοῦς) 9.
Ἰησοῦς (nom.sing.masc.of Ἰησοῦς, subject of λέγει) 3.
λέγει (3d.per.sing.pres.act.ind.of λέγω, historical) 66.
τοῖς (dat.pl.masc.of the article in agreement with μαθηταῖς) 9.
μαθηταῖς (dat.pl.masc.of μαθητής, indirect object of λέγει) 421.
αὐτοῦ (gen.sing.masc.of αὐτός, relationship) 16.
Πῶς (exclamatory adverb) 627.
δυσκόλως (adverbial) 1307.
οἱ (nom.pl.masc.of the article in agreement with ἔχοντες) 9.
τὰ (acc.pl.neut.of the article in agreement with χρήματα) 9.
χρήματα (acc.pl.neut.of χρῆμα, direct object of ἔχοντες) 2637.
ἔχοντες (pres.act.part.nom.pl.masc.of ἔχω, substantival, subject of εἰσελεύσονται) 82.
εἰς (preposition with the accusative of extent) 140.
τὴν (acc.sing.fem.of the article in agreement with βασιλείαν) 9.
βασιλείαν (acc.sing.fem.of βασιλεία, extent) 253.
τοῦ (gen.sing.masc.of the article in agreement with θεοῦ) 9.
θεοῦ (gen.sing.masc.of θεός, description) 124.
εἰσελεύσονται (3d.per.pl.fut.ind.of εἰσέρχομαι, deliberative) 234.

Translation - "And having looked around Jesus said to His disciples, 'With what great difficulty will those who have money enter into the kingdom of God."

Comment: *Cf.* comment on Mt.19;23 and Lk.18:24. Mark's only addition is the participle περιβλεψάμενος. He also used εἰσέρχομαι (#234) instead of εἰσπορεύομαι (#1161).

Verse 24 - "And the disciples were astonished at his words. But Jesus answereth again, and saith unto them, Children, how hard is it for them that trust in riches to enter into the kingdom of God!"

οἱ δὲ μαθηταὶ ἐθαμβοῦντο ἐπὶ τοῖς λόγοις αὐτοῦ. ὁ δὲ Ἰησοῦς πάλιν ἀποκριθεὶς λέγει αὐτοῖς, Τέκνα, πῶς δύσκολόν ἐστιν εἰς τὴν βασιλείαν τοῦ θεοῦ εἰσελθεῖν.

οἱ (nom.pl.masc.of the article in agreement with μαθηταὶ) 9.
δὲ (continuative conjunction) 11.
μαθηταὶ (nom.pl.masc.of μαθητής, subject of ἐθαμβοῦντο) 421.
ἐθαμβοῦντο (3d.per.pl.imp.pass.ind.of θαμβέω, inceptive) 2059.
ἐπὶ (preposition with the instrumental of cause) 47.
τοῖς (instru.pl.masc.of the article in agreement with λόγοις) 9.
λόγοις (instru.pl.masc.of λόγος, cause) 510.
αὐτοῦ (gen.sing.masc.of αὐτός, possession) 16.
ὁ (nom.sing.masc.of the article in agreement with Ἰησοῦς) 9.
δὲ (inferential conjunction) 11.
Ἰησοῦς (nom.sing.masc.of Ἰησοῦς, subject of λέγει) 3.
πάλιν (adverbial) 355.
ἀποκριθεὶς (aor.part.nom.sing.masc.of ἀποκρίνομαι, adverbial, modal) 318.
λέγει (3d.per.sing.pres.act.ind.of λέγω, historical) 66.
αὐτοῖς (dat.pl.masc.of αὐτός, indirect object of λέγει) 16.
Τέκνα (voc.pl.neut.of τέκνον, address) 229.
πῶς (adverb in exclamation) 627.

#2640 δύσκολόν (nom.sing.neut.of δύσκολος, predicate adjective).

hard - Mark 10:24.

*Meaning: Cf.*δυσκόλως (#1307). *κόλον* - "food." Properly, fastidious about food. Hence, hard to please. Only in Mark 10:24 in the New Testament and not in this sense. As a predicate adjective defining an infinitive subject, with reference to the difficulty in entering into the Kingdom of God.

ἐστιν (3d.per.sing.pres.ind.of εἰμί, static) 86.
εἰς (preposition with the accusative of extent) 140.
τὴν (acc.sing.fem.of the article in agreement with βασιλείαν) 9.
βασιλείαν (acc.sing.fem.of βασιλεία, extent) 253.
τοῦ (gen.sing.masc.of the article in agreement with θεοῦ) 9.
θεοῦ (gen.sing.masc.of θεός, description) 124.
εἰσελθεῖν (aor.inf.of εἰσέρχομαι, noun use, subject of ἐστιν) 234.

Translation - "And the disciples were dumbfounded because of what He said. Therefore Jesus repeated what He had said to them, 'Children, how hard it is to enter into the Kingdom of God.' "

Comment: *Cf.* comment on Mt.19:23 and Lk.18:24. Mark alone tells us of the amazed reaction of the disciples to Jesus' words in verse 23. *Cf.*#'s 2059 and 2053. This interesting verb can be translated by something like "rooted to the spot" or "petrified." Apparently they were not too speechless to ask Jesus about it, since we have *ἀποκριθεὶς λέγει αὐτοῖς* - "he said to them in reply. . . *κ.τ.λ.*" Here He uses the adjective (#2640) instead of the adverb (#1307). It was probably the reaction of the disciples that induced Jesus to employ the hyperbole of verse 25 to hammer home His point. The phrase "for them that trust in riches" of the Textus Receptus is not in the more primitive text. Metzger's explanation follows:

"The Western text (D it a,b,d,ff2) has moved ver.25 so as to follow *εἰσελεύσονται* (reading verses 23, 25, 24, 26). The transposition appears to be the work of the Western redactor who sought to improve the sense by making a more gradual sequence (first, it is difficult for rich people to enter the kingdom; then, it is difficult for those who trust in riches (for the addition, see the comment on ver.23) to enter). Although some have preferred the transposed sequence, it is precisely (as Lagrange points out *ad loc.*) the too-logical order of the Western text that renders it suspect as a secondary modification of the more primitive text. The minuscule 235 includes ver.25 twice (reading verses 23, 25, 24, 25, 26).

The rigor of Jesus' saying was softened by the insertion of one or another qualification that limited its generality and brought it into closer connection with the context. Thus, A C D Θ *f1 f13 al* read *ἐστιν τοὺς πεποιθότας ἐπὶ χρήμασιν* ("for those who trust in riches"); W and itc insert *πλούσιον* ("a rich man"); and 1241 reads *οἱ τὰ χρήματα ἔχοντες* ("those who have possession"). (Metzger, *A Textual Commentary on the Greek Testament*, 105, 106).

All of that editing and insertion of explanatory material by Medieval copyists, totally uncalled for, would not have been introduced if those who presumed to improve upon the Holy Spirit's work of inspiration had understood that the point that they were trying so hard to make would be obvious, in any case, to those who understand that the scriptures interpret themselves if they are allowed to do so. We have nothing to fear when we follow the text as it was originally inspired and written. Commentary on the text has its place, but it should always be presented as such, and not inserted into the text as having come from the Holy Spirit. Jesus was in fact speaking of those who trust in riches, instead of in Christ, when He said that they could not enter into the Kingdom of God. This we derive from other scriptures that speak to the subject, no thanks to the copyists who presumed to improve upon the Word of God.

Verse 25 - "It is easier for a camel to go through the eye of a needle, than for a rich man to enter into the kingdom of God."

εὐκοπώτερόν ἐστιν κάμηλον διὰ τρυμαλιᾶς ῥαφίδος διελθεῖν ἢ πλούσιον εἰς τὴν βασιλείαν τοῦ θεοῦ εἰσελθεῖν.

εὐκοπώτερόν (nom.sing.neut.of *εὐκοπώτερος*, predicate adjective) 783.
ἐστιν (3d.per.sing.pres.ind.of *εἰμί*, static) 86.
κάμηλον (acc.sing.masc.of *κάμηλος*, general reference) 262.
διὰ (preposition with the genitive, physically through) 118.

#2641 τρυμαλιᾶς (gen.sing.fem.of τρυμαλιά, place description).

eye - Mark 10:25.

Meaning: from τρύω - "to wear away; to perforate." Hence, the eye, or perforation of a needle - Mark 10:25. *cf.*#1308.

ῥαφίδος (gen.sing.fem.of ῥαφίς, description) 1309.
διελθεῖν (aor.inf.of διέρχομαι, noun use, subject of ἐστιν) 1017.
ἢ (disjunctive particle) 465.
πλούσιον (acc.sing.masc.of πλούσιος, general reference) 1306.
εἰς (preposition with the accusative of extent) 140.
τὴν (acc.sing.fem.of the article in agreement with βασιλείαν) 9.
βασιλείαν (acc.sing.fem.of βασιλεία, extent) 253.
τοῦ (gen.sing.masc.of the article in agreement with θεοῦ) 9.
θεοῦ (gen.sing.masc.of θεός, description) 124.
εἰσελθεῖν (aor.inf.of εἰσέρχομαι, noun use, subject of ἐστιν understood) 234.

Translation - "The passage of a camel through a needle's eye is easier than a rich man's entrance into the Kingdom of God."

Comment: *Cf.* comment on Mt.19:24 and Luke 18:25. Mark uses τρυμαλιά (#2641) rather than τρῆμα (#1308) and διέρχομαι (#1017) instead of εἰσέρχομαι (#234).

Verse 26 - "And they were astonished out of measure, saying among themselves, Who then can be saved?"

οἱ δὲ περισσῶς ἐξεπλήσσοντο λέγοντες πρὸς ἑαυτούς, Καὶ τί δύναται σωθῆναι;

οἱ(nom.pl.masc.of the article, subject of ἐξεπλήσσοντο) 9.
δὲ (continuative conjunction) 11.
περισσῶς (adverbial) 1630.
ἐξεπλήσσοντο (3d.per.pl.imp.pass.ind.of ἐκπλήσσομαι, inceptive) 705.
λέγοντες (pres.act.part.nom.pl.masc.of λέγω, complementary) 66.
πρὸς (preposition with the accusative of extent, after a verb of speaking) 197.
ἑαυτούς (acc.pl.masc.of ἑαυτός, extent after a verb of speaking) 288.
Καὶ (inferential conjunction) 14.
τίς (nom.sing.masc.of τίς, the interrogative pronoun, subject of δύναται, direct question) 281.
δύναται (3d.per.sing.pres.ind.of δύναμαι, static) 289.
σωθῆναι (aor.pass.inf.of σώζω, epexegetical) 109.

Translation - "And they were startled beyond description, saying among themselves, 'Who then can be saved?' "

Comment: *Cf.* comment on Mt.19:25 and Lk.18:26. Again we see the individuality of the synoptic writers. Mark has καὶ. Matthew has ἄρα (#995). Mark describes the disciples' astonishment with περισσῶς (#1630) - "beyond description" or "beyond words" while Matthew has σφόδρα (#185) - "greatly" or "exceedingly."

Verse 27 - "And Jesus looking upon them saith, With men it is impossible, but not with God; for with God all things are possible."

ἐμβλέψας αὐτοῖς ὁ Ἰησοῦς λέγει, Παρὰ ἀνθρώποις ἀδύνατον ἀλλ' οὐ παρὰ θεῷ, πάντα γὰρ δυνατὰ παρὰ τῷ θεῷ.

ἐμβλέψας (aor.act.part.nom.sing.masc.of ἐμβλέπω, adverbial, temporal) 614.
αὐτοῖς (dat.pl.masc.of αὐτός, personal advantage) 16.
ὁ (nom.sing.masc.of the article in agreement with Ἰησοῦς) 9.
Ἰησοῦς (nom.sing.masc.of Ἰησοῦς, subject of λέγει) 3.
Παρὰ (preposition with the locative of sphere) 154.
ἀνθρώποις (loc.pl.masc.of ἄνθρωπος, sphere) 341.
ἀδύνατον (nom.sing.neut.of ἀδύνατος, predicate adjective) 1310.
ἀλλ' (alternative conjunction) 342.
οὐ (summary negative conjunction with the indicative) 130.
παρὰ (preposition with the locative of sphere) 154.
θεῷ (loc.sing.masc.of θεός, sphere) 124.
πάντα (nom.pl.neut.of πᾶς, subject of ἐστιν understood) 67.
γὰρ (causal conjunction) 105.
δυνατὰ (nom.pl.neut.of δυνατός, predicate adjective) 1311.
παρὰ (preposition with the locative of sphere) 154.
τῷ (loc.sing.masc.of the article in agreement with θεῷ) 9.
θεῷ (loc.sing.masc.of θεός, sphere) 124.

Translation - "Having looked upon them, Jesus said, 'In the human sphere - impossible! but not in the divine, because everything is possible with God.' "

Comment: *Cf.* comment on Mt.19:26 and Lk.18:27. Mark makes the statement even more emphatic than do Matthew and Luke, by emphasizing the difference between the human and the divine spheres. Note the absence of the article with θεῷ (first use) and its presence with the last.

Verse 28 - "Then Peter began to say unto him, Lo, we have left all, and have followed thee."

Ἤρξατο λέγειν ὁ Πέτρος αὐτῷ, Ἰδοὺ ἡμεῖς ἀφήκαμεν πάντα καὶ ἠκολουθήκαμέν σοι.

Ἤρξατο (3d.per.sing.aor.mid.ind.of ἄρχω, ingressive) 383.
λέγειν (pres.act.inf.of λέγω, epexegetical) 66.
ὁ (nom.sing.masc.of the article in agreement with Πέτρος) 9.

Πέτρος (nom.sing.masc.of Πέτρος, subject of ἤρξατο) 387.
αὐτῷ (dat.sing.masc.of αὐτός, indirect object of λέγειν) 16.
Ἰδοὺ (exclamation) 95.
ἡμεῖς (nom.pl.masc.of ἐγώ, subject of ἀφήκαμεν and ἠκολουθήκαμέν) 123.
ἀφήκαμεν (1st.per.pl.aor.act.ind.of ἀφίημι, culminative) 319.
πάντα (acc.pl.neut.of πᾶς, direct object of ἀφήκαμεν) 67.
καὶ (adjunctive conjunction joining verbs) 14.
ἠκολουθήκαμεν (1st.per.pl.perf.act.ind.of ἀκολουθέω, iterative) 394.
σοι (dat.sing.masc.of σύ, personal advantage) 104.

Translation - "Peter began to say to Him, 'Look! we have left everything and have been following you.' "

Comment: *Cf.* comment on Mt.19:27 and Lk.18:28. Mark uses the aorist and the perfect in that order. The aorist is culminative, with emphasis upon the finished results of the action. Peter was saying that the disciples had burned their bridges behind them. There was no going back to the fishing boats or the tax collector's table. The perfect tense is iterative. For the past three years the disciples had followed Jesus up and down the land, sharing His fortunes and enduring, to a lesser degree than He, to be sure, His reproach. But Peter is thinking here of the cost of discipleship and perhaps a little too eagerly pointing out to Jesus, as if He did not know, that the disciples should not find the Kingdom of God barred against their entrance. Thus Mark accentuates the continuous nature of the disciples' service for Christ during the past three years.

Before we continue with verse 29 we must review Mt.19:28 and Lk.22:30b, which promises to each of the twelve apostles (except Judas Iscariot) a judgeship in the Kingdom of the Heavens, at the Second Coming of Christ.

Verse 29 - "And Jesus answered and said, Verily I say unto you, There is no man that hath left house, or brethren or sisters, or father, or mother, or wife, or children, or lands, for my sake and the gospel's . . . "

ἔφη ὁ Ἰησοῦς, Ἀμὴν λέγω ὑμῖν, οὐδείς ἐστιν ὃς ἀφῆκεν οἰκίαν ἢ ἀδελφοὺς ἢ ἀδελφὰς ἢ μητέρα ἢ πατέρα ἢ τέκνα ἢ ἀγροὺς ἕνεκεν ἐμοῦ καὶ ἕνεκεν τοῦ εὐαγγελίου, . . . "

ἔφη (3d.per.sing.aor.act.ind.of φημί, constative) 354.
ὁ (nom.sing.masc.of the article in agreement with Ἰησοῦς) 9.
Ἰησοῦς (nom.sing.masc.of Ἰησοῦς, subject of ἔφη) 3.
Ἀμὴν (explicative) 466.
λέγω (1st.per.sing.pres.act.ind.of λέγω, aoristic) 66.
ὑμῖν (dat.pl.masc.of σύ, indirect object of λέγω) 104.
οὐδείς (nom.sing.masc.of οὐδείς, subject of ἐστιν) 446.
ἐστιν (3d.per.sing.pres.ind.of εἰμί, static) 86.
ὃς (nom.sing.masc.of ὅς, the relative pronoun, subject of ἀφῆκεν) 65.
ἀφῆκεν (3d.per.sing.aor.act.ind.of ἀφίημι, culminative) 319.
οἰκίαν (acc.sing.fem.of οἰκία, direct object of ἀφῆκεν) 186.

ἢ (disjunctive particle) 465.
ἀδελφοὺς (acc.pl.masc.of ἀδελφός, direct object of ἀφῆκεν) 15.
ἢ (disjunctive particle) 465.
ἀδελφὰς (acc.pl.fem.of ἀδελφή, direct object of ἀφῆκεν) 1025.
ἢ (disjunctive particle) 465.
μητέρα (acc.sing.fem.of μήτηρ, direct object of ἀφῆκεν) 76.
ἢ (disjunctive particle) 465.
πατέρα (acc.sing.masc.of πάτηρ, direct object of ἀφῆκεν) 238.
ἢ (disjunctive particle) 465.
τέκνα (acc.pl.neut.of τέκνον, direct object of ἀφῆκεν) 229.
ἢ (disjunctive conjunction) 465.
ἀγροὺς (acc.pl.masc.of ἀγρός, direct object of ἀφῆκεν) 626.
ἕνεκεν (improper preposition with the genitive, cause) 435.
ἐμοῦ (gen.sing.masc.of ἐγώ, cause description) 123.
καὶ (adjunctive conjunction joining prepositional phrases) 14.
ἕνεκεν (improper preposition with the genitive, cause) 435.
τοῦ (gen.sing.neut.of the article in agreement with εὐαγγελίου) 9.
εὐαγγελίου (gen.sing.neut.of εὐαγγέλιον, cause) 405.

Translation - "Jesus said, 'Truly I am telling you there is no one who has left house or brothers or sisters or mother or father or children or lands for my sake and for the sake of the gospel . . . "

Comment: *Cf.* comment on Mt.19:29 and Lk.18:29. Matthew and Mark include the entire list of seven items. Luke omits ἀδελφας, μητέρα, πατέρα and ἀγροὺς, but adds γυναῖκα and γονεῖς. Taken together the passage means the one who leaves everything that is precious to him for the sake of ἐμοῦ ὀνόματος (Mt.); ἐμοῦ καὶ τοῦ εὐαγγελίου (Mk.) and τῆς βασιλείας τοῦ θεοῦ (Lk.).

Verse 30 - "But he shall receive an hundredfold now in this time, houses, and brethren, and sisters, and mothers, and children, and lands, with persecutions; and in the world to come eternal life."

ἐὰν μὴ λάβῃ ἑκατονταπλασίονα νῦν ἐν τῷ καιρῷ τούτῳ οἰκίας καὶ ἀδελφοὺς καὶ ἀδελφὰς καὶ μητέρας καί τέκνα καὶ ἀγροὺς μετὰ διωγμῶν, καὶ ἐν τῷ αἰῶνι τῷ ἐρχομένῳ, ζωὴν αἰώνιον.

ἐὰν (conditional particle in a third-class condition) 363.
μὴ (qualified negative conjunction with the subjunctive) 87.
λάβῃ (aor.act.subj.of λαμβάνω, third-class condition) 533.
ἑκατονταπλασίονα (acc.pl.neut.of ἑκατονταπλασίων, proportional adjective) 2200.
νῦν (temporal adverb) 1497.
ἐν (preposition with the locative of time point) 80.
τῷ (loc.sing.masc.of the article in agreement with καιρῷ) 9.
καιρῷ (loc.sing.masc.of καιρός, time point) 767.
τούτῳ (loc.sing.masc.of οὗτος, in agreement with καιρῷ) 93.

οἰκίας (acc.pl.fem.of *οἰκία*, direct object of *λάβῃ*) 186.
καὶ (adjunctive conjunction joining nouns) 14.
ἀδελφοὺς (acc.pl.masc.of *ἀδελφός*, direct object of *λάβῃ*) 15.
καὶ (adjunctive conjunction joining nouns) 14.
ἀδελφὰς (acc.pl.fem.of *ἀδελφή*, direct object of *λάβῃ*) 1025.
καὶ (adjunctive conjunction joining nouns) 14.
μητέρας (acc.pl.fem.of *μήτηρ*, direct object of *λάβῃ*) 76.
καὶ (adjunctive conjunction joining nouns) 14.
τέκνα (acc.pl.neut.of *τέκνον*, direct object ofd *λάβῃ*) 229.
καὶ (adjunctive conjunction joining nouns) 14.
ἀγροὺς (acc.pl.masc.of *ἀγρός*, direct object of *λάβῃ*) 626.
μετὰ (preposition with the genitive of accompaniment) 50.
διωγμῶν (gen.pl.masc.of *διωγμός*, accompaniment) 1047.
καὶ (adjunctive conjunction joining prepositional phrases) 14.
ἐν (preposition with the locative of time point) 80.
τῷ (loc.sing.masc.of the article in agreement with *αἰῶνι*) 9.
αἰῶνι (loc.sing.masc.of *αἰῶν*, time point) 1002.
τῷ (loc.sing.masc.of the article in agreement with *ἐρχομένῳ*) 9.
ἐρχομένῳ (pres.part.loc.sing.masc.of *ἔρχομαι*, adjectival, restrictive, in agreement with *αἰῶνι*) 146.
ζωὴν (acc.sing.fem.of *ζωή*, direct object of *λάβῃ*) 668.
αἰώνιον (acc.sing.fem.of *αἰώνιος*, in agreement with *ζωὴν*) 1255.

Translation - " . . . who shall not receive one hundred times more, now, in this time, houses and brothers and sisters and mothers and children and lands, with persecutions, and in the coming age eternal life."

Comment: *Cf.* comment on Mt.19:29 and Lk.18:30. Mark makes clearer than either Matthew of Luke that the rewards to be received in this life by one who has sacrificed all for Christ, are material as well as spiritual, though he adds that, for all of God's material rewards, there will also be persecution from the unsaved world. The houses, lands and loved ones whom we repudiate, if necessary in order to follow Christ, will be returned to us in abundance even now and, in addition life eternal in the coming age. This was the experience of Job, who was twice as affluent after his trial than before. (Job 1:3; 42:12). Apparently it is not the divine will to reward all who follow Christ in this manner. Perhaps He cannot trust some of us with affluence.

Verse 31 - "But many that are first shall be last, and the last first."

πολλοὶ δὲ ἔσονται πρῶτοι ἔσχατοι καὶ (οἱ) ἔσχατοι πρῶτοι.

πολλοὶ (nom.pl.masc.of *πολύς*, in agreement with *πρῶτοι*) 228.
δὲ (adversative conjunction) 11.
ἔσονται (3d.per.pl.fut.ind.of *εἰμί*, predictive) 86.
πρῶτοι (nom.pl.masc.of *πρῶτος*, subject of *ἔσονται*) 487.
ἔσχατοι (nom.pl.masc.of *ἔσχατος*, predicate nominative) 496.

καὶ (continuative conjunction) 14.
(*οἱ*) (nom.pl. masc.of the article in agreement with *ἔσχατοι*) 9.
ἔσχατοι (nom.pl.masc.of *ἔσχατος*, subject of *ἔσονται* understood) 496.
πρῶτοι (nom.pl.masc.of *πρῶτος*, predicate nominative) 487.

Translation - "But many who are first will be last and the last first."

Comment: *Cf.* comment on Mt.19:30 and Lk.13:30, especially our comment that not all Christians who surrender all to follow Christ receive material compensation in this life. Some do. Peter was worried about this point or he would not have raised the question in Mk.13:28. It is to assure Peter that nothing important is ever lost as a result of a full commitment to Christ, that Jesus made the statement of verses 29 and 30. But lest those Christians who are materially rewarded in this life for the sacrifices which they make for Christ, think that their good fortune proves them superior to others, Jesus warned that many Christians who are first in this life may be last in eternity. We may be sure that the Judge of all the earth will do right (Gen.18:25).

Jesus Foretells His Death and Resurrection

(Matthew 20:17-19; Mark 10:32-34; Luke 18:31-34)

Mark 10:32 - "And they were in the way going up to Jerusalem, and Jesus went before them: and they were amazed; and as they followed they were afraid. And he took again the twelve, and began to tell them what things should happen to him."

Ἦσαν δὲ ἐν τῇ ὁδῷ ἀναβαίνοντες εἰς Ἱεροσόλυμα, καὶ ἦν προάγων αὐτοὺς ὁ Ἰησοῦς, καὶ ἐθαμβοῦντο, οἱ δὲ ἀκολουθοῦντες ἐφοβοῦντο. καὶ παραλαβὼν πάλιν τοὺς δώδεκα ἤρξατο αὐτοῖς λέγειν τὰ μέλλοντα αὐτῷ συμβαίνειν,

Ἦσαν (3d.per.pl.imp.ind.of *εἰμί*, imperfect periphrastic) 86.
δὲ (explanatory conjunction) 11.
ἐν (preposition with the locative of place) 80.
τῇ (loc.sing.fem.of the article, in agreement with *ὁδῷ*) 9.
ὁδῷ (loc.sing.fem.of *ὁδός*, place where) 199.
ἀναβαίνοντες (pres.act.part.nom.pl.masc.of *ἀναβαίνω*, imperfect periphrastic) 323.
εἰς (preposition with the accusative of extent) 140.
Ἱεροσόλυμα (acc.sing.masc.of *Ἱεροσολύμων*, extent) 141.
καὶ (continuative conjunction) 14.
ἦν (3d.per.sing.imp.ind.of *εἰμί*, imperfect periphrastic) 86.
προάγων (pres.act.part.nom.sing.masc.of *προάγω*, imperfect periphrastic) 179.
αὐτοὺς (acc.pl.masc.of *αὐτός*, general reference) 16.
ὁ (nom.sing.masc.of the article in agreement with *Ἰησοῦς*) 9.
Ἰησοῦς (nom.sing.masc.of *Ἰησοῦς*, subject of *ἦν*) 3.
καὶ (continuative conjunction) 14.

ἐθαμβοῦντο (3d.per.pl.imp.mid.ind.of θαμβέω, inceptive) 2059.
οἱ (nom.pl.masc.of the article, subject of ἐφοβοῦντο) 9.
δὲ (adversative conjunction) 11.
ἀκολουθοῦντες (pres.act.part.nom.pl.masc.of ἀκολουθέω, adverbial, concessive) 394.
ἐφοβοῦντο (3d.per.pl.imp.mid.ind.of φοβέομαι, inceptive) 101.
καὶ (inferential conjunction) 14.
παραλαβὼν (aor.act.part.nom.sing.masc.of παραλαμβάνω, adverbial, temporal) 102.
πάλιν (adverbial) 355.
τοὺς (acc.pl.masc.of the article in agreement with δώδεκα) 9.
δώδεκα (acc.pl.masc.of δώδεκα, direct object of παραλαβὼν) 820.
ἤρξατο (3d.per.sing.aor.mid.ind.of ἄρχω, ingressive) 383.
αὐτοῖς (dat.pl.masc.of αὐτος,indirect object of λέγειν) 16.
τὰ (acc.pl.neut.of the article in agreement with μέλλοντα) 9.
μέλλοντα (pres.act.part.acc.pl.neut.of μέλλω, substantival, direct object of λέγειν) 206.
αὐτῷ (dat.sing.masc.of αὐτός, reference) 16.

#2642 συμβαίνειν (pres.act.inf.of συμβαίνω, completes μέλλοντα).

be so - Acts 21:35.
befall - Acts 20:19.
happen - Mark 10:32; Luke 24:14; Acts 3:10; 1 Cor.10:11; 1 Pet.4:12; 2 Pet.2:22.

Meaning: A combination of σύν (#1542) and βαίνω - "to fall." Hence, to fall or come together. In ancient Greek "to walk with the feet close together." To meet at some place. In the New Testament, to happen at the same time. To occur simultaneously. To befall; happen to - With reference to the suffering and death of Jesus - Mark 10:32; Luke 24:14. Of Paul's trials - Acts 20:19; 21:35. Of the healing of the lame man - Acts 3:10. Of the experience of Israel in the wilderness - 1 Cor.10:11. Of the trials of all Christians - 1 Pet.4:12; of the apostasy of end-time apostates - 2 Pet.2:22.

Translation - "Now as they were on the road going up to Jerusalem, Jesus was going ahead of them and they were seized with amazement, but, although they were following (Him) they began to be afraid. Therefore when He had again called the twelve to His side He began to relate to them the things that were going to happen to Him."

Comment: *Cf.* comment on Mt.20:17 and Lk.18:31. Jesus had just finished His teaching about forsaking all to follow Him (Mk.10:17-31). Now He is about to put the Twelve to the test, because, if they continue to follow Him, they must go to Jerusalem, where He is about to die.

They are leaving Perea for the last time, as they thread their way through the hill country, going up to the city where Jesus will die. Note the imperfect periphrastics ἦν ἀναβαίνοντες and ἦν προάγων. It was while they were going up to Jerusalem, and while Jesus was walking ahead of them, "on the road" (ἐν τῇ ὁδῷ). The two main verbs are imperfects with inceptive emphasis. "They were seized with amazement and they began to fear." But their amazement and fear did not prevent them from following Jesus. This is the force of the concessive participle ἀκολουθοῦντες. "Although they were following Him" - a fact which might, to superficial observation, seem to indicate that they were not worried by what He had said about giving up everything for His sake, the fact was that they were seized with fear. Thus the Twelve at this point manifested their bravery. It takes a brave man to walk into a battle, when he has the choice before him to remain behind.

Jesus was walking in front. Normally one would suppose that the one who was to die would lag behind. But not our Lord. His hour was at hand (Mt.26:45; Mk.14:35,41; Lk.22:14; John 7:30; 8:20; 12:23,27,27; 13:1; 17:1). He had been looking forward to it since the day that He raised Lazarus from the dead (John 11:33,38). It was the disciples who were lagging behind, although they were following, not deserting, Him. They were in a state of emotional stress (#2059) and fear (#101).

Jesus, of course,knew how they felt and He acted to help them. He called them again to His side (aorist participle in παραλαβὼν) and began to explain to them that what was about to happen to Him was in conformity to God's eternal plan of redemption. The only fear that the Christian could have that could be justified, is the fear that something could happen that God is helpless to prevent, the consequences of which would prevent the ultimate purpose of God from being realized. If God can be ultimately defeated in His plan, then we, who are identified with Him through Christ, are in eternal trouble. The cure for soul sorrow therefore is the assurance, confidently held and joyously contemplated, that what happened to the Son of God when He arrived in Jerusalem was the perfect outworking of a perfectly conceived plan and that God, not only anticipated the cross, but He planned it. He, Who planned it, also planned a resurrection from the grave for the One who died at Calvary. And He also planned an ascension, a high priestly ministry of intercession for the Heavenly Melchisedek, the coming of the Holy Spirit into the world, the inspiration of the New Testament and the administration of the worldwide missionary enterprise, that would select from every culture of human history the members of the Body of Christ. Finally, God planned that when His missionary work was finished, Christ would return to earth, sit on David's throne as David's Son and Heir, and establish, for the first time in human history, a viable government among redeemed men and women. These things are what the Twelve needed to know if they were to follow Jesus without fear and dread to the Garden of Gethsemane, the kangaroo court of Annas and Caiaphas, the judgment hall of Pilate and to Golgotha.

What Jesus told them now was what He had already told them before (Mt.16:21). Now that the time is at hand, He goes into more detail than before in verses 33 and 34.

Verse 33 - "Saying, Behold we go up to Jerusalem, and the Son of Man shall be delivered unto the chief priests, and unto the scribes; and they shall condemn him to death, and shall deliver him to the Gentiles."

ὅτι Ἰδοὺ ἀναβαίνομεν εἰς Ἱεροσόλυμα, καὶ ὁ υἱὸς τοῦ ἀνθρώπου παραδοθήσεται τοῖς ἀρχιερεῦσιν καὶ τοῖς γραμματεῦσιν, καὶ κατακρινοῦσιν αὐτὸν θανάτῳ καὶ παραδώσουσιν αὐτὸν τοῖς ἔθνεσιν.

ὅτι (recitative) 211.
Ἰδοὺ (exclamation) 95.
ἀναβαίνομεν (1st.per.pl.pres.act.ind.of ἀναβαίνω, futuristic) 323.
εἰς (preposition with the accusative of extent) 140.
Ἱεροσόλυμα (acc.sing.masc.of Ἱεροσολύμων, extent) 141.
καὶ (continuative conjunction) 14.
ὁ (nom.sing.masc.of the article in agreement with υἱὸς) 9.
υἱὸς (nom.sing.masc.of υἱός, subject of παραδοθήσεται and ἀναστήσεται) 5.
τοῦ (gen.sing.masc.of the article in agreement with ἀνθρώπου) 9.
ἀνθρώπου (gen.sing.masc.of ἄνθρωπος, description) 341.
παραδοθήσεται (3d.per.sing.fut.pass.ind.of παραδίδωμι, predictive) 368.
τοῖς (dat.pl.masc.of the article in agreement with ἀρχιερεῦσιν) 9.
ἀρχιερεῦσιν (dat.pl.masc.of ἀρχιερεύς, indirect object of παραδοθήσεται) 151.
καὶ (adjunctive conjunction joining nouns) 14.
τοῖς (dat.pl.masc.of the article in agreement with γραμματεῦσιν) 9.
γραμματεῦσιν (dat.pl.masc.of γραμματεύς, indirect object of παραδοθήσεται) 152.
καὶ (continuative conjunction) 14.
κατακρινοῦσιν (3d.per.pl.fut.act.ind.of κατακρίνω, predictive) 1012.
αὐτὸν (acc.sing.masc.of αὐτός, direct object of κατακρινοῦσιν) 16.
θανάτῳ (instrumental sing.masc.of θάνατος, means) 381.
καὶ (adjunctive conjunction joining verbs) 14.
παραδώσουσιν (3d.per.pl.fut.act.ind.of παραδίδωμι, predictive) 368.
αὐτὸν (acc.sing.masc.of αὐτός, direct object of παραδώσουσιν) 16.
τοῖς (dat.pl.masc.of the article in agreement with ἔθνεσιν) 9.
ἔθνεσιν (dat.pl.masc.of ἔθνος, indirect object of παραδώσουσιν) 376.

Translation - "Look! We are going up to Jerusalem, and the Son of Man will be betrayed into the hands of the chief priests and the scribes, and they will condemn Him to death and deliver Him to the Gentiles."

Comment: ὅτι is recitative introducing the direct discourse. Our Lord's terse statement is a compound sentence consisting of four coordinate clauses tied together by continuative and adjunctive καὶ. They were going to Jerusalem, despite the fact that they knew full well what would happen when they arrived. Jesus would be betrayed by Judas Iscariot to the police who would deliver Him to the chief priests and scribes. They would condemn Him to death, but, because the Jewish court, under Roman law, had no jurisdiction in cases involving the death penalty, they would hand Him over to Pilate, the Roman Governor, whose court was competent in such a case. *Cf.* κατακρίνω in Roman 8:3. The

Jews thought only of condemning Jesus, but in God's plan they brought about the death of the Son of Man and thus condemned "sin in the flesh." *Cf.*#381, III, for all the uses of θάνατος in reference to the death of Christ. The Jews determined to kill Him, little realizing what His death would do to save sinners! Of course, we are not forgetting John 10:16-18. His tormentors did not kill, although they tried hard enough. They were not big enough to kill Him. He laid down His life and He took it again, because He is the Author of Life (Acts 3:15).

Jesus' detailed description of coming events continues in

Verse 34 - "And they shall mock him, and shall scourge him, and shall spit upon him, and shall kill him; and the third day he shall rise again.

καὶ ἐμπαίξουσιν αὐτῷ καὶ ἐμπτύσουσιν αὐτῷ καὶ μαστιγώσουσιν αὐτὸν καὶ ἀποκτενοῦσιν, καὶ μετὰ τρεῖς ἡμέρας ἀναστήσεται.

καὶ (continuative conjunction) 14.
ἐμπαίξουσιν (3d.per.pl.fut.act.ind.of ἐμπαίζω, predictive) 212.
αὐτῷ (dat.sing.masc.of αὐτός, indirect object of ἐμπαίξουσιν) 16.
καὶ (adjunctive conjunction, joining verbs) 14.
ἐμπτύσουσιν (3d.per.pl.fut.act.ind.of ἐμπτύω, predictive) 1606.
αὐτῷ (loc.sing.masc.of αὐτός, place where) 14.
καὶ (adjunctive conjunction joining verbs) 14.
μαστιγώσουσιν (3d.per.pl.fut.act.ind.of μαστιγόω, predictive) 875.
αὐτὸν (acc.sing.masc.of αὐτός, direct object of μαστιγώσουσιν) 16.
καὶ (adjunctive conjunction joining verbs) 14.
ἀποκτενοῦσιν (3d.per.pl.fut.act.ind.of ἀποκτείνω, predictive) 889.
καὶ (adversative conjunction) 14.
μετὰ (preposition with the accusative of time extent) 50.
τρεῖς (acc.sing.fem.of τρεῖς, in agreement with ἡμέρας) 1010.
ἡμέρας (acc.pl.fem.of ἡμέρα, time extent) 135.
ἀναστήσεται (3d.per.sing.fut.pass.ind.of ἀνίστημι, predictive) 789.

Translation - "And they will mock Him and spit upon Him and whip Him and they will kill Him, but after three days He will be raised up."

Comment: The list of coming events continues from verse 33. The Gentiles were to ridicule, spit upon, flog and murder Him. But (adversative καὶ) He was destined to be raised from the dead. Note the passive voice in ἀναστήσεται. God the Father will raise Him from the dead (Eph.1:20). Here Jesus gives credit to the Father, though He, being equal to the Father also had the power to take up His life again (John 10:16-18). No one but the incarnate Son of God who, in counsel with the Father and the Holy Spirit, had conceived redemption's plan, even down to the details, could have foretold the precise details of His suffering. What He predicted to the Disciples on the road to Jerusalem is exactly what happened. Note the sequence - betrayal, insult, torture, death *AND* resurrection! This was all in conformity to His promise of Mark 10:30 - personal denial, their reward, with persecution in this life, followed by eternal life in the coming age. We now examine the parallel account in Luke 18:31-34.

Luke 18:31 - "Then he took unto him the twelve, and said unto them, Behold, we go up to Jerusalem, and all things that are written by the prophets concerning the Son of Man shall be accomplished."

Παραλαβὼν δὲ τοὺς δώδεκα εἶπεν πρὸς αὐτούς, Ἰδοὺ ἀναβαίνομεν εἰς Ἰερουσαλήμ, καὶ τελεσθήσεται πάντα τὰ γεγραμμένα διὰ τῶν προφητῶν τῷ υἱῷ τοῦ ἀνθρώπου.

Παραλαβὼν (aor.act.part.nom.sing.masc.of παραλαμβάνω, adverbial, temporal) 102.
δὲ (continuative conjunction) 11.
τοὺς (acc.pl.masc.of the article in agreement with δώδεκα) 9.
δώδεκα (acc.pl.masc.of δώδεκα, direct object of παραλαβὼν) 820.
εἶπεν (3d.per.sing.aor.act.ind.of εἶπον, constative) 155.
πρὸς (preposition with the accusative of extent, after a verb of speaking) 197.
αὐτούς (acc.pl.masc.of αὐτός, extent, after a verb of speaking) 16.
Ἰδοὺ (exclamation) 95.
ἀναβαίνομεν (1st.per.pl.pres.act.ind.of ἀναβαίνω, futuristic) 323.
εἰς (preposition with the accusative of extent) 140.
Ἰερουσαλήμ (acc.sing.masc.of Ἰεροσολύμων, extent) 141.1
καὶ (continuative conjunction) 14.
τελεσθήσεται (3d.per.sing.fut.pass.ind.of τελέω, predictive) 704.
πάντα (acc.pl.neut.of πᾶς, in agreement with γεγραμμένα) 67.
τὰ (acc.pl.neut.of the article in agreement with γεγραμμένα) 9.
γεγραμμένα (perf.pass.part.acc.pl.neut. of γράφω, substantival, direct object of τελεσθήσεται) 156.
διὰ (preposition with the genitive, intermediate agent) 118.
τῶν (gen.pl.masc.of the article in agreement with προφητῶν) 9.
προφητῶν (gen.pl.masc.of προφητής, intermediate agent) 119.
τῷ (dat.sing.masc.of the article in agreement with υἱῷ) 9.
υἱῷ (dat.sing.masc.of υἱός, reference) 5.
τοῦ (gen.sing.masc.of the article in agreement with ἀνθρώπου) 9.
ἀνθρώπου (gen.sing.masc.of ἄνθρωπος, relationship) 341.

Translation - "And when He had called the Twelve to Him, He said to them, 'Look! We are going up to Jerusalem, and all the things written by the prophets about the Son of Man will be fulfilled.' "

Comment: *Cf.* comment on Mk.10:32,33 and Mt.20:17,18. Matthew and Mark spell out in detail what will be done. Luke refers to these things, not in specific detail, but by saying πάντα τὰ γεγραμμένα διὰ τῶν προφητῶν τῷ υἱῷ τοῦ ἀνθρώπου. Thus Luke points to the fact that the Godhead had not only planned the passion of Christ in detail so that Jesus could announce in advance what was going to happen, but had also inspired the Old Testament prophets to write about it, hundreds of years before the fact. *Cf.*#704 for all the passages where τελέω is used to refer to the death of Christ - Lk.12:50; 18:31; 22:37; John 19:30,38; Acts 13:29. See the account of the events themselves for the Old Testament passages which prophesied the events.

Verse 32 - "For he shall be delivered unto the Gentiles, and shall be mocked, and spitefully entreated, and spitted upon."

παραδοθήσεται γὰρ τοῖς ἔθνεσιν καὶ ἐμπαιχθήσεται καὶ ὑβρισθήσεται καὶ ἐμπτυσθήσεται,

παραδοθήσεται (3d.per.sing.fut.pass.ind.of παραδίδωμι, predictive) 368.
γὰρ (causal conjunction) 105.
τοῖς (dat.pl.masc.of the article in agreement with ἔθνεσιν) 9.
ἔθνεσιν (dat.pl.masc.of ἔθνος, indirect object of παραδοθήσεται) 376.
καὶ (continuative conjunction) 14.
ἐμπαιχθήσεται (3d.per.sing.fut.pass.ind.of ἐμπαίζω, predictive) 212.
καὶ (adjunctive conjunction joining verbs) 14.
ὑβρισθήσεται (3d.per.sing.fut.pass.ind.of ὑβρίζω, predictive) 1403.
καὶ (adjunctive conjunction, joining verbs) 14.
ἐμπτυσθήσεται (3d.per.sing.fut.pass.ind.of ἐμπτύω, predictive) 1606.

Translation - "Because He will be betrayed to the Gentiles, and He will be ridiculed and upbraided and spit upon."

Comment: *Cf.* comment on Mt.20:19 and Mk.10:33,34. Note Luke 11:45. The lawyers accused Jesus of shamefully treating them as they were about to treat Him.

Verse 33 - "And they shall scourge him, and put him to death: and the third day he shall rise again."

καὶ μαστιγώσαντες ἀποκτενοῦσιν αὐτόν, καὶ τῇ ἡμέρᾳ τῇ τρίτῃ ἀναστήσεται.

καὶ (adjunctive conjunction joining verbs) 14.
μαστιγώσαντες (aor.act.part.nom.pl.masc.of μαστιγόω, adverbial, temporal) 875.
ἀποκτενοῦσιν (3d.per.pl.fut.act.ind.of ἀποκτείνω, predictive) 889.
αὐτόν (acc.sing.masc.of αὐτός, direct object of ἀποκτενοῦσιν) 16.
καὶ (adversative conjunction) 14.
τῇ (loc.sing.fem.of the article in agreement with ἡμέρᾳ) 9.
ἡμέρᾳ (loc.sing.fem.of ἡμέρα, time point) 135.
τῇ (loc.sing.fem.of the article in agreement with τρίτῃ) 9.
τρίτῃ (loc.sing.fem.of τρίτος, in agreement with ἡμέρᾳ) 1209.
ἀναστήσεται (3d.per.sing.fut.pass.ind.of ἀνίστημι, predictive) 789.

Translation - "And when they have scourged Him they will murder Him, but on the third day He will be raised up."

Comment: *Cf.*comment on Mk.10:34 and Mt.20:19. Lukes uses the adverbial temporal participle μαστιγώσαντες. Mark uses the future indicative and Matthew has the aorist infinitive. Same idea; differing personal styles. Matthew uses the normal attributive position for τρίτῃ - τῇ τρίτῃ ἡμέρᾳ in the locative of time point phrase. Luke makes it emphatic with τῇ ἡμέρᾳ τῇ τρίτῃ. Mark says, μετὰ τρεῖς ἡμέρας - "after three days." All agree that the resurrection verb is passive, though Matthew uses ἐγερθήσεται (#125) instead of ἀναστήσεται (#789)

Verse 34 - "And they understood none of these things: and this saying was hid from them, neither knew they the things which were spoken."

καὶ αὐτοὶ οὐδὲν τούτων συνῆκαν, καὶ ἦν τὸ ῥῆμα τοῦτο κεκρυμμένον ἀπ' αὐτῶν, καὶ οὐκ ἐγίνωσκον τὰ λεγόμενα.

καὶ (adversative conjunction) 14.
αὐτοὶ (nom.pl.masc.of αὐτός, subject of συνῆκαν) 16.
οὐδὲν (acc.sing.neut.of οὐδείς, direct object of συνῆκαν) 446.
τούτων (gen.pl.neut.of οὗτος, partitive genitive) 93.
συνῆκαν (3d.per.pl.aor.act.ind.of συνίημι, constative) 1039.
καὶ (causal conjunction) 14.
ἦν (3d.per.sing.imp.ind.of εἰμί, pluperfect periphrastic) 86.
τὸ (nom.sing.neut.of the article in agreement with ῥῆμα) 9.
ῥῆμα (nom.sing.neut.of ῥῆμα, subject of ἦν) 343.
τοῦτο (nom.sing.neut.of οὗτος, in agreement with ῥῆμα) 93.
κεκρυμμένον (perf.pass.part.nom.sing.neut.of κρύπτω, pluperfect periphrastic) 451.
ἀπ' (preposition with the ablative of separation) 70.
αὐτῶν (abl.pl.masc.of αὐτός, separation) 16.
καὶ (inferential conjunction) 14.
οὐκ (summary negative conjunction with the indicative) 130.
ἐγίνωσκον (3d.per.pl.imp.act.ind.of γίνώσκω, inceptive) 131.
τὰ (acc.pl.neut.of the article in agreement with λεγόμενα) 9.
λεγόμενα (pres.pass.part.acc.pl.neut.of λέγω, substantival, direct object of ἐγίνωσκον) 66.

Translation - "But they understood none of these things, because this concept had been hidden from them. Therefore they did not begin to graspthe meaning of what was said."

Comment: καὶ is adversative. Despite the clarity of Jesus' words the disciples did not understand. The causal clause introduced by καὶ tells us why. The pluperfect periphrastic (ἦν κεκρυμμένον) speaks of a complete action in the past with durative present results. The meaning of Jesus' words had been hidden from them and the result (inferential καὶ) was that they did not begin to know (inceptive imperfect in ἐγίνωσκον) what was said. The substantival participle λεγόμενα is the object of ἐγίωσκον.

On the subject of "planned obscurity" see Lk.19:42; Mt.11:25; 13:35. *Cf.*#451.

It is difficult to understand why the disciples could not understand such plain language as Jesus had just employed. The words, *παραδίδωμι, ἐμπαίζω, ὑβρίζω, ἐμπτύω, μαστιγόω, ἀποκτείνω, ἀνίστημι* - "betray,mock,insult,spit on, whip,kill, rise" are all clear. It was all so foreign to their idea that Jesus was indeed Messiah, but that He should receive such treatment. Even after He arose the Emmaus disciples could not believe it (Lk.24:16). *Cf.* Lk.9:45. We have the benefit of hindsight as we read the New Testament and enjoy a tradition of two thousands years of church history. We should not therefore take too much credit for understanding the history which to the disciples was not history but prophecy. Yet modern students of the Word of God feel that we have some clear understanding of what the Bible tells us about events which are yet future to us, as we await the Second Coming of Messiah.

It is clear from the next episode that the disciples, particularly James and John, did not understand that there would be no Messianic kingdom at this time.

The Selfish Ambition of James and John Rebuked

(Matthew 20:20-28; Mark 10:35-45)

Mark 10:35 - "And James and John, the sons of Zebedee, come unto him, saying, Master, we would that thou shouldest do for us whatsoever we shall desire."

Καὶ προσπορεύονται αὐτῷ Ἰάκωβος καὶ Ἰωάννης οἱ υἱοὶ Ζεβεδαίου λέγοντες αὐτῷ, Διδάσκαλε, θέλομεν ἵνα ὃ ἐὰν αἰτήσωμέν σε ποιήσῃς ἡμῖν.

Καὶ (continuative conjunction) 14.

#2643 *προσπορεύονται* (3d.per.pl.pres.mid.ind.of *προσπορεύομαι*, historical).

come unto - Mark 10:35.

Meaning: A combination of *πρός* (#197) and *πορεύομαι* (#170). Hence, to approach. With reference to James and John in Mark 10:35.

αὐτῷ (loc.sing.masc.of *αὐτός*, after *πρός* in composition, with a verb of rest) 16.

Ἰάκωβος (nom.sing.masc.of *Ἰάκωβος*, subject of *προσπορεύονται*) 397.

καὶ (adjunctive conjunction joining nouns) 14.

Ἰωάννης (nom.sing.masc.of *Ἰωάννης*, subject of *προσπορεύονται*) 399.

οἱ (nom.pl.masc.of the article in agreement with *υἱοὶ*) 9.

υἱοὶ (nom.pl.masc.of *υἱός*, apposition) 5.

Ζεβεδαίου (gen.sing.masc.of *Ζεβεδαῖος*, relationship) 398.

λέγοντες (pres.act.part.nom.pl.masc.of *λέγω*, adverbial, circumstantial) 66.

αὐτῷ (dat.sing.masc.of *αὐτός*, indirect object of *λέγοντες*) 16.

Διδάσκαλε (voc.sing.masc.of *διδάσκαλος*, address) 742.

θέλομεν (1st.per.pl.pres.act.ind.of *θέλω*, aoristic) 88.

ἵνα (conjunction introducing a consecutive clause with the subjunctive) 114.

ὃ (acc.sing.neut.of *ὅς*, direct object of *ποιήσῃς*) 65.

ἐὰν (conditional particle with the subjunctive in an indefinite relative clause) 363.

αἰτήσωμέν (1st.per.pl.aor.act.subj.of αἰτέω, third-class condition) 537.
σε (acc.sing.masc.of σύ, direct object of αἰτήσωμεν) 104.
ποιήσῃς (2d.per.sing.aor.act.subj.of ποιέω, consecutive clause, result) 127.
ἡμῖν (dat.pl.masc.of ἐγώ, personal advantage) 123.

Translation - "And James and John the sons of Zebedee came to Him, saying, 'Teacher, we want you to do for us whatever we ask.' "

Comment: *Cf.* comment on Mt.20:20. Matthew records that the mother of James and John accompanied them. The ἵνα clause with ποιήσῃς is consecutive. It expresses result. James and John were hoping for a result - that Jesus would do whatever they asked. ἐὰν with the subjunctive αἰτήσωμεν is an indefinite relative clause, introduced by the relative pronoun ὅ. The passage can also be regarded as a third-class condition. "We hope for this result: that if we ask anything, whatever it may be, you will do it for us." The self seeking character of the three is clear when we look at the extent of their request. "Whatever we ask, you want you to do!" This blanket approval of course could not be given. If God agreed, upon His unsullied honor, to grant every request that came to Him from this degenerate race we would drive Him out of His universe.

Jesus asked James and John to be more specific in

Verse 36 - "And he said unto them, What would ye that I should do for you?"

ὁ δὲ εἶπεν αὐτοῖς, Τί θέλετέ (με) ποιήσω ὑμῖν;

ὁ (nom.sing.masc.of the article, subject of εἶπεν) 9.
δὲ (continuative conjunction) 11.
εἶπεν (3d.per.sing.aor.act.ind.of εἶπον, constative) 155.
αὐτοῖς (dat.pl.masc.of αὐτός, indirect object of εἶπεν) 16.
Τί (acc.sing.neut.of τίς, the interrogative pronoun, direct object of θέλετέ) 281.
θέλετέ (2d.per.pl.pres.act.ind.of θέλω, direct question) 88.
(με) (acc.sing.masc.of ἐγώ, general reference) 123.
ποιήσω (1st.per.sing.aor.act.subj.of ποιέω, asyndeton, ἵνα omitted) 127.
ὑμῖν (dat.pl.masc.of σύ, personal advantage) 104.

Translation - "And He said to them, 'What do you want me to do for you?' "

Comment: Mark is guilty of asyndeton here as he omits ἵνα before the subjunctive ποιήσω. Matthew simplifies it with Τί θέλεις;- "what do you want?"

Verse 37 - "They said unto him, Grant unto us that we may sit, one on thy right hand, and the other on thy left hand, in thy glory."

οἱ δὲ εἶπαν αὐτῷ, Δὸς ἡμῖν ἵνα εἷς σου ἐκ δεξιῶν καὶ εἷς ἐξ ἀριστερῶν καθίσωμεν ἐν τῇ δόξῃ σου.

οἱ (nom.pl.masc.of the article, subject of εἶπαν) 9.
δὲ (continuative conjunction) 11.

εἶπαν (3d.per.pl.aor.act.ind.of εἶπον, constative) 155.
αὐτῷ (dat.sing.masc.of αὐτός, indirect object of εἶπαν) 16.
Δὸς (2d.per.sing.2d.aor.aor.act.impv.of δίδωμι, entreaty) 362.
ἡμῖν (dat.pl.masc.of ἐγώ, indirect object of δὸς) 123.
ἵνα (conjunction with the subjunctive in a consecutive clause) 114.
εἷς (nom.sing.masc.of εἷς, antithetic pronoun) 469.
σοῦ (gen.sing.masc.of σύ, possession) 104.
ἐκ (preposition with the genitive of place description) 19.
δεξιῶν (gen.pl.masc.of δεξιός, place description) 502.
καὶ (adjunctive conjunction joining prepositional phrases) 14.
εἷς (nom.sing.masc.of εἷς, antithetic pronoun) 469.
ἐξ (preposition with the genitive of place description) 19.
ἀριστερῶν (gen.pl.masc.of ἀριστερός, place description) 564.
καθίσωμεν (1st.per.pl.aor.act.subj.of καθίζω, result) 420.
ἐν (preposition with the locative of place where) 80.
τῇ (loc.sing.fem.of the article in agreement with δόξῃ) 9.
δόξῃ (loc.sing.fem.of δόξα, place where) 361.
σου (gen.sing.masc.of σύ, possession) 104.

Translation - "And they said to Him, 'Grant to us that we may sit, one at your right and one at your left, in your glory.' "

Comment: *Cf.* comment on Mt.20:21, which represents the mother as making the request on behalf of her sons. *Cf.* Mt.19:28. They were already certain of a judgeship in the Kingdom Age. James and John wanted the two principal thrones. It is a wonder that they were not fighting between themselves for the better of the two positions, if there was a difference. Their request indicates that they did not understand what Jesus had just told them about the events in the future, not too distant, in Jerusalem (Lk.18:34). Failing to grasp the fact of a cross in the future, they were thinking only of a crown. And James and John wanted the two best crowns! How necessary that they should hear what Jesus now asks, in

Verse 38 - "But Jesus said unto them, Ye know not what ye ask: can ye drink of the cup that I drink of? and be baptized with the baptism that I am baptized with?"

ὁ δὲ Ἰησοῦς εἶπεν αὐτοῖς, Οὐκ οἴδατε τί αἰτεῖσθε. δύνασθε πιεῖν τὸ ποτήριον ὃ ἐγὼ πίνω, ἢ τὸ βάπτισμα ὃ ἐγὼ βαπτίζομαι βαπτισθῆναι;

ὁ (nom.sing.masc.of the article, in agreement with Ἰησοῦς) 9.
δὲ (adversative conjunction) 11.
Ἰησοῦς (nom.sing.masc.of Ἰησοῦς, subject of εἶπεν) 3.
εἶπεν (3d.per.sing.aor.act.ind.of εἶπον, constative) 155.
αὐτοῖς (dat.pl.masc.of αὐτός, indirect object of εἶπεν) 16.
Οὐκ (summary negative conjunction with the indicative) 130.
οἴδατε (2d.per.pl.pres.act.ind.of ὁράω, aoristic) 144.
τί (acc.sing.neut.of τίς, direct object of οἴδατε, indirect question) 281.

αἰτεῖσθε (2d.per.pl.pres.mid.ind.of *αἰτέω*, aoristic) 537.
δύνασθε (2d.per.pl.pres.mid.ind.of *δύναμαι*, direct question) 289.
πιεῖν (aor.act.inf.of *πίνω*, epexegetical) 611.
τὸ (acc.sing.neut.of the article in agreement with *ποτήριον*) 9.
ποτήριον (acc.sing.neut.of *ποτήριον*, direct object of *πιεῖν*) 902.
ὃ (acc.sing.neut.of *ὅς*, direct object of *πίνω*) 65.
ἐγὼ (nom.sing.masc.of *ἐγώ*, subject of *πίνω*) 123.
πίνω (1st.per.sing.pres.act.ind.of *πίνω*, futuristic) 611.
ἢ (disjunctive particle) 465.
τὸ (acc.sing.neut.of the article in agreement with *βάπτισμα*) 9.
βάπτισμα (acc.sing.neut.of *βάπτισμα*, general reference) 278.
ὃ (acc.sing.neut.of *ὅς*, general reference) 65.
ἐγὼ (nom.sing.masc.of *ἐγώ*, subject of *βαπτίζομαι*) 123.
βαπτίζομαι (1st.per.sing.pres.pass.ind.of *βαπτίζω*, futuristic) 273.
βαπτισθῆναι (aor.pass.inf.of *βαπτίζω*, completes *δύνασθε*) 273.

Translation - "But Jesus said to them, 'You do not know what you are asking. Are you able to drink the cup which I am going to drink, or to be baptized with the baptism with which I am going to be baptized?' "

Comment: *Cf.* comment on Mt.20:22 and Lk.12:50a. *δὲ* is adversative as Jesus is going to deny their request. Note the present middle in *αἰτεῖσθε* - "what you are asking for yourselves." The cup which He is going to drink - *Cf.* Mt.26:42; John 18:11; Mt.26:39; Mk.14:36; Lk.22:42. Can you drain the cup of sin, agony and death upon a cross? The disciples were looking for a crown without a cross. With reference to baptism in the sense of the suffering of Christ, *cf.* Lk.12:50. The cup symbolizes evil (Ps.11:6), but also good (Ps.23:5). Here it refers to His suffering. Jesus asks a penetrating question and gets almost an offhand reply in

Verse 39 - "And they said unto him, We can. And Jesus said unto them, Ye shall indeed drink of the cup that I drink of; and with the baptism that I am baptized withal shall ye be baptized."

οἱ δὲ εἶπαν αὐτῷ, Δυνάμεθα. ὁ δὲ Ἰησοῦς εἶπεν αὐτοῖς, Τὸ ποτήριον ὃ ἐγὼ πίνω πίεσθε καὶ τὸ βάπτισμα ὃ ἐγὼ βαπτίζομαι βαπτισθήσεσθε,

οἱ (nom.pl.masc.of the article, subject of *εἶπαν*) 9.
δὲ (continuative conjunction) 11.
εἶπαν (3d.per.pl.aor.act.ind.of *εἶπον*, constative) 155.
αὐτῷ (dat.sing.masc.of *αὐτός*, indirect object of *εἶπαν*) 16.
Δυνάμεθα (1st.per.pl.pres.mid.ind.of *δύναμαι*, aoristic) 289.
ὁ (nom.sing.masc.of the article in agreement with *Ἰησοῦς*) 9.
δὲ (adversative conjunction) 11.
Ἰησοῦς (nom.sing.masc.of *Ἰησοῦς*, subject of *εἶπεν*) 3.
εἶπεν (3d.per.sing.aor.act.ind.of *εἶπον*, constative) 155.
αὐτοῖς (dat.pl.masc.of *αὐτός*, indirect object of *εἶπεν*) 16.
Τὸ (acc.sing.neut.of the article in agreement with *ποτήριον*) 9.

ποτήριον (acc.sing.neut.of ποτήριον, direct object of πίεσθε) 902.
ὃ (acc.sing.neut.of ὅς, direct object of πίνω) 65.
ἐγὼ (nom.sing.masc.of ἐγώ, subject of πίνω) 123.
πίνω (1st.per.sing.fut.act.ind.of πίνω, futuristic) 611.
πίεσθε (2d.per.pl.fut.act.ind.of πίνω, predictive) 611.
καὶ (continuative conjunction) 14.
τὸ (acc.sing.neut.of the article in agreement with βάπτισμα) 9.
βάπτισμα (acc.sing.neut.of βάπτισμα, general reference) 278.
ὃ (acc.sing.neut.of ὅς, general reference) 65.
ἐγώ (nom.sing.masc.of ἐγώ, subject of βαπτίζομαι) 123.
βαπτίζομαι (1st.per.sing.pres.mid.ind.of βαπτίζω, futuristic) 273.
βαπτισθήσεσθε (2d.per.pl.fut.pass.ind.of βαπτίζω, predictive) 273.

Translation - "And they said to Him, 'We are able." But Jesus said to them, 'The cup which I will drink, you will drink, and the baptism which I will endure you will undergo.' "

Comment: *Cf.* comment on Mt.20:22,23. Δυνάμεθα. How glib! Jesus, with His exact knowledge of the future hastens to agree with them. They will indeed drink of the cup of death and be baptized (overwhelmed) with the baptism which He will endure. This refers to the persecution which James and John would both endure and the martyrdom of James, though it cannot be pushed to mean that their death would involve what His death did. They were already sinners and could never know Jesus' experience as He became sin for them (2 Cor.5:21) and paid their sin debt (1 Pet.2:24; 3:18; Isa.53:5,6). But from an earthly point of view their future was not a rosy one.

Verse 40 - "But to sit on my right hand and on my left is not mine to give; but it shall be given to them for whom it is prepared.

τὸ δὲ καθίσαι ἐκ δεξιῶν μου ἢ ἐξ εὐωνύμων οὐκ ἔστιν ἐμὸν δοῦναι, ἀλλ' οἷς ἡτοίμασται.

τὸ (nom.sing.neut.of the article in agreement with καθίσαι) 9.
δὲ (adversative conjunction) 11.
καθίσαι (aor.act.inf.of καθίζω, noun use, subject of ἔστιν) 420.
ἐκ (preposition with the genitive of place description) 19.
δεξιῶν (gen.pl.masc.of δεξιός, place description) 502.
μου (gen.sing.masc.of ἐγώ, possession) 123.
ἢ (disjunctive particle) 465.
ἐξ (preposition with the genitive of place description) 19.
εὐωνύμων (gen.pl.masc.of εὐώνυμος, place description) 1329.
οὐκ (summary negative conjunction with the indicative) 130.
ἔστιν (3d.per.sing.pres.ind.of εἰμί, static) 86.
ἐμὸν (acc.sing.masc.of ἐμός, possessive pronoun, general reference) 1267.
δοῦναι (aor.act.inf.of δίδωμι, completes ἔστιν) 362.
ἀλλ' (alternative conjunction) 342.

οἷς (dat.pl.masc.of ὅς, indirect object of δοῦναι) 65.
ἡτοίμασται (3d.per.sing.perf.pass.ind.of ἑτοιμάζω, consummative) 257.

Translation - "But to sit at my right hand or at my left is not mine to give, except to those for whom it has been prepared."

Comment: *Cf.* comment on Mt.20:23, who adds ὑπὸ τοῦ πατρός μου. Τὸ καθίσαι, the articular infinitive in the nominative case is the subject of ἔστιν, which in turn is completed by δοῦναι. δοῦναι, however is qualified. Jesus does not say that the gift of the privilege of sitting beside Him is not His to give at all. He does say that, though He will give these gifts, they will be given to those for whom it has been prepared. The perfect tense in ἡτοίμασται indicates that this preparation decision was made in the past. The throne belongs to Jesus Christ, the King and He will grant these honors to those already designated.

The other disciples were not happy about the presumption of James and John, as we learn in

Verse 41 - "And when the ten heard it they began to be much displeased with James and John."

Καὶ ἀκούσαντες οἱ δέκα ἤρξαντο ἀγανακτεῖν περὶ Ἰακώβου καὶ Ἰωάννου.

Καὶ (continuative conjunction) 14.
ἀκούσαντες (aor.act.part.nom.pl.masc.of ἀκούω, adverbial, temporal/causal) 148.
οἱ (nom.pl.masc.of the article in agreement with δέκα) 9.
δέκα (nom.pl.masc.of δέκα, subject of ἤρξαντο) 1330.
ἤρξαντο (3d.per.pl.aor.mid.ind.of ἄρχω, ingressive) 383.
ἀγανακτεῖν (pres.inf.of ἀγανακτέω, epexegetical) 1331.
περὶ (preposition with the genitive of reference) 173.
Ἰακώβου (gen.sing.masc.of Ἰάκωβον, reference) 397.
καὶ (adjunctive conjunction joining nouns) 14.
Ἰωάννου (gen.sing.masc.of Ἰωάννης, reference) 399.

Translation - "And when (because) they heard, the ten became incensed with James and John."

Comment: The participle is both temporal and causal. It was when and because the ten disciples heard about the ambitious requests of James and John that they became annoyed. Thus they demonstrated that they were as carnal as James and John, whose only superiority was that they thought of it first. The pique was jealousy. This is as sinful as vaulting political ambition. Their attitudes are particularly revolting in view of the fact that they were all within the shadow of the cross. If the ten disciples had understood the love that sent Jesus to Calvary they would have been happy for James and John to be honored with the positions that they sought. They all needed the lesson that Jesus gave them in

Verse 42 - "But Jesus called them to him, and saith unto them, Ye know that they which are accounted to rule over the Gentiles exercise lordship over them; and

their great ones exercise authority upon them."

καὶ προσκαλεσάμενος αὐτοὺς ὁ Ἰησοῦς λέγει αὐτοῖς, Οἴδατε ὅτι οἱ δοκοῦντες ἄρχειν τῶν ἐθνῶν κατακυριεύουσιν αὐτῶν καὶ οἱ μεγάλοι αὐτῶν κατεξουσιάζουσιν αὐτῶν.

καὶ (inferential conjunction) 14.
προσκαλεσάμενος (aor.mid.part.nom.sing.masc.of προσκαλέω, adverbial, temporal) 842
αὐτοὺς (acc.pl.masc.of αὐτός, direct object of προσκαλεσάμενος) 16.
ὁ (nom.sing.masc.of the article in agreement with Ἰησοῦς) 9.
Ἰησοῦς (nom.sing.masc.of Ἰησοῦς, subject of λέγει) 3.
λέγει (3d.per.sing.pres.act.ind.of λέγω, historical) 66.
αὐτοῖς (dat.pl.masc.of αὐτός, indirect object of λέγει) 16.
Οἴδατε (2d.per.pl.pres.act.ind.of ὁράω, aoristic) 144.
ὅτι (conjunction introducing an object clause in indirect discourse) 211.
οἱ (nom.pl.masc.of the article in agreement with δοκοῦντες) 9.
δοκοῦντες (pres.act.part.nom.pl.masc.of δοκέω, substantival, subject of κατακυριεύουσιν) 287.
ἄρχειν (pres.act.inf.of ἄρχω, completes δοκοῦντες) 383.
τῶν (gen.pl.masc.of the article in agreement with ἐθνῶν) 9.
ἐθνῶν (gen.pl.masc.of ἔθνος, description) 376.
κατακυριεύουσιν (3d.per.pl.pres.act.ind.of κατακυριεύω, customary) 1332.
αὐτῶν (gen.pl.masc.of αὐτός, description) 16.
καὶ (continuative conjunction) 14.
οἱ (nom.pl.masc.of the article in agreement with μεγάλοι) 9.
μεγάλοι (nom.pl.masc.of μέγας, subject of κατεξουσιάζουσιν) 184.
αὐτῶν (gen.pl.masc.of αὐτός, relationship) 16.
κατεξουσιάζουσιν (3d.per.pl.pres.act.ind.of κατεξουσιάζω, customary) 1333.
αὐτῶν (gen.pl.masc.of αὐτός, description) 16.

Translation - "And Jesus called them to Him and said to them, 'You know that those who are plotting to rule the Gentiles, lord it over them and their leaders exercise authority over them.' "

Comment: *Cf.*comment on Mt.20:25; Lk.22:25,26.

Verse 43 - "But so shall it not be among you: but whosoever will be great among you, shall be your minister."

οὐχ οὕτως δέ ἐστιν ἐν ὑμῖν, ἀλλ' ὃς ἂν θέλῃ μέγας γενέσθαι ἐν ὑμῖν ἔσται ὑμῶν διάκονος,

οὐχ (summary negative conjunction with the indicative) 130.
οὕτως (demonstrative adverb) 74.
δὲ (adversative conjunction) 11.
ἐστιν (3d.per.sing.pres.ind.of εἰμί, static) 86.
ἐν (preposition with the locative, with plural pronouns) 80.
ὑμῖν (loc.pl.masc.of σύ, association, plural pronouns) 104.

ἀλλ' (alternative conjunction) 342.

ὅς (nom.sing.masc.of ὅς, indefinite relative clause, subject of θέλῃ, more probable condition) 65.

ἂν (contingent particle in an indefinite relative clause) 205.

θέλῃ (3d.per.sing.pres.act.subj.of θέλω, indefinite relative clause) 88.

μέγας (nom.sing.masc.of μέγας, predicate adjective) 184.

γενέσθαι (aor.inf.of γίνομαι, completes θέλῃ) 113.

ἐν (preposition with the locative with plural pronouns) 80.

ὑμῖν (loc.pl.masc.of σύ, association) 104.

ἔσται (3d.per.sing.fut.ind.of εἰμί, imperative) 86.

ὑμῶν (gen.pl.masc.of σύ, relationship) 104.

διάκονος (nom.sing.masc.of διάκονος, predicate nominative) 1334.

Translation - "But it is not like that among you, rather whoever may wish to be great among you must be your servant."

Comment: *Cf.* comment on Mt.20:26; Lk.22:26. The unsaved world plays the game one way (verse 42). Christian disciples, in our fellowship play it exactly oppositively. Jesus recognized that not all Christians would be so self-effacing. The indefinite relative clause ὅς ἂν θέλῃ . . . κ.τ.λ. is a more probable condition. True greatness is found in the lowest, not the highest place. Jesus did not say, "Be a dictator." He said, "Be a deacon." Deacons should find out what the word means.

Verse 44 - "And whosoever of you will be the chiefest, shall be servant of all."

καὶ ὅς ἂν θέλῃ ἐν ὑμῖν εἶναι πρῶτος, ἔσται πάντων δοῦλος.

καὶ (continuative conjunction) 14.

ὅς (nom.sing.masc.of ὅς, in an indefinite relative clause, more probable condition) 65.

ἂν (contingent particle) 205.

θέλῃ (3d.per.sing.pres.act.subj.of θέλω, more probable condition) 88.

ἐν (preposition with the locative with plural pronouns) 80.

ὑμῖν (loc.pl.masc.of σύ, association) 104.

εἶναι (pres.inf.of εἰμί, complementary) 86.

πρῶτος (nom.sing.masc.of πρῶτος, predicate adjective) 487.

ἔσται (3d.per.sing.fut.ind.of εἰμί, imperative) 86.

πάντων (gen.pl.masc.of πᾶς, description) 67.

δοῦλος (nom.sing.masc.of δοῦλος, predicate nominative) 725.

Translation - "And whoever may wish to be first in your fellowship must be a servant of all."

Comment: *Cf.* comment on Mt.20:27. This is good advice because it conforms to the divine example, set by Jesus in

Verse 45 - "For even the Son of Man came not to be ministered unto, but to

minister, and to give his life a ransom for many."

καὶ γὰρ ὁ υἱὸς τοῦ ἀνθρώπου οὐκ ἦλθεν διακονηθῆναι ἀλλὰ διακονῆσαι καὶ δοῦναι τὴν ψυχὴν αὐτοῦ λύτρον ἀντὶ πολλῶν.

καὶ (ascensive conjunction) 14.
γὰρ (causal conjunction) 105.
ὁ (nom.sing.masc.of the article in agreement with *υἱὸς*) 9.
υἱὸς (nom.sing.masc.of *υἱός*, subject of *ἦλθεν*) 5.
τοῦ (gen.sing.masc.of the article in agreement with *ἀνθρώπου*) 9.
ἀνθρώπου (gen.sing.masc.of *ἄνθρωπος*, relationship) 341.
οὐκ (summary negative conjunction with the indicative) 130.
ἦλθεν (3d.per.sing.aor.ind.of *ἔρχομαι*, culminative) 146.
διακονηθῆναι (1st.aor.pass.inf.of *διακονέω*, purpose) 367.
ἀλλὰ (alternative conjunction) 342.
διακονῆσαι (aor.act.inf.of *διακονέω*, purpose) 367
καὶ (adjunctive conjunction joining infinitives) 14.
δοῦναι (aor.act.inf.of *δίδωμι*, purpose) 362.
τὴν (acc.sing.fem.of the article in agreement with *ψυχὴν*) 9.
ψυχὴν (acc.sing.fem.of *ψυχή*, direct object of *δοῦναι*) 233.
αὐτοῦ (gen.sing.masc.of *αὐτός*, possession) 16.
λύτρον (acc.sing.neut.of *λύτρος*, predicate nominative) 1335.
ἀντὶ (preposition with the ablative, substitution) 237.
πολλῶν (abl.pl.masc.of *πολύς*, substitution) 228.

Translation - "Because even the Son of Man is not here to be served, but to serve and to give His life a ransom in behalf of many."

Comment: *καὶ* is ascensive. It points to the limitless superiority of the person of Jesus above the twelve. Yet *even* He did not come to be waited upon. Note the culminative aorist in *ἦλθεν*. *γὰρ* is causal. Jesus came to do two things: (a) to minister to other people, and (2) to give His life in substitution, as a payment for the sin debt of many. Thus He sets the many free. The idea of freedom in *λύτρον* (#1335) fits this context admirably. James and John had ambitions to take the most prominent places. This implies that they would enslave the others. Those who sit at the right and left of the Sovereign are not normally thought of as servants. Rather they expect others to serve them. But even the King did not come to earth to do that.

ἀντί does not always mean "instead of." *Cf.*#237. But here, and in the parallel passage (Mt.20:28) it occurs. "But does it mean *instead of* in Mt.20:28 and Mk.10:45? Either that, or else it means *in exchange for*, and each implies substitution. The obscurity of this passage is not the result of linguistic ambiguity, but of theological controversy." (J.R.Mantey, *A Manual Grammar of the Greek New Testament*, 100). Note the LXX for Gen.22;13; 44:33; Num.3:12. Dr. Faris D. Whitesell has discovered these and 35 other passages in the LXX where *ἀντί* is correctly translated *instead of* in the Revised Version. *Cf.* comment on Mt.20:28.

(4). Towards Jerusalem. Blind Man Healed Near Jericho

(Matthew 20:29-34; Mark 10:46-52; Luke 18:35-43)

Mark 10:46 - "And they came to Jericho: And as he went out of Jericho with his disciples and a great number of people, blind Bartimaeus, the Son of Timaeus, sat by the highway side begging.

Καὶ ἔρχονται εἰς Ἰεριχώ. καὶ ἐκπορευομένου αὐτοῦ ἀπὸ Ἰεριχὼ καὶ τῶν μαθητῶν αὐτοῦ καὶ ὄχλου ἱκανοῦ ὁ υἱὸς Τιμαίου Βαρτιμαῖος τυφλὸς ἐκάθατο παρὰ τὴν ὁδὸν προσαιτῶν.

Καὶ (continuative conjunction) 14.
ἔρχονται (3d.per.pl.pres.ind.of *ἔρχομαι*, historical) 146.
εἰς (preposition with the accusative of extent) 140.
Ἰεριχώ (acc.of extent) 1336.
καὶ (continuative conjunction) 14.
ἐκπορευομένου (pres.mid.part.gen.sing.masc.of *εκπορεύομαι*, genitive absolute) 270.
αὐτοῦ (gen.sing.masc.of *αὐτός*, genitive absolute) 16.
ἀπὸ (preposition with the ablative of separation) 70.
Ἰεριχὼ (abl.sing.of *Ἰεριχώ* indeclin., separation) 1336.
καὶ (adjunctive conjunction joining a pronoun with a noun) 14.
τῶν (gen.pl.masc.of the article in agreement with *μαθητῶν*) 9.
μαθητῶν (gen.pl.masc.of *μαθητής*, genitive absolute) 421.
αὐτοῦ (gen.sing.masc.of *αὐτός*, relationship) 16.
καὶ (adjunctive conjunction joining nouns) 14.
ὄχλου (gen.sing.masc.of *ὄχλος*, genitive absolute) 418.
ἱκανοῦ (gen.sing.masc.of *ἱκανός*, in agreement with *ὄχλου*) 304.
ὁ (nom.sing.masc.of the article in agreement with *υἱὸς*) 9.
υἱὸς (nom.sing.masc.of *υἱός*, subject of *ἐκάθητο*) 5.

#2644 *Τιμαίου* (gen.sing.masc.of *Τιμαῖος*, relationship).

Timaeus - Mark 10:46.

Meaning: Timaeus, the father of Bartimaeus - Mark 10:46.

#2645 *Βαρτιμαῖος* (nom.sing.masc.of *Βαρτιμαῖος*, apposition).

Bartimaeus - Mark 10:46.

Meaning: Bartimaeus, the son of Timaeus, a blind man whom Jesus healed - Mark 10:46.

τῦφλὸς (nom.sing.masc.of *τυφλός*, in agreement with *προσαίτης*) 830.

#2646 *προσαίτης* (nom.sing.masc.of *προσαίτης*, apposition).

beggar - Mark 10:46.

Meaning: *Cf.*προσαιτέω (#2397). Hence, a beggar. Bartimaeus - Mark 10:46.

ἐκάθητο (3d.per.sing.imp.mid.ind.of κάθημαι, progressive description) 377.
παρὰ (preposition with the accusative, "physically alongside") 154.
τὴν (acc.sing.fem.of the article in agreement with ὁδόν) 9.
ὁδόν (acc.sing.fem.of ὁδός, alongside) 199.

Translation - "And they came to Jericho. And as He and His disciples with a large crowd were leaving Jericho, the son of Timaeus, Bartimaeus, a blind man, was sitting by the side of the road."

Comment: Jesus did not remain long in the city of Jericho. *Cf.*#1336 for a description of the city. Having passed through, He, His disciples and a large number of people were on their way out of town. Note the involved genitive absolute with αὐτοῦ, τῶν μαθητῶν αὐτοῦ καὶ ὄχλου ἱκανου all joined to the participle ἐκπορευομένου. As Jesus and His company were leaving the city they passed the blind beggar, identified only in Mark as Bartimaeus, the son of Timaeus and further described as a blind beggar. Matthew 20:30 tells us that he was accompanied by another blind man. *Cf.* also Mt.9:27-31 for a similar earlier occasion when He healed two blind men. Matthew tells us that Jesus picked up the great crowd in the city. In the Mt.20:29-34 account there are two blind men, both of whom are healed. Mark 10:46-52 and Luke 18:35-43 tell essentially the same story, but mention only one, though there is no denial that there was another one also. It should be clear that Mt.9:27-31 records an earlier event.

(*Note: The Greek text which we have printed at the beginning of this verse is preferred by the United Bible Societies' Committee. Because the text which we were following when this verse was worked out originally contains the word* προσαίτης, in its only occurrence in the New Testament, we included it and gave it the appropriate number. The reader will note that we call attention to προσειτέω (#2397), which the Aland Committee text has in its participial form.).

Verse 47 - "And when he heard that it was Jesus of Nazareth, he began to cry out, and say, Jesus, thou Son of David, have mercy on me."

καὶ ἀκούσας ὅτι Ἰησοῦς ὁ Ναζαρηνός ἐστιν ἤρξατο κράζειν καὶ λέγειν, Υἱὲ Δαυὶδ Ἰησοῦ, ἐλέησόν με.

καὶ (continuative conjunction) 14.
ἀκούσας (aor.act.part.nom.sing.masc.of ἀκούω, adverbial, temporal/causal) 148.
ὅτι (conjunction introducing an object clause in indirect discourse) 211.
Ἰησοῦς (nom.sing.masc.of Ἰησοῦς, subject of ἐστιν) 3.
ὁ (nom.sing.masc.of the article in agreement with Ναζαρηνός) 9.
Ναζαρηνός (nom.sing.masc.of Ναζαρηνός, apposition) 245.
ἐστιν (3d.per.sing.pres.ind.of εἰμί, aoristic) 86.
ἤρξατο (3d.per.sing.aor.mid.ind.of ἄρχω, ingressive) 383.
κράζειν (pres.act.inf.of κράζω, completes ἤρξατο) 765.

καὶ (adjunctive conjunction, joining infinitives) 14.
λέγειν (pres.act.infinitive of *λέγω*, completes *ἤρξατο*) 66.
Υἱὲ (voc.sing.masc.of *υἱός*, address) 5.
Δαυὶδ (gen.sing.masc.of *Δαυίδ*, relationship) 5.
Ἰησοῦ (voc.sing.masc.of *Ἰησοῦς*, apposition) 3.
ἐλέησόν (2d.per.sing.aor.act.impv.of *ἐλεέω*, entreaty) 430.
με (acc.sing.masc.of *ἐγώ*, direct object of *ἐλέησόν*) 123.

Translation - "And when he heard that it was Jesus, the Nazarene, he began to cry out and to say, 'Son of David, Jesus, have mercy on me.' "

Comment: *Cf.* comment on Mt.20:30 and Lk.18:37. The participle *ἀκούσας* may be taken both as temporal and causal. *ὅτι* introducing the object clause in indirect discourse. In indirect, the tenses are the same as in direct. The people about the beggar were saying, "It is Jesus, the Nazarene."

Here was a man too blind to see Jesus, perhaps symbolic of many who are too prejudiced and depraved to see Jeses intellectually and spiritually (2 Cor.4:4). But at least Bartimaeus had faith enough in those about him to believe that when he heard them say that Jesus was passing by, such was really the case. If he had not believed them as they shouted their greeting to Jesus, he would never have been healed. Similarly, some unsaved people are so skeptical that they choose to believe nothing that the Christian witness may say about Jesus. Bartimaeus acted upon his faith in the truth of the cry of the people. He cried out for help. The inceptive imperfect in *ἤρξατο* indicates that he began to cry out and did not cease, when he was rebuked, but continued to cry out for help until he got it. The people said that Jesus was there and the blind man believed it. Faith in the testimony of the preacher may result in faith in the One being preached. Faith always means action. He also believed that Jesus could and would heal him, if he could attract our Lord's attention. Hence he continued to call out. Nor would he cease, despite the rebuke of the people in verse 48.

It is interesting that Bartimaeus did exactly what Paul says in Romans 10:13 one must do to be saved. He called upon the name of the Lord, although he added his entreaty, *ἐλέησόν με*.

I remember a poor man in a rescue mission. I had showed him Romans 10:13 and told him that he needed only to "call upon the name of the Lord" if he wanted to be saved. He took my statement literally. He held up his hands to heaven and said, "Lord, Lord! Lord!!!' He was saved. So was Bartimaeus.

Verse 48 - "And many charged him that he should hold his peace; but he cried out the more a great deal, Thou son of David, have mercy on me."

καὶ ἐπετίμων αὐτῷ πολλοὶ ἵνα σιωπήσῃ. ὁ δὲ πολλῷ μᾶλλον ἔκραζεν, Υἱὲ Δαυίδ, ἐλέησόν με.

καὶ (adversative conjunction) 14.
ἐπετίμων (3d.per.pl.imp.act.ind.of *ἐπιτιμάω*, inceptive) 757.

αὐτῷ (loc.sing.masc.of αὐτός, with a verb of emotion) 16.
πολλοὶ (nom.pl.masc.of πολύς, subject of ἐπετίμων) 228.
ἵνα (conjunction with the subjunctive, purpose) 114.
σιωπήσῃ (3d.per.sing.aor.act.subj.of σιωπάω, purpose) 1337.
ὁ (nom.sing.masc.of the article, subject of ἔκραζεν) 9.
δὲ (adversative conjunction) 11.
πολλῷ (instrumental sing.neut.of πολύς, measure) 228.
μᾶλλον (adverbial) 619.
ἔκραζεν (3d.per.sing.imp.act.ind.of κράζω, progressive description) 765.
Υἱὲ (voc.sing.masc.of υἱός, address) 5.
Δαυίδ (gen.sing.masc.of Δαυίδ, relationship) 6.
ἐλέησόν (2d.per.sing.aor.act.impv.of ἐλεέω, entreaty) 430.
με (acc.sing.masc.of ἐγώ, direct object of ἐλέησόν) 123.

Translation - "But many began to order him to stop crying out, but he continued to shout even more, 'Son of David, have mercy on me.' "

Comment: The cries of Bartimaeus annoyed many and they began to order him to be silent. The ἵνα clause with the subjunctive tells us why. But (adversative δὲ) he refused to stop. On the contrary he continued to cry out with increased intensity.

Here was one of Jericho's most poverty stricken outcasts - a blind beggar, too blind to see Jesus physically (βλέπω) but not too blind in terms of his faith to see Him intellectually and with spiritual perception (ὁράω). We recall Helen Keller's remark about those who had eyes and still could not see. *Cf.*#228, for other examples of πολλῷ μᾶλλον.

Verse 49 - "And Jesus stood still, and commanded him to be called. And they call the blind man, saying unto him, Be of good comfort, rise; he calleth thee."

καὶ στὰς ὁ Ἰησοῦς εἶπεν, Φωνήσατε αὐτόν. καὶ φωνοῦσιν τὸν τυφλὸν λέγοντες αὐτῷ, Θάρσει, ἔγειρε, φωνεῖ σε.

καὶ (continuative conjunction) 14.
στὰς (aor.act.part.nom.sing.masc.of ἵστημι, adverbial, temporal) 180.
ὁ (nom.sing.masc.of the article in agreement with Ἰησοῦς) 9.
Ἰησοῦς (nom.sing.masc.of Ἰησοῦς, subject of εἶπεν) 3.
εἶπεν (3d.per.sing.aor.act.ind.of εἶπον, constative) 155.
Φωνήσατε (2d.per.pl.aor.act.impv.of φωνέω, command) 1338.
αὐτόν (acc.sing.masc.of αὐτός, direct object of φωνήσατε) 16.
καὶ (inferential conjunction) 14.
φωνοῦσιν (3d.per.pl.pres.act.ind.of φωνέω, historical) 1338.
τὸν (acc.sing.masc.of the article in agreement with τυφλὸν) 9.
τυφλὸν (acc.sing.masc.of τυφλός, direct object of φωνοῦσιν) 830.
λέγοντες (pres.act.part.nom.pl.masc.of λέγω, adverbial, temporal) 66.
αὐτῷ (dat.sing.masc.of αὐτός, indirect object of λέγοντες) 16.
Θάρσει (2d.per.sing.pres.act.impv.of θαρσέω, command) 780.

ἔγειρε (2d.per.sing.pres.act.impv.of ἐγείρω, command) 125.
φωνεῖ (3d.per.sing.pres.act.ind.of φωνέω, aoristic) 1338.
σε (acc.sing.masc.of σύ, direct object of φωνεῖ) 104.

Translation - "And Jesus paused and said, 'Call him." Therefore they called the blind man and said to him, 'Cheer up! Get up. He is calling you.' "

Comment: Jesus, of course, heard Bartimaeus' cries. He already knew that he was there and that he was blind and a beggar. Note the plural in *φωνοῦσιν*. Many (πολλοὶ) had tried to silence him. Now many, others perhaps as well as those who had tried to silence him, call and encourage him. "Cheer up! Get up. Jesus is calling." (Rom.10:13; John 10:3; Lk.8:54; John 12:17). *Cf.*#1338 for the dynamic nature of the call of the Son of God. The calling of God is without repentance (Rom.11:29).

Verse 50 - "And he, casting away his garment, rose, and came to Jesus."

ὁ δὲ ἀποβαλὼν τὸ ἱμάτιον αὐτοῦ, ἀναπηδήσας ἦλθεν πρὸς τὸν Ἰησοῦν.

ὁ (nom.sing.masc.of the article, subject of ἦλθεν) 9.
δὲ (inferential conjunction) 11.

#2647 ἀποβαλὼν (aor.act.part.nom.sing.masc.of ἀποβάλλω, adverbial, temporal).

cast away - Mark 10:50; Heb.10:35.

Meaning: A combination of ἀπό (#70) and βάλλω (#299). Hence, to throw away; abandon by casting aside. Physically, of a garment - Mark 10:50. Metaphorically in Heb.10:35.

τὸ (acc.sing.neut.of the article in agreement with ἱμάτιον) 9.
ἱμάτιον (acc.sing.neut.of ἱμάτιον, direct object of ἀποβαλὼν) 534.
αὐτοῦ (gen.sing.masc.of αὐτός, possession) 16.

#2648 ἀναπηδήσας (aor.act.part.nom.sing.of of ἀναπηδάω, adverbial, temporal).

rose - Mark 10:50.

Meaning: A combination of ἀνά (#1059) and πηδάω - "to spring" or "to leap." Hence, to spring or leap up. *Cf.*ἀνίστημι (#789). With reference to Bartimaeus, upon being called by Jesus - Mark 10:50.

ἦλθεν (3d.per.sing.aor.ind.of ἔρχομαι, constative) 146.
πρὸς (preposition with the accusative of extent) 197.
τὸν (acc.sing.masc.of the article in agreement with Ἰησοῦν) 9.
Ἰησοῦν (acc.sing.masc.of Ἰησοῦς, extent) 3.

Translation - "And he threw off his coat, leaped up and came to Jesus."

Comment: The two participles provide the order of the action. He threw aside

his coat. Perhaps he had been using it to protect himself from the chill. It was late March or early April. Then he leaped to his feet with alacrity and came to Jesus. When Jesus calls even a blind man can find the way to His side.

Verse 51 - "And Jesus answered and said unto him, What wilt thou that I should do unto thee? The blind man said unto him, Lord, that I might receive my sight."

καὶ ἀποκριθεὶς αὐτῷ ὁ Ἰησοῦς εἶπεν, Τί σοι θέλεις ποιήσω; ὁ δὲ τυφλὸς εἶπεν αὐτῷ, Ραββουνι, ἵνα ἀναβλέψω.

καὶ (continuative conjunction) 14.
ἀποκριθεὶς (aor.part.nom.sing.masc.of *ἀποκρίνομαι*, adverbial, modal) 318.
αὐτῷ (dat.sing.masc.of *αὐτός*, indirect object of *ἀποκριθεὶς*) 16.
ὁ (nom.sing.masc.of the article in agreement with Ἰησοῦς) 9.
Ἰησοῦς (nom.sing.masc.of Ἰησοῦς, subject of *εἶπεν*) 3.
εἶπεν (3d.per.sing.aor.act.ind.of *εἶπον*, constative) 155.
Τί (acc.sing.neut.of *τίς*, interrogative pronoun, direct object of *ποιήσω*) 281.
σοι (dat.sing.masc.of *σύ*, personal advantage) 104.
θέλεις (2d.per.sing.pres.act.ind.of *θέλω*, aoristic) 88.
ποιήσω (1st.per.sing.fut.act.ind.of *ποιέω*, deliberative) 127.
ὁ (nom.sing.masc.of the article in agreement with *τυφλὸς*) 9.
δὲ (continuative conjunction) 11.
τυφλὸς (nom.sing.masc.of *τυφλός*, subject of *εἶπεν*) 830.
εἶπεν (3d.per.sing.aor.act.ind.of *εἶπον*, constative) 155.
αὐτῷ (dat.sing.masc.of *αὐτός*, indirect object of *εἶπεν*) 16.

#2649 Ραββουνι (voc.sing.masc.of Ραββονι, address).

Lord - Mark 10:51.
Rabboni - John 20:16.

Meaning: The highest title of honor in the Jewish schools - Mark 10:51; John 20:16.

ἵνα (conjunction with the subjunctive in a purpose clause) 114.
ἀναβλέψω (1st.per.sing.1st.aor.act.subj.of *ἀναβλέπω*, purpose) 907.

Translation - "And Jesus said to him in reply, 'What do you want me to do for you?' And the blind man said to Him, 'Rabbi, that I may see again.' "

Comment: Jesus, of course knew what the man wanted, but He elicted his request nevertheless. *Cf.* Mt.20:32,33; Lk.18:41. Matthew has the two men saying, "Lord, that our eyes may be opened."

Verse 52 - "And Jesus said unto him, Go thy way; thy faith had made thee whole. And immediately he received his sight, and followed Jesus in the way."

καὶ ὁ Ἰησοῦς εἶπεν αὐτῷ, Ὕπαγε, ἡ πίστις σου σέσωκέν σε. καὶ εὐθὺς ἀνέβλεψεν, καὶ ἠκολούθει αὐτῷ ἐν τῇ ὁδῷ.

καὶ (continuative conjunction) 14.

ὁ (nom.sing.masc.of the article in agreement with Ἰησοῦς) 9.
Ἰησοῦς (nom.sing.masc.of Ἰησοῦς, subject of εἶπεν) 3.
εἶπεν (3d.per.sing.aor.act.ind.of εἶπον, constative) 155.
αὐτῷ (dat.sing.masc.of αὐτός, indirect object of εἶπεν) 16.
Ὕπαγε (2d.per.sing.pres.act.impv.of ὑπάγω, command) 364.
ἡ (nom.sing.fem.of the article in agreement with πίστις) 9.
πίστις (nom.sing.fem.of πίστις, subject of σέσωκέν) 728.
σου (gen.sing.masc.of σύ, possession) 104.
σέσωκέν (3d.per.sing.perf.act.ind.of σῴζω, intensive) 109.
σε (acc.sing.masc.of σύ, direct object of σέσωκέν) 104.
καὶ (continuative conjunction) 14.
εὐθὺς (adverbial) 258.
ἀνέβλεψεν (3d.per.sing.aor.act.ind.of ἀναβλέπω, constative) 907.
καὶ (adjunctive conjunction joining verbs) 14.
ἠκολούθει (3d.per.sing.imp.act.ind.of ἀκολουθέω, inceptive) 394.
αὐτῷ (dat.sing.masc.of αὐτός, personal advantage) 16.
ἐν (preposition with the locative of place) 80.
τῇ (loc.sing.fem.of the article in agreement with ὁδῷ) 9.
ὁδῷ (loc.sing.fem.of ὁδός, place where) 199.

Translation - "And Jesus said to him, 'Go on your way. Your faith has saved you.' And immediately he regained his sight, and he began to follow Him along the road."

Comment: Jesus ordered the man to go away - perhaps back to Jericho, to find employment, now that his sight was restored. He also implied that Bartimaeus was not only healed from blindness, but also given the inner light of salvation from sin. In this case, unlike that of John 9, there is no anointing with clay or order to wash. By His word, Jesus opened Bartimaeus' eyes.

There is nothing mysterious about the last clause. The man now began (inceptive imperfect in ἠκολούθει) to follow Jesus along the road, as He made His way to Jerusalem. We shall see in Luke's account, which follows, that it probably resulted in Bartimaeus sharing in the wealth of another lost man in Jericho, who also could not see Jesus.

Luke 18:35 - "And it came to pass, that as he was come nigh unto Jericho, a certain blind man sat by the way side begging."

Ἐγένετο δὲ ἐν τῷ ἐγγίζειν αὐτὸν εἰς Ἰεριχὼ τυφλός τις ἐκάθητο παρὰ τὴν ὁδὸν ἐπαιτῶν.

Ἐγένετο (3d.per.sing.aor.ind.of γίνομαι, constative) 113.
δὲ (explanatory conjunction) 11.
ἐν (preposition with the locative of time point) 80.
τῷ (loc.sing.neut.of the article, time point) 9.
ἐγγίζειν (pres.act.inf.of ἐγγίζω, temporal clause) 252.
αὐτὸν (acc.sing.masc.of αὐτός, general reference) 16.
εἰς (preposition with the accusative of extent) 140.

Ἰεριχὼ (acc.sing.of Ἰεριχώ, extent) 1336.

τυφλὸς (nom.sing.masc.of τυφλός, subject of ἐκάθητο) 830.

τις (nom.sing.masc.of τις, the indefinite pronoun, in agreement with τυφλὸς) 486.

ἐκάθητο (3d.per.sing.imp.mid.ind.of κάθημαι, progressive description) 377.

παρὰ (preposition with the accusative, "alongside") 154.

τὴν (acc.sing.fem.of the article in agreement with ὁδὸν) 9.

ὁδὸν (acc.sing.fem.of ὁδός, place where) 199.

ἐπαιτῶν (pres.act.part.nom.sing.masc.of ἐπαιτέω, adverbial, circumstantial) 2562.

Translation - "And it happened as He approached Jericho that some blind man was sitting by the road side begging."

Comment: *Cf.* comment on Mt.20:29 and Mk.10:46. Matthew and Mark employ the participial genitive absolutes to denote the time of the event. Luke uses the articular infinitive in the locative case to show time point. Both modes of expression are good Greek.

But Matthew and Mark say that Jesus encountered the blind man as He was leaving Jericho, while Luke says that it was as He entered the city. Mark says, "They came to Jericho and as He was leaving. . . " There is no way to resolve the contradiction. Matthew and Mark on the one hand and Luke on the other cannot both be correct. The Holy Spirit was not concerned about it apparently, since the point has nothing to do with the story. What difference does it make whether Jesus met Bartimaeus as He was entering Jericho (Luke) or, having entered it (Mark), as He was leaving the city (Matthew and Mark)? This is precisely the point in our comment on inspiration in Luke 18:15. Here the Holy Spirit wishes us to know the story about Jesus and Bartimaeus. The exact spot, whether on one side of Jericho or the other, is not important. If exact physical location were essential to our clear understanding of the story, the orthodox view of inspiration would be in trouble. Of course the *Fundamentalist* dictation theory has always been in trouble because it does not conform to the facts.

Verse 36 - "And hearing the multitude pass by, he asked what it meant."

ἀκούσας δὲ ὄχλου διαπορευομένου ἐπυνθάνετο τί εἴη τοῦτο.

ἀκούσας (aor.act.part.nom.sing.masc.of ἀηούω, adverbial, temporal/causal) 148.

δὲ (continuative conjunction) 11.

ὄχλου (gen.sing.masc.of ὄχλος, description) 418.

διαπορευομένου (pres.part.gen.sing.masc.of διαπορεύομαι, adjectival, in agreement with ὄχλου) 2101.

ἐπυνθάνετο (3d.per.sing.imp.mid.ind.of πυνθάνομαι, inceptive) 153.

τί (nom.sing.neut.of τίς, the interrogative pronoun subject of εἴη, indirect question) 281.

εἴη (3d.per.sing.pres.opt.of εἰμί, deliberative) 86.

τοῦτο (nom.sing.neut.of οὗτος, predicate nominative) 93.

Translation - "And when he heard a crowd passing through he began to ask what it meant?"

Comment: Luke alone records the blind man's question. He heard the sound. The participle διαπορευομένου is a verbal adjective, modifying ὄχλου. Note the deliberative optative, the mode of the greatest doubt. "Whatever might this noise be?" *Cf.* Lk.3:15; 8:9, but 15:26 where we have τί ἂν εἴη ταῦτα. The blind man needed to depend upon his friends to tell him what was happening since he could not see. If he had had no faith in their integrity he would not have asked them to explain the commotion, or having asked, would not have believed what they said. Thus he never would have called out for mercy and might never have been healed and saved. Sinners with no faith in Christ might, at least, have faith in the Christian testimony. Otherwise they could never believe in Christ.

Verse 37 - "And they told him, that Jesus of Nazareth passeth by."

ἀπήγγειλαν δὲ αὐτῷ ὅτι Ἰησοῦς ὁ Ναζωραῖος παρέρχεται.

ἀπήγγειλαν (3d.per.pl.aor.act.ind.of ἀπαγγέλλω, constative) 176.
δὲ (continuative conjunction) 11.
αὐτῷ (dat.sing.masc.of αὐτός, indirect object of ἀπήγγειλαν) 16.
ὅτι (conjunction introducing an object clause in indirect discourse) 211.
Ἰησοῦς (nom.sing.masc.of Ἰησοῦς, subject of παρέρχεται) 3.
ὁ (nom.sing.masc.of the article in agreement with Ναζωραῖος) 9.
Ναζωραῖος (nom.sing.masc.of Ναζωραῖος, apposition) 245.
παρέρχεται (3d.per.sing.pres.mid.ind.of παρέρχομαι, historical) 467.

Translation - "And they told him that Jesus, the Nazarene was passing by."

Comment: *Cf.* comment on Mt.20:30 and Mk.10:47. *Cf.*#467 with special attention to Lk.11:42; 15:29, where παρέρχομαι means "to disregard." It is fortunate for Bartimaeus that Jesus was passing by physically and not in the metaphorical sense. Our Lord would never disregard a cry for help, which comes in

Verse 38 - "And he cried saying, Jesus, thou Son of David, have mercy on me."

καὶ ἐβόησεν λέγων, Ἰησοῦ, υἱὲ Δαυίδ, ἐλέησόν με.

καὶ (continuative conjunction) 14.
ἐβόησεν (3d.per.sing.aor.act.ind.of βοάω, ingressive) 256.
λέγων (pres.act.part.nom.sing.masc.of λέγω, recitative) 66.
Ἰησοῦ (voc.sing.masc.of Ἰησοῦς, address) 3.
υἱὲ (voc.sing.masc.of υἱός, apposition) 5.
Δαυίδ (gen.sing.masc.of Δαυίδ, relationship) 6.
ἐλέησόν (2d.per.sing.aor.act.impv.of ἐλεέω, entreaty) 430.
με (acc.sing.masc.of ἐγώ, direct object of ἐλέησόν) 123.

Translation - "And he began to cry out, saying, 'Jesus, Son of David, have mercy on me.' "

Comment: *Cf.* comment on Mt.20:30; Mk.10:47. The student may wish to compare βοάω (#256) with κράζω (#765). Luke uses the former; Matthew and Mark the latter. All four gospel writers use both verbs somewhere. Thayer conjectures, "βοάω, to cry out as a manifestation of feeling; κράζειν, to cry out harshly, often of an inarticulate and brutal sound... βοάω suggests sensibilities; κράζειν instincts. Hence, βοάω, esp. a cry for help." In Classical Greek perhaps. In the New Testament??!

Verse 39 - "And they which went before rebuked him, that he should hold his peace; but he cried so much the more, Thou Son of David, have mercy on me."

καὶ οἱ προάγοντες ἐπετίμων αὐτῷ ἵνα σιγήσῃ. αὐτὸς δὲ πολλῷ μᾶλλον ἔκραξεν, Υἱὲ Δαυίδ, ἐλέησόν με.

καὶ (adversative conjunction) 14.
οἱ (nom.pl.masc.of the article in agreement with προάγοντες) 9.
προάγοντες (pres.act.part.nom.pl.masc.of προάγω, substantival, subject of ἐπετίμων) 179.
αὐτῷ (loc.sing.masc.of αὐτός, with a verb of emotion) 16.
ἵνα (conjunction with the subjunctive, purpose) 114.
σιγήσῃ (3d.per.sing.aor.act.subj.of σιγάω, purpose) 2330.
αὐτὸς (nom.sing.masc.of αὐτός, subject of ἔκραξεν) 16.
δὲ (adversative conjunction) 11.
πολλῷ (instru.sing.neut.of πολύς, measure) 228.
μᾶλλον (adverbial) 619.
ἔκραξεν (3d.per.sing.imp.act.ind.of κράζω, progressive description) 765.
Υἱὲ (voc.sing.masc.of υἱός, address) 5.
Δαυίδ (gen.sing.masc.of Δαυίδ, relationship) 6.
ἐλέησόν (2d.per.sing.aor.act.impv.of ἐλεέω, entreaty) 430.
με (acc.sing.masc.of ἐγώ, direct object of ἐλεησόν) 123.

Translation - "But those who were going in front began to scold him in order that he would be silent, but he began to cry out much more, 'Son of David, have mercy on me.' "

Comment: *Cf.* comment on Mt.20:31; Mk.10:48. καὶ is adversative as the people tried to quiet Bartimaeus. οἱ προάγοντες - those advance men - not in an official sense. Jesus seldom employed them, but the people were so immature that, in the excitement about Jesus, they ran ahead! We often see children do this. Why would an adult who admired Jesus as they apparently did run ahead of Him, rather than remaining close by His side?

That Jesus had come to heal a blind beggar was farthest from their thoughts. They probably did not have a clear idea as to just why He had come. At any rate, He was so important that He could not be bothered with a blind beggar! So they began to insist that Bartimaeus be silent. But we have another adversative in δὲ. Bartimaeus was not about to be silent and allow perhaps the only chance that he would ever have to pass, without asking for Jesus' help. Bartimaeus called out πολλῷ μᾶλλον. *Cf.*#228, IV. Here Luke uses ἔκραξεν rather than ἐβόησεν as in verse 38. Perhaps the distinction referred to *supra* (vs.38) holds here. At first the blind man called (ἐβόησεν); then, when he was ordered to cease, he called frantically (ἔκραξεν, imperfect tense) again and again. Luke's account gives us enough information to fill in the picture. Those who went ahead (οἱ προάγοντες) rebuked him. This means that he first called out before Jesus arrived at the spot on the road directly in front of him. Rebuked, he called again and again, more vigorously and perhaps with a tone of desperation until Jesus moved up. Let us remember that the man was blind, and had no way of knowing where Jesus was in precise relation to where he sat.

Luke uses σιγάω (#2330) while Matthew and Mark use σιωπάω (#1337). σιγάω means to relax psychologically and thus remain speechless. σιωπάω means simply to abstain from speech. (Thayer, *Lexicon*, 281). *Cf.* also ἡσυχάζω (#2519) which means a quiet condition in general, including verbal abstention.

Jesus was now confronted with one of the poorest men in Jericho, too blind physically to see Him, but not too blind spiritually to call for His help. He was soon to be confronted with the richest man in Jericho, who was not too physically blind but too physically short to see Jesus, but who also was not too spiritually short to seek His help. Thus we have the makings of an application of the social gospel to the theological gospel - in the same town and in the same fifteen minutes.

Verse 40 - "And Jesus stood and commanded him to be brought unto him: and when he was come near, he asked him,"

σταθεὶς δὲ ὁ Ἰησοῦς ἐκέλευσεν αὐτὸν ἀχθῆναι πρὸς αὐτόν. ἐγγίσαντος δὲ αὐτοῦ ἐπηρώτησεν αὐτόν,

σταθεὶς (aor.part.nom.sing.masc.of ἵστημι, adverbial, temporal) 180.
δὲ (continuative conjunction) 11.
Ἰησοῦς (nom.sing.masc.of Ἰησοῦς, subject of ἐκέλευσεν) 3.
αὐτὸν (acc.sing.masc.of αὐτός, general reference) 16.
ἀχθῆναι (aor.pass.inf.of ἄγω, noun use, direct object of ἐκέλευσεν) 876.
πρὸς (preposition with the accusative of extent) 197.
αὐτόν (acc.sing.masc.of αὐτός, extent) 16.
ἐγγίσαντος (aor.act.part.nom.sing.masc.of ἐγγίζω, genitive absolute) 252.
δὲ (continuative conjunction) 11.
αὐτοῦ (gen.sing.masc.of αὐτός, genitive absolute) 16.
ἐπηρώτησεν (3d.per.sing.aor.act.ind.of ἐπερωτάω, constative) 973.
αὐτόν (acc.sing.masc.of αὐτός, direct object of ἐπηρώτησεν) 16.

Translation - "And Jesus stood still and ordered that he be brought to Him. And when he came near He asked him,"

Comment: *Cf.* comment on Mt.20:32 and Mk.10:49,50. Luke uses the 1st.aorist passive participle, σταθεὶς, while Matthew and Mark use the 2d.aorist active *στάς*. Jesus ordered him brought. Matthew and Mark say that He called him. The ideas are not incompatible. Luke explains how a blind man found the spot where Jesus stood. He was led there. The object of *ἐκέλευσεν* is *ἀχθῆναι*, with *αὐτὸν*, an accusative of general reference.

Verse 41 - "Saying, What wilt thou that I shall do unto thee? And he said, Lord, that I may receive my sight."

Τί σοι θέλεις ποιήσω; ὁ δὲ εἶπεν, Κύριε, ἵνα ἀναβλέψω.

Τί (acc.sing.neut.of *τίς*, interrogative pronoun, direct object of *ποιήσω*, direct question) 281.
σοι (dat.sing.masc.of *σύ*, personal advantage) 104.
θέλεις (2d.per.sing.pres.act.ind.of *θέλω*, aoristic) 88.
ποιήσω (1st.per.sing.fut.act.ind.of *ποιέω*, deliberative) 127.
ὁ (nom.sing.masc.of the article, subject of *εἶπεν*) 9.
δὲ (continuative conjunction) 11.
εἶπεν (3d.per.sing.aor.act.ind.of *εἶπον*, constative) 155.
Κύριε (voc.sing.masc.of *κύριος*, address) 97.
ἵνα (conjunction with the subjunctive, purpose) 114.
ἀναβλέψω (1st.per.sing.aor.act.subj.of *ἀναβλέπω*, purpose) 907.

Translation - "What do you want me to do for you? And he said, 'Lord, that I may regain my sight.' "

Comment: *Cf.* comment on Mt.20:33; Mk.10:51. Note the deliberative future after *θέλεις* and the *ἵνα* clause of purpose with the subjunctive.

Verse 42 - "And Jesus said unto him, Receive thy sight: thy faith hath saved thee."

καὶ ὁ Ἰησοῦς εἶπεν αὐτῷ, Ἀνάβλεψον. ἡ πίστις σου σέσωκέν σε.

καὶ (continuative conjunction) 14.
ὁ (nom.sing.masc.of the article in agreement with Ἰησοῦς) 9.
Ἰησοῦς (nom.sing.masc.of Ἰησοῦς, subject of *εἶπεν*) 3.
εἶπεν (3d.per.sing.aor.act.ind.of *εἶπον*, constative) 155.
αὐτῷ (dat.sing.masc.of *αὐτός*, indirect object of *εἶπεν*) 16.
Ἀνάβλεψον (2d.per.sing.aor.act.impv.of *ἀναβλέπω*, command) 907.
ἡ (nom.sing.fem.of the article in agreement with *πίστις*) 9.
πίστις (nom.sing.fem.of *πίστις*, subject of *σέσωκέν*) 728.
σου (gen.sing.masc.of *σύ*, possession) 104.
σέσωκέν (3d.per.sing.perf.act.ind.of *σώζω*, intensive) 109.
σε (acc.sing.masc.of *σύ*, direct object of *σέσωκέν*) 104.

Translation - "And Jesus said to him, 'Regain your sight! Your faith has saved you.' "

Comment: *Cf.* comment on Mt.20:34; Mk.10:52. Matthew says that Jesus touched their eyes. Mark says that He said, "Go away." Luke says He said, "Regain your sight." Of course, Jesus did and said all of these things. Luke follows Mark with ἡ πίστις σου σέσωκέν σε.

Verse 43 - "And immediately he received his sight and followed him, glorifying God. And all the people, when they saw it, gave praise unto God."

καὶ παραχρῆμα ἀνέβλεψεν, καὶ ἠκολούθει αὐτῷ δοξάζων τὸν θεόν. καὶ πᾶς ὁ λάος ἰδὼν ἔδωκεν αἶνον τῷ θεῷ.

καὶ (continuative conjunction) 14.
παραχρῆμα (adverbial) 1369.
ἀνέβλεψεν (3d.per.sing.aor.act.ind.of ἀναβλέπω, ingressive) 907.
ἠκολούθει (3d.per.sing.imp.act.ind.of ἀκολουθέω, inceptive) 394.
αὐτῷ (dat.sing.masc.of αὐτός, personal advantage) 16.
δοξάζων (pres.act.part.nom.sing.masc.of δοξάζω, adverbial, complementary) 461.
τὸν (acc.sing.masc.of the article in agreement with θεόν) 9.
θεόν (acc.sing.masc.of θεός, direct object of δοξάζων) 124.
καὶ (continuative conjunction) 14.
πᾶς (nom.sing.masc.of πᾶς, in agreement with λαὸς) 67.
ὁ (nom.sing.masc.of the article in agreement with λαὸς) 9.
λαὸς (nom.sing.masc.of λαός, subject of ἔδωκεν) 110.
ἰδὼν (aor.act.part.nom.sing.masc.of ὁράω, adverbial, temporal/causal) 144.
ἔδωκεν (3d.per.sing.aor.act.ind.of δίδωμι, ingressive) 362.
αἶνον (acc.sing.masc.of αἶνος, direct object of ἔδωκεν) 1362.
τῷ (dat.sing.masc.of the article, in agreement with θεῷ) 9.
θεῷ (dat.sing.masc.of θεός, indirect object of ἔδωκεν) 124.

Translation - "And immediately he began to see and he began to follow him, glorifying God; and all the people when they saw (it) began to praise God."

Comment: *Cf.* comment on Mt.20:34; Mk.10:52. All the reporters say that Bartimaeus followed Jesus on the road after he received his sight. Matthew includes his companion. Luke adds the praise to God, not only from Bartimaeus, but also from all the people who saw the miracle. There is no reason to translate ἀναβλέπω (#907) literally "to look up." For a former blind man to look up, of course his sight needed first to be restored. ἀνά may be thought of in the sense of "again." As he followed Jesus he was praising God. This is the force of the present tense in δοξάζων. He began (inceptive imperfect in ἠκολούθει) a lifetime of followship that day that we may be sure continued as long as he lived. We can well imagine the scene as Jesus proceded on His way to Jerusalem. Immediately behind Him are the beggars, leaping for joy, as they look in every direction, feasting once blinded eyes upon all the sights, none of which they had ever seen before, weeping no doubt for joy, with hearts overflowing with love and gratitude to Him, Who not only restored their eyesight but saved their souls as well. The episode is not yet complete, as it is tied to the next story.

The Conversion of Zacchaeus

(Luke 19:1-10)

Luke 19:1 - "And Jesus entered and passed through Jericho."

Καὶ εἰσελθὼν διήρχετο τὴν Ἰεριχώ.

Καὶ (continuative conjunction) 14.
εἰσελθὼν (aor.act.part.nom.sing.masc.of εἰσέρχομαι, adverbial, temporal) 234.
διήρχετο (3d.per.sing.imp.mid.ind.of διέρχομαι, progressive description) 1017.
τὴν (acc.sing.fem.of the article in agreement with Ἰεριχώ) 9.
Ἰεριχώ (acc.sing.fem.of Ἰεριχώ, extent) 1336.

Translation - "And He entered and was passing through Jericho."

Comment: Jesus entered Jericho and was on His way through the city. Note the imperfect tense with its durative action in progressive description, of διήρχετο. Keep in mind that immediately behind Him are two very happy men. Very happy but very poor. Bartimaeus and his friend, both of whom have just been saved and who have had their eyesight miraculously restored. The presence of these two men is crucial to our understanding of the entire Jericho episode. We have thus far dealt with the poorest man in Jericho. Now we introduce the richest man in the city.

Verse 2 - "And behold there was a man named Zacchaeus, which was the chief among the publicans, and he was rich."

καὶ ἰδοὺ ἀνὴρ ὀνόματι καλούμενος Ζακχαῖος, καὶ αὐτὸς ἦν ἀρχιτελώνης καὶ αὐτὸς πλούσιος.

καὶ (continuative conjunction) 14.
ἰδοὺ (exclamation) 95.
ἀνὴρ (nom.sing.masc.of ἀνήρ,nominative absolute) 63.
ὀνόματι (instru.sing.neut.of ὄνομα, means) 108.
καλούμενος (pres.pass.part.nom.sing.masc.of καλέω, adjectival, restrictive, in agreement with ἀνὴρ) 107.

#2650 Ζακχαῖος (nom.sing.masc.of Ζακχαῖος, appellation).

Zacchaeus - Luke 19:2,5,8.

Meaning: - The Jericho tax collector - Luke 19:2,5,8.
καὶ (explanatory conjunction) 14.
αὐτὸς (nom.sing.masc.of αὐτός, subject of ἦν) 16.
ἦν (3d.per.sing.imp.ind.of εἰμί, progressive description) 86.

#2651 ἀρχιτελώνης (nom.sing.masc.of ἀρχιτελώνης, predicate nominative).

chief among the publicans - Luke 19:2.

Meaning: A combination of ἄρχω (#383) and τελώνης (#550). Hence, chief publican. Supervisor of all tax collectors. With reference to Zacchaeus in Jericho - Luke 19:2.

καὶ (continuative conjunction) 14.
αὐτὸς (nom.sing.masc.of αὐτός, subject of ἦν understood) 16.
πλούσιος (nom.sing.masc.of πλούσιος, predicate adjective) 1306.

Translation - "And Look! A man called Zacchaeuss was the leading tax collector and he was rich."

Comment: Jesus had only just met two of the poorest people in Jericho. Now He is about to meet the richest man in town, the supervisor of the local revenue department. In league with the hated Romans he collected taxes from the local residents and paid to Rome whatever Caesar required, while he kept the remainder for himself. His personal wealth depended upon the amount which he was able to extract from the people since his obligation to Rome was a fixed amount. We may be sure that it was all that the local traffic would bear. A Jew himself, Zacchaeus had sold out to the enemy and was thoroughly despised by the other Jews who hated Rome and longed for the establishment of their own national state under the rule of Messiah. Zacchaeus' business was lucrative and he had made the most of it.

Bartimaeus was a poverty-stricken beggar who had only recently been lost in sin and too blind to see Jesus. Zacchaeus was a wealthy social outcast, also lost in sin and too short to see Jesus, if there was a crowd around. In this case the crowd was present.

Verse 3 - "And he sought to see Jesus who He was, and could not for the press, because he was little of stature."

καὶ ἐζήτει ἰδεῖν τὸν Ἰησοῦν τίς ἐστιν, καὶ οὐκ ἠδύνατο ἀπὸ τοῦ ὄχλου ὅτι τῇ ἡλικίᾳ μικρὸς ἦν.

καὶ (continuative conjunction) 14.
ἐζήτει (3d.per.sing.imp.act.ind.of ζητέω, progressive description) 207.
ἰδεῖν (aor.act.inf.of ὁράω, purpose) 144.
τὸν (acc.sing.masc.of the article in agreement with Ἰησοῦν) 9.
Ἰησοῦν (acc.sing.masc.of Ἰησοῦς, direct object of ἰδεῖν) 3.
τίς (nom.sing.masc.of τίς, interrogative pronoun, subject of ἐστιν, indirect question) 281.
ἐστιν (3d.per.sing.pres.ind.of εἰμί, indirect question) 86.
καὶ (adversative conjunction) 14.
οὐκ (summary negative conjunction with the indicative) 130.
ἠδύνατο (3d.per.sing.imp.mid.ind.of δύναμαι, progressive description) 289.

ἀπὸ (preposition with the ablative, cause) 70.
τοῦ (abl.sing.masc.of the article in agreement with ὄχλου) 9.
ὄχλου (abl.sing.masc.of ὄχλος, cause) 418.
ὅτι (conjunction introducing a subordinate causal clause) 211.
τῇ (loc.sing.fem.of the article in agreement with ἡλικίᾳ) 9.
ἡλικίᾳ (loc.sing.fem.of ἡλικία, sphere) 622.
μικρὸς (nom.sing.masc.of μικρός, predicate adjective) 901.
ἦν (3d.per.sing.imp.ind.of εἰμί, progressive description) 86.

Translation - "And he was trying to see who Jesus was, but he could not because of the crowd, because he was a little man."

Comment: The imperfect tense in ἐζήτει indicates that Zacchaeus did not give up easily. There were a great many people surrounding Jesus, most of whom were taller and bigger than the little tax collector. We can see him dodging in and out, trying to get a front row vantage point, making vain attempts to squeeze through the dense crowd. He probably jumped up if only for a momentary glance. He may have tried to find something upon which to stand. The fact that he was a rich tax collector did not assure that he would receive any cooperation from the people who knew and hated him. They could have asked him with considerable logic what he was doing there, and why he, of all people would be interested in seeing Jesus, because when Jesus took His place on David's throne as their Messiah, Zacchaeus would be out of a job.

That he resorted to his final successful tactic proves how very great the crowd was. It also proves how much Zacchaeus wanted to see Jesus. *Cf.*#70 for other examples of ἀπό with the ablative in a causal context. ὅτι introduces the subordinate clause which explains Zacchaeus' problem. He was small in the sphere of physical size - an interesting use of the locative of sphere. Small - not in intellect, nor in finanical status, nor in any other sphere, but in physical stature.

Just as Bartimaeus could do nothing about the disability which prevented him from seeing Jesus, so neither could Zacchaeus (Mt.6:27).

There is danger lurking in the pages of the inspired Word for the exegete when he is tempted to see symbolic meaning in the text which leads him to doctrines contrary to Scripture, but if his conclusion, suggested symbolically, is supported elsewhere in Scripture by the most severely objective exegesis, he may safely point out the symbolic element. Here we have two men. Both are unregenerate. Neither is able to see Jesus (βλέπω #499), because of disabilities which neither of them were able to overcome. Bartimaeus was too blind and Zacchaeus was too short. So also all unregenerate sinners are unable to see Jesus (ὁράω #144), and to appropriate His salvation, because of the limitations of depravity, which none of us can overcome. This concept is clearly taught elsehwere in unequivocal language and can be supported even though the most severely objective hermeneutical analysis is applied (*e.g.* John 6:44; Eph.2:1-3, *et al*).

Bartimaeus and his beggar friend could do nothing but cry out again and again with tones of increasing frenzy and despair. In doing so unwittingly they did what everyone must do to be saved. They called upon the name of the Lord (Rom.10:13). They said Ἰησοῦ Υἱὲ Δαυίδ, ἐλεησόν με. Unfortunately Zacchaeus made the mistake of trying his own plan before he cried out for help. We shall see that climbing a tree did not help him. Nor do any of our human schemes and efforts, however tireless, to implement them help the sinner to be saved. All men are sinners - too blind and too short to *see* Jesus. And all that we can do to be saved is to do what the blind man did - call for help. Climbing trees, elevating ourselves by our own efforts, philosophically, intellectually, culturally, politically, socially and economically applied, only result in our being self-elevated sinners, now, thanks to our efforts, we believe, in a position to look down on Jesus. This is what Zacchaeus of Jericho did, and that is what the Zacchaeus of the late 20th century is doing. He has climbed so high - even to the moon and beyond - that now he sits astride a sycamore limb and looks down at the Incarnate Son of God, Who stands looking up at him and asking for an invitation to dinner.

Verse 4 - "And he ran before, and climbed up into a sycamore tree to see him: for he was to pass that way."

καὶ προδραμὼν εἰς τὸ ἔμπροσθεν ἀνέβη ἐπὶ συκομορέαν ἵνα ἴδῃ αὐτόν, ὅτι ἐκείνης ἤμελλεν διέρχεσθαι.

καὶ (inferential conjunction) 14.

#2652 προδραμὼν (aor.act.part.nom.sing.masc.of προτρέχω, adverbial, temporal).

run before - Luke 19:4.
outrun - John 20:4.

Meaning: A combination of πρό (#442) and τρέχω (#1655). Hence, to run ahead; to run before someone in the spatial sense. With reference to Zacchaeus - Luke 19:4; of John who outran Peter in a footrace to the empty tomb of Jesus - John 20:4.

εἰς (preposition with the accusative of extent) 140.
τὸ (acc.sing.neut.of the article, extent) 9.
ἔμπροσθεν (adverbial used as a substantive, pleonasm) 459.
ἀνέβη (3d.per.sing.aor.act.ind.of ἀναβαίνω, constative) 323.
ἐπὶ (preposition with the accusative of extent) 47.

#2653 συκομορέαν (acc.sing.fem.of συκομορέα, extent).

sycomore tree - Luke 19:4.

Meaning: A combination of σῦκον (#681) and μορέα - "mulberry tree." - A sycomore tree - Luke 19:4.

ἵνα (conjunction with the subjunctive introducing a final clause of purpose) 114.

ἴδῃ (3d.per.sing.aor.act.subj.of ὁράω, purpose) 144.
αὐτόν (acc.sing.masc.of αὐτός, direct object of ἴδῃ) 16.
ὅτι (conjunction introducing a subordinate causal clause) 211.
ἐκείνης (gen.sing.fem. in agreement with ὁδοῦ understood, description) 246.
ἤμελλεν (3d.per.sing.imp.act.ind.of μέλλω, progressive description) 206.
διέρχεσθαι (pres.mid.inf.of διέρχομαι, completes ἤμελλεν) 1017.

Translation - "So he ran ahead (into the forward area) and climbed upon a sycamore tree, in order that he might see Him, because he was going to pass along that road."

Comment: We have translated literally so that the student can appreciate Luke's idiom. The preposition phrase εἰς τὸ ἔμπροσθεν is really not necessary, since we have πρό in composition in the participle. We mention it because in ἔμπροσθεν we have an example of an improper preposition used like a substantive. We have also an example of pleonasm - the use of more words than is necessary to make the point clear. Since Zacchaeus "ran *ahead*" it is obvious that he ran into a area that was "forward" to Jesus and the crowd, as our Lord passed along the road. We have also in ἐκείνης, an interesting use of the genitive of description (not unusual in itself, but without the noun which it modifies). Thus we are to understand ὁδοῦ - "he was about to pass along that *road*."

καὶ is clearly inferential. The little man's decision to run ahead and climb a tree was based upon the knowledge that he was too short to see Jesus unless he did something drastic. The use of ἐπὶ with the accusative of extent is an example of Luke's precise Greek. One cannot climb "into" a tree, but he can climb "upon" a tree. Zacchaeus did not penetrate the bark of the sycamore. But he sat upon one of the limbs. Hence ἐπί rather than εἰς.

The purpose clause tells us why he climbed the tree and the ὅτι clause tells us why he chose that particular tree. Zacchaeus knew the line of march that Jesus would take. Now his attempt to solve his problem is finished. Now he occupies a vantage point where shortness of stature is no problem. The people cannot prevent him from seeing Jesus any longer. He is in a position to see (βλέπω) Jesus, though not yet in a position to see (ὁράω) Him as Jesus Christ, Messiah and Personal Saviour. Our Lord, of course, knew all of this and He moved to correct the situation in

Verse 5 - "And when Jesus came to the place, He looked up, and saw him, and said unto him, Zacchaeus, make haste, and come down; for today I must abide at thy house."

καὶ ὡς ἦλθεν ἐπὶ τὸν τόπον, ἀναβλέψας ὁ Ἰησοῦς εἶπεν πρὸς αὐτόν, Ζακχαῖε, σπεύσας κατάβηθι, σήμερον γὰρ ἐν τῷ οἴκῳ σου δεῖ με μεῖναι.

καὶ (continuative conjunction) 14.
ὡς (particle introducing a definite temporal clause) 128.
ἦλθεν (3d.per.sing.aor.ind.of ἔρχομαι, definite temporal clause) 146.
ἐπὶ (preposition with the accusative of extent) 47.

τὸν (acc.sing.masc.of the article in agreement with **τόπον**) 9.
τόπον (acc.sing.masc.of **τόπος**, extent) 1019.
ἀναβλέψας (aor.act.part.nom.sing.masc.of **ἀναβλέπω**, adverbial, temporal) 907.
ὁ (nom.sing.masc.of the article in agreement with **Ἰησοῦς**) 9.
Ἰησοῦς (nom.sing.masc.of **Ἰησοῦς**, subject of **εἶπεν**) 3.
εἶπεν (3d.per.sing.aor.act.ind.of **εἶπον**, constative) 155.
πρὸς (preposition with the accusative of extent, after a verb of speaking) 197.
αὐτόν (acc.sing.masc.of **αὐτός**, extent, after a verb of speaking) 16.
Ζακχαῖε (voc.sing.masc.of **Ζακχαῖος**, address) 2650.
σπεύσας (aor.act.part.nom.sing.masc.of **σπεύδω**, adverbial, modal) 1883.
κατάβηθι (2d.per.sing.2d.aor.mid.impv.of **καταβαίνω**, command) 324.
σήμερον (temporal adverb) 579.
γὰρ (causal conjunction) 105.
ἐν (preposition with the locative of place) 80.
τῷ (loc.sing.masc.of the article in agreement with **οἴκῳ**) 9.
οἴκῳ (loc.sing.masc.of **οἶκος**, place where) 784.
σου (gen.sing.masc.of **σύ**, possession) 104.
δεῖ (3d.per.sing.pres.ind.impersonal of **δέω**) 1207.
με (acc.sing.masc.of **ἐγώ**, general reference) 123.
μεῖναι (aor.act.inf.of **μένω**, completes **δεῖ**) 864.

Translation - "And when He came to the place, Jesus looked up and said to him, 'Zacchaeus, come down quickly, because today I am going to stay at your house.' "

Comment: The Creator of the universe, now humbly incarnate in human flesh, comes to the foot of a tree, looks up and speaks to a degenerate Jew sitting astride a limb and looking down upon Him! He is also asking this covetous, greedy little sinner for the privilege of going home with him for a visit. Thus the sinner looks down on God and God incarnate looks up to the sinner.

The symbolism has been discussed in our comment on verse 3. Jesus' first words after the address, involve an order. "Come down quickly," or "Come down at once." σπεύσας refers to Zacchaeus' decision; κατάβηθι to his action. The aorist participle σπεύσας indicates antecendent time, in relation to the time of the imperative κατάβηθι. We can also think of σπεύσας as a modal adverb, indicating how the man is to come down from the tree. The ideas do not conflict. "Do not debate it. Come down." Perhaps in a sharper tone, "Come down out of that tree and hurry up about it!" Jesus did not want any argument out of him about obedience to His command.

One's imagination may be allowed a little freedom as we try to reconstruct the scene. We know that Zacchaeus was short. Most short men are fat, especially if they are also rich and likely to have eaten too much rich food. I have always imagined that Zacchaeus was fat. If so, Jesus must have seen the humorous side of this ridiculous picture. Here, sitting astride the limb of a tree, with his little short fat legs dangling on opposite sides of a limb, is the richest Jew in town. It is easier for a fat man to come down from a tree than to climb it. Zacchaeus promptly complied with Jesus' order - perhaps too promptly!

Why did Jesus order him first to come down? Because Zacchaeus had not yet accepted Christ as His Messiah/Saviour. And why the demand for haste? Because, said Jesus, "there is a sense of divine necessity laid upon me to visit you, so that I can gain your acceptance of me as your Saviour and Lord." *Cf.*#1207, III, for δεῖ in this sense elsewhere. Jesus was saying that the matter of Zacchaeus' salvation was urgent. There should be no delay. "Now is the accepted time" (2 Cor.6:2). Jesus was soon to leave for Jerusalem. In a little while, less than a week, He would be crucified. He was going to Jerusalem to die for Zacchaeus. This was His last visit to Jericho, perhaps the last opportunity for Zacchaeus to see Him. "The king's business requires haste" (1 Samuel 21:8).

The social gospel exponents seem to teach that divine justice dictates that all who are poor on earth will go to heaven and that the rich on earth must suffer in hell. In extreme opposition are the Fundamentalists who shun all social applications of the Christian gospel (which they ought not) and insist that faith in Christ alone saves (which they ought) while insisting that Christ has nothing to say about economic distribution of the wealth after one is saved (in which assertion they are mistaken). But these extreme positions are wrong as this episode makes clear. Bartimaeus was not automatically saved because he was a blind beggar and had been unjustly dispossessed throughout his life, through no fault of his. Nor was Zacchaeus automatically damned because he was a rich tax collector, who had built a fortune out of dishonest and capacious greed. Jesus did not commiserate with Bartimaeus because he was poor, nor condemn Zacchaeus because he was rich. Each man tried to see Jesus, but could not because of inherent disability. One cried out helplessly. The other climbed a tree. Bartimaeus came to Christ when he was called. Zacchaeus came down out of the tree when he was ordered to do so. Both men were saved, only because they believed and received Christ (Acts 16:31; John 1:12; 3:16; 5:24; Rom.10:13 *et al.*). Neither the physical condition of the one nor the financial status of the other had anything to do with either case. Jesus said not one word to either man about possible financial readjustments. He promised no wealth to Bartimaeus. He threatened Zacchaeus with no confiscatory income tax. The two men met at the foot of a sycamore tree with Jesus standing between them (Luke 18:42). Both were saved. Each had believed upon Christ. Each had received Him. Bartimaeus had salvation in his soul, sight in his eyes, and a void in his stomach. Zacchaeus had salvation in his soul, money in the bank and a guilty conscience about his wealth. Redistribution of the wealth took place but without a word from Jesus to either man about it. The extreme Fundamentalists should observe that social justice *comes* after the new birth, and the social gospel preachers should observe that social justice comes *after* the new birth. Social justice as a means to salvation is a dead-end street - a no thoroughfare. A claim to salvation from one who ignores the demands of social justice is the sounding brass and tinkling cymbal of hypocrisy. The Bartimaeus/Zacchaeus episode teaches us what is root and what is fruit, what is cause and what is effect, what is foundation and what is superstructure. Each set of extremists should abandon their positions and find Jesus Christ in the middle.

Verse 6 - "And he made haste, and came down, and received him joyfully."

καὶ σπεύσας κατέβη, καὶ ὑπεδέξατο αὐτὸν χαίρων.

καὶ (continuative conjunction) 14.
σπεύσας (aor.act.part.nom.sing.masc.of *σπεύδω*, adverbial, modal) 1883.
κατέβη (3d.per.sing.aor.act.ind.of *καταβαίνω*, constative) 324.
καὶ (adjunctive conjunction joining verbs) 14.
ὑπεδέξατο (3d.per.sing.aor.mid.ind.of *ὑποδέχομαι*, constative) 2437.
αὐτὸν (acc.sing.masc.of *αὐτός*, direct object of *ὑπεδέξατο*) 14.
χαίρων (pres.act.part.nom.sing.masc.of *χαίρω*, adverbial, modal) 182.

Translation - "And he came down quickly and received Him with joy."

Comment: In compliance with Jesus' order, Zacchaeus decided to come down. *σπεύσας* - having hastened - an act of his will - a quick decision, preceding his action. He determined speedily to come down. Then he came down, suiting the action to the decision. *σπεύσας* cannot be taken as simultaneous with *κατέβη*, since it is aorist tense. The Greek text does not say that he came down speedily. It says that he speedily decided to come down. But we may be sure that he did, in fact, come down speedily, since the descent from a tree of a fat man is likely to be speedy. Then he took Jesus home with him. *Cf.*#2437 for *ὑποδέχομαι*. No doubt he also received Jesus as Saviour (John 1:12), though the word in John 1:12 is *λαμβάνω* (#533). Zacchaeus did not receive Jesus while he was up in the tree. He came down first and then, at the foot of the tree, he received Him joyfully. No man who is up in his tree, occupying an exalted position which he has gained by much effort and who is now looking down on Jesus, is going to accept Him. This is why Jesus ordered Zacchaeus to come down. Note that he received Him with joy. *Cf.*#182. The fruit of the Holy Spirit is joy (Gal.5:22).

Thus the tax collector became a child of God. The chief evidence that when he offered the hospitality of his home to Jesus, he also offered him the hospitality of his heart is his changed attitude toward his wealth (vs.8). But before we can look at the good news about his change of attitude toward his wealth, we must endure the account of the bigotry of the people, in

Verse 7 - "And when they saw it, they all murmured, saying, That he was gone to be guest with a man that is a sinner."

καὶ ἰδόντες πάντες διεγόγγυζον λέγοντες ὅτι Παρὰ ἁμαρτωλῷ ἀνδρὶ εἰσῆλθεν καταλῦσαι.

καὶ (adversative conjunction) 14.
ἰδόντες (aor.act.part.nom.pl.masc.of *ὁράω*, adverbial, temporal/causal) 144.
πάντες (nom.pl.masc.of *πᾶς*,subject of *διεγόγγυζον*) 67.
διεγόγγυζον (3d.per.pl.imp.act.ind.of *διαγογγύζω*, inceptive) 2538.
λέγοντες (pres.act.part.nom.pl.masc.of *λέγω*, adverbial, modal) 66.
ὅτι (recitative) 211.
Παρὰ (preposition with the instrumental of association) 154.

ἁμαρτωλῷ (instru.sing.masc.of ἁμαρτωλός, in agreement with ἀνδρὶ) 791.
ἀνδρὶ (instru.sing.masc.of ἀνήρ, association) 63.
εἰσῆλθεν (3d.per.sing.aor.mid.ind.of εἰσέρχομαι, culminative) 234.
καταλῦσαι (aor.act.inf.of καταλύω, purpose) 463.

Translation - "And when they saw it, they all began to complain, saying, 'He has gone to stay with a sinful man.' "

Comment: καὶ is adversative, as the people in Jericho objected to Jesus' visit. They began to complain bitterly (inceptive imperfect in διεγόγγυζον, #2538). Like spoiled children. καταλῦσαι means to let down, relax. The reaction of the crowd is to be expected from unenlightened people. They had seen Jesus heal the blind beggars. To that they did not object. But they despised Zacchaeus. Their interest in Jesus was not wholly sincere. With some it was a matter of vulgar curiosity. But it was too much when the object of their interest suddenly left them and went home with this hated rich man. Was Jesus selling out to the Establishment? They had no way of knowing about the change in the heart of Zacchaeus which came about by divine grace. The evidence for that comes in verses 8 and 9. While the people were complaining, Zacchaeus was making restitution.

Verse 8 - "And Zacchaeus stood, and said unto the Lord; behold, Lord, the half of my goods I give to the poor; and if I have taken anything from any man by false accusation, I restore him fourfold."

σταθεὶς δὲ Ζακχαῖος εἶπεν πρὸς τὸν κύριον, Ἰδοὺ τὰ ἡμίσειά μου τῶν ὑπαρχόντων, κύριε, τοῖς πτωχοῖς δίδωμι, καὶ εἴ τινός τι ἐσυκοφάντησα ἀποδίδωμι τετραπλοῦν.

σταθεὶς (aor.mid.part.nom.sing.masc.of ἵστημι, adverbial, temporal) 180.
δὲ (continuative conjunction) 11.
Ζακχαῖος (nom.sing.masc.of Ζακχαῖος, subject of εἶπεν) 2650.
πρὸς (preposition with the accusative of extent, after a verb of speaking) 197.
τὸν (acc.sing.masc.of the article in agreement with κύριον) 9.
κύριον (acc.sing.masc.of κύριος, extent after a verb of speaking) 97.
Ἰδοὺ (exclamation) 95.
τὰ (acc.pl.neut.of the article in agreement with ἡμίσια) 9.
ἡμίσια (acc.pl.neut.of ἥμισυ, direct object of δίδωμι) 2259.
μου (gen.sing.masc.of ἐγώ, possession) 123.
τῶν (gen.pl.masc.of the article in agreement with ὑπαρχόντων) 9.
ὑπαρχόντων (pres.act.part.gen.pl.masc.of ὑπάρχω, substantival, description) 1303.
κύριε (voc.sing.masc.of κύριος, address) 97.
τοῖς (dat.pl.masc.of the article in agreement with πτωχοῖς) 9.
πτωχοῖς (dat.pl.masc.of πτωχός, indirect object of δίδωμι) 423.
δίδωμι (1st.per.sing.pres.act.ind.of δίδωμι, futuristic) 362.
καὶ (continuative conjunction) 14.

εἴ (conditional particle in a mixed condition) 337.

τινός (abl.sing.masc.of τις, indefinite pronoun, separation) 486.

τι (acc.sing.neut.of τις, indefinite pronoun, direct object of ἐσυκοφάντησα) 486.

ἐσυκοφάντησα (1st.per.sing.aor.act.ind.of συκοφαντέω, culminative) 1946.

ἀποδίδωμι (1st.per.sing.pres.act.ind.of ἀποδίδωμι, futuristic) 495.

#2654 τετραπλοῦν (acc.sing.neut.of τετραπλοῦς, measure).

fourfold - Luke 19:8.

Meaning: Quadruple; fourfold; on a ratio of four to one - Luke 19:8.

Translation - "And stood and said to the Lord, 'Look, Lord! Half of my assets I will give to the poor, and if I have extorted anything from anyone, I will give back fourfold.' "

Comment: There is nothing in the text to say precisely when this statement was made - whether at the foot of the tree, immediately after Zacchaeus came down and received Jesus, or later in his house. τῷ οἴκῳ τούτῳ of verse 9 may indicate that it was in his home. He stood to make his statement, which may indicate that they had discussed his past life, with its injustice to the people as they reclined at his table.

With a new spiritual experience that changed his life Zacchaeus now had a new ethical sensitivity. His social conscience was now awake. He wanted to make restitution. τὰ ἡμίσεά μου τῶν ὑπαρχόντων - "my halves (pl.) of the goods (pl.)" Perhaps τῶν ὑπαρχόντων refers to the exactions which Caesar demanded that Zacchaeus take from tax payers, on a fifty percent commission. If so, he owned one half of all the money he collected. Thus he was saying that he would give to the poor all of his part of the Roman tax revenue which he had collected in the past. If this is correct, Zacchaeus was giving away all of his past wealth, not half, since the other half had already been paid to the Roman government.

The remainder of the verse is a mixed condition with εἴ and the aorist indicative in the protasis and the futuristic present indicative in the apodosis. The secondary (aorist) tense in the protasis looks like a second-class contrary to fact condition, although we do not have a secondary tense in the result clause. Thus the issue is in doubt as to whether or not Zacchaeus was admitting that he had cheated anyone. If his wealth had been attained by extortion he promised to pay it back on a four for one basis.

Since Zacchaeus promised to give to the poor, and since Bartimaeus and his beggar friend had followed Jesus after their healing (Lk.18:43), it is probable that Jesus now suggested to Zacchaeus that he need not go far to find someone who could use some of his money. Of the three latest converts whom Jesus had won that day, one was rich and the other two were paupers. Did Zacchaeus make perhaps his first distribution of money to the two beggars who were now his brothers in Christ? If so, the social gospel redistribution of wealth occurred as a result of the theological gospel regeneration. Thus the ethics of Christian giving is carried out as the Holy Spirit prompts regenerate hearts to do for love what governments in the name of liberalism do by force. (Eph.4:28; 1 Tim.6:18; Rom.12:13; James 2:15,16; 1 John 3:17). The Modernists, by preaching only the social gospel and sneering at the theological gospel, have perverted God's truth one way, while the Fundamentalists, by preaching *only* "ye must be born again" and attacking social justice movements have perverted it in the other direction.

Regenerate children of God who see both sides of this coin recognize that the theological gospel must come first, and then be inevitably followed by the social gospel, just as Jesus gave the proper priorities in the story before us. The Christian conservative theologian is thus forced to espouse the liberal social and economic policies of the government. One cannot criticize the government for attempting to do for the poor what the church, through the private activities of her individual born again members, should be doing, but has miserably failed to do. To put the proposition the other way around, if the Christians who talk so much about being born again would attend to the social and economic needs of society as they are commanded in Scripture to do, there would be no need for the welfare state. It is disquieting to hear the Fundamentalists attack the government for the welfare state, when they have done little or nothing to alleviate the miseries of the poor who are all about us. Those who fail to understand this assume that the conservative stance in the theological field requires a conservative stance in the social and political field and that those who say, as I do, that they are theological conservatives, and *therefore* political liberals are confused. The confusion grows out of the failure to see that love for God, with the whole heart, soul, mind, and strength must also show love for self and for one's neighbour as for one's self. The first four commandments ask us to love God and ourselves. The last six ask us to love others as much as we love ourselves.

Verse 9 - "And Jesus said unto him, This day is salvation come to this house, forasmuch as he also is a son of Abraham."

εἶπεν δὲ πρὸς αὐτὸν ὁ Ἰησοῦς ὅτι Σήμερον σωτηρία τῷ οἴκῳ τούτῳ ἐγένετο, καθότι καὶ αὐτὸς υἱὸς Ἀβραάμ ἐστιν.

εἶπεν (3d.per.sing.aor.act.ind.of *εἶπον*, constative) 155.
δὲ (continuative conjunction) 11.
πρὸς (preposition with the accusative of extent) 197.
αὐτὸν (acc.sing.masc.of *αὐτός*, extent after a verb of speaking) 16.
ὁ (nom.sing.masc.of the article in agreement with *Ἰησοῦς*) 9.
Ἰησοῦς (nom.sing.masc.of *Ἰησοῦς*, subject of *εἶπεν*) 3.
ὅτι (recitative) 211.
Σήμερον (temporal adverb) 579.
σωτηρία (nom.sing.fem.of *σωτηρία*, subject of *ἐγένετο*) 1852.
τῷ (dat.sing.masc.of the article in agreement with *οἴκῳ*) 9.
οἴκῳ (dat.sing.masc.of *οἶκος*, personal advantage) 784.
τούτῳ (dat.sing.masc.of *οὗτος*, in agreement with *οἴκῳ*) 93.
ἐγένετο (3d.per.sing.aor.ind.of *γίνομαι*,culminative) 113.
καθότι (particle introducing a causal clause) 1783.

καὶ (adjunctive conjunction, joining substantives) 14.
αὐτὸς (nom.sing.masc.of αὐτός, subject of ἐστιν) 16.
υἱὸς (nom.sing.masc.of υἱός, predicate nominative) 5.
Ἀβραάμ (gen.sing.masc.of Ἀβραάμ, relationship) 7.
ἐστιν (3d.per.sing.pres.ind.of εἰμί, aoristic) 86.

Translation - "And Jesus said to him, 'Today, salvation has come to this house, because he also is a son of Abraham.' "

Comment: Our Lord's statement leaves no doubt that Zacchaeus was not only socially rehabilitated, but also spiritually regenerated. The social rehabilitation was the fruit of the spiritual regeneration. καθότι is a causal particle introducing a subordinate causal clause. καὶ is adjunctive, as Jesus is pointing out that although Zacchaeus was indeed a tax collector with political ties with Rome, his professional connection with the Gentiles did not change the fact that he was Jewish and, as such, could lay a claim to the services of the Jewish Messiah. *Cf.* Luke 1:7 for καθότι in the same sense. Also Acts 2:24.

Zacchaeus had in the past repudiated his nationalistic hopes of a coming Messiah and had placed himself in league with Rome. This had nothing to do with his genetics. Abraham's blood flowed in the publican's veins, as much as it did in the veins of those who complained because Jesus went home with him. And he was just as worthy to be saved as any of them, since, in fact,no one in worthy to be saved. Therefore, there is no ground for the discrimination that comes from man. All men are lost be they Jews, Gentiles, sons of Abraham, Levites, priests, scribes, lawyers, publicans - hence Jesus came to seek them all, regardless of their past sins. This is the closing thought of

Verse 10 - "For the Son of Man is come to seek and to save that which was lost."

ἦλθεν γὰρ ὁ υἱὸς τοῦ ἀνθρώπου ζητῆσαι καὶ σῶσαι τὸ ἀπολωλός.

ἦλθεν (3d.per.sing.aor.ind.of ἔρχομαι, culminative) 146.
γὰρ (inferential conjunction) 105.
ὁ (nom.sing.masc.of the article in agreement with υἱὸς) 9.
υἱὸς (nom.sing.masc.of υἱός, subject of ἦλθεν) 5.
τοῦ (gen.sing.masc.of the article in agreement with ἀνθρώπου) 9.
ἀνθρώπου (gen.sing.masc.of ἄνθρωπος, relationship) 341.
ζητῆσαι (aor.act.inf.of ζητέω, purpose) 207.
καὶ (adjunctive conjunction joining infinitives) 14.
σῶσαι (aor.act.inf.of σῴζω, purpose) 109.
τὸ (acc.sing.masc.of the article in agreement with ἀπολωλός) 9.
ἀπολωλός (2d.perf.part.acc.sing.neut.of ἀπόλλυμι, substantival, direct object of ζητῆσαι and σῶσαι) 208.

Translation - "Therefore the Son of Man is here in order to seek and to save that which has been lost."

Comment: Note that ἦλθεν is a culminative aorist. The emphasis is upon the result of the past action. Christ, the Son of Man, came, thirty years before and as a result He was saying, "I came and here I am." *Cf.* Mt.2:2. The two purpose infinitives *ζητῆσαι καὶ σῶσαι* tell us the purpose of His mission - "to seek and save those who are lost." The perfect participle *ἀπολωλὸς* speaks of those who are currently in a state of being lost as a result of a past action that alienated them from the favor of God. It is to restore that lost fellowship that Jesus came.

The Parable of the Pounds

(Luke 19:11-28)

Luke 19:11 - "And as they heard these things, he added and spake a parable, because he was nigh to Jerusalem, and because they thought that the kingdom of God should immediately appear."

Ἀκουόντων δὲ αὐτῶν ταῦτα προσθεὶς εἶπεν παραβολὴν διὰ τὸ ἐγγὺς εἶναι Ἰερουσαλὴμ αὐτὸν καὶ δοκεῖν αὐτοὺς ὅτι παραχρῆμα μέλλει ἡ βασιλεία τοῦ θεοῦ ἀναφαίνεσθαι.

Ἀκουόντων (pres.act.part.gen.pl.masc.of ἀκούω, genitive absolute) 148.
δὲ (continuative conjunction) 11.
αὐτῶν (gen.pl.masc.of αὐτός, genitive absolute) 16.
ταῦτα (acc.pl.neut.of οὗτος, direct object of ἀκουόντων) 93.
προσθεὶς (aor.part.nom.sing.masc.of προστίθημι, adverbial, telic) 621.
εἶπεν (3d.per.sing.aor.act.ind.of εἶπον, constative) 155.
παραβολὴν (acc.sing.fem.of παραβολή, direct object of εἶπεν) 1027.
διὰ (preposition with the accusative of cause) 118.
τὸ (acc.sing.neut.of the article, cause) 9.
ἐγγὺς (nom.sing.neut.of ἐγγύς, predicate adjective) 1512.
εἶναι (pres.inf.of εἰμί, cause) 86.
Ἰερουσαλὴμ (acc.sing.indeclin. of Ἱεροσόλυμα, extent) 141.
αὐτὸν (acc.sing.masc.of αὐτός, general reference) 16.
καὶ (adjunctive conjunction joining infinitives) 14.
δοκεῖν (pres.act.inf.of δοκέω, cause) 287.
αὐτοὺς (acc.pl.masc.of αὐτός, general reference) 16.
ὅτι (conjunction introducing an object clause in indirect discourse) 211.
παραχρῆμα (adverbial) 1369.
μέλλει (3d.per.sing.pres.act.ind.of μέλλω, historical) 206.
ἡ (nom.sing.fem.of the article in agreement with βασιλεία) 9.
βασιλεία (nom.sing.fem.of βασιλεία, subject of μέλλει) 253.
τοῦ (gen.sing.masc.of the article in agreement with θεοῦ) 9.
θεοῦ (gen.sing.masc.of θεός, description) 124.

#2655 ἀναφαίνεσθαι (pres.pass.inf.of ἀναφαίνομαι, completes μέλλει).

appear - Luke 19:11.
discover - Acts 21:3.

Meaning: A combination of ἀνά (#1059) and φαίνω (#100). Hence, to show up; to be manifest; to appear. In the passive, to be made apparent. Of the Kingdom of God in its earthly physical manifestation - Luke 19:11. The island of Cyprus to the mariner - Acts 21:3.

Translation - "And as they were listening to these things, in order to complete (His teaching) he expounded a parable because He was near Jerusalem and they thought that the Kingdom of God was going to appear immediately."

Comment: ἀκουόντων αὐτῶν is a genitive absolute in the present tense. While they were listening to Jesus' remarks in the house of Zacchaeus, (which incidentally proves that the people had followed Jesus and Zacchaeus to the latter's home), Jesus detected that they had misunderstood His statement that Zacchaeus, though Jewish, was lost and that He had come in His role as Messiah to save the Jews. They thought that Jesus meant salvation in a national sense and that soon He, as Messiah, would move against Rome and assert His authority as King of Israel, Son of David. Thus Jesus saw the need to supplement (προσθεὶς, the telic participle) His remarks by adding another parable. Why? The preposition διὰ is followed by the accusative τὸ and two infinitives in the accusative case to show cause. He was near Jerusalem and they thought that . . . κ.τ.λ. Obviously Messiah would make His move against the current Establishment in Israel only in the capitol city. His audience had put together what He said about seeking and saving Jews like Zacchaeus and concluded that the time for Messiah's manifestation had finally arrived. And, since He was not far from the city, they were in a high state of euphoric expectation.

Jesus knew that He must dispossess them of this idea. Note however that He did not deny that the Kingdom of God, in the sense in which they were thinking of it. would ever appear. Indeed, it will, at the end of the current Gentile dispensation. Their mistake was in supposing that it was to be unveiled immediately. Amillenialists and postmillenialists (if there are any of the latter remaining!) can gain scant support for their views from the parable which Jesus is about to give. Jesus does not deny that there is to be an earthly kingdom. He only teaches that it was not scheduled for the *immediate* future.

αὐτὸν and αὐτοὺς, which the uninitiated grammarians describe as "subjects" of the infinitives to which they are joined, are accusatives of general reference. ὅτι introduces the object clause in indirect discourse.

ἐγγὺς - *i.e.* fifteen miles away.

Luke 19:11-28 is similar to the parable of Matthew 25:14-30, though the Matthew parable was spoken at a little later time. Jesus must have often repeated His teachings, particularly when different audiences were involved.

Verse 12 - "He said therefore, A certain nobleman went into a far country to receive for himself a kingdom, and to return."

εἶπεν οὖν, Ἄνθρωπος τις εὐγενὴς ἐπορεύθη εἰς χώραν μακρὰν λαβεῖν ἑαυτῷ βασιλείαν καὶ ὑποστρέψαι.

εἶπεν (3d.per.sing.aor.act.ind.of *εἶπον*, constative) 155.
οὖν (inferential conjunction) 68.
Ἄνθρωπος (nom.sing.masc.of *ἄνθρωπος*, subject of *ἐπορεύθη*) 341.
τις (nom.sing.masc.of *τις*, indefinite pronoun, in agreement with *ἄνθρωπος*) 486.

#2656 *εὐγενὴς* (nom.sing.masc.of *εὐγενής*, in agreement with *ἄνθρωπος*).

noble - Acts 17:11; 1 Cor.1:26; Luke 19:12.

Meaning: *εὐ* plus *γεννάω* (#8). Hence, well bred. Of superior genetic lineage. *Cf.* *γένος* (#1090). With reference to a prince or noble in a sociological and political sense - Luke 19:12; 1 Cor.1:26. Noble minded - of superior intellectual poise and integrity - Acts 17:11.

ἐπορεύθη (3d.per.sing.aor.mid.ind.of *πορεύομαι*, constative) 170.
εἰς (preposition with the accusative of extent) 140.
χώραν (acc.sing.fem.of *χώρα*, extent) 201.
μακρὰν (acc.sing.fem.of *μακρός*, in agreement with *χώραν*) 2546.
λαβεῖν (aor.act.inf.of *λαμβάνω*, purpose) 533.
ἑαυτῷ (dat.sing.masc.of *ἑαυοτός*, possession) 288.
βασιλείαν (acc.sing.fem.of *βασιλεία*, direct object of *λαβεῖν*) 253.
καὶ (adjunctive conjunction joining infinitives) 14.
ὑποστρέψαι (aor.act.inf.of *ὑποστρέφω*, purpose) 1838.

Translation - "Therefore He said, 'A certain nobleman went into a country far away, to take for himself a kingdom and to return."

Comment: *οὖν* is inferential. Luke has just told us in verse 11 that Jesus felt it necessary to add something more in order to correct a wrong impression. Therefore He adds this parable. The nobleman is introduced. It is apparent that Jesus is speaking of Himself. He is about to go into a far country - in His ascension to the right hand of God. The resurrection and ascension is in view (Acts 1:9; Ps.110:1; Eph.1:20; John 14:2,3, etc.). The purpose of His trip? *λαβεῖν ἑαυτῷ βασιλείαν καὶ ὑποστρέψαι.* There is a twofold purpose: (a) to take a kingdom for Himself (Acts 15:14-18), and (b) to return (John 14:3; Acts 1:10,11; 1 Thess.4:16; 2 Thess.2:7,8; Rev.1:7, etc.).

Those who want us to adopt an allegorical interpretation with reference to His return, must be prepared for us to adopt the same interpretation to His departure. If *ὑποστρέψαι* is not to be taken literally, why then should we be literal about *ἐπορεύθη*? He went away bodily. Or did He? To deny that He will return bodily casts doubt upon His bodily departure. One cannot have it both ways. One might wonder if the postmillenialists are quite certain that Jesus ever had an objective historical existence?

Jesus is here assuring the people, who were expecting that soon, perhaps the next day, in Jerusalem, only fifteen miles up the mountain, His Messianic kingdom would be ushered in, that though He must first die, be buried, be raised again and ascended to Heaven, He would, after He has called out His bride, out of every kindred, tongue, people and nation (Rev.5:9,10), return to set up a kingdom - the one which they expected at that time. The people were not wrong about a literal kingdom on earth, and Jesus is not denying that there will be such a kingdom in the literal sense. They were wrong in expecting it to be established at that time. Jesus was telling them that they were dispensationally out of place. They had a chronological "blind spot" which has come to be known as "the church age" but which is more scripturally called "the fulness of the Gentiles" (Rom.11:25) and "the times of the Gentiles" (Luke 21:24). It is a period of time, now extended to more than 1900 years, during which God's promises to Abraham, Isaac, Jacob, Judah and David (Gen.12:1-3; 26:24,25; 28:10-15; 49:8-12; 2 Sam.7:10-17) are being held in abeyance, though by no means repudiated, until the Holy Spirit, at the direction of the ascended Messiah at the Father's right hand, has engineered and completed a worldwide missionary enterprise among the Gentiles (Ps.110:1,4; 2:8). Then He will return (Rev.10:7).

Verse 13 - "And he called his ten servants, and delivered unto them ten pounds, and said unto them, Occupy till I come."

καλέσας δὲ δέκα δούλους ἑαυτοῦ ἔδωκεν αὐτοῖς δέκα μνᾶς καὶ εἶπεν πρὸς αὐούς, Πραγματεύσασθε ἐν ᾧ ἔρχομαι.

καλέσας (aor.act.part.nom.sing.masc.of *καλέω*, adverbial, temporal) 107.
δὲ (continuative conjunction) 11.
δέκα (numeral) 1330.
δούλους (acc.pl.masc.of *δοῦλος*, direct object of *καλέσας*) 725.
ἑαυτοῦ (gen.sing.masc.of *ἑαυτός*, partitive) 288.
ἔδωκεν (3d.per.sing.aor.act.ind.of *δίδωμι*, constative) 362.
αὐτοῖς (dat.pl.masc.of *αὐτός*, indirect object of *ἔδωκεν*) 16.
δέκα (numeral) 1330.

#2657 *μνᾶς* (acc.pl.fem.of *μνᾶ*, direct object of *ἔδωκεν*).

pound - Luke 19:13,16,18,18,20,24,24,25.

Meaning: A unit of money. In the Old Testament equal to one hundred shekels. In Attic Greek equal to one hundred *δράχμαε* (*cf.*#2540). Approximately $16.67 in current American value - Luke 19:13,16,18,18,20,24,24,25.

καὶ (adjunctive conjunction joining verbs) 14.
εἶπεν (3d.per.sing.aor.act.ind.of *εἶπον*, constative) 155.
πρὸς (preposition with the accusative of extent, after a verb of speaking) 197.
αὐτούς (acc.pl.masc.of *αὐτός*, extent, after a verb of speaking) 16.

#2658 *Πραγματεύσασθε* (2d.per.pl.1st.aor.impv.of *πραγματεύομαι*, command).

occupy - Luke 19:13.

Meaning: *Cf.πρᾶγμα* (#1266). Generally, to be busy doing anything; to be practical. Specifically to carry on a business, as a banker or trader. To engage in commercial investment for purposes of making a profit - Luke 19:13.

ἐν (preposition with the relative pronoun in a temporal phrase) 80.
ᾧ (loc.sing.neut.of *ὅς*, in a temporal phrase) 65.
ἔρχομαι (1st.per.sing.pres.ind.of *ἔρχομαι*, temporal phrase) 146.

Translation - "And He called ten of His servants and gave to each of them $16.67 and said to them, 'Invest it until I come.' "

Comment: It is not "His ten servants" but "ten of His servants." A total of ten pounds was distributed to the servants, presumably one pound for each servant. Thus each man received $16.67. The order was that they should invest the money in some way with a view to profit making. For how long? *ἐν ᾧ ἔρχομαι* is an example of a preposition used with a relative pronoun as a temporal phrase. "Thus *ἀφ' οὗ*. In Luke 13:7 *ἀφ' οὗ* is preceded by *τρία ἔτη* as the *terminus quo*. It means "since." *Cf.τρίτην παύτην ἡμέραν ἄγει ἀφ' οὗ* in Lu.24:21. In Rev.16:18 it is the simple equivalent of *ἀπὸ τούτου ὅτε* as in the Attic Greek and Herodotus. In these examples the indicative occurs, but in Lu.13:25, *ἀφ' οὗ ἂν ἐγερθῇ*, the construction of *ἕως* is used for the uncertain future, the subj.with *ἂν*. The conception of *ἀπὸ τούτου ὅτε* has to be appealed to, 'from that moment when,' 'when once' the master arises. In like manner we see *ἀφ' ἧς* used for 'since' in Lu.7:45; Ac.24:11; 2 Pet.3:4. In Col.1:6,9 we have the form *ἀφ' ἧς ἡμέρας*.'Εν *ᾧ* is not always temporal. It may be merely local (Rom.2:1), instrumental (Ro.14:21) or causal (Ro.8:3). The temporal use is much like *ἕως* in the sense of 'while,' as in Mk.2:19 (Lu.5:34) *ἐν ᾧ ὁ νυμφίος μετ' αὐτῶν ἐστίν*. Cf.Jo.5:7, *ἐν ᾧ ἔρχομαι* with *ἕως ἔρχομαι* in Jo.21:22. In Lu.19:13 the Text.Rec.has *ἕως ἔρχομαι*, but *ἐν ᾧ* is the true reading." (Robertson, *Grammar*, 977, 978). "During the time in which I am coming" or "while I am gone."

The nobleman does not wish his servants to be idle during his absence. He gives to each an inventory of "stock in trade" with which to work before he goes away. He tells them that he will return. The implication is that when he returns he will expect them to submit to an audit and account for their activity while he was gone.

To carry out the symbolism of the parable we ask what Jesus gave to His disciples and, through them to the Church, that we can use to trade in the world while He is gone? What we have to sell must be capable of satisfying felt wants in the world, if it is to have the utility that gives it value. Otherwise it cannot command a price in the market.

The world with whom we deal must want these things. At Jesus' last extended conference with His disciples before His death (John 13:1 - 16:33) He gave to them His humility, His love, His home, His way, His truth, His life, His comfort, His peace, His friendship and His victory. For comment on each, *q.v. en loc.* There is no doubt that there is a universal inelastic demand for these commodities in the world market of lost and dying sinners.

Verse 14 - "But his citizens hated him and sent a message after him saying, We will not have this man to reign over us."

οἱ δὲ πολῖται αὐτοῦ ἐμίσουν αὐτόν, καὶ ἀπέστειλαν πρεσβείαν ὀπίσω αὐτοῦ λέγοντες, Οὐ θέλομεν τοῦτον βασιλεῦσαι ἐφ' ἡμᾶς.

οἱ (nom.pl.masc.of the article in agreement with πολῖται) 9.
δὲ (adversative conjunction) 11.
πολῖται (nom.pl.masc.of πολίτης, subject of ἐμίσουν and ἀπέστειλαν) 2548.
αὐτοῦ (gen.sing.masc.of αὐτός, relationship) 16.
ἐμίσουν (3d.per.pl.imp.act.ind.of μισέω, progressive description) 542.
αὐτόν (acc.sing.masc.of αὐτός, direct object of ἐμίσουν) 16.
καὶ (adjunctive conjunction joining verbs) 14.
ἀπέστειλαν (3d.per.pl.aor.act.ind.of ἀποστέλλω, constative) 215.
πρεσβείαν (acc.sing.fem.of πρεσβεία, direct object of ἀπέστειλαν) 2537.
ὀπίσω (adverbial) 302.
αὐτοῦ (gen.sing.masc.of αὐτός, place description) 16.
λέγοντες (pres.act.part.nom.pl.masc.of λέγω, adverbial, complementary) 66.
Οὐ (summary negative conjunction with the indicative) 130.
θέλομεν (1st.per.pl.pres.act.ind.of θέλω, aoristic) 88.
τοῦτον (acc.sing.masc.of οὗτος, general reference) 93.
βασιλεῦσαι (aor.act.inf.of βασιλεύω, noun use, object of θέλομεν) 236.
ἐφ' (preposition with the accusative of place, metaphorical) 47.
ἡμᾶς (acc.pl.masc.of ἐγώ, metaphorical place) 123.

Translation - "But his fellow citizens hated him and they sent a diplomat after him, saying, 'We do not want this man to rule over us.' "

Comment: But (adversative δὲ) the nobleman was not popular. The citizens hated him and sent one of their older men on a diplomatic mission to announce their refusal to be governed by his edicts. Thus the ten servants who have been left behind to trade with the citizens in the noble's country are facing a hostile market. The antipathy of the citizens against the noble is transferred to his servants (Mt.10:22; Lk.6:22; John 15:18). Despite the fact that Christ's servants have been left with the products discussed in verse 13 and that the world desperately needs these products, and deep within, knows that it needs them, yet, because they are products identified with Jesus Christ, they are hard to sell. The world wants love, humility, a home, a sure way to go, the truth, life, comfort, peace, friendship and victory, but not if these things must be accepted from Jesus Christ on His terms. If they could have these qualities without accepting Him, they would be glad to have them. But hatred, pride, uncertainty, falsehood, death, agony, war, antagonism and even defeat without Christ is better than His gifts with Him. Such is the citizen of the world and his prejudice against Jesus Christ. This is Christophobia at its worst. This is why it is difficult for one of Christ's servants to take one pound and parlay it into more than one.

Verse 15 - "And it came to pass, that when he was returned, having received the kingdom, then he commanded these servants to be called unto him, to whom he had given the money, that he might know how much every man had gained by trading."

Καὶ ἐγένετο ἐν τῷ ἐπανελθεῖν αὐτὸν λαβόντα τὴν βασιλείαν καὶ εἶπεν φωνηθῆναι αὐτῷ τοὺς δούλους τούτους οἷς δεδώκει τὸν ἀργύριον, ἵνα γνοῖ τί διεπραγματεύσαντο.

Καὶ (continuative conjunction) 14.
ἐγένετο (3d.per.sing.aor.ind.of *γίνομαι*, constative) 113.
ἐν (preposition with the locative of time point) 80.
τῷ (loc.sing.neut.of the article in agreement with *ἐπανελθεῖν*, time point) 9.
ἐπανελθεῖν (aor.mid.inf.of *ἐπανέρχομαι*, time point) 2435.
αὐτὸν (acc.sing.masc.of *αὐτός*, general reference) 16.
λαβόντα (aor.act.part.acc.sing.masc.of *λαμβάνω*, adverbial, temporal) 533.
τὴν (acc.sing.fem.of the article in agreement with *βασιλείαν*) 9.
βασιλείαν (acc.sing.fem.of *βασιλεία*, direct object of *λαβόντα*) 253.
καὶ (anacoluthon) 14.
εἶπεν (3d.per.sing.aor.act.ind.of *εἶπον*, constative) 155.
φωνηθῆναι (1st.aor.pass.inf.of *φωνέω*, accusative case, object of *εἶπεν*) 1338.
αὐτῷ (dat.sing.masc.of *αὐτός*, personal advantage) 16.
τοὺς (acc.pl.masc.of the article in agreement with *δούλους*) 9.
δούλους (acc.pl.masc.of *δοῦλος*, general reference) 725.
τούτους (acc.pl.masc.of *οὗτος*, in agreement with *δούλους*) 93.
οἷς (dat.pl.masc.of *ὅς*, indirect object of *δεδώκει*) 65.
τὸ (acc.sing.neut.of the article in agreement with *ἀργύριον*) 9.
ἀργύριον (acc.sing.neut.of *ἀργύριον*, direct object of *δεδώκει*) 1535.
ἵνα (conjunction introducing a purpose clause) 114.
γνοῖ (3d.per.sing.2d.aor.act.subj.of *γινώσκω*, purpose clause) 131.
τί (acc.sing.neut.of *τίς*, interrogative pronoun, direct object of *διεπραγματεύσαντο*) 281.

#2659 *διεπραγματεύσαντο* (3d.per.pl.aor.mid.ind.of *διαπραγματεύομαι*, culminative).

gain by trading - Luke 19:15.

Meaning: A combination of *διά* (#118) and *πραγματεύομαι* (#2658). Since #2658 means to trade in a market and receive gross revenue, *διαπραγματεύομαι* would seem to indicate net gain. To show a profit by realizing greater output than input. With reference to the ten servants - Luke 19:15.

Translation - "And it happened that after he had received the kingdom and returned, he ordered those servants to whom he had given the money to be called to him, so that he might know how much profit they had made for themselves.

Comment: The verse is full of interesting tense. The articular infinitive with *ἐν* and the locative of time point is aorist. Thus the time of his return was antecedent to his order that the servants be called. Luke has *ἐν* with the aorist infinitive nine times. We have the same construction twice in Hebrews and once in 1 Corinthians. (Burton, *New Testament Moods and Tenses,* paragraph #109, p.50). "After *ἐν* we naturally expect to find only the Present Infinitive, the preposition by its meaning suggesting an action thought of as in process; and this is indeed the more common usage." (*Ibid.*). In Luke 2:27; 11:37; 19:15; 24:30 and Acts 11:15, where we have ἐν with the aorist infinitive, the action of the infinitive is clearly antecedent to that of the main verb. It is like the aorist indicative with ὅτε. In some cases we can depend upon the context to tell us what temporal relation the infinitive has with the main verb, but the aorist tense indicates antecedent action here, as does the aorist participle λαβόντα. The order of events is clear: (1) the nobleman received his kingdom while he was in the far country, since λαβόντα is aorist, and thus antecedent to the action of ἐπανελθεῖν. (2) He returned, a completed action with the aorist infinitive, which is also antecedent to his order to call the servants. (3) He ordered his servants to be called to him. They are defined by the relative clause οἷς δεδώκει τὸ ἀργύριον - "to whom he had given the money." Why did he want an accounting? The ἵνα purpose clause with γνοῖ tells us - "in order that he might know . . " Know what? The indirect question τί διεπραγματεύσαντο - "what profit they had made" - answers that question.

The kingdom to which reference is made, which the nobleman received while he was in the far country before he returned, is the completion of the calling to salvation of the elect. When Christ has completed His call to the members of His body, the Church, He will return. Then He will call for the judgment seat of Christ, where believers will be judged for their works, after they became members of His body (2 Cor.5:10; 1 Cor.3:10-15; Rev.11:18; Lk.14:14.*Cf.* comment on each of these references. The issue at this judgment will not be salvation. Nobody will be called except those who are already in Christ. The issue is the degree of reward for the saints, whose eternal destiny is already fixed in Christ, by virtue of God's election, Christ's redemption and the effectual call of the Holy Spirit. How have we succeeded in trading in the world market place with the inventory which He left for us before He went away? Will we be able to show a net gain? Our task is not easy. Although the citizens of the world experience a deeply felt need for what we have to offer, they are nursing an implacable hatred for our absent Lord.

The first servant had some success.

Verse 16 - "Then came the first, saying, Lord, thy pound hath gained ten pounds."

παρεγένετο δὲ ὁ πρῶτος λέγων, Κύριε, ἡ μνᾶ σου δέκα προσηργάσατο μνᾶς.

παρεγένετο (3d.per.sing.aor.mid.ind.of παραγίνομαι, constative) 139.
δὲ (continuative conjunction) 11.
ὁ (nom.sing.masc.of the article in agreement with πρῶτος) 9.
πρῶτος (nom.sing.masc.of πρῶτος, subject of παρεγένετο) 487.
λέγων (pres.act.part.nom.sing.masc.of λέγω, recitative) 66.
Κύριε (voc.sing.masc.of κύριος, address) 97.
ἡ (nom.sing.fem.of the article in agreement with μνᾶ) 9.
μνᾶ (nom.sing.fem.of μνᾶ, subject of προσηργάσατο) 2657.

σου (gen.sing.masc.of *σύ*, possession) 104.
δέκα (numeral) 1330.

#2660 *προσηργάσατο* (3d.per.sing.aor.mid.ind.of *προσεργάζομαι*, culminative).

gain - Luke 19:16.

Meaning: A combination of *πρός* (#197) and *ἐργάζομαι* (#691). Hence, to gain beyond; to gain a marginal amount; to yield a profit - Luke 19:16.

μνᾶς (acc.pl.fem.of *μνᾶ* direct object of *προσηργάσατο*) 2657.

Translation - "And the first came, saying, 'Lord, your pound has gained ten pounds.' "

Comment: This report reveals a high degree of efficiency and steadfast application on the part of the first servant. A ten-fold gain is reported. *Cf.* Mt.13:8. This man made a great many contacts, sold his lord's services persuasively and was prudent in the Lord's business.

Verse 17 - "And he said unto him, Well, thou good servant: because thou hast been faithful in a very little, have thou authority over ten cities.' "

καὶ εἶπεν αὐτῷ, Εὖγε, ἀγαθὲ δοῦλε, ὅτι ἐν ἐλαχίστῳ πιστὸς ἐγένου, ἴσθι ἐξουσίαν ἔχων ἐπάνω δέκα πόλεων.

καὶ (continuative conjunction) 14.
εἶπεν (3d.per.sing.aor.act.ind.of *εἶπον*, constative) 155.
αὐτῷ (dat.sing.masc.of *αὐτός*, indirect object of *εἶπεν*) 16.

#26661 Εὖγε (exclamation).

Well! - Luke 19:17.

Meaning: A combination of *εὖ* (#1536) and *γε* (#2449). An adverb of manner. In Luke 19:17 - "well done."

ἀγαθὲ (voc.sing.masc.of *ἀγαθός*, in agreement with *δοῦλε*) 547.
δοῦλε (voc.sing.masc.of *δοῦλος*, address) 725.
ὅτι (conjunction introducing a subordinate causal clause) 211.
ἐν (preposition with the locative of sphere) 80.
ἐλαχίστῳ (loc.sing.neut.of *ἐλάχιστος*, sphere) 159.
πιστὸς (nom.sing.masc.of *πιστός*, predicate adjective) 1522.
ἐγένου (2d.per.sing.2d.aor.ind.of *γίνομαι*, culminative) 113.
ἴσθι (2d.per.sing.pres.impv.of *εἰμί*, command) 86.
ἐξουσίαν (acc.sing.fem.of *ἐξουσία*, direct object of *ἔχων*) 707.
ἔχων (pres.act.part.nom.sing.masc.of *ἔχω*, present periphrastic) 82.
ἐπάνω (adverb of place , metaphorical) 181.
δέκα (numeral) 1330.

πόλεων (gen.pl.fem.of πόλις, description) 243.

Translation - "And he said to him, 'Well done! good servant. Because you were faithful in a little thing, assume authority over ten cities.' "

Comment: εὔγε is an exclamation of approval, such as athletic fans shout to approve exploits on a football field or basketball court. The ὅτι clause tells us why the nobleman was well pleased. The servant had been given supreme authority in an insignificant sphere of activity. There were no instructions from the nobleman about how he was to invest the money. He was free to buy and sell whatever he pleased. He had parlayed $16.67 into $166.70. Εὔγε! Because of his faithfulness and success, not because of the scope of his operation, he now receives a reward. ἴσθι ἐξουσίαν ἔχων ἐπάνω δέκα πόλεων is a present periphrastic, with the present imperative of εἰμί and the present participle of ἔχω. His tenure over the ten cities is to be permanent. *Cf.* #707 for other examples of ἐξουσία in the sense of political authority and administration.

Premillenialists, who interpret the kingdom prophecies with the same literality that we use to view the scriptures in regard to Jesus' first coming, have no hesitancy in applying the Lord's commission to His faithful servant literally. When Christ returns He will reign upon the earth for 1000 years, and after the events of Revelation 20:7-15, the new heaven and the new earth will enjoy His rule forever. There will be an eternal heavenly city. Why not other cities on earth forever? And Jesus Christ, King of heaven and earth, will need subordinate municipal administrators. Ten cities for one man; two for another; other duties, great or small to perform as He wills it (John 5:22). These are rewards, passed out to faithful Christians at the judgment seat of Christ. The Twelve Apostles will be given special judgeships, sitting on twelve thrones, judging the twelve tribes of Israel. Some commentators seem to have a strange antipathy for anything material in prophecy. This is a modern form of Docetic Gnosticism which Paul attacked in Col.2:20-23. Why, indeed is something unethical because it is tangible? πνευματικός (#3791) does not mean immaterial. Those who think it does should try to apply that meaning in Gal.6:1; 1 Cor.2:15; 14:37.

Verse 18 - "And the second came, saying, Lord, thy pound hath gained five pounds."

καὶ ἦλθεν ὁ δεύτερος λέγων, Ἡ μνᾶ σου, κύριε, ἐποίησεν πέντε μνᾶς.

καὶ (continuative conjunction) 14.
ἦλθεν (3d.per.sing.aor.ind.of ἔρχομαι, constative) 146.
ὁ (nom.sing.masc.of the article in agreement with δεύτερος) 9.
δεύτερος (nom.sing.masc.of δεύτερος, subject of ἦλθεν) 1371.
λέγων (pres.act.part.nom.sing.masc.of λέγω, recitative) 66.
Ἡ (nom.sing.fem.of the article in agreement with μνᾶ) 9.
μνᾶ (nom.sing.fem.of μνᾶ, subject of ἐποίησεν) 2657.
σου (gen.sing.masc.of σύ, possession) 104.

κύριε (voc.sing.masc.of *κύριος*, address) 97.
ἐποίησεν (3d.per.sing.aor.act.ind.of *ποιέω*, culminative) 127.
πέντε (numeral) 1119.
μνᾶς (acc.pl.fem.of *μνᾶ*, direct object of *ἐποίησεν*) 2657.

Translation - "And the second came saying, 'Your pound, Lord, made five pounds.' "

Comment: Note that Luke, having used *προσεργάζομαι*, to introduce the concept, uses the more general word *ποιέω* (#127), now that the reader sees what it means. We have efficiency here again, not as great as in the fomer case, but, nevertheless, this servant was not a failure.

Verse 19 - "And he said likewise to him, Be thou also over five cities."

εἶπεν δὲ καὶ τούτῳ, Καὶ *σὺ ἐπάνω γίνου πέντε πόλεων.*

εἶπεν (3d.per.sing.aor.act.ind.of *εἶπον*, constative) 155.
δὲ (continuative conjunction) 11.
καὶ (adjunctive conjunction joining pronouns) 14.
τούτῳ (dat.sing.masc.of *οὗτος*, indirect object of *εἶπεν*) 93.
Καὶ (adjunctive conjunction joining pronouns) 14.
σὺ (nom.sing.masc.of *σύ*, subject of *γίνου*) 104.
ἐπάνω (adverbial) 181.
γίνου (2d.per.sing.pres.impv.of *γίνομαι*, command) 113.
πέντε (numeral) 1119.
πόλεων (gen.pl.fem.of *πόλις*, description) 243.

Translation - "And he said also to this man, 'You may assume authority over five cities.' "

Comment: Rewards at the judgment seat of Christ are in direct ratio to faithfulness while we serve Christ upon earth (2 Cor.5:10; 1 Cor.3:13-15).

Verse 20 - "And another came, saying, Lord, behold, here is thy pound, which I have kept laid up in a napkin."

καὶ ὁ ἕτερος ἦλθεν λέγων, Κύριε, *ἰδοὺ ἡ μνᾶ σου ἣν εἶχον ἀποκειμένην ἐν σουδαρίῳ.*

καὶ (continuative conjunction) 14.
ὁ (nom.sing.masc.of the article in agreement with *ἕτερος*) 9.
ἕτερος (nom.sing.masc.of *ἕτερος*, subject of *ἦλθεν*) 605.
ἦλθεν (3d.per.sing.aor.act.ind.of *ἔρχομαι*, constative) 146.
λέγων (pres.act.part.nom.sing.masc.of *λέγω*, recitative) 66.
Κύριε (voc.sing.masc.of *κύριος*, address) 97.
ἰδοὺ (exclamation) 95.
ἡ (nom.sing.fem.of the article in agreement with *μνᾶ*) 9.
μνᾶ (nom.sing.fem.of *μνᾶ*, nominative absolute) 2657.

σου (gen.sing.masc.of *σύ*, possession) 104.

ἣν (acc.sing.fem.of *ὅς*, relative pronoun, direct object of *εἶχον*) 65.

εἶχον (1st.per.sing.imp.act.ind.of *ἔχω*, progressive description) 82.

#2662 *ἀποκειμένην* (pres.mid.part.acc.sing.fem.of *ἀποκεῖμαι*, adverbial, circumstanital).

be appointed - Heb.9:27.
be laid up - Luke 19:20; Col.1:5; 2 Tim.4:8.

Meaning: A combination of *ἀπό* (#70) and *κεῖμαι* (#295). To be kept *ἀπό*, *i.e.* reserved, or kept away from. Saved from current consumption or use. With reference to the money which the servant kept safely, with *ἐν σουδαρίῳ* - Luke 19:20. Of the hope of reward reserved in heaven, followed by *ὑμῖν* in Col.1:5. The crown of righteousness, with *μοι* in 2 Tim.4:8. In a different sense - appointed, in the plan of God and in the nature of things, that men should die, with *τοῖς ἀνθρώποις* and the infinitive - Heb.9:27.

ἐν (preposition with the locative of place) 80.

σουδαρίῳ (loc.sing.neut.of *σουδάριον*,place where) 2608.

Translation - "And the other man came saying, 'Lord, see here. Your pound, which I have been keeping, put away in a handkerchief,' "

Comment: *ὁ ἕτερος* does not mean that there were only three, for there were ten (vs.13), but Jesus, in telling the story chose only to speak of three representative types. There was an efficient servant whose record merited a great reward. There was a less efficient servant, who merited a somewhat smaller reward. And there was the servant who earned no reward at all, but rather suffered the loss of the money, though no loss of salvation. The other seven are not mentioned. Possibly there could be found among them representatives of all three types. The servant was honest, but inefficient. He did not lose the money. On the contrary he was super cautious and thus he refused to risk it in the market. This man is representative of the Christian who does nothing to employ the gifts which the Holy Spirit has given to him (1 Cor.12:1-11) and which he should have used during his days as a follower of Christ. With a product for which there was great demand he did nothing to sell it.

He tells us why in

Verse 21 - "For I feared thee because thou art an austere man: thou takest up that thou layedst not down, and reapest that thou didst not sow."

ἐφοβούμην γάρ σε, ὅτι ἄνθρωπος αὐστηρὸς εἶ, αἴρεις ὃ οὐκ ἔθηκας καὶ θερίζεις ὃ οὐκ ἔσπειρας.

ἐφοβούμην (1st.per.sing.imp.mid.ind.of *φοβέομαι*, progressive description) 101.

γάρ (causal conjunction) 105.

σε (acc.sing.masc.of σύ, direct object of ἐφοβούμην) 104.
ὅτι (conjunction introducing a subordinate causal clause) 211.
ἄνθρωπος (nom.sing.masc.of ἄνθρωπος, predicate nominative) 341.

#2663 αὐστηρὸς (nom.sing.masc.of αὐστηρός, predicate adjective).

austere - Luke 19:21,22.

Meaning: from αὔω - "to dry up." Hence, harsh, rough, rigid, exacting, demanding, austere. Of the nobleman of Luke 19:21,22.

εἶ (2d.per.sing.pres.ind.of εἰμί, customary) 86.
αἴρεις (2d.per.sing.pres.act.ind.of αἴρω, customary) 350.
ὃ (acc.sing.neut.of ὅς, direct object of αἴρεις) 65.
οὐκ (summary negative conjunction with the indicative) 130.
ἔθυκας (2d.per.sing.1st.aor.act.ind.of τίθημι, constative) 455.
καὶ (adjunctive conjunction joining verbs) 14.
θερίζεις (2d.per.sing.pres.act.ind.of θερίζω, customary) 617.
ὃ (acc.sing.neut.of ὅς, direct object of θερίζεις) 65.
οὐκ (summary negative conjunction with the indicative) 130.
ἔθηκας (2d.per.sing.1st.aor.act.ind.of τίθημι, constative) 455.

Translation - "For I have always been afraid of you, because you are an austere man. You pick up that which you did not lay down, and you reap that which you did not sow.' "

Comment: The servant is trying to justify his lack of trading activity - something which the nobleman had specifically ordered. "I was always in awe of you." Note the imperfect tense, with its linear action in the past. φοβέομαι here does not necessarily mean physical fear, though it can include that. Rather the servant means that his lord would hold him to strict account for any loss which might be incurred. Therefore he balanced the fear of persecution from the citizens who hated his absent lord against the fear of possible recriminations by his returning lord in the event that he lost his money, and decided that, since the lord would accept no excuses for lost money, even though the market was a hostile one, the safest course was to guard the money against loss. Thus he would not arouse the citizens and escape persecution. He was willing to take his chances that his lord would at least understand, since he lost none of the money entrusted to him.

What he should have done was to recognize the superiority of his products and brave any possible persecution as he traded in the market place, in obedience to his lord's express command (vs.13). Had he done this he would have realized some gain, as did the others, and would have received some reward.

ὅτι introduces the causal clause. "You are a stern man. You pick up and reap the returns that result from the hard work of other people. They lay down and sow. You pick up and reap. Theirs is the input. Yours is the output. They incur the risk. You realize the return." He did not understand that the policy which he described is the Lord's prerogative. He also forgot that it was his lord's money in the first place, and that the lord was in a position to reward him handsomely if he had only been faithful. He need not be successful - only faithful. The success for the faithful salesman comes, not from his faithfulness, but from the superiority of the products which he had to sell.

The unwise servant made the following mistakes: (1) he thought too much of his personal safety in the short run; (2) he underestimated the sales appeal of his products, even though the market in which they were to be offered was hostile; (3) he failed to realize the potentiality of eternal gain in return for temporal loss (Rom.8:18; 2 Cor.4:17-18; Mt.5:11,12); (4) he judged the nobleman by his own standards, as though he were the final arbiter of what is right and wrong. Arminians and others who attack the God of the Reformed theology, make this last mistake. The ultimate question is whether or not the Calvinistic conception of decrees is taught in Scripture. If indeed it is, then the objection that God is arbitrary must be admitted, with the counter objection that we are calling God arbitrary only from the standpoint of human reasoning. It is the only standpoint which we have, so let us not quibble about whether or not God is arbitrary. Let us admit that He is. If He is that is how it is and we can do nothing about it. If we object to His "arbitrary" way of running the universe and go away and pout and refuse to do what He has asked us to do, we have no one to blame but ourselves if we hear His condemnation in verses 22-24.

Some or all of the mistakes listed *supra* are the reasons why Chritians are not soul winners.

Verse 22 - "And he saith unto him, Out of thine own mouth will I judge thee, thou wicked servant. Thou knewest that I was an austere man, taking up that I laid not down, and reaping that I did not sow."

λέγει αὐτῷ, Ἐκ τοῦ στόματός σου κρίνω σε, πονηρὲ δοῦλε. ᾔδεις ὅτι ἐγὼ ἄνθρωπος αὐστηρός εἰμι, αἴρων ὃ οὐκ ἔθηκα καὶ θερίζων ὃ οὐκ ἔσπειρα;

λέγει (3d.per.sing.pres.act.ind.of *λέγω*, historical) 66.
αὐτῷ (dat.sing.masc.of *αὐτός*,indirect object of *λέγει*) 16.
Ἐκ (preposition with the ablative of source) 19.
τοῦ (abl.sing.neut.of the article in agreement with *στόματός*) 9.
στόματός (abl.sing.neut.of *στόμα*, source) 344.
σου (gen.sing.masc.of *σύ*, possession) 104.
κρίνω (1st.per.sing.pres.act.ind.of *κρίνω*, futuristic) 531.
σε (acc.sing.masc.of *σύ*, direct object of *κρίνω*) 104.
πονηρὲ (voc.sing.masc.of *πονηρός*, in agreement with *δοῦλε*) 438.
δοῦλε (voc.sing.masc.of *δοῦλος*, address) 725.
ᾔδεις (2d.per.sing.pluperfect indicative of *ὁράω*, intensive) 144.
ὅτι (conjunction introducing an object clause in indirect discourse) 211.
ἐγὼ (nom.sing.masc.of *ἐγώ*, subject of *εἰμι*) 123.
ἄνθρωπος (nom.sing.masc.of *ἄνθρωπος*, predicate nominative) 341.
αὐστηρός (nom.sing.masc.of *αὐστηρός*, predicate adjective) 2663.
εἰμι (1st.per.sing.pres.ind.of *εἰμί*, static) 86.
αἴρων (pres.act.part.nom.sing.masc.of *αἴρω*, adverbial, causal) 350.
ὃ (acc.sing.neut.of *ὅς*, direct object of *αἴρων*) 65.

οὐκ (summary negative conjunction with the indicative) 130.
ἔθηκα (1st.per.sing.aor.act.ind.of τίθημι, constative) 455.
καὶ (adjunctive conjunction joining participles) 14.
θερίζων (pres.act.part.nom.sing.masc.of θερίζω, adverbial, causal) 617.
ὃ (acc.sing.neut.of ὅς, direct object of θερίζων) 65.
οὐκ (summary negative conjunction with the indicative) 130.
ἔσπειρα (1st.per.sing.aor.act.ind.of σπείρω, constative) 616.

Translation - "He said to him, 'Out of your own mouth I am going to judge you, evil servant. So you have always known, have you, that I am an austere man, because I pick up that which I did not lay down and reap that which I did not sow?' "

Comment: ἐκ τοῦ στόματός σου - an ablative of source. The nobleman's statement is a rhetorical question and it demands an affirmative reply, since he is only repeating the servant's words of verse 21. κρίνω is a futuristic present, albeit the judgment was in the immediate future (vss.24-26). The logical conclusion of what the servant offered as an excuse for his failure, is that he was culpable. The servant could not plead that he did not know what sort of judge the nobleman was. ᾔδεις, the pluperfect is intensive, concentrating the thought upon the present result of what he had learned in the past. He could not say that he had only recently come to understand his lord's character and policy. Since he knew that his lord would require a strict accounting and would be furious if he did not show a profit, he faced three alternative policies: (1) he could trade and face the enmity of the hostile world; (2) he could make peace with the world, stay out of the market with his products, and face the displeasure of his returning lord and take his punishment, or (3) he could challenge his lord to combat on the ground that he was arbitrary and unfair. It is not likely that he considered the third possibility. One wonders if the Arminians are going to argue with God at the judgment about the "arbitrary" nature of His decrees. The servant chose to stay out of the market and enjoy a temporary popularity with the hostile world. Nobody likes a salesman who cannot demonstrate that his product is something that the customer really needs, and with which he would be much happier. His decision to disregard the lord's orders shows that he had a higher regard for the world than for the nobleman. This, in itself, is enough to earn for him the epithet, πονηρὲ δοῦλε. Many Christians, unfortunately, view the situation temporally rather than eternally and thus they make the same sad mistake as did the evil servant.

The question was not whether the servant agreed with his lord's stern standard of judgment. The point was that he *knew* that that was how it was. The question therefore becomes this: why did he not conduct himself accordingly. This is the nobleman's question in

Verse 23 - "Wherefore then gavest not thou my money into the bank that at my coming I might have required mine own with usury?"

καὶ διὰ τί οὐκ ἔδωκάς μου τὸ ἀργύριον ἐπὶ τράπεζαν; κἀγὼ ἐλθὼν σὺν τόκῳ *ἂν αὐτὸ ἔπραξα.*

καὶ (inferential conjunction) 14.
διὰ (preposition with the accusative, cause) 118.
τί (acc.sing.neut.of *τίς*, interrogative pronoun, cause) 281.
οὐκ (summary negative conjunction with the indicative in direct question) 130.
ἔδωκάς (2d.per.sing.aor.act.ind.of *δίδωμι*, constative) 362.
μου (gen.sing.masc.of *ἐγώ*, possession) 123.
τὸ (acc.sing.neut.of the article, in agreement with *ἀργύριον*) 9.
ἀργύριον (acc.sing.neut.of *ἀργύριον*, direct object of *ἔδωκάς*) 1535.
ἐπὶ (preposition with the accusative of extent) 47.
τράπεζαν (acc.sing.fem.of *τράπεζα*, extent) 1176.
κἀγὼ (continuative conjunction) 178.
ἐλθὼν (aor.act.part.nom.sing.masc.of *ἔρχομαι*, adverbial, temporal) 146.
σὺν (preposition with the instrumental of association) 1542.
τόκῳ (instrumental sing.masc.of *τόκος*, association) 1543.
ἂν (definite particle of contingency, in an implied second-class condition) 205.

αὐτὸ (acc.sing.neut.of *αὐτός*, direct object of *ἔπραξα*) 16.
ἔπραξα (1st.per.sing.aor.act.ind.of *πράσσω*, implied second-class condition) 1943.

Translation - "Why then did you not put my money into a bank? And when I came back I might possibly withdraw it with interest."

Comment: *καὶ* is inferential. "In view of what you know about me and my demands, why, then . . . *κ.τ.λ.?*" *διὰ τί* - the usual causal construction with *διά* and the accusative. *ἐπὶ τράπεζαν* is interesting - "upon a table" since *τράπεζα* - "table" was the only bank that the Greek bankers had. *Cf.*#1176. The evil servant, who had decided not to invest the money in a saleable inventory of tangible products, could, at least, have put the money into the money market. Here is evidence that in the first century the speculative motive for holding money was understood. Classical economists from Adam Smith and J.B.Say to Alfred Marshall ignored this motive and thought only of the transactions and precautionary motives, despite the fact that Aristotle had condemned the practice of taking money into a speculative money market, rather than investing it in a production process in anticipation of the sale of the product and a profit.

The presence of *ἂν* and the aorist indicative in *ἔπραξα* in the apodosis implies a second-class condition. The lord is expressing some doubt that he would in fact earn an interest rate if his servant had put his money into the bank. There was no doubt that he could have recovered the original amount, but, at least, there was some chance that his original investment would have earned a small increment. There was no possibility that an increment could be gained by hoarding the money as the servant had done. What the lord may have lost as a result of the servant's timidity and conservatism was the interest that *might have* accrued. *Cf.*#1543 for the root of *τόκος*. Today we still say that money *bears* interest.

Christ is concerned about the growth potential of His investment at Calvary. When He arose from the dead he got His investment back. One body crucified -

the same body raised again. But whether marginal gain is received depends upon His servants who must trade in a hostile world market. The grain of wheat falls into the ground and dies, else it must remain forever only one grain of wheat. But since it died it is in a position to bear much fruit. This is τόκος. The whole purpose of Christ's death is τόκος - growth (John 12:24-32 - note "much fruit" in verse 24 and "all men" in verse 32).

The nobleman's indignation was justified and His decision to take away the pound from the inefficient servant and give it to the most efficient servant, who could parlay it into ten pounds, was proper.

Verse 24 - "And he said unto them that stood by, Take from him the pound, and give it to him that hath ten pounds."

καὶ τοῖς παρεστῶσιν εἶπεν,"Αρατε ἀπ' αὐτοῦ τὴν μνᾶν καὶ δότε τῷ τὰς δέκα μνᾶς ἔχοντι.

καὶ (continuative conjunction) 14.
τοῖς (dat.pl.masc.of the article in agreement with παρεστῶσιν) 9.
παρεστῶσιν (perf.act.part.dat.pl.masc.of παρίστημι, indirect object of εἶπεν) 1596.
εἶπεν (3d.per.sing.aor.act.ind.of εἶπον, constative) 155.
"Αρατε (2d.per.pl.aor.act.impv.of αἴρω, command) 350.
ἀπ' (preposition with the ablative of separation) 70.
αὐτοῦ (abl.sing.masc.of αὐτός, separation) 16.
τὴν (acc.sing.fem.of the article in agreement with μνᾶν) 9.
μνᾶν (acc.sing.fem.of μνᾶ, direct object of"Αρατε) 2657.
καὶ (adjunctive conjunction joining verbs) 14.
δότε (2d.per.pl.2d.aor.act.impv.of δίδωμι, command) 362.
τῷ (dat.sing.masc.of the article in agreement with ἔχοντι) 9.
τὰς (acc.pl.fem.of the article in agreement with μνᾶς) 9.
δέκα (numeral) 1330.
μνᾶς (acc.pl.fem.of μνᾶ, direct object of ἔχοντι) 2657.
ἔχοντι (pres.act.part.dat.sing.masc.of ἔχω, indirect object of δότε) 82.

Translation - "And to those standing by he said, 'Take the money away from him and give it to the one who has the $166.70!' "

Comment: As pointed out above, the Lord wants His treasure to be in the hands of an efficient servant who has already demonstrated by his past performance that he is capable of managing and augmenting it. It is not so much a reward given to the ten pound servant, as it is an attempt to maximize profits by putting the assets into the hands of the most efficient producer. Thus the implied objection of verse 25 is totally without point. *Cf.*2 Cor.4:7 for the way that Paul felt about his obligation to be the Lord's wise investor.

Verse 25 - "(And they said unto him, Lord he hath ten pounds.)"

(— καὶ εἶπαν αὐτῷ, Κύριε, ἔχει δέκα μνᾶς).

καὶ (adversative conjunction) 14.
εἶπαν (3d.per.pl.aor.act.ind.of *εἶπον*, constative) 155.
αὐτῷ (dat.sing.masc.of *αὐτός*, indirect object of *εἶπαν*) 16.
Κύριε (voc.sing.masc.of *κύριος*, address) 97.
ἔχει (3d.per.sing.pres.act.ind.of *ἔχω*, aoristic) 82.
δέκα (numeral) 1330.
μνᾶς (acc.pl.fem.of *μνᾶ*, direct object of *ἔχει*) 2657.

Translation - "(But they said to him, 'Lord, he has $166.70.)"

Comment: *καὶ* is adversative as those who stood by seem to be objecting to the lord's decision, by pointing out that the good servant already had ten pounds. Why not give the money to the second best servant who had only five pounds? This would be logical only if the end to be achieved were a more equal distribution of the wealth. But that is not the end in view. The lord's purpose is to maximize returns on his money. Thus he wanted his assets in the hands of the most efficient producer.

The Christian should ask himself this question: How well have I taken the Lord's assets and traded with them in the world? He gave us His humility, His love, His home, His way, His truth, His life, His comfort, His peace, His friendship and His victory. How much of each of these have we been able to distribute to the world. The source of nine is His truth, which we have in His Word, which the Holy Spirit inspired the Apostles to write. If we "preach the Word" (2 Tim.4:2) and teach it wherever we go, we will find that our listeners will find all of the treasures which He has committed unto us.

Verse 26 - "For I say unto you, That unto every one which hath shall be given; and from him that hath not, even that he hath shall be taken away from him."

λέγω ὑμῖν ὅτι παντὶ τῷ ἔχοντι δοθήσεται, ἀπὸ δὲ τοῦ μὴ ἔχοντος καὶ ὃ ἔχει ἀρθήσεται.

λέγω (1st.per.sing.pres.act.ind.of *λέγω*, aoristic) 66.
ὑμῖν (dat.pl.masc.of *σύ*, indirect object of *λέγω*) 104.
ὅτι (conjunction introducing an object clause in indirect discourse) 211.
παντὶ (dat.sing.masc.of *πᾶς*, in agreement with *ἔχοντι*) 67.
τῷ (dat.sing.masc.of the article in agreement with *ἔχοντι*) 9.
ἔχοντι (pres.act.part.dat.sing.masc.of *ἔχω*, substantival, indirect object of *δοθήσεται*) 82.
δοθήσεται (3d.per.sing.fut.pass.ind.of *δίδωμι*, predictive) 362.
ἀπὸ (preposition with the ablative of separation) 70.
δὲ (adversative conjunction) 11.
τοῦ (abl.sing.masc.of the article in agreement with *ἔχοντος*) 9.
μὴ (qualified negative conjunction with the participle) 87.
ἔχοντος (pres.act.part.abl.sing.masc.of *ἔχω*, substantival, separation) 82.
καὶ (ascensive conjunction) 14.
ὃ (nom.sing.neut.of *ὅς*, subject of *ἀρθήσεται*) 65.

ἔχει (3d.per.sing.pres.act.ind.of ἔχω, aoristic) 82.
ἀρθήσεται (3d.per.sing.fut.pass.ind.of αἴρω, predictive) 350.

Translation - "I am telling you that to everyone who has shall be given, but from the one who has not, even that which he has shall be taken away."

Comment: This is a logical directive since the point in the parable is profit maximization. Why should a nonproductive Christian be allowed to handle the Lord's assets when such assets can be transferred to a productive Christian who can make them grow? But it is important that the wicked servant lost only the money which was entrusted to him at the beginning. He did not lose his position as a servant. The nonproductive Christian likewise does not lose his salvation - only his gifts (1 Cor.12:1-11) and the rewards which they could have brought him if he had traded with them. *Cf.* our comments on 1 Cor.9:27; Heb.6:4-8.

Verse 27 clearly reveals the difference between the Lord's treatment of His three servants on the one hand, and His enemies who hated Him, on the other.

Verse 27 - "But those mine enemies which would not that I should reign over them, bring hither, and slay them before me."

πλὴν τοὺς ἐχθρούς μου τούτους τοὺς μὴ θελήσαντάς με βασιλεῦσαι ἐπ' αὐτοὺς ἀγάγετε ὧδε καὶ κατασφάξατε αὐτοὺς ἔμπροσθέν μου.

πλὴν (adversative conjunction) 944.
τοὺς (acc.pl.masc.of the article in agreement with ἐχθρούς) 9.
ἐχθρούς (acc.pl.masc.of ἐχθρός, direct object of ἀγάγετε) 543.
μου (gen.sing.masc.of ἐγώ, relationship) 123.
τούτους (acc.pl.masc.of οὗτος, in agreement with θελήσαντάς) 93.
τοὺς (acc.pl.masc.of the article in agreement with θελήσαντάς) 9.
μὴ (qualified negative conjunction with the participle) 87.
θελήσαντάς (aor.act.part.acc.pl.masc.of θέλω, in apposition) 88.
με (acc.sing.masc.of ἐγώ, general reference) 123.
βασιλεῦσαι (aor.act.inf.of βασιλεύω, noun use, direct object of θελήσαντάς) 236.
ἐπ' (preposition with the accusative of place, metaphorical) 47.
αὐτοὺς (acc.pl.masc.of αὐτός, place, metaphorical) 16.
ἀγάγετε (2d.per.pl.2d.aor.act.impv.of ἄγω, command) 876.
ὧδε (adverb of place) 766.
καὶ (adjunctive conjunction joining verbs) 14.

#2664 κατασφάξατε (2d.per.pl.aor.act.impv.of κατασφάζω, command).

slay - Luke 19:27.

Meaning: A combination of κατά (#98) and σφάζω (#5292). Hence, to kill; to strike down; to cut down with a sword, spear of other weapon. To destroy physically - Luke 19:27.

αὐτοὺς (acc.pl.masc.of αὐτός, direct object of κατασφάξατε) 16.
ἔμπροσθέν (improper preposition with the ablative of separation) 459.

μου (abl.sing.masc.of ἐγώ, separation) 123.

Translation - "However, those enemies of mine, those who did not want me to reign over them, bring here and cut them down in my presence."

Comment: πλὴν introduces further material of a different type than the foregoing. *Cf.*#944. Jesus is going to change the subject. He has been dealing with material that applies to His own servants in verses 16-26. It was to them that He gave the gifts before He went away. Note that Paul refers to himself as ὁ δοῦλος of Jesus Christ (Romans 1:1, *et al.*). Now He is going to deal with His enemies. Hence, πλὴν - "nevertheless", "however" or "but." Note the emphasis upon them as Jesus puts τοὺς ἐχθρούς μου, the object of the verb, ἀγάγετε first. Then, as if to prevent any misunderstanding as to the group of whom He is speaking, He identifies them by the apposition construction τοὺς μὴ θελήσαντάς με βασιλεῦσαι ἐπ' αὐτοὺς - "namely those who did not want me to rule over them."

Our interest in the story of the Lord's dealings with His servants may have caused us to forget about the citizens of the country who hated Him and sent their courier to tell Him that they would not accept His rule. But Jesus had not forgotten them. Having reminded us of them, He now tells us what to do with them - "bring them here and kill them in my presence."

Here is the judgment of Christ at His second coming upon the lost - a very different treatment from that imposed upon His evil servant.

The parable represents the judgment seat of Christ, where believers' works will be evaluated and rewarded (1 Cor.3:11-15; 2 Cor.5:10; Mt.16:27; Rev.11:11-18), as simultaneous with the judgment of Christ upon the unsaved. This is consistent with what we find in Rev.11:15-19. Note particularly Rev.11:18. "Angry nations" (Ps.2:1-3) and the wrath of the returning Christ (Ps.2:4-5); judgment of the saints who have just been raised from the dead, together with the giving of rewards to those who merit them (Luke 19:16-19) and the Judge's wrath upon the end-time enemies of Christ (Luke 19:27). *Cf.* also 2 Thess.1:7-10; Rev.19:11-21 *et al.*.

The parable is finished. Now the disciples should understand that, while there is indeed to be a literal Messianic Kingdom of Christ on earth, it was not to be established in their immediate future. Rather, they, His disciples, were to be given His heavenly stock in trade - humility, love, home, way, truth, life, comfort, peace, friendship and victory, and were to trade with them in a hostile world while He is gone. After that the King will come back.

And now the King leads the way to Jerusalem, and a Roman cross in

Verse 28 - "And when he had thus spoken, he went before, ascending up to Jerusalem."

Καὶ εἰπὼν ταῦτα ἐπορεύετο ἔμπροσθεν ἀναβαίνων εἰς Ἱεροσόλυμα.

Καὶ (continuative conjunction) 14.
εἰπὼν (aor.act.part.nom.sing.masc.of εἶπον, adverbial, temporal) 155.
ταῦτα (acc.pl.neut.of οὗτος, direct object of εἰπὼν) 93.

ἐπορεύετο (3d.per.sing.imp.mid.ind.of πορεύομαι, inceptive) 170.
ἔμπροσθεν (improper preposition used adverbially) 459.
ἀναβαίνων (pres.act.part.nom.sing.masc.of ἀναβαίνω, adverbial, temporal) 323.
εἰς (preposition with the accusative of extent) 140.
Ἱεροσόλυμα (acc.sing.of Ἱεροσόλυμα, extent) 141.

Translation - "And having said these things He led the way up to Jerusalem."

Comment: Note the inceptive imperfect in ἐπορεύετο. Jesus led the way - ἔμπροσθεν. *Cf.* Mark 10:32.

Jesus' Arrival in Bethany

(John 11:55 - 12:1; 9-11)

John 11:55 - "And the Jews' passover was nigh at hand; and many went out of the country up to Jerusalem, before the passover, to purify themselves."

Ἦν δὲ ἐγγὺς τὸ πάσχα τῶν Ἰουδαίων, καὶ ἀνέβησαν πολλοὶ εἰς Ἱεροσόλυμα ἐκ τῆς χώρας πρὸ τοῦ πάσχα ἵνα ἁγνίσωσιν ἑαυτούς.

Ἦν (3d.per.sing.imp.ind.of εἰμί, progressive description) 86.
δὲ (explanatory conjunction) 11.
ἐγγὺς (nom.sing.neut.of ἐγγύς, predicate adjective) 1512.
τὸ (nom.sing.neut.of the article in agreement with πάσχα) 9.
πάσχα (nom.sing.neut.of πάσχα, subject of ἦν) 1553.
τῶν (gen.pl.masc.of the article in agreement with Ἰουδαίων) 9.
Ἰουδαίων (gen.pl.masc.of Ἰουδαῖος, description) 143.
καὶ (continuative conjunction) 14.
ἀνέβησαν (3d.per.pl.aor.act.ind.of ἀναβαίνω, constative) 323.
πολλοὶ (nom.pl.masc.of πολύς, subject of ἀνέβησαν) 228.
εἰς (preposition with the accusative of extent) 140.
Ἱεροσόλυμα (acc.sing.of Ἱεροσόλυμα, extent) 141.
ἐκ (preposition with the ablative of separation) 19.
τῆς (abl.sing.fem.of the article in agreement with χώρας) 9.
χώρας (abl.sing.fem.of χώρα, separation) 201.
πρὸ (preposition with the ablative of time separation) 442.
τοῦ (abl.sing.neut.of the article in agreement with πάσχα) 9.
πάσχα (abl.sing.neut.of πάσχα, time separation) 1553.
ἵνα (conjunction introducing a purpose clause) 114.

#2665 ἁγνίσωσιν (3d.per.pl.aor.act.subj.of ἁγνίζω, purpose).

purify - John 11:55; Acts 21:24,26; 24:18; James 4:8; 1 Pet.1:22; 1 John 3:3.

Meaning: to purify. In the Levitical sense - John 11:55; Acts 21:24,26; 24:18.

Morally - James 4:8; 1 Pet.1:22; 1 John 3:3.

ἑαυτούς (acc.pl.masc.of ἑαυτός, direct object of ἁγνίσωσιν) 288.

Translation - "Now the Passover of the Jews was at hand and many went up to Jerusalem out of the country before the feast in order to purify themselves."

Comment: It is early April. The Passover week is approaching, the most eventful in the history of Israel, since God's lamb is about to be sacrificed (John 1:29). John identifies the feast with τῶν Ἰουδαίων, since he is writing to a Greek audience in the tenth decade of the Christian era. The Ephesians were not particularly familiar with Jewish customs. Many of the Jews went up to Jerusalem early in order to engage in the Levitical ceremonies connected with purification. Jesus of Nazareth, Who for the past three years had startled and electrified the country with His teachings and His miracles was much in the thoughts of many as they toiled up the mountain roads to the Holy City.

Verse 56 - "Then sought they for Jesus, and spake among themselves, as they stood in the temple, What think ye, that he will not come to the feast?"

ἐζήτουν οὖν τὸν Ἰησοῦν καὶ ἔλεγον μετ' ἀλλήλων ἐν τῷ ἱερῷ ἑστηκότες, Τί δοκεῖ ἡμῖν; ὅτι οὐ μὴ ἔλθῃ εἰς τὴν ἑορτήν;

ἐζήτουν (3d.per.pl.imp.act.ind.of ζητέω, progressive description) 207.
οὖν (continuative conjunction) 68.
τὸν (acc.sing.masc.of the article in agreement with Ἰησοῦν) 9.
Ἰησοῦν (acc.sing.masc.of Ἰησοῦς, direct object of ἐζήτουν) 3.
καὶ (adjunctive conjunction joining verbs) 14.
ἔλεγον (3d.per.pl.imp.act.ind.of λέγω, progressive description) 66.
μετ' (preposition with the genitive of accompaniment) 50.
ἀλλήλων (gen.pl.masc.of ἀλλήλος, accompaniment) 1487.
ἐν (preposition with the locative of place) 80.
τῷ (loc.sing.neut.of the article in agreement with ἱερῷ) 9.
ἱερῷ (loc.sing.neut.of ἱερόν, place where) 346.
ἑστηκότες (perf.act.part.nom.pl.masc.of ἵστημι, adverbial, temporal) 180.
Τί (nom.sing.neut.of τίς, the interrogative pronoun, subject of δοκεῖ) 281.
δοκεῖ (3d.per.sing.pres.act.ind.of δοκέω, aoristic) 287.
ὑμῖν (dat.pl.masc.of σύ, indirect object of δοκεῖ) 104.
ὅτι (conjunction introducing an object clause in indirect discourse) 211.
οὐ (summary negative conjunction with μὴ and the deliberative subjunctive) 130.
μὴ (qualified negative conjunction with οὐ and the deliberative subjunctive) 87.
ἔλθῃ (3d.per.sing.2d.aor.subj.of ἔρχομαι, deliberative) 146.
εἰς (preposition with the accusative of extent) 140.
τὴν (acc.sing.fem.of the article in agreement with ἑορτήν) 9.
ἑορτήν (acc.sing.fem.of ἑορτή, extent) 1558.

Translation - "Then after they had taken their place in the temple they began to look for Jesus and to say to one another, 'What do you think? that He will not come to the feast?' "

Comment: The pilgrims went to the temple and took their place there (perfect participle in ἑστηκότες) and began to look for Jesus and to discuss the matter among themselves (imperfect tenses in ἐζήτουν and ἔλεγον. Note the deliberative subjunctive in ἔλθῃ preceded by the double negative, indicating considerable doubt. These were the people from the outlying areas who came up to the feast early. Their speculation was caused by the order of the Establishment in verse 57, pursuant to their conference following the resurrection of Lazarus (John 11:47-53). Verse 57 is retrospective.

Verse 57 - "Now both the chief priests and the Pharisees had given a commandment, that, if any man knew where he were, he should shew it, that they might take him."

δεδώκεισαν δὲ οἱ ἀρχιερεῖς καὶ οἱ Φαρισαῖοι ἐντολὴν ἵνα ἐάν τις γνῷ ποῦ ἐστιν μηνύσῃ, ὅπως πιάσωσιν αὐτόν.

δεδώκεισαν (3d.per.pl.plu.act.ind.of δίδωμι, consummative) 362.
δὲ (explanatory conjunction) 11.
οἱ (nom.pl.masc.of the article in agreement with ἀρχιερεῖς) 9.
ἀρχιερεῖς (nom.pl.masc.of ἀρχιερεύς, subject of δεδωκεισαν) 151.
καὶ (adjunctive conjunction joining nouns) 14.
οἱ (nom.pl.masc.of the article in agreement with Φαρισαῖοι) 9.
Φαρισαῖοι (nom.pl.masc.of Φαρισαῖος, subject of δεδώκεισαν) 276.
ἐντολὴν (acc.sing.fem.of ἐντολή, direct object of δεδώκεισαν) 472.
ἵνα (conjunction introducing a purpose clause with the subjunctive) 114.
ἐὰν (conditional particle in a third-class condition) 363.
τις (nom.sing.masc.of τις,the indefinite pronoun, subject of γνῷ) 486.
γνῷ (3d.per.sing.2d.aor.act.subj.of γινώσκω, third-class condition) 131.
ποῦ (interrogative adverb of place, in indirect question) 142.
ἐστιν (3d.per.sing.pres.ind.of εἰμί, indirect question) 86.

#2666 μηνύσῃ (3d.per.sing.1st.aor.act.subj.of μηνύς).

show - Luke 20:37; John 11:57; 1 Cor.10:28.
tell - Acts 23:30.

Meaning: to inform; make known; reveal. In a forensic sense, with ποῦ ἐστιν in John 11:57; with τινί τι - Acts 23:30. In a didactic sense, to indicate, or intimate, followed by ὅτι in Luke 20:37. To declare, to tell - 1 Cor.10:28.

ὅπως (conjunction introducing a purpose clause with the subjunctive) 177.
πιάσωσιν (3d.per.pl.aor.act.subj.of πιάζω, purpose) 2371.
αὐτόν (acc.sing.masc.of αὐτός, direct object of πιάσωσιν) 16.

Translation - "Now the chief priests and the Pharisees had issued an order that, if anyone knew where He was, he should reveal it, so that they might arrest Him."

Comment: δὲ is explanatory. What follows explains why the people were looking for Jesus and speculating about Him in verse 56. The pluperfect δεδώκεισαν is consummative. It points to an action in the past. The order had been issued by the Sanhedrin at the time of Lazarus' resurrection (John 11:47-53). Note that John uses ἵνα in his first purpose clause, and then, perhaps to avoid repetition, ὅπως in his second. The aorist subjunctive μηνύσῃ in the apodosis is unusual but necessary since it is involved in the purpose clause.

The people were obedient to the orders of the Sanhedrin, either for fear of reprisal from the court, or out of hostility to Jesus, or both. All of that flurry of activity was unnecessary, since Jesus could avoid arrest as long as He wished and would allow Himself to be taken at the proper time. Of course His enemies did not know this.

John 12:1 - "Then Jesus, six days before the passover, came to Bethany, where Lazarus was which had been dead, whom he raised from the dead."

Ὁ οὖν Ἰησοῦς πρὸ ἓξ ἡμερῶν τοῦ πάσχα ἦλθεν εἰς Βηθανίαν, ὅπου ἦν Λάζαρος, ὃν ἤγειρεν ἐκ νεκρῶν Ἰησοῦς.

Ὁ (nom.sing.masc.of the article in agreement with Ἰησοῦς) 9.
οὖν (continuative conjunction) 68.
Ἰησοῦς (nom.sing.masc.of Ἰησοῦς, subject of ἦλθεν) 3.
πρὸ (preposition with the ablative of time separation) 442.
ἓξ (numeral) 1220.
ἡμερῶν (gen.pl.fem.of ἡμέρα time extent) 135.
τοῦ (abl.sing.neut.of the article in agreement with πάσχα) 9.
πάσχα (abl.sing.neut.of πάσχα, time separation) 1553.
ἦλθεν (3d.per.sing.aor.ind.of ἔρχομαι, constative) 146.
εἰς (preposition with the accusative of extent) 140.
Βηθανίαν (acc.sing.fem.of Βηθανία, extent) 1363.
ὅπου (adverb of place introducing a definite local clause) 592.
ἦν (3d.per.sing.imp.ind.of εἰμί, progressive description) 86.
Λάζαρος (nom.sing.masc.of Λάζαρος, subject of ἦν) 2596.
ὃν (acc.sing.masc.of ὅς, direct object of ἤγειρεν) 65.
ἤγειρεν (3d.per.sing.aor.act.ind.of ἐγείρω, culminative) 125.
ἐκ (preposition with the ablative of separation) 19.
νεκρῶν (abl.pl.masc.of νεκρός, separation) 749.
Ἰησοῦς (nom.sing.masc.of Ἰησοῦς, subject of ἤγειρεν) 3.

Translation - "Then Jesus, six days before the passover, came to Bethany, where Lazarus was, whom Jesus had raised from the dead."

Comment: Back from Ephraim and Perea, by way of Jericho, to the suburbs of Jerusalem, the Lamb of God had come to offer Himself - the sacrifice to end all previous sacrifices and accomplish the redemptive purpose. John reintroduces Lazarus to his audience for purposes of continuity. Since John has been speaking of Jesus and His relations with the Jewish Establishment and their attempt to arrest Him, we leave verses 2 - 8 for later treatment and examine verses 9 - 11.

Verse 9 - "Much people of the Jews therefore knew that he was there: and they came not for Jesus' sake only, but that they might see Lazarus also, whom he had raised from the dead."

Ἔγνω οὖν (ὁ) ὄχλος πολὺς ἐκ τῶν Ἰουδαίων ὅτι ἐκεῖ ἐστιν, καὶ ἦλθον οὐ διὰ τὸν Ἰησοῦν μόνον ἀλλ' ἵνα καὶ τὸν Λάζαρον ἴδωσιν ὃν ἤγειρεν ἐκ νεκρῶν.

Ἔγνω (3d.per.sing.2d.aor.act.ind.of *γινώσκω*, constative) 131.
οὖν (continuative conjunction) 68.
(*ὁ*) (nom.sing.masc.of the article in agreement with *ὄχλος*) 9.
ὄχλος (nom.sing.masc.of *ὄχλος*, subject of *ἔγνω* and *ἦλθον*) 418
πολὺς (nom.sing.masc.of *πολύς*, in agreement with *ὄχλος*) 228.
ἐκ (preposition with the partitive ablative) 19.
τῶν (abl.pl.masc.of the article in agreement with *Ἰουδαίων*) 9.
Ἰουδαίων (abl.pl.masc.of *Ἰουδαῖος*, partitive) 143.
ὅτι (conjunction introducing an object clause in indirect discourse) 211.
ἐκεῖ (adverb of place) 204.
ἐστιν (3d.per.sing.pres.ind.of *εἰμί*, aoristic, indirect discourse) 86.
καὶ (adjunctive conjunction joining verbs) 14.
ἦλθον (3d.per.pl.aor.ind.of *ἔρχομαι*, constative) 146.
οὐ (summary negative conjunction with the indicative) 130.
διὰ (preposition with the accusative of cause) 118.
τὸν (acc.sing.masc.of the article in agreement with *Ἰησοῦν*) 9.
Ἰησοῦν (acc.sing.masc.of *Ἰησοῦς*, cause) 3.
μόνον (acc.sing.masc.of *μόνος*, adverbial accusative) 339.
ἀλλ' (alternative conjunction) 342.
ἵνα (conjunction introducing a purpose clause) 114.
καὶ (adjunctive conjunction joining clauses) 14.
τὸν (acc.sing.masc.of the article in agreement with *Λάζαρον*) 9.
Λάζαρον (acc.sing.masc.of *Λάζαρος*, direct object of *ἴδωσιν*) 2596.
ἴδωσιν (3d.per.pl.aor.act.subj.of *ὁράω*, purpose) 144.
ὃν (acc.sing.masc.of *ὅς*,direct object of *ἤγειρεν*) 65.
ἤγειρεν (3d.per.sing.aor.act.ind.of *ἐγείρω*, consummative) 125.
ἐκ (preposition with the ablative of separation) 19.
νεκρῶν (abl.pl.masc.of *νεκρός*, separation) 749.

Translation - "Then a great crowd of Jews knew that He was there, and they came, not because of Jesus alone, but in order that they might also see Lazarus, whom He had raised from the dead."

Comment: The *ὅτι* clause is indirect discourse. Note the present tense in *ἐκεῖ ἐστιν*. That was what the people were saying, "He is there." Indirect discourse maintains the same tense as in direct. The people had two reasons now for coming to Bethany. They had been ordered by the Sanhedrin to find Jesus and report His whereabouts. The rumor was that He was at Bethany. They went out to confirm the rumor, but they were also eager to see Lazarus, who was now alive, thanks to Jesus' miracle. This curiosity on the part of the Jews to see Lazarus created an additional problem for the Establishment, as we shall see in verse 10.

Six days before the Passover would be the last Sabbath before Jesus died, for He died the day before the Sabbath. The Sabbath began at 6:00 p.m. on Friday and ended 24 hours later. If Jesus died on Friday afternoon, then He came to Bethany on the previous Saturday, the Sabbath.

Verse 10 - "But the chief priests consulted that they might put Lazarus also to death.

ἐβουλεύσαντο δὲ οἱ ἀρχιερεῖς ἵνα καὶ τὸν Λάζαρον ἀποκτείνωσιν,

ἐβουλεύσαντο (3d.per.pl.aor.mid.ind.of *βουλεύομαι*, ingressive) 90.
δὲ (inferential conjunction) 11.
οἱ (nom.pl.masc.of the article in agreement with *ἀρχιερεῖς*) 9.
ἀρχιερεῖς (nom.pl.masc.of *ἀρχιερεύς*, subject of *ἐβουλεύσαντο*) 151.
ἵνα (conjunction introducing a purpose clause) 114.
καὶ (adjunctive conjunction joining nouns) 14.
τὸν (acc.sing.masc.of the article in agreement with *Λάζαρον*) 9.
Λάζαρον (acc.sing.masc.of *Λάζαρος*, direct object of *ἀποκτείνωσιν*) 2596.
ἀποκτείνωσιν (3d.per.pl.aor.act.subj.of *ἀποκτείνω*, purpose) 889.

Translation - "Therefore the high priests began to lay a plot so that they might also murder Lazarus."

Comment: We have taken *δὲ* as inferential with the thought that the enthusiasm of the people for seeing Lazarus was the reason for the plot to kill him. Thus we have taken *ἐβουλεύσαντο* as an ingressive aorist. The Sanhedrin wanted to avoid a public uproar over the death of Jesus at all costs. If too many people saw Lazarus alive and in radiant health, they would believe upon Jesus. The Sadducee party, who denied the resurrection of the body, were particularly embarrassed by Lazarus' living presence. He not only gave irrefutable evidence against their views, but he also gave a powerful testimony to the divine power of Jesus.

Verse 11 - "Because that by reason of him many of the Jews went away, and believed on Jesus."

ὅτι πολλοὶ δι' αὐτὸν ὑπῆγον τῶν Ἰουδαίων καὶ ἐπίστευον εἰς τὸν Ἰησοῦν.

ὅτι (conjunction introducing a subordinate causal clause) 211.
πολλοὶ (nom.pl.masc.of *πολύς*, subject of *ὑπῆγον* and *ἐπίστευον*) 228.
δι' (preposition with the accusative of cause) 118.
αὐτὸν (acc.sing.masc.of *αὐτός*, cause) 16.
ὑπῆγον (3d.per.pl.imp.act.ind.of *ὑπάγω*, progressive description) 364.

τῶν (gen.pl.masc.of the article in agreement with Ἰουδαίων) 9.
Ἰουδαίων (gen.pl.masc.of Ἰουδαῖος, partitive) 143.
καὶ (adjunctive conjunction joining verbs) 14.
ἐπίστευον (3d.per.pl.imp.act.ind.of πιστεύω, inceptive) 734.
εἰς (preposition with the accusative of cause) 140.
τὸν (acc.sing.masc.of the article in agreement with Ἰησοῦν) 9.
Ἰησοῦν (acc.sing.masc.of Ἰησοῦς, cause) 3.

Translation - "Because many of the Jews because of him were going away and they were beginning to believe upon Jesus."

Comment: ὅτι and the causal clause explains the murder plot against Lazarus. It was "because of him - δι' αὐτὸν" - a causal construction - that many of the Jews were leaving Bethany with a new faith in Jesus as the Son of God. ὑπῆγον may be interpreted to mean that they were forsaking their previous theological allegiance to the Sanhedrin party, in favor of Jesus. The absence of an object after ὑπῆγον, however argues against it. It is simpler to say that after they saw Lazarus and his radiant good health, that they left Bethany to go back to Jerusalem. Of course the latter idea implies the former.

(Part Eight - A.D.30 - One week. The order of events during the Passion Week in this harmony follows the traditional view of the Church, but is not necessarily, on that account, correct.)

The Closing Events of Jesus' Ministry
(1) Sunday - The Day of Demonstration

The Triumphal Entry into Jerusalem

(Matthew 21:1-9; Mark 11:1-10; Luke 19:29-40; John 12:12-19)

Mark 11:1 - "And when they came nigh to Jerusalem, unto Bethphage and Bethany, at the Mount of Olives, he sendeth forth two of his disciples."

Καὶ ὅτε ἐγγίζουσιν εἰς Ἰεροσόλυμα εἰς Βηθφαγὴ καὶ Βηθανίαν πρὸς τὸ Ὄρος τῶν Ἐλαιῶν, ἀποστέλλει δύο τῶν μαθητῶν αὐτοῦ

Καὶ (continuative conjunction) 14.
ὅτε (conjunction introducing a definite temporal clause) 703.
ἐγγίζουσιν (3d.per.pl.pres.act.ind.of ἐγγίζω, historical) 252.
εἰς (preposition with the accusative of extent) 140.
Ἰεροσόλυμα (acc.sing.masc.of Ἰεροσόλυμα, extent) 141.
εἰς (preposition with the accusative of extent) 140.
Βηθφαγὴ (acc.sing.indeclin.of Βηθφαγή, extent) 1340.
καὶ (adjunctive conjunction joining nouns) 14.
Βηθανίαν (acc.sing.fem.of Βηθανία, extent) 1363.
πρὸς (preposition with the accusative of extent) 197.
τὸ (acc.sing.neut.of the article in agreement with Ὄρος) 9.

Ὄρος (acc.sing.neut.of ὄρος, extent) 357.
τῶν (gen.pl.masc.of the article in agreement with 0Elaiv$n) 9.
Ἐλαιῶν (gen.pl.masc.of ἐλαιών, description) 1341.
ἀποστέλλει (3d.per.sing.pres.act.ind.of ἀποστέλλω, historical) 215.
δύο (acc.sing.masc.of δύο, direct object of ἀποστέλλει) 385.
τῶν (gen.pl.masc.of the article in agreement with Ἐλαιῶν) 9.
μαθητῶν (gen.pl.masc.of μαθητής, partitive) 421.
αὐτοῦ (gen.sing.masc.of αὐτός, relationship) 16.

Translation - "And as they approached Jerusalem, arriving at Bethphage and Bethany, near the Mount of Olives, He sent two of His disciples. . . "

Comment: Two examples of the historical present in ἐγγίζουσιν and ἀποστέλλει. Approaching Jerusalem, by way of Bethphage and Bethnay, near the Mount of Olives, Jesus dispatched two of His disciples on an errand. His purpose was deliberately to fulfill a prophecy. *Cf.* comment on Mt.21:1 and Lk.19:29. Why should not the God of Creation and Inspiration, Who directed the utterance of the prophecy that foretold His behavior in His coming incarnation, now, that He is incarnate, and the hour has arrived, continue to arrange events so that the prophecy is fulfilled? God has all of the advantages and none of the disadvantages. He knows the end from the beginning - thus He is able to predict events with precision. He also directs events as He pleases - thus He directs events in keeping with His prediction. Deists, of course reject the idea that God is active in human history, either in the writing of an inspired body of scripture or in an incarnate visit to earth such as the New Testament describes. It is incumbent upon them to explain how prophecies written hundreds of years before the fact were fulfilled with the precision that is recorded in the New Testament.

Verse 2 - "And saith unto them, Go your way into the village over against you; and as soon as ye be entered into it, ye shall find a colt tied, whereon never man sat; loose him, and bring him."

καὶ λέγει αὐτοῖς, Ὑπάγετε εἰς τὴν κώμην τὴν κατέναντι ὑμῶν, καὶ εὐθὺς εἰσπορευόμενοι εἰς αὐτὴν εὑρήσετε πῶλον δεδεμένον ἐφ' ὃν οὐδεὶς οὔπω ἀνθρώπων ἐκάθισεν. λύσατε αὐτὸν καὶ φέρετε.

καὶ (adjunctive conjunction joining verbs) 14.
λέγει (3d.per.sing.pres.act.ind.of λέγω, historical) 66.
αὐτοῖς (dat.pl.masc.of αὐτός, indirect object of λέγει) 16.
Ὑπάγετε (2d.per.pl.pres.act.impv.of ὑπάγω, command) 364.
εἰς (preposition with the accusative of extent) 140.
τὴν (acc.sing.fem.of the article in agreement with κώμην) 9.
κώμην (acc.sing.fem.of κώμη, extent) 834.
τὴν (acc.sing.fem.of the article in agreement with κατέναντι) 9.
κατέναντι (improper preposition with the genitive of place description) 1342.
ὑμῶν (gen.pl.masc.of σύ, place description) 104.
καὶ (continuative conjunction) 14.

εὐθὺς (adverbial) 258.

εἰσπορευόμενοι (pres.mid.part.nom.pl.masc.of *εἰσπορεύομαι*, adverbial, temporal) 1161.

εἰς (preposition with the accusative of extent) 140.

αὐτὴν (acc.sing.fem.of *αὐτός*, extent) 16.

εὑρήσετε (2d.per.pl.fut.act.ind.of *εὑρίσκω*, predictive) 79.

πῶλον (acc.sing.masc.of *πῶλος*, direct object of *εὑρήσετε*) 1344.

δεδεμένον (perf.pass.part.acc.sing.masc.of *δέω*, adjectival, ascriptive) 998.

ἐφ' (preposition with the accusative of place) 47.

ὃν (acc.sing.masc.of *ὅς*, accusative of place, extent) 65.

οὐδεὶς (nom.sing.masc.of *οὐδείς*, subject of *ἐκάθισεν*) 446.

οὔπω (adverbial) 1198.

ἀνθρώπων (gen.pl.masc.of *ἄνθρωπος*, partitive) 341.

ἐκάθισεν (3d.per.sing.aor.act.ind.of *καθίζω*, constative) 420.

λύσατε (2d.per.pl.aor.act.impv.of *λύω*, command) 471.

αὐτὸν (acc.sing.masc.of *αὐτός*, direct object of *λύσατε*) 16.

καὶ (adjunctive conjunction joining verbs) 14.

φέρετε (2d.per.pl.pres.act.impv.of *φέρω*, command) 683.

Translation - "And He said to them, 'Go into the first village that you come to, and as soon as you enter it, you will find a colt tied, upon which no man has ever sat. Untie and bring him."

Comment: Note *τὴν κατέναντι* in the emphatic attributive position, modifying *τὴν κώμην*. The village, the one "down on across" (*κατά* plus *ἐν* plus *ἀντί*). - "The first one you come to." Directions to the two disciples were explicit. Immediately upon entering the village (*εὐθὺς εἰσπορευόμενοι*), they were told that they would find a colt tied. Note the perfect passive participle, a present condition as a result of a past action. An unbroken colt. No had had ever ridden him. Two imperatives close the directive. Untie the colt and bring him. There are further directions in verse 3. *Cf.* Mt.21:2 and Lk.19:30. Matthew also mentions *ὄνον* as well as *πῶλον*. Luke follows Mary and omits *τὸ ὄνον*.

Verse 3 - "And if any man say unto you, Why do ye this? say ye that the Lord hath need of him; and straightway he will send him hither."

καὶ ἐάν τις ὑμῖν εἴπῃ, Τί ποιεῖτε τοῦτο; εἴπατε,'Ο κύριος αὐτοῦ χρείαν ἔχει, καὶ εὐθὺς αὐτὸν ἀποστέλλει πάλιν ὧδε.

καὶ (continuative conjunction) 14.

ἐάν (conditional particle in a third-class condition) 363.

τις (nom.sing.masc.of *τις*, indefinite pronoun, subject of *εἴπῃ*) 486.

ὑμῖν (dat.pl.masc.of *σύ*, indirect object of *εἴπῃ*) 104.

εἴπῃ (3d.per.sing.aor.act.subj.of *εἶπον*, third-class condition) 155.

Τί (acc.sing.neut.of *τίς*, interrogative pronoun, cause with *διὰ* supplied) 281.

ποιεῖτε (2d.per.pl.pres.act.ind.of *ποιέω*, direct question) 127.

τοῦτο (acc.sing.neut.of *οὗτος*, direct object of *ποιεῖτε*) 93.

εἴπατε (2d.per.pl.aor.act.impv.of εἶπον, command) 155.
Ὁ (nom.sing.masc.of the article in agreement with κύριος) 9.
κύριος (nom.sing.masc.of κύριος, subject of ἔχει) 97.
αὐτοῦ (gen.sing.masc.of αὐτός, description) 16.
χρείαν (acc.sing.fem.of χρεία, direct object of ἔχει) 317.
ἔχει (3d.per.sing.pres.act.ind.of ἔχω, aoristic) 82.
καὶ (continuative conjunction) 14.
εὐθὺς (adverbial) 258.
αὐτὸν (acc.sing.masc.of αὐτός, direct object of ἀποστέλλει) 16.
ἀποστέλλει (3d.per.sing.pres.act.ind.of ἀποστέλλω, futuristic) 215.
πάλιν (adverbial) 355.
ὧδε (adverb of place) 766.

Translation - "And should anyone say to you, 'Why are you doing this?' say, 'The Lord has need of him' and immediately he will send him here."

Comment: *Cf.* Mt.21:3 and Lk.19:31. Note the third-class condition with ἐάν and the subjunctive in the protasis and the aorist imperative in the apodosis. Jesus did not say that anybody would interfere, but He suggested the possibility and gave instructions about what the disciples were to say if they encountered objection. They were to assure the owner that the Lord would send the colt back again when the ride was finished. The last clause is not a statement that the owner will send the animal, in compliance with the disciples' request to borrow him. This makes πάλιν without point. Yet the manuscript authority for πάλιν is impressive. Meyer thinks that to render the disciples' speech, "The Lord needs him and He will send him back here again" lowers the dignity of Jesus! Nonesense!! This is precisely the point of the entire passage - the humility of Christ. Here is the Messiah of Israel, God incarnate, about to present Himself as Messiah to a nation on the verge of crucifying Him. He is so poor that He cannot ride a white horse. He must ride an ass; and one that is borrowed at that. In order to secure the use of the animal He must promise to return it after the parade is over!

Verse 4 - "And they went their way, and found the colt tied by the door without, where two ways met; and they loose him."

καὶ ἀπῆλθον καὶ εὗρον πῶλον δεδεμένον πρὸς θύραν ἔξω ἐπὶ τοῦ ἀμφόδου, καὶ λύουσιν αὐτόν.

καὶ (continuative conjunction) 14.
ἀπῆλθον (3d.per.pl.aor.mid.ind.of ἀπέρχομαι, constative) 239.
καὶ (adjunctive conjunction joining verbs) 14.
εὗρον (3d.per.pl.2d.aor.act.ind.of εὑρίσκω, constative) 79.
πῶλον (acc.sing.masc.of πῶλος, direct object of εὗρον) 1344.
δεδεμένον (perf.pass.part.acc.sing.masc.of δέω, adjectival, ascriptive, in agreement with πῶλον) 998.
πρὸς (preposition with the accusative, place, extent) 197.
θύραν (acc.sing.fem.of θύρα, place, after πρὸς) 571.

Translation - "And should anyone say to you, 'Why are you doing this?' say, 'The Lord needs him, and soon He will send him back here again.' "

ἔξω (adverbial) 449.
ἐπὶ (preposition with the genitive of place description) 47.
τοῦ (gen.sing.neut.of the article in agreement with ἀμφόδου) 9.

#2667 ἀμφόδου (gen.sing.neut.of ἄμφοδον, place description).

place where two ways meet - Mark 11:4.

Meaning: A combination of ἀμφί - "on both sides" and ὁδός (#199). Hence a place at the junction of two roads - Mark 11:4.

καὶ (adjunctive conjunction joining verbs) 14.
λύουσιν (3d.per.pl.pres.act.ind.of λύω, historical) 471.
αὐτόν (acc.sing.masc.of αὐτός, direct object of λύουσιν) 16.

Translation - "And they went away and found a colt tied outside near a door, at a junction of two roads, and they untied him."

Comment: Mark's description is very precise. They went. They found the colt. It had been tied near a door - πρὸς θύραν.ἔξω is really unnecessary. Obviously the colt would be tied near the door on the outside. ἐπὶ τοῦ ἀμφόδου is interesting - "at a place where two roads come together" *i.e.* at a junction. They were near two little towns, Bethphage and Bethany, and they were told to go to the one nearest them. They found the colt tied outside the door of a house that sat at the place where the road divided, one to go to Bethphage and the other to Bethany. Everything was exactly as Jesus had described it, which does not surprize the trinitarian, although the unitarian will have some difficult in explaining it. *Cf.*Mt.21:6. Note that Mt.21:4,5 connect these events with the prophecies of Isa.62:11 and Zech.9:9. Luke 19:32 agrees with Mt.21:6.

Verse 5 - "And certain of them that stood there said unto them, What do ye, loosing the colt?"

καί τινες τῶν ἐκεῖ ἑστηκότων ἔλεγον αὐτοῖς, Τί ποιεῖτε λύοντες τὸν πῶλον;

καί (continuative conjunction) 14.
τινες (nom.pl.masc.of τις, indefinite pronoun, subject of ἔλεγον) 486.
τῶν (gen.pl.masc.of the article in agreement with ἑστηκότων) 9.
ἐκεῖ (adverb of place) 204.
ἑστηκότων (perf.act.part.gen.pl.masc.of ἵστημι, substantival, partitive) 180.
ἔλεγον (3d.per.pl.imp.act.ind.of λέγω, inceptive) 66.
αὐτοῖς (dat.pl.masc.of αὐτός, indirect object of ἔλεγον) 16.
Τί (acc.sing.neut.of τίς, the interrogative pronoun, direct object of ποιεῖτε) 281.
ποιεῖτε (2d.per.pl.pres.act.ind.of ποιέω, aoristic, direct question) 127.
λύοντες (pres.act.part.nom.pl.masc.of λύω, adverbial, modal) 471.
τὸν (acc.sing.masc.of the article in agreement with πῶλον) 9.
πῶλον (acc.sing.masc.of πῶλος, direct object of λύοντες) 1344.

Translation - "And some of those who had been standing there, began to say to them, 'What are you doing?! - untying the colt?' "

Comment: "Some of the bystanders - τινες τῶν ἐκεῖ ἑστηκότων. Note the imperfect in ἔλεγον as the bystanders began to protest - a natural thing since the animal did not belong to the disciples. There is a tone of belligerence in the question - "What are you doing?" In modern parlance - "What are you up to? What's the idea? Who do you think you are?" Since the participle λύοντες is modal, the question can be put more formally, "What do you intend to accomplish *by* untying the colt?" *Cf.* Luke 19:33. Matthew does not record the protest. The disciples were well armed for the occasion. They knew exactly what to say (vs.3).

Verse 6 - "And they said unto them even as Jesus had commanded: and they let them go."

οἱ δὲ εἶπαν αὐτοῖς καθὼς εἶπεν ὁ Ἰησοῦς. καὶ ἀφῆκαν αὐτούς.

οἱ (nom.pl.masc.of the article, subject of εἶπαν) 9.
δὲ (inferential conjunction) 11.
εἶπαν (3d.per.pl.aor.act.ind.of εἶπον, constative) 155.
αὐτοῖς (dat.pl.masc.of αὐτός, indirect object of εἶπαν) 16.
καθὼς (comparative adverb) 1348.
εἶπεν (3d.per.sing.aor.act.ind.of εἶπον, constative) 155.
ὁ (nom.sing.masc.of the article in agreement with Ἰησοῦς) 9.
Ἰησοῦς (nom.sing.masc.of Ἰησοῦς, subject of εἶπεν) 3.
καὶ (continuative conjunction) 14.
ἀφῆκαν (3d.per.pl.aor.act.ind.of ἀφίημι, constative) 319.
αὐτούς (acc.pl.masc.of αὐτός, direct object of ἀφῆκαν) 16.

Translation - "So they replied to them as Jesus had suggested, and they withdrew their objection."

Comment: δέ is inferential, as the disciples met the bystanders' objection with the comment that Jesus had told them to use (vs.3). They probably were expecting opposition as they approached the house and saw the bystanders standing there, and they were ready for it. There was no further objection and the disciples led the colt back to Jesus. *Cf.* Lk.19:33,34.

Verse 7 - "And they brought the colt to Jesus, and cast their garments on him: and he sat upon him."

καὶ φέρουσιν τὸν πῶλον πρὸς τοσν Ἰησοῦν, καὶ ἐπιβάλλουσιν αὐτῷ τὰ ἱμάτια αὐτῶν, καὶ ἐκάθισεν ἐπ' αὐτόν.

καὶ (continuative conjunction) 14.
φέρουσιν (3d.per.pl.pres.act.ind.of φέρω, historical) 683.
τὸν (acc.sing.masc.of the article in agreement with πῶλον) 9.
πῶλον (acc.sing.masc.of πῶλος, direct object of φέρουσιν) 1344.

πρὸς (preposition with the accusative of extent) 197.
τὸν (acc.sing.masc.of the article in agreement with Ἰησοῦν) 9.
Ἰησοῦν (acc.sing.masc.of Ἰησοῦς, extent) 3.
καὶ (continuative conjunction) 14.
ἐπιβάλλουσιν (3d.per.pl.pres.act.ind.of ἐπιβάλλω, historical) 800.
αὐτῷ (loc.sing.masc.of αὐτός, place where, after ἐπί in composition) 16.
τὰ (acc.pl.neut.of the article in agreement with ἱμάτια) 9.
ἱμάτια (acc.pl.neut.of ἱμάτιον, direct object of ἐπιβάλλουσιν) 534.
αὐτῶν (gen.pl.masc.of αὐτός, possession) 16.
καὶ (continuative conjunction) 14.
ἐκάθισεν (3d.per.sing.aor.act.ind.of καθίζω, constative) 420.
ἐπ' (preposition with the accusative of extent, place) 47.
αὐτόν (acc.sing.masc.of αὐτός, extent, place) 16.

Translation - "And they brought the colt to Jesus, and they put upon him their coats, and He sat upon him."

Comment: Mark is not consistent with his use of the historical present. He used it in φέρουσιν and ἐπιβάλλουσιν, but the aorist in ἐκάθισεν. In translation the historical present is rendered as though it were an aorist of complete action in the past. The short trip from the little village back to the spot near the Mount of Olives, where Jesus was waiting, was followed by a brief preparation as they threw their coats over the colt, as a makeshift saddle and Jesus mounted him. The colt made no objection which is unusual for an unbroken animal (verse 2). Jesus never had any difficulty "with the wild beasts" (Mk.1:13) - only with people. He was the Creator of the universe. He came to His own creation (John 1:12a), which received Him, but His own people (John 1:12b) received Him not. *Cf.* Mt.21:7 and Lk.19:35.

Not all of the people who loved Jesus were privileged to participate in the preparation for His coronation as were the disciples. But they found ways to express their enthusiasm in

Verse 8 - "And many spread their garments in the way: and others cut down branches off the trees, and strawed them in the way."

καὶ πολλοὶ τὰ ἱμάτια αὐτῶν ἔστρωσαν εἰς τὴν ὁδόν, ἄλλοι δὲ στιβάδας κόψαντες ἐκ τῶν ἀγρῶν.

καὶ (continuative conjunction) 14.
πολλοὶ (nom.pl.masc.of πολύς, subject of ἔστρωσαν) 228.
τὰ (acc.pl.neut.of the article in agreement with ἱμάτια) 9.
ἱμάτια (acc.pl.neut.of ἱμάτιον, direct object of ἔστρωσαν) 534.
εἰς (preposition with the accusative of extent) 140.
τὴν (acc.sing.fem.of the article in agreement with ὁδόν) 9.
ὁδόν (acc.sing.fem.of ὁδός, extent) 199.
ἄλλοι (nom.pl.masc.of ἄλλος, subject of an omitted verb) 198.
δὲ (continuative conjunction) 11.

#2668 **στιβάδας** (acc.pl.fem.of **στοιβάς**, direct object of **κόψαντες**).

branch - Mark 11:8.

Meaning: from **στείβω** - — "to tread on" - hence, a spread of leaves, rushes, soft grass or flowers, straw, small branches - anything growing in a field that would make a soft bed. That which the people spread upon the road before Jesus in the triumphal entry into Jerusalem - Mark 11:8.

κόψαντες (aor.act.part.nom.pl.masc.of **κόπτω**, adverbial, temporal) 929.
ἐκ (preposition with the ablative of separation) 19.
τῶν (abl.pl.masc.of the article in agreement with **ἀγρῶν**) 9.
ἀγρῶν (abl.pl.masc.of **ἀγρός**, separation) 626.

Translation - "And many people spread their coats in the road, and others when they had cut vegetation out of the fields . . . "

Comment: There was not room on the colt's back for all of the coats in the crowd, so those not privileged to offer their coats for a saddle, spread them upon the roadway. If this seems to some to be undue adulation, let two things be remembered: the man who rode that colt was Incarnate God and Saviour of the world, and destined, before God finishes with world history, to be the Messiah of Israel. Secondly, the high praise of the multitude now serves to balance the wretched indignities perpetrated upon Him a week later. Here were people who had suffered for centuries under the grinding heels of Gentile dictators. For some, the Messianic hope, reduced only shortly before to a flicker, was now burning brightly. They had seen Jesus' miracles and they had listened to His teaching. They were convinced that He was their king. Their only intellectual "blind spot" was their failure to understand that God's plan of salvation involved His suffering and death before it could involve His coronation on David's throne. The Messianic hope, burning brightly now, suffered on the following Thursday night, when He was arrested, insulted and tortured. Those who hailed Him as Messiah now were to turn against Him the following Friday morning when He was crucified. Only those who had the supernatural gift of faith could fit a cross into the pattern of events and still conclude that Jesus was genuine. With them it required foresight. With us it has the benefit of hindsight, which makes all of the difference. There should be no condemnation of these people for their inconsistency, until we ask ourselves how much different we would have been under their circumstances. Enlightened with no more revelation than they had, we would have been as inconsistent.

Others in the crowd went out into the fields and cut down various types of wild vegetation. *Cf.*#2668. The word means anything that grows in a field suitable for a soft bed or pathway. Note that the source is not **δένδρων**, as the AV would indicate, with its "branches," but **ἀγρῶν** - "fields," or "farm land." Hence the word is not necessarily "branches" though it could include small branches. The phrase ". . . and strawed them in the way" does not occur in the text, but, of course that is what they did with the vegetation. Mark, the young man, was so excited (he was probably an eye witness) about the gala event that when he wrote about it, he failed to include a verb to go with ἄλλοι.

The frantic efforts of the people to express their love and devotion for Jesus is contributory to our emotions as we try to visualize the scene.

Verse 9 - "And they that went before, and they that followed, cried, saying, Hosanna; Blessed is he that cometh in the name of the Lord."

καὶ οἱ προάγοντες καὶ οἱ ἀκολουθοῦντες ἔκραζον,'Ωσαννά, Εὐλογημένος ὁ ἐρχόμενος ἐν ὀνόματι κυρίου.

καὶ (continuative conjunction) 14.
οἱ (nom.pl.masc.of the article in agreement with **προάγοντες**) 9.
προάγοντες (pres.act.part.nom.pl.masc.of **προάγω**, substantival, subject of **ἔκραζον**) 179.
καὶ (adjunctive conjunction joining participles) 14.
οἱ (nom.pl.masc.of the article in agreement with **ἀκολουθοῦντες**) 9.
ἀκολουθοῦντες (pres.act.part.nom.pl.masc.of **ἀκολουθέω**, substantival, subject of **ἔκραζον**) 394.
ἔκραζον (3d.per.pl.imp.act.ind.of **κράζω**, inceptive) 765.
'Ωσαννά (exclamation) 1352.
Εὐλογημένος (pres.pass.part.nom.sing.masc.of **εὐλογέω**, predicate adjective) 1120.
ὁ (nom.sing.masc.of the article in agreement with **ἐρχόμενος**) 9.
ἐρχόμενος (pres.mid.part.nom.sing.masc.of **ἔρχομαι**, substantival, subject of **ἐστιν** understood) 146.
ἐν (preposition with the instrumental of means) 80.
ὀνόματι (instrumental sing.neut.of **ὄνομα** means) 108.
κυρίου (gen.sing.masc.of **κύριος**, description) 97.

Translation - "And those who went ahead and those who followed began to cry out, 'Hurrah! Blessed is the One who comes with a lordly name.' "

Comment: The participial substantives **προάγοντες** and **ἀκολουθοῦντες** describe both those who went ahead of the parade and those who brought up the rear as beginning (inceptive imperfect in **ἔκραζον**) a series of shouts. Again and again the shout arose from the throats of hundreds and echoed and reverberated from the surrounding hills. "Hurrah!" in modern English, though Thayer says that the word means "Welcome." He was coming by means of a "lordly name." This is better than the locative of sphere "in the name of the Lord" since **κυρίου** is anarthrous. The genitive without the article is descriptive.

Verse 10 - "Blessed be the kingdom of our father David, that cometh in the name of the Lord: Hosanna in the highest.

Εὐλογημένη ἡ ἐρχομένη βασιλεία τοῦ πατρὸς ἡμῶν Δαυίδ.'Ωσαννὰ ἐν τοῖς ὑψίστοις.

Εὐλογημένη (pres.pass.part.nom.sing.fem.of εὐλογέω, predicate adjective) 1120.

ἡ (nom.sing.fem.of the article in agreement with βασιλεία) 9.

ἐρχομένη (pres.pass.part.nom.sing.fem.of ἔρχομαι, adjectival, ascriptive, in agreement with βασιλεία) 146.

βασιλεία (nom.sing.fem.of βασιλεία, subject of ἐστίν, understood) 253.

τοῦ (gen.sing.masc.of the article in agreement with πατρὸς) 9.

πατρὸς (gen.sing.masc.of πατήρ, possession) 238.

ἡμῶν (gen.pl.masc.of ἐγώ, relationship) 123.

Δαυίδ (gen.sing.indeclin.of Δαυίδ, apposition) 6.

Ὡσαννὰ (exclamation) 1352.

ἐν (preposition with the locative of place) 80.

τοῖς (loc.pl.masc.of the article in agreement with ὑψίστοις) 9.

ὑψίστοις (loc.pl.masc.of ὕψιστος, place where) 1353.

Translation - "Blessed is the coming kingdom of our father, David! Hurrah, in the highest!!"

Comment: The people indicated that they understood quite clearly the Davidic covenant of 2 Sam.7:11-17. God's promise to their forefather, King David, was that he would have an heir who would sit upon his throne forever. Israel had waited a long time, suffering as they had for most of their history since David's death, under the rule of the Gentiles. Some day that servitude would be over. And now in the person of Jesus,the Nazarene, they recognized King David's greater son, the only man in Israel who had a legal right to sit upon David's throne. *Cf.*our comment in *The Renaissance New Testament*, I, 4. And so they continued to shout it out: "Hurrah, up to the highest and from the highest places." In other words "Universal praise and Welcome to the King", even though He rode upon a lowly donkey on His way to a coronation which He deserved, and which, in His second coming, He will have, but which now He was destined to receive only with a crown of thorns as He assumed His throne upon a Roman cross.

We should shake our heads sadly and with some contempt, when we considered Him, except for the fact that we know that He planned the entire series of events, as the only means by which He, a righteous Judge in a moral universe, could bring about the fulfillment of God's promise to David.

We turn now to Luke's account of the triumphal entry, in

Luke 19:29 - "And it came to pass, when he was come nigh to Bethphage and Bethany, at the mount called the mount of Olives, he sent two of his disciples."

Καὶ ἐγένετο ὡς ἤγγισεν εἰς Βηθφαγὴ καὶ Βηθανιὰ πρὸς τὸ ὄρος τὸ καλούμενον Ἐλαιῶν, ἀπέστειλεν δύο τῶν μαθητῶν

Καὶ (continuative conjunction) 14.

ἐγένετο (3d.per.sing.aor.ind.of γίνομαι, constative) 113.

ὡς (temporal adverb introducing a definite temporal clause, contemporaneous time) 128.

ἤγγισεν (3d.per.sing.aor.act.ind.of ἐγγίζω, temporal clause) 252.
εἰς (preposition with the accusative of extent) 140.
Βηθφαγὴ (acc.sing.indeclin.of Βηθφαγή, extent) 1340.
καὶ (adjunctive conjunction joining nouns) 14.
Βηθανιὰ (acc.sing.fem. indeclin.of Βηθανιά, extent) 1363.
πρὸς (preposition with the accusative of extent) 197.
τὸ (acc.sing.neut.of the article in agreement with ὄρος) 9.
ὄρος (acc.sing.neut.of ὄρος, extent) 357.
τὸ (acc.sing.neut.of the article in agreement with καλούμενον) 9.
καλούμενον (pres.pass.part.acc.sing.neut.of καλέω, adjectival, restrictive, in agreement with ὄρος) 107.
Ἐλαιῶν (gen.pl.masc.of Ἐλαιών, description) 1341.
ἀπέστειλεν (3d.per.sing.aor.act.ind.of ἀποστέλλω, constative) 215.
δύο (acc.sing.masc.of δύο, numeral) 385.
τῶν (gen.pl.masc.of the article in agreement with μαθητῶν) 9.
μαθητῶν (gen.pl.masc.of μαθητής, partitive) 421.

Translation - "And it happened as He approached Bethphage and Bethany, near the mountain called Olivet, that He sent two of the disciples . . . "

Comment: *Cf.* comment on Mt.21:1 and Mk.11:1. Note that Luke uses ὡς to introduce the temporal clause instead of ὅτε as in Matthew and Mark.

Verse 30 - "Saying, Go ye into the village over against you; in the which at your entering ye shall find a colt tied, whereon yet never man sat: loose him, and bring him hither."

λέγων, Ὑπάγετε εἰς τὴν κατέναντι κώμην, ἐν ᾗ εἰσπορευόμενοι εὑρήσετε πῶλον δεδεμένον, ἐφ' ὃν οὐδεὶς πώποτε ἀνθρώπων ἐκάθισεν, καὶ λύσαντες αὐτὸν ἀγάγετε.

λέγων (pres.act.part.nom.sing.masc.of λέγω, recitative) 66.
Ὑπάγετε (2d.per.pl.pres.act.impv.of ὑπάγω, command) 364.
εἰς (preposition with the accusative of extent) 140.
τὴν (acc.sing.fem.of the article in agreement with κώμην) 9.
κατέναντι (improper preposition, adverbial) 1342.
κώμην (acc.sing.fem.of κώμη, extent) 834.
ἐν (preposition with the locative of place) 80.
ᾗ (loc.sing.fem.of ὅς, relative pronoun, place where) 65.
εἰσπορευόμενοι (pres.mid.part.nom.pl.masc.of εἰσπορεύομαι, adverbial, temporal) 1161.
εὑρήσετε (2d.per.pl.fut.act.ind.of εὑρίσκω, predictive) 79.
πῶλον (acc.sing.masc.of πῶλος, direct object of εὑρήσετε) 1344.
δεδεμένον (perf.pass.part.acc.sing.masc.of δέω, adjectival, in agreement with πῶλον) 998.
ἐφ' (preposition with the accusative of place, extent) 47.
ὃν (acc.sing.masc.of the relative pronoun ὅς, extent, place) 65.

οὐδεὶς (nom.sing.masc.of οὐδείς, subject of ἐκάθισεν) 446.
πώποτε (temporal adverb) 1701
ἀνθρώπων (gen.pl.masc.of ἄνθρωπος, partitive) 341.
ἐκάθισεν (3d.per.sing.aor.act.ind.of καθίζω, ingressive) 420.
καὶ (adjunctive conjunction joining verbs) 14.
λύσαντες (aor.act.part.nom.pl.masc.of λύω, adverbial, temporal) 471.
αὐτὸν (acc.sing.masc.of αὐτός, direct object of λύσαντες and ἀγάγετε) 16.
ἀγάγετε (2d.per.pl.2d.aor.act.impv.of ἄγω, command) 876.

Translation - "Saying, 'Go into the next village, in which, as you enter, you will find a colt tied, upon which nobody ever yet sat. Untie and bring him.' "

Comment: *Cf.*Mt.21:2 and Mk.11:2. Note that Mark uses οὔπω; Luke uses πώποτε. These are only stylistic differences, which do not obscure the meaning.

Verse 31 - "And if any man ask you, Why do ye loose him? thus shall ye say unto him: Because the Lord hath need of him."

καὶ ἐάν τις ὑμᾶς ἐρωτᾷ, Διὰ τί λύετε; οὕτως ἐρεῖτε ὅτι,'Ο κύριος αὐτοῦ χρείαν ἔχει.

καὶ (continuative conjunction) 14.
ἐάν (conditional particle in the third-class condition) 363.
τις (nom.sing.masc.of τις, indefinite pronoun, subject of ἐρωτᾷ) 486.
ὑμᾶς (acc.pl.masc.of σύ, direct object of ἐρωτᾷ) 104.
ἐρωτᾷ (3d.per.sing.pres.subj.of ἐρωτάω, third-class condition) 1172.
Διὰ (preposition with the accusative, cause) 118.
τί (acc.sing.neut.of τίς, the interrogative pronoun, cause) 281.
λύετε (2d.per.pl.pres.act.ind.of λύω, aoristic, direct question) 471.
οὕτως (demonstrative adverb) 74.
ἐρεῖτε (2d.per.pl.fut.act.ind.of εἶπον, imperative) 155.
ὅτι (recitative) 211.
'Ο (nom.sing.masc.of the article in agreement with κύριος) 9.
κύριος (nom.sing.masc.of κύριος, subject of ἔχει) 97.
αὐτοῦ (gen.sing.masc.of αὐτός, description) 16.
χρείαν (acc.sing.fem.of χρεία, direct object of ἔχει) 317.
ἔχει (3d.per.sing.pres.act.ind.of ἔχω, aoristic) 82.

Translation - "And if anybody says to you, 'Why are you untying the colt?' this is what you must say, 'The Lord needs him.' "

Comment: *Cf.* Mt.21:3 and Mk.11:3. Luke gives us a simplified version.

Verse 32 - "And they that were sent went their way, and found even as he had said unto them."

ἀπελθόντες δὲ οἱ ἀπεσταλμένοι εὗρον καθὼς εἶπεν αὐτοῖς.

ἀπελθόντες (aor.mid.part.nom.pl.masc.of ἀπέρχομαι, adverbial, temporal) 239.

ἀπελθόντες (aor.mid.part.nom.pl.masc.of *ἀπέρχομαι*, adverbial, temporal) 239.

δὲ (continuative conjunction) 11.

οἱ (nom.pl.masc.of the article in agreement with *ἀπεσταλμένοι*) 9.

ἀπεσταλμένοι (perf.pass.part.nom.pl.masc.of *ἀποστέλλω*, substantival, subject of *εὗρον*) 215.

εὗρον (3d.per.pl.aor.act.ind.of *εὑρίσκω*, constative) 79.

καθὼς (demonstrative adverb) 1348.

εἶπεν (3d.per.sing.aor.act.ind.of *εἶπον*, culminative) 155.

αὐτοῖς (dat.pl.masc.of *αὐτός*, indirect object of *εἶπεν*) 16.

Translation - "And when those who were sent had gone away they found it just as He had told them."

Comment: *Cf.*Mt.21:6 and Mk.11:4. Mark gives the original account with the most detail; Luke with the least.

Verse 33 - "And as they were loosing the colt the owners thereof said unto them, Why loose ye the colt?"

λυόντων δὲ αὐτῶν τὸν πῶλον εἶπαν οἱ κύριοι αὐτοῦ πρὸς αὐτούς, Τί *λύετε τὸν πῶλον;*

λυόντων (pres.act.part.gen.pl.masc.of *λύω*, genitive absolute) 471.

δὲ (adversative conjunction) 11.

αὐτῶν (gen.pl.masc.of *αὐτός*, genitive absolute) 16.

τὸν (acc.sing.masc.of the article in agreement with *πῶλον*) 9.

πῶλον (acc.sing.masc.of *πῶλος*, direct object of *λυόντων*) 1344.

εἶπαν (3d.per.pl.aor.act.ind.of *εἶπον*, constative) 155.

οἱ (nom.pl.masc.of the article in agreement with *κύριοι*) 9.

κύριοι (nom.pl.masc.of *κύριος*, subject of *εἶπαν*) 97.

αὐτοῦ (gen.sing.masc.of *αὐτός*, relationship) 16.

πρὸς (preposition with the accusative after a verb of speaking) 197.

αὐτούς (acc.pl.masc.of *αὐτός*, extent, after a verb of speaking) 16.

Τί (acc.sing.neut.of *τίς*, interrogative pronoun, cause) 281.

λύετε (2d.per.pl.pres.act.ind.of *λύω*, aoristic, direct question) 471.

τὸν (acc.sing.masc.of the article, in agreement with *πῶλον*) 9.

πῶλον (acc.sing.masc.of *πῶλος*, direct object of *λύετε*) 1344.

Translation - "But as they were untying the colt, his owners said to them, 'Why are you untying the colt?' "

Comment: *Cf.*Mk.11:5. Luke tells us that *τινες τῶν ἐκεῖ ἑστηκότων* (Mk.11:5) were *οἱ κύριοι αὐτοῦ* - "his lords." Thus the colt had "lords" (*κύριοι*, vs.33), but in verse 34 we learn that the "lords" of the colt also had a *LORD.*

Verse 34 - "And they said, The Lord hath need of him."

οἱ δὲ εἶπαν ὅτι Ὁ κύριος αὐτοῦ χρείαν ἔχει.

οἱ (nom.pl.masc.of the article, subject of εἶπαν) 9.
δὲ (inferential conjunction) 11.
εἶπαν (3d.per.pl.aor.act.ind.of εἶπον, constative) 155.
ὅτι (recitative) 211.
'Ο (nom.sing.masc.of the article in agreement with κύριος) 9.
κύριος (nom.sing.masc.of κύριος, subject of ἔχει) 97.
αὐτοῦ (gen.sing.masc.of αὐτός, description) 16.
χρείαν (acc.sing.fem.of χρεία, direct object of ἔχει) 317.
ἔχει (3d.per.sing.pres.act.ind.of ἔχω, aoristic) 82.

Translation - "So they said, 'The Lord needs him.' "

Comment: The men who objected when the disciples untied the colt could not even claim sole ownership to the animal. They could only claim a part of a joint ownership. There are a great many people whose only property may consist of the ownership of a jackass, in whole or in part, who nevertheless feel that they are the lords of creation and therefore they yield no allegiance to any other Lord. Not these men who owned this colt. A man may be the lord of a jackass with perfect propriety if he recognizes that he is subject to the will of the Lord of the Universe and that when his Lord needs the animal, he is honored to lend or even give him as a gift. When one is so conscious of that over which he exercises lordship (colts, jackasses, *et al)* that he forgets that he too is subject to an overlord in Jesus Christ, he needs repentance. The owners of this animal, fortunately were not in this unfortunate category.

The author recalls a conversation with a friend whose financial position placed him only slightly higher than a pauper, who, upon hearing the story about the time when Henry Ford found it necessary to borrow a dollar in order to pay a taxi fare, said, "I would like to have the opportunity of loaning Henry Ford a dollar." I would rather have had the privilege of loaning the Lord Jesus Christ my colt on that great day.

Verse 35 - "And they brought him to Jesus: and they cast their garments upon the colt, and they set Jesus thereon."

καὶ ἤγαγον αὐτὸν πρὸς τὸν Ἰησοῦν, καὶ ἐπιρίψαντες αὐτῶν τὰ ἱμάτια ἐπὶ τὸν πῶλον ἐπεβίβασαν τὸν Ἰησοῦν.

καὶ (continuative conjunction) 14.
ἤγαγον (3d.per.pl.2d.aor.act.ind.of ἄγω, constative) 876.
αὐτὸν (acc.sing.masc.of αὐτός, direct object of ἤγαγον) 16.
πρὸς (preposition with the accusative of extent) 197.
τὸν (acc.sing.masc.of the article in agreement with Ἰησοῦν) 9.
Ἰησοῦν (acc.sing.masc.of Ἰησοῦς, extent) 3.
καὶ (adjunctive conjunction joining verbs) 14

#2669 ἐπιρίψαντες (aor.act.part.nom.pl.masc.of ἐπιῤῥίπτω, adverbial, temporal).

cast upon - Luke 19:35; 1 Pet.5:7.

Meaning: A combination of ἐπί (#47) and ῥίπτω (#837). Hence, to throw upon, or over. Physically of τὰ ἱμάτια ἐπὶ τὸν πῶλον - Luke 19:35. Metaphorically in 1 Pet.5:7.

αὐτῶν (gen.pl.masc.of αὐτός, possession) 16.
τὰ (acc.pl.neut.of the article in agreement with ἱμάτια) 9.
ἱμάτια (acc.pl.neut.of ἱμάτιον, direct object of ἐπιρίψαντες) 534.
ἐπὶ (preposition with the accusative of extent) 47.
τὸν (acc.sing.masc.of the article in agreement with πῶλον) 9.
πῶλον (acc.sing.masc.of πῶλος, extent) 1344.
ἐπεβίβασαν (3d.per.pl.aor.act.ind.of ἐπιβιβάζω, constative) 2429.
τὸν (acc.sing.masc.of the article in agreement with Ἰησοῦν) 9.
Ἰησοῦν (acc.sing.masc.of Ἰησοῦς, direct object of ἐπεβίβασαν) 3.

Translation - "And they brought him to Jesus and when they had thrown their coats over the colt, they set Jesus upon him."

Comment: *Cf.*Mt.21:6,7 and Mk.11:7. Luke uses ἐπιρίπτω and ἐπιβιβάζω, instead of ἐπιβάλλω (Mark) and ἐπιτίθημι (Matthew). Matthew uses ἐπικαθίζω and Mark καθίζω. Luke also says that they mounted Jesus upon the colt, while Matthew and Mark make Jesus the subject, rather than the object. Of course Jesus was not totally passive. Both ideas are true.

Verse 36 - "And as he went, they spread their clothes in the way."

πορευομένου δὲ αὐτοῦ ὑπεστρώννυον τὰ ἱμάτια αὐτῶν ἐν τῇ ὁδῷ.

πορευομένου (pres.mid.part.gen.sing.masc.of πορεύομαι, genitive absolute) 170
δὲ (continuative conjunction) 11.
αὐτοῦ (gen.sing.masc.of αὐτός, genitive absolute) 16.

#2670 ὑπεστρώννυον (3d.per.pl.imp.act.ind.of ὑποστρώννυμι, progressive description).

spread - Luke 19:36.

Meaning: A combination of ὑπό(#117) and στρώννυμι (#1351). Hence, to spread underfoot - Luke 19:36.

τὰ (acc.pl.neut.of the article in agreement with ἱμάτια) 9.
ἱμάτια (acc.pl.neut.of ἱμάτιον, direct object of ὑπεστρώννυον) 534.
αὐτῶν (gen.pl.masc.of αὐτός, possession) 16.
ἐν (preposition with the locative of place) 80.
τῇ (loc.sing.fem.of the article in agreement with ὁδῷ) 9.
ὁδῷ (loc.sing.fem.of ὁδός, place where) 199.

Translation - "And as He went along, they began to spread their coats on the road."

Comment: *Cf.* Mt.21:8 and Mk.11:18. Luke's statement is much simpler; almost terse. Mark adds vegetation from the fields and Matthew branches from the trees.

Verse 37 - "And when he was come nigh, even now at the descent of the mount of Olives, the whole multitude of the disciples began to rejoice and praise God with a loud voice for all the mighty works that they had seen."

Ἐγγίζοντος δὲ αὐτοῦ ἤδη πρὸς τῇ καταβάσει τοῦ Ὄρους τῶν Ἐλαιῶν ἤρξαντο ἅπαν τὸ πλῆθος τῶν μαθητῶν χαίροντες αἰνεῖν τὸν θεὸν φωνῇ μεγάλῃ περὶ πασῶν ὧν εἶδον δυνάμεων,

Ἐγγίζοντος (pres.act.part.gen.sing.masc.of *ἐγγίζω*, genitive absolute) 252.
δὲ (continuative conjunction) 11.
αὐτοῦ (gen.sing.masc.of *αὐτός*, genitive absolute) 16.
ἤδη (adverbial) 291.
πρὸς (preposition with the locative of place) 197.
τῇ (loc.sing.fem.of the article in agreement with *καταβάσει*) 9.

#2671 *καταβάσει* (loc.sing.fem.of *κατάβασις*, place where).

descent - Luke 19:37.

Meaning: A combination of *κατά* (#98) and *βαίνω*. *Cf.καταβαίνω* (#324). Hence, descent. The point from which one descends. In Luke 19:37 it is followed by a genitive of description - *τοῦ Ὄρους τῶν Ἐλαιῶν*. Hence, the spot reached by Jesus enroute from Bethphage to Jerusalem, as He passed near the Mount of Olives, when He passed *πρὸς τῇ καταβάσει* - "near the road down" without stating that He was at the beginning of the *κατάβασις* at the top of the mountain.

τοῦ (gen.sing.neut.of the article in agreement with *Ὄρους*) 9.
Ὄρους (gen.sing.neut.of *ὄρος*, place description) 357.
τῶν (gen.pl.masc.of the article in agreement with *Ἐλαιῶν*) 9.
Ἐλαιῶν (gen.pl.masc.of *Ἐλαιῶν*, description) 1341.
ἤρξαντο (3d.per.pl.aor.mid.ind.of *ἄρχω*, ingressive) 383.
ἅπαν (nom.sing.neut.of *ἅπας*, in agreement with *πλῆθος*) 639
τὸ (nom.sing.neut.of the article in agreement with *πλῆθος*) 9.
πλῆθος (nom.sing.neut.of *πλῆθος*, subject of *ἤρξαντο*) 1792.
τῶν (gen.pl.masc.of article in agreement with *μαθητῶν*) 9.
μαθητῶν (gen.pl.masc.of *μαθητής*, partitive) 421.
χαίροντες (pres.act.part.nom.pl.masc.of *χαίρω*, adverbial, modal) 182.
αἰνεῖν (pres.act.inf.of *αἰνέω*, complementary) 1881.
τὸν (acc.sing.masc.of the article in agreement with *θεὸν*) 9.
θεὸν (acc.sing.masc.of *θεός*, direct object of *αἰνεῖν*) 124.
φωνῇ (instru.sing.fem.of *φωνή*, means) 222.
μεγάλῃ (instru.sing.fem.of *μέγας*, in agreement with *φωνῃ*) 184.
περὶ (preposition with the genitive of reference) 173.

πασῶν (gen.pl.fem.of πᾶς, in agreement with δυνάμεων) 67.
ὧν (gen.pl.fem.of ὅς, description) 65.
εἶδον (3d.per.pl.aor.act.ind.of ὁράω, constative) 144.
δυνάμεων (gen.pl.fem.of δύναμις, reference) 687.

Translation - "And as He approached (the city) just as He came near the descent of the Mount of Olives, the entire multitude of His disciples began joyfully and loudly to praise God about all of the miracles which they had seen."

Comment: Luke now gives us detail which Matthew and Mark omit. *Cf.* Mt.21:9 and Mk.11:9. As He was approaching Jerusalem (though the text does not say so) He passed near the spot where the road leads down from the Mount of Olives. Luke either questioned Peter and Mark about this with care or personally visited the spot, in order to give us the precise description of the terrain over which Jesus passed. The entire multitude joined in the shout. *Cf.*#639 - the intensive of πᾶς - literally "all." Jesus had no enemies in the crowd that day, although they turned against Him under the brainwashing techniques of the Establishment, six days later. They shouted loudly - φωνῇ μεγάλῃ - "with a loud voice" and joyfully χαίροντες, the modal participle. What were they shouting about. περὶ with the genitive of reference tells us - "with reference to all of the mighty works which they had seen." Many in Israel had accepted Jesus' challenge of John 10:38. Theirs was the pragmatic approach. Not because Jesus said that He was God, but because they had seen Him do things that convinced them that He was God, because what He did only God could do.

Verse 38 - "Saying, Blessed be the king that cometh in the name of the Lord: peace in heaven and glory in the highest."

λέγοντες, Εὐλογημένος ὁ ἐρχόμενος ὁ βασιλεὺς ἐν ὀνόματι κυρίου. ἐν οὐρανῷ εἰρήνη καὶ δόξα ἐν ὑψίστοις.

λέγοντες (pres.act.part.nom.pl.masc.of λέγω, recitative) 66.
Εὐλογημένος (perf.pass.part.nom.sing.masc.of εὐλογέω, adjectival, predicate adjective) 1120.
ὁ (nom.sing.masc.of the article in agreement with βασιλεὺς) 9.
ἐρχόμενος (pres.part.nom.sing.masc.of ἔρχομαι, adjectival, ascriptive, in agreement with βασιλεὺς) 146.
ὁ (nom.sing.masc.of the article in agreement with βασιλεὺς) 9.
βασιλεὺς (nom.sing.masc.of βασιλεύς, subject of ἐστιν understood) 31.
ἐν (preposition with the instrumental of means) 80.
ὀνόματι (instru.sing.neut.of ὄνομα, means) 108.
κυρίου (gen.sing.masc.of κύριος, description) 97.
εν (preposition with the locative of place) 80.
οὐρανῷ (loc.sing.masc.of οὐρανός, place where) 254.
εἰρήνη (nom.sing.fem.of εἰρήνη, subject of the verb understood) 865.
καὶ (continuative conjunction) 14.
δόξα (nom.sing.fem.of δόξα, subject of verb understood) 361.

ἐν (preposition with the locative of place) 80.
ὑψίστοις (loc.pl.masc.of ὕψιστος, place where) 1353.

Translation - "Saying, 'Blessed is He who comes, the King with a lordly name. In heaven peace and glory in the highest.' "

Comment: *Cf.* Mt.21:9 and Mk.11:9,10. Matthew stresses the Son of David; Mark the kingdom of David; Luke the Coming King. Luke adds ἐν οὐρανῷ εἰρήνη . . . not found in the other synoptics.

When Jesus was born, Luke reported the angels to have said ἐπὶ γῆς εἰρήνη ἐν ἀνθρώποις εὐδοκίας (Lk.2:14) - "upon earth peace to men of good will." Now that He is about to die,men of good will surround Him and say ἐν οὐρανῷ εἰρήνη. This can happen only when His atoning death occurs on the cross (Ps.85:10,11) and the results of His sacrifice have been implemented in human history by the Holy Spirit. The multitudes thronging the road that day did not realize that they were predicting what could result only from His death. They were thinking of Christ on a throne. Christ on an earthly throne, without first being Christ on a cross could never bring εἰρήνη ἐν οὐρανῷ.

Verse 39 - "And some of the Pharisees from among the multitude said unto him, Master, rebuke thy disciples."

καί τινες τῶν Φαρισαίων ἀπὸ τοῦ ὄχλου εἶπαν πρὸς αὐτόν, Διδάσκαλε, ἐπιτίμησον τοῖς μαθηταῖς σου.

καί (adversative conjunction) 14.
τινες (nom.pl.masc.of τις, the indefinite pronoun, subject of εἶπαν) 486.
τῶν (gen.pl.masc.of the article in agreement with Φαρισαίων) 9.
Φαρισαίων (gen.pl.masc.of Φαρισαῖος, partitive) 276.
ἀπὸ (preposition with the ablative of source) 70.
τοῦ (abl.sing.masc.of the article in agreement with ὄχλου) 9.
ὄχλου (abl.sing.masc.of ὄχλος, source) 418.
εἶπαν (3d.per.pl.aor.act.ind.of εἶπον, constative) 155.
πρὸς (preposition with the accusative of extent, after a verb of speaking) 197.
αὐτόν (acc.sing.masc.of αὐτός, extent, after a verb of speaking) 16.
Διδάσκαλε (voc.sing.masc.of διδάσκαλος, address) 742.
ἐπιτίμησον (2d.per.sing.aor.act.impv.of ἐπιτιμάω, command) 757.
τοῖς (dat.pl.masc.of the article in agreement with μαθηταῖς) 9.
μαθηταῖς (dat.pl.masc.of μαθητής, indirect object of ἐπιτίμησον) 421.
σου (gen.sing.masc.of σύ, relationship) 104.

Translation - "But some of the Pharisees from the crowd said to Him, 'Teacher, rebuke your disciples.' "

Comment: Matthew and Mark do not record this incident. καὶ is adversative. The Pharisees objected to the demonstration and the enthusiasm of the people. Note that not all of the Pharisees objected. Not all, but some. This is followed by *τοῦ ὄχλου*, which seems contradictory to *ἅπαν* in verse 37, until we note that *ἅπαν* applies to *τὸ πλῆθος τῶν μαθητῶν*, not to everyone in the crowd. Also it is likely that as the procession swept on toward Jerusalem, it picked up some who were not in sympathy with it. The Establishment always gets nervous when an independent thinker who does not fit into the pattern of the Inner Circle arouses public sympathy, enthusiasm and excitement for his cause. The people may shout as much as they please as long as they are shouting for the Establishment, but otherwise they must be put to silence.

Before we draw too many lessons from a supposed similarity between the triumphal entry of Jesus into Jerusalem and the latest demonstration in Lafayette Square, it should be said that the demonstrators who were shouting for Jesus had objective reasons for supporting their demand for a change in administration. Their candidate was the Incarnate Son of God, the only legitimate claimant to David's throne. Unfortunately demonstrators in the late 20th century do not always have Jesus as their candidate, though they insist that their standards are in line with those of our Lord - a position not always unassailable.

But there is one sound parallel. Demonstrators, then and now, were then and are now dissatisfied with the record of the Establishment. Modern society, protected by entrenched and powerful social, economic and social forces, is no more viable than the tottering Sanhedrin in A.D.30 which had only 40 more years to live. That is why Jesus rejected the demand of the Pharisees in

Verse 40 - "And he answered and said unto them, I tell you that, if these should hold their peace, the stones would immediately cry out."

καὶ ἀποκριθεὶς εἶπεν, Λέγω ὑμῖν, ἐὰν οὗτοι σιωπήσουσιν, οἱ λίθοι κράξουσιν.

καὶ (adversative conjunction) 14.
ἀποκριθεὶς (aor.mid.part.nom.sing.masc.of *ἀποκρίνομαι*, adverbial, modal) 318.
εἶπεν (3d.per.sing.aor.act.ind.of *εἶπον*, constative) 155.
Λέγω (1st.per.sing.pres.act.ind.of *λέγω*, aoristic) 66.
ὑμῖν (dat.pl.masc.of *σύ*, indirect object of *λέγω*) 104.
ἐὰν (conditional particle with the future indicative in a first-class condition) 363.
οὗτοι (nom.pl.masc.of *οὗτος*, subject of *σιωπήσουσιν*) 93.
σιωπήσουσιν (3d.per.pl.fut.ind.of *σιωπάω*, first-class condition) 1337.
οἱ (nom.pl.masc.of the article in agreement with *λίθοι*) 9.
λίθοι (nom.pl.masc.of *λίθος*, subject of *κράξουσιν*) 290.
κράξουσιν (3d.per.pl.fut.act.ind.of *κράζω*, predictive) 765.

Translation - "But He said,'I am telling you, if these people are silent,the stones will cry out.' "

Comment: Normally *ἐάν* with the subjunctive in the protasis and the future indicative in the apodosis expresses the third-class less vivid future, where some doubt may be entertained about the fulfillment of the protasis. This is the normal construction in classical Greek as well as in the New Testament. Occasionally, however, as here we have ἐάν with the future indicative in the protasis to express a future supposition with more probability. "If the people become silent (I doubt that they will) the stones will cry out." Robertson says, "In general, the difference between εἰ and ἐάν is considerably lessened in the κοινή, though it must be remembered that ἐάν was never confined to the subj.nor εἰ to the ind.and opt.... Thayer calls it "a somewhat negligent use, met with from the time of Aristotle on." It was just a normal development in the κοινή till in the modern Greek ἄν is used indifferently with either ind.or subj." (Robertson, *Grammar*, 1009, 1010).

It is more likely that the miraculous outcry of the stones beneath their feet would have been heard than that the Messianic kingdom of Christ, so abundantly attested, both by His person and His work, should have gone unrecognized. The stones of the temple (Mt.24:2) were destined to be taken apart, one by one, by the Romans in A.D.70, to cry out in historic protest against the Jewish murder of Jesus. One stone (Mt.27:60,66; 28:2; Mk.15:46; 16:3,4; Lk.24:2; John 20:1) rolled away to avoid collision with the dynamics of His bodily resurrection; other desert stones would indeed have yielded to His command to become bread if He had chosen to order it (Mt.4:3; Lk.4:3). Stones will decorate His throne in heaven (Rev.4:3) and a stone will figure as a weapon in His judgment (Rev.18;21). Finally stones are jewels to decorate the New Jerusalem. Also, if we substitute πέτρα (#695) for λίθος (#290), sinners will cry out to the stones (Rev.6:16) to fall upon them to hide them from the wrath of the Lamb, whereas now (λίθοι) wait to cry out His praises if the people should desist. Thus the stones cry out or are cried out to. We either cry out to praise Him or we cry out to the stones to cover us - the stones that would praise Him if men did not.

We turn now to John's account of the triumphal entry in John 12:12-19.

John 12:12 - "On the next day much people that were come to the feast, when they heard that Jesus was coming to Jerusalem,"

Τῇ ἐπαύριον ὁ ὄχλος πολὺς ὁ ἐλθὼν εἰς τὴν ἑορτήν, ἀκούσαντες ὅτι ἔρχεται ὁ Ἰησοῦς εἰς Ἱεροσόλυμα,

Τῇ (loc.sing.fem.of the article, time point) 9.
ἐπαύριον (adverbial) 1680.
ὁ (nom.sing.masc.of the article in agreement with ὄχλος) 9.
ὄχλος (nom.sing.masc.of ὄχλος, subject of ἔλαβον) 418.
πολὺς (nom.sing.masc.of πολύς, in agreement with ὄχλος) 228.
ὁ (nom.sing.masc.of the article in agreement with ἐλθὼν) 9.
ἐλθὼν (aor.mid.part.nom.sing.masc.of ἔρχομαι, adjectival, in agreement with ὄχλος) 146.
εἰς (preposition with the accusative of extent) 140.
τὴν (acc.sing.fem.of the article in agreement with ἑορτήν) 9.
ἑορτήν (acc.sing.fem.of ἑορτή, extent) 1558.

ἀκούσαντες (aor.act.part.nom.pl.masc.of ἀκούω, adverbial, temporal, causal) 148.
ὅτι (conjunction introducing an object clause in indirect discourse) 211.
ἔρχεται (3d.per.sing.pres.ind.of ἔρχομαι, aoristic) 146.
ὁ (nom.sing.masc.of the article in agreement with Ἰησοῦς) 9.
Ἰησοῦς (nom.sing.masc.of Ἰησοῦς, subject of ἔρχεται) 3.
εἰς (preposition with the accusative of extent) 140.
Ἱεροσόλυμα (acc.sing.masc.of Ἱεροσόλυμα, extent) 141.

Translation - "The next day when the great crowd which came to the feast heard that Jesus was coming to Jerusalem, . . ."

Comment: Τῇ ἐπαύριον refers to the day following the visit of Jesus to the home of Mary, Martha and Lazarus (John 12:1-11). That was six days before the Passover. Hence, the time of John 12:12 is five days before the Passover. If Christ died on Friday, then the triumphal entry was on the Sunday before, *i.e.* the day after the last Sabbath before Christ's death. The people from the outlying regions were already in Jerusalem before Jesus arrived (John 11:55). They heard that Jesus was coming (indirect discourse in ἀκούσαντες ὅτι ἔρχεται ὁ Ἰησοῦς). Hence this is a different group of people from those who followed Him out of Jericho (Lk.18:35-19:40). Those who were with Him when He sent the two disciples to Bethqhage, after the colt, were met by the group John is describing here, who came out to meet Him.

Verse 13 - ". . . took branches of palm trees, and went forth to meet him, and cried Hosanna: Blessed is the King of Israel that cometh in the name of the Lord."

ἔλαβον τὰ βαΐα τῶν φοινίκων καὶ ἐξῆλθον εἰς ὑπάντησιν αὐτῷ, καὶ ἐκραύγαζον, Ὡσαννά, εὐλογημένος ὁ ἐρχόμενος ἐν ὀνόματι κυρίου, καὶ ὁ βασιλεὺς τοῦ Ἰσραήλ.

ἔλαβον (3d.per.pl.aor.act.ind.of λαμβάνω, constative) 533.
τὰ (acc.pl.neut.of the article in agreement with βαΐα) 9.

#2672 βαΐα (acc.pl.neut.of βαΐον, direct object of ἔλαβον).

branch - John 12:13.

Meaning: A Greek derivation from the Egyptian - a palm branch - John 12:13.

τῶν (gen.pl.masc.of the article in agreement with φοινίκων) 9.

#2673 φοινίκων (gen.pl.masc.of φοίνιξ, description).

palm - Rev.7:9.
palm tree - John 12:13.

Meaning: properly, a city in Crete - Phoenix. In the New Testament, a palm tree - John 12:13. The branches of the palm tree in Rev.7:9.

καὶ (adjunctive conjunction) 14.
ἐξῆλθον (3d.per.pl.aor.mid.ind.of ἐξέρχομαι, constative) 161.
εἰς (preposition with the accusative, purpose) 140.
ὑπάντησιν (acc.sing.fem.of ὑπάντησις, purpose) 775.
αὐτῷ (instrumental sing.masc.of αὐτός, association) 16.
καὶ (adjunctive conjunction joining verbs) 14.
ἐκραύγαζον (3d.per.pl.imp.act.ind.of κραυγάζω, inceptive) 984.

Ὡσαννά (exclamation) 1352.
εὐλογημένος (perf.pass.part.nom.sing.masc.of εὐλογέω, adjectival, predicate, in agreement with ἐρχόμενος) 1120.
ὁ (nom.sing.masc.of the article in agreement with ἐρχόμενος) 9.
ἐρχόμενος (pres.mid.part.nom.sing.masc.of ἔρχομαι, substantival, subject of ἐστιν, understood) 146.
ἐν (preposition with the instrumental of means) 80.
ὀνόματι (instru.sing.neut.of ὄνομα, means) 108.
κυρίου (gen.sing.masc.of κύριος, description) 97.
καὶ (adjunctive conjunction joining substantives) 14.
ὁ (nom.sing.masc.of the article in agreement with βασιλεὺς) 9.
βασιλεὺς (nom.sing.masc.of βασιλεύς, subject of ἐστιν, understood) 31.
τοῦ (gen.sing.masc.of the article in agreement with Ἰσραήλ) 9.
Ἰσραήλ (gen.sing.masc.of Ἰσραήλ, description) 165.

Translation - ". . . they took the branches of the palm trees and went out to meet Him and began to shout, 'Hurrah! Blessed is the One Who is coming with a lordly name, even the King of Israel.' "

Comment: *Cf.* Mt.21:8; Mk.11:8 and Lk.19:38. Matthew says branches from the trees without specifying what kind. Mark says cuttings from the vegetation that grew in the fields. John, who is speaking of a different group who came out from Jerusalem to meet Jesus and the crowd coming in from Olivet, says palm branches. *Cf.*#775 for the other uses of εἰς ὑπάντησιν and the instrumental/associative case. *Cf.* #984, a different word from #765 used by Matthew and Mark. What they said is not essentially different from the shouts of the incoming group. As the two crowds met and blended into one, everyone tended to repeat the cry, either in his own formulation or in that which he heard others use. The essence is that Jesus was the Messiah, the Son of God, the King of Israel.

Verse 14 - "And Jesus when he had found a young ass, sat thereon, as it is written, . . . "

εὑρὼν δὲ ὁ Ἰησοῦς ὀνάριον ἐκάθισεν ἐπ' αὐτό, καθώς ἐστιν γεγραμμένον,

εὑρὼν (aor.act.part.nom.sing.masc.of εὑρίσκω, adverbial, temporal) 79.
δὲ (continuative conjunction) 11.
ὁ (nom.sing.masc.of the article in agreement with Ἰησοῦς) 9.
Ἰησοῦς (nom.sing.masc.of Ἰησοῦς, subject of ἐκάθισεν) 3.

#2674 ὀνάριον (acc.sing.neut.of ὀνάριον, direct object of εὑρὼν).

young ass - John 12:14.

Meaning: diminutive of ὄνος (#1343). The colt of an ass - John 12:14.

ἐκάθισεν (3d.per.sing.aor.act.ind.of καθίζω, ingressive) 420.
ἐπ' (preposition with the accusative of extent, place) 47.
αὐτό (acc.sing.neut.of αὐτός, extent, place) 16.
καθώς (adverbial) 1348.
ἐστιν (3d.per.sing.pres.ind.of εἰμί, perfect periphrastic) 86.
γεγραμμένον (perf.pass.part.acc.sing.neut.of γράφω, perfect periphrastic) 156.

Translation - "And when Jesus had found a young ass He mounted it, as it is written, . . . "

Comment: *Cf.* Mt.21:1-7; Mk.11:1-7; Lk.19:29-35. The synoptics tell the story of Jesus' acquisition of the animal in vivid detail. John reduces the story to seven words - εὑρὼν δὲ ὁ Ἰησοῦς ὀνάριον ἐκάθισεν ἐπ' αὐτό and adds that this action is in conformity to prophetic scripture. Note the perfect periphrastic in ἐστιν γεγραμμένον. The citation is Zechariah 9:9, which John quotes in

Verse 15 - "Fear not, daughter of Zion: behold thy King cometh, sitting on an ass's colt."

Μὴ φοβοῦ, θυγάτηρ Σιών, ἰδοὺ ὁ βασιλεύς σου ἔρχεται, καθήμενος ἐπὶ πῶλον ὄνου.

Μὴ (qualified negative conjunction with the imperative) 87.
φοβοῦ (2d.per.sing.pres.mid.impv.of φοβέομαι, command) 101.
θυγάτηρ (voc.sing.fem.of θυγάτηρ, address) 817.
Σιών (gen.sing.masc.of Σιών, relationship) 1345.
ἰδοὺ (exclamation) 95.
ὁ (nom.sing.masc.of the article in agreement with βασιλεύς) 9.
σου (gen.sing.masc.of σύ, relationship) 104.
ἔρχεται (3d.per.sing.pres.ind.of ἔρχομαι, aoristic) 146.
καθήμενος (pres.mid.part.nom.sing.masc.of κάθημαι, adverbial, modal) 377.
ἐπὶ (preposition with the accusative of extent, place) 47.
πῶλον (acc.sing.masc.of πῶλος, extent, place) 1344.
ὄνου (gen.sing.masc.of ὄνος, relationship) 1343.

Translation - "Do not go on fearing, Daughter of Zion. Look! Your King is coming, riding on the colt of an ass."

Comment: The LXX for Zechariah 9:9 has χαῖρε σφόδρα, θύγατερ Σειών. Κήρυσσε, θύγατερ Ἰερουσαλήμ, ἰδοὺ ὁ βασιλεύς σου ἔρχεταί σοι δίκαιος καὶ σώζων αὐτός, πραῢς καὶ ἐπιβεβηκὼς ἐπὶ ὑποζύγιον καὶ πῶλον νέον - "Rejoice greatly, Daughter of Zion; Shout, Daughter of Jerusalem; Behold, your king is coming to you; just and saving the same: meek and mounted upon an ass, even a new colt."

"Thy King - " *Cf.* Ps.2:6; 45:1,6,7; Isa.32:1; 9:6; Ps.72:1-4; 72:7; Isa.11:2-4.

Verse 16 - "These things understood not his disciples at the first: but when Jesus was glorified, then remembered they that these things were written of him, and that they had done these things unto him."

ταῦτα οὐκ ἔγνωσαν αὐτοῦ οἱ μαθηταὶ τὸ πρῶτον, ἀλλ' ὅτε ἐδοξάσθη Ἰησοῦς τότε ἐμνήσθησαν ὅτι ταῦτα ἦν ἐπ' αὐτῷ γεγραμμένα καὶ ταῦτα ἐποίησαν αὐτῷ.

ταῦτα (acc.pl.neut.of *οὗτος*, direct object of *ἔγνωσαν*) 93.
οὐκ (summary negative conjunction with the indicative) 130.
ἔγνωσαν (3d.per.pl.aor.act.ind.of *γινώσκω*, constative) 131.
αὐτοῦ (gen.sing.masc.of *αὐτός*, relationship) 16.
οἱ (nom.pl.masc.of the article in agreement with *μαθηταὶ*) 9.
μαθηταὶ (nom.pl.masc.of *μαθητής*, subject of *ἔγνωσαν*, *ἐμνήσθησαν* and *ἐποίησαν*) 421.
τὸ (acc.sing.neut.of the article in agreement with *πρῶτον*) 9.
πρῶτον (acc.sing.neut.of *πρῶτος*, adverbial accusative) 487.
ἀλλ' (adversative conjunction) 342.
ὅτε (conjunction introducing a definite temporal clause) 703.
ἐδοξάσθη (3d.per.sing.aor.pass.ind.of *δοξάζω*, definite temporal clause) 461.
Ἰησοῦς (nom.sing.masc.of *Ἰησοῦς*, subject of *ἐδοξάσθη*) 3.
τότε (temporal adverb) 166.
ἐμνήσθησαν (3d.per.pl.aor.pass.ind.of *μιμνήσκω*, ingressive) 485.
ὅτι (conjunction introducing an object clause in indirect discourse) 211.
ταῦτα (nom.pl.neut.of *οὗτος*, subject of *ἦν*) 93.
ἦν (3d.per.sing.imp.ind.of *εἰμί*, pluperfect periphrastic) 86.
ἐπ' (preposition with the dative of reference) 47.
αὐτῷ (dat.sing.masc.of *αὐτός*, reference) 16.
γεγραμμένα (perf.pass.part.nom.pl.neut.of *γράφω*, pluperfect periphrastic) 156.
καὶ (adjunctive conjunction joining object clauses) 14.
ταῦτα (acc.pl.neut.of *οὗτος*, direct object of *ἐποίησαν*) 93.
ἐποίησαν (3d.per.pl.aor.act.ind.of *ποιέω*, culminative) 127.
αὐτῷ (dat.sing.masc.of *αὐτός*, personal advantage) 16.

Translation - "His disciples did not understand these things at first, but when Jesus had been glorified, then they began to remember that these things had been written about Him and that they had done these things for Him."

Comment: *ταῦτα* refers to all of the events of the triumphal entry, beginning with Jesus' order to the disciples to go find the colt. At the time the disciples did not understand that they were fulfilling prophecy. But this realization dawned upon them (ingressive aorist in ἐμνήσθησαν) after Jesus was resurrected and had ascended to glory. Then they remembered that the events were in accord with what had been written about Him. Note ἐπί with the dative of reference. Then too they realized that what they did in terms of getting the colt, placing their coats on him, helping Jesus to mount and participating in the parade were all in fulfillment of the prophetic scriptures.

In view of Ephesians 2:10 which teaches that every Christian has had assigned to him by our risen Lord, "the head over all things to the church" (Eph.1:22), specific "good works that we should walk in them," the Christian who lives the victorious life and enjoys the leadership of the residing and presiding Holy Spirit, has the daily assurance that what he is doing every day is in accord with the divine purpose, even though it was not included in the Old Testament prophecies. The details about where we go and what we do and say have all been planned by our Lord in eternity past. If we allow the Holy Spirit to direct our lives our path will never deviate from the assigned path and what we say and do will never deviate from the script for the scenario.

John adds two verses to give a natural explanation of the behavior of the rest of the crowd, other than the disciples. *Cf.* Ps.118:25,26.

Verse 17 - "The people therefore that was with him when he called Lazarus out of his grave, and raised him from the dead, bare record."

ἐμαρτύρει οὖν ὁ ὄχλος ὁ ὢν μετ' αὐτοῦ ὅτε τὸν Λάζαρον ἐφώνησεν ἐκ τοῦ μνημείου καὶ ἤγειρεν αὐτὸν ἐκ νεκρῶν.

ἐμαρτύρει (3d.per.sing.imp.act.ind.of μαρτυρέω, inceptive) 1471.
οὖν (inferential conjunction) 68.
ὁ (nom.sing.masc.of the article in agreement with ὄχλος) 9.
ὄχλος (nom.sing.masc.of ὄχλος, subject of ἐμαρτύρει) 418.
ὁ (nom.sing.masc.of the article in agreement with ὢν) 9.
ὢν (pres.part.nom.sing.masc.of εἰμί, substantival, in apposition) 86.
μετ' (preposition with the genitive of accompaniment) 50.
αὐτοῦ (gen.sing.masc.of αὐτός, accompaniment) 16.
ὅτε (conjunction introducing a definite temporal clause) 703.
τὸν (acc.sing.masc.of the article in agreement with Λάζαρον) 9.
Λάζαρον (acc.sing.masc.of Λάζαρος, direct object of ἐφώνησεν) 2596.
ἐφώνησεν (3d.per.sing.aor.act.ind.of φωνέω, definite temporal clause) 1338.
ἐκ (preposition with the ablative of separation) 19.
τοῦ (abl.sing.neut.of the article in agreement with μνημείου) 9.
μνημείου (abl.sing.neut.of μνημεῖον, separation) 763.
καὶ (adjunctive conjunction joining verbs) 14.
ἤγειρεν (3d.per.sing.aor.act.ind.of ἐγείρω, constative) 125.
αὐτὸν (acc.sing.masc.of αὐτός, direct object of ἤγειρεν) 16.
ἐκ (preposition with the ablative of separation) 19.
νεκρῶν (abl.pl.masc.of νεκρός, separation) 749.

Translation - "Therefore the crowds who were with Him when He called Lazarus out of the tomb and raised him from the dead began to tell it."

Comment: Note John's emphasis as he puts the verb ahead of everything else. The procession formed near Bethphage and Bethany and a part of it was composed of people from Bethany who had witnessed the resurrection of Lazarus. In addition to the shouts of Hurrah which the text records they added their accounts of His miracle at Lazarus' tomb. Thus we have further evidence that as Jesus met the crowd coming out from Jerusalem to meet Him, He already had a large body of people who had followed him out of Bethany and Bethphage. The news of the miracle spread as we see in

Verse 18 - "For this cause the people also met him, for that they heard that he had done this miracle."

διὰ τοῦτο (καὶ) ὑπήντησεν αὐτῷ ὁ ὄχλος ὅτι ἤκουσαν τοῦτο αὐτὸν πεποιηκέναι τὸ σημεῖον.

διὰ (preposition with the accusative of cause) 118.
τοῦτο (acc.sing.neut.of οὗτος, cause) 93.
(καὶ) (adjunctive conjunction) 14.
ὑπήντησεν (3d.per.sing.aor.act.ind.of ὑπαντάω, constative) 762.
αὐτῷ (instru.sing.masc.of αὐτός, association) 16.
ὁ (nom.sing.masc.of the article in agreement with ὄχλος) 9.
ὄχλος (nom.sing.masc.of ὄχλος, subject of ὑπήντησεν) 418.
ὅτι (conjunction introducing a subordinate causal clause) 211.
ἤκουσαν (3d.per.pl.aor.act.ind.of ἀκούω, culminative) 148.
τοῦτο (acc.sing.neut.of οὗτος, in agreement with σημεῖον) 93.
αὐτὸν (acc.sing.masc.of αὐτός, general reference) 16.
πεποιηκέναι (perf.act.inf.of ποιέω, noun use, object of ἤκουσαν) 127.
τὸ (acc.sing.neut.of the article in agreement with σημεῖον) 9.
σημεῖον (acc.sing.neut.of σημεῖον, direct object of πεποιηκέναι) 1005.

Translation - "Because of this also the crowd met Him, because they had heard that He had performed this miracle."

Comment: τοῦτο in the διὰ τοῦτο causal phrase, refers to ἐμαρτύρει in verse 17. The witnesses who had been present and had seen Lazarus come from the tomb at the command of Jesus had joined the procession and were spreading the news about the miracle. The reports had already reached Jerusalem through the testimony of others who had carried the news back to the city on the day that Jesus raised him from the dead (John 11:46). Now others, perhaps those who ran ahead (Mk.11:9), continued to tell the story. Jesus, Who raised Lazarus, was approaching the city, riding a colt and surrounded by hundreds of His admirers who were shouting His praises to the heavens. Was Lazarus with Jesus? The text does not tell us. When the crowd from the city met Him, they retraced their steps and as the procession neared the city gate it continued to increase in size, enthusiasm and noise. This explains the reaction of the Pharisees in

Verse 19 - "The Pharisees therefore said among themselves, Perceive ye how ye prevail nothing? Behold, the world is gone after Him."

οἱ οὖν Φαρισαῖοι εἶπαν πρὸς ἑαυτούς, Θεωρεῖτε ὅτι οὐκ ὠφελεῖτε οὐδέν. ἴδε ὁ κόσμος ὀπίσω αὐτοῦ ἀπῆλθεν.

οἱ (nom.pl.masc.of the article in agreement with Φαρισαῖοι) 9.
οὖν (inferential conjunction) 68.
Φαρισαῖοι (nom.pl.masc.of Φαρισαῖος, subject of εἶπαν) 276.
εἶπαν (3d.per.pl.aor.act.ind.of εἶπον, constative) 155.
πρὸς (preposition with the accusative of extent, after a verb of speaking) 197.
ἑαυτούς (acc.pl.masc.of ἑαυτός, extent, after a verb of speaking) 288.
Θεωρεῖτε (2d.per.pl.pres.act.ind.of θεωρέω, aoristic) 1667.
ὅτι (conjunction introducing an object clause) 211.
ὠφελεῖτε (2d.per.pl.pres.act.ind.of ὠφελέω, aoristic) 1144.
οὐδέν (acc.sing.neut.of οὐδείς, direct object of ὠφελεῖτε) 446.
ἴδε (2d.per.sing.aor.act.impv.of ὁράω, command) 144.
ὁ (nom.sing.masc.of the article in agreement with κόσμος) 9.
κόσμος (nom.sing.masc.of κόσμος, subject of ἀπῆλθεν) 360.
ὀπίσω (adverb of time and place) 302.
αὐτοῦ (abl.sing.masc.of αὐτός, separation) 16.
ἀπῆλθεν (3d.per.sing.aor.mid.ind.of ἀπέρχομαι, culminative) 239.

Translation - "Therefore the Pharisees said to each other, 'You see that you are making no progress. Look! The world has gone after Him.' "

Comment: It is idle to speculate about what might have happened if Jesus had suddenly resorted to military tactics. The Sanhedrin had not the police power to stop Him. Even Pilate did not have enough troops in Jerusalem to stop the mob who later were determined to kill Jesus. But the plan of God for world redemption, of which Jesus was coauthor and major participant, called for His humiliation and death. But not until He had had His Palm Sunday moment of glory. The officers could not arrest Him that day, nor on any day following until after the Paschal supper on Thursday evening, and then, only with the sovereign permission and willing cooperation of the victim.

Crowds are basically irrational. There is not a great deal of difference between democracy and a crowd. Some of the same voices, perhaps, who shouted His praises on Sunday, called for His blood on the Friday following.

The Pharisees said ruefully, "The world has gone after Him." The following Friday Jesus went after the world.

Prediction Over Jerusalem

(Luke 19:41-44)

Luke 19:41 - "And when he was come near, he beheld the city, and wept over it."

Καὶ ὡς ἤγγισεν, ἰδὼν τὴν πόλιν ἔκλαυσεν ἐπ' αὐτήν,

Καὶ (continuative conjunction) 14.
ὡς (temporal particle introducing a definite temporal clause) 128.
ἤγγισεν (3d.per.sing.aor.act.ind.of ἐγγίζω, definite temporal clause) 252.
ἰδὼν (aor.act.part.nom.sing.masc.of ὁράω, adverbial, temporal/causal) 144.
τὴν (acc.sing.fem.of the article in agreement with πόλιν) 9.
πόλιν (acc.sing.fem.of πόλις, direct object of ἰδὼν) 243.
ἔκλαυσεν (3d.per.sing.aor.act.ind.of κλαίω, ingressive) 225.
ἐπ (preposition with the accusative, cause) 47.
αὐτήν (acc.sing.fem.of αὐτός, cause) 16.

Translation - "And as He approached He saw the city and burst into tears because of it."

Comment: The road from the Mount of Olives descends westward into the Valley of the Kidron ("The Valley of Jehoshaphat") and climbs up into the city. The text is not clear as to how high upon Olivet Jesus' route took Him. Bethany is almost due east of the southern end of the escarpment and Bethphage is west of Bethany just south of the mountain. The procession was making its way northwest toward the city. It is probable that they entered Jerusalem at or near the Pool of Siloam. From the bottom of the valley, as He crossed the brook of Kidron He was looking up at the city. A short time before that He gazed at it from the same altitude, and a short time before that He looked down upon the city. When he looked (and because He looked) He suddenly burst into tears (ingressive aorist in ἔκλαυσεν). *Cf.*#47 for other examples of ἐπί with the accusative in a causal context.

Verse 42 - "Saying, If thou hadst known, even thou, at least in this thy day, the things which belong unto thy peace! But now they are hid from thine eyes."

λέγων ὅτι Εἰ ἔγνως ἐν τῇ ἡμέρᾳ ταύτῃ καὶ σὺ τὰ πρὸς εἰρήνην — νῦν δὲ ἐκρύβη ἀπὸ ὀφθαλμῶν σου.

λέγων (pres.act.part.nom.sing.masc.of λέγω, adverbial, complementary) 66.
ὅτι (recitative) 211.
Εἰ (conditional particle in an elliptical second-class condition) 337.
ἔγνως (2d.per.sing.2d.aor.act.ind.of γινώσκω, second-class condition) 131.
ἐν (preposition with the locative of time point) 80.
τῇ (loc.sing.fem.of the article in agreement with ἡμέρᾳ) 9.
ἡμέρᾳ (loc.sing.fem.of ἡμέρα, time point) 135.
ταύτῃ (loc.sing.fem.of οὗτος, in agreement with ἡμέρᾳ) 93.
καὶ (ascensive conjunction) 14.
σὺ (nom.sing.fem.of σύ, emphatic) 104.
τὰ (acc.pl.neut.of the article, direct object of ἔγνως) 9.
πρὸς (preposition with the accusative of purpose) 197.
εἰρήνην (acc.sing.fem.of εἰρήνη, purpose) 865.
νῦν (temporal adverb) 1497.
δὲ (adversative conjunction) 11.
ἐκρύβη (3d.per.sing.2d.aor.pass.ind.of κρύπτω, culminative) 451.

ἀπὸ (preposition with the ablative of separation) 70.
ὀφθαλμῶν (abl.pl.masc.of ὀφθαλμός, separation) 501.
σου (gen.sing.masc.of σύ, possession) 104.

Translation - ". . . saying, 'If you had known on this day, especially you, the things which make for peace — but now it has been hidden from your eyes.' "

Comment: Overcome by His sudden burst of emotion Jesus left unfinished the conditional sentence - an elliptical condition or aposiopesis. The condition in the protasis was of the second-class, contrary to fact. "If you had known . . . " But she did not know. The ascensive καὶ with the emphatic σὺ - "especially you." "You of all people. . . . "If any city had a tradition that should have prepared her for the coming of her Messiah, it was Jerusalem. Jesus omitted the apodosis because Jerusalem could not fulfill the condition in the protasis. Jerusalem had been the most favored of all of Israel's cities. She had been the city of David. She was the capitol of Solomon's kingdom at the height of its glory. In her streets the Prophets had preached the messages that should have pointed her forward to this very day - when her Messiah would appear. In her temple the sacrifices had been offered which pointed her forward to the Lamb of God who would shed, not the blood of bulls and of goats, but His own precious blood for her sins. Her high priests offered her sacrifices here, but they died. One was to come Who would rule, not on the basis of a carnal commandment but by the power of an endless life (Heb.7:16). If any city on earth should have recognized in the Nazarene Carpenter, astride an unbroken colt, their Eternal King, it should have been Jerusalem. ἐν τῇ ἡμέρᾳ ταύτῃ - "on this day of all days." In bondage to Rome, Jerusalem had presented to her the King, Son of David, the only Jew Who held the throne rights to David's throne. He alone could have rescued her from Caesar. If Jesus is not the Jewish Messiah then Israel has no Messiah (*cf.*comment on Mt.1:1). Her peace depended upon her acceptance of Him, but this involved her repentance and her acceptance of all of His ethical interpretations of Moses' law. This she was unwilling to do. Unwilling to fulfill the divine requirements for peace, she could have no peace. So it is with all who cry, "Peace, Peace!" when there can be no peace (Numbers 6:26; Ps.4:8; 29:11; 85:8; 122:6; Isa.26:3; 32:17; 57:21; Rom.3:17; Jer.6:14; 18:11; Lk.1:79; 2:14; John 14:27; 16:33; Rom.5:1; Eph.4:19; Phil.4:7).

The popularity of Antichrist, when he comes, will rest in his promise of peace without any necessary commitment to righteousness (Rev.6:1-2). But Jerusalem could not perceive the things which were prerequisite to her peace. Jesus tells her why this is so. They have been hidden from her eyes (culminative aorist in ἐκρύβη) This is similar to a perfect construction. Robertson asks, "But was the aorist used *for* the perfect? Clyde says, "The aorist was largely used for the perfect." Winer replies, 'There is no passage in which it can be certainly proved that the aorist stands for the perfect." Gildersleeve more correctly says, "The aorist is very often used where we should expect the perfect," *i.e.* in English." (Robertson, *Grammar,* 843). Moulton finds the following resultant aorists in Matthew: Mt.9:18; 5:28; 14:15; 17:12; 6:12; 12:28; 14:2; 16:17; 18:15; 20:12;

26:10,13,25,64,65; 27:19; 28:7,18. Add Mt.12:26 says Robertson, who comments, "These all can be translated by the English 'have.' " (*Ibid.*, 842).

It was not God's plan that Israel should accept Jesus as Messiah at that time. Had she done so nationally, there would have been no cross, and thus no redemption or salvation for anyone, Jew or Gentile. But there was no reason why individuals in Jerusalem could not accept Jesus as Saviour. Many did. Most did not. Therefore Jesus now foretells the judgment which fell upon her with totally annihilative force forty years later in A.D.70.

Verse 43 - "For the days shall come upon thee, that thine enemies shall cast a trench about thee, and compass thee round, and keep thee in on every side."

ὅτι ἥξουσιν ἡμέραι ἐπὶ σὲ καὶ παρεμβαλοῦσιν οἱ ἐχθροί σου χάρακά σοι καὶ περικυκλώσουσίν σε καὶ συνέξουσίν σε πάντοθεν,

ὅτι (causal conjunction) 211.
ἥξουσιν (3d.per.pl.fut.act.ind.of ἥχω, predictive) 730.
ἡμέραι (nom.pl.fem.of ἡμέρα, subject of ἥξουσιν) 135.
ἐπὶ (preposition with the accusative of extent, metaphorical) 47.
σὲ (acc.sing.masc.of σύ, extent, metaphorical) 104.
καὶ (continuative conjunction) 14.

#2675 παρεμβαλοῦσιν (3d.per.pl.fut.act.ind.of παρεμβάλλω, predictive).

cast about - Luke 19:43.

Meaning: A combination of παρά (#154) and ἐμβάλλω (#2575). Hence to cast in and beside. From Polybius on, a term in military usage. To install a military emplacement - Luke 19:43.

οἱ (nom.pl.masc.of the article in agreement with ἐχθροί) 9.
ἐχθροί (nom.pl.masc.of ἐχθρός, subject of παρεμβαλοῦσιν) 543.
σου (gen.sing.masc.of σύ, relationship) 104.

#2676 χάρακά (acc.sing.masc.of χάραξ, direct object of παρεμβαλοῦσιν).

trench - Luke 19:43.

Meaning: a rampart or palisade. A series of posts driven into the ground between which earthworks are thrown up to provide an entanglement of earth, stones, tree, etc., such as an army would use in besieging a city - Luke 19:43.

σοι (loc.sing.masc.of σύ, place where, after παρά in composition) 104.
καὶ (adjunctive conjunction joining verbs) 14.

#2677 περικυκλώσουσίν (3d.per.pl.fut.act.ind.of περικυκλύω, predictive).

compass round - Luke 19:43.

Meaning: A combination of περί (#173) and κυκλόω (#2509). Hence, to encircle;

to surround with a circle - Luke 19:43.

σε (acc.sing.masc.of *σύ*, direct object of *περικυκλώσουσίν*) 104.
καὶ (adjunctive conjunction joining verbs) 14.
συνέξουσίν (3d.per.pl.fut.act.ind.of *συνέχω*, predictive) 414.
σε (acc.sing.masc.of *σύ*, direct object of *συνέξουσίν*) 104.
πάντοθεν (adverbial) 2073.

Translation - "Because the days will come upon you when your enemies will build a siege wall around you and they will encompass you and enclose you on every side,"

Comment: Thus Jesus predicts with total accuracy the siege of Titus and his Roman army in A.D.70. The language indicates massive military fortification and encirclement, similar to that prophesied in Isa.29:3. Some have argued for a late date for Luke - after A.D.70, so that he is accused of putting into Jesus' mouth words of prophecy, when in reality, they are the detailed description, written after the event. But Matthew also recorded similar prophecy by Jesus (Mt.24:1-2). Titus built a palisade, which was burned by the Jews and afterward replaced with a wall.

Verse 44 - "And shall lay thee even with the ground, and thy children with thee; and they shall not leave in thee one stone upon another; because thou knowest not the time of thy visitation."

καὶ ἐδαφιοῦσίν σε καὶ τὰ τέκνα σου ἐν σοί, καὶ οὐκ ἀφήσουσιν λίθον ἐπὶ λίθον ἐν σοί, ἀνθ' ὧν οὐκ ἔγνως τὸν καιρὸν τῆς ἐπισκοπῆς σου.

καὶ (adjunctive conjunction) 14.

#2678 *ἐδαφιοῦσίν* (3d.per.pl.fut.act.ind.of *ἐδαφίζω*, predictive).

lay even with the ground - Luke 19:44.

Meaning: Cf.ἔδαφος (#3578 in Acts 22:7). Hence, to flatten; to knock down; to level with the ground. In zeugmatic usage here, applying both to the buildings in the city and to its inhabitants - Luke 19:44.

σε (acc.sing.masc.of *σύ*, direct object of *ἐδαφιοῦσίν*) 104.
καὶ (adjunctive conjunction joining a pronoun with a noun) 14.
τὰ (acc.pl.neut.of the article in agreement with *τέκνα*) 9.
τέκνα (acc.pl.neut.of *τέκνον*, direct object of *ἐδαφιοῦσίν*) 229.
σου (gen.sing.masc.of *σύ*, relationship) 104.
ἐν (preposition with the instrumental of association) 80.
σοί (instru.sing.masc.of *σύ*, association) 104.
καὶ (adjunctive conjunction, joining verbs) 14.
οὐκ (summary negative conjunction with the indicative) 130.
ἀφήσουσιν (3d.per.pl.fut.act.ind.of *ἀφίημι*, predictive) 319.
λίθον (acc.sing.masc.of *λίθος*, direct object of *ἀφήσουσιν*) 290.
ἐπὶ (preposition with the accusative of extent, place) 47.

λίθον (acc.sing.masc.of λίθος, extent, place) 290.
ἐν (preposition with the locative of place where) 80.
σοί (loc.sing.masc.of σύ, place where) 104.
ἀνθ' (preposition with the genitive, cause) 237.
ὧν (gen.pl.masc.of ὅς, cause) 65.
οὐκ (summary negative conjunction with the indicative) 130.
ἔγνως (2d.per.sing.aor.act.ind.of γινώσκω, constative) 131.
τὸν (acc.sing.masc.of the article in agreement with καιρὸν) 9.
καιρὸν (acc.sing.masc.of καιρός, direct object of ἔγνως) 767.
τῆς (gen.sing.fem.of the article in agreement with ἐπισκοπῆς) 9.

#2679 **ἐπισκοπῆς** (gen.sing.fem.of ἐπισκοπή, description).

bishopric - Acts 1:20.
office of bishop - 1 Tim.3:1.
visitation - Luke 19:44; 1 Pet.2:12.

*Meaning: Cf.*ἐπισκοπέω (#5072) and ἐπίσκοπος (#3531). Visitation for the purpose of inspection and overseership. A function of superintendance that certain standards of faith and practise may be maintained. The office of one who exercises such superintendance - Acts 1:20; 1 Tim.3:1. The day of visitation - ἐν ἡμέρᾳ ἐπισκοπῆς (1 Pet.2:12), *i.e.* the time when God will visit the Gentiles with the gospel to win converts; the era or time of visitation - τὸ καιρὸν τῆς ἐπισκοπῆς (Luke 19:44), *i.e.* the period in the history of Jerusalem when Messiah visited them and offered them eternal salvation as well as earthly glory.

σου (gen.sing.masc.of σύ, possession) 104.

Translation - ". . . and they shall level you and your children with you to the ground, and they will not leave stone upon stone in you, because you did not know the time of your visitation."

Comment: Jesus continues to describe the tragic events of the coming Jewish war. The erection of the fortification, the encirclement of troops and the closing of the trap (verse 43) will be accomplished by wholesale destruction of life and property and the utter destruction of all of the buildings. The Romans brought to the ground both the buildings and the people. This is regarded by some as zeugma, but the verb ἐδαφίζω (#2678) can apply as well to a human being as to a building, though normally it means to raze a building. The destruction of the city was to be complete οὐκ ἀφήσουσιν λὶθον ἐπὶ οίθον ἐν σοί (*Cf.*Mt.24:1,2). *Cf.* #237 for ἀνθ ὧν meaning "because."

The purpose of Jesus' ministry was hidden from them (verse 42). The result will be (ὅτι, verse 43) the tragic events described, because (ἀνθ' ὧν, in verse 44) they did not recognize that Jesus came to earth to help Israel. Jesus' ministry of 33 years was the time of Israel's inspection. The Shepherd and Bishop of Souls (1 Pet.2:25) inspected Israel officially for three years and He did not like what He saw. Meanwhile they were unaware that they were being inspected. Hence, there was no remedy for them at the national level but judgment, though individual Jews were invited to accept Jesus, as many in fact did.

Jesus in the City and the Temple and Retirement to Bethany

(Matthew 21:10,11; Mark 11:11)

Mark 11:11 - "And Jesus entered into Jerusalem, and into the temple: and when He had looked round about upon all things, and now the eventide was come, he went out unto Bethany with the twelve.

Καὶ εἰσῆλθεν εἰς Ἰεροσόλυμα εἰς τὸ ἱερόν, καὶ περιβλεψάμενος πάντα, ὀψίας ἤδη οὔσης τῆς ὥρας, ἐξῆλθεν εἰς Βηθανίαν μετὰ τῶν δώδεκα.

Καὶ (continuative conjunction) 14.
εἰσῆλθεν (3d.per.sing.aor.mid.ind.of εἰσέρχομαι, constative) 234.
εἰς (preposition with the accusative of extent) 140.
Ἰεροσόλυμα (acc.sing.masc.of Ἰεροσολυμα, extent) 141.
εἰς (preposition with the accusative of extent) 140.
τὸ (acc.sing.neut.of the article in agreement with ἱερόν) 9.
ἱερόν (acc.sing.neut.of ἱερόν, extent) 346.
καὶ (adjunctive conjunction joining verbs) 14.
περιβλεψάμενος (aor.mid.part.nom.sing.masc.of περιβλέπομαι, adverbial, temporal) 2107.
πάντα (acc.pl.neut.of πᾶς, direct object of περιβλεψάμενος) 67.
ὀψίας (gen.sing.fem.of ὄψιος, description) 739.
ἤδη (temporal adverb) 291.
οὔσης (pres.part.gen.sing.fem.of εἰμί, genitive absolute) 86.
τῆς (nom.sing.fem.of the article in agreement with ὥρας) 9.
ὥρας (gen.sing.fem.of ὥρα, genitive absolute) 735.
ἐξῆλθεν (3d.per.sing.aor.mid.ind.of ἐξέρχομαι, constative) 161.
εἰς (preposition with the accusative of extent) 140.
Βηθανίαν (acc.sing.fem.of Βηθανία, extent) 1363.
μετὰ (preposition with the genitive of accompaniment) 50.
τῶν (gen.pl.masc.of the article in agreement with δώδεκα) 9.
δώδεκα (numeral, genitive of accompaniment) 820.

Translation - "And He entered Jerusalem and came into the temple. And after He had looked around at everything, since the hour was already late, He went out to Bethany with the Twelve."

Comment: The procession which began at Bethphage ended at the entrance of the temple. Jesus went in and looked around. It was a thorough inspection. He seemed to be in no hurry. One gets the impression that His presence there was in contempt of the police who had been ordered to arrest Him. Jesus gave them every opportunity. His hour, though but five days away, was not yet come. The genitive absolute ὀψίας ἤδη οὔσης τῆς ὥρας - "the hour of evening having already arrived" is causal. It was getting late. Jesus left the temple and returned to Bethany with the Twelve. It had been a big day. *Cf.*comment on Mt.21:10,11.

Thirty years before a company of Oriental philosophers had come to Jerusalem and asked, "Where is the King?" Their question had agitated the city (Mt.2:1-3). Now, four days before His arrest, another company comes into Jerusalem and says, "Here is the King!" Once again Jerusalem is shaken. Jesus was introduced as the King from Nazareth (Mt.21:10,11) - an incongruity, though, of course, He was born in Bethlehem and was thus qualified as Messiah. Jerusalem had been put to sleep, spiritually and intellectually as a result of which the truth was hidden from her. What a price she paid for her blindness! But, oh, how the plan of God was fulfilled!!

Monday, The Day of Authority. A Fig Tree Cursed

(Matthew 21:18,19; Mark 11:12-14)

Mark 11:12 - "And on the morrow, when they were come from Bethany, he was hungry."

Καὶ τῇ ἐπαύριον ἐξελθόντων αὐτῶν ἀπὸ Βηθανίας ἐπείνασεν.

Καὶ (continuative conjunction) 14.
τῇ (loc.sing.fem.of the article, time point) 9.
ἐπαύριον (adverbial) 1680.
ἐξελθόντων (aor.mid.part.gen.pl.masc.of ἐξέρχομαι, genitive absolute) 161.
αὐτῶν (gen.pl.masc.of αὐτός, genitive absolute) 16.
ἀπὸ (preposition with the ablative of separation) 70.
Βηθανίας (abl.sing.fem.of Βηθανία, separation) 1363.
ἐπείνασεν (3d.per.sing.aor.act.ind.of πεινάω, ingressive) 335.

Translation - "And the next day, after they had left Bethany, He became hungry."

Comment: ἐξελθόντων αὐτῶν, the genitive absolute is in the aorist tense, indicating that it was after Jesus and the Twelve had left Bethany and were returning to Jerusalem that He became hungry. ἐπείνασεν is ingressive.

Verse 13 - "And seeing a fig tree afar off having leaves, he came, if haply he might find anything thereon: and when he came to it, he found nothing but leaves: for the time of figs was not yet."

καὶ ἰδὼν συκῆν ἀπὸ μακρόθεν ἔχουσαν φύλλα ἦλθεν εἰ ἄρα τι εὑρήσει ἐν αὐτῇ, καὶ ἐλθὼν ἐπ' αὐτὴν οὐδὲν εὗρεν εἰ μὴ φύλλα, ὁ γὰρ καιρὸς οὐκ ἦν σύκων.

καὶ (continuative conjunction) 14.
ἰδὼν (aor.act.part.nom.sing.masc.of ὁράω, adverbial, temporal/causal) 144.
συκῆν (acc.sing.fem.of συκέα, direct object of ἰδὼν) 1366.
ἀπὸ (preposition with the adverb, separation) 70.
μακρόθεν (adverbial) 1600.
ἔχουσαν (pres.act.part.acc.sing.fem.of ἔχω, adverbial, circumstantial) 82.

φύλλα (acc.pl.neut.of φύλλον, direct object of ἔχουσαν) 1367.
ἦλθεν (3d.per.sing.aor.mid.ind.of ἔρχομαι, constative) 146.
εἰ (conditional particle in an elliptical condition, indirect question) 337.
ἄρα (illative particle in a first-class elliptical condition, indirect question) 995.
τι (acc.sing.neut.of τις, indefinite pronoun, direct object of εὑρήσει) 486.
εὑρήσει (3d.per.sing.fut.act.ind.of εὑρίσκω, indirect question) 79.
ἐν (preposition with the locative of place) 80.
αὐτῇ (loc.sing.fem.of αὐτός, place where) 16.
καὶ (adversative conjunction) 14.
ἐλθὼν (aor.part.nom.sing.masc.of ἔρχομαι, adverbial, temporal) 146.
ἐπ' (preposition with the accusative of extent) 47.
αὐτὴν (acc.sing.fem.of αὐτός, extent) 16.
οὐδὲν (acc.sing.neut.of οὐδείς, direct object of εὗρεν) 446.
εὗρεν (3d.per.sing.2d.aor.act.ind.of εὑρίσκω, constative) 79.
εἰ (conditional particle in an ellipticial second-class condition) 337.
μὴ (qualified negative particle in an elliptical second-class condition, with εἰ) 87.
φύλλα (acc.pl.neut.of φύλλον, direct object of εὗρεν) 1367.
ὁ (nom.sing.masc.of the article in agreement with καιρὸς) 9.
γὰρ (causal conjunction) 105.
καιρὸς (nom.sing.masc.of καιρός, subject of ἦν) 767.
οὐκ (summary negative conjunction with the indicative) 130.
ἦν (3d.per.sing.imp.ind.of εἰμί, progressive description) 86.
σύκων (gen.pl.neut.of σῦκον, description) 681.

Translation - "And when He saw a fig tree with leaves, some distance away, He came in the hope perhaps that He might find something on it, but when He arrived, He found nothing on it except leaves, because it was not the time for figs."

Comment: ἰδὼν is both temporal (antecedent) and causal. The circumstantial participle ἔχουσα tells us that the fig tree had leaves. Jesus saw it from a distance and varied His course enough to reach the tree. His purpose? εἰ ἄρα τι εὑρήσει ἐν αὐτῇ is an indirect question. There is doubt that the trip will be worth His time. ἄρα is an illative particle and there is also implicit doubt in the future εὑρήσει. Jesus seemed to be assuming that since the tree had leaves it also had figs. καὶ is adversative. But it did not. The second-class condition means that if Jesus had not found leaves on the tree He would not have found anything on it. Everything is contrary to fact. If He had not found leaves (but He did) He would not have found anything. Mark explains why. The fig season had not yet come. *Cf.* Mt.21:18,19.

Verse 14 - "And Jesus answered and said unto it, No man eat fruit of thee, hereafter forever. And his disciples heard it."

καὶ ἀποκριθεὶς εἶπεν αὐτῇ, Μηκέτι εἰς τὸν αἰῶνα ἐκ σοῦ μηδεὶς καρπὸν φάγοι. καὶ ἤκουον οἱ μαθηταὶ αὐτοῦ.

καὶ (continuative conjunction) 14.
ἀποκριθεὶς (aor.part.nom.sing.masc.of ἀποκρίνομαι, adverbial, modal) 318.
εἶπεν (3d.per.sing.aor.act.ind.of εἶπον, constative) 155.
αὐτῇ (dat.sing.fem.of αὐτός, indirect object of εἶπεν) 16.
Μηκέτι (negative temporal adverb) 1368.
εἰς (preposition with the accusative, time extent) 140.
τὸν (acc.sing.masc.of the article in agreement with αἰῶνα) 9.
αἰῶνα (acc.sing.masc.of αἰῶν, time extent) 1002.
ἐκ (preposition with the ablative of source) 19.
σοῦ (abl.sing.fem.of σύ, source) 104.
μηδεὶς (nom.sing.masc.of μηδείς, subject of φάγοι) 713.
καρπὸν (acc.sing.masc.of καρπός, direct object of φάγοι) 284.
φάγοι (3d.per.sing.2d.aor.act.opt.of ἐσθίω, voluntative) 610.
καὶ (continuative conjunction) 14.
ἤκουον (3d.per.pl.imp.act.ind.of ἀκούω, progressive description) 148.
οἱ (nom.pl.masc.of the article in agreement with μαθηταὶ) 9.
μαθηταὶ (nom.pl.masc.of μαθητής, subject of ἤκουον) 421.
αὐτοῦ (gen.sing.masc.of αὐτός, relationship) 16.

Translation - "And He responded to it by saying, 'May no man ever again throughout eternity eat fruit from you.' And His disciples were listening."

Comment: The negatives are present! μηκέτι, μηδείς and the optative mode in φάγοι - "never again. . . not one man . . . shall ever eat, κ.τ.λ." "The optative is the ordinary form of the verb used in the expression of a wish. This is the most extensive use in the New Testament." (Mantey, *Manual*, 173). *Cf.*2 Thess.3:5; Acts 8:20; 1 Pet.1:2 as other examples of the voluntative optative.

Matthew records that the tree died immediately. The reference to Israel as a nation is reasonably clear. The tree was not cursed for being barren, but for being false. Since it was not the time for figs, neither was it the time for leaves. Fig trees produce fruit before they produce leaves. This tree produced leaves before fruit. Hence it was hypocritical, like the House of Israel. There is danger, however, that we push μηκέτι, μηδείς and εἰς τὸν αἰῶνα too far. They apply to that particular fig tree which withered under Jesus' curse. But the nation Israel, which may be suggested by the fig tree, though cut down and driven to the ends of the earth in exile in the first century, is destined to grow again from the roots. John the Baptist had predicted that the tree would be cut down but that the roots would remain (Mt.3:10). The tree is burned, but not the roots. From those roots Israel will flourish again at the end of the age (Rom.11:15-27).

The amillenial position, that national Israel forfeited all future participation in the economy of God because she rejected her King, when He presented Himself, ignores the fact that God is under obligations to Abraham, Isaac, Jacob, Judah and David to set their Son, Jesus, on an eternal throne over the nations of earth (Gen.12:1-3; 2 Sam.7:10-15, *et al*). Who believed these promises? Abraham, Isaac, Jacob, Judah, David and millions of others who had been long since dead when this incident occurred. Who disbelieved, rejected and crucified their King? Only a very small minority of the seed of Abraham. Can the unconditional promise of God to men, long since dead, who along with millions of their descendants believed, be abrogated because of the unbelief of a few, on the day when the King appears? That particular generation of Israel (γενεά, #922, not γένος #1090) murdered the Son of God and went to hell. But the entire nation is not cast aside (Rom.11:1,2). To argue that any reference to Israel is to be interpreted symbolically to mean the Church and not the nation composed of the physical seed of Abraham, is the kind of eisegesis indulged in by those who are determined to make the Bible teach what they believe. The Bible cannot be made to teach what we believe. We must believe what the Bible teaches. The Bible teaches its lesson without regard to whether or not we believe it. We need not fear that the truths of the Word of God will be destroyed because we misunderstand and/or deny them. We should fear for all of us who get it wrong and must pay in terms of loss of reward at the judgment seat of Christ.

The disciples were listening to what Jesus told the fig tree, and thus they added one more conundrum to the long list already collected which they were to solve in the years following Pentecost and the inspiration of the New Testament literature.

Second Cleansing of the Temple

(Matthew 21:12,13; Mark 11:15-19; Luke 19:45-48)

Mark 11:15 - "And they came to Jerusalem: and Jesus went into the temple, and began to cast out them that sold and bought in the temple and overthrew the tables of the money changers, and the seats of them that sold doves."

Καὶ ἔρχονται εἰς Ἱεροσόλυμα. καὶ εἰσελθὼν εἰς τὸ ἱερὸν ἤρξατο ἐκβάλλειν τοὺς πωλοῦντας καὶ τοὺς ἀγοράζοντες ἐν τῷ ἱερῷ, καὶ τὰς τραπέζας τῶν κολλυβιστῶν καὶ τὰς καθέδρας τῶν πωλούντων τὰς περιστερὰς κατέστρεψεν,

Καὶ (continuative conjunction) 14.
ἔρχονται (3d.per.pl.pres.mid.ind.of ἔρχομαι, historical) 146.
εἰς (preposition with the accusative of extent) 140.
Ἱεροσόλυμα (acc.sing.masc.of Ἱεροσόλυμα, extent) 141.
καὶ (adjunctive conjunction joining verbs) 14.
εἰσελθὼν (aor.part.nom.sing.masc.of εἰσέρχομαι, adverbial, temporal) 234.
εἰς (preposition with the accusative of extent) 140.
τὸ (acc.sing.neut.of the article in agreement with ἱερὸν) 9.
ἱερὸν (acc.sing.neut.of ἱερόν, extent) 346.
ἤρξατο (3d.per.sing.aor.mid.ind.of ἄρχω) 383.
ἐκβάλλειν (pres.act.inf.of ἐκβάλλω, complementary) 649.
τοὺς (acc.pl.masc.of the article in agreement with πωλοῦντας) 9.
πωλοῦντας (pres.act.part.acc.pl.masc.of πωλέω, substantival, direct object of ἐκβάλλειν) 892.
καὶ (adjunctive conjunction joining participles) 14.
τοὺς (acc.pl.masc.of the article in agreement with ἀγοράζοντας) 9.

ἀγοράζοντας (pres.act.part.acc.pl.masc.of ἀγοράζω, substantival, direct object of ἐκβάλλειν) 1085.

ἐν (preposition with the locative of place) 80.

τῷ (loc.sing.neut.of the article in agreement with ἱερῷ) 9.

ἱερῷ (loc.sing.neut.of ἱερόν, place where) 346.

καὶ (adjunctive conjunction joining a participle with a noun) 14.

τὰς (acc.pl.fem.of the article in agreement with τραπέζας) 9.

τραπέζας (acc.pl.fem.of τράπεζα, direct object of κατέστρεφεν) 1176.

τῶν (gen.pl.masc.of the article in agreement with κολλυβιστῶν) 9.

κολλυβιστῶν (gen.pl.masc.of κολλυβιστής, possession) 1355.

καὶ (adjunctive conjunction joining verbs) 14.

τὰς (acc.pl.fem.of the article in agreement with καθέδρας) 9.

καθέδρας (acc.pl.fem.of καθέδρα, direct object of κατέστρεφεν) 1357.

τῶν (gen.pl.masc.of the article in agreement with πωλούντων) 9.

πωλούντων (pres.act.part.gen.pl.masc.of πωλέω, substantival, possession) 892.

τὰς (acc.pl.fem.of the article in agreement with περιστεράς) 9.

περιστερὰς (acc.pl.fem.of περιστερά, direct object of πωλούντων) 326.

κατέστρεφεν (3d.per.sing.aor.act.ind.of καταστρέφω, constative) 1356.

Translation - "And they came to Jerusalem. And when He had gone into the temple, He began to throw out the merchants and the customers in the temple, and He upset the tables of the money changers and the seats of those who were selling the doves."

Comment: Mark likes the historical present, but he is not consistent in its use. He uses it in ἔρχονται and then follows with the two aorists. The scene is one of chaos. Buyers and sellers flee from the temple. Tables, used as banks for the money changers and the seats of the dove salesmen are overturned while their owners flee with precipitation for the exists. Physical safety is at a premium. Doves fly about, liberated from their cages. Coins of all descriptions, including the official silver coin, are scattered about the floor, while little boys scurry to retrieve them. Jesus is in a rage of holy indignation. The country folk stand with open mouths. Some applaud our Lord's efforts and call their encouragement. The disciples are amused. Peter especially and James and John, the Sons of Thunder enjoy it. The temple officials mutter helplessly and shake their fists. *Cf.*#1355 for the reason for the presence of the money changers. *Cf.* comment on Mt.21:12 and Lk.19:45.

occasion Jesus had just returned from Capernaum for a short visit, immediately following His water-to-wine miracle in Cana of Galilee (John 2:11-13). There were no sheep or oxen in the second cleansing, nor any mention of a scourge of small cords. There was no challenge of Jesus' authority as in the first event.

Verse 16 - "And would not suffer that any man should carry any vessel through the temple."

καὶ οὐκ ἤφιεν ἵνα τις διενέγκῃ σκεῦος διὰ τοῦ ἱεροῦ.

καὶ (continuative conjunction) 14.
οὐκ (summary negative conjunction with the indicative) 130.
ἤφιεν (3d.per.sing.imp.act.ind.of ἀφίημι, progressive description) 319.
ἵνα (conjunction with the subjunctive, sub-final) 114.
τις (nom.sing.masc.of τις, the indefinite pronoun, subject of διενέγκῃ) 486.
διενέγκῃ (3d.per.sing.aor.act.subj.of διαφέρω, purpose/result) 620.
σκεῦος (acc.sing.neut.of σκεῦος, direct object of διενέγκῃ) 997.
διὰ (preposition with the genitive, through, physically) 118.
τοῦ (gen.sing.neut.of the article in agreement with ἱεροῦ) 9.
ἱεροῦ (gen.sing.neut.of ἱερόν, physically through) 346.

Translation - "And He would not permit anyone to carry a vessel through the temple."

Comment: Note that the word here is ἱερόν (#346) not ναός (#1447). The outer court of the building is in view here - not the Holy of Holies behind the Inner Veil. τὸ ἱερόν was called the Court of the Gentiles. Even it was considered sacred. The Rabbis considered it a sacrilege if anyone carried any common property, such as a pot or a pan or a piece of equipment through the temple court. Possibly in this case the equipment of the merchants and money changers was involved. This taboo extended even to the synagogues. The Rabbis had written, "What reverence is due to the temple? That no one go into the mountain of the house (the court of the Gentiles) with his staff, shoes, purse, or dust on his feet. Let no one make a crossing through it, or degrade it into a place of spitting." (Babyl. Jevamoth, in Lightfoot, *ad loc*, as cited in *The Expositors' Greek Testament*, I, 418).

Verse 17 - "And he taught, saying unto them, Is it not written, My house shall be called of all nations, the house of prayer? But ye have made it a den of thieves."

καὶ ἐδίδασκεν καὶ ἔλεγεν αὐτοῖς, Οὐ γέγραπται ὅτι Ὁ οἶκός μου οἶκος προσευχῆς κληθήσεται πᾶσιν τοῖς ἔθνεσιν; ὑμεῖς δὲ πεποιήκατε αὐτὸν σπήλαιον λῃστῶν.

καὶ (continuative conjunction) 14.
ἐδίδασκεν (3d.per.sing.aor.act.ind.of διδάσκω, ingressive) 403.
καὶ (adjunctive conjunction joining verbs) 14.
ἔλεγεν (3d.per.sing.imp.act.ind.of λέγω, inceptive) 66.
αὐτοῖς (dat.pl.masc.of αὐτός, indirect object of ἔλεγεν) 16.
Οὐ (summary negative conjunction with the indicative in rhetorical question, expecting an affirmative reply) 130.
γέγραπται (3d.per.sing.perf.pass.ind.of γράφω, rhetorical question) 156.
ὅτι (recitative) 211.
Ὁ (nom.sing.masc.of the article in agreement with οἶκός) 9.
οἶκός (nom.sing.masc.of οἶκος, subject of κληθήσεται) 784.
μου (gen.sing.masc.of ἐγώ, possession) 123.
οἶκος (nom.sing.masc.of οἶκος, appellation) 784.

προσευχῆς (gen.sing.fem.of προσευχή, description) 1238.
κληθήσεται (3d.per.sing.fut.pass.ind.of καλέω, predictive) 107.
πάσιν (dat.pl.masc.of πᾶς, in agreement with ἔθνεσιν) 67.
τοῖς (dat.pl.masc.of the article in agreement with ἔθνεσιν) 9.
ἔθνεσιν (dat.pl.masc.of ἔθνος, personal advantage) 376.
ὑμεῖς (nom.pl.masc.of σύ, subject of πεποιήκατε) 104.
δὲ (adversative conjunction) 11.
πεποιήκατε (2d.per.pl.perf.act.ind.of ποιέω, intensive) 127.
αὐτὸν (acc.sing.masc.of αὐτός, direct object of πεποιήκατε) 16.
σπήλαιον (acc.sing.neut.of σπήλαιον, double accusative) 1358.
λῃστῶν (gen.pl.masc.of λῃστής, description) 1359.

Translation - "And He began to teach them, saying, 'It is written is it not, 'My house will be called a house of prayer for all nations?' But you have turned it into a den of robbers.' "

Comment: *Cf.* comment on Mt.21:13 and Lk.19:46. The quotation ὁ . . . ἔθνεσιν is from Isa.56:7, while ὑμεῖς . . . λῃστῶν is from Jer.7:11. πᾶσιν τοῖς ἔθνεσιν can be taken as a dative of personal advantage, a locative of place where and an instrumental of agent. All of these ideas are true. In the Kingdom Age, following Messiah's return, Jerusalem and the rebuilt temple will be so considered, in, by and for the benefit of all of the nations of the earth (Micah 4:1-2). Jesus was reminding His audience that, despite His death in only four more days, the Kingdom prophecies will yet be fulfilled. Directly from Isaiah, Jesus pointed to the universal appeal of Messiah to all the Gentiles as well as the Jews and thus He destroyed the Pharisaic exclusivism of official Jewry. Why had Israel failed? The adversative clause with δὲ explains - "But you have already turned it into a robber's lair." Note that He emphasized ὑμεῖς, as no doubt He turned to glare at the Pharisees. Note also the perfect tense in πεποιήκατε - they had already accomplished this change from a house of prayer, in which all men of all nations could find their way to God, to an institution for the fleecing of all who came there. He did not say κλέπτης (#595) but λῃστής (#1359), *i.e.* those who rob openly. Jeremiah had complained about the same desecration and highway robbery in the name of religion in Jeremiah 7:11. Thus Jesus, who had observed the mess that the commercial interests had left in the court the night before (Mk.11:11) cleansed the temple and analyzed the reason why Israel, in a position to be a supreme blessing to all the world, had become a stench in the nostrils of God and a reproach, even in the eyes of the Gentiles.

Our Lord's revolutionary action and His stern denunciation of the practices which, under Pharisaic rule, had become commonplace, could have far reaching effects if He were not stopped. This the scribes and chief priests understood completely. Hence their increased efforts to destroy Him in

Verse 18 - "And the scribes and chief priests heard it, and sought how they might destroy him; for the feared him, because all the people were astonished at his doctrine."

καὶ ἤκουσαν οἱ ἀρχιερεῖς καὶ οἱ γραμματεῖς, καὶ ἐζήτουν πῶς αὐτὸν *ἀπολέσωσιν, ἐφοβοῦντο γὰρ αὐτόν, πᾶς γὰρ ὁ ὄχλος ἐξεπλήσσετο ἐπὶ τῇ διδαχῇ αὐτοῦ.*

καὶ (continuative conjunction) 14.
ἤκουσαν (3d.per.pl.aor.act.ind.of *ἀκούω*, constative) 148.
οἱ (nom.pl.masc.of the article in agreement with *ἀρχιερεῖς*) 9.
ἀρχιερεῖς (nom.pl.masc.of *ἀρχιερεύς*, subject of *ἤκουσαν* and *ἐζήτουν*) 151.
καὶ (adjunctive conjunction joining nouns) 14.
οἱ (nom.pl.masc.of the article in agreement with *γραμματεῖς*) 9.
γραμματεῖς (nom.pl.masc.of *γραμματεύς*, subject of *ἤκουσαν*, *ἐζήτουν* and *ἐφοβοῦντο*) 152.
καὶ (adjunctive conjunction joining verbs) 14.
ἐζήτουν (3d.per.pl.imp.act.ind.of *ζητέω*, progressive description) 207.
πῶς (interrogative conjunction introducing indirect question with the subjunctive) 627.
αὐτὸν (acc.sing.masc.of *αὐτός*, direct object of *ἀπολέσωσιν*) 16.
ἀπολέσωσιν (3d.per.pl.1st.aor.act.subj.of *ἀπόλλυμι*, deliberative subjunctive in indirect question) 208.
ἐφοβοῦντο (3d.per.pl.imp.ind.of *φοβέομαι*, progressive description) 101.
γὰρ (causal conjunction) 105.
αὐτόν (acc.sing.masc.of *αὐτός*, direct object of *ἐφοβοῦντο*) 16.
πᾶς (nom.sing.masc.of *πᾶς*, in agreement with *ὄχλος*) 67.
γὰρ (causal conjunction) 105.
ὁ (nom.sing.masc.of the article in agreement with *ὄχλος*) 9.
ὄχλος (nom.sing.masc.of *ὄχλος*, subject of *ἐξεπλήσσετο*) 418.
ἐξεπλήσσετο (3d.per.sing.imp.pass.ind.of *ἐκπλήσσομαι*, progressive description) 705.
ἐπὶ (preposition with the instrumental, means) 47.
τῇ (instru.sing.fem.of the article in agreement with *διδαχῇ*) 9.
διδαχῇ (instru.sing.fem.of *διδαχή*, means) 706.
αὐτοῦ (gen.sing.masc.of *αὐτός*, possession) 16.

Translation - "And the chief priests and the scribes heard and they were seeking how they might destroy Him, because they were afraid of Him, for all the people were astonished at His teaching."

Comment: *Cf.* comment on Mt.21:15,16; 22:33; Lk.19:47,48. This kind of teaching, *viz.* that universal blessings were destined to flow from Israel to the ends of the earth, following as it did Jesus' violence in dealing with the "robbers," had impacted upon the crowd in two ways: they saw the Temple Court and all that it had represented under the administration of the Establishment as a thing of exploitation and dictatorship and they had feelings of distrust, scorn and revulsion toward it. But when Jesus painted the picture of the Temple being the center from which God's blessings might flow to the entire world, the people were astonished and delighted. Here was a positive program for their national religious hope. The Establishment noted these attitudes among the people with hatred and consternation. Pause to appreciate the contrast between the scene now, on Monday, and the scene only 24 hours before. Then it was hurry scurry, rush, push, short, argue prices. As the country people tried to get ready for the Passover there was extortion and recriminations from the exploited subjects of the system. Helpless against the Establishment they could only submit with sullen rage or hopeless resignation. Now they gathered about Jesus and heard His castigation of the Establishment. With a skillful use of their Old Testament scriptures He told of a time when all nations would gather there for prayer. It is no wonder that *πᾶς ὁ ὄχλος ἐξεπλήσσετο ἐπὶ τῇ διδαχῇ αὐτοῦ* and that the little children went about shouting *Ὡσαννὰ τῷ υἱῷ Δαυίδ* (Mt.21:15). All of this added up in the minds of the chief priests and scribes to a Messianic *coup d'etat* which they lacked the police power to put down. *Cf.*#'s 208,101,705 and 706 for cross-indexed references that suggest much good sermon material. The *πῶς* clause has the deliberative subjunctive. The chief priests and scribes wanted to kill Jesus, but they had great doubts about how to go about it, in view of His great popularity with the people, whom the Establishment considered a mob. The attitude of the religious leaders on this occasion recalls Marie Antoinnette at Versailles, looking down from the balcony at a courtyard full of hungry Parisians who were asking for bread and saying, "Let them eat cake."

Verse 19 - "And when even was come He went out of the city."

Καὶ ὅταν ὀψὲ ἐγένετο, ἐξεπορεύοντο ἔξω τῆς πόλεωσ.

Καὶ (continuative conjunction) 14.
ὅταν (temporal conjunction with the indicative in a definite temoral clause) 436.
ὀψὲ (adverbial) 1687.
ἐγένετο (3d.per.sing.aor.ind.of *γίνομαι*, constative) 113.
ἐξεπορεύοντο (3d.per.pl.imp.mid.ind.of *ἐκπορεύομαι*, inceptive) 270.
ἔξω (adverbial) 449.
τῆς (abl.sing.fem.of the article in agreement with *πόεως*) 9.
πόλεως (abl.sing.fem.of *πόλις*, separation) 243.

Translation - "And when evening came, they started out of the city."

Comment: *Cf.*comment on Mt.21:17 and Lk.21:37. *ὅταν* suggests the subjunctive with its element of doubt, but *ἐγένετο* is aorist indicative. "When at last (as though it would never come) evening came, they left the city. There was no need to hurry out of town after He had driven the merchants out of the temple. Who was afraid of the police? Jesus remained in the temple area and its environs all day, preaching and teaching the people in full view of His enemies. He made no effort to hide or flee. When at last the day was over He and the Twelve went back to Bethany (Mt.21:17).

It was as though Jesus, in the manner of a military commander in the field, was making a series of lightning thrusts at the enemy. On Sunday there was the Triumph and then the withdrawal to Bethany. Now, on Monday, the cleansing of the temple area and the eloquent condemnation of Jewish graft and another casual withdrawal to Bethany. The Son of God is immortal - safe from arrest, torture and death until His hour has come, which is Friday. What will He do on Tuesday? We must examine first Luke's account of the temple cleansing in Luke 19:45-48.

Luke 19:45 - "And He went into the temple, and began to cast out them that sold therein, and them that bought."

Καὶ εἰσελθὼν εἰς τὸ ἱερὸν ἤρξατο ἐκβάλλειν τοὺς πωλοῦντας,

Καὶ (continuative conjunction) 14.
εἰσελθὼν (aor.part.nom.sing.masc.of εἰσέρχομαι, adverbial, temporal) 234.
εἰς (preposition with the accusative of extent) 140.
τὸ (acc.sing.neut.of the article in agreement with ἱερὸν) 9.
ἱερὸν (acc.sing.neut.of ἱερόν, extent) 346.
ἤρξατο (3d.per.sing.aor.mid.ind.of ἄρχω, ingressive) 383.
ἐκβάλλειν (pres.act.inf.of ἐκβάλλω, complementary) 649.
τοὺς (acc.pl.masc.of the article in agreement with πωλοῦντας) 9.
πωλοῦντας (pres.act.part.acc.pl.masc.of πωλέω, substantival, direct object of ἐκβάλλειν) 892.

Translation - "And when He had gone into the temple court He began to throw out those who were selling things."

Comment: *Cf.* Mt.21:12 and Mk.11:15. The best manuscript authority does not contain the phrase "and them that bought."

Verse 46 - ". . . saying unto them, It is written, My house is the house of prayer; but ye have made it a den of thieves."

λέγων αὐτοῖς, Γέγραπται, Καὶ ἔσται ὁ οἶκός μου οἶκος προσευχῆς, ὑμεῖς δὲ αὐτὸν ἐποιήσατε σπήλαιον λῃστῶν.

λέγων (pres.act.part.nom.sing.masc.of λέγω, adverbial, complementary) 66.
αὐτοῖς (dat.pl.masc.of αὐτός, indirect object of λέγων) 16.
Γέγραπται (3d.per.sing.perf.pass.ind.of γράφω, intensive) 156.
Καὶ (continuative conjunction) 14.
ἔσται (3d.per.sing.fut.ind.of εἰμί, predictive) 86.
ὁ (nom.sing.masc.of the article in agreement with οἶκός) 9.
οἶκός (nom.sing.masc.of οἶκος, subject of ἔσται) 784.
μου (gen.sing.masc.of ἐγώ, possession) 123.
οἶκος (nom.sing.masc.of οἶκος, predicate nominative) 784.
προσευχῆς (gen.sing.fem.of προσευχή, description) 1238.
ὑμεῖς (nom.pl.masc.of σύ,subject of ἐποιήσατε) 104.
δὲ (adversative conjunction) 11.
αὐτὸν (acc.sing.masc.of αὐτός, direct object of ἐποιήσατε) 16.

ἐποιήσατε (2d.per.pl.aor.act.ind.of ποιέω culminative) 127.
σπήλαιον (acc.sing.neut.of σπήλαιον, double accusative) 1358.
λῃστῶν (gen.pl.masc.of λῃστής, description) 1359.

Translation - ". . . as He said to them, 'It is written, And my house will be a house of prayer; but you have made it a den of robbers.' "

Comment: *Cf.* Mt.21:13; Mk.11:17. Note that Mark uses the intensive perfect πεποιήκατε, Matthew the durative present ποιεῖτε and Luke the culminative aorist ἐποιήσατε. All three constructions tell the same story - a present condition. Mark and Luke point to the fact that this commercial corruption of the temple had been going on for some time, a fact that Matthew does not deny.

Verse 47 - "And he taught daily in the temple. But the chief priests and the scribes and the chief of the people sought to destroy him."

Καὶ ἦν διδάσκων τὸ καθ' ἡμέραν ἐν τῷ ἱερῷ. οἱ δὲ ἀρχιερεῖς καὶ οἱ γραμματεῖς ἐζήτουν αὐτὸν ἀπολέσαι καὶ οἱ πρῶτοι τοῦ λαοῦ.

Καὶ (continuative conjunction) 14.
ἦν (3d.per.sing.imp.ind.of εἰμί, imperfect periphrastic) 86.
διδάσκων (pres.act.part.nom.sing.masc.of διδάσκω, imperfect periphrastic) 403.
τὸ (acc.sing.neut.of the article in agreement with ἡμέραν) 9.
καθ' (preposition with the adverbial accusative) 98.
ἡμέραν (acc.sing.fem.of ἡμέρα, adverbial accusative) 135.
ἐν (preposition with the locative of place) 80.
τῷ (loc.sing.neut.of the article in agreement with ἱερῷ) 9.
ἱερῷ (loc.sing.neut.of ἱερόν, place where) 346.
οἱ (nom.pl.masc.of the article in agreement with ἀρχιερεῖς) 9.
δὲ (adversative conjunction) 11.
ἀρχιερεῖς (nom.pl.masc.of ἀρχιερεύς, subject of ἐζήτουν) 151.
καὶ (adjunctive conjunction joining nouns) 14.
οἱ (nom.pl.masc.of the article in agreement with γραμματεῖς) 9.
γραμματεῖς (nom.pl.masc.of γραμματεύς, subject of ἐζήτουν) 152.
ἐζήτουν (3d.per.pl.imp.act.ind.of ζητέω, progressive description) 207.
αὐτὸν (acc.sing.masc.of αὐτός, direct object of ἀπολέσαι) 16.
ἀπολέσαι (aor.act.inf.of ἀπόλλυμι, complementary) 208.
καὶ (adjunctive conjunction joining substantives) 14.
οἱ (nom.pl.masc.of the article in agreement with πρῶτοι) 9.
πρῶτοι (nom.pl.masc.of πρῶτος, subject of ἐζήτουν) 487.
τοῦ (gen.sing.masc.of the article in agreement with λαοῦ) 9.
λαοῦ (gen.sing.masc.of λαός, description) 110.

Translation - "And He continued to teach day by day in the temple. But the chief priests, the scribes and the most influential people were trying to destroy Him."

Comment: *Cf.* Mt.21:15,16; Mk.11:18. In Luke we have an imperfect periphrastic - ἦν διδάσκων. It is decidedly durative. Jesus continued His teaching ministry in the temple day by day. καθ' with the accusative is an adverbial prepositional phrase. Jesus was there in the temple on Sunday, Monday and Tuesday of the last week, despite the fact that the Establishment, whom Luke identifies as οἱ ἀρχιερεῖς καὶ γραμματεῖς . . . καὶ οἱ πρῶτοι τοῦ λαοῦ - "the high priests, the scribes and the first among the people" - the religious, academic and political communities in Israel found no area of agreement with Jesus in their philosophy. The idea that an adversary relationship between those who do not agree can be stimulating and helpful if full and free dialogue is encouraged was, of course, foreign to the fanatics who were occupying the seats of power in Jerusalem. Fanatics have always believed that the only way to dispose of an adversary is to kill him. Thus the Jerusalem Establishment - thus Adolf Hitler - thus the Ku Klux Klan - thus Ayatollah Ruhollah Khomeini. There is a little bit of this psychology and philosophy in a small segment of American Fundamentalism. If the fanatic really loved and trusted the *truth* as much as he says he does, he would not fear a full and free discussion of error, since error carries within it the seeds of its own destruction and will destroy itself only when it is given complete freedom of expression. This is what Gamaliel tried to tell his colleagues in Acts 5:33-40. But Gamaliel was a "doctor of the law" and therefore more sophisticated than his intolerant colleagues.

The urge to kill Jesus was not lacking among those who were threatened by His presence. How to arrest, indict, try, convict and execute Him without arousing the people was their big problem.

Verse 48 - "And could not find what they might do: for all the people were very attentive to hear him."

καὶ οὐχ εὕρισκον τὸ τί ποιήσωσιν, ὁ λαὸς γὰρ ἅπας ἐξεκρέματο αὐτοῦ ἀκούων.

καὶ (adversative conjunction) 14.
οὐχ (summary negative conjunction with the indicative) 130.
εὕρισκον (3d.per.pl.imp.act.ind.of εὑρίσκω, progressive description) 79.
τὸ (acc.sing.neut.of the article to emphasize the indirect question) 9.
τί (acc.sing.neut.of τίς, the interrogative pronoun, direct object of ποιήσωσιν) 281.
ποιήσωσιν (3d.per.pl.aor.act.subj.of ποιέω, deliberative subjunctive) 127.
ὁ (nom.sing.masc.of the article in agreement with λαὸς) 9.
γὰρ (causal conjunction) 105.
ἅπας (nom.sing.masc.of ἅπας, in agreement with λαὸς) 639.

#2680 ἐξεκρέματο (3d.per.sing.imp.ind.of ἐκκρέμαμαι, progressive description).

be very attentive - Luke 19;48.

Meaning: A combination of ἐκ (#19) and κρεμάννυμι (#1249). Hence, to hang from, or upon. Followed by αὐτοῦ ἀκούων in Luke 19:48. To hang upon every word. To give rapt attention to what is being said - Luke 19:48

αὐτοῦ (gen.sing.masc.of αὐτός, description) 16.
ἀκούων (pres.act.part.nom.sing.masc.of ἀκούω, adverbial, instrumental) 148.

Translation - "But they could not decide what they should do because all the people were hanging on His words."

Comment: *Cf.* Mt.22:33; Mk.11:18. Luke does not mention the fear of the Establishment but he mentions their search for a way to arrest and kill Jesus without exciting the people who, at that point, were solidly behind Him. ἅπας (#639) - the intensive πᾶς. "All of the people by listening to Him (instrumental participle in ἀκούων) were paying rapt attention to what He said." Four days later most of the people had been brainwashed into a murderous mob. But this could happen only when His hour had come.

At this point the student should review Matthew 21:14-17 for a record of Jesus' miracles and His justification of the praise of Himself.

Tuesday. The Day of Conflict. The Fig Tree Withered and Jesus' Remarks Thereon

(Matthew 21:19-22; Mark 11:20-26)

Mark 11:20 - "And in the morning, as they passed by, they saw the fig tree dried up from the roots."

Καὶ παραπορευόμενοι πρωῒ εἶδον τὴν συκῆν ἐξηραμμένην ἐκ ῥιζῶν.

Καὶ (continuative conjunction) 14.
παραπορευόμενοι (pres.mid.part.nom.pl.masc.of παραπορεύομαι adverbial, temporal) 1649.
πρωῒ (temporal adverb) 1192.
εἶδον (3d.per.pl.aor.act.ind.of ὁράω, constative) 144.
τὴν (acc.sing.fem.of the article in agreement with συκῆν) 9.
συκῆν (acc.sing.fem.of συκέα, direct object of εἶδον) 1366.
ἐξηραμμένην (perf.pass.part.acc.sing.fem.of ξηραίνω, intensive, adjectival, ascriptive) 1033.
ἐκ (preposition with the ablative of source) 19.
ῥιζῶν (abl.pl.fem.of ῥίζα, source) 293.

Translation - "And as they passed by in the morning, they saw the fig tree withered from the roots."

Comment: *Cf.* Mt.21:18,20. It is Tuesday morning and they are on their way back to Jerusalem, where on Monday morning He had driven the merchants from the temple. It was on Monday morning that Jesus had cursed the fig tree.

Now, twenty four hours later, as they passed the spot they saw that the fig tree was dead, having been withered (perfect passive participle) from the roots upward. Note that the roots were not dead. *Cf.* our comments on Mark 11:14. *Cf.* Mt.13:6; Mk.4:6; Lk.8:6; John 15:6; Jam.1:11; 1 Pet.1:24 for references to the spiritual decline of believers and others. *Cf.*#293 for a study of *ῥίζα*, particularly as it relates to Israel.

Verse 21 - "And Peter calling to remembrance saith unto him, Master, behold the fig tree which thou cursedst in withered away."

καὶ ἀναμνησθεὶς ὁ Πέτρος λέγει αὐτῷ, Ῥαββί, ἴδε ἡ συκῆ ἣν κατηράσω ἐξήρανται.

καὶ (continuative conjunction) 14.

#2681 *ἀναμνησθεὶς* (aor.mid.part.nom.sing.masc.of *ἀναμιμνήσκω*, adverbial, causal).

bring into remembrance - 1 Cor.4:17.
call to mind - Mark 4:72.
call to remembrance - Heb.10:32.
put in remembrance - Mark 11:21; 2 Tim.1:6.
remember - 2 Cor.7:15.

Meaning: To call to remembrance; remind. Absolutely - Mark 11:21, where the context tells us what was recalled. Followed by the accusative of person or thing - Mark 14:72; 2 Tim.1:6. To consider; to weigh well what one already knows - 1 Cor.4:17; Heb.10:32; 2 Cor.7:15.

ὁ (nom.sing.masc.of the article in agreement with *Πέτρος*) 9.
Πέτρος (nom.sing.masc.of *Πέτρος*, subject of *λέγει*) 387.
λέγει (3d.per.sing.pres.act.ind.of *λέγω*, historical) 66.
αὐτῷ (dat.sing.masc.of *αὐτός*, indirect object of *λέγει*) 16.
Ῥαββί (voc.sing.masc.of *Ῥαββί*, address) 1443.
ἴδε (2d.per.sing.aor.act.impv.of *ὁράω*, entreaty) 144.
ἡ (nom.sing.fem.of the article in agreement with *συκῆ*) 9.
συκῆ (nom.sing.fem.of *συκῆ*, contraction of *συκέα*, subject of *ἐξήρανται*) 1366.
ἣν (acc.sing.fem.of *ὅς*, relative pronoun, direct object of *κατηράσω*) 65.
κατηράσω (2d.per.sing.1st.aor.ind.of *καταράομαι*, constative) 1550.
ἐξήρανται (3d.per.sing.perf.pass.ind.of *ξηραίνω*, intensive) 1033.

Translation - "And Peter, because he remembered, said to Him, 'Rabbi, look at the fig tree which you cursed. It has withered.' "

Comment: The participle *ἀναμνησθεὶς* is causal. The events of the morning before flashed across Peter's memory and he called Jesus' attention to the dead fig tree. *Cf.* Matthew 21:20 where we learn that the sudden death of the fig tree was the source of some surprize to the disciples - which sets the stage for Jesus' comments on prayer and faith in verses 22-25.

Verse 22 - "And Jesus answering saith unto them, Have faith in God."

καὶ ἀποκριθεὶς ὁ Ἰησοῦς λέγει αὐτοῖς, Ἔχετε πίστιν θεοῦ.

καὶ (continuative conjunction) 14.
αποκριθεὶς (aor.mid.part.nom.sing.masc.of *ἀποκρίνομαι*, adverbial, modal) 318.
ὁ (nom.sing.masc.of the article in agreement with Ἰησοῦς) 9.
Ἰησοῦς (nom.sing.masc.of Ἰησοῦς,subject of *λέγει*) 3.
αὐτοῖς (dat.pl.masc.of *αὐτός*, indirect object of *λέγει*) 16.
Εχετε (2d.per.pl.pres.act.impv.of *ἔχω*, command) 82.
πίστιν (acc.sing.fem.of *πίστις*, direct object of *ἔχετε*) 728.
θεοῦ (gen.sing.masc.of *θεός*, objective genitive) 124.

Translation - "And Jesus said to them in reply, 'Have faith in God.' "

Comment: Note that *θεοῦ* is without the article and that anarthrous nouns in the genitive may be construed as descriptive. If this be the construction the translation is "Have divine faith." But since God is the object of our faith, we can also construe it as an objective genitive, in which case the translation is as we have it above.

One of the prerequisites for the ability to exercise faith in God is the full assurance that we are completely obedient to God's will, even though such obedience may cost us our lives. Had Jesus been fleeing from Jerusalem the day before instead of moving with deliberation toward Calvary, He could not have called God's wrath down upon the fig tree with the assurance that God would hear and comply with His request. This is the key to the requirements for successful prayer in

Verse 23 - "For verily I say unto you, That whosoever shall say unto this mountain, Be thou removed and be thou cast into the sea, and shall not doubt in his heart, but shall believe that those things which he saith, shall come to pass, he shall have whatsoever he saith."

ἀμὴν λέγω ὑμῖν ὅτι ὃς ἂν εἴπῃ τῷ ὄρει τούτῳ,Ἄρθητι καὶ βλήθητι εἰς τὴν θάλασσαν, καὶ μὴ διακριθῇ ἐν τῇ καρδίᾳ αὐτοῦ ἀλλὰ πιστεύῃ ὅτι ὃ λαλεῖ γίνεται, ἔσται αὐτῷ.

ἀμὴν (explicative) 466.
λέγω (1st.per.sing.pres.act.ind.of *λέγω*, aoristic) 66.
ὑμῖν (dat.pl.masc.of *σύ*, indirect object of *λέγει*) 104.
ὅτι (conjunction introducing an object clause in indirect discourse) 211.
ὃς (nom.sing.masc.of the relative pronoun *ὅς*, in a more probable condition) 65.
ἂν (contingent particle in a more probable condition relative clause) 205.
εἴπῃ (3d.per.sing.aor.act.subj.of *εἶπον*, more probable condition relative clause) 155.
τῷ (dat.sing.neut.of the article in agreement with *ὄρει*) 9.

ὄρει (dat.sing.neut.of ὄρος, indirect object of εἴπῃ) 357.
τούτῳ (dat.sing.neut.of οὗτος, in agreement with ὄρει) 93.
Ἄρθητι (2d.per.sing.aor.pass.impv.of αἴρω, command) 350.
καὶ (adjunctive conjunction joining verbs) 14.
βλήθητι (2d.per.sing.aor.pass.impv.of βάλλω, command) 299.
εἰς (preposition with the accusative of extent) 140.
τὴν (acc.sing.fem.of the article in agreement with θάλασσαν) 9.
θάλασσαν (acc.sing.fem.of θάλασσα, extent) 374.
καὶ (adjunctive conunction joining relative clauses) 14.
μὴ (qualified negative conjunction with the subjunctive in a relative clause) 87.
διακριθῇ (3d.per.sing.aor.pass.subj.of διακρίνω, in a more probable condition relative clause) 1195.
ἐν (preposition with the instrumental of means) 80.
τῇ (instru.sing.fem.of the article in agreement with καρδίᾳ) 9.
καρδίᾳ (instru.sing.fem.of καρδία, means) 432.
αὐτοῦ (gen.sing.masc.of αὐτός, possession) 16.
ἀλλὰ (alternative conjunction) 342.
πιστεύῃ (3d.per.sing.pres.act.subj.of πιστεύω, more probable condition relative clause) 734.
ὅτι (conjunction introducing an object clause in indirect discourse) 211.
ὃ (nom.sing.neut.of ὅς, subject of γίνεται) 65.
λαλεῖ (3d.per.sing.pres.act.ind.of λαλέω, aoristic) 815.
γίνεται (3d.per.sing.pres.ind.of γίνομαι, aoristic) 113.
ἔσται (3d.per.sing.fut.ind.of εἰμί, predictive) 86.
αὐτῷ (dat.sing.masc.of αὐτός, personal advantage) 16.

Translation - "Truly I am telling you that whoever shall say to this mountain, 'Be picked up and thrown into the sea' and shall not be made to doubt in his heart, but shall believe that what he is saying will happen, it will happen for him."

Comment: Here we have a long and involved more probable condition relative clause. Jesus is describing one who (a) gives a preposterous command, (b) is not overcome with doubt, but (c) believes that his command will be obeyed. Such a prayer warrior, if he should ever be found can have anything he demands. Jesus indicates that we may never find an example. ὅς ἂν and the subjunctives εἴπῃ, μὴ διακριθῇ and πιστεύῃ. It is not statistically probable that we will ever encounter a Christian who meets all three of these requirements. First of all not many will wish to uproot the mountains and have them removed to the seas. How many, if he did issue such an order could do so without some doubt in his heart that it would be done, but could believe without a shred of doubt? But though we may never see the protasis fulfilled, if we did there is no doubt that we would see the result in the apodosis. ἔσται αὐτῷ is final and conclusion. "It will be for him." διακριθῇ and πιστεύῃ are the negative and positive sides of the same idea. If there is no doubt, then there is faith, and if there is faith that the asking is identified with the achieving, then the desired result is forthcoming. To what sort of requests does this promise extent? To everything and anything. This is the reason for the exaggeration. Even if one should wish to see a mountain uprooted and thrown into the sea (!) - even that, or anything else of equal improbability is covered by the promise, because with God nothing is impossible except that which is inconsistent with His own will and nature. God may or may not wish to do those things which are consistent with His nature, but He never wishes to do those things which violate His nature. For He is a moral God and He runs a moral universe. If something is not impossible, neither is it improbable if God, in His wisdom choses to do it. Which brings us down to the heart of the problem. What sort of request can a rational Christian make that generates no doubt in his mind, but rather faith that it will be done? Only a request coming from a heart that desires only the will of God for His life and who believes (a) that what he asks will enable him to do God's will, and (b) that what he asks is necessary before he can do God's will. To ask for the ability to disobey God's revealed will for his life is to generate inevitable doubt in the Christian's mind and thus short-circuits the promise. To ask for the ability to do God's will, but through extraordinary means, when the same results can be achieved in a more ordinary and less dramatic manner, also creates doubt in a rational mind and also short circuits the promise. If I feel that I must fly to San Francisco to preach the Word of God in order to do God's will, but do not have the money for the air fare, I can pray without doubt for the money and receive it. I could also pray that I might be given the supernatural power to fly to San Francisco without the airplane. This would be more dramatic and would not require the money, but it is not likely that such a prayer could be offered with much confidence. God could indeed answer the prayer either way. The latter request would create no greater problem for Him than the former, but God is not in the business of titillating the media. He would find it more sensible to give me the money so that I might go to the coast in a more conventional manner.

Suppose that a Christian young man in the university correctly assumes that God wants him to be a lawyer. Assume, however, that he wants to be a surgeon, despite what he feels to be God's will for his life. He lacks the money to continue his education. Could he pray for money to go to medical school, without a doubt in his mind, when he knows that if he got the money he would use it to pursue a pre-medical, not a pre-legal education? Now let us suppose that he repents and agrees to pursue a legal education, and prays for God to send him the money from an unknown source in a plain envelope. This indeed would be a miracle - like moving a mountain. Can he pray such a prayer without doubt? Certainly not. But he can pray for enough money to allow him to finish law school, because he knows that God wants him to be a lawyer. He will leave the method by which God will answer His prayer up to the higher intelligence at the throne of grace. This prayer he can pray without any doubt in his mind, since it facilitates his progress along the path that God has pointed out for his life. So he believes, and it is done in heaven (present tense in *γίνεται*) and will be done on earth (future tense in *ἔσται*). He may get a scholarship or a job in a service station or grocery store, or he may find it possible to arrange a low interest loan at the bank. God will work only to fulfill His will; never against it. And God will work through ordinary channels in most cases; in extraordinary channels only when there is no other way. The superficial student who scans this verse and fails to understand it, will misapply it and then conclude that Jesus lied to us! Preachers had better explain this principle to the saints very carefully.

Verse 24 - "Therefore I say unto you, What things soever ye desire, when ye pray, believe that you receive them, and ye shall have them."

διὰ τοῦτο λέγω ὑμῖν, πάντα ὅσα προσεύχεσθε καὶ αἰτεῖσθε, πιστεύετε ὅτι ἐλάβετε, καὶ ἔσται ὑμῖν.

διὰ (preposition with the accusative, cause) 118.
τοῦτο (acc.sing.neut.of οὗτος, cause) 93.
λέγω (1st.per.sing.pres.act.ind.of λέγω, aoristic) 66.
ὑμῖν (dat.pl.masc.of σύ, indirect object of λέγω) 104.
πάντα (acc.pl.neut.of πᾶς, direct object of ἐλάβετε) 67.
ὅσα (acc.pl.neut.of ὅσος, direct object of αἰτεῖσθε) 660.
προσεύχεσθε (2d.per.pl.pres.mid.ind.of προσεύχομαι) 544.
καὶ (adjunctive conjunction joining verbs) 14.
αἰτεῖσθε (2d.per.pl.pres.mid.ind.of αἰτέω) 537.
πιστεύετε (2d.per.pl.pres.act.impv.of πιστεύω, command) 734.
ὅτι (conjunction introducing an object clause) 211.
ἐλάβετε (2d.per.pl.aor.act.ind.of λαμβάνω, culminative) 533.
καὶ (continuative conjunction) 14.
ἔσται (3d.per.sing.fut.ind.of εἰμί, predictive) 86.
ὑμῖν (dat.pl.masc.of σύ, personal advantage) 104.

Translation - "It is because of this principle that I am telling you that all things, whatever they may be for which you pray and ask, believe that you have received them, and they will be yours."

Comment: The διὰ τοῦτο phrase refers to verse 23. On the basis of the principle expounded in verse 23 the promise of verse 24 is made. It is only a simplified restatement of the previous promise. Note the present tense in the imperative πιστεύετε. At the time that we pray and ask, we are to believe *then* (not before or after). What are we to believe? The ὅτι object clause follows - "that *we have already received them*" (this is the force of the culminative aorist in ἐλάβετε). The resultant aorist describes present possession as a result of a past reception. This is a construction similar to the intensive perfect tense. *Cf.* Luke 19:42 where we have ἐκρύβη. This use of the aorist is strongly in support of the doctrine of decrees. The prayer of faith, offered in fulfillment of the strict conditions laid down by Jesus in verses 23-24, only ratifies on earth what God has already done in heaven. The protasis in the conditional clause is missing and the imperative πιστεύετε ὅτι ἐλάβετε is substituted in its place. Thus we have an implied conditional clause. We would get the same idea if Mark had said ἐὰν πιστεύητε ὅτι ἐλάβετε . . . ἔσται ὑμῖν. *Cf.* other implied conditions in Mk.1:7; Mt.7:7; 11:28; 19:21; Lk.7:7; John 2:19; 14:16; James 4:7.

Verse 25 - "And when ye stand praying, forgive, if ye have ought against any: that your Father also which is in heaven may forgive you your trespasses."

καὶ ὅταν στήκετε προσευχόμενοι, ἀφίετε εἴ τι ἔχετε κατά τινος, ἵνα καὶ ὁ πατὴρ ὑμῶν ὁ ἐν τοῖς οὐρανοῖς ἀφῇ ὑμῖν τὰ παραπτώματα ὑμῶν.

καὶ (continuative conjunction) 14.
ὅταν (temporal conjunction in a temporal clause) 436.
στήκετε (2d.per.pl.pres.act.ind.of στήκω, definite temporal clause) 1957.
προσευχόμενοι (pres.mid.part.nom.pl.masc.of προσεύχομαι, adverbial, telic) 544.
ἀφίετε (2d.per.pl.pres.act.impv.of ἀφίημι, command) 319.
εἴ (conditional particle in a first-class condition) 337.
τι (acc.sing.neut.of τις, indefinite pronoun, direct object of ἔχετε) 486.
ἔχετε (2d.per.pl.pres.act.ind.of ἔχω, first-class condition) 82.
κατὰ (preposition with the genitive, opposition) 98.
τινος (gen.sing.masc.of τις, indefinite pronoun, opposition) 486.
ἵνα (conjunction with the subjunctive, purpose clause) 114.
καὶ (adjunctive conjunction joining a pronoun and a noun) 14.
ὁ (nom.sing.masc.of the article in agreement with πατὴρ) 9.
πατὴρ (nom.sing.masc.of πατήρ, subject of ἀφῇ) 238.
ὑμῶν (gen.pl.masc.of σύ, relationship) 104.
ὁ (nom.sing.masc.of the article, introducing a prepositional phrase) 9.
ἐν (preposition with the locative of place) 80.
τοῖς (loc.pl.masc.of the article in agreement with οὐρανοῖς) 9.
οὐρανοῖς (loc.pl.masc.of οὐρανός, place where) 254.
ἀφῇ (3d.per.sing.aor.act.subj.of ἀφίημι, purpose clause) 319.
ὑμῖν (dat.pl.masc.of σύ, personal advantage) 104.
τὰ (acc.pl.neut.of the article in agreement with παραπτώματα) 9.
παραπτώματα (acc.pl.neut.of παράπτωμα, direct object of ἀφῇ) 585.
ὑμῶν (gen.pl.masc.of σύ, possession) 104.

Translation - "And when you stand in order to pray, if you have anything against anyone, forgive him, in order that your Father, the one in the heavens, may also forgive your trespasses."

Comment: ὅταν with the indicative seems a little strange as we normally see it with the subjunctive, since it is a combination of ὅτε and ἄν, the particle of contingency. ". . . a number of examples occur of ὅταν with the indicative. (cf. ἐάν and ὅπου ἄν with the indicative). . . A good many manuscripts likewise have ὅταν with the future indicative in Mt.10:19 and 1 Tim.5:11. Cf. ὅταν ἔσται in Clem., *Cor.* 2,12, 1. Moulton (*Prol.*, p.168) notes in the papyri only a small number of examples of ἄν with temporal clauses and the indicative." (Robertson, *Grammar*, 972). Jesus seems to imply some doubt (ὅταν) that we would ever stand to pray, but not enough doubt to warrant the subjunctive στήκητε. When we pray we are to be in a mood of forgiveness. He expressed no doubt that when we stand to pray we will have been offended by others. *εἴ τι ἔχετε κατά τινος*, is the protasis of a first-class condition. Few Christians, even praying Christians, do not harbor in their hearts the thoughts of injustice real or imagined, perpetrated upon them by other people. Thus we have another condition attached to the formula for victorious prayer. For he who does not forgive cannot know the will of God for his life. Refusal to forgive others involves judgment upon others, and this is strictly forbidden (Mt.7:1-5; John 5:22). The Christian who refuses to forgive others arrogates to himself the right to judge. Thus he preempts the position of His resurrected Lord. Such a saint is blind to his own faults and thus his prayers are short-circuited (1 Pet.3:7; Ps.66:18).

Verse 26 in the AV is not found in the most ancient manuscripts and is therefore not included in the text of the United Bible Societies' text. "Although it might be thought that the sentence was accidentally omitted because of homoeoteleuton, its absence from early witnesses that represent all text-types makes it highly probable that the words were inserted by copyists in imitation of Mt.6:15. (Metzger,*A Textual Commentary on the Greek New Testament*, 110).

Controversy With the Priests, Scribes and Elders About His Authority

(Matthew 21:23-22:14; Mark 11:27-12:12; Luke 20:1-19)

Mark 11:27 - "And they come again to Jerusalem: and as he was walking in the temple, there come to Him the chief priests, and the scribes and the elders."

Καὶ ἔρχονται πάλιν εἰς Ἱεροσόλυμα. καὶ ἐν τῷ ἱερῷ περιπατοῦντος αὐτοῦ ἔρχονται πρὸς αὐτὸν οἱ ἀρχιερεῖς καὶ οἱ γραμματεῖς καὶ οἱ πρεσβύτεροι

Καὶ (continuative conjunction) 14.
ἔρχονται (3d.per.pl.pres.mid.ind.of ἔρχομαι, historical) 146.
πάλιν (adverbial) 355
εἰς (preposition with the accusative of extent) 140.
Ἱεροσόλυμα, (acc.sing.masc.of Ἱεροσόλυμα, extent) 141.
καὶ (continuative conjunction) 14.
ἐν (preposition with the locative of place) 80.
τῷ (loc.sing.neut.of the article in agreement with ἱερῷ) 9.
ἱερῷ (loc.sing.neut.of ἱερόν, place where) 346.
περιπατοῦντος (pres.act.part.gen.sing.masc.of περιπατέω, genitive absolute) 384.
αὐτοῦ (gen.sing.masc.of αὐτός, genitive absolute) 16.
ἔρχονται (3d.per.pl.pres.mid.ind.of ἔρχομαι, historical) 146.
πρὸς (preposition with the accusative of extent) 197.
αὐτὸν (acc.sing.masc.of αὐτός, extent) 16.
οἱ (nom.pl.masc.of the article in agreement with ἀρχιερεῖς) 9.

ἀρχιερεῖς (nom.pl.masc.of ἀρχιερεύς, subject of ἔρχονται) 151.
καὶ (adjunctive conjunction joining nouns) 14.
οἱ (nom.pl.masc.of the article in agreement with γραμματεῖς) 9.
γραμματεῖς (nom.pl.masc.of γραμματεύς, subject of ἔρχονται) 152.
καὶ (adjunctive conjunction joining nouns) 14.
οἱ (nom.pl.masc.of the article in agreement with πρεσβύτεροι) 9.
πρεσβύτεροι (nom.pl.masc.of πρεσβύτερος, subject of ἔρχονται) 1141.

Translation - "And they came again into Jerusalem, and as He was walking around in the temple the high priests, the scribes and the elders came to Him,"

Comment: The historical present again as is so common in Mark, in ἔρχονται (both places). Once again Jesus demonstrated His contempt for the police power of the Establishment who had been plotting to kill Him since the day He raised Lazarus from the dead. He was there in the temple on Sunday evening, following the Triumphal parade, surveying the scene after a busy day by the commercial interests as they exploited the pilgrims (Mk.11:11). He came again on Monday and drove the merchants and bankers from the temple (Mk.11:12-19). Now, on Tuesday, He is back in the temple court, in plain sight of all the people, including His detractors. The genitive absolute is in the present tense, indicating time simultaneous with the main verb ἔρχονται. It was while Jesus was strolling about ἐν τῷ ἱερῷ - "in the temple" that His enemies approached Him. Jesus was not out in the suburbs, slinking about,hiding behind trees and staying out of sight, but He in the Temple Court, as though daring the police to interfere.

Verse 28 - "And say unto him, By what authority doest thou these things? And who gave thee this authority to do these things?"

καὶ ἔλεγον αὐτῷ, Ἐν ποίᾳ ἐξουσίᾳ ταῦτα ποιεῖς; ἢ τίς σοι ἔδωκεν τὴν ἐξουσίαν ταύτην ἵνα ταῦτα ποιῇς;

καὶ (adjunctive conjunction joining verbs) 14.
ἔλεγον (3d.per.pl.imp.act.ind.of λέγω, inceptive) 66.
αὐτῷ (dat.sing.masc.of αὐτός, indirect object of ἔλεγον) 16.
Ἐν (preposition with the instrumental of cause) 80.
ποίᾳ (instru.sing.fem.of ποῖος, in agreement with ἐξουσίᾳ) 1298.
ἐξουσίᾳ (instru.sing.fem.of ἐξουσία, cause) 707.
ταῦτα (acc.pl.neut.of οὗτος, direct object of ποιεῖς) 93.
ποιεῖς (2d.per.sing.pres.act.ind.of ποιέω, static) 127.
ἢ (disjunctive particle) 465.
τίς (nom.sing.masc.of τίς, the interrogative pronoun, subject of ἔδωκεν) 281.
σοι (dat.sing.masc.of σύ, indirect object of ἔδωκεν) 104.
ἔδωκεν (3d.per.sing.aor.act.ind.of δίδωμι, constative) 362.
τὴν (acc.sing.fem.of the article in agreement with ἐξουσίαν) 9.
ἐξουσίαν (acc.sing.fem.of ἐξουσία, direct object of ἔδωκεν) 707.
ταύτην (acc.sing.fem.of οὗτος, in agreement with ἐξουσίαν) 93.
ἵνα (conjunction with the subjunctive in a sub-final clause) 114.

ταῦτα (acc.pl.neut.of οὗτος, direct object of ποιῇς) 93.
ποιῇς (2d.per.sing.pres.act.subj.of ποιέω, purpose/result) 127.

Translation - "And they began to say to Him, 'By what authority are you doing these things?' or 'Who gave you this authority so that you are doing these things?' "

Comment: The self-appointed leaders of the temple are insistent as they begin and continue to demand that Jesus show His credentials. Some asked the question in one way and the others in another. "By what authority and who gave it to you?" Since the Establishment always thought that what they thought and did was moral, they were asking by what moral as well as legal right Jesus had to drive them from the temple. The idea that their legal right might not have a moral base was not in their thinking. *Cf.*#707 for other uses of the word in this sense. The final clause is sub-final, expressing both purpose and result. Whoever gave to Jesus the authority to cleanse the temple did so, both for the purpose (final) and with the result (consecutive) that He cleansed it. God's purpose is always consistent with the result (Eph.1:11). To deny this is to say that God is not big enough to do all that He would like to do, which leaves us with a God no better than those who inhabited the Pantheon in pagan Rome.

Forty-five days later Jesus was to give an answer to the question asked now by the temple officials (Mt.28:18). How much authority is *πᾶσα ἐξουσία ἐν οὐρανῷ καὶ ἐπὶ τῆς γῆς*!? For this group of religious bigots, who had no authority at all to ask the Sovereign of the Universe, the Incarnate Messiah and Son of God this impertinent question, the answer was never to be submitted except as, by faith, they accepted the testimony of those who saw Him after He arose from the dead and later wrote it down in the New Testament.

But they had a subtle motive. Jesus was not yet risen from the dead, and hence not yet *officially* ratified as the One to Whom all authority in heaven and upon earth had been given. He could not yet, therefore, give a categorical reply to their question without appearing presumptuous. On the other hand, if He said that He had no authority, He would have been admitting that He was a disturber of the public peace.

We have here another evidence that this incident is not the same as the one recorded in John 2:13-21, where He gave them an answer that became clear to Christian believers, after the fact, but was *at that time* equivocal. Now Jesus shows that He too can play the game of asking difficult questions.

Verse 29 - "And Jesus answered and said unto them, I will also ask of you one question, and answer me, and I will tell you by what authority I do these things."

ὁ δὲ Ἰησοῦς εἶπεν αὐτοῖς, Ἐπερωτήσω ὑμᾶς ἕνα λόγον, καὶ ἀποκρίθητέ μοι, καὶ ἐρῶ ὑμῖν ἐν ποίᾳ ἐξουσίᾳ ταῦτα ποιῶ.

ὁ (nom.sing.masc.of the article in agreement with Ἰησοῦς) 9.
δὲ (adversative conjunction) 11.
Ἰησοῦς (nom.sing.masc.of Ἰησοῦς, subject of εἶπεν) 3.

εἶπεν (3d.per.sing.aor.act.ind.of *εἶπον*, constative) 155.
αὐτοῖς (dat.pl.masc.of *αὐτός*, indirect object of *εἶπεν*) 16.
'Επερωτήσω (1st.per.sing.fut.act.ind.of *ἐπερωτάω*, predictive) 973.
ὑμῖν (dat.pl.masc.of *σύ*, indirect object of *ἐρῶ*) 104.
ἕν (acc.sing.masc.of *εἷς*, in agreement with *λόγον*) 469.
λόγον (acc.sing.masc.of *λόγος*, direct object of *ἐπερωτήσω*, double accusative) 510.
καὶ (continuative conjunction) 14.
ἀποκρίθητέ (2d.per.pl.1st.aor.mid.impv.of *ἀποκρίνομαι*, command) 318.
μοι (dat.sing.masc.of *ἐγώ*, indirect object of *ἀποκρίητέ*) 123.
καὶ (continuative conjunction) 14.
ἐρῶ (1st.per.sing.fut.act.ind.of *εἶπον*, predictive) 155.
ὑμῖν (dat.pl.masc.of *σύ*, indirect object of *ἐρῶ*) 104.
ἐν (preposition with the instrumental of cause) 80.
ποίᾳ (instru.sing.fem.of *ποῖος*, in agreement with *ἐξουσίᾳ*) 1298.
ἐξουσίᾳ (instru.sing.fem.of *ἐξουσία*, cause) 707.
ταῦτα (acc.pl.neut.of *οὗτος*, direct object of *ποιῶ*) 93.
ποιῶ (1st.per.sing.pres.act.ind.of *ποιέω*, customary) 127.

Translation - "But Jesus said to them, 'I will ask you for a statement, and you must reply to me. Then I will tell you by what authority I am doing these things."

Comment: *Cf.* Mt.21:24; Lk.20:3. Mark's greek is far more *κοινή* than Matthew's. Luke short-cuts the repartee. Jesus confronted His enemies with a fair proposition. Note that the object of *'Επερωτήσω* is *λόγον*. "I will ask you to make a one statement." That is what they had demanded of Him. They wanted to trap Him into making a categorical statement about His authority that they could cash against Him, regardless of what His statement might be. They did not expect Him to demand that they also make a categorical statement which He could use against them. Jesus challenged them to reply to His question and then promised that, if they did, He would also make His statement. Jesus was proving to them that two could play this game of extracting incriminating statements. His question, which follows in verse 30, was as embarrasing to them as their question was to Him. Indeed it was more embarrassing, as we shall see.

Verse 30 - "The baptism of John, was it from heaven, or of men? Answer me."

τὸ βάπτισμα τὸ 'Ιωάννου ἐξ οὐρανοῦ ἦν ἢ ἐξ ἀνθρώπων; ἀποκρίητέ μοι.

τὸ (nom.sing.neut.of the article in agreement with *βάπτισμα*) 9.
βάπτισμα (nom.sing.neut.of *βάπτισμα*, subject of *ἦν*) 278.
τὸ (nom.sing.neut.of the article in agreement with *βάπτισμα*) 9.
'Ιωάννου (gen.sing.masc.of *'Ιωάννης*, description) 247.
ἐξ (preposition with the ablative of source) 19.
οὐρανοῦ (abl.sing.masc.of *οὐρανός*, source) 254.
ἦν (3d.per.sing.imp.ind.of *εἰμί*, progressive description) 86.
ἢ (disjunctive particle) 465.

ἐξ (preposition with the ablative of source) 19.
ἀνθρώπων (abl.pl.masc.of ἄνθρωπος, source) 341.
ἀποκρίθητέ (2d.per.pl.aor.mid.impv.of ἀποκρίνομαι, command) 318.
μοι (dat.sing.masc.of ἐγώ, indirect object of ἀποκρίθητέ) 123.

Translation - "The baptism of John - was it of heaven or of men? Answer me!"

Comment: Jesus emphasized the subject τὸ βάπτισμα τὸ Ἰωάννου ahead of the verb - a fact which is reflected in our translation. It was as though Jesus was eager to bring to their attention as quickly as possible this embarrassing issue that had plagued them for the past three years. A smoother translation, as Goodspeed has it, is "Was John's baptism from heaven or from men?" This is faithful to the Greek text, but it fails to bring to the English student the emphasis that Jesus placed upon the subject. He was laboring a sore point. Often they had been impaled upon the sharp horns of this dillema. Their problem was that (a) they had rejected the baptism of John and ignored his message, and (b) that John the Baptist was held in high regard by the common people in Israel, as the prophet of God. If John was God's prophet,then his message was true. What was his message? That Jesus was the Messiah. Did the Messiah have authority over the temple and over everything else in Israel? No one dared deny that. Then if John was God's prophet, Jesus was the Messiah, and the Establishment had the answer to their question about His authority to cleanse the temple. But the Establishment denied that Jesus had such authority, which, as we reason backward, means that they rejected John's message and his baptism. This, in fact,they had done, but why did they not say so openly? Because it was impolitic to do so, since such a statement would be the cause for a revolution in Israel, since the common people regarded John as a prophet of God. Thus we see that the high priests, scribes and elders, like all politicians, were more interested in their tenure in office than they were in the truth.

They had not only rejected John's message, but they had acquiesced in his murder, if not secretly applauding it. They had been stung to the quick by John's castigation of them and their hypocrisy and had declined his challenge to prove their repentance by changing their lifestyle (Mt.3:7,8). He had demanded confession of sin, repentance and conversion as prerequisite to his baptism; he had called Israel's leaders "snakes" and he had predicted the nation's decline and fall, in language that anticipated Jesus' curse upon the fig tree (Mt.3:1-12). Yet they had rejected him. Thus we have the dilemma which Jesus presented to them. They were not stupid - only perverse, as we see in

Verse 31 - "And they reasoned with themselves, saying, If we shall say, From heaven, he will say, Why then did ye not believe him?"

καὶ διελογίζοντο πρὸς ἑαυτοὺς λέγοντες, Ἐὰν εἴπωμεν, Ἐξ οὐρανοῦ, ἐρεῖ, Διὰ τί (οὖν) οὐκ ἐπιστεύσατε αὐτῷ;

καὶ (continuative conjunction) 14.
διελογίζοντο (3d.per.pl.imp.mid.ind.of διαλογίζομαι, inceptive) 1197.

πρὸς (preposition with the accusative of extent, after a verb of speaking) 197.
ἑαυτοὺς (acc.pl.masc.of ἑαυτός, extent after a verb of speaking) 288.
λέγοντες (pres.act.part.nom.pl.masc.of λέγω, recitative) 66.
Ἐὰν (conditional particle in a third-class condition) 363.
εἴπωμεν (1st.per.pl.aor.act.subj.of εἶπον, third-class condition) 155.
Ἐξ (preposition with the ablative of source) 19.
οὐρανοῦ (abl.sing.masc.of οὐρανός, source) 254.
ἐρεῖ (3d.per.sing.fut.act.ind.of εἶπον, predictive) 155.
Διὰ (preposition with the accusative of cause) 118.
τί (acc.sing.neut.of τίς, the interrogative pronoun, cause) 281.
οὖν (inferential conjunction) 68.
οὐκ (summary negative conjunction with the indicative) 140.
ἐπιστεύσατε (2d.per.pl.aor.act.ind.of πιστεύω, constative) 734.
αὐτῷ (dat.sing.masc.of αὐτός, reference) 16.

Translation - "And they began to reason among themselves, saying, 'If we should say, From heaven, He will say, Why, then did you not believe Him?' "

Comment: The argument among the scholars was a thorough one. *Cf.*#1197 for its basic meaning, and note that it is in the imperfect tense. They began a discussion that continued for some time. Note that Mark uses πρὸς ἑαυτοὺς while Matthews says it with ἐν ἑαυτοῖς. They discussed it together (Matthew) by throwing arguments back and forth at each other (Mark). Both ideas are true. It is another example of unity of thought and diversity of personal expression. Thus the Holy Spirit gave us a verbally inspired record without robbing fallible men of their individuality. ἐὰν . . . αὐτῷ - a third-class condition with the subjunctive of doubt in the protasis and some certainty in the prediction of the future indicative in the apodosis. "If we should say (and therefore we are not going to say it) From heaven, He will say. . . (what we do not want Him to say). ἐξ οὐρανοῦ - John's message had heaven as its source. διὰ τί οὖν - "on account of what (why?) therefore . . . κ.τ.λ." These scholars wanted the reputation that they were in such complete touch with heaven that anyone who came with a message from heaven would certainly and readily be believed and received with open arms. Yet they had rejected John the Baptist and his message and they were plotting to kill the One who John said was the Messiah. Therefore if they were going to be logical they should say to Jesus, 'John the Baptist was a false prophet with no heavenly authority." But this reply also carried with it its dangers.

Verse 32 - "But if we shall say, of men; they feared the people; for all men counted John, that he was a prophet indeed."

ἀλλὰ εἴπωμεν,'Εξ ἀνθρώπων; — ἐφοβοῦντο τὸν ὄχλον, ἅπαντες γὰρ εἶχον τὸν Ἰωάννην ὄντως ὅτι προφήτης ἦν.

ἀλλὰ (alternative conjunction) 342.
εἴπωμεν (1st.per.pl.aor.act.subj.of εἶπον, third-class condition) 155.

Ἐξ (preposition with the ablative of source) 19.

ἀνθρώπων (abl.pl.masc.of ἄνθρωπος, source) 341.
ἐφοβοῦντο (3d.per.pl.imp.mid.ind.of φοβέομαι, progressive description) 101.
τὸν (acc.sing.masc.of the article in agreement with ὄχλον) 9.
ὄχλον (acc.sing.masc.of ὄχλος, direct object of ἐφοβοῦντο) 418.
ἅπαντες (nom.pl.masc.of ἅπας, subject of εἶχον) 639.
γὰρ (causal conjunction) 105.
εἶχον (3d.per.pl.imp.act.ind.of ἔχω, progressive description) 82.
τὸν (acc.sing.masc.of the article in agreement with Ἰωάννην) 9.
Ἰωάννην (acc.sing.masc.of Ἰωάννης, direct object of εἶχον) 247.
ὄντως (adverbial) 2486.
ὅτι (conjunction introducing an object clause in indirect discourse) 211.
προφήτης (nom.sing.masc.of προφήτης, predicate nominative) 119.
ἦν (3d.per.sing.imp.ind.of εἰμί, indirect discourse) 86.

Translation - "But (if) we should say, 'Of men. . .' — they were afraid of the people, because everyone held the view that John was indeed a prophet."

Comment: ἀλλὰ, the alternative conjunction introduces the alternate statement that they might make, since they had decided that they could not say that John's message was from heaven. I have taken εἴπωμεν as the verb in the protasis of a second third-class condition. This requires that we understand ἐὰν before it. It is also possible to take εἴπωμεν as a deliberative subjunctive and translate, "But shall we say, 'Of men?' " If this is the construction then we do not have an elliptical condition. Robertson lists Mk.11:32 as an example of aposiopesis - ". . . a conscious suppression of part of a sentence under the influence of a strong emotion like anger, fear, pity." (Robertson, *Grammar*, 1203). In either case we have the Establishment admitting that they are in a dilemma. Having ruled out the possibility of admitting that John the Baptist had God's message, since such an admission would leave them open to Jesus' charge that they had therefore rejected the heavenly message, they now ponder what will happen if they say that John was only a man, with no heavenly authority. Should they say it? If they should say it, — — — the consequences were too dreadful for them to contemplate. They were not prepared to face the wrath of the public, since everyone believed in John.

Thus the argument ended in a draw, except that had Jesus told them that His authority was from heaven, He would have been speaking the truth, whereas their position was wholly inconsistent. If John's message was heavenly they should have said so and they should have repented of their previous refusal to follow him. But if they did that they would become disciples of the Lord Jesus. If John was a false prophet then it was their duty, as leaders of Israel, to expose him as such, despite the fact that such an attack upon John would have been unpopular with the people.

Normally ". . . the imperfect in indirect discourse represents an imperfect of the direct discourse. But sometimes with verbs of perception it is relative time and refers to a time previous to the perception" (Robertson, *Grammar*, 887). So it is here. The tense of the indirect discourse in ἦν in this case, refers to a time antecedent to that of *εἶχον*. The people *on that day* were of the opinion that John *had been* a prophet in the time previous to that day when he was yet alive.

Here is a good illustration that in some cases democracy is better than oligarchy. All of the people (#639) believed the truth about John while their leaders believed otherwise. Not that the people as a whole were holier than their leaders, but they were less sophisticated and poorer. Hence they were babes, and as such able to receive God's message (Mt.11:25). Being poorer they had no vested interest in the perpetuation of the political, social and economic *status quo,* which had done nothing but exploit them. They had nothing to lose temporally and everything to gain eternally by accepting both John and Jesus.

Verse 33 - "And they answered and said unto Jesus, We cannot tell. And Jesus answering saith unto them, Neither do I tell you by what authority I do these things."

καὶ ἀποκριθέντες τῷ Ἰησοῦ λέγουσιν, Οὐκ οἴδαμεν. καὶ ὁ Ἰησοῦς λέγει αὐτοῖς, Οὐδὲ ἐγὼ λέγω ὑμῖν ἐν ποίᾳ ἐξουσίᾳ ταῦτα ποιῶ.

καὶ (inferential conjunction) 14.
ἀποκριθέντες (aor.mid.part.nom.pl.masc.of *ἀποκρίνομαι*, adverbial, modal) 318.
τῷ (dat.sing.masc.of the article in agreement with *Ἰησοῦ*) 9.
Ἰησοῦ (dat.sing.masc.of *Ἰησοῦς*, indirect object of *λέγουσιν*) 3.
λέγουσιν (3d.per.pl.pres.act.ind.of *λέγω*,historical) 66.
Οὐκ (summary negative conjunction with the indicative) 130.
οἴδαμεν (1st.per.pl.aor.act.ind.of *ὁράω*, culminative) 144.
καὶ (continuative conjunction) 14.
ὁ (nom.sing.masc.of the article in agreement with *Ἰησοῦς*) 9.
Ἰησοῦς (nom.sing.masc.of *Ἰησοῦς*, subject of *λέγει*) 3.
λέγει (3d.per.sing.pres.act.ind.of *λέγω*, historical) 66.
αὐτοῖς (dat.pl.masc.of *αὐτός*, indirect object of *λέγει*) 16.
Οὐδὲ (disjunctive particle) 452.
ἐγὼ (nom.sing.masc.of *ἐγώ*, subject of *λέγω*) 123.
λέγω (1st.per.sing.pres.act.ind.of *λέγω*, aoristic) 66.
ὑμῖν (dat.pl.masc.of *σύ*, indirect object of *λέγω*) 104.
ἐν (preposition with the instrumental of agency) 80.
ποίᾳ (instru.sing.fem.of *ποῖος*, in agreement with *ἐξουσίᾳ*) 1298.
ἐξουσίᾳ (instru.sing.fem.of *ἐξουσία*, agency) 707.
ταῦτα (acc.pl.neut.of *οὗτος*, direct object of *ποιῶ*) 93.
ποιῶ (1st.per.sing.pres.act.ind.of *ποιέω*, aoristic) 127.

Translation - "Therefore they replied to Jesus by saying, 'We do not know.' And Jesus said to them, 'Neither am I telling you by what authority I am doing these things.' "

Comment: Note their mendacity - *οὐκ οἴδαμεν*! None are so ignorant as those who cannot afford to be honest. They should have said, "We know but we dare not say." The disjunctive with οὐκ (#452) makes it clear that Jesus' statement is not in the same category as theirs. He did not say, "I also do not know with what authority . . . κ.τ.λ." He said, "I will not tell." If they were not going to be honest with Jesus, why should He tell them the truth and give them a chance to twist His truth into a lie which they would then use against Him? This is what is meant by casting genuine pearls before genuine swine (Mt.7:6).

The Parable of the Vineyard and the Tenants

(Matthew 21:33-46; Mark 12:1-12; Luke 20:9-19)

Mark 12:1 - "And he began to speak unto them by parables. A certain man planted a vineyard, and set an hedge about it, and digged a place for the winefat, and built a tower, and let it out to husbandmen, and went into a far country."

Καὶ ἤρξατο αὐτοῖς ἐν παραβολαῖς λαλεῖν, 'Αμπελῶνα ἄνθρωπος ἐφύτευσεν, καὶ περιέθηκεν φραγμὸν καὶ ὤρυξεν ὑπολήνιον καὶ ᾠκοδόμησεν πύργον, καὶ ἐξέδετο αὐτὸν γεωργοῖς, καὶ ἀπεδήμησεν.

Καὶ (continuative conjunction) 14.
ἤρξατο (3d.per.sing.aor.mid.ind.of ἄρχω, ingressive) 383.
αὐτοῖς (dat.pl.masc.of αὐτός, indirect object of λαλεῖν) 16.
ἐν (preposition with the instrumental of means) 80.
παραβολαῖς (instru.pl.fem.of παραβολή, means) 1027.
λαλεῖν (pres.act.inf.of λαλέω, completes ἤρξατο) 815.
'Αμπελῶνα (acc.sing.masc.of ἀμπελών, direct object of ἐφύτευσεν) 1316.
ἄνθρωπος (nom.sing.masc.of ἄνθρωπος, subject of ἐφύτευσεν) 341.
ἐφύτευσεν (3d.per.sing.aor.act.ind.of φυτεύω, constative) 1154.
καὶ (adjunctive conjunction joining verbs) 14.
περιέθηκεν (3d.per.sing.aor.act.ind.of περιτίθημι, constative) 1376.
φραγμὸν (acc.sing.masc.of φραγμός, direct object of περιέθηκεν) 1375.
καὶ (adjunctive conjunction joining verbs) 14.
ὤρυξεν (3d.per.sing.aor.act.ind.of ὀρύσσω, constative) 1377.

#2682 ὑπολήνιον (acc.sing.neut.of ὑπολήνιον, direct object of ὤρυξεν).

winefat - Mark 12:1.

Meaning: A combination of ὑπό (#117) and ληνός (#1378). Hence, under the wine press. A pit dug directly under a wine press to hold a vessel to catch the juice of the grape - Mark 12:1.

καὶ (adjunctive conjunction joining verbs) 14.
ᾠκοδόμησεν (3d.per.sing.aor.act.ind.of οἰκοδομέω, constative) 694.
πύργον (acc.sing.masc.of πύργος, direct object of ᾠκοδομήσεν) 1379.
καὶ (adjunctive conjunction joining verbs) 14.
ἐξέδετο (3d.per.sing.2d.aor.mid.ind.of ἐκδίδωμι, constative) 1380.
αὐτὸν (acc.sing.masc.of αὐτός, direct object of ἐξέδετο) 16.
γεωργοῖς (dat.pl.masc.of γεωργός, indirect object of ἐξέδετο) 1381.

καὶ (adjunctive conjunction joining verbs) 14.
ἀπεδήμησεν (3d.per.sing.aor.act.ind.of ἀποδημέω, constative) 1382.

Translation - "And He began to speak to them in parables. A man planted a vineyard and built a hedge around it and dug a wine vat and built a tower and leased it to some farmers and went away."

Comment: Note the plural in παραβολαῖς despite the fact that Jesus used only one parable. It is an idiomatic use, indicating Jesus' choice of method for His teaching. The constative aorists and their objects follow in paratactic succession, joined by adjunctive καὶ in each case. He planted a vineyard, built a fence around it, dug a pit, built a tower and leased it to farmers and went away.

The elements in the story are easily identified. The man is God; the vineyard is Israel in her covenant relations with God in history; the servants who came to collect the harvest are the prophets and others whom God sent to Israel in the Old Testament period, whom they shamefully mistreated and in some cases killed. The Son is Christ, the Messiah. The Chief Priests, Scribes and Elders come into the story personally in verse 7. Verse 9 describes the judgment of the Romans in A.D.70. The "others" of verse 9 are the Gentiles who make up the Church.

Note the hedge (φραγμόν) which God built around Israel, designed to isolate her from the corrupting influences of the Gentile world. It consisted of the elements in her monotheism - in terms of the ceremonialism of the Aaronic Priesthood and the dietary, social, economic and political directives to Moses in the law, along with specially anointed kings and priests. Consider also the unique advantage which Israel had over the Gentiles in the inspired revelations of the Prophets who came periodically to preach to them. Also the miraculous deliverances and provision for Israel from Abraham to Christ. This is special treatment for a special people under an exclusive covenant with God. *Cf.* Eph.2:14. This hedge which God built around Israel, behind which she was protected from the world is now broken down in Christ.

In verses 2 - 5 we have the picture of God's ministry to Israel in the Old Testament age, as He sent prophets, priests and kings to them for their guidance and protection.

Verse 2 - "And at the season he sent to the husbandmen a servant, that he might receive from the husbandmen of the fruit of the vineyard.

καὶ ἀπέστειλεν πρὸς τοὺς γεωργοὺς τῷ καιρῷ δοῦλον, ἵνα παρὰ τῶν γεωργῶν λάβῃ ἀπὸ τῶν καρπῶν τοῦ ἀμπελῶνος.

καὶ (continuative conjunction) 14.
ἀπέστειλεν (3d.per.sing.aor.act.ind.of ἀποστέλλω, constative) 215.
πρὸς (preposition with the accusative of extent) 197.
τοὺς (acc.pl.masc.of the article in agreement with γεωργοὺς) 9.
γεωργοὺς (acc.pl.masc.of γεωργός, extent) 1381.
τῷ (loc.sing.masc.of the article in agreement with καιρῷ) 9.
καιρῷ (loc.sing.masc.of καιρός, time point) 767.
δοῦλον (acc.sing.masc.of δοῦλος, direct object of ἀπέστειλεν) 725.
ἵνα (conjunction introducing a purpose clause with the subjunctive) 114.

παρὰ (preposition with the ablative of source) 154.
τῶν (abl.pl.masc.of the article in agreement with γεωργῶν) 9.
γεωργῶν (abl.pl.masc.of γεωργός, source) 1381.
λάβῃ (3d.per.sing.aor.act.subj.of λαμβάνω, purpose) 533.
ἀπὸ (preposition with the ablative of source) 70.
τῶν (abl.pl.masc.of the article in agreement with καρπῶν) 9.
καρπῶν (abl.pl.masc.of καρπός, source) 284.
τοῦ (gen.sing.masc.of the article in agreement with ἀμπελῶνος) 9.
ἀμπελῶνος (gen.sing.masc.of ἀμπελών, description) 1316.

Translation - "And at harvest time he sent a servant to the farmers in order that he might receive from them some of the fruit of the vineyard."

Comment: *Cf.* comment on Mt.21:33,34; Lk.20:9,10. Note παρά with the ablative in a source construction. παρά with the ablative is joined to persons only; also with the locative. With the accusative, with a few exceptions, it is joined to things. God sent His appointed servants to Israel often in the Old Testament age.

Verse 3 - "And they caught him, and beat him, and sent him away empty."

καὶ λαβόντες αὐτὸν ἔδειραν καὶ ἀπέστειλαν κενόν.

καὶ (adversative conjunction) 14.
λαβόντες (aor.act.part.nom.pl.masc.of λαμβάνω, adverbial, temporal) 533.
αὐτὸν (acc.sing.masc.of αὐτός, direct object of λαβόντες, ἔδειραν and ἀπεστειλαν) 16.
ἔδειραν (3d.per.pl.aor.act.ind.of δέρω, constative) 1383.
καὶ (adjunctive conjunction joining verbs) 14.
ἀπέστειλαν (3d.per.pl.aor.act.ind.of ἀποστέλλω, constative) 215.
κενόν (acc.sing.masc.of κενός, predicate adjective) 1836.

Translation - "But they took him and beat and sent him back with nothing."

Comment: The servant represented the owner's interests and spoke in his name. But he was taken, beaten and sent back empty handed. *Cf.* Luke 1:52,53 where we have ἐξαποστέλλω with κενός (#'s 835, 1836). When Messiah reigns on earth He will preside over a political, social and economic revolution in which those who once mistreated Him will be the ones to be sent away empty handed (Rom.12:19). All Old Testament material which relates to Israel's maltreatment of God's prophets, judges, priests and kings is pertinent to this passage.

Verse 4 - "And again he sent unto them another servant; and at him they cast stones, and wounded him in the head, and sent him away shamefully handled."

καὶ πάλιν ἀπέστειλεν πρὸς αὐτοὺς ἄλλον δοῦλον, κἀκεῖνον ἐκεφαλίωσαν καὶ ἠτίμασαν.

καὶ (continuative conjunction) 14.

πάλιν (adverbial) 355.
ἀπέστειλεν (3d.per.sing.aor.act.ind.of *ἀποστέλλω*, constative) 215.
πρὸς (preposition with the accusative of extent) 197.
αὐτοὺς (acc.pl.masc.of *αὐτός*, extent) 16.
ἄλλον (acc.sing.masc.of *ἄλλος*, in agreement with *δοῦλον*) 198.
δοῦλον (acc.sing.masc.of *δοῦλος*, direct object of *ἀπέστειλεν*) 725.
κακεῖνον (acc.sing.masc.of *κακεῖνος*, direct object of *ἐκεφαλίωσαν* and *ἠτίμασαν*) 1164.

#2683 *ἐκεφαλίωσαν* (3d.per.pl.aor.act.ind.of *κεφαλαιόω*, constative).

wound in the head - Mark 12:4.

Meaning: Cf.κεφαλή (#521). To beat on the head - Mark 12:4.

καὶ (adjunctive conjunction joining verbs) 14.
ἠτίμασαν (3d.per.pl.aor.act.ind.of *ἀτιμάζω*, constative) 2390.

Translation - "And again he sent to them another servant; but they struck him on the head and treated him shamefully."

Comment: *Cf.* comment on Mt.21:36 and Lk.20:11. *κακεῖνον* is an example of crasis, the *καὶ* in the combination being adversative and *ἐκεῖνος* being deictic, pointing to *δοῦλον*. They treated him without honor (#2390). The second servant received treatment no better than the first. Verse 3 - *ἔδειραν* - "to strike or pummel" without designating what part of the body was attacked. Verse 4 - *ἐκεφαλαιόω* - "to strike upon the head" - blows that could possibly inflict greater injury if not death. There was no mention of insult in verse 3. Neither servant brought back the owner's share of the crop.

Verse 5 - "And again he sent another; and him they killed, and many others; beating some and killing some."

καὶ ἄλλον ἀπέστειλεν, κἀκεῖνον ἀπέκτειναν, καὶ πολλοὺς ἄλλους, οὓς μὲν δέροντες οὓς δὲ ἀποκτέννοντες.

καὶ (continuative conjunction) 14.
ἄλλον (acc.sing.masc.of *ἄλλος*, direct object of *ἀπέστειλεν*) 198.
ἀπέστειλεν (3d.per.sing.aor.act.ind.of *ἀποστέλλω*, constative) 215.
κἀκεῖνον (acc.sing.masc.of *κἀκεῖνος*, direct object of *ἀπέκτειναν*) 1164.
ἀπέκτειναν (3d.per.pl.aor.act.ind.of *ἀποκτείνω*, constative) 889.
καὶ (continuative conjunction) 14.
πολλοὺς (acc.pl.masc.of *πολύς*, in agreement with *ἄλλους*) 228.
ἄλλους (acc.pl.masc.of *ἄλλος*, direct object of *ἀπέστειλεν*, understood) 198.
οὓς (acc.pl.masc.of *ὅς*, direct object of *δέροντες*) 65.
μὲν (particle of affirmation and emphasis) 300.
δέροντες (pres.act.part.nom.pl.masc.of *δέρω*, adverbial, circumstantial) 1383.
οὓς (acc.pl.masc.of *ὅς*, direct object of *ἀποκτέννοντες*) 65.

δὲ (continuative conjunction) 11.

ἀποκτέννοντες (pres.act.part.nom.pl.masc.of ἀποκτείνω, adverbial, circumstantial) 889.

Translation - "And he sent another; they killed him too. And many others — some of whom they beat and others they killed."

Comment: *Cf.* Luke 20:12. Just as κακεῖνον may be construed adversatively in verse 4, here it can be taken adjunctively. He sent one servant, *but* him they beat and insulted (verse 4). He sent another, *and* him they killed. All of the servants were receiving progressively rougher treatment from the farmers. Robertson observes that the principal verb must be drawn from the idea of the two participles δέροντες and ἀποκτέννοντες. (Robertson, *Grammar*, 394). It was not the owner of the vineyard who did the beating and the killing; it was the farmers. The non-classical style is strictly Markan, but the thought comes through with clarity.

Israel's degenerate behavior across history from Abraham to Christ, is seen as becoming progressively worse. They never treated God's messengers, be they law givers, judges, kings, priests or prophets with the respect that a servant of their covenant God deserved. Every century saw more malice in the Jewish heart toward God and greater cruelty to His messengers. But — (and here is the point that the amillenialists overlook) not all of the people of Israel rejected God's covenant and mistreated His messengers. In every era of her history Israel had those elect believers, who believed God, as Abraham did, and to whom, therefore it was counted unto them for righteousness (Rom.4:3; Gal.3:9). These people will not only be saved personally, but they also inherit God's promise to Abraham, with reference to an everlasting earthly kingdom for Messiah. God is under obligation to fulfill His promise to Abraham, in behalf of all of Abraham's seed who believed. Even in Jesus' day the hatred of official Israel, in line with the teaching of the parable under discussion, was not shared by all of the people. What of those who were on Jesus' side in the controversy? In their eagerness to prove their point and abolish a literal earthly kingdom, with a literally resurrected Messiah reigning over a literal earthly nation, the amillenialists have denied to every faithful son and daughter of Abraham their right to a fulfillment of God's millenial kingdom promises to Abraham, Isaac, Jacob, Judah and David. Jesus was speaking this parable against the Chief Priests, Scribes and Elders, not against the Jews who two days before had waved the palm branches and cried out, 'Hosanna to the Son of David."

Amillenialism, with its objection to a literal earthly kingdom, pursues their line of thought as though there were something inherently wicked about matter. This is a form of Neo-Manichaeanism, the Gnostic heresy with which the Arians and the Docetists denied the essential deity of Jesus in the former case and His essential humanity in the latter.

Israel's hatred for God culminates in verses six and seven.

Verse 6 - "Having yet therefore one son, his wellbeloved, he sent him also last unto them, saying, They will reverence my son."

ἔτι ἕνα εἶχεν, υἱὸν ἀγαπητόν, ἀπέστειλεν αὐτὸν ἔσχατον πρὸς αὐτοὺς λέγων ὅτι Ἐντραπήσονται τὸν υἱόν μου.

ἔτι (adverbial) 448.
ἕνα (acc.sing.masc.of εἷς, in agreement with υἱὸν) 469.
εἶχεν (3d.per.sing.imp.act.ind.of ἔχω, progressive description) 82.
υἱὸν (acc.sing.masc.of υἱός, direct object of εἶχεν) 5.
ἀγαπητόν (acc.sing.masc.of ἀγαπητός, in agreement with υἱὸν) 327.
ἀπέστειλεν (3d.per.sing.aor.act.ind.of ἀποστέλλω, constative) 215.
αὐτὸν (acc.sing.masc.of αὐτός, direct object of ἀπέστειλεν) 16.
ἔσχατον (acc.sing.neut.of ἔσχατος, adverbial) 496.
πρὸς (preposition with the accusative of extent) 197.
αὐτοὺς (acc.pl.masc.of αὐτός, extent) 16.
λέγων (pres.act.part.nom.sing.masc.of λέγω, complementary) 66.
ὅτι (recitative) 211.
Ἐντραπήσονται (3d.per.pl.2d.fut.pass.ind.of ἐντρέπω, predictive) 1385.
τὸν (acc.sing.masc.of the article in agreement with υἱόν) 9.
υἱόν (acc.sing.masc.of υἱός, direct object of ἐντραπήσονται) 5.
μου (gen.sing.masc.of ἐγώ, relationship) 123.

Translation - "He still had one beloved son. Finally he sent him to them saying, 'They will respect my son.' "

Comment: ἔτι as applied to the present *cf.*#448. The imperfect in εἶχεν is descriptive. All of his servants had been sent and rejected, beaten or killed. All who returned were empty handed. But he still had a son whom he could send. He had received no return to date on his investment in the vineyard. As a last resort (ἔσχατον) he sent his son. Christ, God's well beloved Son (John 3:16) was the last messenger that national Israel was to receive from the God of Abraham. Those individuals who received Christ personally when He came were to receive still another messenger from God, *viz.* the Holy Spirit. But the Holy Spirit did not come to any of those who rejected Christ. Had they received God's Son and rendered due respect to Him, their previous mistreatment of God's other servants in the Old Testament age would have been forgiven. But when they killed the Son of God, all further appeal to the nation Israel *of that day* was to be denied. When He comes again, it will not be to the nation as such, as it was then constituted, but to the 144,000 elect representatives, 12,000 from each of twelve tribes, who will have been sealed for Him (Rev.7:1-8). From this representative group of virgin Jews (presumably 72,000 young couples) He will build a new national Israel and rule over them as their Messiah, and through them the entire world.

It is interesting to note that the judges of these twelve newly constituted tribes of Israel, in the millenial kingdom will be the twelve apostles, who also are the first Christians, and as such members of the body of Christ (Mt.19:28; Luke 22:30; Eph.2:20; 4:16). Thus we have the coordination of the activities of the members of the body of Christ, which is the Church, with the political administration of the earth as carried out through the nation Israel.

Amillenialists will object to our literal interpretation of these passages, and must face our question: "If the Bible does not mean what it says, why does not the Bible say what it means, unless we are willing to advance the theory that God is deliberately seeking to mislead us?" Some exegete once said, "When the plain sense of the Bible makes good sense, seek no other sense." When we arbitrarily decide that certain language is allegorical or figurative, we open the door for a method of interpretation which will permit us to make the Bible teach anything and everything, in which case it teaches nothing. When literalists apply the figurative method of interpretation to passages which the figurative interpreters wish to take literally, they protest. For example the angel Gabriel predicted that the virgin Mary would conceive, bear a son, and name Him Jesus. He went on to say that He would be great and be called the Son of the Highest. Gabriel then added that the Lord God would give unto Him the throne of His father David, that He would reign over the house of Jacob forever, and that of his kingdom there would be no end (Luke 1:30-33). There are eight predictions: (1) that she would conceive, and (2) bear a son, and (3) name Him Jesus, and (4) that He would be great, and (5) that He would be called the Son of the Highest. The angel added that (6) the Lord God would give to Him the throne of His father David, (7) that He would reign over the house of David forever, in a (8) kingdom that would have no end. Amillenialists choose to interpret the first five predictions literally and the last three figuratively. They do not deny that Mary had a baby. They do deny that He will sit upon David's throne forever. Why should they object if I choose to interpret the entire passage figuratively? Perhaps the virgin Mary never had a baby. Perhaps, as I once heard a so-called Christian Scientist say, "Mary conceived the idea of God." I hasten to assure the reader that I do indeed believe that a literal virgin named Mary had a literal conception and gave a literal birth to a literal baby whom she named Jesus. That He was great and called the Son of the Highest goes without saying. I also believe that Gabriel was still speaking literally when he enunciated the last three-eighths of his prophecy.

God has not bothered to communicate with Israel since they nailed His beloved Son on a cross. Because they murdered Him Who came to the vineyard to collect the Father's due, they were scattered to the ends of the earth in A.D.70. Since Calvary God hears prayer only when it is mediated through His risen and exalted Son. Rabbinical prayer in a synagogue, however orthodox from a Jewish point of view, not unlike the prayer of the Unitarian is nothing more than ritualistic cant. God will not permit any lost sinner to bypass His crucified, risen and ascended son.

There was real finality in the cry of the mob before Pilate, "We have no king but Caesar." *ἐντραπήσονται* is one of a number of future passives without a passive sense. *Cf.* Mt.8:11, among others, which see *en loc.*

Israel cannot be excused for rejecting God's Old Testament servants. How much less can we excuse her for rejecting One, Who, by every pragmatic evidence proved beyond reasonable doubt that He was indeed the Son of God. A group of political Establishmentarians who would crucify Jesus of Nazareth, after His public record had been reviewed are indeed incorrigible. For such there is no remedy but judgment. But we repeat that they did not represent all of Abraham's seed. They did not represent Peter, James, John and the other eight

Apostles, who with Paul, who came late to the fold, will occupy judicial posts during the kingdom ages.

Verse 7 - "But those husbandment said among themselves, This is the heir; come, let us kill him, and the inheritance shall be ours."

ἐκεῖνοι δὲ οἱ γεωργοὶ πρὸς ἑαυτοὺς εἶπαν ὅτι Οὗτος ἐστιν ὁ κληρονόμος. δεῦτε ἀποκτείνωμεν αὐτόν, καὶ ἡμῶν ἔσται ἡ κληρονομία.

ἐκεῖνοι (nom.pl.masc.of *ἐκεῖνος*, in agreement with *γεωργοὶ*) 246.
δὲ (adversative conjunction) 11.
οἱ (nom.pl.masc.of the article in agreement with *γεωργοὶ*) 9.
γεωργοὶ (nom.pl.masc.of *γεωργός*, subject of *εἶπαν*) 1381.
πρὸς (preposition with the accusative of extent, after a verb of speaking) 197.
ἑαυτοὺς (acc.pl.masc.of *ἑαυτός*, extent, after a verb of speaking) 288.
εἶπαν (3d.per.pl.aor.act.ind.of *εἶπον*, constative) 155.
Οὗτος (nom.sing.masc.of *οὗτος*, predicate nominative) 93.
ἔστιν (3d.per.sing.pres.ind.of *εἰμί*, static) 86.
ὁ (nom.sing.masc.of the article in agreement with *κληρονόμος*) 9.
κληρονόμος (nom.sing.masc.of *κληρονόμος*, subject of *ἔστιν*) 1386.
δεῦτε (particle of exhortation and incitement) 391.
ἀποκτείνωμεν (1st.per.pl.pres.act.subj.of *ἀποκτείνω*, hortatory) 889.
αὐτόν (acc.sing.masc.of *αὐτός*, direct object of *ἀποκτείνωμεν*) 16.
καὶ (continuative conjunction) 14.
ἡμῶν (gen.pl.masc.of *ἐγώ*, possession) 123.
ἔσται (3d.per.sing.fut.ind.of *εἰμί*, predictive) 86.
ἡ (nom.sing.fem.of the article in agreement with *κληρονομία*) 9.
κληρονομία (nom.sing.fem.of *κληρονομία*, subject of *ἔσται*) 1387.

Translation - "But those farmers said to one another, 'This man is the heir. Come, Let us kill him and ours will be the inheritance.' "

Comment: *δὲ* is adversative. The father in the parable had supposed that his son would be respected. We have already pointed out that this detail of the story cannot be pushed, since God the Father had no such illusions about the reception which would be afforded His Son when Christ came into the world. "This man is the heir!" They were so right. Not only of the vineyard but *κληρονόμον πάντων* (Heb.1:2). *δεῦτε ἀποκτείνωμεν* is a case of what Robertson calls "original parataxis." He cites other examples in Mt.7:4; 27:49; 28:6; Acts 7:34; Jam.5:1; Mk.15:36 (Robertson, *Grammar*, 430). These are cases where the conjunction has dropped out. Hortatory subjunctive in *δεῦτε ἀποκτείνωμεν* - "Come on, let us kill him." The end to be achieved is then predicted - *καὶ ἡμῶν ἔσται ἡ κληρονομία*. Note the emphasis of *ἡμῶν*, the point that was uppermost in their minds.

Theirs was a most illogical deduction. Just why they thought if they killed the heir that the owner would meekly submit to their murderous confiscation is not clear! No more clear than the thinking of the Chief Priests that if they crucified the Messiah they would be permitted by God to inherit the national hegemony of

Israel! The Establishment in Jerusalem wanted the kingdom for themselves, but this involved murdering the King. What they failed to see was that their *coup d'etat* brought God the Father into the fight in flaming judgment. He used Titus, the Roman in A.D.70 as His battle-axe. The members of the Establishment, were scattered abroad throughout the world, but not until many of their colleagues died on crosses similar to the one upon which they murdered their king. Israel can never have the kingdom without the King. Had God not raised from the dead the only man in Israel who had a legal right to the throne of David, Israel would never have either the kingdom or the King. Jesus was not married and left no legal heir to the throne. Thus the Davidic line was terminated when He died. "But God raised Him from the dead" (Acts 13:30) and He will yet be King, but not for those who murdered Him (verse 9). *Cf.*#1387, particularly Gal.3:18; Eph.1:14,18; 5:5; Col.3:24; Heb.9:15 and 1 Pet.1:4. Because He died, we who believe that His death was that of the Son of God, in expiation for our sins, shall have the inheritance. But those who murdered Him in order to take His inheritance will never have an inheritance. If the Jews had said, "Come, let us kill Him and the inheritance will belong to every true believer, be he Jew or Gentile" they would have told the truth. It is another irony, similar to "He saved others; Himself He cannot save" (Mk.15:31). God makes the wrath of men to praise Him (Ps.76:10).

Verse 8 - "And they took him and killed him, and cast him out of the vineyard."

καὶ λαβόντες ἀπέκτειναν αὐτόν, καὶ ἐξέβαλον αὐτὸν ἔξω τοῦ ἀμπελῶνος.

καὶ (continuative conjunction) 14.
λαβόντες (2d.aor.act.part.nom.pl.masc.of λαμβάνω, adverbial, temporal) 533.
ἀπέκτειναν (3d.per.pl.aor.act.ind.of ἀποκτείνω, constative) 889.
αὐτόν (acc.sing.masc.of αὐτός, direct object of ἀπέκτειναν) 16.
καὶ (adjunctive conjunction joining verbs) 14.
ἐξέβαλον (3d.per.pl.aor.act.ind.of ἐκβάλλω, constative) 649.
αὐτὸν (acc.sing.masc.of αὐτός, direct object of ἐξέβαλον) 16.
ἔξω (adverbial) 449.
του (abl.sing.masc.of the article in agreement with ἀμπελῶνος) 9.
ἀμπελῶνος (abl.sing.masc.of ἀμπελών, separation, after ἐκ in composition) 1316.

Translation - "And they seized him and killed him and cast him out of the vineyard."

Comment: *Cf.* Mt.21:39 and Lk.20:15. Matthew and Luke say that they threw him out of the vineyard and killed Him. Mark reverses the order. The Holy Spirit is not here concerned with precise chronological detail. The point is that the tenants killed the heir. *Cf.*#649, paragraphs 2 and 3 for all of the references on ἐκβάλλω that may provide correlative sermon material, *e.g.* Gal.4:30. There are others. Christ is going to do some "casting out" of His own in the judgment. The sad story is nearly ended. Jesus asks a logical question in conclusion in

Verse 9 - "What shall therefore the Lord of the vineyard do? He will come and destroy the husbandmen, and will give the vineyard unto others."

τί (οὖν) ποιήσει ὁ κύριος τοῦ ἀμπελῶνος; ἐλεύσεται καὶ ἀπολέσει τοὺς γεωργούς, καὶ δώσει τὸν ἀμπελῶνα ἄλλοις.

τί (acc.sing.neut.of τίς, interrogative pronoun, direct object of ποιήσει) 281.
ποιήσει (3d.per.sing.fut.act.ind.of ποιέω, deliberative) 127.
ὁ (nom.sing.masc.of the article in agreement with κύριος) 9.
κύριος (nom.sing.masc.of κύριος, subject of ποιήσει) 97.
τοῦ (gen.sing.masc.of the article in agreement with ἀμπελῶνος) 9.
ἀμπελῶνος (gen.sing.masc.of ἀμπελών, description) 1316.
ἐλεύσεται (3d.per.sing.fut.ind.of ἔρχομαι, predictive) 146.
καὶ (adjunctive conjunction joining verbs) 14.
ἀπολέσει (3d.per.sing.fut.act.ind.of ἀπόλλυμι, predictive) 208.
τοὺς (acc.pl.masc.of the article in agreement with γεωργούς) 9.
γεωργούς (acc.pl.masc.of γεωργός, direct object of ἀπολέσει) 1381.
καὶ (adjunctive conjunction joining verbs) 14.
δώσει (3d.per.sing.fut.act.ind.of δίδωμι predictive) 362.
τὸν (acc.sing.masc.of the article in agreement with ἀμπελῶνα) 9.
ἀμπελῶνα (acc.sing.masc.of ἀμπελών, direct object of δώσει) 1316.
ἄλλοις (dat.pl.masc.of ἄλλος, indirect object of δώσει) 198.

Translation - "What will the lord of the vineyard do? He will come and He will destroy the farmers, and He will give the vineyard to others."

Comment: Note that despite the farmers' murderous design, the man who planted it is still the lord of the vineyard, and He is in complete control. Future action in response to the death of His Son is His prerogative and His alone. What will He do? The answer is in three parts, set forth by three predictive future tense verbs. He will come; He will destroy some; and He will give the vineyard to others. In view of verses 10 - 12, it is clear that this part of the parable does not refer to the second coming of Christ, but to the Jewish war in A.D.70. The parable was spoken against the Chief Priests who were present that day. They were marked for destruction in retaliation for their part in the murder of Jesus, the Heir. God sent His representative - a pagan Roman Emperor. Titus came and destroyed the very men who stood there that day. "Let His blood be on us and on our children" became a prayer that had a complete answer. The kingdom was given to others. Palestine has been under Gentile rule from that day until 1948, and will be overrun by the Gentile powers until the "times of the Gentiles be fulfilled" (Luke 21:24).

However, we can say that since Christ is the corner stone of His Building, the Church (Eph.2:20), the vineyard has become a spiritual garden of the Lord, as the Holy Spirit calls out from the Gentiles a people for His name (Acts 15:14). There is a sense in which all members of the Body of Christ are γεωργοί in the vineyard of the Lord. It has been given to us. But the national Jewish idea is not dead. It is only being held in abeyance. At the second coming of Christ, 144,000 elect Jews (Rev.7:1-8) who had nothing to do with the murder of their Messiah, but who have Abraham's blood flowing in their veins, and who therefore are heirs of God's promise to Abraham, will be given the rule over God's vineyard. Indeed the twelve Apostles will sit upon twelve thrones judging the nation that will be born in a day (Isa.66:8).

Verse 10 - "And have ye not read this scripture; The stone which the builders rejected is become the head of the corner?"

οὐδὲ τὴν γραφὴν ταύτην ἀνέγνωτε, Λίθον ὃν ἀπεδοκίμασαν οἱ οἰκοδομοῦντες, οὗτος ἐγενήθη εἰς κεφαλὴν γωνίας.

οὐδὲ (disjunctive particle) 452.
τὴν (acc.sing.fem.of the article in agreement with *γραφὴν*) 9.
γραφὴν (acc.sing.fem.of *γραφή*, direct object of *ἀνέγνωτε*) 1389.
ταύτην (acc.sing.fem.of *οὗτος*, in agreement with *γραφὴν*) 93.
ἀνέγνωτε (2d.per.pl.2d.aor.act.ind.of *ἀναγινώσκω*, rhetorical question) 967.
Λίθον (acc.sing.masc.of *λίθος*, inverse attraction to *ὃν*, subject of *ἐγενήθη*) 290.
ὃν (acc.sing.masc.of *ὅς*, direct object of *ἀπεδοκίμασαν*) 65.
ἀπεδοκίμασαν (3d.per.pl.aor.act.ind.of *ἀποδοκιμάζω*, culminative) 1390.
οἱ (nom.pl.masc.of the article in agreement with *οἰκοδομοῦντες*) 9.
οἰκοδομοῦντες (pres.act.part.nom.pl.masc.of *οἰκοδομέω*, substantival, subject of *ἀπεδοκίμασαν*) 694.
οὗτος (nom.sing.masc.of *οὗτος*, subject of *ἐγενήθη*) 93.
ἐγενήθη (3d.per.sing.aor.pass.ind.of *γίνομαι*, culminative) 113.
εἰς (preposition with the predicate accusative) 140.
κεφαλὴν (acc.sing.fem.of *κεφαλή*, predicate accusative) 521.
γωνίας (gen.sing.fem.of *γωνία*, description) 567.

Translation - "You have read this scripture, have you not - 'The stone which the builders rejected - that one has been made the cornerstone?' "

Comment: *Λίθον*, the subject of *ἐγενήθη* is attracted to its relative pronoun *ὃν* in a case of inverse attraction. This idiom is rare in the New Testament. Normally, if attraction occurs, the relative pronoun is attracted to its antecedent to which it refers. The quotation is from Psalm 118:22 and is cited in the New Testament, in addition to the synoptic parallels, Mt.21:42; Mk.10:12 and Lk.20:17 in Acts 4:11 and 1 Pet.2:7. Thus Christ is the cornerstone of the building associated with the Church, which, in other imagery, is referred to as the Body of Christ. The cornerstone is the most important stone in the building and therefore it must be the best. It is the stone, in conformity with the angles of which all other parts of the building must be installed. If all stones of the building are laid in conformity to it, we have a building/body "fitly joined together and compacted by that which every joint supplieth, according to the effectual working in the measure of every part. . . " (Eph.4:16). Any carpenter knows that when he builds a building in total conformity with this principle the more pieces he builds into the building the more compact the structure becomes. The Jewish leaders rejected the best stone available as one which did not comport with their building plans. Contrary to their evaluation, He is the corner stone of all of the building that God will ever do, whether He is building with Jews or Gentiles. Jesus alluded to His rejection elsewhere. *Cf.* Mk.8:31; Lk.9:22; 17:25. Since the Jews did not want Jesus as a stone fit for their building, God would give the building operation to others who would not only use Him but make Him the head of the corner. Thus Jesus is saying that God's building plans, which make for permanence, are different from those of the Chief Priests, Scribes and Elders whose building could not survive.

Verse 11 - "This was the Lord's doing, and it is marvelous in our eyes."

παρὰ κυρίου ἐγένετο αὕτη, καὶ ἔστιν θαυμαστὴ ἐν ὀφθαλμοῖς ἡμῶν;

παρὰ (preposition with the ablative of agent) 154.
κυρίου (abl.sing.masc.of *κύριος*, agent) 97.
ἐγένετο (3d.per.sing.aor.ind.of *γίνομαι*, culminative) 113.
αὕτη (nom.sing.fem.of *οὗτος*, subject of *ἐγένετο*) 93.
καὶ (continuative conjunction) 14.
ἔστιν (3d.per.sing.pres.ind.of *εἰμί*, static) 86.
θαυμαστὴ (nom.sing.fem.of *θαυμαστός*, predicate adjective) 1391.
ἐν (preposition with the locative of sphere) 80.
ὀφθαλμοῖς (loc.pl.masc.of *ὀφθαλμός*, sphere) 501.
ἡμῶν (gen.pl.masc.of *ἐγώ*, possession) 123.

Translation - "This was the Lord's policy and it is marvelous in our eyes."

Comment: Normally we would have *τοῦτο* instead of the feminine *αὕτη*. Note the ablative of agent after *παρά*. *Cf.*#154. Note the locative of sphere in *ἐν ὀφθαλμοῖς ἡμῶν*. *Cf.*#80,V. In re *θαυμαστός* *cf.* 1 Pet.2:9. *cf.* Mt.21:42-45. Matthew goes on to record further dire prophecies against Israel, not recorded by Mark. *cf.* Luke 20:18.

Verse 12 - "And they sought to lay hold on him, but feared the people; for they knew that he had spoken the parable against them: and they left him and went their way."

Καὶ ἐζήτουν αὐτὸν κρατῆσαι, καὶ ἐφοβήθησαν τὸν ὄχλον, ἔγνωσαν γὰρ ὅτι πρὸς αὐτοὺς τὴν παραβολὴν εἶπεν. καὶ ἀφέντες αὐτὸν ἀπῆλθον.

Καὶ (continuative conjunction) 14.
ἐζήτουν (3d.per.pl.imp.act.ind.of *ζητέω*, inceptive) 207.
αὐτὸν (acc.sing.masc.of *αὐτός*, direct object of *κρατῆσαι*) 16.
κρατῆσαι (aor.act.inf.of *κρατέω*, completes *ἐζήτουν*) 828.
καὶ (adversative conjunction) 14.
ἐφοβηθήσαν (3d.per.pl.aor.mid.ind.of *φοβέομαι*, constative) 101.
τὸν (acc.sing.masc.of the article in agreement with *ὄχλον*) 9.

ὄχλον (acc.sing.masc.of *ὄχλος*, direct object of *ἐφοβηθήσαν*) 418.
ἔγνωσαν (3d.per.po.aor.act.ind.of *γινώσκω*, constative) 131.
γὰρ (causal conjunction) 105.
ὅτι (conjunction introducing an object clause in indirect discourse) 211.
πρὸς (preposition with the accusative of extent, with a verb of speaking, opposition) 197.
αὐτοὺς (acc.pl.masc.of *αὐτός*, extent with a verb of speaking, opposition) 16.
τὴν (acc.sing.fem.of the article in agreement with *παραβολὴν*) 9.
παραβολὴν (acc.sing.fem.of *παραβολή*, direct object of *εἶπεν*) 1027.
εἶπεν (3d.per.sing.aor.act.ind.of *εἶπον*, constative) 155.
καὶ (continuative conjunction) 14.
ἀφέντες (aor.act.part.nom.pl.masc.of *ἀφίημι*, adverbial, temporal) 319.
αὐτὸν (acc.sing.masc.of *αὐτός*, direct object of *ἀφέντες*) 16.
ἀπῆλθον (3d.per.pl.aor.ind.of *ἀπέρχομαι*, constative) 239.

Translation - "And they were trying to arrest Him, but they were afraid of the people, because they knew that He had spoken the parable against them. And they withdrew from Him and went away."

Comment: The Establishment understood perfectly well what Jesus meant by the parable and the application of Psalm 118:22 with which He climaxed it. He had sketched Jewish history in a quick succession of brilliant brush strokes on a broad canvas and had painted the picture into the future to reveal Israel's doom. They still wanted very much to arrest Him but were deterred by their fear of the people. Since *ὄχλον* is singular (though it can refer to a plurality of people) we have chosen to join *ἔγνωσαν* and *πρὸς αὐτοὺς* to the chief priests to whom both *ἐζήτουν* and *ἐφοβήθησαν* refer. It was the chief priests who knew that Jesus' parable was spoken at their expense, although it is very probable that the people (*ὄχλον*) also understood the parable in that light. The point cannot be established from the grammar. Luke 20:19 gives no help since Luke uses *τὸν λαόν* which also is singular in form but plural in meaning.

We now examine Luke's account of the controversy in Luke 20:1-19.

The Authority of Jesus Questioned

(Matthew 21:23-27; Mark 11:27-33; Luke 20:1-8)

Luke 20:1 - "And it came to pass, that on one of those days as he taught the people in the temple, and preached the gospel, the chief priests and the scribes came upon him with the elders,"

Καὶ ἐγένετο ἐν μιᾷ τῶν ἡμερῶν διδάσκοντος αὐτοῦ τὸν λαὸν ἐν τῷ ἱερῷ καὶ εὐαγγελιζομένου ἐπέστησαν οἱ ἀρχιερεῖς καὶ οἱ γραμματεῖς σὺν τοῖς πρεσβυτέροις,

Καὶ (continuative conjunction) 14.
ἐγένετο (3d.per.sing.aor.ind.of *γίνομαι*, constative) 113.

ἐν (preposition with the locative of time point) 80.
μιᾷ (loc.sing.fem.of *εἷς*, time point) 469.
τῶν (gen.pl.fem.of the article in agreement with *ἡμερῶν*) 9.
ἡμερῶν (gen.pl.fem.of *ἡμέρα*, partitive) 135.
διδάσκοντος (pres.act.part.gen.sing.masc.of *διδάσκω*, genitive absolute) 403.
αὐτοῦ (gen.sing.masc.of *αὐτός*, genitive absolute) 16.
τὸν (acc.sing.masc.of the article in agreement with *λαὸν*) 9.
λαὸν (acc.sing.masc.of *λαός*, direct object of *διδάσκοντος*) 110.
ἐν (preposition with the locative of place where) 80.
τῷ (loc.sing.neut.of the article in agreement with *ἱερῷ*) 9.
ἱερῷ (loc.sing.neut.of *ἱερόν*, place where) 346.
καὶ (adjunctive conjunction joining participles) 14.
εὐαγγελιζομένου (pres.mid.part.gen.sing.masc.of *εὐαγγελίζομαι*, genitive absolute) 909.
ἐπέστησαν (3d.per.pl.aor.act.ind. of *ἐπίστημι*, constative) 1877.
οἱ (nom.pl.masc.of the article in agreement with *ἀρχιερεῖς*) 9.
ἀρχιερεῖς (nom.pl.masc.of *ἀρχιερεύς*, subject of *ἐπέστησαν*) 151.
καὶ (adjunctive conjunction joining nouns) 14.
οἱ (nom.pl.masc.of the article in agreement with *γραμματεῖς*) 9.
γραμματεῖς (nom.pl.masc.of *γραμματεύς*, subject of *ἐπέστησαν*) 152.
σὺν (preposition with the instrumental of association) 1542.
τοῖς (instru.pl.masc.of the article in agreement with *πρεσβυτέροις*) 9.
πρεσβυτέροις (instru.pl.masc.of *πρεσβύτερος*, association) 1141.

Translation - "And it happened that, on one of the days when He was teaching the people and preaching in the temple, the chief priests and the scribes, accompnied by the elders, confronted Him,"

Comment: *Cf.* comment on Mt.21:23 and Mk.11:27. It was Tuesday. Luke writes as though he was not certain which day, so he spoke generally - *ἐν μιᾷ τῶν ἡμερῶν* - "on one of the days." The double genitive absolute tells us what Jesus was doing when the chief priests, scribes and elders approached Him. He was in the temple area preaching the gospel and teaching the people. Within the shadow of His cross, Jesus was proclaiming the good news of the gospel. If He had not died there would be no good news for man - ever, in any age or in any place. Luke uses a stronger word - *ἐπέστησαν* than Matthew and Mark. Matthew says *προσῆλθον αὐτῷ* - "they came to him" and Mark has *ἔρχονται πρὸς αὐτόν* - "they came to him." Luke says that "they stood up to him" or "they confronted him." There is a bit more belligerence in Luke's description.

Verse 2 - "And spoke unto him, saying, Tell us, by what authority doest thou these things? or who is he that giveth thee this authority?"

καὶ εἶπαν λέγοντες πρὸς αὐτόν Εἰπὸν ἡμῖν ἐν ποίᾳ ἐξουσίᾳ ταῦτα ποιεῖς, ἢ τίς ἐστιν ὁ δούς σοι τὴν ἐξουσίαν ταύτην.

καὶ (adjunctive conjunction joining verbs) 14.
εἶπαν (3d.per.pl.aor.act.ind.of *εἶπον*, constative) 155.

λέγοντες (pres.act.part.nom.pl.masc.of λέγω, recitative) 66.
πρὸς (preposition with the accusative of extent, after a verb of speaking) 197.
αὐτόν (acc.sing.masc.of αὐτός, extent after a verb of speaking) 16.
Εἰπὸν (2d.per.sing.aor.act.impv.of εἶπον, command) 155.
ἡμῖν (dat.pl.masc.of ἐγώ, indirect object of Εἰπὸν) 123.
ἐν (preposition with the instrumental of agent) 80.
ποίᾳ (instru.sing.fem.of ποῖος, in agreement with ἐξουσίᾳ) 1298.
ἐξουσίᾳ (instru.sing.fem.of ἐξουσία, agent) 707.
ταῦτα (acc.pl.neut.of οὗτος, direct object of ποιεῖς) 93.
ποιεῖς (2d.per.sing.pres.act.ind.of ποιέω, customary) 127.
ἢ (disjunctive particle) 465.
τίς (nom.sing.masc.of τίς, the interrogative pronoun, predicate nominative, direct question) 281.
ἐστιν (3d.per.sing.pres.ind.of εἰμί, aoristic) 86.
ὁ (nom.sing.masc.of the article in agreement with δούς) 9.
δούς (2d.aor.act.part.nom.sing.masc.of δίδωμι, substantival, subject of ἐστιν) 362.
σοι (dat.sing.masc.of σύ, indirect object of δούς) 104.
τὴν (acc.sing.fem.of the article in agreement with ἐξουσίαν) 9.
ἐξουσίαν (acc.sing.fem.of ἐξουσία, direct object of δούς) 707.
ταύτην (acc.sing.fem.of οὗτος, in agreement with ἐξουσίαν) 93.

Translation - "And they said to Him, 'Tell us by what authority you are doing these things, or Who is the one who gave you this authority?' "

Comment: *Cf.*comment on Mt.21:23 and Mk.11:28. Edersheim (*The Life and Times of Jesus, II,* 380-383) says that the chief priests, scribes and elders were well within their rights to demand Jesus' credentials, since no one was to teach in the temple courts without a syllabus of the course of study from one of the established schools of thought, or by special permission from some recognized authority.

Verse 3 - "And he answered and said unto them, I will also ask you one thing: and answer me."

ἀποκριθεὶς δὲ εἶπεν πρὸς αὐτούς, Ἐρωτήσω ὑμᾶς κἀγὼ λόγον, καὶ εἴπατέ μοι.

ἀποκριθεὶς (aor.mid.part.nom.sing.masc.of ἀποκρίνομαι, adverbial, modal) 318.
δὲ (adversative conjunction) 11.
εἶπεν (3d.per.sing.aor.act.ind.of εἶπον, constative) 155.
πρὸς (preposition with the accusative of extent after a verb of speaking) 197.
αὐτούς (acc.pl.masc.of αὐτός, extent after a verb of speaking) 16.
Ἐρωτήσω (1st.per.sing.fut.act.ind.of ἐρωτάω, predictive) 1172.
ὑμᾶς (acc.pl.masc.of σύ, direct object of Ἐρωτήσω) 104.
κἀγὼ (continuative conjunction, crasis, subject of Ἐρωτήσω) 178.

λόγον (acc.sing.masc.of *λόγος*, direct object of'*Ερωτήσω*, double accusative) 510.

καὶ (continuative conjunction) 14.
εἴπατέ (2d.per.pl.aor.act.impv.of *εἶπον*, command) 155.
μοι (dat.sing.masc.of *ἐγώ*, indirect object of *εἴπατέ*) 123.

Translation - "But Jesus thought about it a moment and said to them, 'I also will ask you a question, and you tell me. . .' "

Comment: *Cf.* comment on Mt.21:24 and Mk.11:29. Luke shortens our Lord's response by leaving out His promise to answer their question if they would answer one for Him. We can consider *ἀποκριθεὶς* as redundant, as it comes out in the AV - "Jesus answered and said. . . " In which case we leave it untranslated, or we can construe it as indicating an intellectual evaluation of the demand of the officials and an appropriate response. It is in this sense that we have translated it. *ἀποκρίνομαι* (#318) means "to judge (*κρίνω*) from or in return (*ἀπό*). Jesus is prepared to put the temple officials "on the spot" as they had tried to embarrass Him.

Verse 4 - "The baptism of John, was it from heaven, or of men?"

Τὸ *βάπτισμα* '*Ιωάννου ἐξ οὐρανοῦ ἦν ἢ ἐξ ἀνθρώπων*;

Τὸ (nom.sing.neut.of the article in agreement with *βάπτισμα*) 9.
βάπτισμα (nom.sing.neut.of *βάπτισμα*, subject of *ἦν*) 278.
'*Ιωάννου* (gen.sing.masc.of '*Ιωάννης*, description) 247.
ἐξ (preposition with the ablative of source) 19.
οὐρανοῦ (abl.sing.masc.of *οὐρανός*, source) 254.
ἦν (3d.per.sing.imp.ind.of *εἰμί*, progressive description) 86.
ἢ (disjunctive particle) 465.
ἐξ (preposition with the ablative of source) 19.
ἀνθρώπων (abl.pl.masc.of *ἄνθρωπος*, source) 341.

Translation - "The baptism of John — was it from heaven or from men?"

Comment: *Cf.* comment on Mt.21:25 and Mk.11:30. We have a direct double question, a rare idiom in the New Testament, with *ἢ*, but with the verb *ἦν* missing from the second half of the question.

Verse 5 - "And they reasoned with themselves, saying, If we shall say, from heaven, he will say, Why then believed ye not him?"

οἱ δὲ συνελογίσαντο πρὸς ἑαυτοὺς λέγοντες ὅτι 'Εὰν εἴπωμεν, 'Εξ οὐρανοῦ, ἐρεῖ, Διὰ τί οὐκ ἐπιστεύσατε αὐτῷ;

οἱ (nom.pl.masc.of the article, subject of *συνελογίσαντο*) 9.
δὲ (inferential conjunction) 11.

#2684 *συνελογίσαντο* (3d.per.pl.aor.mid.ind.of *συλλογίζομαι*, ingressive).

reason with - Luke 20:5.

Meaning: A combination of σύν (#1542) and λογίζομαι (#2611). Hence, to reckon, compute, bring together accounts (in an accounting sense). To compare arguments; to take a mental inventory of one's logical position. Of the chief priests assessing their position in argument with Jesus - Luke 20:5.

πρὸς (preposition with the accusative of extent, after a verb of speaking) 197.
ἑαυτοὺς (acc.pl.masc.of ἑαυτός, extent after a verb of speaking) 288.
λέγοντες (pres.act.part.nom.pl.masc.of λέγω, adverbial, modal) 66.
ὅτι (recitative) 211.
'Εὰν (conditional particle in a third-class condition) 363.
εἴπωμεν (1st.per.pl.aor.act.subj.of εἶπον, third-class condition) 155.
'Εξ (preposition with the ablative of source) 19.
οὐρανοῦ (abl.sing.masc.of οὐρανός, source) 254.
ἐρεῖ (3d.per.sing.fut.act.ind.of εἶπον, predictive) 155.
Διὰ (preposition with the accusative of cause) 118.
τί (acc.sing.neut.of τίς, interrogative pronoun, cause) 281.
οὐκ (summary negative conjunction with the indicative) 130.
ἐπιστεύσατε (2d.per.pl.aor.act.ind.of πιστεύω, culminative) 734.
αὐτῷ (dat.sing.masc.of αὐτός, reference) 16.

Translation - "But they began to reason among themselves, saying, 'If we say, From heaven, He will say, Why did you not believe him.' "

Comment: *Cf.* comment on Mt.21:25 and Mk.11:31. No change except that Luke uses συλλογίζομαι (#2684) instead of διαλογίζομαι (#1197). The reaction of the Establishment to Jesus' question reveals that Jesus has indeed already answered their question by asking one. If they admitted that John's baptism and ministry was from a heavenly source they had the answer to their question about where Jesus got His authority, since it was obvious that John had predicted Jesus' arrival (Mt.3:11,12; John 1:19-27) and that the Baptist endorsed Him when He came (Mt.3:13-15; John 1:29-34). But they dared not admit that John was God's messenger since they had not believed him and were not permitted to participate in his baptism, since they were unwilling to meet the conditions which he laid down. To reject John was also to reject Jesus. The only consistency of which they could boast was that they rejected both John and Jesus.

But this put them in jeopardy with the masses - something that a politician dare not do. That is the behavior of a statesman and the chief priests, scribes and elders did not qualify. A politician does not mind being inconsistent, so long as he does not offend the people. In fact most politicians are intellectually incapable of recognizing inconsistency. So the Establishment wished to appear favorable to John, who was dead, but antagonistic to Jesus, who was very much alive - in the temple, with a message that would, if accepted, mean the end of their regime in the position of national power.

Verse 6 - "But and if we say, Of men, all the people will stone us: for they be persuaded that John was a prophet."

ἐὰν δὲ εἴπωμεν, Ἐξ ἀνθρώπων, ὁ λαὸς ἅπας καταλιθάσει ἡμᾶς, πεπεισμένος γάρ ἐστιν Ἰωάννην προφήτην εἶναι.

ἐὰν (conditional particle in a third-class condition) 363.
δὲ (adversative conjunction) 11.
εἴπωμεν (1st.per.pl.aor.act.subj.of εἶπον, third-class condition) 155.
Ἐξ (preposition with the ablative of source) 19.
ἀνθρώπων (abl.pl.masc.of ἄνθρωπος, source) 341.
ὁ (nom.sing.masc.of the article in agreement with λαὸς) 9.
λαὸς (nom.sing.masc.of λαός, subject of καταλιθάσει) 110.
ἅπας (nom.sing.masc.of ἅπας, in agreement with λαὸς) 639.

#2685 καταλιθάσει (3d.per.sing.fut.act.ind.of καταλιθάζω, predictive).

stone - Luke 20:6.

Meaning: A combination of κατά (#98) and λιθάζω (#2377). Hence to stone down, or completely. To knock one down with stones; to prostrate, and even kill with stones - Luke 20:6.

ἡμᾶς (acc.pl.masc.of ἐγώ, direct object of καταλιθάσει) 123.
πεπεισμένος (perf.pass.part.nom.sing.masc.of πείθω, perfect periphrastic) 1629.
γάρ (causal conjunction) 105.
ἐστιν (3d.per.sing.pres.ind.of εἰμί, perfect periphrastic, intensive) 86.
Ἰωάννην (acc.sing.masc.of Ἰωάννης, general reference) 247.
προφήτην (acc.sing.masc.of προφήτης, predicate accusative) 119.
εἶναι (pres.inf.of εἰμί, noun use in an object clause in indirect discourse) 86.

Translation - "But if we say, 'Of men,' all the people will stone us, because they are persuaded that John was a prophet."

Comment: *Cf.* comment on Mt.21:26 and Mk.11:32. We have a third-class condition with ἐὰν and the subjunctive in the protasis and the future indicative in the apodosis. "If we say . . . κ.τ.λ. (which we are most certainly not going to do) they will probably stone us to death." We may be certain that the chief priests and their colleagues were not going to say that John's ministry was authorized only by a human source. Why not? The causal clause with γάρ tells us why. *All* of the people (ἅπας) were firmly convinced (the intensive force in the perfect periphrastic) of what? We have an object clause without ὅτι in indirect discourse with the noun use of the infinitive εἶναι in the accusative case and Ἰωάννην the accusative of general reference. This is a typical and beautiful Lukan use of the classical Greek idiom with which he and Paul were familiar.

Normally present tense (in εἶναι) in indirect discourse stands for present tense in direct, but this is an exception. The direct discourse was, "John *was* a prophet," not "John *is* a prophet," since John was long since dead. Thus here the present tense in indirect discourse stands for the imperfect in direct. "The present infinitive in indirect discourse in the New Testament stands for the present indicative of the direct form," (Burton, *Moods and Tenses,* 52). This is true generally, but Luke 20:6 is an exception to the rule. The Greek grammar rule book, which the sophomores pore over and which must be mastered if we are to translate effectively, must nevertheless yield to the context, which is always the final arbiter. Of course we can interpret it to mean that even though John was dead, the people were still saying, "John *is* a prophet" in the sense that he had the standing of a prophet, though he was no longer living. And yet it is doubtful that when the people talked about John they said, "He is a prophet." They most likely said, "He was a prophet."

The contrast between Jesus and His enemies is startlingly realistic. They knew what to say and what not to say in order to stay alive. And they said the right things and refrained from saying the wrong things at all times. As a result, they stayed alive in the short run. Jesus also knew how to avoid death in the short run, but He told the truth, regardless of the shadow of an impending cross and therefore He died (short run) only to live forever (long run). What does a politican care about truth and consistency? The name of the game is to survive. Talleyrand was once asked what he did during the French Revolution. He replied, "I survived." John Maynard Keynes once said, "In the long run we are all dead." Not my Lord. He was not a politician. He was a statesman and He knew that the only way to live in the long run is to tell and act upon the truth in the short run.

Verse 7 - "And they answered that they could not tell whence it was."

καὶ ἀπεκρίθησαν μὴ εἰδέναι πόθεν.

καὶ (inferential conjunction) 14.
ἀπεκρίθησαν (3d.per.pl.aor.mid.ind.of *ἀποκρίνομαι*, constative) 318.
μὴ (qualified negative conjunction with the infinitive) 87.
εἰδέναι (perf.inf.of *ὁράω*, in an object clause in indirect discourse) 144.
πόθεν (interrogative conjunction) 1061.

Translation - "Therefore they replied that they had never been able to decide where it came from."

Comment: *καὶ* is inferential. What they said in verse 7 was upon the basis of what they said to each other in verses 5 and 6. They dared not say, "From heaven" (verse 5). They dared not say, "From men" (verse 6). But they had to say something. So they said that they had never been able to decide (verse 7). The perfect infinitive in indirect discourse stands for the perfect indicative in direct. What had they always said, at least according to what they are telling Jesus now? "We have not in the past been able to make up our minds about John and his ministry and therefore we have never known; nor do we know now." Thus they revealed the extent to which prejudice blinds the minds of the unsaved (2 Cor.4:4). They did not know? Even in the face of all of the evidence?!

Verse 8 - "And Jesus said unto them, Neither tell I you by what authority I do these things."

καὶ ὁ Ἰησοῦς εἶπεν αὐτοῖς, Οὐδὲ ἐγὼ λέγω ὑμῖν ἐν ποίᾳ ἐξουσίᾳ ταῦτα ποιῶ.

καὶ (inferential conjunction) 14.
ὁ (nom.sing.masc.of the article in agreement with *Ἰησοῦς*) 9.
Ἰησοῦς (nom.sing.masc.of *Ἰησοῦς*, subject of *εἶπεν*) 3.
εἶπεν (3d.per.sing.aor.act.ind.of *εἶπον*, constative) 155.
αὐτοῖς (dat.pl.masc.of *αὐτός*, indirect object of *εἶπεν*) 16.
Οὐδὲ (disjunctive particle) 452.
ἐγὼ (nom.sing.masc.of *ἐγώ*, subject of *λέγω*) 123.
λέγω (1st.per.sing.pres.act.ind.of *λέγω*, futuristic) 66.
ὑμῖν (dat.pl.masc.of *σύ*, indirect object of *λέγω*) 104.
ἐν (preposition with the instrumental of agent) 80.
ποίᾳ (instru.sing.fem.of *ποῖος*, in agreement with *ἐξουσίᾳ*) 1298.
ἐξουσίᾳ (instru.sing.fem.of *ἐξουσία*, agent) 707.
ταῦτα (acc.pl.neut.of *οὗτος*, direct object of *ποιῶ*) 93.
ποιῶ (1st.per.sing.pres.act.ind.of *ποιέω*, aoristic) 127.

Translation - "So Jesus said to them, 'Neither am I going to tell you by what authority I am doing these things.' "

Comment: *Cf.* comment on Mt.21:27; Mk.11:33. He had already told them indirectly, by His question to them, and they knew it. They withdrew from the argument in silent confusion, but not out of earshot, as Jesus continued with a parable in

Verse 9 - "Then began he to speak to the people this parable; a certain man planted a vineyard and let it forth to husbandment, and went into a far country for a long time."

The Parable of the Vineyard and the Tenants

(Matthew 21:33-46; Mark 12:1-12; Luke 20:9-19)

Luke 20:9 - "Then began he to speak to the people this parable: A certain man planted a vineyard and let it forth to husbandmen, and went into a far country for a long time."

Ἤρξατο δὲ πρὸς τὸν λαὸν λέγειν τὴν παραβολὴν ταύτην, Ἄνθρωπός (τις) ἐφύτευσεν ἀμπελῶνα, καὶ ἐξέδετο αὐτὸν γεωργοῖς, καὶ ἀπεδήμησεν χρόνους ἱκανούς.

Ἤρξατο (3d.per.sing.aor.mid.ind.of *ἄρχω*, ingressive) 383.
δὲ (continuative conjunction) 11.
πρὸς (preposition with the accusative of extent, with a verb of speaking) 197.
τὸν (acc.sing.masc.of the article in agreement with *λαὸν*) 9.
λαὸν (acc.sing.masc.of *λαός*, extent with a verb of speaking) 110.
λέγειν (pres.act.inf.of *λέγω*, completes *Ἤρξατο*) 66.
τὴν (acc.sing.fem.of the article in agreement with *παραβολὴν*) 9.
παραβολὴν (acc.sing.fem.of *παραβολή*, direct object of *λέγειν*) 1027.

ταύτην (acc.sing.fem.of οὗτος, in agreement with παραβολὴν) 93.
Ἄνθρωπος (nom.sing.masc.of ἄνθρωπος, subject of ἐφύτευσεν, ἐξέδετο and ἀπεδήμησεν) 341.
(τις) (nom.sing.masc.of τις, the indefinite pronoun, in agreement with Ἄνθρωπος) 486.
ἐφύτευσεν (3d.per.sing.aor.act.ind.of φυτεύω, constative) 1154.
ἀμπελῶνα (acc.sing.masc.of ἀμπελών, direct object of ἐφύτευσεν) 1316.
καὶ (adjunctive conjunction joining verbs) 14.
ἐξέδετο (3d.per.sing.aor.mid.ind.of ἐκδίδωμι, constative) 1380.
αὐτὸν (acc.sing.masc.of αὐτός, direct object of ἐξέδετο) 16.
γεωργοῖς (dat.pl.masc.of γεωργός, indirect object of ἐξέδετο) 1381.
καὶ (adjunctive conjunction joining verbs) 14.
ἀπεδήμησεν (3d.per.sing.aor.act.ind.of ἀποδημέω, constative) 1382.
χρόνους (acc.pl.masc.of χρόνος, time extent) 168.
ἱκανούς (acc.pl.masc.of ἱκανός, in agreement with χρόνους) 304.

Translation - "And He began to narrate this parable to the people: Some man planted a vineyard and leased it to farmers and went away for a long time."

Comment: *Cf.* comment on Mt.21:33; Mk.12:1. Luke leaves out some of the detail included in Matthew and Mark but adds the accusative phrase of time extent at the end - χρόνους ἱκανούς. He went away to a far country and was gone a long time. Matthew records another parable before the parable of the vineyard in Mt.21:28-32, *q.v.* It is at the expense of the Jewish leaders as is the one before us.

Verse 10 - "And at the season he sent a servant to the husbandmen, that they should give him the fruit of the vineyard; but the husbandmen beat him and sent him away empty."

καὶ καιρῷ ἀπέστειλεν πρὸς τοὺς γεωργοὺς δοῦλον, ἵνα ἀπὸ τοῦ καρποῦ τοῦ ἀμπελῶνος δώσουσιν αὐτῷ, οἱ δε γεωργοὶ ἐξαπέστειλαν αὐτὸν δείραντες κενόν .

καὶ (continuative conjunction) 14.
καιρῷ (loc.sing.masc.of καιρός, time point) 767.
ἀπέστειλεν (3d.per.sing.aor.act.ind.of ἀποστέλλω, constative) 215.
πρὸς (preposition with the accusative of extent) 197.
τοὺς (acc.pl.masc.of the article in agreement with γεωργοὺς) 9.
γεωργοὺς (acc.pl.masc.of γεωργός, extent) 1381.
δοῦλον (acc.sing.masc.of δοῦλος, direct object of ἀπέστειλεν) 725.
ἵνα (conjunction introducing the future indicative in a final clause) 114.
ἀπὸ (preposition with the ablative of source) 70.
τοῦ (abl.sing.masc.of the article in agreement with καρποῦ) 9.
καρποῦ (abl.sing.masc.of καρπός, source) 284.
τοῦ (gen.sing.masc.of the article in agreement with ἀμπελῶνος) 9.
ἀμπελῶνος (gen.sing.masc.of ἀμπελών, description) 1316.
δώσουσιν (3d.per.pl.fut.act.ind.of δίδωμι, final clause) 362.

αὐτῷ (dat.sing.masc.of *αὐτός*, indirect object of *δώσουσιν*) 16.
οἱ (nom.pl.masc.of the article in agreement with *γεωργοὶ*) 9.
δὲ (adversative conjunction) 11.
γεωργοὶ (nom.pl.masc.of *γεωργός*, subject of *ἐξαπέστειλαν*) 1381.
αὐτὸν (acc.sing.masc.of *αὐτός*, direct object of *ἐξαπέστειλαν* and *δείραντες*) 16.
δείραντες (aor.act.part.nom.pl.masc.of *δέρω*, adverbial, temporal) 1383.
κενόν (acc.sing.neut.of *κενός*, adverbial accusative) 1836.

Translation - "And at harvest time he sent to the farmers a servant, in order that they might give him some of the fruit of the vineyard, but after they had beaten him the farmers sent him away empty handed."

Comment: *Cf.* comment on Mt.21:34,35; Mk.12:2,3. Note *ἵνα* with the future indicative in a final clause. "In classical Greek *ἵνα* was not used with the future indicative. (Goodwin, *Moods and Tenses*, 115, as cited in Robertson, *Grammar*, 984). It was not common even with *ὅπως*, *ὡς* and *μή* (*Ibid*). "The future indicative is not merely a tense in the true sense of that term, expressing the state of the action. It is almost a mode on a par with the subjunctive and imperative. Gildersleeve puts the matter plainly when he says, "The future was originally a mood." (Gildersleeve, *Syntax*, 115, as cited in *Ibid.*,872). In both Greek and Latin the forms of the future come for the most part from the subj. and it must be treated as a mode as well as a tense. . . It partakes, as a matter of fact, of the qualities of both mood and tense, and both need to be considered." (*Ibid.*, 872).

Verse 11 - "And again he sent another servant: and they beat him also, and entreated him shamefully, and sent him away empty."

καὶ προσέθετο ἕτερον πέμψαι δοῦλον, οἱ δὲ κἀκεῖνον δείραντες καὶ ἀτιμάσαντες ἐξαπέστειλαν κενόν.

καὶ (continuative conjunction) 14.
προσέθετο (3d.per.sing.2d.aor.mid.ind.of *προστίθημι*, constative) 621.
ἕτερον (acc.sing.masc.of *ἕτερος*, in agreement with *δοῦλον*) 605.
πέμψαι (aor.act.inf.of *πέμπω*, completes *προσέθετο*) 169.
δοῦλον (acc.sing.masc.of *δοῦλος*, direct object of *πέμψαι*) 725.
οἱ (nom.pl.masc.of the article, subject of *ἐξαπέστειλαν*) 9.
δὲ (adversative conjunction) 11.
κἀκεῖνον (acc.sing.masc.of *κἀκεῖνος*, direct object of *ἐξαπέστειλαν*, *δείραντες* and *ἀτιμάσαντες*) 1164.
δείραντες (aor.act.part.nom.pl.masc.of *δέρω*, adverbial, temporal) 1383.
καὶ (adjunctive conjunction joining participles) 14.
ἀτιμάσαντες (aor.act.part.nom.pl.masc.of *ἀτιμάζω*, adverbial, temporal) 2390.
ἐξαπέστειλαν (3d.per.pl.aor.act.ind.of *ἐξαποστέλλω*, constative) 1835.
κενόν (acc.sing.neut.of *κενός*, adverbial accusative) 1836.

Translation - "And he proceeded to send another servant, but when they had beaten and insulted him,they sent him away empty handed."

Comment: προσέθετο . . . πέμψαι is an interesting idiom. *Cf.*#621 and see it followed by an infinitive also in Luke 20:12 and Acts 12:3. δὲ is adversative. The farmers were no more disposed to share the crop with the second servant than with the first. The participles indicate their treatment of him before they sent him back, as they had the first, empty handed. *Cf.*Mt.21:36; Mk.12:4.

Verse 12 - "And again he sent a third: and they wounded him also and cast him out."

καὶ προσέθετο τρίτον πέμψαι, οἱ δὲ καὶ τοῦτον τραυματίσαντες ἐξέβαλον.

καὶ (continuative conjunction) 14.
προσέθετο (3d.per.sing.2d.aor.act.ind.of προστίθημι, constative) 621.
τρίτον (acc.sing.masc.of τρίτος, direct object of πέμψαι) 1209.
πέμψαι (aor.act.inf.of πέμπω, completes προσέθετο) 169.
οἱ (nom.pl.masc.of the article, subject of ἐξέβαλον) 9.
δὲ (adversative conjunction) 11.
καὶ (adjunctive conjunction joining pronouns) 14.
τοῦτον (acc.sing.masc.of οὗτος, direct object of ἐξέβαλον) 93.

#2686 τραυματίσαντες (aor.act.part.nom.pl.masc.of τραυματίζω, adverbial, temporal).

wound - Luke 20:12; Acts 19:16.

Meaning: To inflict a wound. In the parable of the vineyard - Luke 20:12; of the sons of Sceva - Acts 19:16.

ἐξέβαλον (3d.per.pl.aor.act.ind.of ἐκβάλλω, constative) 649.

Translation - "And he proceeded to send a third, but after they had wounded him also they cast him out."

Comment: *Cf.* comment on Mt.21:36; Mk.12:5. Luke's new word τραυματίζω (#2686) is general. Mark 12:5 says that they wounded the second servant in the head.

Verse 13 - "Then said the lord of the vineyard, What shall I do? I will send my beloved son: it may be they will reverence him when they see him."

εἶπεν δὲ ὁ κύριος τοῦ ἀμπελῶνος, Τί ποιήσω; πέμψω τὸν υἱόν μου τὸν ἀγαπητόν. ἴσως τοῦτον ἐντραπήσονται.

εἶπεν (3d.per.sing.aor.act.ind.of εἶπον, constative) 155.
δὲ (continuative conjunction) 11.
ὁ (nom.sing.masc.of the article in agreement with κύριος) 9.
κύριος (nom.sing.masc.of κύριος, subject of εἶπεν) 97.
τοῦ (gen.sing.masc.of the article in agreement with ἀμπελῶνος) 9.
ἀμπελῶνος (gen.sing.masc.of ἀμπελών, description) 1316.

Tί (acc.sing.neut.of *τίς*, interrogative pronoun, direct object of *ποιήσω*) 281.
ποιήσω (1st.per.sing.fut.act.ind.of *ποιέω*, deliberative) 127.
πέμψω (1st.per.sing.fut.act.ind.of *πέμπω*, predictive) 169.
τὸν (acc.sing.masc.of the article in agreement with *υἱόν*) 9.
υἱόν (acc.sing.masc.of *υἱός*, direct object of *πέμψω*) 5.
μου (gen.sing.masc.of *ἐγώ*, relationship) 123.
τὸν (acc.sing.masc.of the article in agreement with *ἀγαπητόν*) 9.
ἀγαπητόν (acc.sing.masc.of *ἀγαπητός*, in agreement with *υἱόν*) 327.

#2687 *ἴσως* (adverbial).

it may be - Luke 20:13.

Meaning: Cf.ἴσος (#1323). From Sophocles down - "it may be." Perhaps, agreeably to expectation - Luke 20:13.

τοῦτον (acc.sing.masc.of *οὗτος*, direct object of *ἐντραπήσονται*) 93.
ἐντραπήσονται (3d.per.pl.fut.pass.ind.of *ἐντρέπω*, deliberative) 1385.

Translation - "And the owner of the vineyard said, 'What shall I do? I will send my son, the beloved one. Perhaps they will respect him.' "

Comment: *Cf.* comment on Mt.21:37; Mk.12:6. Here again, as in the parallel accounts, we have *ἐντραπήσονται*, a future passive, but without a passive sense. Except for the fact that *τοῦτον* is accusative, the object of the verb, we might translate "Perhaps they will be overawed (shamed) by him."

Verse 14 - "But when the husbandmen saw him, they reasoned among themselves, saying, This is the heir: come, let us kill him, that the inheritance may be ours."

ἰδόντες δὲ αὐτὸν οἱ γεωργοὶ διελογίζοντο πρὸς ἀλλήλους λέγοντες, Οὗτός ἐστιν ὁ κληρονόμος, ἀποκτείνωμεν αὐτόν, ἵνα ἡμῶν γένηται ἡ κληρονομία.

ἰδόντες (aor.act.part.nom.pl.masc.of *ὁράω*, adverbial, temporal) 144.
δὲ (adversative conjunction) 11.
αὐτὸν (acc.sing.masc.of *αὐτός*, direct object of *ἰδόντες*) 16.
οἱ (nom.pl.masc.of the article in agreement with *γεωργοὶ*) 9.
γεωργοὶ (nom.pl.masc.of *γεωργός*, subject of *διελογίζοντο*) 1381.
διελογίζοντο (3d.per.pl.imp.mid.ind.of *διαλογίζομαι*, inceptive) 1197.
πρὸς (preposition with the accusative of extent after a verb of speaking) 197.
ἀλλήλους (acc.pl.masc.of *ἀλλήλων*, after a verb of speaking) 1487.
λέγοντες (pres.act.part.nom.pl.masc.of *λέγω*, adverbial, modal) 66.
Οὗτός (nom.sing.masc.of *οὗτος*, predicate nominative) 93.
ἐστιν (3d.per.sing.pres.ind.of *εἰμί*, static) 86.
ὁ (nom.sing.masc.of the article in agreement with *κληρονόμος*) 9.
κληρονόμος (nom.sing.masc.of *κληρονόμος*, subject of *ἐστιν*) 1386.
ἀποκτείνωμεν (1st.per.pl.pres.act.subj.of *ἀποκτείνω*, hortatory) 889.
αὐτόν (acc.sing.masc.of *αὐτός*, direct object of *ἀποκτείνωμεν*) 16.

ἵνα (conjunction introducing the subjunctive in a purpose clause) 114.
ἡμῶν (gen.pl.masc.of ἐγώ, possession) 123.
γένηται (3d.per.sing.aor.subj.of γίνομαι, purpose) 113.
ἡ (nom.sing.fem.of the article in agreement with κληρονομία) 9.
κληρονομία (nom.sing.fem.of κληρονομία, subject of γένηται) 1387.

Translation - "But when they saw him the farmers began to reason with one another saying, 'This is the heir. Let us kill him so that the inheritance may become ours.' "

Comment: *Cf.* comment on Mt.21:38; Mk.12:7. Note ἡμῶν as a predicate genitive denoting possession as in Mk.12:7. *Cf.* 1 Thess.5:5,6,8; 1 Cor.1:12; 6:19. Others will be discussed *en loc.* Here it is also placed in emphasis, indicating the dominant desire of the tenants to own the vineyard.

Verse 15 - "So they cast him out of the vineyard and killed him. What therefore shall the lord of the vineyard do unto them?"

καὶ ἐκβαλόντες αὐτὸν ἔξω τοῦ ἀμπελῶνος ἀκέκτειναν. τί οὖν ποιήσει αὐτοῖς ὁ κύριος τοῦ ἀμπελῶνος;

καὶ (inferential conjunction) 14.
ἐκβαλόντες (aor.act.part.nom.pl.masc.of ἐκβάλλω, adverbial, temporal) 649.
αὐτὸν (acc.sing.masc.of αὐτός, direct object of ἐκβαλόντες and ἀπέκτειναν) 16.
ἔξω (adverbial) 449.
τοῦ (abl.sing.masc.of the article in agreement with ἀμπελῶνος) 9.
ἀμπελῶνος (abl.sing.masc.of ἀμπελών, separation) 1316.
ἀπέκτειναν (3d.per.pl.aor.act.ind.of ἀποκτείνω, constative) 889.
τί (acc.sing.neut.of τίς, the interrogative pronoun, direct object of ποιήσει) 281.
οὖν (inferential conjunction) 68.
ποιήσει (3d.per.sing.fut.act.ind.of ποιέω, deliberative) 127.
αὐτοῖς (dat.pl.masc.of αὐτός, personal disadvantage) 16.
ὁ (nom.sing.masc.of the article in agreement with κύριος) 9.
κύριος (nom.sing.masc.of κύριος, subject of ποιήσει) 97.
τοῦ (gen.sing.masc.of the article in agreement with ἀμπελῶνος) 9.
ἀμπελῶνος (gen.sing.masc.of ἀμπελών, description) 1316.

Translation - "So they threw him out of the vineyard and killed him. What, then, will the lord of the vineyard do to them?"

Comment: "The future indicative is sometimes used in questions of deliberation, asking not what will happen, but what can or ought to be done. Such questions may be real questions asking information, or rhetorical questions taking the place of a direct assertion." (Burton, *Moods and Tenses*, 36). We have such a rhetorical question here. Jesus was not asking for information, since He answered His own question in the next verse. *Cf.*John 6:68. The deliberative subjunctive also serves in this capacity. *Cf.* Lk.3:10. For other deliberative futures, *cf.* Rom.3:5; 6:1; Mk.12:9; Mt.21:40.

Verse 16 - "He shall come and destroy these husbandmen, and shall give the vineyard to others. And when they heard it, they said, God forbid."

ἐλεύσεται καὶ ἀπολέσει τοὺς γεωργοὺς τούτους, καὶ δώσει τὸν ἀμπελῶνα ἄλλοις. ἀκούσαντες δὲ εἶπαν, Μὴ γένοιτο.

ἐλεύσεται (3d.per.sing.fut.mid.ind.of ἔρχομαι, predicitve) 146.
καὶ (adjunctive conjunction joining verbs) 14.
ἀπολέσει (3d.per.sing.fut.act.ind.of ἀπόλλυμι, predictive) 208.
τοὺς (acc.pl.masc.of the article in agreement with γεωργοὺς) 9.
γεωργοὺς (acc.pl.masc.of γεωργός, direct object of ἀπολέσει) 1381.
τούτους (acc.pl.masc.of οὗτος, in agreement with γεωργοὺς) 93.
καὶ (adjunctive conjunction joining verbs) 14.
δώσει (3d.per.sing.fut.act.ind.of δίδωμι, predictive) 362.
τὸν (acc.sing.masc.of the article in agreement with ἀμπελῶνα) 9.
ἀμπελῶνα (acc.sing.masc.of ἀμπελών, direct object of δώσει) 1316.
ἄλλοις (dat.pl.masc.of ἄλλος, indirect object of δώσει) 198.
ἀκούσαντες (aor.act.part.nom.pl.masc.of ἀκούω, adverbial, temporal/causal) 148.
δὲ (adversative conjunction) 11.
εἶπαν (3d.per.pl.aor.act.ind.of εἶπον,constative) 155.
Μὴ (qualified negative conjunction with the optative) 87.
γένοιτο (3d.per.sing.2d.aor.optative of γίνομαι, protest) 113.

Translation - "He will come and he will destroy those farmers and he will give the vineyard to others. But when they heard it they said, 'May it never be!' "

Comment: *Cf.* comment on Mt.21:41; Mk.12:9. Note that Matthew records that the lord would expect better things of those to whom he had entrusted the vineyard. Luke alone adds the exclamation of dismay Μὴ γένοιτο, which fell from the lips of the chief priests who had withdrawn, but not far enough to be out of hearing (Mk.12:12). They understood that Jesus was saying that they were the descendants of those who had killed the prophets and were soon to murder the heir. Now He says that they will lose the vineyard to others. This is clear evidence that the hidden meaning of the parable was not lost on Jesus' audience. For this strong negation, μὴ γένοιτο, *cf.*#113 in all references where the English translation is "forbid." Grammarians refer to it as a volitive optative. Modern Greeks say ὁ θεὸς νὰ φυλάξῃ - "may God guard against it" instead of μὴ γένοιτο - "may God forbid." Of the 38 instances of the optative in the New Testament, 15 are used with μὴ in μὴ γένοιτο - one here, in Luke 20:16 and the other 14 in the Pauline epistles. The Establishment leaders were horrified at the thought that they should lose control of the kingdom.

Verse 17 - "And he beheld them and said, What is this then that is written, The stone which the builders rejected, the same is become the head of the corner."

ὁ δὲ ἐμβλέψας αὐτοῖς εἶπεν, Τί οὖν ἐστιν τὸ γεγραμμένον τοῦτο, Λίθον ὃν ἀπεδοκίμασαν οἱ οἰκοδομοῦντες, οὗτος ἐγενήθη εἰς κεφαλὴν γωνίας;

ὁ (nom.sing.masc.of the article, subject of εἶπεν) 9.
δὲ (adversative conjunction) 11.
ἐμβλέψας (aor.act.part.nom.sing.masc.of ἐμβλέπω, adverbial, temporal) 614.
αὐτοῖς (dat.pl.masc.of αὐτός, indirect object of εἶπεν) 16.
εἶπεν (3d.per.sing.aor.act.ind.of εἶπον, constative) 155.
Τί (nom.sing.neut.of τίς, the interrogative pronoun, predicate nominative, direct question) 281.
οὖν (inferential conjunction) 68.
ἐστιν (3d.per.sing.pres.ind.of εἰμί, static) 86.
τὸ (nom.sing.neut.of the article in agreement with γεγραμμένον) 9.
γεγραμμένον (perf.pass.part.nom.sing.neut.of γράφω, subject of ἐστιν) 156.
τοῦτο (nom.sing.neut.of οὗτος, in agreement with γεγραμμένον, deictic) 93.
Λίθον (acc.sing.masc.of λίθος, inverse attraction to ὃν, subject of ἐγενήθη) 290.
ὃν (acc.sing.masc.of ὅς, direct object of ἀπεδοκίμασαν) 65.
ἀπεδοκίμασαν (3d.per.pl.aor.act.ind.of ἀποδοκιμάζω, culminative) 1390.
οἱ (nom.pl.masc.of the article in agreement with οἰκοδομοῦντες) 9.
οἰκοδομοῦντες (pres.act.part.nom.pl.masc.of οἰκοδομέω, substantival, subject of ἀπεδοκίμασαν) 694.
οὗτος (nom.sing.masc.of οὗτος, subject of ἐγενήθη, deictic) 93.
ἐγενήθη (3d.per.sing.aor.pass.ind.of γίνομαι, culminative) 113.
εἰς (preposition with the predicate accusative) 140.
κεφαλὴν (acc.sing.fem.of κεφαλή, predicate accusative) 521.
γωνίας (gen.sing.fem.of γωνία, description) 567.

Translation - "And He looked up and said to them, 'What then does this scripture mean, 'The stone which the builders rejected - that one has become the corner stone?' "

Comment: *Cf.* comment on Mt.21:42; Mk.12:10.

Verse 18 - "Whosoever shall fall upon that stone shall be broken; but on whomsoever it shall fall, it will grind him to powder."

πᾶς ὁ πεσὼν ἐπ' ἐκεῖνον τὸν λίθον συνθλασθήσεται, ἐφ' ὃν δ' ἂν πέσῃ, λικμήσει αὐτόν.

πᾶς (nom.sing.masc.of πᾶς, in agreement with πεσὼν) 67.
ὁ (nom.sing.masc.of the article in agreement with πεσὼν) 9.
πεσὼν (2d.aor.act.part.nom.sing.masc.of πίπτω, substantival, subject of συνθλασθήσεται) 187.
ἐπ' (preposition with the accusative of extent) 47.

ἐκεῖνον (acc.sing.masc.of ἐκεῖνος, in agreement with λίον, deictic) 246.
τὸν (acc.sing.masc.of the article in agreement with λίθον) 9.
λίθον (acc.sing.masc.of λίθος, extent) 290.
συνθλασθήσεται (3d.per.sing.fut.pass.ind.of συνθλάω, predictive) 1392.
ἐφ' (preposition with the accusative of extent) 47.
ὃν (acc.sing.masc.of ὅς, extent, in a more probable relative clause) 65.
δ' (adversative conjunction) 11.
ἂν (contingent particle in a more probable relative clause) 205.
πέσῃ (3d.per.sing.2d.aor.act.subj.of πίπτω, in a more probable relative clause) 187.
λικμήσει (3d.per.sing.fut.act.ind.of λικμάω, predictive) 1393.
αὐτόν (acc.sing.masc.of αὐτός, direct object of λικμήσει) 16.

Translation - "Everyone who falls upon that stone will be broken, but upon whom it may fall - it will pulverize him."

Comment: *Cf.*Mt.21:44.

Verse 19 - "And the chief priests and the scribes the same hour sought to lay hands on him; and they feared the people: for their perceived that he had spoken this parable against them."

Καὶ ἐζήτησαν οἱ γραμματεῖς καὶ οἱ ἀρχιερεῖς ἐπιβαλεῖν ἐπ' αὐτὸν τὰς χεῖρος ἐν αὐτῇ τῇ ὥρᾳ, καὶ ἐφοβήθησαν τὸν λαόν, ἔγνωσαν γὰρ ὅτι πρὸς αὐτοὺς εἶπεν τὴν παραβολὴν ταύτην.

Καὶ (continuative conjunction) 14.
ἐζήτησαν (3d.per.pl.aor.act.ind.of ζητέω, ingressive) 207.
οἱ (nom.pl.masc.of the article in agreement with γραμματεῖς) 9.
γραμματεῖς (nom.pl.masc.of γραμματεύς, subject of ἐζήτησαν, ἐφοβήθησαν and ἔγνωσαν) 152.
καὶ (adjunctive conjunction joining nouns) 14.
οἱ (nom.pl.masc.of the article in agreement with ἀρχιερεῖς) 9.
ἀρχιερεῖς (nom.pl.masc.of ἀρχιερεύς, subject of ἐζήτησαν, ἐφοβήτησαν and ἔγνωσαν) 151.
ἐπιβαλεῖν (2d.aor.act.inf.of ἐπιβάλλω, completes ἐζήτησαν) 800.
ἐπ' (preposition with the accusative of extent) 47.
αὐτὸν (acc.sing.masc.of αὐτός, extent) 16.
τὰς (acc.pl.fem.of the article in agreement with χεῖρας) 9.
χεῖρας (acc.pl.fem.of χείρ, direct object of ἐπιβαλεῖν) 308.
ἐν (preposition with the locative of time point) 80.
αὐτῇ (loc.sing.fem.of αὐτός, in agreement with ὥρᾳ, emphatic) 16.
τῇ (loc.sing.fem.of the article in agreement with ὥρᾳ) 9.
ὥρᾳ (loc.sing.fem.of ὥρα, time point) 735.
καὶ (adversative conjunction) 14.
ἐφοβήθησαν (3d.per.pl.aor.mid.ind.of φοβέομαι, constative) 101.
τὸν (acc.sing.masc.of the article in agreement with λαόν) 9.
λαόν (acc.sing.masc.of λαός, direct object of ἐφοβήθησαν) 110.

ἔγνωσαν (3d.per.pl.aor.act.ind.of γινώσκω, ingressive) 131.
γὰρ (causal conjunction) 105.
ὅτι (conjunction introducing an object clause in indirect discourse) 211.
πρὸς (preposition with the accusative with persons, opposition) 197.
αὐτοὺς (acc.pl.masc.of αὐτός, opposition) 16.
εἶπεν (3d.per.sing.aor.act.ind.of εἶπον, culminative) 155.
τὴν (acc.sing.fem.of the article in agreement with παραβολὴν) 9.
παραβολὴν (acc.sing.fem.of παραβολή, direct object of εἶπεν) 1027.
ταύτην (acc.sing.fem.of οὗτος, in agreement with παραβολὴν, deictic) 93.

Translation - "And the scribes and the chief priests began to try to lay their hands on Him at that time, but they were afraid of the people, because they realized that He had spoken this parable against them."

Comment: Robertson calls πρὸς αὐτοὺς an accusative of general reference, - "He had spoken this parable with reference to them." This, of course is true, and perhaps closer to the text. The idea of opposition is supplied by the context. *Cf.* Acts 23:30b; Eph.6:11b, 12a,b,c,d,e; Col.3:13,19.

Controversy With the Pharisees and Herodians About Paying Tribute to Caesar

(Matthew 15:15-22; Mark 12:13-17; Luke 20:20-26)

Mark 12:13 - "And they send unto him certain of the Pharisees and of the Herodians, to catch him in his words."

Καὶ ἀποστέλλουσιν πρὸς αὐτόν τινας τῶν Φαρισαίων καὶ τῶν Ἡρῳδιανῶν ἵνα αὐτὸν ἀγρεύσωσιν λόγῳ.

Καὶ (continuative conjunction) 14.
ἀποστέλλουσιν (3d.per.pl.pres.act.ind.of ἀποστέλλω, historical) 215.
πρὸς (preposition with the accusative of extent) 197.
αὐτόν (acc.sing.masc.of αὐτός, extent) 16.
τινας (acc.pl.masc.of τις, the indefinite pronoun, direct object of ἀποστέλλοῦσιν) 486.
τῶν (gen.pl.masc.of the article in agreement with Φαρισαῖων) 9.
Φαρισαῖων (gen.pl.masc.of Φαρισαῖος, partitive) 276.
καὶ (adjunctive conjunction joining nouns) 14.
τῶν (gen.pl.masc.of the article in agreement with Ἡρῳδιανῶν) 9.
Ἡρῳδιανῶν (gen.pl.masc.of Ἡρῳδιανοί, partitive) 1414.
ἵνα (conjunction introducing the subjunctive in a purpose clause) 114.
αὐτὸν (acc.sing.masc.of αὐτός, direct object of ἀγρεύσωσιν) 16.

#2688 ἀγρεύσωσιν (3d.per.pl.1st.aor.act.subj.of ἀγρεύω, purpose).

catch - Mark 12:13.

Meaning: properly, to catch in a trap as with animals or fish. In Mark 12:13, followed by *λόγῳ*, a locative of sphere. Hence, to entrap in some illogical statement.

λόγῳ (loc.sing.masc.of *λόγος*, sphere) 510.

Translation - "And they sent to Him some of the Pharisees and the Herodians, in order to trap Him in an argument."

Comment: *Cf.* Mt.22:15,16; Lk.20:20. The argument with the chief priests, scribes and elders over His authority to cleanse the temple, was followed by His parables of the vineyard (Mk.12:1-12) and the parable of the two sons (Mt.21:28-32). Now the Establishment, embarrassed by the exchange, have withdrawn in confusion (Mk.12:12). In order to recoup some of their losses, they picked a select group of their colleagues from among the Pharisees and Herodians to attack Jesus. Note again Mark's historical present in *ἀποστέλλουσιν*. They did not pick just anyone, but *τινας τῶν Φαρ. καὶ Ἡρ.* No doubt they chose skillful lawyers who were adept at cross examination.

Verse 14 - "And when they were come, they say unto him, Master, we know that thou art true and carest for no man: for thou regardest not the person of men, but teachest the way of God in truth. It is lawful to give tribute to Caesar or not?"

καὶ ἐλθόντες λέγουσιν αὐτῷ, Διδάσκαλε, οἴδαμεν ὅτι ἀληθὴς εἶ καὶ οὐ μέλει σοι περὶ οὐδενός, οὐ γὰρ βλέπεις εἰς πρόσωπον ἀνθρώπων, ἀλλ' ἐπ' ἀληθείας τὴν ὁδὸν τοῦ θεοῦ διδάσκεις. ἔξεστιν δοῦναι κῆνσον Καίσαρι *ἢ οὔ; δῶμεν ἢ μὴ δῶμεν;*

καὶ (continuative conjunction) 14.
ἐλθοντες (aor.part.nom.pl.masc.of *ἔρχομαι*, adverbial, temporal) 146.
λέγουσιν (3d.per.pl.pres.act.ind.of *λέγω*, historical) 66.
αὐτῷ (dat.sing.masc.of *αὐτός*, indirect object of *λέγουσιν*) 16.
Διδάσκαλε (voc.sing.masc.of *διδάσκαλος*, address) 742.
οἴδαμεν (1st.per.pl.pres.act.ind.of *ὁράω*, aoristic) 144.
ὅτι (conjunction introducing an object clause in indirect discourse) 211.
ἀληθὴς (nom.sing.masc.of *ἀληθής*, predicate adjective) 1415.
εἶ (2d.per.sing.pres.ind.of *εἰμί*, static) 86.
καὶ (adjunctive conjunction joining clauses) 14.
οὐ (summary negative conjunction with the indicative) 130.
μέλει (3d.per.sing.pres.act.ind.of *μέλω*, aoristic) 1417.
σοι (dat.sing.masc.of *σύ*, personal interest) 104.
περὶ (preposition with the genitive of reference) 173.
οὐδενός (gen.sing.masc.of *οὐδεις*, reference) 446.
οὐ (summary negative conjunction with the indicative) 130.
γὰρ (causal conjunction) 105.
βλέπεις (2d.per.sing.pres.act.ind.of *βλέπω*, customary) 499.
εἰς (preposition with the accusative of extent) 140.
πρόσωπον (acc.sing.neut.of *πρόσωπον*, extent) 588.

ἀνθρώπων (gen.pl.masc.of ἄνθρωπος, description) 341.
ἀλλ' (alternative conjunction) 343.
ἐπ' (preposition with the genitive, adverbial) 47.
ἀληθείας (gen.sing.fem.of ἀλήθεια, adverbial) 1416.
τὴν (acc.sing.fem.of the article in agreement with ὁδὸν) 9.
ὁδὸν (acc.sing.fem.of ὁδός,direct object of διδάσκεις) 199.

τοῦ (gen.sing.masc.of the article in agreement with θεοῦ) 9.
θεοῦ (gen.sing.masc.of θεός, definition) 124.
διδάσκεις (2d.per.sing.pres.act.ind.of διδάσκω, customary) 403.
ἔξεστιν (impersonal verb in direct question) 966.
δοῦναι (aor.act.inf.of δίδωμι, completes ἔξεστιν) 362.
κῆνσον (acc.sing.masc.of κῆνσος, direct object of δοῦναι) 1243.
Καίσαρι (dat.sing.masc.of Καίσαρι, indirect object of δοῦναι) 1418.
ἢ (disjunctive particle) 465.
οὐ (summary negative conjunction with the indicative) 130.
δῶμεν (1st. per.pl. 2d.aor.act.subj.of δίδωμι, deliberative) 363.
ἢ (disjunctive particle) 465.
μὴ (qualified negative conjunction with the subjunctive) 87.
δῶμεν (1st.per.pl.2d.aor.act.subj.of δίδωμι, deliberative) 362.

Translation - "And they came and said to Him, 'Teacher, we know that you are true and (that) you are not afraid of anybody, because you do not look at the human face; - instead you always teach the way of God truthfully. Is it proper to pay taxes to Caesar or not? Shall we give or shall we not give?' "

Comment: *Cf.*comment on Mt.22:16; Lk.20:21. I have translated literally, in part. The comment reveals what was meant by οὐμέλει σοι περὶ οὐδενός and οὐ . . . βλέπεις εἰς πρόσωπον ἀνθρώπων.

The speech drips with insincerity. Jesus' enemies were about as subtle as a freight train. Herein lies the insult - that they should presume that such an oily Uriah Heep approach would deceive the perceptive Son of God. They admitted that Jesus' gaze penetrated behind the face of mankind; *i.e.* that He could look into the mind and heart of man and tell what he was really thinking, in order to distinguish it from the outer appearance. Jesus could never be gulled. Yet they expected Jesus to fawn upon them because of all of this insincere praise. "You are true." "You are not concerned about anybody" - *i.e.* you belong to no political party; you are not a lobbyist for any particular pressure group. They indeed were . The Herodians were extreme nationalists who wanted Herod to consolidate his hegemony over all of Israel, which thus unified under Herod, might gain independence from Rome. The Pharisees and Herodians normally were at odds, but they were united on this day by their mutual hatred for Jesus. οὐ γὰρ βλέπεις . . .ἀνθρώπων. "You are not deceived by appearances. In modern terms they were saying that Jesus had a great deal of sales resistance. Why then did they suppose that they could trap Him? ἀλλα is strongly alternative. On the contrary "You teach God's way by telling the truth." *Cf.* Acts 4:27a; 10:34 for ἐπ' ἀληθείας in an adverbial sense, as we have it here.

They were wrong when they said, οὐ μέλει σοι περὶ οὐδενός. Jesus cares for all the saints (1 Pet.5:7), but they meant the phrase in a different sense.

Their question implied that they would never think of doing anything unlawful or improper. Was it lawful for a Jew to pay taxes to a Gentile government. Should they pay it or not? The implication was that if Jesus said that it was unlawful they would never pay it again. This is the hypocrsiy to which Jesus referred in verse 15. The question was another of those designed to put Jesus in a position such that no matter what He said they could cash it against Him. If He said that the tax should be paid, they would accuse Him to the San Heḑrin of being friendly to a Gentile power. If He said that it should not be paid, they would accuse Him of sedition before Pilate.

The last clause **δῶμεν ἢ μὴ δῶμεν** is in verse 14 but translated by the KJV in verse 15.

Verse 15 - "Shall we give, or shall we not give? But he, knowing their hypocrisy, said unto them, Why tempt ye me? bring me a penny, that I may see it."

ὁ δὲ εἰδὼς αὐτῶν τὴν ὑπόκρισιν εἶπεν αὐτοῖς, Τί με πειράζετε; φέρετέ μοι δηνάριον ἵνα ἴδω.

ὁ (nom.sing.masc.of the article, subject of **εἶπεν**) 9.
δὲ (adversative conjunction) 11.
εἰδὼς (pres.act.part.nom.sing.masc.of **ὁράω**, adverbial, causal) 144.
αὐτῶν (gen.pl.masc.of **αὐτός**, possession) 16.
τὴν (acc.sing.fem.of the article in agreement with **ὑπόκρισιν**) 9.
ὑπόκρισιν (acc.sing.fem.of **ὑπόκρισις**, direct object of **εἰδὼς**) 1469.
εἶπεν (3d.per.sing.aor.act.ind.of **εἶπον**, constative) 155.
αὐτοῖς (dat.pl.masc.of **αὐτός**, indirect object of **εἶπεν**) 16.
Τί (acc.sing.neut.of **τίς**, interrogative pronoun, cause) 281.
με (acc.sing.masc.of **ἐγώ**, direct object of **πειράζετε**) 123.
πειράζετε (2d.per.pl.pres.act.ind.of **πειράζω**, progressive) 330.
φέρετέ (2d.per.pl.pres.act.impv.of **φέρω**, command) 683.
μοι (dat.sing.masc.of **ἐγώ**, indirect object of **φέρετέ**) 123.
δηνάριον (acc.sing.neut.of **δηνάριον**, direct object of **φέρετέ**) 1278.
ἵνα (conjunction with the subjunctive in a final clause) 114.
ἴδω (1st.per.sing.aor.act.subj.of **ὁράω**, final) 144.

Translation - "But since He saw through their hypocrisy, He said to them, 'Why are you cross examining me? Bring me a denarius so that I can examine it.'"

Comment: *Cf.* comment on Mt.22:18,19; Mk.20:23,24. **δὲ** is adversative as it is obvious that Jesus was not going to fall for their pretense. The participle is causal. They had asked Him a devious question designed to bring Him into judgment, either from the San Hedrin or from Pilate. Also His answer, whether yes or no, would have polarized the political parties in Israel itself. In fact the Pharisees and Herodians were divided on this question. The Pharisees said, "Yes, pay it." The Herodians said, "No." Thus they thought that by forcing Jesus to answer they could ruin His influence, either with one party or the other. But they had already said that they knew that Jesus was impervious to adverse public opinion - that He always told the truth, and cared nothing about the reactions which might result from what He said. Why, then, did they think that they could embarrass Him with their question? "Yes" would be blasphemy from the Jewish point of view. "No" would be treason in Rome's view.

Jesus replied with the straightest question of the day - Τί με πειράζετε; This should have unmasked them utterly. On defense now, meekly they obeyed His curt imperative - *φέρετέ μοι δηνάριον*. Jesus wanted to examine it, as though He did not already know what He would find! *Cf.*#330 for all of the attempts to trap Jesus.

Verse 16 - "And they brought it. And he saith unto them, Whose is this image and superscription? And they said unto him, Caesar's."

οἱ δὲ ἤνεγκαν. καὶ λέγει αὐτοῖς, Τίνος ἡ εἰκὼν αὕτη καὶ ἡ ἐπιγραφή; οἱ δὲ εἶπαν αὐτῷ Καίσαρος.

οἱ (nom.pl.masc.of the article, subject of ἤνεγκαν) 9.
δὲ (inferential conjunction) 11.
ἤνεγκαν (3d.per.pl.aor.act.ind.of φέρω, constative) 683.
καὶ (continuative conjunction) 14.
λέγει (3d.per.sing.pres.act.ind.of λέγω, historical) 66.
αὐτοῖς (dat.pl.masc.of αὐτός, indirect object of λέγει) 16.
Τίνος (gen.sing.masc.of τίς, the interrogative pronoun, possession) 281.
ἡ (nom.sing.fem.of the article in agreement with εἰκὼν) 9.
εἰκὼν (nom.sing.fem.of εἰκών, subject of ἐστιν understood) 1421.
αὕτη (nom.sing.fem.of οὗτος, in agreement with εἰκὼν, deictic) 93.
καὶ (adjunctive conjunction joining nouns) 14.
ἡ (nom.sing.fem.of the article in agreement with ἐπιγραφή) 9.
ἐπιγραφή (nom.sing.fem.of ἐπιγραφή, subject of ἐστιν understood) 1422.
οἱ (nom.pl.masc.of the article, subject of εἶπαν) 9.
δὲ (continuative conjunction) 11.
εἶπαν (3d.per.pl.aor.act.ind.of εἶπον, constative) 155.
αὐτῷ (dat.sing.masc.of αὐτός, indirect object of εἶπαν) 16.
Καίσαρος (gen.sing.masc.of Καίσαρι, possession) 1418.

Translation - "Therefore they brought (it). And He said to them, 'Of whom is this picture and the superscription?' And they said to Him, 'It is Caesar's.' "

Comment: *Cf.* comment on Mt.22:20; Lk.20:24. Note the absence of the object after ἤνεγκαν. Also the copulative verb in Jesus' question is missing. It was a rapid exchange. Jesus demanded to see a coin; they produced one. He took it and pointed to both sides with the question - "Whose and what - heads and tails?" They said, "Caesar's." The word means, "Emperor. Supreme Ruler. Augustus !" Jesus could have said to them, "It is a graven image. What are you doing with it?" When money is involved Moses' law doesn't count.

Verse 17 - "And Jesus answering said unto them, Render to Caesar the things that are Caesar's, and to God, the things that are God's. And they marvelled at him."

ὁ δὲ Ἰησοῦς εἶπεν αὐτοῖς, Τὰ Καίσαρος ἀπόδοτε Καίσαρι καὶ τὰ τοῦ θεοῦ τῷ θεῷ. καὶ ἐξεθαύμαζον ἐπ' αὐτῷ.

ὁ (nom.sing.masc.of the article in agreement with Ἰησοῦς) 9.
δὲ (continuative conjunction) 11.
Ἰησοῦς (nom.sing.masc.of Ἰησοῦς, subject of εἶπεν) 3.
εἶπεν (3rd.per.sing.aor.act.ind.of εἶπον, constative) 155.
τὰ (acc.pl.neut.of the article, direct object of ἀπόδοτε) 9.
Καίσαρος (gen.sing.masc.of Καίσαρι, possession) 1418.
ἀπόδοτε (2d.per.pl.aor.act.impv.of ἀποδίδωμι, command) 495.
Καίσαρι (dat.sing.masc.of Καίσαρι, indirect object of ἀπόδοτε) 1418.
καὶ (adjunctive conjunction joining clauses) 14.
τὰ (acc.pl.neut.of the article, direct object of ἀπόδοτε) 9.
τοῦ (gen.sing.masc.of the article in agreement with θεοῦ) 9.
θεοῦ (gen.sing.masc.of θεός, possession) 124.
τῷ (dat.sing.masc.of the article in agreement with θεῷ) 9.
θεῷ (dat.sing.masc.of θεός, indirect object of ἀπόδοτε) 124.
καὶ (continuative conjunction) 14.

#2689 ἐξεθαύμαζον (3d.per.pl.imp.act.ind.of ἐκθαυμάζω, inceptive).

marvel - Mark 12:17.

Meaning: A combination of ἐκ (#19) and θαυμάζω (#726). Hence, to marvel; to wonder; to be amazed. Perhaps a more intense emotion than θαυμάζω in Mark 12:17, which is perfective.

ἐπ' (preposition with the locative, with a verb of emotion) 47.
αὐτῷ (locative sing masc.of αὐτός, cause) 16.

Translation - "And Jesus said to them, 'Give back to Caesar that which is Caesar's and that which is God, give to God.' And they were seized with utter amazement."

Comment: *Cf.* comment on Mt.22:21,22; Lk.20:25,26. Jesus here distinguished between the spiritual and the secular sphere and said that the two spheres coexist. They should not be antagonistic, each to the other, nor will they be as long as the secular sphere does not impose its unholy demands upon those who are also subject to the spiritual sphere. Eventually, after the second coming of Messiah, there will be no distinction. World government will be in the hands of Messiah who will also direct all spiritual worship. But in the interim, Christ rules the minds and hearts of men while secular governments of whatever sort - democracies, oligarchies, monarchies, dictatorships - rule their bodies (Rom.13:1-7; 1 Pet.2:13-18). All men have an obligation to support human government since human depravity meakes anarchy impractical. Governments perform services which demand and merit support. Caesar was not all bad. "It is his image and superscription. It is his. Give it to him. You bear the image and superscription of God, your Creator. Give yourself, therefore to God." (Gen.1:26,27; Rom.8:29; 1 Cor.15:49b; 2 Cor.3:18; Col.3:10, 1 Cor.11:7). In the creation sense all men bear the image of God. In the greater recreation sense all Christians are destined to bear His image, just as our Lord bore His image (Col.1:15; 2 Cor.4:4).

Jesus had escaped their trap and laid down, once and for all time, the principle upon which the separation of church and state rests. The Pharisees and Herodians could only stand in silent amazement and then withdraw from the field of verbal battle as had their predecessors (Mt.22:22; Mk.12:12). Robertson says that ἐκ in composition here with θαυμάζω is perfective; *i.e.* it heightens the intensity of their amazement.

We now examine Luke's account of this episode in Luke 20:20-26.

Luke 20:20 - "And they watched him, and sent forth spies, which should feign themselves just men that they might take hold of his words, that so they might deliver him unto the power and authority of the governor."

Καὶ παρατηρήσαντες ἀπέστειλαν ἐγκαθέτους ὑποκρινομένους ἑαυτοὺς δικαίους εἶναι ἵνα ἐπιλάβωνται αὐτοῦ λόγου, ὥστε παραδοῦναι αὐτὸν τῇ ἀρχῇ καὶ τῇ ἐξουσίᾳ τοῦ ἡγεμόνος.

Καὶ (continuative conjunction) 14.
παρατηρήσαντες (aor.act.part.nom.pl.masc.of παρατηρέω, adverbial, temporal) 2104.
ἀπέστειλαν (3d.per.pl.aor.act.ind.ofd ἀποστέλλω, constative) 215.

#2690 ἐγκαθέτους (acc.pl.masc.of ἐγκάθετος, direct object of ἀπέστειλαν).

spy - Luke 20:20.

Meaning: One who is suborned by others to trap a man with crafty words. A spy, skilled in repartee - with reference to the Pharisees and Herodians - Luke 20:20.

#2691 ὑποκρινομένους (pres.mid.part.acc.pl.masc.of ὑποκρίνομαι, adverbial, complementary).

feign — Luke 20:20.

Meaning: A combination of ὑπό (#117) and κρίνομαι (#531). To reply to the speech of another. To play a part as upon a stage. To impersonate. To act. To pretend to be something that one is not. To feign. With reference to the Pharisees and Herodians - Luke 20:20.

ἑαυτοὺς (acc.pl.masc.of ἑαυτός, direct object of ὑποκρινομένους) 288.
δικαίους (acc.pl.masc.of δίκαιος, predicate adjective) 85.
εἶναι (pres.inf.of εἰμί, completes ὑποκρινομένους) 86.
ἵνα (conjunction introducing the subjunctive in a purpose clause) 114.
ἐπιλάβωνται (3d.per.pl.aor.mid.subj.of ἐπιλαμβάνω, purpose) 1133.

αὐτοῦ (gen.sing.masc.of αὐτός, possession) 16.
λόγου (gen.sing.masc.of λόγος, description with a verb of seizing) 510.
ὥστε (conjunction with the infintive in a result clause) 752.
παραδοῦναι (aor.act.inf.of παραδίδωμι, result clause) 368.
αὐτὸν (acc.sing.masc.of αὐτός, direct object of παραδοῦναι) 16.
τῇ (loc.sing.fem.of the article in agreement with ἀρχῇ) 9.
ἀρχῇ (loc.sing.fem.of ἀρχή, sphere) 1285.
καὶ (adjunctive conjunction joining nouns) 14.
τῇ (loc.sing.fem.of the article in agreement with ἐξουσίᾳ) 9.
ἐξουσίᾳ (loc.sing.fem.of ἐξουσία, sphere) 707.
τοῦ (gen.sing.masc.of the article in agreement with ἡγεμένος) 9.
ἡγεμένος (gen.sing.masc.of ἡγεμών, description) 160.

Translation - "And after they had observed Him, they sent interviewers who pretended that they were upright men, in order that they might seize upon His views, so that they could deliver Him to the jurisdiction and the authority of the governor."

Comment: *Cf.* comment on Mt.22:15; Mk.12:13. Luke's account is more detailed than either of the synoptic writers. They were watching Him closely - literally, "keeping by His side" so as to listen to His speeches in an attempt to spot a weakness in Jesus' philosophy that they might exploit. The genitive in λογοῦ is explained by the fact that we have it here in connection with a verb of seizing or grasping. ὥστε with the infinitive is the most frequent form for a result clause. Burton (*Moods and Tenses*, 148) says that purpose is "intended result." Burton continues by saying, "that the line of distinction between them" *i.e.* purpose and result "has become correspondingly indistinct." "It is hard to draw a line between conceived result and intended result. . . The line of distinction is often very faint, if not wholly gone." (Robertson, *Grammar*, 1089). Robertson counts only seven cases of ὥστε with the infinitive expressing purpose in the W/H text - eight, if we include Acts 20:24 which W/H omits. *Cf.* Lk.9:52; Mt.10:1; Lk.4:29; Mt.15:33; 27:1; Lk.20:20. The student will examine these passages and decide for himself.

The action of the spies, ὑποκρινομένους ἑαυτοὺς δικαίους εἶναι - "pretending to be righteous" was for the purose - ἵνα ἐπιλάβωνται αὐτοῦ λόγου - of finding in Jesus' words something to seize upon for the conceived result, and therefore purpose, that they could indict Him in Pilate's court. Obviously the ὥστε clause with the anarthrous infinitive is both purpose and result. If they accomplished their purpose, the result would be what they started out to achieve. The basic sense is the same, so we will allow the grammarians to fight it out while the exegete goes on his way. Note the infinitive and the accusative in indirect discourse. Accusatives in connection with infinitives in indirect discourse are accusatives of general reference, unless there are other syntactical adjuncts to explain them. τῇ ἀρχῇ καὶ τῇ ἐξουσίᾳ τοῦ ἡγεμόνος - is an example of a locative of sphere. The Jews knew enough Roman law to realize that since they wanted Jesus dead, He would have to be tried in a Roman court, since Jewish courts had no jurisdiction in cases involving the death penalty. Thus they must trap Him into an utterance that violated Roman law. Pilate would never have tried Jesus in a case which involved nothing more than a theological dispute among the Jews, so long as the Roman position was not threatened. It was not illegal under Roman law for schools of Jewish thought to differ on theological or philosophical points. The question, however, about tax liability could, if fumbled by Jesus, give them grounds for filing a complaint in Pilate's jurisdiction.

Verse 21 - "And they asked him saying, Master, we know that thou sayest and teachest rightly, neither acceptest thou the person of any, but teachest the way of God truly."

καὶ ἐπηρώτησαν αὐτὸν λέγοντες, Διδάσκαλε, οἴδαμεν ὅτι ὀρθῶς λέγεις καὶ διδάσκεις καὶ οὐ λαμβάνεις πρόσωπον, ἀλλ' ἐπ ἀληθείας τὴν ὁδὸν τοῦ θεοῦ διδάσκεις.

καὶ (continuative conjunction) 14.
ἐπηρώτησαν (3d.per.pl.aor.act.ind.of ἐπερωτάω, constative) 973.
αὐτὸν (acc.sing.masc.of αὐτός, direct object of ἐπηρώτησαν) 16.
λέγοντες (pres.act.part.nom.pl.masc.of λέγω, adverbial, modal) 66.
Διδάσκαλε (voc.sing.masc.of διδάσκαλος, address) 742.
οἴδαμεν (1st.per.pl.pres.act.ind.of ὁράω, aoristic) 144.
ὅτι (conjunction introducing an object clause in indirect discourse) 211.
ὀρθῶς (adverbial) 2174.
λέγεις (2d.per.sing.pres.act.ind.of λέγω, customary) 66.
καὶ (adjunctive conjunction joining verbs) 14.
διδάσκεις (2d.per.sing.pres.act.ind.of διδάσκω, customary) 402.
καὶ (adjunctive conjunction joining verbs) 14.
οὐ (summary negative conjunction, with the indicative) 130.
λαμβάνεις (2d.per.sing.pres.act.ind.of λαμβάνω, customary) 533.
πρόσωπον (acc.sing.neut.of πρόσωπον, direct object of λαμβάνεις) 588.
ἀλλ' (alternative conjunction) 343.
ἐπ' (preposition with the genitive, adverbial) 47.
ἀληθείας (gen.sing.fem.of ἀλήθεια, adverbial) 1416.
τὴν (acc.sing.fem.of the article in agreement with ὁδὸν) 9.
ὁδὸν (acc.sing.fem.of ὁδός, direct object of διδάσκεις) 199.
τοῦ (gen.sing.masc.of the article in agreement with θεοῦ) 9.
θεοῦ (gen.sing.masc.of θεός, definition) 124.
διδάσκεις (2d.per.sing.pres.act.ind.of διδάσκω, customary) 403.

Translation - "And they asked Him saying, 'Teacher, we know that you always speak and teach correctly and you never receive a face, but you always truthfully teach the way of God.' "

Comment: *Cf.* comment on Mt.22:16; Mk.12:14. In the college campus language of the 1970's the Pharisees and Herodians approached Jesus and said, "Right

On!" In view of verse 20 and their attempt to appear righteous, they oversold their case, because this clumsy bit of palaver was obviously insincere. Everything they said to Jesus about Himself was true, but they did not really believe it. Or, if they did, they thought that, for all of His sincerity, He was incredibly stupid not to notice their obvious insincerity.

Verse 22 - "Is it lawful for us to give tribute unto Caesar, or no?"

ἔξεστιν ὑμᾶς Καίσαρι φόρον δοῦναι ἢ οὔ;

ἔξεστιν (impersonal verb in direct question) 966.
ἡμᾶς (acc.pl.masc.of ἐγώ, general reference) 123.
Καίσαρι (dat.sing.masc.of Καίσαρι, indirect object of δοῦναι) 1418.

#2692 φόρον (acc.sing.masc.of φόρος, direct object of δοῦναι).

tribute - Luke 20:22; 23:2; Rom.13:6,7,7.

Meaning: An annual tax levied upon houses, lands and persons. In the Roman tax structure - Luke 20:22; 23:2; generally to any duly constituted authority, but specifically in context to the Romans in Romans 13:6,7,7.

δοῦναι (aor.act.inf.of δίδωμι, noun use, subject of ἔξεστιν) 362.
ἢ (disjunctive particle) 465.
οὔ (summary negative conjunction with the indicative) 130.

Translation - "Is it lawful for us to pay taxes to Caesar or not?"

Comment: *Cf.* comment on Mt.22:17; Mk.12:14,15.

Verse 23 - "But he perceived their craftiness, and said unto them, Why tempt ye me?"

κατανοήσας δὲ αὐτῶν πανουργίαν εἶπεν πρὸς αὐτούς,

κατανοήσας (aor.act.part.nom.sing.masc.of κατανοέω, adverbial, causal) 648.
δὲ (adversative conjunction) 11.
αὐτῶν (gen.pl.masc.of αὐτός, possession) 16.
τὴν (acc.sing.fem.of the article in agreement with πανουργίαν) 9.

#2693 πανουργίαν (acc.sing.fem.of πανουργία, direct object of κατανοήσας).

craftiness - Luke 20:23; 1 Cor.3:19; 2 Cor.4:2.
cunning craftiness - Eph.4:14.
subtilty - 2 Cor.11:3.

*Meaning: Cf.*πανοῦγος (#4403), from πᾶς (#67) and ἐργάζομαι (#691). Hence, to manipulate everything. In a devious sense - crafty reasoning, which is specious and therefore false. In a good sense, though not in this sense in the New Testament. In this sense, prudent and with careful consideration of everything involved. A holistic approach. Always in an evil sense in the New Testament - Luke 20:23; 1 Cor.3:19; 2 Cor.4:2; 11:3; Eph.4:14.

εἶπεν (3d.per.sing.aor.act.ind.of εἶπον, constative) 155.
πρὸς (preposition with the accusative of extent, after a verb of speaking) 197.
αὐτούς (acc.pl.masc.of αὐτός, extent after a verb of speaking) 16.

Translation - "But because He was aware of their insidious intent, He said to them, . . . "

Comment: *Cf.* comment Mt.22:18; Mk.12:15. The question in the KJV, "Why tempt ye me?" does not occur in the best text. Matthew says, γνοὺς . . . τὴν πονηρίαν αὐτῶν. Mark has εἰδὼς αὐτῶν τὴν ὑπόκρισιν; while Luke has κατανοήσας αὐτῶν τὴν πανουργίαν. "Having known (Mt.), seeing (Mk.), and having perceived (Lk.) their evil (Mt.), their hypocrisy (Mk.), their craftiness (Lk.). Thus we get a full orbed picture of the incident. They were evil, hypocritical and crafty. Jesus was knowledgeable, observant and perceptive. Chesterfield called such a crafty approach "the dark sanctuary of incapacity," and John Locke called it "the ape of wisdom." We may be sure that it was a futile gesture when employed upon our Lord.

Verse 24 - "Shew me a penny. Whose image and superscription hath it? They answered and said, Caesar's."

Δείξατέ μοι δηνάριον. τίνος ἔχει εἰκόνα καὶ ἐπιγραφήν; οἱ δὲ εἶπαν, Καίσαρος.

Δείξατέ (2d.per.pl.aor.act.impv.of δείκνυμι, command) 359.
μοι (dat.sing.masc.of ἐγώ, indirect object of δείξατέ) 123.
δηνάριον (acc.sing.neut.of δηνάριον, direct object of δείξατέ) 1278.
τίνος (gen.sing.masc.of τίς, the interrogative pronoun, possession) 281.
ἔχει (3d.per.sing.pres.act.ind.of ἔχω, aoristic) 82.
εἰκόνα (acc.sing.masc.of εἰκών, direct object of ἔχει) 1421.
καὶ (adjunctive conjunction joining nouns) 14.
ἐπιγραφήν (acc.sing.fem.of ἐπιγραφή, direct object of ἔχει) 1422.
οἱ (nom.pl.masc.of the article, subject of εἶπαν) 9.
δὲ (continuative conjunction) 11.
εἶπαν (3d.per.pl.aor.act.ind.of εἶπον, constative) 155.
Καίσαρος (gen.sing.masc.of Καίσαρι, possession) 1418.

Translation - "Show me a denarius. Whose image and superscription does it have? And they said, 'Caesar's.' "

Comment: *Cf.* comment on Mt.22:19,20; Mk.12:15,16.

Verse 25 - "And he said unto them, Render therefore unto Caesar, the things which be Caesar's; and unto God the things which be God's."

ὁ δὲ εἶπεν πρὸς αὐτούς, Τοίνυν ἀπόδοτε τὰ Καίσαρος Καίσαρι καὶ τὰ τοῦ θεοῦ τῷ θεῷ.

ὁ (nom.sing.masc.of the article, subject of εἶπεν) 9.
δὲ (continuative conjunction) 11.
εἶπεν (3d.per.sing.aor.act.ind.of εἶπον, constative) 155.
πρὸς (preposition with the accusative of extent, after a verb of speaking) 197.
αὐτούς (acc.pl.masc.of αὐτός, extent after a verb of speaking) 16.

#2694 Τοίνυν (inferential conjunction).

therefore - Luke 20:25; 1 Cor.9:26; Heb.13:13.

Meaning: A combination of τοί and νῦν (#1497). Therefore, then (in an inferential sense), accordingly. Similar to γάρ (#105). Post positive in 1 Cor.9:26, though not in Luke 20:25 and Heb.13:13.

ἀπόδοτε (2d.per.pl.aor.act.impv.of ἀποδίδωμι, command) 495.
τὰ (acc.pl.neut.of the article, direct object of ἀπόδοτε) 9.
Καίσαρος (gen.sing.masc.of Καίσαρος, possession) 1418.
Καίσαρι (dat.sing.masc.of Καίσαρος, indirect object of ἀπόδοτε) 1418
καὶ (adjunctive conjunction joining clauses) 14.
τὰ (acc.pl.neut.of the article, direct object of ἀπόδοτε) 9.
τοῦ (gen.sing.masc.of the article in agreement with θεοῦ) 9.
θεοῦ (gen.sing.masc.of θεός, possession) 124.
τῷ (dat.sing.masc.of the article in agreement with θεῷ) 9.
θεῷ (dat.sing.masc.of θεός, indirect object of ἀπόδοτε) 124.

Translation - "And He said to them, 'Then give Caesar's things to Caesar and God's things to God.'"

Comment: *Cf.* Mt.22:21 where he uses post positive οὖν. Mk.12:17.

Verse 26 - "And they could not take hold of his words before the people: and they marvelled at his answer and held their peace."

καὶ οὐκ ἴσχυσαν ἐπιλαβέσθαι αὐτοῦ ῥήματος ἐναντίον τοῦ λαοῦ, καὶ θαυμάσαντες ἐπὶ τῇ ἀποκρίσει αὐτοῦ ἐσίγησαν.

καὶ (continuative conjunction) 14.
οὐκ (summary negative conjunction with the indicative) 130.
ἴσχυαν (3d.per.pl.aor.act.ind.of ἰσχύω, constative) 447.
ἐπιλαβέσθαι (2d.aor.mid.inf.of ἐπιλαμβάνω, completes ἴσχυσαν) 1133.
αὐτοῦ (gen.sing.masc.of αὐτός, possession) 16.
ῥήματος (gen.sing.neut.of ῥῆμα, with a verb of seizing) 343.
ἐναντίον (improper preposition with a genitive of description) 1780.
τοῦ (gen.sing.masc.of the article in agreement with λαοῦ) 9.
λαοῦ (gen.sing.masc.of λαός, description) 110.
καὶ (emphatic conjunction) 14.
θαυμάσαντες (aor.act.part.nom.pl.masc.of θαυμάζω, adverbial, causal) 726.
ἐπὶ (preposition with the locative with a verb of emotion) 47.

τῇ (loc.sing.fem.of the article in agreement with ἀποκρίσει) 9.
ἀποκρίσει (loc.sing.fem.of ἀπόκρισις, cause) 1919.
αὐτοῦ (gen.sing.masc.of αὐτός, possession) 16.
ἐσίγησαν (3d.per.pl.aor.act.ind.of σιγάω, ingressive) 2330.

Translation - "And they were not able to lay hold of His remark in the presence of the people; in fact because they were amazed at his answer, they became silent."

Comment: *Cf.* comment Mt.22:22; Mk.12:17. They came to trap Him with their cunning craftiness. They flattered Him and then, because they thought that they had prepared Him psychologically for the "kill" they asked Him the trick question. He not only answered it. He turned the episode into an object lesson. He borrowed a Roman coin from them. The fact that they had one proved that they hated Rome and its money only in abstract theory - not in practise. Then He pointed out that they were violating one of their own rules by carrying an image around with them, in violation of their interpretation of the Mosaic code. Then He answered their question with a statement that they could not use against Him either in Pilate's court or before Herod or the San Hedrin. All that they could do was to turn His answer over and over in their minds and remain silent. *Cf.*#726. *Cf.* Luke 18:39. Jesus makes those who are commanded to be silent to cry out and those, who wish to speak, He compels to remain silent! Bartimaeus' cry for help and the Herodian's confused silence both attest that this incarnate Son of God is no ordinary mortal! A fight with His enemies about His authority (Mk.11:27-12:12; Mt.21:23-22:14; Lk.20:19) is followed by a fight over paying taxes to Caesar (Mk.12:13-17; Mt.22:15-22; Lk.20:20-26). Now we have an argument with the Sadducees about the resurrection (Mk.12:18-27; Mt.22:23-33; Lk.20:27-40). Jesus is having quite a busy day.

Controversy With the Sadducees About the Resurrection

(Matthew 22:23-33; Mark 12:18-27; Luke 20:27-40)

Mark 12:18 - "Then cometh unto him the Sadducees, which say there is no resurrection; and they asked him, saying, . . . "

Καὶ ἔρχονται Σαδδουκαῖοι πρὸς αὐτόν, οἵτινες λέγουσιν ἀνάστασιν μὴ εἶναι, καὶ ἐπηρώτων αυτὸν λέγοντες,

Καὶ (continuative conjunction) 14.
ἔρχονται (3d.per.pl.pres.mid.ind.of ἔρχομαι,historical) 146.
Σαδδουκαῖοι (nom.pl.masc.of Σαδδουκαῖος, subject of ἔρχονται) 277.
πρὸς (preposition with the accusative of extent) 197.
αὐτόν (acc.sing.masc.of αὐτός, extent) 16.
οἵτινες (nom.pl.masc.of ὅστις, subject of λέγουσιν) 163.
λέγουσιν (3d.per.pl.pres.act.ind.of λέγω, customary) 66.
ἀνάστασιν (acc.sing.fem.of ἀνάστασις, general reference) 1423.

μὴ (qualified negative conjunction with the infinitive) 87.
εἶναι (pres.inf.of εἰμί, indirect discourse) 86.
καὶ (adjunctive conjunction joining verbs) 14.
ἐπηρώτων (3d.per.pl.imp.act.ind.of ἐπερωτάω, inceptive) 973.
αὐτὸν (acc.sing.masc.of αὐτός, direct object of ἐπηρώτων) 16.
λέγοντες (pres.act.part.nom.pl.masc.of λέγω, adverbial, modal) 66.

Translation - "And the Sadducees who say that there is no resurrection came to Him and began to question Him, saying, . . . "

Comment: Now that we are back with Mark we can expect to see the historical present again as we have it here in ἔρχονται. Note the indirect discourse in the relative clause *οἵτινες λέγουσιν ἀνάστασιν μὴ εἶναι*, with the infinitive carrying the same tense as in the direct. The Sadducees customarily said "There is no resurrection." This cardinal denial by the Sadducees placed them at odds with the Pharisees, who believed both in the resurrection and the end time judgment. Therefore the Pharisees were not involved in this phrase of the battle of words between Jesus and His enemies on this last Tuesday of His passion week. The Pharisees had joined the Herodians, whom they despised, against Jesus on the taxation question and they were to enter the fray again on the question about the greatest commandment (Mt.22:34). Once again we note that chief priests, scribes, elders, Pharisees, Sadducees and Herodians, all personally at odds with each other, were drawn together by their mutual hatred of Jesus.

Now the Sadducees are in the ring with Jesus with a story that boggles the mind of any normal person. It would appear that the first Ananias Club was organized in Jerusalem! Here is their story in

Verse 19 - "Master, Moses wrote unto us, If a man's brother die, and leave his wife behind him, and leave no children, that his brother should take his wife, and raise up seed unto his brother."

Διδάσκαλε, Μωϋσῆς ἔγραψεν ἡμίν ὅτι ἐάν τινος ἀδελφὸς ἀποθάνῃ καὶ καταλίπῃ γυναῖκα καὶ μὴ ἀφῇ τέκνον, ἵνα λάβῃ ὁ ἀδελφὸς αὐτοῦ τὴν γυναῖκα καὶ ἐξαναστήσῃ σπέρμα τῷ ἀδελφῷ αὐτοῦ.

Διδάσκαλε (voc.sing.masc.of διδάσκαλος, address) 742.
Μωϋσῆς (nom.sing.masc.of Μωϋσῆς, subject of ἔγραψεν) 715.
ἔγραψεν (3d.per.sing.aor.act.ind.of γράφω, culminative) 156.
ἡμῖν (dat.pl.masc.of ἐγώ, indirect object of ἔγραψεν) 123.
ὅτι (conjunction introducing an object clause in indirect discourse) 211.
ἐάν (conditional particle in a third-class mixed condition) 363.
τινος (gen.sing.masc.of τις, the indefinite pronoun, relationship) 486.
ἀδελφὸς (nom.sing.masc.of ἀδελφός, subject of ἀποθάνῃ, καταλίπῃ and ἀφῇ) 15.
ἀποθάνῃ (3d.per.sing.aor.act.subj.of ἀποθνήσκω, third-class condition) 774.
καὶ (adjunctive conjunction joining verbs) 14.
καταλίπῃ (3d.per.sing.aor.act.subj.of καταλείπω, third-class condition) 369.

γυναῖκα (acc.sing.fem.of γυνή, direct object of καταλίπῃ) 103.
καὶ (adjunctive conjunction joining verbs) 14.
μὴ (qualified negative conjunction with the subjunctive) 87.
ἀφῇ (3d.per.sing.aor.act.subj.of ἀφίημι, third-class condition) 319.
τέκνον (acc.sing.neut.of τέκνον, direct object of ἀφῇ) 229.
ἵνα (conjunction introducing a purpose clause) 114.
λάβῃ (3d.per.sing.aor.act.subj.of λαμβάνω, purpose) 533.
ὁ (nom.sing.masc.of the article in agreement with ἀδελφὸς) 9.
ἀδελφὸς (nom.sing.masc.of ἀδελφός, subject of λάβῃ and ἐξαναστήσῃ) 15.
αὐτοῦ (gen.sing.masc.of αὐτός, relationship) 16.
τὴν (acc.sing.fem.of the article in agreement with γυναῖκα) 9.
γυναῖκα (acc.sing.fem.of γυνή, direct object of λάβῃ) 103.
καὶ (adjunctive conjunction joining verbs) 14.

#2695 ἐξαναστήσῃ (3d.per.sing.1st.aor.act.subj.of ἐξανίστημι, purpose.

raise up - Mark 12:19; Luke 20:28.
rise up - Acts 15:5.

Meaning: A combination of ἐκ (#19) and ἵστημι (#180). Hence to rise. Properly of seated persons who stand up and come forward to protest - Acts 15:5. Of begetting children - "to raise up seed" - Mark 12:19; Luke 20:28.

σπέρμα (acc.sing.neut.of σπέρμα, direct object of ἐξαναστήσῃ) 1056.
τῷ (dat.sing.masc.of the article in agreement with ἀδελφῷ) 9.
ἀδελφῷ (dat.sing.masc.of ἀδελφός, personal advantage) 15.
αὐτοῦ (gen.sing.masc.of αὐτός, relationship) 16.

Translation - "Teacher, Moses wrote to us that if a brother of any man die and leave a wife, and not leave a son, that his brother should take the wife and raise up an heir for his brother."

Comment: Both Mark and Luke have written it in awkward Greek. Matthew expresses it much better. *Cf.* Luke 20:28; Mt.22:24. Mark begins the indirect discourse as a third-class condition with ἐάν and the subjunctives in ἀποθάνῃ, καταλίπῃ and ἀφῇ and then forsakes the future indicative or the imperative in favor of ἵνα and the subjunctives of purpose in λάβῃ and ἐξαναστήσῃ. *Cf.* comment on Mt.22:24 for the legal discussion of the Mosaic tradition.

The motive of the Sadducees however was not to discuss the Mosaic law as such but to pose what for them was an impossible question for Jesus.

Verse 20 - "Now there were seven brethren; and the first took a wife, and dying left no seed."

ἑπτὰ ἀδελφοὶ ἦσαν, καὶ ὁ πρῶτος ἔλαβεν γυναῖκα, καὶ ἀποθνήσκων οὐκ ἀφῆκεν σπέρμα.

ἑπτὰ (numeral) 1024.

ἀδελφοὶ (nom.pl.masc.of ἀδελφός, subject of ἦσαν) 15.
ἦσαν (3d.per.pl.imp.ind.of εἰμί, progressive description) 86.
καὶ (continuative conjunction) 14.
ὁ (nom.sing.masc.of the article in agreement with πρῶτος) 9.
πρῶτος (nom.sing.masc.of πρῶτος, subject of ἔλαβεν) 487.
ἔλαβεν (3d.per.sing.aor.act.ind.of λαμβάνω, constative) 533.
γυναῖκα (acc.sing.fem.of γυνή, direct object of ἔλαβεν) 103.
καὶ (adjunctive conjunction joining verbs) 14.
ἀποθνήσκων (pres.act.part.nom.sing.masc.of ἀποθνήσκω, adverbial, temporal) 774.
οὐκ (summary negative conjunction with the indicative) 130.
ἀφῆκεν (3d.per.sing.aor.act.ind.of ἀφίημι, culminative) 319.
σπέρμα (nom.sing.neut.of σπέρμα, direct object of ἀφῆκεν) 1056.

Translation - "There were seven brothers. And the first took a wife, and when he died, he had left no heir."

Comment: *Cf.* comment on Luke 20:29; Matthew 22:24,25. ὁ πρῶτος does not necessarily mean the oldest, but it is probable that it did, under the ancient law of priogeniture. He married but he died without a legal heir.

Verse 21 - "And the second took her, and died, neither left he any seed; and the third likewise."

καὶ ὁ δεύτερος ἔλαβεν αὐτήν, καὶ ἀπέθανεν μὴ καταλιπὼν σπέρμα, καὶ ὁ τρίτος ὡσαύτως.

καὶ (continuative conjunction) 14.
ὁ (nom.sing.masc.of the article in agreement with δεύτερος) 9.
δεύτερος (nom.sing.masc.of δεύτερος, subject of ἔλαβεν and ἀπέθανεν) 1371.
ἔλαβεν (3d.per.sing.aor.act.ind.of λαμβάνω, constative) 533.
αὐτήν (acc.sing.fem.of αὐτός, direct object of ἔλαβεν) 16.
καὶ (adjunctive conjunction joining verbs) 14.
ἀπέθανεν (3d.per.sing.aor.act.ind.of ἀποθνήσκω, constative) 774.
μὴ qualified negative conjunction with the participle) 87.
καταλιπὼν (aor.act.part.nom.sing.masc.of καταλείπω, adverbial, concessive) 369.
σπέρμα (acc.sing.neut.of σπέρμα, direct object of καταλιπὼν) 1056.
καὶ (continuative conjunction) 14.
ὁ (nom.sing.masc.of τρίτος, subject understood) 1209.
ὡσαύτως (adverbial) 1319.

Translation - "And the second took her, and he died although he left no heir. And the third likewise."

Comment: *Cf.* comment on Mt.22:26; Lk.20:30.

Verse 22 - "And the seven had her, and left no seed; last of all the woman died also."

καὶ οἱ ἑπτὰ οὐκ ἀφῆκαν σπέρμα. ἔσχατον πάντων καὶ ἡ γυνὴ ἀπέθανεν.

καὶ (adversative conjunction) 14.
οἱ (nom.pl.masc.of the article in agreement with *ἑπτὰ*) 9.
οὐκ (summary negative conjunction with the indicative) 130.
ἀφῆκαν (3d.per.pl.aor.act.ind.of *ἀφίημι*, culminative) 319.
σπέρμα (acc.sing.neut.of *σπέρμα*, direct object of *ἀφῆκαν*) 1056.
ἔσχατον (acc.sing.neut.of *ἔσχατος*, adverbial) 496.
πάντων (gen.pl.masc.of *πᾶς*, partitive) 67.
καὶ (adjunctive conjunction joining substantives) 14.
ἡ (nom.sing.fem.of the article in agreement with *γυνὴ*) 9.
ἀπέθανεν (3d.per.sing.aor.act.ind.of *ἀποθνήσκω*, culminative) 774.

Translation - "But none of the seven left an heir, and last of all the woman died."

Comment: *Cf.* comment on Mt.22:26,27; Lk.20:31,32. The first clause in the KJV does not occur in the Greek text. The seven brothers each married the woman and preceded her in death but without begetting an heir to the first brother's estate. *ἔσχατον πάντων* is adverbial - "finally" or, literally, "last of all . . . " the woman also died. This outlandish story indicates what vivid imaginations the Sadducees had and to what ridiculous lengths they were willing to go to establish their point that the resurrection of the body was not a sensible doctrine. Having told their story they now raise the question, which, like the previous question about paying taxes to Caesar, they thought would embarrass Jesus.

Verse 23 - "In the resurrection therefore, when they shall rise, whose wife shall she be of them? for the seven had her to wife."

ἐν τῇ ἀναστάσει (, ὅταν ἀναστῶσιν,) τίνος αὐτῶν ἔσται γυνή; οἱ γὰρ ἑπτὰ ἔσχον αὐτὴν γυναῖκα.

ἐν (preposition with the locative of time point) 80.
τῇ (loc.sing.fem.of the article in agreement with *ἀναστάσει*) 9.
ἀναστάσει (loc.sing.fem.of *ἀνάστασις*, time point) 1423.
τίνος (gen.sing.masc.of *τίς*, the interrogative pronoun, relationship) 281.
αὐτῶν (gen.pl.masc.of *αὐτός*, partitive) 16.
ἔσται (3d.per.sing.fut.ind.of *εἰμί*, deliberative) 86.
γυνή (nom.sing.fem.of *γυνή*, subject of *ἔσται*) 103.
οἱ (nom.pl.masc.of the article in agreement with *ἑπτὰ*) 9.
γὰρ (causal conjunction) 105.
ἑπτὰ (numeral, subject of *ἔσχον*) 1024.
ἔσχον (3d.per.pl.2d.aor.act.ind.of *ἔχω*, progressive description) 82.
αὐτὴν (acc.sing.fem.of *αὐτός*, direct object of *ἔσχον*) 16.
γυναῖκα (acc.sing.fem.of *γυνή*, double accusative in the predicate) 103.

Translation - "In the resurrection of which of them will she be wife? Because the seven each had her as his wife."

Comment: *Cf.* comment on Mt.22:28; Lk.20:33. *ἐν τῇ ἀναστάσει* - a locative of time point. There is considerable doubt that the indefinite temporal clause *ὅταν ἀναστῶσιν*, which we have enclosed in parentheses, belongs in the text. Metzger's comment follows: "The absence of *ὅταν ἀναστῶσιν* from Sinaiticus, B C* D L W Δ Φ *al* is probably deliberate, having been omitted by copyists as superfluous (Matthew and Luke also omitted the words, probably for the same reason). It is hard to imagine that a copyist would have been tempted to gloss *ἐν τῇ ἀναστάσει*, and the pleonasm is in accord with Mark's style (cf.13.19f.). At the same time, however, in deference to the generally high reputation of the witnesses that attest the omission, the Committee thought it right to enclose the words within square brackets.

In order to suggest more clearly that ver.23 constitutes the nub of the query, copyists inserted *οὖν* at various places in various witnesses." (Metzger, *A Textual Commentary on the Greek New Testament*, 110,111).

In view of the fact that the Sadducees did not believe in the resurrection of the body, it is not unreasonable to suppose that they might have added *ὅταν ἀναστῶσιν*, since it is an indefinite temporal clause, and might be translated, "at the resurrection, *if in fact/whenever they rise. . .*" *ὅταν* with the subjunctive reflects the skepticism of the Sadducees on the point. The clause is not necessary to the exegesis of the passage. The point is made without it, and if it is genuine it only makes the point more vivid.

The Sadducees' assumption is that the marriage relationship is perpetuated in eternity. If this were true, and if we assume that resurrection of the body is to be expected, then it follows that heaven will be a place where polyandry is practised, something forbidden by the Mosaic law. The dilemma, then, which the Sadducees supposed that they presented to Jesus was one in which He must either deny the resurrection or repudiate the Mosaic law, something which He had previously said He would not do (Mt.5:17).

Verse 24 - "And Jesus answering said unto them, Do ye not therefore err, because ye know not the scriptures, neither the power of God?"

ἔφη αὐτοῖς ὁ Ἰησοῦς, Οὐ διὰ τοῦτο πλανᾶσθε μὴ εἰδότες τὰς γραφὰς μηδὲ τὴν δύναμιν τοῦ θεοῦ;

ἔφη (3d.per.sing.aor.act.ind.of *φημί*, constative) 354.
αὐτοῖς (dat.pl.masc.of *αὐτός*, indirect object of *ἔφη*) 16.
ὁ (nom.sing.masc.of the article in agreement with *Ἰησοῦς*) 9.
Ἰησοῦς (nom.sing.masc.of *Ἰησοῦς*, subject of *ἔφη*) 3.
Οὐ (summary negative conjunction with the indicative in a rhetorical question which expects an affirmative reply) 130.
διὰ (preposition with the accusative, cause) 118.
τοῦτο (acc.sing.neut.of *οὗτος*, cause) 93.
πλανᾶσθε (2d.per.pl.pres.mid.ind.of *πλανάω*, aoristic) 1257.
μὴ (qualified negative conjunction with the participle) 87.
εἰδότες (aor.part.nom.pl.masc.of *ὁράω*, adverbial, causal) 144.
τὰς (acc.pl.fem.of the article in agreement with *γραφὰς*) 9.
γραφὰς (acc.pl.fem.of *γραφή*, direct object of *εἰδότες*) 1389.

μηδὲ (negative continuative conjunction) 612.
τὴν (acc.sing.fem.of the article in agreement with δύναμιν) 9.
δύναμιν (acc.sing.fem.of δύναμις, direct object of εἰδότες) 687.
τοῦ (gen.sing.masc.of the article in agreement with θεοῦ) 9.
θεοῦ (gen.sing.masc.of θεός, possession) 124.

Translation - "Jesus said to them, 'Are you not deluding yourselves in this matter, because you know neither the scriptures nor the power of God?' "

Comment: *Cf.* comment on Mt.22:29. Why were they deceiving themselves (or being deceived)? πλανᾶσθε can be either middle or passive voice. The διὰ τοῦτο idiom tells us. τοῦτο refers to the hypothetical story of verses 20 -23. Self deception is a tragedy - the logical outcome of ignorance of the scriptures and a lack of experimental contact with the power of God. Their ignorance of the scriptures led them to a false assumption which is the ground of what, to them, appeared to be a logical argument. It is a bad piece of rationalization. To seduce someone else is bad, but to seduce oneself is unspeakable. The participle εἰδότες is causal. Note the μὴ . . . μηδὲ sequence. "The neither knew the scriptures, nor the power of God." *Cf.*#612 for other examples.

Jesus went on in verse 25 to point out to the Sadducees what was wrong with their reasoning.

Verse 25 - "For when they shall rise from the dead, they neither marry, nor are given in marriage; but are as the angels which are in heaven."

ὅταν γὰρ ἐκ νεκρῶν ἀναστῶσιν, οὔτε γαμοῦσιν οὔτε γαμίζονται, ἀλλ' εἰσὶν ὡς ἄγγελοι ἐν τοῖς οὐρανοῖς.

ὅταν (conjunction with the subjunctive in an indefinite temporal clause) 436.
γὰρ (causal conjunction) 105.
ἐκ (preposition with the ablative of separation) 19.
νεκρῶν (abl.pl.masc.of νεκρός, separation) 749.
ἀναστῶσιν (3d.per.pl.2d.aor.act.subj.of ἀνίστημι, indefinite temporal clause) 789.
οὔτε (negative copulative conjunction) 598.
γαμοῦσιν (3d.per.pl.pres.act.ind.of γαμέω. customary) 512.
οὔτε (negative copulative conjunction) 598.
γαμίζονται (3d.per.pl.pres.pass.ind.of γαμίζω, customary) 1426.
ἀλλ' (alternative conjunction) 343.
εἰσὶν (3d.per.pl.pres.ind.of εἰμί, futuristic) 86.
ὡς (relative adverb introducing a comparative clause) 128.
ἄγγελοι (nom.pl.masc.of ἄγγελος, subject of εἰσίν, understood) 96.
ἐν (preposition with the locative of place) 80.
τοῖς (loc.pl.masc.of the article in agreement with οὐρανοῖς) 9.
οὐρανοῖς (loc.pl.masc.of οὐρανός, place where) 254.

Translation - "Because when they rise from the dead, they neither marry nor are they given in marriage, but they are as angels in the heavens."

Comment: *Cf.* comment on Mt.22:30; Lk.20:35. *ὅταν* and the subjunctive does not cast doubt about the fact of the resurrection but about the time when it will occur. *γὰρ* is causal as it introduces the reason for the self seduction of the Sadducees. Note the *οὔτε . . οὔτε* "neither. . nor" sequence with the indicative mode in *γαμοῦσιν* and *γαμίζονται*, just as we had *μὴ . . . μηδέ* is verse 24. At the resurrection, sex is a thing of the past. Jesus did not deny that other aspects of the marriage relationship would continue after the resurrection. There is no reason to suppose that men and women will cease to love each other as man and wife, in other aspects of their relationship. It is only that in the sphere of sexual relationships, they will be as the angels. Jesus also did not say that in heaven the saints would be angels, or even that we would be like angels, except in this one aspect. No other lessons should be drawn from this exchange between Jesus and the Sadducees, except those connected with the Sadducees' theory that bi-sexual relationships on earth make the fact of the bodily resurrection impossible.

The saints should be immensely grateful that we will not be angels in heaven. Angels have never known the joy of redemption from sin, nor will they ever know the intimacy of the fellowship which we enjoy with the Godhead, in Christ (John 17:21).

Having answered their argument against the resurrection, Jesus then moved in on offense, to show that the argument of the Sadducees would not stand the light of Old Testament scripture.

Verse 26 - "And as touching the dead that they rise, have ye not read in the book of Moses, how in the bush, God spake unto him saying, I am the God of Abraham, and the God of Isaac and the God of Jacob?"

περὶ δὲ τῶν νεκρῶν ὅτι ἐγείρονται οὐκ ἀνέγνωτε ἐν τῇ βίβλῳ Μωϋσέως *ἐπὶ τοῦ βάτου πῶς εἶπεν αὐτῷ ὁ θεὸς λέγων,* Ἐγὼ *ὁ θεὸς* Ἀβραὰμ *καὶ (ὁ) θεὸς* Ἰσαάκ *καὶ (ὁ) θεὸς* Ἰακώβ;

περὶ (preposition with the genitive of reference) 173.
δὲ (explanatory conjunction) 11.
τῶν (gen.pl.masc.of the article in agreement with *νεκρῶν*) 9.
νεκρῶν (gen.pl.masc.of *νεκρός*, reference) 749.
ὅτι (conjunction in indirect question) 211.
ἐγείρονται (3d.per.pl.pres.pass.ind.of *ἐγείρω*, futuristic) 125.
οὐκ (summary negative conjunction with the indicative in rhetorical question expecting an affirmative reply) 130.
ἀνέγνωτε (2d.per.pl.2d.aor.act.ind.of *ἀναγινώσκω*, culminative) 967.
ἐν (preposition with the locative of place) 80.
τῇ (loc.sing.fem.of the article in agreement with *βίβλῳ*) 9.
βίβλῳ (loc.sing.masc.of *βίβλος*, place where) 1.
Μωϋσέως (gen.sing.masc.of Μωϋσῆς, description) 715.
ἐπὶ (preposition with the locative of place, ellipsis) 47.
τοῦ (gen.sing.masc.of the article, joined to *βάτου*) 9.

βάτου (gen.sing.fem.of βάτος, reference) 2138. .
πῶς (conjunction introducing indirect discourse) 627.
εἶπεν (3d.per.sing.aor.act.ind.of εἶπον, constative) 155.
αὐτῷ (dat.sing.masc.of αὐτός, indirect object of εἶπεν) 16.
ὁ (nom.sing.masc.of the article in agreement with θεὸς) 9.
θεὸς (nom.sing.masc.of θεός, subject of εἶπεν) 124.
λέγων (pres.act.part.nom.sing.masc.of λέγω, recitative) 66.
'Εγὼ (nom.sing.masc.of ἐγώ, subject of εἰμί understood) 123.
ὁ (nom.sing.masc.of the article in agreement with θεὸς) 9.
θεὸς (nom.sing.masc.of θεός, predicate nominative) 124.
'Αβραὰμ (gen.sing.masc.of'Αβραάμ, relationship) 7.
καὶ (adjunctive conjunction joining nouns) 14.
(ὁ) (nom.sing.masc.of the article in agreement with θεὸς) 9.
θεὸς (nom.sing.masc.of θεός, predicate nominative) 124.
'Ισαὰκ (gen.sing.masc.of'Ισαάκ, relationship) 10.
καὶ (adjunctive conjunction joining nouns) 14.
(ὁ) (nom.sing.masc.of the article in agreement with'Ιακώβ) 9.
'Ιακώβ (gen.sing.masc.of'Ιακώβ, relationship) 12.

Translation - "Now with reference to the (fact) that the dead will be raised, have you not read in the book of Moses, at the place about the bush, how God spoke to him, saying, 'I am the God of Abraham and the God of Isaac and the God of Jacob'?"

Comment: *Cf.*comment on Mt.22:31,32; Lk.20:37,38. ὅτι introduces an object clause with reference to which the περὶ . . . τῶν νεκρῶν phrase points. ἐν τῇ βίβλῳ is a simple locative but note Mark's feminine article τῇ with the masculine βίβλῳ! ἐπὶ with the genitive is rare. It is better to view it as a result of an ellipsis, with τοῦ βάτου as a genitive of reference. "At the place with reference to (about) the bush. . . κ.τ.λ." Note that the copulative verb is missing after'Εγὼ in the direct discourse. The quotation is from Exodus 3:6.

Here is another ἐγὼ εἰμί passage, indicating the eternal presence of the Eternal God. *Cf.* John 4:26 and our comments (*The Renaissance New Testament, 4*, 483). The point is that in the fifteenth century B.C. God, speaking in the present tense to Moses at the bush, referred to Himself as "the God of Abraham, Isaac and Jacob" who were at that time long since dead. If there is no resurrection, then God was representing Himself as a God of those who had long since gone back to the dust, never to return. The conclusion of the matter is in

Verse 27 - "He is not the God of the dead, but the God of the living: ye therefore do greatly err."

οὐκ ἔστιν θεὸς νεκρῶν ἀλλὰ ζώντων. πολὺ πλανᾶσθε.

οὐκ (summary negative conjunction with the indicative) 130.
ἔστιν (3d.per.sing.pres.ind.of εἰμί, static) 86.
θεὸς (nom.sing.masc.of θεός, predicate nominative) 124.

νεκρῶν (gen.pl.masc.of *νεκρός*, description) 749.
ἀλλὰ (alternative conjunction) 343.
ζώντων (pres.act.part.gen.pl.masc.of *ζάω*, substantival, description) 340.
πολὺ (acc.sing.neut.of *πολύς*, adverbial) 228.
πλανᾶσθε (2d.per.pl.pres.mid.ind.of *πλανάω*, aoristic) 1257.

Translation - "He is not a God of the dead, but of those who are alive. You greatly deceive yourselves."

Comment: *Cf.* comment on Mt.22:32; Lk.20:38. Having pointed out to the Sadducees that the source of error is ignorance of the teaching of scripture, as well as lack of experiential knowledge of the power of God, Jesus then cited Exodus 3:6 - a passage that is utterly without point if the Sadducee position is correct. Was Abraham, Isaac and Jacob dead or alive on the day that God spoke to Moses at the bush? In order to support the Sadducee position God should have said, "I *was* the God of Abrham, Isaac and Jacob, and I promised each of them that they would possess a land of their own forever, but unfortunately they are dead and gone, so I cannot keep my promise to them." To put it another way, God should never have made an eternal covenant with men whom He knew would die and never again live to see His promise fulfilled. The same promise that God made to Abraham, is made in the covenant of grace to all who, of faith are "the children of Abraham" (Gal.3:7). He has promised us that we will live forever, even though, in the meantime, like Lazarus, we die. If there is no resurrection of the body of the saints, then all of these promises are empty and destined to remain unfulfilled.

It is prolix, redundant and tautological (and these adjectives do not *quite* mean the same thing) to speak of the resurrection *of the body,* although most of us fall into the habit, particularly when speaking to the point that the resurrection, if there is to be one at all, must be the resurrection of the body, since the body is the only component of the human being that ever died. Death must precede resurrection. To speak therefore of the resurrection *of the spirit* is nonesense. The spirit is the non-material part of man that is not subject to the thermodynamic equilibrium, which we call death. Thermodynamic death, which physicists call "heat death" does not occur until after positive entropy has advanced to the point where the vital functions of the body cease. At this point we have a funeral and bury the body. But it continues to be reduced to its most elemental components after burial. In fact, hair, beard and finger and toe nails continue to grow as they exploit the remaining chemical disequilibrium of their environment, as any mortician knows who has ever reopened a grave. Thus resurrection can apply only to that which has been subject to decomposition up to the point that we refer to as death. It does not take long as John 11:39 attests.

We turn now to Luke's account of Jesus' confrontation with the Sadducees in Luke 20:27-40.

Luke 20:27 - "Then came to him certain of the Sadducees which deny that there is any resurrection; and they asked him, . . . "

Προσελθόντες δέ τινες τῶν Σαδδουκαίων, οἱ ἀντιλέγοντες ἀνάστασιν μὴ εἶναι, ἐπηρώτησαν αὐτὸν . . .

Προσελθόντες (aor.mid.part.nom.pl.masc.of προσέρχομαι, adverbial, temporal) 336.

δὲ (continuative conjunction) 11.

τινες (nom.pl.masc.of τις, the indefinite pronoun, subject of ἐπηρώτησαν) 486.

τῶν (gen.pl.masc.of the article in agreement with Σαδδουκαίων) 9.

Σαδδουκαίων (gen.pl.masc.of Σαδδουκαῖος, partitive) 277.

οἱ (nom.pl.masc.of the article in agreement with ἀντιλέγοντες) 9.

ἀντιλέγοντες (pres.act.part.of ἀντιλέγω, apposition) 1903.

ἀνάστασιν (acc.sing.fem.of ἀνάστασις, general reference) 1423.

μὴ (qualified negative conjunction with the infinitive in indirect discourse) 87.

εἶναι (pres.inf.of εἰμί, indirect discourse) 86.

ἐπηρώτησαν (3d.per.pl.aor.act.ind.of ἐπερωτάω, constative) 973.

αὐτὸν (acc.sing.masc.of αὐτός, direct object of ἐπηρώτησαν) 16.

Translation - "And some of the Sadducees, who deny that there is a resurrection, came up and asked Him, . . . "

Comment: *Cf.* comment on Mt.22:23; note the nominative in οἱ ἀντιλέγοντες, which indicates that it is in apposition with τινες, not with τῶν Σαδδουκαίων. The infinitive εἶναι with μὴ in indirect discourse represents the same tense as in the direct.

Verse 28 - "Saying, Master, Moses wrote unto us, If any man's brother die, having a wife, and he die without children, that his brother should take his wife, and riase up seed unto his brother."

λέγοντες, Διδάσκαλε, Μωϋσῆς ἔγραψεν ὑμῖν, ἐάν τινος ἀδελφὸς ἀποθάνῃ ἔχων γυναῖκα, καὶ οὗτος ἄτεκνος ᾖ, ἵνα λάβῃ ὁ ἀδελφὸς αὐτοῦ τὴν γυναῖκα καὶ ἐξαναστήσῃ σπέρμα τῷ ἀδελφῷ αὐτοῦ.

λέγοντες (pres.act.part.nom.pl.masc.of λέγω, recitative) 66.

Διδάσκαλε (voc.sing.masc.of διδάσκαλος, address) 742.

Μωϋσῆς (nom.sing.masc.of Μωϋσῆς, subject of ἔγραψεν) 715.

ἔγραψεν (3d.per.sing.aor.act.ind.of γράφω, culminative) 156.

ἡμῖν (dat.pl.masc.of ἐγώ, indirect object of ἔγραψεν) 123.

ἐάν (conditional particle in a third-class condition) 363.

τινος (gen.sing.masc.of τις, relationship) 486.

ἀδελφὸς (nom.sing.masc.of ἀδελφός, subject of ἀποθάνῃ) 15.

ἀποθάνῃ (3d.per.sing.aor.act.subj.of ἀποθνήσκω, third-class condition) 774.

ἔχων (pres.act.part.nom.sing.masc.of ἔχω, adverbial, circumstantial) 82.

γυναῖκα (acc.sing.fem.of γυνή, direct object of ἔχων) 103.

καὶ (adversative conjunction) 14.

οὗτος (nom.sing.masc.of οὗτος, subject of ᾖ) 93.

#2696 ἄτεκνος (nom.sing.masc.of ἄτεκνος, predicate adjective).

childless - Luke 20:30.
without children - Luke 20:28,29.

Meaning: A combination of α privative and τέκνον (#229). Hence, childless. In the Sadducees' encounter with Jesus - Luke 20:28,29.

ᾖ (3d.per.sing.pres.subj.of εἰμί, third-class condition) 86.
ἵνα (conjunction with the subjunctive, purpose) 114.
λάβῃ (3d.per.sing.aor.act.subj.of λαμβάνω, purpose) 533.
ὁ (nom.sing.masc.of the article in agreement with ἀδελφὸς) 9.
ἀδελφὸς (nom.sing.masc.of ἀδελφός, subject of λάβῃ and ἐξαναστήσῃ) 15.
αὐτοῦ (gen.sing.masc.of αὐτός, relationship) 16.
τὴν (acc.sing.fem.of the article in agreement with γυναῖκα) 9.
γυναῖκα (acc.sing.fem.of γυνή, direct object of λάβῃ) 103.
καὶ (adjunctive conjunction joining verbs) 14.
ἐξαναστήσῃ (3d.per.sing.aor.act.subj.of ἐξανίστημι, purpose) 2695.
σπέρμα (acc.sing.neut.of σπέρμα, direct object of ἐξαναστήσῃ) 1056.
τῷ (dat.sing.masc.of the article in agreement with ἀδελφῷ) 9.
ἀδελφῷ (dat.sing.masc.of ἀδελφός, personal advantage) 16.
αὐτοῦ (gen.sing.masc.of αὐτός, relationship) 16.

Translation - "saying, 'Teacher, Moses wrote to us that if the brother of someone died, who, though he had a wife, was without children, that his brother should take the wife and raise up an heir for his brother."

Comment: *Cf.*comment on Mt.22:24; Mk.12:19. The peculiarities of the mixed conditional clause have already been discussed in the parallel passage in Mark 12:19.

Verse 29 - "There were therefore seven brethren: and the first took a wife and died without children."

ἑπτὰ οὖν ἀδελφοὶ ἦσαν. καὶ ὁ πρῶτος λαβὼν γυναῖκα ἀπέθανεν ἄτεκνος.

ἑπτὰ (numeral) 1024.
οὖν (explanatory conjunction) 68.
ἀδελφοὶ (nom.pl.masc.of ἀδελφός, subject of ἦσαν) 15.
ἦσαν (3d.per.pl.imp.ind.of εἰμί, progressive description) 86.
καὶ (continuative conjunction) 14.
ὁ (nom.sing.masc.of the article, in agreement with πρῶτος) 9.
πρῶτος (nom.sing.masc.of πρῶτος, subject of ἀπέθανεν) 487.
λαβὼν (aor.act.part.nom.sing.masc.of λαμβάνω, adverbial, temporal) 533.
γυναῖκα (acc.sing.fem.of γυνή, direct object of λαβὼν) 103.
ἀπέθανεν (3d.per.sing.aor.act.ind.of ἀποθνήσκω, constative) 774.
ἄτεκνος (nom.sing.masc.of ἄτεκνος, predicate adjective) 2696.

Translation - "Now there were seven brothers. And the first got married and died without children."

Comment: *Cf.* comment on Mt.22:24,25; Mk.12:20.

Verse 30 - "And the second took her to wife, and he died childless."

καὶ ὁ δεύτερος

καὶ (continuative conjunction) 14.
ὁ (nom.sing.masc.of the article in agreement with *δεύτερος*) 9.
δεύτερος (nom.sing.masc.of *δεύτερος*, subject of the verbs understood) 1371.

Translation - "And the second — . . . "

Comment: The KJV "took her to wife, and he died childless" does not occur in the Greek text.

Verse 31 - "And the third took her; and in like manner the seven also; and they left no children, and died."

καὶ ὁ τρίτος ἔλαβεν αὐτήν, ὡσαύτως δὲ καὶ οἱ ἑπτὰ οὐ κατέλιπον τέκνα καὶ ἀπέθανον.

καὶ (continuative conjunction) 14.
ὁ (nom.sing.masc.of the article in agreement with *τρίτος*) 9.
τρίτος (nom.sing.masc.of *τρίτος*, subject of *ἔλαβεν*) 1209.
ἔλαβεν (3d.per.sing.aor.act.ind.of *λαμβάνω*, constative) 533.
αὐτήν (acc.sing.fem.of *αὐτός*, direct object of *ἔλαβεν*) 16.
ὡσαύτως (adverbial) 1319.
δὲ (continuative conjunction) 11.
καὶ (adjunctive conjunction joining substantives) 14.
οἱ (nom.pl.masc.of the article in agreement with *ἑπτὰ*) 9.
ἑπτὰ (numeral, subject of *κατέλιπον* and *ἀπέθανον*) 1024.
οὐ (summary negative conjunction with the indicative) 130.
κατέλιπον (3d.per.pl.aor.act.ind.of *καταλείπω*, culminative) 369.
τέκνα (acc.pl.neut.of *τέκνον*, direct object of *κατέλιπον*) 299.
καὶ (adjunctive conjunction joining verbs) 14.
ἀπέθανον (3d.per.pl.aor.act.ind.of *ἀποθνήσκω*, culminative) 774.

Translation - "And the third took her, and likewise also the seven and they left no children and died."

Comment: *Cf.* comment on Mt.22:26; Mk.12:21. Luke shortens the sentence structure, but gives the same detail found in Matthew and Mark.

Verse 32 - "Last of all the woman died also."

ὕστερον καὶ ἡ γυνὴ ἀπέθανεν.

ὕστερον (acc.sing.neut.of *ὕστερος*, adverbial) 334.
καὶ (adjunctive conjunction joining substantives) 14.
ἡ (nom.sing.fem.of the article in agreement with *γυνὴ*) 9.
γυνὴ (nom.sing.fem.of *γυνή*, subject of *ἀπέθανεν*) 103.
ἀπέθανεν (3d.per.sing.aor.act.ind.of *ἀποθνήσκω*, culminative) 774.

Translation - "At last also the woman died."

Comment: *Cf.* comment on Mt.22:27; Mk.12:22. Luke brings this bizarre and vulgar story to a merciful end. One can almost see the leer on the faces of the Sadducees as they ask the question in

Verse 33 - "Therefore in the resurrection whose wife of them is she? For seven had her to wife."

ἡ γυνὴ οὖν ἐν τῇ ἀναστάσει τίνος αὐτῶν γίνεται γυνή; οἱ γὰρ ἑπτὰ ἔσχον αυτὴν γυναῖκα.

ἡ (nom.sing.fem.of the article in agreement with γυνὴ) 9.
γυνὴ (nom.sing.fem.of γυνή, subject of γίνεται) 103.
οὖν (inferential conjunction) 68.
ἐν (preposition with the locative of time point) 80.
τῇ (loc.sing.fem.of the article in agreement with ἀναστάσει) 9.
ἀναστάσει (loc.sing.fem.of ἀνάστασις, time point) 1423.
τίνος (gen.sing.masc.of τίς, interoggative pronoun, relationship) 281.
αὐτῶν (gen.pl.masc.of αὐτός, partitive) 16.
γίνεται (3d.per.sing.pres.ind.of γίνομαι futuristic) 113.
γυνή (nom.sing.fem.of γυνή, predicate nominative) 103.
οἱ (nom.pl.masc.of the article in agreement with ἑπτὰ) 9.
γὰρ (causal conjunction) 104.
ἑπτὰ (numeral, subject of ἔσχον) 1024.
ἔσχον (3d.per.pl.2d.aor.act.ind.of ἔχω, culminative) 82.
αὐτὴν (acc.sing.fem.of αὐτός, direct object of ἔσχον) 16.
γυναῖκα (acc.sing.fem.of γυνή, double accusative, predicate accusative) 103.

Translation - "Therefore of which of these will the woman be the wife in the resurrection? Because all seven had married her."

Comment: *Cf.* comment on Mt.22:28; Mk.12:23.

Verse 34 - "And Jesus answering said unto them, The children of this world marry, and are given in marriage."

καὶ εἶπεν αὐτοῖς ὁ Ἰησοῦς, Οἱ υἱοὶ τοῦ αἰῶνος τούτου γαμοῦσιν καὶ γαμίσκονται,

καὶ (continuative conjunction) 14.
εἶπεν (3d.per.sing.aor.act.ind.of εἶπον, constative) 155.
αὐτοῖς (dat.pl.masc.of αὐτός, indirect object of εἶπεν) 16.
ὁ (nom.sing.masc.of the article in agreement with Ἰησοῦς) 9.
Ἰησοῦς (nom.sing.masc.of Ἰησοῦς, subject of εἶπεν) 3.
Οἱ (nom.pl.masc.of the article in agreement with υἱοὶ) 9.
υἱοὶ (nom.pl.masc.of υἱός, subject of γαμοῦσιν and γαμίσκονται) 5.
τοῦ (gen.sing.masc.of the article in agreement with αἰῶνος) 9.
αἰῶνος (gen.sing.masc.of αἰών, description) 1002.

τούτου (gen.sing.masc.of οὗτος, in agreement with αἰῶνος) 93.
γαμοῦσιν (3d.per.pl.pres.act.ind.of γαμέω, customary) 512.
καὶ (adjunctive conjunction joining verbs) 14.

#2697 γαμίσκονται (3d.per.pl.pres.mid.ind.of γαμίσκω, customary).

give in marriage - Luke 20:34.

Meaning: *Cf.*γαμίζω (#1426). To give in marriage - Luke 20:34. This is really only a different spelling of #1426, although Thayer lists the two words separately. Liddell & Scott say, "—ίσκω, equals γαμίζω."

Comment: At this point Luke departs from the pattern set by Mark and followed by Matthew to give us his own formulation. "The sons of this age" - *οἱ υἱοὶ τοῦ αἰῶνος τούτου* - refers to the human race upon earth prior to the second coming of Messiah and the kingdom age which He will establish, as opposed to the future, heavenly and eternal age. In this life it is customary for men and women to marry.

Verse 35 - "But they which shall be accounted worthy to obtain that world and the resurrection from the dead, neither marry nor are given in marriage."

οἱ δὲ καταξιωθέντες τοῦ αἰῶνος ἐκείνου τυχεῖν καὶ τῆς ἀναστάσεως τῆς ἐκ νεκρῶν οὔτε γαμοῦσιν οὔτε γαμίζονται.

οἱ (nom.pl.masc.of the article in agreement with καταξιωθέντες) 9.
δὲ (adversative conjunction) 11.

#2698 καταξιωθέντες (1st.aor.pass.part.nom.pl.masc.of καταξιόω, substantival, subject of γαμοῦσιν and γαμίζονται).

account worthy - Luke 20:35.
count worthy - Acts 5:41; 2 Thess.1:5.

Meaning: A combination of κατά (#98) and ἀξιόω (#2151). To judge one worthy of some reward. Followed by a genitive of reference in 2 Thess.1:5. Followed by an infinitive - Luke 20:35; Acts 5:41.

τοῦ (gen.sing.masc.of the article in agreement with αἰῶνος) 9.
αἰῶνος (gen.sing.masc.of αἰών, with a verb of obtaining) 1002.
ἐκείνου (gen.sing.masc.of ἐκεῖνος, in agreement with αἰῶνος) 246.

#2699 τυχεῖν (2d.aor.act.inf.of τυγχάνω, completes καταξιωθέντες).

be - 1 Cor.14:10; 16:6.
chance - 1 Cor.15:37.
enjoy - Acts 24:2.
obtain - Luke 20:35; Acts 26;22; 1 Tim.2:10; Heb.8:6; 11:35.
no little - Acts 28:2.
refresh self - Acts 27:3.

special - Acts 19:11.

Meaning: A transitive verb, prop. - "to hit the mark." In this sense opposed to ἁμαρτάνω (#1260). Trop.to achieve a goal, reach, attain, get, become master of, earn - followed by the genitive as are other verbs of getting, grasping,obtaining, etc. (Robertson, *Grammar,* 509), in Luke 20:35; Acts 24:2; 26:22; 27:3; 2 Tim.2:10; Heb.8:6; 11:35. Used intransitively - "to happen, come to pass, chance to be true," etc. in 1 Cor.14:10; 15:37; 16:6; Acts 19:11; 28:2.

καὶ (adjunctive conjunction joining nouns) 14.
τῆς (gen.sing.fem.of the article in agreement with ἀναστάσεως) 9.
ἀναστάσεως (gen.sing.fem.of ἀνάστασις, with a verb of obtaining) 1423.
τῆς (gen.sing.fem.of the article in agreement with ἀναστάσεως, introducing a prepositional phrase) 9.
ἐκ (preposition with the ablative of separation) 19.
νεκρῶν (abl.pl.masc.of νεκρός, separation) 749.
οὔτε (negative copulative conjunction) 598.
γαμοῦσιν (3d.per.pl.pres.act.ind.of γαμέω, futuristic) 512.
οὔτε (negative copulative conjunction) 598.
γαμίζονται (3d.per.pl.pres.pass.ind.of γαμίζω, futuristic) 1426.

Translation - "But those who have been accounted worthy to attain that age and the resurrection from the dead, neither marry nor are they given in marriage."

Comment: δὲ is adversative. The contrast is between the practice of this and the coming age. Now it is customary to marry; then it is not. Note the contrast between αἰῶνος τούτου (verse 34) and αἰῶνος ἐκείνου (verse 35) - "this age" as opposed to "that age." The former refers to "man's day" (1 Cor.4:3); the latter to "the day of the Lord." *Cf.*#1002 for a contrast study between the two ages. There is some good preaching material in this study of contrast. In this life we indulge in sex; in the life following the resurrection we do not. It is important to recognize in τυγκάνω (#2699) a verb that properly is transitive, although used in transitively five times in the New Testament.

Note that καταξιωθέντες is aorist. This reckoning of worth is a past decision. The subject of salvation is not directly in view here. No conclusion can be drawn to support the Arminian theology that citizenship in that coming age and participation in the resurrection is obtained upon the basis of accounted worth. If that were true the accounting decision would come in the future, not as a completed decision of the past. There is an implied suggestion that the philosophy of materialism, with its hedonistic glorification of sex and the assumption that it will extend into eternity is unworthy of the next age. The Sadducees, with their rejection of the resurrection were materialistic. Unable to get their minds off of sex long enough to think of heaven, they were unworthy of heaven's philosophy. Moslem philosophy is rebuked by this point. Jesus went on to show the superiority of life in the next age over that of the present.

Verse 36 - "Neither can they die any more: for they are equal unto the angels; and are the children of God, being the children of the resurrection."

οὐδὲ γὰρ ἀποθανεῖν ἔτι δύνανται, ἰσάγγελοι γάρ εἰσιν, καὶ υἱοί εἰσιν θεοῦ, τῆς ἀναστάσεως υἱοὶ ὄντες.

οὐδὲ (disjunctive particle) 452.
γὰρ (emphatic conjunction) 105.
ἀποθανεῖν (aor.act.inf.of ἀποθνήσκω, completes δύνανται) 774.
ἔτι (adverbial) 448.
δύνανται (3d.per.pl.pres.ind.of δύναμαι, futuristic) 289.

#2700 ἰσάγγελοι (nom.pl.masc.of ἰσάγγελος, predicate adjective).

equal unto the angels - Luke 20:36.

Meaning: A combination of ἴσος (#1323) and ἄγγελος (#96). Hence, equal to the angels - Luke 20:36, the sphere of the equality being supplied by the context. *Cf.* ἰσόψυχος (#4560), ἰσότης (#4338), ἰσότιμος (#5226), ἰσόθεος, ἰσάστερος, ἰσάδελφος, etc.

γὰρ (causal conjunction) 105.
εἰσιν (3d.per.pl.pres.ind.of εἰμί, futuristic) 86.
καὶ (continuative conjunction) 14.
υἱοί (nom.pl.masc.of υἱός, predicate nominative) 5.
εἰσιν (3d.per.pl.pres.ind.of εἰμί, futuristic) 86.
θεοῦ (gen.sing.masc.of θεός, relationship) 124.
τῆς (gen.sing.fem.of the article in agreement with ἀναστάσεως) 9.
ἀναστάσεως (gen.sing.fem.of ἀνάστασις, description) 1423.
υἱοὶ (nom.pl.masc.of υἱός, predicate nominative) 5.
ὄντες (pres.act.part.nom.pl.masc.of εἰμί, adverbial, complementary) 86.

Translation - "In fact neither will they any longer be able to die, because they will be equal to the angels, and they will be sons of God, being sons of the resurrection.

Comment: Jesus is describing life in the coming age. Thus the present tense verbs are all futuristic. After the resurrection the problem which the Sadducees raised about a husband dying and leaving his widow without an heir will not arise in any case. Those who participate in the first resurrection owe their presence in the kingdom age to their resurrection. It is in this sense that they are "sons of the resurrection." They are deathless (1 Cor.15:26; John 11:25,26), and, in this respect, they are like the angels. The participle ὄντες is not causal, but complementary. We are not the sons of God because we are going to rise from the dead. Rather, one of the results of the believer's sonship to God is his resurrection from the dead (John 5:24). On τῆς ἀναστάσεως υἱοὶ ὄντες *cf.* Rom.1:4. All of this is taught in scripture and the Sadducees should have known it, but for their ignorance of the scriptures (Mk.12:24).

Verse 37 - "Now that the dead are raised, even Moses shewed at the bush, when he calleth the Lord the God of Abraham, and the God of Isaac, and the God of Jacob."

ὅτι δὲ ἐγείρονται οἱ νεκροὶ καὶ Μωϋσῆς ἐμήνυσεν ἐπὶ τῆς βάτου, ὡς λέγει κύριον τὸν θεὸν Ἀβραὰμ καὶ θεὸν Ἰσαὰκ καὶ θεὸν Ἰακώβ.

ὅτι (conjunction introducing an object clause in indirect discourse) 211.
δὲ (explanatory conjunction) 11.
ἐγείρονται (3d.per.pl.pres.pass.ind.of *ἐγείρω*, futuristic) 125.
οἱ (nom.pl.masc.of the article in agreement with *νεκροὶ*) 9.
νεκροὶ (nom.pl.masc.of *νεκρός*, subject of *ἐγείρονται*) 749.
καὶ (ascensive conjunction) 14.
Μωϋσῆς (nom.sing.masc.of Μωϋσῆς, subject of *ἐμήνυσεν*) 715.
ἐμήνυσεν (3d.per.sing.aor.act.ind.of *μηνύω*, constative) 2666.
ἐπὶ (preposition with the locative of place, ellipsis) 47.
τῆς (gen.sing.fem.of the article, joined to *βάτου*) 9.
βάτου (gen.sing.masc.of *βάτος*, reference) 2138.
ὡς (particle introducing a temporal clause) 128.
λέγει (3d.per.sing.pres.act.ind.of λέγω, historical) 66.
κύριον (acc.sing.masc.of *κύριος*, direct object of λέγει) 97.
τὸν (acc.sing.masc.of the article in agreement with *θεὸν*) 9.
θεὸν (acc.sing.masc.of *θεός*, predicate accusative) 124.
Ἀβραὰμ (gen.sing.masc.of Ἀβραάμ, relationship) 7.
καὶ (adjunctive conjunction joining nouns) 14.
θεὸν (acc.sing.masc.of *θεός*, predicate accusative) 124.
Ἰσαὰκ (gen.sing.masc.of Ἰσαάκ, relationship) 10.
καὶ (adjunctive conjunction joining nouns) 14.
θεὸν (acc.sing.masc.of *θεός*, predicate accusative) 124.
Ἰακώβ (gen.sing.masc.of Ἰακώβ, relationship) 12.

Translation - "Now that the dead will be raised even Moses made clear in the passage about the bush, when he called the Lord the God of Abraham and (the) God of Isaac,and (the) God of Jacob."

Comment: *δὲ* is explanatory and the first *καὶ* is ascensive or adjunctive. The *ὅτι* clause is indirect discourse. Where did Moses indicate this? "In the passage about the bush" in Exodus 3:1-6. *Cf.* our comment on Mark 12:26, with reference to the ellipsis following *ἐπὶ*. But Luke has *τῆς*, the feminine article joined properly with the feminine *βάτος*, not to be confused with the masculine *βάτος* (#2565).

How did Moses indicate in the Exodus passage that the dead would rise? *ὡς* introduces the temporal clause. He did it "when he called . . .*κ.τ.λ.*" If Abraham, Isaac and Jacob, who were dead when God met Moses at the bush, had no prospect of resurrection, such language was without meaning. *Cf.* our comment on Mark 12:26,27; Mt.22:31,32. The conclusion of verse 38 therefore follows.

Verse 38 - "For he is not a God of the dead, but of the living: for all live unto him."

θεὸς δὲ οὐκ ἔστιν νεκρῶν ἀλλὰ ζώντων, πάντες γὰρ αὐτῷ ζῶσιν.

θεὸς (nom.sing.masc.of θεός, predicate nominative) 124.
δὲ (inferential conjunction) 11.
οὐκ (summary negative conjunction with the indicative) 86.
ἔστιν (3d.per.sing.pres.ind.of εἰμί, static) 86.
νεκρῶν (gen.pl.masc.of νεκρός, description) 749.
ἀλλὰ (alternative conjunction) 342.
ζώντων (pres.act.part.gen.pl.masc.of ζάω, substantival, description) 340.
πάντες (nom.pl.masc.of πᾶς, subject of ζῶσιν) 67.
γὰρ (causal conjunction) 105.
αὐτῷ (loc.sing.masc.of αὐτός, sphere) 16.
ζῶσιν (3d.per.pl.pres.act.ind.of ζάω, futuristic) 340.

Translation - "Therefore He is not a God of the dead but of the living, because all in Him will live."

Comment: δὲ seems inferential, as Jesus uses the quotation from Exodus 3 as a final rebuttal against the argument of the Sadducees. If He was the God of Abraham, in Moses' day, since He is not a God of the dead, but of the living, Abraham, Isaac and Jacob must have been alive (though not physically) in Moses' day, and since they were alive, they were destined to rise from the grave at the last day. αὐτῷ can be taken as a dative of personal advantage or reference. It can also be construed as a locative of sphere, as we have chosen to do. Those who live within the sphere of the salvation provided by Him will live. Otherwise the passage could be construed to teach universalism, which other passages clearly refute.

Verse 39 - "Then certain of the scribes answering said, Master thou hast well said."

ἀποκριθέντες δέ τινες τῶν γραμματέων εἶπαν, Διδάσκαλε, καλῶς εἶπας.

ἀποκριθέντες (aor.part.nom.pl.masc.of ἀποκρίνομαι, adverbial, modal) 319.
δὲ (continuative conjunction) 11.
τινες (nom.pl.masc.of τις, the indefinite pronoun, subject of εἶπαν) 486.
τῶν (gen.pl.masc.of the article in agreement with γραμματέων) 9.
γραμματέων (gen.pl.masc.of γραμματεῖς, partitive) 152.
εἶπαν (3d.per.pl.aor.act.ind.of εἶπον, constative) 155.
Διδάσκαλε (voc.sing.masc.of διδάσκαλος, address) 742.
καλῶς (adverbial) 977.
εἶπας (2d.per.sing.aor.act.ind.of εἶπον,culminative) 155.

Translation - "And some of the Scribes said, 'Teacher, you have spoken well.'"

Comment: Approbation from the Scribes who knew the Old Testament scriptures well enough to recognize the soundness of Jesus' argument, discouraged any further attempt on the part of the Jews to argue with Him.

Verse 40 - "And after that they durst not ask him any question at all."

οὐκέτι γὰρ ἐτόλμων ἐπερωτᾶν αὐτὸν οὐδέν.

οὐκέτι (temporal adverb) 1289.
γὰρ (inferential conjunction) 105.
ἐτόλμων (3d.per.pl.imp.ind.of τολμάω, progressive duration) 1430.
ἐπερωτᾶν (pres.act.inf.of ἐπερωτάω, completes ἐτόλμων) 973.
αὐτὸν (acc.sing.masc.of αὐτός, direct object of ἐπερωτᾶν) 16.
οὐδέν (acc.sing.neut.of οὐδείς, double accusative, object of ἐπερωτᾶν) 446.

Translation - "Therefore never again did they dare to ask Him a single thing."

Comment: Note the double accusative after ἐπερωτᾶν in αὐτὸν οὐδέν. It had been a long and busy day for Jesus. The Elders challenged His authority. The Pharisees and Herodians tried to compromise Him about the taxes. The Sadducees attacked His view of the resurrection. In each case Jesus had been more than a match for His enemies. They seemed to know when they were defeated and were ready to quit, but for a lawyer who had a sincere question. Luke's statement of verse 40 does not include the question of Mark 12:28, since Luke meant that Jesus' enemies dared not ask Him a hostile question. The question of Mark 12:28 was not a hostile question.

Controversy With a Lawyer About the Commandments

(Matthew 22:34-40; Mark 12:28-34)

Mark 12:28 - "And one of the scribes came, and having heard them reasoning together, and perceiving that he had answered them well, asked him, Which is the first commandment of all?"

Καὶ προσελθὼν εἷς τῶν γραμματέων ἀκούσας αὐτῶν συζητούντων, ἰδὼν ὅτι καλῶς ἀπεκρίθη αὐτοῖς, ἐπηρώτησεν αὐτόν, Ποία ἐστὶν ἐντολὴ πρώτη πάντων;

Καὶ (continuative conjunction) 14.
προσελθὼν (aor.mid.part.nom.sing.masc.of προσέρχομαι, adverbial, temporal) 336.
εἷς (nom.sing.masc.of εἷς, subject of ἐπηρώτησεν) 469.
τῶν (gen.pl.masc.of the article in agreement with γραμματέων) 9.
γραμματέων (gen.pl.masc.of γραμματεύς, partitive) 152.
ἀκούσας (aor.act.part.nom.sing.masc.of ἀκούω, adverbial, causal) 148.
αὐτῶν (gen.pl.masc.of αὐτός, description) 16.
συζητούντων (pres.act.part.gen.pl.masc.of συζητέω, adverbial, circumstantial) 2060.
ἰδὼν (aor.act.part.nom.sing.masc.of ὁράω, adverbial, causal) 144.

ὅτι (conjunction introducing an object clause in indirect discourse) 211.
καλῶς (adverbial) 977.
ἀπεκρίθη (3d.per.sing.aor.ind.of ἀποκρίνομαι, culminative) 318.
αὐτοῖς (dat.pl.masc.of αὐτός, indirect object of ἀπεκρίθη) 16.
ἐπηρώτησεν (3d.per.sing.aor.act.ind.of ἐπερωτάω, constative) 973.
αὐτόν (acc.sing.masc.of αὐτός, direct object of ἐπηρώτησεν) 16.
Ποία (nom.sing.fem.of ποῖος, in agreement with ἐντολή) 1298.
ἐστὶν (3d.per.sing.pres.ind.of εἰμί, static) 86.
ἐντολή (nom.sing.fem.of ἐντολή, subject of ἐστὶν) 472.
πρώτη (nom.sing.fem.of πρῶτος, predicate adjective) 487.
πάντων (gen.pl.fem.of πᾶς, partitive) 67.

Translation - "And one of the Scribes approached and because he heard them arguing and saw that Jesus answered them well, he asked Him, 'Which commandment is first of all?' "

Comment: *Cf.* comment on Mt.22:34-36. The verse is full of participles, all of them adverbial. προσελ. . is temporal, ἀκούσας is causal as is ἰδών.συζούντων is circumstantial. After the scribe came up, and because he heard the argument and saw that Jesus had given them the proper response, he was motivated to ask a question, which apparently came from an honest heart. The action of all of these participles is antecedent to the action of the main verb ἐπηρώτησεν. "Which of the ten commandmends is the most important?" Matthew 22:35 says that he was a lawyer as well as a scribe and that he asked the question in a manner of court room cross examination - πειράζων (#330).

To ask the Heavenly Lawgiver, incarnate in human flesh, which of His ten commandments is most important is like asking a mother which of her ten children she loves the most. Had Jesus selected one of the ten He would have taught, by implication, that the other nine were of less importance. Yet it should not be thought that the lawyer was not sincere with his question. *cf.* verse 34.

Verse 29 - "And Jesus answered him, The first of all the commandments is, Hear, O Israel, the Lord our God is one Lord."

ἀπεκρίθη ὁ Ἰησοῦς ὅτι Πρώτη ἐστίν, Ἄκουε, Ἰσραήλ, κύριος ὁ θεὸς ἡμῶν κύριος εἷς ἐστιν.

ἀπεκρίθη (3d.per.sing.aor.mid.ind.of ἀποκρίνομαι, constative) 318.
ὁ (nom.sing.masc.of the article in agreement with Ἰησοῦς) 9.
Ἰησοῦς (nom.sing.masc.of Ἰησοῦς, subject of ἀπεκρίθη) 3.
ὅτι (recitative) 211.
Πρώτη (nom.sing.fem.of πρῶτος, subject of ἐστίν) 487.
ἐστίν (3d.per.sing.pres.ind.of εἰμί, static) 86.
Ἄκουε (2d.per.sing.pres.act.impv.of ἀκούω, command) 148.
Ἰσραήλ (voc.sing.masc.of Ἰσραήλ, address) 165.
κύριος (nom.sing.masc.of κύριος, subject of ἐστιν) 97.
ὁ (nom.sing.masc.of the article in agreement with θεός) 9.

θεὸς (nom.sing.masc.of θεός, apposition) 124.
ἡμῶν (gen.pl.masc.of ἐγώ, relationship) 123.
κύριος (nom.sing.masc.of κύριος, predicate nominative) 97.
εἷς (nom.sing.masc.of εἷς, in agreement with κύριος) 469.
ἐστιν (3d.per.sing.pres.ind.of εἰμί, static) 86.

Translation - "Jesus answered, 'The first is, Hear, Israel! The Lord our God is one Lord.' "

Comment: The quotation is from Deut.6:4. The lawyer's question seemed to emphasize diversity. There were many commandments - ten in the Decalogue and many others in the Levitcal code. Which one, of all of these, is greatest? In reply, Jesus emphasized unity, as if to say that the source of all the commandments, though the Godhead consists of a trinity of personalities, operates as a unit. Hence, to begin with, it is a mistake to imagine that one of His commandments could compete with any of the others. Just as God, being three, yet is one, so His commandments, being many, are essentially one from an eternal point of view. Further, just as God is One and the commandments are essentially one, so we must love Him with a unified personality. This is the thought of

Verse 30 - "And thou shalt love the Lord thy God with all thy heart and with all thy soul, and with all thy mind, and with all thy strength; this is the first commandment."

καὶ ἀγαπήσεις κύριον τὸν θεόν σου ἐξ ὅλης τῆς καρδίας σου καὶ ἐξ ὅλης τῆς ψυχῆς σου καὶ ἐξ ὅλης τῆς διανοίας σου καὶ ἐξ ὅλης τῆς ἰσχύος σου.

καὶ (continuative conjunction) 14.
ἀγαπήσεις (2d.per.sing.fut.act.ind.of ἀγαπάω, imperative) 540.
κύριον (acc.sing.masc.of κύριος, direct object of ἀγαπήσεις) 97.
τὸν (acc.sing.masc.of the article in agreement with θεόν) 9.
θεόν (acc.sing.masc.of θεός, apposition) 124.
σου (gen.sing.masc.of σύ, relationship) 104.
ἐξ (preposition with the ablative of source) 19.
ὅλης (abl.sing.fem.of ὅλος, in agreement with καρδίας) 112.
τῆς (abl.sing.fem.of the article in agreement with καρδίας) 9.
καρδίας (abl.sing.fem.of καρδία, source) 432.
σου (gen.sing.masc.of σύ, possession) 104.
καὶ (adjunctive conjunction joining prepositional phrases) 14.
ἐξ (preposition with the ablative of source) 19.
ὅλης (abl.sing.fem.of ὅλος, in agreement with ψυχῆς) 112.
τῆς (abl.sing.fem.of the article in agreement with ψυχῆς) 9.
ψυχῆς (abl.sing.fem.of ψυχή, source) 233.
σου (gen.sing.masc.of σύ, possession) 104.
καὶ (adjunctive conjunction joining prepositional phrases) 14.
ἐξ (preposition with the ablative of source) 19.

ὅλης (abl.sing.fem.of ὅλος, in agreement with διανοίας) 112.
τῆς (abl.sing.fem.of the article in agreement with διανοίας) 9.
διανοίας (abl.sing.fem.of διάνοια, source) 1428.
σου (gen.sing.masc.of σύ, possession) 104.
καὶ (adjunctive conjunction joining prepositional phrases) 14.
ἐξ (preposition with the ablative of source) 19.
ὅλης (abl.sing.fem.of ὅλος, in agreement with ἰσχύος) 112.
τῆς (abl.sing.fem.of the article in agreement with ἰσχύος) 9.
ἰσχύος (abl.sing.fem.of ἰσχύς, source) 2419.
σου (gen.sing.masc.of σύ, possession) 104.

Translation - "And you will love the Lord your God from your whole heart and from your whole soul, and from your whole mind and from your entire strength."

Comment: Note the imperative future in ἀγαπήσεις. Our love for God has its sources in (1) the heart, symbolically used to refer to the emotions; (2) the soul - the sociologically developed self which makes us conscious of God and our earthly environment; (3) the mind - the intellectual capacity to reason and philosophize, and (4) the strength - the bodily prowess measured in physical strength and vigor. Every asset is to be devoted to God. Thus when we love God with the total capacity of our being, we automatically keep the first four commandments of the decalogue. *Cf.* Mt.22:37 and Lk.10:27.

Verse 31 - "And the second is like, namely this, Thou shalt love thy neighbour as thyself. There is none other commandment greater than these."

δευτέρα αὕτη, Ἀγαπήσεις τὸν πλησίον σου ὡς σεαυτόν. μείζων τούτων ἄλλη ἐντολὴ οὐκ ἔστιν.

δευτέρα (nom.sing.fem.of δεύτερας, in agreement with ἐντολή, understood) 1371.
αὕτη (nom.sing.fem.of οὗτος, predicate nominative) 93.
Ἀγαπήσεις (2d.per.sing.fut.act.ind.of ἀγαπάω, imperative) 540.
τὸν (acc.sing.masc.of the article in agreement with πλησίον) 9.
πλησίον (acc.sing.masc.of πλησίος, direct object of ἀγαπήσεις) 541.
σου (gen.sing.masc.of σύ, possession) 104.
ὡς (adverb introducing a comparative clause) 128.
σεαυτόν (acc.sing.masc.of σεαυτός, direct object of ἀγαπήσεις understood) 347.
μείζων (nom.sing.masc.of μείζων, predicate adjective) 916.
τούτων (abl.pl.neut.of οὗτος, comparison) 93.
ἄλλη (nom.sing.fem.of ἄλλος, in agreement with ἐντολή) 198.
ἐντολὴ (nom.sing.fem.of ἐντολή, subject of ἔστιν) 472.
οὐκ (summary negative conjunction with the indicative) 130.
ἔστιν (3d.per.sing.pres.ind.of εἰμί, static) 86.

Translation - "The second is this: You will love your neighbour as yourself.

There is no other commandment greater than these."

Comment: δευτέρα αὕτη - The copula ἔστιν is missing. The second commandment is second only in the order of listing. It is of equal importance with the first. Some miss the point that the second commandment tells us to love ourselves and then adds that we are to love others with the same intense devotion with which we love ourselves. Self love is not selfish, when the love we lavish upon ourselves is also lavished upon all others. Selfish love is the love that is exhausted upon ourselves, until there is none for others.

Love of self is required if we are to keep the fourth commandment, which enjoins rest and relaxation one day in seven. The Sabbath is not a day of worship, except in the sense that all days are days of worship. It is a day of rest. The inveterate worker who drives himself beyond physical endurance violates this commandment. Since we must love God with all of our strength we should allow our bodies to rehabilitate by rest from exertion on the sabbath.

He who loves himself must also love his neighbour as much. Thus he keeps the last six commandments. To love God is to keep the first three commandments. To love oneself is to keep the fourth. To love one's neightbour as much is to keep the last six. This leaves no need for any other greater commandment. *Cf.* Gal.5:14; Rom.13:9,10.

Verse 32 - "And the scribe said unto him, Well, Master, thou hast said the truth: for there is one God; and there is none other but he."

καὶ εἶπεν αὐτῷ ὁ γραμματεύς, Καλῶς, διδάσκαλε, ἐπ' ἀληθείας εἶπες ὅτι εἷς ἐστιν καὶ οὐκ ἔστιν ἄλλος πλὴν αὐτοῦ.

εἶπεν (3d.per.sing.aor.act.ind.of εἶπον, constative) 155.
αὐτῷ (dat.sing.masc.of αὐτός, indirect object of εἶπεν) 16.
ὁ (nom.sing.masc.of the article in agreement with γραμματεύς) 9.
γραμματεύς (nom.sing.masc.of γραμματεύς, subject of εἶπεν) 152.
Καλῶς (adverbial) 977.
διδάσκαλε (voc.sing.masc.of διδάσκαλος, address) 742.
ἐπ' (preposition with the genitive, adverbial) 47.
ἀληθείας (gen.sing.fem.of ἀλήθεια, adverbial) 1416.
εἶπες (2d.per.sing.aor.act.ind.of εἶπον, culminative) 155.
ὅτι (conjunction introducing an object clause in indirect discourse) 211.
εἷς (nom.sing.masc.of εἷς, predicate nominative) 469.
ἐστιν (3d.per.sing.pres.ind.of εἰμί, static) 86.
καὶ (continuative conjunction) 14.
οὐκ (summary negative conjunction with the indicative) 130.
ἔστιν (3d.per.sing.pres.ind.of εἰμί, static) 86.
ἄλλος (nom.sing.masc.of ἄλλος, subject of ἔστιν) 198.
πλὴν (adversative conjunction) 944.
αὐτοῦ (gen.sing.masc.of αὐτός, reference) 16.

Translation - "The scribe said to Him, 'Splendid, Teacher! You have spoken truthfully that He is one and there is no other except Him."

Comment: ἐπ' with the genitive in ἀληθείας can be thought of as an indication of contact. "You spoke *in contact* with the truth." Thus it is adverbial - "You spoke truthfully." In the 1970's the university term was "Right On!" This is why the lawyer began by saying, "Splendid, Teacher." The lawyer then emphasized the monotheistic unity of God. Only one God exists. There should therefore be a single guiding principle in all matters of worship and ethics.

Verse 33 - "And to love him with all the heart and with all the understanding, and with all the soul, and with all the strength, and to love his neighbour as himself, is more than all whole burnt offerings and sacrifices."

καὶ τὸ ἀγαπᾶν αὐτὸν ἐξ ὅλης τῆς καρδίας καὶ ἐξ ὅλης τῆς συνέσεως καὶ ἐξ ὅλης τῆς ἰσχύος καὶ τὸ ἀγαπᾶν τὸν πλησίον ὡς ἑαυτὸν περισσότερόν ἐστιν πάντων τῶν ὁλοκαυτωμάτων καὶ θυσιῶν.

καὶ (continuative conjunction) 14.
τὸ (nom.sing.neut.of the article in agreement with ἀγαπᾶν) 9.
ἀγαπᾶν (pres.act.inf.of ἀγαπάω, noun use, nom.sing.neut.,subject of ἐστιν) 540.
αὐτὸν (acc.sing.masc.of αὐτός, direct object of ἀγαπᾶν) 16.
ἐξ (preposition with the ablative of source) 19.
ὅλης (abl.sing.fem.of ὅλος, in agreement with καρδίας) 112.
τῆς (abl.sing.fem.of the article in agreement with καρδίας) 9.
καρδίας (abl.sing.fem.of καρδία, source) 432.
καὶ (adjunctive conjunction joining prepositional phrases) 14.
ἐξ (preposition with the ablative of source) 19.
ὅλης (abl.sing.fem.of ὅλος, in agreement with συνέσεως) 112.
τῆς (abl.sing.fem.of the article in agreement with συνέσεως) 9.
συνέσεως (abl.sing.fem.of σύνεσις, source) 1918.
καὶ (adjunctive conjunction joining prepositional phrases) 14.
ὅλης (abl.sing.fem.of ὅλος, in agreement with ἰσχύος) 112.
τῆς (abl.sing.fem.of the article in agreement with ἰσχύος) 9.
ἰσχύος (abl.sing.fem.of ἰσχύς, source) 2419.
καὶ (adjunctive conjunction joining infinitives) 14.
τὸ (nom.sing.neut.of the article in agreement with ἀγαπᾶν) 9.
ἀγαπᾶν (pres.act.inf.of ἀγαπάω, noun use, nom.sing.neut., subject of ἐστιν) 540.

τὸν (acc.sing.masc.of the article in agreement with πλησίον) 9.
πλησίον (acc.sing.masc.of πλήσιος, direct object of ἀγαπᾶν) 541.
ὡς (adverb introducing a comparative clause) 128.
ἑαυτὸν (acc.sing.masc.of ἑαυτός, direct object of ἀγαπᾶν) 288.
περισσότερόν (acc.sing.neut.of περισσός, comp.degree, predicate adjective) 525.
ἐστιν (3d.per.sing.pres.ind.of εἰμί, static) 86.
πάντων (abl.pl.masc.of πᾶς in agreement with ὁλοκαυτωμάτων and θυσιῶν) 67.
τῶν (abl.pl.masc.of the article in agreement with ὁλοκαυτωμάτων and θυσιῶν) 9.

#2701 ὁλοκαυτωμάτων (abl.pl.masc.of ὁλοκαύτωμα, comparison).

burnt offering - Heb.10:6,8.
whole burnt offering - Mark 12:33.

Meaning: Cf. ὁλοκαυτόω - "to burn whole." With reference to the Levitical burnt offering - Mark 12:33; Heb.10:6,8.

καὶ (adjunctive conjunction joining nouns) 14.
θυσιῶν (abl.pl.fem.of θυσία, comparison) 796.

Translation - "And to love Him out of the whole heart, and out of the complete understanding, and out of the entire strength, and to love your neighbour as yourself is more than all the burnt offerings and sacrifices."

Comment: Two identical subjects, τὸ ἀγαπᾶν, articular infinitives in the nominative case are joined to the same verb ἐστιν. The predicate adjective is περισσότερόν. "To love is better. . . " To love how and whom? And better than what? The first question is answered with the series of prepositional phrases in the ablative of source - "from (out of, with) the entire emotional, intellectual and physical resources." That is how. Whom? Our neighbour. How should we love him? As we love ourselves. Better than what? All of the burnt offerings and sacrifices of the Levitical priesthood. Note that the love for God which is here described leaves no conflict better the emotional and intellectual sides of our experience. The Christian whose head and heart do not agree is remiss somewhere . Some Christians love God with all of their emotional drive, or so they say, but they are too intellectually lazy to lay their intellects on the line.

Thus this lawyer took his stand with the school of thought that held that the ethical essence of the law was of greater importance than the ritualistic and ceremonial directives. Judaism is essentially a spiritual experience, based upon a monotheistic view of God and demanding our *total* devotion to Him, as a by-product of which comes peaceable and profitable relations with man. The altitude of the theological equilateral triangle determines the breadth of the social base. A lofty theological view of the one God means a broad and loving pro-social view of man. Ghenghis Khan, Attila the Hun, Tamerlane, the Ku Klux Klan, Cain, Ahab and Zezebel, Adolph Hitler and the Ayatollah Khomeni, among other misanthropes, apparently have a low opinion of God.

Verse 34 - "And when Jesus saw that he answered discreetly, he said unto him, Thou art not far from the kingdom of God. And no man after that durst ask him any question."

καὶ ὁ Ἰησοῦς ἰδὼν (αὐτὸν) ὅτι νουνεχῶς ἀπεκρίθη εἶπεν αὐτῷ, Οὐ μακρὰν εἶ ἀπὸ τῆς βασιλείας τοῦ θεοῦ. καὶ οὐδεὶς οὐκέτι ἐτόλμα αὐτὸν ἐπερωτῆσαι.

καὶ (continuative conjunction) 14.
ὁ (nom.sing.masc.of the article in agreement with Ἰησοῦς) 9.
Ἰησοῦς (nom.sing.masc.of Ἰησοῦς, subject of εἶπεν) 3.
ἰδὼν (aor.act.part.nom.sing.masc.of ὁράω, adverbial, temporal/causal) 144.
(αὐτὸν) (acc.sing.masc.of αὐτός, direct object of ἰδὼν) 16.

ὅτι (conjunction introducing an object clause in indirect discourse) 211.

#2702 νουνεχῶς (adverbial).

discreetly - Mark 12:34.

Meaning: A combination of νοῦς (#2928) and ἔχω (#82). Hence, "having a mind." Thus, thoughtfully, exercising discretion, prudence and judgment. The thought of a thorough, original and independent thinker. With reference to the lawyer and the question about the law - Mark 12:34.

ἀπεκρίθη (3d.per.sing.aor.mid.ind.of ἀποκρίνομαι, constative) 318.
εἶπεν (3d.per.sing.aor.act.ind.of εἶπον, constative) 155.
αὐτῷ (dat.sing.masc.of αὐτός, indirect object of εἶπεν) 16.
Οὐ (summary negative conjunction with the indicative) 130.
μακρὰν (an adverb of place) 768.
εἶ (2d.per.sing.pres.ind.of εἰμί, aoristic) 86.
ἀπὸ (preposition with the ablative of separation) 70.
τῆς (abl.sing.fem.of the article in agreement with βασιλείας) 9.
βασιλείας (abl.sing.fem.of βασιλεία, separation) 253.
τοῦ (gen.sing.masc.of the article in agreement with θεοῦ) 9.
θεοῦ (gen.sing.masc.of θεός, description) 124.
καὶ (continuative conjunction) 14.
οὐδεὶς (nom.sing.masc.of οὐδείς, subject of ἐτόλμα) 446.
οὐκέτι (adverbial) 1289.
ἐτόλμα (3d.per.sing.imp.act.ind.of τολμάω, progressive description) 1430.
αὐτὸν (acc.sing.masc.of αὐτός, direct object of ἐπερωτῆσαι) 16.
ἐπερωτῆσαι (aor.act.inf.of ἐπερωτάω, completes ἐτόλμα) 973.

Translation - "And when (because) Jesus perceived him, that he replied thoughtfully, He said to him, 'You are not far from the kingdom of God.' And no one dared to question Him further."

Comment: The aorist participle ἰδὼν is both temporal and causal. Of course, in the nature of the case, since cause always precedes result, all causal participles are also temporal. The objective clause with ὅτι introduces indirect discourse.

The lawyer answered Jesus in a way that indicated that he was an independent thinker who reacted to the Pharisees and their traditions in very much the same way that Jesus did. The outer ritualistic forms, without the inner spiritual and ethical content, is worthless. (1 Samuel 15:22; Mal.1:7,8; Amos 5:21-27). How often this scribe must have noted with sadness and some contempt the hypocrisy of those who observed the Levitical rules with fanatical zeal only to deny in their life styles all that the law of God really demands. One who thinks about theology for himself, and is critical of the religious *status quo*, who "puts his mind to it" and forms his own conclusions, indicates that he is an earnest seeker after truth, and thus he is not far from the kingdom of God. God is morally obligated to give more light to one who honestly uses the light that he has. Marknow adds what Luke says in Luke 20:40, though Luke does not mention the material in Mark 12:28-34. There is no contradiction since Luke was referring to hostile questions.

Christ's Unanswerable Question About David's Son

(Matthew 22:41-46; Mark 12:35-37; Luke 20:41-44)

Mark 12:35 - "And Jesus answered and said, while he taught in the temple, How say the scribes that Christ is the Son of David?"

Καὶ ἀποκριθεὶς ὁ Ἰησοῦς ἔλεγεν διδάσκων ἐν τῷ ἱερῷ, Πῶς λέγουσιν οἱ γραμματεῖς ὅτι ὁ Χριστὸς υἱὸς Δαυίδ ἐστιν;

Καὶ (continuative conjunction) 14.
ἀποκριθεὶς (aor.mid.part.nom.sing.masc.of ἀποκρίνομαι, adverbial, modal) 318.
ὁ (nom.sing.masc.of the article in agreement with Ἰησοῦς) 9.
Ἰησοῦς (nom.sing.masc.of Ἰησοῦς, subject of ἔλεγεν) 3.
ἔλεγεν (3d.per.sing.imp.act.ind.of λέγω, inceptive) 66.
διδάσκων (pres.act.part.nom.sing.masc.of διδάσκω, adverbial, temporal) 403.
ἐν (preposition with the locative of place) 80.
τῷ (loc.sing.neut.of the article in agreement with ἱερῷ) 9.
ἱερῷ (loc.sing.neut.of ἱερόν, place where) 346.
Πῶς (interrogative conjunction in direct question) 627.
λέγουσιν (3d.per.pl.pres.act.ind.of λέγω, customary) 66.
οἱ (nom.pl.masc.of the article in agreement with γραμματεῖς) 9.
γραμματεῖς (nom.pl.masc.of γραμματεύς,subject of λέγουσιν) 152.
ὅτι (conjunction introducing an object clause in indirect discourse) 211.
ὁ (nom.sing.masc.of the article in agreement with Χριστὸς) 9.
Χριστὸς (nom.sing.masc.of Χριστός, subject of ἐστιν) 4.
υἱὸς (nom.sing.masc.of υἱός, predicate nominative) 5.
Δαυίδ (gen.sing.masc.of Δαυίδ, relationship) 6.
ἐστιν (3d.per.sing.pres.ind.of εἰμί, static) 86.

Translation - "And as Jesus taught in the temple, He said in reply, 'Why do the Scribes say that the Messiah is a son of David?' "

Comment: ἀποκριθεὶς here must be considered as an answer by Jesus, not to any further hostile questions, for there were no more (vs.34), but as a continuation of the dialogue. The purpose of the controversies generally, all day long, had been to put Jesus on defense while His enemies plied Him with hard questions. Thus now it is Jesus' time to ask them a question that truly has no answer from one who does not accept Him as David's son and the Messiah. Note ἔλεγεν, indicating that Jesus was pressing the point. Πῶς in the sense of "Why?" as often. *Cf.*#627. Jesus is assuming that His enemies are correct as He poses the question, thus to place them in a dilemma. The scribes did indeed say that Christ was the son of David. And they were correct in saying so. Luke 3:23-31 traces the line from Jesus, through Heli (Mary's father) back to David. Thus Jesus, genetically descended from Mary, was a son of David. That His throne rights were protected under the law of inheritance (Numbers 27:1-8; 36:1-13) is clear from Mt.1:1-16 which proves that Joseph, whom Mary later married, was also from the family of David. Hence Mary was engaged to a man within her tribe and thus she kept inviolate her throne rights to pass down to her first-born son, Jesus. Messiah must be David's Son in order to claim the kingdom throne rights vested in David in the covenant of 2 Samuel 7:12-17. Note that 2 Samuel 7;14 is applied to Jesus in Heb.1:5. *Cf.* our full discussion of this matter in *The Renaissance New Testament, I,4.*

Having called attention to what the Scribes were teaching, Jesus now quotes David in

Verse 36 - "For David himself said by the Holy Ghost, The Lord said to my Lord, Sit thou on my right hand, till I make thine enemies thy footstool."

αὐτὸς Δαυὶδ εἶπεν ἐν τῷ πνεύματι τῷ ἁγίῳ, Εἶπεν *κύριος τῷ κυρίῳ μου,* Κάθου *ἐκ δεξιῶν μου ἕως ἂν θῶ τοὺς ἐχθρούς σου ὑποκάτω τῶν ποδῶν σου.*

αὐτὸς (nom.sing.masc.of *αὐτός*, intensive predicate use) 16.
Δαυὶδ (nom.sing.masc.of *Δαυίδ*, subject of *εἶπεν*) 6.
εἶπεν (3d.per.sing.aor.act.ind.of *εἶπον*, constative) 155.
ἐν (preposition with the instrumental of means) 80.
τῷ (instru.sing.neut.of the article in agreement with *πνεύματι*) 9.
πνεύματι (instru.sing.neut.of *πνεῦμα*, means) 83.
τῷ (instru.sing.neut.of the article in agreement with *ἁγίῳ*) 9.
ἁγίῳ (instru.sing.neut.of *ἅγιος*, in agreement with *πνεύματι*) 84.
εἶπεν (3d.per.sing.aor.act.ind.of *εἶπον*, constative) 155.
κύριος (nom.sing.masc.of *κύριος*, subject of *εἶπεν*) 97.
τῷ (dat.sing.masc.of the article in agreement with *κυρίῳ*) 9.
κυρίῳ (dat.sing.masc.of *κύριος*, indirect object of *εἶπεν*) 97.
μου (gen.sing.masc.of *ἐγώ*, relationship) 123.
Κάθου (2d.per.sing.pres.act.impv.of *καθίζω*, command) 420.
ἐκ (preposition with the ablative, where *ἐν* and the locative could have been used) 19.
δεξιῶν (abl.pl.masc.of *δεξιός*, place) 502.
μου (gen.sing.masc.of *ἐγώ*, possession) 123.
ἕως (conjunction with the subjunctive in an indefinite temporal, with future reference) 71.
ἂν (particle in an indefinite temporal clause, future reference) 205.
θῶ (1st.per.sing.2d.aor.act.subj.of *τίθημι*, indefinite temporal clause) 455.
τοὺς (acc.pl.masc.of the article in agreement with *ἐχθρούς*) 9.
ἐχθρούς (acc.pl.masc.of *ἐχθρός*, direct object of *θῶ*) 543.
σου (gen.sing.masc.of *σύ*, relationship) 104.
ὑποκάτω (improper preposition with the ablative of place separation) 1429.
τῶν (abl.pl.masc.of the article in agreement with *ποδῶν*) 9.
ποδῶν (abl.pl.masc.of *πούς*, place separation) 353.
σου (gen.sing.masc.of *σύ*, possession) 104.

Translation - "David himself, with the guidance of the Holy Spirit, said, 'The Lord said to my Lord, Sit at my right hand until I put your enemies under your feet.' "

Comment: αὐτὸς in the predicate position in an intensive sense, a rare use in the N.T. ἐν τῷ . . . ἁγίῳ - as Jesus puts His stamp of approval upon the divine inspiration by the Holy Spirit of the writers of the scriptures (2 Pet.1:21). Goodspeed rightly translates ". . . under the influence of the Holy Spirit." Speaking by the divine inspiration of the Holy Spirit, David, in Psalm 110:1, said, "The Lord (God the Father) said to my Lord (God the Son). . . " Note that David gave equal dignity to the Father, the speaker, and to the Son, the one spoken to. Note the present imperative, κάθου - "be always sitting . . . until. . . " ἕως with ἂν and the subjunctive in θῶ comprise an indefinite temporal clause, with a future reference. The contingency in the construction does not refer to the fact, but rather to the time, which is unannounced, when God the Father will put Christ's enemies under His feet. Note ἐξ with a genitive of place description in a construction where ἐν and the locative could have served. *Cf.*#19 for other examples, *viz.*, Mt.20:21,21,23,23; 21:19; 25:33,33,34; Lk.1:11, etc.

Christ will not always sit at the Father's right hand. The subjugation of Christ's enemies under His feet is not in doubt - only the time of such subjugation. Hence ἂν with the subjunctive. *Cf.*#455 for a list of quotations of Psalm 110:1, elsewhere. New Testament theology is proud of the fact that our Lord is exalted to the right hand of God and that His ultimate superiority over all things is promised. This makes good preaching material. Especially note Heb.1:13 in the same context that links Jesus (Heb.1:5) with 2 Samuel 7:14, the Davidic covenant.

Our Lord's main purpose here is not to point to His exaltation to the Father's right hand, which was destined to take place soon, nor to His ultimate victory over His enemies, but to the fact that David, under divine inspiration called his *son* his *Lord.* Who is τῷ κυρίῳ μου of our verse? It is Messiah, destined to proceed from David's loins, and hence, physically speaking, his son. This is Jesus' point in

Verse 37 - "David therefore himself calleth him, Lord; and whence is he then his son? And the common people heard him gladly."

αὐτὸς Δαυὶδ λέγει αὐτὸν κύριον, καὶ πόθεν αὐτοῦ ἐστιν υἱός; καὶ (οἱ) πολὺς ὄχλος ἤκουεν αὐτοῦ ἡδέως.

αὐτὸς (nom.sing.masc.of αὐτός, intensive) 16.
Δαυὶδ (nom.sing.masc.of Δαυὶδ, subject of λέγει) 6.
λέγει (3d.per.sing.pres.act.ind.of λέγω, historical) 66.
αὐτὸν (acc.sing.masc.of αὐτός, direct object of λέγει) 16.
κύριον (acc.sing.masc.of κύριος, double accusative, object of λέγει) 97.
καὶ (inferential conjunction) 14.
πόθεν (interrogative conjunction) 1061.
αὐτοῦ (gen.sing.masc.of αὐτός, relationship) 16.
ἐστιν (3d.per.sing.pres.ind.of εἰμί, aoristic) 86.
υἱός (nom.sing.masc.of υἱός, predicate nominative) 5.

καὶ (inferential conjunction) 14.
(ὁ) (nom.sing.masc.of the article in agreement with ὄχλος) 9.
πολὺς (nom.sing.masc.of πολύς, in agreement with ὄχλος) 228.
ὄχλος (nom.sing.masc.of ὄχλος, subject of ἤκουεν) 418.
ἤκουεν (3d.per.sing.imp.act.ind.of ἀκούω, progressive description) 148.
αὐτοῦ (gen.sing.masc.of αὐτός, subjective genitive) 16.
ἡδέως (adverbial) 2255.

Translation - "David himself called him Lord. How then is He his Son? And the great crowd was listening to Him gladly."

Comment: Again we have αὐτὸς in an intensive sense as in the previous verse. Note the double accusative in αὐτὸν κύριον - "He called (historical present) Him Lord" both being objects of the verb. καὶ is inferential. πόθεν here in the sense of "why/ from what cause/ by what reasoning" - *Cf.* Lk.1:43; John 1:48; James 4:1. Jesus was demanding an explanation. What logic is involved in the fact that David, speaking of one to be born his grandchild after 700 years, whom the Scribes called the Messiah, refers to Him as his Lord? The answer is that David's Son is God, the Messiah, incarnate in human flesh for purposes of redemption and Messiahship. The Scribes offered no explanation, but the great crowds of people were delighted. *Cf.* comment on Mt.22:41-46; Lk.20:41-44.

We turn now to Luke's account of the episode in Luke 20:41-44.

Luke 20:41 - "And he said unto them, How say they that Christ is David's son?"

Εἶπεν δὲ πρὸς αὐτούς, Πῶς λέγουσιν τὸν Χριστὸν εἶναι Δαυὶδ υἱόν;

Εἶπεν (3d.per.sing.aor.act.ind.of εἶπον, constative) 155.
δὲ (continuative conjunction) 11.
πρὸς (preposition with the accusative of extent, after a verb of speaking) 197.
αὐτούς (acc.pl.masc.of αὐτός, extent after a verb of speaking) 16.
Πῶς (interrogative conjunction) 627.
λέγουσιν (3d.per.pl.pres.act.ind.of λέγω, customary) 66.
τὸν (acc.sing.masc.of the article in agreement with Χριστὸν) 9.
Χριστὸν (acc.sing.masc.of Χριστός, general reference) 4.
εἶναι (pres.act.inf.of εἰμί, object clause in indirect discourse) 86.
Δαυὶδ (gen.sing.masc.of Δαυίδ, relationship) 6.
υἱόν (acc.sing.masc.of υἱός, predicate accusative) 5.

Translation - "And He said to them, 'Why do they say that the Messiah is David's son?' "

Comment: The infinitive εἶναι in indirect discourse carries the same time as the indicative in direct discourse. They were saying, "Messiah is David's Son." Why were they saying this? This was Jesus' question. *Cf.* comment on Mt.22:41,42; Mk.12:35.

Verse 42 - "And David himself saith in the book of Psalms, The Lord said unto my Lord, Sit thou on my right hand."

αὐτὸς γὰρ Δαυὶδ λέγει ἐν βίβλῳ ψαλμῶν, Εἶπεν κύριος τῷ κυρίῳ μου, Κάθου ἐκ δεξιῶν μου . . ."

αὐτὸς (nom.sing.masc.of αὐτός, intensive use) 16.
γὰρ (causal conjunction) 105.
Δαυὶδ (nom.sing.masc.of Δαυίδ, subject of λέγει) 6.
λέγει (3d.per.sing.pres.act.ind.of λέγω, historical) 66.
ἐν (preposition with the locative of place) 80.
βίβλῳ (loc.sing.masc.of βίβλος, place where) 1.

#2703 ψαλμῶν (gen.pl.masc.of ψαλμός, description).

psalm - Acts 1:20; 13:33; 1 Cor.14:26; Eph.5:19; Col.3:16.
Psalms - Luke 20:42; 24:44.

Meaning: Cf. ψάλλω (#4047) - to strike chords on an instrument of strings. Hence ψαλμός is the result of such music. It came to mean a pious song. Specifically of Psalm 110 - Luke 20:42; Psalm 69 - Acts 1:20; Psalm 2 - Acts 13:33. In the Psalmody of the Old Testament, as distinct from the Law and the Prophets - Luke 24:44. Generally, of a song indited in a Christian heart - 1 Cor.14:26; Eph.5:19; Col.3:16.

Εἶπεν (3d.per.sing.aor.act.ind.of εἶπον, constative) 155.
κύριος (nom.sing.masc.of κύριος, subject of εἶπεν) 97.
τῷ (dat.sing.masc.of the article in agreement with κυρίῳ) 9.
κυρίῳ (dat.sing.masc.of κύριος, indirect object of εἶπεν) 97.
μου (gen.sing.masc.of ἐγώ, relationship) 123.
Κάθου (2d.per.sing.pres.act.impv.of καθίζω, command) 420.
ἐκ (preposition with the genitive of place description, where ἐν with the locative could have served) 19.
δεξιῶν (gen.pl.masc.of δεξιός, place where) 502.
μου (gen.sing.masc.of ἐγώ, possession) 123.

Translation - "For David himself said in a book of Psalms, 'The Lord said to my Lord, Sit at my right hand' " . . .

Comment: γὰρ is causal, as Jesus pursues His point. Intensive in αὐτὸς. *Cf.* the parallel passages. Luke omits ἐν τῷ πνεύματι τῷ ἁγίῳ, which Mark includes. Otherwise the passages are identical. *Cf.* Mark 12:36; Matthew 22:44.

Verse 43 - " . . . till I make thine enemies thy footstool."

ἕως ἂν θῶ ἐχθρούς σου ὑποπόδιον τῶν ποδῶν σου.

ἕως (conjunction with ἂν in an indefinite temporal clause of future reference) 71.
ἂν (particle in an indefinite temporal clause of future reference) 205.
θῶ (1st.per.sing.2d.aor.act.subj.of τίθημι, indefinite temporal clause) 455.

τοὺς (acc.pl.masc.of the article in agreement with ἐχθρούς) 9.
ἐχθρούς (acc.pl.masc.of ἐχθρός, direct object of θῶ) 543.
σου (gen.sing.masc.of σύ, relationship) 104.
ὑποπόδιον (acc.sing.neut.of ὑποπόδιον, direct object of θῶ, double accusative) 520.
τῶν (gen.pl.masc.of the article in agreement with ποδῶν) 9.
ποδῶν (gen.pl.masc.of πούς, description) 353.
σου (gen.sing.masc.of σύ, possession) 104.

Translation ". . . until I make your enemies a footstool beneath your feet."

Comment: *Cf.* comment on Mt.22:44; Mk.12:36, who say, ". . . until I place your enemies under your feet." Luke's idea is the same, but he uses ὑποπόδιον with a genitive of description.

Verse 44 - "David therefore calleth him, Lord. How is he then his son?"

Δαυὶδ οὖν κύριον αὐτὸν καλεῖ, καὶ πῶς αὐτοῦ υἱός ἐστιν;

Δαυὶδ (nom.sing.masc.of Δαυίδ, subject of καλεῖ) 6.
οὖν (inferential conjunction) 68.
αὐτὸν (acc.sing.masc.of αὐτός, direct object of καλεῖ, double accusative) 16.
κύριον (acc.sing.masc.of κύριος, object of καλεῖ) 97.
καλεῖ (3d.per.sing.pres.act.ind.of καλέω,historical) 107.
καὶ (inferential conjunction) 14.
πῶς (interrogative conjunction) 627.
αὐτοῦ (gen.sing.masc.of αὐτός, relationship) 16.
υἱός (nom.sing.masc.of υἱός, predicate nominative) 5.
ἐστιν (3d.per.sing.pres.ind.of εἰμί, static) 86.

Translation - "David therefore called him, Lord. How then is He a son of his?"

Comment: *Cf.* comment on Mt.22:45; Mk.12:37. Jesus had not only spent the day in victorious verbal combat with the best that the Jerusalem Establishment could send against Him, but He has had the last word with an exegetical question that they cannot answer without accepting Him as their Messiah. Now comes His fiery denunciation of the Scribes and Pharisees, recorded at length by Matthew 23:1-39, and briefly by Mark and Luke.

Denunciation of the Scribes and Pharisees

(Matthew 23:1-39; Mark 12:38-40; Luke 20:45-47)

Mark 12:38 - "And he said unto them in his doctrine, Beware of the scribes, which love to go in long clothing, and love salutations in the market places."

Καὶ ἐν τῇ διδαχῇ αὐτοῦ ἔλεγεν, Βλέπετε ἀπὸ τῶν γραμματέων τῶν θελόντων ἐν στολαῖς περιπατεῖν καὶ ἀσπασμοὺς ἐν ταῖς ἀγοραῖς.

Καὶ (continuative conjunction) 14.

ἐν (preposition with the locative of time point) 80.
τῇ (loc.sing.fem.of the article in agreement with διδαχῇ) 9.
διδαχῇ (loc.sing.fem.of διδαχή, time point) 706.
αὐτοῦ (gen.sing.masc.of αὐτός, possession) 16.
ἔλεγεν (3d.per.sing.imp.act.ind.of λέγω, progressive description) 66.
Βλέπετε (2d.per.pl.pres.act.impv.of βλέπω, command) 499.
ἀπὸ (preposition with the ablative of source) 70.
τῶν (abl.pl.masc.of the article in agreement with γραμματέων) 9.
γραμματέων (abl.pl.masc.of γραμματεύς, source) 152.
τῶν (abl.pl.masc.of the article in agreement with θελόντων) 9.
θελόντων (pres.act.part.abl.pl.masc.of θέλω, adjectival, restrictive) 88.
ἐν (preposition with the instrumental of manner) 80.
στολαῖς (instru.pl.fem.of στολή, manner) 2552.
περιπατεῖν (pres.act.inf.of περιπατέω, completes θελόντων) 384.
καὶ (adjunctive conjunction joining substantives) 14.
ἀσπασμοὺς (acc.pl.masc.of ἀσπασμός, direct object of θελόντων) 1442.
ἐν (preposition with the locative of place) 80.
ταῖς (loc.pl.fem.of the article in agreement with ἀγοραῖς) 9.
ἀγοραῖς (loc.pl.fem.of ἀγορά, place where) 924.

Translation - "And during His discourse He was saying, 'Beware of the Scribes who want to walk around in robes and to be greeted in the shopping centers.' "

Comment: *Cf.* Luke 20:46. ἐν τῇ διδαχῇ can be construed, either as an instrumental of means or a locative of time point - "by means of His teaching" (instrumental) or "during His teaching" (locative of time). Jesus warned the people against the Scribes. We have chosen the latter, although both are admissible and they are not contradictory. Goodspeed, in agreement, says, "And in the course of His teaching He said, . . . κ.τ.λ." ἀπό with the ablative of source. "Look out for the evil influences which comes from the scribes." He tells us why they are dangerous. The character sketch which follows reveals men of small intellectual stature who are therefore insecure and seek to compensate by ostentation. They love to walk about in their doctoral robes. Think of that the next time you attend a university graduation ceremony, but keep in mind that many in the procession are there only in reluctant obedience to the orders from the President! The Scribes were seeking popularity. They wanted to be noticed. Such men like attention and imagine the worst if they do not get it. Paranoid personalities, these compulsive politicians are a pernicious breed. We should all submit to some honest introspection when we find outselves unduly delighted because the newspaper printed our name. Not all of the scribes died when the Romans sacked Jerusalem.

Verse 39 - "And the chief seats in the synagogues and the uppermost rooms at feasts."

καὶ πρωτοκαθεδρίας ἐν ταῖς συναγωγαῖς καὶ προτοκλισίας ἐν τοῖς δείπνοις.

καὶ (adjunctive conjunction joining nouns) 14.
πρωτοκαθεδρίας (acc.pl.fem.of πρωτοκαθεδρία, direct object of θελόντων) 1441.
ἐν (preposition with the locative of place) 80.
ταῖς (loc.pl.fem.of the article in agreement with συναγωγαῖς) 9.
συναγωγαῖς (loc.pl.fem.of συναγωγή, place where) 404.
καὶ (adjunctive conjunction joining nouns) 14.
πρωτοκλισίας (acc.pl.fem.of πρωτοκλισία, direct object of θελόντων) 1439.
ἐν (preposition with the locative of place where) 80.
τοῖς (loc.pl.neut.of the article in agreement with δείπνοις) 9.
δείπνοις (loc.pl.neut.of δεῖπνον, place where) 1440.

Translation - ". . . and front seats in the synagogues and most important couches at the feasts."

Comment: They loved their long robes, the greetings which came their way in the markets, the front seats in the synagogues and the places of honor at the dinner parties. Two verses describe the fatal flaws in the personalities of the scribes. Such personality disorder is associated in verse 40 with anti-social behavior. Note that those who desire the places of honor at banquets on earth will not be present at the marriage supper of the Lamb (Rev.19:9).

Verse 40 - "Which devour widow's houses, and for a pretense make long prayers: those shall receive greater damnation."

οἱ κατεσθίοντες τὰς οἰκίας τῶν χηρῶν καὶ προφάσει μακρὰ προχευχόμενοι, οὗτοι λήμψονται περισσότερον κρίμα.

οἱ (nom.pl.masc.of the article in agreement with κατεσθίοντες) 9.
κατεσθίοντες (pres.act.part.nom.pl.masc.of κατεσθίω,appellation) 1028.
τὰς (acc.pl.fem.of the article in agreement with οἰκίας) 9.
οἰκίας (acc.pl.fem.of οἰκία, direct object of κατεσθίοντες) 186.
τῶν (gen.pl.fem.of the article in agreement with χηρῶν) 9.
χηρῶν (gen.pl.fem.of χήρα, possession) 1910.
καὶ (adjunctive conjunction joining participles) 14.

#2704 προφάσει (dat.sing.fem.of πρόφασις, advantage).

cloak - John 15:22; 1 Thess.2:5.
colour - Acts 27:30.
pretence - Mark 12:40; Phil.1:18.
show - Luke 20:47.

*Meaning: Cf.*προφαὶνω - "to cause to shine before." Hence, anything that is designed to be conspicuous. A pretext. A show of pretence. Play acting; a form of hypocrisy. Jesus' coming destroyed the world's rationalization for living in sin; *i.e.* before He came they could plead the lack of understanding for their behavior, instead of the real reason. Now that Jesus has come they can no longer plead ignorance as their excuse - John 15:22. Paul refused to use his apostolic office as an excuse for collecting money - 1 Thess.2:5. The sailors on an imperiled ship tried to launch a boat to escape, pretending that they were casting an anchor overboard - Acts 27:30. With reference to long prayers as a way to display sanctity - Mark 12:40; Luke 20:47. Sometimes the gospel is preached εἴτε προφάσει (whether in pretense) εἴτε ἀληθείᾳ (or truth) - Phil.1:18, where πρόφασις is used in contradistinction to ἀληθεία.

μακρὰ (acc.pl.neut.of μακρός, adverbial) 2546.

προσευχόμενοι (pres.mid.part.nom.pl.masc.of προσεύχομαι, appellation) 544.

οὗτοι (nom.pl.masc.of οὗτος, subject of λήμψονται) 93.

λήμψονται (3d.per.pl.fut.mid.ind.of λαμβάνω, predictive) 533.

περισσότερον (acc.sing.neut.of περισσότερος, comparative degree, in agreement with κρίμα) 525.

κρίμα (acc.sing.neut.of κρίμα, direct object of λήμψονται) 642.

Translation - "Devourers of widows' houses and for purposes of ostentation sonorous prayer orators! These will receive greater condemnation."

Comment: We can call the participle substantives οἱ κατεσθίοντες and προσευχόμενοι nominative absolutes. They cannot be construed in apposition with τῶν θελόντων of verse 38 because they do not agree in case (ablative in θελόντων and nominative in κατεσθίοντες and προσευχόμενοι. Orwe can explain it as a case of anacoluthon. Robertson calls it apposition with anacoluthon on one page (Robertson, *Grammar,* 1106) and adds that "It is possible . . . to explain (as nominative absolutes, *our comment)* some examples of anacolutha in ancient Greek and the N.T.. . . " (*Ibid*, 1130) and go ones to cite Mark 12:40 as an example. We have translated the participles as nominative absolute appellations, as Jesus holds this kind of hypocrisy up to public ridicule.

The character sketch which Jesus gave is not flattering. They walked about in long robes; they sought public recognition in the markets; they occupied the front seats at the synagogue and the places of highest honor at the dinner parties. They exploited the real estate holdings of widows and they prayed long pretentious prayers. Then came the prediction of their greater condemnation. These shall receive greater condemnation than those who sinned with less knowledge. All who do not repent and believe will be condemned, but religious pretenders will come in for greater punishment.

Note that their narrow sociological base revealed in their exploitation of poor widows, is related to their short theological altitude. Thus we have an illustration of the principle set forth in Mark 12:28-34. The Scribes and Pharisees majored in the commandments of ritual rather than in the underlying principle of love for God, self and neighbour. *Cf.*#1028 for other uses of κατεσθίω - especially Rev.20:9. Those who devour the fortunes of widows will be devoured by the judgment fires of God.

We turn now to Luke's account of Jesus' remarks in Luke 20:45-47.

Luke 20:45 - "Then in the audience of all the people he said unto his disciples,"

Ἀκούοντος δὲ παντὸς τοῦ λαοῦ εἶπεν τοῖς μαθηταῖς (αὐτοῦ).

Ἀκούοντος (pres.act.part.gen.sing.masc.of ἀκούω, genitive absolute) 148.
δὲ (continuative conjunction) 11.
παντὸς (gen.sing.masc.of πᾶς, genitive absolute) 67.
τοῦ (gen.sing.masc.of the article in agreement with λαοῦ) 9.
λαοῦ (gen.sing.masc.of λαός, description) 110.
εἶπεν (3d.per.sing.aor.act.ind.of εἶπον, constative) 155.
τοῖς (dat.pl.masc.of the article in agreement with μαθηταῖς) 9.
μαθηταῖς (dat.pl.masc.of μαθητής, indirect object of εἶπεν) 421.
(αὐτοῦ) (gen.sing.masc.of αὐτός, relationship) 16.

Translation - "And as all the people listened, He said to His disciples. . . "

Comment: The genitive absolute is in the present tense, indicating simultaneous action. As all of the people listened, Jesus spoke directly to His disciples and denounced the scribes in verses 46 and 47.

Verse 46 - "Beware of the scribes, which desire to walk in long robes, and love greetings in the markets, and the highest seats in the synagogues, and the chief room at feasts;"

Προσέχετε ἀπὸ τῶν γραμματέων τῶν θελόντων περιπατεῖν ἐν στολαῖς καὶ φιλούντων ἀσπασμοὺς ἐν ταῖς ἀγοραῖς καὶ πρωτοκαθεδρίας ἐν ταῖς συναγωγαῖς καὶ πρωτοκλισίας ἐν τοῖς δείπνοις,

Προσέχετε (2d.per.pl.pres.act.impv.of προσέχω, command) 555.
ἀπὸ (preposition with the ablative of source) 70.
τῶν (abl.pl.masc.of the article in agreement with γραμματέων) 9.
γραμματέων (abl.pl.masc.of γραμματεύς, source) 152.
τῶν (abl.pl.masc.of the article in agreement with θελόντων) 9.
θελόντων (pres.act.part.abl.pl.masc.of θέλω, adjectival, restrictive) 88.
περιπατεῖν (pres.act.inf.of περιπατέω, completes θελόντων) 384.
ἐν (preposition with the instrumental of manner) 80.
στολαῖς (instru.pl.fem.of στολή, manner) 2552.
καὶ (adjunctive conjunction joining participles) 14.
φιλούντων (pres.act.part.abl.pl.masc.of φιλέω, adjectival, restrictive) 566.
ἀσπασμοὺς (acc.pl.masc.of ἀσπασμός, direct object of φιλούντων) 1442.
ἐν (preposition with the locative of place) 80.
ταῖς (loc.pl.fem.of the article in agreement with ἀγοραῖς) 9.
ἀγοραῖς (loc.pl.fem.of ἀγορά, place where) 924.
καὶ (adjunctive conjunction joining nouns) 14.
πρωτοκαθεδρίας (acc.pl.fem.of πρωτοκαθεδρία, direct object of φιλούντων) 1441
ἐν (preposition with the locative of place) 80.
ταῖς (loc.pl.fem.of the article in agreement with συναγωγαῖς) 9.

συναγωγαῖς (loc.pl.fem.of συναγωγή, place where) 404.
καὶ (adjunctive conjunction joining nouns) 14.
πρωτοκλισίας (acc.pl.fem.of πρωτοκλισία, direct object of φιλούντων) 1439.
ἐν (preposition with the locative of place) 80.
τοῖς (loc.pl.neut.of the article in agreement with δείπνοις) 9.

δείπνοις (loc.pl.neut.of δεῖπνον, place where) 1440.

Translation - "Beware of the scribes who like to walk about in long robes, and who love greetings in the shopping centers and front seats in the synagogues and places of honor at the dinner parties."

Comment: *Cf.* comment on Mk.12:38. Lukes uses προσέχετε (#555) instead of Mark's βλέπετε (#499). He also uses φιλούντων as another participle while Mark makes θελόντων serve for the entire sentence.

Verse 47 - "Which devour widows' houses, and for a shew make long prayers; the same shall receive greater damnation."

οἱ κατεσθίουσιν τὰς οἰκίας τῶν χηρῶν καὶ προφάσει μακρὰ προσεύχονται. οὗτοι λήμψονται περισσότερον κρίμα.

οἱ (nom.pl.masc.of the article, subject of κατεσθίουσιν and προσεύχονται) 9.
κατεσθίουσιν (3d.per.pl.pres.act.ind.of κατεσθίω, customary) 1028.
τὰς (acc.pl.fem.of the article in agreement with οἰκίας) 9.
οἰκίας (acc.pl.fem.of οἰκία, direct object of κατεσθίουσιν) 186.
τῶν (gen.pl.fem.of the article in agreement with χηρῶν) 9.
χηρῶν (gen.pl.fem.of χήρα, possession) 1910.
καὶ (adjunctive conjunction joining verbs) 14.
προφάσει (dat.sing.fem.of πρόφασις, advantage) 2704.
μακρὰ (acc.pl.neut.of μακρός, adverbial) 2546.
προσεύχονται (3d.per.pl.pres.mid.ind.of προσεύχομαι, customary) 544.
οὗτοι (nom.pl.masc.of οὗτος, subject of λήμψονται) 93.
λήμψονται (3d.per.pl.fut.pass.ind.of λαμβάνω, predictive) 533.
περισσότερον (acc.sing.neut.of πέρισσος, in agreement with κρίμα) 525.
κρίμα (acc.sing.neut.of κρίμα, direct object of λήμψονται) 642.

Translation - "They devour the houses of the widows and for the sake of display they pray interminably. They will be given greater condemnation."

Comment: *Cf.* comment on Mark 12:40. It is interesting that Luke, with a greater grasp of the language than Mark avoids the anacolutha, which we pointed out in Mark, by using the indicative in κατεσθίουσιν and προσεύχονται.

Note the intensive effect of the compound verb κατεσθίουσιν (#1028) - "to eat down," "to eat up (completely)" "to eat away at" indicating the constant drain on the financial resources of widows, until all had been taken.

The fuller account of Jesus' castigation of the Scribes, Pharisees and others in the Jewish Establishment is found in Matthew 23:1-39 *q.v.*.

Jesus Commends the Liberality of a Poor Widow

(Mark 12:41-44; Luke 21:1-4)

Mark 12:41 - "And Jesus sat over against the treasury and beheld how the people cast money into the treasury; and many that were rich cast in much."

Καὶ καθίσας κατέναντι τοῦ γαζοφυλακίου ἐθεώρει πῶς ὁ ὄχλος βάλλει χαλκὸν εἰς τὸ γαζοφυλάκιον, καὶ πολλοὶ πλούσιοι ἔβαλλον πολλά.

Καὶ (continuative conjunction) 14.
καθίσας (aor.act.part.nom.sing.masc.of καθίζω, adverbial, temporal) 420.
κατέναντι (improper preposition with the genitive of place description) 1342.
τοῦ (gen.sing.neut.of the article in agreement with γαζοφυλακίου) 9.
γαζοφυλακίου (gen.sing.neut.of γαζοφυλάκιον, place description) 2383.
ἐθεώρει (3d.per.sing.imp.act.ind.of θεωρέω, progressive description) 1667.
πῶς (adverb introducing an object clause in indirect assertion) 627.
ὁ (nom.sing.masc.of the article in agreement with ὄχλος) 9.
ὄχλος (nom.sing.masc.of ὄχλος, subject of βάλλει) 418.
βάλλει (3d.per.sing.pres.act.ind.of βάλλω, indirect assertion) 299.
χαλκὸν (acc.sing.masc.of χαλκός, direct object of βάλλει) 861.
εἰς (preposition with the accusative of extent) 140.
τὸ (acc.sing.neut.of the article in agreement with γαζοφυλάκιον) 9.
γαζοφυλάκιον (acc.sing.neut.of γαζοφυλάκιον, extent) 2383.
καὶ (continuative conjunction) 14.
πολλοὶ (nom.pl.masc.of πολύς, in agreement with πλούσιοι) 228.
πλούσιοι (nom.pl.masc.of πλούσιος, subject of ἔβαλλον) 1306.
ἔβαλλον (3d.per.pl.imp.act.ind.of βάλλω, progressive description) 299.
πολλά (acc.pl.neut.of πολύς, direct object of ἔβαλλον) 228.

Translation - "And He sat down opposite the treasury and began to watch how the people were casting money into the treasury. And many rich people were putting in large sums."

Comment: *Cf.* comment on Luke 21:1. *Cf.*#1342 for this interesting improper preposition with the genitive of place description. The imperfect is inceptive. He began to watch the people to see how much they contributed to the temple treasury. Robertson calls the imperfect "the descriptive tense in narrative." It presents us with "a moving panorama" . . . "a moving picture show." Jesus sat quietly watching while the people came by and dropped their contributions into the treasury. Many rich people were contributing a great deal. ἔβαλλον could be an iterative imperfect. If so, it means that the same rich man returned again and again to drop in his money. If not, it refers to all of the rich people, who filed by, one at a time, to contribute. Or perhaps both. It is difficult to tell. In view of what Jesus had just said about the pretentious scribes, no doubt, in some cases, at least, there was fanfare. But not in the case of the poor widow in

Verse 42 - "And there came a certain poor widow, and she threw in two mites, which make a farthing."

καὶ ἐλθοῦσα μία χήρα πτωχὴ ἔβαλεν λεπτὰ δύο, ὅ ἐστιν κοδράντης.

καὶ (continuative conjunction) 14.
ἐλθοῦσα (aor.act.part.nom.sing.fem.of *ἔρχομαι*, adverbial, temporal) 146.
μία (nom.sing.fem.of *εἷς*, in agreement with *χήρα*) 469.
χήρα (nom.sing.fem.of *χήρα*, subject of *ἔβαλεν*) 1910.
πτωχὴ (nom.sing.fem.of *πτωχός*, in agreement with *χήρα*) 423.
ἔβαλεν (3d.per.sing.aor.act.ind.of *βάλλω*, constative) 299.
λεπτὰ (acc.pl.neut.of *λεπτόν*, direct object of *ἔβαλεν*) 2498.
δύο (numeral) 385.
ὅ (nom.sing.neut.of *ὅς*, subject of *ἐστιν*) 65.
ἐστιν (3d.per.sing.pres.ind.of *εἰμί*, static) 86.
κοδράντης (nom.sing.masc.of *κοδράντης*, predicate nominative) 497.

Translation - "And a poor widow came and dropped in two little brass coins which equals a penny."

Comment: *Cf.* comment on Luke 21:2. The widow's offering was insignificant when compared on an absolute basis with the gifts of the rich, but Jesus is about to point out that the comparison must be made, not on an absolute, but on a relative basis. We may be sure that there was no show of ostentation as the widow made her offering.

Verse 43 - "And he called unto him his disciples and saith unto them, Verily I say unto you, That this poor widow hath cast more in, than all they which hath cast into the treasury."

καὶ προσκαλεσάμενος τοὺς μαθητὰς αὐτοῦ εἶπεν αὐτοῖς, Ἀμὴν λέγω ὑμῖν ὅτι ἡ χήρα αὕτη ἡ πτωχὴ πλεῖον πάντων ἔβαλεν τῶν βαλλόντων εἰς τὸ γαζοφυλάκιον.

καὶ (continuative conjunction) 14.
προσκαλεσάμενος (aor.mid.part.nom.sing.masc.of *προσκαλέω*, adverbial, temporal) 842.
τοὺς (acc.pl.masc.of the article in agreement with *μαθητὰς*) 9.
μαθητὰς (acc.pl.masc.of *μαθητής*, direct object of *προσκαλεσάμενος*) 421.
αὐτοῦ (gen.sing.masc.of *αὐτός*, relationship) 16.
εἶπεν (3d.per.sing.aor.act.ind.of *εἶπον*, constative) 155.
αὐτοῖς (dat.pl.masc.of *αὐτός*, indirect object of *εἶπεν*) 16.
Ἀμὴν (explicative) 466.
λέγω (1st.per.sing.pres.act.ind.of *λέγω*, aoristic) 66.
ὑμῖν (dat.pl.masc.of *σύ*, indirect object of *λέγω*) 104.
ὅτι (conjunction introducing an object clause in indirect discourse) 211.
ἡ (nom.sing.fem.of the article in agreement with *χήρα*) 9.
χήρα (nom.sing.fem.of *χήρα*, subject of *ἔβαλεν*) 1910.
αὕτη (nom.sing.fem.of *οὗτος*, in agreement with *χήρα*, deictic) 93.
ἡ (nom.sing.fem.of the article in agreement with *πτωχὴ*) 9.
πτωχὴ (nom.sing.fem.of *πτωχός*, in agreement with *χήρα*) 423.

πλεῖον (acc.sing.neut.of πλείων, direct object of ἔβαλεν) 474.
πάντων (abl.pl.masc.of πᾶς, in agreement with βαλλόντων) 67.
ἔβαλεν (3d.per.sing.aor.act.ind.of βάλλω, culminative) 299.
τῶν (abl.pl.masc.of the article in agreement with βαλλόντων) 9.
βαλλόντων (pres.act.part.abl.pl.masc.of βάλλω, substantival, comparison) 299.
εἰς (preposition with the accusative of extent) 140.
τὸ (acc.sing.neut.of the article in agreement with γαζοφυλάκιον) 9.
γαζοφυλάκιον (acc.sing.neut.of γαζοφυλάκιον, extent) 2382.

Translation - "And He called His disciples to Him and said to them, 'Truly, I am telling you that this poor widow dropped in more than all those contributing to the treasury."

Comment: *Cf.* comment on Luke 21:3. We have indirect discourse, following οτι within the direct discourse. Note that Jesus emphasized the poverty of the woman with ἡ χηρα αὕτη ἡ παρωχή. πλεῖον is also out of position for emphasis. Note the ablative of comparison.

The woman who gave only two brass coins gave more than all the rich who gave much. This, of course, is true only on a relative basis. After her gift she had nothing left. The rich gave only a very small proportion of their total wealth. This helps to explain how the scribes fulfilled their function as οἱ κατεσθίοντες τὰς οἰκίας τῶν χηρῶν. The tithe as a guide for giving is a proportional tax, and, as such, very regressive. It places the heaviest burden on those least able to bear it. In any temple, synagogue or church where there is a wide and unequal distribution of wealth, the lion's share of the financial support comes from the numerous poor, upon whom it imposes an intolerable burden, while the relatively small number of rich, escape the burden, even though their tithe in absolute amount is much greater than that of the poor. Thus is the institutional church financed. Jesus explains this kind of economics in

Verse 44 - "For all they did cast in of their abundance; but she of her want did cast in all that she had, even all her living."

πάντες γὰρ ἐκ τοῦ περισσεύοντος αὐτοῖς ἔβαλον, αὕτη δὲ ἐκ τῆς ὑστερήσεως αὐτῆς πάντα ὅσα εἶχεν ἔβαλεν, ὅλον τὸν βίον αὐτῆς.

πάντες (nom.pl.masc.of πᾶς, subject of ἔβαλον) 67.
γὰρ (causal conjunction) 105.
ἐκ (preposition with the ablative of source) 19.
τοῦ (abl.sing.masc.of the article in agreement with περισσεύοντος) 9.
περισσεύοντος (pres.act.part.abl.sing.masc.of περισσεύω, substantival, source) 473.
αὐτοῖς (dat.pl.masc.of αὐτός, personal advantage) 16.
ἔβαλον (3d.per.pl.aor.act.ind.of βάλλω, culminative) 299.
αὕτη (nom.sing.fem.of οὗτος, subject of ἔβαλεν) 93.
δὲ (adversative conjunction) 11.
ἐκ (preposition with the ablative of source) 19.

τῆς (abl.sing.fem.of the article in agreement with ὑστερήσεως) 9.

#2705 ὑστερήσεως (abl.sing.fem.of ὑστέρησις, source).

want - Mark 12:44; Phil.4:11.

Meaning: Cf. ὑστερέω (#1302). Hence, want, poverty. With reference to the widow - Mark 12:44. Of Paul - Phil.4:11.

αὐτῆς (gen.sing.fem.of αὐτός, possession) 16.
πάντα (acc.pl.neut.of πᾶς, direct object of ἔβαλεν) 67.
ὅσα (acc.pl.neut.of ὅσος, direct object of εἶχεν) 660.
εἶχεν (3d.per.sing.imp.ind.of ἔχω, progressive description) 82.
ἔβαλεν (3d.per.sing.aor.act.ind.of βάλλω, culminative) 299.
ὅλον (acc.sing.masc.of ὅλος, in agreement with βίον) 112.
τὸν (acc.sing.masc.of the article in agreement with βίον) 9.
βίον (acc.sing.masc.of βίος, in apposition with πάντα) 2202.
αὐτῆς (gen.sing.fem.of αὐτός, possession) 16.

Translation - "Because all contributed out of their abundant resources, but she from her poverty, dropped in all that she had, - all she had to live on."

Comment: The contrast lies between πάντες and αὕτη - "all the others" as opposed to "she" - the poor widow. The widow stood alone in her class. There is another contrast - ἐκ τοῦ περισσεύοντος and ἐκ τῆς ὑστερήσεως - "out of their abundance" as opposed to "out of her poverty." She gave πάντα ὅσα εἶχεν, with a further definition in apposition ὅλον τὸν βίον αὐτῆς. The rich gave large absolute amounts, but had large amounts left for themselves after the gift. She gave only one penny, but she had nothing left. The measure of our devotion to God is the measure of our sacrifice. It is only since economists have understood marginal analysis (in the mid 19th century), which, in this case says that as wealth decreases, the pain suffered by continuing decreases becomes greater, that we are in a position to see Jesus' point. How much pain did the rich suffer when they gave their gifts? How much did the widow suffer?

We look now at Luke's account of the widow's gift in Luke 21:1-4.

Luke 21:1 - "And he looked up, and saw the rich men casting their gifts into the treasury."

Ἀναβλέψας δὲ εἶδεν τοὺς βάλλοντας εἰς τὸ γαζοφυλάκιον τὰ δῶρα αὐτῶν πλουσίους.

Ἀναβλέψας (aor.act.part.nom.sing.masc.of ἀναβλέπω, adverbial, temporal) 907.
δὲ (continuative conjunction) 11.
εἶδεν (3d.per.sing.aor.act.ind.of ὁράω, constative) 144.
τοὺς (acc.pl.masc.of the article in agreement with βάλλοντας) 9.
βάλλοντας (pres.act.part.acc.pl.masc.of βάλλω, substantival, direct object

εἰς (preposition with the accusative of extent) 140.
τὸ (acc.sing.neut.of the article in agreement with γαζοφυλάκιον) 9.
γαζοφυλάκιον (acc.sing.neut.of γαζοφυλάκιον, extent) 2383.
τὰ (acc.pl.neut.of the article in agreement with δῶρα) 9.
δῶρα (acc.pl.neut.of δῶρον, direct object of βάλλοντας) 191.
αὐτῶν (gen.pl.masc.of αὐτός, possession) 16.
πλουσίου (acc.pl.masc.of πλούσιος, in agreement with βάλλοντας) 1306.

Translation - "And He looked up and saw the rich men dropping their gifts into the treasury."

Comment: *Cf.*comment on Mk.12:41. Note that Jesus was seated καθίσας (Mk.12:41). Hence, he looked up - ἀναβλέψας (Lk.21:1) to see the activity across the way at the treasury. Mark tells us that there were many rich men who came, which serves to spotlight the poor widow in

Verse 2 - "And he saw also a certain poor widow casting in thither two mites."

εἶδεν δέ τινα χήραν πενιχρὰν βάλλουσαν ἐκεῖ λεπτὰ δύο,

εἶδεν (3d.per.sing.aor.act.ind.of ὁράω, constative) 144.
δέ (continuative conjunction) 11.
τινα (acc.sing.fem.of τις, indefinite pronoun, in agreement with χήραν) 486.
χήραν (acc.sing.fem.of χήρα, direct object of εἶδεν) 1910.

#2706 πενιχρὰν (acc.sing.fem.of πενιχρός, in agreement with χήραν).

poor - Luke 21:2.

Meaning: Cf. πένομαι, πένης (#4353). Hence, needy, poor, poverty stricken. One who is forced to work for a living. With reference to the widow at the treasury - Luke 21:2.

βάλλουσαν (pres.act.part.acc.sing.fem.of βάλλω, adverbial, circumstantial) 299.
ἐκεῖ (adverb of place) 204.
λεπτὰ (acc.pl.neut.of λεπτόν, direct object of βάλλουσαν) 2498.
δύο (numeral) 385.

Translation - "And He saw there a certain widow dropping in two brass coins."

Comment: *Cf.* comment on Mk.12:42. Luke's adjective is more descriptive than Mark's. *Cf.*#2706. This woman, without a husband, was forced to work for a living. She may have approached furtively, ashamed of the size of her gift, and hastened away hoping that no one would notice her there among the tycoons who threw their money in with a flourish.

Verse 3 - "And he said, Of a truth I say unto you, that this poor widow hath cast in more than they all."

καὶ εἶπεν, Ἀληθῶς λέγω ὑμῖν ὅτι ἡ χήρα αὕτη ἡ πτωχὴ πλεῖον πάντων ἔβαλεν.

καὶ (inferential conjunction) 14.
εἶπεν (3d.per.sing.aor.act.ind.of εἶπον, constative) 155.
Ἀληθῶς (adverbial) 1136.
λέγω (1st.per.sing.pres.act.ind.of λέγω, aoristic) 66.
ὑμῖν (dat.pl.masc.of σύ, indirect object of λέγω) 104.
ὅτι (conjunction introducing an object clause in indirect discourse) 211.
ἡ (nom.sing.fem.of the article in agreement with χήρα) 9.
χήρα (nom.sing.fem.of χήρα, subject of ἔβαλεν) 1910.
αὕτη (nom.sing.fem.of οὗτος, in agreement with χήρα) 93.
ἡ (nom.sing.fem.of the article in agreement with πτωχὴ) 9.
πτωχὴ (nom.sing.fem.of πτωχός, in agreement with χήρα) 423.
πλεῖον (acc.sing.neut.of πλείων, direct object of ἔβαλεν) 474.
πάντων (abl.pl.masc.of πᾶς, comparison) 67.
ἔβαλεν (3d.per.sing.aor.act.ind.of βάλλω, culminative) 299.

Translation - "Therefore He said, 'Truly I tell you that this poor widow has contributed more than all."

Comment: The emphatic attributive position of πτωχὴ is to be noted. Also, as in Mark 12:43, πλεῖον is emphasized.

Verse 4 - "For all these have of their abundance cast in unto the offerings of God: but she of her penury hath cast in all the living that she had."

πάντες γὰρ οὗτοι ἐκ τοῦ περισσεύοντος αὐτοῖς ἔβαλον εἰς τὰ δῶρα, αὕτη δὲ ἐκ τοῦ ὑστερήματος αὐτῆς πάντα τὸν βίον ὃν εἶχεν ἔβαλεν.

πάντες (nom.pl.masc.of πᾶς, in agreement with οὗτοι) 67.
γὰρ (causal conjunction) 105.
οὗτοι (nom.pl.masc.of οὗτος, subject of ἔβαλον) 93.
ἐκ (preposition with the ablative of source) 19.
τοῦ (abl.sing.masc.of the article in agreement with περισσεύοντος) 9.
περισσεύοντος (pres.act.part.abl.sing.masc.of περισσεύω, substantival, source) 473.
αὐτοῖς (dat.pl.masc.of αὐτός, personal advantage) 16.
ἔβαλον (3d.per.pl.aor.act.ind.of βάλλω, culminative) 299.
εἰς (preposition with the accusative of extent) 140.
τὰ (acc.pl.neut.of the article in agreement with δῶρα) 9.
δῶρα (acc.pl.neut.of δῶρον, extent) 191.
αὕτη (nom.sing.fem.of οὗτος, subject of ἔβαλεν) 93.
δὲ (adversative conjunction) 11.
ἐκ (preposition with the ablative of source) 19.
τοῦ (abl.sing.neut.of the article in agreement with ὑστερήματος) 9.

\# **2707** ὑστερήματος (abl.sing.neut.of ὑστέρμα, source).

lack - Phil.2:30.
penury - Luke 21:4.

that which is behind - Col.1:24.
that which is lacking - 1 Cor.16:17; 2 Cor.11:9; 1 Thess.3:10.
want - 2 Cor.8:14,14; 9:12.

*Meaning: Cf.*ὑστερέω (#1302); ὑστέρησις (#2705). Hence, a deficiency; a lack; a shortage. In terms of money or property - Luke 21:4; 2 Cor.8:14,14; 9:12; 11:9. Of personal gifts of the Philippian church to Paul - Phil.2:30; with reference to the Christian's ministry of suffering - Col.1:24. Of gifts of the Corinthian church to the poor saints - 1 Cor.16:17. With reference to the deficiency in the faith of the Thessalonians - 1 Thess.3:10.

αὐτῆς (gen.sing.fem.of αὐτός, possession) 16.
πάντα (acc.sing.neut.of πᾶς, in agreement with βίον) 67.
τὸν (acc.sing.masc.of the article in agreement with βίον) 9.
βίον (acc.sing.masc.of βίος, direct object of ἔβαλεν) 2202.
ὃν (acc.sing.masc.of ὅς, direct object of εἶχεν) 65.
εἶχεν (3d.per.sing.imp.act.ind.of ἔχω, progressive description) 82.
ἔβαλεν (3d.per.sing.aor.act.ind.of βάλλω, culminative) 299.

Translation - "For all these dropped in their offerings out of the surplus available to them, but this widow, out of her poverty dropped in all the resources which she had."

Comment: γὰρ is causal as Jesus explains the rationale of His statement of verse 3. Relatively she gave more than any, although in absolute terms, hers was the smallest gift of all. Note that Luke uses a different noun (ὑστέρμα, #2707) than Mark (ὑστέρσις #2705).

"Commentators are agreed in thinking that the reference is to the treasury in the court of the women, consisting of thirteen brazen trumpet-shaped receptacles, each destined for its distinctive gifts, indicated by an inscription, so many for the temple tribute, and money gifts for sacrifice; others for incense, wood, etc: all the gifts have reference to the service carried on. The gifts were people's offerings, generally moderte in amount: "the Peter's pence of the Jews." (Holtzman, H.C., as cited in *The Expositors' Greek Testament, I,* 427).

Greeks Desire to see Jesus, and His Following Discourse

(John 12:20-36)

John 12:20 - "And there were certain Greeks among them that came up to worship at the feast."

Ἦσαν δὲ Ἕλληνές τινες ἐκ τῶν ἀναβαινόντων ἵνα προσκυνήσωσιν ἐν τῇ ἑορτῇ.

Ἦσαν (3d.per.pl.imp.ind.of εἰμί, progressive description) 86.
δὲ (explanatory conjunction) 11.
Ἕλληνές (nom.pl.masc.of ἑλλήν, subject of ἦσαν) 2373.
τινες (nom.pl.masc.of τις, the indefinite pronoun, in agreement with Ελληνές) 486.
ἐκ (preposition with the genitive, partitive) 19.

τῶν (gen.pl.masc.of the article in agreement with *ἀναβαινόντων*) 9.
ἀναβαινόντων (pres.act.part.gen.pl.masc.of *ἀναβαίνω*, substantival, partitive genitive) 323.
ἵνα (conjunction with the subjunctive in a purpose clause) 114.
προσκυνήσωσιν (3d.per.pl.1st.aor.act.subj.of *προσκυνέω*, purpose) 147.
ἐν (preposition with the locative of time point) 80.
τῇ (loc.sing.fem.of the article in agreement with *ἑορτῇ*) 9.
ἑορτῇ (loc.sing.fem.of *ἑορτή*, time point) 1558.

Translation - "Now there were some Greeks among those who were going up to worship at the feast."

Comment: *δὲ* is explanatory. These men (*cf.*2373) were either Greeks by nationality or Gentiles who came to be Greeks culturally, as a result of the spread of the Hellenistic culture throughout the Mediterranean world following the conquest of Alexander the Great and his death in 323 B.C. The fact that they were coming up to Jerusalem to worship during the Passover festival indicates that they may have been Jewish prosylytes. *ἐν τῇ ἑορτῇ* can be construed either as a locative of time point - "during the feast" or a locative of place - "at the feast." The ideas blend; hence they are both correct.

Verse 21 - "The same came therefore to Philip, which was of Bethsaida of Galilee, and desired him saying, Sir, we would see Jesus."

οὗτοι οὖν προσῆλθον Φιλίππῳ τῷ ἀπὸ Βηθσαϊδὰ τῆς Γαλιλαίας, καὶ ἠρώτων αὐτὸν λέγοντες, Κύριε, θέλομεν τὸν Ἰησοῦν ἰδεῖν.

οὗτοι (nom.pl.masc.of *οὗτος*, subject of *προσῆλθον* and *ἠρώτων*) 93.
οὖν (continuative conjunction) 68.
προσῆλθον (3d.per.pl.aor.ind.of *προσέρχομαι*, constative) 336.
Φιλίππῳ (loc.sing.masc.of *Φίλιππος*, after *πρός* in composition, with a verb of rest) 845.
τῷ (loc.sing.masc.of the article, in apposition with *Φιλίππῳ*) 9.
ἀπὸ (preposition with the ablative of source) 70.
Βηθσαϊδὰ (abl.sing.fem.of *Βηθσαιδάν*, source) 938.
τῆς (gen.pl.fem.of the article in agreement with *Γαλιλαίας*) 9.
Γαλιλαίας (gen.sing.fem.of *Γαλιλαία* , description) 241.
καὶ (adjunctive conjunction joining verbs) 14.
ἠρώτων (3d.per.pl.imp.act.ind.of *ἐρωτάω*, inceptive) 1172.
αὐτὸν (acc.sing.masc.of *αὐτός*, direct object of *ἠρώτων*) 16.
λέγοντες (pres.act.part.nom.pl.masc.of *λέγω*, recitative) 66.
Κύριε (voc.sing.masc.of *κύριος*, address) 97.
θέλομεν (1st.per.pl.pres.act.ind.of *θέλω*, aoristic) 88.
τὸν (acc.sing.masc.of the article in agreement with *Ἰησοῦν*) 9.
Ἰησοῦν (acc.sing.masc.of *Ἰησοῦς*, direct object of *ἰδεῖν*) 3.
ἰδεῖν (aor.act.inf.of *ὁράω*, completes *θέλομεν*) 144.

Translation - "And these men came to Philip, the man from Bethsaida of Galilee, and they began to ask him, 'Sir, we want to see Jesus.' "

Comment:οὗτοι has Ἕλληνές of verse 20 as its antecedent. John, for some reason known perhaps only to the Holy Spirit, gives us Philip's background. κύριε - a term of great respect, not often applied except to Deity. *Cf.*#97. While ὁράω (#144) also means intellectual and spiritual perception, and always means that when used in contradistinction to βλέπω, it carries the idea of physical sight as well and is used primarily in that sense here. The Greeks, however, would not have been satisfied only by seeing Jesus in the βλέπω sense, since they could have accomplished that without asking Philip for an interview. Their reasons for a personal interview were probably varied. Curiosity was a part of it. The prestige factor entered in. Being Greeks, they may have been of a philosophical bent who wished help in understanding the deeper meanings of God's plan of redemption.

But these people were Gentiles. Philip immediately entertained a doubt as to whether Jesus was willing to see them at this crucial time, though Jesus had, by this time, made it abundantly clear that national Israel was going to reject Him and that His spiritual kingdom was to include representatives of all of the human race.

Verse 22 - "Phillip cometh and telleth Andrew: and again Andrew and Phillip tell Jesus."

ἔρχεται ὁ Φίλιππος καὶ λέγει τῷ Ἀνδρέᾳ. ἔρχεται Ἀνδρέας καὶ Φίλιππος καὶ λέγουσιν τῷ Ἰησοῦ.

ἔρχεται (3d.per.sing.pres.ind.of ἔρχομαι, historical) 146.
ὁ (nom.sing.masc.of the article in agreement with Φίλιππος) 9.
Φίλιππος (nom.sing.masc.of Φίλιππος, subject of ἔρχεται and λέγει) 845.
καὶ (adjunctive conjunction joining verbs) 14.
λέγει (3d.per.sing.pres.act.ind.of λέγω, historical) 66.
τῷ (dat.sing.masc.of the article in agreement with Ἀνδρέᾳ) 9.
Ἀνδρέᾳ (dat.sing.masc.of Ἀνδρέας, indirect object of λέγει) 388.
ἔρχεται (3d.per.sing.pres.ind.of ἔρχομαι, historical) 146.
Ἀνδρέας (nom.sing.masc.of Ἀνδρέας, subject of ἔρχεται and λέγει) 388.
καὶ (adjunctive conjunction joining nouns) 14.
Φίλιππος (nom.sing.masc.of Φίλιππος, subject of ἔρχεται and λέγει) 845.
καὶ (adjunctive conjunction joining verbs) 14.
λέγουσιν (3d.per.pl.pres.act.ind.of λέγω, historical) 66.
τῷ (dat.sing.masc.of the article in agreement with Ἰησοῦ) 9.
Ἰησοῦ (dat.sing.masc.of Ἰησοῦς, indirect object of λέγουσιν) 3.

Translation - "Phillip went and told Andrew; Andrew went with Phillip and they told Jesus."

Comment: The meaning is perfectly clear whether we translate literally or take liberties with the grammar in the interest of smooth English. We cannot literally translate "Andrew and Phillip went and told Jesus" because ἔρχεται, joined to Ἀνδρέας, is singular. There is no verb joined to Phillip in the second clause, though it is clearly understood. John should have written ἔρχονται, the plural form in the last clause. Actually it is not an important point. Note John's use of the historical present throughout.

Does the fact that'Ἀνδρέας is mentioned first in the second clause, with Phillip included almost as an afterthought, indicate that Andrew took the initiative to carry the request to Jesus? If Phillip had had the initiative to carry the request to Jesus in the first place, he would not have gone to Andrew for advice. In any case the two men from Bethsaida carried the report to Jesus. It is interesting that Phillip went to Andrew, one of the three disciples from Bethsaida, rather than to Peter, Andrew's brother, who was so often the self-appointed leader of the Twelve. Did Phillip resent Peter's leadership? The text does not so indicte and we must beware of *eisegesis!*

Verse 23 - "And Jesus answered them, saying, The hour is come, that the Son of Man should be glorified."

ὁ δὲ'Ἰησοῦς ἀποκρίνεται αὐτοῖς λέγων,'Ἐλήλυθεν ἡ ὥρα ἵνα δοξασθῇ ὁ υἱὸς τοῦ ἀνθρώπου.

ὁ (nom.sing.masc.of the article in agreement with'Ἰησοῦς) 9.
δὲ (adversative conjunction) 11.
'Ἰησοῦς (nom.sing.masc.of'Ἰησοῦς, subject of ἀποκρίνεται) 9.
ἀποκρίνεται (3d.per.sing.pres.mid.ind.of ἀποκρίνομαι, historical) 318.
αὐτοῖς (dat.pl.masc.of αὐτός, indirect object of ἀποκρίνεται) 16.
λέγων (pres.act.part.nom.sing.masc.of λέγω, recitative) 66.
'Ἐλήλυθεν (3d.per.sing.2d.perf.mid.ind.of ἔρχομαι, intensive) 146.
ἡ (nom.sing.fem.of the article in agreement with ὥρα) 9.
ὥρα (nom.sing.fem.of ὥρα, subject of ἐλήλυθεν) 735.
ἵνα (conjunction with the subjunctive in a sub-final clause) 114.
δοξασθῇ (3d.per.sing.aor.pass.subj.of δοξάζω, purpose/result) 461.
ὁ (nom.sing.masc.of the article in agreement with υἱὸς) 9.
υἱὸς (nom.sing.masc.of υἱός, subject of δοξασθῇ) 5.
τοῦ (gen.sing.masc.of the article in agreement with ἀνθρώπου) 9.
ἀνθρώπου (gen.sing.masc.of ἄνθρωπος, description) 341.

Translation - "But Jesus replied to them by saying, 'The hour has come that the Son of Man should be glorified."

Comment: δὲ is adversative. Jesus is not going to grant the interview except on His own terms. It is as though He was saying, "If they want to see me, let them go to the cross, because that is where I am going." ἐλήλυθεν is an example of what Robertson calls the Extensive present perfect, which describes a complete state of being. It denotes a durative action in the past, which finally achieves a punctiliar state. *Cf.* John 17:6. *Cf.*#735 for other references to that hour - as not having come as yet in John 2:4; 7:30; 8:20; as being in the immediate offing - Mt.26:45; Mk.14:35,41; Lk.22:14; John 12:23,27,27; 13:1; 17:1. It is the hour, fixed in the predestinating eternal counsels of the Godhead, when the incarnate Λόγος would offer Himself without spot to God in vicarious expiation for the elect. The hour had been in the process of coming since that eternal moment. As time flowed forward (in the terms in which mortals think of it) the hour continuously drew nearer. Now His hour was less than three days away. In an accommodated sense Jesus refers to it as having already come, though, strictly speaking it came at three o'clock on Friday afternoon. Having moved out of eternity and through Old Testament time it was now "come" - a complete state of being. God does what He has chosen to do "on time." He cannot be anticipated, hurried, delayed or thwarted. Though it was to be an hour of His death, it was also to be an hour of His glorification. ἵνα and the subjunctive in δοξασθῇ is neither all purpose or all result, but all of both. Thus we call it sub-final. It was an hour established in order that Christ might be glorified (purpose) and also one as a result of which He would be glorified (result).

This glorification, which of course includes His resurrection, can be represented also as not yet having been accomplished. *Cf.*#461, and the following passages: John 7:39; 8:54b; 12:16,23; 13:31. It can also be represented as having been accomplished already (Acts 3:13). Thus the hour delivers Him both to death because of our sins and to glorification because of our justification (Rom.4:25).

We have noted Robertson's description of Ἐλήλυθεν as an extensive present perfect, which points to the durative action of the past which has produced a completed state of being. Another way of looking at it emphasizes the existing results. Mantey, not in rebuttal to what Robertson has said, but in confirmation says, ". . . it is distinctively the tense of the 'finished product.' When special attention is thus directed to the results of the action, stress upon the existing fact is intensified. This is the emphatic method in Greek of presenting a fact or condition. It is the strong way of saying that a thing *is.*" (Mantey, *Manual,* 202).

The Calvary event is looked upon by the natural, unenlightened world as a major tragedy, perhaps the greatest blunder in human history. The gospel of Jesus Christ represents it as the moment of His greatest triumph, to be followed in three days by His breathtaking glorification. On this Rock Unitarianism and Trinitarianism, Deism and Theism are forever split asunder, never to be united. This truth forever separates those who are eternally saved from those who are eternally lost.

That death and glorification are inseparably united is the truth set forth in the next verse.

Verse 24 - "Verily, verily I say unto you, Except a corn of wheat fall into the ground and die, it abideth alone; but if it die, it bringeth forth much fruit."

ἀμὴν ἀμὴν λέγω ὑμῖν, ἐὰν μὴ ὁ κόκκος τοῦ σίτου πεσὼν εἰς τὴν γῆν ἀποθάνῃ, αὐτὸς μόνος μένει, ἐὰν δὲ ἀποθάνῃ, πολὺν καρπὸν φέρει.

ἀμὴν (explicative) 466.
ἀμὴν (explicative) 466.
λέγω (1st.per.sing.pres.act.ind.of λέγω, aoristic) 66.
ὑμῖν (dat.pl.masc.of σύ, indirect object of λέγει) 104.
ἐὰν (conditional particle in a third-class condition) 363.

μή (qualified negative conjunction with the subjunctive in a third-class condition) 87.

ὁ (nom.sing.masc.of the article in agreement with κόκκος) 9.

κόκκος (nom.sing.masc.of κόκκος, subject of ἀποθάνῃ) 1067.

τοῦ (gen.sing.masc.of the article in agreement with σίτου) 9.

σίτου (gen.sing.masc.of σῖτος, description) 311.

πεσὼν (aor.act.part.nom.sing.masc.of πίπτω, adverbial, temporal) 187.

εἰς (preposition with the accusative of extent) 140.

τὴν (acc.sing.fem.of the article in agreement with γῆν) 9.

γῆν (acc.sing.fem.of γῆ, extent) 157.

ἀποθάνῃ (3d.per.sing.aor.act.subj.of ἀποθνήσκω, third-class condition) 774.

αὐτὸς (nom.sing.masc.of αὐτός, subject of μένει) 16.

μόνος (nom.sing.masc.of μόνος, predicate adjective) 339.

μένει (3d.per.sing.pres.act.ind.of μένω, customary) 864.

ἐὰν (conditional particle in a third-class condition) 363.

δὲ (adversative conjunction) 11.

ἀποθάνῃ (3d.per.sing.aor.act.subj.of ἀποθνήσκω, third-class condition) 774.

πολὺν (acc.sing.masc.of πολύς, in agreement with καρπὸν) 228.

καρπὸν (acc.sing.masc.of καρπός, direct object of φέρει) 284.

φέρει (3d.per.sing.pres.act.ind.of φέρω, customary) 683.

Translation - "Truly, truly I am telling you, 'If a grain of wheat, after it falls into the soil does not die, it always remains alone, but, if it dies, it always bears much fruit.' "

Comment: We have two third-class conditions with ἐὰν and the subjunctive in the protases of both and the present indicative in each result clause. These present indicatives are customary presents. A grain of wheat which does not die will always remain only one grain of wheat. A grain of wheat that dies, after it is planted will always reproduce itself with a marginal gain. Some might wish to consider these present tenses as futuristic. In the sense that the result is always future to the cause (the sowing of the grain is the cause and the result follows) we might consider them futuristic, except for the fact that the future tense implies some doubt about the final result. This we cannot have in this passage. There is no doubt about the future conclusion in either of these conditional clauses. Thus we have construed the result clauses as customary presents. There is doubt that a grain of wheat will be sown. There is the possibility that it will be used for other purposes than as seed wheat. There is also doubt that, if sown, it will decompose. The birds may eat it (Mt.13:4). But there is no doubt about the conclusion which follows the conditional clause. If it does not die (nothing dogmatic as to whether it will or not) it will remain only one grain of wheat. If it dies (again, no dogma about it, one way or the other) it will produce a stalk of wheat bearing many grains.

The second conditional clause, with adversative δὲ, is adverse to the first. The first grain sown did not die. The second one did.

This biological fact, used here to illustrate the truth of verse 23, explains why

Christ's hour, so near at hand, was at once His hour of greatest degradation and the hour of His greatest glorification. His hour, having been in the process of "coming" from all eternity, and now within 72 hours or less of fulfillment, is for the *purpose* of His glorification and it will also *result* in His glorification. Purpose is anticipated result. We have a present general supposition. (Burton, *Moods and Tenses*, 260, p.107). *Cf.*John 11:9; 2 Tim.2:5; Mark 3:24; John 7:51; 12:24; 1 Cor.7:39,40 for other examples. The hour was to be an hour of death, but its purpose and its result was His resurrection and glorification. Of what does this glorification consist? It was not only His own personal victory over death and corruption (Ps.16:10), but much more, the multiplication of His own divine life in millions of redeemed saints.

Verse 23 points through His death to His glorification. Verse 24 points through the death of one grain of wheat to its multiplication. πολὺν καρπόν - "many grains." If there is no death, the grain of wheat abides in all of its beauty and perfection and with its potential for life giving undiminished, but αὐτὸς μόνος μένει - "it lives on alone." So, if Christ had not died, He would have lived on eternally alone - beautiful, noble, altogether lovely, all powerful, Teacher, Miracle Worker - in short, everything that He demonstrated Himself to be during His incarnation, but eternally alone. With His potential for multiplying His eternal life, with all of its quantity and quality, for millions of saints, He would have gone on forever with this potential unused.

It is reported by botanists that the grains of wheat buried in the Pyramid tombs of Egyptian kings were intact after 2500 years of entombment, and that, when they were planted, they decomposed and yielded their harvest of grain. So Christ would have remained alone, a Divine Monopolist of all of His virtues if He had not died (Rom.8;29). He "is the first-born of many creatures," but, without His death in His "hour" He would have been the "only born." In bringing many sons into glory, God must make the Captain of our Salvation perfect through suffering (Heb.2:10). Without the suffering of the Captain, there were be no sons in glory.

Having made clear that "the path(s) of glory led but" past a cross and "to the grave" (with apologies to Thomas Gray), Jesus next insisted that what is true of the Captain of our Salvation, is also true of the soldiers of the cross. For those saints who follow in His train, "the path to the grave" can lead only to "the glory that shall be revealed in us" (Rom.8:18).

Verse 25 - "He that loveth his life shall lose it; and he that hateth his life in this world shall keep it unto life eternal."

ὁ φιλῶν τὴν ψυχὴν αὐτοῦ ἀπολλύει αὐτήν, καὶ ὁ μισῶν τὴν ψυχὴν αὐτοῦ ἐν τῷ κόσμῳ τούτῳ εἰς ζωὴν αἰώνιον φυλάξει αὐτήν.

ὁ (nom.sing.masc.of the article in agreement with φιλῶν) 9.

φιλῶν (pres.act.part.nom.sing.masc.of φιλέω, substantival, subject of ἀπολλύει) 566.

τὴν (acc.sing.fem.of the article in agreement with ψυχὴν) 9.

ψυχὴν (acc.sing.fem.of ψυχή, direct object of φιλῶν) 233.

αὐτοῦ (gen.sing.masc.of αὐτός, possession) 16.
ἀπολλύει (3d.per.sing.fut.act.ind.of ἀπόλλυμι, predictive) 208.
αὐτήν (acc.sing.fem.of αὐτός, direct object of ἀπολλύει) 16.
καὶ (adversative conjunction) 14.
ὁ (nom.sing.masc.of the article in agreement with μισῶν) 9.
μισῶν (pres.act.part.nom.sing.masc.of μισέω, substantival, subject of φυλάξει) 542.
τὴν (acc.sing.fem.of the article in agreement with ψυχὴν) 9.
ψυχὴν (acc.sing.fem.of ψυχή, direct object of μισῶν) 233.
αὐτοῦ (gen.sing.masc.of αὐτός, possession) 16.
ἐν (preposition with the locative of time point) 80.
τῷ (loc.sing.masc.of the article in agreement with κόσμῳ) 9.
κόσμῳ (loc.sing.masc.of κόσμος, time point) 360.
τούτῳ (loc.sing.masc.of οὗτος, in agreement with κόσμῳ) 93.
εἰς (preposition with the accusative of time extent) 140.
ζωὴν (acc.sing.fem.of ζωή, time extention) 668.
αἰώνιον (acc.sing.fem.of αἰώνιος, in agreement with ζωὴν) 1255.
φυλάξει (3d.per.sing.fut.act.ind.of φυλάσσω, predictive) 1301.
αὐτήν (acc.sing.fem.of αὐτός, direct object of φυλάξει) 16.

Translation - "He who prizes his life will lose it, but the one who cares nothing for his life in this age will preserve it unto eternal life."

Comment: The participial substantives, ὁ φιλῶν and ὁ μισῶν, form the subjects of the two clauses - "the life lover" and the "life in this age hater." To the modern audience "love" and "hate" may convey the wrong ideas. Since Christianity is not a popular philosophy in this age and Chritians will be hated and persecuted as was Jesus (John 15:18), the attitudes which the Christian may take toward the value of life in this age are in view. Do we prize them to the point that we are willing to make any concession with the unchristian world in order to preserve them? Or do we look upon life during this short age and in this unhappy world with the contempt that it deserves, in view of the fact that we are certain that we are going to spend eternity in the perfect environment, physically and socially, which will be provided by the Messiah when He returns to reign forever on David's throne?

The Christian, who, due to his lack of Bible study and therefore his lack of commitment to its message, entertains a dim view of the heavenly society where he is destined to spend eternity. Thus, by comparison, he overvalues his life in this world in the here and now. To be oversold on the virtues of the world and this age is to be willing to compromise the commitment to Christ. On the other hand, the more we know about the Christian *weltanschauung*, the less value we place upon life as it must now be lived. The only reason why the child of God should wish to remain in this world is that he might finish the work which God, in His wisdom has appointed him to do (Eph.2:10). Thus we value our lives in this age and in this world society. When the Christian's appointed work on earth is finished, he has no further desire to remain here. This explains why the

Christian martyrs,helpless in the clutches of their murderers, looked upon the occasion in triumph. No Christian looks upon his life of service for the Lord in this world with contempt or disdain. But, were it not for the fact that he is here for the divine purpose, and for the fact that he understands why he is here, he would be utterly contemptuous of a world society, where policy is made by the unregenerate, who walk in their rejection of the Light of the World and stumble in the darkness (John 8:12; 11:10). Unregenerate man, who has nothing but his flesh, which profits nothing, to guide him (John 6:63) is working at night (John 9:4) and that is the time when no man can work to show a profit. Physicists know that work requires energy and that the second law of thermodynamics, the entropy principle, dictates that the amount of available energy, as more work is done, steadily decreases in a process that is irreversible. Thus conservation of available energy would be the proper policy if the rulers of this age wanted to avoid complete failure in what the physicists refer to as "heat death." But sinners think of their task in this age as one of the production of more and more utility. Thus the industrial revolution demanded a technological infrastructure to produce more and more creature comforts, which uses up the available energy in exponential degree. This trend will not be reversed. The capitol of the world, the city of the Antichrist, when our Lord returns, reveals a tempo of industrial and commercial activity that will have been pushed to its frenetic limits (Rev. 18:1-24, with special attention to verses 11-19). When sinful man murdered the Light of the World on a cross,they put out the light and the night settled upon this age - night when no man can work (John 9:4). Yet they did work - more and more. And the more they worked the less energy is available for the work which they still intend to do. Thus the price of production rises and as prices rise, and the value of money lessens, poverty abounds exponentially and with it, the misery of the masses. Why should any sensible person be proud of life in this age. Science, for all of its short-run accomplishments, has painted the human race into a corner, and the chemists are going to get us all killed with their tinkering and the pollution that results from it.

Unsaved sinners can never agree that their mission on earth is not to make society the place which the Bible describes as the New Jerusalem, and they will do this without the help of Him Who is "the stone which the builders rejected" (Mt.21:42). Thus the word is progress, and the result is not progress, but change. Men who have rejected Christ can stumble about in the dark and fumble their way through a policy of change, but their assumption, that since the change was their idea, it is also progress, cannot be sustained, in the light of the evidence, to say nothing of the evaluation which the Word of God puts upon their efforts. Sinners can change the world, but they cannot make it better. The Polly Anna singers of sweet songs have not recently driven through the Bronx or the slums of Washington, D.C. Of course politicians could never admit that we have failed in this age to sustain life in decency, because voters will not retain in office those who fail.

Thus the Christian does not "hate" his life. He only regrets that in order to do the will of God he must live a portion of it in this unfortunate world and in this era of darkness. We despise our present lives because we look forward to eternal living in the glory of the perfect environment, where the true scientists who are aware of the fact that there is but One complete Scientist, in whom are hid "all of the treasures of wisdom and knowledge" (Col.2:3), will have the entire universe as their laboratory in which to discover and implement those principles which, because they are true principles, will be devoid of destructive ripple effects and will make for viability in a regime in which "they shall not hurt nor destroy in all my holy kingdom: for the earth shall be full of the knowledge of the Lord, as the waters cover the sea" (Isa.11:9).

The point is that those who look forward to the perfect life in eternal glory, find much that is despicable in the lives which we are compelled now to live. Here is a paradox. The only way to live forever in eternity is to die temporarily in time. Note the present tense in ὁ φιλῶν. "The one who is now (at the time that Jesus said this) always loving his life. . . " - this means those who would take steps to avoid a cross. The disciples took many rapid steps! "They all forsook Him and fled" (Mark 14:50). Be it said to the everlasting credit of the eleven disciples that they thought better of it and later despised their lives in this world and thus preserved them in glory. The life despisers (ὁ μισῶν, present tense) are those committed permanently to eternal values, even though the cost in this world and during this era, be a cross.

So Jesus was saying to Phillip and Andrew, "Go tell those Greeks that this is a dual universe. There is good and evil. There is light and darkness. There is love and hatred. There is earth and heaven. There is a temporal and an eternal point of view. There is a short and a long run analysis. We have Plato's black horses and white horses. There is spirit and flesh. There is id, ego and superego. The Greeks must choose. If they want to understand me forever, let them come with me to a Roman cross. I am good, light, love, heaven, eternal, long run. I am what Plato meant by the white horse. I am his real substance, not the shadow on the wall of the darkened cave. I am on the outside of the cave in the brilliant light of the sun. Indeed I am the Son. But if I do not die, then, like a preserved grain of wheat, I will always be alone. And if they are not willing to despise this life and this world and die with me, they will lose their lives and spend eternity in the utter frustration that is called Hell."

Jesus pursues the thought in

Verse 26 - "If any man serve me, let him follow me; and where I am, there shall also my servant be: if any man serve me, him will my Father honor."

ἐὰν ἐμοί τις διακονῇ, ἐμοὶ ἀκολουθείτω, καὶ ὅπου εἰμὶ ἐγὼ ἐκεῖ καὶ ὁ διάκονος ὁ ἐμὸς ἔσται. ἐάν τις ἐμοὶ διακονῇ τιμήσει αὐτὸν ὁ πατήρ.

ἐὰν (conditional particle in a third-class condition) 363.
ἐμοί (dat.sing.masc.of ἐμός, personal advantage) 1267.
τις (nom.sing.masc.of τις, indefinite pronoun, subject of διακονῇ) 486.
διακονῇ (3d.per.sing.pres.act.subj.of διακονέω, third-class condition) 367.
ἐμοὶ (dat.sing.masc.of ἐμός, personal advantage) 1267.
ἀκολουθείτω (3d.per.sing.pres.act.impv.of ἀκολουθέω, command) 394.
καὶ (continuative conjunction) 14.
ὅπου (adverb introducing a definite local clause) 592.

εἰμὶ (1st.per.sing.pres.ind.of εἰμί, definite local clause) 86.
ἐγὼ (nom.sing.masc.of ἐγώ, subject of εἰμί) 123.
ἐκεῖ (adverb of place) 204.
καὶ (adjunctive conjunction joining a pronoun with a noun) 14.
ὁ (nom.sing.masc.of the article in agreement with διάκονος) 9.
διάκονος (nom.sing.masc.of διάκονος, subject of ἔσται) 1334.
ὁ (nom.sing.masc.of the article in agreement with ἐμὸς) 9.
ἐμὸς (nom.sing.masc.of ἐμός, possessive pronoun, in agreement with διάκονος) 1267.
ἔσται (3d.per.sing.fut.ind.of εἰμί, predictive) 86.
ἐάν (conditional particle in a third-class condition) 363.
τις (nom.sing.masc.of τις, indefinite pronoun, subject of διακονῇ) 486.
ἐμοὶ (dat.sing.masc.of ἐμός, personal advantage) 1267.
διακονῇ (3d.per.sing.pres.act.subj.of διακονέω, third-class condition) 367.
τιμήσει (3d.per.sing.fut.act.ind.of τιμάω, predictive) 1142.
αὐτὸν (acc.sing.masc.of αὐτός, direct object of τιμήσει) 16.
ὁ (nom.sing.masc.of the article in agreement with πατήρ) 9.
πατήρ (nom.sing.masc.of πατήρ, subject of τιμήσει) 238.

Translation - "If anyone will serve me let him follow me, and where I am, there also my servant will be. If anyone will serve me my Father will value him highly."

Comment: We have two third-class conditions, the first with the imperative and the second with the future indicative in the result clauses. They are undetermined, as to whether the condition in the protasis will be met, but there is a prospect of determination. It is logical that if we would serve Christ, we must follow Him always (present imperative in ἀκολουθείτω). The verb διακονέω (#367) is the function of ὁ διάκονος (#1334), not of δοῦλος (#725). ὁ δοῦλος is a slave who performs his function whether in the presence of his master or not. But ὁ διάκονος is a personal servant, such as a valet, whose function can be carried out only in the presence of his Lord. Hence, Jesus is saying that if we are going to serve Him (διακονέω) we must perforce be where He is at all times, which involves following Him constantly. The statement of the next clause is by definition, a truism. ὅπου εἰμὶ ἐγὼ ἐκεῖ καὶ ὁ διάκονος ὁ ἐμὸς ἔσται. Since ὁ διάκονος is not a servant unless he is serving his Lord *in His presence*, it follows that the two, master and servant, must be always together. The thrust of the passage is that if the Greeks were sincere in seeking an interview with Jesus in order to become His διάκονοι, they must understand that the servant must always follow His Lord so as to be ever at His side. The cost of servitude is followship, but the reward of followship is fellowship.

Now, where was Jesus going? To His death. Because only when and because He died, could the glorification of resurrection and self-multiplication (the grain of wheat figure) take place. "Therefore if the Greeks want to see me, tell them to come along with me to Calvary." The fortunes of the servant are always tied up with the fortunes of the one whom he serves. Whatever, if anything, is beyond Calvary for the Lord, is also beyond Calvary for the servant.

In the last clause, Jesus promised His servants the honor of future glorification in a third-class condition with ἐάν and the present subjunctive followed by the future indicative - "If anyone will always serve me, the Father will always honor him." *Cf.*#1142 for the basic meaning of τιμάω. God will highly evaluate the servant who is always at Jesus' side and obedient to His commands. Servants like that are hard to find, so God will take special care of them. When physical death comes to such a servant, we may be sure that the Father, Who values him highly, will not allow him to remain in the grave. Resurrection, the glorification which came for Jesus after His death, will come also for His servants, after which, at the judgment seat of Christ, the faithful servant will be rewarded in a manner to indicate the degree of the Father's desire to honor him. This is not to say that resurrection of the body of the Christian is a reward for faithful service, to be denied to those less than faithful, "for if we have been planted together in the likeness of his death, we shall be also in the likeness of his resurrection" (Rom.6:5). A special reward however awaits the faithful servant whom the Father regards as especially worthy of honor.

Jesus was offering discipleship to the Greeks in the spirit of *caveat emptor*. "If you really mean it, come on, but count the cost. However, if you come, on my terms, I guarantee future honor from the Father." This was the same approach that He used once before when the Jews announced their desire to follow Him (Mt.8:18-22).

The thought now moves on to the sombre aspects of the coming ordeal in

Verse 27 - "Now is my soul troubled; and what shall I say? Father, save me from this hour: but for this cause came I unto this hour."

Νῦν ἡ ψυχή μου τετάρακται. καὶ τί εἴπω; Πάτερ, σῶσόν με ἐκ τῆς ὥρας ταύτης; ἀλλὰ διὰ τοῦτο ἦλθον εἰς τὴν ὥραν ταύτην.

Νῦν (temporal adverb) 1497.
ἡ (nom.sing.fem.of the article in agreement with ψυχή) 9.
ψυχή (nom.sing.fem.of ψυχή, subject of τετάρακται) 233.
μου (gen.sing.masc.of ἐγώ, possession) 123.
τετάρακται (3d.per.sing.perf.pass.ind.of ταράσσω, intensive) 149.
καὶ (adversative conjunction) 14.
τί (acc.sing.neut.of τίς, the interrogative pronoun, direct object of εἴπω) 281.
εἴπω (1st.per.sing.pres.act.subj.of εἶπον, deliberative) 155.
Πάτερ (voc.sing.masc.of πατήρ, address) 238.
σῶσόν (2d.per.sing.aor.act.impv.of σώζω, entreaty) 109.
με (acc.sing.masc.of ἐγώ, direct object of σῶσόν) 123.
ἐκ (preposition with the ablative of separation) 19.
τῆς (abl.sing.fem.of the article in agreement with ὥρας) 9.
ὥρας (abl.sing.fem.of ὥρα, separation) 735.
ταύτης (abl.sing.fem.of οὗτος, in agreement with ὥρας) 93.
ἀλλὰ (adversative conjunction) 342.
διὰ (preposition with the accusative of cause) 118.
τοῦτο (acc.sing.neut.of οὗτος, cause) 93.

ἦλθον (1st.per.sing.aor.ind.of ἔρχομαι, dramatic/culminative) 146.
εἰς (preposition with the accusative of time extent) 140.
τὴν (acc.sing.fem.of the article in agreement with ὥραν) 9.
ὥραν (acc.sing.fem.of ὥρα, time extent) 735.
ταύτην (acc.sing.fem.of οὗτος, in agreement with ὥραν) 93.

Translation - "Now my soul continues to be troubled. But what shall I say? Father, save me from this hour? But this is why I have come to this hour."

Comment: τετάρακται is an intensive present perfect, one in which the punctiliar force of the perfect is dropped, leaving only the durative force. The trouble of His soul had been going on in the past and it was still going on. "My soul, having been continuously troubled,is still in distress." ἦλθον is a Dramatic aorist - referring to what is in the immediate past, and exercising an effect upon the present. "I have in the immediate past come to this hour and here I am." It has a culminative force. Moulton thinks that "we have probably to do here with one of the most ancient uses of the aorist" (Moulton, *Prolegomena to the Grammar of New Testament Greek*, 135, as cited in Mantey, *Manual*, 199) and Robertson agrees, describing this idiom as "possibly the oldest use of the tense" (Robertson, *Grammar*, 841, as cited in *Ibid.*). εἴπω is a deliberative subjunctive. Jesus was standing in the shadow of the cross upon which His physical agony and spiritual horror would be indescribable. What should He say? In His distress, the thought crossed His mind that perhaps at this, almost the last moment, He might ask the Father to allow Him to abandon the plan of redemption. Thus He would be spared the agony of the cross. ἀλλὰ, the alternative conjunction is used here to indicate a sudden break in the thought, as Jesus rejects out of hand the thought that He could escape crucifixion. Of course He could not, because it was for this very purpose of dying for our sins that He had been brought to this hour.

The soul sorrow of Jesus, as He contemplated His death, was not something which He had only recently experienced. Indeed, as the sinless Son of God, with perfect unbroken fellowship from all eternity with the Father and the Holy Spirit, He had been shrinking from this unspeakably horrible experience of becoming sin (2 Cor.5:21; 1 Pet.2:24; Isa.53:5,6) upon the cross and suffering the consequent alienation from the Godhead. Since His incarnation He had also dreaded the physical agony of the Roman cross and all its its preliminary insults, indignities and tortures. Thus He had been and still was suffering from soul sorrow. From the human point of view, He feared it, and from the divine point of view He dreaded and abhorred it. Does this fact grade Him down? Critics have said, "Socrates drank the cup of hemlock without a murmer, but Jesus asked His Father to let Him off." Some superficial theologians have attempted to rescue Jesus from this odious comparison by seeking to show that Jesus did not fear the coming ordeal. Fortunately, they have failed to disprove the fact that He feared the cross and its physical and spiritual consequences. If they could have proved that He did not, they would have proved too much and thus would have "thrown out the baby with the bath water." For if He did not fear the cross He was not qualified to be our "merciful and faithful High Priest" (Heb.4:15; 5:1-7) and thus not qualified, He would not have been raised from the dead. The glorification which is the result of His "hour" was contingent upon His total qualification as our heavenly High Priest. And one essential element in this qualification was His common experience with the race which we call fear. When, in Jesus' life, prior to this time, have we evidence that He ever feared anything? Alone in the wilderness with the wild beasts? During the storm at sea? In the tombs at Gadara? On any of the many occasions when they took up stones to stone Him? In none of these incidents is there evidence that Jesus was anything less than the complete master of the situation. He took these events in stride. But having previously been hungry, thirsty, cold, miserable, lonely, poor, misunderstood, insulted and spurned - in short, having experienced every human trial common to man, except the sinful inducement to evil (Heb.4:15), and thus qualified to sympathize with the saints in these distresses, finally, in the shadow of the cross, He said that He had been contiunally troubled in His soul and was still distressed by fear, until, in His deliberations about a possible escape, He wondered if He should pray, "Father, save me from this hour."

Here we have what some have called "Little Gethsamane" on Tuesday, prior to the Thursday night, when He fulfilled Heb.5:7. We shall never know what He would have added after *Πάτερ σῶσόν με ἐκ τῆς ὥρας ταύτης* because He broke off abruptly with *ἀλλὰ* and observed that it was *διὰ τοῦτο* - "on account of this" that He had just come to this hour.

To what does *τοῦτο* refer? On account of what? Not only that the purpose of the hour was that He should die, but also that the result of the hour was that He would be glorified. And He could not be glorified in resurrection if He did not fear the hour. So He came to this hour in order that He might fear it. And fear it, He did. Thus He was made "perfect through suffering" (Heb.2:10). But although He feared it, He did not flee from it. On the contrary He walked straight into it. No soldier was ever decorated for doing what he did not fear to do, but the frightened soldier, who, in spite of his mortal terror, walked into the teeth of death, is a brave man. Did Socrates dread the cup of hemlock? Have other executed criminals, who seemed to face death without flinching, feared the ordeal? Many have died without expressing fear, but no one ever died without fear. Death is an enemy to every rational man (1 Cor.15:26). Why then, did Jesus express the fear that He felt, when others, just as fearful, did not? Because we must be assured that Jesus is qualified to be our "merciful and faithful High Priest." Others were not destined for glorification. Jesus was. If the scriptures had been silent about Jesus' fear, the saints would never know beyond doubt that He fulfilled all of the requirements. As it is, there is no doubt. *Cf.*John 13:21; 11:33 for previous distress in the experience of our Lord.

Verse 28 - "Father, glorify thy name. Then came a voice from heaven, saying, I have both glorified it, and will glorify it again."

πάτερ, δόξασόν σου τὸ ὄνομα. ἦλθεν οὖν φωνὴ ἐκ τοῦ οὐρανοῦ, Καὶ ἐδόξασα καὶ πάλιν δοξάσω.

πάτερ (voc.sing.masc.of πατήρ, address) 238.
δόξασόν (2d.per.sing.aor.act.impv.of δοξάζω, entreaty) 461.
σου (gen.sing.masc.of σύ, possession) 104.
τὸ (acc.sing.neut.of the article in agreement with ὄνομα) 9.
ὄνομα (acc.sing.neut.of ὄνομα, direct object of δόξασόν) 108.
ἦλθεν (3d.per.sing.aor.ind.of ἔρχομαι, constative) 146.
οὖν (continuative conjunction) 68.
φωνὴ (nom.sing.fem.of φωνή, subject of ἦλθεν) 222.
ἐκ (preposition with the ablative of source) 19.
τοῦ (abl.sing.masc.of the article in agreement with οὐρανοῦ) 9.
οὐρανοῦ (abl.sing.masc.of οὐρανός, source) 254.
Καὶ (emphatic conjunction) 14.
ἐδόξασα (1st.per.sing.aor.act.ind.of δοξάζω, culminative) 461.
καὶ (adjunctive conjunction joining verbs) 14.
δοξάσω (1st.per.sing.fut.act.ind.of δοξάζω, predictive) 461.

Translation - " 'Father, glorify your name.' Then there came a voice out of heaven, 'I have already glorified (it) and I will glorify (it) again.' "

Comment: Here was a prayer that Jesus could pray with perfect confidence that it was compatible with the divine purpose. That God could glorify His name in the death, burial and resurrection of His Son, is a fact of trinitarian theology to be grasped only by the recipients, by divine grace, of a supernatural revelation. Immediately and inferentially God spoke from heaven with an aorist, ἐδόξασα, that relates to the present perfect. "I have been glorifying it at all times in the past and I am glorifying it now." The emphatic force of the first καὶ with the adjunctive force of the second, makes it possible to translate as though ἤδη had been used. "I have, in fact, already been in the process of glorifying . . . and I will glorify it (future tense in δοξάσω) again, and again, and again, and again, and . . . again, ag, a." Everything that Jesus had even done in His incarnation had glorified God's name, including His qualification as a fearful sacrifice and the spontaneous and wholly human cry, πάτερ, σῶσόν με ἐκ τῆς ὥρας ταύτης.(John 8:29).

God's future glorification of His name, specifically would occur, when, among other things, He reconciled the world unto Himself in the death of His Son (2 Cor.5:19); when He raised Him from the dead (Acts 13:30) and seated Him at His own right hand (Eph.1:20-23) and made Him utterly sovereign. The student should examine #461 for all of the occasions when God's name was glorified. The leader of the Roman squad who supervised the crucifixion of Jesus glorified God on that occasion (Luke 23:47).

The sound of the Father's voice, speaking from heaven had the effect of dividing the people who heard it into the two categories that have always divided the human race with reference to Christian theology.

Verse 29 - "The people therefore, that stood by, and heard it, said that it thundered: others said, An angel spoke to him."

ὁ οὖν ὄχλος ὁ ἑστὼς καὶ ἀκούσας ἔλεγεν βροντὴν γεγονὲναι. ἄλλοι ἔλεγον, Ἄγγελος αὐτῷ λελάληκεν.

ὁ (nom.sing.masc.of the article in agreement with *ὄχλος*) 9.
οὖν (inferential conjunction) 68.
ὄχλος (nom.sing.masc.of *ὄχλος*, subject of *ἔλεγεν*) 418.
ὁ (nom.sing.masc.of the article in agreement with *ἑστὼς*) 9.
ἑστὼς (perf.act.part.nom.sing.masc.of *ἵστημι*, adjectival, restrictive, in agreement with *ὄχλος*) 180.
καὶ (adjunctive conjunction joining participles) 14.
ἀκούσας (aor.act.part.nom.sing.masc.of *ἀκούω*, adjectival, restrictive, in agreeement with *ὄχλος*) 148.
ἔλεγεν (3d.per.sing.imp.act.ind.of *λέγω*,inceptive) 66.
βροντὴν (acc.sing.fem.of *βροντή*, general reference) 2117.
γεγονέναι (2d.perf.inf.of *γίνομαι*, indirect discourse) 113.
ἄλλοι (nom.pl.masc.of *ἄλλος*, subject of *ἔλεγον*) 198.
ἔλεγον (3d.per.pl.imp.act.ind.of *λέγω*, inceptive) 66.
Ἄγγελος (nom.sing.masc.of *ἄγγελος*, subject of *λελάληκεν*) 96.
αὐτῷ (dat.sing.masc.of *αὐτός*, indirect object of *λελάληκεν*) 16.
λελάληκεν (3d.per.sing.perf.act.ind.of *λαλέω*, consummative) 815.

Translation - "Therefore the people who had been standing there and had heard it began to say, 'It has thundered.' Others were saying, 'An angel has spoken to Him.' "

Comment: The sound of the Father's voice was heard by the bystanders, though not understood. Thus, their comments. Note the 2d.perfect infinitive in indirect discourse. Other examples of the perfect infinitive in indirect discourse, representing the perfect indicative in direct discourse are Luke 22:34; Acts 14:19; 2 Tim.2:18.

The sound of the Father's voice brought reactions at three levels of spiritual perception. Jesus heard it and clearly understood who spoke, what was said and what was meant by what was said. There is nothing in the text to suggest that any other, even among the disciples, shared with our Lord the total appreciation of what the Father said. Others, less perceptive, recognized that it was a voice and that words had been spoken, though they supposed that the speaker was an angel. A third group was so lacking in perceptivity that they heard only a sound which they assumed to be thunder.

It is the fate of the materialist that he is committed to the philosophy that everything in human history has a naturalistic explanation. He always looks within natural science for an explanation, because he is already committed, *a fortiori* to the view that there is no other force at work in the universe. We need not seek to impress him with the extraordinary nature of an event, in the hope that he will be forced to admit that after all there must be a supernatural God in the universe who sometimes moves in the affairs of men. He seeks his explanation within the scope of his craft, or, if he cannot explain the event, he will deny that it ever occurred. Either Lazarus was not really dead, or his resurrection was caused by some scientific principle as yet undiscovered, or the story is a fabrication, devised by some unprincipled holy man - some unscrupulous Rasputin to fleece the unwary. The preacher who wrote that Jesus fed the five thousand with the little lad's lunch, to be sure, but that it was "an extra large lunch" is the type who would always mistake the voice of God for a thunderstorm. The Red Sea did not divide and the axe head did not swim, because these things are not possible for those who understand the positivism of Auguste Comte. God did not speak from heaven to His Son for there is no God and He has no Son.

Perhaps had we been standing there that day we too would have said that it thundered, but if so, this would have been our reaction in the days of our lives before we were touched by the matchless grace of God and called irresistibly by His Holy Spirit. Now by divine grace the child of God has no difficulty in accepting the fact that Jesus and the Heavenly Father were carrying on an important conversation that day - the Father speaking from His throne in heaven and His Son standing within the shadow of a cross. We should pray that, just as the Holy Spirit called us, He will also attune the ears of the unsaved to hear the voice of God, open the eyes of the blind to behold the wondrous workings of His way in human history and sharpen the perceptivity of the skeptics to understand that in the universe which God created and which He sustains, though nothing is unscientific there is much that is superscientific.

Verse 30 - "Jesus answered and said, This voice came not because of me, but for your sakes."

ἀπεκρίθη καὶ εἶπεν Ἰησοῦς, Οὐ δι' ἐμὲ ἡ φωνὴ αὕτη γέγονεν ἀλλὰ δι' ὑμᾶς.

ἀπεκρίθη (3d.per.sing.aor.mid.ind.of ἀποκρίνομαι, constative) 318.
καὶ (adjunctive conjunction joining verbs) 14.
εἶπεν (3d.per.sing.aor.act.ind.of εἶπον, constative) 155.
Ἰησοῦς (nom.sing.masc.of Ἰησοῦς, subject of ἀπεκρίθη and εἶπεν) 3.
Οὐ (summary negative conjunction with the indicative) 130.
δι' (preposition with the accusative of cause) 118.
ἐμὲ (acc.sing.masc.of ἐμός, cause) 1267.
ἡ (nom.sing.fem.of the article in agreement with φωνὴ) 9.
φωνὴ (nom.sing.fem.of φωνή, subject of γέγονεν) 222.
αὕτη (nom.sing.fem.of οὗτος, in agreement with φωνὴ) 93.
γέγονεν (3d.per.sing.perf.ind.of γίνομαι, dramatic) 113.
ἀλλὰ (alternative conjunction) 342.
δι' (preposition with the accusative of cause) 118.
ὑμᾶς (acc.pl.masc.of σύ, cause) 104.

Translation - "Jesus responded, 'It was not for my sake that this voice came, but for yours.' "

Comment: The Father spoke at His baptism (Mt.3:17), at His transfiguration (Mt.17:5) and now on this occasion. It was always for the benefit of the human audience. Those who stood by and heard Jesus talking about His coming hour of death and the glorification which would follow needed supernatural assurance that these events were not uncontrolled and unplanned tragedies, but deliberately executed historic events, designed especially for the glory of God.

There are many true Christian believers who,for one reason or another, cannot accept the Reformed theology. The alternative for them must be that, to some degree we live in a random universe in which random causes produce ripple effect results. For them, and for Reformed theologians as well, Ephesians 1:11 is strong medicine. The Arminian rejects the passage, at least in part, and is left with the conclusion that we have a random universe. The Calvinist accepts the passage and is left with the doctrine that God is the author of our sins! There are difficulties on both sides of the dispute. How far from the perfect will of God can we go before He intervenes, lest His universe become a shambles? William James may have been of some help with his circle diagram, in which he indicates focal truth in the center of the circle and peripheral truth on its circumference. Somewhere between the center and the circumference is where most Christians operate most of the time. It would appear that all would agree that God will permit no one of His elect to go outside the circle. The Christian experience, with its Holy Spirit inspired repentance and faith begins at the center. There was at least one time in our lives when we were wholly within the perfect will of God. That was the moment when, drawn by His Holy Spirit we made our cordial commitment to His Son and accepted Him as our Saviour. The ideal Christian experience would place us at the focal point at all times. We lessen our effectiveness for Him as we stray toward the periphery.

To reject the immanent control of events applied by the transcendant deity is to return to Spinoza's block universe, which is also a form of determinism. The difference is that Spinoza's determinism has blind natural forces at the controls, whereas the determinism of Ephesians 1:11 has at the controls One Who knows everything, loves us too much to inflict upon us an injury and is powerful enough, despite all the obstacles which Satan can devise, to bring the scenario to a conclusion that demonstrates His point of view above that of all of His foes. If there is no God who controls His universe then we are moving on an exponential course that cannot be reversed toward the heat death of the second law of thermodynamics. When that time comes, time will be no more and everything will have moved back to the chemical simplicity which the grave diggers call decomposition. It is a ghastly prospect. If this is true all moral precepts are nonesense, since all of us, those who are good and those who are evil are unalterably headed for the same end.

For the Christian thinker who is not afraid to entertain thoughts like this, one of the brightest prospects of heaven, second only to the thrill of meeting our lovely Lord in person, will be the conversation with Him in which He will explain all of this to us, at which time, we will probably say, "Of course. Why did I not think of that?"

Verse 31 - "Now is the judgment of this world: now shall the prince of this world be cast out."

νῦν κρίσις ἐστὶν τοῦ κόσμου τούτου, νῦν ὁ ἄρχων τοῦ κόσμου τούτου ἐκβαληθήσεται ἔξω.

νῦν (explanatory adverb) 1497.
κρίσις (nom.sing.fem.of κρίσις, subject of ἐστὶν) 478.
ἐστὶν (3d.per.sing.pres.ind.of εἰμί, futuristic) 86.
τοῦ (gen.sing.masc.of the article in agreement with κόσμου) 9.
κόσμου (gen.sing.masc.of κόσμος, description) 360.
τούτου (gen.sing.masc.of οὗτος, in agreement with κόσμου) 93.
νῦν (explanatory adverb) 1497.
ὁ (nom.sing.masc.of the article in agreement with ἄρχων) 9.
ἄρχων (nom.sing.masc.of ἄρχων, subject of ἐκβληθήσεται) 816.
τοῦ (gen.sing.masc.of the article in agreement with κόσμου) 9.
κόσμου (gen.sing.masc.of κόσμος, description) 360.
τούτου (gen.sing.masc.of οὗτος, in agreement with κόσμου) 93.
ἐκβληθήσεται (3d.per.sing.fut.pass.ind.of ἐκβάλλω, predictive) 649.
ἔξω (adverbial) 449.

Translation - "Now the sentence of this world will be handed down. Now the ruler of this world will be cast out."

Comment: We face a difficulty if we construe νῦν as a temporal adverb indicating simultaneous time with the statement of Jesus, because the present tense which it implies conflicts with the futuristic present in ἐστὶν and in the second clause with the future tense in ἐκβληθήσεται. Obviously Jesus did not mean that *at that moment* the judgment of the world took place and that *at that moment* "the evil genius" (Goodspeed) was cast out. The judgment of the world and the eternal condemnation of Satan took place at the cross when Christ died (Heb.2:14). νῦν may be taken here in an explanatory sense, or perhaps Jesus was including all of the closing events of the Passion Week in His remark. Note that Jesus did not say that the execution of the sentence which was issued when He died would take place forthwith. Satan and his dupes have already been condemned to eternal separation from God, but the sentence will not be carried out until the appointed time at the close of the kingdom age.

The world has gone on its wicked way for nearly two thousand years since Jesus spoke these words. In what sense then did Jesus mean to point to its judgment as about to occur at that time? *Cf.*#478 carefully for all of the ways the Holy Spirit has used the word in the New Testament. It means, among other things, an evaluation. A discriminating examination of the world leads to a judgment as to its moral value, as a judge in a contest judges between the contestants to determine to what extent they attain to a desired standard of excellence. The evidence that God examined the world and found it wanting was revealed in Christ's hour of death. The extent of the world's depravity was measured in direct ratio to the extremity of the end employed to save it. A world that can be saved only by the curcifixion of the incarnate Son of God and its accompanying sacrifice of His life, is indeed totally depraved. The price that God demanded and that Jesus paid was infinite and could have been paid only by an infinite Christ capable of infinite suffering. Thus the judgment of the world is that it was infinitely evil. κρίσις is also used to convey the idea that the official judgment upon the world was handed down when Jesus died. *Cf.* the verses listed in this category. Heaven's court, with its Judge upon the cross, decreed in that hour that the world was from thenceforth under a judicial sentence of death. Since then the world has been waiting on death row, pending the execution on a day still future.

It is in this sense also that we are to understand the banishment of ὁ ἄρχων τοῦ κόσμου τούτου. The banishment of Satan was decreed, though he will not actually be banished until the final judgment at the end of the millenium (Rev.20:10). It is this fact which the Holy Spirit in His convincing ministry impresses upon the elect, along with the facts of the glorification of Christ and the sin of rejecting Him (John 16:7-11). *Cf.*#816 for the passages where ἄρχων is applied to Satan. The Devil's power to seduce the elect and make them his victims was broken at Calvary. It was "through death (Jesus) destroyed him that had the power of death, that is, the devil, and delivered them, who, through fear of death were all of their lifetime subject to bondage" (Heb.2:14). When Christ died He bound the strong man and proceded to rob him of his property (Mt.12:29).*Cf.* our comment *en loc.* Satan is the "god of this world" (2 Cor.4:4). He is not the god of the elect.

Jesus went on in verses 32 and 33 to predict the physical mode of His death and the spiritual results that would flow from it.

Verse 32 - "And I, if I be lifted up from the earth, will draw all men unto me."

κἀγὼ ἐὰν ὑψωθῶ ἐκ τῆς γῆς, πάντας ἑλκύσω πρὸς ἐμαυτόν.

κἀγὼ (continuative conjunction, crasis) 178.
ἐὰν (conditional particle in a third-class condition) 363.
ὑψωθῶ (1st.per.sing.1st.aor.pass.subj.of υήφόω, third-class condition) 946.
ἐκ (preposition with the ablative of separation) 19.
τῆς (abl.sing.fem.of the article in agreement with γῆς) 9.
γῆς (abl.sing.fem.of γῆ, separation) 157.
πάντας (acc.pl.masc.of πᾶς, direct object of ἑλκύσω) 67.
ἑλκύσω (1st.per.sing.fut.act.ind.of ελκύω, predictive) 2289.
πρὸς (preposition with the accusative of extent) 197.
ἐμαυτόν (acc.sing.masc.of ἐμαυτός, extent) 723.

Translation - "And I, if I be lifted up from the earth, will draw all men to myself."

Comment: We have the typical third-class condition with ἐὰν and the subjunctive in the protasis and the future indicative in the apodosis. The condition (if clause) is undetermined, but with a prospect of fulfillment, as though Jesus had some small doubt about the certainty of His death. "If I am lifted up (though I am certain to be lifted up) I will draw all men to myself (and there isn't any doubt about that)."

While we can take ἐκ τῆς γῆς simply as an ablative of separation, as though it were ἀπὸ τῆς γῆς - "away from the earth" instead of "out of the earth," the fact still remains that the Holy Spirit used ἐκ (out of) and not ἀπό (away from). A study of ἐκ (#19) and ἀπό (#70) reveals that while each is used with the ablative, which basicly means separation, the idea of separation can also mean source. Thus when a difference, made clear by the context, exists, we translate ἐκ by "out of" and ἀπό by "away from." Now there is no doubt that Jesus was lifted up *away from* the earth in a spatial sense. And perhaps this is all that the Holy Spirit intended to say. But if we are justified in translating "if I be lifted up *out of* the earth," we have the separation concept (away from) and something more. Is there a hint here of Jesus' earthly humanity in the sense of Isa.53:2? His body, in a very true biological sense, was "out of" the earth, since He and His mother were nourished throughout their entire earthly lives out of the terrestrial sphere. The humanity of our Lord was descended through His mother from all of their ancestors back to Adam. As the Eternal Λόγος He had no source. Indeed 'Ο Λόγος is the unproduced Source of all, but as "the Son of Man," the perfect human sacrifice for sin, He came "out of the earth" in a source sense, and was then lifted up "away from the ground" in a directional sense (ἀπὸ with the ablative) when He was crucified.

The physical act of lifting the body of Jesus up from the earth upon a cross, was preceded by the preparation of that body "out of the earth" as a "root (the source of life) out of dry ground" (Isa.53:2). *Cf.* Heb.10:5; Ps.40:6.

The conclusion is clear in the result clause - πάντας ἑλκύσω πρὸς ἐμαυτόν. Note that the Father, Who sent Jesus into the world for the suffering of death, cooperates with His Son, in an eternally planned division of divine labor, by drawing men to Him (John 6:44). No man can come unless he be drawn to Christ, and the Father attracts to the Son, while the Son also attracts men to Himself. Who are these people who will be attracted to the Son? They are those whom the Father has given to the Son (John 6:37; 17:6,9,11,12,20,24; Mt.1:21). Since all that the Father has given to the Son will come to Him, and since all who come will be accepted by Him, it is clear that we cannot push πάντας to mean the quantitative one hundred per cent of the human race. To do so, in the light of John 6:37, is to conclude on a Univeralist basis that all men will be saved. Let me say that if that is what the Father, Son and Holy Spirit want to do, it is all right with me! But that is not what He indicates in His word. Note that πάντας, an adjective is not joined in the text by a substantive. πάντας, the adjective serves. "All kinds of men." Men of all classes, races, colors, tongues (Rev.5:9). 2 Peter 1:21 directs us to avoid building a theology upon an isolated verse of scripture. No scripture verse *means anything* until we have allowed the light of every other verse to shine upon it. To say it another way, one passage cannot be pushed literally to a position which other passages *just as literally* deny. The principle of hermeneutics is that if the literal interpretation is *the only one possible*, it must be accepted and the truth that it reveals must serve as a guide to all other passages involved. If more than one interpretation is possible, we must accept the one which avoids a collision with passages that offer no alternative to a literal acceptance. Our passage, in isolation, admits two interpretations. We can say that all of the human family will be drawn to Christ and saved, or we can say that men, women and children "... out of every kindred and tongue and people and nation" (Rev.5:9) will be saved. The former interpretation conflicts, while the latter conforms with many passages which clearly, literally and imperiously teach that some individuals will be lost, and which offer no other alternative to their interpretation than the literal one.

It is obvious that a valid interpretative *gestalt*, from which we can derive objective truth need not involve all of the other verses in the Bible. We must, however, take into account all of the verses that are involved in the problem which the exegete is trying to solve. To make the point with an extreme example Job.6:1 which reads, "But Job answered and said. . . " sheds little light on our task of interpreting John 12:33. Verse John 12:33 does.

Verse 33 - "This he said, signifying what death he should die."

τοῦτο δὲ ἔλεγεν σημαίνων ποίῳ θανάτῳ ἤμελλεν ἀποθνήσκειν.

τοῦτο (acc.sing.neut.of *οὗτος*, direct object of *ἔλεγεν*) 93.
δὲ (explanatory conjunction) 11.
ἔλεγεν (3d.per.sing.imp.act.ind.of *λέγω*, progressive description) 66.

#2708 *σημαίνων* (pres.act.part.nom.sing.masc.of *σημαίνω*, adverbial, telic).

signify -John 12:33; 18:32; 21:19; Acts 11:28; 25:27; Rev.1:1.

Meaning: Cf.σῆμα - "a sign." To indicate by giving a sign. To signify. Followed by indirect discourse in John 12:33; 18:32; 21:19. Absolutely in Rev.1:1. As an infinitive with an object - Acts 25:27; with an infinitive in indirect discourse - Acts 11:28.

ποίῳ (instru.sing.masc.of *ποῖος*, in agreement with *θανάτῳ*) 1298.
θανάτῳ (instru.sing.masc.of *θάνατος*, means) 381.
ἤμελλεν (3d.per.sing.imp.act.ind.of *μέλλω*, inceptive) 206.
ἀποθνήσκειν (pres.act.inf.of *ἀποθνήσκω*, epexegetical) 774.

Translation - "Now this He was saying in order to indicate by what death He was going to die."

Comment: The antecedent of *τοῦτο* is the protasis of the conditional clause of verse 32. So we have upon the face of the text of verse 33, the primary meaning of His figure of speech *ὑψωθῶ ἐκ τῆς γῆς*. He was saying that His death would be carried out by crucifixion. There is no denial however of our possible interpretation of why the Holy Spirit used *ἐκ* instead of *ἀπό*. The ablative indicates separation and that is the point of verse 33. It was to be by crucifixion. The preposition with the ablative indicates source, which points to the fact that the One to be lifted up "away from the earth" on a cross, was *the man* Christ Jesus (1 Tim.2:5).

Jesus' clear-cut description of His impending ignominious death created a problem for the audience, as we see in

Verse 34 - "The people answered him, We have heard out of the law that Christ abideth forever: and how sayest thou, The Son of Man must be lifted up? Who is

ἀπεκρίθη οὖν αὐτῷ ὁ ὄχλος, Ἡμεῖς ἠκούσαμεν ἐκ τοῦ νόμου ὅτι ὁ Χριστὸς μένει εἰς τὸν αἰῶνα, καὶ πῶς σὺ λέγεις ὅτι δεῖ ὑψωθῆναι τὸν υἱὸν τοῦ ἀνθρώπου; τίς ἐστιν οὗτος ὁ υἱὸς τοῦ ἀνθρώπου;

ἀπεκρίθη (3d.per.sing.aor.mid.ind.of ἀποκρίνομαι, constative) 318.
οὖν (continuative conjunction) 68.
αὐτῷ (dat.sing.masc.of αὐτός, indirect object of ἀπεκρίθη) 16.
ὁ (nom.sing.masc.of the article in agreement with ὄχλος) 9.
ὄχλος (nom.sing.masc.of ὄχλος, subject of ἀπεκρίθη) 418.
Ἡμεῖς (nom.pl.masc.of ἐγώ, subject of ἠκούσαμεν) 123.
ἠκούσαμεν (1st.per.pl.aor.act.ind.of ἀκούω, culminative) 148.
ἐκ (preposition with the ablative of source) 19.
τοῦ (abl.sing.masc.of the article in agreement with νόμου) 9.
νόμου (abl.sing.masc.of νόμος, source) 464.
ὅτι (conjunction introducing an object clause in indirect discourse) 211.
ὁ (nom.sing.masc.of the article in agreement with Χριστὸς) 9.
Χριστὸς (nom.sing.masc.of Χριστός, subject of μένει) 4.
μένει (3d.per.sing.pres.act.ind.of μένω, static) 864.
εἰς (preposition with the accusative of time extent) 140.
τὸν (acc.sing.masc.of the article in agreement with αἰῶνα) 9.
αἰῶνα (acc.sing.masc.of αἰών, time extent) 1002.
καὶ (adversative conjunction) 14.
πῶς (interrogative conjunction) 627.
λέγεις (2d.per.sing.pres.act.ind.of λέγω, aoristic) 66.
σὺ (nom.sing.masc.of σύ, subject of λέγεις) 104.
ὅτι (conjunction introducing an object clause in indirect discourse) 211.
δεῖ (3d.per.sing.pres.ind.of the impersonal verb) 1207.
ὑψωθῆναι (aor.pass.inf.of ὑψόω, epexegetical) 946.
τὸν (acc.sing.masc.of the article in agreement with υἱὸν) 9.
υἱὸν (acc.sing.masc.of υἱός, general reference) 5.
τοῦ (gen.sing.masc.of the article in agreement with ἀνθρώπου) 9.
ἀνθρώπου (gen.sing.masc.of ἄνθρωπος, description) 341.
τίς (nom.sing.masc.of τίς, the interrogative pronoun, predicate nominative) 281.
ἐστιν (3d.per.sing.pres.ind.of εἰμί, aoristic) 86.
οὗτος (nom.sing.masc.of οὗτος, in agreement with υἱὸς, contemptuous use) 93.
ὁ (nom.sing.masc.of the article in agreement with υἱὸς) 9.
υἱὸς (nom.sing.masc.of υἱός, subject of ἐστιν) 5.
τοῦ (gen.sing.masc.of the article, in agreement with ἀνθρώπου) 9.
ἀνθρώπου (gen.sing.masc.of ἄνθρωπος, description) 341.

Translation - "Then the people answered, 'We have always understood from the law that the Messiah will remain into the ages; but why are you saying that it is necessary for the Son of Man to be lifted up? Who is this man, the Son of Man?'"

Comment: Jesus' remarks presented the people with a dilemma. If He was the Messiah, as He said, why should He be crucified? It was natural that they should respond like this. They stated a clear-cut proposition. The law taught them that the Messiah's reign would go on forever. The question, introduced by *πῶς* is therefore one that we would expect them to ask. The law says - - - *ὅτι* with indirect discourse, but (adversative *καὶ*) you say - - - another *ὅτι* with indirect discourse. *Cf.*#1207, 5. This sounded to the people like a collision of ideas. Therefore comes the contemptuous question *τίς ἐστιν οὗτος ὁ υἱὸς τοῦ ἀνθρώπου*?

It is important to note that Jesus had not used the phrase *ὁ υἱὸς τοῦ ἀνθρώπου* - "the son of man" to refer to Himself since verse 23. All of the soliloquy which followed, including the excitement of the Father's voice from heaven, and the argument about that, had not erased from the minds of the people the fact that He had called Himself "the Son of Man" and yet had spoken of the divine necessity involved in His going to the cross. The real question in the minds of the people is the question at the heart of the trinitarian theology of redemption - *viz.* the hypostatic union of deity and humanity in Jesus Christ, the Messiah. If He is Messiah, He must be God. Then how can He also be man? Must God die on a cross? If so how can He be the Messiah? This may lend some credence to my suggestion that *ἐκ τῆς γῆς* of verse 32 may point first to His humanity, as well as to the physical manner in which He was lifted up *away from* the earth. Who was lifted up? The Messiah. From whence came He? From heaven for the purpose of incarnation. But as "the Son of Man" He came *out of the earth* (Isa.53:2) in order that He might be lifted up *away from the earth* upon a cross.

Verse 35 - "Then Jesus said unto them, Yet a little while is the light with you. Walk while ye have the light, lest darkness come upon you: for he that walketh in darkness knoweth not whither he goeth."

εἶπεν οὖν αὐτοῖς ὁ Ἰησοῦς, Ἔτι μικρὸν χρόνον τὸ φῶς ἐν ὑμῖν ἐστιν. περιπατεῖτε ὡς τὸ φῶς ἔχετε, ἵνα μὴ σκοτία ὑμᾶς καταλάβῃ. καὶ ὁ περιπατῶν ἐν τῇ σκοτίᾳ οὐκ οἶδεν ποῦ ὑπάγει.

εἶπεν (3d.per.sing.aor.act.ind.of *εἶπον*, constative) 155.
οὖν (inferential conjunction) 68.
αὐτοῖς (dat.pl.masc.of *αὐτός*, indirect object of *εἶπεν*) 16.
ὁ (nom.sing.masc.of the article in agreement with *Ἰησοῦς*) 9.
Ἰησοῦς (nom.sing.masc.of *Ἰησοῦς*, subject of *εἶπεν*) 3.
ἔτι (temporal adverb) 448.
μικρὸν (acc.sing.masc.of *μικρός*, in agreement with *χρόνον*) 901.
χρόνον (acc.sing.masc.of *χρόνος*, time extent) 168.
τὸ (nom.sing.neut.of the article in agreement with *φῶς*) 9.
φῶς (nom.sing.neut.of *φῶς*, subject of *ἐστιν*) 379.
ἐν (preposition with the locative of place where) 80.
ὑμῖν (loc.pl.masc.of *σύ*, "among" with plural pronouns) 104.
ἐστιν (3d.per.sing.pres.ind.of *εἰμί*, aoristic) 86.
περιπατεῖτε (2d.per.pl.pres.act.impv.of *περιπατέω*, command) 384.

ὡς (particle introducing a definite temporal clause) 128.
τὸ (acc.sing.neut.of the article in agreement with φῶς) 9.
φῶς (acc.sing.neut.of φῶς, direct object of ἔχετε) 379.
ἔχετε (2d.per.pl.pres.act.ind.of ἔχω, definite temporal clause) 82.
ἵνα (conjunction with the subjunctive, negative purpose) 114.
μὴ (qualified negative conjunction with the subjunctive) 87.
σκοτία (nom.sing.fem.of σκοτία, subject of καταλάβῃ) 378.
ὑμᾶς (acc.pl.masc.of σύ, direct object of καταλάβῃ) 104.
καταλάβῃ (3d.per.sing.aor.act.subj.of καταλαμβάνω, purpose) 1694.
καὶ (causal conjunction) 14.
ὁ (nom.sing.masc.of the article, in agreement with περιπατῶν) 9.
περιπατῶν (pres.act.part.nom.sing.masc.of παρεπατέω, substantival, subject of οἶδεν) 384.
ἐν (preposition with the locative of place) 80
τῇ (loc.sing.fem.of the article in agreement with σκοτίᾳ) 9.
σκοτίᾳ (loc.sing.fem.of σκοτία, place where) 378.
οὐκ (summary negative conjunction with the indicative) 130.
οἶδεν (3d.per.sing.pres.ind.of ὁράω, customary) 144.
ποῦ (interrogative abverb of place) 142.
ὑπάγει (3d.per.sing.pres.act.ind.of ὑπάγω, customary) 364.

Translation - "So Jesus said to them, 'The light is still in your midst for a short time. Walk while you have the light, lest darkness envelope you, because the one who is walking in the darkness does not know where he is going.' "

Comment: Their question, with its contemptuous reference to the Son of Man, motivated Jesus' answer. Thus οὖν is inferential. *Cf.* Luke 17:21, where ἐντὸς ὑμῶν ἐστιν, for "in your midst" is similar to ἐν ὑμῖν - "in the midst of/with you" for the same reason, *viz.* that the pronoun is plural. Jesus did not say, "the light is in you." He was referring to Himself and the fact that they had only two more days in which to see Him and hear Him teach.

The people had reason to believe that Jesus was their Messiah. In this they were correct. They were also correct that Messiah, when He came as Messiah, not as Suffering Saviour, would establish a permanent reign. Jesus advises them to go on walking in the light that they had. To the extent that they had any intellectual light about Him, Who is the Light of the world (John 8:12) they were advised to walk in accord with it. Otherwise the darkness would overcome them. Here is an analysis that is in line with Plato's teaching. In every man there is light and darkness. Some things we understand; some things we do not. Thus it was with the people who analyzed the problem before them. They were trying to put together what they knew in a consistent manner. Truth one: Jesus said He was the Messiah. Truth two: Messiah is eternal. Truth three: Jesus, who says that He is Messiah also says that He is about to be crucified. All three of these were true. Where was the darkness? They did not know how to fit the three together because they did not understand that Messiah was there on earth, in His first coming, for purposes of redemption and resurrection, and that there was to be a future second coming of Messiah, when He would fulfill all of their nationalistic hopes. This was the darkness - the blind spot. Jesus promised them that if they would walk in the light to the extent that they had it and during the time that He, the Light, was still with them, they would have more light. The alternative was to reject the light and to walk in the dark. Such a man does not know where he is going.

This last statement by our Lord explains why the unregenerate world cannot tell the difference between change and progress as they tinker with world society and make their frenetic efforts, through change to improve it. If one does not know where he is going, how can he be sure that he is going in the direction where he believes his Utopia lies?

Verse 36 - "While ye have the light, believe in the light, that ye may be the children of light. These things spake Jesus, and departed, and did hide himself from them."

ὡς τὸ φῶς ἔχετε, πιστεύετε εἰς τὸ φῶς ἵνα υἱοὶ φωτὸς γένησθε. Ταῦτα ἐλάλησεν Ἰησοῦς, καὶ ἀπελθὼν ἐκρύβη ἀπ' αὐτῶν.

ὡς (particle introducing a definite temporal clause) 128.
τὸ (acc.sing.neut.of the article in agreement with φῶς) 9.
φῶς (acc.sing.neut.of φῶς, direct object of ἔχετε) 379.
ἔχετε (2d.per.pl.pres.act.ind.of ἔχω, aoristic) 82.
πιστεύετε (2d.per.pl.pres.act.impv.of πιστεύω, command) 734.
εἰς (preposition with the accusative, cause) 140.
τὸ (acc.sing.neut.of the article in agreement with φῶς) 9.
φῶς (acc.sing.neut.of φῶς, cause) 379.
ἵνα (conjunction introducing a purpose clause) 114.
υἱοὶ (nom.pl.masc.of υἱός, predicate nominative) 5.
φωτὸς (gen.sing.neut.of φῶς, description) 379.
γένησθε (2d.per.pl.aor.subj.of γίνομαι, purpose) 113.
Ταῦτα (acc.pl.neut.of οὗτος, direct object of ἐλάλησεν) 93.
ἐλάλησεν (3d.per.sing.aor.act.ind.of λαλέω, constative) 815.
Ἰησοῦς (nom.sing.masc.of Ἰησοῦς, subject of ἐλάλησεν and ἐκρύβη) 3.
καὶ (adjunctive conjunction joining verbs) 14.
ἀπελθὼν (aor.mid.part.nom.sing.masc.of ἀπέρχομαι, adverbial, temporal) 239.
ἐκρύβη (3d.per.sing.aor.mid.ind.of κρύπτω;, constative) 451.
ἀπ' (preposition with the ablative of separation) 70.
αὐτῶν (abl.pl.masc.of αὐτός, separation) 16.

Translation - "While you have the light believe in the light in order that you may become sons of light. Jesus said these things and went away and hid Himself from them."

Comment: Jesus repeats the definite temporal clause ὡς τὸ φῶς ἔχετε of verse 35. Then He told them to walk according to the light while they had Him. Now He adds that while they have Him they are to believe upon (because of) Him. The penalty for rejection is a confused, stumbling, frustrating fiasco in the *cul de sac* of utter darkness. The reward for acceptance is that we are the υἱοὶ φωτὸς - "the sons of light." It is a Hebraism. Literally, "enlightened sons."

The moral responsibility associated with entertaining light is great. We must believe in it and walk according to it or lose it and fall victim to our enemy, the opposite of light - darkness. To walk in the darkness is not to know where one is going. This philosophy is what William James called "tender mindedness." Jesus urges us to believe as much as we understand, despite the fact that there are areas of darkness, in the hope that belief in all the light that is currently available, will bring more light and rescue us from the frustration of the remaining darkness. Jesus placed a premium on knowing something and denied that the agnostic's boast that he knows nothing is a virtue. *Cf.* John 7:17 - "If any man will do His will he shall know. . . " The same thought is found here. Have you some light? Walk by it. Believe in it. The result? You will become enlightened sons and know. Here is Jesus' challenge. He was not suggesting that intellectual progress alone will lead to salvation. He was saying that He was the Light and that certitude in anything begins really and only when we accept Him as Saviour and Lord.

With this He left them and went into seclusion. Did the Greeks try to find Him? Did they follow His advice? *Cf.* John 1:5 with John 12:35. The darkness does not overcome the light so long as we walk by it and believe in it. Otherwise light gives way to darkness. *Cf.* Matthew 6:23; John 8:12. Thus the prevailing agnosticism, a by-product of radical empiricism, is deadly to society.

Verse 37 - "But though he had done so many miracles before them, yet they believed not on him.

Τοσαῦτα δὲ αὐτοῦ σημεῖα πεποιηκότος ἔμπροσθεν αὐτῶν οὐκ ἐπίστευον εἰς αὐτόν.

Τοσαῦτα (acc.pl.neut.of τοσοῦτος, in agreement with σημεῖα) 727.
δὲ (adversative conjunction) 11.
αὐτοῦ (gen.sing.masc.of αὐτός, genitive absolute) 16.
σημεῖα (acc.pl.neut.of σημεῖον, direct object of πεποιηκότος) 1005.
πεποιηκότος (perf.act.part.gen.sing.masc.of ποιέω, genitive absolute) 127.
ἔμπροσθεν (improper preposition with the ablative of separation) 459.
αὐτῶν (abl.pl.masc.of αὐτός, separation) 16.
οὐκ (summary negative conjunction with the indicative) 130.
ἐπίστευον (3d.per.pl.imp.act.ind.of πιστεύω, inceptive) 734.
εἰς (preposition with the accusative of cause) 140.
αὐτόν (acc.sing.masc.of αὐτός, cause) 16.

Translation - "But, despite the fact that He had performed so many miracles before them,they refused to make a commitment to Him."

Comment: Here we have in the genitive absolute a concessive participle. Despite all of the evidence that He was God in human flesh, as abundantly attested by the miracles which He performed, they rejected Him. They had all of the empirical evidence that any scientist, however fanatically committed to the scientific method, could desire, that Jesus was no ordinary human being. We could not expect them to understand Jesus as clearly as we, who have the advantage of God's full New Testament revelation. But they did have some light. They refused to walk by it or to believe in it and the result was that, like all blind men, they did not know where they were going. Why? Because Isaiah had prophesied that it would be that way.

Verse 38 - "That the saying of Esaias the prophet might be fulfilled, which he spake, Lord, who hath believed our report? And to whom hath the arm of the Lord been revealed?"

ἵνα ὁ λόγος Ἠσαΐου τοῦ προφήτου πληρωθῇ ὃν εἶπεν, Κύριε, *τίς ἐπίστευσεν τῇ ἀκοῇ ἡμῶν; καὶ ὁ βραχίων κυρίου τίνι ἀπεκαλύφθη;*

ἵνα (conjunction with the subjunctive in a purpose clause) 114.
ὁ (nom.sing.masc.of the article in agreement with *λόγος*) 9.
λόγος (nom.sing.masc.of *λόγος*, subject of *πληρωθῇ*) 510.
Ἠσαΐου (gen.sing.masc.of Ἠσαΐας, description) 255.
τοῦ (gen.sing.masc.of the article in agreement with *προφήτου*) 9.
προφήτου (gen.sing.masc.of *προφήτης*, apposition) 119.
πληρωθῇ (3d.per.sing.aor.pass.subj.of *πληρόω*, purpose) 115.
ὃν (acc.sing.masc.of *ὅς*, general reference) 65.
εἶπεν (3d.per.sing.aor.act.ind.of *εἶπον*, constative) 155.
Κύριε (voc.sing.masc.of *κύριος*, address) 97.
τίς (nom.sing.masc.of *τίς*, interrogative pronoun, subject of *ἐπίστευσεν*) 281.
ἐπίστευσεν (3d.per.sing.aor.act.ind.of *πιστεύω*, constative) 734.
τῇ (dat.sing.fem.of the article in agreement with *ἀκοῇ*) 9.
ἀκοῇ (dat.sing.fem.of *ἀκοή*, reference) 409.
ἡμῶν (gen.pl.masc.of *ἐγώ*, possession) 123.
καὶ (continuative conjunction) 14.
ὁ (nom.sing.masc.of the article in agreement with *βραχίων*) 9.
βραχίων (nom.sing.masc.of *βραχίων*, subject of *ἀπεκαλύφθη*) 1829.
κυρίου (gen.sing.masc.of *κύριος*, description) 97.
τίνι (dat.sing.masc.of *τίς*, indirect object of *ἀπεκαλύφθη*) 281.
ἀπεκαλύφθη (3d.per.sing.aor.pass.ind.of *ἀποκαλύπτω*, culminative) 886.

Translation - "In order that the prophecy of Isaiah,the prophet, might be fulfilled, with reference to which he said, 'Lord, who has believed our report, and to whom has your sovereign arm been revealed."

Comment: Let us remember that purpose is predicted result . The *ἵνα* clause is joined to *οὐκ ἐπίστευον εἰς αὐτόν* of verse 37. There is no way to escape the Calvinistic tone of this passage. The historic facts stand out. Isaiah spoke this prophecy 700 years B.C. It is recorded in Isa.53:1. Seven hundred years later, despite all of the abundant evidence in terms of miracles and subline teachings from the most winsome personality in history, Jesus' auditors still did not believe in Him. Sixty five years later the Holy Spirit inspired John to say that their unbelief (fact two) resulted in the fulfillment of the prophecy (fact one). God, Who, of course, lives in the eternal present, viewed it all without chronological limitations. God made the prediction; God presided over its fulfillment. The scripture does not say that some wished to believe but were forced by divine decree not to believe, in order that the prophecy might not fail. All who were drawn by God (John 6:44) and wanted to believe on Christ, did so and they were saved. Those who did not, who walked not in the light and rejected Him Who is the Light (John 8:12) failed to become enlightened sons (verse 36), but were overwhelmed by the darkness (verse 35), with the result that they never knew, after that, where they were going. And they have never known since where they are going, any more than present unbelievers know where they are going, although most insist that they are leading world society forward in a progress that will bring the kingdom of heaven, but without the help of the King. How great indeed is their darkness! (Mt.6:23).

Study carefully #409 for its connection with saving faith. It will lead you back to Mt.13:14 and its context. Acts 28:26. Faith results when we believe what we hear - Rom.10:16,17; Gal.3:2,5; Heb.4:2. The saints, no less than the unregenerate, must react with humility when we hear the Word of God, if we are to grow and escape the destruction, not of the souls, but of their rewards (Heb.5:11-6:8). Those who hear but do not believe, or are "dull of hearing" (Heb.5:11) reject because partial light seems not to be enough for them. As long as there is *any* doubt, they choose to reserve judgment. In their view, they must understand all before personal commitment is made. This is basic sinful egotism. They imply that their mental capacity is sufficient to absorb *all* of God's truth, so they intend to wait until the entire *gestalt* is there for their considertion. There must be no danda; only empirically established data. These skeptics, who in reality are quite naive, pride themselves on their "tough mindedness." The sovereign arm of the Lord is never revealed to people like this. God is not in the business of casting pearls before swine. Mary did not understand everything that she heard (Lk.1:34), but she walked in the light that she had and the arm of the Lord was revealed unto her (Lk.1:51) Israel did not understand all that God was doing in Egypt, but she accepted and obeyed what she did understand and the arm of the Lord was revealed to her also (Acts 13:17), but only because she passed under the blood. *Cf.*#886 for a complete study of ἀποκαλύπτω. There is much rich preaching material here.

Verse 39 - "Therefore they could not believe, because that Esaias said again, . . ."

διὰ τοῦτο οὐκ ἠδύναντο πιστεύειν, ὅτι πάλιν εἶπεν Ἠσαΐας.

διὰ (preposition with the accusative of cause) 118.
τοῦτο (acc.sing.neut.of οὗτος, cause) 93.
οὐκ (summary negative conjunction with the indicative) 130.
ἠδύναντο (3d.per.pl.imp.mid.ind.of δύναμαι, Attic for ἐδύναντο) 289.
πιστεύειν (pres.act.inf.of πιστεύω, epexegetical) 734.

ὅτι (causal conjunction) 211.
πάλιν (adverbial) 355.
εἶπεν (3d.per.sing.aor.act.ind.of εἶπον, constative) 155.
Ἠσαΐας (nom.sing.masc.of Ἠσαΐας, subject of εἶπεν) 255.

Translation - "Therefore they were not able to believe, because Isaiah said again, . . . "

Comment: διὰ τοῦτο refers to what Isaiah had said. The result was their inability to believe. Then Jesus links another of Isaiah's prophecies into the analysis, from Isaiah 6:10.

Verse 40 - "He hath blinded their eyes, and hardened their heart; that they should not see with their eyes, nor understand with their heart, and be converted, and I should heal them."

Τετύφλωκεν αὐτῶν τοὺς ὀφθαλμοὺς καὶ ἐπώρωσεν αὐτῶν τὴν καρδίαν, ἵνα μὴ ἴδωσιν τοῖς ὀφθαλμοῖς καὶ νοήσωσιν τῇ καρδίᾳ καὶ στραφῶσιν, καὶ ἰάσομαι αὐτούς.

#2709 Τετύφλωκεν (3d.per.sing.perf.act.ind.of τυφλόω, intensive).

blind - John 12:40; 1 John 2:11; 2 Cor.4:4.

Meaning: Cf. τυφλός (#830). To make blind; to render sightless. Always in the New Testament in a spiritual and intellectual sense. Followed by τοὺς ὀφθαλμοὺς in a metaphorical sense - John 12:40; 1 John 2:11. Followed by τὰ νοήματα τῶν ἀπίστων in a metaphorical sense - 2 Cor.4:4.

αὐτῶν (gen.pl.masc.of αὐτός, possession) 16.
τοὺς (acc.pl.masc.of the article in agreement with ὀφθαλμοὺς) 9.
ὀφθαλμοὺς (acc.pl.masc.of ὀφθαλμός, direct object of τετύφλωκεν) 501.
καὶ (adjunctive conjunction joining verbs) 14.
ἐπώρωσεν (3d.per.sing.aor.act.ind.of πωρόω, culminative) 2282.
αὐτῶν (gen.pl.masc.of αὐτός, possession) 16.
τὴν (acc.sing.fem.of the article in agreement with καρδίαν) 9.
καρδίαν (acc.sing.fem.of καρδία, direct object of ἐπώρωσεν) 432.
ἵνα (conjunction introducing the subjunctive in a negative purpose clause) 114.
μὴ (qualified negative conjunction with the subjunctive) 87.
ἴδωσιν (3d.per.pl.aor.act.subj.of ὁράω, negative purpose) 144.
τοῖς (instru.pl.masc.of the article in agreement with ὀφθαλμοῖς) 9.
ὀφθαλμοῖς (instru.pl.masc.of ὀφθαλμός, means) 501.
καὶ (adjunctive conjunction joining verbs) 14.
νοήσωσιν (3d.per.pl.aor.act.subj.of νοέω, negative purpose) 1160.
τῇ (instru.sing.fem.of the article in agreement with καρδίᾳ) 9.
καρδίᾳ (instru.sing.fem.of καρδία, means) 432.
καὶ (adjunctive conjunction joining verbs) 14.
στραφῶσιν (3d.per.pl.2d.aor.pass.subj.of στρέφω, negative purpose) 530.

καὶ (adjunctive conjunction joining verbs) 14.
ἰάσομαι (1st.per.sing.fut.ind.of ἰάομαι, gnomic) 721.
αὐτούς (acc.pl.masc.of αὐτός, direct object of ἰάσομαι) 16.

Translation - "He has blinded their eyes and hardened their heart, lest they see with their eyes and understand with their heart and be converted and I would heal them."

Comment: *Cf.*#2709. Note ἐτύφλωσεν in 1 John 2:11 and 2 Cor.4:4. Hatred surrounds the walk of the sinner with darkness, and the darkness robs him of the awareness that he is being destroyed (John 12:35). Darkness also blinds his eyes (1 John 2:11). Blinded eyes prevent conversion, yet only conversion can cure hatred. Hence the unregenerate is caught up in a vicious circle from which there is no escape except by the gift of divine grace. Thus, also, the true source of his confusion is not the will of God, but the hatred of his unregenerate heart, a legacy from Adam's fall. Note also in 2 Cor.4:4 that Satan has blinded the understanding of those who do not believe, lest they be enlightened. Once again we see the vicious circle of cause and effect that keeps the sinner in the dark.

Cf.#2282 and run the references on πωρόω, especially Rom.11:7; 2 Cor.3:14; Mk.6:52; 8:17. The ἵνα clause of negative purpose follows - "lest they see (intellectually) with their eyes (metaphorically) and understand in their heart. *Cf.*#1160 and run all of the references. Notice in Romans 1:20 that understanding of the abstract truths about God comes by observation about the concrete objects of His creation in the physical realm. The data will lead us to the danda. God's eternal power and deity can be grasped, but only if we follow the partial light which we gain by the scientific method of observation of sense data. Heb.11:3 teaches the same thing in reverse. We look at the worlds that are made; we thus have some light. We walk in the light and thus we escape being defeated by the darkness and become enlightened sons. Thus we gain faith, and by faith we come to understand that the physical world came from God's eternal power and deity. Thus we have a glorious circle with exponential growth of perception: - empirical observation of data, leads to partial knowledge, which leads to intellectual humility, with its willingness and desire to know more. With the acceptance of the partial truth, we have more light, with its saving faith and a complete understanding of the danda that relates to God and our salvation. This glorious circe matches the vicious circle which begins with Adamic depravity, hatred, the darkened walk, the meaningless journey, the blinded eye, the rejection of all light and damnation. How does a sinner get rescued from the slavery of the vicious circle to the freedom of the glorious circle? By divine grace.

Francis Bacon wrote, "I had rather beleeve all the fables in the Legend, and the Talmud, and the Alcoran, then that this universall frame is without a minde. And therefore God never wrought miracle, to convince Atheisme, because his ordinary works convince it. It is true, that a little philosophy inclineth man's minde to Atheisme; but depth in philosophy bringeth men's mindes about to religion. For while the minde of man looketh upon second causes scattered, it may sometimes rest in them, and goe no further: but when it beholdeth the chaine of them, confederate and linked together, it must needs flie to Providence and Deitie." (Francis Bacon, *Of Atheisme,* in *Essays,* Collector's Edition, The

Easton Press, 52).

Isaiah revealed the circumstances under which he made the observations of verse 40 in

Verse 41 - "These things said Esaias, when he saw his glory and spoke of him."

ταῦτα εἶπεν Ἠσαΐας, ὅτι εἶδεν τὴν δόξαν αὐτοῦ, καὶ ἐλάλησεν περὶ αὐτοῦ.

ταῦτα (acc.pl.neut.of *οὗτος*, direct object of *εἶπεν*) 93.
εἶπεν (3d.per.sing.aor.act.ind.of *εἶπον*, constative) 155.
Ἠσαΐας (nom.sing.masc.of *Ἠσαΐας*, subject of *εἶπεν*, *εἶδεν* and *ἐλάλησεν*) 255.
ὅτι (causal conjunction) 211.
εἶδεν (3d.per.sing.aor.act.ind.of *ὁράω*, constative) 144.
τὴν (acc.sing.fem.of the article in agreement with *δόξαν*) 9.
δόξαν (acc.sing.fem.of *δόξα*, direct object of *εἶδεν*) 361.
αὐτοῦ (gen.sing.masc.of *αὐτός*, possession) 16.
καὶ (adjunctive conjunction joining verbs) 14.
ἐλάλησεν (3d.per.sing.aor.act.ind.of *λαλέω*, constative) 815.
περὶ (preposition with the genitive of reference) 173.
αὐτοῦ (gen.sing.masc.of *αὐτός*, reference) 16.

Translation - "These things Isaiah said, because he saw His glory and spoke about Him."

Comment: *ὅτι* is causal. Isaiah saw God's glory. Read his description of the experience in Isa.6:1-13. He wrote the passage under discussion (Isa.6:9,10) in obedience to God's explicit direction. Hence the message came not from the prophet's unenlightened brain and his uninspired and unclean lips. It came straight from the throne of God. The majesty of the sight was so great that Isaiah's only comment was "Woe is me" and that followed by his confession of uncleanness. He added that he was no different than all of mankind.

The argument over Calvinism and Arminianism would suddenly cease if the theologians on both sides of the dispute could glimpse for only a moment what Isaiah saw. The wonder is not that God should rescue some from the vicious circle and transplant them into the glorious circle, while leaving others to their own deliberately hateful and self-chosen and unregenerate designs. The wonder is that God should save any of us. This is hard theology, but with our basic assumption that the Word of God is His true revelation and hence the only true source of our theology, we are stuck with it. The alternative is to substitute human reason which leads in one direction to Gnosticism or in the other direction to Agnosticism with its disavowal of the possibility of any knowledge. Calvinists do not understand these plain statements of scripture any better than Arminians. But they are not afraid to believe and teach what they do not understand. Let us all remember Jesus' advice in John 12:35. The only way to come to understand what we do not understand is to accept by faith what we do understand. The promise that we will be *υἱοὶ φωτός* - "enlightened sons" is a promise to a Christian who wishes to become a mature child of God after he is saved. The Christian must grow up (2 Pet.3:18) if he wishes to understand God (Mt.5:8). None of us have arrived but we have a glorious eternity in which to learn (1 Cor.13:9-13).

Verse 42 - "Nevertheless among the chief rulers also many believed on him; but because of the Pharisees they did not confess him, lest they should be put out of the synagogue."

ὅμως μέντοι καὶ ἐκ τῶν ἀρχόντων πολλοὶ ἐπίστευσαν εἰς αὐτόν, ἀλλὰ διὰ τοὺς Φαρισαίους οὐχ ὡμολόγουν ἵνα μὴ ἀποσυνάγωγοι γένωνται.

#2710 *ὅμως* (adversative particle).

and even - 1 Cor.14:7.
though it be but - Gal.3:15.
nevertheless - John 12:42.

Meaning: an adversative particle with *μέντοι* in John 12:42; with a participle in 1 Cor.14:7; Gal.3:15 to accent the concessive force of the passage.

μέντοι (particle of affirmation) 2013.
καὶ (ascensive conjunction) 14.
ἐκ (preposition with the partitive genitive) 19.
τῶν (gen.pl.masc.of the article in agreement with *ἀρχόντων*) 9.
ἀρχόντων (gen.pl.masc.of *ἄρχων*, partitive) 816.
πολλοὶ (nom.pl.masc.of *πολύς*, subject of *ἐπίστευσαν*) 228.
ἐπίστευσαν (3d.per.pl.aor.act.ind.of *πιστεύω*, constative) 734.
εἰς (preposition with the accusative of general reference/cause) 140.
αὐτόν (acc.sing.masc.of *αὐτός*, general reference/cause) 16.
ἀλλὰ (adverative conjunction) 342.
διὰ (preposition with the accusative of cause) 118.
τοὺς (acc.pl.masc.of the article in agreement with *Φαρισαίους*) 9.
Φαρισαίους (acc.pl.masc.of *Φαρισαῖος*, cause) 276.
οὐχ (summary negative conjunction with the indicative) 130.
ὡμολόγουν (3d.per.pl.imp.act.ind.of *ὁμολογέω*, progressive duration) 688.
ἵνα (conjunction with the subjunctive, negative purpose) 114.
μὴ (qualified negative conjunction with the subjunctive, negative purpose) 87.
ἀποσυνάγωγοι (nom.pl.masc.of *ἀποσυνάγωγος*, predicate nominative) 2401.
γένωνται (3d.per.pl.2d.aor.subj.of *γίνομαι*, negative purpose) 113.

Translation - "Nevertheless in fact even many of the public officials began to believe on Him, but, because of the Pharisees they were not confessing Him, lest they be expelled from the synagogue."

Comment: *ὅμως* is strengthened here, both by the affirmative *μέντοι* and ascensive *καὶ*. *εἰς* with the accusative when associated in the text with faith in

Christ is an accusative of general reference expressing causation. To believe εἰς τὸν Ἰησοῦν is to believe "in reference to Jesus," and the reason we believe *about, in reference to* Him is *because* of Him. The text does not say that these believers did not confess Jesus as Saviour at all, but they did not continue to confess Him to the point that their confession attracted the animosity of the Pharisees who would have cast them out of the synagogue. That this would have been no great loss is clear from

Verse 43 - "For they loved the praise of men more than the praise of God."

ἠγάπησαν γὰρ τὴν δόξαν τῶν ἀνθρώπων μᾶλλον ἤπερ τὴν δόξαν τοῦ θεοῦ.

ἠγάπησαν (3d.per.pl.aor.act.ind.of ἀγαπάω, constative) 540.
γὰρ (causal conjunction) 105.
τὴν (acc.sing.fem.of the article in agreement with δόξαν) 9.
δόξαν (acc.sing.fem.of δόξα, direct object of ἠγάπησαν) 361.
τῶν (gen.pl.masc.of the article in agreement with ἀνθρώπων) 9.
ἀνθρώπων (gen.pl.masc.of ἄνθρωπος, description) 341.
μᾶλλον (comparative adverb) 619.

#2711 ἤπερ (intensive disjunctive particle).

than - John 12:43.

Meaning: The comparative of ἤ (#465). With μᾶλλον - John 12:43.
τὴν (acc.sing.fem.of the article in agreement with δόξαν) 9.
δόξαν (acc.sing.fem.of δόξα, direct object of ἠγάπησαν) 361.
τοῦ (gen.sing.masc.of the article in agreement with θεοῦ) 9.
θεοῦ (gen.sing.masc.of θεός, description) 124.

Translation - "Because they loved the praise of men more than the praise of God."

Comment: γὰρ is causal. John is explaining why the new believers on Jesus were not more active and vocal in His support. If they had understood what He added in verse 44, they might have been more willing to be identified with Him. No one in Jerusalem would be cast out of the synagogue if he identified himself with God. Indeed faith in God was prerequisite for participation in any of the temple services and in the life of the nation itself. The mistake, widely held, was that one could honor God without honoring His Son, Jesus. Or, to put it the other way, the only way to honor God was to receive and honor His Son, Jesus. This is the thought of

Verse 44 - "Jesus cried and said, He that believeth on me, believeth not on me, but on Him that sent me."

Ἰησοῦς δὲ ἔκραξεν καὶ εἶπεν, Ὁ πιστεύων εἰς ἐμὲ οὐ πιστεύει εἰς ἐμὲ ἀλλὰ εἰς τὸν πέμψαντά με,

Ἰησοῦς (nom.sing.masc.of Ἰησοῦς, subject of ἔκραξεν and εἶπεν) 3.
δὲ (adversative conjunction) 11.
ἔκραξεν (3d.per.sing.imp.act.ind.of κράζω, inceptive) 765.
καὶ (adjunctive conjunction joining verbs) 14.
εἶπεν (3d.per.sing.aor.act.ind.of εἶπον, constative) 155.
Ὁ (nom.sing.masc.of the article in agreement with πιστεύων) 9.
πιστεύων (pres.act.part.nom.sing.masc.of πιστεύω, substantival, subject of πιστεύει) 734.
εἰς (preposition with the accusative of general reference/cause) 140.
ἐμὲ (acc.sing.masc.of ἐμός, general reference/cause) 1267.
οὐ (summmary negative conjunction with the indicative) 130.
πιστεύει (3d.per.sing.pres.act.ind.of πιστεύω, static) 734.
εἰς (preposition with the accusative of general reference/cause) 140.
ἐμὲ (acc.sing.masc.of ἐμός, general referece/cause) 1267.
ἀλλὰ (alternative conjunction) 342.
εἰς (preposition with the accusative of general reference) 140.
τὸν (acc.sing.masc.of the article in agreement with πέμψαντά) 9.
πέμψαντά (aor.act.part.acc.sing.masc.of πέμπω, substantival, general reference) 169.
με (acc.sing.masc.of ἐγώ, direct object of πέμψαντά) 123.

Translation - "And Jesus began to cry out and said, 'The one who believes on me is not believing on me, but upon the One who has sent me.' "

Comment: Thus Jesus identified Himself with God the Father as He had done previously, and thus He pointed out the inconsistency of those who professed to worship God but rejected God's Son Whom He had sent. Put in the opposite form He meant that whoever rejected Him rejected the God of Israel, whom the rulers of the synagogue professed to serve. This being true those who had believed on Him but refused to say so openly for fear of retribution from the Pharisees were making a grave error.

Verse 45 - "And he that seeth me seeth him that sent me."

καὶ ὁ θεωρῶν ἐμὲ θεωρεῖ τὸν πέμψαντά με.

καὶ (continuative conjunction) 14.
ὁ (nom.sing.masc.of the article in agreement with θεωρῶν) 9.
θεωρῶν (pres.act.part.nom.sing.masc.of θεωρέω, substantival, subject of θεωρεῖ) 1667.
ἐμὲ (acc.sing.masc.of ἐμός, direct object of θεωρῶν) 1267.
θεωρεῖ (3d.per.sing.pres.act.ind.of θεωρέω, static) 1667.
τὸν (acc.sing.masc.of the article in agreement with πέμψαντά) 9.
πέμψαντά (aor.act.part.acc.sing.masc.of πέμπω substantival, direct object of θεωρεῖ) 169.
με (acc.sing.masc.of ἐγώ, direct object of πέμψαντά) 123.

Translation - "And the one who sees me sees the one who sent me."

Comment: A repetition of the thought of verse 44. θεωρέω is the sense of a personal relationship.

Verse 46 - "I am come a light into the world that whosoever believeth on me should not abide in darkness."

ἐγὼ φῶς εἰς τὸν κόσμον ἐλήλυθα, ἵνα πᾶς ὁ πιστεύων εἰς ἐμὲ ἐν τῇ σκοτίᾳ μὴ μείνῃ.

ἐγὼ (nom.sing.masc.of *ἐγώ*, subject of *ἐλήλυθα*) 123.
φῶς (nom.sing.neut.of *φῶς*, predicate nominative) 379.
εἰς (preposition with the accusative of extent) 140.
τὸν (acc.sing.masc.of the article in agreement with *κόσμον*) 9.
κόσμον (acc.sing.masc.of *κόσμος*, extent) 360.
ἐλήλυθα (1st.per.sing.perf.mid.ind.of *ἔρχομαι*, intensive) 146.
ἵνα (conjunction with the subjunctive in a negative purpose clause) 114.
πᾶς (nom.sing.masc.of *πᾶς*, in agreement with *πιστεύων*) 67.
ὁ (nom.sing.masc.of the article in agreement with *πιστεύων*) 9.
πιστεύων (pres.act.part.nom.sing.masc.of *πιστεύω*, substantival, subject of *μείνῃ*) 734.
εἰς (preposition with the accusative of general reference/cause) 140.
ἐμὲ (acc.sing.masc.of *ἐμός*, general reference/cause) 1267.
ἐν (preposition with the locative of sphere) 80.
τῇ (loc.sing.fem.of the article in agreement with *σκοτίᾳ*) 9.
σκοτίᾳ (loc.sing.fem.of *σκοτία*, sphere) 378.
μὴ (qualified negative conjunction with the subjunctive) 87.
μείνῃ (3d.per.sing.1st.aor.act.subj.of *μένω*, negative purpose) 864.

Translation - "I am a light, come into the world in order that no one who believes on me will remain in the dark."

Comment: Since Jesus has come into the world as the Light of the World (John 8:12) the vicious circle of darkness that we discussed (1 John 2:11 and John 12:35) is now broken and there is a way of escape. Depravity produces hatred, which produces the walk in the dark with the ever deepening darkness of ignorance and its final horrible fruitage - damnation. How does one escape the walk in the sphere of darkness? By believing upon Christ (John 12:46). But this introduction to the sphere of light is only by divine enablement (John 6:44).

Verse 47 - "And if any man hear my words and believe not, I judge him not: for I came not to judge the world but to save the world."

καὶ ἐάν τίς μου ἀκούσῃ τῶν ῥημάτων καὶ μὴ φυλάξῃ, ἐγὼ οὐ κρίνω αὐτόν, οὐ γὰρ ἦλθον ἵνα κρίνω τὸν κόσμον ἀλλ' ἵνα σώσω τὸν κόσμον.

καὶ (continuative conjunction) 14.
ἐάν (conditional particle in a third-class condition) 363.
τίς (nom.sing.masc.of *τις*, indefinite pronoun, subject of *ἀκούσῃ* and *φυλάξῃ*) 486.
μου (gen.sing.masc.of *ἐγώ*, possession) 123.

ἀκούσῃ (3d.per.sing.aor.act.subj.of ἀκούω, third-class condition) 148.
τῶν (gen.pl.neut.of the article in agreement with ῥημάτων) 9.
ῥμάτων (gen.pl.neut.of ῥῆμα, objective genitive) 343.
καὶ (adversative conjunction) 14.
μὴ (qualified negative conjunction with the subjunctive) 87.
φυλάξῃ (3d.per.sing.1st.aor.act.subj.of φυλάσσω, third-class condition) 1301.
ἐγὼ (nom.sing.masc.of ἐγώ, subject of κρίνω) 123.
οὐ (summary negative conjunction with the indicative) 130.
κρίνω (1st.per.sing.pres.act.ind.of κρίνω, futuristic) 531.
αὐτόν (acc.sing.masc.of αὐτός, direct object of κρίνω) 16.
οὐ (summary negative conjunction with the indicative) 130.
γὰρ (causal conjunction) 105.
ἦλθον (1st.per.sing.aor.act.ind.of ἔρχομαι, culminative) 146.
ἵνα (conjunction with the subjunctive, purpose) 114.
κρίνω (1st.per.sing.pres.act.subj.of κρίνω, purpose) 531.
τὸν (acc.sing.masc.of the article in agreement with κόσμον) 9.
κόσμον (acc.sing.masc.of κόσμος, direct object of κρίνω) 360.
ἀλλ' (alternative conjuncton) 342.
ἵνα (conjunction with the subjunctive, purpose) 114.
σώσω (1st.per.sing.aor.act.subj.of σώζω, purpose) 109.
τὸν (acc.sing.masc.of the article in agreement with κόσμον) 9.
κόσμον (acc.sing.masc.of κόσμον direct object of σώσω) 360.

Translation - "And if anyone hears my words, but does not keep them, I am not going to judge him, because I did not come to judge the world, but to save the world."

Comment: ἐάν with a double protasis in ἀκούσῃ and φυλᾶξῃ with the present indicative in the apodosis. Nothing is said about whether or not any would hear His words and refuse to keep them, but if such did in fact transpire, the conclusion is that Jesus is not going to judge him. *Cf.*#1301 for φυλάσσω in this sense. The rich young ruler did keep God's word - Mt.19:20; Lk.18:21; Mk.10:20. Israel as a nation did not (Acts 7;13). Paul did (Acts 21:24). The Gentiles sometimes do (Rom.2:26). The Judaizers did not (Gal.6:13). Paul admonishes Timothy to do so (2 Tim.1:14; 1 Tim.5:21). Some, who heard Jesus did; others did not (John 12:47. Why does Jesus not judge those who reject His word? Because judgment at His first coming is dispensationally out of place. Jesus will indeed judge them at His second coming. Jesus did not say that He never would judge them. Indeed He will (2 Thess.1:7-10). His function in His first coming was not judgment but salvation. Thus when He could have called for twelve legions of avenging angels as He hung upon the cross, He prayed, "Father, forgive them. . . " (Lk.23:34).

Jesus' real meaning in this otherwise cryptic statement is clarified in

Verse 48 - "He that rejecteth me, and receiveth not my words, hath one that judgeth him: the word that I have spoken, the same shall judge him in the last day."

ὁ ἀθετῶν ἐμὲ καὶ μὴ λαμβάνων τὰ ῥήματά μου ἔχει τὸν κρίνοντα αὐτόν. ὁ λόγος ὃν ἐλάλησα ἐκεῖνος κρινεῖ αὐτὸν ἐν τῇ ἐσχάτῃ ἡμέρᾳ.

ὁ (nom.sing.masc.of the article in agreement with *ἀθετῶν*) 9.
ἀθετῶν (pres.act.part.nom.sing.masc.of *ἀθετέω*, substantival, subject of *ἔχει*) 2164.
ἐμὲ (acc.sing.masc.of *ἐμός*, direct object of *ἀθετῶν*) 1267.
καὶ (adjunctive conjunction joining participles) 14.
μὴ (qualified negative conjunction with the participle) 87.
λαμβάνων (pres.act.part.nom.sing.masc.of *λαμβάνω*, substantival, subject of *ἔχει*) 533.
τὰ (acc.pl.neut.of the article in agreement with *ῥήματά*) 9.
ῥήματά (acc.pl.neut.of *ῥῆμα*, direct object of *λαμβάνων*) 343.
μου (gen.sing.masc.of *ἐγώ*, possession) 123.
ἔχει (3d.per.sing.pres.act.ind.of *ἔχω*, static) 82.
τὸν (acc.sing.masc.of the article, in agreement with *κρίνοντα*) 9.
κρίνοντα (acc.sing.masc.of *κρίνω*, substantival, direct object of *ἔχει*) 531.
αὐτόν (acc.sing.masc.of *αὐτός*, direct object of *κρίνοντα*) 16.
ὁ (nom.sing.masc.of the article in agreement with *λόγος*) 9.
λόγος (nom.sing.masc.of *λόγος*, subject of *κρινεῖ*) 510.
ὃν (acc.sing.masc.of *ὅς*, direct object of *ἐλάλησα*) 65.
ἐλάλησα (1st.per.sing.aor.act.ind.of *λαλέω*, culminative) 815.
ἐκεῖνος (nom.sing.masc.of *ἐκεῖνος*, in agreement with *λόγος*) 246.
κρινεῖ (3d.per.sing.fut.act.ind.of *κρίνω*, predictive) 531.
αὐτὸν (acc.sing.masc.of *αὐτός*, direct object of *κρινεῖ*) 16.
ἐν (preposition with the locative of time point) 80.
τῇ (loc.sing.fem.of the article in agreement with *ἡμέρᾳ*) 9.
ἐσχάτῃ (loc.sing.fem.of *ἔσχατος*, in agreement with *ἡμέρᾳ*) 496.
ἡμέρᾳ (loc.sing.fem.of *ἡμέρα*, time point) 135.

Translation - "The one who rejects me and does not receive my words has one who is judging him. That word which I have spoken will judge him on the last day."

Comment: We have a good study in substantival participles here. Two participial subjects of *ἔχει* have a participial direct object of the verb. He who rejects Christ also rejects His message. Modernists have denied to Jesus His words, but they have tried to capture Him for their institutions in order to exploit His name and personality. To accept Jesus as a great and good man who was mistaken about what He said, constitutes a collision of ideas that could occur only in the unregenerate mind. Those who do this have their own judge. Note the present tense of *κρίνοντα*. Christ's word is eternal as He is eternal and therefore stands in constant judgment against those who reject Him and His word. Heb.13:8; Mt.24:35. *Cf.*#2164 for *ἀθετέω* in all its other uses. Some did - Mk.7:9; Lk.7:30; Jude 8. Paul did not - Gal.2:21. Note also 1 Cor.1:19. God rejects and destroys man's wisdom which has seen fit to reject God's word. He who rejects Christ and His word is destined to see his own philosophic house come crashing down in flames at the last day. Eternal truth is constantly sitting in judgment upon human error. ὁ λόγος ὃν ἐλάλυσα - Christ's spoken record during His incarnation stands as a record upon the books of heaven. Note the deictic ἐκεῖνος for emphasis. The locative of time point in τῇ ἐσχάτῃ ἡμέρᾳ makes the judgment day a definite historic event in the future, as definite as the reader's next birthday anniversary or Independence Day. Judgment for the rejector rides potentially upon his head continuously. Kinetically it will fall on the last day.

What Jesus has just said in this passage is only the raving of a maniacal paranoid, unless it is coming from the lips of the incarnate Son of God. The language of verse 48 in the mouth of Alexander the Great, Napoleon or any other "great man" would be ridiculous. The thing that dignifies it here is the person of Jesus Christ. Jesus recognized this fact and closes His remarks by identifying His words with those of His Father.

Verse 49 - "For I have not spoken of myself; but the Father which sent me, he gave me a commandment, what I should say and what I should speak."

ὅτι ἐγὼ ἐξ ἐμαυτοῦ οὐκ ἐλάλησα, ἀλλ' ὁ πέμψας με πατὴρ αὐτός μοι ἐντολὴν δέδωκεν τί εἴπω καὶ τί λαλήσω.

ὅτι (causal conjunction) 211.
ἐγὼ (nom.sing.masc.of ἐγώ, subject of ἐλάλησα) 123.
ἐξ (preposition with the ablative of source) 19.
ἐμαυτοῦ (abl.sing.masc.of ἐμαυτός, source) 723.
οὐκ (summary negative conjunction with the indicative) 130.
ἐλάλησα (1st.per.sing.aor.act.ind.of λαλέω, culminative) 815.
ἀλλ' (alternative conjunction) 342.
ὁ (nom.sing.masc.of the article in agreement with πέμψας) 9.
πέμψας (aor.act.part.nom.sing.masc.of πέμπω, substantival, subject of δέδωκεν) 169.
με (acc.sing.masc.of ἐγώ, direct object of πέμψας) 123.
πατὴρ (nom.sing.masc.of πατήρ, apposition) 238.
αὐτός (nom.sing.masc.of αὐτός, intensive) 16.
μοι (dat.sing.masc.of ἐγώ, indirect object of δέδωκεν) 123.
ἐντολὴν (acc.sing.fem.of ἐντολή, direct object of δέδωκεν) 472.
δέδωκεν (3d.per.sing.perf.act.ind.of δίδωμι, intensive) 362.
τί (acc.sing.neut.of τίς, general reference) 281.
εἴπω (1st.per.sing.aor.subj.of εἶπον, indirect question) 155.
καὶ (adjunctive conjunction joining pronouns) 14.
τί (acc.sing.neut.of τίς, general reference) 281.
λαλήσω (1st.per.sing.aor.act.subj.of λαλέω, indirect question) 815.

Translation - "Because I have not spoken from my own resources, but the One Who sent me - the Father Himself has given to me a commandment with reference to what I should say and what I should speak."

Comment: Why should Jesus' words have such eternal impact upon history? The ὅτι clause is causal - "Because He is not the source of them. The Father has sent the Son into the world with a specific commandment, not only the philosophy of which was dictated, but even the precise phraseology. There is collaboration between the Father and the Son as to what Jesus should say. They share mutual responsibility for it. It is established in the mouth of two witnesses. After a statement like that, if God the Father ever had cause to repudiate Jesus, it was now, after Jesus had charged God with responsibility for what He (Jesus) had said during the past three years. God's agreement with and ratification of all that Jesus said is demonstrated when He raised Him from the dead (Heb.5:5,6; Ps.2:7; 110:1; Eph.1:19-23; Rom.1:4).

Verse 50 - "And I know that his commandment is life everlasting: whatsoever I speak therefore, even as the Father said unto me, so I speak."

καὶ οἶδα ὅτι ἡ ἐντολὴ αὐτοῦ ζωὴ αἰώνιός ἐστιν. ἃ οὖν ἐγὼ λαλῶ, καθὼς εἴρηκέν μοι ὁ πατήρ, οὕτως λαλῶ.

καὶ (continuative conjunction) 14.
οἶδα (1st.per.sing.pres.act.ind.of ὁράω, aoristic) 144.
ὅτι (conjunction introducing an object clause in indirect discourse) 211.
ἡ (nom.sing.fem.of the article in agreement with ἐντολὴ) 9.
ἐντολὴ (nom.sing.fem.of ἐντολή, subject of ἐστιν) 472.
αὐτοῦ (gen.sing.masc.of αὐτός, possession) 16.
ζωὴ (nom.sing.fem.of ζωή, predicate nominative) 668.
αἰώνιός (nom.sing.fem.of αἰώνιος, in agreement with ζωὴ) 1255.
ἐστιν (3d.per.sing.pres.ind.of εἰμί, aoristic) 86.
ἃ (acc.pl.neut.of ὅς, direct object of λαλῶ) 65.
οὖν (inferential conjunction) 68.
ἐγὼ (nom.sing.masc.of ἐγώ, subject of λαλῶ) 123.
λαλῶ (1st.per.sing.pres.act.ind.of λαλέω, customary) 815.
καθὼς (adverbial) 1348.
εἴρηκέν (3d.per.sing.perf.act.ind.of ῥέω, consummative) 116.
μοι (dat.sing.masc.of ἐγώ, indirect object of εἴρηκέν) 123.
ὁ (nom.sing.masc.of the article in agreement with πατήρ) 9.
πατήρ (nom.sing.masc.of πατήρ, subject of εἴρηκέν) 238.
οὕτως (demonstrative adverb) 74.
λαλῶ (1st.per.sing.pres.act.ind.of λαλέω, customary) 815.

Translation - "And I know that His commandment means eternal life. So whatever I say, I say only as the Father has spoken it to me."

Comment: Here is a strong statement by Jesus in support of plenary verbal divine inspiration. He begins by saying that He knows that the Father's words mean eternal life to Him who accepts them. They are, therefore, most important. Jesus is therefore careful to transmit them accurately. *ἃ οὖν ἐγὼ λαλῶ* - that is what He is speaking. How is He speaking them? *καθὼς . . . οὕτως* - "just as . . . even so. . ." *Cf.*#'s 1348 and 74 for a list of passages where the two words occur together. Note #116 as coming from *ῥέω*, and used overwhelmingly in the New Testament to denote "God breathing." Exactly as the Father had spoken to Jesus, just so exactly was He speaking.

Discourse Concerning the Destruction of Jerusalem

And the End of the Age

(Matthew 24:1 - 25:46; Mark 13:1-37; Luke 21:5-38)

Mark 13:1 - "And as he went out of the temple, one of his disciples saith unto him, Master, see what manner of stones and what buildings are here!"

Καὶ ἐκπορευομένου αὐτοῦ ἐκ τοῦ ἱεροῦ λέγει αὐτῷ εἷς (ἐκ) τῶν μαθητῶν αὐτοῦ, Διδάσκαλε, ἴδε ποταποὶ λίθοι καὶ ποταπαὶ οἰκοδομαί.

Καὶ (continuative conjunction) 14.
ἐκπορευομένου (pres.mid.part.gen.sing.masc.of ἐκπορεύομαι, genitive absolute) 270.
αὐτοῦ (gen.sing.masc.of αὐτός, genitive absolute) 16.
ἐκ (preposition with the ablative of separation) 19
τοῦ (abl.sing.neut.of the article in agreement with ἱεροῦ) 9.
ἱεροῦ (abl.sing.neut.of ἱερόν, separation) 346.
λέγει (3d.per.sing.pres.act.ind.of λέγω, historical) 66.
αὐτῷ (dat.sing.masc.of αὐτός, indirect object of λέγει) 16.
εἷς (nom.sing.masc.of εἷς, subject of λέγει) 469.
τῶν (gen.pl.masc.of the article in agreement with μαθητῶν) 9.
μαθητῶν (gen.pl.masc.of μαθητής, partitive) 421.
αὐτοῦ (gen.sing.masc.of αὐτός, relationship) 16.
Διδάσκαλε (voc.sing.masc.of διδάσκαλος, address) 742.
ἴδε (2d.per.sing.aor.act.impv.of ὁράω, entreaty) 144.
ποταποὶ (nom.pl.masc.of ποταπός, in agreement with λίθοι) 759.
λίθοι (nom.pl.masc.of λίθος, subject of verb understood) 290.
καὶ (adjunctive conjunction joining nouns) 14.
ποταπαὶ (nom.pl.fem.of ποταπός, in agreement with λἰκοδομαί) 759.
οἰκοδομαί (nom.pl.fem.of οἰκοδομή, subject of verb understood) 1481.

Translation - "And as He was leaving the temple court, one of His disciples said to Him, 'Teacher, look! What stones and buildings!"

Comment: The genitive absolute in the present tense indicates simultaneity with the action of λέγει, which Mark put in the historical present. One of His disciples called His attention to the wonder of the quarried stones and the architectural splendor of the buildings. It was a demonstration of Chamber of Commerce pride in the Establishment that forgot, for the moment, that within there was "nothing but dead men's bones" and moral, philosophical and spiritual corruption. The disciple, who was manifesting a bit of nationalistic pride knew that, for all of the magnificance of the temple buildings, the leaders were soon to reject the Stone which was to become the Head of the Corner.

Therefore admiration for the stones, when the leaders were about to murder the Cornerstone was ill advised. *Cf.* Mt.24:1; Lk.21:5.

Verse 2 - "And Jesus answering said unto him, Seest thou these great buildings? There shall not be left one stone upon another, that shall not be thrown down."

καὶ ὁ Ἰησοῦς εἶπεν αὐτῷ, Βλέπεις ταύτας τὰς μεγάλας οἰκοδομάς; οὐ μὴ ἀφεθῇ ὧδε λίθος ἐπὶ λίθον ὃς οὐ μὴ καταλυθῇ.

καὶ (adversative conjunction) 14.
ὁ (nom.sing.masc.of the article in agreement with Ἰησοῦς) 9.
Ἰησοῦς (nom.sing.masc.of Ἰησοῦς, subject of *εἶπεν*) 3.
αὐτῷ (dat.sing.masc.of *αὐτός*, indirect object of *εἶπεν*) 16.
βλέπεις (2d.per.sing.pres.act.ind.of *βλέπω*, direct question) 499.
ταύτας (acc.pl.fem.of *οὗτος*, in agreement with *οἰκοδομάς*) 93.
τὰς (acc.pl.fem.of the article in agreement with *οἰκοδομάς*) 9.
μεγάλας (acc.pl.fem.of *μέγας*, in agreement with *οἰκοδομάς*) 184.
οἰκοδομάς (acc.pl.fem.of *οἰκοδομή*, direct object of *βλέπεις*) 1481.
οὐ (summary negative conjunction, with *μὴ* and the subjunctive, emphatic negation) 130.
μὴ (qualified negative conjunction with *οὐ* and the subjunctive, emphatic negation) 87.
ἀφεθῇ (3d.per.sing.1st.aor.pass.subj.of *ἀφίημι*, emphatic negation) 319.
ὧδε (adverb of place) 766.
λίθος (nom.sing.masc.of *λίθος*, subject of *ἀφεθῇ*) 290.
ἐπὶ (preposition with the accusative of extent) 47.
λίθον (acc.sing.masc.of *λίθος*, extent) 290.
ὃς (nom.sing.masc.of *ὅς*, relative pronoun, subject of *καταλυθῇ*) 65.
οὐ (summary negative conjunction with *μὴ* and the subjunctive, emphatic negation) 130.
μὴ (qualified negative conjunction with *οὐ* and the subjunctive, emphatic negation) 87.
καταλυθῇ (3d.per.sing.1st.aor.pass.subj.of *καταλύω*, emphatic negation) 463.

Translation - "But Jesus said to him, 'You see these great buildings don't you? There will be left here not one stone upon another, which will not be torn down."

Comment: *καὶ* is adversative. Instead of joining with His disciple in his admiration for the temple buildings, Jesus abruptly prophesied their total destruction. The rhetorical question seems to imply, "You had better look at them while you can." The double negatives with the subjunctives is emphatic negation. *Cf.*Heb.13:5; Mt.5:18; Mk.13:30; Lk.9:27. *Cf.* also Lk.18:7 and Rev.15:4 where *οὐ μὴ* and the subjunctive is used in a rhetorical question (Burton, *Moods and Tenses*, 78). Not a single stone left upon a single stone. This is wholesale disintegration. *Cf.* Lk.19:41-44; Mt.24:2; Lk.21:6.

Verse 3 - "And as He sat upon the Mount of Olives over against the temple, Peter and James, and John and Andrew asked him privately. . . "

Καὶ καθημένου αὐτοῦ εἰς τὸ Ὄρος τῶν Ἐλαιῶν κατέναντι τοῦ ἱεροῦ ἐπηρώτα αὐτὸν κατ' ἰδίαν Πέτρος καὶ Ἰάκωβος καὶ Ἰωάννης καὶ Ἀνδρέας,

Καὶ (continuative conjunction) 14.
καθημένου (pres.mid.part.gen.sing.masc.of κάθημαι, genitive absolute) 377.
αὐτοῦ (gen.sing.masc.of αὐτός, genitive absolute) 16.
εἰς (preposition with the accusative, where ἐν and the locative would be expected) 140.
τὸ (acc.sing.neut.of the article in agreement with Ὄρος) 9.
Ὄρος (acc.sing.neut.of ὄρος, place where) 357.
τῶν (gen.pl.fem.of the article in agreement with Ἐλαιῶν) 9.
Ἐλαιῶν (gen.pl.fem.of ἐλαία, description) 1341.
κατέναντι (improper preposition with the genitive of place description) 1342.
τοῦ (gen.sing.neut.of the article in agreement with ἱεροῦ) 9.
ἱεροῦ (gen.sing.neut.of ἱερόν, place description) 346.
ἐπηρώτα (3d.per.sing.imp.act.ind.of ἐπερωτάω, inceptive) 973.
αὐτὸν (acc.sing.masc.of αὐτός, direct object of ἐπηρώτα) 16.
κατ' (preposition with the accusative, adverbial) 98.
ἰδίαν (acc.sing.masc.of ἴδιος, adverbial) 778.
Πέτρος (nom.sing.masc.of Πέτρος, subject of ἐπηρώτα) 387.
καὶ (adjunctive conjunction joining nouns) 14.
Ἰάκωβος (nom.sing.masc.of Ἰάκωβος, subject of ἐπηρώτα) 397.
καὶ (adjunctive conjunction joining nouns) 14.
Ἰωάννης (nom.sing.masc.of Ἰωάννης, subject of ἐπηρώτα) 399.
καὶ (adjunctive conjunction joining nouns) 14.
Ἀνδρέας (nom.sing.masc.of Ἀνδρέας, subject of ἐπηρώτα) 388.

Translation - "And while He was seated upon the Mount of Olives across the way from the temple, Peter, James, John and Andrew, began privately to ask Him, . . . "

Comment: We have εἰς with the accusative here in its original static use, where in κοινή times we would expect, either ἐν with the locative, or ἐπί with the accusative. It is difficult to tell whether the disciples came to Jesus, as a group, but apart from the others to ask their questions, or whether each came to Him alone and one at a time. The former idea is favored due to the plural ἡμῖν in verse 4. Their three questions motivated the long discourse, the full exposition of which we have given from Matthew's account. *Cf.* Mt.24:3; Lk.21:7.

Verse 4 - "Tell us, when shall these things be? And what shall be the sign when all these things shall be fulfilled?"

Εἰπὸν ἡμῖν πότε ταῦτα ἔσται, καὶ τί τὸ σημεῖον ὅταν μέλλῃ ταῦτα συντελεῖσθαι πάντα.

Εἰπὸν (2d.per.sing.aor.act.impv.of εἶπον, entreaty) 155.

ἡμῖν (dat.pl.masc.of ἐγώ, indirect object of εἶπον) 123.
πότε (temporal interrogative adverb) 1233.
ταῦτα (nom.pl.neut.of οὗτος, subject of ἔσται) 93.
ἔσται (3d.per.sing.fut.ind.of εἰμί, deliberative, in direct question) 86.
καὶ (continuative conjunction) 14.
τί (nom.sing.neut.of τίς, predicate nominative) 281.
τὸ (nom.sing.neut.of the article in agreement with σημεῖον) 9.
σημεῖον (nom.sing.neut.of σημεῖον, subject of ἔσται, understood) 1005.
ὅταν (adverb with the subjunctive in an indefinite temporal clause) 436.
μέλλῃ (3d.per.sing.pres.act.subj.of μέλλω, indefinite temporal clause) 206.
ταῦτα (acc.pl.neut.of οὗτος, general reference) 93.
συντελεῖσθαι (pres.pass.inf.of συντελέω, epexegetical) 1952.
πάντα (acc.pl.neut.of πᾶς, in agreement with ταῦτα) 67.

Translation - "Tell us when these things will be, and what will be the sign when all these things will be fulfilled?"

Comment: ταῦτα refers to Jesus' prediction about the destruction of the temple. The disciples, as reported by Mark, asked when the impendinging destruction of the temple would occur and what sign, if any, would herald the fact that the prophecy was about to be fulfilled. Matthew 24:3 says that they also asked about Messiah's second coming and the end of the age. *Cf.* also Lk.21:7. Jesus begins to answer by warning them against deception.

Verse 5 - "And Jesus answering them began to say, Take heed lest any man deceive you."

ὁ δὲ Ἰησοῦς ἤρξατο λέγειν αὐτοῖς, Βλέπετε μή τις ὑμᾶς πλανήσῃ.

ὁ (nom.sing.masc.of the article in agreement with Ἰησοῦς) 9.
δὲ (continuative conjunction) 11.
Ἰησοῦς (nom.sing.masc.of Ἰησοῦς, subject of ἤρξατο) 3.
λέγειν (pres.act.inf.of λέγω, completes ἤρξατο) 66.
αὐτοῖς (dat.pl.masc.of αὐτός, indirect object of λέγειν) 16.
Βλέπετε (2d.per.pl.pres.act.impv.of βλέπω, command) 499.
μή (qualified negative conjunction with the subjunctive, negative purpose) 87.
τις (nom.sing.masc.of τις, the indefinite pronoun, subject of πλανήσῃ) 486.
ὑμᾶς (acc.pl.masc.of σύ, direct object of πλανήσῃ) 104.
πλανήσῃ (3d.per.sing.aor.act.subj.of πλανάω, negative purpose) 1257.

Translation - "And Jesus began to say to them, 'Beware, lest anyone lead you astray."

Comment: *Cf.* Mt.24:4; Lk.21:8.

Verse 6 - "For many shall come in my name, saying, I am Christ; and shall deceive many."

πολλοὶ ἐλεύσονται ἐπὶ τῷ ὀνόματί μου λέγοντες ὅτι Ἐγώ εἰμι, καὶ πολλοὺς πλανήσουσιν.

πολλοὶ (nom.pl.masc.of πολύς, subject of ἐλεύσονται) 228.
ἐλεύσονται (3d.per.pl.fut.mid.ind.of ἔρχομαι, predictive) 146.
ἐπὶ (preposition with the instrumental, means) 47.
τῷ (instru.sing.neut.of the article in agreement with ὀνόματι) 9.
ὀνόματί (instru.sing.neut.of ὄνομα, means) 108.
μου (gen.sing.masc.of ἐγώ, possession) 123.
λέγοντες (pres.act.part.nom.pl.masc.of λέγω, adverbial, instrumental) 66.
ὅτι (recitative) 211.
Ἐγώ (nom.sing.masc.of ἐγώ, subject of εἰμι) 123.
εἰμι (1st.per.sing.pres.ind.of εἰμί, aoristic) 86.
καὶ (continuative conjunction) 14.
πολλοὺς (acc.pl.masc.of πολύς, direct object of πλανήσουσιν) 228.
πλανήσουσιν (3d.per.pl.fut.act.ind.of πλανάω, predictive) 1257.

Translation - "Many will come in my name, saying, 'I Am.' And they will lead many astray."

Comment: To come ἐπὶ τῷ ὀνόματί μου - "in my name" is to claim the name of Christ as the basis for their plea for acceptance. As they come they will say'Εγώ εἰμι. - "I Am." *Cf.*John 4:26 for the list of verses where this name appears. The name, without the accompanying circumstances which Jesus will go on to list, will only serve to deceive many into believing a false Christ, of whom there will be many, to be the true Messiah. There is no reason why a true Christian, sufficiently informed by what follows should fail to detect the falsity of all such claims. *Cf.* Mt.24:5; Lk.21:8.

The followers of the Watchtower Bible and Tract Society, commonly referred to as "Jehovah's Witnesses" who reject the claim of Jesus to Messiahship and Sonship with God, are compelled to reject the argument that'Εγώ εἰμι, the name by which God identified Himself to Moses at the bush (Exodus 3:14) refers to Jesus the Messiah. Yet in our passage Jesus told His disciples that when the false Messiahs will come to deceive their dupes, they will come ἐπὶ τῷ ὀνόματί μου - "in my name" and that they will be saying'Εγώ εἰμι. Jesus here clearly says that His name is'Εγώ εἰμι.

Verse 7 - "And when ye shall hear of wars and rumors of wars, be ye not troubled: for such things must needs be; but the end is not yet."

ὅταν δὲ ἀκούσητε πολέμους καὶ ἀκοὰς πολέμων, μὴ θροεῖσθε, δεῖ γενέσθαι, ἀλλ' οὔπω τὸ τέλος.

ὅταν (conjunction with the subjunctive introducing an indefinite temporal clause) 436.
δὲ (continuative conjunction) 11.
ἀκούσητε (2d.per.pl.aor.act.subj.of ἀκούω, indefinite temporal clause) 148.
πολέμους (acc.pl.masc.of πόλεμος, general reference) 1483.
καὶ (adjunctive conjunction joining nouns) 14.
ἀκοὰς (acc.pl.fem.of ἀκοή, general reference) 409.
πολέμων (gen.pl.masc.of πολεμος, description) 1483.

μὴ (qualified negative conjunction with the imperative, prohibition) 87.
θροεῖσθε (2d.per.pl.pres.pass.impv.of *θροέω*, prohibition) 1484.
δεῖ (3d.per.sing.pres.ind., imperson) 1207.
γενέσθαι (aor.inf.of *γίνομαι*, completes *δεῖ*) 113.
ἀλλ' (adversative conjunction) 342.
οὔπω (temporal adverb) 1198.
τὸ (nom.sing.neut.of the article in agreement with *τέλος*) 9.
τέλος (nom.sing.neut.of *τέλος*, subject of the verb understood) 881.

Translation - "And when you hear the sound of fighting and reports of wars, stop being alarmed. Such things will happen, but the it is not yet the end."

Comment: The sounds of warfare and rumors of war might reasonably be expected to signal the fast approaching end of the age. But Jesus denies that such will be the case. Such things are characteristic of human history. "Man's day (1 Cor.4:2) is the period of history after man has rejected the Son of God. Wars arise as a result of the frustrations that are always found in the unbalanced personality (James 4:1,2). Wars have characterized every century since the Son of God ascended to heaven and therefore they are not proof, in themselves, that the second coming of Christ is near. Paul had similar advice for the Thessalonians (2 Thess.2:1-3). *Cf.* Mt.24:6; Lk.21:9.

Verse 8 - "For nation shall rise against nation, and kingdom against kingdom; and there shall be earthquakes in divers places, and there shall be famines and troubles: these are the beginnings of sorrows."

ἐγερθήσεται γὰρ ἔθνος ἐπ' ἔθνος καὶ βασιλεία ἐπὶ βασιλείαν, ἔσονται σεισμοὶ κατὰ τόπους, ἔσονται λιμοί, ἀρχὴ ὠδίνων ταῦτα.

ἐγερθήσεται (3d.per.sing.fut.pass.ind.of *ἐγείρω*, predictive) 125.
γὰρ (causal conjunction) 105.
ἔθνος (nom.sing.neut.of *ἔθνος*, subject of *ἐγερθήσεται*) 376.
ἐπ' (preposition with the accusative, hostility) 47.
ἔθνος (acc.sing.neut.of *ἔθνος*, hostility) 376.
καὶ (continuative conjunction) 14.
βασιλεία (nom.sing.fem.of *βασιλεία*, subject of *ἐγερθήσεται*) 253.
ἐπὶ (preposition with the accusative, hostility) 47.
βασιλείαν (acc.sing.fem.of *βασιλεία*, hostility) 253.
ἔσονται (3d.per.pl.fut.ind.of *εἰμί*, predictive) 86.
σεισμοὶ (nom.pl.masc.of *σιεσμός*, subject of *ἔσονται*) 751.
κατὰ (preposition with the accusative, distributive) 98.
τόπους (acc.pl.masc.of *τόπος*, distributive) 1019.
ἔσονται (3d.per.pl.fut.ind.of *εἰμί*, predicitve) 86.
λιμοί (nom.pl.masc.of *λιμός*, subject of *ἔσονται*) 1485.
ἀρχὴ (nom.sing.fem.of *αχή*, predicate nominative) 1285.
ὠδίνων (gen.pl.fem.of *ὠδίν*, description) 1486.
ταῦτα (nom.pl.neut.of *οὗτος*, subject of verb understood) 93.

Translation - "Because nation shall be raised up against nation and kingdom against kingdom. There will be earthquakes in various places. There will be famines. These things are the beginning of the sufferings."

Comment: *Cf.* Mt.24:7; Lk.21:10,11. γὰρ is causal, since it introduces material to explain why those who witness the growing militarism upon earth should not be unduly influenced by it (verse 7). Nation against nation and kingdom against kingdom in blood conflict is the predicted course of events from Calvary to the second coming of our Lord. He pointed forward also to earthquakes here and there and repeated food shortages. Such things herald the birthpangs of a new age.

These predictions are more easily understood by economists who study the economic history of the planet, especially in the western world since the rise of the Industrial Revolution. There were wars before the 18th century, but when the world shifted the productive emphasis from foods and fibers in an agricultural culture to the industrial paradigm, with its factory system, the separation of the worker from his tools, business cycles with their problems of inflation and unemployment, crowded slums of the great cities, with all of the social ills which they produce, and the struggle for raw materials and markets throughout the world, wars have become the order of the day, rather than the exception. Famines occur more frequently as the world population explodes out of control.

Things worse than wars, earthquakes and famines will follow as the age draws to a close. At precisely what point in Mark's account Jesus ceases to speak of world conditions generally throughout the church age and begins to speak specifically of world conditions during the last seven years (Daniel's 70th week - Daniel 9:27; Rev.1:4-22:5) is not clear. At verse 14 we are clearly in the middle of the week, just three and one half years, 42 months or 1260 days (Rev.12:14; 13:5; 12:6) from the second coming. So far in Mark 13:6-8, Jesus has not described anything that is uniquely characteristic of world history during the final seven years. There have always been wars, earthquakes and famines. The persecution of Christians is nothing new either. Following the false peace of the first seal (Rev.6:1-2) we have war in the second seal (Rev.6:3-4) and famine in the third (Rev.6:5-6), before Antichrist appears at the fourth seal (Rev.6:7-8). It seems clear that Rev.6:5-17 is parallel to Mark 13:14-27. Thus we have two differing descriptions of the same period, which is called "the great tribulation", the last half of Daniel's 70th week.

Mark 13:14 is parallel to Matthew 24:15. Jesus' remarks in Mk.13:1-13 apply to world conditions generally, with nothing specific about where we may be on God's clock, just as does the material in Mt.24:1-14. There is no doubt where we are on God's clock from Mk.13:14 to Mk.13:27. These verses describe events during the last three and one half years immediately prior to the second coming of Christ.

Verse 9 - "But take heed to yourselves: for they shall deliver you up to councils; and in the synagogues ye shall be beaten: and ye shall be brought before rulers and kings for my sake, for a testimony against them."

βλέπετε δὲ ὑμεῖς ἑαυτούς, παραδώσουσιν ὑμᾶς εἰς συνέδρια καὶ εἰς συναγωγὰς δαρήσεσθε καὶ ἐπὶ ἡγεμόνων καὶ βασιλέων σταθήσεσθε ἕνεκεν ἐμοῦ εἰς μαρτύριον αὐτοῖς.

βλέπετε (2d.per.pl.pres.act.impv.of βλέπω, command) 499.
δὲ (continuative conjunction) 11.
ὑμεῖς (nom.pl.masc.of σύ, subject of βλέπετε) 104.
ἑαυτούς (acc.pl.masc.of ἑαυτός, direct object of βλέπετε) 288.
παραδώσουσιν (3d.per.pl.fut.act.ind.of παραδίδωμι, predictive) 368.
ὑμᾶς (acc.pl.masc.of σύ, direct object of παραδώσουσιν) 104.
εἰς (preposition with the accusative of extent) 140.
συνέδρια (acc.pl.neut.of συνέδριον, extent) 481.
καὶ (continuative conjunction) 14.
εἰς (preposition with the accusative, static use) 140.
συναγωγὰς (acc.pl.fem.of συναγωγή, static use, place where) 404.
δαρήσεσθε (2d.per.pl.2d.fut.pass.ind.of δέρω, predictive) 1383.
καὶ (continuative conjunction) 14.
ἐπὶ (preposition with the genitive of place description) 47.
ἡγεμόνων (gen.pl.masc.of ἡγεμών, place description) 160.
καὶ (adjunctive conjunction joining nouns) 14.
βασιλέων (gen.pl.masc.of βασιλεύς, place description) 31.
σταθήσεσθε (2d.per.pl.fut.pass.ind.of ἵστημι, predictive) 180.
ἕνεκεν (improper preposition with the genitive) 435.
ἐμοῦ (gen.sing.masc.of ἐμός, reference) 1267.
εἰς (preposition with the accusative, purpose) 140.
μαρτύριον (acc.sing.neut.of μαρτύριον, purpose) 716.
αὐτοῖς (dat.pl.masc.of αὐτός, personal advantage) 16.

Translation - "But watch yourselves! They will betray you to courts and you will be beaten in synagogues, and you will be arraigned before governors and kings for my sake in order to witness to them."

Comment: Betrayed to religious leaders, beaten in synagogues and arraigned before judges - This was the history of the early Christian apostles and disciples. Why? ἕνεκεν ἐμοῦ. For what purpose? As a witness to them. One recalls Paul's great speeches before Felix, Festus and Agrippa. This prophecy finds its fulfillment in the Book of Acts and beyond, as Christians in every age have suffered for the organic union with Jesus Christ. *Cf.* Mt.24:9-10; Lk.21:12. Review my comments on Matthew carefully in the light of what we have just written.

(Note: Since this work has occupied the author's attention for more than forty years, the comments on Matthew were written long before those in regard to the parallel passages in Mark, Luke and John. The reader may find slight differences of opinion between these comments. I have chosen not to change comments written previously unless later research and interpretation revealed gross errors in earlier comments. Since we have no desire to be unreasonably dogmatic, perhaps it is helpful to leave the evidences of the author's evolution in thought across forty years unedited.)

Verse 10 - "And the gospel must first be published among all nations."

καὶ εἰς πάντα τὰ ἔθνη πρῶτον δεῖ κηρυχθῆναι τὸ εὐαγγέλιον.

καὶ (continuative conjunction) 14.
εἰς (preposition with the accusative of extent) 140.
πάντα (acc.pl.neut.of *πᾶς*, in agreement with *ἔθνη*) 67.
τὰ (acc.pl.neut.of the article in agreement with *ἔθνη*) 9.
ἔθνη (acc.pl.neut.of *ἔθνος*, extent) 376.
πρῶτον (acc.sing.neut.of *πρῶτος*, adverbial) 487.
δεῖ (3d.per.sing.pres.impersonal) 1207.
κηρυχθῆναι (1st.aor.pass.inf.of *κηρύσσω*, epexegetical) 249.
τὸ (nom.sing.neut.of the article in agreement with *εὐαγγέλιον*) 9.
εὐαγγέλιον (nom.sing.neut.of *εὐαγγέλιον*, subject of *κηρυχθῆναι*) 405.

Translation - "And the gospel must first be preached to all the nations."

Comment: Winer (*A Treatise on the Grammar of New Testament Greek*, Moulton edition, 267) thinks that *εἰς* here with *κηρυχθῆναι* is a New Testament use of *εἰς* with the accusative, like a dative of personal advantage, and should be translated "among all of the nations." The accusative of extent idea is not greatly different. Mt.24:14 identifies this *εὐαγγέλιον* as *τὸ εὐαγγέλιον τῆς βασιλείας*, which is the same gospel that John the Baptist preached (Mt.3:2) to the effect that the Kingdom of Messiah was the next event on God's prophetic calendar - a message which he withdrew in favor of the gospel of the blood of Christ, which he preached "the next day" after he baptized Jesus (John 1:29). *Cf.* our comments on Mt.3:2 and John 1:29.

The gospel of the kingdom - "Repent for the kingdom of the heavens is at hand" cannot be preached again until we are in Daniel's 70th week, during which time we can for the first time, truthfully predict that the inauguration of Messiah's kingdom is immanent. Given the confirmation of the covenant with national Israel, gathered in unbelief in their home land, by Antichrist (Dan.9:27), Christians upon the earth at that time will *add to* the present gospel of blood redemption and the grace of God, the gospel of the kingdom, which will announce when Messiah is coming back. This gospel will cover the earth - *εἰς πάντα τὰ ἔθνη* - during the 70th Week of Daniel's prophecy. When it is preached it will arouse great hostility and result in great persecution to the saints, since it will repudiate the claims of Antichrist, to whom the entire unsaved world will be offering its worship (Rev.13:8). Jesus goes on to point out in verses 11-13 that this future period will be one of persecution for the Christians. It seems from this analysis that, beginning with verse 10, at least, Jesus' analysis applies to the time of the end, which is yet future to us today (August 25, 1980).

Verse 11 - "But when they shall lead you, and deliver you up, take no thought beforehand what ye shall speak, neither do ye premeditate; but whatsoever shall be given you in that hour, that speak ye: for it is not ye that speak but the Holy Ghost."

καὶ ὅταν ἄγωσιν ὑμᾶς παραδιδόντες, μὴ προμεριμνᾶτε τί λαλήσητε, ἀλλ' ὃ ἐὰν δοθῇ ὑμῖν ἐν ἐκείνῃ τῇ ὥρᾳ τοῦτο λαλεῖτε, οὐ γάρ ἐστε ὑμεῖς οἱ λαλοῦντες ἀλλὰ τὸ πνεῦμα τὸ ἅγιον.

καὶ (continuative conjunction) 14.
ὅταν (conjunction with the subjunctive introducing an indefinite temporal clause) 436.
ἄγωσιν (3d.per.pl.pres.act.subj.of *ἄγω*, indefinite temporal clause) 876.
ὑμᾶς (acc.pl.masc.of *σύ*, direct object of *ἄγωσιν*) 104.
παραδιδόντες (pres.act.part.nom.pl.masc.of *παραδίδωμι*, adverbial, telic) 368.

μὴ (qualified negative conjunction with the imperative, prohibition) 87.

#2712 *προμεριμνᾶτε* (2d.per.pl.pres.act.impv.of *προμεριμνάω*, prohibition).

take thought beforehand - Mark 13:11.

Meaning: A combination of *πρό* (#442) and *μεριμνάω* (#609). Hence, to think ahead of time; to premeditate. In Mark 13:11 in a context which means to think about what one will say in court.

τί (acc.sing.neut.of *τίς*, interrogative pronoun, direct object of *λαλήσητε*) 281.
λαλήσητε (2d.per.pl.1st.aor.act.subj.of *λαλέω*, deliberative) 815.
ἀλλ' (alternative conjunction) 342.
ὃ (nom.sing.neut.of *ὅς*, subject of *δοθῇ*) 65.
ἐὰν (conditional particle in a third-class condition) 363.
δοθῇ (3d.per.sing.1st.aor.pass.subj.of *δίδωμι*, third-class condition) 362.
ὑμῖν (dat.pl.masc.of *σύ*, indirect object of *δοθῇ*) 104.
ἐν (preposition with the locative of time point) 80.
ἐκείνῃ (loc.sing.fem.of *ἐκεῖνος*, in agreement with *ὥρᾳ*) 246.
τῇ (loc.sing.fem.of the article in agreement with *ὥρᾳ*) 9.
ὥρᾳ (loc.sing.fem.of *ὥρα*, time point) 735.
τοῦτο (acc.sing.neut.of *οὗτος*, direct object of *λαλεῖτε*) 93.
λαλεῖτε (2d.per.pl.pres.act.impv.of *λαλέω*, command) 815.
οὐ (summary negative conjunction with the indicative) 130.
γάρ (causal conjunction) 105.
ὑμεῖς (nom.pl.masc.of *σύ*, predicate nominative) 104.
ἐστε (2d.per.pl.pres.ind.of *εἰμί*, futuristic) 86.
οἱ (nom.pl.masc.of the article in agreement with *λαλοῦντες*) 9.
λαλοῦντες (pres.act.part.nom.pl.masc.of *λαλέω*, substantival, subject of *ἔστε*) 815.
ἀλλὰ (alternative conjunction) 342.
τὸ (nom.sing.neut.of the article in agreement with *πνεῦμα*) 9.
πνεῦμα (nom.sing.neut.of *πνεῦμα*, subject of *ἐστί* understood) 83.
τὸ (nom.sing.neut.of the article in agreement with *ἅγιον*) 9.
ἅγιον (nom.sing.neut.of *ἅγιος*, in agreement with *πνεῦμα*) 84.

Translation - "And when in order to betray they arrest you, stop planning in advance what you are going to say, but say that which will be given to you at that time, because the one speaking will not be you, but the Holy Spirit."

Comment: The indefinite temporal clause with ὅταν and the subjunctive leaves no doubt that the Christian will be betrayed and arraigned in the court, but it leaves open to question only the precise date of the arrest. The participle παραδιδόντες is telic. They will arrest the Christian in order that they may deliver him to the court for judgment. Whenever it happens, we are to stop thinking about what we are going to say in our defense. The present tense in the prohibition μὴ προμεριμνᾶτε - "do not go on thinking," or "stop thinking. . . " indicates what we would normally expect. In that day of widespread persecution of the Christians, as the unsaved world worships Antichrist, the saints will expect to be arrested and naturally think about what they will say when their time in court comes. Jesus here orders us to stop thining about it. What then will we say? We are ordered to say whatever is given us to say in that hour. How can we be sure that what seems impromptu will be the proper thing to say? The γάρ clause is causal. It tells us why. It is because we are not the one who will be speaking. It will be the Holy Spirit.

This passage does not teach that public speakers should speak without proper preparation. This instruction applies to a specific situation in the seven year tribulation period. The defendant will have been preaching the gospel of the kingdom (Mk.13:10; Mt.24:14). His message, so far from endorsing Antichrist, who will at that time be receiving universal acclaim among the unsaved (Rev.13:3,4,8,12) will be denouncing him and it will be clearly prediciting, not only God's judgment upon him (Rev.19:20) but also the precise day of that judgment - 2560 days from the time of Daniel 9:27; 42 months or 1260 days from his mid-week restoration (Rev.13:5) and the imposition of his mark upon the unsaved. Obviously this preaching will not be popular and will result in the Christian's arrest and arraignment in the court. It is this specific occasion of which Jesus is speaking, when He counsels against prior preparation of our defense. Why? Because we will be only the mouthpiece for the real speaker - the Holy Spirit. The gift of prophecy will be bestowed upon the defendant in that day (1 Cor.12:8,10). The court, hopelessly prejudiced against the defendant, will hear some supernaturally directed defense from his lips. Thus the court will receive the witness of the gospel (Mk.13:9) which is the divine purpose of the entire procedure (Mk.13:9).

Verse 12 - "Now the brother shall betray the brother to death, and the father the son; and the children shall rise up against their parents, and shall cause them to be put to death."

καὶ παραδώσει ἀδελφὸς ἀδελφὸν εἰς θάνατον καὶ πατὴρ τέκνον, καὶ ἐπαναστήσονται τέκνα ἐπὶ γονεῖς καὶ θανατώσουσιν αὐτούς.

καὶ (continuative conjunction) 14.
παραδώσει (3d.per.sing.fut.act.ind.of παραδίδωμι, predictive) 368.

ἀδελφὸς (nom.sing.masc.of ἀδελφός, subject of παραδώσει) 15.
ἀδελφὸν (acc.sing.masc.of ἀδελφός, direct object of παραδώσει) 15.
εἰς (preposition with the accusative, purpose) 140.
θάνατον (acc.sing.masc.of θάνατος, purpose) 381.
καὶ (continuative conjunction) 14.
πατὴρ (nom.sing.masc.of πατήρ, subject of παραδώσει) 238.
τέκνον (acc.sing.neut.of τέκνον, direct object of παραδώσει) 229.
καὶ (continuative conjunction) 14.
ἐπαναστήσονται (3d.per.pl.fut.mid.ind.of ἐπανίστημι, predictive) 877.
τέκνα (nom.pl.neut.of τέκνον, subject of ἐπαναστήσονται) 229.
ἐπὶ (preposition with the accusative, hostility) 47.
γονεῖς (acc.pl.masc.of γονεύς, hostility) 878.
καὶ (adjunctive conjunction joining verbs) 14.
θανατώσουσιν (3d.per.pl.fut.act.ind.of θανατόω, predictive) 879.
αὐτούς (acc.pl.masc.of αὐτός, direct object of θανατώσουσιν) 16.

Translation - "And brother will betray brother to death, and father his child, and children will stand up in accusation against parents and demand their death."

Comment: *Cf.* Mt.24:20,21; Lk.21:16,17. The passage recalls Micah 7:6. *Cf.* Mt.10:34,35,36. The Light of the World came not to bring peace but a sword. Electing grace chooses some while eternal justice operates on others. The same sun that melts wax hardens clay.

The old expression which says that "blood is thicker than water" is untrue. The spiritual ties that bind the believer to Christ and the darkness that blinds the eyes of the unbeliever creates the hostility on the part of the lost that ignores even the close blood ties that bind parent and child and brother and brother.

There have been periods in history when in certain areas of the globe the persecution of the Christian has been observed. But the fulfillment of our Lord's prophecy will wait for its greatest fulfillment for the last seven years of the "times of the Gentiles." Then the gospel message of the kingdom will be seen in such diametric opposition to the regime of Antichrist that he will answer it with the social and economic pressures that unsaved parents and children will be unable to resist, blood ties to the contrary notwithstanding.

Verse 13 - "And ye shall be hated of all men for my name's sake: but he that shall endure unto the end, the same shall be saved."

καὶ ἔσεσθε μισούμενοι ὑπὸ πάντων διὰ τὸ ὄνομά μου. ὁ δὲ ὑπομείνας εἰς τέλος οὗτος σωθήσεται.

καὶ (continuative conjunction) 14.
ἔσεσθε (2d.per.pl.fut.ind.of εἰμί, future passive periphrastic) 86.
μισούμενοι (pres.pass.part.nom.pl.masc.of μισέω, future passive periphrastic) 542.
ὑπὸ (preposition with the ablative of agent) 117.
πάντων (abl.pl.masc.of πᾶς, agent) 67.

διὰ (preposition with the accusative, cause) 118.
τὸ (acc.sing.neut.of the article in agreement with ὄνομά) 9.
ὄνομά (acc.sing.neut.of ὄνομα, cause) 108.
μου (gen.sing.masc.of ἐγώ, possession) 123.
ὁ (nom.sing.masc.of the article in agreement with ὑπομείνας) 9.
δὲ (adversative conjunction) 11.
ὑπομείνας (1st.aor.act.part.nom.sing.masc.of ὑπομένω, substantival, subject of σωθήσεται) 880.
εἰς (preposition with the accusative of time extent) 140.
τέλος (acc.sing.neut.of τέλος, time extent) 881.
οὗτος (nom.sing.masc.of οὗτος, deictic) 93.
σωθήσεται (3d.per.sing.fut.pass.ind.of σῴζω, predictive) 109.

Translation - "And you will be hated by all, because of my name, but the one who survives until the end will be rescued."

Comment: The future periphrastic is decidedly durative in force. It points to the unrelenting hatred of the unsaved for the child of God who bears the name of Christ. Note the aorist tense in the substantival participle ὁ ὑπομείνας. Jesus is talking about those Christians who, at the end of the tribulation period, can say "I have survived." Having lived through the period of hatred and persecution, he will be delivered from any further persecution. *Cf.* 1 Thess.4:17. The statement, taken from context, has been interpreted by some Arminians to mean that salvation is the reward to those who remain faithful in an ethical sense. For them, "to *hold out faithful* means to live one's life by one's own efforts in a way that is acceptable to God until the day of one's death. Thus the born again alcoholic may say, "Pray that I may *hold out faithful* and never take another drink." Thus - salvation by works. In its context our Lord's statement has no reference to ethical fidelity. Physical, not moral continuance, is in view here. The phrase εἰς τέλος refers to the end of the tribulation period, not to the end of one's normal life span. He who has managed to stay alive until the end of the tribulation period will be raptured.

Suppose, under torture, a Christian denies Christ? In such a case Mt.10:32,33 applies. But since the Holy Spirit is the speaker, directing the message through the lips of a tortured Christian (Mk.13:11) this could not happen. Furthermore, denial before the Father by the Son could never be in terms of repudiation, but only in terms of lack of fidelity to His name, under extenuating circumstances. There is nothing in scripture to say that a Christian who was later "denied" by Christ, has lost his soul; only his reward. *Cf.* Mt.24:10-13; Lk.21:17-19.

The Great Tribulation

(Matthew 24:15-28; Mark 13:14-23; Luke 21:17-19).

Mark 13:14 - "But when ye shall see the abomination of desolation, spoken of by Daniel the prophet, standing where it ought not, (let him that readeth understand), then let them that be in Judea flee to the mountains."

Ὅταν δὲ ἴδητε τὸ βδέλυγμα τῆς ἐρημώσεως ἑστηκότα ὅπου οὐ δεῖ, ὁ ἀναγινώσκων νοείτω, τότε οἱ ἐν τῇ Ἰουδαίᾳ φευγέτωσαν εἰς τὰ ὄρη,

Ὅταν (conjunction with the subjunctive introducing an indefinite temporal clause) 436.

δὲ (inferential conjunction) 11.

ἴδητε (2d.per.pl.aor.act.subj.of *ὁράω*, indefinite temporal clause) 144.

τὸ (acc.sing.neut.of the article in agreement with *βδέλυγμα*) 9.

βδέλυγμα (acc.sing.neut.of *βδέλυγμα*, direct object of *ἴδητε*) 1492.

τῆς (gen.sing.fem.of the article in agreement with *ἐρημώσεως*) 9.

ἐρημώσεως (gen.sing.fem.of *ἐρήμωσις*, description) 1493.

ἑστηκότα (perf.act.part.acc.sing.neut.of *ἵστημι*, adverbial, circumstantial) 180.

ὅπου (adverb introducing a definite local clause) 592.

οὐ (summary negative conjunction with the indicative) 130.

δεῖ (3d.per.sing.impersonal of *δεῖ*, in a definite local clause) 1207.

ὁ (nom.sing.masc.of the article in agreement with *ἀναγινώσκων*) 9.

ἀναγινώσκων (pres.act.part.nom.sing.masc.of *ἀναγινώσκω*, substantival, subject of *νοείτω*) 967.

νοείτω (3d.per.sing.pres.act.impv.of *νοέω*, command) 1160.

τότε (temporal adverb) 166.

οἱ (nom.pl.masc.of the article, subject of *φευγέτωσαν*) 9.

ἐν (preposition with the locative of place where) 80.

τῇ (loc.sing.fem.of the article in agreement with *Ἰουδαίᾳ*) 9.

Ἰουδαίᾳ (loc.sing.fem.of *Ἰουδαῖος*, place where) 134.

φευγέτωσαν (3d.per.pl.pres.act.impv.of *φεύγω*, command) 202.

εἰς (preposition with the accusative of extent) 140.

τὰ (acc.pl.neut.of the article in agreement with *ὄρη*) 9.

ὄρη (acc.pl.neut.of *ὄρος*, extent) 357.

Translation - "Therefore when you see the Abomination of Desolation standing where he should not, (let the reader understand), then those in Judea must flee unto the mountains."

Comment: *Cf.*Mt.24:15,16; Lk.21:20. There is no need to repeat here the exposition of Mt.24:15,16 but the student should read it now. The passages are parallel. There may have been a first century application of this prophecy in A.D. 70 when Titus, the Roman Emperor destroyed Jerusalem, but the true application is end-time. Daniel 9:27 deals with the last seven year period marked out for Daniel and including 490 years in which God will have been dealing with Israel to bring her to the Kingdom Age (Dan.9:24-27). Note that Daniel 9:24 carries us to the millenial period when "everlasting righteousness" will be established and the "Most Holy" will be anointed. The Abomination of Desolation appears in the middle of the last week (Dan.9:27). This could not mean Titus or anyone else standing *ἐν τῷ ναῷ* because three and one half years after the middle of the week brings us to Messiah's kingdom. It has been 1900 years since Jerusalem was destroyed and the temple torn down as Jesus prophesied in Mark 13:2. That occurred in A.D. 70. Furthermore the events of Mark 13:24-27 did not occur in the first century.

The principle of double imagery will permit us to say that Jews in Jerusalem in A.D.70 did flee to the surrounding mountains to escape the Romans, but Titus is not the final fulfillment of Jesus' words. They point to a day yet future to us in 1980. Daniel's 70th week has not yet begun. When it does begin we can expect the Abomination of Desolation three and one half years later, when Mark 13:14 will be literally fulfilled. A similar double imagery is found in Peter's remark concerning the behavior of the Christians at Pentecost in Acts 2:16-21. He said, "This is that" but he did not say, "This is *all* of that." A part of what Joel prophesied was fulfilled at Pentecost, but verses 19 and 20 were not. Joel's prophecy also relates to end time events. So it is with Mark 13:14-27. Our timeless God often associates events, separated by 2000 years of human history, as though they came together. *e.g.* Lk.1:30-33; Isa.9:6,7; Isa.61:1-2; Lk.4:17-21, where Jesus in the synagogue in Nazareth read the part that applied to His first coming, stopped reading in the middle of the second verse, and closed the book. This scriptural precedent for the view that there is a time gap between the close of Daniel's 69th week and the beginning of the 70th is overlooked by amillenialists and historical premillenialists, who deny to the Revelation a futuristic interpretation. *Cf.* our comments on the opening verses of the Revelation.

It is incumbent upon those who see no time gap in the Daniel 9 prophecy, and who agree that the end of the 69th week brings us to the death of Messiah, to find the fulfillment of the 70th week within the time frame of the next seven years following the death, burial, resurrection and ascension of Christ. The establishment of "everlasting righteousness" must be assigned to some event in the next seven years after Pentecost. This forces them into an allegorical approach. When we resort to allegory as a substitutionary means of interpretation to the literal acceptance of plain statements of good Greek, we have opened the door for the policy of denying to any scripture what it says unequivocally, when its unequivocal sense contradicts the theory that we are trying to prove! With this method of interpretation anyone can make the Word of God teach anything he wishes. And to say that the Bible teaches anything is to say that it teaches everything, and therefore that it teaches nothing.

When the Antichrist stands in the Holy Place and demands the worship of all, at pain of death for those who refuse, those who will refuse to worship him will exercise haste in their flight to safety in the mountains. This is the thought of verses 15-18.

Verse 15 - "And let him that is on the housetop not go down into the house, neither enter therein, to take anything out of his house."

ὁ (δὲ) ἐπὶ τοῦ δώματος μὴ καταβάτω μηδὲ εἰσελθάτω ἆραί τι ἐκ τῆς οἰκίας αὐτοῦ,

ὁ (nom.sing.masc.of the article, subject of καταβάτω and εἰσελθάτω) 9.

(δὲ) (inferential conjunction) 11.
ἐπὶ (preposition with the genitive of place description) 47.
τοῦ (gen.sing.neut.of the article in agreement with δώματος) 9.
δώματος (gen.sing.neut.of δῶμα, place description) 888.
μὴ (qualified negative conjunction with the imperative) 87.
καταβάτω (3d.per.sing.2d.aor.act.impv.of καταβαίνω, prohibition) 324.
μηδὲ (negative continuative particle) 612.
εἰσελθάτω (3d.per.sing.2d.aor.mid.impv.of εἰσέρχομαι, prohibition) 234.
ἆραί (aor.act.inf.of αἴρω, purpose) 350.
τι (acc.sing.neut.of τις,the indefinite pronoun, direct object of ἆραί) 486.
ἐκ (preposition with the ablative of separation) 19.
τῆς (abl.sing.fem.of the article in agreement with οἰκίας) 9.
οἰκίας (abl.sing.fem.of οἰκία, separation) 186.
αὐτοῦ (gen.sing.masc.of αὐτός, possession) 16.

Translation - "He who is upon the housetop must not go down nor go in to carry anything out of his house."

Comment: Note the article here joined with the prepositional phrase ἐπὶ τοῦ δώματος as the subject of the sentence. He is forbidden to descend into his house in order to carry with him his valuables. Rather he must avail himself of the outside exist for the fast get away. The thought here is the speed necessary for escape, since Antichrist will have revealed himself in his true colors, not as a White Horse Rider bringing peace, as he appeared three and one half years before, but as a murderous, blasphemous enemy of God and the saints. Divine rescue for God's elect will come three and one half years in the future for those who survive (Mk.13:13). In the meantime the only hope of survival is flight and all haste is required. The extra time required to enter the house and collect valuables is forbidden. The encumberances of personal property, however slight, would hinder rapid flight. *Cf.*Mt.24:17; Lk.17:31.

Verse 16 - "And let him that is in the field not turn back again for to take up his garment."

καὶ ὁ εἰς τὸν ἀγρὸν μὴ ἐπιστρεψάτω εἰς τὰ ὀπίσω ἆραι τὸ ἱμάτιον αὐτοῦ.

καὶ (continuative conjunction) 14.
ὁ (nom.sing.masc.of the article, subject of ἐπιστρεψάτω) 9.
εἰς (preposition with the accusative, static use) 140.
τὸν (acc.sing.masc.of the article in agreement with ἀγρὸν) 9.
ἀγρὸν (acc.sing.masc.of ἀγρός, static use, like ἐν with the locative) 626.
μὴ (qualified negative conjunction with the imperative) 87.
ἐπιστρεψάτω (3d.per.sing.aor.act.impv.of ἐπιστρέφω, prohibition) 866.
εἰς (preposition with the accusative of extent) 140.
τὰ (acc.pl.neut.of the article, extent) 9.
ὀπίσω (adverb of place) 302.
ἆραι (aor.act.inf.of αἴρω, purpose) 350.

τὸ (acc.sing.neut.of the article in agreement with ἱμάτιον) 9.
ἱμάτιον (acc.sing.neut.of ἱμάτιον, direct object of ἆραι) 534.
αὐτοῦ (gen.sing.masc.of αὐτός, possession) 16.

Translation - "And the man in the field must not turn back to get his coat."

Comment: Note Mark's use of the original static use of εἰς with the accusative, for the locative of place which we normally expect to see with ἐν. In the parallel passage, Matthew has ἐν τῷ ἀγρῷ. This variation in the text, as two writers each report the same statement of our Lord, constitutes no problem, except for those who expouse a dictation theory of inspiration. If the Holy Spirit intended to dictate every word, then one of these two writers is wrong. But the thought is totally conveyed and the interpretation is the same, whether we read it from Matthew or Mark. Here we have the evidence in the text that the Holy Spirit allowed each writer to write His total message into the text in his own way, so long as, in the Holy Spirit's sovereign judgment, the exegete would not be misled to interpret something different or something more or something less. *Cf.* our discussion of this problem in *The Renaissance New Testament*, I, xix *ff.*

The picture here is one with which any farm boy is totally familiar. Early morning chill is enough to demand a coat. Mid morning heat demands that he take it off and hang it on the fence post while he goes on ploughing. If the Antichrist should strike when the farmer is halfway down the furrow he should not even take the time to return to the end of the furrow to retrieve his coat. Again, the picture is one of haste to escape. *Cf.* Mt.24:18.

Verse 17 - "But woe to them that are with child, and to them that give suck in those days."

οὐαὶ δὲ ταῖς ἐν γαστρὶ ἐχούσαις καὶ ταῖς θηλαζούσαις ἐν ἐκείναις ταῖς ἡμέραις.

οὐαὶ (exclamation) 936.
δὲ (adversative conjunction) 11.
ταῖς (dat.pl.fem.of the article in agreement with ἐχούσαις) 9.
ἐν (preposition with the locative of place) 80.
γαστρὶ (loc.sing.fem.of γαστήρ, place where) 81.
ἐχούσαις (pres.act.part.dat.pl.fem.of ἔχω, substantival, personal disadvantage) 82.
καὶ (adjunctive conjunction joining participles) 14.
ταῖς (dat.pl.fem.of the article in agreement with θηλαζούσαις) 9.
θηλαζούσαις (pres.act.part.dat.pl.fem.of θηλάζω, personal disadvantage) 1361.
ἐν (preposition with the locative of time point) 80.
ἐκείναις (loc.pl.fem.of ἐκεῖνος, in agreement with ἡμέραις) 246.
ταῖς (loc.pl.fem.of the article in agreement with ἡμέραις) 9.
ἡμέραις (loc.pl.fem.of ἡμέρα, time point) 135.

Translation - "But alas for those who are pregnant and for those who are nursing their babies in those days."

Comment: The idiom ταῖς ἐν γαστρὶ ἐχούσαις, literally translated is "to those having in the womb." *Cf.* Mt.1:82 and #82. ταῖς θηλαζούσιας - for a mother who is nursing her baby. Women thus hindered will find it harder to escape the agents of the Antichrist. *Cf.* Mt.24:19.

Verse 18 - "And pray ye that your flight be not in the winter."

προσεύχεσθε δὲ ἵνα μὴ γένηται χειμῶνος.

προσεύχεσθε (2d.per.pl.pres.mid.impv.of προσεύχομαι, command) 544.
δὲ (continuative conjunction) 11.
ἵνα (conjunction introducing the subjunctive in a negative purpose clause) 114.
μὴ (qualified negative conjunction in a negative purpose clause) 87.
γένηται (3d.per.sing.aor.subj.of γίνομαι, negative purpose) 113.
χειμῶνος (gen.sing.masc.of χειμών, time description) 1193.

Translation - "And pray that it won't happen during bad weather."

Comment: *Cf.* Mt.24:20, which adds μηδὲ σαββάτῳ.

Verse 19 - "For in those days shall be affliction such as was not from the beginning of the creation which God created, unto this time, neither shall be."

ἔσονται γὰρ αἱ ἡμέραι ἐκεῖναι θλῖψις οἵα οὐ γέγονεν τοιαύτη ἀπ' ἀρχῆς κτίσεως ἣν ἔκτισεν ὁ θεὸς ἕως τοῦ νῦν καὶ οὐ μὴ γένηται.

ἔσονται (3d.per.pl.fut.ind.of εἰμί, predictive) 86.
γὰρ (causal conjunction) 105.
αἱ (nom.pl.fem.of the article in agreement with ἡμέραι) 9.
ἡμέραι (nom.pl.fem.of ἡμέρα, subject of ἔσονται) 135.
ἐκεῖναι (nom.pl.fem.of ἐκεῖνος, in agreement with ἡμέραι) 246.
θλῖψις (nom.sing.fem.of θλῖψις, predicate nominative) 1046.
οἵα (nom.sing.fem.of οἷος, attracted to θλῖψις) 1496.
οὐ (summary negative conjunction with the indicative) 130.
γέγονεν (3d.per.sing.perf.ind.of γίνομαι, consummative) 113.
τοιαύτη (nom.sing.fem.of τοιοῦτος, in agreement with οἵα) 785.
ἀπ' (preposition with the ablative of time separation) 70.
ἀχῆς (abl.sing.fem.of ἀρχή, time separation) 1285.
κτίσεως (gen.sing.fem.of κτίσις, description) 2633.
ἣν (acc.sing.fem.of ὅς, direct object of ἔκτισεν) 65.
ἔκτισεν (3d.per.sing.aor.act.ind.of κτίζω, culminative) 1284.
ὁ (nom.sing.masc.of the article in agreement with θεὸς) 9.
θεὸς (nom.sing.masc.of θεός, subject of ἔκτισεν) 124.
ἕως (preposition with the ablative of time separation) 71.
τοῦ (abl.sing.neut.of the article, time separation) 9.
νῦν (adverbial substantive, time separation) 1497.
καὶ (emphatic conjunction) 14.

οὐ (summary negative conjunction with μὴ and the subjunctive, emphatic negation) 130.

μὴ (qualified negative conjunction with the subjunctive, emphatic negation) 87.

γένηται (3d.per.sing.aor.subj.of γίνομαι, emphatic negation) 113.

Translation - "Because those days will be days of tribulation, the like of which has not been from the beginning of that which God created until now. In fact will never be."

Comment: *Cf.* Mt.24:21; Lk.21:23. The language is taken from Daniel 12:1, which supports the view that Jesus is referring to events yet future, which lie between the beginning of Daniel's 70th week (Dan.9:27) and the Second Coming of Messiah. The description of this time forbids the interpretation that Jesus was only describing the war in A.D.70, when the Romans sacked the city and destroyed the temple. Many eras of human history have seen greater affliction than occurred then. Never before nor after this specific time of trouble will there be a greater. Note ἕως τοῦ νῦν - an adverb used like a substantive. *Cf.* John 8:23; 2 Cor.1:17; Col.3:1; Acts 5:38; Lk.1:48 and many others.

Verse 20 - "And except that the Lord had shortened those days, no flesh should be saved: but for the elect's sake, whom he hath chosen, he hath shortened the days."

καὶ εἰ μὴ ἐκολόβωσεν κύριος τὰς ἡμέρας, οὐκ ἂν ἐσώθη πᾶσα σάρξ. ἀλλὰ διὰ τοὺς ἐκλεκτοὺς οὓς ἐξελέξατο ἐκολόβωσεν τὰς ἡμέρας.

καὶ (continuative conjunction) 14.

εἰ (conditional particle in a negative second-class condition) 337.

μὴ (qualified negative conjunction in a second-class condition) 87.

ἐκολόβωσεν (3d.per.sing.aor.act.ind.of κολοβόω, second-class condition) 1498.

κύριος (nom.sing.masc.of κύριος, subject of ἐκολόβωσεν) 97.

τὰς (acc.pl.fem.of the article in agreement with ἡμέρας) 9.

ἡμέρας (acc.pl.fem.of ἡμέρα, direct object of ἐκολόβωσεν) 135.

οὐκ (summary negative conjunction in a second-class condition) 130.

ἂν (contingent particle in a second-class condition) 205.

ἐσώθη (3d.per.sing.1st.aor.pass.ind.of σώζω, second-class condition) 109.

πᾶσα (nom.pl.fem.of πᾶς, in agreement with σάρξ) 67.

σάρξ (nom.sing.fem.of σάρξ, subject of ἐσώθη) 1202.

ἀλλὰ (adversative conjunction) 342.

διὰ (preposition with the accusative, cause) 118.

τοὺς (acc.pl.masc.of the article in agreement with ἐκλεκτοὺς) 9.

ἐκλεκτοὺς (acc.pl.masc.of ἐκλεκτός, cause) 1412.

οὓς (acc.pl.masc.of ὅς, direct object of ἐξελέξατο) 65.

ἐξελέξατο (3d.per.sing.1st.aor.mid.ind.of ἐκλέγω, culminative) 2119.

ἐκολόβωσεν (3d.per.sing.aor.act.ind.of κολοβόω, culminative) 1498.

τὰς (acc.pl.fem.of the article in agreement with ἡμέρας) 9.
ἡμέρας (acc.pl.fem.of ἡμέρα, direct object of ἐκολόβωσεν) 135.

Translation - "And if the Lord had not shortened the days, no flesh would have been saved. But because of the elect, whom He has chosen, He shortened the days."

Comment: We should be careful to distinguish between οὐ πᾶς, written together, which means "not all," which is the same as "some" and what we have here - οὐκ . . . πᾶς where the negative οὐκ goes with the verb ἐσώθη, with the subject being πᾶσα σάρξ - "all flesh will not be saved" which can be written, "all flesh will be lost" or "no flesh will be saved."

Until the advent of Madison Avenue's destruction of good English on the television screen, we had no problem with this. Now more and more people are saying it wrong. When the commercial says, "All aspirins are not alike" they do not mean that "all aspirins are different" because that means that all of their Bayers are different from all other Bayers. If that is what they mean they should tell me which Bayer in the box that I buy is better than all of the others. Greeks were never confused on points like this; nor were Englishmen until recently.

Note that the shortening of these days of affliction is a past tense. The verb ἐκολόβωσεν is aorist indicative in both cases. The fact that is is aorist does not mean that it refers to a past event, but the augment does. The aorist is culminative. The shortening of the days was done in the eternal counsels of God in eternity past and declared in the Word to be exactly 2520 days, which is equal to 84 months or 7 years. This is fixed. In any longer period Antichrist would have had time to murder all of God's people. "For the sake of the elect, whom He chose for Himself." διὰ with the accusative in a causal sense. *Cf.*#'s 1412 and 2119 and satisfy yourself that the words are used of all of the elect members of the Gentile body of Christ, as well as of elect Israel. Both elect groups will be upon the earth during this period. There is nothing in the exegesis of the inspired text to support a pretribulation rapture of the Church. Those who say that there is, of course, apply the word ἐκλεκτός solely to Israel. This view runs into trouble in verse 27. The shortened days will run their course, and, though Antichrist and his henchmen will murder many saints (Rev.6:9-11) some will be alive and will remain unto the coming of the Lord (1 Thess.4:17). The endtime Christian who lives to see this seven year period begin, may enjoy the experience of going to heaven without dying. All he must do, by God's grace, is to stay alive until the last day. "O Joy, O Delight! Should we go without dying!!" Those, of course, who died first, will be raised first (1 Cor.15:51-58).

Verse 21 - "And then, if any man shall say to you, Lo, here is Christ: or, lo, he is there; believe him not."

καὶ τότε ἐάν τις ὑμῖν εἴπῃ, Ἴδε ὧδε ὁ Χριστός, Ἴδε ἐκεῖ, μὴ πιστεύετε.

καὶ (continuative conjunction) 14.
τότε (temporal adverb) 166.

ἐάν (conditional particle in a third-class condition) 363.
τις (nom.sing.masc.of τις, the indefinite pronoun, subject of εἴπῃ) 486.
ὑμῖν (dat.pl.masc.of σύ, indirect object of εἴπῃ) 104.
εἴπῃ (3d.per.sing.aor.act.subj.of εἶπον, third-class condition) 155.
Ἴδε (2d.per.sing.aor.act.impv.of ὁράω, command) 144.
ὧδε (local adverb) 766.
ὁ (nom.sing.masc.of the article in agreement with Χριστός) 9.
Χριστός (nom.sing.masc.of Χριστός, nominative absolute) 4.
Ἴδε (2d.per.sing.aor.act.impv.of ὁράω, command) 144.
ἐκεῖ (local adverb) 204.
μὴ (qualified negative conjunction with the imperative, prohibition) 87.
πιστεύετε (2d.per.pl.pres.act.impv.of πιστεύω, prohibition) 734.

Translation - "And then if anyone says to you, 'Look! Here is the Messiah!' 'Look! There He is!' do not believe it."

Comment: The third-class condition with ἐάν and the subjunctive in εἴπῃ indicates little doubt that false prophets will announce false Messiahs here and there, though the time when this will occur is not known. In the apodosis we have the prohibition with μὴ and the present imperative. If the action has already begun, μὴ means to desist. If it has not yet begun the imperative forbids the action to begin (Burton, *Moods and Tenses*, 75). *Cf.* Mt.24:23; Lk.17:23.

The reason for this prohibition is the prediction of

Verse 22 - "For false Christs and false prophets shall rise, and shall show signs and wonders, to seduce, if it were possible, even the elect."

ἐγερθήσονται γὰρ ψευδόχριστοι καὶ ψευδοπροφῆται καὶ δώσουσιν σημεῖα καὶ τέρατα πρὸς τὸ ἀποπλανᾶν, εἰ δυνατόν, τοὺς ἐκλεκτούς.

ἐγερθήσονται (3d.per.pl.fut.pass.ind.of ἐγείρω, predictive) 125.
γὰρ (causal conjunction) 105.
ψευδόχριστοι (nom.pl.masc.of ψευδόχριστος, subject of ἐγερθήσονται) 1499.
καὶ (adjunctive conjunction joining nouns) 14.
ψευδοπροφῆται (nom.pl.masc.of ψευδοπροφήτης, subject of ἐγερθήσονται) 670.
καὶ (adjunctive conjunction joining verbs) 14.
δώσουσιν (3d.per.pl.fut.act.ind.of δίδωμι, predictive) 362.
σημεῖα (acc.pl.neut.of σημεῖον, direct object of δώσουσιν) 1005.
καὶ (adjunctive conjunction joining nouns) 14.
τέρατα (acc.pl.neut.of τέρας, direct object of δώσουσιν) 1500.
πρὸς (preposition with the accusative and an infinitive of purpose) 197.
τὸ (acc.sing.neut.of the article, purpose, joined to the infinitive) 9.

#2713 ἀποπλανᾶν (pres.act.inf.of ἀποπλανάω, purpose).

seduce - Mark 13:22.

err - 1 Tim.6:10.

Meaning: A combination of ἀπό (#70) and πλανάω (#1257). Hence, to lead away from, by deception. To seduce from a proper path. To divert the worship of a Christian from the true Messiah to a false one - Mark 13:22. Followed by ἀπὸ τῆς πίστεως in 1 Tim.6:10.

εἰ (conditional particle in an elliptical second-class condition) 337.
δυνατόν (nom.sing.neut.of δυνατός, predicate adjective) 1311.
τοὺς (acc.pl.masc.of the article in agreement with ἐκλεκτούς) 9.
ἐκλεκτούς (acc.pl.masc.of ἐκλεκτός, direct object of ἀποπλανᾶν) 1412.

Translation - "Because false Messiahs and false prophets will be raised up and they will produce signs and wonders, in order, if possible, to deceive the elect."

Comment: *Cf.*Mt.24:24; Deut.13:1-3.*Cf.*#670 for references to the ψευδοπροφῆται - Rev.16:13; 19:20; 20:10 and his signs (#1005) - 2 Thess.2:9; Rev.13:13,14; 16:14; 19:20 and his seduction (#'s 2713, 1257). Note πρὸς τὸ ἀποπλανᾶν, the articular infinitive in the accusative case, denoting purpose. *Cf.* Mt.5:28; 6:1; 13:30; 23:5; Lk.18:1; Mk.13:22. Obviously the elect cannot be deceived to the point where they would receive Antichrist's mark and number and be lost (Rev.19:20), although that there is danger that some will be temporarily confused is obvious. Otherwise there is no point in this warning from the lips of our Lord. The end-time revival in the true church will recall the backslidden saints to a study of the Word, at which time Jesus' warnings will alert the elect to the machinations of the enemy. To be told in advance about Antichrist and his deceptive tactics, and to also learn what his fate will be, when the true Messiah comes again, is to be forearmed with the resistance which will stand us in good stead in that time of trial.

Verse 23 - "But take ye heed: behold, I have foretold you all things."

ὑμεῖς δὲ βλέπετε. προείρηξκα ἡμῖν πάντα.

ὑμεῖς (nom.pl.masc.of σύ, subject of βλέπετε) 104.
δὲ (adversative conjunction) 11.
βλέπετε (2d.per.pl.pres.act.impv.of βλέπω, command) 499.
προείρηκα (1st.per.sing.perf.act.ind.of προεῖπον, intensive) 1501.
ὑμῖν (dat.pl.masc.of σύ, indirect object of προείρηκα) 104.
πάντα (acc.pl.neut.of πᾶς, direct object of προείρηκα) 67.

Translation - "But you must always be alert. I have told you all about it in advance."

Comment: δὲ is adversative. Jesus offered a counterforce to the inducements of the Beast. Note ὑμεῖς in emphasis. Our Lord's prediction of everything (πάντα) is for the advantage of the Christian who will be alive at that time and faced with the problem. Since the Disciples, to whom Jesus spoke this, did not live to face Antichrist and his false prophet, they did not need this advice for themselves. But they recorded it for the benefit of the elect upon the earth during the tribulation who will face Antichrist. If it had been true, which it is not, that the elect would be raptured out of the world before Antichrist is revealed, which they will not, then all of this teaching by Jesus would be pointless, which it is not. Note our second-class contrary to fact conditional sentence. *Cf.* Mt.24:25.

Verse 24 - "But in those days, after that tribulation the sun shall be darkened, and the moon shall not give her light."

Ἀλλὰ ἐν ἐκείναις ταῖς ἡμέραις μετὰ τὴν θλῖψιν ἐκείνην, ὁ ἥλιος σκοτισθήσεται, καὶ ἡ σελήνη οὐ δώσει τὸ φέγγος αὐτῆς,

Ἀλλὰ (adversative conjunction) 342.
ἐν (preposition with the locative of time point) 80.
ἐκείναις (loc.pl.fem.of ἐκεῖνος, in agreement with ἡμέραις) 246.
ταῖς (loc.pl.fem.of the article in agreement with ἡμέραις) 9.
ἡμέραις (loc.pl.fem.of ἡμέρα, time point) 135.
μετὰ (preposition with the accusative of time extent) 50.
τὴν (acc.sing.fem.of the article in agreement with θλῖψιν) 9.
θλῖψιν (acc.sing.fem.of θλῖψις, time extent) 1046.
ἐκείνην (acc.sing.fem.of ἐκεῖνος, in agreement with θλῖψιν) 246.
ὁ (nom.sing.masc.of the article in agreement with ἥλιος) 9.
ἥλιος (nom.sing.masc.of ἥλιος, subject of σκοτισθήσεται) 546.
σκοτισθήσεται (3d.per.sing.fut.pass.ind.of σκοτίζω, predictive) 1504.
καὶ (continuative conjunction) 14.
ἡ (nom.sing.fem.of the article in agreement with σελήνη) 9.
σελήνη (nom.sing.fem.of σελήνη, subject of δώσει) 1505.
οὐ (summary negative conjunction with the indicative) 130.
δώσει (3d.per.sing.fut.act.ind.of δίδωμι, predictive) 362.
τὸ (acc.sing.neut.of the article in agreement with φέγγος) 9.
φέγγος (acc.sing.neut.of φέγγος, direct object of δώσει) 1506.
αὐτῆς (gen.sing.fem.of αὐτός, description) 16.

Translation - "But during those days after that time of trouble, the sun will be darkened and the moon will not give its light, . . . "

Comment: *Cf.* Mt.24:29; Lk.21:25; Isa.13:10. None of these meteorological disturbances occurred after Titus' destruction of Jerusalem in A.D.70. Nor have they occurred since in connection with the events of verse 26. Jesus was describing the events of His second coming. We see double imagery in Isaiah 13, where the prophet is foretelling the destruction of Babylon by the Medes, but in a way that was not totally fulfilled when Babylon fell. The rest of Isaiah's picture will be seen at the second coming of Christ.

Verse 25 - "And the stars of heaven shall fall, and the powers that are in heaven shall be shaken."

καὶ οἱ ἀστέρες ἔσονται ἐκ τοῦ οὐρανοῦ πίπτοντες, καὶ αἱ δυνάμεις αἱ ἐν τοῖς *οὐρανοῖς σαλευθήσονται.*

καὶ (continuative conjunction) 14.
οἱ (nom.pl.masc.of the article in agreement with *ἀστέρες*) 9.
ἀστέρες (nom.pl.masc.of *ἀστήρ*, subject of *ἔσονται*) 145.
ἔσονται (3d.per.pl.fut.pass.ind.of *εἰμί*, future periphrastic) 86.
ἐκ (preposition with the ablative of separation) 19.
τοῦ (abl.sing.masc.of the article in agreement with *οὐρανοῦ*) 9.
οὐρανοῦ (abl.sing.masc.of *οὐρανός*, separation) 254.
πίπτοντες (pres.act.part.nom.pl.masc.of *πίπτω*, future periphrastic) 187.
καὶ (continuative conjunction) 14.
αἱ (nom.pl.fem.of the article in agreement with *δυνάμεις*) 9.
δυνάμεις (nom.pl.fem.of *δύναμις*, subject of *σαλευθήσονται*) 687.
αἱ (nom.sing.fem.of the article in agreement with *δυνάμεις*) 9.
ἐν (preposition with the locative of place) 80.
τοῖς (loc.pl.masc.of the article in agreement with *οὐρανοῖς*) 9.
οὐρανοῖς (loc.pl.masc.of *οὐρανός*, place where) 254.
σαλευθήσονται (3d.per.pl.fut.pass.ind.of *σαλεύω*, predictive) 911.

Translation - "And the stars will be falling out of heaven, and the powers in the heavens will be shaken."

Comment: *ἔσονται . . . πίπτοντες* is a future periphrastic indicating continuous action in the future. Since the future cannot convey durative action by itself, the resort is to the periphrastic construction, which adds the present participle *πίπτοντες* to the future of *εἰμί*. A star shower will occur when our Lord returns. Note the emphatic attributive position of the prepositional phrase *ἐν τοῖς οὐρανοῖς* to define *δυνάμεις*. *Cf.* Isa.13:10; 34:4. Mt.24:29.

The last clause about the "powers of the heavens" being shaken, may have a reference to the second law of thermodynamics - the entropy principle, with its irreversible conversion of matter to the energy which is then no longer available to perform work. Astronomers are studying the "black hole" into which matter is pulled and, as it falls, loses mass, with the result that there is an increasing concentration of energy. Some scientists believe that this development will result in another "big bang" similar to the one of the original creation. The layman should be careful not to dogmatize, where the scientists are reluctant to speak with certainty. After the event in which the powers of the heavens will be shaken we will be in a better position to understand precisely what happened. The event described will be unprecedented because in connection with it we will see the second coming of our Lord, as set forth in

Verse 26 - "And then shall they see the Son of Man coming in the clouds with great power and glory."

καὶ τότε ὄψονται τὸν υἱὸν τοῦ ἀνθρώπου ἐρχόμενον ἐν νεφέλαις μετὰ δυνάμεως πολλῆς καὶ δόξης.

καὶ (continuative conjunction) 14.
τότε (temporal conjunction) 166.

ὄψονται (3d.per.pl.fut.act.ind.of ὁράω, predictive) 144.
τὸν (acc.sing.masc.of the article in agreement with υἱὸν) 9.
υἱὸν (acc.sing.masc.of υἱός, direct object of ὄψονται) 5.
τοῦ (gen.sing.masc.of the article in agreement with ἀνθρώπου) 9.
ἀνθρώπου (gen.sing.masc.of ἄνθρωπος, description) 341.
ἐρχόμενον (pres.part.acc.sing.masc.of ἔρχομαι, adverbial, temporal) 146.
ἐν (preposition with the locative of place) 80.
νεφέλαις (loc.pl.fem.of νεφέλη, place) 1225.
μετὰ (preposition with the genitive, adverbial) 50.
δυνάμεως (gen.sing.fem.of δύναμις, adverbial) 687.
πολλῆς (gen.sing.fem.of πολύς, in agreement with δυνάμεως) 228.
καὶ (adjunctive conjunction joining nouns) 14.
δόξης (gen.sing.fem.of δόξα, adverbial) 361.

Translation - "And then they will see the Son of Man coming in clouds with great power and glory."

Comment: Note that Jesus changed to the third person in ὄψονται from the second person in ἴδητε (vs.14), νοείτω (vs.14), ὑμῖν (vs.21), πιστεύετε (vs.21), ὑμεῖς δὲ βλέπετε (vs.23), ὑμῖν (vs.23). All of the events described through verse 23 can have a local application to the disciples and other Christians in the first century. Even verse 14, in the sense that many βδελύγμα have profaned the Holy places, although the ultimate profanation is yet to come (2 Thess.2:3,4). But with verse 24 we are clearly at the end of the age. Jesus, therefore, changed to the third person ὄψονται - "they will see . . . κ.τ.λ." rather than ὄψεσθε - "you will see." The audience to whom Jesus spoke these words have been in their graves for centuries. Of course, at His coming, everybody will see Him (Rev.1:7), but Jesus seems to be speaking from the point of view of those upon the earth who have survived the great tribulation. *Cf.*#1225 for the references to the clouds, both at His ascension and at His return. δυνάμεως πολλῆς καὶ δόξης (Mt.28:18-20; Eph.1:19-23).

The connection that exists between Mark 13:14, with its parallel passage in Matthew 24:15, and Mark 13:26,27 makes impossible the view that the Daniel 9 prophecy was totally fulfilled in the first century of the Christian era and that there is no time gap between the first sixty-nine and the seventieth week.

Verse 27 - "And then shall he send his angels, and shall gather his elect from the four winds, from the uttermost part of the earth to the uttermost part of heaven."

καὶ τότε ἀποστελεῖ τοὺς ἀγγέλους καὶ ἐπισυνάξει τοὺς ἐκλεκτοὺς (αὐτοῦ) ἐκ τῶν τεσσάρων ἀνέμων ἀπ' ἄκρου γῆς ἕως ἄκρου οὐρανοῦ.

καὶ (continuative conjunction) 14.
τότε (temporal adverb) 166.
ἀποστελεῖ (3d.per.sing.fut.act.ind.of ἀποστέλλω, predictive) 215.
τοὺς (acc.pl.masc.of the article in agreement with ἀγγέλους) 9.
ἀγγέλους (acc.pl.masc.of ἄγγελος, direct object of ἀποστελεῖ) 96.

καὶ (continuative conjunction) 14.
ἐπισυνάξει (3d.per.sing.fut.act.ind.of *ἐπισυνάγω*, predicitve) 1476.
τοὺς (acc.pl.masc.of the article in agreement with *ἐκλεκτοὺς*) 9.
ἐκλεκτοὺς (acc.pl.masc.of *ἐκλεκτός*, direct object of *ἐπισυνάξει*) 1412.
(*αὐτοῦ*) (gen.sing.masc.of *αὐτός*, possession) 16.
ἐκ (preposition with the ablative of source) 19.
τῶν (abl.pl.masc.of the article in agreement with *ἀνέμων*) 9.
τεσσάρων (abl.pl.masc.of *τέσσαρες*, in agreement with *ἀνέμων*) 1508.
ἀνέμων (abl.pl.masc.of *ἄνεμος*, source) 698.
ἀπ' (preposition with the ablative of source) 70.
ἄκρου (abl.sing.neut.of *ἄκρον*, source) 1509.
γῆς (gen.sing.fem.of *γῆ*, description) 157.
ἕως (preposition with the genitive of description) 71.
ἄκρου (gen.sing.neut.of *ἄκρον*, description) 1509.
οὐρανοῦ (gen.sing.masc.of *οὐρανός*, description) 254.

Translation - "And then He will send forth the angels, and He will gather together to Himself His chosen ones from the four winds from the end of the earth to the end of heaven."

Comment: *Cf.*Zech.2:6; Deut.30:4. *Cf.*Mt.24:13 for a full discussion. Christ will send the angels as direct agents of the gathering of the elect, but He is the indirect gatherer as the singular number in *ἐπισυνάξει* indicates. *ἐκ τῶν . . . οὐρανοῦ* is a double expression of universality. The elect, for whom Christ died, will have been scattered universally. Most of them will have died and their bodies buried in graves scattered throughout the earth, will be resurrected. One thinks of those who died and were buried at sea. The living saints at His coming will be scattered to the remotest parts of earth. The souls of the saints who have died will be with the Lord in the heavens. Wherever He is they will be. Because when He comes again, He will be just above and descending to the Mount of Olives, where He was then sitting as He spoke these words, there will be a universal concentration of the bodies and souls, now reunited upon that mountain.

There is a gruesome side to the picture because rebellion against God and His universal moral law is ghastly and produces macabre results. Another universal gathering will occur as the vultures circle in and descend upon the carrion of the bodies of the unsaved, wherever they may fall (Lk.17:37).

The glorious rapture of the elect and the divine judgment upon the lost are associated in 2 Thess.1:7-10, where the angels appear in verse 7, with judgment upon the unsaved in verses 8 and 9 and the rapture of the saints in verse 10 - all of it happening "in that day" (verse 10).

The Lesson of the Fig Tree

(Matthew 24:32-35; Mark 13:28-31; Luke 21:29-33)

Mark 13:28 - "Now learn a parable of the fig tree; when her branch is yet tender, and putteth forth leaves, ye know that summer is near."

Ἀπὸ δὲ τῆς συκῆς μάθετε τὴν παραβολήν. ὅταν ἤδη ὁ κλάδος αὐτῆς ἁπαλὸς γένηται καὶ ἐκφύῃ τὰ φύλλα, γινώσκετε ὅτι ἐγγὺς τὸ θέρος ἐστίν.

Ἀπὸ (preposition with the ablative of source) 70.
δὲ (explanatory conjunction) 11.
τῆς (gen.sing.fem.of the article in agreement with συκῆς) 9.
συκῆς (gen.sing.fem.of συκέα, description) 1366.
μάθετε (2d.per.pl.aor.act.impv.of μανθάνω, command) 794.
τὴν (acc.sing.fem.of the article in agreement with παραβολήν) 9.
παραβολήν (acc.sing.fem.of παραβολή, direct object of μάθετε) 1027.
ὅταν (conjunction introducing an indefinite temporal clause) 436.
ἤδη (temporal adverb) 291.
ὁ (nom.sing.masc.of the article in agreement with κλάδος) 9.
κλάδος (nom.sing.masc.of κλάδος, subject of γένηται) 1071.
αὐτῆς (gen.sing.fem.of αὐτός, possession) 16.
ἁπαλὸς (nom.sing.masc.of ἁπαλός, predicate adjective) 1510.
γένηται (3d.per.sing.aor.subj.of γίνομαι, indefinite temporal clause) 113.
καὶ (adjunctive conjunction joining verbs) 14.
ἐκφύῃ (3d.per.sing.pres.act.subj.of ἐκφύω, indefinite temporal clause) 1511.
τὰ (acc.pl.neut.of the article in agreement with φύλλα) 9.
φύλλα (acc.pl.neut.of φύλλον, direct object of ἐκφύῃ) 1367.
γινώσκετε (2d.per.pl.pres.act.ind.of γινώσκω, customary) 131.
ὅτι (conjunction introducing an object clause in indirect discourse) 211.
ἐγγὺς (nom.sing.neut.of ἐγγύς, predicate adjective) 1512.
τὸ (nom.sing.neut.of the article in agreement with θέρος) 9.
θέρος (nom.sing.neut.of θέρος, subject of ἐστίν) 1513.
ἐστίν (3d.per.sing.pres.ind.of εἰμί, aoristic) 86.

Translation - "Now learn the lesson from the fig tree. When the branch has become tender and is growing leaves, you know that summer is near."

Comment: δὲ is explanatory. The fig tree will be the basis for an object lesson. ὅταν with its two subjunctives, γένηται and ἐκφῦῃ comprise the indefinite temporal clause. When the branch of the fig tree has already grown soft and when it begins to put forth leaves (no definite time is predicted) it is then possible to know. . . κ.τ.λ. This is definite. Note the indirect discourse with the object clause introduced by ὅτι. He who lives to see the fig tree bud and grow leaves will live also to see the summer season, unless, of course, he should die an untimely death. The point is that there is very little time, much less than a year, between the budding of the fig tree and the beginning of summer. *Cf.* Mt.24:32; Lk.21:30. Sooooo?! The application of the parable follows in

Verse 29 - "So ye in like manner, when ye shall see these things come to pass, know that it is nigh, even at the doors."

οὕτως καὶ ὑμεῖς, ὅταν ἴδητε ταῦτα γινόμενα, γινώσκετε ὅτι ἐγγύς ἐστιν ἐπὶ θύραις.

οὕτως (demonstrative adverb) 74.
καὶ (adjunctive conjunction joining indefinite temporal clauses) 14.
ὑμεῖς (nom.pl.masc.of *σύ*, emphatic subject of *γινώσκετε*) 104.
ὅταν (conjunction introducing an indefinite temporal clause) 436.
ἴδητε (2d.per.pl.aor.act.subj.of *ὁράω*, indefinite temporal clause) 144.
ταῦτα (acc.pl.neut.of *οὗτος*, direct object of *ἴδητε*) 93.
γινόμενα (pres.part.acc.pl.neut.of *γίνομαι*, adverbial, circumstantial) 113.
γινώσκετε (2d.per.pl.pres.act.impv.of *γινώσκω*, command) 131.
ὅτι (conjunction introducing an object clause in indirect discourse) 211.
ἐγγύς (nom.sing.neut..of *ἐγγύς*, predicate adjective) 1512.
ἐστιν (3d.per.sing.pres.ind.of *εἰμί*, aoristic) 86.
ἐπὶ (preposition with the locative in a metaphorical time expression) 47.
θύραις (loc.pl.fem.of *θύρα*, time expression) 571.

Translation - "And as you see these things happening, know that it is near - at the doors."

Comment: *Cf.*#74 for the use of *οὕτως* here. *καὶ* joins together the two indefinite temporal clauses - "when the fig tree . . . *κ.τ.λ.*" of verse 28 and "when you see these things. . . *κ.τ.λ.*" of verse 29. The new growth of the fig tree announces the coming of summer, and the occurrence of *ταῦτα* - "these things" announces the the second coming of Messiah. *ὅταν ἴδητε* does not suggest to every Christian who heard Jesus say this or who read these words that he would be certain to live to witness the second coming, but endtime Christians will. If and when we do - - - the conclusion contains real certitude - you are commanded to know. . . put it down as established. . . you can be certain that. What? The *ὅτι* object clause tells us. It is near. How near? At the doors. Verse 30 will answer this question more specifically.

To what does *ταῦτα* refer? The events of vss.14-23. Even if we did not have verse 30, we could not conclude that the Abomination of Desolation had a local and first century reference to Titus in A.D.70, since what is described in verse 14 is tied to vss.24-27. Nothing like that happened in A.D.70, nor has it yet occured at this writing (l980). So we are still to look for the prophetic signs that our Lord's coming is near. Perhaps this is as good a time as any to observe that, as of this date (September 4, 1980) there is no specific scriptural warrant for predicting that the second coming of Messiah will occur on any specific date. We still do not know. But Jesus nowhere said that no one would *ever* know the day. *Cf.* Mt.24:33; Lk.21:31.

Verse 30 - "Verily I say unto you, that this generation shall not pass, till all these things be done."

ἀμὴν λέγω ὑμῖν ὅτι οὐ μὴ παρέλθῃ ἡ γενεὰ αὕτη μέχρις οὗ ταῦτα πάντα γένηται.

ἀμὴν (explicative) 466.

λέγω (1st.per.sing.pres.act.ind.of λέγω, aoristic) 66.

ὑμίν (dat.pl.masc.of σύ, indirect object of λέγω) 104.

ὅτι (conjunction introducing an object clause in indirect discourse) 211.

οὐ (summary negative conjunction with μὴ and the subjunctive, emphatic negation) 130.

μὴ (qualified negative conjunction with οὐ and the subjunctive, emphatic negation) 87.

παρέλθῃ (3d.per.sing.aor.mid.subj.of παρέρχομαι, emphatic negation) 467.

ἡ (nom.sing.fem.of the article in agreement with γενεὰ) 9.

γενεὰ (nom.sing.fem.of γενεά, subject of παρέλθῃ) 922.

αὕτη (nom.sing.fem.of οὗτος, in agreement with γενεὰ) 93.

μέχρις (improper preposition with the genitive of time description) 948.

οὗ (gen.sing.masc.of ὅς, time description) 65.

ταῦτα (nom.pl.neut.of οὗτος, subject of γένηται) 93.

πάντα (nom.pl.neut.of πᾶς, in agreement with ταῦτα) 67.

γένηται (3d.per.sing.aor.subj.of γίνομαι, indefinite temporal clause) 113.

Translation - "I am telling you truly that this generation will not pass away until such time as all these things have been done."

Comment: Montgomery translates ". . . the present generation shall not pass until all these things begin to happen." Apparently she means that the generation to whom Jesus was speaking in A.D.33 would live to see the *beginning* of *all these things*, including happenings described in verses 24-27. Goodspeed has, "These things will *all* (our emphasis) happen before the present age passes away" by which it may be assumed that he understood by γενεά the church age - a period of time from Calvary to 1980 and beyond. Montgomery's translation is open to question since she makes γένηται in the indefinite relative temporal clause ingressive. A more serious objection is that since she correctly translates *all these things* Jesus must have had reference also to the events of verses 24-27. The generation to whom Jesus spoke these words did not live to see the beginning of *all these things*, since they include the darkened sun, the failing moon, the falling stars, the quaking heavens, the coming of the Son of Man and the gathering of the saints. To make γένηται ingressive - "begin to happen" makes no sense since it would stretch the events of the second coming across a long period of time. History thus belies her interpretation.

Goodspeed is wrong because γενεά does not mean "age" in the sense of a period of time of undetermined extent. Montgomery is correct in interpreting γενεά to mean a single generation of human beings, whose parents belonged to the immediately preceding generation and whose children belong to the generation immediately following. It is in the proper sense of γενεά (#922) that we speak of grandfather, father and son as representing three generations. This is the consistent meaning of γενεά in the New Testament. The student should examine all of the references (#922) and satisfy himself. Montgomery's translation suggests that there was something in the lifetime of that generation to whom Jesus spoke which was the "beginning" of the events of verses 24-27. The

Son of Man has not yet *begun* to come in the clouds, nor have the angels yet *begun* to translate the saints. Nor have the celestial events of verse 25 begun, for when they do begin they will not cease until the show is over as the future periphrastic in verse 25 makes clear. Some multiplied billions ofthe stars are still up there as we write. Goodspeed's statement is correct, but it is not a translation of the Greek text!

The problem boils down to two questions: (1) What does γενεά (#922) mean? *Cf.* comments *supra*, and (2) What is meant by αὕτη (#93) which modifies it? Which generation is Jesus talking about? The antecedent of αὕτη is the people of verse 29. Hence we translate, "The *same* generation, *viz.* the generation which lives to see "these things happening" (vs.29) is the generation that will see all of the things (Mk.13:14-27) finished. How much time will elapse between the Abomination of Desolation (Mk.13:14) spoken of by Daniel's prophecy (Mt.24:15) and the coming of the Son of Man in the clouds, the ministry of the angels and the celestial events which are a part of the final drama? Both Daniel 9:27 and Rev.13:5 tell us that it will be forty two months. Thus the people who belong to the generation alive to witness the middle of Daniel's last week, will be alive only three and one half years later.

This of course, makes date setting possible for Christians of that last generation. No problem. Noah was a date setter. Simeon was and Jesus only said in Mt.24:36 that on that day when He sat upon the Mount of Olives and answered the three-fold question of Peter, James, John and Andrew, no one knew the day, except the Father in heaven. He even said that He did not know *at that time.* He did not say that no one would ever know. He did not deny that the last generation of living Christians would know, and Paul said that in fact they would know (1 Thess.5:4,5).

Does the present generation as this is being written (September 4, 1980) know? Are we the generation that Jesus referred to in verse 30? *At present* we cannot qualify under the terms of verse 29 and therefore we are not necessarily the generation of verse 30. The budding of the fig tree refers specifically to the events of Mk.14:14 and those that follow, not to the rise of Jewish nationalism in 1948 as some prophecy teachers, in our opinion, erroneously teach. At any moment we may qualify and if we do we will then be able to predict the day, though not the hour, when He will come. When some internationally powerful diplomat "confirms" the Abrahamic Covenant with Israel for a period of seven years (Dan.9:27) and the other correlative events of Rev.6:1-6; 8:7-11 corroborate our conclusion, we will know that our generation, who lived to see the beginning will live to see the end, although no one individual in that generation will have any personal assurance that he will not die before the great day comes.

The reader is urged to shake off preconceived ideas about endtime eschatology, stop worshipping big names at prophetic Bible conferences and prestigious Biblical footnotes, stop gazing at multicolored charts and, in substitution for all of this, start searching the scriptures. Those who refuse to search for themselves and choose rather to follow some other Christian's interpretation is, to that degree a slave.

Verse 31 - "Heaven and earth shall pass away; but my words shall not pass away."

ὁ οὐρανὸς καὶ ἡ γῆ παρελεύσονται, οἱ δὲ λόγοι μου οὐ μὴ παρελεύσονται.

ὁ (nom.sing.masc.of the article in agreement with οὐρανὸς) 9.
οὐρανὸς (nom.sing.masc.of οὐρανός, subject of παρελεύσονται) 254.
καὶ (adjunctive conjunction joining nouns) 14.
ἡ (nom.sing.fem.of the article in agreement with γῆ) 9.
γῆ (nom.sing.fem.of γῆ, subject of παρελεύσονται) 157.
παρελεύσονται (3d.per.pl.fut.mid.ind.of παρέρχομαι, predictive) 467.
οἱ (nom.pl.masc.of the article in agreement with λόγοι) 9.
δὲ (adversative conjunction) 11.
λόγοι (nom.pl.masc.of λόγος, subject of παρελεύσονται) 510.
μου (gen.sing.masc.of ἐγώ, possession) 123.
οὐ (summary negative conjunction with μὴ and the predictive future) 130.
μὴ (qualified negative conjunction with οὐ and the predictive future) 87.
παρελεύσονται (3d.per.pl.fut.mid.ind.of παρέρχομαι, predictive) 467.

Translation - "The heaven and the earth will pass away, but my words will not pass away."

Comment: *Cf.*comment on Mt.24:35; Lk.21:33. Note that Matthew uses the subjunctive of emphatic negation with οὐ μὴ, while Mark and Luke have οὐ μὴ with the predictive future. In Mk.13:30 we have οὐ μὴ παρέλθῃ, the subjunctive of emphatic negation.

The Unknown Day and Hour

(Matthew 24:36-44; Mark 13:32-37)

Mark 13:32 - "But of that day and that hour knoweth no man, no, not the angels which are in heaven, neither the Son, but the Father."

Περὶ δὲ τῆς ἡμέρας ἐκείνης ἢ τῆς ὥρας οὐδεὶς οἶδεν, οὐδὲ οἱ ἄγγελοι ἐν οὐρανῷ οὐδὲ ὁ υἱός, εἰ μὴ ὁ πατήρ.

Περὶ (preposition with the genitive of reference) 173.
δὲ (adversative conjunction) 11.
τῆς (gen.sing.fem.of the article in agreement with ἡμέρας) 9.
ἡμέρας (gen.sing.fem.of ἡμέρα, reference) 135.
ἐκείνης (gen.sing.fem.of ἐκεῖνος, in agreement with ἡμέρας) 246.
ἢ (disjunctive particle) 465.
τῆς (gen.sing.fem.of the article in agreement with ὥρας) 9.
ὥρας (gen.sing.fem.of ὥρα, reference) 735.
οὐδεὶς (nom.sing.masc.of οὐδείς, subject of οἶδεν) 446.
οἶδεν (3d.per.sing.pres.act.ind.of ὁράω, aoristic) 144.
οὐδὲ (disjunctive particle) 452.
οἱ (nom.pl.masc.of the article in agreement with ἄγγελοι) 9.
ἄγγελοι (nom.pl.masc.of ἄγγελος, subject of οἶδεν) 96.
ἐν (preposition with the locative of place) 80.

οὐρανῷ (loc.sing.masc.of οὐρανός, place where) 254.
οὐδὲ (disjunctive particle) 452.
ὁ (nom.sing.masc.of the article in agreement with υἱός) 9.
υἱός (nom.sing.masc.of υἱός, subject of οἶδεν) 5.
εἰ (conditional particle in an elliptical first-class condition) 337.
μὴ (qualified negative conjunction in an elliptical condition) 87.
ὁ (nom.sing.masc.of the article in agreement with πατήρ) 9.
πατήρ (nom.sing.masc.of πατήρ, subject of the verb understood) 238.

Translation - "But with reference to that day or to the hour, not one man knows, neither the angels in heaven, nor even the Son, except the Father."

Comment: *Cf.* Mt.24:36. Leopold von Ranke, the German historian, taught his students that the task of the historian, when evaluating a document, was to put himself back into the time and place when and where the document was created. Viewed in its provenance (where, by whom and under what circumstances did it originate?) and in its time (*zeitgeist*) its meaning would be clear. For example "Man the lifeboats!" cannot be evaluated until we know whether a sea captain is announcing that the Titanic is going to the bottom or that the children are enjoying a water fight at the beach. The attempt to achieve *zeitgeist* ("the spirit of the time") is difficult, but essential to sound exegesis. Where, when and under what circumstances did our Lord make the disclaimer of our passage?

The place was the Mount of Olives. The time was about two days before the crucifixion. The circumstance? Peter, James, John and Andrew had asked Him three questions about the order and time of certain events to which Jesus had alluded. What precisely did He say about it? The statement of Jesus about the day and hour of the second coming of Messiah was that ". . . no man at that time and in that place knew the hour." He added that the angels did not know and that even He did not know. Only the Father knew.

Jesus was not yet officially declared to be the Son of God (Rom.1:4), nor appointed High Priest (Heb.5:5; Ps.2:7; Acts 13:33; Heb.5:10; Ps.110:4), nor was He yet exalted to the Father's right hand (Psa.110:1), nor invited to direct a worldwide missionary enterprise (Ps.2:8). He was still in the period of His κενόσις (Phil.2:7,8). He knew that He was to die and He had prophesied that He would be raised from the dead (Mt.16:21), that He would ascend to the Father (John 14:3; Mt.26:64) and that He would return to earth (John 14:3; Mk.13:26,27). But He did not, *at that time*, know the precise day when He would return. That is what He said and that is all that He said.

The effort to torture His statement in order to support a doctrine that Christians at the end of the age of grace will not know when to expect Him, and will therefore be overtaken by an unannounced coming, as a thief surprizes his victim, is totally reprehensible. This view is urged upon us, because it is an essential component of the Plymouth Brethren eschatology model which is based upon the concept of a pretribulation rapture of the church. This is perhaps the most tragic bit of eisegesis to mar the otherwise good record of the modern evangelical movement.

After Jesus ascended to heaven He received the entire Revelation, which contains the key to the story of the last days, by showing us the connection between Daniel and the Revelation. The Father gave it to Jesus Christ, His Son, Who in turn gave it to John who delivered it to the churches, who incorporated it into the New Testament canon. John "... bare record of the word of God, and of the testimony of Jesus Christ, and of all things that he saw. Blessed is he that ... *κ.τ.λ.*" (Rev.1:1-3).

Verse 33 - "Take ye heed, watch and pray: for ye know not when the time is."

βλέπετε ἀγρυπνεῖτε. οὐκ οἴδατε γὰρ πότε ὁ καιρός ἐστιν.

βλέπετε (2d.per.pl.pres.act.impv.of *βλέπω*, command) 499.

#2714 *ἀγρυπνεῖτε* (2d.per.pl.pres.act.impv.of *ἀγρυπνέω*, command).

watch - Mark 13:33; Luke 21:36; Eph.6:18; Heb.13:17.

Meaning: Cf.ἀγρυπνία (#4314). To stay awake; to be alert; to watch so as not to be surprized - so as to learn when the Lord is coming back to earth - Mk.13:33; Lk.21:36. As a general attitude for the victorious Christian - Eph.6:18. As an attitude of watch-care of a pastor over his flock - Heb.13:17.

οὐκ (summary negative conjunction with the indicative) 130.
οἴδατε (2d.per.pl.pres.act.ind.of *ὁράω*, aoristic) 144.
γὰρ (causal conjunction) 105.
πότε (temporal conjunction with the indicative in a definite temporal clause) 1233.
ὁ (nom.sing.masc.of the article in agreement with *καιρός*) 9.
καιρός (nom.sing.masc.of *καιρός*, subject of *ἐστιν*) 767.
ἐστιν (3d.per.sing.pres.ind.of *εἰμί*, definite temporal clause) 86.

Translation - "Take heed! Stay awake! Because you do not know when the time is."

Comment: If it is God's will that the saints shall never know when our Lord will return, this admonition to keep looking and to stay alert is without point. It is precisely because (causal *γὰρ*) we do not know now that Jesus tells us to make an effort to find out. Two dramatic imperatives follow the statement that the day of the second coming is known but to God the Father. Look out! Stay awake! Watch! Be alert! The football fans call their advice to the defense - "Look out for a pass!" If the Father did not intend ever to reveal the day to His children, this admonition to watch is meaningless. Why watch for it if we are not suppose to know when it comes? The reason for watchfullness is given - "Because you do not know the time." We are not to watch for the Lord's return but we are to watch for the events that will tell us the time. "You do not know the time. Find out!" How? By watching. Once we know when He will come, there will be no further need for the Lord to admonish us to be watching. Can one imagine a persecuted Christian during the tribulation, looking forward to the day of his redemption, as it drew ever nearer, being indifferent to the event on the appointed day?

If the pretribulation rapturist continues to cling to his view, all persuasion to the contrary notwithstanding, that nothing more of prophetic significance is to take place before the rapture of the church, he will fail to recognize the fulfillment of Daniel 9:27 when it comes and perhaps, three and one half years later, even fail to recognize the Antichrist. We can be sure that, rather than receive the mark and number of the Beast, he will finally admit that his views had been mistaken. If tomorrow's media reported the signing of an agreement between Antichrist and Israel confirming for seven years Israel's claim to Palestine, on the strength of the Zionist interpretation of the Abrahamic Covenant, the announcement would not appear to be significant to one who is unalterably committed to the idea that Daniel's 70th week cannot begin until the rapture has taken place.

Our Lord's orders to watch and be alert are in the present tense, indicating a state of constant watching. We must not take our eyes from the sky for a moment. Obedience to these orders is impossible now even for the most ardent premillenialist. No one watches the heavens for the unannounced coming of the Lord *all of the time.* If we did we could neither eat nor sleep and there would be a rash of traffic accidents. But it is not at all unreasonable to believe that the Christian who is alert to the signs of the times and who will know when he will come, will do nothing else but watch when the time comes. One cannot imagine Noah and his family being indifferent to the weather on the seventh day (Gen.7:4, 11-13) after God told him when the rain would begin. But the day before they did not watch, because they already knew when the flood would come. The only way to prevent the coming of the Lord from being a surprize to the saints is for them to know when He is coming. Are there no golfers who are saved? For it is not likely that a golfer is thinking about the rapture when he is trying to hit a tee shot!

Verse 34 - "For the Son of Man is as a man taking a far journey, who left his house, and gave authority to his servants, and to every man his work, and commanded the porter to watch."

ὡς ἄνθρωπος ἀπόδημος ἀφεὶς τὴν οἰκίαν αὐτοῦ καὶ δοὺς τοῖς δούλοις αὐτοῦ τὴν ἐξουσίαν, ἑκάστῳ τὸ ἔργον αὐτοῦ, καὶ τῷ θυρωρῷ ἐνετείλατο ἵνα γρηγορῇ.

ὡς (comparative adverb) 128.
ἄνθρωπος (nom.sing.masc.of *ἄνθρωπος*, nominative absolute) 341.

#2715 *ἀπόδημος* (nom.sing.masc.of *ἀπόδημος*, in agreement with *ἄνθρωπος*).

taking a far journey - Mark 13:34.

Meaning: A combination of *ἀπό* (#70) and *δῆμος* (#3264). Hence, one absent from the people. One taking a journey. One who is abroad - Mark 13:34.

ἀφεὶς (aor.act.part.nom.sing.masc.of *ἀφίημι*, adverbial, temporal) 319.
τὴν (acc.sing.fem.of the article in agreement with *οἰκίαν*) 9.

οἰκίαν (acc.sing.fem.of οἰκία, direct object of ἀφεὶς) 186.
αὐτοῦ (gen.sing.masc.of αὐτός, possession) 16.
καὶ (adjunctive conjunction joining participles) 14.
δοὺς (aor.act.part.nom.sing.masc.of δίδωμι, adverbial, temporal) 362.
τοῖς (dat.pl.masc.of the article in agreement with δούλοις) 9.
δούλοις (dat.pl.masc.of δοῦλος, indirect object of δοὺς) 725.
αὐτοῦ (gen.sing.masc.of αὐτός, possession) 16.
τὴν (acc.sing.fem.of the article in agreement with ἐξουσίαν) 9.
ἐξουσίαν (acc.sing.fem.of ἐξουσία, direct object of δοὺς) 707.
ἑκάστῳ (dat.sing.masc.of ἕκαστος, indirect object of δοὺς) 1217.
τὸ (acc.sing.neut.of the article in agreement with ἔργον) 9.
ἔργον (acc.sing.neut.of ἔργον, direct object of δοὺς) 460.
αὐτοῦ (gen.sing.masc.of αὐτός, possession) 16.
καὶ (continuative conjunction) 14.
τῷ (dat.sing.masc.of the article in agreement with θυρωρῷ) 9.
θυρωρῷ (dat.sing.masc.of θυρωρός, indirect object of ἐνετείλατο) 2405.
ἐνετείλατο (3d.per.sing.1st.aor.mid.ind.of ἐντ ἐλλομαι, constative) 349.
ἵνα (conjunction with the subjunctive introducing a purpose clause) 114.
γρηγορῇ (3d.per.sing.pres.act.subj.of πρηγορέω, purpose) 1520.

Translation - "Like a man leaving on a long trip, who after he left his house and gave to his servants the authority - to each to do his work, commanded the porter to be on the alert."

Comment: Jesus has ordered the disciples to assume an attitude of intelligent, scripturally guided watchfullness, so that, since they did not know the time of Messiah's advent, they might be apprized of it, if it should come during their lifetime. Now He illustrates His point with a story. A man planned to take a long trip away from home. He left his house, but not until he had assigned specific work to each of his servants and gave them the authority to carry it out while he was gone. Just before he left he assigned to the porter the task of keeping careful watch over the affairs of the household and to watch for his return. The ἵνα clause is an object clause of purpose after a verb of exhorting - in this case ἐνετείλατο (Burton, *Moods and Tenses*, 83), although it is neither pure purpose nor pure result but ". . . a bridge, in a sense, between the two extremes" (Robertson, *Grammar*, 991). Mark has allowed an ellipsis to creep into his sentence structure. There is no main verb joined to the participles ἀφεὶς and δοὺς. There would have been no problem if Mark had omitted καὶ, the continuative adverb, which introduces the last clause. "Having left . . . and given . . . he commanded. . κ.τ.λ." *Cf.* Mt.25:14.

The assignment given to each of the servants, with authority to carry out specific tasks recalls Ephesians 2:10. We are saved by the grace of God in order to do the "good works which He hath before ordained that we should walk in them." The porter may be thought of as the pastor of a church or other Bible student, who, while the servants are busy with their appointed tasks, keeps a close watch on events which will herald the return of the owner.

Verse 35 - "Watch ye therefore: for ye know not when the master of the house cometh, at even, or at midnight, or at the cock crowing, or in the morning."

γρηγορεῖτε οὖν, οὐκ οἴδατε γὰρ πότε ὁ κύριος τῆς οἰκίας ἔρχεται, ἢ ὀψὲ ἢ μεσονύκτιον ἢ ἀλεκτοροφωνίας ἢ πρωΐ,

γρηγορεῖτε (2d.per.pl.pres.act.impv.of *πρηγορέω*, command) 1520.
οὖν (inferential conjunction) 68.
οὐκ (summary negative conjunction with the indicative) 130.
οἴδατε (2d.per.pl.pres.act.ind.of *ὁράω*, aoristic) 144.
γὰρ (causal conjunction) 105.
πότε (temporal conjunction with the indicative in a definite temporal clause) 1233.
ὁ (nom.sing.masc.of the article in agreement with *κύριος*) 9.
κύριος (nom.sing.masc.of *κύριος*, subject of *ἔρχεται*) 97.
τῆς (gen.sing.fem.of the article in agreement with *οἰκίας*) 9.
οἰκίας (gen.sing.fem.of *οἰκία*, description) 186.
ἔρχεται (3d.per.sing.pres.act.ind.of *ἔρχομαι*, definite temporal clause) 146.
ἢ (disjunctive particle) 465.
ὀψὲ (adverbial) 1687.
ἢ (disjunctive particle) 465.
μεσονύκτιον (acc.sing.neut.of *μεσονύκτιος*, adverbial, time point) 2446.
ἢ (disjunctive particle) 465.

#2716 *ἀλεκτοροφωφνίας* (gen.sing.fem.of *ἀλεκτοροφωνία*, time description).

cock crowing - Mark 13:35.

Meaning: A combination of *ἀλέκτωρ* (#1581) and *φωνή* (#222). The crowing of the cock. Under Roman rule the third watch of the night, preceded by *ὀψέ* and *μεσονύκτιον* and followed by *πρωΐ* - Mark 13:35.

ἢ (disjunctive particle) 465.
πρωΐ (adverbial) 1192.

Translation - "Watch therefore, because you do not know when the master of the house is coming - whether in the evening or at midnight or when the cock crows or in the morning."

Comment: The four time points correspond to the four watches of the night as divided by the Romans and observed by the Jews, beginning respectively at 9:00 p.m., midnight, 3:00 a.m. and 6:00 a.m. Who is to watch? Every Christian, but especially *ὁ θυρωρός* of verse 34, although each of the servants had specific tasks assigned to him to be performed during the absence of his lord. The porter's task to stay awake and look for the events that will presage the second coming is the task of all Christian disciples. We are to teach, preach, sing, farm, buy or sell, work in an office or a factory or whatever else He has appointed us to do, but with one eye out to the signs of the times. The penalty for failing to watch is given in

Verse 36 - "Lest coming suddenly he find you sleeping."

μὴ ἐλθὼν ἐξαίφνης εὕρῃ ὑμᾶς καθεύδοντας.

μὴ (qualifed negative conjunction with the subjunctive, negative purpose) 87.
ἐλθὼν (aor.part.nom.sing.masc.of ἔρχομαι, adverbial, temporal) 146.
ἐξαίφνης (adverbial) 1879.
εὕρῃ (3d.per.sing.aor.act.subj.of εὑρίσκω, negative purpose) 79.
ὑμᾶς (acc.pl.masc.of σύ, direct object of εὕρῃ) 104.
καθεύδοντας (pres.act.part.acc.pl.masc.of καθεύδω, adverbial, circumstantial) 755.

Translation - "So that when he comes unexpectedly he will not find you asleep."

Comment: Negative purpose here with μὴ and the subjunctive in εὕρῃ. It is interesting to note that the porter is to watch, not for the day, because the Christian to whom the porter corresponds in the parable, who will be alive at the coming of the Lord will already have come to understand on what *day* the Lord will come. This porter is to watch in order to know the *hour* of the day. There is nothing in the prophecies of Daniel, nor in the Revelation to tell us the hour when He will come, although the precise day will be understood at that time. In that day He may come at any one of the times mentioned - 9:00 p.m., midnight, 3:00 a.m. or 6:00 a.m. or at any moment in between. Hence the need to watch, not for the day but for the hour of the day. No Christian is going to be embarrassed by being found asleep when He comes.

The view that the rapture of the church is immanent and unannounced means that some Christians, despite their utmost devotion to His cause and enthusiasm for His return, are going to be asleep when He comes. How often have we arrived at our homes, late and night and unannounced, to find our loved ones asleep? Did we censure them for their apparent unconcern for our coming? How could they lose sleep indefinitely in order to be awake if and when we came? The only way to assure that every Christian upon earth who is alive and remains (1 Thess.4:17) to the coming of the Lord shall be watching and waiting for Him in eager anticipation for His return, rather than asleep, is for all of the saints at that time to know precisely when He will appear. It is difficult to imagine an endtime Christian who has endured persecution for seven years and who has the great day marked in his mind and on his calendar, asleep in his bed when our Lord comes! He might try to get a little extra sleep the night before so as to be alert for His Lord's return. Does one suppose that Noah was able to sleep on the day that the rain began and he entered the ark? (Gen.7:4, 11-13). Pretribulation rapture teachers should be disturbed about this verse. It poses no problems for those of us who look for the rapture on the same day as the revelation.

Verse 37 - "And what I say unto you, I say unto all, Watch."

ὃ δὲ ὑμῖν λέγω, πᾶσιν λέγω, γρηγορεῖτε.

ὃ (acc.sing.neut.of ὅς, direct object of λέγω) 66.
δὲ (continuative conjunction) 11.
ὑμῖν (dat.pl.masc.of σύ, indirect object of λέγω) 104.
λέγω (1st.per.sing.pres.act.ind.of λέγω, aoristic) 66.
πᾶσιν (dat.pl.masc.of πᾶς, indirect object of λέγω) 67.
λέγω (1st.per.sing.pres.act.ind.of λέγω, aoristic) 66.
γρηγορεῖτε (2d.per.pl.pres.act.impv.of γρηγορέω, command) 1520.

Translation - "That which I am telling you, I am telling to all: Watch!"

Comment: This verse definitely applies the entire passage to all the saints, of whatever age, not only to the Twelve disciples and others seated that day with Jesus upon the Mount of Olives. Let every Christian stay alert. Let him study his Bible and watch the events of human history. An intelligent evaluation of events that might possibly be "signs of the times" with prophetic significance, can be made only by those who understand the biblical *weltanschauung*. Those who fail to understand the purpose of God in this age and who thus expect a political, social and economic system of government to be established on the ethical principles of the gospel of Christ, solely by the ethical acculturation of the church, will misread the signs, just as Jesus accused the Pharisees and Sadducees (Mt.16:3). Millions of Christians have watched in vain for the harbingers of the second coming. And yet their watch was not in vain, since they were obeying His command and trying to be patient (Heb.10:36,37). They lived out their lives, performed the tasks assigned to them by their Lord, finished their course, kept the faith (2 Tim.4:5-8) and died without knowing precisely where they were on God's time clock. Indeed, this may be the role of the generations who live in the 20th century of the Christian era. But we are commanded to watch nonetheless. There will be one generation of Christians who some day will see upon this earth the events that will clearly mark the beginning of Daniel's 70th week. That generation will live to see the day when He will descend in the clouds to rescue them. That is the day when the last of the seven trumpets will sound (1 Cor.15:52; Rev.10:7; 11:15-19), the last elect soul for whom Christ died will be saved and the dead in Christ, in company with those who are yet alive will be caught up to meet Him in the air. Can we imagine that any of them will be asleep when He comes?

We turn now to Luke's parallel account in Luke 21:5-38.

The Destruction of the Temple Foretold

(Matthew 24:1-2; Mark 13:1-2; Luke 21:5,6)

Luke 21:5 - "And as some spake of the temple, how it was adorned with goodly stones and gifts, he said . . . "

Καί τινων λεγόντων περὶ τοῦ ἱεροῦ, ὅτι λίθους καλοῖς καὶ ἀναθήμασιν κεκόσμηται, εἶπεν,

Καί (continuative conjunction) 14.

τινων (gen.pl.masc.of τις, indefinite pronoun, genitive absolute) 486
λεγόντων (pres.act.part.gen.pl.masc.of λέγω, genitive absolute) 66.
περὶ (preposition with the genitive of reference) 173.
τοῦ (gen.sing.neut.of the article in agreement with ἱεροῦ) 9.
ἱεροῦ (gen.sing.neut.of ἱερόν, reference) 346.
ὅτι (conjunction introducing an object clause in indirect discourse) 211.
λίθοις (instru.pl.masc.of λίθος, means) 290.
καλοῖς (instru.pl.masc.of καλός, in agreement with λίθοις) 296.
καὶ (adjunctive conjunction joining nouns) 14.

#2717 ἀναθήμασιν (instru.pl.neut.of ἀνάθημα, means).

gift - Luke 21:5.

*Meaning: Cf.*ἀνατίθημι (#3639). A gift, dedicated to God and laid up in the temple. A votive offering - Luke 21:5.

κεκόσμηται (3d.per.sing.perf.pass.ind.of κοσμέω, intensive) 1023.
εἶπεν (3d.per.sing.aor.act.ind.of εἶπον, constative) 155.

Translation - "And as some were speaking about the Temple court to the effect that it had been decorated with beautiful stones and votive offerings, He said, . . . "

Comment: *Cf.* Mt.24:1; Mk.13:1. Luke gives us the details of the construction and adornment of the temple - λίθοις καλοῖς καὶ ἀναθήμασιν. The disciples were speaking about the stones to the Stone, which was about to be rejected by the builders of a Christless society, and was destined to become the Cornerstone of Messiah's kingdom. The stones which the disciples so much admired would be thrown down in divine judgment upon an Establishment which majored in architecture and formality and neglected the weightier matters of the law. *Cf.*#290.

Verse 6 - "As for these things which ye behold, the days will come, in the which there shall not be left one stone upon another, that shall not be thrown down."

Ταῦτα ἃ θεωρεῖτε, ἐλεύσονται ἡμέραι ἐν αἷς οὐκ ἀφεθήσεται λίθος ἐπὶ λίθῳ ὃς οὐ καταλυθήσεται.

Ταῦτα (nom.pl.neut.of οὗτος, nominative absolute) 93.
ἃ (acc.pl.neut.of ὅς, direct object of θεωρεῖτε) 65.
θεωρεῖτε (2d.per.pl.pres.act.ind.of θεωρέω, aoristic) 1667.
ἐλεύσονται (3d.per.pl.fut.ind.of ἔρχομαι, predictive) 146.
ἡμέραι (nom.pl.fem.of ἡμέρα, subject of ἐλεύσονται) 135.
ἐν (preposition with the locative of time point) 80.
αἷς (loc.pl.fem.of ὅς, time point) 65.
οὐκ (summary negative conjunction with the indicative) 130.
ἀφεθήσεται (3d.per.sing.fut.pass.ind.of ἀφίημι, predictive) 319.
λίθος (nom.sing.masc.of λίθος, subject of ἀφεθήσεται) 290.

ἐπὶ (preposition with the locative of place where) 47.
λίθῳ (loc.sing.masc.of λίθος, place where) 290.
ὃς (nom.sing.masc.of ὅς, subject of καταλυθήσεται) 65.
οὐ (summary negative conjunction with the indicative) 130.
καταλυθήσεται (3d.per.sing.fut.pass.ind.of καταλύω, predictive) 463.

Translation - "These things which you see — the days will come in which not a stone will be left upon another stone that will not be torn down."

Comment: Ταῦτα ἃ θεωρεῖτε may be viewed as a nominative absolute or as an ordinary anacoluthon or aposiopesis. If the former, there is grammatical *non sequitur*, that is, there is nothing following to which it can be joined grammatically. It needs a verb which does not occur. If aposiopesis, it represents a deliberate break in the sentence, as our Lord is overcome with some emotion - sorrow or disgust, or both, and He breaks off the thought and takes a different tack. ἃ is attracted to its antecedent ταῦτα, though αἷς is locative by virtue of its use in its own clause. Note that Luke says λίθος ἐπὶ λίθῳ, while Matthew 24:2 and Mark 13:2 have λίθος ἐπὶ λίθον. There is no conflict. The accusative indicates extension - "stone up against stone" while the locative indicates place where "stone upon stone." Here are words, divinely inspired in the sense that they convey the total thought which God wished to convey, although they are not precisely dictated words. In this case the parallel passages which report the same speech enhance rather than destroy or diminish the meaning. Which way did Jesus say it? The dictation theorists have the problem and must decide, in which case they must accuse either Luke on the one hand or Matthew and Mark on the other of having written error into the text. The Holy Spirit is not concerned that we know the precise formulation of Jesus' remark. If we needed to know precisely how He said it, in order to gain what the Holy Spirit wishes to convey, then He would have dictated the passage to all three writers and no conflict in wording would occur. But this was not the Holy Spirit's concern. He wants us to know that Jesus predicted the total disintegration of that building. Precisely how Jesus said it, in this case, is therefore not important. *Cf.* Mt.24:2; Mk.13:2.

Signs and Persecutions

(Matthew 24:3-14; Mark 13:3-13; Luke 21:7-19)

Luke 21:7 - "And they asked him saying, Master, but when shall these things be? And what sign will there be when these things shall come to pass?"

Ἐπηρώτησαν δὲ αὐτὸν λέγοντες, Διδάσκαλε, πότε οὖν ταῦτα ἔσται, καὶ τί τὸ σημεῖον ὅταν μέλλῃ ταῦτα γίνεσθαι;

Ἐπηρώτησαν (3d.per.pl.aor.act.ind.of ἐπερωτάω, constative) 973.
δὲ (continuative conjunction) 11.
αὐτὸν (acc.sing.masc.of αὐτός, direct object of ἐπηρώτησαν) 16.
λέγοντες (pres.act.part.nom.pl.masc.of λέγω, recitative) 66.
Διδάσκαλε (voc.sing.masc.of διδάσκαλος, address) 742.

πότε (interrogative adverb in direct question) 1233.
οὖν (inferential conjunction) 68.
ταῦτα (nom.pl.neut.of οὗτος, subject of ἔσται) 93.
ἔσται (3d.per.sing.fut.ind.of εἰμί, deliberative) 86.
καὶ (continuative conjunction) 14.
τί (nom.sing.neut.of the interrogative pronoun, predicate nominative) 281.
τὸ (nom.sing.neut.of the article in agreement with σημεῖον) 9.
σημεῖον (nom.sing.neut.of σημεῖον, subject of ἔσται, understood) 1005.
ὅταν (temporal conjunction with the subjunctive in an indefinite temporal clause) 436.
μέλλῃ (3d.per.sing.pres.act.subj.of μέλλω, indefinite temporal clause) 206.
ταῦτα (nom.pl.neut.of οὗτος, subject of μέλλῃ) 93.
γίνεσθαι (pres.inf.of γίνομαι, complementary) 113.

Translation - "And they asked Him, 'But, Teacher, when will these things happen, and what will be the sign (to show) when they are about to take place?'"

Comment: *Cf.* Mt.24:3; Mk.13:4. Note that the question is for a sign that will tell the observer when the events which Jesus described in verses 5 and 6 will transpire? When? How shall we know that the time is near at hand? Note Luke's precise classical Greek as he is careful to join the singular verbs with the neuter plural subjects.

Verse 8 - "And he said, Take heed that ye be not deceived: for many shall come in my name, saying, I am Christ; and the time draweth near: go ye not therefore after them."

ὁ δὲ εἶπεν, Βλέπετε μὴ πλανηθῆτε. πολλοὶ γὰρ ἐλεύσονται ἐπὶ τῷ ὀνόματί μου λέγοντες, 'Εγώ εἰμι, καί, 'Ο καιρὸς ἤγγικεν. μὴ πορευτῆτε ὀπίσω αὐτῶν.

ὁ (nom.sing.masc.of the article, subject of εἶπεν) 9.
δὲ (continuative conjunction) 11.
εἶπεν (3d.per.sing.aor.act.ind.of εἶπον, constative) 155.
Βλέπετε (2d.per.pl.pres.act.impv.of βλέπω, command) 499.
μὴ (qualified negative conjunction with the subjunctive in a prohibition) 87.
πλανηθῆτε (2d.per.pl.aor.pass.subj.of πλανάω, prohibition) 1257.
πολλοὶ (nom.pl.masc.of πολύς, subject of ἐλεύσονται) 228.
γὰρ (causal conjunction) 105.
ἐλεύσονται (3d.per.pl.fut.mid.ind.of ἔρχομαι, predictive) 146.
ἐπὶ (preposition with the instrumental, means) 47.
τῷ (instru.sing.neut.of the article in agreement with ὀνόματί) 9.
ὀνόματί (instru.sing.neut.of ὄνομα, means) 108.
μου (gen.sing.masc.of ἐγώ, possession) 123.
λέγοντες (pres.act.part.nom.pl.masc.of λέγω, adverbial, complementary) 66.
'Εγώ (nom.sing.masc.of ἐγώ, subject of εἰμι) 123.
εἰμι (1st.per.sing.pres.ind.of εἰμι, aoristic) 86.

καί (adjunctive conjunction joining clauses in direct quotation) 14.
Ὁ (nom.sing.masc.of the article in agreement with καιρὸς) 9.
καιρὸς (nom.sing.masc.of καιρός, subject of ἤγγικεν) 767.
ἤγγικεν (3d.per.sing.perf.act.ind.of ἐγγίζω, intensive) 252.
μὴ (qualified negative conjunction with the subjunctive in a prohibition) 87.
πορευθῆτε (2d.per.pl.aor.mid.subj.of πορεύομαι, prohibition) 170.
ὀπίσω (adverbial, time and place) 302.
αὐτῶν (gen.pl.masc.of αὐτός, time and place description) 16.

Translation - "And He said, 'Look out! Do not be deceived! Because many will come in my name saying, 'I AM' and 'The time has arrived.' Do not follow after them.' "

Comment: We need not accuse Luke of omitting ἵνα before μὴ as though he were writing a negative purpose clause. He has written a command (imperative in βλέπετε) and followed it paratactically with a prohibition (μὴ with the subjunctive in πλανηθῆτε). Βλέπετε is a positive command and μὴ πλανηθῆτε is a negative command. Thus our translation. If we think of it the other way there is no damage done as the concept is the same. Thus, "Look out (Be careful) lest you be deceived" as we would translate if he had written Βλέπετε ἵνα μὴ πλανηθῆτε. Burton lends his support to our analysis. "It is true that βλέπω does not take an objective clause in classical Greek, that in the New Testament only the imperative of this verb is followed by a clause defining the action to be done or avoided, and that in a few instances the second verb is an aorist subjunctive in the second person with μὴ and might therefore be regarded as a Prohibitory Subjunctive." (Burton, *Moods and Tenses,* 89). *Cf.* Gal.5:15; Heb.12:25 for two other examples.

The danger is that the Christian will be led astray from time to time by the appearance of various demagogues who will come in the name of Christ, flashing the famous phrase Ἐγώ εἰμι and adding Ὁ καιρὸς ἤγγικεν. This will happen often, with a variety of personalities in the spotlight.

Josephus bears out Jesus' prophecy in his account of the days shortly before Titus' destruction of Jerusalem in A.D. 70. The latest example was Jim Jones. Jesus' solution to the problem is simple. We are to ignore them. *Cf.* Mt.24:4,5; Mk.13:5,6.

Verse 9 - "But when ye shall hear of wars and commotions, be not terrified: for these things must first come to pass; but the end is not by and by."

ὅταν δὲ ἀκούσητε πολέμους καὶ ἀκαταστασίας, μὴ πτοηθῆτε. δεῖ γὰρ ταῦτα γενέσθαι πρῶτον, ἀλλ' οὐκ εὐθέως τὸ τέλος.

ὅταν (adverb with the subjunctive introducing an indefinite temporal clause) 436.
δὲ (continuative conjunction) 11.
ἀκούσητε (2d.per.pl.aor.act.subj.of ἀκούω, indefinite temporal clause) 148.
πολέμους (acc.pl.masc.of πόλεμος, general reference) 1483.
καὶ (adjunctive conjunction joining nouns) 14.

#2718 ἀκαταστασίας (acc.pl.fem.of ἀκαταστασία, general reference).

commotion - Luke 21:9.
confusion - 1 Cor.14:33; James 3:16.
tumult - 2 Cor.6:5; 12:20.

*Meaning: Cf.*ἀκτάστατος (#5097). Instability, disorder, confusion, commotion, tumult. With reference to public violence - Luke 21:9. Mob action - 2 Cor.6:5. Confusion within a church body due to differences of opinion - 2 Cor.12:20; James 3:16, and the confusion caused by an indiscriminate and unscriptural exercise of the gift of tongues - 1 Cor.14:33.

μὴ (qualified negative conjunction with the subjunctive in a prohibition) 87.

#2719 πτοηθῆτε (2d.per.pl.aor.pass.subj.of πτοέω, prohibition).

terrify - Luke 21:9; 24:37.

Meaning: From πτόα - "terror." To be startled, made afraid, terrified. Because of wars and commotions - Luke 21:9. The reaction of the disciples at a post-resurrection appearance of Jesus - Luke 24:37.

δεῖ (pres.act.ind.imperson.) 1207.
γὰρ (causal conjunction) 105.
ταῦτα (acc.pl.neut.of οὗτος, general reference) 93.
γενέσθαι (aor.inf.of γίνομαι, noun use, subject of δεῖ) 113.
πρῶτον (acc.sing.neut.of πρῶτος, adverbial) 487.
ἀλλ' (negative conjunction) 342.
οὐκ (summary negative conjunction with the indicative understood) 130.
εὐθέως (temporal adverb) 392.
τὸ (nom.sing.neut.of the article in agreement with τέλος) 9.
τέλος (nom.sing.neut.of τέλος, subject of ἐστί, understood) 881.

Translation - "And when you hear about wars and violence, do not be afraid, because it is necessary for these things to happen first, but the end is not about to come."

Comment: False Messiahs are no evidence of an immediate end of the age (verse 8). Nor are wars and incidents of public violence. Examples of ἀκαταστασίας (#2718) in recent years can be found in the conflicts in Ireland between Catholics and Protestants, border skirmishes between Israel and the Arabs in the Middle East, race riots in Watts, on Hough Avenue or in Miami. Note the accusative in πολέμους and ἀκαταστασίας after ακούσητε.The accusative after a verb of hearing means "this and no more" whereas the genitive means "this and no other." These things must not be allowed to frighten us. Jesus tells us why with the γὰρ causal clause. They have always happened in the course of human history. They are the evidence of man's depraved inability to get along with himself or with others. They are charactertistic of an economic interpretation of history in a world composed of sinners with a materialistic point of view. These things must first occur, but the consummation of the age, which will feature the glorious return of Messiah to sit on David's throne and to rule the world in righteousness, as predicted by the Old Testament prophets, is not necessarily telegraphed by these events. *Cf.* Mt.24:6; Mk.13:7.

Verse 10 - "Then said he unto them, Nation shall rise against nation, and kingdom against kingdom."

Τότε ἔλεγεν αὐτοῖς, Ἐγερθήσεται ἔθνος ἐπ' ἔθνος καὶ βασιλεία ἐπὶ βασιλείαν,

Τότε (continuative conjunction) 166.
ἔλεγεν (3d.per.sing.imp.act.ind.of *λέγω*, progressive duration) 66.
αὐτοῖς (dat.pl.masc.of *αὐτός*, indirect object of *ἔλεγεν*) 16.
Ἐγερθήσεται (3d.per.sing.fut.pass.ind.of *ἐγείρω*, predictive) 125.
ἔθνος (nom.sing.neut.of *ἔθνος*, subject of *ἐγερθήσεται*) 376.
ἐπ' (preposition with the accusative, hostility) 47.
ἔθνος (acc.sing.neut.of *ἔθνος*, hostility) 376.
καὶ (adjunctive conjunction joining prepositional phrases) 14.
βασιλεία (nom.sing.fem.of *βασιλεία*, subject of *ἐγερθήσεται*) 253.
ἐπὶ (preposition with the accusative, hostility) 47.
βασιλείαν (acc.sing.fem.of *βασιλεία*, hostility) 253.

Translation - "And He added, 'Nation will rise up against nation and kingdom against kingdom.' "

Comment: *Cf.* Mt.24:7; Mk.13:8; Isa.19:2.

Verse 11 - "And great earthquakes shall be in divers places, and famines, and pestilences, and fearful sights and great signs shall there be from heaven."

σεισμοί τε μεγάλοι καὶ κατὰ τόπους λιμοὶ καὶ λοιμοὶ ἔσονται, φόβητρά τε καὶ ἀπ' οὐρανοῦ σημεῖα μεγάλα ἔσται.

σεισμοί (nom.pl.masc.of *σεισμός*, subject of *ἔσονται*) 751.
τε (correlative conjunction) 1408.
μεγάλοι (nom.pl.masc.of *μέγας*, in agreement with *σεισμοί*) 184.
καὶ (adjunctive conjunction joining nouns) 14.
κατὰ (preposition with the accusative, distributive) 98.
τόπους (acc.pl.masc.of *τόπος*, distributive) 1019.
λιμοὶ (nom.pl.masc.of *λιμός*, subject of *ἔσονται*) 1485.
καὶ (adjunctive conjunction joining nouns) 14.

#2720 *λοιμοὶ* (nom.pl.masc.of *λοιμός*, subject of *ἔσονται*).

pestilence - Luke 21:11.
pestilent fellow - Acts 24:5.

Meaning: pestilence. As a noun - Luke 21:11. With reference to Paul by his enemies in Acts 24:5.

ἔσονται (3d.per.pl.fut.ind.of εἰμί, predictive) 86.

#2721 φόβητρά (nom.pl.neut.of φόβητρον, subject of ἔσται).

fearful sight - Luke 21:11.

Meaning: *Cf.*φοβέομαι (#101), φοβερός (#5016), φόβος (#1131). That which strikes terror; a terrible sight. With reference to end time phenomena - Luke 21:11.

τε (correlative conjunction) 1408.
καὶ (adjunctive conjunction joining nouns) 14.
ἀπ' (preposition with the ablative of source) 70.
οὐρανοῦ (abl.sing.masc.of οὐρανός, source) 254.
σημεῖα (nom.pl.neut.of σημεῖον, subject of ἔσται) 1005.
μεγάλα (nom.pl.neut.of μέγας, in agreement with σημεῖα) 184.
ἔσται (3d.per.sing.fut.ind.of εἰμί, predictive) 86.

Translation - "Both great earthquakes in various places and famines and pestilences will occur, and there will be both terrifying sights and great signs from heaven."

Comment: Earthquakes, famines, pestilences and terrifying and supernatural signs from heaven will produce a little preview of hell on earth for the unsaved. But the saints will not be touched by any of these fearful judgments. The student should now read Psalm 91 and apply the entire Psalm to the saints on earth during the tribulation period. Note especially vss.5-14 and *cf.* Mt.24:7; Mk.13:8. A good question to ask might be: When, since Psalm 91 was written have we had a literal fulfillment?

In Luke 21:5-11 Jesus has given an overview of the tribulation period with mention of false Christs, war, earthquakes, famines, pestilence and supernatural signs from heaven. This parallels the seal and trumpet judgments of Revelation. Then in verse 12, being very careful to say πρὸ δὲ τούτων πάντων, He carries the description back to the first century and events that could and did apply in the lives of the disciples who sat with Him that day on the Mount of Olives. This description runs through verse 17. Verses 18-28 carry us forward into Daniel's 70th week, to and including the second coming of Messiah in verse 28.

Verse 12 - "But before all these, they shall lay their hands on you, and persecute you, delivering you up to the synagogues, and into prisons, being brought before kings and rulers for my name's sake."

πρὸ δὲ τούτων πάντων ἐπιβαλοῦσιν ἐφ' ὑμᾶς τὰς χεῖρας αὐτῶν καὶ διώξουσιν, παραδιδόντες εἰς τὰς συναγωγὰς καὶ φυλακάς, ἀπαγομένους ἐπὶ βασιλεῖς καὶ ἡγεμόνας ἕνεκεν τοῦ ὀνόματός μου.

πρὸ (preposition with the ablative of time comparison) 442.

δὲ (adversative conjunction) 11.
τούτων (abl.pl.neut.of *οὗτος*, time comparison) 93.
πάντων (abl.pl.neut.of *πᾶς*, in agreement with *τούτων*) 67.
ἐπιβαλοῦσιν (3d.per.pl.fut.act.ind.of *ἐπιβάλλω*, predictive) 800.
ἐφ' (preposition with the accusative of extent) 47.
ὑμᾶς (acc.pl.masc.of *σύ*, extent) 104.
τὰς (acc.pl.fem.of the article in agreement with *χεῖρας*) 9.
χεῖρας (acc.pl.fem.of *χείρ*, direct object of *ἐπιβαλοῦσιν*) 308.
αὐτῶν (gen.pl.masc.of *αὐτός*, possession) 16.
καὶ (adjunctive conjunction joining verbs) 14.
διώξουσιν (3d.per.pl.fut.act.ind.of *διώκω*, predictive) 434.
παραδιδόντες (pres.act.part.nom.pl.masc.of *παραδίδωμι*, adverbial, telic) 368.
εἰς (preposition with the accusative of extent) 140.
τὰς (acc.pl.fem.of the article in agreement with *συναγωγὰς*) 9.
συναγωγὰς (acc.pl.fem.of *συναγωγή*, extent) 404.
καὶ (adjunctive conjunction joining nouns) 14.
φυλακάς (acc.pl.fem.of *φυλακή*, extent) 494.
ἀπαγομένοὺς (pres.pass.part.acc.pl.masc.of *ἀπάγω*, adverbial, temporal) 665.
ἐπὶ (preposition with the accusative of extent) 47.
βασιλεῖς (acc.pl.masc.of *βασιλεύς*, extent) 31.
καὶ (adjunctive conjunction joining nouns) 14.
ἡγεμόνας (acc.pl.masc.of *ἡγεμών*, extent) 160.
ἕνεκεν (improper preposition with the genitive - "in behalf of. . ") 435.
τοῦ (gen.sing.neut.of the article in agreement with *ὀνόματος*) 9.
ὀνόματός (gen.sing.neut.of *ὄνομα*, reference) 108.
μου (gen.sing.masc.of *ἐγώ*, possession) 123.

Translation - "But before all of this happens, they are going to pursue and lay their hands on you in order to conduct you into the synagogies and prisons as you are led before kings and governors for my name's sake."

Comment: The antecedent of *τούτων* is the list of phenomena in verse 11, which are clearly descriptive of the events of Daniel's 70th week. Thus events *πρὸ τούτων πάντων* are prophetic of the period beginning with Pentecost and extending to the beginning of the last seven years of the church age. Jesus was speaking of the persecutions that fell upon the early church, immediately after Pentecost and which continue to be imposed upon Christians. Pursuit, arrest, arraignment and prosecution in ecclesiastical and civil courts for no reason other than that the defendant bears the name of Christ is here foretold. History in every age since the first century amply attests the accuracy of this prophecy. Jesus is not saying that persecution of Christians is a sign of the immediate end of the age. All of the material covered in verses 12-24 has found and will continue to find fulfillment before the great tribulation. Verse 24 extends from the day that Jesus spoke these words to the day of His second coming.

Verse 13 - "And it shall turn to you for a testimony."

ἀποβήσεται ὑμῖν εἰς μαρτύριον.

ἀποβήσεται (3d.per.sing.fut.mid.ind.of ἀποβαίνω, predictive) 2042.
ὑμῖν (dat.pl.masc.of σύ, personal advantage) 104.
εἰς (preposition with the accusative, purpose) 140.
μαρτύριον (acc.sing.neut.of μαρτύριον, purpose) 716.

Translation - "It will work for your advantage as a chance to give your testimony."

Comment: *Cf.* comment on Mt.10:18; Mk.13:10. Note Phil.1:19 as an example of ἀποβαίνω in this same sense. What begins as an action against the Christian will result in an opportunity for him to give his testimony in court as to the saving grace and sovereign power of God.

Verse 14 - "Settle it therefore in your hearts, not to meditate before what ye shall answer."

θέτε οὖν ἐν ταῖς καρδίαις ὑμῶν μὴ προμελετᾶν ἀπολογηθῆναι,

θέτε (2d.per.pl.2d.aor.act.impv.of τίθημι, command) 455.
οὖν (inferential conjunction) 68.
ἐν (preposition with the locative of sphere) 80.
ταῖς (loc.pl.fem.of the article in agreement with καρδίαις) 9.
καρδίαις (loc.pl.fem.of καρδία, sphere) 432.
υμῶν (gen.pl.masc.of σύ, possession) 104.
μὴ (qualified negative conjunction with the infinitive, negative purpose) 87.

#2722 προμελετᾶν (pres.act.inf.of προμελετάω, negative purpose).

meditate before - Luke 21:14.

Meaning: A combination of πρό (#442) and μελετάω (#3041). Hence, to think ahead; to make plans for some future need. In Luke 21:14 to plan and rehearse a speech of defense before a court.

ἀπολογηθῆναι (aor.mid.inf.of ἀπολογέομαι, noun use, object of προμελετᾶν) 2476.

Translation - "Determine therefore in your hearts not to plan ahead how to defend yourself."

Comment: *Cf.* comment on Mt.10:19; Mk.13:11. Note again how the writers use different words, Matthew (#609), Mark (#2712) and Luke (#2722) to transmit the same thought. But the Holy Spirit has guarded the concept and the full meaning of what Jesus said is clear. This is the real meaning of plenary verbal inspiration.

Verse 15 - "For I will give you a mouth and wisdom, which all your adversaries shall not be able to gainsay nor resist."

ἐγὼ γὰρ δώσω ὑμῖν στόμα καὶ σοφίαν ᾗ οὐ δυνήσονται ἀντιστῆναι ἢ ἀντειπεῖν ἅπαντες οἱ ἀντικείμενοι ὑμῖν.

ἐγὼ (nom.sing.masc.of *ἐγώ*, subject of *δώσω*) 123.
γὰρ (causal conjunction) 105.
δώσω (1st.per.sing.fut.act.ind.of *δίδωμι*, predictive) 362.
ὑμῖν (dat.pl.masc.of *σύ*, indirect object of *δώσω*) 104.
στόμα (acc.sing.neut.of *στόμα*, direct object of *δώσω*) 344.
καὶ (adjunctive conjunction joining nouns) 14.
σοφίαν (acc.sing.fem.of *σοφία*, direct object of *δώσω*) 934.
ᾗ (dat.sing.fem.of *ὅς*, personal disadvantage) 65.
οὐ (summary negative conjunction with the indicative) 130.
δυνήσονται (3d.per.pl.fut.mid.ind.of *δύναμαι*, predictive) 289.
ἀντιστῆναι (aor.act.inf.of *ἀνθίστημι*, completes *δυνήσονται*) 527.
ἢ (disjunctive particle) 465.

#2723 *ἀντειπεῖν* (aor.act.inf.of *ἀντεῖπον*, completes *δυνήσονται*).

gainsay - Luke 21:15.
say against - Acts 4:14.

Meaning: A combination of *ἀντί* (#237) and *εἶπον* (#155). Hence, to gainsay; rebut; offer a counter argument. With reference to an adversary in court attempting to reply to a defense argument - Luke 21:15. Of the Jews who were unable to answer Peter and John - Acts 4:14.

ἅπαντες (nom.pl.masc.of *ἅπας*, in agreement with *ἀντικείμενοι*) 639.
οἱ (nom.pl.masc.of the article in agreement with *ἀντικείμενοι*) 9.
ἀντικείμενοι (pres.mid.part.nom.pl.masc.of *ἀντίκειμαι*, substantival, subject of *δυνήσονται*) 2506.
ὑμῖν (dat.pl.masc.of *σύ*, personal disadvantage) 104.

Translation - "Because I will give to you mouth and wisdom which none of those arrayed against you will be able to stand against or rebut."

Comment: *Cf.* comment on Mt.10:19,20; Mk.13:11. Luke's statement is much more dramatic and colorful than those of the other synoptics. I have chosen to translate *στόμα καὶ σοφίαν* literally. Goodspeed, with total fidelity to the text, has "wisdom of utterance." The persecuted Christian will need the ability to think quickly and articulate his repartee with eloquence and devastating logic. In Acts 4:14 we see the fulfillment of this promise to Peter and John. Note the compound verbs with *ἀντί*.

The student, as always, should study the analysis of each word and note how the Holy Spirit has used it elsewhere in the New Testament. Much interesting and profitable cross-fertilization of ideas, hidden in scripture, can be uncovered only in this way. The research requires time and effort but it is extremely rewarding.

Verse 16 - "And ye shall be betrayed, both by parents, and brethren, and kinsfolks, and friends; and some of you shall they cause to be put to death."

παραδοθήσεσθε δὲ καὶ ὑπὸ γονέων καὶ ἀδελφῶν καὶ συγγενῶν καὶ φίλων, καὶ θανατώσουσιν ἐξ ὑμῶν.

παραδοθήσεσθε (2d.per.pl.fut.pass.ind.of παραδίδωμι, predictive) 368.
δὲ (continuative conjunction) 11.
καὶ (adjunctive conjunction) 14.
ὑπὸ (preposition with the ablative of agent) 117.
γονέων (abl.pl.masc.of γονεύς, agent) 878.
καὶ (adjunctive conjunction) 14.
ἀδελφῶν (abl.pl.masc.of ἀδελφός, agent) 15.
καὶ (adjunctive conjunction joining nouns) 14.
συγγενῶν (abl.pl.masc.of συγγενής, agent) 1815.
καὶ (adjunctive conjunction joining nouns) 14.
φίλων (abl.pl.masc.of φίλος, agent) 932.
καὶ (continuative conjunction) 14.
θανατώσουσιν (3d.per.pl.fut.act.ind.of θανατόω, predictive) 879.
ἐξ (preposition with the partitive genitive) 19.
ὑμῶν (gen.pl.masc.of σύ, partitive) 104.

Translation - "And you will be betrayed both by parents and brothers and relatives and friends, and they will put some of you to death."

Comment: *Cf.* comment on Mt.24:21; Mk.13:12. Luke uses the passive voice. Matthew and Mark the active.

Verse 17 - "And ye shall be hated of all men for my name's sake."

καὶ ἔσεσθε μισούμενοι ὑπὸ πάντων διὰ τὸ ὄνομά μου.

καὶ (continuative conjunction) 14.
ἔσεσθε (2d.per.pl.fut.ind.of εἰμί, future periphrastic) 86.
μισούμενοι (pres.pass.part.nom.pl.masc.of μισέω, future passive periphrastic) 542.
ὑπὸ (preposition with the ablative of agent) 117.
πάντων (abl.pl.masc.of πᾶς, agent) 67.
διὰ (preposition with the accusative, cause) 118.
τὸ (acc.sing.neut.of the article in agreement with ὄνομά) 9.
ὄνομά (acc.sing.neut.of ὄνομα, cause) 108.
μου (gen.sing.masc.of ἐγώ, possession) 123.

Translation - "And you will always be hated by everyone because of my name."

Comment: *Cf.* comment on Mt.24:9; Mk.13:13. *Cf.* John 15:18. The prediction of betrayal and death in verse 16 and of universal hatred in verse 17 seems inconsistent with verse 18. It would seem that Luke's account throws together descriptions that apply both in the first century and following and in Daniel's

70th week. Beginning in verse 18 and continuing through verse 28 we seem clearly to be looking at the tribulation, during which time the saints will be protected,not from the wrath of men, but from the judgments of God. Such are the interesting exegetical problems connected with double imagery.

Verse 18 - "But there shall not an hair of your head perish."

καὶ θρὶξ ἐκ τῆς κεφαλῆς ὑμῶν οὐ μὴ ἀπόληται.

καὶ (adversative conjunction) 14.
θρὶξ (nom.sing.fem.of θρίξ, subject of ἀπόληται) 261.
ἐκ (preposition with the ablative of source) 19.
τῆς (abl.sing.fem.of the article in agreement with κεφαλῆς) 9.
κεφαλῆς (abl.sing.fem.of κεφαλή, source) 521.
ὑμῶν (gen.pl.masc.of σύ, possession) 104.
οὐ (summary negative conjunction with μὴ and the subjunctive, emphatic negation) 130.
μὴ (qualified negative conjunction with οὐ and the subjunctive, emphatic negation) 87.
ἀπόληται (3d.per.sing.2d.aor.mid.subj.of ἀπόλλυμι, emphatic negation) 208.

Translation - "But not a hair of your head will perish."

Comment: καὶ is adversative, translated "but," "yet" or "nevertheless." Despite universal hatred and persecution from men, no harm will befall the Christian as a result of God's divine judgments which will fall upon the earth during the tribulation. While the scriptures make clear that the church will go through the tribulation, she will go through it safely, insofar as God's judgments are concerned. Scripture nowhere promises the Christian immunity from persecution by the unsaved world. Quite the contrary. But the child of God is safe "under the blood" from the wrath of God. Israel remained in Egypt while the ten plagues were visited upon the Egyptians, but Israel did not suffer from the plagues (Exodus 8:22,23; 9:4,6,7,26; 10:23; 12:13; 11:7). God did not find it necessary to "rapture" Israel out of Egypt before the plagues fell upon the land in order to protect His covenant people. Nor need God remove the church from the earth before He rains down judgment upon the unsaved upon the earth, in order to protect the church from those plagues. We are saved from God's wrath through Jesus Christ (1 Thess.5:9; Rom.5:9). The 91st Psalm has never yet had a literal fulfillment but we will see such fulfillment as the Bride of Christ lives out the last seven years of her ministry during Daniel's 70th week. Col.3:3 is parallel to Psalm 91:1. Psalm 91:1-10 is a fuller exposition of Luke 21:18. "Not a hair of your head will perish" as a result of divine judgment upon the unsaved, though unsaved men may give the saint a chance to gain a martyr's crown.

Verse 19 - "In your patience possess ye your souls."

ἐν τῇ ὑπομονῇ ὑμῶν κτήσασθε τὰς ψυχὰς ὑμῶν.

ἐν (preposition with the instrumental of means) 80.
τῇ (instru.sing.fem.of the article in agreement with ὑπομονῇ) 9.
ὑπομονῇ (instru.sing.fem.of ὑπομονή, means) 2204.
ὑμῶν (gen.pl.masc.of σύ, possession) 104.
κτήσασθε (2d.per.pl.1st.aor.impv.of κτάομαι, command) 859.
τὰς (acc.pl.fem.of the article in agreement with ψυχὰς) 9.
ψυχὰς (acc.pl.fem.of ψυχή, direct object of κτήσασθε) 233.
ὑμῶν (gen.pl.masc.of σύ, possession) 104.

Translation - "By means of your endurance you must attain your self-control."

Comment: *Cf.* comment on Mt.24:13; Mk.13:13b. #859 in the sense of "make secure," "achieve," "attain." #233 means one's self-consciousness. Thus Jesus was telling the Christian how to cope with the situation in which he will find himself, as the object of the world's persecution. There is danger of personality disorientation and disintegration for anyone who must live in a society that despises him and seeks his death. It is easy for a Christian to lose his bearings and be cast adrift on a sea of troubles without a compass. How can the Christian, under fire from the unsaved world achieve and maintain his sanity? Jesus suggests the means which he must use to make the adjustments which must be made. He is to use his patience. Note the genitive of possession in ὑμῶν, following ὑπομονῇ. This patience belongs to the Christian. How did he acquire it? The same tribulation that the world has brought down upon him is the source of the patience which he must have to react in a mature Christian manner to the tribulation (Rom.5:3-5; James 1:2-4). Under fire from the world the Christian will be in dire need of patience (Heb.10:36,37), and that is precisely the quality which the tribulation provides for him. One can endure anything if he knows that his tribulation is temporary. As he looks to the future for relief and reward he finds himself with a holistic view of the situation. A comprehensive view of any situation means mental and psychological maturity, if the view includes the assurance of the love of God and salvation and the promise that the tribulation which one is called upon to endure is of relatively short duration. One does not lose his mind in a dentist chair as long as he remembers that the dentist will not drill forever. It should be added that there is no promise that tribulation develops patience for anyone except regenerated children of God. The unsaved church member, for all of his societal adjustment and "good moral character" (as though such can be developed apart from Christ), will be unable to understand the course of events during the tribulation and will thus become a drifting ship without anchor or compass in a sea of troubles to which he cannot react with maturity because he cannot understand them.

"The aorist imperative, which is attested by Sinaiticus D K L W X Δ Φ *f1 al*, seems to be slightly preferable, for copyists would have perhaps been likely to conform it to the future tense, used several times in the preceding context." (Metzger, *A Textual Commentary on the Greek New Testament*, 173).

Verse 20 - "And when ye shall see Jerusalem compassed with armies, then know that the destruction thereof is nigh."

Ὅταν δὲ ἴδητε κυκλουμένην ὑπὸ στρατοπέδων Ἰερουσαλήμ, τότε γνῶτε ὅτι ἤγγικεν ἡ ἐρήμωσις αὐτῆς.

Ὅταν (conjunction introducing the subjunctive in an indefinite temporal clause) 436.

δὲ (continuative conjunction) 11.

ἴδητε (2d.per.pl.aor.subj.of ὁράω, indefinite temporal clause) 144.

κυκλουμένην (pres.pass.part.acc.sing.fem.of κυκλόω, adjectival, ascriptive, attributive) 2509.

ὑπὸ (preposition with the ablative of agent) 117.

#2724 στρατοπέδων (abl.pl.neut.of στρατόπεδον, agent).

army - Luke 21:20.

Meaning: A combination of στρατός - "people" and πέδον - "ground, land." Hence, a military camp; soldiers in camp; an assembled and encamped military expedition. With reference to the Roman army under Titus in A.D. 70 and prophetically to the armies of all Gentile nations (Zech.14:2) - Luke 21:20.

Ἰερουσαλήμ (acc.sing.of Ἰεροσολύμων, direct object of ἴδητε) 141.

τότε (temporal adverb) 166.

γνῶτε (2d.per.pl.2d.aor.act.impv.of γινώσκω, command) 131.

ὅτι (conjunction introducing an object clause in indirect discourse) 211.

ἤγγικεν (3d.per.sing.perf.act.ind.of ἐγγίζω, intensive) 252.

ἡ (nom.sing.fem.of the article in agreement with ἐρήμωσις) 9.

ἐρήμωσις (nom.sing.fem.of ἐρήμωσις, subject of ἤγγικεν) 1493.

αὐτῆς (gen.sing.fem.of αὐτός, description) 16.

Translation - "And when you see Jerusalem being surrounded by armies then you will conclude that her destruction is at hand."

Comment: *Cf.* comment on Mt.24:15; Mk.13:14. There is no doubt that Matthew and Mark have the mid-point in Daniel's 70th week in view. Through the use of double imagery, Luke also means this, yet there is nothing to deny the view that in His primary application Jesus was referring to the Roman war of A.D.70. Everything that Jesus said in this verse occurred in A.D.70. Josephus attests that Jerusalem was encircled by the armed camps of the Romans. There may be significance in the fact that Jesus here used the word ἐρήμωσις - "destruction, desolation, a thorough sacking" which occured in the first century whereas Jerusalem will not be totally destroyed at the Second Coming of Christ (Rev.16:19; Zech.14:1-4).

Those with a theological stance that denies the supernatural, owe to us who believe in it an explanation as to how Jesus knew all about these things in advance.

Verse 21 - "Then let them which are in Judea flee to the mountains; and let them which are in the midst of it, depart out; and let not them that are in the countries enter thereinto."

τότε οἱ ἐν τῇ Ἰουδαίᾳ φευγέτωσαν εἰς τὰ ὄρη, καὶ οἱ ἐν μέσῳ αὐτῆς ἐκχωρείτωσαν, καὶ οἱ ἐν ταῖς χώραις μὴ εἰσερχέσθωσαν εἰς αὐτήν,

τότε (temporal adverb) 166.
οἱ (nom.pl.masc.of the article, subject of *φευγέτωσαν*) 9.
ἐν (preposition with the locative of place where) 80.
τῇ (loc.sing.fem.of the article in agreement with *Ἰουδαίᾳ*) 9.
Ἰουδαίᾳ (loc.sing.fem.of *Ἰουδαίας*, place where) 134.
φευγέτωσαν (3d.per.pl.aor.act.impv.of *φεύγω*, command) 202.
εἰς (preposition with the accusative of extent) 140.
τὰ (acc.pl.neut.of the article in agreement with *ὄρη*) 9.
ὄρη (acc.pl.neut.of *ὄρος*, extent) 357.
καὶ (continuative conjunction) 14.
οἱ (nom.pl.masc.of the article, subject of *ἐκχωρείτωσαν*) 9.
ἐν (preposition with the locative of place where) 80.
μέσῳ (loc.sing.masc.of *μέσος*, place where) 873.
αὐτῆς (gen.sing.fem.of *αὐτός*, description) 16.

#2725 *ἐκχωρείτωσαν* (3d.per.pl.aor.act.impv.of *ἐκχωρέω*, command).

depart out - Luke 21:21.

Meaning: A combination of *ἐκ* (#19) and *χωρέω* (#1162). Hence, to make room for something or someone else by leaving. To leave; depart - Luke 21:21.

καὶ (continuative conjunction) 14.
οἱ (nom.pl.masc.of the article, subject of *εἰσερχέσθωσαν*) 9.
ἐν (preposition with the locative of place where) 80.
ταῖς (loc.pl.fem.of the article in agreement with *χώραις*) 9.
χώραις (loc.pl.fem.of *χώρα*, place where) 201.
μὴ (qualified negative conjunction with the imperative in a prohibition) 87.
εἰσερχέσθωσαν (3d.per.pl.pres..mid.impv.of *εἰσέρχομαι*, prohibition) 234.
εἰς (preposition with the accusative of extent) 140.
αὐτήν (acc.sing.fem.of *αὐτός*, extent) 16.

Translation - "Then those who are in Judea must flee unto the mountains, and those who are in the interior must get out, and those who are in the country must not enter into the city."

Comment: *Cf.* comment on Mt.24:16; Mk.13:14. Luke makes his report of Jesus' statement a little stronger. The idea is that of escape from persecution and death. I have translated the middle clause literally, even though it is clear that it refers to the city of Jerusalem. This is clear from the contrast in the last clause between *χώραις* ("countryside/rural areas") and *αὐτήν*, which has *αὐτῆς* as its antecedent.

Verse 22 - "For these be the days of vengeance, that all things which are written may be fulfilled."

ὅτι ἡμέραι ἐκδικήσεως αὗταί εἰσιν τοῦ πλησθῆναι πάντα τὰ γεγραμμένα.

ὅτι (conjunction introducing a subordinate causal clause) 211.
ἡμέραι (nom.pl.fem.of ἡμέρα, predicate nominative) 135.
ἐκδικήσεως (gen.sing.fem.of ἐκδίκησις, description) 2625.
αὗταί (nom.pl.fem.of οὗτος, subject of εἰσιν) 93.
εἰσιν (3d.per.pl.pres.ind.of εἰμί, aoristic) 86.
τοῦ (gen.sing.neut.of the article, with the infinitive of purpose) 9.
πλησθῆναι (1st.aor.pass.inf.of πίμπλημι, articular infinitive of purpose) 1409.
πάντα (acc.pl.neut.of πᾶς, in agreement with γεγραμμένα) 67.
τὰ (acc.pl.neut.of the article in agreement with γεγραμμένα) 9.
γεγραμμένα (perf.pass.part.acc.pl.neut.of γράφω, direct object of πλησθῆναι) 156.

Translation - "Because these will be days of vengeance, in order to fulfill all that has been written."

Comment: ὅτι introduces the subordinate causal clause. It is subordinate to Jesus' warning of verse 21 that if God's people are to escape with their lives they must flee the city. These days He describes as "days of vengeance." The articular infinitive in the genitive case is purpose. "The O.T. shows the idiom in great abundance, though the construction is classic. It was used especially by Thucydides, 'who was the first to use τοῦ and the inf.for purpose.' (Berklein, *Entwickelungsgesch*, 58, as cited by Moulton, *Prol.*, 216, in Robertson, *Grammar*, 1080). This was the normal use.... Paul makes little, if any use of this idiom (Moulton , *Ibid.*, 217). It is possible in Ro.6:6; Ph.3:10. Indeed Votaw (Votaw, *The Use of the Infinitive in Biblical Greek*, 21, as cited in Robertson, *Grammar*, Ibid.,) notes only 33 instances of τοῦ and the inf.of purpose in the N.T., and these are chiefly in Matthew, Luke and Acts. Note Mt.2:13; 13:3; Lk.21:22; 24:29; Acts 3:2; 5:31; 26:18; 1 Cor.10:7; Gal.3:10; Heb.10:7, etc." (Robertson, *Ibid.*).

On those days all that was written in scripture about the destruction of Jerusalem was to be fulfilled. *Cf.* Hosea 9:7, where the same phrase in the LXX occurs, *viz.* ἡμέραι ἐκδικήσεως. *Cf.* 2 Thess.1:8; Lk.18:7,8; Rom.12:19; Heb.10:30.

Verse 23 - "But woe unto them that are with child and to them that give suck in those days! For there shall be great distress in the land, and wrath upon this people."

οὐαὶ ταῖς ἐν γαστρὶ ἐχούσαις καὶ ταῖς θηλαζούσαις ἐν ἐκείναις ταῖς ἡμέραις ἔσται γὰρ ἀνάγκη μεγάλη ἐπὶ τῆς γῆς καὶ ὀργὴ τῷ λαῷ τούτῳ,

οὐαὶ (exclamation) 936.
ταῖς (dat.pl.fem.of the article in agreement with ἐχούσαις) 9.
ἐν (preposition with the locative of place where) 80.
γαστρὶ (loc.sing.fem.of γαστήρ, place where) 81.
ἐχούσαις (pres.act.part.dat.pl.fem.of ἔχω, substantival, personal disadvantage) 82.

καὶ (adjunctive conjunction joining participles) 14.
ταῖς (dat.pl.fem.of the article in agreement with *θηλαζούσαις*) 9.
θηλαζούσαις (pres.act.part.dat.pl.fem.of *θηλάζω*, substantival, personal disadvantage) 1361.
ἐν (preposition with the locative of time point) 80.
ἐκείναις (loc.pl.fem.of *ἐκεῖνος*, in agreement with *ἡμέραις*) 246.
ταῖς (loc.pl.fem.of the article in agreement with *ἡμέραις*) 9.
ἡμέραις (loc.pl.fem.of *ἡμέρα*, time point) 135.
ἔσται (3d.per.sing.fut.ind.of *εἰμί*, predictive) 86.
γὰρ (inferential conjunction introducing a coordinate causal clause) 105.
ἀνάγκη (nom.sing.fem.of *ἀνάγκη*, subject of *ἔσται*) 1254.
μεγάλη (nom.sing.fem.of *μέγας*, in agreement with *ἀνάγκη*) 184.
ἐπὶ (preposition with the genitive of place description) 47.
τῆς (gen.sing.fem.of the article in agreement with *γῆς*) 9.
γῆς (gen.sing.fem.of *γῆ*, place description) 157.
καὶ (adjunctive conjunction joining nouns) 14.
ὀργὴ (nom.sing.fem.of *ὀργή*, subject of *ἔσται*) 283.
τῷ (loc.sing.masc.of the article in agreement with *λαῷ*) 9.
λαῷ (loc.sing.masc.of *λαός*, place where) 110.
τούτῳ (loc.sing.masc.of *οὗτος*, in agreement with *λαῷ*) 93.

Translation - "Alas for the pregnant and those who are nursing babies in those days, because there will be great distress upon the earth and wrath upon this people."

Comment: *Cf.* comment on Mt.24:19; Mk.13:17. *Cf.*#1254 for other uses of *ἀνάγκη* in this classical sense. Distress upon the land of Palestine and wrath against the children of Israel. The double imagery of Luke's account makes it difficult to separate Jesus' remarks which were fulfilled in the first century from those which are to see fulfillment at the end of the church age. There is nothing in verse 23 that did not apply in A.D. 70 and it will all apply again during the tribulation. It is significant that Luke did not use the expression *τῆς θλίψεως τῆς μεγάλης* as we have it in Rev.7:14 or *θλῖψαις μεγάλη* as in Mt.24:21, nor the formulation of Mark 13:19 - *θλῖψις οἵα οὐ γέγονεν ποιαύτη ἀπ' ἀρχῆς κτίτεως*, all of which refer to the reign of Antichrist at the end of the age. It is also to be noted that our Lord spoke of *ὀργὴ τῷ λαῷ τούτῳ* - "anger against *this people,*" where the use of deictic *τούτω* seems to indicate that He was speaking about the generation of Jews who were alive at that time, against whom Titus and the Romans visited their anger. As if to clinch the point verse 24 makes it undeniable that our Lord was speaking of the events of A.D. 70.

Verse 24 - "And they shall fall by the edge of the sword, and shall be led away captive into all nations; and Jerusalem shall be trodden down of the Gentiles, until the times of the Gentiles be fulfilled."

καὶ πεσοῦνται στόματι μαχαίρης καὶ αἰχμαλωτισθήσονται εἰς τὰ ἔθνη πάντα, καὶ Ἰερουσαλὴμ ἔσται πατουμένη ὑπὸ ἐθνῶν, ἄχρι οὗ πληρωθῶσιν καιροὶ ἐθνῶν.

καὶ (continuative conjunction) 14.
πεσοῦνται (3d.per.pl.fut.act.ind.of *πίπτω*, predictive) 187.
στόματι (instru.sing.neut.of *στόμα*, means) 344.
μαχαίρης (gen.sing.fem.of *μάχαιρα*, description) 896.
καὶ (adjunctive conjunction joining verbs) 14.

#2726 *αἰχμαλωτισθήσονται* (3d.per.pl.fut.pass.ind.of *αἰχμαλωτίζω*, predictive).

bring into captivity - Rom.7:23; 2 Cor.10:5.
lead away captive - Luke 21:24.
lead captive - 2 Tim.3:6.

Meaning: to lead away captive; to captivate; to bring under subjection. In a physical and spatial sense - Luke 21:24. To make all thoughts captive/obedient to Christ - 2 Cor.10:5; to captivate the will and lead the victim into the captivity to sin - Rom.7:23; 2 Tim.3:6.

εἰς (preposition with the accusative of extent) 140.
τὰ (acc.pl.neut.of the article in agreement with *ἔθνη*) 9.
ἔθνη (acc.pl.neut.of *ἔθνος*, extent) 376.
πάντα (acc.pl.neut.of *πᾶς*, in agreement with *ἔθνη*) 67.
καὶ (continuative conjunction) 14.
Ἰερουσαλὴμ (nom.sing.of *Ἰερουσαλήμ*, subject of *ἔσται*) 141.
ἔσται (3d.per.sing.fut.ind.of *εἰμί*, future passive periphrastic) 86.
πατουμένη (pres.pass.part.nom.sing.fem.of *πατέω*, future passive periphrastic) 2415.
ὑπὸ (preposition with the ablative of agent) 117.
ἐθνῶν (abl.pl.neut.of *ἔθνος*, agent) 376.
ἄχρι (preposition introducing the relative clause in the ablative, time separation) 1517.
οὗ (abl.sing.neut.of *ὅς*, in an indefinite temporal clause, time separation) 65.
πληρωθῶσιν (3d.per.pl.1st.aor.pass.subj.of *πληρόω*, indefinite temporal clause) 115.
καιροὶ (nom.pl.masc.of *καιρός*, subject of *πληρωθῶσιν*) 767.
ἐθνῶν (gen.pl.neut.of *ἔθνος*, description) 376.

Translation - "And they will fall by the edge of the sword, and they will be carried away captive into all the nations, and Jerusalem will always be trodden down by Gentiles until such time as the Gentile era has been terminated."

Comment: This is the Lord's picture of what happened when the Romans came in A.D. 70. Many Jews were slaughtered and the survivors were carried into captivity. The Jew became on that day a man without a country, to live under Gentile rule until 1948 when Israel was reestablished and recognized, first by the United States, and later by other Gentile powers, and admitted to the United Nations. Jesus then added that Jerusalem and Palestine would continue under Gentile domination until a specific future event - *ἄχρι οὗ πληρωθῶσιν καιροὶ* *εκθνῶν*. The phrase, *καιροὶ ἐθνῶν* - "the Gentile era/period" - refers to the time beginning with the rejection of Jesus as the Messiah, at Calvary, and extending to the day of His second coming, when He comes again to take His rightful place on David's throne (2 Samuel 7:10-17; Luke 1:30-33). *Cf.* Rom.11:25 - "the fullness of the Gentiles" which means the completion of the Gentile bride of Christ, at which time Israel, formerly partially blind, will recover her total capacity to understand. On the day that the last elect Gentile is saved and the Bride of Christ is thus complete, Israel will look upon Him whom they pierced and a nation will be born in a day (Zech.12:10; 13:6; Isa.66:8). These events are simultaneous with the sound of the last trumpet, the completion of the mystery, the rapture of the living saints, the resurrection of the dead in Christ, the judgment seat of Christ and Christ's judgment upon the Antichrist and his dupes (Rev.10:7; 1 Cor.15:51; Lk.14:14; Eph.3:4-6; 1 Thess.4:13-18; 2 Thess.1:7-10; Rev.19:11-21). The city of Jerusalem will have been dominated, not by the Zionists, but by Gentile power until that day. This leads to the conclusion that Zionist attempts by Prime Minister Begin and his colleagues to make Jerusalem the capitol of the nation, with complete freedom from the interference of Gentile powers will not be permitted.

Verse 24 presages the history of Israel from the beginning of the diaspora in A.D. 70 until the Second Coming of Christ.

The Coming of the Son of Man

(Matthew 24:29-31; Mark 13:24-27; Luke 21:25-28)

Luke 21:25 - "And there shall be signs in the sun, and in the moon, and in the stars; and upon the earth distress of nations, with perplexity; the seas and waves roaring;"

Καὶ ἔσονται σημεῖα ἐν ἡλίῳ καὶ σεληνῃ καὶ ἄστροις, καὶ ἐπὶ τῆς γῆς συνοχὴ ἐθνῶν ἐν ἀπορίᾳ ἤχους θαλάσσης καὶ σάλου,

Καὶ (continuative conjunction) 14.
ἔσονται (3d.per.pl.fut.ind.of εἰμί, predictive) 86.
σημεῖα (nom.pl.neut.of σημεῖον, subject of ἔσονται) 1005.
ἐν (preposition with the locative of place where) 80.
ἡλίῳ (loc.sing.masc.of ἥλιος, place where) 546.
καὶ (adjunctive conjunction joining nouns) 14.
σελήνῃ (loc.sing.fem.of σελήνη, place where) 1505.
καὶ (adjunctive conjunction joining nouns) 14.
ἄστροις (loc.pl.masc.of ἀστήρ, place where) 145.
καὶ (adjunctive conjunction joining prepositional phrases) 14.
ἐπὶ (preposition with the genitive of place description) 47.
τῆς (gen.sing.fem.of the article in agreement with γῆς) 9.
γῆς (gen.sing.fem.of γῆ, place description) 157.

#2727 συνοχὴ (nom.sing.fem.of συνοχή, subject of ἔσται, understood).

anguish - 2 Cor.2:4.
distress - Luke 21:25.

Meaning: *Cf.* συνέχω (#414). Hence, a feeling of being compressed; squeezed; pressured. Hence, consternation, distress, anguish. The distress that results from facing a dilemma. With ἀπορίᾳ in Luke 21:25. Followed by καρδίας in 2 Cor.2:4.

ἐθνῶν (gen.pl.neut.of ἔθνος, description) 376.
ἐν (preposition with the instrumental, cause) 80.

#2728 ἀπορίᾳ (instru.sing.fem.of ἀπορία, cause).

perplexity - Luke 21:25.

Meaning: *Cf.*ἀπορέομαι (#2254), from α privative and πάρος. Hence, without resources; no way to go; inability to procede due to lack of money. ἀπορία therefore means perplexity. In Luke 21:25 - συνοχὴ ἐθνῶν ἐν ἀπορίᾳ - "distress due to pressure, because of the lack of means to solve problems" and hence, perplexity. The United Nations illustrates this state of mind constantly.

ἤχους (nom.sing.neut.of ἦχος, nominative absolute) 2064.
θαλάσσης (gen.sing.fem.of θάλασσα, description) 374.
καὶ (adjunctive conjunction joining nouns) 14.

#2729 σάλου (gen.sing.masc.of σάλος, description).

waves - Luke 21:25.

Meaning: The tossing or swell of the sea in agitation. Billows - Luke 21:25.

Translation - "And there will be signs in sun and moon and stars, and upon the earth national distress because of perplexity - the roaring of the sea and its billows."

Comment: *Cf.*comment on Mt.24:29; Mk.13:24,25. The 26th verse continues in this vein and leads directly (καὶ τότε) to the actual second coming of Messiah in verse 27. Hence it seems that we have a description of events in the final days of the tribulation period. The heavenly phenomena are described in parallel passages in the Revelation. *Cf.* Psalm 65:7.

Verse 26 - "Men's hearts failing them for fear, and for looking after these things which are coming on the earth: for the powers of heaven shall be shaken."

ἀποψυχόντων ἀνθρώπων ἀπὸ φόβου καὶ προσδοκίας τῶν ἐπερχομένων τῇ οἰκουμένῃ, αἱ γὰρ δυνάμεις τῶν οὐρανῶν σαλευθήσονται.

#2730 ἀποψυχόντων (pres.act.part.gen.pl.masc.of ἀποψύχω, genitive absolute).

hearts failing them - Luke 21:26.

Meaning: A combination of ἀπό (#70) and ψύχω (#1489). To breathe away one's life. To sorrow; faint; succomb to death. As a result of φόβος - Luke 21:26.

ἀνθρώπων (gen.pl.masc.of ἄνθρωπος, genitive absolute) 341.
ἀπὸ (preposition with the albative, cause) 70.
φόβος (abl.sing.masc.of φόβος, cause) 1131.
καὶ (adjunctive conjunction joining nouns) 14.

#2731 προσδοκίας (gen.sing.fem.of προσδοκία, cause).

expectation - Acts 12:11.
looking after - Luke 21:26.

Meaning: A combination of πρός (#197) and δοκέω (#287). A looking toward, expectation and consideration of any situation, resulting in an expected result. Followed by a subjective genitive in Luke 21:26; with ἐκ and the ablative in Acts 12:11.

τῶν (gen.pl.neut.of the article in agreement with ἐπερχομένων) 9.
ἐπερχομένων (pres.mid.part.gen.pl.neut.of ἐπέρχομαι, substantival, subjective genitive) 1814.
τῇ (loc.sing.fem.of the article in agreement with οἰκουμένῃ) 9.
οἰκουμένῃ (loc.sing.fem.of οἰκομένη, place where) 1491.
αἱ (nom.pl.fem.of the article in agreement with δυνάμεις) 9.
δυνάμεις (nom.pl.fem.of δύναμις, subject of σαλευθήσονται) 687.
τῶν (gen.pl.masc.of the article in agreement with οὐρανῶν) 9.
οὐρανῶν (gen.pl.masc.of οὐρανός, description) 254.
σαλευθήσονται (3d.per.pl.fut.pass.ind.of σαλεύω, predictive) 911.

Translation - "Men dying from fright and from anticipation of events coming upon society, for the powers of the heavens will be shaken."

Comment: A long list of substantives follow ἔσονται in verse 25 - σημεῖα, συνοχή, ἦχος, - each with its modifying adjuncts. Now Luke adds a genitive absolute, ἀποψυχόντων ἀνθρώπων, and finally the list is complete and a new subject, αἱ δυνάμεις is joined to a new verb σαλευθήσονται. "There will be signs . . . distress. . . sound. . . heart failure. . . " In addition, and as an explanation for the fear of coming phenomena he adds that the "powers of the heavens will be shaken." *Cf.* Isa.34:4; Mt.24:29; Mk.13:25; Acts 2:25. The powers of the heavens may be shaken but the Lord of the heavens and those who trust Him will not be shaken.

Verse 27 - "And then shall they see the Son of Man coming in a cloud with power and great glory."

καὶ τότε ὄψονται τὸν υἱὸν τοῦ ἀνθρώπου ἐρχόμενον ἐν νεφέλῃ μετὰ δυνάμεως καὶ δόξης πολλῆς.

καὶ (continuative conjunction) 14.

τότε (temporal adverb) 166.
ὄψονται (3d.per.pl.fut.ind.of ὁράω, predictive) 144.
τὸν (acc.sing.masc.of the article in agreement with υἱὸν) 9.
υἱὸν (acc.sing.masc.of υἱός, direct object of ὄψονται) 5.
τοῦ (gen.sing.masc.of the article in agreement with ἀνθρώπου) 9.
ἀνθρώπου (gen.sing.masc.of ἄνθρωπος, description) 341.
ἐρχόμενον (pres.part.acc.sing.masc.of ἔρχομαι, adjectival, ascriptive, attributive) 146.
ἐν (preposition with the locative of place where) 80.
νεφέλῃ (loc.sing.fem.of νεφέλη, place where) 1225.
μετὰ (preposition with the genitive, adverbial) 50.
δυνάμεως (gen.sing.fem.of δύναμις, adverbial) 687.
καὶ (adjunctive conjunction joining nouns) 14.
δόξης (gen.sing.fem.of δόξα, adverbial) 361.
πολλῆς (gen.sing.fem.of πολύς, in agreement with δόξης) 228.

Translation - "And then they will see the Son of Man coming on a cloud with power and great glory."

Comment: The future always carries the time element regardless of the mode in which it occurs. It "is primarily an indicative tense, and hence the element of time is very pronounced. . . Outside the indicative the future is but rarely used in the New Testament. The future optative does not occur at all - in fact, it has disappeared entirely from the Koine Greek. The future infinitive is rare; the future participles more frequent, but not abundant." (Mantey, *Manual*, 191, 192). Here it is absolute, not gnomic. There is going to be a time when men upon the earth will look up into the sky and see Jesus Christ, Son of God and Son of Man, coming back to earth. He is a coming Son of Man. Note the adjectival participle ἐρχόμενον with its ascriptive definition of Him. Two prepositional phrases serve adverbially to tell how He will come. "On a cloud/in association with a cloud" and "with power and great glory." The sight will beggar description. *Cf.* Rev.1:7; 2 Thess.1:7-10; Acts 1:11; 1 Thess.4:13-18; 1 Cor.15:51-58; Phil.3:20,21; Rev.19:11-16. He is Plato's Philosopher-King (Plato, *Republic*, V, 473, D) - too intelligent to err; too loving to injure us; powerful enough to see that His total will is carried out. He is the Legislative, Judicial and Executive Sovereign. Smart Man, Good Man, Strong Man. Until He takes His place on David's throne, earth's agonies will only exacerbate. His coming will mean redemption in its fullest sense for the elect.

O, Lord Jesus, how long? how long?
E'er we hear the glad song?
Christ returneth, Hallelujah, Hallelujah, Amen.
Hallelujoh, Amen.

Verse 28 - "And when these things begin to come to pass, then look up, and lift up your heads

ἀρχομένων δὲ τούτων γίνεσθαι ἀνακύψατε καὶ ἐπάρατε τὰς κεφαλὰς ἡμῶν, διότι ἐγγίζει ἡ ἀπολύτρωσις ὑμῶν.

ἀρχομένων (pres.pass.part.gen.pl.masc.of ἄρχω, genitive absolute) 383.
δὲ (continuative conjunction) 11.
τούτων (gen.pl.masc.of οὗτος, genitive absolute) 93.
γίνεσθαι (pres.pass.inf.of γίνομαι, completes ἀρχομένων) 113.
ἀνακύψατε (2d.per.pl.aor.act.impv.of ἀνακύπτω, command) 2380.
καὶ (adjunctive conjunction joining verbs) 14.
ἐπάρατε (2d.per.pl.aor.act.impv.of ἐπαίρω, command) 1227.
τὰς (acc.pl.fem.of the article in agreement with κεφαλὰς) 9.
κεφαλὰς (acc.pl.fem.of κεφαλή, direct object of ἐπάρατε) 521.
ὑμῶν (gen.pl.masc.of σύ, possession) 104.
διότι (conjunction introducing a subordinate causal clause) 1795.
ἐγγίζει (3d.per.sing.pres.act.ind.of ἐγγίζω, aoristic) 252.
ἡ (nom.sing.fem.of the article in agreement with ἀπολύτρωσις) 9.

#2732 ἀπολύτρωσις (nom.sing.fem.of ἀπολύτρωσις, subject of ἐγγίζει).

deliverance - Heb.11:35.
redemption - Luke 21:28; Rom.3:24; 8:23; 1 Cor.1:30; Eph.1:7,14; 4:30; Col.1:14; Heb.9:15.

Meaning: A combination of ἀπό (#70) and λύτρωσις (#1850). *Cf.* also #'s 1335, 2902, 3133. Hence, the state of having been set free by the payment of a price. A ransom. Redemption. The verb means to pay the full penalty charged judicially against a defendant or debtor in order to secure his immediate freedom. The noun therefore means deliverance; rescue. With reference to deliverance from physical torture - Heb.11:35. The spiritual and physical deliverance from the penalty of God's broken law which is secured by the death of Christ - Rom.3:24; Eph.1:7; Col.1:14; Heb.9;15; 1 Cor.1:30. Including the previous idea, but with special reference to the redemption of the bodies of the saints, either in rapture or resurrection - Luke 21:28; Rom.8;23; Eph.1:14; 4:30. Luke 21:28 also includes the concept of physical rescue from the persecution of Antichrist.

ὑμῶν (gen.pl.masc.of σύ, possession) 104.

Translation - "And when these things are introduced, look up and lift up your heads because your redemption is coming soon."

Comment: Luke alone records these words of Jesus. Our translation attempts to reflect the fact that both ἀρχομένων and γίνεσθαι are passive. The genitive absolute is in the present tense, thus indicating simultaneous time with the two imperatives. The antecedent of τούτων obviously is the coming of the Son of Man in verse 27. The upward look and the uplifted head will be characteristic of the Christian who has studied his Bible and who understands what he reads. *Cf.*#2732 and note the three meanings of ἀπολύτρωσις - deliverance from physical danger, from the wrath of God and from the curse upon our physical bodies. Those who will be caught up on that day will already have been redeemed in the soteriological sense. They have no fear of the wrath of God (1 Thess.5:9), but they need redemption from the corruptibility and mortality of their physical bodies.

The world on that day, full of wrath and hatred for God, Christ and Christianity, must stand helplessly by as we are raptured into Christ's presence as He descends to earth. In that moment, in an instantaneous miracle of physical redemption we will shed our corruptible bodies and be transformed into His physical image. (1 Cor.15:51,52; 1 Thess.4:13-17; 2 Cor.5:1,2; Phil.3:31; Rom.8:23) *Cf.* comment on Eph.4:30; Rom.8:23.

The Lesson of the Fig Tree

(Matthew 23:32-35; Mark 13:28-31; Luke 21:29-33)

Luke 21:29 - "And he spake to them a parable; behold the fig tree and all the trees."

Καὶ εἶπεν παραβολὴν αὐτοῖς, Ἴδετε τὴν συκῆν καὶ πάντα τὰ δένδρα.

Καὶ (continuative conjunction) 14.
εἶπεν (3d.per.sing.aor.act.ind.of *εἶπον*, constative) 155.
παραβολὴν (acc.sing.fem.of *παραβολή*, direct object of *εἶπεν*) 1027.
αὐτοῖς (dat.pl.masc.of *αὐτός*, indirect object of *εἶπεν*) 16.
Ἴδετε (2d.per.pl.aor.act.impv.of *ὁράω*, command) 144.
τὴν (acc.sing.fem.of the article in agreement with *συκῆν*) 9.
συκῆν (acc.sing.fem.of *συκέα*, direct object of *Ἴδετε*) 1366.
καὶ (adjunctive conjunction joining nouns) 14.
πάντα (acc.pl.neut.of the article in agreement with *δένδρα*) 67.
τὰ (acc.pl.neut.of the article in agreement with *δένδρα*) 9.
δένδρα (acc.pl.neut.of *δένδρον*, direct object of *Ἴδετε*) 294.

Translation - "And he gave them an illustration. Consider the fig tree and all the trees."

Comment: *Cf.* comment on Mt.24:32; Mk.13:28. Luke indicates that the truth which Jesus intended to convey can be drawn from any tree as well as from the fig tree, which indicates that we are not necessarily warranted in drawing any conclusions from a supposed relation between Israel as a nation and the fig tree in particular. This is the type of hermeneutics that has led the uninitiated astray on many points. Any tree that puts forth leaves in the spring telegraphs the fact that summer is near. *Cf.* our discussion of Mt.24:33.

Verse 30 - "When they now shoot forth, ye see and know of your own selves that summer is nigh at hand."

ὅταν προβάλωσιν ἤδη, βλέποντες ἀφ' ἑαυτῶν γινώσκετε ὅτι ἤδη ἐγγὺς τὸ θέρος ἐστίν.

ὅταν (conjunction with the subjunctive introducing an indefinite temporal clause) 436.

#2733 προβάλωσιν (3d.per.pl.aor.act.subj.of προβάλλω, indefinite temporal clause).

put forward - Acts 19:33.
shoot forth - Luke 21:30.

Meaning: A combination of πρό (#442) and βάλλω (#299). Hence, to thrust forward. To push a man forward through a crowd that he might make a speech - Acts 19:33. With reference to the budding of a tree - Luke 21:30.

ἤδη (adverbial) 291.
βλέποντες (pres.act.part.nom.pl.masc.of βλέπω, adverbial, causal) 499.
ἀφ' (preposition with the ablative of agent) 70.
ἑαυτῶν (abl.pl.masc.of ἑαυτός, agent) 288.
γινώσκετε (2d.per.pl.pres.act.ind.of γινώσκω, customary) 131.
ὅτι (conjunction introducing a subordinate clause in indirect discourse) 211.
ἤδη (adverbial) 291.
ἐγγὺς (nom.sing.masc.of ἐγγύς, predicate adjective) 1512.
τὸ (nom.sing.neut.of the article in agreement with θέρος) 9.
θέρος (nom.sing.neut.of θέρος, subject of ἐστίν) 1513.
ἐστίν (3d.per.sing.pres.ind.of εἰμί, aoristic) 86.

Translation - "When they have already begun to bud, because you see it for yourselves, you conclude that the summer season is already near."

Comment: *Cf.* comment on Mt.24:32; Mk.13:28. The ablative reflexive pronoun phrase ἀφ' ἑαυτῶν means that those who see the trees begin to bud do not need to be told.

Verse 31 - "So likewise ye, when ye see these things come to pass, know ye that the kingdom of God is nigh at hand."

οὕτως καὶ ὑμεῖς, ὅταν ἴδητε ταῦτα γινόμενα, γινώσκετε ὅτι ἐγγύς ἐστιν ἡ βασιλεία τοῦ θεοῦ.

οὕτως (demonstrative adverb) 74.
καὶ (adjunctive conjunction joining pronouns) 14.
ὑμεῖς (nom.pl.masc.of σύ, subject of γινώσκετε) 104.
ὅταν (conjunction with the subjunctive introducing an indefinite temporal clause) 436.
ἴδητε (2d.per.pl.aor.act.subj.of ὁράω, indefinite temporal clause) 144.
ταῦτα (acc.pl.neut.of οὗτος, direct object of ἴδητε) 93.
γινόμενα (pres.part.acc.pl.neut.of γίνομαι, adjectival, ascriptive, predicate position, in agreement with ταῦτα) 113.
γινώσκετε (2d.per.pl.pres.act.impv.of γινώσκω, command) 131.
ὅτι (conjunction introducing a subordinate clause in indirect discourse) 211.
ἐγγύς (adverbial) 1512.
ἐστιν (3d.per.sing.pres.ind.of εἰμί, aoristic) 86.

ἡ (nom.sing.fem.of the article in agreement with βασιλεία) 9.
βασιλεία (nom.sing.fem.of βασιλεία, subject of ἐστιν) 253.
τοῦ (gen.sing.masc.of the article in agreement with θεοῦ) 9.
θεοῦ (gen.sing.masc.of θεός, description) 124.

Translation - "So also will it be with you - when you see these things taking place, understand that the Kingdom of God is near."

Comment: *Cf.* comment on Mt.24:33; Mk.13:29. Note that Luke refers to the Kingdom of Messiah on David's throne, which is imminent to the events just described, as the Kingdom of God. *Cf.* the note joined to #253. God's sovereign jurisdiction over His creation in whatever age and place exercised can be called the Kingdom of God.

Verse 32 - "Verily I say unto you, This generation shall not pass away until all be fulfilled."

ἀμὴν λέγω ὑμῖν ὅτι οὐ μὴ παρέλθῃ ἡ γενεὰ αὕτη ἕως ἂν πάντα γένηται.

ἀμὴν (explicative) 466.
λέγω (1st.per.sing.pres.act.ind.of λέγω, aoristic) 66.
ὑμῖν (dat.pl.masc.of σύ, indirect object of λέγω) 104.
ὅτι (conjunction introducing a subordinate clause in indirect discourse) 211.
οὐ (summary negative conjunction with μὴ and the subjunctive, emphatic negation) 130.
μὴ (qualified negative conjunction with the subjunctive, emphatic negation) 87.
παρέλθῃ (3d.per.sing.aor.mid.subj.of παρέρχομαι, emphatic negation) 467.
ἡ (nom.sing.fem.of the article in agreement with γενεὰ) 9.
γενεὰ (nom.sing.fem.of γενεά, subject of παρέλθῃ) 922.
αὕτη (nom.sing.fem.of οὗτος, in agreement with γενεὰ) 93.
ἕως (conjunction introducing an indefinite temporal clause) 71.
ἂν (particle in an indefinite temporal clause) 205.
πάντα (nom.pl.neut.of πᾶς, subject of γένηται) 67.
γένηται (3d.per.sing.aor.subj.of γίνομαι, indefinite temporal clause) 113.

Translation - "Truly, I am telling you that this generation shall not pass away until all things have been done."

Comment: The key to the passage lies in the question as to what generation Jesus meant. ἡ γενεὰ αὕτη refers to the generation of verse 31 who sees ταῦτα γινόμενα - "these things happening." And to what do ταῦτα γινόμενα refer? Obviously to the events of verses 25-27. The generation which is alive to see the beginning of end-time events, will not pass away until everything that Jesus described, including His personal return (vs.27) has taken place. *Cf.* Mt.24:34; Mk.13:30. To Christians in the 20th century who may read these words and who live prior to the beginning of Daniel's 70th week, these matters may seem remote. Our Lord has delayed His coming for almost two thousand years. Is He really ever coming back? We need the advice of Heb.10:36. But to the end time believers who live to see what in our Lord's illustration corresponds to the budding of the trees, it will be a great thrill to know that the history of the imminently ensuing seven years, described in detail between Revelation 1:4 and Revelation 20:6 will be enacted before their eyes and that on the appointed day, 2520 days from the beginning, Jesus will come. Thus the day of our Lord's return will not come upon them as a thief (1 Thess.5:4).

As if to assure us that there is no doubt about the fulfillment of these prophecies, our Lord adds in

Verse 33 - "Heaven and earth shall pass away: but my words shall not pass away."

ὁ οὐρανὸς καὶ ἡ γῆ παρελεύσονται, οἱ δὲ λόγοι μου οὐ μὴ παρελεύσονται.

ὁ (nom.sing.masc.of the article in agreement with *οὐρανὸς*) 9.
οὐρανὸς (nom.sing.masc.of *οὐρανός*, subject of *παρελεύσονται*) 254.
καὶ (adjunctive conjunction joining nouns) 14.
ἡ (nom.sing.fem.of the article in agreement with *γῆ*) 9.
γῆ (nom.sing.fem.of *γῆ*, subject of *παρελεύσονται*) 157.
παρελεύσονται (3d.per.pl.fut.mid.ind.of *παρέρχομαι*, predictive) 467.
οἱ (nom.pl.masc.of the article in agreement with *λόγοι*) 9.
δὲ (adversative conjunction) 11.
λόγοι (nom.pl.masc.of *λόγος*, subject of *παρελεύσονται*) 510.
μου (gen.sing.masc.of *ἐγώ*, possession) 123.
οὐ (summary negative conjunction with *μὴ* and the future) 130.
μὴ (qualified negative conjunction with *οὐ* and the future) 87.
παρελεύσονται (3d.per.pl.fut.mid.ind.of *παρέρχομαι*, predictive) 467.

Translation - "The heaven and the earth will pass away, but my words will not pass away."

Comment: *Cf.* comment on Mt.24:35; Mk.13:31. "Sometimes (very rarely) *οὐ μὴ* occurs with the predictive fut. (cf. the usual aorist subj.) as in *οὐ μὴ παρελεύσονται* (Lu.21:33); *οὐ μὴ εὑρήσουσιν* (Rev.9:6); *οὐκέτι οὐ μὴ εὑρήσουσιν* (18:14; cf. *ἀπῆλθεν, ἀπώλετο*).The construction of *οὐ μὴ* with the fut.ind.is "moribund" in the N.T., (Moulton, *Prol.*,p.190) only 14 and some of these doubtful (MSS.vary greatly between aorist subj.and fut.ind.). Some of the 14 are examples of the volitive future. In Mt.15:5, *οὐ μὴ τιμήσει* is probably volitive, (Burton, *N.T. Moods and Tenses*, p.35) though some hold it predictive." (Robertson, *Grammar*, 873, 874).

There will be a new heaven and a new earth, for the former heaven and earth will pass away (Rev.21:1), but never a new and different message from Christ. It was and is inerrant and it abides forever.

Verse 34 - "And take heed to yourselves, lest at any time your hearts are overcharged with surfeiting and drunkenness, and cares of this life, and so that day come upon you unawares as a snare."

Προσέχετε δὲ ἑαυτοῖς μήποτε βαρηθῶσιν ὑμῶν αἱ καρδίαι ἐν κραιπάλῃ καὶ μέθῃ καὶ μερίμναις βιωτικαῖς, καὶ ἐπιστῇ ἐφ' ὑμᾶς αἰφνίδιος ἡ ἡμέρα ἐκείνη.

Προσέχετε (2d.per.pl.pres.act.impv.of προσέχω, command) 555.
δὲ (adversative conjunction) 11.
ἑαυτοῖς (dat.pl.masc.of ἑαυτός, reference) 288.
μήποτε (conjunction introducing the subjunctive in a negative purpose clause) 351.
βαρηθῶσιν (3d.per.pl.aor.pass.subj.of βαρέομαι, negative purpose) 1589.
αἱ (nom.pl.fem.of the article in agreement with καρδίαι) 9.
καρδίαι (nom.pl.fem.of καρδία, subject of βαρηθῶσιν) 432.
ὑμῶν (gen.pl.masc.of σύ, possession) 104.
ἐν (preposition with the instrumental of means) 80.

#2734 κραιπάλῃ (instru.sing.fem.of κραιπάλη, means).

surfeiting - Luke 21:34.

Meaning: from κράς, a poetic form of κάρα - "head" and πάλλω - "to toss or shake" ' hence, the giddiness or nausea of a sick headache as a result of drunkenness. A hangover - Luke 21:34.

καὶ (adjunctive conjunction joining nouns) 14.

#2735 μέθῃ (instrumental sing.fem.of μέθη, means).

drunkenness - Luke 21:34; Rom.13:13; Gal.5:21.

*Meaning: Cf.*μεθύω (#1527). μέθυ - "any intoxicating drink." Hence, drunkenness, intoxication. Listed as one of the ἔργα τῆς σαρκός in Gal.5:21. Warned against in Rom.13:13. A foe to watchfulness - Luke 21:34.

καὶ (adjunctive conjunction joining nouns) 14.
μερίμναις (instru.pl.fem.of μέριμνα, means) 1048.

#2736 βιωτικαῖς (dat.pl.fem.of βιωτικός, reference).

of things pertaining to this life - LUke 21:34; 1 Cor.6:3,4.

Meaning: first used by Aristotle to denote things that have relevance in this life as opposed to the eternal and spiritual world - Luke 21:34; 1 Cor.6:3,4.

καὶ (adjunctive conjunction joining negative purpose clauses) 14.
ἐπιστῇ (3d.per.sing.aor.act.subj.of ἐφίστημι, negative purpose) 1877.
ἐφ' (preposition with the accusative of extent) 47.
ὑμᾶς (acc.pl.masc.of σύ, extent) 104.

#2737 ἐφνίδιος (for αἰφνίδιος, predicate adjective).

sudden - 1 Thess.5:3.
unawares - Luke 21:34.

Meaning: *Cf.*αἴφνης, ἀφανής (#4947), ἄφνω (#2957), from α privative and φαίνω (#100). Hence, unseen and therefore unexpected. Sudden. With reference to the coming of the Lord - 1 Thess.5:3; Luke 21:34.

ἡ (nom.sing.fem.of the article in agreement with ἡμέρα) 9.
ἡμέρα (nom.sing.fem.of ἡμέρα, subject of ἀπιστῇ) 135.
ἐκείνη (nom.sing.fem.of ἐκεῖνος, in agreement with ἡμέρα) 246.

Translation - "But watch yourselves, lest your hearts be overburdened with self indulgence and intoxication and frustrations in this life and that day come upon you when you do not expect it."

Comment: προσέχετε ἑαυτοῖς - "keep a close watch upon yourselves." The negative purpose clause introduced by μήποτε follows. Hearts burdened down by the sick headaches that result from over indulgence (#2734) and intoxication (#2735) and the distractions, frustrations and petty annoyances (#1048) that are a part of life in the here and now, would prevent the watchfulness of the alert Christian who, by diligent Bible study, can otherwise understand when Christ will return. Thus the day of His return would come upon such a burdened Christian unannounced and unpremeditated (#2737), like a trap that suddenly springs and fastens itself upon its unsuspecting prey.

The KJV translates ὡς παγίς as a part of verse 34. The editors of the United Bible Societies' Committee have it in verse 35, joining the comparative clause to ἐπελεύσεται.

There is no comfort here for the pretribulationists, since we have it from 1 Thess.5:3 that this unannounced destruction will come upon the unsaved, while in the following verse (1 Thess.5:4) the Thessalonian Christians, who are referred to as "brethren" are promised that that day will not come upon them as a thief. All that Jesus is saying in our passage is that an unannounced coming of Christ is something to be avoided by those who are otherwise likely to be surprized because of being burdened down with hangovers, overindulgence and incidental frustrations of this life. The clear implication is that Jesus wants His saints to be victorious over the fate of the unsaved in this verse. The reward for faithfulness is his alert expectation of the great event.

Verse 35 - "For as a snare shall it come on all them that dwell on the face of the whole earth."

ὡς παγὶς γὰρ ἐπελεύσεται ἐπὶ πάντας τοὺς καθημένους ἐπὶ πρόσωπον πάσης τῆς γῆς.

ὡς (particle introducing a comparative clause) 128.

#2738 παγὶς (nom.sing.fem.of παγίς, subject of verb understood).

snare - Luke 21:35; Rom.11:9; 1 Tim.3:7; 6:9; 2 Tim.2:26.

Meaning: *Cf.*πήγνυμι (#4997). Hence, that which holds secure; that which catches and retains. A trap, snare. A device to take an animal unexpectedly. Prop.with ὡς in a comparative clause. The Second Coming of Christ being unexpected to the backslidden Christian would catch him as a snare catches an animal - Luke 21:35. trop. associated with θήρα (#3988) in Rom.11:9. Joined to an ablative of source τοῦ διαβόλου in 1 Tim.3:7; 2 Tim.2:26. Joined with πειρασμόν, ἐπιθυμίας πολλὰς ἀνοήτους καὶ βλαβεράς in 1 Tim.6:9.

γὰρ (inferential conjunction in a coordinate causal clause) 105.

#2739 ἐπελεύσεται (3d.per.sing.fut.mid.ind.of ἐπεισέρχομαι, predictive).

come on - Luke 21:35.

Meaning: A combination of ἐπί (#47), εἰς (#140) and ἔρχομαι (#146). Hence to come in and upon. Followed by ἐπί and the accusative in Luke 21:35.

ἐπὶ (preposition with the accusative of extent) 47.
πάντας (acc.pl.masc.of πᾶς, in agreement with καθημένους) 67.
τοὺς (acc.pl.masc.of the article in agreement with καθημένους) 9.
καθημένους (pres.mid.part.acc.pl.masc.of κάθημαι, substantival, extent) 377.
ἐπὶ (preposition with the accusative of extent) 47.
πρόσωπον (acc.sing.neut.of πρόσωπον, extent) 588.
πάσης (gen.sing.fem.of πᾶς, in agreement with γῆς) 67.
τῆς (gen.sing.fem.of the article in agreement with γῆς) 9.
γῆς (gen.sing.fem.of γῆ, description) 157.

Translation - "Because like a trap it will seize upon all who live upon the face of all the earth."

Comment: The antecedent of "it," implicit in ἐπελεύσεται, the subject of the verb, is ἡ ἡμέρα ἐκείνη of verse 34. That day, when it comes, will come upon the entire earth, a rather obvious observation. What our Lord means is that the events that occur on that day will be experienced throughout the earth. The coming of the Lord will be universal. *Cf.* Mt.24:27,28. It will come, unexpectedly, as a thief comes, and it will spring like a trap, upon the unsuspecting unsaved, but not upon the saved, who will be watching (1 Thess.5:3-5).

Verse 36 - "Watch ye, therefore, and pray always, that ye may be accounted worthy to escape all these things that shall come to pass, and to stand before the Son of Man."

ἀγρυπνεῖτε δὲ ἐν παντὶ καιρῷ δεόμενοι ἵνα κατισχύσητε ἐκφυγεῖν ταῦτα πάντα τὰ μέλλοντα γίνεσθαι, καὶ σταθῆναι ἔμπροσθεν τοῦ υἱοῦ τοῦ ἀνθρώπου.

ἀγρυπνεῖτε (2d.per.pl.pres.act.impv.of ἀγρυπνέω, command) 2714.
δὲ (inferential conjunction) 11.

ἐν (preposition with the locative of time point) 80.
παντὶ (loc.sing.masc.of πᾶς, in agreement with καιρῷ) 67.
καιρῷ (loc.sing.masc.of καιρός, time point) 767.
δεόμενοι (pres.mid.part.nom.pl.masc.of δέομαι, adverbial, complementary) 841.
ἵνα (conjunction introducing the subjunctive in a purpose clause) 114.
κατισχύσητε (2d.per.pl.aor.pass.subj.of κατισχύω, purpose) 1205.

#2740 ἐκφυγεῖν (aor.act.inf.of ἐκφεύγω, completes κατισχύσητε).

escape - Luke 21:36; Acts 16:27; 19;16; 1 Thess.5:3; Heb.2:3; Rom.2:3; Heb.12:25; 2 Cor.11:33.

Meaning: A combination of ἐκ (#19) and φεύγω (#202). Hence, to flee away from; to escape. To escape divine judgments at the second coming of Christ - Luke 21:36; 1 Thess.5:3; from a jail - Acts 16:27; from personal assault - Acts 19:16; Paul from capture - 2 Cor.11:33; the judgments of God - Rom.2:3; Heb.2:3; 12:25.

ταῦτα (acc.pl.neut.of οὗτος, direct object of ἐκφυγεῖν) 93.
πάντα (acc.pl.neut.of πᾶς, in agreement with ταῦτα) 67.
τὰ (acc.pl.neut.of the article in agreement with μέλλοντα) 9.
μέλλοντα (pres.act.part.acc.pl.neut.of μέλλω, adjectival, ascriptive, in agreement with ταῦτα) 206.
γίνεσθαι (pres.inf.of γίνομαι, completes μέλλοντα) 113.
καὶ (adjunctive conjunction joining infinitives) 14.
σταθῆναι (aor.pass.inf.of ἵστημι, completes κατισχύσητε) 180.
ἔμπροσθεν (improper preposition with the ablative of place separation) 459.
τοῦ (abl.sing.masc.of the article in agreement with υἱοῦ) 9.
υἱοῦ (abl.sing.masc.of υἱός, place separation) 5.
τοῦ (gen.sing.masc.of the article in agreement with ἀνθρώπου) 9.
ἀνθρώπου (gen.sing.masc.of ἄνθρωπος, description) 341.

Translation - "Therefore be alert at all times, praying that you may succeed in escaping all these things which are about to happen, and to be presented before the Son of Man."

Comment: The admonition to be alert at all times is coupled with the complementary participle δεόμενοι. Thus the watching and the praying go together. For what are we to pray? The ἵνα clause of purpose follows: that we may succeed in escaping all of the judgments that are about to come upon the earth. We must pray also that we may be presented in the presence of the Son of Man. The KJV translation of κατισχύσητε - "accounted worthy" is unfortunate. It leaves the impression that escape on that day is a matter of ethical worth. The prevailing which leads to escape is watchfulness and prayer. The unsaved in that day will not escape (1 Thess.5:3), but Paul adds ". . . ye brethren are not in darkness that that day should overtake you as a thief." (1 Thess.5:4).

Verse 37 - "And in the day time he was teaching in the temple; and at night he went out and abode in the mount that is called the Mount of Olives."

Ἦν δὲ τὰς ἡμέρας ἐν τῷ ἱερῷ διδάσκων, τὰς δὲ νύκτας ἐξερχόμενος ηὐλίζετο εἰς τὸ ὄρος τὸ καλούμενον Ἐλαιῶν.

Ἦν (3d.per.sing.imp.ind.of εἰμί, imperfect periphrastic) 86.
δὲ (continuative conjunction) 11.
τὰς (acc.pl.fem.of the article in agreement with ἡμέρας) 9.
ἡμέρας (acc.pl.fem.of ἡμέρα, time extent) 135.
ἐν (preposition with the locative of place where) 80.
τῷ (loc.sing.neut.of the article in agreement with ἱερῷ) 9.
ἱερῷ (loc.sing.neut.of ἱερόν, place where) 346.
διδάσκων (pres.act.part.nom.sing.masc.of διδάσκω, imperfect periphrastic) 403.
τὰς (acc.pl.fem.of the article in agreement with νύκτας) 9.
δὲ (adversative conjunction) 11.
νύκτας (acc.pl.fem.of νύξ, time extent) 209.
ἐξερχόμενος (pres.mid.part.nom.sing.masc.of ἐξέρχομαι, adverbial, temporal) 161.
ηὐλίζετο (3d.per.sing.imp.mid.ind.of αὐλίζομαι, progressive description) 1364.
εἰς (preposition with the accusative, static use) 140.
τὸ (acc.sing.neut.of the article in agreement with ὄρος) 9.
ὄρος (acc.sing.neut.of ὄρος, place where, static use of εἰς with the accusative) 357.
τὸ (acc.sing.neut.of the article in agreement with καλούμενον) 9.
καλούμενον (pres.pass.part.acc.sing.neut.of καλέω, adjectival, restrictive) 107.
Ἐλαιῶν (gen.pl.fem.of ἐλαία, designation) 1341.

Translation - "And He continued to teach during the days in the temple court, but at night He went out and bedded down upon the Mount of Olives."

Comment: The imperfect periphrastic Ἦν . . . διδάσκων indicates a continuing action, which is supported by the accusative of time extent in τὰς ἡμέρας. He preached during the days in the temple. He spent the nights upon the Mount of Olives. Apparently the people observed His schedule of activity and adjusted to it as we see in

Verse 38 - "And all the people came early in the morning to him in the temple, for to hear him."

καὶ πᾶς ὁ λαὸς ὤρθριζεν πρὸς αὐτὸν ἐν τῷ ἱερῷ ἀκούειν αὐτοῦ.

καὶ (inferential conjunction) 14.
πᾶς (nom.sing.masc.of πᾶς, in agreement with λαὸς) 67.
ὁ (nom.sing.masc.of the article in agreement with λαὸς) 9.
λαὸς (nom.sing.masc.of λαός, subject of ὤρθριζεν) 110.

#2741 ὤρθριζεν (3d.per.sing.imp.act.ind.of ὀρθρίζω, progressive description).

come early in the morning - Luke 21:38.

*Meaning: Cf.*ὄρθρος (#2375); to rise early in the morning - Luke 21:38.

πρὸς (preposition with the accusative of extent) 197.
αὐτὸν (acc.sing.masc.of αὐτός, extent) 16.
ἐν (preposition with the locative of place where) 80.
τῷ (loc.sing.neut.of the article in agreement with ἱερῷ) 9.
ἱερῷ (loc.sing.neut.of ἱερόν, place where) 346.
ἀκούειν (pres.act.inf.of ἀκούω, purpose) 148.
αὐτοῦ (gen.sing.masc.of αὐτός, description) 16.

Translation - "Therefore all the people were coming to Him early in the morning in order to hear Him."

Comment: The action of the people was adjusted to Jesus' habit described in verse 37. He had established a routine which they observed. The fact that they came to the temple court early in the morning indicates their interest in His teaching. They did not wish to miss a word.

Jesus Predicts His Death As At Hand

(Matthew 26:1-5; Mark 14:1-2; Luke 22:1-2)

Mark 14:1 - "After two days was the feast of the Passover, and of unleavened bread; and the chief priests and scribes sought how they might take him by craft, and put him to death."

Ἦν δὲ τὸ πάσχα καὶ τὰ ἄζυμα μετὰ δύο ἡμέρας, καὶ ἐζήτουν οἱ ἀρχιερεῖς καὶ οἱ γραμματεῖς πῶς αὐτὸν ἐν δόλῳ κρατήσαντες ἀποκτείνωσιν.

Ἦν (3d.per.sing.imp.ind.of εἰμί, progressive description) 86.
δὲ (explanatory conjunction) 11.
τὸ (nom.sing.neut.of the article in agreement with πάσχα) 9.
πάσχα (nom.sing.neut.of πάσχα, subject of ἦν) 1553.
καὶ (adjunctive conjunction joining nouns) 14.
τὰ (acc.pl.neut.of the article in agreement with ἄζυμα) 9.
ἄζυμα (acc.pl.neut.of ἄζυμος, subject of ἦν) 1571.
μετὰ (preposition with the accusative of time extent) 50.
δύο (numeral) 385.
ἡμέρας (acc.pl.fem.of ἡμέρα, time extent) 135.
καὶ (continuative conjunction) 14.
ἐζήτουν (3d.per.pl.imp.act.ind.of ζητέω, progressive description) 207.
οἱ (nom.pl.masc.of the article in agreement with ἀρχιερεῖς) 9.
ἀρχιερεῖς (nom.pl.masc.of ἀρχιερεύς, subject of ἐζήτουν) 151.
καὶ (adjunctive conjunction joining nouns) 14.

οἱ (nom.pl.masc.of the article in agreement with γραμματεῖς) 9.
γραμματεῖς (nom.pl.masc.of γραμματεύς, subject of ἐζήτουν) 152.
πῶς (interrogative conjunction with the deliberative subjunctive) 627.
αὐτὸν (acc.sing.masc.of αὐτός, direct object of ἀποκτείνωσιν) 16.
ἐν (preposition with the instrumental of means) 80.
δόλῳ (instrumental sing.masc.of δόλος, means) 1557.
κρατήσαντες (aor.act.part.nom.pl.masc.of κρατέω, adverbial,temporal) 828.
ἀποκτείνωσιν (3d.per.pl.pres.act.subj.of ἀποκτείνω, deliberative) 889.

Translation - "Now in two days the Passover and the Feasts of Unleavened Bread would be observed, and the Chief Priests and the Scribes were seeking how, after they had arrested Him by guile, they might kill Him."

Comment: δὲ is explanatory. The Paschal meal and, in its connection the Feasts of Unleavned Bread, were only two days in the offing. If in fact the time point here is still Tuesday evening, then two days would bring us to Thursday evening. At six o'clock the Passover would begin. This puts the Last Supper on Thursday evening and our Lord's arrest later than night with the crucifixion on Friday morning, which is the traditional date. If we take our Lord's statement of Mt.12:40 in the sense in which it would be understood today, we have a conflict. If Jesus was dead at 3:00 p.m. on Friday and buried before 6:00 p.m., thus to avoid a violation of the Sabbath, then He was in "the heart of the earth" a part of Friday (3:00 to 6:00 p.m.), all of Saturday and a part of Sunday. This accounts for three days but only for two nights. If He was crucified on Thursday, then Thursday, Friday and Saturday (not Sunday, since He arose as it began to dawn toward the first day of the week) accounts for three days, while Thursday, Friday and Saturday nights also accounts for three nights. This does not total 72 hours, because it was only a part of Thursday, followed by two full days. The view that He was crucified on Wednesday means three full days - Thursday, Friday and Saturday and a part of a fourth (Wednesday) and four nights. The view that Jesus died on Thursday is thought by some to comport with Mt.12:40 most easily. A.T.Robertson offers the following explanation:

"But how about the prediction of Jesus, repeatedly made, and once illustrated in the case of Jonah, that he would rise after three days? Are two nights and a day and two pieces of days three days? Let us see.

(a) The well-known custom of the Jews was to count a part of a day as a whole day of twenty-four hours. Hence a part of a day or night would be counted as a whole day, the term day obviously having two senses, as night and day, or day contrasted with night. So then the part of Friday would count as one day, Saturday another, and the part of Sunday the third day. This method of reckoning gives no trouble to a Jew or to modern men, for that matter. In free vernacular we speak the same way today. . . .

(b) Besides, the phrase "on the third day" is obliged to mean that the resurrection took place on that day, for, if it occurred after the third day, it would be on the fourth day and not on the third. Now it so happens that this term "third day" is applied seven times to the resurrection of Christ (Matt.16:21; Matt.17:23; Matt.20:19; Luke 27:7,21,46; 1 Cor.15:4). These numerous passages of Scripture, both prophecy and statement of history, agree with the record of the fact that Jesus did rise

on the third day. (Luke 24:7).

(c) Moreover, the phrase "after three days" is used by the same writers (Matthew and Luke) in connection with the former one, "the third day," as meaning the same thing. Hence the definite and clear expressions must explain the one that is less so. The chief priests and Pharisees remember (Matt. 27:63) that Jesus said, after three days I rise again. (sic). *Hence they urge Pilate to keep a guard over the tomb until the* third day *(Matt.27:64). This is their own interpretation of the Saviour's words. Besides, in parallel passages in the different Gospels, one will have one expression and another the other, naturally suggesting that they regarded them as equivalent. (Cf. Mark 8:31 with Matt.16:21, Luke 9:22 with Mark 10:34). On the third day cannot mean on the fourth day, while after three days can be used as meaning on the third day.*

(d) Matthew 12:40 is urged as conclusive the other way. But the "three days and three nights" may be nothing more than a longer way of saying three days, using day in its long sense. And we have already seen that the Jews counted any part of this full day (day and night) as a whole day (day and night). Hence this passage may mean nothing more than the common "after three days" above mentioned, and, like that expression, must be interpreted in accordance with the definite term "on the third day" and with the clear chronological data given by Luke and the rest. They seemed to be conscious of no discrepancy in these various expressions. Most likely they understood them as well as we do at any rate."

A.T.Robertson, *A Harmony of the Gospels,* 290,291.

The chief priests and Pharisees were constantly planning (imperfect tense in ἐζήτουν) how to kill Him. Note πῶς with the deliberative subjunctive. The problem was how to arrest Him without arousing popular indignation against themselves, since at that time public opinion was high in Jesus' favor. *Cf.*#1557 for other uses of δόλος. Once the officials had arrested Jesus and the San Hedrin had Him in custody, public opinion could be swayed to favor His death.

Verse 2 - "But they said, Not on the feast day, lest there be an uproar of the people."

ἔλεγον γάρ, Μὴ ἐν τῇ ἑορτῇ, μήποτε ἔσται θόρυβος τοῦ λαοῦ.

ἔλεγον (3d.per.pl.imp.act.ind.of λέγω, progressive description) 66.

γάρ (inferential conjunction introducing a coordinating causal clause) 105.

Μὴ (qualified negative conjunction in an elliptical clause with the hortatory subjunctive understood) 87.

ἐν (preposition with the locative of time point) 80.

τῇ (loc.sing.fem.of the article in agreement with ἑορτῇ) 9.

ἑορτῇ (loc.sing.fem.of ἑορτή, time point) 1558.

μήποτε (negative particle with the future indicative in a negative final clause) 351.

ἔσται (3d.per.sing.fut.indicative of εἰμί, negative final clause) 86.

θόρυβος (nom.sing.masc.of θόρυβος, subject of ἔσται) 1559.

τοῦ (gen.sing.masc.of the article in agreement with λαοῦ) 9.

λαοῦ (gen.sing.masc.of λαός, description) 110.

Translation - "But they were saying, 'Not on the feast day lest there be a popular uprising.' "

Comment: We have an ellipsis in Μὴ ἐν τῇ ἑορτῃ. . κ.τ.λ." They were saying, "Let us not arrest Him on the feast day . . . κ.τ.λ." but they omitted the hortatory subjunctive verb. Note μήποτε here with the future indicative in a negative final clause. The San Hedrin wished to avoid mob violence (Mk.14:2) just as Pilate, who wanted to protect Jesus, could not do so because of the mob (Mt.27:24). Willing to fight to protect Jesus on Tuesday afternoon the mob was demanding His death on the Friday morning following.

We turn now to the parallel passage in

Luke 22:1 - "Now the feast of unleavened bread drew nigh, which is called the Passover."

Ἤγγιζεν δὲ ἡ ἑορτὴ τῶν ἀζύμων ἡ λεγομένη πάσχα.

Ἤγγιζεν (3d.per.sing.imp.act.ind.of ἐγγίζω, progressive description) 252.
δὲ (explanatory conjunction) 11.
ἡ (nom.sing.fem.of the article in agreement with ἑορτὴ) 9.
ἑορτὴ (nom.sing.fem.of ἑορτή, subject of ἤγγιζεν) 1558.
τῶν (gen.pl.masc.of the article in agreement with ἀζύμων) 9.
ἀζύμων (gen.pl.masc.of ἄζυμος, description) 1571.
ἡ (nom.sing.fem.of the article in agreement with λεγομένη) 9.
λεγομένη (pres.pass.part.nom.sing.fem.of λέγω, apposition) 66.
πάσχα (nom.sing.fem.of πάσχα, appellation) 1553.

Translation - "Now the feast of Unleavened Breads, the one called Passover, was approaching."

Comment: δὲ is explanatory. Note ἡ λεγομένη πάσχα in apposition. *Cf.* Mt.26:2; Mk.14:1.

Verse 2 - "And the chief priests and scribes sought how they might kill him; for they feared the people."

καὶ ἐζήτουν οἱ ἀρχιερεῖς καὶ οἱ γραμματεῖς τὸ πῶς ἀνέλωσιν αὐτόν, ἐφοβοῦντο γὰρ τὸν λαόν.

καὶ (inferential conjunction introducing a coordinate causal clause) 105.
ἐζήτουν (3d.per.pl.imp.act.ind.of ζητέω, progressive description) 207.
οἱ (nom.pl.masc.of the article in agreement with ἀρχιερεῖς) 9.
ἀρχιερεῖς (nom.pl.masc.of ἀρχιερεύς, subject of ἐζήτουν) 151.
καὶ (adjunctive conjunction joining nouns) 14.
οἱ (nom.pl.masc.of the article in agreement with γραμματεῖς) 9.
γραμματεῖς (nom.pl.masc.of γραμματεύς, subject of ἐζήτουν) 152.
τὸ (acc.sing.neut.of the article, introducing the object clause, πῶς ἀνέλωσιν αὐτόν) 9.
πῶς (interrogative conjunction introducing indirect question) 627.

ἀνέλωσιν (3d.per.pl.2d.aor.act.subj.of ἀναιρέω, deliberative subjunctive) 216.

αὐτόν (acc.sing.masc.of αὐτός, direct object of ἀνέλωσιν) 16.

ἐφοβοῦντο (3d.per.pl.imp.mid.ind.of φοβέομαι, progressive description) 101.

γὰρ (inferential conjunction introducing a coordinate causal clause) 105.

τὸν (acc.sing.masc.of the article in agreement with λαόν) 9.

λαόν (acc.sing.masc.of λαός, direct object of ἐφοβοῦντο) 110.

Translation - "Therefore the chief priests and the scribes were seeking the way to kill Him, because they were afraid of the people."

Comment: τὸ πῶς ἀνέλωσιν αὐτόν is a substantival use of a hypotactic clause in the accusative case as the direct object of ἐζήτουν. It has the subjunctive mode to indicate the fact that they had doubts, not that they wanted to kill him, but as to how they might arrest Him without arousing the wrath of the people. *Cf.* Mt.26:1-5; Mk.14:1-2.

Anointing of Jesus by Mary of Bethany

(Matthew 26:6-13; Mark 14:3-9; John 12:2-8)

Mark 14:3 - "And being in Bethany in the house of Simon the leper, as he sat at meat, there came a woman having an alabaster box of ointment of spikenard very precious; and she brake the box, and poured it on his head."

Καὶ ὄντος αὐτοῦ ἐν Βηθανίᾳ ἐν τῇ οἰκίᾳ Σίμωνος τοῦ λεπροῦ κατακειμένου αὐτοῦ ἦλθεν γυνὴ ἔχουσα ἀλάβαστρον μύρου νάρδου πιστικῆς πολυτελοῦς, συντρίψασα τὴν ἀλάβαστρον κατέχεεν αὐτοῦ τῆς κεφαλῆς.

Καὶ (continuative conjunction) 14.

ὄντος (pres.part.gen.sing.masc.of εἰμί, genitive absolute) 86.

αὐτοῦ (gen.sing.masc.of αὐτός, genitive absolute) 16.

ἐν (preposition with the locative of place where) 80.

Βηθανίᾳ (loc.sing.fem.of Βηθανία, place where) 1363.

ἐν (preposition with the locative of place where) 80.

τῇ (loc.sing.fem.of the article in agreement with οἰκίᾳ) 9.

οἰκίᾳ (loc.sing.fem.of οἰκία, place where) 186.

Σίμωνος (gen.sing.masc.of Σίμων, possession) 1560.

τοῦ (gen.sing.masc.of the article in agreement with λεπροῦ) 9.

λεπροῦ (gen.sing.masc.of λεπρός, apposition) 708.

κατακειμένου (pres.mid.part.gen.sing.masc.of κατάκειμαι, genitive absolute) 2065.

αὐτοῦ (gen.sing.masc.of αὐτός, genitive absolute) 16.

ἦλθεν (3d.per.sing.aor.ind.of ἔρχομαι, constative) 146.

γυνὴ (nom.sing.fem.of γυνή, subject of ἦλθεν) 103.

ἔχουσα (pres.act.part.nom.sing.fem.of ἔχω, adjectival, restrictive) 82.

ἀλάβαστρον (acc.sing.neut.of ἀλάβαστρον, direct object of ἔχουσα) 1561.

μύρου (gen.sing.neut.of *μύρον*, description) 1562.

#2742 *νάρδου* (gen.sing.masc.of *νάρδος*, description).

spikenard - Mark 14:3; John 12:3.

Meaning: nard, the head or spike of a fragrant East Indian plant, belonging to the genus of Valeriana. The juice has a delicious odor. Used in the anointing of Jesus - Mark 14:3; John 12:3.

#2743 *πιστικῆς* (gen.sing.masc.of *πιστικός*, in agreement with *νάρδου*).

(not translated) - Mark 14:3; John 12:3.

Meaning: Cf.pisto1w (#1522). Hence, genuine, pure, unadulterated. An as adjective to modify *νάρδου* in Mk.14:3; John 12:3, it means "pure." Not translated in the K.J.V.

#2744 *πολυτελοῦς* (gen.sing.fem.of *πολυτελής*, joined to *μύρου*).

costly - 1 Tim.2:9.
of great price - 1 Peter 3:4.
very precious - Mark 14:3.

Meaning: A combination of *πολύς* (#228) and *τέλος* (#881). Hence, costly, expensive. With reference to female attire - 1 Tim.2:9. Of the ointment used in Jesus' anointing - Mark 14:3. Metaphorically - a humble and quiet spirit - 1 Peter 3:4.

συντρίψασα (aor.act.part.nom.sing.fem.of *συντρίβω*, adverbial, temporal) 985.
τὴν (acc.sing.fem.of the article, joined to *ἀλάβαστρον*) 9.
ἀλάβαστρον (acc.sing.neut.of *ἀλάβαστρον*, direct object of *συντρίφαςα*) 1561.
κατέχεεν (3d.per.sing.1st.aor.actind.of *καταχέω*, constative) 1564.
αὐτοῦ (gen.sing.masc.of *αὐτός*, possession) 16.
τῆς (gen.sing.fem.of the article in agreement with *κεφαλῆς*) 9.
κεφαλῆς (gen.sing.fem.of *κεφαλή*, genitive of description) 521.

Translation - "And while He was in Bethany in the home of Simon, the Leper, as He was sitting at the table, a woman came who had an alabaster box of pure nard ointment, very expensive. When she had broken the box in pieces she poured the ointment upon His head."

Comment: We have two genitive absolute constructions. The first tells us where Jesus was when the action of the main verb (*ἦλθεν*) occurred, and the second what He was doing. Both are in the present tense, indicating simultaneous time with that of the main verb. Note the adjectival participle *ἔχουσα* defining *γυνή*. The aorist participle *συντρίψασα* is temporal. Its action is antecedent to *κατέχεεν*. She broke the box and poured its contents upon Jesus' head. It is a dramatic scene. The dinner party is a progress. Jesus is the guest of honor. A woman enters, carrying an alabaster box full of pure nard - very costly and delightfully aromatic. Without hesitation she breaks the box and pours the ointment upon His head. The identity of the woman is clear. It is Mary, the sister of Lazarus, as the parallel passage in John 12 indicates. A former prostitute, who had been saved as a result of Jesus' ministry, had performed a similar service before. *Cf.* Luke 7:36-50. This occurred before Jesus' second tour of Galilee. When we compare Luke 7:36-50 with John 12:1-8 and Mark 14:1-3 we must conclude that the Lukan incident is not the same one as is recorded by Mark and John. The first woman was a woman of the street. The last was Mary of Bethany. The first incident occurred earlier in Jesus' ministry. The last only a day or two before His death.

Note the various uses of *συντρίβω* (#985). Mary broke the alabaster box in order to honor her Lord (Mark 14:3). The Roman soldiers intended to break the bones of Jesus in order to hasten His death (John 19:36). Jesus will rule with a rod of iron (Rev.2:27) Note also Isaiah's description of the ministry of Messiah (Mt.12:20). Messiah will bruise Satan under our feet (Rom.16:20). *Cf.* Mt.26:6,7.

Note Mark's grammatical blunders as *πιστικῆς*, a genitive form, fails to conform either to *μύρου* (neuter) or *νάρδου* (masculine), and the feminine article *τὴν* is joined to the neuter *ἀλάβαστρον*. We will excuse Mark. He was only a very young man. Those who contend for a dictation theory of inspiration must accuse the Holy Spirit of not knowing His Greek grammar!

Verse 4 - "And there were some that had indignation within themselves, and said, Why was this waste of the ointment made?"

ἦσαν δέ τινες ἀγανακτοῦντες πρὸς ἑαυτους, Εἰς τί ἡ ἀπώλεια αὔτη τοῦ μύρου γέγονεν;

ἦσαν (3d.per.pl.imp.ind.of *εἰμί*, progressive description) 86.
δέ (adversative conjunction) 11.

τινες (nom.pl.masc.of *τις*, indefinite pronoun, subject of *ἦσαν*) 281.
ἀγανακτοῦντες (pres.act.part.nom.pl.masc.of *ἀγανακτέω*, adjectival, ascriptive) 1331.

πρὸς (preposition with the accusative with persons) 197.
ἑαυτούς (acc.pl.masc.of *ἑαυτός*, extent) 288.
Εἰς (preposition with the accusative, cause) 140.
τί (acc.sing.neut.of *τίς*, cause) 281.
ἡ (nom.sing.fem.of the article in agreement with *ἀπώλεια*) 9.
ἀπώλεια (nom.sing.fem.of *ἀπώλεια*, subject of *γέγονεν*) 666.
αὔτη (nom.sing.fem.of *οὗτος*, in agreement with *ἀπώλεια*) 93.
τοῦ (gen.sing.neut.of the article in agreement with *μύρου*) 9.
μύρου (gen.sing.neut.of *μύρον*, description) 1562.

γέγονεν (3d.per.sing.2d.perf.ind.of γίνομαι, intensive) 113.

Translation - "But certain ones were annoyed and said to themselves, 'Why has this waste of the ointment occurred?' "

Comment: *Cf. comment on Matthew 26:8.*

Verse 5 - "For it might have been sold for more than three hundred pence, and have been given to the poor. And they murmured against her."

ἠδύνατο γὰρ τοῦτο τὸ μύρον πραθῆναι ἐπάνω δηναρίων τριακοσίων καὶ δοθῆναι τοῖς πτωχοῖς. καὶ ἐνεβριμῶντο αὐτῇ.

ἠδύνατο (3d.per.sing.imp.ind.of δύναμαι, voluntative) 289.
γὰρ (inferential conjunction introducing a coordinate causal clause) 105.
τοῦτο (nom.sing.neut.of οὗτος, in agreement with μύρον) 93.
τὸ (nom.sing.neut.of the article in agreement with μύρον) 9.
μύρον (nom.sing.neut.of μύρον, subject of ἠδύνατο) 1562.
πραθῆναι (1st.aor.pass.inf.of πιπράσκω, completes ἠδύνατο) 1088.
ἐπάνω (adverbial) 181.
δηναρίων (abl.pl.neut.of δηνάριον, comparison) 1278.

#2745 τριακοσίων (abl.pl.neut.of τριακόσιοι, with δηναρίων).

three hundred - Mark 14:5; John 12:5.

Meaning: The numeral three hundred. Defining δηναρίων in Mark 14:5; John 12:5.

καὶ (adjunctive conjunction joining infinitives) 14.
δοθῆναι (aor.pass.inf.of δίδωμι, completes ἠδύνατο) 362.
τοῖς (dat.pl.masc.of the article in agreement with πτωχοῖς) 9.
πτωχοῖς (dat.pl.masc.of πτωχός, indirect object of δοθῆναι) 423.
καὶ (continuative conjunction) 14.
ἐνεβριμῶντο (3d.per.pl.imp.mid.ind.of ἐμβριμάομαι, inceptive) 831.
αὐτῇ (dat.sing.fem.of αὐτός, reference) 16.

Translation - "Because it is possible that this ointment could have been sold for more than fifty dollars and given to the poor.' And they began to grumble at her."

Comment: *Cf.* comment on Mt.26:9. We have here one of the rare uses of the voluntative imperfect in the Greek New Testament. "The want of attainment in the imperfect prepares it to submit quite easily to the expression of a desire or disposition, since the statement of a wish itself implies the lack of realization. There are but a few instances of this usage in the New Testament, but adequate grammatical treatment requires that they be recognized as a distinct class." (Mantey, *Manual*, 190).

ἐπάνω (#181), an improper preposition, a combination of ἐπί (#47) and ἀνά

(#1059), has no effect upon the case of the substantive which follows it. Ablative of comparison here in δηναρίων, but the instrumental of measure in 1 Cor.15:6.

The disciples were snorting in disgust at the woman. *Cf.*#831. The insensitivity of the disciples on this occasion makes the reader want to "snort" at them. In the shadow of a Roman cross, a saved woman comes to the incarnate Son of God, Who is about to give His life for the elect, and anoints His head with the ointment, at great personal sacrifice. The disciples suddenly get excited about the welfare state! If they had been sincere they would have sold some of their own possessions at a sacrifice to themselves in order to help the poor. The crass insensitivity and inhumanity of sinful men often comes to the surface in loud, stinking bubbles of inner depravity and gross disregard for the finer things of life. The disciples looked as bad on this occasion as the woman looked good. Yet Jesus' rebuke is gentle.

Verse 6 - "And Jesus said, Let her alone. Why trouble ye her? She hath wrought a good work on me."

ὁ δὲ Ἰησοῦς εἶπεν, Ἄφετε αὐτήν. τί αὐτῇ κόπους παρέχετε; καλὸν ἔργον ἠργάσατο ἐν ἐμοί.

ὁ (nom.sing.masc.of the article in agreement with Ἰησοῦς) 9.
δὲ (adversative conjunction) 11.
Ἰησοῦς (nom.sing.masc.of Ἰησοῦς, subject of εἶπεν) 3.
εἶπεν (3d.per.sing.aor.act.ind.of εἶπον, constative) 155.s
Ἄφετε (2d.per.pl.aor.act.impv.of ἀφίημι, command) 319.
αὐτήν (acc.sing.fem.of αὐτός, direct object of ἄφετε) 16.
τί (acc.sing.neut.of τίς, interrogative pronoun, cause) 281.
αὐτῇ (dat.sing.fem.of αὐτός, personal disadvantage) 16.
κόπους (acc.pl.masc.of κόπος, direct object of παρέχετε) 1565.
παρέχετε (2d.per.pl.pres.act.ind.of παρέχω, direct question) 1566.
καλὸν (acc.sing.neut.of καλός, in agreement with ἔργον) 296.
ἔργον (acc.sing.neut.of ἔργον, direct object of ἠργάσατο) 460.
ἠργάσατο (3d.per.sing.aor.mid.ind.of ἐργάζομαι, culminative) 691.
ἐν (preposition with the dative of personal advantage) 80.
ἐμοί (dat.sing.masc.of ἐμός, personal advantage) 1267.

Translation - "But Jesus said, 'Let her alone. Why are you adding to her troubles? She has done something beautiful for me.' "

Comment: Note the difference between ἐν ἐμοί in Mark and εἰς ἐμέ in the parallel passage in Mt.26:10. δὲ is adversative, as Jesus expressed His objection to the attitude of the disciples. I remember a Sunday School song I sang as a boy in the Methodist church that went, "It's just like Jesus . . . κ.τ.λ." It is "just like Jesus" that two days after the disciples objected to the anointing of Jesus' head and feet by a grateful woman, who loved Him, He washed the feet of the disciples (John 13:1-10). ἄφετε αὐτήν is abrupt. The question follows, perhaps with a bit of asperity. "Why are you piling trouble upon her?" Then His words of commendation. *Cf.* Matthew 26:10.

Verse 7 - "For ye have the poor with you always, and whensoever ye will, ye may do them good: but me ye have not always."

πάντοτε γὰρ τοὺς πτωχοὺς ἔχετε μεθ' ἑαυτῶν, καὶ ὅταν θέλητε δύνασθε αὐτοῖς εὖ ποιῆσαι, ἐμὲ δὲ οὐ πάντοτε ἔχετε.

πάντοτε (adverbial) 1567.
γὰρ (inferential conjunction introducing a coordinate causal clause) 105.
τοὺς (acc.pl.masc.of the article in agreement with *πτωχοὺς*) 9.
πτωχοὺς (acc.pl.masc.of *πτωχός*, direct object of *ἔχετε*) 423.
ἔχετε (2d.per.pl.pres.act.ind.of *ἔχω*, static) 82.
μεθ' (preposition with the genitive of accompaniment) 50.
ἑαυτῶν (gen.pl.masc.of *ἑαυτός*, accompaniment) 288.
καὶ (continuative conjunction) 14.
ὅταν (conjunction introducing the subjunctive in an indefinite temporal clause) 436.
θέλητε (2d.per.pl.pres.act.subj.of *θέλω*, indefinite temporal clause) 88.
δύνασθε (2d.per.pl.pres.mid.ind.of *δύναμαι*, futuristic) 289.
αὐτοῖς (dat.pl.masc.of *αὐτός*, personal advantage) 16.
πάντοτε (adverbial) 1567.
εὖ (adverbial) 1536.
ποιῆσαι (aor.act.inf.of *ποιέω*, completes *δύνασθε*) 127.
ἐμὲ (acc.sing.masc.of *ἐμός*, direct object of *ἔχετε*) 1267.
οὐ (summary negative conjunction with the indicative) 130.
πάντοτε (adverbial) 1567.
ἔχετε (2d.per.pl.pres.act.ind.of *ἔχω*, futuristic) 82.

Translation - "Because you always have the poor with you, and when you wish, you will always be able to do good for them,but you will not always have me."

Comment: *Cf.* comment on Mt.26:11. Luke adds the clause *καὶ ὅταν. . . ποιῆσαι* which Matthew omits. Jesus did not deny that caring for the poor was an act of Christian charity, even though He noticed that the disciples were not sincere in their loud protestations of concern for the poor. Indeed Jesus suggests that during a long future the disciples would have ample opportunity to do for the poor whatever good thing they might wish. But He reminded the disciples of something that apparently they had forgotten, though Mary had not forgotten. He was soon to leave them.

Verse 8 - "She hath done what she could: she is come aforehand to anoint my body to the burying."

ὃ ἔσχεν ἐποίησεν. προέλαβεν μυρίσαι τὸ σῶμά μου εἰς τὸν ἐνταφιασμόν.

ὃ (acc.sing.neut.of *ὅς*, direct object of *ἐποίησεν*) 65.
ἔσχεν (3d.per.sing.2d.aor.act.ind.of *ἔχω*, constative) 82.

ἐποίησεν (3d.per.sing.aor.act.ind.of *ποιέω*, culminative) 127.

#2746 *προέλαβεν* (3d.per.sing.aor.act.ind.of *προλαμβάνω*, culminative).

come beforehand - Mark 14:8.
overtake - Gal.6:1.
take before - 1 Cor.11:21.

Meaning: A combination of *πρό* (#442) and *λαμβάνω* (#533). Hence, to take in advance; to take ahead of time. With reference to eating a meal before others at church - 1 Cor.11:21; to anticipate in order to perform a function before the time - with reference to anointing a body for burial - Mark 14:8. In Gal.6:1 to be surprized by and thus overtaken or defeated spiritually. To fall unexpectedly into sin. To be overcome by evil.

#2747 *μυρίσαι* (aor.act.inf.of *μυρίζω*, purpose).

anoint - Mark 14:8.

Meaning: To anoint by pouring on ointment. *Cf.μύρον* (#1562) - Mark 14:8.

τὸ (acc.sing.neut.of the article in agreement with *σῶμά*) 9.
σῶμά (acc.sing.neut.of *σῶμα*, direct object of *μυρίσαι*) 507.
μου (gen.sing.masc.of *ἐγώ*, possession) 123.
εἰς (preposition with the accusative, purpose) 140.
τὸν (acc.sing.masc.of the article in agreement with *ἐνταφιασμόν*) 9.

#2748 *ἐνταφιασμόν* (acc.sing.masc.of *ἐνταφιασμός*, purpose).

burying - Mark 14:8; John 12:7.

Meaning: Cf. ἐνταφιάζω (#1568). Preparation of a body for burial - Mark 14:8; John 12:7.

Translation - "That which she had she has brought in advance in order to anoint my body for the burial."

Comment: *Cf.* comment on Mt.26:12. Note that Matthew expressed the purpose with *πρὸς* and the articular infinitive in its noun use with *με*, the accusative of general reference. Mark uses the simpler formulation - *εἰς* with the accusative of purpose. Mary brought what she had, and apparently did not hesitate to make what was, for her, a notable financial sacrifice. She had taken seriously her Lord's words of Matthew 6:19-21.

Verse 9 - "Verily, I say unto you. Wheresoever this gospel shall be preached throughout the whole world, this also that she hath done shall be spoken of for a memorial of her."

ἀμὴν δὲ λέγω ὑμῖν, ὅπου ἐὰν κηρυχθῇ τὸ εὐαγγέλιον εἰς ὅλον τὸν κόσμον, καὶ ὃ ἐποίησεν αὕτη λαληθήσεται εἰς μνημόσυνον αὐτῆς.

ἀμὴν (explicative) 466.
δὲ (continuative conjunction) 11.
λέγω (1st.per.sing.pres.act.ind.of λέγω, aoristic) 66.
ὑμῖν (dat.pl.masc.of σύ, indirect object of λέγω) 104.
ὅπου (local adverb with the subjunctive in an indefinite local clause, pointing to the future) 592.
ἐὰν (contingent particle with the subjunctive in an indefinite local clause) 363.
κηρυχθῇ (3d.per.sing.aor.pass.subj.of κηρύσσω, indefinite local clause, pointing to the future) 249.
τὸ (nom.sing.neut.of the article in agreement with εὐαγγέλιον) 9.
εὐαγγέλιον (nom.sing.neut.of εὐαγγέλιον, subject of κηρυχθῇ) 405.
εἰς (preposition with the accusative, static use) 140.
ὅλον (acc.sing.masc.of ὅλος, in agreement with κόσμον) 112.
τὸν (acc.sing.masc.of the article in agreement with κόσμον) 9.
κόσμον (acc.sing.masc.of κόσμος, like a locative of place) 360.
καὶ (adjunctive conjunction joining substantives) 14.
ὅ (acc.sing.neut.of ὅς, direct object of λαληθήσεται) 65.
ἐποίησεν (3d.per.sing.aor.act.ind.of ποιέω, culminative) 127.
αὕτη (nom.sing.fem.of οὗτος, subject of ἐποίησεν, deictic) 93.
λαληθήσεται (3d.per.sing.fut.pass.ind.of λαλέω, predictive) 815.
εἰς (preposition with the accusative, purpose) 140.
μνημόσυνον (acc.sing.neut.of μνημόσυνον, purpose) 1569.
αὐτῆς (gen.sing.fem.of αὐτός, designation) 16.

Translation - "Truly I am telling you, Wherever the gospel is preached throughout the entire world, that which this woman has done will also be told as a memorial to her."

Comment: *Cf.* comment on Mt.26:13. We turn now to the parallel passage in John 12:2-8.

John 12:2 - "There they made him a supper; and Martha served: but Lazarus was one of them that sat at the table with him."

ἐποίησαν οὖν αὐτῷ δεῖπνον ἐκεῖ, καὶ ἡ Μάρθα διηκόνει, ὁ δὲ Λάζαρος εἷς ἦν ἐκ τῶν ἀνακειμένων σὺν αὐτῷ.

ἐποίησαν (3d.per.pl.aor.act.ind.of ποιέω, constative) 127.
οὖν (continuative conjunction) 68.
αὐτῷ (dat.sing.masc.of αὐτός, personal advantage) 16.
δεῖπνον (acc.sing.neut.of δεῖπνον, direct object of ἐποίησαν) 1440.
ἐκεῖ (local adverb) 204.
καὶ (continuative conjunction) 14.
ἡ (nom.sing.fem.of the article in agreement with Μάρθα) 9.
Μάρθα (nom.sing.fem.of Μάρθα, subject of διηκόνει) 2436.
διηκόνει (3d.per.sing.imp.act.ind.of διακονέω, progressive description) 367.
ὁ (nom.sing.masc.of the article in agreement with Λάζαρος) 9.
δὲ (continuative conjunction) 11.

Λάζαρος (nom.sing.masc.of Λάζαρος, subject of ἦν) 2596.
εἷς (nom.sing.masc.of εἷς, predicate nominative) 469.
ἦν (3d.per.sing.imp.ind.of εἰμί, progressive description) 86.
ἐκ (preposition with the partitive genitive) 19.
τῶν (gen.pl.masc.of the article in agreement with ἀνακειμένων) 9.
ἀνακειμένων (pres.mid.part.gen.pl.masc. substantival, partitive genitive) 790.
σὺν (preposition with the instrumental of association) 1542.
αὐτῷ (instru.sing.masc.of αὐτός, association) 16.

Translation - "And they prepared a dinner for Him there; and Martha was serving; and Lazarus was one of those sitting at the table with Him."

Comment: John uses σύν (#1542) only three times in the gospel: here, in John 18:1 and 21:3. Not at all in the Epistles or the Revelation. We can take οὖν here as inferential, on the basis that Jesus' visit to Bethany precipitated the dinner party, or merely as continuative. The time was two days before the Passover (Mk.14:1). Hence it was the fourth day of Jesus' last visit to Bethany. This is the same event as that described in Mark 14:3-9. Martha, always concerned with being a good hostess (Luke 10:38-42) began (inceptive imperfect) and continued (progressive description) to serve Jesus and the others who were sitting with Him at the table, among whom was her brother Lazarus. Once before when Jesus had visited Mary, Martha and Lazarus in Bethany, as Martha attended to her duties as hostess, Mary had sat at His feet, listening to His conversation, and had received His commendation. Now Mary goes even further in her devotion to Him in

Verse 3 - "Then took Mary a pound of ointment of spikenard, very costly, and anointed the feet of Jesus and wiped his feet with her hair; and the house was filled with the odour of the ointment."

ἡ οὖν Μαριὰμ λαβοῦσα λίτραν μύρου νάρδου πιστικῆς πολυτίμου ἤλειψεν τοὺς πόδας τοῦ Ἰησοῦ καὶ ἐξέμαξεν ταῖς θριξὶν αὐτῆς τοὺς πόδας αὐτοῦ. ἡ δὲ οἰκία ἐπληρώθη ἐκ τῆς ὀσμῆς τοῦ μύρου.

ἡ (nom.sing.fem.of the article in agreement with Μαριὰμ) 9.
οὖν (continuative conjunction) 68.
Μαριὰμ (nom.sing.fem.of Μαριάμ, subject of ἤλειψεν and ἐξέμαξεν) 2439.
λαβοῦσα (2d.aor.act.part.nom.sing.fem.of λαμβάνω, adverbial, temporal) 533.

#2749 λίτραν (acc.sing.fem.of λίτρα, direct object of λαβοῦσα).

pound - John 12:3; 19:39.

Meaning: a weight of 12 ounces. Used by Mary in John 12:3; by Nicodemus in John 19:39.

μύρου (gen.sing.neut.of μύρον, description) 1562.
νάρδου (gen.sing.masc.of νάρδος, description) 2742.

πιστικῆς (gen.sing.fem.of *πιστικός*, in agreement with *λίτραν*) 2743.
πολυτίμου (gen.sing.masc.of *πολύτιμος*, in agreement with *νάρδου*) 1087.
ἤλειψεν (3d.per.sing.aor.act.ind.of *ἀλείφω*, ingressive) 589.
τοὺς (acc.pl.masc.of the article in agreement with *πόδας*) 9.
πόδας (acc.pl.masc.of *πούς*, direct object of *ἤλειψεν*) 353.
τοῦ (gen.sing.masc.of the article in agreement with *Ἰησοῦς*) 9.
Ἰησοῦ (gen.sing.masc.of *Ἰησοῦς*, possession) 3.
καὶ (adjunctive conjunction joining verbs) 14.
ἐξέμαξεν (3d.per.sing.aor.act.ind.of *ἐκμάσσω*, ingressive) 2167.
ταῖς (instru.pl.fem.of the article in agreement with *θριξὶν*) 9.
θριξὶν (instru.pl.fem.of *θρίξ*, means) 261.
αὐτῆς (gen.sing.fem.of *αὐτός*, possession) 16.
τοὺς (acc.pl.masc.of the article in agreement with *πόδας*) 9.
πόδας (acc.pl.masc.of *πούς*, direct object of *ἐξέμαξεν*) 353.
αὐτοῦ (gen.sing.masc.of *αὐτός*, possession) 16.
ἡ (nom.sing.fem.of the article in agreement with *οἰκία*) 9.
δὲ (continuative conjunction) 11.
οἰκία (nom.sing.fem.of *οἰκία*, subject of *ἐπληρώθη*) 186.
ἐπληρώθη (3d.per.sing.aor.pass.ind.of *πληρόω*, ingressive) 115.
ἐκ (preposition with the ablative of agency) 19.
τῆς (abl.sing.fem.of the article in agreement with *ὀσμῆς*) 9.

#2750 *ὀσμῆς* (abl.sing.fem.of *ὀσμή*, agency) .

odour - John 12:3; Phil.4:18.
savour - 2 Cor.2:14,16,16; Eph.5:2.

Meaning: Cf.ὄζω (#2604). Hence, odor. The odor that came from *τοῦ νάρδου* - John 12:3. Metaphorically, with reference to that which is well pleasing to God - Phil.4:18; Eph.5:2; 2 Cor.2:14,16b; the odor of death - 2 Cor.2:16a.

τοῦ (gen.sing.neut.of the article in agreement with *μύρου*) 9.
μύρου (gen.sing.neut.of *μύρον*, description) 1562.

Translation - "Then Mary took twelve ounces of pure nard ointment, very costly, and began to anoint the feet of Jesus and to wipe His feet with her hair. And the house began to be filled with the fragrance of the ointment."

Comment: *Cf.* comment on Mark 14:3. It is the same event, but details, while not contradictory,are different.John tells us that the woman was Mary; Mark leaves her unidentified. Mark says that the dinner party was in the home of Simon, the Leper. John does not tell us who the host was. The fact that Martha was serving does not prove that the dinner party was in her home. Mark says that she poured the ointment on Jesus' head. John says that she also anointed His feet. There are no conflicts, but a richer story comes out when both accounts are read together. I have translated the aorist verbs as ingressive, due to the nature of the action involved in each case. Mary did not pour all of the perfume on either Jesus' feet or His head. It was a process that took a little time. Also the house was not immediately filled with the odor of the perfume. Two nights later Jesus would wipe His disciples' feet with a towel as Mary had wiped His with her hair. Since a woman's hair is her glory (1 Cor.11:15), Mary was laying her glory at the feet of her Master. Such devotion resulted in the fragrance that permeated the entire house.

We learn from Mark 14:4 that Judas Iscariot was not the only one present who objected to Mary's act, but he acted as the spokesman in giving expression to their feeling, in

Verse 4 - "Then saith one of his disciples, Judas Iscariot, Simon's son, which should betray him, "

λέγει δὲ Ἰούδας ὁ Ἰσκαριώτης εἷς τῶν μαθητῶν αὐτοῦ, ὁ μέλλων αὐτὸν παραδιδόναι,

λέγει (3d.per.sing.pres.act.ind.of *λέγω*, historical) 66.
δὲ (adversative conjunction) 11.
Ἰούδας (nom.sing.masc.of *Ἰούδας*, subject of *λέγει*) 853.
ὁ (nom.sing.masc.of the article in agreement with *Ἰσκαριώτης*) 9.
Ἰσκαριώτης (nom.sing.masc.of *Ἰσκαριώτης*, apposition) 854.
εἷς (nom.sing.masc.of *εἷς*, apposition) 469.
τῶν (gen.pl.masc.of the article in agreement with *μαθητῶν*) 9.
μαθητῶν (gen.pl.masc.of *δμαθήτης*, partitive) 421.
αὐτοῦ (gen.sing.masc.of *αὐτός*, relationship) 16.
ὁ (nom.sing.masc.of the article in agreement with *μέλλων*) 9.
μέλλων (pres.act.part.nom.sing.masc.of *μέλλω*, substantival, apposition) 206.
αὐτὸν (acc.sing.masc.of *αὐτός*, direct object of *παραδιδόναι*) 16.
παραδιδόναι (pres.act.inf.of *παραδίδωμι*, completes *μέλλων*) 368.

Translation - "But Judas, the Iscariot, one of His disciples, the one who was about to betray Him, said, . . . "

Comment: Note the historical present in *λέγει*. *Ἰούδας* is identified by three appositional constructions: he was *ὁ Ἰσκαριώτης*; he was also one of Jesus' disciples, and he was the one about to betray Him. Note *ὁ παραδώσων αὐτόν* in John 6:64, as contrasted with *ὁ μέλλων αὐτὸν παραδιδόναι* here. Future intention with the participle in John 6:64 and the same idea with *μέλλων* and the present infinitve in John 12:4. *Cf.* Mark 14:4,5 and Matthew 26:8,9. The other disciples also must bear the responsibility for having criticized Mary for this spontaneous act of devotion. John singled out Judas and followed with his analysis of Judas' motive for his objection.

Verse 5 - "Why was not this ointment sold for three hundred pence, and given to the poor?"

Διὰ τί τοῦτο τὸ μύρον οὐκ ἐπράθη τριακοσίων δηναρίων καὶ ἐδόθη πτωχοῖς;

Διὰ (preposition with the accusative, cause) 118.
τί (acc.sing.neut.of *τίς*, interrogative pronoun, cause) 281.
τοῦτο (nom.sing.neut.of *οὗτος*, in agreement with *μύρον*) 93.
τὸ (nom.sing.neut.of the article in agreement with *μύρον*) 9.
μύρον (nom.sing.neut.of *μύρον*, subject of *ἐπράθη*) 1562.
οὐκ (summary negative conjunction with the indicative, direct question) 130.
ἐπράθη (3d.per.sing.aor.pass.ind.of *πιπράσκω*, direct question) 1088.
τριακοσίων (gen.pl.neut.of *τριακόσιοι*, in agreement with *δηναρίων*) 2745.
δηναρίων (gen.pl.neut.of *δηνάριον*, description) 1278.
καὶ (continuative conjunction) 14.
ἐδόθη (3d.per.sing.aor.pass.ind.of *δίδωμι*, direct question) 362.
πτωχοῖς (dat.pl.masc.of *πτωχός*, indirect object of *ἐδόθη*) 423.

Translation - "Why was not this ointment sold for fifty dollars and (the money) given to the poor?"

Comment: *Cf.*comment on Mt.26:9; Mk.14:5. *Διὰ τί* - "on account of what?" Hence, "Why?" The subject for *ἐδόθη* is omitted. We have supplied it in parentheses in the translation. This sounds noble *prima facie*, but Judas' real motive is revealed in

Verse 6 - "This he said, not that he cared for the poor; but because he was a thief, and had the bag, and bare what was put therein."

εἶπεν δὲ τοῦτο οὐχ ὅτι περὶ τῶν πτωχῶν ἔμελεν αὐτῷ ἀλλ' ὅτι κλέπτης ἦν καὶ τὸ γλωσσόκομον ἔχων τὰ βαλλόμενα ἐβάσταζεν.

εἶπεν (3d.per.sing.aor.act.ind.of *εἶπον*, constative) 155.
δὲ (adversative conjunction) 11.
τοῦτο (acc.sing.neut.of *οὗτος*, direct object of *εἶπεν*) 93.
οὐχ (summary negative conjunction with the indicative) 130.
ὅτι (conjunction introducing a subordinate causal clause) 211.
περὶ (preposition with the genitive of reference) 173.
τῶν (gen.pl.masc.of the article in agreement with *πτωχῶν*) 9.
πτωχῶν (gen.pl.masc.of *πτωχός*, reference) 1417.
ἔμελεν (3d.per.sing.imp.act.ind.of *μέλω*, inceptive) 1417.
αὐτῷ (dat.sing.masc.of *αὐτός*, personal interest) 16.
ἀλλ' (alternative conjunction) 342.
ὅτι (conjunction introducing a subordinate causal clause) 211.
κλέπτης (nom.sing.masc.of *κλέπτης*, predicate nominative) 595.
ἦν (3d.per.sing.imp.ind.of *εἰμί*, inceptive) 86.
καὶ (adjunctive conjunction joining verbs) 14.
τὸ (acc.sing.neut.of the article in agreement with *γλωσσόκομον*) 9.

#2751 *γλωσσόκομον* (acc.sing.neut.of *γλωσσόκομον*, direct object of *ἔχων*).

bag - John 12:6; 13:29.

Meaning: Originally a case in which to keep the mouth pieces of wind instruments. *Cf.* γλῶσσα (#1846). In later Greek, a small box for other uses also, such as a purse - John 12:6; 13:29.

ἔχων (pres.act.part.nom.sing.masc.adverbial, causal) 82.
τὰ (acc.pl.neut.of the article, in agreement with βαλλόμενα) 9.
βαλλόμενα (pres.pass.part.acc.pl.neut.of βάλλω, substantival, direct object of ἐβάσταζεν) 299.
ἐβάσταζεν (3d.per.sing.imp.act.ind.of βαστάζω, progressive description) 306.

Translation - "But he said this, not because he was worried about the poor, but because he had become a thief, and, since he had the bag, he carried the money that was put in it."

Comment: δὲ is adversative. Judas' reason for his protest ostensibly was his concern for the poor, but John immediately tells us that such was not the case. Note the first subordinate causal clause introduced by οὐχ and followed by the second introduced by ἀλλα. "Not because . . . but because . . . κ.τ.λ." Note also that we have a causal participle within the second causal clause - a causal construction within another. Judas protested because (a) he had become a thief, and (b) because he had the bag (adverbial, causal ἔχων), he therefore carried what was placed in it. The implication is that since Judas was a thief he also stole the money that was put into the bag, although βαστάζω (#306) does not mean "to steal." Thus Montgomery has ". . . and, carrying the purse, used to purloin what was put in it." Goodspeed translates, ". . . and when he had charge of the purse he used to take what was put in it." The implication is present but such a translation depends upon the fact that Judas was a thief, not upon the meaning of the words in the passage. Since a thief had been appointed as treasurer who carried the common purse of Jesus and the twelve, he was in a strong position to steal its contents. I have chosen to take the imperfect tense verbs as inceptive, although they can be taken as imperfects of progressive description. If they are inceptive it means that Judas had not acquired a concern for the poor, but that he had *become* a thief. It is doubtful that Judas had always been a thief. In any case John has pointed out that Judas' motives were not pure when he protested about the waste of the ointment.

Verse 7 - "Then said Jesus, Let her alone: against the day of my burying hath she kept this."

εἶπεν οὖν ὁ Ἰησοῦς, Ἄφες αὐτήν, ἵνα εἰς τὴν ἡμέραν τοῦ ἐνταφιασμοῦ μου τηρήσῃ αὐτό.

εἶπεν (3d.per.sing.aor.act.ind.of εἶπον, constative) 155.
οὖν (inferential conjunction) 68.
ὁ (nom.sing.masc.of the article in agreement with Ἰησοῦς) 9.
Ἰησοῦς (nom.sing.masc.of Ἰησοῦς, subject of εἶπεν) 3.
Ἄφες (2d.per.sing.aor.act.impv.of ἀφίημι, command) 319.
αὐτήν (acc.sing.fem.of αὐτός, direct object of ἄφες) 16.

ἵνα (conjunction introducing the subjunctive in a sub-final clause) 114.
εἰς (preposition with the accusative, purpose) 140.
τὴν (acc.sing.fem.of the article in agreement with ἡμέραν) 9.
ἡμέραν (acc.sing.fem.of ἡμέρα, purpose) 135.
τοῦ (gen.sing.masc.of the article in agreement with ἐνταφιασμοῦ) 9.
ἐνταφιασμοῦ (gen.sing.masc.of ἐνταφιασμός, description) 2748.
μου (gen.sing.masc.of ἐγώ, possession) 123.
τηρήσῃ (3d.per.sing.aor.act.subj.of τηρέω, purpose/result) 1297.
αὐτό (acc.sing.neut.of αὐτός, direct object of τηρήσῃ) 16.

Translation - "Therefore Jesus said, 'Let her alone, so that she can keep it for the day of my burial.' "

Comment: *Cf.* comment on Mt.26:10; Mk.14:6. ἵνα . . . τηρήσῃ is a volitive subjunctive, following the imperative in Ἄφες, or the ἵνα clause can be taken as a sub-final clause, expressing both purpose and result. Mary had not yet used all of the ointment as she anointed the feet and head of Jesus. They were arguing about what she might have left. Judas wanted to sell it and put the money into the bag over which he had control. Jesus told him to let her keep what was left until they buried Him, when it would be needed.

Verse 8 - "For the poor always ye have with you, but me ye have not always."

τοὺς πτωχοὺς γὰρ πάντοτε ἔχετε μεθ' ἑαυτῶν, ἐμὲ δὲ οὐ πάντοτε ἔχετε.

τοὺς (acc.pl.masc.of the article in agreement with πτωχοὺς) 9.
πτωχοὺς (acc.pl.masc.of πτωχός, direct object of ἔχετε) 423.
γὰρ (inferential conjunction introducing a coordinate causal clause) 105.
πάντοτε (adverbial) 1567.
ἔχετε (2d.per.pl.pres.act.ind.ofd ἔχω, futuristic) 82.
μεθ' (preposition with the genitive of accompaniment) 50.
ἑαυτῶν (gen.pl.masc.of ἑαυτός, accompaniment) 288.
ἐμὲ (acc.sing.masc.of ἐμός, direct object of ἔχετε) 1267.
δὲ (adversative conjunction) 11.
οὐ (summary negative conjunction with the indicative) 130.
πάντοτε (adverbial) 1567.
ἔχετε (2d.per.pl.pres.act.ind.of ἔχω, futuristic) 82.

Translation - "Because you will always have the poor with you, but you will not always have me."

Comment: *Cf.* comment on Mt.26:11; Mk.14:7.

Judas Arranges to Betray Jesus

(Matthew 26:14-16; Mark 14:10-11; Luke 22:3-6)

Mark 14:10 - "And Judas Iscariot, one of the twelve, went unto the chief priests, to betray him unto them."

Καὶ Ἰούδας Ἰσκαριὼθ ὁ εἷς τῶν δώδεκα ἀπῆλθεν πρὸς τοὺς ἀρχιερεῖς ἵνα αὐτὸν παραδοῖ (αὐτοῖς).

Καὶ (continuative conjunction) 14.
Ἰούδας (nom.sing.masc.of Ἰούδας, subject of ἀπῆλθεν) 853.
Ἰσκαριὼθ (nom.sing.masc. for Ἰσκαρλιώτης, apposition) 854.
ὁ (nom.sing.masc.of the article in agreement with εἷς) 9.
εἷς (nom.sing.masc.of εἷς, apposition) 469.
τῶν (gen.pl.masc.of the article, partitive genitive) 9.
δώδεκα (indeclinable, partitive) 820.
ἀπῆλθεν (3d.per.sing.aor.mid.ind.of ἀπέρχομαι, constative) 239.
πρὸς (preposition with the accusative of extent) 197.
τοὺς (acc.pl.masc.of the article in agreement with ἀρχιερεῖς) 9.
ἀρχιερεῖς (acc.pl.masc.of ἀρχιερεύς, extent) 151.
ἵνα (conjunction with the subjunctive, purpose) 114.
αὐτὸν (acc.sing.masc.of αὐτός, direct object of παραδοῖ) 16.
παραδοῖ (3d.per.sing.2d.aor.act.subj.of παραδίδωμι, purpose) 368.
(αὐτοῖς) (dat.pl.masc.of αὐτός, indirect object of παραδοῖ) 16.

Translation - "And Judas Iscariot, one of the Twelve, went away to the chief priests in order that he might betray Him to them."

Comment: Note that Mark has the article ὁ with εἷς. Robertson says that εἷς here, should be considered as a pronoun. The article, which in Greek is always definite (there is no indefinite article in Greek) serves to call attention to Judas, as the *only one* of the Twelve who would betray Jesus. (Robertson, *Grammar,* 675). Judas' purpose was to betray Jesus to the authorities, as the ἵνα clause with παραδοῖ makes clear. *Cf.* comment on Mt.26:14; Lk.22:3,4. Note that Luke points to Satan as the motivator of Judas' betrayal. *Cf.* John 6:70,71. Also Luke adds that Judas talked both with the high priests and the soldiers.

There has been much speculation about the motives of Judas Iscariot, none of which can be supported by scripture. A popular theory is that he was an extreme nationalist, perhaps a Zealot, who believed that Jesus was the Messiah, but who failed, as did the other disciples, to see that Messiah's first coming to earth was for purposes of death and redemption, while His Kingly functions as Messiah would be seen at a second coming. The theory then goes on to suppose that Judas, impatient that Jesus had not yet made His move to march against the Romans, sought to force His hand by betraying Him to the Jewish authorities. If this is true (the question cannot be decided on the basis of Scripture interpretation) then Judas fully expected Jesus to assert His Messianic power in the Garden at the time of His arrest and carry out the *coup d'etat* that would have placed Him upon David's throne. We are warned to respect the divine reticencies of the Holy Spirit and to refrain from speculation about matters about which He has chosen to remain silent. Judas found the authorities eager to cooperate as we see in

Verse 11 - "And when they heard it, they were glad, and promised to give him money. And he sought how he might conveniently betray him."

οἱ δὲ ἀκούσαντες ἐχάρησαν καὶ ἐπηγγείλαντο αὐτῷ ἀργύριον δοῦναι. καὶ ἐζήτει πῶς αὐτὸν εὐκαίρως παραδοῖ.

οἱ (nom.pl.masc.of the article in agreement with *ἀκούσαντες*) 9.
δὲ (continuative conjunction) 11.
ἀκούσαντες (aor.act.part.nom.pl.masc.of *ἀκούω*, substantival, subject of *ἐχάρησαν*) 148.
ἐχάρησαν (3d.per.pl.aor.act.ind.of *χαίρω*, ingressive) 182.
καὶ (adjunctive conjunction joining verbs) 14.

#2752 *ἐπηγγείλαντο* (3d.per.pl.aor.mid.ind.of *ἐπαγγέλλομαι*, constative).

make promise - Mark 14:11.
profess - 1 Tim.2:10; 6:21; Acts 7:5; Rom.4:21; Gal.3:19.
promise - Titus 1:2; Heb.6:13; 10:23; 11;11; 12:26; James 1:12; 2:5; 2 Peter 2:19; 1 John 2:25.

Meaning: A combination of *ἐπί* (#47) and *ἀγγέλλω* - "to promise." Hence, to make a commitment; to pledge to do something. Followed by an infinitive - *δοῦναι* - money - Mark 14:11; Acts 7:5. Followed by a direct object - godliness - 1 Tim.2:10; 2 Pet.2:19, *ἐλευθερίασν*; with a definite relative pronoun - *ἣν* - 1 Tim.6:21; Tit.1:2; 1 John 2:25; *ὃν* - James.1:12; *ἣ* - James 2:5; *ὃ* - Rom.4:21; *ᾧ* - Gal.3:19. Followed by *λέγω* and direct discourse - Heb.12:26; absolutely in Heb.6:13; 10:23; 11:11.

αὐτῷ (dat.sing.masc.of *αὐτός*, indirect object of *δοῦναι*) 16.
ἀργύριον (acc.sing.neut.of *ἀργύριον*, direct object of *δοῦναι*) 1535.
καὶ (inferential conjunction) 14.
ἐζήτει (3d.per.sing.imp.act.ind.of *ζητέω*, inceptive) 207.
πῶς (interrogative conjunction introducing the deliberative subjunctive) 627.
αὐτὸν (acc.sing.masc.of *αὐτός*, direct object of *παραδοῖ*) 16.

#2753 *εὐκαίρως* (adverbial).

conveniently - Mark 14:11.
in season - 2 Tim.4:2.

Meaning: A combination of *εὐ* (#1536) and *καιρός* (#767). *Cf.* also #'s 2263, 1570, 2256 and 783. An adverb - conveniently - To betray Jesus - Mark 14:11; to preach the Word, (with *ἀκαίρως*) - 2 Tim.4:2.

παραδοῖ (3d.per.sing.2d.aor.act.subj.of *παραδίδωμι*, deliberative subjunctive) 368.

Translation - "And those who heard were seized with delight, and they promised to give money to him. Therefore he began to seek how he might conveniently betray Him."

Comment: Judas' perfidious offer delighted the chief priests and the soldiers (ingressive aorist in ἐχάρησαν) and they entered into an agreement with him forthwith. He would deliver Jesus to them, in a way and at a time and place that would not excite the people whom they feared were still on Jesus' side. They would pay him money. Judas began immediately (inceptive imperfect in ἐζήτει) to solve his problem. πῶς . . . παραδοῖ - "how to betray Him?" The adverb εὐκαίρως refers to the fact that the Establishment wanted as little publicity about it as possible - as though they could bring off the most important event in human history secretly, and as though they had something to fear from Jesus' fickle followers! *Cf.* Mt.26:15,16; Lk.22:5,6.

We turn now to Luke's account of Judas' betrayal efforts in

Luke 22:3 - "Then entered Satan into Judas, surnamed Iscariot, being of the number of the twelve."

Εἰσῆλθεν δὲ Σατανᾶς εἰς Ἰούδαν τὸν καλούμενον Ἰσκαριώτην, ὄντα ἐκ τοῦ ἀριθμοῦ τῶν δώδεκα.

Εἰσῆλθεν (3d.per.sing.aor.mid.ind.of εἰσέρχομαι, constative) 234.
δὲ (continuative conjunction) 11.
Σατανᾶς (nom.sing.masc.of Σατανᾶς, subject of εἰσῆλθεν) 365.
εἰς (preposition with the accusative of extent) 140.
Ἰούδαν (acc.sing.masc.of Ἰούδας, extent) 853.
τὸν (acc.sing.masc.of the article in agreement with καλούμενον) 9.
καλούμενον (pres.pass.part.acc.sing.masc.of καλέω, substantival, apposition) 107.
Ἰσκαριώτνη (acc.sing.masc.of Ἰσκαριώτης, appellation) 854.
ὄντα (pres.part.acc.sing.masc.of εἰμί, adverbial, causal) 86.
ἐκ (preposition with the partitive genitive) 19.
τοῦ (gen.sing.masc.of the article in agreement with ἀριθμοῦ) 9.
ἀριθμοῦ (gen.sing.masc.of ἀριθμός, partitive genitive) 2278.
τῶν (gen.pl.masc.of the article, description) 9.
δώδεκα (indeclinable, description) 820.

Translation - "And Satan entered into Judas, the one called Iscariot, because he was numbered among the Twelve."

Comment: *Cf.* comment on Mt.26:14; Mk.14:10. Luke alone records the Satanic motivation that prompted Judas, although John had written of Jesus' allusion to it (John 6:70,71).

Satan overplayed his hand here as always. The scheme was to liquidate Jesus quietly - perhaps a stab in the back or a blow on the head in a dark alley. The idea that He should be tried in an ecclesiastical court, where witnesses for the prosecution could not agree, and that ultimately He should be tried in a Roman court, where a Roman judge, in the tradition of the famous Roman record for legal objectivity, would declare Him not guilty, but that, due to the overwhelming threat of mob violence, He would be put to death by the Roman method, which involved bruising His heel, although not breaking a single bone, was not in Satan's plan. But it was in God's plan. For thus He would fulfill the Old Testament prophecies (Gen.3:15; Ex.12:46; Ps.34:20, etc.,etc.) and destroy Satan (Heb.2:14,15).

Satan tried to kill Him when He was a baby (Mt.2:16-18). He tried again to drown Him when He was asleep on a pillow (Mt.8:23-27). He tried again to throw Jesus off a cliff (Lk.4:29) and on numerous occasions tried to stone Him (John 8:59). Satan is nothing if not persistent. Any murderous device would do except by death on a cross, by which, and only by which, our Lord would complete God's eternal plan of redemption. If Satan had been wiser (thanks be to God he was not!) he would have directed Judas to protect Jesus until He died of old age!

The idea, of course, that Satan, Judas, Annas, Caiphas, Pilate, Herod or anyone else could have forestalled in the slightest detail the execution of the eternal plan of salvation as decreed by the Sovereign Triune God, is preposterous. Judas could say, in the language of a current comedian, "The devil made me do that" but he did not thus absolve himself of moral responsibility. He made a mistake. The Devil made a mistake. From Hell's point of view the death of Christ on the cross was a mistake - a tragedy. It ought never to have happened. And this is precisely what the Modernists say about it. From Heaven's point of view it had to happen in precisely the manner in which it did, in fact, happen. Satan and Judas, so far from being the primary contributory causes of the event, were the chief victims of the results that flowed from the event. If Jesus had followed Satan's suggestion on the mount of temptation, three years before (Mt.4:8-10) His death would have been avoided and the entire universe, men and fallen angels would have been banished in hell by this time. But the scenario which Satan and Judas carried out proceeded according to plan as we see in

Verse 4 - "And he went his way, and communed with the chief priests and captains, how he might betray him unto them."

καὶ ἀπελθὼν συνελάλησεν τοῖς ἀρχιερεῦσιν καὶ στρατηγοῖς τὸ πῶς αὐτοῖς παραδῷ αὐτόν.

καὶ (continuative conjunction) 14.

ἀπελθὼν (aor.mid.part.nom.sing.masc.of *ἀπέρχομαι*, adverbial, temporal) 239.

συνελάλησεν (3d.per.sing.aor.act.ind.of *συλλαλέω*, ingressive) 1223.

τοῖς (dat.pl.masc.of the article in agreement with *ἀρχιερεῦσιν*) 9.

ἀρχιερεῦσιν (dat.pl.masc.of *ἀρχιερεύς*, indirect object of *συνελάλησεν*) 151.

καὶ (adjunctive conjunction joining nouns) 14.

#2754 *στρατηγοῖς* (dat.pl.masc.of *στρατηγός*, indirect object of *συνελάλησεν*).

captain - Luke 22:4,52; Acts 4:1; 5:24,26.
magistrate - Acts 16:20,22,35,36,38.

Meaning: A combination of *στρατός* - "army" and *ἄγω* (#876). Hence, a leader of an army. A captain. A minor military official. Among the Jews (Levites) -

στραγηγοὶ τοῦ ἱεροῦ - Luke 22:4,52; Acts 4:1; 5:24,26. Among Gentiles - specifically in the N.T. in Philippi - Acts 16:20,22,35,36,38, where it appears that they also had some political and national authority, as in a case of martial law.

τὸ (acc.sing.neut.of the article with indirect question) 9.
πῶς (interrogative conjunction in indirect question) 627.
αὐτοῖς (dat.pl.masc.of αὐτός, indirect object of παραδῷ) 16.
παραδῷ (3d.per.sing.aor.act.subj.of παραδίδωμι, indirect question) 368.
αὐτόν (acc.sing.masc.of αὐτός, direct object of παραδῷ) 16.

Translation - "And he went away and began to discuss with the chief priests and captains how he might deliver Him to them."

Comment: The article with indirect questions is a ". . . classical idiom (which) appears in Luke and Paul." (Robertson, *Grammar,* 1045, 1046). *Cf.* Luke 1:62; 9:46; 22:4; 1 Thess.4:1; Rom.8:26; Luke 22:23; Acts 4:21; 22:30. It emphasizes the substantival character of the clause τὸ πῶς αὐτοῖς παραδῷ αὐτόν, which is in the accusative case. As Judas discussed his problem with the authorities in direct discourse they put the verb in the subjunctive, since they were deliberating about something about which they had some doubt. Thus the subjunctive appears also in indirect discourse.

What was their problem? Why the need for all of the deliberation between Judas and the Establishment? If they wanted Jesus, why did Judas not lead them to Him in the broad light of day? *Quem Juppiter vult perdere dementat prius* - "Whom God would destroy He first sends mad." (Sophocles, *Antigone*, as quoted by James Duport).

Verse 5 - "And they were glad and convenanted to give him money."

καὶ ἐχάρησαν καὶ συνέθεντο αὐτῷ ἀργύριον δοῦναι.

καὶ (continuative conjunction) 14.
ἐχάρησαν (3d.per.pl.aor.act.ind.of χαίρω, ingressive) 182.
καὶ (adjunctive conjunction joining verbs) 14.
συνέθεντο (3d.per.pl.2d.aor.mid.ind.of συντίθημι, constative) 2400.
αὐτῷ (dat.sing.masc.of αὐτός, indirect object of δοῦναι) 16.
ἀργύριον (acc.sing.neut.of ἀργύριον, direct object of δοῦναι) 1535.
δοῦναι (aor.act.inf.of δίδωμι, completes συνέθεντο) 362.

Translation - "And they were filled with delight and they agreed to give him money."

Comment: *Cf.* comment on Mt.26:15; Mk.14:11.

Verse 6 - "And he promised, and sought opportunity to betray him unto them in the absence of the multitude."

καὶ ἐξωμολόγησεν, καὶ ἐζήτει εὐκαιρίαν τοῦ παραδοῦναι αὐτὸν ἄτερ ὄχλου αὐτοῖς.

καὶ (continuative conjunction) 14.
ἐξωμολόγησεν (3d.per.sing.aor.act.ind.of *ἐξομολογέω*, constative) 275.
καὶ (adjunctive conjunction joining verbs) 14.
ἐζήτει (3d.per.sing.imp.act.ind.of *ζητέω*, inceptive) 207.
εὐκαιρίαν (acc.sing.fem.of *εὐκαιρία*, direct object of *ἐζήτει*) 1570.
τοῦ (gen.sing.neut.of the article, purpose) 9.
παραδοῦναι (aor.act.inf.of *παραδίδωμι*, purpose) 368.
αὐτὸν (acc.sing.masc.of *αὐτός*, direct object of *παραδοῦναι*) 16.

#2755 *ἄτερ* (improper preposition with the ablative of separation).

in the absence of - Luke 22:6.
without - Luke 22:35.

Meaning: An improper (not found in composition with verbs) preposition with the ablative of separation. With persons - Luke 22:6; with things - Luke 22:35.

ὄχλου (abl.sing.masc.of *ὄχλος*, separation) 418.
αὐτοῖς (dat.pl.masc.of *αὐτός*, indirect object of *παραδοῦναι*) 16.

Translation - "And he promised and began to look for a good chance to deliver Him to them, when the crowd was not present."

Comment: *καὶ* in the first clause can be taken as inferential as also in verse 5. Judas approached the chief priests with his offer to betray. *Therefore* they were glad and promised to pay him for his services. *Therefore* he promised. Inferential *καὶ* of course, can always be taken as continuative. The context determines which translation is better. Note the articular infinitive in the genitive case, indicating purpose. *Cf.* Mt.26:16; Mk.14:11.

(4) Wednesday — The Day of Silence
(5) Thursday — The Day of Preparation
Preparation For The Paschal Meal

(Matthew 26:17-19; Mark 14:12-16; Luke 22:7-13)

Mark 14:12 - "And the first day of unleavened bread, when they killed the passover, his disciples said unto him, Where wilt thou that we go and prepare that thou mayest eat the passover?"

Καὶ τῇ πρώτῃ ἡμέρᾳ τῶν ἀζύμων, ὅτε τὸ πάσχα ἔθυον, λέγουσιν αὐτῷ οἱ μαθηταὶ αὐτοῦ, Ποῦ θέλεις ἀπελθόντες ἑτοιμάσωμεν ἵνα φάγῃς τὸ πάσχα;

Καὶ (continuative conjunction) 14.
τῇ (loc.sing.fem.of the article in agreement with *ἡμέρᾳ*) 9.
πρώτῃ (loc.sing.fem.of *πρῶτος*, in agreement with *ἡμέρᾳ*) 487.
ἡμέρᾳ (loc.sing.fem.of *ἡμέρα*, time point) 135.

τῶν (gen.pl.fem.of the article in agreement with ἀζύμων) 9.
ἀζύμων (gen.pl.fem.of ἄζυμος, description) 1571.
ὅτε (conjunction introducing the indicative in a definite temporal clause) 703.
τὸ (acc.sing.neut.of the article in agreement with πάσχα) 9.
πάσχα (acc.sing.neut.of πάσχα, direct object of ἔθυον) 1553.
ἔθυον (3d.per.pl.imp.act.ind.of θύω, definite temporal clause) 1398.
λέγουσιν (3d.per.pl.pres.act.ind.of λέγω, historical) 66.
αὐτῷ (dat.sing.masc.of αὐτός, indirect object of λέγουσιν) 16.
οἱ (nom.pl.masc.of the article in agreement with μαθηταὶ) 9.
μαθηταὶ (nom.pl.masc.of μαθητής, subject of λέγουσιν) 421.
αὐτοῦ (gen.sing.masc.of αὐτός, relationship) 16.
Ποῦ (interrogative adverb of place in direct question) 142.
θέλεις (2d.per.sing.pres.act.ind.of θέλω, direct question) 88.
ἀπελθόντες (aor.mid.part.nom.pl.masc.of ἀπέρχομαι, adverbial, temporal) 239.
ἑτοιμάσωμεν (1st.per.pl.aor.act.subj.of ἑτοιμάζω, contemplated result) 257.
ἵνα (conjunction introducing the subjunctive, purpose) 114.
φάγῃς (2d.per.sing.aor.act.subm.of ἐσθίω, purpose) 610.
τὸ (acc.sing.neut.of the article in agreement with πάσχα) 9.
πάσχα (acc.sing.neut.of πάσχα, direct object of φάγῃς) 1553.

Translation - "And on the first day of the Feasts of Unleavened Bread, when they were preparing to slay the Paschal Lamb, His disciples said to Him, 'Where shall we go to prepare for you to eat the Passover?' "

Comment: The definite temporal clause with ὅτε describes the day when it was customary for the Jews to kill the lamb in preparation for the Passover meal in the evening. This puts the time of the story on Thursday evening, the eve of the day of His death. The participle ἀπελθόντες is adverbial and temporal, indicating time prior to that of the verb ἑτοιμάσωμεν. They were asking where, after they had gone to the place which they asked Jesus to designate, they were to prepare the meal, in order that (purpose clause in ἵνα φάγῃς) He might eat it. "It is not always easy to distinguish purpose and result in the mind of the writer or speaker. The very word *finis* may be the end aimed at (purpose) or attained (result). My colleague, Prof. W. O. Carver, D.D., has suggested grouping these ideas all under result, either contemplated, feared or attained. Some such idea is near the true analysis and synthesis. The later Greek showed a tendency to gather most of these ideas under ἵνα" (Robertson, *Grammar,* 980). Thus, following Carver's suggestion I have taken ἑτοιμάσωμεν as contemplated result. πάσχα is used here in two senses: the first refers to the Paschal Lamb; the second to the supper where the lamb was eaten. *Cf.* Mt.26:17; Lk.22:7,8. Note that Matthew follows ἑτοιμάσωμεν with φαγεῖν, the infinitive of purpose, rather than with the ἵνα clause in Mark. Luke identifies the disciples as Peter and John. They little understood that this "Last Supper" had special significance and that the lamb which they would slay that evening was typical of God's Lamb (John 1:29) whose blood was to speak better things than that of Abel's lamb (Heb.12:24).

Verse 13 - "And he sendeth forth two of his disciples and saith unto them, Go ye into the city, and there shall meet you a man bearing a pitcher of water: follow him."

καὶ ἀποστέλλει δύο τῶν μαθητῶν αὐτοῦ καὶ λέγει αὐτοῖς, Ὑπάγετε εἰς τὴν πόλιν, καὶ ἀπαντήσει ὑμῖν ἄνθρωπος κεράμιον ὕδατος βαστάζων. ἀκολουθήσατε αὐτῷ,

καὶ (continuative conjunction) 14.
ἀποστέλλει (3d.per.sing.pres.act.ind.of ἀποστέλλω, historical) 215.
δύο (acc.pl. indeclin.of δύο, direct object of ἀποστέλλει) 385.
τῶν (gen.pl.masc.of the article in agreement with μαθητῶν) 9.
μαθητῶν (gen.pl.masc.of μαθητής, partitive genitive) 421.
αὐτοῦ (gen.sing.masc.of αὐτός, relationship) 16.
καὶ (adjunctive conjunction joining verbs) 14.
λέγει (3d.per.sing.pres.act.ind.of λέγω, historical) 66.
αὐτοῖς (dat.pl.masc.of αὐτός, indirect object of λέγει) 16.
Ὑπάγετε (2d.per.pl.pres.act.impv.of ὑπάγω, command) 364.
εἰς (preposition with the accusative of extent) 140.
τὴν (acc.sing.fem.of the article in agreement with πόλιν) 9.
πόλιν (acc.sing.fem.of πόλις, extent) 243.
καὶ (continuative conjunction) 14.
ἀπαντήσει (3d.per.sing.fut.act.ind.of ἀπαντάω, predictive) 2613.
ὑμῖν (dat.pl.masc.of σύ, personal interest) 104.
ἄνθρωπος (nom.sing.masc.of ἄνθρωπος, subject of ἀπαντήσει) 341.

#2756 κεράμιον (acc.sing.neut.of κεράμιον, direct object of βαστάζων).

pitcher - Mark 14:13; Luke 22:10.

*Meaning: Cf.*κεραμεύς (#1620), κεραμικός (#5332) and κέραμος (#2080). dimin.of κέραμος. A small earthen vessel; a pot, jar, jug or pitcher. Followed by a genitive of description - Mark 14:13; Luke 22:10.

ὕδατος (gen.sing.neut.of ὕδωρ, description) 301.
βαστάζων (pres.act.part.nom.sing.masc.of βαστάζω, adjectival, restrictive) 306.
ἀκολουθήσατε (2d.per.pl.aor.act.impv.of ἀκολουθέω, command) 394.
αὐτῷ (dat.sing.masc.of αὐτός, direct object of ἀκολουθήσατε) 16.

Translation - "And He sent two of His disciples and He said to them, 'Go into the city, and a man carrying a water pitcher will meet you. Follow him."

Comment: κεράμιον ὕδατος, without the article means "a water pitcher," while κεράμιον τοῦ ὕδατος would translate "a pitcher of water."

Some commentators think that since carrying water was normally considered as women's work, a man carrying a water pitcher would be conspicuous and easy to detect.

Verse 14 - "And wheresoever he shall go in, say ye to the goodman of the house, The Master saith, Where is the guestchamber, where I shall eat the passover with my disciples?"

καὶ ὅπου ἐὰν εἰσέλθῃ εἴπατε τῷ οἰκοδεσπότῃ ὅτι Ὁ διδάσκαλος λέγει, Ποῦ ἐστιν τὸ κατάλυμά μου ὅπου τὸ πάσχα μετὰ τῶν μαθητῶν μου φάγω;

καὶ (continuative conjunction) 14.
ὅπου (local adverb introducing the subjunctive in an indefinite local clause, future expectation) 592.
ἐὰν (contingent particle in an indefinite local clause, future expectation) 363.
εἰσέλθῃ (3d.per.sing.aor.mid.subj.of *εἰσέρχομαι*, indefinite local clause, future expectation) 234.
εἴπατε (2d.per.pl.aor.act.impv.of *εἶπον*, command) 155.
τῷ (dat.sing.masc.of the article in agreement with *οἰκοδεσπότῃ*) 9.
οἰκοδεσπότῃ (dat.sing.masc.of *οἰκοδεσπότης*, indirect object of *εἴπατε*) 882.
ὅτι (recitative) 211.
Ὁ (nom.sing.masc.of the article in agreement with *διδάσκαλος*) 9.
διδάσκαλος (nom.sing.masc.of *διδάσκαλος*, subject of *λέγει*) 742.
λέγει (3d.per.sing.pres.act.ind.of *λέγω*, historical) 66.
Ποῦ (interrogative adverb of place, in direct question) 142.
ἐστιν (3d.per.sing.pres.ind.of *εἰμί*, aoristic) 86.
τὸ (nom.sing.neut.of the article in agreement with *κατάλυμά*) 9.
κατάλυμά (nom.sing.neut.of *κατάλυμα*, subject of *ἐστιν*) 1875.
μου (gen.sing.masc.of *ἐγώ*, possession) 123.
ὅπου (interrogative adverb of place with the deliberative subjunctive in direct question) 592.
τὸ (acc.sing.neut.of the article in agreement with *πάσχα*) 9.
πάσχα (acc.sing.neut.of *πάσχα*, direct object of *φάγω*) 1553.
μετὰ (preposition with the genitive of accompaniment) 50.
τῶν (gen.pl.masc.of the article in agreement with *μαθητῶν*) 9.
μαθητῶν (gen.pl.masc.of *μαθητής*, accompaniment) 421.
μου (gen.sing.masc.of *ἐγώ*, relationship) 123.
φάγω (1st.per.sing.aor.act.subj.of *ἐσθίω*, deliberative subjunctive) 610.

Translation - "And wherever he goes in, say to the man of the house, 'The Master said, 'Where is my guest room where I may eat the passover with my disciples?' ' "

Comment: *Cf.*comment on Lk.22:10,11; Mt.26:18. The subjunctive with *ἐάν* or *ἄν* is used in an indefinite local clause "when the action is expected to take place in the future." (Mantey, *Manual*, 278). *ὅτι* introduces *oratio recta* (direct discourse) within *oratio recta*. Contained within the direct discourse which the disciples were ordered to give is the direct discourse in which they quote to the man of the house what Jesus had said. Note that Jesus calls *τὸ κατάλυμά μου* "*my* guest room."

This is the second instance where Jesus sent His disciples on a specific errand and predicted what they would find and told them what they should do and say.

Cf. Mark 11:1-3; Luke 19:29-31; Matthew 21:1-3.

Verse 15 - "And he will shew you a large upper room furnished and prepared: there make ready for us."

καὶ αὐτὸς ὑμῖν δείξει ἀνάγαιον μέγα ἐστρωμένον ἕτοιμον, καὶ ἐκεῖ ἑτοιμάσατε ἡμῖν.

καὶ (continuative conjunction) 14.
αὐτὸς (nom.sing.masc.of αὐτός, subject of δείξει) 16.
ὑμῖν (dat.pl.masc.of σύ, indirect object of δείξει) 104.
δείξει (3d.per.sing.fut.act.ind.of δείκνυμι, predictive) 359.

#2757 ἀνάγαιον (acc.sing.neut.of ἀνώγεον, direct object of δείξει).

upper room - Mark 14:15; Luke 22:12.

Meaning: A combination of ἀνά (#1059) and γῆ (#157). Hence, anything above the ground. Upper room. The scene of the Last Supper - a second floor guest room - Mark 14:15; Luke 22:12.

μέγα (acc.sing.neut.of μέγας, in agreement with ἀνάγαιον) 184.
ἐστρωμένον (perf.pass.part.acc.sing.neut.of στρώννυμι, adjectival, ascriptive) 1351.
ἕτοιμον (acc.sing.neut.of ἕτοιμος, in agreement with ἀνάγαιον) 1399.
καὶ (continuative conjunction) 14.
ἐκεῖ (adverb of place) 204.
ἑτοιμάσατε (2d.per.pl.aor.act.impv.of ἑτοιμάζω, command) 257.
ἡμῖν (dat.pl.masc.of ἐγώ, personal advantage) 123.

Translation - "And he will show you a large upper room, already furnished and prepared. And there you will make ready for us."

Comment: αὐτὸς, the third personal pronoun, the subject of δείξει. The second floor room is described by two adjectives, μέγα and ἕτοιμον and an adjectival participle ἐστρωμένον. It was large, furnished and prepared. Just as Jesus had arranged to have the colt tied at Bethphage and waiting for His use, so here He has a room furnished and prepared for His use. All that Peter and John had to do was to prepare the meal. *Cf.*Mt.26;19; Luke 22:12. It is thought by some that the place was the home of Mark, and that when Jesus and the disciples left the house later that evening and went to the Garden of Gethsemane, Mark accompanied them. If true, this would explain why Mark was with Jesus at the time of His arrest.

Verse 16 - "And his disciples went forth and came into the city, and found as he had said unto them: and they made ready the passover."

καὶ ἐξῆλθον οἱ μαθηταὶ καὶ ἦλθον εἰς τὴν πόλιν καὶ εὗρον καθὼς εἶπεν αὐτοῖς, καὶ ἡτοίμασαν τὸ πάσχα.

καὶ (continuative conjunction) 14.
ἐξῆλθον (3d.per.pl.aor.mid.ind.of ἐξέρχομαι, constative) 161.
οἱ (nom.pl.masc.of the article in agreement with μαθηταὶ) 9.
μαθηταὶ (nom.pl.masc.of μαθητής, subject of ἐξῆλθον, ἦλθον, εὗρον and ἡτοίμασαν) 421.
καὶ (adjunctive conjunction joining verbs) 14.
ἦλθον (3d.per.sing.aor.ind.of ἔρχομαι, constative) 146.
εἰς (preposition with the accusative of extent) 140.
τὴν (acc.sing.fem.of the article in agreement with πόλιν) 9.
πόλιν (acc.sing.fem.of πόλις, extent) 243.
καὶ (adjunctive conjunction joining verbs) 14.
εὗρον (3d.per.pl.2d.aor.act.ind.of εὑρίσκω, constative) 79.
καθὼς (adverb introducing a comparative clause) 1348.
εἶπεν (3d.per.sing.aor.act.ind.of εἶπον, culminative) 155.
αὐτοῖς (dat.pl.masc.of αὐτός, indirect object of εἶπεν) 16.
καὶ (adjunctive conjunction joining verbs) 14.
ἡτοίμασαν (3d.per.pl.aor.act.ind.of ἑτοιμάζω, constative) 257.
τὸ (acc.sing.neut.of the article in agreement with πάσχα) 9.
πάσχα (acc.sing.neut.of πάσχα, direct object of ἡτοίμασαν) 1553.

Translation - "And the disciples left and went into the city and they found it just as He had said to them, and they prepared the Passover supper."

Comment: Jesus' instructions to them had been explicit. Peter and John found everything exactly as He had told them it would be. *Cf.*comment on Mt.26:19; Lk.22:13.

We look now at Luke's account in Luke 22:7-13.

Luke 22:7 - "Then came the day of unleavened bread, when the passover must be killed."

Ἦλθεν δὲ ἡ ἡμέρα τῶν ἀζύμων, (ἐν) ᾗ ἔδει θύεσθαι τὸ πάσχα.

Ἦλθεν (3d.per.sing.aor.ind.of ἔρχομαι, culminative) 146.
δὲ (explanatory conjunction) 11.
ἡ (nom.sing.fem.of the article in agreement with ἡμέρα) 9.
ἡμέρα (nom.sing.fem.of ἡμέρα, subject of ἦλθεν) 135.
τῶν (gen.pl.masc.of the article in agreement with ἀζύμων) 9.
ἀζύμων (gen.pl.masc.of ἄζυμος, description) 1571.
(ἐν) (preposition with the locative of time point) 80.
ᾗ (loc.sing.fem.of ὅς, time point) 65.
ἔδει (3d.per.sing.imp.ind.of δέω, unmet obligation) 1207.
θύεσθαι (pres.pass.inf.of ξύω, completes ἔδει) 1398.
τὸ (acc.sing.neut.of the article in agreement with πάσχα) 9.
πάσχα (acc.sing.neut.of πάσχα, direct object of θύεσθαι) 1553.

Translation - "Now the day of Unleavened Bread came on which it was necessary that the Passover Lamb be killed."

Comment: ἔδει is a verb of obligation. Such verbs are written in the imperfect if the obligation has not yet been met. Robertson says that Greek and Latin begin with the fact of a past obligation and the reader, comparing that with the present facts, determines that what must be done has not yet been done. (Robertson, *Grammar*,886). This principle also applies to verbs of possibility or propriety. Note the locative of time point in the definite relative pronoun ᾗ. *Cf.* Mt.26:17; Mk.14:12.

On many occasions Jesus had spoken of His hour as not having yet come (John 2:4) or as coming in the immediate future (John 12:23). For a complete list *cf.*#735. Now the day has arrived. It began at 6:00 p.m. on Thursday. The Passover Supper with His disciples in the upper room, the betrayal and arrest in the Garden, mock trials, torture and crucifixion at 9:00 a.m. on Friday and death at 3:00 p.m. are now in the immediate future.

Verse 8 - "And He sent Peter and John, saying, Go and prepare us the passover, that we may eat."

καὶ ἀπέστειλεν Πέτρον καὶ Ἰωάννην εἰπών, Πορευθέντες ἑτοιμάσατε ἡμῖν τὸ πάσχα ἵνα φάγωμεν.

καὶ (continuative conjunction) 14.
ἀπέστειλεν (3d.per.sing.aor.act.ind.of ἀποστέλλω, constative) 215.
Πέτρον (acc.sing.masc.of Πέτρος, direct object of ἀπέστειλεν) 387.
καὶ (adjunctive conjunction joining nouns) 14.
Ἰωάννην (acc.sing.masc.of Ἰωάννης, direct object of ἀπέστειλεν) 399.
εἰπών (aor.act.part.nom.sing.masc.of εἶπον, adverbial, temporal) 155.
Πορευθέντες (aor.mid.part.nom.pl.masc.of πορεύομαι, adverbial, temporal) 170.
ἑτοιμάσατε (2d.per.pl.aor.act.impv.of ἑτοιμάζω, command) 257.
ἡμῖν (dat.pl.masc.of ἐγώ, personal advantage) 123.
τὸ (acc.sing.neut.of the article in agreement with πάσχα) 9.
πάσχα (acc.sing.neut.of πάσχα, direct object of ἑτοιμάσατε) 1553.
ἵνα (conjunction introducing the subjunctive in a purpose clause) 114.
φάγωμεν (1st.per.pl.aor.act.subj.of ἐσθίω, purpose) 610.

Translation - "And He sent forth Peter and John, having said, 'Go and prepare for us the Passover Supper that we may eat."

Comment: *Cf.* Mt.26:17-19; Mk.14:12-16. Luke alone tells us Peter and John were the disciples to whom Jesus gave this directive. Their question follows in

Verse 9 - "And they said unto him, Where wilt thou that we prepare?"

οἱ δὲ εἶπαν αὐτῷ, Ποῦ θέλεις ἑτοιμάσωμεν;

οἱ (nom.pl.masc.of the article, subject of εἶπαν) 9.
δὲ (inferential conjunction) 11.
εἶπαν (3d.per.pl.aor.act.ind.of εἶπον, constative) 155.

αὐτῷ (dat.sing.masc.of *αὐτός*, indirect object of *εἶπαν*) 16.
Ποῦ (interrogative adverb introducing deliberative subjunctive in direct question) 142.
θέλεις (2d.per.sing.pres.act.ind.of *θέλω*, direct question) 88.
ἑτοιμάσωμεν (1st.per.pl.aor.act.subj.of *ἑτοιμάζω*, deliberative subjunctive) 257.

Translation - "Therefore they said to Him, 'Where do you want us to prepare?'"

Comment: Note the deliberative subjunctive after *θέλεις*, a verb of wishing. Ποῦ in the direct question. *Cf.* Mt.26:17; Mk.14:12.

Verse 10 - "And he said unto them, Behold when ye are entered into the city, there shall a man meet you, bearing a pitcher of water; follow him into the house where he entereth in."

ὁ δὲ εἶπεν αὐτοῖς, Ἰδοὺ εἰσελθόντων ὑμῶν εἰς τὴν πόλιν συναντήσει ὑμῖν ἄνθρωπος κεράμιον ὕδατος βαστάζων. ἀκολουθήσατε αὐτῷ εἰς τὴν οἰκίαν εἰς ἣν εἰσπορεύεται.

ὁ (nom.sing.masc.of the article, subject of *εἶπεν*) 9.
δὲ (continuative conjunction) 11.
εἶπεν (3d.per.sing.aor.act.ind.of *εἶπον*, constative) 155.
αὐτοῖς (dat.pl.masc.of *αὐτός*, indirect object of *εἶπεν*) 16.

Ἰδοὺ (exclamation) 95.
εἰσελθόντων (aor.mid.part.gen.pl.masc.of *εἰσέρχομαι*, genitive absolute) 234.
ὑμῶν (gen.pl.masc.of *σύ*, genitive absolute) 104.
εἰς (preposition with the accusative of extent) 140.
τὴν (acc.sing.fem.of the article in agreement with *πόλιν*) 9.
πόλιν (acc.sing.fem.of *πόλις*, extent) 243.
συναντήσει (3d.per.sing.fut.act.ind.of *συναντάω*, predictive) 2340.
ὑμῖν (instru.pl.masc.of *σύ*, association, after *σύν* in composition) 104.
ἄνθρωπος (nom.sing.masc.of *ἄνθρωπος*, subject of *συναντήσει*) 341.
κεράμιον (acc.sing.neut.of *κεράμιον*, direct object of *βαστάζων*) 2756.
ὕδατος (gen.sing.neut.of *ὕδωρ*, description) 301.
βαστάζων (pres.act.part.nom.sing.masc.of *βαστάζω*, adjectival, restrictive) 306.
ἀκολουθήσατε (2d.per.pl.aor.act.impv.of *ἀκολουθέω*, command) 394.
αὐτῷ (dat.sing.masc.of *αὐτός*, object of *ἀκολουθήσατε*) 16.
εἰς (preposition with the accusative of extent) 140.
τὴν (acc.sing.fem.of the article in agreement with *οἰκίαν*) 9.
οἰκίαν (acc.sing.fem.of *οἰκία*, extent) 186.
εἰς (preposition with the accusative of extent) 140.
ἣν (acc.sing.fem.of *ὅς*, extent) 65.
εἰσπορεύεται (3d.per.sing.pres.mid.ind.of *εἰσπορεύομαι*, futuristic) 1161.

Translation - "And He said to them, 'Look! After you have entered the city, a man carrying a water pitcher will meet you. Follow him into the house into which he enters,' "

Comment: *Cf.* comment on Mt.26:18; Mk.14:13. The thought conveyed is identical, though the grammar and syntax are Luke's, not those of Matthew or Mark.

Verse 11 - "And ye shall say unto the goodman of the house, The Master saith unto thee, Where is the guestchamber, where I shall eat the passover with my disciples?' "

καὶ ἐρεῖτε τῷ οἰκοδεσπότῃ τῆς οἰκίας, Λέγει σοι ὁ διδάσκαλος, Ποῦ ἐστιν τὸ κατάλυμα ὅπου τὸ πάσχα μετὰ τῶν μαθητῶν μου φάγω;' "

καὶ (continuative conjunction) 14.
ἐρεῖτε (2d.per.pl.fut.act.ind.of *εἶπον*, imperative) 155.
τῷ (dat.sing.masc.of the article in agreement with *οἰκοδεσπότῃ*) 9.
οἰκοδεσπότῃ (dat.sing.masc.of *οἰκοδεσπότης*, indirect object of *ἐρεῖτε*) 882.
τῆς (gen.sing.fem.of the article in agreement with *οἰκίας*) 9.
οἰκίας (gen.sing.masc.of *οἰκία*, description) 186.
Λέγει (3d.per.sing.pres.act.ind.of *λέγω*, historical) 66.
σοι (dat.sing.masc.of *σύ*, indirect object of *Λέγει*) 104.
ὁ (nom.sing.masc.of the article in agreement with *διδάσκαλος*) 9.
διδάσκαλος (nom.sing.masc.of *διδάσκαλος*, subject of *Λέγει*) 742.
Ποῦ (interrogative adverb in direct question) 142.
ἐστιν (3d.per.sing.pres.ind.of *εἰμί*, aoristic) 86.
τὸ (nom.sing.neut.of the article in agreement with *κατάλυμα*) 9.
κατάλυμα (nom.sing.neut.of *κατάλυμα*, subject of *ἐστιν*) 1875.
ὅπου (adverb introducing the subjunctive in an indefinite local clause) 592.
τὸ (acc.sing.neut.of the article in agreement with *πάσχα*) 9.
πάσχα (acc.sing.neut.of *πάσχα*, direct object of *φάγω*) 1553.
μετὰ (preposition with the genitive of accompaniment/fellowship) 50.
τῶν (gen.pl.masc.of the article in agreement with *μαθητῶν*) 9.
μαθητῶν (gen.pl.masc.of *μαθητής*, accompaniment/fellowship) 421.
μου (gen.sing.masc.of *ἐγώ*, relationship) 123.
φάγω (1st.per.sing.aor.act.subj.of *ἐσθίω*, indefinite local clause) 610.

Translation - "And you must say to the man of the house, 'The Master says to you, 'Where is the guestroom where I may eat the Passover with my disciples?' ' "

Comment: *Cf.* comment on Mt.26:18; Mk.14:14.

Verse 12 - "And he shall show you a large upper room furnished: there make ready."

κἀκεῖνος ὑμῖν δείξει ἀνάγαιον μέγα ἐστρωμένον, ἐκεῖ ἑτοιμάσατε.

κἀκεῖνος (nom.sing.masc.of *κἀκεῖνος*, subject of *δείξει*) 1164.
ὑμῖν (dat.pl.masc.of *σύ*, indirect object of *δείξει*) 104.

δείξει (3d.per.sing.fut.act.ind.of δείκνυμι, predictive) 359.
ἀνάγαιον (acc.sing.neut.of ἀνάγαιον, direct object of δείξει) 2757.
μέγα (acc.sing.neut.of μέγας, in agreement with ἀνάγαιον) 184.
ἐστρωμένον (perf.pass.part.acc.sing.neut.of στρώννυμι, adjectival, ascriptive) 1351.
ἐκεῖ (local adverb) 204.
ἑτοιμάσατε (2d.per.pl.aor.act.impv.of ἑτοιμάζω, command) 257.

Translation - "And that man will show you a large, furnished upper room. There make preparation."

Comment: *Cf.* comment on Mt.26:19; Mk.14:15.

Verse 13 - "And they went, and found as he had said unto them; and they made ready the passover."

ἀπελθόντες δὲ εὗρον καθὼς εἰρήκει αὐτοῖς, καὶ ἡτοίμασαν τὸ πάσχα.

ἀπελθόντες (aor.mid.part.nom.pl.masc.of ἀπέρχομαι, adverbial, temporal) 239.
δὲ (continuative conjunction) 11.
εὗρον (3d.per.pl.aor.act.ind.of εὑρίκω, constative) 79.
καθὼς (adverb introducing a comparative clause) 1348.
εἰρήκει (3d.per.sing.pluperf.act.ind.of εἶπον, consummative) 155.
αὐτοῖς (dat.pl.masc.of αὐτός, indirect object of εἰρήκει) 16.
καὶ (continuative conjunction) 14.
ἡτοίμασαν (3d.per.pl.aor.act.ind.of ἑτοιμάζω, constative) 257.
τὸ (acc.sing.neut.of the article in agreement with πάσχα) 9.
πάσχα (acc.sing.neut.of πάσχα, direct object of ἡτοίμασαν) 1553.

Translation - "And they went away and found it as He had said to them. And they prepared the Passover meal."

Comment: *Cf.* comment on Mt.26:19; Mk.14:16.

Jesus Partakes of the Passover with His Apostles

(Matthew 26:20; Mark 14:17; Luke 22:14-16)

Mark 14:17 - "And in the evening he cometh with the twelve."

Καὶ ὀψίας γενομένης ἔρχεται μετὰ τῶν δώδεκα.

Καὶ (continuative conjunction) 14.
ὀψίας (gen.sing.fem.of ὄψιος, genitive absolute) 739
γενομένης (aor.part.gen.sing.fem.of γίνομαι, genitive absolute) 113.
ἔρχεται (3d.per.sing.pres.ind.of ἔρχομαι, historical) 146.
μετὰ (preposition with the genitive of accompaniment) 50.
τῶν (gen.pl.masc.of the article, accompaniment) 9.
δώδεκα (gen.pl.masc.indeclin., accompaniment) 820.

Translation - "And when evening had come, He came with the Twelve."

Comment: The genitive absolute participle is aorist indicating that Jesus and the Twelve came to the Upper Room after 6:00 p.m. The Passover day had at last arrived. Less than twenty four hours later Jesus' body will be in Joseph's tomb, and His soul, in Sheol, in the heart of the earth (Mt.12:40; Eph.4:8-10). *Cf.*comment on Mt.26:20; Lk.22:14.

Luke 22:14 - "And when the hour was come, he sat down, and the twelve apostles with him."

Καὶ ὅτε ἐγένετο ἡ ὥρα, ἀνέπεσεν καὶ οἱ ἀπόστολοι σὺν αὐτῷ.

Καὶ (continuative conjunction) 14.
ὅτε (conjunction introducing the indicative in a definite temporal clause) 703.
ἐγένετο (3d.per.sing.aor.ind.of γίνομαι, definite temporal clause) 113.
ἡ (nom.sing.fem.of the article in agreement with ὥρα) 9.
ὥρα (nom.sing.fem.of ὥρα, subject of ἐγένετο) 735.
ἀνέπεσεν (3d.per.sing.aor.act.ind.of ἀναπίπτω, constative) 1184.
καὶ (continuative conjunction) 14.
οἱ (nom.pl.masc.of the article in agreement with ἀπόστολοι) 9.
ἀπόστολοι (nom.pl.masc.of αποστολος, subject of ἀνέπεσαν, understood) 844.
σὺν (preposition with the instrumental of association) 1542.
αὐτῷ (instru.sing.masc.of αὐτός, association) 16.

Translation - "And when the hour had come, He sat down and the Apostles with Him."

Comment: *Cf.* comment on Mt.26:20; Mk.14:17. Luke uses the aorist indicative in ἐγένετο, while Matthew and Mark use the aorist participle γενομένης in the genitive absolute. All agree, (by their use of the aorist) that it was after 6:00 p.m. Note Luke's use of ἀναπίπτω (#1184) while Matthew has ἀνάκειμαι (#790).

Verse 15 - "And he said unto them, With desire I have desired to eat this passover with you before I suffer."

καὶ εἶπεν πρὸς αὐτούς,'Επιθυμίᾳ ἐπεθύμησα τοῦτο τὸ πάσχα φαγεῖν μεθ' υμῶν πρὸ τοῦ με παθεῖν.

καὶ (continuative conjunction) 14.
εἶπεν (3d.per.sing.aor.act.ind.of εἶπον, constative) 155.
πρὸς (preposition with the accusative of extent, after a verb of speaking) 197.
αὐτούς (acc.pl.masc.of αὐτός, extent after a verb of speaking) 16.
'Επιθυμίᾳ (instrumental sing.fem.of ἐπιθυμία, manner, cognate instrumental) 2186.
ἐπεθύμησα (1st.per.sing.aor.act.ind.of ἐπιθυμέω, dramatic) 500.
τοῦτο (acc.sing.neut.of οὗτος, in agreement with πάσχα) 93.
τὸ (acc.sing.neut.of the article in agreement with πάσχα) 9.
πάσχα (acc.sing.neut.of πάσχα, direct object of φαγεῖν) 1553.

φαγεῖν (aor.act.inf.of ἐσθίω, completes ἐπεθύμησα) 610.
μεθ' (preposition with the genitive of accompaniment/fellowship) 50.
ὑμῶν (gen.pl.masc.of σύ, accompaniment/fellowship) 104.
πρὸ (preposition with the ablative of time separation) 442.
τοῦ (abl.sing.neut.of the article, time separation) 9.
με (acc.sing.masc.of ἐγώ, general reference) 123.
παθεῖν (2d.aor.act.inf.of πάσχω, noun use, ablative of separation) 1208.

Translation - "And He said to them, 'I have wanted very much to eat this Passover supper with you before I suffer.' "

Comment: The most intense desire is expressed both by #2186 and #500. We have in ἐπιθυμίᾳ ἐπεθύμησα a cognate construction. A cognate relation exists when a word is related in derivation to the verb to which it is joined. Mt.2:10 - ἐχάρησαν χαράν, 1 John 5:16 - ἁμαρτάνοντα ἁμαρτίαν, and φυλάσσοντες φυλακάς (Luke 2:8) are examples of the cognate accusative. There are many more. "The cognate is not very common in the papyri (Moulton, "The Classical Review," 1901, 436, as cited in Robertson, *Grammar*, 477, 478) but in the Hebrew the idiom is very frequent.(Conybeare and Stock, *Selections from the LXX*, as cited in *Ibid.*) It is perfectly good Greek to have this "playing with paronymous terms," as a passage from Plato's *Protagoras* 326 D illustrates, ὑπογράφαντες γραμμὰς τῇ γραφίδι οὕτω τὸ γραμματεῖον. Cf. τίς ποιμαίνει ποίμνην (1 Cor.9:7). So also in Lu.8:5, ἐξῆλθεν ὁ σπείρων τοῦ σπεῖραι τὸν σπόρον." (*Ibid.*,478). But here we have what might be called an instrumental cognate. This is ". . . one usage in the N.T. that has caused some trouble. It is called "Hebraic" (Moulton, *Prolegomena*, 75, as cited in *Ibid.*,) by some of the grammarians. The instances are rather numerous in the N.T., though nothing like so common as in the LXX (Conybeare and Stock,*Selections*, 60f). Conybeare and Stock quote Plato to show that it is, however, an idiom in accordance with the genius of the Greek language. Thus λόγῳ λέγειν, φεύγων φυγῇ, φύσει πεφυκυῖαν, etc. They call it the "cognate dative." That will do if instrumental is inserted in the place of dative." (Robertson, *Ibid.*,531). Other instances of the cognate instrumental, as listed by Robertson, are Mt.13:14; Acts 23:14; 2:17; Luke 22:15; Mt.15:4; Acts 2:30; Mk.5:42; Acts 5:28; Jam.5:17; John 3:29.

Note πρὸ τοῦ με παθεῖν, the articular infinitive in the ablative case with πρό introducing a subordinate clause of antecedent time. There are nine such instances in the N.T. of which Lk.2:21; 22:15 and John 1:48 are examples.

The reason for Jesus' desire to eat the Passover Supper with His disciples is explained in the verses which follow.

Verse 16 - "For I say unto you, I will not any more eat thereof, until it be fulfilled in the Kingdom of God."

λέγω γὰρ ὑμῖν ὅτι οὐ μὴ φάγω αὐτὸ ἕως ὅτου πληρωθῇ ἐν τῇ βασιλείᾳ τοῦ θεοῦ.

λέγω (1st.per.sing.pres.act.ind.of λέγω, aoristic) 66.

γὰρ (inferential conjunction introducing a coordinate causal clause) 105.

ὑμῖν (dat.pl.masc.of σύ, indirect object of λέγω) 104.

ὅτι (conjunction introducing a subordinate causal clause in indirect discourse) 211.

οὐ (summary negative conjunction with μὴ and the subjunctive, emphatic negation) 130.

μὴ (qualified negative conjunction with οὐ and the subjunctive, emphatic negation) 87.

φάγω (1st.per.sing.2d.aor.act.subj.of ἐσθίω, emphatic negation) 610.

αὐτὸ (acc.sing.neut.of αὐτός, direct object of φάγω) 16.

ἕως (conjunction introducing an indefinite temporal clause, future reference) 71.

ὅτου (Attic for οὗτινος, gen.sing.neut.of ὅστις, time description) 163.

πληρωθῇ (3d.per.sing.aor.pass.subj.of πληρόω, indefinite temporal clause, future reference) 115.

ἐν (preposition with the locative of time point) 80.

τῇ (loc.sing.fem.of the article in agreement with βασιλείᾳ) 9.

βασιλείᾳ (loc.sing.fem.of βασιλεία, time point) 253.

τοῦ (gen.sing.masc.of the article in agreement with θεοῦ) 9.

θεοῦ (gen.sing.masc.of θεός, description) 124.

Translation - "Because I am telling you that I will never again eat this until it be fulfilled in the Kingdom of God."

Comment: On the occasion of this last observance of the Passover Supper, which was held in connection with the slaughter of the Paschal Lamb, Jesus was about to give to it its typical significance, and establish it as an ordinance of memorial to be observed by His church periodically, while we await the completion of His worldwide missionary enterprise and His subsequent return to earth. The Supper, as observed by His church, points back to Calvary and forward to the Second Coming of Messiah (1 Cor.11:26). The type will not be fulfilled completely until the last elect soul for whom the Lamb was slain, is in the Body. When the redemption project is complete (πληρωθῇ) He will return and once again eat the Passover Supper with His church (Rev.19:9). Had Jesus not observed this Passover with His disciples and endowed it with the specialized significance, the Church would not have had the privilege of its observance, with its ethical considerations, mentioned by Paul in 1 Cor.11:20-34. This is why our Lord was so eager to establish the ordinance.

Jesus Washes the Feet of the Apostles

(John 13:1-20)

John 13:1 - "Now before the feast of the passover, when Jesus knew that his hour was come that he should depart out of this world unto the Father, having loved

His own which were in the world, He loved them unto the end."

Πρὸ δὲ τῆς ἑορτῆς τοῦ πάσχα εἰδὼς ὁ Ἰησοῦς ὅτι ἦλθεν αὐτοῦ ἡ ὥρα ἵνα μεταβῇ ἐκ τοῦ κόσμου τούτου πρὸς τὸν πατέρα, ἀγαπήσας τοὺς ἰδίους τοὺς ἐν τῷ κόσμῳ, εἰς τέλος ἠγάπησεν αὐτούς.

Πρὸ (preposition with the ablative of time separation) 442.
δὲ (explanatory conjunction) 11.
τῆς (abl.sing.fem.of the article in agreement with *ἑορτῆς*) 9.
ἑορτῆς (abl.sing.fem.of *ἑορτή*, time separation) 1558.
τοῦ (gen.sing.neut.of the article in agreement with *πάσχα*) 9.
πάσχα (gen.sing.neut.of *πάσχα*, description) 1553..
εἰδὼς (pres.act.part.nom.sing.masc.of *ὁράω*, adverbial, causal) 144.
ὁ (nom.sing.masc.of the article in agreement with Ἰησοῦς) 9.
Ἰησοῦς (nom.sing.masc.of Ἰησοῦς, subject of *ἠγάπησεν*) 3.
ὅτι (conjunction introducing an object clause, after *εἰδὼς*, in indirect discourse) 211.
ἦλθεν (3d.per.sing.aor.ind.of *ἔρχομαι*, culminative) 146.
αὐτοῦ (gen.sing.masc.of *αὐτός*, possession) 16.
ἡ (nom.sing.fem.of the article in agreement with *ὥρα*) 9.
ὥρα (nom.sing.fem.of *ὥρα*, subject of *ἦλθεν*) 735.
ἵνα (conjunction introducing the subjunctive in a consecutive clause) 114.
μεταβῇ (3d.per.sing.aor.act.subj.of *μεταβαίνω*, result) 776.
ἐκ (preposition with the ablative of separation) 19.
τοῦ (abl.sing.masc.of the article in agreement with *κόσμου*) 9.
κόσμου (abl.sing.masc.of *κόσμος*, separation) 360.
τούτου (abl.sing.masc.of *οὗτος*, in agreement with *κόσμου*) 93.
πρὸς (preposition with the accusative of extent) 197.
τὸν (acc.sing.masc.of the article in agreement with *πατέρα*) 9.
πατέρα (acc.sing.masc.of *πατήρ*, extent) 238.
ἀγαπήσας (aor.act.part.nom.sing.masc.of *ἀγαπάω*, adverbial, causal) 540.
τοὺς (acc.pl.masc.of the article in agreement with *ἰδίους*) 9.
ἰδίους (acc.pl.masc.of *ἴδιος*, direct object of *ἀγαπήσας*) 778.
τοὺς (acc.pl.masc.of the article, in agreement with *ἰδίους*) 9.
ἐν (preposition with the locative of place where) 80.
τῷ (loc.sing.masc.of the article, in agreement with *κόσμῳ*) 9.
κόσμῳ (loc.sing.masc.of *κόσμος*, place where) 360.
εἰς (preposition with the accusative of time extent) 140.
τέλος (acc.sing.neut.of *τέλος*, time extent) 881.
ἠγάπησεν (3d.per.sing.aor.act.ind.of *ἀγαπάω*, constative) 540.
αὐτούς (acc.pl.masc.of *αὐτός*, direct object of *ἠγάπησεν*) 16.

Translation - "Now before the feast of the Passover, because Jesus knew that His hour had come that He should depart out of this world (and go) to the Father, because He had always loved His own in the world, He loved them to the end."

Comment: *δὲ* is explanatory. *πρὸ* with the ablative of time separation. It was "before the feast of the *Passover* but after the *supper*. (vs.2). The distinction here is between the meal and that part of it when Jesus gave new significance to the bread and wine. This part John does not mention. *Cf.*Mt.26:26*ff.* The εἰδὼς clause is causal. It extends through τὸν πατέρα. It contains the ὅτι object clause in indirect discourse and the ἵνα consecutive clause. Because Jesus knew that His hour had come, as a result of which He was about (a) to leave this world, and (b) go back to the Father. The main verb is ἠγάπησεν. It is preceded by another causal participle - ἀγαπήσας. Because He had always loved those whom the Father had given Him, He loved them to the end. Verse 2 begins a long sentence which finally closes in verse 5. The statement, once we have noted all of the anacolutha, is that ὁ Ἰησοῦς (verse 1) ἤρξατο νίπτειν . . . κ.τ.λ." (verse 5).

Jesus knew that His death and departure from this world was immanent. Note that He was going back to the same position that He left when He became incarnate. He was soon to go πρὸς τὸν πατέρα, and that is where He was before He came to earth. *Cf.*πρὸς τὸν πατέρα in 1 John 1:2. Before the incarnation the Λόγος was πρὸς τὸν θεόν (John 1:1) and πρὸς τὸν πατέρα (1 John 1:2). Now He is about to return to that position of close intimate relationship, but not until He pays the wages for our sins, which involved His separation from the Father (Mt.27:46).

When He came to earth - εἰς τὰ ἴδια- (John 1:11) οἱ ἴδιοι did not receive Him. He is their King Messiah, but they chose a bandit named Barabbas (Mk.15:7) and said, "We have no king but Caesar" (John 19:15). But though His own nation rejected Him the Father gave to Him some whom John now calls "His own." He had always loved them and He loved them unto the end. The greatest expression of His love was at the end of His life, when He delivered up His spirit (Mt.27:50). A lesser, but no less eloquent expression of His love for them was given when He washed their feet. And that act of devotion included the feet of Judas who had the betrayal money in his pocket.

Verse 2 - "And supper being ended, the devil having now put into the heart of Judas Iscariot, Simon's son, to betray him, . . . "

καὶ δείπνου γινομένου, τοῦ διαβόλου ἤδη βεβληκότος εἰς τὴν καρδίαν ἵνα παραδοῖ αὐτὸν Ἰούδας Σίμωνος Ἰσκαριώτης,

καὶ (continuative conjunction) 14.
δείπνου (gen.sing.neut.of δεῖπνον, genitive absolute) 1440.
γινομένου (pres.mid.part.gen.sing.neut.of γίνομαι, genitive absolute) 113.
τοῦ (gen.sing.masc.of the article in agreement with διαβόλου) 9.
διαβόλου (gen.sing.masc.of διάβολος, genitive absolute) 331.
ἤδη (adverbial) 291.
βεβληκότος (perf.act.part.gen.sing.masc.of βάλλω, genitive absolute) 299.
εἰς (preposition with the accusative of extent) 140.
τὴν (acc.sing.fem.of the article in agreement with καρδίαν) 9.
καρδίαν (acc.sing.fem.of καρδία, metaphorical extent) 432.
ἵνα (conjunction introducing the subjunctive in a purpose clause) 114.
παραδοῖ (3d.per.sing.2d.aor.act.subj.of παραδίδωμι, purpose) 368.

αὐτὸν (acc.sing.masc.of αὐτός, direct object of παραδοῖ) 16.
Ἰούδας (gen.sing.masc.of Ἰούδας, possession) 853.
Σίμωνος (gen.sing.masc.of Σίμων, relationship) 2294.
Ἰσκαριώτης (gen.sing.masc.of Ἰσκαριώτης, apposition) 854.

Translation - "And during supper, the devil having already put into the heart of Judas Iscariot, the son of Simon, to betray Him, . . . "

Comment: This begins the long convoluted sentence which ends with verse 5. It was during supper - the genitive absolute δείπνου γινομένου is in the present tense, thus indicating when Jesus performed the acts indicated by the verbs in verses 4 and 5. It was while the meal was in progress and before the institution of the bread and wine ordinance. Now John adds another circumstantial clause which occupies the remainder of verse 2. It is another genitive absolute, except that the participle is in the perfect tense, and the completed action in the past is supported by the adverb ἤδη. The devil had already put it into the heart of Judas to betray Jesus (Luke 22:3). Satan is in complete control of Judas, a domination which was being permitted only "in order that the scriptures might be fulfilled" (John 17:12).

Verse 3 returns to the recital of all of that which Jesus knew, begun in verse 1 and interrupted by the account of Satan's work in the heart of Judas Iscariot. It is significant that John should remind us that despite Satan's work, there is no doubt that God the Father, Son and Holy Spirit, are in total control of the events of the next twenty four hours, as indeed they are of all the hours of what men call time.

Verse 3 - "Jesus knowing that the Father had given all things into his hands, and that he was come from God, and went to God, . . . "

εἰδὼς ὅτι πάντα ἔδωκεν αὐτῷ ὁ πατὴρ εἰς τὰς χεῖρας καὶ ὅτι ἀπὸ θεοῦ ἐξῆλθεν καὶ πρὸς τὸν θεὸν ὑπάγει,

εἰδὼς (pres.act.part.nom.sing.masc.of ὁράω, adverbial, causal) 144.
ὅτι (conjunction introducing an object clause in indirect discourse) 211.
πάντα (acc.pl.neut.of πᾶς, direct object of ἔδωκεν) 67.
ἔδωκεν (3d.per.sing.aor.act.ind.of δίδωμι, culminative) 362.
αὐτῷ (dat.sing.masc.of αὐτός, indirect object of ἔδωκεν) 16.
ὁ (nom.sing.masc.of the article in agreement with πατὴρ) 9.
πατὴρ (nom.sing.masc.of πατήρ, subject of ἔδωκεν) 238.
εἰς (preposition with the accusative of extent) 140.
τὰς (acc.pl.fem.of the article in agreement with χεῖρας) 9.
χεῖρας (acc.pl.fem.of χείρ, metaphorical extent) 308.
καὶ (adjunctive conjunction joining object clauses) 14.
ὅτι (conjunction introducing an object clause in indirect discourse) 211.
ἀπὸ (preposition with the ablative of source) 70.
θεοῦ (abl.sing.masc.of θεός, source) 124.
ἐξῆλθεν (3d.per.sing.aor.ind.of ἐξέρχομαι, culminative) 161.

καὶ (adjunctive conjunction joining prepositional phrases) 14.
πρὸς (preposition with the accusative of extent) 197.
τὸν (acc.sing.masc.of the article in agreement with θεὸν) 9.
θεὸν (acc.sing.masc.of θεός, extent) 124.
ὑπάγει (3d.per.sing.pres.act.ind.of ὑπάγω, futuristic) 364.

Translation - ". . . because He knew that the Father had given everything to Him, and that He had come out from God and was going back to God, . . . "

Comment: Another causal participle, like the one in verse 1,- this one followed by two ὅτι object clauses. Let us review what He knew as recorded in verse 1. He knew (a)that His hour had come,and (b) that He was going to leave the earth and go back to the Father. Now we add (c) that the Father had given everything into His hands, which is another way of saying that our Lord had everything under His control. He also knew (d) that He had come from God and (e) that He would soon be going back πρὸς τὸν θεόν (John 1:1).

What we have here in verses 1 and 3 is an exposition of Phil.2:6-8, upon which passage *cf.* comment *en loc.* Since our Lord knew all of this about Himself He could afford to play the role of the humble servant as He does in verses 4 and 5.

Everything was for His benefit (dative of personal advantage in αὐτῷ) and also under His control, as the phrase εἰς τὰς χεῖρας indicates. (Mt.28:18-20). A benefactor may put a fortune into a bank for the benefit of his heir, but, by legal means, deprive the heir of its control. Not in this case. Everything is Christ's and He will have total control of all of the resources of heaven in the future (Eph.1:20-23; Phil.2:9-11).

Our Lord also was fully aware of the divine source of His mission to earth and of His eternal destiny as He would soon (futuristic present in ὑπάγει) return to the Father. Since the fortunes of the Christian are eternally identified with those of Jesus Christ (John 17:21) we too can afford to wash the feet, even of those who are about to deny or even betray us. "Let his mind be in you which was also in Christ Jesus" (Phil.2:6).

Verse 4 - "He riseth from supper, and laid aside his garments; and took a towel, and girded himself."

ἐγείρεται ἐκ τοῦ δείπνου καὶ τίθησιν τὰ ἱμάτια, καὶ λαβὼν λέντιον διέζωσεν ἑαυτόν.

ἐγείρεται (3d.per.sing.pres.mid.ind.of ἐγείρω, historical) 125.
ἐκ (preposition with the ablative of separation) 19.
τοῦ (abl.sing.neut.of the article in agreement with δείπνου) 9.
δείπνου (abl.sing.neut.of δεῖπνον, separation) 1440.
καὶ (adjunctive conjunction joining verbs) 14.
τίθησιν (3d.per.sing.pres.act.ind.of τίθημι, historical) 455.
τὰ (acc.pl.neut.of the article in agreement with ἱμάτια) 9.
ἱμάτια (acc.pl.neut.of ἱμάτιον, direct object of τίθησιν) 534.
καὶ (adjunctive conjunction joining verbs) 14.
λαβὼν (aor.act.part.nom.sing.masc.of λαμβάνω, adverbial, temporal) 533.

#2758 λέντιον (acc.sing.neut.of λέντιον, direct object of λαβὼν).

towel - John 13:4,5.

Meaning: an apron (John 13:4),which also served as a towel (John 13:5).

#2759 διέζωσεν (3d.per.sing.aor.act.ind.of διαζώννυμι, constative).

gird - John 13:4,5.
gird unto one's self - John 21:7.

Meaning: To bind around; to gird; to wrap around the body. Of the towel that Jesus used at the foot washing episode - John 13:4,5. With reference to Peter's coat - John 21:7.

ἑαυτόν (acc.sing.masc.of ἑαυτός, direct object of διέζωσεν) 288.

Translation - "He arose from the supper and took off His tunic and took a towel and fastened it about His waist."

Comment: Note the historical present tenses in ἐγείρεται and τίθησιν. *Cf.*#534.

Verse 5 - "After that he poureth water into a basin, and began to wash the disciples' feet, and to wipe them with the towel wherewith he was girded."

εἶτα βάλλει ὕδωρ εἰς τὸν νιπτῆρα καὶ ἤρξατο νίπτειν τοὺς πόδας τῶν μαθητῶν καὶ ἐκμάσσειν τῷ λεντίῳ ᾧ ἦν διεζωσμένος.

εἶτα (an adverb of time) 2185.
βάλλει (3d.per.sing.pres.act.ind.of βάλλω, historical) 299.
ὕδωρ (acc.sing.neut.of ὕδωρ, direct object of βάλλει) 301.
εἰς (preposition with the accusative of extent) 140.
τὸν (acc.sing.masc.of the article in agreement with νιπτῆρα) 9.

#2760 νιπτῆρα (acc.sing.masc.of νιπτήρ, extent).

basin - John 13:5.

*Meaning: Cf.*νίπτω (#590). Hence, a basin for washing - John 13:5.

καὶ (adjunctive conjunction joining verbs) 14.
ἤρξατο (3d.per.sing.aor.mid.ind.of ἄρχω, ingressive) 383.
νίπτειν (pres.act.inf.of νίπτω, completes ἤρξατο) 590.
τοὺς (acc.pl.masc.of the article in agreement with πόδας) 9.
πόδας (acc.pl.masc.of πούς, direct object of νίπτειν) 353.
τῶν (gen.pl.masc.of the article in agreement with μαθητῶν) 9.
μαθητῶν (gen.pl.masc.of μαθητής, possession) 421.
καὶ (adjunctive conjunction joining infinitives) 14.
ἐκμάσσειν (pres.act.inf.of ἐκμάσσω, completes ἤρξατο) 2167.
τῷ (instru.sing.neut.of the article in agreement with λεντίῳ) 9.
λεντίῳ (instru.sing.neut.of λέντιον, means) 2758.

ᾧ (instru.sing.neut.of *ὅς*, means) 65.
ἦν (3d.per.sing.imp.ind.of *εἰμί*, pluperfect periphrastic) 86.
διεζωσμένος (perf.pass.part.nom.sing.masc.of *διαζώννυμι*, pluperfect periphrastic) 2759.

Translation - "Then He poured water into the basin and began to wash the feet of the disciples and to wipe with the towel which He had wrapped about Himself."

Comment: We may translate *εἶτα* as "then" in the sense of "after that." Again the historical present in *βάλλει*. The pluperfect periphrastic is itensive. Note the absence of an object after *ἐκμάσσειν*.

Verse 6 - "Then cometh he to Simon Peter; and Peter saith unto him, Lord, dost thou wash my feet?"

ἔρχεται οὖν πρὸς Σίμωνα Πέτρον. λέγει αὐτῷ, Κύριε, σύ μου νίπτεις τοὺς πόδας;

ἔρχεται (3d.per.sing.pres.mid.ind.of *ἔρχομαι*, historical) 146.
οὖν (continuative conjunction) 68.
πρὸς (preposition with the accusative of extent) 197.
Σίμωνα (acc.sing.masc.of *Σίμων*, extent) 386.
Πέτρον (acc.sing.masc.of *πέτρος*, extent) 387.
λέγει (3d.per.sing.pres.act.ind.of *λέγω*, historical) 66.
αὐτῷ (dat.sing.masc.of *αὐτός*, indirect object of *λέγει*) 16.
Κύριε (voc.sing.masc.of *κύριος*, address) 97.
σύ (nom.sing.masc.of *σύ*, subject of *νίπτεις*, emphatic) 104.
μου (gen.sing.masc.of *ἐγώ*, possession, emphatic) 123.
νίπτεις (2d.person sing.pres.act.ind.of *νίπτω*, in rhetorical question, inchoative) 590.
τοὺς (acc.pl.masc.of the article in agreement with *πόδας*) 9.
πόδας (acc.pl.masc.ofd *πούς*, direct object of *νίπτεις*) 353.

Translation - "Then He came to Simon Peter. He said to Him, 'Lord, **you** *are going to wash* **my** *feet?' "*

Comment: *νίπτεις* is a conative or inchoative present tense, used to describe an act, either just about to begin or one begun but interrupted. Note that both *σύ* and *μου* are in emphasis. Peter's question is rhetorical. He was expressing his objection on the grounds that the Lord should not be serving the servant in such a menial task - that it ought to be the other way around. It is the same concept as that expressed by John the Baptist in Matthew 3:14. That the incarnate Son of God, Sovereign Lord of the universe, should stoop to wash the feet of a fast talking and inconsistent Galilean fisherman, seemed incredible. Peter's humility comes through clearly here. Also his lack of understanding, as is clear in the next verse. Apparently Jesus had washed the feet of some of the others before reaching Peter. Why did they not protest? Was Peter's protest sincere, or was it intended as a rebuke to the others who had not protested? Why did not Peter protest when Jesus washed the feet of the other disciples before reaching him? We can only speculate. The record does not tell us. Perhaps Peter's incredulous question was humility on parade?!

Verse 7 - "Jesus answered and said unto him, What I do thou knowest not now; but thou shalt know hereafter."

ἀπεκρίθη Ἰησοῦς καὶ εἶπεν αὐτῷ Ὃ ἐγὼ ποιῶ σὺ οὐκ οἶδας ἄρτι, γνώσῃ δὲ μετὰ ταῦτα.

ἀπεκρίθη (3d.per.sing.aor.mid.ind.of *ἀποκρίνομαι*, constative) 318.
Ἰησοῦς (nom.sing.masc.of Ἰησοῦς, subject of *ἀπεκρίθη* and *εἶπεν*) 3.
καὶ (adjunctive conjunction joining verbs) 14.
εἶπεν (3d.per.sing.aor.act.ind.of *εἶπον*, constative) 155.
αὐτῷ (dat.sing.masc.of *αὐτός*, indirect object of *εἶπεν*) 16.
Ὃ (acc.sing.neut.of *ὅς*, direct object of *οἶδας*) 65.
ἐγὼ (nom.sing.masc.of *ἐγώ*,subject of *ποιῶ*) 123.
ποιῶ (1st.per.sing.pres.act.ind.of *ποιέω*, inchoative) 127.
σὺ (nom.sing.masc.of *σύ*, subject of *οἶδας*) 104.
οὐκ (summary negative conjunction with the indicative) 130.
ἄρτι (temporal adverb) 320.
γνώσῃ (2d.per.sing.fut.act.ind.of *γινώσκω*, predictive) 131.
δὲ (adversative conjunction) 11.
μετὰ (preposition with the accusative of time extent) 50.
ταῦτα (acc.pl.neut.of *οὗτος*, time extent) 93.

Translation - "In reply Jesus said to him, 'That which I am going to do you do not understand now, but you will know later.' "

Comment: Ὃ, the definite relative pronoun is the object of *οἶδας*. It is idle to attempt to make a distinction between *οἶδας* and *γνώσῃ*, on the basis of the meaning of the two verbs. The context however helps us. Peter *knew* what Jesus was about to do, but he did not *understand* the significance of it. He knew that Jesus was about to wash his feet. What he lacked was the reason for Jesus' act and what spiritual application our Lord would make of it. In keeping with Jesus' prediction Peter came later to understand. This promise that he would understand it better later, should have been enough to cause the irrepressible fisherman to subside. His sensitivity and humility up to this point had been commendable if, in fact, it was sincere. Now his attitude changes to stubborn resistance, as though he knew more about the matter than Jesus did. This is not commendable. Thus, as almost always, was our friend, Peter.

Verse 8 - "Peter saith unto him, Thou shalt never wash my feet. Jesus answered him, If I wash thee not, thou hast no part with me."

λέγει αὐτῷ Πέτρος, Οὐ μὴ νίψῃς μου τοὺς πόδας εἰς τὸν αἰῶνα. ἀπεκρίθη Ἰησοῦς αὐτῷ, Ἐὰν μὴ νίψω σε, οὐκ ἔχεις μέρος μετ' ἐμοῦ.

λέγει (3d.per.sing.pres.act.ind.of *λέγω*, historical) 66.

αὐτῷ (dat.sing.masc.of *αὐτός*, indirect object of *λέγει*) 16.

Πέτρος (nom.sing.masc.of *Πέτρος*, subject of *λέγει*) 387.

Οὐ (summary negative conjunction with *μὴ* and the subjunctive, emphatic negation) 130.

μὴ (qualified negative conjunction with *οὐ* and the subjunctive, emphatic negation) 87.

νίψῃς (2d.per.sing.aor.act.subj.of *νίπτω*, emphatic negation) 590.

μου (gen.sing.masc.of *ἐγώ*, possession, emphatic) 123.

τοὺς (acc.pl.masc.of the article in agreement with *πόδας*) 9.

πόδας (acc.pl.masc.of *πούς*, direct object of *νίψῃς*) 353.

εἰς (preposition with the accusative of time extent) 140.

τὸν (acc.sing.masc.of the article in agreement with *αἰῶνα*) 9.

αἰῶνα (acc.sing.masc.of *αἰών*, time extent) 1002.

ἀπεκρίθη (3d.per.sing.aor.mid.ind.of *ἀποκρίνομαι*, constative) 318.

Ἰησοῦς (nom.sing.masc.of *Ἰησοῦς*, subject of *ἀπεκρίθη*) 3.

αὐτῷ (dat.sing.masc.of *αὐτός*, indirect object of *ἀπεκρίθη*) 16.

Ἐὰν (conditional particle in a third-class condition) 363.

μὴ (qualified negative conjunction, with the subjunctive in a third-class condition) 87.

νίψω (1st.per.sing.aor.act.subj.of *νίπτω*, third-class condition) 590.

σε (acc.sing.masc.of *σύ*, direct object of *νίψω*) 104.

οὐκ (summary negative conjunction with the indicative) 130.

ἔχεις (2d.per.pl.pres.act.ind.of *ἔχω*, futuristic) 82.

μέρος (acc.sing.neut.of *μέρος*, direct object of *ἔχεις*) 240.

μετ' (preposition with the genitive, fellowship) 50.

ἐμοῦ (gen.sing.masc.of *ἐμός*, fellowship) 1267.

Translation - "Peter said to Him, 'You shall never wash my feet, not in all eternity.' Jesus answered him, 'If I do not wash you, you will never have fellowship with me.' "

Comment: *Οὐ μὴ νίψῃς* is a volitive subjunctive prohibition, strengthened by the double negative *Οὐ μὴ*. Peter is expressing the strongest of wishes that Jesus should never wash his feet. He adds *εἰς τὸν αἰῶνα* - "throughout eternity" - for emphasis. The clear implication of Peter's emphatic negation is that whatever reason Jesus may have had for washing the disciples' feet (verse 7) it was not sufficient to justify the act. Jesus was making a bad mistake and Peter was determined to stop it. He was unwilling to wait for understanding of the act, which Jesus promised them in verse 7. Speaking out of his ignorance of its significance, Peter ruled himself out of participation in it. This was a presumptive insult to Jesus, although Peter did not intend it to be so. Jesus then laid before Peter the choice with the third-class condition, in which Jesus suggested doubt about whether or not the condition would be fulfilled, but no doubt about the result in the event that the condition remained unfilfilled. "Whether you permit me to wash your feet or not, I will not say. That is up to you. But if you do not permit it, I must say that you will have no part with me."

Cf.#240 for μέρος and the Christian's part with Christ. What about Judas? He had not yet gone out to betray Jesus before the foot washing began. *Cf.*# 590 and λούω (#2761). Jesus' meaning becomes clear in verse 10. Note the historical present in λέγει.

Verse 9 - "Simon Peter saith unto him, Lord, not my feet only, but also my hands and my head."

λέγει αὐτῷ Σίμων Πέτρος, Κύριε, μὴ τοὺς πόδας μου μόνον ἀλλὰ καὶ τὰς χεῖρας καὶ τὴν κεφαλήν.

λέγει (3d.per.sing.pres.act.ind.of λέγω, historical) 66.
αὐτῷ (dat.sing.masc.of αὐτός, indirect object of λέγει) 16.
Σίμων (nom.sing.masc.of Σίμων, subject of λέγει) 386.
Πέτρος (nom.sing.masc.of Πέτρος, apposition) 387.
Κύριε (voc.sing.masc.of κύριος, address) 97.
μὴ (qualified negative conjunction with the imperative mode understood) 87.
τοὺς (acc.pl.masc.of the article in agreement with πόδας) 9.
πόδας (acc.pl.masc.of πούς, direct object of νίψαι understood) 353.
μου (gen.sing.masc.of ἐγώ, possession) 123.
μόνον (acc.sing.neut.of μόνος, adverbial) 339.
ἀλλὰ (alternative conjunction) 342.
καὶ (adjunctive conjunction joining nouns) 14.
τὰς (acc.pl.fem.of the article in agreement with χεῖρας) 9.
χεῖρας (acc.pl.fem.of χείρ, direct object of νίψαι understood) 308.
καὶ (adjunctive conjunction joining nouns) 14.
τὴν (acc.sing.fem.of the article in agreement with κεφαλήν) 9.
κεφαλήν (acc.sing.fem.of κεφαλή, direct object of νίψαι understood) 521.

Translation - "Simon Peter said to Him, 'Lord, not my feet only but also my hands and my head.' "

Comment: Note μὴ μόνον . . . ἀλλὰ καὶ - "not only . . . but also" sequence. The verb νίψαι is to be supplied from verse 8.

Here we have the erratic swing of the pendulum of Peter's inconsistent and impatient mind, from no washing at all to a complete bath. Peter persisted in being wrong because he was too impatient to wait for our Lord's teaching about what the ceremony was intended to signify. He was unwilling for Jesus to perform this beautiful act without the benefit of his misguided and unsolicited advice. Even after Jesus quietly told Peter that, although he did not grasp the significance of the event at the moment, he would understand it later, Peter had to talk. Any normal person, upon hearing Jesus' promise of verse 7, would have withheld any further comment and waited patiently for further light in God's own good time. Not Peter. This man, who, before the night had passed, would deny with curses that he even knew Jesus, was now feeding the flames of his own personal insecurity by his unseemly comments about that which he knew nothing.

Verse 10 - "Jesus saith unto him, He that is washed needeth not save to wash his feet, but is clean every whit: and ye are clean, but not all."

λέγει αὐτῷ ὁ Ἰησοῦς, Ὁ λελουμένος οὐκ ἔχει χρείαν εἰ μὴ τοὺς πόδας νίψασθαι, ἀλλ' ἔστιν καθαρὸς ὅλος. καὶ ὑμεῖς καθαροί ἐστε, ἀλλ' οὐχὶ πάντες.

λέγει (3d.per.sing.pres.act.ind.of λέγω, historical) 66.
αὐτῷ (dat.sing.masc.of αὐτός, indirect object of λέγει) 16.
ὁ (nom.sing.masc.of the article in agreement with Ἰησοῦς) 9.
Ἰησοῦς (nom.sing.masc.of Ἰησοῦς, subject of λέγει) 3.
Ὁ (nom.sing.masc.of the article in agreement with λελουμένος) 9.

#2761 λελουμένος (perf.pass.part.nom.sing.masc.of λούω, substantival, subject of ἔχει and ἔστιν).

wash - John 13:10; Acts 9:37; 16:33; Heb.10:22; 2 Pet.2:22; Rev.1:5 (mgn.).

Meaning: to wash the entire body. To bathe a corpse - Acts 9:37; one who has been beaten - Acts 16:33l. Ceremonially and metaphorically - Heb.10:22; with reference to an animal - 2 Pet.2:22; spiritually - John 13:10. In Rev.1:5, where some mss.have λούσαντι instead of λύσαντι - to be cleansed by the blood of Christ - Rev.1:5.

οὐκ (summary negative conjunction with the indicative) 130.
ἔχει (3d.per.sing.pres.act.ind.of ἔχω, static) 82.
χρείαν (acc.sing.fem.of χρεία, direct object of ἔχει) 317.
εἰ (conditional particle in an elliptical condition, second-class, contrary to fact) 337.
μὴ (qualified negative conjunction in an elliptical second-class condition) 87.
τοὺς (acc.pl.masc.of the article in agreement with πόδας) 9.
πόδας (acc.pl.masc.of πούς, direct object of νίψασθαι) 353.
νίψασθαι (aor.mid.inf.of νίπτω, in apposition with χρείαν) 590.
ἀλλ' (alternaitve conjunction) 342.
ἔστιν (3d.per.sing.pres.ind.of εἰμί, static) 86.
καθαρὸς (nom.sing.masc.of καθαρός, predicate adjective) 431.
ὅλος (nom.sing.masc.of ὅλος, adverbial) 112.
καὶ (emphatic conjunction) 14.
ὑμεῖς (nom.pl.masc.of σύ, subject of ἐστε) 104.
καθαροὶ (nom.pl.masc.of καθαρός, predicate adjective) 431.
ἐστε (2d.per.pl.pres.ind.of εἰμί, aoristic) 86.
ἀλλ' (adversative conjunction) 342.
οὐχὶ (summary negative conjunction) 130.
πάντες (nom.pl.masc.of πᾶς, subject of εἰσί understood) 67.

Translation - "Jesus said to him, 'The one who has been washed has no further need, except (the need) to wash the feet, but is clean throughout. As a matter of fact you disciples are clean, but not all (of you)."

Comment: The perfect passive participle ὁ λελουμένος indicates one who is now clean as a result of a past completed washing. The reference to Rev.1:5 (#2761) is to a marginal reading. The better manuscript authorities have λύσαντι (from λύω (#471) in the text. Neither λούω (#2761) nor νίπτω (#590) is used in a clear connection with the cleansing from sin in the blood of Christ, but πλύνω (#2043) in Rev.7:14 is, where the robes of the redeemed are washed (ἔπλυναν) "in the blood of the Lamb - ἐν τῷ αἵματι τοῦ'Αρνίου. The distinction in John 13:10 between λούω and νίπτω is one of permanent cleansing (ὁ λελουμένος) as a result of which one has no further need of washing, except the periodic washing of the feet (εἰ μὴ τοὺς πόδας νίψασθαι), which are soiled as we, who have been permanently cleansed in the soteriological sense, walk in the sinful world and thus require periodic foot cleansing. Once washed (λούω) we need no further washing (λούω),but our feet need continuous cleansing (νίπτω). Otherwise "he is totally cleansed (ἀλλ' ἔστιν καθαρὸς ὅλος).ὅλος here does not apply to the disciples as a group, which would include Judas Iscariot, since it is singular to conform to ὁ λελουμένος, which is also singular. Each individual who is cleansed is cleansed throughout, from top to bottom, inside and outside. Thus it seems that λούω here refers to salvation by grace through faith in Christ's blood. How many of those present were thus cleansed? Eleven, but not all (πάντες). One - Judas Iscariot, was not washed (λούω) and thus was not cleansed throughout (ὅλος). As a matter of fact he was not cleansed at all in any sense, except that his feet were temporarily physically clean as a result of Jesus' ministration. And those feet were destined to get dirty quite soon as Judas soon left and went out into the night to mingle his footsteps with those who paid him to betray Jesus. So the formal foot washing meant nothing to Judas, because at that very moment he had the price of Jesus' betrayal in his pocket and Satan in his heart. He submitted to the foot washing with no spiritual appreciation of its significance, while Peter first asked for none and then for too much, because, though he did not understand from an intellectual point of view what Jesus was doing, his regenerated heart was right with his Lord. The eleven disciples, like all true believers were clean throughout, but they had walked in the world and collected its godless dust on their feet and they would do so again. Thus they needed the "washing of water by the word" (Eph.5:26; John 15:3). *Cf.* also 1 Cor.6:11, where we have ἀπολούω and Acts 22:16 *q.v.en loc.*

Foot washing suggests cleansing as the result of walking. The student should consult #384 for the list of verses where περιπατέω is used to refer to the Christian's ethical walk in the world. In the epistles of Paul and John it is always used in this sense.

That Jesus referred to Judas in the last clause of verse 10 is clear from

Verse 11 - "For he knew who should betray him; therefore said he, Ye are not all clean."

ᾔδει γὰρ τὸν παραδιδόντα αὐτόν. διὰ τοῦτο εἶπεν ὅτι Οὐχὶ πάντες καθαροί ἐστε.

ᾔδει (3d.per.sing.pluperfect ind.of ὁράω, intensive) 144.

γὰρ (inferential conjunction introducing a coordinating causal clause) 105.
τὸν (acc.sing.masc.of the article in agreement with παραδιδόντα) 9.
παραδιδόντα (pres.act.part.acc.sing.masc. of παραδίδωμι, substantival, direct object of ᾔδει) 368.
αὐτόν (acc.sing.masc.of αὐτός, direct object of παραδιδόντα) 16.
διὰ (preposition with the accusative, cause) 118.
τοῦτο (acc.sing.neut.of οὗτος, cause) 93.
εἶπεν (3d.per.sing.aor.act.ind.of εἶπον, constative) 155.
ὅτι (recitative) 211.
Οὐχὶ (summary negative conjunction with the indicative, joined with πάντες) 130.
πάντες (nom.pl.masc.of πᾶς, subject of ἐστε) 67.
καθαροί (nom.pl.masc.of καθηρός, predicate adjective) 431.
ἐστε (2d.per.pl.pres.ind.of εἰμί, aoristic) 86.

Translation - "Because He had always known the one who was about to betray Him. For that reason He said, 'Not all are clean.' "

Comment: γὰρ, the inferential conjunction introduces the coordinate clause which follows, which is causal. It explains Jesus' statement of verse 10. Note the pluperfect intensive in ᾔδει. The Eternal Λόγος had always known about Judas. Οὐχὶ is joined to πάντες, as in verse 10, not to καθαροὶ. He did not say, "All are not clean" which is another way of saying, "All are dirty." He did say, "Not all are clean," which is another way of saying, "Some (or in this case, One) (are) is dirty. The pluperfect ᾔδει makes our Lord's knowledge of the fact of the betrayal antecedent to the fact itself, which was in the process of being carried out at that very moment, since Judas had just returned from his conference with the authorities. Hence the present tense in the participle παραδιδόντα. διὰ τοῦτο in a causal sense. *Cf.*#118 for other instances.

Eleven disciples, though, unlike Judas, faithful to our Lord, were in great need of the foot washing, as are all of God's children.

Verse 12 - "So after he had washed their feet, and had taken his garments, and was set down again, he said unto them, Know ye what I have done to you?"

Ὅτε οὖν ἔνιψεν τοὺς πόδας αὐτῶν (καὶ) ἔλαβεν τὰ ἱμάτια αὐτοῦ καὶ ἀνέπεσεν πάλιν, εἶπεν αὐτοῖς, Γινώσκετε τί πεποίηκα ὑμῖν;

Ὅτε (conjunction introducing the indicative in a definite temporal clause) 703.
οὖν (continuative conjunction) 68.
ἔνιψεν (3d.per.sing.aor.act.ind.of νίπτω, culminative) 590.
τοὺς (acc.pl.masc.of the article in agreement with πόδας) 9.
πόδας (acc.pl.masc.of πούς, direct object of ἔνιψεν) 353.
αὐτῶν (gen.pl.masc.of αὐτός, possession) 16.
(καὶ) (adjunctive conjunction joining verbs) 14.
ἔλαβεν (3d.per.sing.aor.act.ind.of λαμβάνω, culminative) 533.
τὰ (acc.pl.neut.of the article in agreement with ἱμάτια) 9.

ἱμάτια (acc.pl.neut.of ἱμάτιον, direct object of ἔλαβεν) 534.
αὐτοῦ (gen.sing.masc.of αὐτός, possession) 16.
καὶ (adjunctive conjunction joining verbs) 14.
ἀνέπεσεν (3d.per.sing.aor.act.ind.of ἀναπίπτω, culminative) 1184.
πάλιν (adverbial) 355.
εἶπεν (3d.per.sing.aor.act.ind.of εἶπον, constative) 155.
αὐτοῖς (dat.pl.masc.of αὐτός, indirect object of εἶπεν) 16.
Γινώσκετε (2d.per.pl.pres.act.ind.of γινώσκω, direct question) 131.
τί (acc.sing.neut.of τίς, direct object of γινώσκετε) 281.
πεποίηκα (1st.per.sing.perf.act.ind.of ποιέω, consummative) 127.
ὑμῖν (dat.pl.masc.of σύ, personal advantage) 104.

Translation - "Then after He had washed their feet and taken His garments and sat down again, He said to them, 'Do you know what I have done for you?' "

Comment: ὅτε introduces a definite temporal clause with three verbs in paratactic arrangement with καὶ . . . καὶ . . . καὶ. These aorist tense verbs are culminative. Jesus finished washing their feet and took again His garments which He had laid aside before the washing and sat down at the table again. Then came His question. He did not refer to the physical act of foot washing. Of course they knew what He had been doing. The question was whether or not they understood the significance of it? Did they grasp the lesson which He was trying to teach them? Obviously not.

Clyde (*Greek Syntax*, 76, as cited in Robertson, *Grammar*, 840) says, "The Greeks neglected to mark the priority of one event to another, leaving that to be gathered from the context." And Robertson adds, "Strictly therefore the aorist is not used for the past perfect." But by considering ἔνιψεν, ἔλαβεν and ἀνέπεσεν as culminative aorists, and εἶπεν as constative, we arrive at the same effect. The context here makes it plain that the action of the three aorists before εἶπεν was antecedent to it. Thus, when the context demands it, we can take the aorist tense as culminative and translate it as those it were either perfect, when the situation is present to the writer or speaker, or pluperfect when the situation is relatively past. "The culminative aorist is employed in this meaning when it is wished to view an event in its entirety, but to regard it from the viewpoint of its existing results. Here we usually find verbs which signify effort or process, the aorist denoting the attainment of the end of such effort or process. . . This idiom may be best translated by the English perfect when it affects a situation present to the writer, and by the pluperfect when relatively past." (Mantey, Manual, 196, 197). What Mantey calls the culminative aorist is called effective aorist by Robertson, although he admits that "The name is not particularly good and 'resultant aorist' is suggested by some scholars. Gildersleeve suggests "upshot aorist." Giles calls it aorist of the "culminating point," following Monro. But the idea is that emphasis is laid on the end of the action as opposed to the beginning (ingressive). This is done (if done) by the verb itself (*Aktionsart*)" (Robertson, *Grammar*, 834, 835).

Verse 13 - "Ye call me Master and Lord; and ye say well: for so I am."

ὑμεῖς φωνεῖτέ με Ὁ διδάσκαλος καὶ Ὁ κύριος, καὶ καλῶς λέγετε, εἰμὶ γάρ.

ὑμεῖς (nom.pl.masc.of *σύ* subject of *φωνεῖτέ*) 104.
φωνεῖτέ (2d.per.pl.pres.act.ind.of *φωνέω*, customary) 1338.
με (acc.sing.masc.of *ἐγώ*, direct object of *φωνεῖτέ*) 123.
Ὁ (nom.sing.masc.of the article in agreement with *διδάσκαλος*) 9.
διδάσκαλος (nom.sing.masc.of *διδάσκαλος*, appellation) 742.
καὶ (adjunctive conjunction joining nouns) 14.
Ὁ (nom.sing.masc.of the article in agreement with *κύριος*) 9.
κύριος (nom.sing.masc.of *κύριος*, appellation) 97.
καὶ (adjunctive conjunction joining verbs) 14.
καλῶς (adverbial) 977.
λέγετε (2d.per.pl.pres.act.ind.of *λέγω*, progressive description) 66.
εἰμὶ (1st.per.sing.pres.ind.of *εἰμί*, static) 86.
γάρ (inferential conjunction with a coordinate causal clause) 105.

Translation - "You call me Master and Lord; and you are right, because that is what I am."

Comment: *ὑμεῖς* is emphasized, since it is not needed otherwise, being implicit in *φωνεῖτέ*. He commends them for their view of Him and uses the point upon which to build His argument of

Verse 14 - "If I then, your Lord and Master, have washed your feet, ye also ought to wash one another's feet."

εἰ οὖν ἐγὼ ἔνιψα ὑμῶν τοὺς πόδας ὁ κύριος καὶ ὁ διδάσκαλος, καὶ ὑμεῖς ὀφείλετε ἀλλήλων νίπτειν τοὺς πόδας.

εἰ (conditional particle in a first-class condition) 337.
οὖν (inferential conjunction) 68.
ἐγὼ (nom.sing.masc.of *ἐγώ*, subject of *ἔνιψα*) 123.
ἔνιψα (1st.per.sing.aor.act.ind.of *νίπτω*, culminative) 590.
ὑμῶν (gen.pl.masc.of *σύ*, possession) 104.
τοὺς (acc.pl.masc.of the article in agreement with *πόδας*) 9.
πόδας (acc.pl.masc.of *πούς*, direct object of *ἔνιψα*) 353.
ὁ (nom.sing.masc.of the article in agreement with *κύριος*) 9.
κύριος (nom.sing.masc.of *κύριος*, in apposition with *ἐγὼ*) 97.
καὶ (adjunctive conjunction joining nouns) 14.
ὁ (nom.sing.masc.of the article in agreement with *διδάσκαλος*) 9.
διδάσκαλος (nom.sing.masc.of *διδάσκαλος*, in apposition with *ἐγὼ*) 742.
καὶ (adjunctive conjunction joining pronouns) 14.
ὀφείλετε (2d.per.pl.pres.act.ind.of *ὀφείλω*, static) 1277.
ἀλλήλων (gen.pl.masc.of *ἀλλήλων*, possession) 1487.
νίπτειν (pres.act.inf.of *νίπτω*, completes *ὀφείλετε*) 590.
τοὺς (acc.pl.masc.of the article in agreement with *πόδας*) 9.
πόδας (acc.pl.masc.of *πούς*, direct object of *νίπτειν*) 353.

Translation - "Since therefore I, your Lord and Master, have washed your feet, you also ought to wash the feet of one another."

Comment: The first-class condition with εἰ and the indicative mode leaves no doubt about the condition in the protasis. Jesus had just finished (culminative aorist in ἔνιψα) washing the disciples' feet. οὖν is inferential. Note the words in emphasis, either because otherwise they are unnecessary, being implicit in the verb, like ἐγὼ and ὑμεῖς, or out of position, like ὑμῶν. "*I* have washed *your* feet. . *you* ought to wash . . κ.τ.λ." The argument is that Jesus, Sovereign Lord and Teacher, had given to them an example. I have already discussed this point in comment on John 13:3, *q.v.* Since He was God He needed not to play the role, as if to convince Himself and others. Christians who are sure they are saved should follow in His footsteps. Phil.2:5-8. The ostentation afforded to certain members of the clergy, of whom possibly it can be said that they "think of (themselves) more highly than (they) ought to think" (Rom.12:3) is an indication that we need more foot washing in the house of God, if not literally, as least symbolically in terms of the lesson which Jesus sought to teach. Some congregations have chosen to follow Jesus' orders literally. There is nothing in Scripture to forbid them, just as there is nothing in Scripture to mandate a literal practice of the rite. What is mandated is that Christians should be humble and self-effacing. The more the child of God becomes convinced in his own soul that his eternal fortunes are inextricably bound up with those of the Father, Son and Holy Spirit (John 17:21), the easier it is to take the back seat in the synagogue, and the less interest he has in the telephone call from a newspaper reporter who asks for an interview. Headlines are for insecure people. God bless them, they need them.

If the virtue of humility can be developed without literal foot washing, good. If one Christian must literally wash the feet of another in order to be humble, so be it. If the practice of foot washing contributes to one's spiritual pride, the child of God should beware. Humility on parade may be an expression of the fact that the parader is certain that he is a better Christian than the brother on the curb.

Satan is subtle. A Methodist preacher reported that when he formerly belonged to a congregation that prohibited neckware for men, he found himself proud of the fact that he did not wear a tie and considered himself a better Christian than those men who did.

Some so-called charismatics consider their particular gift superior to those of others and some even contend that others who lack their gift are not regenerate. For them a careful study of 1 Corinthians 12-14 and Romans 12 would be helpful.

The same principle can be observed outside the field of religion. Patriotism on parade, evident in an undue display of the American flag and an undue regard for the playing of "The Star Spangled Banner" makes the skeptic wonder whether the "patriot" stands at rigid attention with his hand over his heart when the national anthem is played and the flag is displayed at 1:00 A.M. when the television station goes off the air? I do not, because there is nobody there to see how patriotic I am.

Verse 15 - "For I have given you an example, that ye should do as I have done to you."

ὑπόδειγμα γὰρ δέδωκα ὑμῖν ἵνα καθὼς ἐγὼ ἐποίησα ὑμῖν καὶ ὑμεῖς ποιῆτε.

#2762 ὑπόδειγμα (acc.sing.neut.of ὑπόδειγμα, direct object of δέδωκα).

ensample - 2 Peter 2:6.
example - John 13:15; Heb.4:11; 8:5; James 5:10.
pattern - Heb.9:23.

Meaning: ***Cf.*ὑποδείκνυμι (#282). Hence, an example, pattern, similitude. Followed by ἵνα and the subjunctive in a purpose clause - John 13:15; of Sodom and Gomorrah, examples of God's judgment on sin - 2 Peter 2:6. Followed by a genitive of description of what we are to avoid - Heb.4:11. With σκιᾷ and a genitive of description - Heb.8;5; Jam.5:10; Heb.9:23.**

γὰρ (inferential conjunction introducing a coordinate causal clause) 105.
δέδωκα (1st.per.sing.perf.act.ind.of δίδωμι, dramatic) 362.
ὑμῖν (dat.pl.masc.of σύ, indirect object of δέδωκα) 104.
ἵνα (conjunction introducing the subjunctive in a purpose clause) 114.
καθὼς (adverb introducing a comparative clause) 1348.
ἐγὼ (nom.sing.masc.of ἐγώ, subject of ἐποίησα) 123.
ἐποίησα (1st.per.sing.or.act.ind.of ποιέω, culminative) 127.
ὑμῖν (dat.pl.masc.of σύ, personal advantage) 104.
καὶ (adjunctive conjunction joining pronouns) 14.
ὑμεῖς (nom.pl.masc.of σύ, subject of ποιῆτε) 104.
ποιῆτε (2d.per.pl.pres.act.subj.of ποιέω, purpose) 127.

Translation - "Because I have given you an object lesson, in order that you will do as I have done for you."

Comment: Some object lessons suggest what we should do. Others warn against what we should not do. *Cf.*#2762. It is interesting to note that in verse 12 John used the culminative aorist in ἔνιψεν, ἔλαβεν and ἀνέπεσεν, to indicate antecedent action to that of εἶπεν, just as he here uses the perfect δέδωκα to show antecedent action to that of λέγω in verse 16. Also note that in verse 15 we have ἐποίησα, another culminative aorist, serving in the same way as the perfect δέδωκα. If the context demands it, the culminative aorist can serve for the intensive perfect. It is always the context that decides. Again we have ὑμεῖς in emphasis.

This verse seems strongly to support the foot washing practice though there is no Scripture to support the idea that it is an ordinance of the church, to be practised regularly and formally. On the other hand congregations who do so should not be censured. The deeper thought is that the saints, secure in the knowledge of their status in Christ, as He was of His in God (verse 3), should assume the humble role of a servant. Proper subordination is essential to Christian happiness. This is the thought of verses 16 and 17.

Verse 16 - "Verily, verily, I say unto you, The servant is not greater than his lord; neither he that is sent greater than he that sent him."

ἀμὴν ἀμὴν λέγω ὑμῖν, οὐκ ἔστιν δοῦλος μείζων τοῦ κυρίου αὐτοῦ οὐδὲ ἀπόστολος μείζων τοῦ πέμψαντος αὐτόν.

ἀμὴν (explicative) 466.
ἀμὴν (explicative) 466.
λέγω (1st.per.sing.pres.act.ind.of *λέγω*,aoristic) 66.
ὑμῖν (dat.pl.masc.of *σύ*, indirect object of *λέγω*) 104.
οὐκ (summary negative conjunction with the indicative) 130.
ἔστιν (3d.per.sing.pres.ind.of *εἰμί*, static) 86.
δοῦλος (nom.sing.masc.of *δοῦλος*, subject of *ἔστιν*) 725.
μείζων (nom.sing.masc.of *μείζων*, predicate adjective) 916.
τοῦ (abl.sing.masc.of the article in agreement with *κυρίου*) 9.
κυρίου (abl.sing.masc.of *κύριος*, comparison) 97.
αὐτοῦ (gen.sing.masc.of *αὐτός*, relationship) 16.
οὐδὲ (disjunctive particle) 452.
ἀπόστολος (nom.sing.masc.of *ἀπόστολος*, subject of *ἔστιν*, understood) 844.
μείζων (nom.sing.masc. of *μείζων*, predicate adjective) 916.
τοῦ (abl.sing.masc.of the article in agreement with *πέμψαντος*) 9.
πέμψαντος (aor.act.part.abl.sing.masc.of *πέμπω*, substantival, comparison) 169.
αὐτόν (acc.sing.masc.of *αὐτός*, direct object of *πέμψαντος*) 16.

Translation - "Truly, truly I am telling you that a servant is not greater than his Lord, nor is an apostle greater than the One Who sent him."

Comment: Note the ablatives of comparison following the comparative adjective *μείζων*. The first statement describes the relation of the disciples to Jesus. He is Lord. They are servants, and, as such, they are not greater than He, despite the fact that He washed their feet. The last statement describes Jesus' relation to the Father (vs.3b). Jesus took a subordinate, or at least, a coordinate position with God, the Father, and reminded His disciples that they should take a subordinate position to Him. There is something else here. The Lord, since He is the Lord, can afford to take the menial position, such as that of a foot washer. Anyone who is certain that he is superior should assume the subordinate role, and, if he does, he will find happiness. This is in complete reversal to unregenerate philosophy. One cannot imagine the Pharisees, Scribes, Chief Priests and Lawyers with this philosophy.

Verse 17 - "If ye know these things, happy are ye if ye do them."

εἰ ταῦτα οἴδατε, μακάριοί ἐστε ἐὰν ποιῆτε αὐτά.

εἰ (conditional particle in a first-class condition) 337.
ταῦτα (acc.pl.neut.of *οὗτος*, direct object of *οἴδατε*) 93.
οἴδατε (2d.per.pl.pres.act.ind.of *ὁράω*, first-class condition) 144.

μακάριοί (nom.pl.masc.of μακάριος, predicate adjective) 422.
ἐστε (2d.per.pl.pres.ind.of εἰμί, futuristic) 86.
ἐὰν (conditional particle in a third-class condition) 363.
ποιῆτε (2d.per.pl.pres.act.subj.of ποιέω, third-class condition) 127.
αὐτά (acc.pl.neut.of αὐτός, direct object of ποιῆτε) 16.

Translation - "Since you understand these principles, you will be happy if you practise them."

Comment: We have here an interesting combination of conditional clauses of the first and third class. εἰ ταῦτα οἴδατε is a first-class condition. The disciples did understand the principles which our Lord had expounded, both by practice and precept in verses 1-16. The conclusion in the apodosis, μακάριοί ἐστε - "you will be happy" however does not follow necessarily. Happiness does not depend upon our understanding that the servant is subordinate to his lord. The conclusion depends upon the protasis of the third-class condition, ἐὰν ποιῆτε - "if you do them." And there is doubt about this as the third-class condition (ἐάν and the subjunctive in ποιῆτε) indicates. Jesus was assuming the truth of the protasis in the first-class condition. The disciples certainly must have understood the lesson that He was trying to teach them. But our Lord was in some doubt about the premise in the third-class condition. To understand a principle is one thing; to put it into practice is another. *Since* they knew and *if* they did, the conclusion would be certain - they would be happy. "If you do what you should do (about which there is some doubt), in the light of what, without doubt, you know to do, there is no doubt that you are going to find happiness."

Here is a sure formula for happiness. It consists of two parts: (1) be assured that you are God's child, saved by His grace, redeemed by the blood of Christ, indwelt by the Holy Spirit, geared with perfect synchronization into God's eternal plan and destined to enjoy eternal victory in Him. (2) Thus assured, take the place of a servant and play out the role in total sincerity. Wash feet, if the occasion demands it, even those of one who, like Judas, is about to get you killed. Perhaps a third condition should be added: (3) Do not become proud of your humility!

Verse 18 - "I speak not of you all: I know whom I have chosen: but that the scripture may be fulfilled, He that eateth bread with me hath lifted up his heel against me."

οὐ περὶ πάντων ὑμῶν λέγω. ἐγὼ οἶδα τίνας ἐξελεξάμην. ἀλλ' ἵνα ἡ γραφὴ πληρωθῇ, Ὁ τρώγων μου τὸν ἄρτον ἐπῆρεν ἐπ' ἐμὲ τὴν πτέρναν αὐτοῦ.

οὐ (summary negative conjunction with the indicative) 130.
περὶ (preposition with the genitive of reference) 173.
πάντων (gen.pl.masc.of πᾶς, reference) 67.
ὑμῶν (gen.pl.masc.of σύ, partitive) 104.
λέγω (1st.per.sing.pres.act.ind.of λέγω, aoristic) 66.
ἐγὼ (nom.sing.masc.of ἐγώ, subject of οἶδα) 123.

οἶδα (1st.per.sing.pres.act.ind.of ὁράω, aoristic) 144.
τίνας (acc.pl.masc.of τίς, direct object of οἶδα) 281.
ἐξελεξάμην (1st.per.sing.1st.aor.mid.ind.of ἐκλέγω, culminative) 2119.
ἀλλ' (adversative conjunction) 342.
ἵνα (conjunction introducing a purpose clause) 114.
ἡ (nom.sing.fem.of the article in agreement with γραφὴ) 9.
γραφὴ (nom.sing.fem.of γραφή, subject of πληρωθῇ) 1389.
πληρωθῇ (3d.per.sing.pass.pass.subj.of πληρόω, purpose) 115.
'Ο (nom.sing.masc.of the article in agreement with τρώγων) 9.
τρώγων (pres.act.part.nom.sing.masc.of τρώγω, substantival, subject of ἐπῆρεν) 1516.
μου (gen.sing.masc.of ἐγώ, possession) 123.
τὸν (acc.sing.masc.of the article in agreement with ἄρτον) 9.
ἄρτον (acc.sing.masc.of ἄρτος, direct object of τρώγων) 338.
ἐπῆρεν (3d.per.sing.aor.act.ind.of ἐπαίρω, culminative) 1227.
ἐπ' (preposition with the accusative of extent, hostility) 47.
ἐμὲ (acc.sing.masc.of ἐμός, extent, hostility) 1267.
τὴν (acc.sing.fem.of the article in agreement with πτέρναν) 9.

#2763 πτέρναν (acc.sing.fem.of πτέρνα, direct object of ἐπῆρεν).

heel - John 13:18.

Meaning: heel. In the figure of speech in John 13:18; to injure by kicking or to trip as in a wrestling match. Hence to injure by trickery. In Judas' case to betray Jesus to arrest, trial and death - John 13:18. This analysis is based upon the entire figure ἐπῆρεν ἐπ' ἐμὲ τὴν πτέρναν αὐτοῦ.

αὐτοῦ (gen.sing.masc.of αὐτός, possession) 16.

Translation - "I am not talking about all of you. I know whom I have chosen, but, in order that the Scripture might be fulfilled - the one eating my bread has lifted up his heel against me."

Comment: οὐ περὶ πάντων ὑμῶν is emphasized. In fact Jesus was speaking about all of them except Judas. We have another culminative aorist in ἐξελεξάμην serving like a perfect tense. Jesus knew *whom* He had chosen and He also knew *why* He had chosen Judas, not for apostleship but for discipleship. Eleven were chosen (#2119), not only as disciples and apostles, but to salvation as well. Judas was chosen as a disciple (John 6:70,71). *Cf.* also John 15:16,19; 17:12; Acts 1:2. *Cf.*#2119 for passages where spiritual salvation is the object of election. Out Lord's total control of the situation comes out here. To sit down with friends at the table to enjoy a meal and then rise to wash the feet of his betrayer would grade Jesus down as one who was incredibly naive, if He had been unaware of Judas' intent. But these events took place with Jesus' full knowledge of who they were and what their individual destinies would be. Indeed the destiny of each was a result of the will of Him who sat with them at the table. Judas and his perfidy was no surprize to Jesus. Why then did He choose Judas? The ἵνα clause of purpose with the aorist subjunctive tells us why. "In order that the Scripture" - specifically Psalm 41:9 (verse 10 in the LXX) - "might be fulfilled. . . " He did it. We have here an example of breviloquent brachylogy - the result of a faster progress of mind than speech. The mind races ahead and compressed words do not always follow syntactical principles. Jesus did not finish the sentence. Instead He broke off, after πληρωθῇ to quote the passage to which He referred - "The one eating my food tripped me up." He, Who inspired the writing of Psalm 41:9 in the first place was thus aware of its contents and He chose Judas, in conformity to His own prophecy.

Hugh J. Schonfield in *The Passover Plot* has argued that Jesus had nothing to do with the inspiration of the Scriptures, but that He studied them with remarkable diligence and then deliberately maneuvered events with the result that they were fulfilled. However, Schonfield denies that his theory applies to the death and resurrection of Jesus, Who is accused of having feigned the former in order also to play-act the latter. This is the old "Swoon theory" - that Jesus fainted upon the cross and appeared to be dead, and that regained consciousness in the tomb and walked out to create His Messianic image among the credulous, from the roster of which latter group, Schonfield, of course, exempts himself. What he has said is neither new nor startling, which makes the sale of his book all the more remarkable, until we remember that unregenerates in the closing days of the age despise Jesus and find that the best way to damn Him is with faint praise. The stage production "Jesus Christ - Super Star" is another example, in which our Lord is praised as a great man, but in which His resurrection is denied. The Swoon theory of the crucifixion and resurrection has long since been destroyed and need not occupy us here.

Verse 19 - "Now I tell you before it come, that,when it is come to pass, ye may believe that I am he."

ἀπ' ἄρτι λέγω ὑμῖν πρὸ τοῦ γενέσθαι, ἵνα πιστεύσησατε ὅταν γένηται ὅτι ἐγώ εἰμι.

ἀπ' (preposition with a temporal adverb in a time expression) 70.
ἄρτι (temporal adverb) 320.
λέγω (1st.per.sing.pres.act.ind.of λέγω, futuristic) 66.
ὑμῖν (dat.pl.masc.of σύ, indirect object of λέγω) 104.
πρὸ (preposition with the ablative of time separation) 442.
τοῦ (abl.sing.neut.of the article, time separation) 9.
γενέσθαι (aor.mid.inf.of γίνομαι, noun use, articular, time separation) 113.
ἵνα (conjunction with the subjunctive in a purpose clause) 114.
πιστεύητε (2d.per.pl.pres.act.subj.of πιστεύω, purpose) 734.
ὅταν (conjunction introducing an indefinite temporal clause) 436.
γένηται (3d.per.sing.aor.mid.subj.of γίνομαι, indefinite temporal clause).
ὅτι (conjunction introducing an object clause in indirect discourse) 211.
ἐγώ (nom.sing.masc.of ἐγώ, subject of εἰμι) 123.
εἰμι (1st.per.sing.pres.ind.of εἰμί, static) 86.

Translation - "From now on I am going to tell you before it happens in order that, when it happens, you will believe that I AM."

Comment: ἀπ' ἄρτι - "from this time on" where we have the preposition of the ablative with a temporal adverb. *Cf.* Mt.26:58; 27:55 where it occurs with a spatial adverb. There are nine instances of πρὸ τοῦ and the infinitive in the New Testament, *viz.,* Mt.6:8; Lk.2:21; 22:15; John 1:48; 13:19; 17:5; Acts 23:15; Gal.2:12; 3:23. There are only three articular infinitives in John's gospel, listed above. Note the futuristic present in λέγω. Jesus is promising that from that time forward, He is going to tell His disciples what is going to heppen. Why? The ἵνα clause of purpose tells us. "In order that they will continue to believe" (present tense in the infinitive). When will they find it possible to begin to believe? The ὅταν indefinite temporal clause tells us. "When (and if) it happens. . . " then His disciples would remember that He had already told them that it would happen and they would come to the conclusion in the object clause, introduced by ὅτι - "that I AM" the One Who first introduced Himself to Moses on Mount Sinai (Exodus 3:14). Here is another of the ἐγὼ εἰμί passages that identify Jesus as the Messiah. *Cf.* John 4:26 for a partial list. *Cf.* John 8:58 and comment.

The disciples came to understand what Jesus was talking about, only with the benefit of hindsight and the reception and filling of the Holy Spirit (*Cf.* John 13:29; Acts 1:15-26). At the moment they did not know, even after Jesus gave the sop to Judas, who then left the room (John 13:21-30).

The relation of Judas to God's plan of redemption is a difficult problem. Efforts to make the Calvinism of the matter more palatable to the reasonable man fall short. We must only bow our heads like little children and say that we do not know, but that our faith assures that our Sovereign God makes no blunders and is guilty of nothing unethical or unjust.

Verse 20 - "Verily, verily I say unto you, He that receiveth whomsoever I send receiveth me; and he that receiveth me, receiveth him that sent me."

ἀμὴν ἀμὴν λέγω ὑμῖν, ὁ λαμβάνων ἄν τινα πέμψω ἐμὲ λαμβάνει, ὁ δὲ ἐμὲ λαμβάνων λαμβάνει τὸν πέμψαντά με.

ἀμὴν (explicative) 466.
ἀμὴν (explicative) 466.
λέγω (1st.per.sing.pres.act.ind.of λέγω, aoristic) 66.
ὑμῖν (dat.pl.masc.of σύ, indirect object of λέγω) 104.
ὁ (nom.sing.masc. of the article in agreement with λαμβάνων) 9.
λαμβάνων (pres.act.part.nom.sing.masc.of λαμβάνω, substantival, subject of λαμβάνει) 533.
ἄν (contingency particle in an indefinite conditional clause) 205.
τινα (acc.sing.masc.of τις, direct object of λαμβάνων) 486.
πέμψω (1st.per.sing.aor.act.subj.of πέμπω, conditional clause) 169.
ἐμὲ (acc.sing.masc.of ἐμός, direct object of λαμβάνει) 1267.
λαμβάνει (3d.per.sing.pres.act.ind.of λαμβάνω, static) 533.
ὁ (nom.sing.masc.of the article in agreement with λαμβάνων) 9.
δὲ (continuative conjunction) 11.

ἐμὲ (acc.sing.masc.of *ἐμός*, direct object of *λαμβάνων*) 1267.

λαμβάνων (pres.act.part.nom.sing.masc.of *λαμβάνω*, substantival, subject of *λαμβάνει*) 533.

λαμβάνει (3d.per.sing.pres.act.ind.of *λαμβάνω*, static) 533.

τὸν (acc.sing.masc.of the article in agreement with *πέμψαντά*) 9.

πέμψαντά (aor.act.part.acc.sing.masc.of *πέμπω*, substantival, direct object of *λαμβάνει*) 169.

με (acc.sing.masc.of *ἐγώ*, direct object of *πέμψαντά*) 123.

Translation - "Truly, truly I am telling you that the one who receives whom I send, receives me, and the one reciving me, receives him who sent me."

Comment: The object of *λαμβάνων* is the conditional clause *ἄν τινα πέμψω - ἄν* and the subjunctive in *πέμψω* indicates doubt as to whom will be sent, but no doubt that someone will be sent. The reception of the one sent, who is not greater than the sender (vs.16), calls for faith on the part of the receiver, since he is in doubt as to who the one sent is.But the faith of the receiver is not in the one who is sent, but in the greater sender. Thus whoever receives Christ also receives the One Who sent Christ. The Christian's faith in God dictates that He will send only someone whom it it safe for us to receive. Hence we receive Christ only if we are convinced that He truly was sent from God. This work of convincing the Christian as to Who Christ is and why He came is that of the Holy Spirit (John 16:7-11).

In the same way, my faith in Christ dictates that He Who was sent from God, will, in turn, send to me only a faithful messenger. Hence I accept His messenger if I am convinced that the messenger truly came from Him. I settle the first question by pointing to His resurrection. Jesus truly came from God or He would not have risen from the dead (Rom.1:4). I settle the second question about the alleged messenger from Christ by what he says about the Christ whom he says has sent him. If he denies what Christ taught, I conclude that Christ did not send him. If Christ had not risen from the dead I would have concluded that God did not send Him, and would thus be under no moral obligation to receive Him, just as I am under no moral obligation to receive one who denies the claims of Christ as He Himself set them forth. To reason the proposition in reverse, if the human messenger who claims to speak for Christ tells me that Christ rose from the dead on the third day and presents all of the other biblical evidence about Christ that He Himself presented, I conclude that Christ sent Him, and am willing to accept him. So I trust in Christ,the resurrected Son of God, confident that Jesus is indeed God's Son because, had He not been, God would not have raised Him from the dead. But God did raise Him from the dead and my faith now is in the God Who sent Christ and proved it to me by raising Him from the dead.

The Betrayer is Pointed Out

(Matthew 26:21-25; Mark 14:18-21; Luke 22:21-23; John 13:21-30)

Mark 14:18 - "And as they sat and did eat Jesus said, Verily I say unto you, One of you which eateth with me shall betray me."

καὶ ἀνακειμένων αὐτῶν καὶ ἐσθιόντων ὁ Ἰησοῦς εἶπεν, Ἀμὴν λέγω ὑμῖν ὅτι εἷς ἐξ ὑμῶν παραδώσει με, ὁ ἐσθίων μετ' ἐμοῦ.

καὶ (continuative conjunction) 14.
ἀνακειμένων (pres.mid.part.gen.pl.masc.of *ἀνάκειμαι*, genitive absolute) 790.
αὐτῶν (gen.pl.masc.of *αὐτός*, genitive absolute) 16.
καὶ (adjunctive conjunction joining participles) 14.
ἐσθιόντων (pres.act.part.gen.pl.masc.of *ἐσθίω*, genitive absolute) 610.
ὁ (nom.sing.masc.of the article in agreement with *Ἰησοῦς*) 9.
Ἰησοῦς (nom.sing.masc.of *Ἰησοῦς*, subject of *εἶπεν*) 3.
εἶπεν (3d.per.sing.aor.act.ind.of *εἶπον*, constative) 155.
Ἀμὴν (explicative) 466.
λέγω (1st.per.sing.pres.act.ind.of *λέγω*, aoristic) 66.
ὑμῖν (dat.pl.masc.of *σύ*, indirect object of *λέγω*) 104.
ὅτι (conjunction introducing an object clause in indirect discourse) 211.
εἷς (nom.sing.masc.of *εἷς*, subj.of *παραδώσει*) 469.
ἐξ (preposition with the partitive genitive) 19.
ὑμῶν (gen.pl.masc.of *σύ*, partitive) 104.
παραδώσει (3d.per.sing.fut.act.ind.of *παραδίδωμι*, predictive) 368.
με (acc.sing.masc.of *ἐγώ*, direct object of *παραδώσει*) 123.
ὁ (nom.sing.masc.of the article in agreement with *ἐσθίων*) 9.
ἐσθίων (pres.act.part.nom.sing.masc.of *ἐσθίω*, substantival, apposition) 610.
μετ' (preposition with the genitive of accompaniment) 50.
ἐμοῦ (gen.sing.masc.of *ἐμός*, accompaniment) 1267.

Translation - "And as they were sitting at the table and eating, Jesus said to them, 'Truly I am telling you that one of you who is eating with me will betray me.' "

Comment: He had said before that He would be betrayed (Mt.17:22; 20:18; 26:2; John 6:70,71; Mt.20:19; Mk.9:31; 10:33; Lk.9:44; 18:32. Now for the first time Jesus revealed that the traitor was one of the Twelve, one who, at that moment, was eating with Him at the table. *Cf.* Mt.26:21; Lk.22:21.

Verse 19 - "And they began to be sorrowful and to say unto him, one by one, Is it I? And another said, Is it I?"

ἤρξαντο λυπεῖσθαι καί λέγειν αὐτῷ εἷς κατὰ εἷς, Μήτι ἐγώ;

ἤρξαντο (3d.per.pl.aor.mid.ind.of *ἄρχω*, ingressive) 383.
λυπεῖσθαι (pres.pass.inf.of *λυπέω*, epexegetical) 1113.
καὶ (adjunctive conjunction joining infinitives) 14.
λέγειν (pres.act.inf.of *λέγω*, epexegetical) 66.
αὐτῷ (dat.sing.masc.of *αὐτός*, indirect object of *λέγειν*) 16.

εἷς (nom.sing.masc.of εἷς, parenthetic nominative, distributive use) 469.
κατὰ (preposition with the nominative, used adverbially, distributive) 98.
εἷς (nom.sing.masc.of εἷς, parenthetic nominative, distributive) 469.
Μήτι (negative conjunction, direct question, expecting a negative reply) 676.
ἐγώ (nom.sing.masc.of ἐγώ, subject of εἰμί understood) 123.

Translation - "Their feelings were hurt and they began to say to Him, one at a time, 'I am not the one am I?' "

Comment: *Cf.* comment on Mt.26:22. These men were Galileans, not cowards under ordinary circumstances, but perhaps cowed by the pomp and circumstance of the capitol city and the police power of the Jewish Establishment. Perhaps each one had entertained some personal misgivings about his loyalty to Jesus, when the critical issue was finally joined. Their questions, "Not I . . . ?!" which call for a negative reply reflected the fear which they were unwilling to express that Jesus might say to them, "Yes."

Verse 20 - "And he answered and said unto them, It is one of the twelve, that dippeth with me in the dish."

ὁ δὲ εἶπεν αὐτοῖς, Εἷς *(ἐκ) τῶν δώδεκα, ὁ ἐμβαπτόμενος μετ' ἐμοῦ εἰς τὸ τρύβλιον.*

ὁ (nom.sing.masc.of the article, subject of εἶπεν) 9.
δὲ (continuative conjunction) 11.
εἶπεν (3d.per.sing.aor.act.ind.of εἶπον, constative) 155.
αὐτοῖς (dat.pl.masc.of αὐτός, indirect object of εἶπεν) 16.
Εἷς (nom.sing.masc.of εἷς, predicate nominative, with subject and copula understood) 469.
τῶν (gen.pl.masc.of the article in agreement with δώδεκα, partitive) 9.
δώδεκα (indeclin., partitive genitive) 820.
ὁ (nom.sing.masc.of the article in agreement with ἐμβαπτόμενος) 9.
ἐμβαπτόμενος (pres.mid.part.nom.sing.masc.of ἐμβάπτω, substantival, apposition) 1573.
μετ' (preposition with the genitive of accompaniment) 50.
ἐμοῦ (gen.sing.masc.of ἐμός, accompaniment) 1267.
εἰς (preposition with the accusative of extent) 140.
τὸ (acc.sing.neut.of the article in agreement with τρύβλιον) 9.
τρύβλιον (acc.sing.neut.of τρύβλιον, extent) 1574.

Translation - "And He said to them, 'One of the Twelve, dipping with me into the dish.' "

Comment: There is no subject or copulative verb here, to go with the predicate nominative Εἷς, in Jesus' response to their Μήτι ἐγώ. No crucial point is involved, but, in order to sharpen the wits of the beginning Greek grammarian, we note that John has used ἐν in composition with the verb ἐμβαπτόμενος and εἰς with the accusative of extent in the phrase that follows. Whether τρύβλιον is an accusative of extent, after εἰς, or a case of εἰς with the accusative, in its original static use, serving for ἐν with the locative of place is the question. Jesus and Judas Iscariot were not "in the dish" dipping "into" its contents. But the act of dipping "into" the contents of the dish was certainly "in" the dish. We do not enter into a dish and then dip in it. Orginally there was only ἐν with the accusative. Later εἰς evolved from ἐν, through the intermediate states of ἐνς, ἐσ and finally εἰς, while ἐν persisted from Homer down. When the oblique cases developepd ἐν came to be used with the locative, instrumental and dative and the more recently developed εἰς with the original accusative. The original static use of εἰς with the accusative for ἐν with the locative is found with some frequence in the κοινή of the New Testamentd.

A variant reading has ἓν before τρύβλιον on the basis of which Goodspeed and Montgomery have translated "in the same dish with me" (Goodspeed) while Montgomery has "into the same dish with me." Metzger and his colleagues have opted for εἰς τὸ τρύβλιον with a B degree of certitude. "The reading ἓν seems to have arisen from assimilation either to the Matthean parallel (26.23) or to the ἐν in composition with the participle. The reading εἰς τὸ ἓν πρύβλιον ("into the same dish"), which emphasizes the baseness of the act, appears to be a secondary heightening of the passage." (Metzger, *A Textual Commentary on the Greek New Testament*, 113). *Cf.* comments on Mt.26:23.

Verse 21 - "The Son of Man indeed goeth, as it is written of him: but woe to that man by whom the Son of Man is betrayed! Good were it for that man if he had never been born."

ὅτι ὁ μὲν υἱὸς τοῦ ἀνθρώπου ὑπάγει καθὼς γέγραπται περὶ αὐτοῦ, οὐαὶ δὲ τῷ ἀνθρώπῳ ἐκείνῳ δι' οὗ ὁ υἱὸς τοῦ ἀνθρώπου παραδίδοται. καλὸν αὐτῷ εἰ οὐκ ἐγεννήθη ὁ ἄνθρωπος ἐκεῖνος.

ὅτι (conjunction introducing a causal clause) 211.
ὁ (nom.sing.masc.of the article in agreement with υἱὸς) 9.
μὲν (particle of affirmation) 300.
υἱὸς (nom.sing.masc.of υἱός, subject of ὑπάγει) 5.
τοῦ (gen.sing.masc.of the article in agreement with ἀνθρώπου) 9.
ἀνθρώπου (gen.sing.masc.of ἄνθρωπος, designation) 341.
ὑπάγει (3d.per.sing.pres.act.ind.of ὑπάγω, futuristic) 364.
καθνὼς (adverbial) 1348.

γέγραπται (3d.per.sing.perf.pass.ind.of γράφω, intensive) 156.
περὶ (preposition with the genitive of reference) 173.
αὐτοῦ (gen.sing.masc.of αὐτός, reference) 16.
οὐαὶ (exclamation) 936.
δὲ (adversative conjunction) 11.
τῷ (dat.sing.masc.of the article in agreement with ἀνθρώπῳ) 9.
ἀνθρώπῳ (dat.sing.masc.of ἄνθρωπος, personal disadvantage) 341.
ἐκείνῳ (dat.sing.masc.of ἐκεῖνος, in agreement with ἀνθρώπῳ) 246.

δι' (preposition with the genitive, intermediate agent) 118.
οὗ (gen.sing.masc.of ὅς, intermediate agent) 65.
ὁ (nom.sing.masc.of the article in agreement with υἱὸς) 9.
υἱὸς (nom.sing.masc.of υἱός, subject of παραδίδοται) 5.
τοῦ (gen.sing.masc.of the article in agreement with ἀνθρώπου) 9.
ἀνθρώπου (gen.sing.masc.of ἄνθρωπος, designation) 341.
παραδίδοται (3d.per.sing.pres.pass.ind.of παραδίδομαι, futuristic) 368.
καλὸν (acc.sing.neut.of καλός, predicate adverb) 296.
αὐτῷ (dat.sing.masc.of αὐτός, reference) 16.
εἰ (conditional particle in a second-class, contrary to fact condition, elliptical) 337.
οὐκ (summary negative conjunction with the indicative) 130.
ἐγεννήθη (3d.per.sing.aor.pass.ind.of γεννάω, second-class condition) 8.
ὁ (nom.sing.masc.of the article in agreement with ἄνθρωπος) 9 .
ἄνθρωπος (nom.sing.masc.of ἄνθρωπος, subject of ἐγεννήθη) 341.
ἐκεῖνος (nom.sing.masc.of ἐκεῖνος, in agreement with ἄνθρωπος) 246.

Translation - "Because the Son of Man indeed is going away, just as it is written, about Him, but woe to that man by whom the Son of Man is going to be betrayed! It would have been good for him if that man had not been born."

Comment: ὅτι here is causal. Jesus had just said that one of His twelve dinner guests would betray Him, because when He goes He must go in complete accord with prophetic Scriptures which, in Psalm 41:9, predicted these precise events. μὲν strengthens the affirmation. καθὼς γέγραπται - "exactly as it was written and therefore now a part of the inspired record." περὶ αὐτοῦ - a genitive of reference, which is proof that Psalm 41:9 must be applied to the Son of Man. Following the adversative (δὲ) and Jesus' pronouncement of doom, we have a second-class contrary to fact condition, with εἰ and the aorist indicative in the protasis, although the apodosis lacks a verb. It is all contrary to fact - "If that man had not been born (but he was) it would be better for him (which it will not be)." The form of the condition (εἰ οὐκ ἐγεννήθη) has to do only with the statement, not with the facts. Judas had been born, unfortunately for him. Jesus is saying that it would have been better for him if that were not true.

Judas, when viewed from our human viewpoint, is an object of pity, but let us not charge God with folly when we plead his defense. The problem of Judas Iscariot and of Pharaoh (Rom.9:17-20) is one of the inscrutabilities which confronts the Calvinist. The seminaries are full of young Ph.D's in the philosophy of religion and theology who are eager to eisegete scripture in order to bring the divine revelation into line with their human reason. When they have it all figured out, the are the wise and prudent, from whom the truth is hidden, rather than the babes, to whom it is revealed (Mt.11:25: Lk.10:21). *Cf.* Mt.26:24. In order to keep the parallel accounts together, we go now to Luke 22:21-23 and return to Luke 22:17-20 later.

Luke 22:21 - "But behold the hand of him that betrayeth me is with me on the table."

πλὴν ἰδοὺ ἡ χεὶρ τοῦ παραδιδόντος με μετ' ἐμοῦ ἐπὶ τῆς τραπέζης.

πλὴν (adversative conjunction) 944.
ἰδοὺ (exclamation) 95.
ἡ (nom.sing.fem.of the article in agreement with χεὶρ) 9.
χεὶρ (nom.sing.fem.of χείρ, subject of ἐστίν understood) 308.
τοῦ (gen.sing.masc.of the article in agreement with παραδιδόντος) 9.
παραδιδόντος (pres.act.part.gen.sing.masc.of παραδίδωμι, substantival, possession) 368.
με (acc.sing.masc.of ἐγώ, direct object of παραδιδόντος) 123.
μετ' (preposition with the genitive of accompaniment) 50.
ἐμοῦ (gen.sing.masc.of ἐμός, accompaniment) 1267.
ἐπὶ (preposition with the genitive of place description) 47.
τῆς (gen.sing.fem.of the article in agreement with τραπέζης) 9.
τραπέζης (gen.sing.fem.of τράπεζα, place description) 1176.

Translation - "But, Look! The hand of the one who will betray me with me upon the table!"

Comment: πλὴν, the strong adversative reveals the irony in the situation. Jesus had just spoken of the cup of the new covenant which would be in force by means of His blood, which He would soon shed for His disciples. Now, as if in surprize, though the omniscient God can never be surprized, He points to the hand of Judas upon the table not far from his own - the betrayer's hand upon the table with the hand destined to be nail pierced.

Jesus had a great desire to eat the last supper with His disciples in order to fulfill the prophecy of Psalm 41:9, and to endow the meal with its spiritual significance for the saints, pointing them back to Calvary and forward to His second coming (verse 17). The irony was that the traiterous hand of Judas had already reached out and grasped and pocketed the purchase price of thirty pieces of silver. Add to this the fact that Jesus had washed Judas' feet and was soon to designate him as the honored guest with the sop. Such irony justifies Jesus' strong statement in verse 22. *Cf.* Mt.26:21; Mk.14:18.

Verse 22 - "And truly the Son of Man goeth as it was determined; but woe unto that man by whom he is betrayed!"

ὅτι ὁ υἱὸς μὲν τοῦ ἀνθρώπου κατὰ τὸ ὡρισμένον πορεύεται, πλὴν οὐαὶ τῷ ἀνθρώπῳ ἐκείνῳ δι' οὗ παραδίδοται.

ὅτι (conjunction introducing a coordinate causal clause) 211.
ὁ (nom.sing.masc.of the article in agreement with υἱὸς) 9.
μὲν (particle of affirmation) 300.
τοῦ (gen.sing.masc.of the article in agreement with ἀνθρώπου) 9.
ἀνθρώπου (gen.sing.masc.of ἄνθρωπος, designation) 341.
κατὰ (preposition with the accusative, standard rule) 98.
τὸ (acc.sing.neut.of the article in agreement with ὡρισμένον) 9.

#2764 ὡρισμένον (perf.pass.part.acc.sing.neut.of ὁρίζω, substantival, standard

determine - Luke 22:22; Acts 17:26; 11:29.
limit - Heb.4:7.
deliver - Acts 2:23.
ordain - Acts 17:31; 10:42.
declare - Rom.1:4.

Meaning: To ordain, decree, establish by sovereign order that specific events will occur - To appoint a day or time when something shall take place - Heb.4:7; Acts 17:26. With reference to the death of Christ for our sins - Acts 2:23; Lk.22:22. Christ is ordained as Judge - Acts 17:31; 10:42. Christ, the Son of God was ratified as such by the resurrection - Rom.1:4. With reference to the decision of the apostles to send relief to the brethren - Acts 11:29.

πορεύεται (3d.per.sing.pres.mid.ind.of πορεύομαι, futuristic) 170.
πλὴν (adversative conjunction, antithetical with μὲν) 944.
οὐαὶ (exclamation) 936.
τῷ (dat.sing.masc.of the article in agreement with ἀνθρώπῳ) 9.
ἀνθρώπῳ (dat.sing.masc.of ἄνθρωπος, personal disadvantage) 342.
ἐκείνῳ (dat.sing.masc.of ἐκεῖνος, in agreement with ἀνθρώπῳ) 246.
δι' (preposition with the genitive of intermediate agent) 118.
οὗ (gen.sing.masc.of ὅς, intermediate agent) 65.
παδαδίδοται (3d.per.sing.pres.pass.ind.of παραδίδωμι, futuristic) 368.

Translation - "Because the Son of Man will surely go in keeping with that which has been decreed, but woe to that man through whom He will be betrayed."

Comment: *Cf.* Mt.26:24; Mk.14:21. Matthew and Mark mention the fact that the Scripture contains the prophecy. Luke goes behind the inspiration of Scripture to the decree of the Godhead itself, on the basis of which the Scripture foretold the event which Christ was about to go out to fulfill. Jesus was saying in effect, "I am going out to obey the eternal decree (Luke 22:22) and thus fulfill the Scritpures (Mt.26:24; Mk.14:21)." κατὰ followed by a substantival participle in the accusative case is interesting and a little rare.

The study of ὁρίζω (#2764) is rich in support of the doctrine of divine decree. The times and seasons are marked out in advance; the judgment day has already been set with specificity. Christ was specifically marked for death and then to be raised from the dead after which He will act as the Judge of all the earth. There is much wonderful preaching material here for those who shudder to think of a random universe and who thus are able to believe in Eph.1:11b, as the only viable alternative. It is true that on the surface Jesus means here that He is going to His death. This He means, but He means much more. For it has been ordained (perfect tense in ὡρισμένον), not only that He should die for our sins (Acts 2:23; Lk.22:22) but also that He should rise from the dead (Rom.1:4), and judge the world (Acts 10:42; 17:31). The entire redemptive process is in view here, not His death only. Had Jesus died only and not been resurrected and elevated to the judgment throne, Judas' betrayal would have gone unpunished. Judas betrayed a Galilean carpenter, Who was also the incarnate Son of God, the Redeeming

Lamb, the Victor over death, the Judge of all (John 5:22) and the Eternal Sovereign of all eternity. Those who plan to betray someone had better select a victim a little nearer their size. Not only *οὐαὶ τῷ ἀνθρώπῳ ἐκείνῳ δι' οὗ παραδίδοται*, but also *οὐαὶ τῷ ἀνθρώπῳ ἐκείνῳ ὁ οὐκ πιστεύων εἰς τὸ ὄνομα αὐτοῦ*. They will all share a place in hell together. How humble should the saints be who, by His grace, have been drawn by the Holy Spirit to Him and have been enabled to believe.

Verse 23 - "And they began to enquire among themselves, which of them it was that should do this thing."

καὶ αὐτοὶ ἤρξαντο συζητεῖν πρὸς ἑαυτοὺς τὸ τίς ἄρα εἴη ἐξ αὐτῶν ὁ τοῦτο μέλλων πράσσειν.

καὶ (continuative conjunction) 14.
αὐτοὶ (nom.pl.masc.of *αὐτός*, subject of *ἤρξαντο*) 16.
ἤρξαντο (3d.per.pl.aor.mid.ind.of *ἄρχω*, ingressive) 383.
συζητεῖν (pres.act.inf.of *συζητέω*, epexegetical) 2060.
πρὸς (preposition with the accusative, after a verb of speaking) 197.
ἑαυτοὺς (acc.pl.masc.of *ἑαυτός*, extent after a verb of speaking) 288.
τὸ (acc.sing.neut.of the article, introducing the indirect question) 9.
τίς (nom.sing.masc.of *τίς*, subject of *εἴη*) 281.
ἄρα (illative particle in indirect question) 995.
εἴη (3d.per.sing.pres.opt.of *εἰμί*, in indirect question, deliberative) 86.
ἐξ (preposition with the partitive genitive) 19.
αὐτῶν (gen.pl.masc.of *αὐτός*, partitive genitive) 16.
ὁ (nom.sing.masc.of the article in agreement with *μέλλων*) 9.
τοῦτο (acc.sing.neut.of *οὗτος*, direct object of *πράσσειν*) 93.
μέλλων (pres.act.part.nom.sing.masc.of *μέλλω*, substantival, predicate nominative) 206.
πράσσειν (pres.act.inf.of *πράσσω*, epexegetical) 1943.

Translation - "And they began to inquire among themselves which one of them might be the one who was about to do this."

Comment: Note the personal use of *αὐτοὶ*. The two infinitives are epexegetical, *i.e.* they complete the verbs with which they are joined. The disciples "began *to inquire*" about who was "about *to do* this." Note the indirect question, introduced by *τὸ*. The neuter article in the accusative with indirect question is common in the N.T. *ἄρα* heightens the speculation, already present in the deliberative optative in *εἴη*. *Cf.* Mt.26;22; Mk.14:19. They not only asked each other, but they also asked Jesus.

We turn now to John's account of this episode in John 13:21-30.

John 13:21 - "When Jesus had thus said, he was troubled in spirit, and testified, and said, Verily, verily, I say unto you, that one of you shall betray me."

Ταῦτα εἰπὼν ὁ Ἰησοῦς ἐταράχθη τῷ πνεύματι καὶ ἐμαρτύρησεν καὶ εἶπεν,

Ἀμὴν ἀμὴν λέγω ὑμῖν ὅτι εἷς ἐξ ὑμῶν παραδώσει με.

Ταῦτα (acc.pl.neut.of οὗτος, direct object of εἰπὼν) 93.
εἰπὼν (aor.act.part.nom.sing.masc.of εἶπον, adverbial, temporal) 155.
ὁ (nom.sing.masc.of the article in agreement with Ἰησοῦς) 9.
Ἰησοῦς (nom.sing.masc.of Ἰησοῦς, subject of ἐταράχθη, ἐμαρτύρησεν, εἶπεν and λέγω) 3.
ἐταράχθη (3d.per.sing.aor.pass.ind.of ταράσσω, constative) 149.
τῷ (loc.sing.neut.of the article in agreement with πνεύματι) 9.
πνεύματι (loc.sing.neut.of πνεῦμα, sphere) 83.
καὶ (adjunctive conjunction joining verbs) 14.
ἐμαρτύρησεν (3d.per.sing.aor.act.ind.of μαρτυρέω, ingressive) 1471.
καὶ (adjunctive conjunction joining verbs) 14.
εἶπεν (3d.per.sing.aor.act.ind.of εἶπον, constative) 155.
Ἀμὴν (explicative) 466.
ἀμὴν (explicative) 466.
λέγω (1st.per.sing.pres.act.ind.of λέγω, aoristic) 66d.
ὑμῖν (dat.pl.masc.of σύ, indirect object of λέγω) 104.
ὅτι (conjunction introducing an object clause in indirect discourse) 211.
εἷς (nom.sing.masc.of εἷς, subject of παραδώσει) 469.
ἐξ (preposition with the partitive genitive) 19.
ὑμῶν (gen.pl.masc.of σύ, partitive genitive) 104.
παραδώσει (3d.pers.sing.fut.act.ind.of παραδίδωμι predictive) 368.
με (acc.sing.masc.of ἐγώ, direct object of παραδώσει) 123.

Translation - "When Jesus had said these things, He became emotionally upset and He began to witness and said, 'Truly, truly I am telling you that one of you is going to betray me.' "

Comment: Ταῦτα refers to Jesus' remarks in verses 18-20, in which He had said that the supper scene was being acted out to fulfill scripture in Psalm 41:9. That statement was followed by an emotional upset - ἐταράχθη τῷ πνεύματι - *Cf.*#149 for the basic meaning of ταράσσω, in this case followed by a locative of sphere. The agitation was not physical, but intellectual and emotional. He had experienced this at the tomb of Lazarus (John 11:33) and as He reflected on His coming passion (John 12:27). These episodes are evidence of His real humanity. Fear, sorrow, disappointment - - fear of the agonies of Calvary, sorrow because of the death of His dear friend, Lazarus, disappointment that Judas, one of His own disciples should turn against Him.

And yet Jesus was the Coauthor of redemption's plan which involved His death upon a cross, His conquest over death at the tomb of Lazarus, and now the prediction of Judas' perdidy. The hypostatic union of deity and humanity in the incarnate Christ is something to be accepted *a priori* if we are to be Christians. We cannot provide a logical rationale, but evidences of both humanity and deity are juxtaposed in the divine text on many occasions.

Note pleonasm in ἐμαρτύρησεν καὶ εἶπεν - a redundant peculiarity of the Greek. We see it often in ἀποκριθεὶς ὁ Ἰησοῦς εἶπεν.

The fact that Jesus understood the scenario that would be enacted during the ensuing twenty four hours, indeed He had ordained it, and that it involved Judas and his sad fate, did not prevent Jesus from being disturbed when He reflected upon it. There is no Scripture to indicate that Judas did what he did unwillingly or under coercion.

Verse 22 - "Then the disciples looked one on another, doubting of whom he spake."

ἔβλεπον εἰς ἀλλήλους οἱ μαθηταὶ ἀπορούμενοι περὶ τίνος λέγει.

ἔβλεπον (3d.per.pl.imp.act.ind.of βλέπω, inceptive) 499.
εἰς (preposition with the accusative of extent) 140.
ἀλλήλους (acc.pl.masc.of ἀλλήλων, extent) 1487.
οἱ (nom.pl.masc.of the article in agreement with μαθηταὶ) 9.
μαθηταὶ (nom.pl.masc.of μαθητής, subject of ἔβλεπον) 421.
ἀπορούμενοι (pres.mid.part.nom.pl.masc.of απορέομαι, adverbial, causal) 2254.
περὶ (preposition with the genitive of reference) 173.
τίνος (gen.sing.masc.of τίς, reference) 281.
λέγει (3d.per.sing.pres.act.ind.of λέγω, historical) 66.

Translation - "The disciples began to look at each other because they were in doubt about the identity of the one to whom He had reference."

Comment: Note the inceptive imperfect in ἔβλεπον. The participle is causal. Jesus' remark was clear about the betrayal but cryptic about who the betrayer would be, except to say that it would be one of the twelve. Because none of them, except Judas, knew whom He meant, they began to look at each other, perhaps hoping to find a clue on the face of the guilty one. Around and around the table the questioning and troubled glances flitted. There was no way to tell of whom Jesus was speaking. Note the basic concept in ἀπορούμενοι (#2254). *Cf.* Mat.26:22; Mk.14:19; Lk.22:23.

Verse 23 - "Now there was leaning on Jesus' bosom one of his disciples, whom Jesus loved."

ἦν ἀνακείμενος εἷς ἐκ τῶν μαθητῶν αὐτοῦ ἐν τῷ κόλπῳ τοῦ Ἰησοῦ, ὃν ἠγάπα ὁ Ἰησοῦς.

ἦν (3d.per.sing.imp.ind.of εἰμί, imperfect periphrastic) 86.
ἀνακείμενος (pres.mid.part.nom.sing.masc.of ἀνάκειμαι, imperfect periphrastic) 790.
εἷς (nom.sing.masc.of εἷς, subject of ἦν) 469.
ἐκ (preposition with the partitive genitive) 19.
τῶν (gen.pl.masc.of the article in agreement with μαθητῶν) 9.
μαθητῶν (gen.pl.masc.of μαθητής, partitive genitive) 421.
αὐτοῦ (gen.sing.masc.of αὐτός, relationship) 16.
ἐν (preposition with the locative of place where) 80.

τῷ (loc.sing.masc.of the article in agreement with κόλπῳ) 9.
κόλπῳ (loc.sing.masc.of κόλπος, place where) 1702.
τοῦ (gen.sing.masc.of the article in agreement with Ἰησοῦ) 9.
Ἰησοῦ (gen.sing.masc.of Ἰησοῦς, possession) 3.
ὅν (acc.sing.masc.of ὅς, direct object of ἠγάπα) 65.
ἠγάπα (3d.per.sing.imp.act.ind.of ἀπαγάω, progressive description) 540.
ὁ (nom.sing.masc.of the article in agreement with Ἰησοῦς) 9.
Ἰησοῦς (nom.sing.masc.of Ἰησοῦς, subject of ἠγάπα) 3.

Translation - "One of His disciples, whom Jesus loved, was reclining at the table at His right."

Comment: ἦν ἀνακείμενος is an imperfect periphrastic construction, consisting of the imperfect of εἰμί and the present participle. It refers to the fact that when they took their places at the table, this disciple , presumably the writer, John, took the place next to Jesus. ἐν τῷ κόλπῳ (*cf.* John 1:18, which has εἰς τὸν κόλπον)does not mean "on" but "near" the bosom of Jesus. See the discussion (#1702). We might say that Washington D.C. is "on" the Potomac River when we mean that it is on the bank, "beside" or "near" the river. Apparently Jesus was especially fond of John, though He loved them all with the divine love He sheds abroad upon all of us. During the entire evening John had occupied this place near to Jesus.

Verse 24 - "Simon Peter therefore beckoned to him, that he should ask who it should be of whom he spake."

νεύει οὖν τούτῳ Σίμων Πέτρος πυθέσθαι τίς ἂν εἴη περὶ οὗ λέγει.

#2765 νεύει (3d.per.sing.pres.act.ind.of νεύω, historical).

beckon - John 13:24; Acts 24:10.

Meaning: To nod the head; to signify or beckon by nodding. Followed by the dative of person in John 13:24; followed by an infinitive in Acts 24:10, when the governor signalled to Paul to speak.

οὖν (inferential conjunction) 68.
τούτῳ (dat.sing.masc.of οὗτος, indirect object of νεύει) 93.
Σίμων (nom.sing.masc.of Σίμων, subject of νεύει) 386.
Πέτρος (nom.sing.masc.of Πέτρος, subject of νεύει) 387.
πυθέσθαι (2d.aor.mid.inf.of πυνθάνομαι, purpose) 153.
τίς (nom.sing.masc.of τίς,interrogative pronoun in indirect question, subject of εἴη) 281.
ἂν (contingent particle in indirect question with the deliberative optative) 205.
εἴη (3d.per.sing.pres.optative in indirect question, deliberative) 86.
περὶ (preposition with the genitive of reference) 173.
οὗ (gen.sing.masc.of ὅς, reference) 65.
λέγει (3d.per.sing.pres.act.ind.of λέγω, historical) 66.

Translation - "Simon Peter therefore nodded to him to ask with reference to whom He spoke."

Comment: οὖν is inferential. It explains Peter's action as he nodded to John who was in the best position to speak to Jesus. We have the deliberative optative in the indirect question following the purpose infinitive πυθέσθαι. A variant reading has Peter asking John to tell the other disciples of whom Jesus was speaking. "The reading adopted by a majority of the Committee contains the only instance of the optative mode in John, and therefore might be considered non-Johannine; nevertheless,on the basis of age and diversity of textual witnesses the construction with εἴη (p66 A D K W Δ Π *f1 f13* 28 565 700 *Byz*) was regarded as superior to the simpler construction attested by several Alexandrian witnesses (B C L X 068 33 892 1071 *al*). The reading of Sinaiticus is conflate, showing the antiquity of both readings." (Metzger, *A Textual Commentary on the Greek New Testament*, 240,241).

Verse 25 - "He then lying on Jesus' breast saith unto him, Lord, who is it?"

ἀναπεσὼν οὖν ἐκεῖνος οὕτως ἐπὶ τὸ στῆθος τοῦ Ἰησοῦ λέγει αὐτῷ, Κύριε, τίς ἐστιν;

ἀναπεσὼν (2d.aor.act.part.nom.sing.masc.of ἀναπίπτω, adjectival, restrictive) 1184.
ἐκεῖνος (nom.sing.masc.of ἐκεῖνος, subject of λέγει, deictic) 246.
οὕτως (demonstrative adverb) 74.
ἐπὶ (preposition with the accusative of extent) 47.
τὸ (acc.sing.neut.of the article in agreement with στῆθος) 9.
στῆθος (acc.sing.neut.of στῆθος, extent) 2631.
τοῦ (gen.sing.masc.of the article in agreement with Ἰησοῦ) 9.
Ἰησοῦς (gen.sing.masc.of Ἰησοῦς, possession) 3.
λέγει (3d.per.sing.pres.act.ind.of λέγω, historical) 66.
αὐτῷ (dat.sing.masc.of αὐτός, indirect object of λέγει) 16.
Κύριε (voc.sing.masc.of κύριος, address) 97.
τίς (nom.sing.masc.of τίς, the interrogative pronoun, subject of ἐστιν) 281.
ἐστιν (3d.per.sing.pres.ind.of εἰμί, aoristic) 86.

Translation - "Therefore that one who had been reclining near the bosom of Jesus said to Him, 'Lord, who is it?'"

Comment: ἐκεῖνος of verse 25 refers to τούτῳ of verse 24, *i.e.* to John, the beloved disciple. John indicates again that he had occupied this favored position near Jesus from the beginning of the meal. *Cf.* ἦν ἀνακειμένος of verse 23 and now the aorist adjectival participle ἀναπεσὼν which defines ἐκεῖνος. He was the logical one to ask the question, since he could do so only by lifting his head, turning slightly to the left and whispering to Jesus. This is the sense of οὕτως. ἐπὶ τὸ στῆθος τοῦ Ἰησοῦ means not literally "on" but "near to".

Verse 26 - "Jesus answered, He it is to whom I shall give a sop, when I have dipped it. And when he had dipped the sop, he gave it to Judas Iscariot, the son of Simon."

ἀποκρίνεται Ἰησοῦς, Ἐκεῖνός ἐστιν ᾧ ἐγὼ βάψω τὸ ψωμίον καὶ δώσω αὐτῷ. βάψας οὖν τὸ ψωμίον (λαμβάνει καὶ) δίδωσιν Ἰούδα Σίμωνος Ἰσκαριώτου.

ἀποκρίνεται (3d.per.sing.pres.mid.ind.of *αποκρίνομαι*, historical) 318.
Ἰησοῦς (nom.sing.masc.of *Ἰησοῦς*, subject of *ἀποκρίνεται*) 3.
Ἐκεῖνός (nom.sing.masc.of *ἐκεῖνος*, subject of *ἐστιν*) 246.
ἐστιν (3d.per.sing.pres.ind.of *εἰμί*, aoristic) 86.
ᾧ (loc.sing.masc.of *ὅς*, time point) 65.
ἐγὼ (nom.sing.masc.of *ἐγώ*, subject of *βάψω*) 123.
βάψω (1st.per.sing.fut.act.ind.of *βάπτω*, definite temporal clause) 2584.
τὸ (acc.sing.neut.of the article in agreement with *ψωμίον*) 9.

#2766 *ψωμίον* (acc.sing.neut.of *ψωμίον*, direct object of *βάψω*).

sop - John 13:26,26,27,30.

Meaning: Cf.ψωμίζω (#4030). dimin.of *ψωμός*, hence, a small bit of food; a bit; a morsel, *hors d' oeuvre*. Of the morsel which Jesus gave to Judas at the last supper - John 13:26,26,27,30.

καὶ (adjunctive conjunction joining verbs) 14.
δώσω (1st.per.sing.fut.act.ind.of *δίδωμι*, predictive) 362.
αὐτῷ (dat.sing.masc.of *αὐτός*, indirect object of *δώσω*) 16.
βάψας (aor.act.part.nom.sing.masc.of *βάπτω*, adverbial, temporal) 2584.
οὖν (continuative conjunction) 68.
τὸ (acc.sing.neut.of the article in agreement with *ψωμίον*) 9.
ψωμίον (acc.sing.neut.of *ψωμίον*, direct object of *βάψας*) 2766.
(*λαμβάνει*) (3d.per.sing.pres.act.ind.of *λαμβάνω*, historical) 533.
(*καὶ*) (adjunctive conjunction joining verbs) 14.
δίδωσιν (3d.per.sing.pres.act.ind.of *δίδωμι*, historical) 362.
Ἰούδα (dat.sing.masc.of *Ἰοῦδας*, indirect object of *δίδωσιν*) 853.
Σίμονος (gen.sing.masc.of *Σίμων*, relationship) 2294.
Ἰσκαριώτου (gen.sing.masc.of *Ἰσκαριώτης*, apposition) 854.

Translation - "Jesus replied, 'It is that one, when I dip the sop, to whom I will give it. Then, when He had dipped the sop, He took it and gave it to Judas, the son of Simon, the Iscariot."

Comment: *Ἐκεῖνος* is deictic. It points directly to him to whom it refers. Note the temporal clause with *ᾧ ἐγὼ βάψω* with the future indicative.

The tid-bit which, according to Oriental custom is offered by the host to the favored and most honored guest, was Jesus' gentle way of identifying Judas for the benefit of the other disciples. It was Jesus' last appeal to the better nature of the man who would go out and betray Him. (*Expositors' Greek Testament*, I, 819). No one but John understood the significance of the act. *Cf.* John 13:28,29.

Verse 27 - "And after the sop Satan entered into him, Then said Jesus unto him, That thou doest do quickly."

*καὶ μετὰ τὸ ψωμίον τότε εἰσῆλθεν εἰς ἐκεῖνον ὁ Σατανᾶς. λέγει οὖν αὐτῷ ὁ Ἰησοῦς,*Ὃ ποιεῖς ποίησον τάχιον.*

καὶ (continuative conjunction) 14.
μετὰ (preposition with the accusative of time extent) 50.
τὸ (acc.sing.neut.of the article in agreement with ψωμίον) 9.
ψωμίον (acc.sing.neut.of ψωμίον, time extent) 2766.
τότε (temporal adverb) 166.
εἰσῆλθεν (3d.per.sing.aor.ind.of εἰσέρχομαι, constative) 234.
εἰς (preposition with the accusative of extent) 140.
ἐκεῖνον (acc.sing.neut.of ἐκεῖνος, extent) 246.
ὁ (nom.sing.masc.of the article in agreement with Σατανᾶς) 9.
Σατανᾶς (nom.sing.masc.of Σατανᾶς, subject of εἰσῆλθεν) 365.
λέγει (3d.per.sing.pres.act.ind.of λέγω, historical) 66.
οὖν (continuative conjunction) 68.
αὐτῷ (dat.sing.masc.of αὐτός, indirect object of λέγει) 16.
ὁ (nom.sing.masc.of the article in agreement with Ἰησοῦς) 9.
Ἰησοῦς (nom.sing.masc.of Ἰησοῦς, subject of λέγει) 3.
Ὃ (acc.sing.neut.of ὅς, direct object of ποίησον) 65.
ποιεῖς (2d.per.sing.pres.act.ind.of ποιέω, futuristic) 127.
ποίησον (2d.per.sing.aor.act.impv.of ποιέω, command) 127.

#2767 τάχειον (adverbial).

quickly - John 13:27.
shortly - 1 Tim.3:14; Heb.13:23.
the sooner - Heb.13:19.
(not translated) - John 20:4.

Meaning: in chronological terms - John 13:27; Heb.13:19,23; 1 Tim.3:14. In a spatial sense - "a little bit ahead of " - Peter - John 20:4, because he ran more swiftly. In John 13:27 - "without any further delay."

Translation - "And after (he took) the bit of bread, then Satan entered into him. Then Jesus said to him, 'That which you are going to do, do quickly.' "

Comment: This is the second time that Satan personally took over in Judas' heart and mind (Luke 22:3). First to motivate his child! (John 6:70) to plot the betrayal; now to stiffen his resistance against the charm of Jesus' personality. Satan motivates the unregenerate whenever and however he wishes (Eph.2:2; 2 Cor.4:4; 1 John 5:19). What B.F. Skinner (*Beyond Dignity and Freedom)* calls the contingencies of environment, the New Testament, in some cases, calls Satan. Whether Satan is directly involved in causation, the victim is not autonomous. The Christian doesn't need Skinner's assist, but he can be grateful for it. Skinner came a little late with his controversial book. The New Testament anticipated him by 1900 years. Even Karl Marx said it before Skinner did. What Robertson (*Grammar*, 880) calls the inchoative present in ποιεῖς, Mantey (*Manual*, 185) calls futuristic, since it relates to an act about to begin. Winer (*Grammar of the Idiom of the New Testament*, 7th ed., Thayer's translation of Luneman's revision, 265) explains that while the present is thus used "in appearance for the future," it in reality retains it own temporal and essential force, being employed to denote a future action "either because it is already firmly resolved upon or because it follows because of some unalterable law." Jesus, thus, is cast here in the role, not of the victim of the plot, but the director of the drama, as He said to Judas, "What you are about to do, do at once." This means that had Judas not been given the sop, he might have gone about his perfidy with more relaxed deliberation. Jesus was saying in effect, "You are committed to a policy and an action. What are you waiting for? Get on with it!" Judas complied (vs.30), not under motivation from Satan, but in obedience to his former Lord, Who is to be victimized by his deed.

No greater evidence of Jesus' sovereignty can be found than in this incident. It is idle to speculate about what did not happen, but it is interesting to reflect upon what Judas would have done had Jesus forbidden him to leave the room! Of this much we can be sure - God's redemptive plan would have failed of execution and the entire race would be justly condemned in hell.

Verse 28 - "Now no man at the table knew for what intent he spake this unto him."

τοῦτο (δὲ) οὐδεὶς ἔγνω τῶν ἀνακειμένων πρὸς τί εἶπεν αὐτῷ.

τοῦτο (acc.sing.neut.of οὗτος, direct object of εἶπεν) 93.
(δὲ) (explanatory conjunction) 11.
οὐδεὶς (nom.sing.masc.of οὐδείς, subject of ἔγνω) 446.
ἔγνω (3d.per.sing.2d.aor.act.ind.of γινώσκω, constative) 131.
τῶν (gen.pl.masc.of the article in agreement with ἀνακειμένων) 9.
ἀνακειμένων (pres.act.part.gen.pl.masc.of ἀνάκειμαι, substantival, partitive genitive) 790.
πρὸς (preposition with the accusative, cause) 197.
τί (acc.sing.neut.of τίς, cause) 281.
εἶπεν (3d.per.sing.aor.act.ind.of εἶπον, constative) 155.
αὐτῷ (dat.sing.masc.of αὐτός, indirect object of εἶπεν) 16.

Translation - "Now not one of those sitting there knew why He said this to him."

Comment: δὲ is explanatory. Despite the fact that Jesus had just told John that Judas was the betrayer, Jesus' further remark to Judas (vs.27) was obscure even to John. The text is not clear that the other ten heard what Jesus said to John about the sop. If so, they knew, as John did, that Judas was the guilty man. Even if so, there is nothing to indicate to them that Jesus meant what Judas, of course, well understood Him to mean. Even John could have interpreted Jesus' remark to Judas in terms of the theories of verse 29. Note πρὸς τί here to denote purpose. *Cf.*#197.

Verse 29 - "For some of them thought, because Judas had the bag, that Jesus had said unto him, Buy these things that we have need of against the feast; or, that he should give something to the poor."

τινὲς γὰρ ἐδόκουν ἐπεὶ τὸ γλωσσόκομον εἶχεν Ἰούδας, ὅτι λέγει αὐτῷ (ὁ) Ἰησοῦς, Ἀγόρασον ὧν χρείαν ἔχομεν εἰς τὴν ἑορτήν, ἢ τοῖς πτωχοῖς ἵνα τι δῷ.

τινὲς (nom.pl.masc.of τις, indefinite pronoun, subject of ἐδόκουν) 486.
γὰρ (inferential conjunction introducing a coordinate causal clause) 105.
ἐδόκουν (3d.per.pl.imp.act.ind.of δοκέω, inceptive) 287.
ἐπεὶ (subordinating conjunction introducing a causal clause) 1281.
τὸ (acc.sing.neut.of the article in agreement with γλωσσόκομον) 9.
γλωσσόκομον (acc.sing.neut.of γλωσσόκομον, direct object of εἶχεν) 2751.
εἶχεν (3d.per.sing.imp.act.ind.of ἔχω, progressive duration) 82.
Ἰούδας (nom.sing.masc.of Ἰούδας, subject of εἶχεν) 853.
ὅτι (conjunction introducing an object clause in indirect discourse) 211.
λέγει (3d.per.sing.pres.act.ind.of λέγω, historical) 66.
αὐτῷ (dat.sing.masc.of αὐτός, indirect object of λέγει) 16.
(ὁ) (nom.sing.masc.of the article in agreement with Ἰησοῦς) 9.
Ἰησοῦς (nom.sing.masc.of Ἰησοῦς, subject of λέγει) 3.
Ἀγόρασον (2d.per.sing.aor.act.impv.of ἀγοράζω, command) 1085.
ὧν (gen.pl.neut.of ὅς, description) 65.
χρείαν (acc.sing.fem.of χρεία, direct object of ἔχομεν) 317.
ἔχομεν (1st.per.pl.pres.act.ind.of ἔχω, futuristic) 82.
εἰς (preposition with the accusative, purpose) 140.
τὴν (acc.sing.fem.of the article in agreement with ἑορτήν) 9.
ἑορτήν (acc.sing.fem.of ἑορτή, purpose) 1558.
ἢ (disjunctive particle) 465.
τοῖς (dat.pl.masc.of the article in agreement with πτωχοῖς) 9.
πτωχοῖς (dat.pl.masc.of πτωχός, indirect object of δῷ) 423.
ἵνα (conjunction introducing the subjunctive in a purpose clause) 114.
τι (acc.sing.neut.of τις, the indefinite pronoun, direct object of δῷ) 486.
δῷ (3d.per.sing.aor.act.subj.of δίδωμι, purpose) 362.

Translation - "Because some began to think, since Judas always carried the purse, that Jesus said to him, 'Buy what we need for the feast," or that he should give something to the poor."

Comment: γὰρ, the inferential conjunction, introduces the coordinate clause in which John is telling us why the disciples did not understand Jesus' remark to Judas in verse 27. They all began to think (inceptive imperfect in ἐδόκουν) about it and arrived at different conclusions.Note the indirect discourse in the object clause introduced by ὅτι. Some thought that Jesus had ordered Judas to go out and buy food for the Festival which was to be held the following evening. This was a logical deduction, since (ἐπεὶ and the subordinate causal clause) Judas was the treasurer of the group. Others thought that Jesus had told Judas to go out and give something to the poor. Both conclusions were based upon the fact that Judas was the treasurer and carried the purse.

The thrust of the passage is that the disciples, caught up in the celebration of the Passover, were insensitive to the eternal purport and consequences of the events in which they were participating. They were thinking that things were going on very much as usual, despite the fact that Jesus had said that His hour had come and that His "hour" meant the hour of His death.

Verse 30 - "He then, having received the sop, went immediately out: and it was night."

λαβὼν οὖν τὸ ψωμίον ἐκεῖνος ἐξῆλθεν εὐθύς. ἦν δὲ νύξ.

λαβὼν (aor.act.part.nom.sing.masc.of λαμβάνω, adverbial, temporal) 533.
οὖν (inferential conjunction) 68.
τὸ (acc.sing.neut.of the article in agreement with ψωμίον) 9.
ψωμίον (acc.sing.neut.of ψωμίον, direct object of λαβὼν) 2766.
ἐκεῖνος (nom.sing.masc.of ἐκεῖνος, subject of ἐξῆλθεν) 246.
ἐξῆλθεν (3d.per.sing.aor.ind.of ἐξέρχομαι, constative) 161.
εὐθύς (adverbial) 258.
ἦν (3d.per.sing.imp.ind.of εἰμί, progressive description) 86.
δὲ (explanatory conjunction) 11.
νὺξ (nom.sing.fem.of νύξ, subject of ἦν) 209.

Translation - "Therefore when he had taken the sop he left immediately. Now it was night."

Comment: οὖν is inferential. It introduces Judas' response to Jesus' command of verse 27. When Jesus ordered him out Judas promptly obeyed, but not until he had gone through the charade involving the sop. There is symbolic significance in ἦν δὲ νύξ - "Night had fallen." It was certainly *night* for Judas Iscariot and all unbelievers, as well as for Satan and his fallen demons. But the text simply says that by the time Judas left the upper room, darkness had fallen. The night had come when "no man can work." *Cf.* comment on John 9:4.

INDEX

* In Volume 8

* In Volume 8

RICH INTERNET APPLICATIONS WITH ADOBE® FLEX™ & JAVA™

SECRETS OF THE MASTERS

First Edition

WRITTEN BY YAKOV FAIN, DR. VICTOR RASPUTNIS & ANATOLE TARTAKOVSKY

SYS-CON Media
Woodcliff Lake, NJ 07677

Rich Internet Applications with Adobe® Flex™ & Java™

Secrets of the Masters

1st Edition

SYS-CON Books/2007

Managing Editor: Nancy Valentine

Cover Design: Abraham Addo

Layout and Design: Abraham Addo

Produced by SYS-CON Media

ISBN 0-9777622-2-X

Published and printed in the United States of America

0 9 8 7 6 5 4 3 2

To Dongli
from Victor
with confidence in your
success!

Victor [illegible]

About the Authors

Yakov Fain is a Managing Principal of Farata Systems. He's responsible for the enterprise architecture and emerging technologies. Yakov has authored several Java books, dozens of technical articles, and his blog is hugely popular. Sun Microsystems has awarded Yakov with the title Java Champion. He leads the Princeton Java Users Group. Yakov holds a BS and an MS in Applied Math and is an Adobe Certified Flex Instructor. You can reach him at yfain@faratasystems.com.

Dr. Victor Rasputnis is a Managing Principal of Farata Systems. He's responsible for providing architectural design, implementation management, and mentoring to companies migrating to XML Internet technologies. He holds a PhD in computer science from the Moscow Institute of Robotics. You can reach him at vrasputnis@faratasystems.com.

Anatole Tartakovsky is a Managing Principal of Farata Systems. He's responsible for the creation of frameworks and reusable components. Anatole has authored a number of books and articles on AJAX, XML, the Internet, and client/server technologies. He holds an MS in mathematics. You can reach him at atartakovsky@faratasystems.com.

Ben Stucki is a software engineer at Atellis, a Washington, D.C., based firm that specializes in developing rich Internet applications and products. As part of the core development team at Atellis, Ben mixes his knowledge of back-end application development and interactive user interfaces to engineer next-generation Flex applications and components. Ben is also an active member of the Flash and Flex communities and manages a number of open source projects.

The authors frequently blog at the following locations:

- Flex Blog: http://flexblog.faratasystems.com/
- Yakov Fain's blog: http://yakovfain.javadevelopersjournal.com/
- Ben Stucki's blog: http://blog.benstucki.net/

CONTENTS

TABLE OF CONTENTS

Acknowledgments

Writing a technical book requires dedication, discipline and wish power. But most important, it requires support from family members, and we'd like to thank our families for understanding and especially our children, who got used to the fact that their fathers were glued to their computers, even in the evenings.

We'd like to thank all members of the vibrant and very active online Flex community for their drive, energy, and eagerness to contribute to the success of the tool of their choice.

We'd like to thank the top-notch Flex professional Valery Silaev for his valuable input to the chapter on integration with external applications, which is one of the most complex chapters in this book.

We'd like to thank a charting guru Vadim Sokolovsky from GreenPoint for his help in writing the chapter about developing custom charting components.

We'd like to thank our contributing author Ben Stucki for creating a very good slideshow component and writing a chapter for our book.

And mainly, we thank you, our readers, for considering this book.

—Yakov Fain, Victor Rasputnis, and Anatole Tartakovsky

FOREWORD

It's risky to try to define Web 2.0 (which may or may not be a trademark of O'Reilly Media Inc.), but the description I've heard that makes the most sense is that Web 1.0 always required a visit to a server to make any changes to what the user sees, whereas Web 2.0 downloads some code to the client so that, for some transactions, data can be sent to the client instead of a whole page. The result is a richer and faster user experience. I like this definition because it gives me something concrete to evaluate.

This is a logical next step now that the primitive, page-at-a-time Web has proven its success. At the same time, it's ridiculous that we should have to do this all over again. After all, before the Web there was a lot of brouhaha about client/server, where the server runs code that makes sense on the server, and the client runs code that makes sense on the client. The idea was a lot simpler than all the marketing noise would have you believe, but it was still a good idea.

If the definition above is valid, then one could argue that the genesis of Web 2.0 is AJAX (Asynchronous JavaScript And XML). Of course, JavaScript has been around since, effectively, the beginning of the Web, but the browser wars made JavaScript inconsistent and thus painful to use. A key part of AJAX is that someone has gone to the trouble of figuring out cross-platform JavaScript issues so that you can ignore differences between browsers.

There are two problems with this approach. The first is that JavaScript is limited in what it can do. AJAX is an excellent hack that gets the last bit of mileage out of JavaScript, but it's a hack nonetheless, and the end is in sight. The second problem is that you're relying on AJAX libraries to handle cross-browser issues, and if you want to write your own code, you have to become an expert on these issues, and at that point AJAX's leverage goes out the door. It's too much trouble and a waste of time to have to know all the gratuitous differences between different versions of what is supposed to be the same programming language.

You could argue that the solution is Java, because Java is designed to be the same on all platforms. In theory this is true. In theory, Java should be the ubiquitous client-side platform. In theory, Lear Jets and bumblebees shouldn't be able to fly, and lots of other things should be true as well, but for various reasons Java applets, after 10 years, don't dominate client-side automation, and it seems unlikely that they will anytime soon.

In practice, Java dominates on the server, so this book takes the practical attitude that most people will want to continue writing the server side using Java. But for a rich client, this book assumes that you've seen that other technologies will either run out of gas or involve an installation process that consumers resist (regardless of how "simple" that installation process claims to be). Because the Flash player is installed on some 98% of all machines and is transparently cross-platform, and because people are comfortable with the idea of Flash and don't resist installing or upgrading it, this book assumes that you want to create your rich client interfaces in Flash.

The only drawback to this approach is that, historically, Flash applications have been built with tools that make more sense to artists and Web designers than they do to programmers. This is where Flex comes in. Flex is a programming system that produces compiled Flash applications. The programming language in Flex, called ActionScript, is based on ECMAScript, the ECMA-standard version of JavaScript, so any JavaScript knowledge you might have isn't lost. You can learn a single programming language and ignore cross-platform issues.

Flex comes with a library of UI widgets, with a potential marketplace for third-party widgets. As you'll see if you look at the Flex demos and tours on www.adobe.com, these widgets can be very functional as well as appealing, so it's possible to assemble a very attractive and professional rich client without much effort.

One of the main reasons that you might not have tried an earlier version of Flex is that the original pricing model meant that you couldn't experiment with the tool without paying a hefty fee upfront. A big change has occurred since then, because with Flex 2 and beyond, you can use any plain text editor along with the free Adobe compiler and Flex Framework components to create your rich Internet applications. This includes the ability to host static Flash applications on your server. Adobe makes its money on the more powerful dynamic application server (which dynamically creates and delivers Flex applications) and the Eclipse-based Flex Builder environment, which simplifies the creation of Flex applications.

I'd like to think that I had something to do with the migration to the free command-line compiler for Flex, since I spent an hour or so on the phone trying to convince a Flash VP (before Adobe bought Macromedia) that to become popular, programmers needed to be able to experiment with the platform freely. However, the result is more than I hoped for.

I think that Flex for rich Internet client applications can become a major player. Its easy cross-platform support removes many programmer headaches, the component model offers powerful library reuse, and the result produces a very comfortable and appealing interface for the client to use. Because this book teaches you how to use Flex along with the dominant server-side development tool (Java), it's an ideal introduction if you want to learn how to leverage these technologies.

Bruce Eckel
Author, *Thinking in Java 4th Edition*
www.MindView.net

FOREWORD

At the beginning of the decade Macromedia coined the term rich Internet application (RIA) to describe the future of applications. An RIA is a Web experience that's engaging, interactive, lightweight, and flexible. RIAs offer the flexibility and ease of use of an intelligent desktop application and add the broad reach of traditional Web applications. Adobe Flex 2 has established itself as the premiere platform for delivering these experiences.

The Flash Player is an ideal runtime for a rich Internet application. Installed on 98% of Web-enabled desktops, the Player has a reach far beyond any individual Web browser or other client technology. For years, developers took advantage of this by using the Macromedia Flash tool to build compelling, data-driven applications. But the Flash programming model wasn't for everyone. When building what would become Flex 1.0, we geared the programming model towards developers who had more of a programming background, especially Java Web application developers. We designed a tag-based language called MXML and influenced the evolution of ActionScript 2.0 to appeal to developers used to object-oriented programming. Flex 1.0 and Flex 1.5 were very successful for Macromedia, reaching hundreds of customers in 18 months, impressive for a v1 product with an enterprise price tag.

But we realized that to reach our goal of a million Flex developers we needed to make some drastic changes in the platform. Our first change was to rewrite the virtual machine in the Flash Player from scratch and improve the language at the same time. The AVM2 inside Flash Player 9 is orders of magnitude faster than the previous virtual machine and uses less memory. The ActionScript 3.0 language is now on a par with other enterprise development languages like Java and C#. We then re-architected the Flex Framework to take advantage of the improvements our underlying foundation exposed.

Next, as Adobe, we decided to make the Flex SDK completely free. Developers can now create, debug, and deploy Flex 2 applications at no cost. The Flex SDK provides tools for compiling MXML and ActionScript into deployable applications, building reusable libraries, a command-line debugger, and a documentation generator. We made this move to remove all the pricing barriers to becoming a Flex developer. We hope that this jump-starts the growth of the Flex community, and we know it's already paying off as we watch the increase in traffic on our forums, blog postings, and mailing list participation.

Of course any development experience is improved if you have a robust development environment, and we built the Flex Builder IDE for that purpose. We decided to leverage the Eclipse platform for Flex Builder because it's familiar to many of the developers we envision using Flex, and also gave us a great starting point to building an enterprise-quality IDE. Flex Builder provides project management, code hinting, compilation, visual debugging, and perhaps, most important, a Design View for rapid development of your user interface. While using Flex Builder is certainly not required to build your Flex applications, we think your experience will be more enjoyable if you do.

All of the enhancements mentioned so far address the development of the Flex application, but don't mention one of the true innovations in the Flex 2 release, Flex Data Services. Flex Data Services is designed so you can easily integrate a Flex application into a new or existing J2EE system. The remoting service lets your Flex application make calls to POJOs or EJBs. The messaging service lets your Flex application connect to JMS message queues and topics and lets those systems push messages to all Flex clients. The Data Management Service manages data synchronization between data on the server and your Flex applications. When you make a change to data in one Flex application, it's immediately reflected in other applications and persisted to your server. The system is scalable, highly configurable, and integrates well into any transaction management you might have, making this system a must for data-intensive applications.

This was certainly the largest project I've ever worked on. We had engineers on both coasts of the U.S. as well as Bangalore, India, working together on this immense system. At any hour during a 24-hour day someone on our team was actively developing. Of course it's not just the engineers, or even just Adobe employees who contributed to the development of Flex 2. From the moment we released our public alpha we've been getting great feedback from the larger community.

The principals of Farata Systems have been key contributors to Flex's success via their participation in our beta programs, posts to community forums, public presentations, and blog postings. And now, Yakov Fain, Victor Rasputnis, and Anatole Tartakovsky are capping those contributions with *Rich Internet Applications with Adobe Flex and Java: Secrets of the Masters*. This may not be the only resource for learning how to experiment with Flex, but it will be an important one for building real-world Flex applications.

The Flex product team spent almost two years taking what we learned from Flex 1 to build a technology that would revolutionize the way developers create applications that engage with their users and with information. Now that technology is here in the form of Flex 2 and this book is here to help you take advantage of all that power. There's a lot to learn, but Yakov, Victor, and Anatole have done an excellent job introducing you to everything you need to know to build a robust application. We at Adobe can't wait to see what you create.

Matt Chotin
Product Manager
Adobe Systems, Inc.
October 2006

CHAPTER

1

Architecture of Rich Internet Applications

Architecture of Rich Internet Applications

What is a rich Internet application?

Historically there have been major shifts in the software industry. We moved from mainframes with dumb terminals to client/server. Users gained in convenience and productivity, and mainframe systems were patronizingly labeled as legacy. With the availability of the World Wide Web industry, visionaries turned the tables; vendors and corporate IT had been eager to get rid of the complexity of client/server version management and technologists were sold on multi-tier computing. This time client/server was called legacy. And to rub it in, good old desktop applications were labeled "fat." Excited with server multi-threading, messaging, persistence, and similar toys, we pretend not to think that, at the end of the day, we'd have to trade user experience and productivity for the transparency of application deployment. And to make us feel better, we proudly called the new breed of applications "thin client."

Meet the new challenge: we're entering an era of rich Internet applications (RIA), which restores the power of desktop applications…inside downloadable Web page. RIAs run in a virtual machine (i.e., Adobe Flash Player or Java VM) and have the potential of becoming a full-featured desktop application soon. As opposed to just simply displaying Web pages delivered from some server machine, RIA really run on the client. Many of the data manipulation tasks (sorting, grouping, and filtering) are done locally like in the old client/server days. Déjà vu indeed! Industry analysts predict that in three or four years most newly developed projects will include RIA technologies.

A rich Internet application combines the benefits of using the Web as a low-cost deployment model with a rich user experience that's at least as good as today's desktop applications. And, since RIAs don't require that the entire page be refreshed to update their data, the response time is much faster and the network load much lower. Think of a globally available client/server application.

Let's illustrate the difference between "legacy" Web and RIA with a shopping cart example. Non-RIA Web applications are page-based. Since HTTP is a stateless protocol, when the user moves from one page to another, a Web browser doesn't "remember" the user's actions on the previous page. As a common treatment of this "amnesia," a user state is stored on the server side in the form of the HTTP session.

Consider the case of an online shopping session. It can go as follows:

1. The user initiates a search for an item on Web page #1.
2. The server processes this request and returns page #2 that may (or may not) contain the required item.
3. The user adds an item to a shopping cart that takes yet another trip to the server to create the shopping cart and store it on the server side. Then the server responds with page #3 so the user can either continue shopping (repeating the first three steps) or proceed to the checkout – page #4.

At the checkout the server retrieves selected items from the session object and sends page #5 to the user for shipping info. The data entered travels back to the server for storage, and the client gets back page #6 for billing information. After that page #7 will confirm the order and only then goes to the order completion page.

This simplest of online purchases consisted of seven roundtrips to the server. In a striking difference to desktop applications, a few-seconds-per-page refresh is considered fast(!) for a typical Web application, and the commonly acceptable delay is up to eight seconds. Is the user motivated enough to complete the purchase? Think again, because your system gave him a chance to reconsider seven times in a row. Now assume that the network and/or server are slow. Result? Your potential buyer went elsewhere.

Rich Internet applications eliminate the roundtrips and substantially improve system performance by doing a lot more of the processing on the client than a thin client Web application. Besides, RIAs are stateful: they accumulate the information right on the client! To put it simply, RIA isn't a set of pages controlled by the server; they are actual applications running on the client's computer and communicating with servers primarily to process and exchange data.

Both consumer-facing and enterprise applications benefit from being RIAs. It's a well-known fact that e-commerce Web sites such as online ticket reservation systems and online retailers are losing revenue because users abandon shopping carts on non-responsive Web sites during the checkout process. Such Web sites result in lots of calls to the call center, a major operational expense in and of itself. The performance of any system operated by employees is critical to company productivity and RIAs provide a performance boost over HTML applications, while reducing operating and infrastructure costs. Finally, introducing well-designed RIAs lets companies build better "mousetraps."

Macromedia introduced the expression rich Internet applications back in 2002 in contrast to the bleak condition of the "legacy" Web, known today as Web 1.0. And yet the first RIA applications were born as early as 1995 when Java was created. Java's initial popularity manifested itself in a wave of small downloadable programs called Java applets. Applets, created with Java AWT (and later Swing) libraries, were run by the browsers' Java Virtual Machine (JVM). Ironically, the very technology that made Java popular wasn't exploited and today Java shines mostly on the server side and in mobile devices.

In 2004 Tim O'Reilly coined the catchy term *Web 2.0*. Which sites qualify for Web 2.0 status has never been clearly defined. If someone sees a cool-looking Web site, it's invariably called Web 2.0. Labeling better-looking Web products "2.0" is pretty popular these days. Often it refers to social engineering sites that let people collaborate and build the site's content themselves. Wikipedia has a lengthy article on Web 2.0 that may give you some idea what this term means. See http://en.wikipedia.org/wiki/Web_2.0.

There's now Web 3.0 too, which refers to the Semantic Web…but let's stop playing this name game and return to the main acronym of this book: RIA.

RIA Platforms: The Major Choices

It's not hard to guess that there's more than one way to create RIAs. As we said earlier, RIAs run in the client's browser with the help of some kind of client engine.

For example, these are the most popular products or technologies:

Using Flex you can create an ActionScript application for the ubiquitous Flash Player, a high-performance multimedia virtual machine that runs bytecode files in the SWF format (pronounced swif). The player's JIT compiler converts the SWF bytecode to native machine code for fast performance. The later facility is specific to Flex 2, available since 2006. Although early versions of Flex were out in 2004, they didn't support just-in-time compilation.

A Java programmer can create Java applets. As mentioned, this solution has been available since 1995.

Windows Presentation Foundation (WPF) was released as part of .NET 3.0 in November of 2006 and can be used to create both Internet and desktop applications.

Finally, there's AJAX, aka DHTML, circa 1998. This solution was recently boosted with XMLHttpRequest API support for all major browsers. AJAX served as a wake-up call for the user and developer communities. It is often the first step on the migration path from the legacy Web to the world of RIA despite being seriously handicapped by having to support browser incompatibilities and a poor programming model.

Adobe Flex 2

Flex 2 applications run cross-platform in a ubiquitous Flash Player 9 that's a lightweight virtual machine. The platform includes:

- An XML-based language called MXML that supports the declarative programming of GUI components targeting designers
- The standard object-oriented programming language, ActionScript 3.0, based on the latest ECMAScript specification
- Server-side integration via Flex Data Services (FDS) giving client applications transparent access to the world of J2EE

- Charting components, access to multimedia controls, etc.
- An Eclipse-based full-featured IDE with automated deployment, debugging, and tracing facilities

The Flex 2 platform is easily extendable and integrates well with server-side Java, ColdFusion, PHP, Ruby, ASP, and the like. The upcoming release of Adobe Apollo will allow the creation of a desktop application based on Flash Player, Flex, PDF, and HTML.

The SWF file format is open, and there are third-party open source products that offer tools for creating RIAs delivered by Flash Player like OpenLaszlo from Laszlo Systems.

As opposed to the last version, Flex 2 offers a way to create RIAs without incurring hefty licensing fees. This is what comes at no cost:

- **MXML:** An XML-based declarative programming language for creating a GUI
- **ActionScript 3.0**: An object-oriented language similar to Java
- **Flash Player 9**: A virtual machine with a tiny footprint that lives inside a Web browser and runs your compiled bytecode (.SWF)
- **Command-line compilers and debugger**
- **Flex Framework**: Includes a library of well-designed GUI component: buttons, tab folders, data grids, tree controls, animated effects, and more
- **Flex Data Services Express**: Template Web application deployed in a J2EE server to communicate with an ActionScript client application run by Flash Player. FDS Express is limited to a single CPU and is not supposed to be used in a high-availability (24x7) configuration

The following Flex tools require a purchased license:

- Flex Builder – the Eclipse-based IDE
- Charting component
- Flex Data Services Departmental, 24x7, 100 concurrent users
- Flex Data Services Enterprise, 24x7, unlimited users

The process of creating a basic Flex 2 application consists of the following steps:

1. Design the application by adding MXML components like this button:

```
<mx:Button  label="Place Order" click="processOrder(event)"/>
```

If you use the Flex Builder IDE, you can apply drag-and-drop techniques. Alternatively, you can write the MXML as text.

2. Write the code in ActionScript per your functional specification, for example:

```
private function processOrder (event:Event):void{
```

```
//The business logic goes here
}
```

3. Compile the code. Flex compiler automatically converts MXML into ActionScript and creates bytecode output in the form of an SWF file to be run in Flash Player 9 or above. You'll enjoy a fully automatic compilation process if you use the Flex Builder IDE.
4 Deploy the SWF file and the wrapping HTML page in the Web server of your choice. The deployment process and creating the wrapped can be completely transparent if you use the Flex Builder IDE.

There is a Flex Online Compiler Web site where you can try writing Flex code online without installing anything on your computer. There are even code snippets ready to be modified and run. See http://try.flex.org/.

More advanced Flex applications can include interaction with the server-side systems through Flex Data Services, which provides remote access to server-side Java objects and Java EE components, extensive messaging support (including JMS integration), synchronization with persisted data, and integration with other persistent technologies.

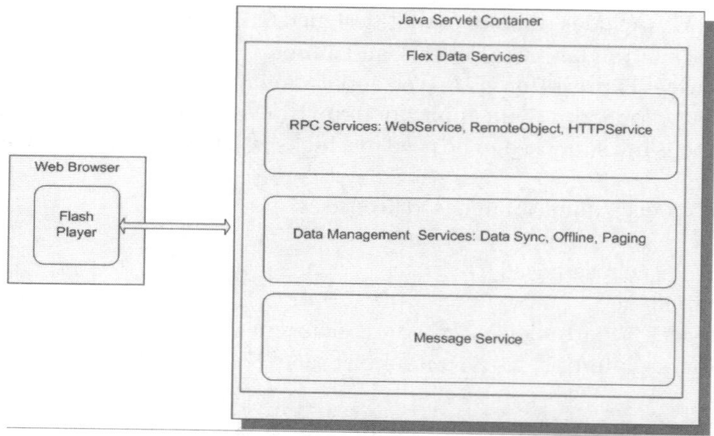

Figure 1.1 Flash Player and Flex Data Services

Java

Even though the Java programming language became popular largely because of applets and the famous dancing Duke (http://java.com/en/download/help/testvm.xml), applets haven't become Java's main use pattern. The main reason: the large footprint of the required JVM (currently 16MB). And there are other drawbacks. For instance, although Java Swing was meant for a platform-independent look-and-feel, absent any good-looking off-the-shelf GUI widgets it was hard selling it to the public. In this regard the Flash and Flex creators did a much better job with their eye-candy components. Or take audio and video integration. Today people are used to having streaming audio and video components embedded in Web pages. But the multimedia Java API remains rudimentary, to say the least.

There are some efforts to minimize the size of the JVM used by Web browsers and the Java Browser Edition project now needs "only" about 3MB to run a primitive Hello World applet. But this can't compete with Flash Player 9, which managed to accommodate two virtual machines in a 1.2MB download that can run any RIA, however complex.

Another issue with Java applets is that they don't offer a seamless download of the proper version of the JVM along with the applet. Flash Player's express install does precisely that.

Having said that, we must acknowledge that Java Swing is a very mature and robust technology for creating GUI applications delivered either over the Web or installed on the desktop. You can do literally anything with Java Swing – if you can afford it. No, you don't pay licensing fees, but because of the longer development cycle and the need to engage expert programmers, industrial-size Swing projects are usually quite expensive to build and maintain.

WPF

Microsoft's Windows Foundation Platform, or WPF, become available with the release of Vista (http://msdn2.microsoft.com/en-us/netframework/aa663326.aspx). It uses an XML-based declarative programming language called XAML to create GUIs and C# as a general-purpose programming language. WPF is suitable for creating both RIA and desktop applications. XBAP stands for XAML Browser Application and it's a WPF way of creating RIAs that run in Internet Explorer. Microsoft is planning to release a version called WPF/E that will run on some non-Windows platforms. While living in a sandbox, XBAP will have access to all .NET 3.0 functionality but WPF/E won't. WPF/E uses XAML and JavaScript (no C#). Common Language Runtime (CLR) is the client's WPF engine.

To create WPF applications, developers can use Microsoft's Visual Studio 2005 IDE with installed .NET 3.0 extensions. The next version of this IDE, called Orcas, will include a visual GUI designer. WPF developers use the same code base for writing XBAP and desktop applications: they just enclose the code sections that aren't allowed in XBAP into the ifdef blocks.

Microsoft XAML code resembles Adobe's MXML. Even though today's Flex 2 is a lot more mature than WPF, Microsoft has an established developer base, while Adobe traditionally catered to designers. Its main goal today is to convince enterprise developers (particularly the Java camp) that Flex can be a tool of choice for creating business RIAs.

AJAX

While the term AJAX was coined by Jesse James Garret in February of 2005 and is partly rooted in the asynchronous XmlHttpRequest implemented by Mozilla, lots of developers have used Microsoft's version of XMLHttpRequest and alternative techniques like IFrame since 1999. These techniques facilitate synchronous and asynchronous communications between the script in a page and server-side code. The main problem with AJAX is that despite its popularity, it has no technical foundation. While the other solutions we mention here are based on rock-solid virtual machines, there's no standard VM for AJAX. Each browser implements AJAX building blocks differently. There's a chance that a deployed AJAX application will require code changes with each new browser release. Wait, let's rephrase that: there's a chance that deployed AJAX apps may run as is on a new browser release. Do you want to take chances with your business?

That said, Internet giants like Google, Yahoo, and Amazon are building AJAX apps on top of their own abstraction layers such as Google Web Toolkit (GWT). Because of the immature level of the technology, these abstract layers need constant vendor attention as soon as changes appear.

AJAX Shortcomings

An ability to create flicker-free Web apps without buying more software is AJAX's big appeal. You may have heard the chant, "AJAX is free." Here's the simple translation: no commercial AJAX tool is worth paying for. There are hundreds of libraries, toolkits, and control sets that give you the impression that AJAX applications are cheap to develop and strategically safe since there's no vendor lock-in. Actually, there is vendor locking because you won't manually write JavaScript code and will have to pick an AJAX library of some vendor. Now think about it: starting from the ground up you need a communication layer, messaging and remoting mechanisms, an HTTP sniffer, a library of UI components with shared objects and event models, a visual IDE that understands these components in design time, and a debugger that accommodates all this stuff. On top of that, there's internationalization support, accessibility for the disabled, and support for automated testing tools.

You really think you're safe with mix-and-match from different vendors? If the answer is yes, you must be working for a software company in the RIA business. Coming to reality; a long development cycle; lack of free, quality GUI components; and the shortcomings listed below make AJAX less appealing and, actually, the most expensive way of creating RIAs.

These are some of AJAX's current drawbacks:

- JavaScript development tools are limited due to the dynamic nature of the language, and debugging any DHTML/JavaScript mix is a pain. Yes, Google's GWT can spare you from writing JavaScript manually, but at the end of the day, it's still JavaScript that has to be deployed in production. When the system isn't working and time is limited, what are you going to use to debug it – the real page of Java mock-up?

- Tons of JavaScript source code has to go over the wire to the client to be interpreted by the browser. We're talking about business applications, not some proof-of-concept demo.

- Web browsers will happily display your application even if a piece of JavaScript didn't arrive at the client. You won't know if a problem exists until you execute the particular use case.

- A simple right-click followed by the "View Source code" menu option would reveal your business application code. Better yet, all this code resides as plain text in the browser cache on disk. Because of this, you have to drop all the code comments and use obfuscators to protect your code from being stolen.

- HTML rendering is slow: think of a data grid that contains 5,000 records. Where's your mutual fund report?

- Any data manipulation by JavaScript is inherently slow because JavaScript is an interpreted, not a compiled language. We're talking thousand of times slow.

- The code is more vulnerable to hacker attack, a fact that was proved recently by a worm that stole a bunch of mail addresses from Yahoo address books.

- AJAX doesn't support server push. The server-side application can't publish the data directly to the client. AJAX applications have to poll the data from the server at specified time intervals without knowing if the data is there or not.

Dion Hinchcliffe, the editor-in-chief of *AJAXWorld Magazine*, listed some of the important things every AJAX developer should know (see http://web2.wsj2.com/seven_things_every_software_project_needs_to_know_about_AJAX.htm):

- Browsers were never meant to handle AJAX.
- You won't need as many Web Services as you think.
- AJAX is harder than traditional Web design and development.
- AJAX tooling and components are immature and there is no clear leader today.
- Good AJAX programmers are hard to find.
- It takes real work to make up for AJAX's shortcomings.
- AJAX is only one element of a successful RIA strategy.

Hinchcliffe says, "The addition of RIA platforms such as Flex, OpenLaszlo, and WPF/E to a RIA strategy is virtually required to properly exploit the range of capabilities you'll want capable online applications to have. This is particularly true around rich media support such as audio and video – which AJAX is virtually incapable of – but even such mundane things as good printing support. These are all things that the more sophisticated Flash-based RIA platforms really shine at and are easier to program in to boot. AJAX will increasingly get a serious run for its money from these platforms, particularly as they provide back-end server support for things like server-side push, formal Web Services, enterprise environments, and more."

Interestingly enough, the future of AJAX in the enterprise application space may not be as bleak as it appears, and we'll tell you why a little bit later in this chapter.

Finally, the browser's golden days are almost over. All leading software vendors are looking beyond the browser for the next Web application platform.

To summarize, if you're developing a new enterprise RIA from scratch, AJAX may not be the way to go. Choose a solid application development environment that offers a virtual machine at runtime like Flex/Flash, Java, or WPF. Any of these environments is more productive than AJAX. If you already have AJAX applications, you can nicely integrate new Flex RIAs in existing AJAX applications using tools like FABridge from Adobe for communicating between AJAX and Flex.

During AJAX's first year of life, every article or book on the subject mentioned Google Maps and Gmail, and various type-ahead samples: you enter the first zip code digit in a text field, and it suggests your possible choices based on your input without a page refresh. Today, you can read about a number of AJAX applications, including ones that work with photo images loaded from the popular flickr.com Web site. If you run into one of these samples, compare it with the slideshow application in Chapter 13. This is probably the easiest way to see the difference between the rich and just a little richer Internet applications.

Last, we'd like to make it clear that popular comparisons of Flex versus AJAX are simply wrong, since Flex is a framework and a complete development platform, while AJAX is a set of techniques. To compare apples to apples, you should compare products like Flex against GWT (Google) and the like.

Other RIA Solutions

In this section we've included short descriptions of several other players in the RIA space.

OpenLaszlo

OpenLaszlo (http://www.openlaszlo.org) from Laszlo Systems is an open source product that lets you create applications that can be deployed as DHTML or Flash Player files (check out the project called Legals at http://www.openlaszlo.org/legals). The ability to generate DHTML code made it a good candidate for developing applications for mobile devices, and Sun Microsystems has recently partnered with Laszlo Systems to bring this technology to the Java mobile space. This is direct competition for Adobe Flash Lite.

Flash Player is becoming a de-facto standard in the delivery of multimedia applications, and OpenLaszlo is already used by thousands of RIA developers. Like Flex and WPF, you define the GUI widgets in a declarative XML-based language called LZX. The processing logic is coded in JavaScript.

One of OpenLaszlo's selling points, besides being an open source solution, is that you can create applications for versions of Flash Player as old as 6.0, which you can't do with Flex 2. But the high speed of penetration and adoption of the latest version of Flash Player diminishes the value of this benefit.

GWT

GWT stands for Google Web Toolkit (http://code.google.com/webtoolkit/). It lets you write programs in Java, which are automatically converted to JavaScript so they can be delivered as AJAX

Web applications. This isn't the first attempt to offer a tool that converts Java to JavaScript. Take the open source project Java2Script (http://j2s.sourceforge.net/), an Eclipse plug-in that implements an Eclipse SWT library in JavaScript. But GWT's success is another illustration of how important it is to have support from a commercial software vendor, such as Google, for any AJAX initiative. GWT is not an open source product, but it is free.

An interesting GWT feature is that it compiles Java into various versions of JavaScript to accommodate the specific needs of different Web browsers. GWT comes with a library of extensible components. When this chapter was written, the number of these components was limited, but that will probably change soon, because it's Google. Its UI components are Java classes (i.e., MenuBar, HiperLink, Tree, and FileUpload), which can be combined into containers (i.e., HTMLTable, SimplePanel, and ComplexPanel).

GWT's hosted Web browser lets Java developers create and test their applications without converting them to JavaScript until the application is ready for real-world deployment. So, if a Java developer for whatever reason has to work on AJAX applications, he should definitely consider using the GWT framework.

Nexaweb

Nexaweb (http://www.nexaweb.com) offers a Java-based thin client that doesn't require any additional installation on the user's desktop. The application's state is controlled by a small Java applet running on the client. This applet communicates with the Nexaweb Java EE application as needed. To avoid issues related to the version of the Java Runtime Environment installed with the Web browser, Nexaweb uses JRE 1.1 for its applet. It's supported by every major browser. This applet partially updates the Web page when the state of the application changes. The user interface is defined using a declarative XML-based language, and the application logic is programmed in Java. It comes with an Eclipse-based visual editor.

Canoo

Canoo (http://www.canoo.com/) offers a so-called UltraLightClient, which is a Java library of server-side proxy classes similar to the Swing API, providing, for example, ULCTable instead of JTable. Basically each of these classes has two peers – one for the server and the other for the client's JRE. The library takes care of the split between client and server, including synchronization and communication of these halves using a proprietary protocol. A small presentation engine runs on the client, while the application runs on the server. The client's presentation layer can be deployed as a Java applet or application using Java Web Start technology. The server-side application can be deployed as a Java servlet or a stateful session bean.

Backbase

Backbase (http://www.backbase.com) includes a very light engine written entirely in JavaScript. It loads seamlessly at the beginning of the client session and brings in the client-side presentation framework, which includes tools to maintain state on the client, client/server synchronization, and incremental data load. The presentation framework supports drag-and-drop, data binding, styling, skinning, and multimedia. Backbase also steps away from typical page-based Web applications and lets you create a so-called Single-Page Interface. It comes with a library of more than 50 off-the-shelf GUI components written using DHTML, JavaScript, CSS, and XML.

Apollo, Desktop 2.0, and the Bright Future

We've been closely following the progress of Adobe's Apollo project (http://labs.adobe.com/wiki/index.php/Apollo), which will make people switch from pure Web applications to disconnected or partially disconnected ones. Apollo will integrate Flash Player, Flex, HTML, JavaScript, and eventually PDF, and it'll provide access to all desktop resources (file system, ports, et al). This means that pretty soon Web applications will spill from the Web browser right on your desktop. Yes, we're moving to desktop applications again – this time "Desktop 2.0."

As history repeats itself, let's recap.

Desktop 1.0 arrived more that 20 years ago as an intelligent and jazzy replacement for dumb mainframe terminals. For the first few years, one of its main functions was terminal emulation. A few killer apps (Lotus 1-2-3 and WordStar) changed the way people envisioned using computers. They realized that they could have their own private data store saved on a home computer! After a while a set of client/server technologies emerged. The main selling point of client/server was the ease in getting server data to the end user in an online mode as opposed to the batch mode, which delivered the data requested the next day or later. Mainframe terminals with their green-on-black-text-only user interface were sentenced to oblivion.

Visual Basic, Visual C++, and PowerBuilder were the tools of choice during the rapid growth of the client/server system. As the world's appetite for computer applications grew, deploying and versioning became more and more costly.

Then the Web with its Web 1.0 thin client started reminding us of the dumb terminal again, but this time the background was white. A semi-intelligent Web browser provided online access to a plethora of J2EE, LAMP, or .NET servers located around the world. The applications were all one big shopping card and users were reduced to the OK and Cancel buttons, but that was an affordable way for everyone to sell their services on the Web. Later on, businesses began creating more sophisticated Web applications and even converted the complete client/server system into DHTML/XmlHttpRequest, albeit not labeled AJAX yet. (Seriously what took Jesse James Garrett so long?) And now we're approaching the "client/Web" revolution – this time making all the data in the world available and personal at the same time with the eye-candy look-and-feel of rich Internet applications.

The world should now come up with new killer apps and revisit old ones but in a Web/Desktop 2.0 context. In the case of word processor or spreadsheet collaboration, privacy can be more important than the ability to do a spell check.

Making application development simpler will get us halfway there. Small teams of developers will be able to create Office-like components in Flex and Apollo. We see another trend here: putting the end user in charge of the GUI experience. For example, many browser shortcomings were "fixed" by adding toolbars and components. Creating a RIA platform and applications capable of cross-integration is going to be vital.

Porting Google Maps into a desktop Apollo application was demo'd at the MAX 2006 conference. Expect to see a number of "webified" desktop applications by mid-2007. The authors of this book are working hard on Flex/Apollo applications and, hopefully, you'll see the result at www.faratasystems.com when Apollo is officially released.

The birth of Apollo has an interesting twist: both Flex and HTML/JavaScript applications can be ported to Apollo, which means that AJAX applications will find their new home in Apollo too. Not only they will be ported, they'll be upgraded and turned into desktop systems. Basically, Apollo will offer AJAX a lifeline.

Some Pragmatic Flex/Java Considerations

Cool technologies come and go. Only some of them settle down in the toolbox of a professional programmer working on enterprise business applications. The technical excellence of any software is important, but it's not the only component in its success.

The Learning Curve: Reuse of Skills and Code

One important concern of any development manager is the availability of a large pool of people who know a particular software. There are plenty of Java programmers with the skills required to develop Web applications, and the good news is that enterprise Java developers with servlet/Java EE programming skills or Java Swing experience will find the Flex path very easy. Java and ActionScript 3.0 are very similar; Eclipse is a familiar environment for many Java developers. Since Flex piggybacks on Java EE and browser technologies, a server-side Java programmer should be able to correlate his current skills with the development process in Flex. Java Swing developers will instantly spot similarities to Java event and layout models. In our experience, the typical ramp-up time for motivated Java developer is two weeks. The best part is that Flex seamlessly integrates with existing Java server code of any flavor – POJO, EJB, Hibernate/Spring, or JMS, so the server-side part can literally remain unchanged.

Application Security

Another important consideration is the security of Flex/Java applications. Flex server-side security management is quite extensive, and it lets you use either container offerings or custom security providers via declarative XML binding. There are a couple of challenges since Flex supports multiple protocols, so Java EE security that relies only on HTTP sessions has to be extended, but it's a simple and well-documented process. On the client side, it builds on Flash Player security that's known for its lack of serious security flaws. You have a built-in security manager that has all the standard protection for cross-domain and zone access. Corporations can further restrict the code they get from third parties by wrapping the code loaders in additional security managers.

Flex GUI Performance

Java Swing is a tried and true tool for developing responsive GUIs in demanding applications like stock trading and online auctions. Flex is capable of providing near-real-time data rendering to the GUI and very high refresh rates on large data sets. Flash Player 9 is the high-performance modern virtual machine with precompiled optimized code and a just-in-time (JIT) machine code compiler.

Shorter Development Cycle

It's very possible to build the client side of a real-time portfolio display integrated with news feeds and graphs in about 200 lines of Flex 2 code. A similar Swing program (even if it's created with commercial IDEs) would be several times larger.

The real selling point becomes obvious on the second or third day of the proof-of-concept phase. A decent Flex developer should be able to prototype (short of server processing) most of the UI for a specific trading system by the end of the first week. If you're lucky and system integration went okay, you can add the collaboration features and multimedia – with the total client code base for the whole project coming within 1,000-1,500 lines. This is definitely not possible with Swing. Of course, some people will say modern Java IDEs generate lots of boilerplate code automatically, but this is still the code that someone has to read, understand, and fix if need be.

Room for Improvement

While many programmers who dealt with previous versions of Flex are really happy now that they have a professional Eclipse-based IDE, Java programmers are spoiled by the variety of excellent and responsive IDEs. Flex Builder is a truly RAD tool, and it helps tremendously in writing Flex code, but when this was written it worked a bit slower than the Eclipse IDE for Java. One of the reasons Flex seems slower than Java is that it does so much more than the Java compiler. It uses a number of code generators behind the scenes, a multi-pass compiler/linker, and a deployment optimizer. It also embeds a full-fledged Flash "projector" in Eclipse.

Connection Management

Flex provides an extensive infrastructure for managing connections between the Web browser and the server. It lets you specify all the protocol details for the Real Time Messaging Protocol (RTMP), HTTP, HTTPS, as well as plain socket connections. You can then specify the order in which the protocols should be tried due to availability/firewall issues. Flex also automatically bundles multiple requests going over the same transport, striving for maximum performance out-of-the-box. Since any Web browser, by default, maintains only two connections with the server, Flex gives you much better use of these two connections if you limit yourself to HTTP. You also get alternative real-time push or pull connections on additional protocols, a direct socket API, and tons of low-level hooks that let you build any protocol you want.

We worked on AJAX-like frameworks during 1999-2005 and can say that Flex is a lot more robust in code and data delivery fields than any cross-browser AJAX solution known today. Robustness is an even bigger showstopper for large AJAX applications than performance. Flex/Flash really gives back the control over communications that is very important for enterprise applications.

Flex and Agile Development

In the mid-'90s PowerBuilder and Visual Basic were the tools of choice in the client/server field. Software developers didn't really worry about what was under the hood, but more importantly, they were business users' best friends. They could do stuff quickly, or using the modern jargon, they were agile programmers without even knowing it. They'd ask the business user Joe, "How do you usually do your business? What would you like to have on this screen? Describe the steps of your business process." Most likely Joe wouldn't know all the answers, but this was okay, because developers could come back to the user the next day with a working prototype. This was easy with PowerBuilder's DataWindow. When Joe-the-user saw the prototype, his glassy look all of a sudden would become friendly and understanding. Now Joe was back in control: "No, you did this part wrong, I wanted it different." No problem, developers would return with the changes the next day (not next month, but the next day!).

Developers didn't really know how the DataWindow worked, but they trusted this component. PowerBuilder used an event-driven programming model, which was clean and simple. Object A triggers event XYZ on object B, and this event can carry a payload – the data that object B needs to operate. Using modern jargon it's called Inversion of Control or Dependency Injection design pattern. What's important is that object B doesn't know about object A. On the same note, if object B needs to return the result of some internal function back, it would broadcast this result "to whom it may concern" by triggering one of its own events (we'll explain this in the section on custom events in Chapter 4). This is loose coupling in action.

The mentality of many Java programmers was different. They'd assign lower priority to the user's windows and spend most of their time designing a multi-tier system that didn't depend on any specific look-and-feel and could be universal. Meetings with Joe would be rare because they couldn't create a decent prototype fast. Fancy IDEs with GUI designers like Matisse weren't in the picture yet and, more importantly, Java programmers were thinking big: UML, design patterns, application servers, and clustering. They enjoyed the programming process for itself. They didn't like the mindset of old-fashioned PowerBuilder or Visual Basic programmers who were thinking windows and screens.

With Flex you started to care about the business users again. You can change the prototype twice a day, and Joe can do the same with his business requirements. No pile of project documentation is needed. The napkin is back and it works. Flex architects can give the server-side Java team the final okay only after Joe is 100% happy.

Besides, with Flex we can have the best of both worlds: the source code of the Flex framework is available, we can learn how it works inside, and override some functionality with what suits our needs better.

Working with Flex promotes agile development, where the people we build the software for are the driving force. Agile development methodology suggests minimizing each development cycle to mitigate the risk of delivering something to the users that they don't want. Agile development encourages frequent face-to-face meetings with the end users as opposed to preparing and sending documents back and forth.

The main page of the Manifesto for Agile Software Development (http://www.agilemanifesto.org/) prioritizes:

- Individuals and interactions over processes and tools
- Working software over comprehensive documentation
- Customer collaboration over contract negotiation
- Responding to change over following a plan

In this book we tried to use agile development methodologies. When you follow the examples, do a "reverse analysis" of the code you've written in the past to see if it could be done simpler using the techniques we describe.

Summary

In this chapter we've presented you with a quick overview of major RIA-enabling technologies and various approaches to making Web applications richer. It's by no means a complete list: new commercial and open source RIA frameworks and components arise every day. However, given the overall business and technical value, there's not a single RIA vendor that the authors of this book would put anywhere near Adobe's position with Flex. Adobe Flex 2 is an excellent tool for creating commercial-strength rich Internet applications. It integrates with various back ends and elegantly accommodates the complexities of an enterprise technology setup. If you're thinking strategically, if you'd like to keep your business competitive, you need to innovate.

CHAPTER

2

Getting Familiar with Flex

Getting Familiar with Flex

Even though this book is not a Flex tutorial, we need to spend some time introducing this RIA tool. While Flex comes with an Integrated Development Environment (IDE) called Flex Builder (see Chapter 3), in this chapter we'll gently introduce you to Flex programming by writing a couple of simple Flex programs using only the tools and components that are available for free. We've also included a brief comparison of the Java and ActionScript languages and some good-to-know topics: frame rates, the application initialization process, and display lists.

Working with text editors and command-line compilers is not the most productive way of developing with Flex, but command-line compilers definitely have their use. In a typical real-world scenario, developers working on a decent-size project would use both – Flex Builder IDE to create and test their applications, and then build tools like Ant or Maven to invoke Flex command-line compilers to create and deploy the application. This is especially important because Flex applications are often used in a mixed environment where an application build consists of multiple steps of compiling and deploying modules written in more than one language, for example, Flex for the GUI part and Java for the server-side components.

Free Flex 2 Ingredients

This is a brief overview of what comprises Flex and what's available for free:

MXML: An XML-based markup language that lets you define GUI components using declarative programming. You add tags to your program that represent visible and invisible Flex objects. For example, the MXML tag <mx:Label text="Enter password:" x="20" y="40" /> will display the text "Enter password:" in 20 pixels to the right from the top left corner of the Flash Player's window and 40 pixels down.

ActionScript 3.0: An object-oriented language with a syntax similar to Java's. ActionScript classes and MXML tags are interchangeable. Most ActionScript classes can be represented by MXML tags and vice versa. Even if you create your application only in MXML, it'll be converted to ActionScript and then compiled into bytecode for execution in Flash Player.

Flex framework: A library of extensible components located in multiple packages. You can create your own classes and new MXML tags as needed. Just write a piece of MXML code, save it in a file called MyCode.mxml and you've got a new tag: <MyCode>. Or create the new class MyCode.as and use it either with other ActionScript classes or as an MXML tag.

mxmlc: A program that launches MXML and the ActionScript compiler located in a Java archive called mxmlc.jar. This command-line compiler generates Flex applications as .swf (pronounced swif) files.

compc[1]: A program that generates Flex component libraries as .swc (pronounced swick) files. An swc file contains an swf, catalog.xml, and asset files if needed. We'll discuss the use of component libraries in Chapter 10.

fdb: A command-line Flex debugging utility that you can start from a command line. It requires the debugger version of Flash Player that comes with the Flex framework.

asdoc: A documentation tool that runs through files containing Flex source code and creates online documentation similar to the one that comes with the standard Flex API.

Flex Data Services 2 Express: Deployed as a standard Java EE application, it provides high-performance connectivity with existing server-side data and business logic. Based on messaging architecture, Flex Data Services integrates with existing common middleware and provides services that automatically synchronize data between client and server, supports real-time data push and publish/subscribe messaging, and facilitates the creation of collaborative applications.

Flash Player 9: A runtime environment for your Flex 2 applications (.swf and .swc files). A debug version of Flash Player can output a trace message to a console or into a file.

Downloading the Flex 2 Framework

All Flex 2 components can be downloaded from the URL: http://www.adobe.com/cfusion/tdrc/index.cfm?product=flex.

Flex Builder IDE comes with command-line compilers and the Flex framework. But since this chapter is about working with free Flex components, we'll assume for a moment that you're not planning to use Flex Builder and will just get the Flex SDK from the section called the Free Flex 2 SDK and Language Pack.

After the download is complete, unzip the archive file into a separate directory. For example, in Windows create a folder c:\FreeFlex and add c:\FreeFlex\bin to the system variable PATH on your computer. Open the command window and type *mxmlc –version*. If you did everything right, your screen may look like Figure 2.1:

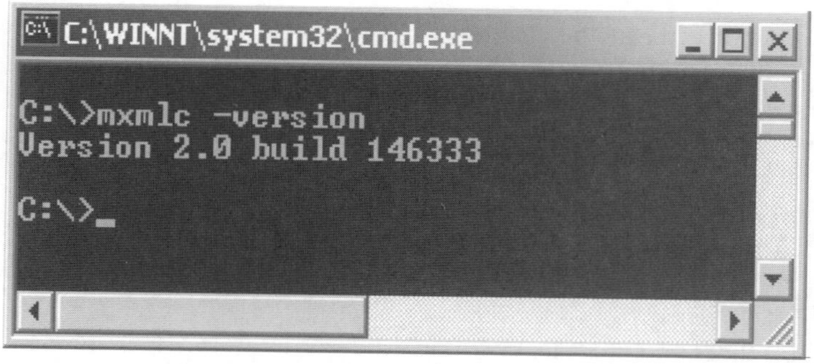

Figure 2.1 Checking the version of mxmlc compiler

Since the mxmlc compiler is written in Java, it uses the Java Runtime Environment (JRE) during the compilation process. Flex Framework comes with its own JRE (when this was written version 1.4.2). You can also download a more current version of JRE at http://www.java.com/en/download/manual.jsp. Having the latest JRE on your PC may increase the speed of the compilation process.

After installing the Flex Framework, you'll find the configuration file jvm.config and, if you have a Windows machine, you can edit this file to use the latest JRE[2]. If you're not using Windows, you can modify the compiler's shell script to point it to the right JRE.

If you don't have Flash Player 9 installed, get it from the same Web page. The debug version of Flash Player 9 is located under your Flex install in the directory Player.

We are now ready to write our first Flex program. Guess what its name will be.

Hello World in MXML

It says in Wikipedia that "Hello World is a software program that prints Hello World on a display device. It is used in many introductory tutorials for teaching a programming language and many students use it as their first programming experience in a language." (See http://en.wikipedia.org/wiki/Hello_world.)

After seeing these two magic words "Hello World" on the system console or a graphical window, you'll get this warm feeling of knowing that your software is installed and configured properly, compilers work, the runtime environment operates, and you're ready to learn the tool, which in our case is Flex.

Ladies and gentlemen, please welcome, Hello World in MXML.

```
<?xml version="1.0" encoding="utf-8"?>
<mx:Application xmlns:mx="http://www.adobe.com/2006/mxml" layout="absolute">
```

```
    <mx:Label text="Hello World"/>
</mx:Application>
```

Listing 2.1 Hello World program: HelloWorld.mxml

Type this code into your favorite plain text editor and save it in a separate directory. In a command window, switch to this directory and compile this application by entering mxmlc HelloWorld.mxml. It should create the new file HelloWorld.swf.

By default, .swf files are associated with Flash Player – just double-click on HelloWorld.swf in Windows Explorer and it'll run our HelloWorld program:

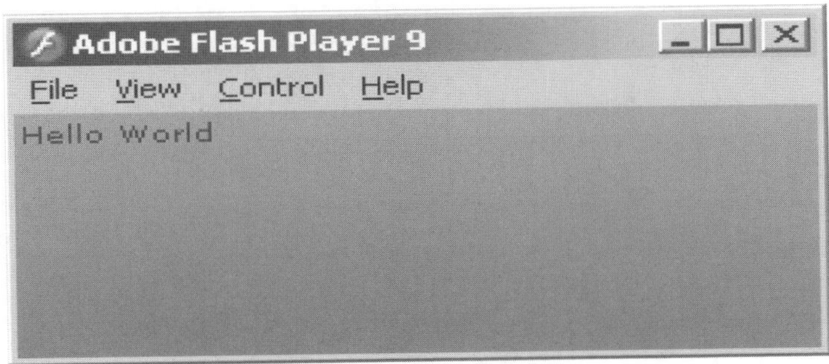

Figure 2.2 HelloWorld in Flash Player

The MXML file has translated HelloWorld into ActionScript and compiled it into the .swf file. During the first pass, the name of your MXML file becomes the name of the main generated ActionScript class, for example, with the virtual wave of a magic wand the MXML tag <mx:Application> turns into the ActionScript code:

```
class HelloWorld extends Application {…}
```

All other MXML tags will undergo a similar procedure. For example, the markup code

```
<mx:Label text="Hello World"/>
```

leads to the generation of an instance of the ActionScript class Label and calls its setter function to assign the text "Hello World" to an attribute called text.

```
<mx:Label text="Hello World"/ >
```

Typically, you deploy a swf file on your Web server as a part of an HTML page[3]. If you're using a command-line Flex compiler, you'll have to create such an HTML file manually, as opposed to Flex Builder, which automatically creates these wrappers for you. But even the process of manually creating HTML wrappers is greatly simplified by using the so-called HTML templates that come with Flex located in the folder resources. Currently, there are six HTML templates of various flavors that can detect the client's version of Flash Player, offer an express install of the player, and support history management. The process of creating HTML wrappers is described in the product manual, "Building and Deploying Flex 2 Applications."

Specifying Compiler Options

The Flex compiler comes with a number of useful options. For example, you can request that the generated ActionScript code not be deleted after compilation. To see which compiler options are available, type the following at the command prompt:

```
mxmlc -help list advanced
```

One option is keep-generated-actionscript. Let's recompile HelloWorld with this option:

```
mxmlc -keep-generated-actionscript HelloWorld.mxml
```

Now the Flex compiler will not only produce the .swf file, but will also create a subdirecory called generated and you will be able to browse the source code of more than two-dozen ActionScript HelloWorld-supporting files.

The speed of the command-line compilation may be improved if you use the option -incremental=true (in Flex Builder this option is on by default).

You can read more about Flex compiler options in the section "Using the Flex Compilers" in the product manual "Building and Deploying Flex 2 Applications."

You can also specify compiler options in a special configuration file named flex-config.xml or in a custom configuration file whose name should be specified in the load-config compiler's option. Just keep in mind that the compilation options from flex-config.xml file affects all your projects.

Another way of specifying some Flex compiler options from an ActionScript class, namely width, height, frameRate, and backgroundColor, is through a special meta tag SWF that you put above the class declaration line. For example:

```
[SWF(frameRate="50", backgroundColor="#FFFFFF")]
public class SomeApp {
}
```

If compilation fails, you'll see a short error description, but if you're still not sure what this error means, consult http://livedocs.adobe.com/labs/as3preview/langref/compilerErrors.html for a more detailed description of the compilation errors. This Web page also has a link to a page describing runtime errors.

Building and Deploying Applications with Ant

Unless your project is as simple as the HelloWorld application, compilation and deployment has to be automated. Creating a build script for any decent-size application (i.e., hundreds of files in Flex and server-side Java) is a project on its own. Java programmers typically use an open source build tool such as Ant or Maven to formally describe and execute all the steps required to build and deploy their projects.

If you haven't had a chance to use any of the build tools before, this section is for you. This is a mini-primer on how to use Ant, the popular Java-based build tool from Apache.

Even deploying such a simple application as HelloWorld consists of several steps. For example:

1. Use mxmlc to compile HelloWorld.mxml into a swf file.
2. Create an HTML wrapper file(s) from one of the HTML templates.
3. Create or clean the directory in your Web server where HelloWorld files will be deployed.
4. Copy or ftp HelloWorld.swf and supporting files to this directory.

Now imagine that your HelloWorld application is part of a larger application that includes Java modules that also have to be compiled and deployed in some server location. The deployment of even a small project usually involves at least a dozen dependent tasks that have to execute in a particular order. Creating and maintaining a build script is well worth the effort.

Building HelloWorld with Ant

With Ant, you describe your project in a build file written in XML (it's typically called build.xml). An Ant project consists of targets (i.e., compile) that, in turn, consist of tasks (i.e., mkdir, exec). Listing 2.2 shows a build.xml that will create an output directory bin and compile our HelloWorld application into this directory. This Ant build file has two targets: *init* and *compile*.

```
<project name="HelloWorld" default="compile">
    <property name="flex.mxmlc" location="C:\Program Files\Adobe\Flex Builder 2 Plug-in\
Flex SDK 2\bin\mxmlc.exe" />
    <property name="dest.dir" value="bin" />

   <target name="init">
      <delete dir="${dest.dir}" />
      <mkdir dir="${dest.dir}" />
      <attrib file="${dest.dir}" readonly="false"/>
   </target>

   <target name="compile" depends="init">
      <exec executable="${flex.mxmlc}" failonerror="true">
        <arg line="-output '${dest.dir}/HelloWorld.swf'"/>
        <arg line="HelloWorld.mxml"/>
```

```
        </exec>
    </target>
</project>
```

Listing 2.2 Ant project - build.xml

The init target consists of two tasks: delete and create the directory called bin.

The compile target will compile HelloWorld.mxml, producing bin\HelloWorld.swf. If we have to write a command manually that compiles HelloWorld.mxml into the bin directory, it would look like this:

```
mxmlc -output bin/HelloWorld.swf HelloWorld.mxml
```

Besides targets and tasks, our build.xml contains two property tags. One of them defines a property called dest.dir that has a value bin that is the name of the output directory for our compiled HelloWorld.swf:

```
<property name="dest.dir" value="bin" />
```

This means that wherever Ant encounters dest.dir surrounded with ${ and }, it'll substitute it with the value of this property. In our case this is bin.

The project in Listing 2.2 also defines a property called flex.mxmlc that tells Ant where the mxmlc compiler is located. The target compile uses Ant's task *exec*, which will run the mxmlc compiler, passing it the arguments specified in the <arg> tags.

Let's download Ant[4] from http://ant.apache.org/. Installation is simple: just unzip the archive and add the path to its bin directory (i.e. C:\apache-ant-1.6.5\bin) to the environment variable *path* of your operating system.

Now we can open a command window, get into the directory where HelloWorld.mxml and build.xml are located, and enter the command *ant* that will start executing the default target of our project, which is compile. But since compile target is marked as a dependent on init, Ant will execute the init target first.

Figure 2.3 shows how the Windows XP command window may look after running this project:

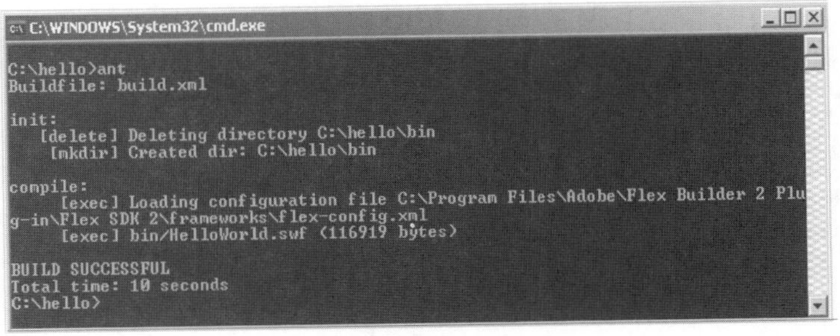

```
C:\WINDOWS\System32\cmd.exe

C:\hello>ant
Buildfile: build.xml

init:
   [delete] Deleting directory C:\hello\bin
    [mkdir] Created dir: C:\hello\bin

compile:
     [exec] Loading configuration file C:\Program Files\Adobe\Flex Builder 2 Plu
g-in\Flex SDK 2\frameworks\flex-config.xml
     [exec] bin/HelloWorld.swf (116919 bytes)

BUILD SUCCESSFUL
Total time: 10 seconds
C:\hello>
```

Figure 2.3 Running an Ant Build

Ant has an extensive set of predefined tasks like copy, zip, jar, War, FTP, Mail, Condition, and many more described at http://ant.apache.org/manual/.

For example, to make our build file work in both Windows and Unix environments, we can specify the location of the mxmlc compiler as follows:

```
<condition property=”flex.mxmlc” value=”${sdkdir}/bin/mxmlc”>
   <os family=”unix”/>
</condition>
<condition property=”flex.mxmlc” value=”${sdkdir}/bin/mxmlc.exe”>
   <os family=”windows”/>
</condition>
```

You can pass values of the properties from the Ant command line using the –Dpropery=value option. For example, if we use the code snippet above, the property sdkdir can be passed from a command line:

```
ant -Dsdkdir=/opt/usr/freeflex
```

You can write more sophisticated Ant scripts. For example, you can automate the creation of an HTML wrapper for swf files with a replace *regex* task applied to one of the HTML templates provided. You can write build scripts that will merge Flex-generated artifacts with Java Web applications. Automating builds with Ant can get you pretty far.

There are lots of online articles and books on Ant, but don't miss *Ant in Anger* by Steve Loughran in which he discusses some Ant core practices, naming conventions, and team development processes. (See http://ant.apache.org/ant_in_anger.html.)

Frame Rate

Flash Player renders its GUI objects (display list) at a specified frame rate. As opposed to Flash movies that consist of multiple frames displayed over a timeline, Flex applications don't have multiple frames, but the frame rate plays an important role in Flex programs. The display list (your GUI components) is rendered at the specified frame rate and applications with higher frame rates can have a better performing GUI, but it doesn't come free.

The Flex compiler builds an swf file with a default frame rate of 24 frames a second, unless another value is specified during compilation. For example:

```
mxmlc -default-frame-rate 50 HelloWorld.mxml
```

This command will build an swf file with the frame rate of 50 frames a second. The display list rendering and ActionScript execution take turns, hence the frame rate can affect your application performance.

Setting the frame rate to 50 doesn't mean that each frame will be displayed in exactly 20 milliseconds (1,000 divided by 50), since there is some OS/browser overhead. Besides, some browsers may impose restrictions on plugins to lower CPU utilization on the user's machine.

To see how the compile time setting of the default-frame-rate option affects program execution, consider the following program that on each enterFrame event makes a simple calculation of the actual frame rate.

```
<?xml version="1.0" encoding="utf-8"?>
<mx:Application xmlns:mx="http://www.adobe.com/2006/mxml"
   enterFrame="enterFrameHandler()">
   <mx:Script>
      <![CDATA[
      var lastTime:int;
      function enterFrameHandler():void{
               trace(int(1000/(getTimer()-lastTime)));
               lastTime=getTimer();
      }
      ]]>
   </mx:Script>
   <mx:Button label="Button"/>
   <mx:TextInput/>
</mx:Application>
```

Listing 2.3 Testing frame rate

We ran this program in the Internet Explorer and Firefox browsers on a Windows XP laptop with a single 1.8GHz CPU. Tables 2.1 and 2.2 show the difference between requested and actual frame rates and how hard the CPU works based on the frame rate settings.

Default-frame-rate	10	24	50	100
Actual frame rate	9-10	18-26	35-52	50-110
CPU utilization	15-17%	15-20%	18-20%	26-28%

Table 2.1 Frame rates with Internet Explorer 6

Default-frame-rate	10	24	50	100
Actual frame rate	9-10	16-22	41-50	70-100
CPU utilization	16-20%	18-20%	22-25%	30-33%

Table 2.2 Frame rates with Firefox 1.5

While results vary slightly, they are self-explanatory – lower frame rates translate into lower CPU utilization. You should experiment with frame rates in your application to find the right balance between GUI performance and CPU use. Remember that your users may be running several programs at the same time, and you don't want to bring their CPUs to their knees just because you've enjoyed super-smooth graphics rendering. If you're not creating a movie, keep the frame rate as low as you can.

Namespaces in MXML

In XML, namespaces are used to avoid potential naming conflicts with other components with the same names. So far we've only seen the xmlns property in our MXML sample programs:

```
<mx:Application xmlns:mx="http://www.adobe.com/2006/mxml" layout="absolute">
```

The namespace mx:xmlns refers to the URI http://www.adobe.com/2006/mxml that lists valid MXML tags. Open the file flex-config.xml and you'll find an XML element there that links this URI to the file mxml-manifest.mxl that lists all the MXML components. Here's an extract from this manifest file:

```
    <component id="ButtonBar" class="mx.controls.ButtonBar"/>
    <component id="Canvas" class="mx.containers.Canvas"/>
    <component id="CheckBox" class="mx.controls.CheckBox"/>
    <component id="ColorPicker" class="mx.controls.ColorPicker"/>
    <component id="ComboBox" class="mx.controls.ComboBox"/>
```

If you want to use one of the standard MXML components, specify the prefix mx for each of them. For example, to use an MXML Label, you write the following:

```
<mx:Label x="111" y="81" text="Hello World"/>
```

Later in this book, we'll show you how to create custom components and keep them in a separate namespace to avoid naming conflicts. We'll introduce another namespace with the URI com.theriabook.controls.*. For example, in Chapter 9 we'll be developing a custom Tree component and Listing 9.10 includes the following MXML code:

```
<mx:Application   xmlns:mx="http://www.adobe.com/2006/mxml"
  xmlns:lib="com.theriabook.controls.*" >
   …
  <lib:Tree id="tree" width="50%"  height="100%"…>
   </lib:Tree>
</mx:Application>
```

This sample defines two namespaces: mx and lib. The <lib:Tree> notation means that we're planning to use a Tree component from the namespace called lib. As you can guess, we're going to program this Tree component in the ActionScript's package com.theriabook.controls and will have to provide either the code of our Tree component or the SWC library that includes this Tree.

The namespace URI tells Flex where to look for the file implementing this component. You can either create a com/theriabook/controls subdirectory in the application's directory or – preferably – keep it in a separate location included in the classpath of your application (read about the flex-config.xml file and the source-path tag in the Flex documentation). Since we've defined two namespaces here, we can use components available in any of them.

You can also specify a so-called local namespace using notations like xmlns="*" or xmlns:mylocal="*" that tells Flex to look for components that are located in the same directory as the MXML file or, in case of Flex Data Services, in the /WEB-INF/flex/user-classes directory.

Chapter 4 includes a section that shows how to use namespaces in ActionScript.

From Hello World to a Calculator

The Hello World application uses just a Label tag put directly inside the parent application tag. But typical MXML code has a hierarchical structure. The application may include containers that in turn can consist of other containers or individual components. For example, a calculator can consist of two panels: the top one will be used for displaying results and the bottom one will hold the buttons with digits. We'll put both of these panels inside the tag VBox – the vertical box (Java programmers can think of it as a Swing BoxLayout).

```
<?xml version="1.0" encoding="utf-8"?>
<mx:Application xmlns:mx="http://www.adobe.com/2006/mxml"
                                           layout="absolute">
   <mx:VBox x="23" y="22" height="350">
      <mx:Panel width="250" height="70" layout="absolute">
      </mx:Panel>
```

```
    <mx:Panel width="250" height="220" layout="absolute">
    </mx:Panel>
  </mx:VBox>
</mx:Application>
```

Listing 2.4 Calculator1.mxml - A VBox with two panels

After saving the code above in the file Calculator1.mxml, we'll compile it with mxmlc and run it in Flash Player:

Figure 2.4 Running Calculator1.mxml in Flash Player

The calculator's panels are ready and after adding a text tag to the top panel and several button tags to the bottom one, the code will looks like this:

```
<?xml version="1.0" encoding="utf-8"?>
<mx:Application xmlns:mx="http://www.adobe.com/2006/mxml"
                                          layout="absolute">
     <mx:VBox x="23" y="22" height="350">
     <mx:Panel width="250" height="70" layout="absolute">
       <mx:Text x="0" y="-14" text="Text" width="144"/>
     </mx:Panel>
     <mx:Panel width="250" height="220" layout="absolute">
       <mx:Button x="0" y="0" label="1" width="36"/>
       <mx:Button x="40" y="0" label="2" width="36"/>
       <mx:Button x="80" y="0" label="3" width="36"/>
       <mx:Button x="0" y="30" label="4" width="36"/>
```

```
        <mx:Button x="40" y="30" label="5" width="36"/>
        <mx:Button x="80" y="30" label="6" width="36"/>
      </mx:Panel>
   </mx:VBox>
</mx:Application>
```

Listing 2.5 Calculator2.mxml – Adding controls

Compile and run this code and you'll see the following screen:

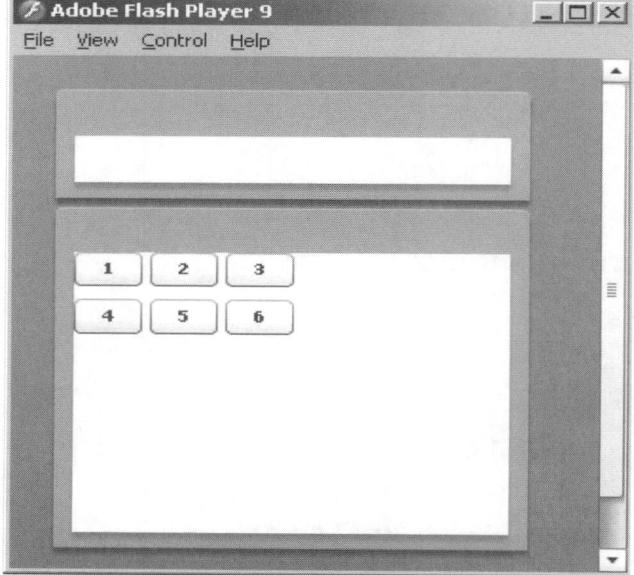

Figure 2.5 Running Calculator2.mxml in Flash Player

It's not the prettiest calculator you've ever seen, but it's not bad for two minutes of coding. The structure of the program in Listing 2.5 is simple, readable, and elegant.

The panels can include either standard Flex containers or custom components that you or other developers created. Table 2.3 provides the widgets that come with the Flex 2 framework.

Layouts	ApplicationControlBar, Canvas, ControlBar, Form, FormHeading, FormItem, Grid, HBox, HDividedBox, HRule, Panel, Spacer, Tile, TitleWindow, VBox, VDividedBox , VRule
Navigators	Accordion, ButtonBar, LinkBar, MenuBar, TabBar, TabNavigator, ToggleButtonBar, ViewStack
Controls	Button, CheckBox, ColorPicker, ComboBox, DataGrid, DateChooser, DateField, HSlider, HorizontalList, Image, Label, Link, List, Loader, NumericStepper, PopUpButton, ProgressBar, RadioButton, RadioButtonGroup, RichTextEditor, Text, TextArea, TextInput, TileList, Tree, VSlider, VideoDisplay

Table 2.3 Flex widgets

You can create custom components by combining these widgets. For example, you can create a custom login component with two Label controls for ID and password, two TextInputs, two Buttons, and a Link for the "Forgot Password?" function. Such custom components can be reused by multiple applications. Starting in Chapter 6 we'll show you how to create custom controls.

Adding Some ActionScript

MXML takes care of the GUI, but where's the processing logic? What will happen when a user presses a button on our calculator? Nothing will happen at this point. The processing logic has to be written using ActionScript 3, which is an object-oriented language with a syntax similar to Java's, and both of these languages can be integrated quite nicely in distributed Internet applications.

ActionScript was first introduced in August of 2000 as a programming language for Flash Player 5. ActionScript 2 came into the picture in September of 2003 with Flash Player 7. ActionScript 3 (June 2006) is a full rewrite of this language that can be used for creating applications (even without using MXML) for Flash Player 9. ActionScript 3 is based on the third edition of ECMAScript, which is an international standardized programming language for scripting.

Flex Framework is written in ActionScript 3. Readers familiar with previous versions of this language may want to check out "ActionScript 3: Learning Tips" at http://www.adobe.com/devnet/actionscript/articles/actionscript_tips.html.

We'll be using ActionScript 3 in every chapter of this book, but for detailed coverage of this language please consult the product manual "Programming ActionScript 3.0" available for download at www.flex.org.

In Flex, you link MXML components with the ActionScript processing logic using one of the following methods:

- Embed ActionScript code in mxml files using the tag <mx:Script>
- Include external ActionScript files into mxml, for example :

```
<mx:Script source="calculateTax.as">
```

- Import ActionScript classes
- Import ActionScript compiled components

A typical Flex project consists of .mxml files with declared components since the files containing ActionScript code, .swc files with compiled components, .css files with presentation style info, and other assets like image files, if needed. All of these components can be compiled into one .swf file, or a number of swc libraries, and run by Flash Player 9. Only one MXML file should have the <mx:Application> tag; the rest of the MXML files usually start with other tags.

The First Date with Events

Calculator2 displays GUI components using MXML. For the processing logic we'll use ActionScript, and the only missing link is how these components can initiate this processing logic. In Flex this is done using events. For example:

```
<mx:Button x="0" y="0" label="1" width="36" click="displayDigit();"/>
```

The displayDigit() is a function written in ActionScript that can contain some processing logic and displays the digit. Chapter 4 will offer more details on using standard and custom events.

Event-driven programming is about identifying important events that may happen to your application and writing event handlers to process these events. If a particular event never happened, the code from the corresponding event handler (aka listener) isn't called.

Not all events are triggered by the user's actions. Some system events may be triggered by your application code or other processes such as the arrival of the database query result set or the return of the Web Services call. Your applications can define its own events and trigger them from MXML or ActionScript code. Writing event listeners that contain code-handling events is automated in Flex, but you have a means of writing such listeners on your ActionScript code.

For example, adding a simple MXML attribute to process a mouseOver event

```
<mx:Label text="Hello World" mouseOver="changeTextColor()" />
```

requires the compiler to work harder as now it needs to do the following:

- Generate an event listener for the Label object
- Create an object to process the mouseOver event in the user-defined function changeTextColor()
- Wire this listener with the instance of the Label

Java compilers work faster because their job is a lot easier – a Java programmer creates all these instances and listeners manually so the javac compiler spends most of its time merely translating the Java source code into bytecode.

The third version of the calculator adds several samples of processing the button-click event. In Listing 2.6 the b1 button uses inline ActionScript to concatenate digit 1 to the text field result:

```
click="result.text+='1'"
```

A click on button 2 calls an ActionScript displayDigit() function defined in the section <mx:Script>.

A click on button 3 concatenates the label of the button to the result field.

In the fourth button, we just fool around to illustrate using more than one ActionScript inline statements – first replace the label of the button to 9 and then display it. Even though it's not recommended, you can use multi-line inline ActionScript code by surrounding it with curly braces.

```
<?xml version="1.0" encoding="utf-8"?>
<mx:Application xmlns:mx="http://www.adobe.com/2006/mxml" layout="absolute">

        <mx:VBox x="23" y="22" height="350">
        <mx:Panel width="250" height="70" layout="absolute">
          <mx:Text id="result" x="0" y="0" width="230" height="30" textAlign="right"/>
        </mx:Panel>
        <mx:Panel width="250" height="220" layout="absolute">
          <mx:Button id="b1" x="0" y="0" label="1" width="36" click="result.text+='1'" />
          <mx:Button id="b2" x="40" y="0" label="2" width="36"
                                                      click="displayDigit(b2.label)"/>
          <mx:Button id="b3" x="80" y="0" label="3" width="36"
                                                       click="result.text+=b3.label"/>
          <mx:Button id="b4" x="0" y="30" label="4" width="36"
                                            click="b4.label='9';result.text+=b4.label"/>
          <mx:Button id="b5" x="40" y="30" label="5" width="36"
                               click="mx.controls.Alert.show('Someone clicked on 5');"/>
          <mx:Button id="b6" x="80" y="30" label="6" width="36"/>
        </mx:Panel>
     </mx:VBox>
     <mx:Script>
        <![CDATA[
           import mx.controls.Alert;
           private function displayDigit(digit:String):void{
              result.text+=digit;
           }
        ]]>
     </mx:Script>
   </mx:Application>
```

Listing 2.6 Calculator3.mxml – Adding event processing

A click on the fifth button shows how to display a message box, and Figure 2.6 depicts a snapshot of Calculator 3's program after pressing the first five buttons.

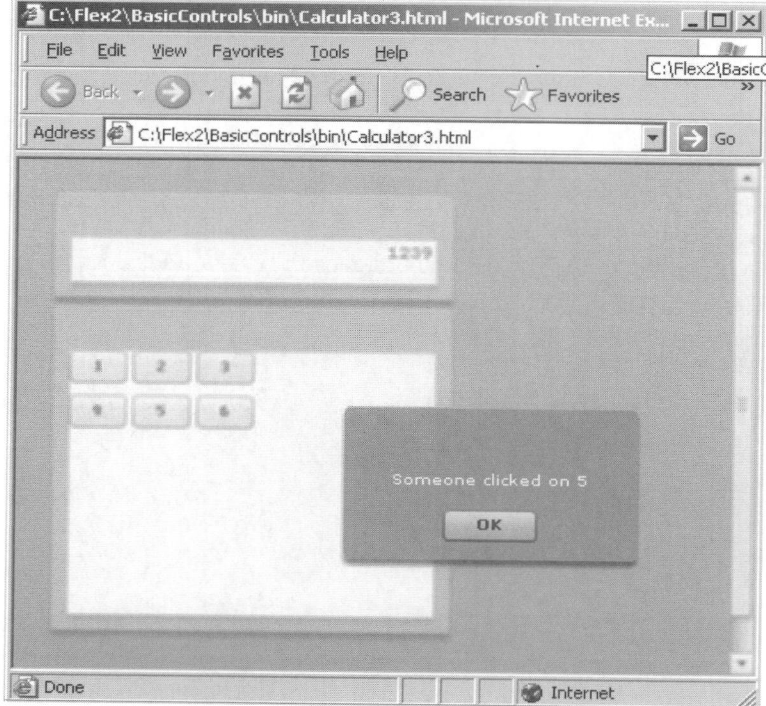

Figure 2.6: Calculator 3 after pressing 1, 2, 3, 4, and 5

Why ActionScript 3.0?

If you have any experience with other programming languages, the natural question is why would you start programming Web applications in ActionScript 3 as opposed to Java or JavaScript?

The simple answer is that an object-oriented language like ActionScript 3 combined with MXML makes GUI programming easier. Java Enterprise Edition (Java EE) with its multi-threading features, plus reliable and scalable application servers, is a great choice for server-side applications. Java Swing, the library for GUI development is powerful but complicated. Dealing with event-dispatch thread and synchronization issues, lack of data binding, and the need to program multiple event listeners manually makes programming in Java Swing a lot less productive.

ActionScript uses a single-threaded model (at least from the developer's perspective) and avoids many of the Java Swing issues by making all client/server communications asynchronous. A client program sends a request to the server specifying the name of the callback handler, and the user can immediately continue working with the screen, which never "freezes." When the result comes back, this handler will process it.

One of the ways to categorize programming languages is by how strict they are with variable types: some languages use static and others dynamic data typing. In statically typed languages (Java, C++, C#) you must declare a variable of a particular type, the compiler will ensure that your program uses this variable properly, and you should not expect any data type-related surprises at runtime. In dynamic languages (Perl, Python, ECMAScript, JavaScript) you don't have to declare the variables upfront.

ActionScript offers you a balance between static and dynamic languages by allowing you to program in both Java and JavaScript styles. But the freedom of not declaring variables comes with a price tag: any runtime environment can more efficiently allocate required resources if the types of program elements are known in advance. ActionScript 3 gives you the choice of writing highly efficient, statically typed code, highly dynamic and loosely typed code, or a combination of the two.

ActionScript 3 is a compiled object-oriented language and its performance has been substantially improved compared to previous versions of the language. Its code is compiled into bytecode and runs in the ActionScript Virtual Machine (AVM) in Flash Player 9. Strictly speaking, Flash Player 9 includes two AVMs: AVM1 executes the code written in the older version of the language, while AVM2 runs the code produced by ActionScript 3. Having two VMs in Flash Player has increased the size of Flash Player to about 1.2MB, but it ensures that existing applications won't break and users won't need to keep the older version of Flash Player.

In AVM2, most of the code goes through a Just-in-Time compiler that converts the bytecode into machine code and substantially improves performance.

Another notable feature of AS3 (and MXML) is their support of ECMAScript for XML (E4X), which makes working with XML a breeze. You'll see many examples of E4X usage in this book starting with Chapter 4.

Comparing ActionScript 3.0 and Java 5

We can't provide a detailed description of either language in this book, but a short comparison table of the major elements/concepts of these two languages may serve as a quick reference. You can read Table 2.4 either left-to-right or right-to-left depending on what your primary programming language is.

Concept/Language Construct	Java 5.0	ActionScript 3.0
Class library packaging	.jar	.swc
Inheritance	Class Employee extends Person{…}	Class Employee extends Person{…}

Variable declaration & initialization	String firstName="John";
	Date shipDate=new Date();
	int i;
	int a, b=10;
	double salary;
		Var firstName:String="John";
		var shipDate:Date=new Date();
		var i:int;
		var a:int, b:int=10;
		var salary:Number;

Undeclared variables	n/a	It's the equivalent of wild card-type notation *. If you declare a variable but don't specify its type, the * type will apply A default value is: undefined var myVar:*;
Variable scopes	block: declared in curly braces, local: declared in a method or block member: declared on the class level no global variables	No block scope: the minimal scope is a function local: declared within a function member: declared on the class level If a variable is declared outside of any function or class definition, it has a global scope.
Strings	Immutable, store sequences of two-byte Unicode characters	Immutable, store sequences of two-byte Unicode characters
Terminating statements with semicolons	A must	If you write one statement per line you can omit it
Strict equality operator (comparing objects without the type conversion)	n/a	=== for strict non-equality use !==
Constant qualifier	The keyword final final int STATE="NY";	The keyword const const STATE:int ="NY";
Type checking	Static (checked at compile time)	Dynamic (checked at runtime) and static (it's so-called 'strict mode,' which is the default in Flex Builder)
Type check operator	instanceof	is – checks data type, i.e., if (myVar is String){…} The is operator is a replacement for older instanceof

The as operator	n/a	Similar to is operator, but returns not Boolean, but the result of expression:
		
		var orderId:String="123";
		var orderIdN:Number=orderId as Number;
		trace(orderIdN);//prints 123

Primitives	byte, int, long, float, double,short, boolean, char	all primitives in ActionScript are objects. Boolean, int, uint, Number, String
		
		The following lines are equivalent;
		var age:int = 25;
		var age:int = new int(25);

Complex types	n/a	Array, Date, Error, Function, RegExp, XML, and XMLList
Array declaration and instantiation	int quarterResults[]; quarterResults = new int[4]; int quarterRe- sults[]={25,33,56,84};	Arrays in ActionScript resemble Java ArrayList: var quarterResults:Array =new Array(); or var quarterResults:Array=[]; var quarterResults:Array= [25, 33, 56, 84]; AS3 also has associative arrays that use named elements instead of numeric indexes (similar to Hashtable).
The top class in the inheritance tree	Object	Object

Casting syntax: cast the class Object to Person:	Person p=(Person) myObject;	var p:Person= Person(myObject);
		or
		var p:Person= myObject as Person;

Upcasting	class Xyz extends Abc{} Abc myObj = new Xyz();	class Xyz extends Abc{} var myObj:Abc=new Xyz();
Un-typed variable	n/a	var myObject:* var myObject:

Packages	package com.xyz;
	class myClass {...}
		package com.xyz{
		class myClass{...}
		}
		ActionScript packages can include not only classes, but separate functions as well

Class access levels	public, private, protected if none is specified, classes have package access level	public, private, protected if none is specified, classes have an internal access level (similar to the package access level in Java)

Custom access levels: namespaces	n/a	Similar to XML namespaces. namespace abc; abc function myCalc(){} or abc::myCalc(){} use namespace abc;

Console output	System.out.println();	// in debug mode only
		trace();

Imports	import com.abc.*; import com.abc.MyClass;	import com.abc.*; import com.abc.MyClass; packages must be imported even if the class names are fully qualified in the code.

Unordered key-value pairs	Hashtable, Map
	
	Hashtable friends = new Hashtable();
	
	friends.put("good", "Mary");
	friends.put("best", "Bill");
	friends.put("bad", "Masha");
	
	String bestFriend= friends.get("best");
	// bestFriend is Bill
		Associative Arrays
		
		Allows referencing its elements by names instead of indexes.
		var friends:Array=new Array();
		friends["good"]="Mary";
		friends["best"]="Bill";
		friends["bad"]="Masha";
		
		var bestFriend:String= friends["best"];
		
		friends.best="Alex";
		
		Another syntax:
		var car:Object = {make:"Toyota", model:"Camry"};
		trace (car["make"], car.model);
		// Output: Toyota Camry

Hoisting	n/a	The compiler moves all variable declarations to the top of the function so you can use a variable name even before it's been explicitly declared in the code

Instantiation objects from classes	Customer cmr = new Customer();
	
	Class cls = Class.forName("Customer");
	Object myObj= cls.newInstance();
		var cmr:Customer = new Customer();
		
		var cls:Class = flash.util.getClassByName("Customer");
		var myObj:Object = new cls();

Private classes	private class myClass{…}	There are no private classes in AS3.
Private constructors	Supported. Typical use: singleton classes	Not available. The implementation of private constructors is postponed since they aren't part of the ECMAScript standard yet. To create a Singleton use the public static method getInstance(). In the public constructor check if the instance already exists, throw an error.
Class and file names	A file can have multiple class declarations, but only one of them can be public, and the file must have the same name as this class.	A file can have multiple class declarations, but only one of them can be put inside the package declaration, and the file must have the same name as this class.
What can be put in a package	Classes and interfaces	Classes, interfaces, variables, functions, namespaces, and executable statements

Dynamic classes (define an object that can be altered at runtime by adding or changing properties and methods).	n/a	dynamic class Person {
		  var name:String;
		}
		//Dynamically add a variable // and a function
		Person p= new Person();
		p.name="Joe";
		p.age=25;
		p.printMe = function () {
		  trace (p.name, p.age);
		}
		p.printMe(); // Joe 25

Function closures	n/a. Closures support is a proposed addition to Java 7	myButton.addEventListener("click," myMethod); A closure is an object that represents a snapshot of a function with its lexical context (variable's values, objects in the scope). A function closure can be passed as an argument and executed without being a part of any object
Abstract classes	Supported	There is no mechanism to mark class methods with the abstract keyword that would enforce implementation of these methods in the descendents
Function overriding	Supported	Supported. You must use the override qualifier

Method/constructor overloading	Supported	Not supported. You can use a workaround with ...rest parameter:
		
		public function MyCLass(...args) {
		switch (args.length) {
		case 0: constructor1(); return;
		case 1: constructor2(args[0]);
		return;
		case 2: constructor3(args[0],
		args[1]); return;
		...
		}}
		This sample covers the case of constructors having a different number of parameters. To make it work with functions having the same number of parameters but different types, you'd have to add the type check to each of the cases above, i.e., if(args[0] is String) {
		//do one thing
		}else if (args[0] is Number){
		// do another thing
		}

Interfaces	class A implements B{...} interfaces can contain method declarations and final variables	class A implements B{...} interfaces can contain only function declarations
Exception handling	Keywords: try, catch, throw, finally, throws Uncaught exceptions are propagated to the calling method	Keywords: try, catch, throw, finally A method doesn't have to declare exceptions. Can throw not only Error objects, but also numbers: throw 25.3; Flash Player terminates the script in case of uncaught exception
Regular expressions	Supported	Supported

Table 2.4 Java/ActionScript cheat sheet

Flex Framework API Documentation

Flex Framework comes with a fully documented API in a format similar to Java's javadoc. We recommend you download and install the Flex Framework documentation and create a bookmark in your Web browser to have it handy. For example, if you've unzipped the document files in the directory C:\Flex2\doc\flex2docs\langref, bookmark the following URI: file:///C:/Flex2/doc/flex2docs/langref/index.html.

The Web browser's screen will look like Figure 2.7.

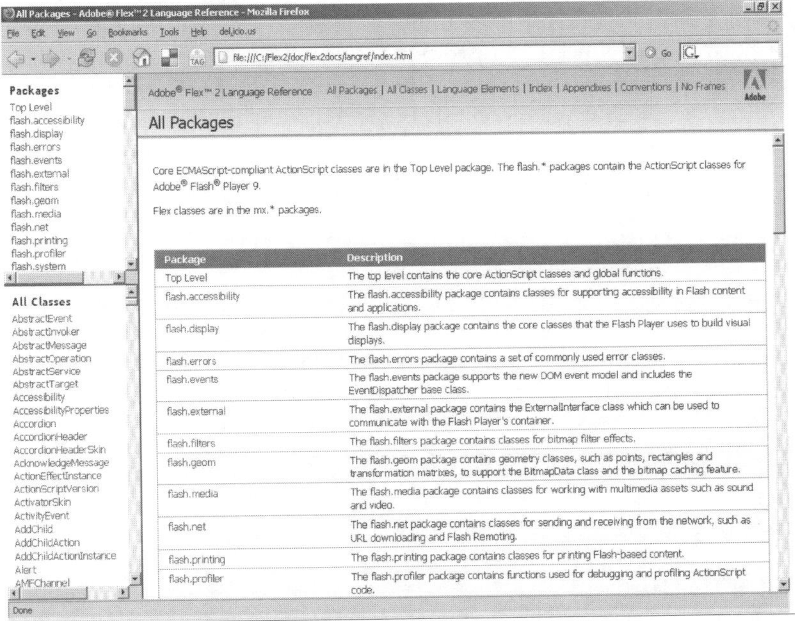

Figure 2.7 Documentation on the Flex 2 API

To create similarly looking documentation for your own classes and components, get the ASDoc tool at: http://labs.adobe.com/wiki/index.php/ASDoc:Using_ASDoc. For more advanced documenting functionality, check the Flex2Doc utility at myflex.org.

Separating Design and Development

We've already learned that a typical Flex program consists of MXML, a markup language for creating a GUI, and the programming language ActionScript. This opens up an opportunity to separate design and development responsibilities between different people, at least in enterprise project development. Mid-size and large organizations can have a group of UI designers that know how to prototype good-looking and intuitive Web sites.

In a perfect world, professional designers would create such prototypes using MXML; professional software developers would just write programs in ActionScript. In reality though your MXML files will have some amount of ActionScript. Try to keep it to a minimum but don't kill yourself trying to achieve the perfect separation of responsibilities.

Besides MXML, Web designers will find themselves at home with Cascading Style Sheets (CSS), which in Flex play the same role and have the same syntax as CSS in HTML. Your firm-specific fonts, coloring, and other styles should be done with CSS.

There is a slight difference in CSS use: in HTML pages, you can change the CSS file, press the Refresh button in your browser, and the appearance of the Web page will change accordingly. In Flex, if you assign CSS statically either by providing the name of a .css file or by using an <mx:Style> object, they are embedded into SWF, so if you decide to change the look of your GUI components, you have to modify the CSS file and recompile the application.

You can also create and assign styles to Flex components dynamically from within your ActionScript code by creating an instance of the StyleSheet object, assigning values to its properties, and then calling the setStyle method on the required UI component.

Flex Style Explorer is a handy tool that automates the process of writing CSS (see http://examples.adobe.com/flex2/consulting/styleexplorer/Flex2StyleExplorer.html). Select the kind of component or container that you want to make "stylish," pick applicable parameters on the left, see how it looks in the middle, and copy the CSS from the right into your <mx:style> tag:

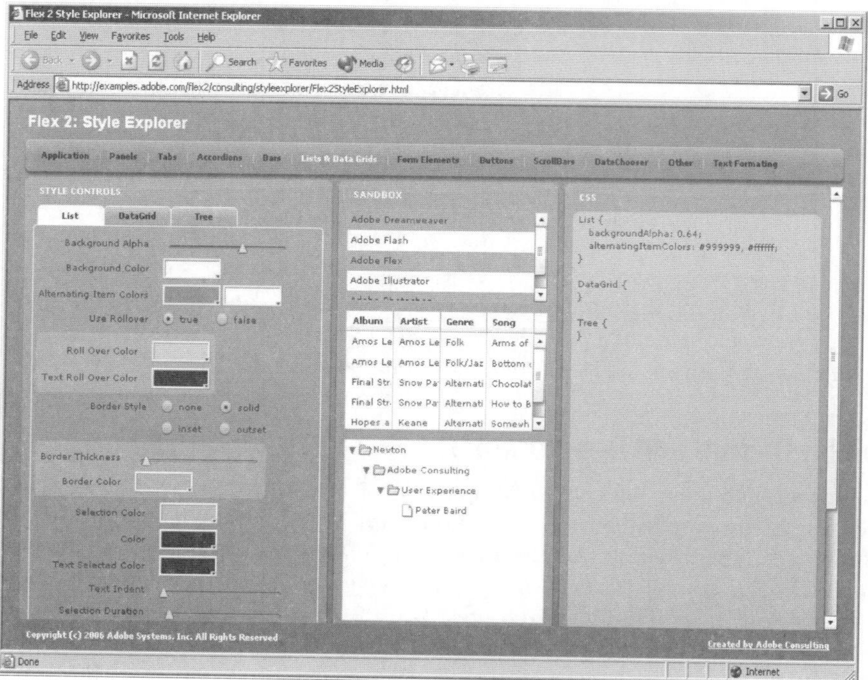

Figure 2.8 Flex-style Explorer

Working with Display Objects in ActionScript

Flash Player shows your application's objects in a display area that is known as "stage" and is represented by the class Stage. When a program renders display objects to the stage, Flash Player uses a display list to manage them. In other words, your ActionScript program has to add required subclasses of the DisplayObject to one of the containers so they can be rendered and displayed. Since the DisplayObject class is inherited from EventDispatcher, all GUI components are capable of processing events.

Each Flex application has at least one default container that is represented by a class Application that corresponds to the mxml tag <mx:Application>.

If you're going to program in ActionScript, you should be aware of the fact that you can't instantiate DisplayObject, but you can create instances of its subclasses (Shape, SimpleButton, and others) and add them to the display list. Flash Player renders changes to DisplayObject to the stage for each video frame (also called keyframe).

You can add several display objects to a display list of one of the subclasses of DisplayObjectContainer. For example, the class Sprite is a direct descendant of DisplayObjectContainer, and flash.display.MovieClip is a subclass of Sprite.

While MovieClip is a suitable class for Flash programs that display a sequence of frames over a timeline, for business applications it's the Sprite class, a lighter container that doesn't include the timeline support. In ActionScript, Sprite represents a display object in a display list node. As an example, you can create an ActionScript class that extends Sprite, and add one or more display objects to your class with a series of the method called addChild(). Flash Player finds classes through the root of the display list. Only after calling addChild() will a component be added to the display list and the SystemManager assigned to it.

The Application Loading Process

Flex defines a number of so-called manager classes located in the package mx.managers. These classes control the mouse cursor, drag-and-drop operations, history (similar to the Web browsers' Back/Forward buttons), pop-up windows, tool tips, and other things.

When Flash Player loads and starts your Flex application, the SystemManager controls the application window; creates and parents the Application instance, pop-ups, and cursors; and manages the classes in the ApplicationDomain. The SystemManager is the first class instantiated by Flash Player for your application. It stores the size and position of the main application window and keeps track of its children, such as floating pop-ups and modal windows. Using SystemManager you can access embedded fonts, styles, and the document object.

SystemManager also controls application domains, which are used to partition classes by the security domains (see the description of the ApplicationDomain class in the Flex Language Reference).

If you'll be developing custom visual components (descendents of the UIComponent class), keep in mind that initially such components aren't connected to any display list and SystemManager=null. Only after the first call of the addChild() will a SystemManager be assigned. You shouldn't access SystemManager from the constructor of your component, because it can still be null at the moment.

In general, when the Application object is created, the following steps are being performed:

1. Instantiation of the application object begins.
2. Initialization of the Application.systemManager property.
3. The application dispatches the pre-initialize event at the beginning of the initialization process.
4. The createChildren()method is called on the application object. At this point each of the application's components is being constructed, and each component's createChildren() will also be called.
5. The application dispatches the initialize event, which indicates that all the application's components have been initialized.
6. A creationComplete event is being dispatched.
7. The application object is added to the display list.
8. The applicationComplete event is being dispatched.

In most cases, you'll be using the MXML tag <mx:Application> to create the application object, but if you need to create it in ActionScript, don't create components in its constructor – use createChildren() for this (for performance reasons).

Flex SWF files have only two frames. The SystemManager, Preloader, DownloadProgressBar, and a handful of other helper classes live in the first frame. The rest of the Flex Framework, your application code, and embedded assets like fonts and images reside in the second frame. When Flash Player initially starts downloading your SWF, as soon as enough bytes come for the first frame, it instantiates a SystemManager that creates a Preloader, which in turn creates a DownloadProgressBar and these two objects are watching the rest of the byte streaming-in process.

When all bytes for the first frame are in, SystemManager sends the enterFrame to the second frame and then dispatches other events. Eventually, the application object dispatches the applicationComplete event.

You may by wondering why you need to know what's happening before the application loads. This knowledge may come in handy especially if your application is large and users experience unpleasant delays during the initial load. You can use this time productively, for example, to let the user log on to this application. This will also give the user a perception that your application loads faster. Farata Systems has created an open source logon component that can be used in Preloader (see http://flexblog.faratasystems.com/?p=88).

You can also create a splash screen that fades away with an image of your choice by substituting the standard Flex Preloader and the DownloadProgressBar objects with the custom ones. Ted Patrick from Adobe has provided sample applications that display a splash screen using an image from PNG, SWF, or GIF files (see http://www.onflex.org/ted/2006/07/flex-2-preloaders-swf-png-gif-examples.php). While your splash screen is displayed, you can download some other system resources and/or libraries and then the splash screen fades away.

Here's another idea. During the loading process, your ActionScript code may interact with the "outside world" aka Web browser. The class ExternalInterface has a method addCallback() that lets you register an ActionScript method as callable from the container. After a successful invocation of addCallBack(), the registered function in Flash Player can be called by the JavaScript or ActiveX code in the container. You'll find more on the ExternalInterface in Chapter 15.

One more suggestion: your application may need to load another application(s) from an SWF. If you have to do it in ActionScript, you can use the SWFLoader class from the applicationComplete event (see more on SWFLoader in Chapter 10).

Summary

In this chapter, we first created simple applications and peeked under Flex's hood. The most important feature of Flex 2 is that it's an open and extendable framework. If you are accustomed to being in complete control with Java, Flex doesn't tie your hands either. In the next chapter we'll get familiar with the Eclipse-based IDE called Flex Builder.

Endnotes

1. Besides mxmlc and compc Flex has one more compiler called the Web tier compiler. This compiler comes with Flex Data Services and lets you create swf files during the runtime on the server side. This compiler runs in a Java EE servlet container.

2. Flex compiler itself is just a wrapper that internally calls the Java archive called mxmlc.jar (or compc.jar). This compilation process can be initiated from a Java program if needed. See http://livedocs.macromedia.com/flex/2/docs/wwhelp/wwhimpl/common/html/wwhelp.htm?context=LiveDocs_Parts&file=00001489.html.

3. If you're using a Web-tier compiler, your user can specify a URL of the remote MXML file, which will be compiled into the swf file and delivered without an HTML wrapper.

4. You can skip this step if you have Eclipse installed – Ant is located in its plug-ins directory.

CHAPTER
3

Flex Builder Development Environment

Flex Builder Development Environment

Installing and Configuring Flex Builder

The Flex Builder IDE is based on Eclipse and it's a more productive environment compared to programming with Flex in a text editor. This IDE comes in two flavors: a standalone version and an Eclipse plug-in. You'll have to choose one of these versions during the installation process. But the standalone version of Flex Builder 2.0 doesn't contain Java Development plug-ins, also known as JDT (Java Development Tools). You need JDT to support Java projects, perspectives, etc., so we recommend installing the plug-in version of Flex Builder on top of the pre-installed Eclipse 3.2. During the Flex Builder install process, you'll have to specify the directory where your Eclipse resides (the one that has a sub-directory called plugins).

After Flex Builder is installed, start Eclipse, select the menus Window | Open Perspective | Other, and open the Flex Development perspective. The Flex Debugging perspective will be automatically added to the Eclipse IDE. The Flex Builder comes with great help content, which in the plug-in version is located under the menu Help | Help Contents | Adobe Flex 2 Help or Help>Flex Start Page.

Yet Another Hello World

We're not going to bore you with all the little details of the Eclipse-based Flex Builder, because they're covered pretty well in the product manual *Using Flex Builder 2*. You can also read the section on Flex Builder using its help menu. We'd rather walk you through the process of creating a simple Flex project with several basic applications. While building these applications, we'll touch on various areas of the Flex Builder's workbench to give you a quick feel for the functionality.

Always start by creating a new project. Select the *File>Flex Project* menu item to open the *New Project* wizard. The first decision you'll have to make is to choose the way your application (in fact, all the applications in this project) is going to access remote data:

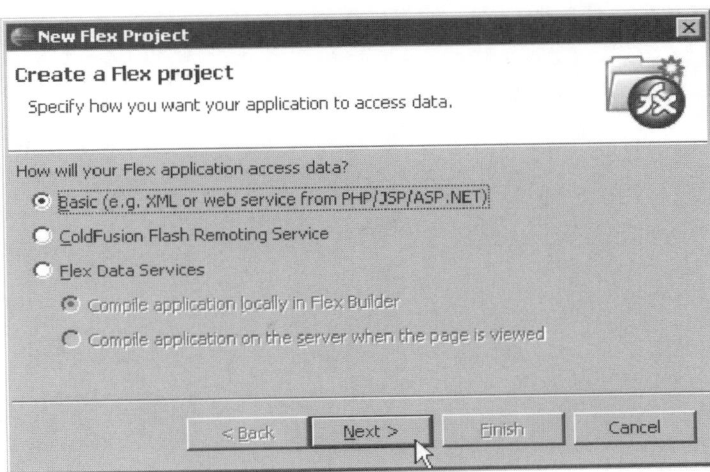

Figure 3.1 Creating the Flex project – project type selection

We'll discuss Flex Builder's project types later in this chapter in the section "Project Types and Data Access." Since we're not going to use any server-side technology in this chapter, the Basic type is our choice so just press the *Next* button. Now you'll have to pick the name and location of the project:

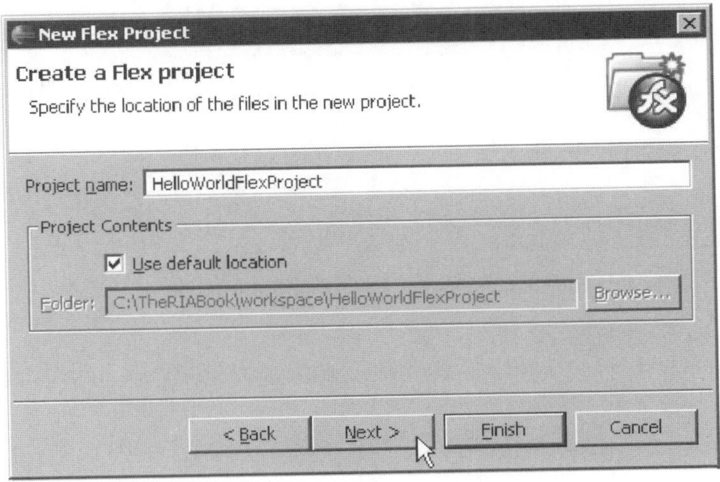

Figure 3.2 Naming the project

Once you're done, click *Next* and, in the following screen, specify the name of the main application file and output folder:

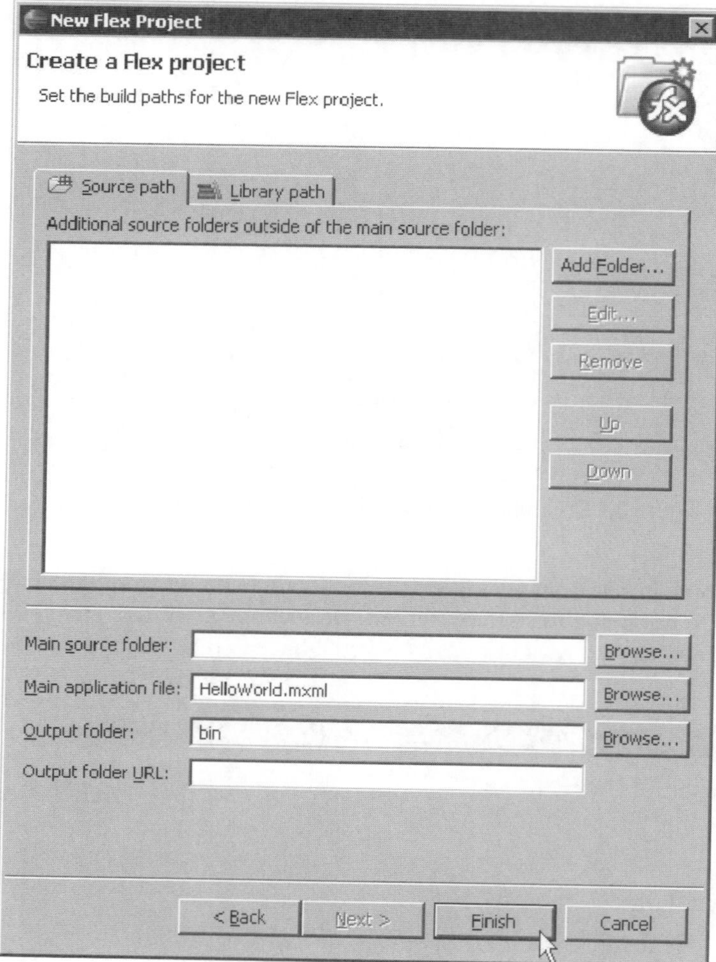

Figure 3.3 Naming the main application file

Enter *HelloWorld.mxml* as the name of the main application file. The compiled application will be saved in the *bin* directory unless you specify another output folder. Click *Finish* to complete the project creation.

After the project is created, you'll see a screen similar to Figure 3.4 with the pre-generated file HelloWorld.mxml.

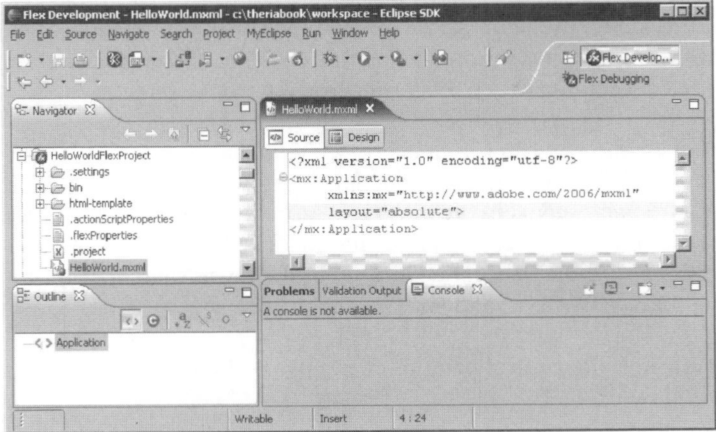

Figure 3.4 A new project has been created

The application may also include other MXML and ActionScript files with application logic as well as images and other resources commonly referred to as "assets."

Have you noticed the two tabs above the code editor? By default, FlexBuilder displays the source code view, but since we have to design our HelloWorld screen, we'll start working in the design mode (as you become more experienced, you'll be using the design mode mostly for quickly prototyping your screen), so click on the Design tab and let the fun begin.

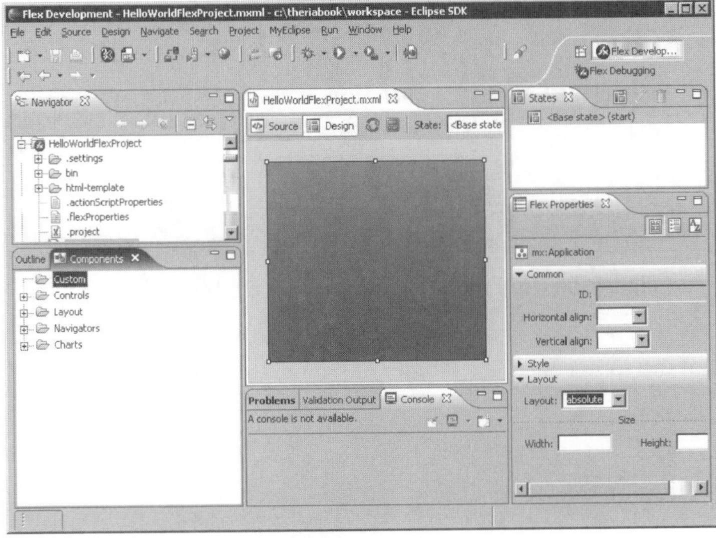

Figure 3.5 A design mode tab

In the middle of the screen in Figure 3.5 you'll see how your future window will look. All folders with predefined Flex components are located on the left: layouts, navigators, standard and custom controls. Select the Label control, then drag-and-drop it onto the screen.

In the middle of the screen you can see canvas of the Application container. Available Flex framework components (as well as custom ones that you develop for your project) are presented in the tree view in the *Components* panel in the lower left. Select the *Label* control parented by *Controls*, then drag-and-drop it onto the screen. Change the label's text to "Hello, World!" Now, switch to the *Category View* in the *Flex Properties* panel, located in the lower right corner of the screen. In the *Styles* category set the *fontSize* to 22 and *fontWeight* to bold.

If you didn't select a specific control prior to changing the font attributes, it would affect all the controls of this window.

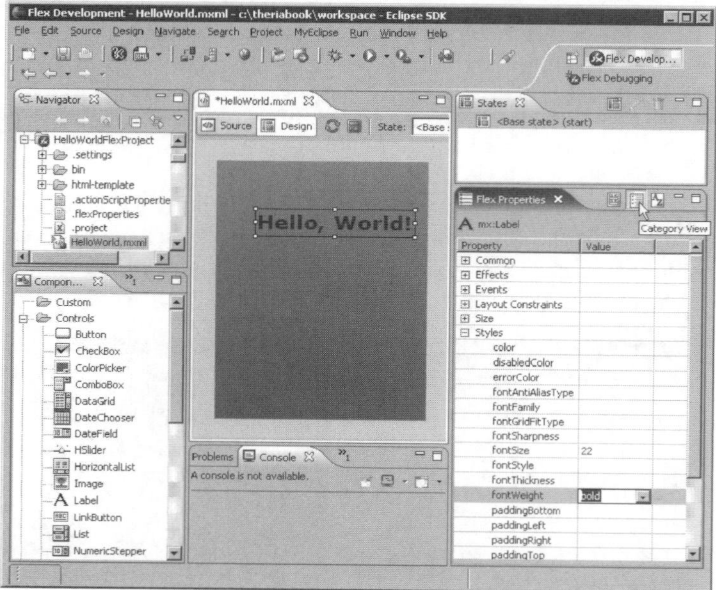

Figure 3.6 Drop the label component on the design panel

Now take a peek at the source tab. Flex Builder has generated a line similar to this one:

```
<mx:Label x=”41” y=”51” text=”Hello, World!” fontWeight=”bold” fontSize=”22”/>
```

and the entire application now looks like:

```
<?xml version=”1.0” encoding=”utf-8”?>
<mx:Application xmlns:mx=”http://www.adobe.com/2006/mxml” layout=”absolute”>
```

```
    <mx:Label x="41" y="51" text="Hello, World!" fontWeight="bold" fontSize="22"/>

</mx:Application>
```

Listing 3.1 HelloWorld.mxml

Working with the Source Panel

Type the space anywhere inside the <mx:Label> tag and enjoy instant access to all the attributes including *fontSize* and *fontWeight*:

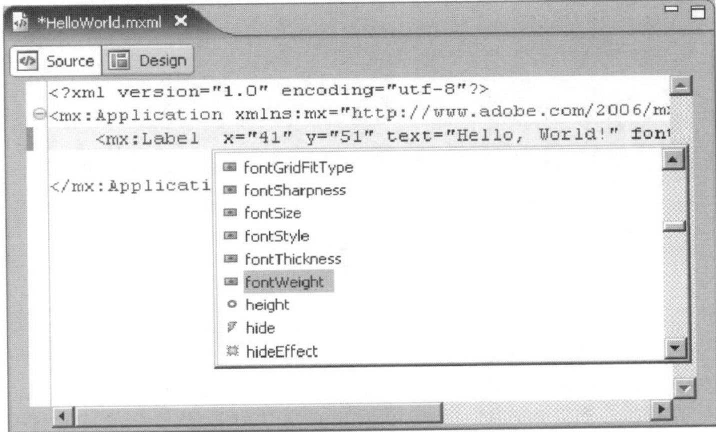

Figure 3.7 Tag attributes code hinting

In fact, you could have just typed the letter "f" and the list of attributes would be conveniently limited to the ones starting with "f."

Similarly, were you to type "<mx:Bu", you'd be prompted with all the MXML components that start with "Bu":

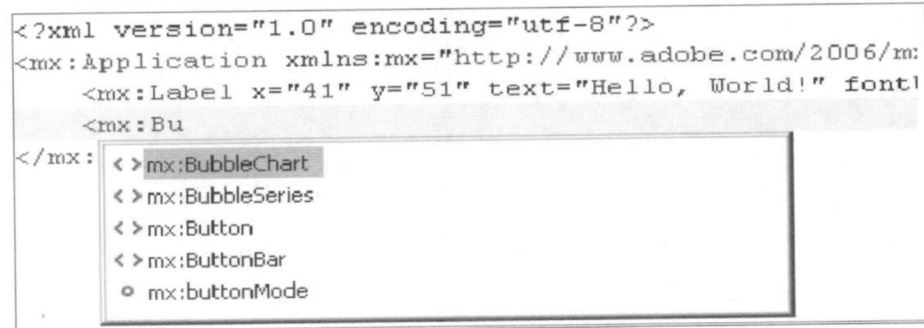

Figure 3.8 Code completion

As you can see, the *Source Panel* is as effective in creating and modifying MXML elements as the *Design Panel*.

Running HelloWorld

Press the right mouse on the HelloWorld.mxml in the *Navigator Panel* on the upper left portion of the screen. Select *RunAs…>Flex Application* and you should see a screen like this:

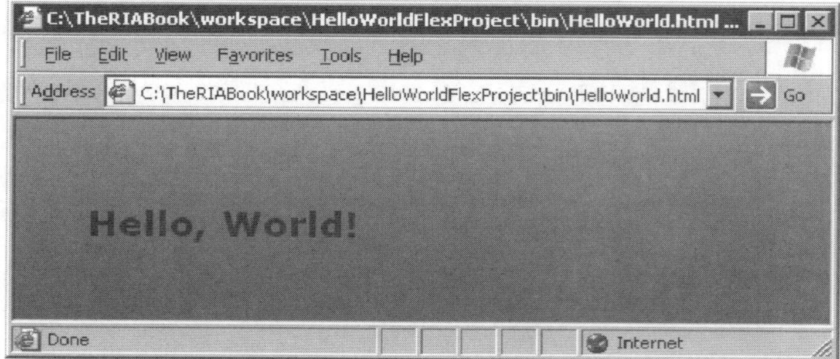

Figure 3.9 Running HelloWorld in a Web browser

Congratulations! Your first Flex Builder program is up and running.

Right-click inside this window. You'll see the pop-up menu without the View Page Source option. No wonder, your application has been compiled and launched inside the virtual machine called Flash Player, that's why you can't see its source code. Actually, at the end of this chapter we'll show you how you can enable this View Source option and make your project's source code available to the general public.

But you can also open the *bin* directory, double-click on the Flash movie SWF file, and your Flash player will run your program without the browser. Now the Flash Player will run your application independently of the Web browser:

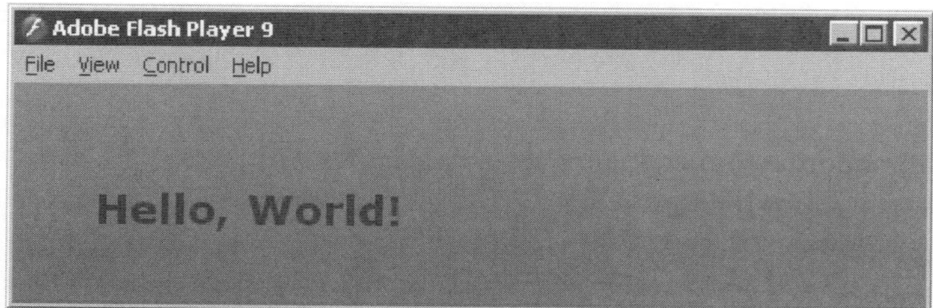

Figure 3.10 Running HelloWorld in the Flash player

Building the Project

To build simple applications like ours, the code is compiled into a single compressed archive with an .swf extension, which is saved in the output directory based on the Flex Builder settings of your project, which is bin by default. You can change this using the menus Project | Preferences | Flex Build Path. During the project build, Flex Builder also creates a handy HTML wrapper for your .swf file, so you can test it in a Web browser.

Your project can be built either automatically (every time you save code changes) or manually based on the Build Automatically setting in the menu Project. Typically, builds are done incrementally based on the data you've modified since the last build. But if you'd like to rebuild the entire project from scratch, just use the menu item Project | Clean.

If you specified that your project depends on other ones (see the Project References screen in the Properties menu), Flex Builder will figure out the order of the project builds, or you can specify the order using the menus Windows | Preferences | General | Workspace | Build Order.

For more sophisticated projects, builds may consist of multiple steps including invocating additional programs, copying files, etc. Flex Builder supports using the Apache Ant tool, and we'll use Ant in Chapter 10.

Flex Builder-Generated Files

When your application, say, HelloWorld.mxml, is compiled for the first time, you'll find the following freshly generated application-specific files in your output folder:

HelloWorld.swf : The byte code (113Kb) ready to run in the Flash Player
HelloWorld.html: An HTML wrapper (5Kb) to run in the Web browser
HelloWorld-debug.swf: The byte code with debug information (180Kb) to run in the debug version of Flash Player (this version of the player is installed automatically with Flex Builder).
HelloWorld-debug.html: An HTML wrapper (5Kb) to run the debug version of HelloWorld.swf in your Web browser

In the output directory you'll also find some files that are shared by all the applications from your project:

AC_OETags.js: A bunch of JavaScript functions used by the HTML wrapper, i.e., the user's Flash Player's version detection
playerProductInstall.swf: A small (1Kb) used by the HTML wrapper to upgrade the user's Flash Player plugin to version 9, if needed
history.* : The Flex's implementation of the history functionality (7Kb total), similar to the history in Web browsers

To deploy your application under a Web server, you'll need to copy there all of the above files except the debug ones and provide your user with the URL of the file HelloWorld.html.

While building a wrapper is an automated process, chances are you'll have to tweak it to set certain options in the browser/application integration like history management or setting the DHTML objects for Flex/JavaScript interaction. You will need to review the files in the html-template used to generate the HTML wrapper and customize them to fit your needs.

Your resulting SWF file may use some of the external resources, for example, image files, which may either be embedded in your SWF files with an [EMBED] tag, or remain external. In the latter case you can replace the image files without needing to recompile your SWF. Just make sure that the option *Copy non-embedded files to output directory* is selected in the project properties screen below. You can also turn off the generation of the HTML wrapper.

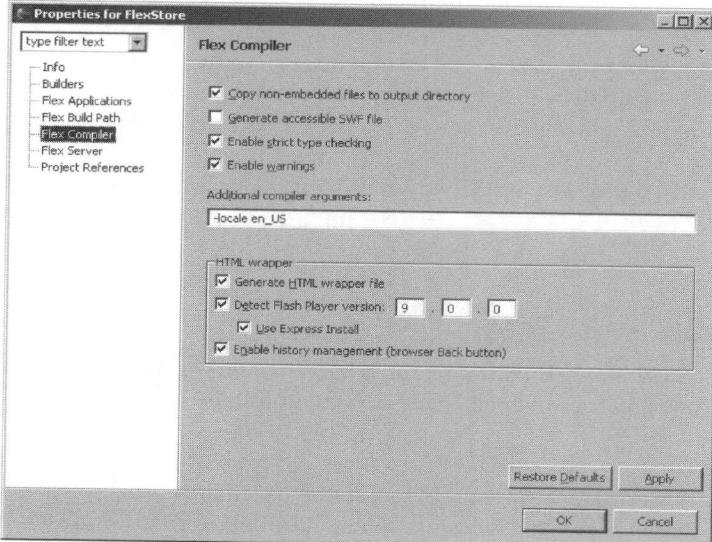

Figure 3.11 Configuring compiler properties

Running Applications in Flex Builder

A typical project consists of multiple MXML and ActionScript files and only one of them should be created as an application by including the <mx:Application> tag as opposed to MXML components that don't need it. On a similar note, Java projects consist of multiple classes, but only one of them should have the method main() that makes the class executable. During the development stage, though, you might want to have more than one MXML file with the <mx:Application> tag, which raises the question: which one of these files will be considered the main one when you run your project? To set the default application file of the project, right-click on the file and select the option *Set as the Default Application* from a pop-up menu.

You can also run non-default MXML files from your project as long as they have the Application tag. Just right-click on the file and select the menu option *Run as a Flex Application*. You can always check which MXML files can run by selecting the Project Properties menu and the option Flex Applications. You'll see a pop-up screen that will list all current runnable files and will let you add (remove) more MXML files to this list.

Simple Event Processing

The next goal is to start getting familiar with Flex event processing and understand the relations between MXML and ActionScript languages.

We're going to create a new application called HelloBasil that will contain three components: a text field, a button, and a label. The user will enter a name in the text field (i.e., Basil), press the button, and the label component will display today's date and a greeting (i.e., "May 1, 2006: Hello, Basil"). This application will have to process the button-click events with the help of ActionScript.

A Pure MXML Version

In the Flex Builder's menu select File | New | Flex Application and enter HelloBasil as the application name. Using the dropdown at the bottom of the dialog, select the vertical layout and press *Finish.*

Drag and now drop the TextInput component from the Components view on the left onto the design area. Enter *input_*1 as the *ID* of this component.

Next, add a Button component and set its *ID* to *btn_1* and its *label* to "Greet Me", then put the Text component under the button. Remove the default text and set its *ID* to *output_1.*

Switch to the Source Pane to see the generated mxml:

```
<?xml version="1.0" encoding="utf-8"?>
<mx:Application xmlns:mx="http://www.adobe.com/2006/mxml" layout="vertical">
   <mx:TextInput id="input_1" />
   <mx:Button id="btn_1" label="Greet me" />
   <mx:Text id="output_1" />
</mx:Application>
```

Listing 3.2 HelloBasil.mxml

Run the program. If you press the "Greet me" button, it won't do much since there's no code yet for processing the button click event:

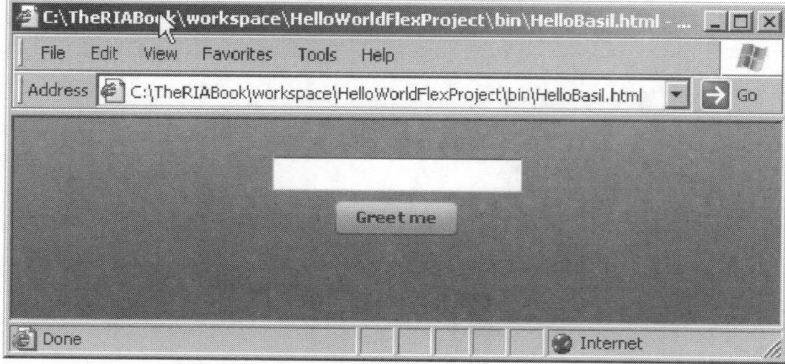

Figure 3.12 Running HelloBasil

Specifying Events Handlers

Let's add the processing of a button *click* event. Type a space before the forward slash in the <mx: Button> line to activate the list of tag attributes, and type "c" to accelerate navigation to attributes that start with "c":

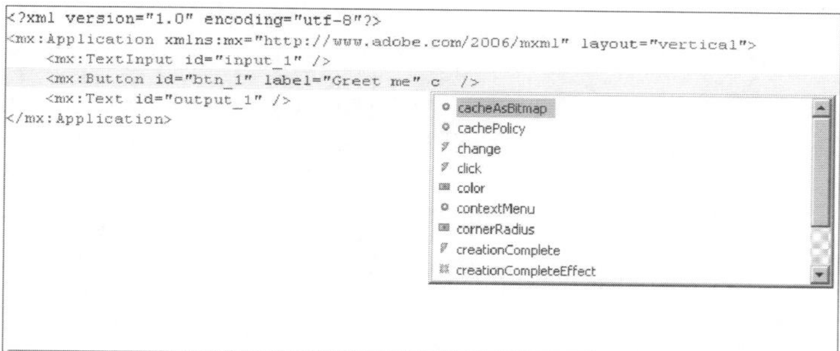

Figure 3.13 A sample of Flex Builder code hinting

Select the click attribute and press Enter. Alternatively, you could have just typed *click=""*. We're going to fill in the blank value of the click attribute with the script, corresponding to the action this button will perform: we want to set the text property of *output_1_* to the concatenated "Hello" and the text of *input_1*. Flex Builder will keep helping you by suggesting available properties of the screen components as you type. The new version of our button's code will look like this:

```
<mx:Button id="btn_1" label="Greet me"
  click="output_1.text='Hello,' + input_1.text"  />
```

Run the program, type in the name, click the button, and if your name is Basil, your screen will look like this:

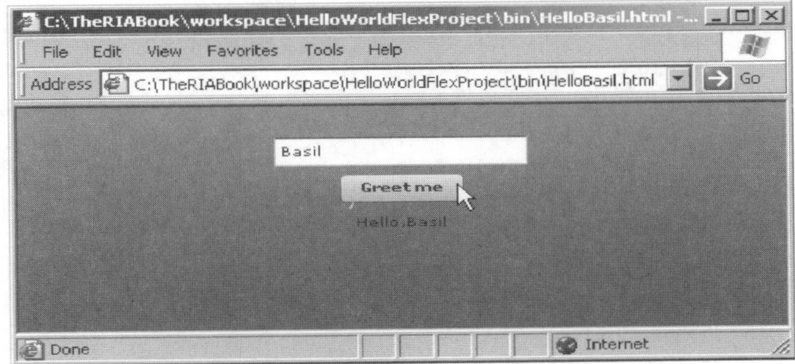

Figure 3.14 After clicking the Greet Me button

As alternative to coding the script directly inside the click attribute, we could have moved this script to an application-level function and called it:

```
<?xml version="1.0" encoding="utf-8"?>
<mx:Application xmlns:mx="http://www.adobe.com/2006/mxml" layout="vertical"   >
   <mx:Script>
      <![CDATA[
         private function greetMe():void {
            output_1.text='Hello,' + input_1.text;
         }
      ]]>
   </mx:Script>
   <mx:TextInput id="input_1" />
   <mx:Button id="btn_1" label="Greet me" click="greetMe()"  />

   <mx:Text id="output_1" />

</mx:Application>
```

Listing 3.3 HelloBasil.mxml with ActionScript

Flex MXML supports embedding ActionScript as the literal value of the <mx:Script> tag. Generally speaking, it's safer to safeguard your code in the CDATA section since it may contain symbols such as "<", which will break the well-formness of MXML.

Layouts

Flex GUI components live in so-called containers that let you arrange these components, provide a consistent view of your application regardless of the current size of the window, and navigate from one view to another.

Let's look at the layouts using our sample HelloBasil.mxml. Switch to the Design View in Flex Builder and change the layout from *vertical* to *horizontal* in the Flex Properties view. Your components will be immediately rearranged horizontally and, if you run the application, it'll look as follows (compare with Figure 3.14):

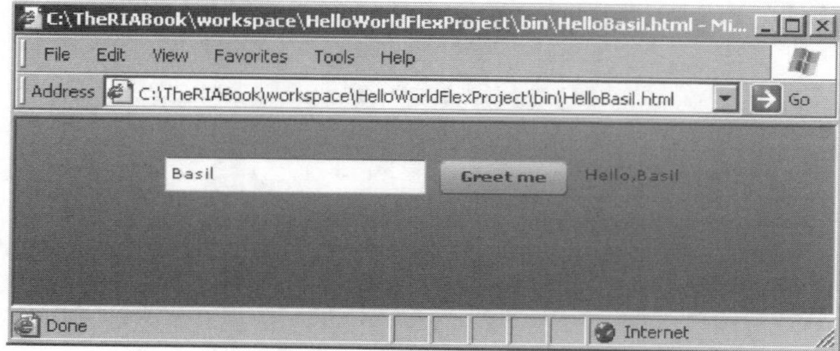

Figure 3.15 HelloBasil with the horizontal layout

Even if you start resizing the browser's window, the relative positioning of the components in the container will remain the same. In Java Swing, a *BoxLayout* class provides a similar functionality.

Change the layout to *absolute*, rerun the application, and resize the browser's window. You'll see that HelloBasil has lost its flexibility: now all the container's components are glued to their positions regardless of the size of the visible portion of the browser. You should use the absolute layout only if you're sure that your GUI application doesn't have to be resizable. The Flash Player renders the components for the containers with absolute layouts slightly faster than with horizontal or vertical layouts.

To relieve a bit the stiffness of the absolute layout, Flex lets you specify so-called *constraints*. In a container with an absolute layout, you can specify top, bottom, and center anchors (the distances from the components to the edges or the center). Instead of using *x* and *y* coordinates, you can use the *right, left, top,* and *bottom* attributes. This so-called *constraint-based layout* will resize the screen components if the user starts resizing the window. In Flex Builder's design mode, select one or more of the components and you'll be able to specify the anchors. For example, the setting shown in Figure 3.16 forces selected component(s) to be "pinned" at a distance of 150 pixels from the right edge of the container and 60 pixels from the bottom even if the browser's window is being resized.

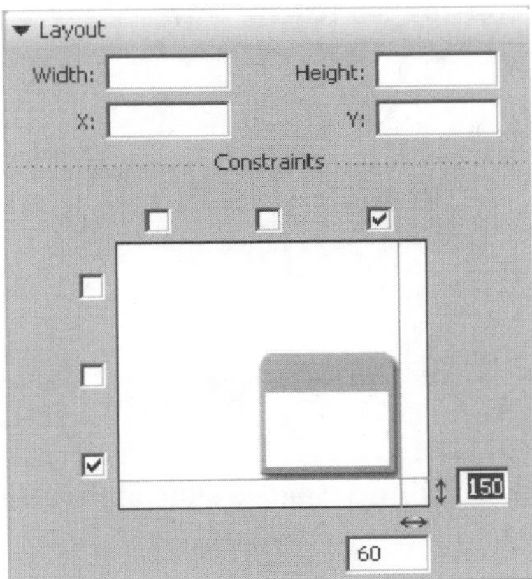

Figure 3.16 Specifying layout constraints

Basically we can say that Flex's constraint-based layout is a simplified version of *Java SpringLayout*.

In the real world the GUI is more complex than in HelloBasil and you'll have to combine containers with different layouts in the same application. For example, you can put horizontal (*HBox*) and vertical (*VBox*) containers in your application. Containers can be nested and arranged in other containers called *Panels* that also support layouts. Besides these flexible containers you can add another one called *Canvas*, which keeps its components in absolute positions relative to the top left corner of the *Canvas*.

In addition to the layout containers, Flex supports navigation containers (i.e., *ViewStack*, *ButtonBar*, and others) that let you switch from one container to another. This topic is out of the scope of this chapter, but we'll use all of these containers in Chapter 5 in a more realistic application.

View States and Transitions

Another noteworthy feature of Flex Builder is related to Flex *View States*. For example, we could have added a checkbox to the HelloBasil application so that when the checkbox is checked, the application reveals an additional *Panel* with some extra information (perhaps the messages that were left for Basil by the nightshift production support crew). The screen of the running application would look like Figure 3.17.

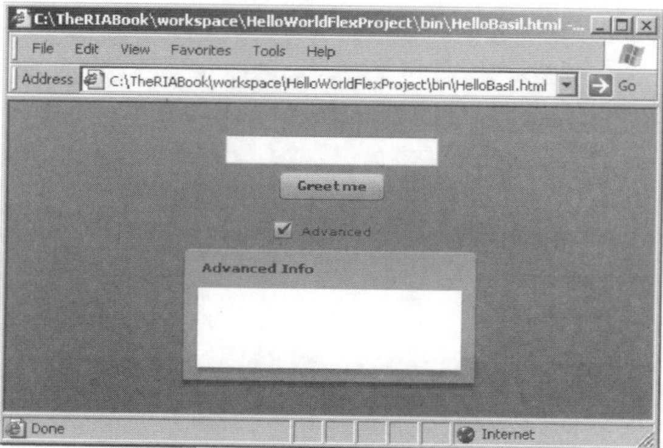

Figure 3.17 An advanced state of HelloBasil

To achieve this, we could have written the checkbox's click script to manipulate the visibility of the panel. Alternatively, we can define a *view state*, named *advanced*, and prescribe that in this state the width and height of the panel will be 50% and 75%, while in the default state they will be set to 0.

Flex Builder allows visually creating multiple states and maintaining state properties via the *States View*, usually displayed at the top right corner of the Flex Builder workbench. If you don't see this view, bring it up by using the menus Windows | Show View | States. Figure 3.18 is an illustration of a modified Hello Basil with the "advanced" state. Please note that using the States View you can navigate from state-to-state and instantly see the changes to the application.

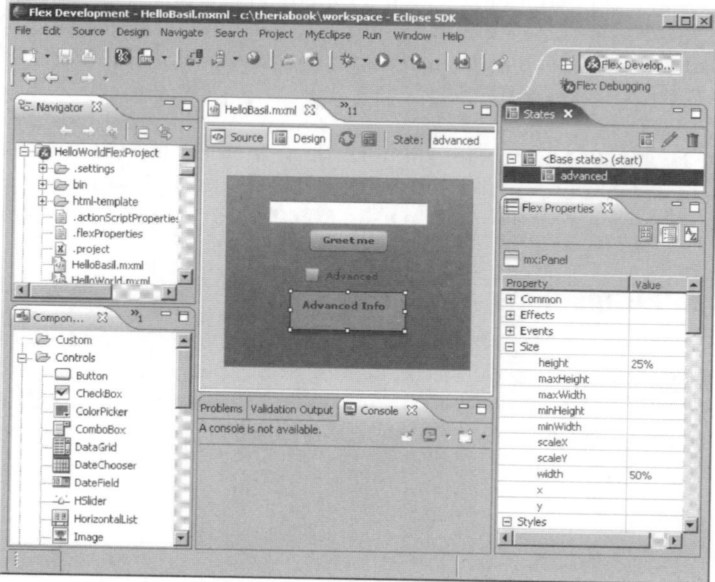

Figure 3.18 Designing a state called advanced

The code of the corresponding version of HelloBasil is in Listing 3.4:

```
<?xml version="1.0" encoding="utf-8"?>
<mx:Application xmlns:mx="http://www.adobe.com/2006/mxml" layout="vertical"   >
   <mx:TextInput id="input_1" />
   <mx:Button id="btn_1" label="Greet me" click="output_1.text='Hello,' + input_1.text"
/>

   <mx:Text id="output_1" />
   <mx:CheckBox id="cbx_1"  label="Advanced"
         click="currentState=cbx_1.selected?'advanced':''"  />

   <mx:transitions>
         <mx:Transition  fromState="*" toState="advanced">
               <mx:Resize target="{advanced_panel}" duration="400"/>
         </mx:Transition>
    </mx:transitions>
   <mx:states>
         <mx:State name="advanced">
         <mx:SetProperty target="{advanced_panel}" name="width" value="50%"/>

         <mx:SetProperty target="{advanced_panel}" name="height" value="75%"/>

         </mx:State>
    </mx:states>
   <mx:Panel id="advanced_panel" title="Advanced Info"  width="0" height="0"/>
</mx:Application>
```

Listing 3.4. HelloBasil.mxml with states and a transition

To make the switch between two states smoother, we've used a special Flex element called Transition. In this particular example we've used a transition with a special effect, Resize, requesting Flex to make a transition from the base to the advanced state gradually during a time interval of 400 milliseconds.

Fine Tuning Flex Builder

Flex Builder consumes system resources and its performance depends on your system configuration and the amount of memory installed in your computer. As your projects grow, FlexBuilder will require more memory to build and navigate them. If it works slowly, try to reserve more heap memory. If you start Flex Builder using an icon on your desktop, request more memory in eclipse.ini (for the plug-in version) or in FlexBuilder.ini (for a standalone version). Specify the minimum and maximum of the reserved heap memory using parameters of the Java Virtual Machine (JVM):

- vmargs
- Xms 128M
- Xmx512M

In the sample above, Xms requests a minimum of 128MB of heap memory that can grow to 512MB (Xmx).

If you start Eclipse in Flex Builder from a command line, you can achieve the same effect by entering these parameters manually in a command line, which in the Windows OS may look like:

```
"c:\eclipse\eclipse.exe" -vmargs -Xms128M -Xmx512M
```

These parameters may improve the responsiveness of Flex Builder and the build time of your projects if you're using the same VM for builds. The larger minimum heap delays the moment when the Java garbage collector kicks in for the first time. Other parameters to fine tune the garbage collection of Flex Builder are –XX:MinHeapFreeRatio and –XX:MaxHeapFreeRatio, which will control the minimum and maximum amount of heap space after garbage collection.

Please note that these parameters only affect the performance of the Flex Builder ID; your compiled programs will run at the same speed as before. When this chapter was written, Flex 2 did not provide tools for fine tuning garbage collection, which is done internally by the Flash Player.

Remember that by reserving too much memory for Flex Builder, you're decreasing the amount of memory left in your system for other applications.

To monitor your Eclipse memory consumption, download the plugin from KyrSoft (http://www.kyrsoft.com/opentools/memmon.html) and unzip it in your Eclipse installation directory. The excellent plugin not only allows you to monitor memory, but also request garbage collection when memory reaches specified thresholds (see Eclipse menu Window | Preferences | Java | Memory Monitor).

Some people recommend closing an unused project; some suggest replacing the JRE that comes with Flex Builder (see the JRE folder under your Flex Builder installation directory) to a newer one. While Flex Builder is a huge leap forward compared to an older Flex development environment, at the time of this writing Flex Builder is slower than Java Eclipse IDE, which will hopefully change in future releases of Flex.

Debugging with Flex Builder

Flex comes with two ways to error-proof your application. First, there's a full-featured debugger that lets you set breakpoints and see variables and walk through the execution stack. This is great for debugging your application logic. To debug the GUI, we use tracing since it lets us dump any information we need to the console/log file without interrupting and potentially changing the application flow. The debugger provides a Console window that automatically displays the trace output, so we usually trace our programs in debug mode.

Let's illustrate how to use the Flex Builder debugger with our HelloBasil application. Let's modify the greetMe() function to display today's date. We'll declare and initialize the ActionScript variable of type Date and concatenate the current date to the greeting.

```
<?xml version="1.0" encoding="utf-8"?>

<?xml version="1.0" encoding="utf-8"?>
<mx:Application xmlns:mx="http://www.adobe.com/2006/mxml" layout="vertical"   >
  <mx:Script>
    <![CDATA[
      private function assert(condition:Boolean, text:String) :void {
        if(condition) trace(text);
      }
      private function greetMe():void {
          var dt : Date = new Date();
          assert(dt.hours>20, "time to go home");
          output_1.text='Hello,' + input_1.text;
          trace("greetMe:" + output_1.text);
      }
    ]]>
  </mx:Script>
  <mx:TextInput id="input_1" />
  <mx:Button id="btn_1" label="Greet me" click="greetMe()"  />

  <mx:Text id="output_1" />
</mx:Application>
```

Listing 3.5 Adding assertions and tracing for debugging

To toggle a breakpoint just double-click on the gray area to the left of the line where you want a program to stop, and Flex Builder will mark this line with a blue bullet. We'll put a breakpoint at the last line of the greetMe() method. To run the program in the debug mode, select the application in the Navigator view and select "Debug As…" in the context menu.

As soon as you press the "Greet me" button, your program will reach the breakpoint and Flex Builder will pause to give you a chance to analyze the values in the variables you're interested in. To step through the execution of your program, you can use the little yellow arrows at the top of the debug view.

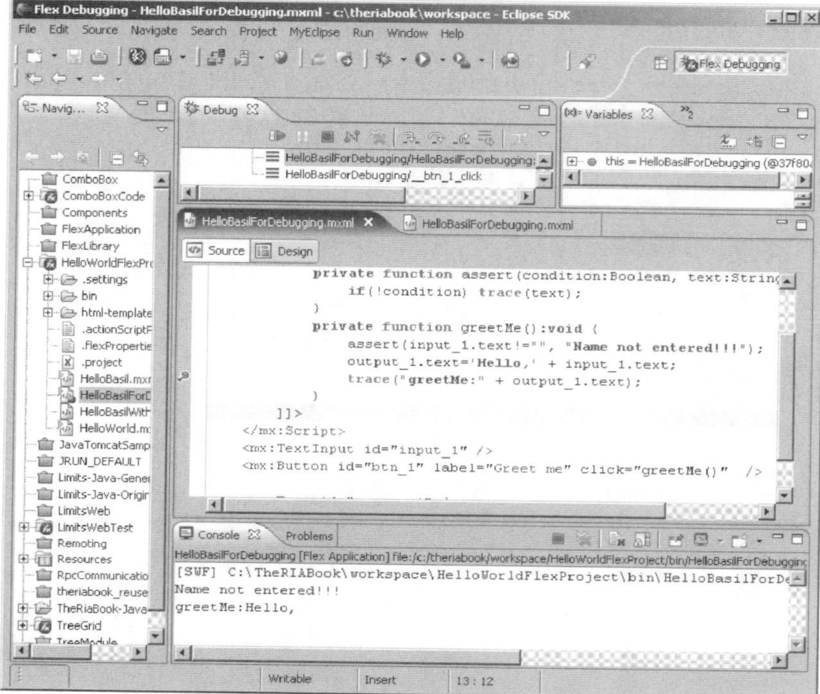

Figure 3.19 Debugging with Flex Builder

The *Variables* view lets you check and change the values of your program variables. If a variable represents a composite object, you can easily see its content by pressing the little plus sign on the right. For example, the variable *this* represents the object you're in – your main application instance. In the Console window we can see the results of our trace statements. Please note the *assert()* method – this technique is often used to reduce the amount of trace output if the entries comply with the listed assertions.

Flex Builder allows you to perform conditional debugging instead of setting up the breakpoints. Just call the method enterDebugger():

```
if (myVar > 25)
    enterDebugger();
```

You still need to run your application in the debug mode, but if myVar is not greater than 25, Flex Builder will execute your program without stopping in the debugger.

Project Types and Data Access

One of the major differences between Flex 2 and previous versions is its ability to compile your code on a standalone client machine without using any servers. All the samples in this chapter where compiled locally on the client machine and they didn't rely on any data located on external servers, so our project is basic. However, your application can directly talk to a remote Web Service despite the fact that your project is basic.

On the other hand, in Chapters 5 and 6 we'll be using Flex remote objects and data services, and we'll select an optional Flex Data Services that assumes you already have it installed and deployed under the Java EE servlet container of your choice. For these types of projects, you'll be asked to specify the URL of your Flex Data Services install (we'll do this in Chapter 5), and after compiling, your project will be embedded into your SWF file.

If you select Flex Data Services as your project type, you'll have to specify if you're planning to compile your project locally using Flex Builder or on the server when the page is viewed.

Generated ActionScript

As we've mentioned before, the Flex compiler converts MXML into ActionScript source code and then compiles it into an swf or swc file. If you'd like to see this ActionScript code, add an additional compiler argument – keep-generated-actionscript in the screen shown below and recompile your project. Flex Builder will create a sub-directory called generated, where you can find the source code of all the generated ActionScript files.

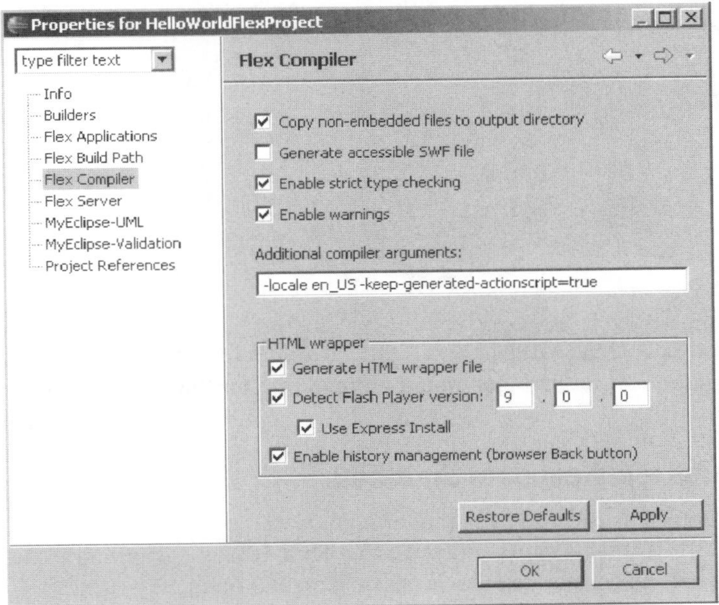

Figure 3.20 Asking the compiler to keep generated ActionScript files

After closing the dialog, you'll also see the new "generated" folder in Flex Builder's project tree containing about 50 ActionScript files. Those files are used to initialize a framework, provide CSS support, and divide our application into resources, classes that have to be initialized on the applications load, etc. We highly recommend that you spend some time reviewing the generated code after learning a new feature/control to get familiar with the dependencies and intercommunications with the Flex framework.

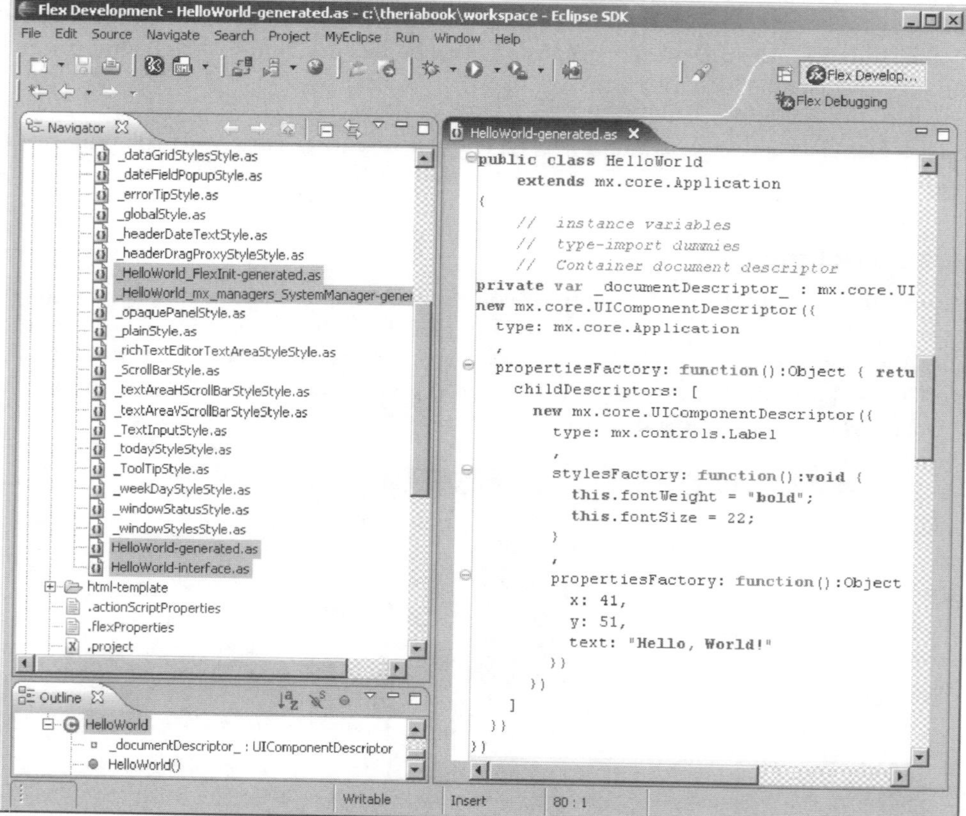

Figure 3.21 An auto-generated ActionScript for HelloWorld.mxml

Flex Builder Tips and Keyboard Shortcuts

Flex Builder has many convenient keyboard commands that make your programming faster. For the complete list of all available shortcuts, press Ctrl-Shift-L. We've listed some of the Flex Builder tips and the keyboard shortcuts here that we use on a regular basis:

- If you see a little asterisk in the tab with the file name, this means that this file has some unsaved code changes.

- Highlight the name of the class or a function and press the button F3 on your keyboard. This will take you to the source code of this class.
- If some of the lines are marked with red error circles, move the mouse over the circle and Flex Builder will display the text describing this error.
- Press Ctrl-Space to get context-sensitive help.
- Alt + / will complete the name of the variable or a class after you typed in a couple of its first letters.
- Press Ctrl-F11 to run the last launched program again. Hit the F11 key alone to run the program in debug mode.
- Place the cursor after a curly brace and Eclipse will mark the matching brace.
- Highlight a line or a block of code and press Alt-ArrowUp or Alt-ArrowDown. The selected code will move up or down.
- Ctrl-H will open a popup to search on multiple files, and Ctrl-F will let you find text in the open file.
- Highlight the MXML tag or ActionScript class and press Shift-F2. This will open the screen with the language reference help on the selected element.
- Highlight a block of code and press Ctrl-Shift-C to comment out the selected block of code.
- To select surrounding containers, select a GUI control and press F4.
- Keep the Control key down while moving the mouse over MXML tags. Flex Builder will show a tool tip with the name of the corresponding ActionScript class. If the tag turns into a hyperlink and the source code is available, click on the link to open the source code of the class.
- As you change your code in the editor, Flex Builder puts a vertical purple bar on the left of each modified line. This is quite handy if you'd like to have a quick look at the new code before pressing the button Save.
- If you want to test your application in different browsers installed on your computer, select the menu Windows | Preferences | General | Web Browser and select the browser to be used by Flex Builder for launching your application.
- If you see an error message that reads "…Check the Error Log file", this log file is located in your workspace, in directory called .metadata.

Publishing the Application Source Code

If you'd like to make the source code available to the users of your deployed applications (similar to the View Source option in the Web browsers in thin clients), use the menu Project | Publish Application Source.

This menu item will quickly build a set of files in the sub-folder srcview in the output folder with the source code of your project ready to be published on the Web as in Figure 3.23.

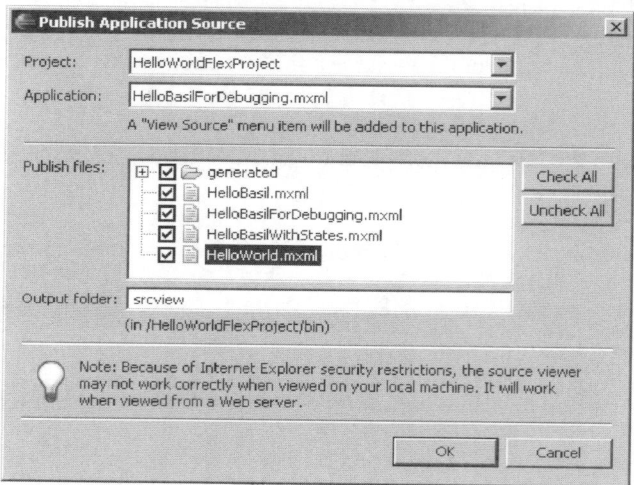

Figure 3.22 Selecting the source code to be published

Besides preparing the source files for publication, Flex Builder will also add to the *Application* the attribute *viewSourceURL* pointing at the location of the source code:

```
<?xml version="1.0" encoding="utf-8"?>
<mx:Application xmlns:mx="http://www.adobe.com/2006/mxml" layout="absolute"
                                                    viewSourceURL="srcview/index.html">
   <mx:Label x="41" y="51" text="Hello, World!" fontWeight="bold" fontSize="22"/>
</mx:Application>
```

Listing 3.6 Enabling the View Source option

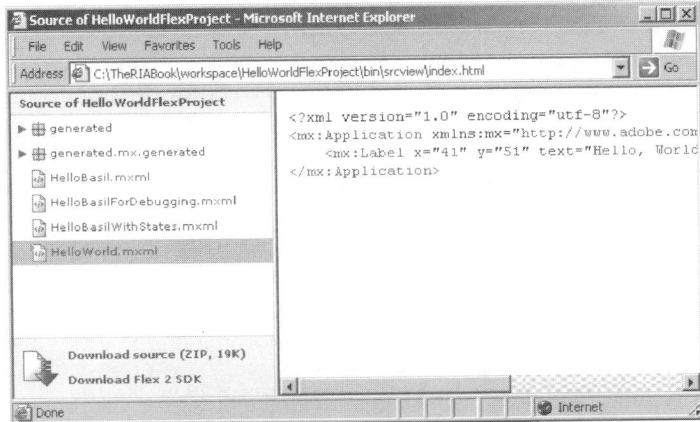


```
<?xml version="1.0" encoding="utf-8"?>
<mx:Application xmlns:mx="http://www.adobe.com
    <mx:Label x="41" y="51" text="Hello, World
</mx:Application>
```

Figure 3.23 Published source code in the folder bin/srcview

Next time you run this application, right-clicking the mouse will open up a menu with one extra item: View Source. Something you got accustomed to in the HTML/JSP-based application, but a lot better organized.

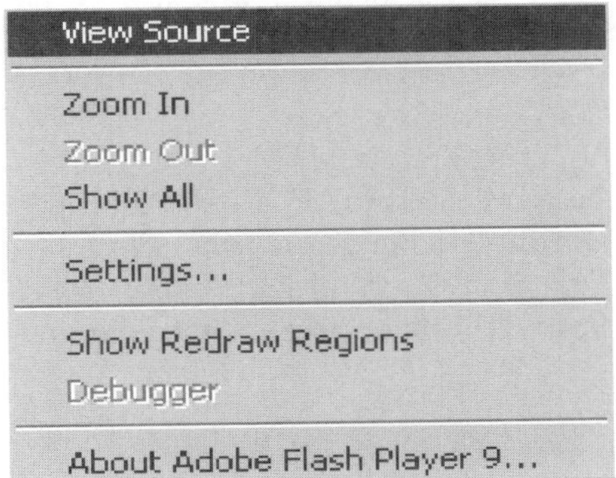

Figure 3.24 The run-time menu displayed on right-click

Using the Subversion Version Control System

Eclipse and hence Flex Builder come with a pre-installed CVS plug-in that you can use as your version control system without any additional client installations. Open the menus Window | Open Perspective | Other and you'll see the CVS Repository Exploring (see Figure 3.25).

But CVS isn't your only choice. Subversion is another popular open source version control system that's easier to administer, allows versioning support for directories, and has some other advantages. Subversion is available for free at http://subversion.tigris.org/. You can also download and install one of the plug-ins for Eclipse (i.e., Subversive or Subclipse), which puts your repository just one click away from your Flex Builder projects. A free online version of the Subversion book is available at http://svnbook.red-bean.com/ and here we'll just provide the information relevant for configuring the Flex Builder client to be used with Subversion repositories.

We assume that you already have the Subversion server installed, the source code repository for your project configured, and the proper permissions to access this repository.

Start by downloading and installing the Subversion client, which will let you to do all the version control operations from the command line. While most of the time you may be using some Subversion plug-in from Flex Builder, this client software will become handy if you decide to automate your application's build process. For example, you may write an Ant build script that will start by running Subversion commands cleanly, checking out all the files from the repository.

You can download and install prepackaged binaries of Subversion at http://subversion.tigris.org/project_packages.html.

After installing your client make sure that the system variable APR_ICONV_PATH is defined and points at the iconv directory in your Subversion client directory. If your Subversion server is located on the Unix box accessed using ssh, also define a variable SVN_SSH that points to the location of your ssh client. For example:

```
SVN_SSH=C:\\my_ssh_client\\ssh2.exe
```

The next step is to install the Subversion plug-in (we use Subclipse here) so you can use the Subversion repository right from your Flex Builder projects. Select the menu Help | Software Updates | Find and Install, and in the pop-up screen pick the option *Search for new features to install.* In the next screen enter Subclipse in the name field and the following URL in http://subclipse.tigris.org/update_1.0.x.

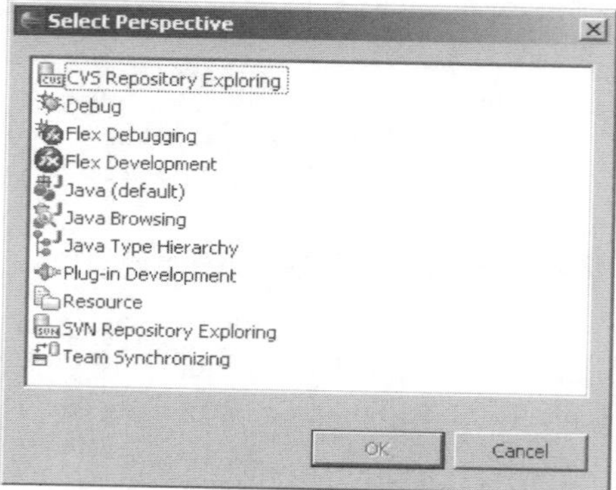

Figure 3.25 Eclipse perspectives including the Subversion plug-in

Check the Subclipse box in the next screen and finish the install.

After a successful install, you'll find a new perspective called SVN Repository Exploring as in Figure 3.25. Now the Eclipse Help menu will have a new section on using Subclipse.

Finally, you need to specify the location of the Subversion repository of your project: the system administrator who installed and configured the repository will give you the parameters of the Subversion server. After getting this information, right-click in the Navigator view, select New | SVN Repository, and enter its URL. The Eclipse help menu has a section on it.

If you're connected to your repository, right-click on your project and select the Team item from the menu. It should open a pop-up window with the typical version control options: Checkout, Update, Commit, Diff, etc.

If you'd like to add an existing project to the repository, use the menu Team | Share Project. To get the project from repository into Flex Builder, open your SVN Repository Exploring perspective, right-click on a project, and select the option Check Out as Project. The rest of the commands are pretty intuitive (don't forget about committing your changes) and are well described in the Subversion documentation.

If for any reason you're not happy with the Subclipse plug-in, try the Subversive client, which is available at http://www.polarion.org/.

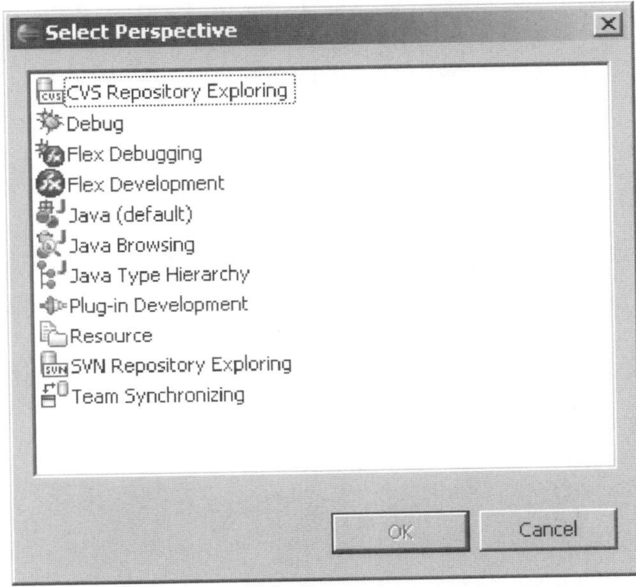

Figure 3.26 Select Perspective with Subclipse plug-in

Summary

In this chapter we've introduced you to a developer-friendly Flex Builder tool. Even though our sample applications were very basic, you've had a chance to see and enjoy the ease of developing in Flex Builder. You can find a detailed description of all Flex Builder features in the manual using Flex Builder 2, which is available for download at www.flex.org. In the following chapters we'll gradually increase the complexity of the examples, so fasten your seat belts, please.

CHAPTER 4

Learning Flex Through Applications

Learning Flex Through Applications

In this chapter we'll roll up our sleeves and build several mini-applications to illustrate the use of various elements and techniques of both ActionScript 3.0 (AS3) and MXML that you'll be using in real-world projects. But this is not a tutorial and we'll be introducing these elements on an as-needed basis. Our goal is to give you the big picture, but you should study the product documentation for detailed coverage of each of these elements.

In particular, this chapter contains:

- A description of some of the AS3 features that may seem unusual to Java programmers
- A review of object-oriented programming techniques in AS3
- A short description of ECMAScript for XML, which offers simplified processing of the XML sources
- An overview of the Flex event model
- An application that uses namespaces in AS3
- A program that uses Flex data binding and regular expressions
- An application illustrating the communication between Flex and JavaServer Pages
- A sample application showing different ways of achieving the same results by people with different programming backgrounds
- An application illustrating the use of collections, filters, and timers

ActionScript Dynamic Classes

Like ActionScript 2 and JavaScript, AS3 lets you add and remove properties on-the-fly. In particular, it's possible to add properties programmatically and add or redefine methods during runtime.

Let's consider the following Person class:

```
dynamic class Person {
   public var firstName:String="Joe";
   public var lastName:String="Doe";
}
```

We can create an instance of Person, add the property age, and override the default method *to-String()*:

```
var p:Person = new Person():
p.age=25; // dynamic property
p.toString = function():String { // overridden method
     return p.lastName + "." + p.firstName + "-" + age;
}

trace(p); // Doe.Joe-25
```

Note that dynamically added or redefined functions can't access private members of the dynamic class: had we declared Person's lastName as private, trace(p) would result in "undefined,Joe-25."

Adding or redefining a method isn't any different from that of any different property type. After all, a function is just a property with a type Function.

Suppose the JavaProgrammer class is defined as:

```
  public class JavaProgrammer {
    public var lastName:String="Mr. Interface";
    public function learnFlex():void {
      trace(lastName + " is ready for RIA work!"):
    }
}
```

Then an instance of Person can "attach" the method learnFlex():

```
var p:Person=new Person():
var jp:JavaProgrammer = new JavaProgrammer();
p.boostCareer = jp.learnFlex;
```

and then invoke the method:

```
p.boostCareer();  // Mr. Interface is ready for RIA work!
```

The attached function retains the scope of the original instance of JavaProgrammer: it prints "Mr. Interface is ready for RIA work!" –not "Doe is ready for RIA work."

Most importantly, however, is that the definition of Person starts with the keyword *dynamic*. What makes AS3, as a scripting language, stand out from its peers is the optional strong typing and, first of all, the just-in-time (JIT) compilation of strongly typed code blocks into native machine code. Having bet on performance, AS3 changed the rules of engagement: now instead of assuming that the class allows dynamic properties or methods, it defaults to the opposite. Regular classes, as they are known in Java, are called *sealed* in AS3. To take advantage of dynamic properties and methods you have to prefix the class definition with the magic word *dynamic*.

What happens if you don't? For starters, the default mode of the Flex Builder compiler is strict and unless you turn it into a so-called standard (strict="false"), you won't be able to compile the above snippet. Then, having turned off the compile-time type checking of AS3, you'd get hit by runtime type checking.

In full compliance with AS2 and JavaScript, it's also possible to add/modify the property or method on the entire dynamic class via its prototype object:

```
Person.prototype.age = 46;
Person.prototype.fullName = function():String {
     return this.lastName + "," + this.firstName ;
}

trace(p.fullName()); // Doe,Joe46
```

Notice how the value of age has been effectively modified on the instance p that's already been created.

The delete operator destroys the property of the dynamic object and makes it eligible for garbage collection:

```
delete p.age;
trace(p);    // Doe,Joe-undefined
```

Some of the Flex classes are intentionally defined as dynamic, those being Object, Array, MovieClip, NetConnection, and AsyncToken. When this chapter was written, the subclasses of the dynamic classes were not dynamic by default. Because of this, you may run into a runtime error: imagine a sealed class S that extends a dynamic class D. If you create an object as

```
var dynObj:D =  new S(),
```

an attempt to add a property to dynObj will produce a runtime error because the variable dynObj points to a sealed object. So,

```
  dynObj.favoriteBand="Beatles";
```

would cause

```
ReferenceError: Error #1056 Can't create a property. favoriteBand…
```

You should be aware of the tradeoff: natively compiled code performs faster in the order of magnitude; it's also significantly more efficient in terms of memory consumption. On the other hand, dynamic classes bring lots of flexibility to programming. For instance, they help you get away from marshaling incompatibilities during remote calls. Compare this with Java RMI. For the successful serialization of a class between two JVMs, the definition of the class has to be present on each end[1]. Importantly it has to be exactly the same definition. But with dynamic classes it's not a must. And, as far as object-oriented terms go, you could say that dynamic classes offer "O-O on steroids" (use at your own risk).

Methods, Functions, and Closures

In addition to the methods of a particular class, ActionScript supports user-defined functions, such as application-level functions and package-level functions. It's a bit unusual for Java programmers that not all user-defined functions should be parts of some class definition, but, hey, in scripting languages a function is an object of itself!

You can define a function using either function statements or function expressions. A function statement declaration of the function calcTax() that returns a number may look like:

```
public function calcTax(income:Number):Number{
       return income*0.28;
}
var myTax:Number=calcTax(70000);
```

Alternatively you may use a function expression. One typical use case for a function expression, aka an anonymous function, is assigning it to some property of an object. That's exactly what we've done in the prior section when we defined the fullName method:

```
Person.prototype.fullName = function():String {
     return this.lastName + "," + this.firstName ;
}
```

Here's another example:

```
var calcFunc:Function = function (income:Number):Number{
    return income*0.28;
}

 var myTax:Number=calcFunc(88000);
```

There's no fundamental difference between the latter use cases and a regular function statement, because a function declaration is equivalent to defining a variable of the type Function and assigning it a function expression. There's a nuisance, however, when an anonymous function is attached to a property of an dynamic object: when the property gets deleted (fullName), the lifespan of the function is over[2].

Another popular use case for anonymous functions is the event handler function:

```
remoteObject.addEventListener(
      "fault",
      function(event:FaultEvent):void {
         // .. .. ..
      }
)
```

Note that the syntax above can cause memory leaks since it requires the VM to make a reference to *this* object and place it inside a global anonymous function that makes garbage collection unavailable on "this." Proper application techniques say to use a bound method and a weak reference/removeEventListener method to simplify memory de-allocation.

Function Parameters

In AS3, primitive parameters are passed by values, and non-primitives are passed by reference. You can include default values for the function parameters. For example:

```
public function calcTax(income:Number, dependents:int=1):Number{
   return (income*0.28 - dependents*500); //Give 500 credit for each dependent
}

var tax=calcTax(10000);   // tax is equal to 2300
```

Within the function body AS3 supports special objects called arguments. These are arrays that include actual arguments passed to the function. The length of these arrays may be different from the number arguments the function declares. The additional property arguments.callee contains a reference to the function itself.

Also, the AS3-specific way of supporting a variable number of function arguments is the so-called ... (rest) parameter. Ellipses followed by the name represent an array that accommodates any number of arguments that you pass in excess of the declared parameters, which always precede the rest parameter:

```
public static function calcTax(… taxParams):Number{
   for (uint i=0; i< taxParams.length; i++){
         trace(taxParams[i]);
   }
}
```

Java programmers may find the ... (rest) similar to a varargs notation. You can mix the ... (rest) with other function parameters so long as it's the last parameter of the function.

Here's an idea for using the ... (rest) parameter to overcome the absence of overloaded functions and constructors in AS3: use a *switch case* operator to branch on the number of actual arguments:

```
Class MyClass {
public function MyCLass(...args) {
  switch (args.length) {
   case 0: constructor1(); return;
   case 1: constructor2(args[0]); return;
   case 2: constructor3(args[0], args[1]); return;
...
}}
```

To ensure proper processing in cases where the number of arguments is the same but the types are different, you'd have to complement this with type checks:

```
if(args[0] is String) {
  // process as String
} else if (args[0] is Number){
   // process as Number
}
```

Getters and Setters

AS3 getters and setters form an alternative mechanism for defining object properties. Unlike Java, where getters and setters are part of the JavaBeans specification, AS3 getters and setters are first-class language citizens. Accordingly, rather than relying on the convention of set/get prefixes for function names, AS3 offers set-and-get modifiers to follow the *function* keyword. Here is an example of the class Tax with the read/write property income:

```
public class Tax extends EventDispatcher  {
   private var myIncome:Number;

   public  function set income(inc:Number):void{
      myIncome=inc;
      // perform related actions, dispatchEvents, etc.
   }

   public function get income():Number{
      return myIncome;
   }
}
```

Listing 4.1 Class Tax

The code snippet below instantiates the class Tax and assigns and prints the income using the getter and setter of the class Tax:

```
var tx:Tax=new Tax();
tx.income=5000.00;
trace("The income is " + tx.income);
```

Functions as Objects

Java programmers may find this concept a bit unusual, but AS3 functions are objects of the type Function, and they can have their own properties and internal methods and can be passed to other functions as arguments. A Function type can't be extended since it's defined as "final" so you can't manipulate it in an OO way. Functions are used in either a *bound* or *closure* mode. Bound functions are identical to Java ones in that they are defined within the class and their lexical environment is the instance of the enclosing class.

```
public class MyClass extends Label {
   public function addNumbers(a:Number, b:Number) : void {
      text = a + b;
   }….
}
```

To use the addNumber method you have to provide a reference to an instance of the MyClass object. It's a direct call to the instance and the context of the instance is available to the function.

You can find other examples of using a function object in some of the ActionScript methods. For example, when you add a listener to process an event, you register in ObjectProxy.addEventListener ("myEvent," myEventHandler) and call a name of the event to process and a function that will handle this event. Note that the name of the myEventHandler function is not followed by parentheses here because we're not calling the function myEventHandler, but are passing a reference to its code, which will be called if and only if the myEvent event in the ObjectProxy object occurs.

The fact that you can pass just the name of the function as a parameter makes it impossible for the compiler to check that this passed function is called with proper parameters, which may potentially lead to runtime errors. Thorough testing of Flex applications is even more important than in Java.

Closures

Closures play a cornerstone role in dynamic languages. They're essential for implementing features like OO or building frameworks. At the same time, the formal definition of closures doesn't really help in understanding them. Let's go through a few examples. First, we'll show what closures look like and then we'll give you their use patterns.

It all starts with the use of an anonymous function that has access to variables in the outer lexical scope:

```
<?xml version="1.0"?>
<mx:Application xmlns:mx="http://www.adobe.com/2006/mxml"
        layout="vertical" creationComplete="doInit(event)">
<mx:Script>
import mx.controls.Alert;
private var greeting:String="Hello";
private function doInit(evt:Event) : void {
   btn.addEventListener("click", function(evt:Event):void {
      Alert.show( greeting + ", " + txt.text);
   });
}
</mx:Script>
<mx:Button id="btn" label="closure" />
<mx:TextInput id="txt"/>
</mx:Application>
```

Listing 4.2 Anonymous function accessing outer scope variables

Compile and run this code – it shows a message box with the value of txt.text that was not defined in the closure.

Here's an oversimplified three-part description of closures:

1. Closures are functions that are defined in a class or function context and passed to another object for execution at a later time.
2. A closure's "attachment" happens at runtime (and can be executed multiple times during an application run). It's just the stack-frame allocation where all context variables ("greeting," in our case) are being saved for later use. In most cases it's about surrounding variables of the hosting function and current runtime class instance.
3. Finally, closure's execution can happen at any time, and can also have parameters when it's called. A standard convention is to have an Event object passed in with information from the calling object.

It seems you can use closures to "snapshot" any number of parameters. Unfortunately, that's true for some dynamic languages, but not for ECMAScript ones like ActionScript and JavaScript. Let's illustrate the difference with a few examples. First, let's make sure that the ActionScript closures are compile-time artifacts rather than true dynamically interpreted counterparts. Just swap the order of the closure and greetings definition statements.

```
<?xml version="1.0"?>
```

```
<mx:Application xmlns:mx="http://www.adobe.com/2006/mxml"
        layout="vertical" creationComplete="doInit(event)">
<mx:Script>
import mx.controls.Alert;
private var myClosure :Function = function(evt:Event) {
      Alert.show( greeting + ", " + txt.text);
   }
private function doInit(evt:Event) : void {
   btn.addEventListener("click", myClosure);
}
private var greeting:String="Hello";
</mx:Script>
<mx:Button id="btn" label="closure"/>
<mx:TextInput id="txt"/>
</mx:Application>
```

Listing 4.3 Closures are compile-time artifacts

It still works even though "greeting" should have been undefined at the time of the closure definition – proving that just the reference is being used. Also, unlike Java, the scope of an object is the stack-frame content of the enclosing function or class. Here is an example that wouldn't compile in Java, but is perfectly legal in AS3:

```
private function aaa():void{
    { var a = 1; } //in Java a is not visible outside of the block
    Alert.show(a);
}
```

Flash is a stack machine. A closure is a stack variable in the enclosing function, and this stack-frame approach greatly simplifies the implementation of closures and code optimizers based on the stack, even though it requires some adjustments in coding style. Another issue is that we don't have object values here – everything is done by reference. Let's modify the greeting's value right before the call:

```
<mx:Button label="closure" click="greeting='good morning'"/>
```

As you can see, the greeting was replaced on an alert screen with the new value – it wouldn't happen if the "closure" used a greeting reference by value at the time of definition.

Closures are first-class citizens of ActionScript. Every method in your class is a closure. That's how it knows the instance variables of the class. Essentially every class is a big closure. You can write a function with closures inside that would be very much a class for all practical purposes.

Closures are unavoidable when you use asynchronous operations or need to process an event on the other object. Almost any non-trivial action in Flex – communication with the server, say, or getting input from a user – is asynchronous. Using closure automatically gives you the reference to the class instance in which you have your function to the external object processing the event. That's sufficient for processing the asynchronous method's results in most cases. Automatic pointing of *this* context to the instance defining the function greatly simplifies the coding since it's natural to the developer.

Before Flex 2, in Flex 1.5 developers were responsible for supplying context to the closure. The ability to replace the closure context gives greater flexibility to the code and makes it truly dynamic.

The next code sample shows a closure on an arbitrary object to provide a custom context object:

```
public class Closure extends Object {
   public static function create(context:Object, func:Function, ... pms):Function {
        var f:Function = function():*
        {
           var target:*  = arguments.callee.target;
           var func:*    = arguments.callee.func;
           var params:*  = arguments.callee.params;

           var len:Number = arguments.length;
           var args:Array = new Array(len);
           for(var i:Number=0; i<len; i++){
              args[i] = arguments[i];

           args["push"].apply(args, params);
           return func.apply(target, args);
        };

        var _f:Object = f;
        _f.target  = context;
        _f.func    = func;
        _f.params  = pms;
        return f;
     }
  }
```

Listing 4.4 A closure and a custom context object

The following code illustrates how to call this closure:

```
<?xml version="1.0" encoding="utf-8"?>
<mx:Application xmlns:mx="http://www.adobe.com/2006/mxml" layout="absolute" creationComp
lete="onCreationComplete(event)">
```

```
<mx:Script>
   <![CDATA[
      import mx.controls.Alert;
      private var myClosure:Function ;
      private function onCreationComplete (evt:Event):void {
         myClosure = Closure.create({greeting:"Good evening"},function(name:String):void
{
            Alert.show( this.greeting + ", " + name);
         },"world");
         var greeting:String;
         greeting ="Hello";
      }
   ]]>
</mx:Script>
<mx:Button id="btn" label="closure" click="myClosure()" />
</mx:Application>
```

Listing 4.5 Testing a closure

Now the alert shows "Good evening, world" because the method has been applied using a different context. Often this methodology is called "delegation" and is used by business frameworks to centralize the processing of certain events.

The example above illustrates the relationship between context, functions, and closures. Using this technique lets you implement dynamic inheritance, polymorphism, and other OO concepts.

Java 6 doesn't support closures, but they may be introduced in Java 7. Closure functions weren't included in the original Java specification because back then the plan was to allow object creation only in the heap memory if a *new* operator was called. But Java 5 introduced auto-boxing, the first violation of this principle because objects were created dynamically behind the scenes. If you find the concept of closures appealing, we'd recommend taking a look at products like BeanShell for Java and other Java interpreters that let you define whole classes or just methods as closures.

The closest constructs to closures in Java are anonymous inner classes (see section 15.9.5 of the Java Language Specification).

Let's consider an example of an event listener in Java Swing where you define an anonymous class at the moment a listener is added. The following Java code snippet adds an event listener to a button:

```
JButton myButton = new JButton("Place Order");
myButton.addActionListener(new ActionListener(){
    public void actionPerformed(ActionEvent ae){
       //your code to place an order goes here...
```

```
    }
  } // end of anonymous class declaration
);
```

This code means that the addActionListener() method in Java requires an instance of the listener class as an argument. But since this listener will only be used by this button, why bother even naming the class? The code above (starting with new and ending with a curly brace) defines and creates an instance of an anonymous class and overrides the method actionPerformed() that processes a clicked event. Looks a bit convoluted, doesn't it?

In AS3, you just define a function and pass it to the listener as an argument for an execution. For example:

```
myButton.addEventListener("click", placeOrder);
```

Here placeOrder is a function closure that defines the business logic; it's passed to the method addEventListener() and is executed as soon as the button is clicked.

To pass a closure to another method and execute it, Flex creates a dynamic object behind the scenes and wraps the closure up. In the example below, we define the following function closure:

```
gotoWebPage(theURL: String) {
  // open a specified Web page in a new Web browser's window
  getURL(theURL, "_blank");
}
```

Let's pass the reference to this to a timer function. The next line will execute the function gotoWebPage() in five seconds while passing it the target URL as an argument:

```
setTimeout(gotoWebPage, 5000, "http://www.theriabook.com");
```

Interestingly enough, the utility function setTimeout() is itself a closure. Adobe's language reference suggests using the Timer object instead for efficiency reasons: when you create an instance of an object yourself (as opposed to the dynamic objects that are used with closures), the garbage collector's work becomes a bit easier. So setTimeout() and some other timing utility functions exist in AS3 only for backward compatibility/simplicity reasons.

Asynchronous Programming

Traditional Java programmers have to get used to the fact that when a client makes an RPC call to a server, it actually just requests the execution of this method, allowing the user to continue working with the application. It doesn't block until the result comes back. After some time, which could be as long as several seconds, the result or error message can come back to the client, and it needs to remember which component has sent this request and process it accordingly. You'll see an example of such an application in Chapter 5. Meanwhile, we'll walk you through a high-level overview of the communication process.

ActionScript doesn't have an explicit multithreading API. It can be emulated by running multiple instances of the player within the hosting page, but it's not a trivial task. On the bright side, Flex makes standard tasks that require multithreading much simpler. Instead of explicit multithreading, the classes that need to be executed asynchronously use pre-built Flash player components that handle all the tracking and optimization.

A financial news service from Yahoo accessed via an HTTPService is a good example of asynchronous communication:

```
<mx:HTTPService id="newsFeed" destination="YahooFinancialNews" /> ...
var token: AsyncToken = newsFeed.send({security:"ADBE"});
token.responder = new Responder(processBusinessNews, processBusinessNewsErrors);
```

The last two lines mean the following: request the news about Adobe (ADBE), and expect the result to come back as an instance of the AsyncToken object.

Flash Player takes care of tracking multiple requests and the invocation of the responders' methods upon completion. A responder specifies that upon return, Flash Player calls processBusinessNews when successful and processBusinessNewsErrors if it fails. The processBusinessNews function is also known as an event handler and must be present in the code.

The processBusinessNews function may look like this:

```
public function processBusinessNews(evt:Event):void {
    myNewsCollection.addNews(evt.result.businessnews);
    // code to display the news on the screen goes here
}
```

Data Binding

The Flex Developers Guide states that "Data binding is the process of tying the data in one object to another object. It provides a convenient way to pass data around in an application."

We'd like to offer you another definition: data binding is the ability of one object to watch the changes of a specified property(ies) on another object, expression, or a function that returns a value.

To watch such changes in Java, you'd need to write and register listeners in one object, while another object has to fire appropriate events when the property in question changes. Even though AS3 has similar language constructs, there's a much easier way to do this in Flex.

Flex offers you several ways of binding data between the objects using a very simple syntax and the job of creating listeners will be done for you automatically without having to write such code manually. You can review the listeners and other generated code by using the compiler option –keep-generated-actionscript=true.

Binding in MXML

Just to give you a quick peek into data binding in its simplest form, look at the sample application in Listing 4.6 that consists of a TextInput field and a label. The text of the label is bound to the text of the input field by a simple use of curly braces:

```
text="{myTextField.text}"
```

This line "tells" myLabel: "Watch the text property of the object called myTextField and as soon as it gets modified, update yourself."

You won't find any listener declaration or firing events in the code below. The very fact that we've put the text property in curly braces will force the Flex compiler to generate all the required AS3 listeners, event dispatchers, and binding automatically.

```
<?xml version="1.0" encoding="utf-8"?>
<mx:Application xmlns:mx="http://www.adobe.com/2006/mxml" layout="absolute">
   <mx:TextInput id="myTextField" x="59" y="41" />
   <mx:Label id="myLabel" text="{myTextField.text}" x="69" y="89" width="150" />
</mx:Application>
```

Listing 4.6 BindingTextFieldAndLabel.mxml

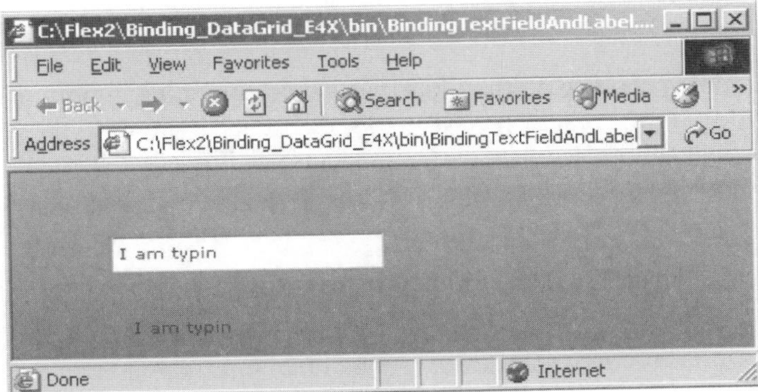

Figure 4.1 Typing in a text field is reflected in the label

This application may seem pretty useless, but we'll give you plenty of real-world examples that demonstrate the power of data bindings in every chapter in this book. These are just some of the nearest examples:

- Watching a panel state as in Listing 4.13
- Binding a data collection to the DataGrid as in Listing 4.28
- Displaying errors as in Listing 5.10
- Implementing master-detail relations between components as in Listing 5.21

But to understand these and other examples, we have to cover some data binding basics.

In each pair of bound objects there's a source, destination, and triggering event. In our example myTextField is the source, myLabel is the destination, and the "change" of the text in the myTextfield is the triggering event. You can bind more than two objects by creating a so-called bindable property chain: object A is a source for destination B, which in turn is a source for destination C and so on.

To specify binding in MXML, you can use either the curly braces as we did before, or a dedicated <mx:Binding> Tag. The previous example can be rewritten as follows:

```
<mx:TextInput id="myTextField" x="59" y="41" />
<mx:Label id="myLabel" x="69" y="89" width="150" />
<mx:Binding source="myTextField.text" destination="myLabel.text" />
```

Your program can have multiple <mx:Binding> tags using the same destinations and/or sources.

Binding Expressions

To complicate our example a little bit, we'll add one more destination:

```
<mx:Label id="myTwoPlusTwoLabel"
     text="{2+2+ Number(myTextField.text)}" x="69" y="109" width="150" />
```

Now we have one source and two destinations (two labels). But more importantly, we've included an expression inside the curly braces. If you run this program, it'll show 4 as the value of the second label. Start typing digits in the text field and both labels will immediately reflect the changes and the value in the second label will be greater by 4.

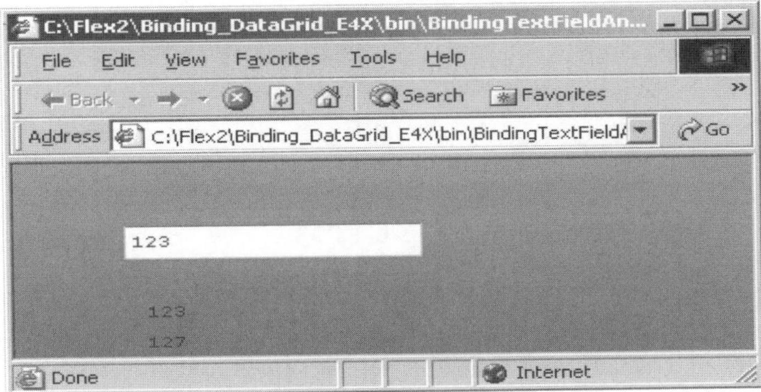

Figure 4.2 One source, two destinations

Entering an alpha character will display NaN (not a number) as the result of our expression evaluation.

On the same note, you can use an AS3 function in the binding expression as long as it returns a value.

What's Under the Hood?

Obviously, using curly braces is just the tip of the iceberg. How does this binding magic work internally?

The Flex compiler generates bindable wrappers in AS3 for each property or expression that is being watched (i.e., PropertyWatcher), and it'll generate all the required AS3 code for event processing (see the section on events later in this chapter). And of course, it'll create an instance of an mx.binding.Binding object that ties everything together.

Metatags are a way of providing compilers/linkers with information that's not part of the language. In the Java universe, annotations are peers of AS3 metatags. For data binding, AS3 offers the metatag [Bindable]. The information in the metatags is used to generate additional framework code and instruct the compiler to use the generated code whenever the annotated properties/methods are used.

For example, let's see the inner workings of our TextImput/Label binding example (the code is generated by the Flex compiler). We start in the source code of the TextInput control and analyze the declaration there. This is what we find:

```
[DefaultBindingProperty(source="text", destination="text")]
[DefaultTriggerEvent("change")]
[Bindable("textChanged")]
[NonCommittingChangeEvent("change")]
```

These binding declarations cause the compiler to generate the following data structures:

```
binding = new mx.binding.Binding(this,
            function():String
            {
                var result:* = (myTextField.text);
                var stringResult:String = (result == undefined ? null :
String(result));
                return stringResult;
            },
            function(_sourceFunctionReturnValue:String):void
            {

                myLabel.text = _sourceFunctionReturnValue;
            },
            "myLabel.text");
        _bindings[0] = binding;
...
        watchers[1] = new mx.binding.PropertyWatcher("myTextField",
            {
                propertyChange: true
            }
                                                                );

        watchers[2] = new mx.binding.PropertyWatcher("text",
            {
                textChanged: true,
                change: false
            }
        );
        watchers[1].addListener(bindings[0]);
        watchers[1].propertyGetter = propertyGetter;
        watchers[1].updateParent(target);

        watchers[2].addListener(bindings[0]);
        watchers[1].addChild(watchers[2]);

        bindings[0].uiComponentWatcher = 1;
        bindings[0].execute();
```

What about watching not just the properties but the expressions? Consider this one:

```
2+2+ Number(myTextField.text)
```

It works the same way. The Flex compiler automatically generates an anonymous wrapper function for the source of the event, which is an expression:

```
function():String {
var result:* = (2+2+ Number(myTextField.text));
var stringResult:String = (result == undefined ? null : String(result));
return stringResult;
}
```

If you'd like to learn more about binding internals read the section in the Flex Developer's Guide called "About the Binding Mechanism."

Binding in ActionScript

You can put the [Bindable] metatag above one or more properties of an AS3 class, but if you'd like all the properties of the class to be bindable, just add one [Bindable] metatag above the class definition:

```
[Bindable]
public class myClass{
...
}
```

If you don't specify which event should trigger an update of the destination, Flex will use propertyChange by default. But this metatag allows another syntax that lets you specify any other applicable event name.

For example, if the variable price should trigger some actions when the stock price changes, you can define a custom event priceChanged (described later in this chapter) and use the following syntax:

```
[Bindable(event="priceChanged")]
var price:Number;
```

A quick peek at the generated folder reveals that the [Bindable] metatag causes the compiler to generate a shadow class with getters/setters for each bindable property. In the setter method the compiler adds a dispatch event to notify listeners of the object change. Also, the destination object automatically gets a binding/watcher for the respective source.

In some cases it is beneficial to provide dynamic binding.

For details, check out the documentation for the classes BindingUtils and ChangeWatcher.

Binding Inside a String and Application Parameters

In this little section we'll kill two birds with one stone.First, we'll show you how to pass parameters to a Flex application from the HTML wrapper generated by Flex Builder, and then you'll see how to use the binding inside a text string.

Our next assignment will be to write a Flex application that will run against different servers (dev, uat, prod) without having to recompile SWF. It doesn't take a rocket scientist to figure out that the URL of the server should be passed to SWF as a parameter, and we'll do this by using a special flashVars variable in the HTML wrapper. Flex's documentation suggests including flashVars parameters in the Object and Embed tags and reading them using Application.application.parameters in AS3 code. As this was written, this doesn't work. But as the ancient saying goes, "Adobe closes one door but opens another one." But first, let's get familiar with Flex code:

```
<?xml version="1.0" encoding="utf-8"?>
<mx:Application xmlns:mx="http://www.adobe.com/2006/mxml" layout="absolute"
   applicationComplete="initApp()">

  <mx:Label text=
"Will run the app deployed at http://{serverURL}:{port}/MyGreatApp.html" />
  <mx:Script>
   <![CDATA[
      [Bindable]
      var serverURL:String;

      [Bindable]
      var port:String;

      function initApp():void{
         serverURL=Application.application.parameters.serverURL;
         port=Application.application.parameters.port
      }
   ]]>
  </mx:Script>
</mx:Application>
```

Listing 4.7 BindingWithString.mxml

The script portion of this code gets the values of parameters serverURL and port (defined by us) using the Application object. We'll add the values of these parameters to the HTML file as described below. These values are bound to the MXML label as a part of the text string.

If you'll open the HTML file generated, you'll find the JavaScript function AC_FL_RunContent that includes flashVars parameters in the form of key-value pairs. For example, in our sample application it looks like this:

```
"flashvars",'historyUrl=history.htm%3F&lconid=' + lc_id +''
```

Add our parameters serverURL and port to this string:

```
"flashvars",'serverURL=MyDevelopmentServer&port=8181&historyUrl=history.
htm%3F&lconid=' + lc_id
```

Run the Application and it'll display the URL of the server it connects to. If you'd like to test your application against a QA server, just change the values of the flashVars parameters in the HTML file.

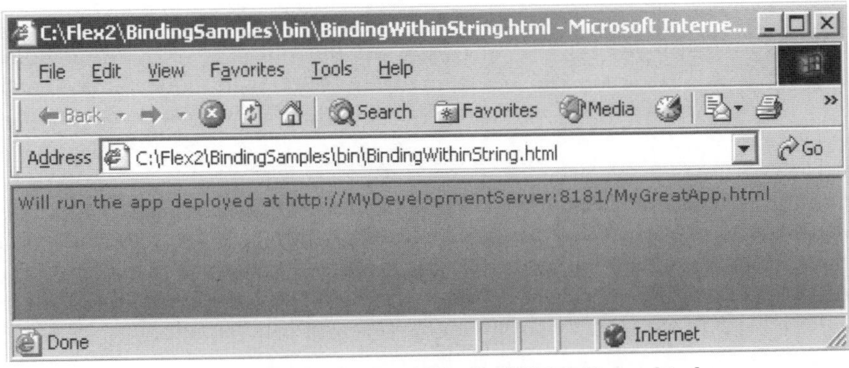

Figure 4.3 The output of BindingWithinString.html

We have one last little wrinkle to iron out: if you manually change the content of the generated HTML file, next time you clean the project in Flex Builder, its content will be overwritten and you'll lose the added flashVars parameters. There's a simple solution to this problem: instead of adding flashVars parameters to the generated HTML, add them to the file index.template.html from the html-template directory, which Flex Builder uses to generate the run and debug versions of the HTML wrapper.

Of course, this little example doesn't connect to any server, but it gives you an idea of how to pass the server URL (or any other value) as a Flash parameter, and how to assemble the URL from a mix of text and bindings

Is Data Binding a Silver Bullet?

The ease of use of Flex data binding is very addictive, but there are cases when using data binding isn't recommended. For example, if a number of changes is done on various properties of a class and you want to display the final state only when all the changes are complete, making each data item bindable would generate unnecessary event firing after each data change.

The other drawback to using binding to tie together properties of different components is that it assumes some knowledge about the component internals. It makes application design a bit complex because it statically links components together and makes changes interdependent. It also requires the compiler to generate a lot of cross-referencing code that consumes both time and memory.

Alternative architecture is to use loosely bound components. You can read about them in the section on Custom Events below.

Program in Style or an Elevator Pitch

We usually run Flex training for our private clients, but once in a while we teach public classes for people with different programming backgrounds, and each of them comes with a different understanding of how to do things right.

We'll tell you a story that might have happened in real life, but first, we'll remind you of the old Indian tale about seven blind men and an elephant. One blind man touched the elephant's head, another one the tail, another was by the leg and each of them visualized the elephant differently based on what he touched.

Students usually arrive in the classroom early, but this time three seats were empty. Five minutes later the instructor got a phone call from one person explaining that the three had gotten stuck in the elevator and would be there for another 15 minutes until the serviceman arrived. Needless to say each of them had a laptop (do not leave home without one), so the instructor gave them a short assignment to help them use the time productively. Here's the assignment:

Create a window with a panel that can resize itself with the click of a +/- button located in the right-hand corner of the panel. One click should minimize the panel's height to 20 pixels, and a subsequent one should maximize to 100 pixels, and so on. For example, these are the two states of such a panel:

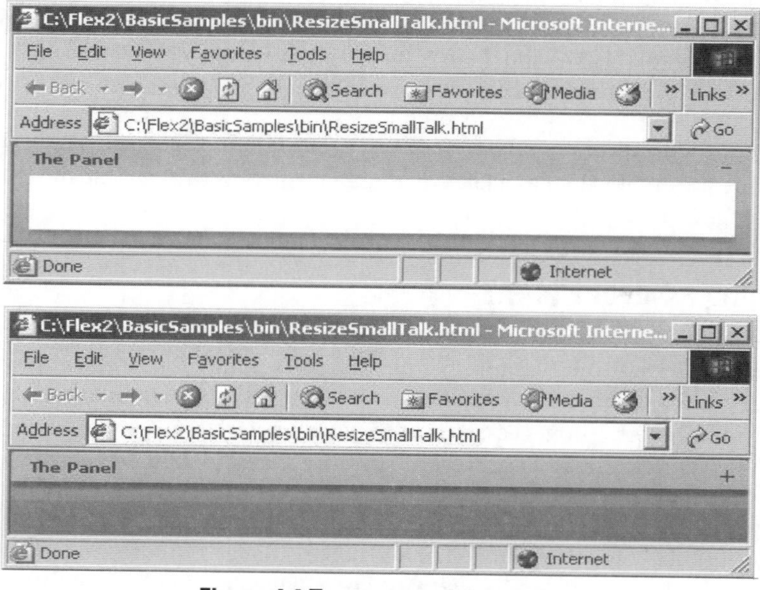

Figure 4.4 Two states of the panel

From COBOL to Flex

A COBOL programmer thought to himself, "We used to write long programs because during job interviews they usually ask how many lines of code I wrote. These guys are different, so to earn a good grade, this program should be small." He finished the program on time and this is what it looked like:

```
<?xml version="1.0" encoding="utf-8"?>
<mx:Application xmlns:mx="http://www.adobe.com/2006/mxml" layout="absolute">
     <mx:Panel id="thePanel" title="The Panell" height="90" width="100%" headerHe-
ight="20" />
     <mx:HBox width="100%" horizontalAlign="right" paddingRight="2">
       <mx:Label text="-"  fontSize="16" width="20" height="17" fontWeight="bold"
              id="minimizeActions"
              click="{if (minimizeActions.text=='+'){
                          minimizeActions.text='-';
                          thePanel.height=100;
                      } else {
                         minimizeActions.text='+';
                          thePanel.height=20;
                      }
                     }" />
     </mx:HBox>
</mx:Application>
```

Listing 4.8 The "Cobol" version

From Java to Flex

The Java programmer thought, "The standard Flex Panel class doesn't have a property that remembers the current state of the panel, but Flex components are easily extendable, so I'll create a descendent of the panel in ActionScript, add a private state flag (minimized), a public setter and getter, and a resize function. That way my new panel class will be reusable and self-contained." This is his reusable AS3 class called ResizableJPanel:

```
package {
          import mx.containers.Panel;
          public class ResizableJPanel extends Panel   {
                   // state of the panel
                  private  var isPanelMinimized:Boolean;

                   public function get minimized():Boolean{
                       return isPanelMinimized;
                   }

                  public function set minimized(state:Boolean){
```

```
                        isPanelMinimized=state;
                    }

                    public function resizeMe():void{
                         if (minimized){
                            minimized=false;
                            height=maxHeight;
                         } else {
                             minimized=true;
                             height=minHeight;
                         }
            }
    }
}
```

Listing 4.9 The "Java" version of the panel class

This is the Javist's MXML code:

```
<?xml version="1.0" encoding="utf-8"?>

<mx:Application xmlns:mx="http://www.adobe.com/2006/mxml" xmlns:local="*"
layout="absolute">
     <local:ResizableJPanel id="aPanel"  height="90" width="100%"
                  title="The Panel" minHeight="20" maxHeight="100" headerHeight="20" />

       <mx:HBox width="100%" horizontalAlign="right" paddingRight="2">
              <mx:Label text="-"  fontSize="16" width="20" height="17" fontWeight="bold"
                                        id="minimizeActions" click="resizePanel(aPanel)" />
        </mx:HBox>

  <mx:Script>
           <![CDATA[
       function resizePanel(thePanel:ResizableJPanel):void{
               if (thePanel.minimized){
                    minimizeActions.text="-";
                    thePanel.resizeMe();
               } else {
                    minimizeActions.text="+";
                    thePanel.resizeMe();
               }
       }
           ]]>
  </mx:Script>
```

```
</mx:Application>
```

Listing 4.10 The MXML from a Java student

From Smalltalk to Flex

The Smalltalk guy thought, "Let me see if the standard panel is a dynamic class. If not, I'll extend it just to make it dynamic and assign the panel's state on-the-fly. I hope the instructor isn't one of those object-oriented Nazis." This is his panel AS3 class that just adds a dynamic behavior to the panel:

```
package{
            import mx.containers.Panel;
    public dynamic class ResizableSmtPanel extends Panel
            {
    }
}
```

Listing 4.11 Dynamic subclass of a panel

His MXML class looked like this:

```
<?xml version="1.0" encoding="utf-8"?>
<mx:Application xmlns:mx="http://www.adobe.com/2006/mxml" xmlns="*" layout="absolute">
     <ResizableSmtPanel title="The Panel" id="thePanel"  height="90" width="100%"
                             minHeight="20" maxHeight="100" headerHeight="20">
     </ResizableSmtPanel>
     <mx:HBox width="100%" horizontalAlign="right" paddingRight="2">
           <mx:Label text="-"  fontSize="16" width="20" height="17" fontWeight="bold"
             id="minimizeActions" click="resizePanel()" />
      </mx:HBox>
  <mx:Script>

            <![CDATA[

        function resizePanel():void{
             if (thePanel.minimized){
                  minimizeActions.text="-";
                  thePanel.minimized=false;
                 thePanel.height=thePanel.maxHeight;
         } else {
                   minimizeActions.text="+";
                   thePanel.minimized=true;
                   thePanel.height=thePanel.minHeight;
         }
```

```
        }
              ]]>
  </mx:Script>
```

Listing 4.12. The "Smalltalk" version of MXML

Fifteen minutes later, the three students were in the classroom, and each got an "A" for this elevator job. And here's the Flex version:

```
<?xml version="1.0" encoding="utf-8"?>

<mx:Application xmlns:mx="http://www.adobe.com/2006/mxml" xmlns="*" layout="absolute">
<mx:Component className="ResizablePanel">
   <mx:Panel>
    <mx:Script>

     [Bindable]
     public var minimized:Boolean = false;
    </mx:Script>
 </mx:Panel>
</mx:Component>

<ResizablePanel title="The Panel" id="thePanel"  minimized="false" height="{thePanel.
minimized?thePanel.minHeight:thePanel.maxHeight}" width="99%"
                            minHeight="20" maxHeight="100" headerHeight="20"/>
     <mx:HBox width="99%" horizontalAlign="right" paddingRight="2">
           <mx:Label text="{thePanel.minimized?'+':'-'}"  fontSize="16" width="20"
                                                     height="17" fontWeight="bold"
             id="minimizeActions" click="{thePanel.minimized=!thePanel.minimized}" />
      </mx:HBox>
</mx:Application>
```

Listing 4.13 The instructor's version of the solution

There's another simple solution to this particular assignment and we'll let the reader try to figure it out (hint: use states).

What's the moral of this story? Learn ANOTHER language, no matter what your current background is. Initially you'll try to bring your own culture to this new language, but eventually your horizons will broaden and you'll become a better programmer.

Object-Oriented ActionScript

You know the drill: a language is called object-oriented if it supports inheritance, encapsulation, and polymorphism. The first two notions can be easily defined:

Inheritance lets you design a class by deriving it from an existing one. This feature allows you to reuse existing code without copying and pasting. AS3 provides the keyword *extends* for declaring inheritance.

```
package com.theriabook.oop{
   public class Person {
     var name:String;
   }
}

package com.theriabook.oop{
   public class Consultant extends Person{
       var dailyRate:Number;
   }
}

package com.theriabook.oop{
   public class Employee extends Person{
       var salary:Number;
   }
}
```

Listing 4.14. The ancestor and two descendents

Encapsulation is an ability to hide and protect data. AS3 has access-level qualifiers such as public, private, protected, and internal to control the access class variables and methods. Besides Java-like public, private, protected, and package access levels, you can also create namespaces in AS3 that will give you another way to control access to properties and methods. This chapter includes some basic samples of namespaces, and you may want to read about the component manifest tiles in Chapter 11.

However, if Java enforces an object-oriented style of programming, this isn't the case with AS3, because it's based on the scripting language standard. Object-oriented purists may not like the next code snippet, but this is how a HelloWorld program can look in AS3:

```
trace("Hello, world");
```

That's it. No class declaration is required for such a simple program, and the debug function trace() can live its own class-independent life, as opposed to Java's println() doubly wrapped in the System and PrintStream classes. You can write your own functions, attach them to dynamic objects, and pass them as parameters to other functions. AS3 supports a regular inheritance chain as well as so-called prototype inheritance where you can add new properties to the class definitions and they become available to all instances of the class. Moreover, you can disable the validation of the properties and methods during compilation by turning off the "strict" mode. In Java, behind every object instance there's an entity of the type Class. This is not an object itself, but it's put in memory by class loaders.

Program Design with Interfaces and Polymorphism

As in Java, AS3 interfaces are special entities that define the behavior (methods) that can be implemented by classes using the keyword implement. After explaining what's crucial to OOP interfaces, we'll discuss how to write generic code without them.

To illustrate how you can design AS3 programs with interfaces, we'll add some behavior to the classes from Listing 4.14. Let's work on the following assignment.

A company has employees and consultants. Design classes to represent the people working in this company. The classes can have the following methods: changeAddress, giveDayOff, increasePay. Promotion can mean a day off and a salary raised a specified percentage. For employees, the increasePay method should raise the yearly salary and, for consultants, it should increase their hourly rate.

First, we'll add all the common methods that are applicable to both employees and consultants to the Person class.

```
package com.theriabook.oop {
   public class Person {
     var name:String;

     public function changeAddress(address: String): String {
         return "New address is"  + address;
      }

      private function giveDayOff(): String {
         return "Class Person: Giving an extra a day off";
      }
   }
}
```

Listing 4.15. The Ancestor class: Person

In the next step, we'll add a new behavior that can be reused by multiple classes: the ability to increase the amount of a person's paycheck. Let's define a Payable interface:

```
package com.theriabook.oop
{
   public interface Payable
```

```
    {
        function increasePay(percent:Number): String;
    }
}
```

Listing 4.16. Interface Payable

More than one class can implement this interface:

```
package com.theriabook.oop
{
    public class Employee extends Person implements Payable
    {
        public function  increasePay(percent:Number):String {
          // Employee-specific code goes here …
         return "Class Employee:Increasing the salary by "+ percent + "%\n";
        }
    }
}
```

Listing 4.17 The AS3 class Employee implementing the Payable interface

```
package com.theriabook.oop
{
    public class Consultant extends Person  implements Payable {

        public function increasePay(percent:Number): String{
         // Consultant-specific code goes here …
         return   "Class Consultant: Increasing the hourly rate by " +  percent + "%\n";

        }
    }
}
```

Listing 4.18 The Consultant class implementing Payable

When the Consultant class declares that it implements a Payable interface, it "promises" to provide implementation for all the methods declared in this interface – in our case there's just one increasePay()method. Why is it so important that the class "keeps the promise" and implements all the interface's methods? An interface is a description of some behavior(s). In our case the Payable behavior means the existence of a method with the signature boolean increasePay(int percent).

If any other class knows that Employee implements Payable, it can safely call any method declared in the Payable interface (see the interface example in the Promoter class in Listing 4.19).

In Java, besides method declarations, interfaces can contain final static variables, but AS3 doesn't allow anything in the interfaces except method declarations.

Interfaces are another workaround for adjusting to the absence of multiple inheritance. A class can't have two independent ancestors, but it can implement multiple interfaces, it just has to implement all the methods declared in all the interfaces. One way to implement multiple inheritance (that we often use but don't recommend it) is to use an "include" statement with the complete implementation of all classes implementing interface:

```
  public class Consultant extends Person  implements Payable {
  include "payableImplementation.as"
  }
public class Employee extends Person  implements Payable {
  include "payableImplementation.as"
}
```

For example, a Consultant class can be defined as:

```
class Consultant extends Person
     implements Payable, Sueable {…}
```

But if a program such as Promoter.mxml (see Listing 4.19) is interested only in Payable functions, it can cast the object only to those interfaces it intends to use. For example:

```
var emp:Employee = new Employee();
var con:Consultant = new Consultant();
var person1:Payable = emp as Payable;
var person2:Payable = con as Payable;
```

Now we'll write an MXML program Promoter that will use the Employee and Consultant classes defined in Listings 4.17 and 4.18. Click on the button and it'll create an array with a mix of employees and consultants. Iterate through this array and cast it to the Payable interface, then call the increasePay()method on each object in this collection.

```
<?xml version="1.0" encoding="utf-8"?>
<mx:Application xmlns:mx="http://www.adobe.com/2006/mxml" layout="absolute">
   <mx:Label y="10" text="Inheritance, Interfaces and Polymorphysm" width="398"
height="35" fontWeight="bold" horizontalCenter="-16" fontSize="16"/>
   <mx:Button x="93" y="66" label="Increase Pay" width="172" fontSize="16"
click="startPromoter()" id="starter"/>
   <mx:TextArea x="26" y="114" width="312" height="133" id="output" wordWrap="true"
editable="false" borderStyle="inset"/>

   <mx:Script>
```

```
<![CDATA[
    import com.theriabook.oop.*;
   function startPromoter():void{
       output.text="Starting global promotions...\n";

        var  workers:Array = new Array();
        workers.push(new Employee());
        workers.push(new Consultant());
        workers.push(new Employee());
        workers.push(new Employee());

        for(var i: int = 0; i < workers.length; i++) {
         // Raise the compensation of every worker using Payable
         //   interface
         var p: Payable = workers[i] as Payable;
         output.text+= p.increasePay(5);

         //p.giveDayOff(); would not work. Payable does not know
         //                  about this function
        }

       output.text+="Finished global promotions...";
   }
  ]]>
 </mx:Script>
</mx:Application>
```

Listing 4.19 Promoter.mxml

The output of this program will look like:

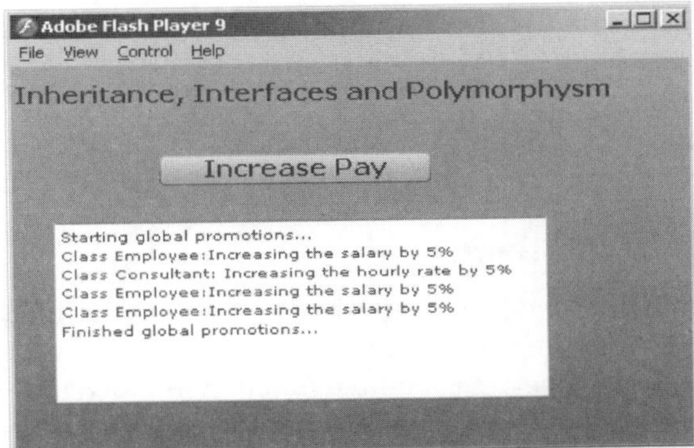

Figure 4.5 The output of Promoter.mxml

The line p.increasePay(5) in the listing above may look a little confusing. How can we call a concrete increasePay method on a variable of an interface type? Actually we call a method on a concrete instance of the Employee or a Consultant object, but by casting this instance to the Payable type we're just letting the AVM know that we're only interested in methods that were declared in this particular interface.

Polymorphism – When you look at our Promoter from Listing 4.19, it looks like it calls the same increasePay()method on different types of objects, and it generates different outputs for each type. This is an example of polymorphic behavior.

In the real world, array *workers* would be populated from some external data source. For example, a program could get a person's work status from the database and instantiate an appropriate concrete class. The loop in Promoter.mxml will remain the same even if we add some other types of workers inherited from the Person class! For example, to add a new category of worker – a foreign contractor, we'll have to create a ForeignContractor class that implements the increasePays method and might be derived from the Person class. Our Promoter will keep casting all these objects to the Payable type during runtime and call the increasePay method of the current object from the array.

Polymorphism allows you to avoid using *switch* or if statements with the checking type operator is. Below is a bad (non-polymorphic) alternative to our loop from Promoter.mxml that checks the type of the object and calls the type-specific methods increaseSalary() and increaseRate() (assuming that these methods were defined):

```
for(var i: int = 0; i < workers.length; i++) {
   var p: Person = workers[i] as Person;
   if (p is Employee){
      increaseSalary(5);
   } else if (p is Consultant) {
      increaseRate(5);
   }
}
```

Listing 4.20 A bad practice example

You'd have to modify the code above each time you add a new worker type.

Polymorphism Without Interfaces

If this was a Java book, we could have patted ourselves on the back for providing a nice example of polymorphism. Let's think of a more generic approach – do we even need to use interfaces to ensure that a particular object instance has a required function like increasePay? Of course not. Java has a powerful introspection and reflection mechanism that analyzes which methods exist in the class in question. It's important to remember though that in Java, object instances have only those methods that were defined in their classes (blueprints). This is not the case with AS3.

There is another urban myth that reflection is slow, and you should use it only if you have to. But this consideration isn't valid in programs that run on the client's PCs, because we don't have to worry about hundreds of threads competing for a slice of time on the same server's CPU(s). Using reflection on the client is fine. Even on the server proper the combination of reflection with caching allows you to avoid any performance penalties.

AS3 provides very short and elegant syntax for introspection, and we'd like to spend some time illustrating polymorphism without the typecasting and strict Java-style coding.

Let's revisit our sample application. Workers get pay and benefits and vacations; consultants are paid hourly wages. But retirees may have some form of receiving pensions, the board of directors might get paid but no benefits – are they workers? No, they're not and their objects may not necessarily implement the Payable interface, which means that the typecasting from Listing 4.19 would cause a runtime exception.

How about raising the compensation of every Person even if it doesn't implement Payable? If one of these objects sneaks into the *workers* array , simple casting to Payable as shown below will throw an exception:

```
Payable p = Payable(workers[i]);
```

Let's rewrite the loop from Listing 4.19 as follows:

```
for(var i:uint = 0; i < workers.length; i++) {
 var p:* = workers[i]["increasePay"];
 output.text+=p==undefined?"no luck":p(5);
}
```

This short loop deserves an explanation. First, we've declared a variable p of type *. This declaration means that p can be any type. Using an asterisk a bit more open than var p:Object; allows the variable p to have a special value of an undefined type as used in the above code sample.

Let's dissect the following line:

```
var p:* = worker[i]["increasePay"];
```

It means "Get a reference to the increasePay()function from the array element workers[i]." You may ask, "Why use the brackets around increasePay instead of the dot notation?" The reason is that dot notation would ask the compiler to find and validate this function, while the brackets tell the compiler not to worry about it, the program will take care of this little something inside the brackets during runtime.

Basically, the single line above performs the introspection and gets a pointer to the increasePay function for future execution in the line:

```
output.text+=p ==undefined?"no luck":p(5);
```

If this particular element of the workers array doesn't have increasePay defined (its class must be declared dynamic), add "no luck" to the text field. Otherwise execute this object's version of increasePay, passing the number five as its argument. The line above is still a potential problem if the class doesn't have the increasePay function, but has a property with the same name. The better version looks like this:

```
output.text+=!(p is Function)?"no luck":p(6);
```

Let's emphasize that again: this increasePay method doesn't have be defined in any interface.

Java programmers would call this wild anarchy. Of course, adhering to strict rules and contracts in Java leads to more predictable code and less surprises at runtime. But modern Java moves toward dynamic scripting, adding implicit typecasting, runtime exceptions, etc. Overuse of interfaces, private, protected, and other "nice clean object-oriented techniques" doesn't promote creative thinking in software developers. We hope all code samples in this chapter break the OOP spell that Java developers live under.

Namespaces in ActionScript

Namespaces in AS3 as in MXML are used to limit the scope (visibility) of methods, properties, or constants. They're also used to avoid naming conflicts in cases where you create your own custom components that may have the same names as the Flex Framework or other vendor's counterparts.

You can think of access control keywords – public, private, protected, and internal – as built-in namespaces. If a method has been declared as

```
protected calculateTax(){}
```

you can say that the calculateTax()method has a protected namespace. But AS3 lets you define your own namespaces to use instead of these standard language qualifiers.

To introduce your own namespace, you need to take the following steps:

- Declare a namespace
- Apply the namespace
- Reference the namespace

Let's write a simple program for an accountant who calculates taxes, but customers who belong to the Mafia would pay only half the amount. To do this, we'll start by declaring two namespaces: *regular* and *riabook*.

```
package com.theriabook.namespaces {
   public namespace mafia="http://www.theriabook.com/namespaces";
}
```

Listing 4.21 riabook.as

Please note that using a URI in the namespace declaration is optional. The listing below doesn't use any explicit URI, but the compiler will generate one.

```
package com.theriabook.namespaces {
   public namespace regular;
}
```

Listing 4.22 regular.as

To apply the namespaces, we'll define a Tax class with two calcTax()methods that will differ in their namespace access attributes and the amount of tax "calculated":

```
package com.theriabook.tax{
   import com.theriabook.namespaces.*;
   public class Tax
   {
      regular static function calcTax():Number{
         return 3500;
      }
      riabook  static function calcTax():Number{
         return 1750;
      }
   }
}
```

Listing 4.23 The AS3 class Tax

```
package com.theriabook.test
{
    import com.theriabook.namespaces.*;
    import com.theriabook.tax.Tax;
    import mx.controls.Alert;

   use namespace regular;
   // use namespace mafia;
   public class TestTax
   {
     public static function myTax():void {
```

```
            var tax:Number;
            tax=Tax.calcTax();
            Alert.show("Your tax is "+ tax,"Calculation complete");
        }
    }
}
```

Listing 4.24 TestTax.as

Since we apply the namespace for the regular customer, s/he will have to pay a tax of $3,500. The MXML code that uses TestTax is shown below:

```
<?xml version="1.0" encoding="utf-8"?>
<mx:Application xmlns:mx="http://www.adobe.com/2006/mxml"
   layout="absolute" creationComplete="initApp();">
   <mx:Script>
      <![CDATA[
        import com.theriabook.test.TestTax;
         public function initApp():void {
              TestTax.myTax();
         }
      ]]>
   </mx:Script>
</mx:Application>
```

Listing 4.25 TestTax.mxml

The output of this program looks like Figure 4.6. Switch to another namespace by changing the use statement to look like

```
use namespace riabook;
```

and the amount of the tax to be paid will be substantially lower. Besides the directive use that affects the entire block of code, AS3 permits finer-grained notation to refer to a specific namespace with a name qualifier (a double colon). In our example, this may look like:

```
tax = Tax.riabook::calcTax();
```

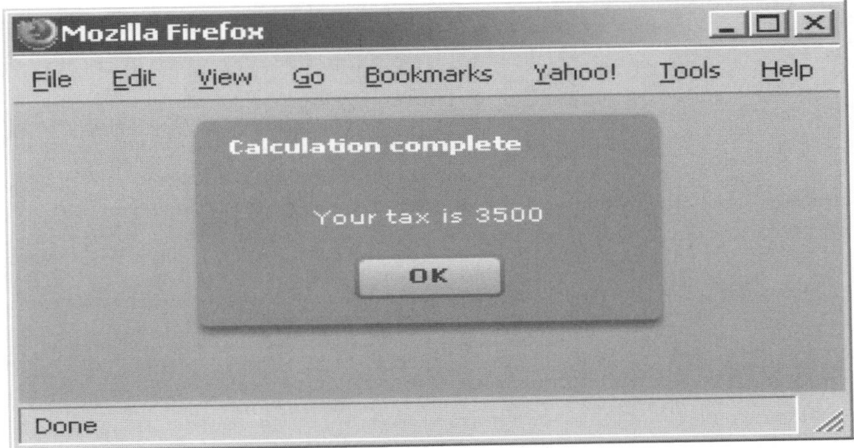

Figure 4.6 The output of the TextTax.mxml for regular customers

Using namespaces provides an additional means of visibility control. The methods, class properties of the constants, can be physically located in different packages, but marked with the same namespace qualifier, and a one-line namespace change can engage a completely different set of methods/properties across the entire application.

Using Flex with JavaServer Pages

In Chapter 5, we'll use Flex Data Services to connect a Flex client with plain old Java objects (POJO) on the server using the object <mx:RemoteObject>. FDS is great software, but you may already have some Web applications written in another technology and just want to put a pretty Flash Player face on your existing Java Web applications that use JavaServer Pages (JSP). So the next couple of pages will show you how to "teach" Flash Player to communicate with a JSP without having to use FDS.

Retrieving Data from JSP

We'll be using JSP here, but you can replace JSP with any technology you're comfortable with: servlets, Active Server Pages, Python, PHP, et al. Whatever can spit out the data to a Web browser should work the same way.

We'll show you a really simple application written in Flex 2 that talks to a JSP that generates XML with the information about employees:

```
<people>
  <person>
      <name>Alex Olson</name>
      <age>22</age><skills>java, HTML, SQL</skills>
```

```
  </person>
 ...
</people>
```

Listing 4.26 A fragment of the XML employees data

Let's just hardcode this XML (we've got three persons) into a JSP that consists of one out.println() statement, where the XML goes between the double quotes:

```
<%out.println("..."); %>
```

The complete JSP looks like this (just put your XML in one line so you won't be bothered with string concatenations):

```
<%
out.println("<?xml version=\"1.0\" encoding=\"UTF-8\"?><people><person><name>Alex Ol-
son</name><age>22</age><skills>java, HTML, SQL</skills></person><person><name>Brandon
Smith</name><age>21</age><skills>PowerScript, JavaScript, ActionScript</skills></person>
<person><name>Jeremy Plant</name><age>20</age><skills>SQL, C++, Java</skills></person></
people>");
%>
```

Listing 4.27 employees.jsp

Deploy this JSP under some servlet container. In the popular Apache Tomcat this means to save it as employees.jsp under the webapp\test directory. As a sanity check we make sure that we've deployed this JSP correctly: entering http://localhost:8080/test/employees.jsp in the Web browser has to return the employee data. Now open Flex Builder and create the application:

```
<?xml version="1.0" encoding="utf-8"?>
<mx:Application xmlns:mx="http://www.adobe.com/2006/mxml"
                        applicationComplete="employees.send()">
    <mx:HTTPService id="employees" useProxy="false"  method="POST"
        url="http://localhost:8080/test/employees.jsp" />

    <mx:DataGrid  dataProvider="{employees.lastResult.people.person}" width="60%">
          <mx:columns>
            <mx:DataGridColumn dataField="name" headerText="Name"/>
            <mx:DataGridColumn dataField="age" headerText="Age"/>
            <mx:DataGridColumn dataField="skills" headerText="Skills"/>

        </mx:columns>
    </mx:DataGrid>
</mx:Application>
```

Listing 4.28 DataGrid_E4X_JSP.mxml

This code uses the <mx:HTTPService> component that lets you connect to a specified URL either directly or through a proxy. The HttpService object is designed to communicate with any URI that understands HTTP requests and responses. In the code above we've just specified the URL for the JSP from Listing 4.24. The data provider of our data grid uses binding (see the curly braces) and E4X syntax to parse the XML and populate this table with the elements located under the <person> XML tag that's coming from our employees.jsp. In the next section we'll explain Flex data binding in more detail.

On the applicationComplete event, the code employees.send() makes an HTTP request to the URL specified in the HTTPService, and our JSP readily returns the XML that's bound to the data grid.

Compile and run this program, and it'll show you the following:

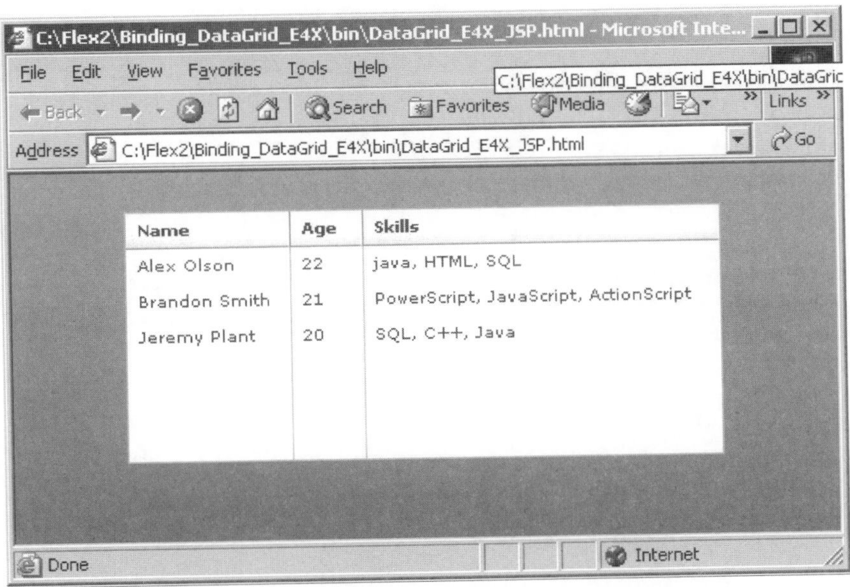

Figure 4.7 The output of DataGrid_E4X_JSP.mxml

Keep in mind that such a direct connection from HTTPService to a JSP is only permitted if your JSP and Flex application are coming from the same domain, or if the Web server you're connecting to has the *crossdomain.xml* file specifying a cross-domain connection policy with the appropriate permission for yours or all domains. You can read more about configuring crossdomain.xml in the product manual under "Building and Deploying Flex 2 Applications."

Sending Data from Flex to JSP

In the next version of our Flex-JSP application we'll show you how to post data from a Flex form to JSP. We'll put a simple form under the data grid above to enter the data about the new employee as in Figure 4.8. Pressing the Add Employee button will submit the entered data to the JSP, which will attach them to existing employees and return back so the data grid can be repopulated to include the newly inserted employee.

To design the form, we'll be using the <mx:Form> Flex objects container, which differs from the HTML tag <form>. The latter is an invisible container that holds some data, while <mx:Form> is used to arrange the input controls on the screen with their labels. We'll also use <mx:Model> to store the data bound to our <mx:Form>. Let's also make the employee's name a required field and add a so-called validator to prevent the user from submitting the form without entering the name. It will look like:

```
<mx:StringValidator id="empNameVld" source="{empName}" property="text" />

  <mx:Model id="employeeModel">
   <root>
     <empName>{empName.text}</empName>
     <age>{age.text}</age>
     <skills>{skills.text}</skills>
   </root>
  </mx:Model>

<mx:Form width="100%" height="100%">
  <mx:FormItem label="Enter name:" required="true">
     <mx:TextInput id="empName" />
  </mx:FormItem>
    <mx:FormItem label="Enter age:">
     <mx:TextInput id="age" />
  </mx:FormItem>
  <mx:FormItem label="Enter skills">
     <mx:TextInput id="skills" />
  </mx:FormItem>
  <mx:Button label="Add Employee" click="submitForm()"/>
</mx:Form>
```

Listing 4.29 The employee entry form and its model

The *required=true* attribute displays a red asterisk by the required field but doesn't do any validation. The <mx:StringValidator> displays the prompt "This field is required" and makes the border of the required field red if you move the cursor out of the name field while it's empty, and shows a prompt when you return to this field again as in Figure 4.8. But we'd like to turn this default validation off by adding the triggerEvent property with a blank value:

```
<mx:StringValidator id="empNameValidator" source="{empName}"
                              property="text"  triggerEvent=""/>
```

We'll also add our own AS3 validateEmpName()function. Now the click event of the Add Employee button will call validateName(), which in turn will either call the submitForm()function if the name was entered or display a message box "Employee name can not be blank".

Validators are outside the scope of this chapter, and so we'll just mention that Flex comes with a number of pre-defined classes that derive from the base class Validator. They ensure that the input data meet certain rules. The names of these classes are self-explanatory: DateValidator, EmailValidator, PhoneNumberValidater, NumberValidator, RegExValidator, CreditCardValidator, ZipCodeValidator, and StringValidator. These validators work on the client side, and round-trips to the server aren't required. A program initiates the validation process either as a response to an event or by a direct call to the method validate() of the appropriate validator instance as in Listing 4.30

The final version of the Flex portion of our application is shown below.

```
<?xml version="1.0" encoding="utf-8"?>
<mx:Application xmlns:mx="http://www.adobe.com/2006/mxml"
                        applicationComplete="employees.send()">
    <mx:HTTPService id="employees" useProxy="false"  method="POST"
     url="http://localhost:8080/test/employees.jsp" result="onResult(event)" />

   <mx:DataGrid dataProvider="{employees.lastResult.people.person}" width="100%">
      <mx:columns>
         <mx:DataGridColumn dataField="name" headerText="Name" />
         <mx:DataGridColumn dataField="age" headerText="Age"/>
         <mx:DataGridColumn dataField="skills" headerText="Skills"/>

      </mx:columns>
   </mx:DataGrid>

   <mx:StringValidator id="empNameValidator" source="{empName}"
                              property="text"  triggerEvent=""/>
   <mx:Model id="employeeModel">
    <root>
      <empName>{empName.text}</empName>
      <age>{age.text}</age>
      <skills>{skills.text}</skills>
    </root>
   </mx:Model>

  <mx:Form width="100%" height="100%">
   <mx:FormItem label="Enter name:" required="true">
```

```
        <mx:TextInput id="empName" />
    </mx:FormItem>
       <mx:FormItem label="Enter age:">
        <mx:TextInput id="age" />
    </mx:FormItem>
    <mx:FormItem label="Enter skills">
        <mx:TextInput id="skills" />
    </mx:FormItem>
    <!--mx:Button label="Add Employee" click="submitForm()"/-->
    <mx:Button label="Add Employee" click="validateEmpName()"/>
</mx:Form>

 <mx:Script>
 <![CDATA[

   import mx.events.ValidationResultEvent;
   import mx.controls.Alert;
   private function validateEmpName():void{
    if (empNameValidator.validate().type == ValidationResultEvent.VALID){
         submitForm();
    } else{
        Alert.show("Employee name can not be blank");
    }
   }

 private function submitForm():void {
  employees.cancel();
  employees.send(employeeModel);
 }

private function onResult(event:Event):void{
    trace('Got the result'); // works only in the debug mode
    return;
  }
 ]]>
 </mx:Script>
</mx:Application>
```

Listing 4.30 DataGrid_EX4-JSP2.mxml

When the user hits the Add Employee button on the form, our HTTPService will submit the employeeModel to a modified employees.jsp, which will now get the parameters from the HTTPRequest object, prepare the new XML element newNode from the received data, concatenate it to the original three employees, and return it back to the client, which will display all the employees in the datagrid:

```
<%
String employees="<?xml version=\"1.0\" encoding=\"UTF-8\"?><people><person><name>Alex
Olson</name><age>22</age><skills>java, HTML, SQL</skills></person><person><name>Brandon
Smith</name><age>21</age><skills>PowerScript, JavaScript, ActionScript</skills></person>
<person><name>Jeremy Plant</name><age>20</age><skills>SQL, C++, Java</skills></person>";

   // Get the parameters entered in the GUI form
   String name=request.getParameter("empName");
   String age=request.getParameter("age");
   String skills=request.getParameter("skills");
   String newEmployee="<person><name>" + name+ "</name><age>" + age + "</age><skills>"
                                   + skills +"</skills></person>";

   if (name == null){
      newEmployee="";
   }
   // the xml goes back to the Web browser via HTTPResponse
   out.println(employees + newEmployee + "</people>");
%>
```

Listing 4.31 The new version of employee.jsp

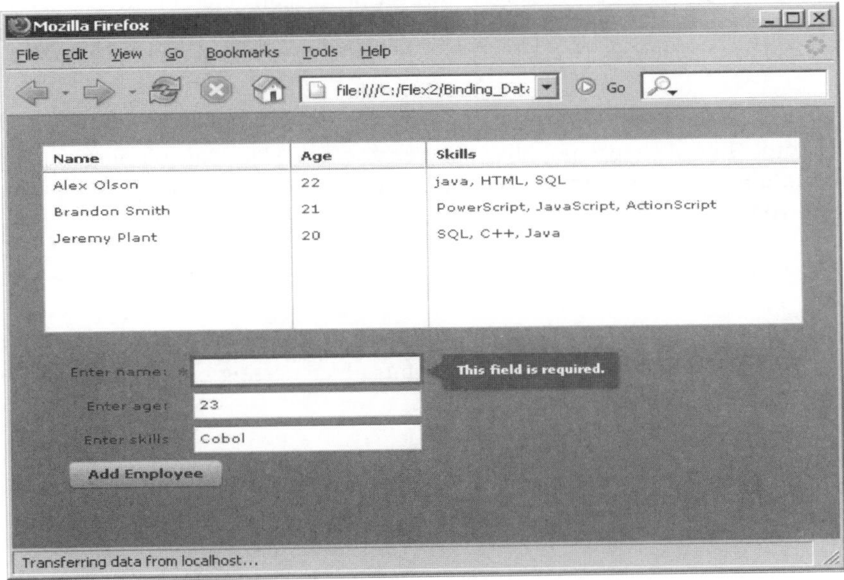

Figure 4.8 The employee form and default validator's message

You'll see more examples of the use of HTTPService object in Chapter 5, where we'll retrieve financial news from Yahoo!, and in Chapter 13, where we'll download photos from the popular Flickr.

com. In Chapter 5 we'll also use HTTPService through a proxy configured with FDS.

Note: There are other ways to pass the data from Flex to a server-side Web application. For example, you can create an instance of the URLVariables object, create the data to be passed as its properties, attach URLVariables to URLRequest.data, and call navigateToURL().

E4X, Data Binding, and Regular Expressions

Parsing XML has never been fun. Java programmers use way too many different parsers and APIs. Java 6 includes Java Architecture for XML Binding (JAXB 2.0) and the implementation of the XML Data Binding Specification (JSR 31) that maps JavaBeans and XML data. To be more accurate, JAXB 2.0 offers two-directional mapping between JavaBeans and XML Schema (see the javax.xml.bind package). Java 6 comes with a new tool called xjc that takes an XML Schema as an input and generates the required JavaBeans as an output.

ActionScript 3.0 supports E4X, which is an ECMA standard for working with XML (see http://www.ecma-international.org/publications/files/ECMA-ST/ECMA-357.pdf). It's very powerful and yet simple to use. You can forget about these SAX and DOM parsers. E4X is a step towards making XML a programming language.

For example, an MXML program can read the XML file people.xml (or any other XML source) shown in Listing 4.23 into a variable with only one line (without worrying about error processing):

```
<mx:XML id="myXmlFile" source="people.xml"/>
```

You'll need another line of code to populate the data grid using Flex data binding (remember, tying the data from a source to a destination). In our case myXmlFile is the source that populates the data grid aka destination:

```
<mx:DataGrid  dataProvider="{myXmlFile.person}">
```

This line means that each element <person> will populate one row in the data grid. Let's make the XML from Listing 4.23 a bit more complex: we'll introduce nesting in the name element. Now it consists of separate <first> and <last> elements.

```
<?xml version="1.0" encoding="UTF-8"?>
<people>
 <person>
 <name>
   <first>Yakov</first>
   <last>Fain</last>
 </name>
 <age>22</age>
 <skills>java, HTML, SQL</skills>
```

```
</person>
 <person>
 <name>
   <first>Victor</first>
   <last>Rasputnis</last>
 </name>
 <age>21</age>
 <skills>PowerScript, JavaScript, ActionScript</skills>
</person>
 <person>
 <name>
   <first>Anatole</first>
   <last>Tartakovsky</last>
 </name>
 <age>20</age>
 <skills>SQL, C++, Java</skills>
</person>
</people>
```

Listing 4.32 The XML file FarataSystems_skills.xml

Our goal is to produce a window that looks like this:

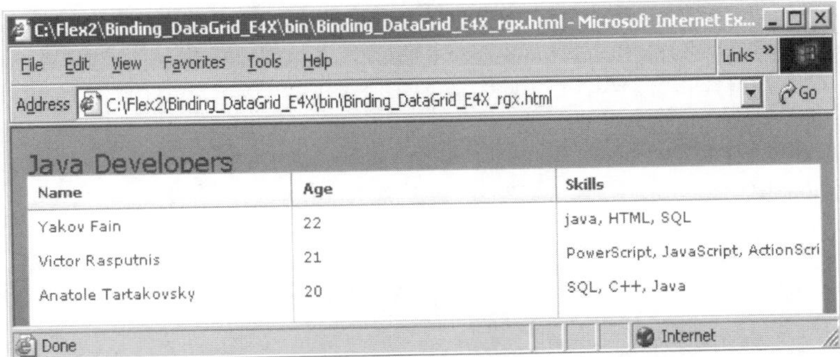

Figure 4.9 A data grid populated from people.xml

Please note that we also want to concatenate the values from the <first> and <last> XML elements for the data grid's Name column. A small program in Listing 4.30 does exactly this. The fullName method concatenates the first and last names, and since we specified the labelFunction property in the name column, the data rendering will be controlled by the fullName() function. We'll return to labelFunction in Chapter 11.

```
<?xml version="1.0" encoding="utf-8"?>
<mx:Application xmlns:mx="http://www.adobe.com/2006/mxml">
```

```
    <mx:XML id="myXmlFile" source="FarataSystems_Skills.xml"/>
    <mx:Label text="Java Developers"  fontSize="18"/>
    <mx:DataGrid  dataProvider="{myXmlFile.person}" width="500">
       <mx:columns>
          <mx:DataGridColumn dataField="name" headerText="Name" labelFunction="fullName"/>
          <mx:DataGridColumn dataField="age" headerText="Age"/>
          <mx:DataGridColumn dataField="skills" headerText="Skills"/>
    </mx:columns>
    </mx:DataGrid>
    <mx:Script>
     <![CDATA[
       private function fullName(item:Object, column:DataGridColumn):String {
        return item.name.first + " " + item.name.last;
       }
     ]]>
    </mx:Script>
</mx:Application>
```

Listing 4.33 Populating a data grid from an XML file

The next step is to add regular expressions to filter the data while populating the data grid. There's a nice example of predicate filtering with E4X and RegExp in Darron Schall's blog at http://www.darronschall.com/weblog/archives/000214.cfm.

Let's imagine that a recruiter wants to do a quick search in our XML file to identify people with Java skills. A small one-line change will do this trick, or at least will be a step in the right direction.

The RegExp class lets you create an instance of the object per the specified pattern, and then find the substring(s) with this pattern and perform the manipulations with the found substrings, if any.

In AS3, you can create an instance of the RegExp by using a familiar syntax with a constructor. For example:

```
var javaPattern:RegExp = new RegExp("Java", "i");
```

This is a pattern for finding occurrences of "Java," ignoring the letter case.

Here's another way of creating this instance:

```
var javaPattern:RegExp = /Java/i;
```

We'll use the latter syntax by feeding the E4X output to this RegExp instance and the result will be used as a data provider for the data grid. Let's modify the MXML code for the <mx:DataGrid> tag to apply this regular expression to the XML element called skills:

```
<mx:DataGrid  dataProvider="{myXmlFile.person.(/Java/.test( skills ))}" >
```

In the line above, /Java/ creates an instance of the RegEx object and the test(skills) method will ensure that only those XML elements that contain Java are included in the myXmlFile. Now the resulting window will look as follows:

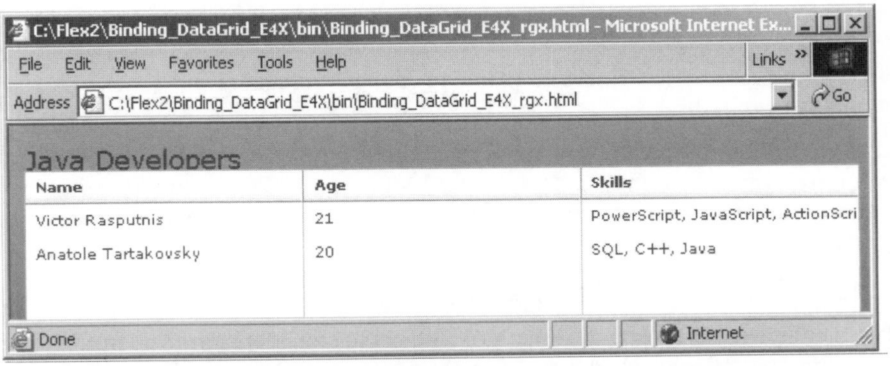

Figure 4.10 Displaying FarataSystems_skills.xml with Java skills

We still don't like a couple of things here. First, this output didn't include Yakov Fain because the word Java was written in lower case in his skills element. Adding the ignore case option "i" to our RegExp instance will help:

```
<mx:DataGrid  dataProvider="{myXmlFile.person.(/Java/i.test(skills))}" >
```

The output will again look like Figure 4.9.

The next step is to filter out people who were included in this list just because of JavaScript, which has very little to do with Java. One of the ways to do this is by requesting that there should be a space or a comma in the regular expression after the word Java:

```
<mx:DataGrid
        dataProvider="{myXmlFile.person.(/Java? ?,/i.test(skills))}" >
```

Now we've lost both Victor and Anatole. Even though Anatole knows Java, there's no space or comma after the word Java in his list of skills. Adding an OR (|) condition that means we're also interested in people with the word Java as the last word in the string will help.

```
<mx:DataGrid
     dataProvider="{myXmlFile.person.(/Java? ?, | Java$/i.test(skills))}"
```

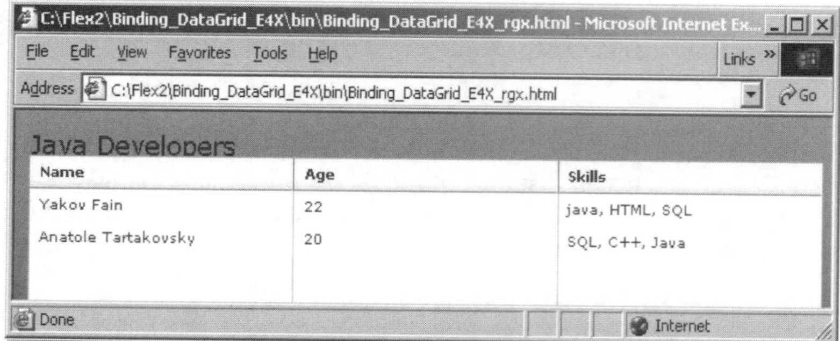

Figure 4.11 Finding Java programmers

Today, E4X doesn't support XML Schema, and all the XML elements are returned as text, but it'll change in future versions of the ECMAScript for XML. Meanwhile, the implementation of E4X by any programming language makes it more appealing to developers who have to deal with XML.

Collections, Filters, and Master-Detail

In the last section, we were using the <mx:XML> object to store data retrieved from the people.xml file (see Listing 4.33). We also used this object as a data provider for the data grid control. But that example used static data, where the content of the XML file didn't change during runtime. In real-world scenarios, data change frequently, and we have to display the latest values on the user (think of an auction or stock exchange displaying the latest prices).

Flex comes with a mx.collections package that contains collection classes that have convenient methods to sort and filter the objects from the underlying collection like XML or array, and they also fire events when the data in the collection change. This makes collection classes very convenient data providers for Flex visual controls – as soon as the data change, visual controls that are bound to this collection immediately reflect the change without any special programming required.

In this section we'll build a small gas station application that will monitor daily operations like gasoline sales. While building this application, you'll get familiar with the XMLListCollection class and learn how to filter the data in these collections.

The window output in this application will look like Figure 4.12. We'll read the initial "gas station activities" data from the following XML:

```
<messages>
 <message msgType="sale">
   <transID>1234</transID>
   <octane>87</octane>
   <price>2.50</price>
   <gallons>10.2</gallons>
   <paidby>MC</paidby>
```

```
  </message>
  <message msgType="sale">
    <transID>1035</transID>
    <octane>89</octane>
    <price>2.69</price>
    <gallons>14.5</gallons>
    <paidby>Cash</paidby>
  </message>
  <message msgType="spill">
    <transID>2301</transID>
    <octane>93</octane>
    <price>2.99</price>
    <paidby></paidby>
    <gallons>17.3</gallons>
  </message>
</messages>
```

Listing 4.34 GSActivities.xml

The final version of our application will include a timer with a random data generator that will add new messages to the window from Figure 4.12, emulating the data feed of messages like sale, purchase, and spill.

The first version of GasStation.mxml reads and parses the data from GSActivities.xml using this one-liner:

```
<mx:XML id="activities" source="GSactivity.xml" />
```

Behind the scenes, Flex creates an object with the reference variable activities used as a data provider for the data grid as follows:

```
<mx:DataGrid  id="messageBook" dataProvider="{activities.message}" width="100%"
height="100%">
```

The dataProvider activities.message represents the XML <message> element from GSActivity.xml, which is displayed as a row in the data grid.

The AS3 paid() function is called for each datagrif row and calculates the amount by multiplying the number of gallons and the price per gallon. The <mx:CurrencyFormatter> ensures that the calculated "paid" column is displayed as a dollar amount.

The rest of the code below just displays other controls that we'll use for filtering and illustrating master-detail relations later in this section.

```
<?xml version="1.0" encoding="utf-8"?>
```

```
<mx:Application xmlns:mx="http://www.adobe.com/2006/mxml" backgroundColor="#e0e0FF">

<mx:XML id="activities" source="GSactivity.xml" />
   <mx:Canvas x="10" y="10" width="100%" height="100%">
      <mx:HBox x="10" y="20" width="100%" height="30">
         <mx:CheckBox id="cbx93" label="93"/>
         <mx:CheckBox id="cbx89" label="89"/>
         <mx:CheckBox id="cbx87" label="87"/>
         <mx:Label text="Msg.Type" />
         <mx:ComboBox id="cbMsgTypes" width="117"
                                    dataProvider="{messageType}"></mx:ComboBox>
      </mx:HBox>
      <mx:VBox x="10" y="64" height="100%" width="100%">
         <mx:Label text="Activity" width="100%" fontSize="15"/>
         <mx:DataGrid  id="messageBook" dataProvider="{activities.message}" width="100%"
                                                                    height="100%">
            <mx:columns>
               <mx:DataGridColumn headerText="Message Type" dataField="@msgType"/>
            <mx:DataGridColumn headerText="Transaction ID" dataField="transID"/>
         <mx:DataGridColumn headerText="Octane" dataField="octane"/>
               <mx:DataGridColumn headerText="Price per gal." dataField="price"/>
               <mx:DataGridColumn headerText="Amount(gal.)" dataField="gallons"/>
            <mx:DataGridColumn headerText="Paid" labelFunction="paid"/>
            </mx:columns>
         </mx:DataGrid>
         <mx:Label text="Required actions" fontSize="15" />
         <mx:TextArea id="txtAction" width="100%"/>
      </mx:VBox>
   </mx:Canvas>

   <!--Defining USD formatting -->
   <mx:CurrencyFormatter id="usdFormatter" precision="2"
       currencySymbol="$" useThousandsSeparator="false" alignSymbol="left" />

    <mx:Script>
   <![CDATA[
      //Data for the Message type  combo
      [Bindable]
      private var messageType: Array = ["all","sale", "spill", "purchase"];

    private function paid(item:Object, column:DataGridColumn):String {
      // calculate total gain/loss
         var total:Number=Number(item.gallons)* Number(item.price);
         if (item.@msgType!="sale"){
```

```
            total*=-1;
          }
          return ""+usdFormatter.format(total); //USD formatting
      }
    ]]>
  </mx:Script>
</mx:Application>
```

Listing 4.35 GasStation1.mxml

Please note that the combobox cbMsgTypes is populated from a messageType array that is marked [Bindable] and will be used below for filtering the messages in the data grid. Also, since we didn't define the Paid By data grid column in this version of the gas station application, the corresponding data from the data provider aren't shown.

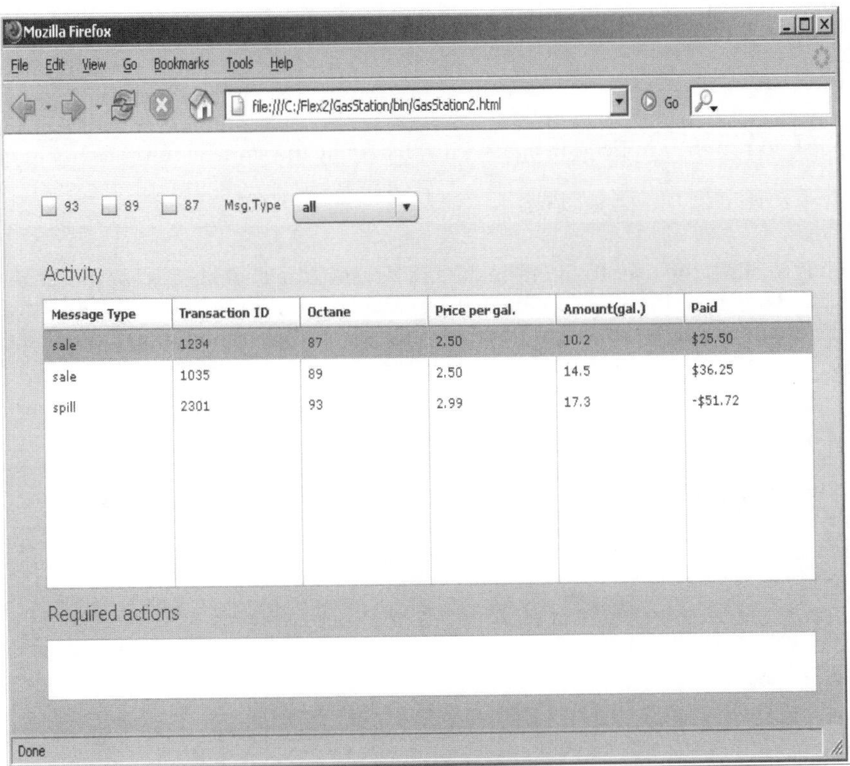

Figure 4.12 Running GasStation1

Adding XMLListCollection

Flex collection classes implement the Ilist and ICollectionView interfaces that let you add, remove, and update items in a collection. These interfaces also have methods for dispatching events when the data in the underlying collection change. This becomes handy when you use a collection as a data provider of one of the list-based controls – just add a new element to such collection and the data in these controls automatically reflect the change.

Using collections (see the mx.collections package) as data providers is well described at http://www.adobe.com/devnet/flex/quickstart/using_data_providers/. We'll just show you one of the ways to deal with collections in our gas station application.

Basically we'll add a middleman between the XML object and the data grid. Now the data grid's provider will become an XMLListCollection (built on top of XML activities):

```
<mx:XML id="activities" source="GSactivity.xml" />
<mx:XMLListCollection id="msgList" source="{activities.message}" />

<mx:DataGrid  id="messageBook" dataProvider="{msgList}">
```

Just recompile and run the application again – it will display the same window as in Figure 4.11.

Filtering

The next step is to allow the user to filter the data by octane (the checkboxes) or message type (the combo box). We'll add an init() function that will be called on the applicationComplete event, when all the objects are constructed to assign the filterMessages() filter function to the collection to do the filtering:

```
msgList.filterFunction=filterMessages;
```

The actual filtering will happen when we call the refresh()function on the collection.

```
<mx:Application xmlns:mx="http://www.adobe.com/2006/mxml"
   backgroundColor="#e0e0FF" applicationComplete="init()">
      // some code is omitted here
    private function init():void {
         // assign the filter function
            msgList.filterFunction=filterMessages;
            // perform filtering
            msgList.refresh();
    }

       private function filterMessages(item:Object):Boolean{
           // Check every checkbox and the combobox and
```

```
        // populate the datagrid with rows that match
        // selected criteria
      if (item.octane=="87"  && this.cbx87.selected)
         return true;
      if (item.octane=="89"  && this.cbx89.selected)
         return true;
      if (item.octane=="93"  && this.cbx93.selected)
         return true;

        return false;
    }
```

If you need to remove the filter, just set the filterFunction property to null.

Run the application after making these changes and you'll see an empty table on the screen. When the creation of the application was complete, Flash VM called the init method, which assigned the filter function to our XMLListCollection, and called refresh(), which applied this filter to each XML node of our collection. Since none of the checkboxes was selected, the filterMessages function correctly returned false to each node leaving the data grid empty. To fix this, let's make a slight change in the checkboxes so they'll be checked off during creation.

```
<mx:CheckBox id="cbx93" label="93" selected="true"/>
<mx:CheckBox id="cbx89" label="89" selected="true"/>
<mx:CheckBox id="cbx87" label="87" selected="true"/>
```

Now the program will show all the rows again. Try to uncheck the boxes – nothing happens because the application doesn't know that it needs to reapply the filter function to the msgList again. This is an easy fix – let's refresh the msgList on each click on the checkbox:

```
<mx:CheckBox id="cbx93" label="93" selected="true" click="msgList.refresh()"/>
<mx:CheckBox id="cbx89" label="89" selected="true" click="msgList.refresh()"/>
<mx:CheckBox id="cbx87" label="87" selected="true" click="msgList.refresh()"/>
```

The filtering by octane number works fine. Adding the code snippet below to the beginning of the filterMessages() function will engage the filtering by message type according to the combo box selection:

```
if (cbMsgTypes.selectedLabel !="all" &&
                              item.@msgType!=cbMsgTypes.selectedLabel ){
   return false;
}
```

Master-Detail Relationships

We took care of the basic functionality of the data grid control. Since the turnover rate at gas stations is pretty high, let's add some help to new employees by populating the Required Actions text area based on the selected message type. This is a typical master-detail relationships task, where the data grid with messages is "the master" and the text box shows the details.

We'll start by creating an actions.xml file where we store the recommended actions for each message type.

```
<MessageTypes>
  <message type="sale">
    <description>Sale of gasoline products</description>
    <actions>Sale is good news. No action required
    </actions>
  </message>
  <message type="purchase">
    <description>Purchase of gasoline products from suppliers</description>
    <actions>If the gas station owner is not on premises, please call him at 212-
             123-4567. Otherwise no actions is required
    </actions>
  </message>
  <message type="spill">
    <description>Spill of gasoline products on the ground</description>
    <actions> Get a bucket of sand and cover the mess. Expect to receive smaller
             pay check this week.
    </actions>
  </message>
</MessageTypes>
```

Listing 4.36 MessageTypes.xml

To read and parse this file into an XML object, we just have to write one line (thanks to E4X):

```
<mx:XML id="msgTypes" source="MessageTypes.xml" />
```

The next step is to specify that a selection of a different row in the data grid should call the function that finds and displays the appropriate message from MessageTypes.xml. And again, E4X makes this job a breeze:

```
private function getAction():void {
  txtAction.text=
    msgTypes.message.(@type==messageBook.selectedItem.@msgType).actions;
}
```

The expression

```
msgTypes.message.(@type==messageBook.selectedItem.@msgType )
```

means select the XML <message> element that has an attribute type that is the same as in the selected row in the @msgType column in the data grid. When this XML element is identified, we assign its <actions> value to the txtAction text area.

As we said earlier, changing the selected row in the data grid should initiate the getAction() function call. Let's modify the declaration of the data grid and add the change event processing:

```
<mx:DataGrid  id="messageBook" dataProvider="{msgList}" width="100%"
                    height="100%" change="getAction()">
```

Compile and run this program, select a row in the data grid, and the action text box will be populated:

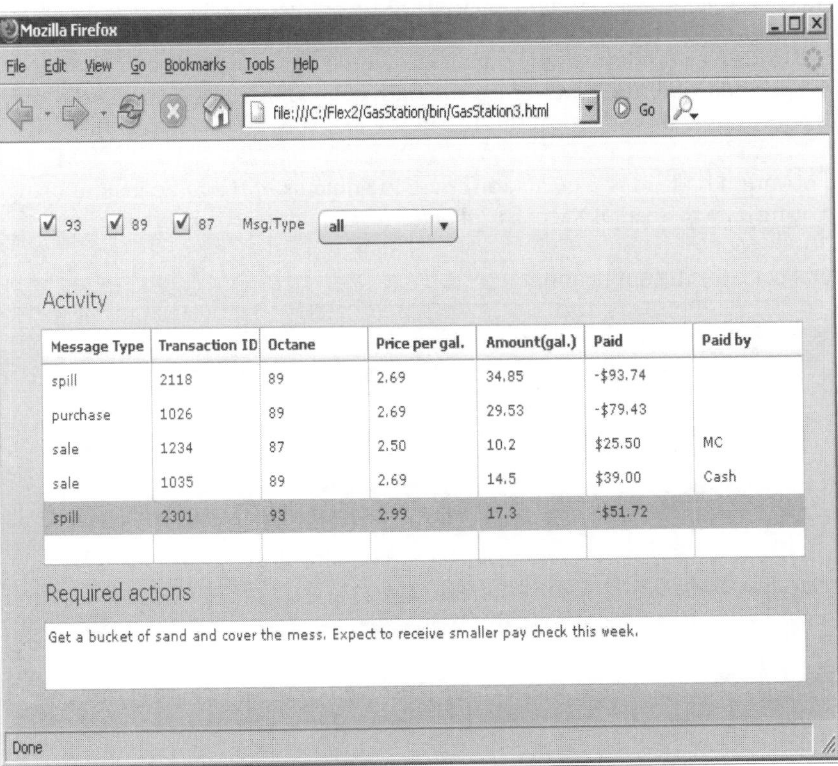

Figure 4.13 Populating the required actions field

We're almost there. Why almost? Because if the user starts filtering the data by octane or a message type, the action text field won't be cleaned. To fix this, let's create a refreshData() function that will not only refresh the XMLListCollection, but also clean the text field:

```
private function refreshData():void{
        msgList.refresh();
        txtAction.text="";
}
```

Don't forget to replace all calls to msgList.refresh() with refreshData().

Adding a Data Feed

In the real world, all the messages should be pushed to our application by some kind of messaging program. Another possibility is to have the gas station front end poll the data at some specified interval by some kind of a server-side program that can be written in JSP, ASP, PHP, or whatever else can bake an HTTPResponse. In coming chapters of this book, you'll learn about various ways to communicate with remote programs. But at this point, for simplicity's sake, we'll emulate a real-time data feed by using a random-number generator and a timer that will add items to our msgList collection at specified time intervals. Since the data collection will be constantly receiving new data, the output window should reflect this by adding new rows to the data grid.

If the speed of your data feed is crucial, don't pass the data as XML, and consider using ArrayCollection for storing data instead of XMLListCollection.

Here's the final code for the application:

```
<?xml version="1.0" encoding="utf-8"?>
<mx:Application xmlns:mx="http://www.adobe.com/2006/mxml"
   backgroundColor="#e0e0FF" applicationComplete="init()">

<mx:XML id="msgTypes" source="MessageTypes.xml" />
<mx:XML id="activities" source="GSactivity.xml" />
<mx:XMLListCollection id="msgList" source="{activities.message}" />
   <mx:Canvas x="10" y="10" width="100%" height="100%">
      <mx:HBox x="10" y="20" width="100%" height="30">
         <mx:CheckBox id="cbx93" label="93" selected="true" click="refreshData()"/>
         <mx:CheckBox id="cbx89" label="89" selected="true" click="refreshData()"/>
         <mx:CheckBox id="cbx87" label="87" selected="true" click="refreshData()"/>
         <mx:Label text="Msg.Type" />
         <mx:ComboBox id="cbMsgTypes" width="117" dataProvider="{messageType}">
               <mx:change>refreshData()</mx:change>
         </mx:ComboBox>
      </mx:HBox>
```

```
  <mx:VBox x="10" y="64" height="100%" width="100%">
    <mx:Label text="Activity" width="100%" fontSize="15"/>
    <mx:DataGrid  id="messageBook" dataProvider="{msgList}" width="100%"
                              height="100%" change="getAction()">
      <mx:columns>
        <mx:DataGridColumn headerText="Message Type" dataField="@msgType"/>

        <mx:DataGridColumn headerText="Transaction ID" dataField="transID"/>

        <mx:DataGridColumn headerText="Octane" dataField="octane"/>
        <mx:DataGridColumn headerText="Price per gal." dataField="price"/>
        <mx:DataGridColumn headerText="Amount(gal.)" dataField="gallons"/>

        <mx:DataGridColumn headerText="Paid" labelFunction="paid"/>
        <mx:DataGridColumn headerText="Paid by" dataField="paidby"/>

      </mx:columns>
    </mx:DataGrid>
    <mx:Label text="Required actions" fontSize="15" />
    <mx:TextArea id="txtAction" width="100%"/>
  </mx:VBox>
</mx:Canvas>

 <!--Defining USD formatting -->
 <mx:CurrencyFormatter id="usdFormatter" precision="2"
    currencySymbol="$" useThousandsSeparator="false" alignSymbol="left" />

 <!-- Gallons Amount formating with 2 digits after dec.point -->
 <mx:NumberFormatter id="numberFormatter" precision="2"/>

<mx:Script>
 <![CDATA[

     //Message type  combo data
     [Bindable]
     private var messageType: Array = ["all","sale", "spill", "purchase"];

     import mx.collections.*;
     private var sortMessages:Sort;

     [Bindable]
     private var grandTotalSale:Number=0;

   private function init():void {
```

```
// assign the filter function
    msgList.filterFunction=filterMessages;
    // perform filtering
    refreshData();

    // emulating message feed in specified intervals
    var myTimer:Timer = new Timer(5000, 0); // every 5 sec
    myTimer.addEventListener("timer", addMessage);
    myTimer.start();
}

  private function filterMessages(item:Object):Boolean{

      // filter by message types
        if (cbMsgTypes.selectedLabel !="all" &&
                    item.@msgType!=cbMsgTypes.selectedLabel ){
          return false;
      }

      // Check every checkbox and the combobox and
      // populate the datagrid with rows that match
      // selected criteria
    if (item.octane=="87"  && this.cbx87.selected)
       return true;
    if (item.octane=="89"  && this.cbx89.selected)
       return true;
    if (item.octane=="93"  && this.cbx93.selected)
       return true;

       return false;
  }

private function paid(item:Object, column:DataGridColumn):String {
   // calculate total gain/loss. Label function is not
   // the best place for calculations as it's being called
   // on each change of the underlying collection
     var total:Number=Number(item.gallons)* Number(item.price);
     if (item.@msgType!="sale"){
      total*=-1;
     }

     return ""+usdFormatter.format(total); //USD formatting
}
private function getAction():void {
```

```
            txtAction.text=msgTypes.message.(@type==messageBook.selectedItem.@msgType).
actions;
      }

      private function refreshData():void{
            msgList.refresh();
            txtAction.text="";
      }

         private function addMessage(event:TimerEvent):void{
         // create and add one message with randomly-generated
         // values to the collection
            var newNode:XML = new XML();
            var transID:String=Math.round(Math.random()*5000).toString();
            var octanes: Array = ["87", "89", "93" ];
            var octaneIndex:Number=Math.round(Math.random()*2);
            var octane:String=octanes[octaneIndex];
            var prices: Array = [2.49, 2.69, 2.99 ];
            var price:Number=prices[octaneIndex];

            var msgTypes: Array = ["sale", "purchase", "spill"];
            var msgType:String=msgTypes[Math.round(Math.random()*2)];

            var payTypes: Array = ["MC", "Visa", "Cash" ];
            var payType:String=msgType=="sale"?payTypes[Math.round(Math.random()*2)]:"";

            var gals:String=(numberFormatter.format(Math.random()*50).toString());

           newNode=<message msgType={msgType}>
                  <transID>{transID}</transID>
                  <octane>{octane}</octane>
                  <price>{price}</price>
                  <gallons>{gals}</gallons>
                  <paidby>{payType}</paidby>
                </message>;

          // adding new messages always on top
          activities.insertChildBefore( activities.message[0], newNode);
         }
     ]]>
    </mx:Script>
  </mx:Application>
```

Listing 4.37 GasStation3.mxml

We've chosen an XML data feed in this application just to introduce the reader to the ease of XML parsing with E4X. In this case, the better performing solution would be to move the data from XML to an AS3 data transfer object and use ArrayCollection instead of XMLListCollection. This AS3 object should define getters that provide data to all the data grid columns, including the calculated amount for the Paid column. Keeping calculations in the labelFunction paid() is not a good idea because the label function is called for each visible row when the new XML element is inserted into the underlying XML collection. Flash Player repaints each visible data grid row when each new gas transaction is inserted, which means that the paid amounts for each visible row will be recalculated.

While using XML and E4X may look very attractive, you shouldn't forget that when you're creating your own AS3 classes, there's less data to push over the wire.

All of the code for our gas station application fits in three pages of this book. You can create simple prototype applications in Flex with a relatively small number of lines of code, but let's not fool ourselves: making efficient real-world applications still requires of programming in good old Java.

Events

In object-oriented languages, if object A needs to notify object B about some important event, it's done using a so-called Observer design pattern; Java implements this pattern in the Observer interface and Observable class. An observable object may have something interesting going on, and other objects that want to know about this implement the Observer interface and register themselves with the observable class.

AS3 implements this design pattern using an event model. Objects can trigger events to each other. System events are triggered by the AVM, while others are triggered as a result of user interactions with your application, such as a click on a button or a mouse move. Below are some situations when events can be dispatched (triggered):

- When Flash Player finishes creating a component, it dispatches a creationComplete event. The DisplayObject class is a subclass of the EventDispatcher class, which means that each of the display objects can register an event listener and process events as they occur.
- User-defined classes can dispatch events according to the business logic of the application.
- The EnterFrame event is triggered by the AVM at the application's frame rate. In movie-type applications it's being dispatched when the playhead is entering a new frame. Even though Flex applications don't have multiple frames, this event is continuously dispatched. This makes it a good candidate to check if some important action has occurred, i.e., a Boolean flag indicating the status of some business transaction is set to true.
- The objects of your application can send custom events to each other.

In an MXML application you'd just specify the name of the event and its handler function (or inline code) in the attribute of the component without worrying too much about the underlying

AS3 code. But all Flex events are subclasses of flash.events.Event, and in AS3 programs you should register an event listener to "listen" to this event and write a function to handle this event when it arrives. For example, the next code snippet specifies that Flash Player has to call a method onEnteringFrame (written by you) on each EnterFrame event:

```
addEventListener(Event.ENTERFRAME, onEnteringFrame);
```

In Java, event listeners are objects, but in AS3 only functions or methods can listen to the events.

If you need to trigger an event from the ActionScript class, it has to be either a subclass of EventDispatcher or implement the IEventDispatcher interface. The latter is the more preferred way because AS3 doesn't support multiple inheritance, and your class may need to extend another class. The other reason to use a lighter interface is that you may not need all the functionality that was defined in the EventDispatcher class and implement the required interface method as you see fit. For example:

```
class  MyClass extends HisClass implements IEventDispatcher{

}
```

Event Flow

When the event listener calls an event handler function, it receives an event object as a parameter, which contains various attributes of the event, and the most important one is the event's target. This terminology might be a little confusing to Java developers since they refer to the component that generates an event as an event source. But here we say that all events are generated by the Flash Player. They are initiated at the stage level and flow to the target component (capturing the stage), i.e., Button, Shape, etc.. After reaching the target, the event "bubbles" its way through to the parents. So, when you click on a button, we can say that a button is the event target. If a button is located on a panel, this event will flow from the stage to the panel and then to the button – and then all the way back.

Flash Player 9 implements an event model based on the World Wide Web Consortium's (W3C) specification entitled Document Object Model Events available at http://www.w3.org/TR/DOM-Level-3-Events/events.html. According to this document, the lifecycle of an event that deals with display objects consists of three phases: capture, target, and bubbling.

- **Capture**: During this phase, Flash Player makes a first pass to check every object from the root of the display list to the target component to see if any parent component might be interested in processing this event. By default, events are ignored by the parents of the target component at the capture phase.

- **Target**: At this phase, event object properties are set for the target and all registered event listeners for this target will get this event.

- **Bubbling**: Finally, the event flows back from the target component all the way up to the root to notify all interested parties identified during the capture phase. Not all events have a bubbling phase and you should consult the AS3 language reference for the events you're interested in.

The three event phases described above don't apply to the user-defined events because Flash Player 9 doesn't know about parent-child relations between user-defined event objects. But AS3 developers can create custom event dispatchers, if they want to arrange event processing in three phases.

Event Propagation or Bubbling

Consider the following sample MXML code with a button in a panel.

```
<?xml version="1.0" encoding="utf-8"?>
<mx:Application xmlns:mx="http://www.adobe.com/2006/mxml" >
   <mx:Panel x="17.5" y="20" width="209" height="142"  layout="absolute"
        click="trace('click event in the Panel')" title="Just a Panel">
   <mx:Button label="ClickMe" x="60.5" y="38"
        click="trace('click event in the Button')"/>
   </mx:Panel>

</mx:Application>
```

Listing 4.38 Events.mxml

Run this simple program in the debug mode to enable trace and it'll show you the following output:

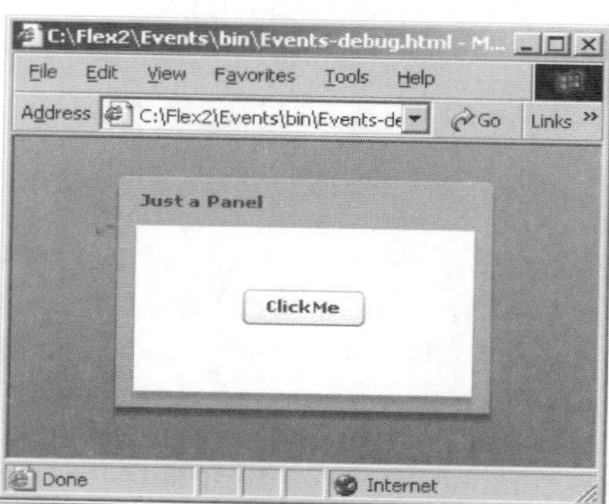

Figure 4.14 Output of the Events.mxml

Clicking on the button in the Flex Builder's console will show the following:

```
click event in the Button
click event in the Panel
```

This illustrates events propagation or bubbling: the click event bubbles up from the target (button) to its parent (panel).

Now let's create another version of this application, where the button and the panel as well as the event processing are coded in AS3. This way you'll see and appreciate all the legwork that MXML did for us:

```
<?xml version="1.0" encoding="utf-8"?>
<mx:Application xmlns:mx="http://www.adobe.com/2006/mxml"
    creationComplete="onCreationComplete();" >

    <mx:Script>
        <![CDATA[
            import mx.controls.Button;
            import mx.containers.Panel;

            private var myButton:Button;
            private var myPanel:Panel;

            // An event handler for  creationComplete event
            private function onCreationComplete():void {

                myPanel=new Panel();
                myPanel.width=200;
                myPanel.height=150;
                myPanel.title="Just a Panel";
                addChild(myPanel);

                myButton = new Button();
                myButton.label = "Click me";
                addChild (myButton);
            }
        ]]>
    </mx:Script>
</mx:Application>
```

Listing 4.39 Creating a button and a panel in ActionScript

If you run this code, the output will look like this:

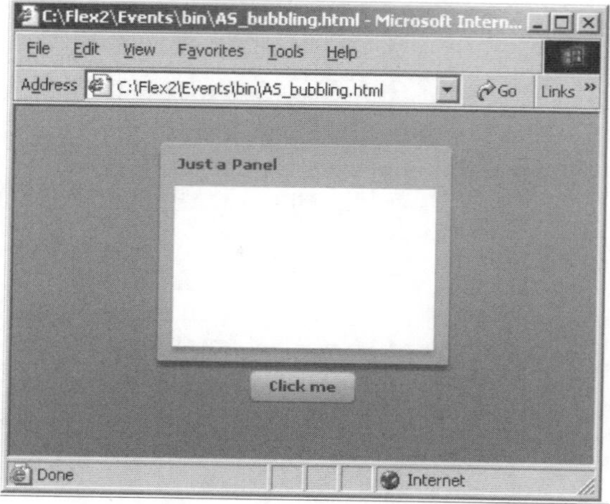

Figure 4.15 A button and a panel without nesting

This is not exactly the result we were looking for and the reason is simple: both the panel and the button were added to the application's display list independently. Let's fix this by adding the button to the panel by replacing addChild(myButton) with myPanel.addChild(myButton).

Now the hierarchy of the nodes in the display list will be different, and the node representing the button will be created under the parent node of the panel as shown in Figure 4.16.

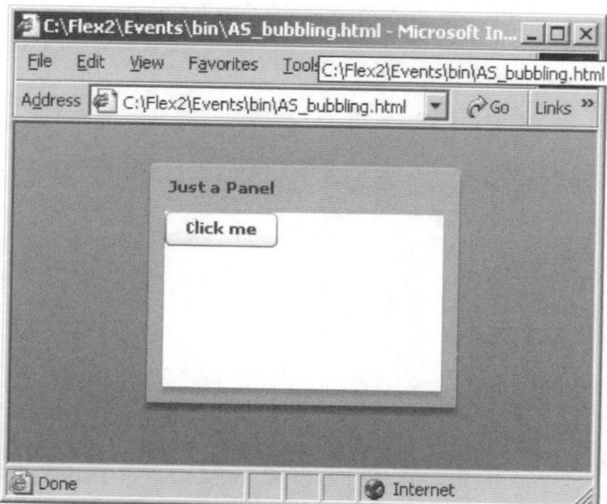

Figure 4.16 A button and a panel with nesting

This is much better, but still not exactly the same as Figure 4.14. Let's try to set the coordinate of the button to values from Listing 4.38:

```
myButton.x=60.5;
myButton.y=38;
```

It did not help because, by default, the panel container uses the vertical layout (see Chapter 3) and ignores the absolute coordinates. Let's add one line to change it into an absolute layout:

```
myPanel.layout="absolute";
```

Now if you run the application it'll look the same as in Figure 4.13.

We've written a lot of ActionScript code, and we haven't even processed the click events yet! We still need to add event listeners and event handlers to the button and the panel:

```
<?xml version="1.0" encoding="utf-8"?>
<mx:Application  xmlns:mx="http://www.adobe.com/2006/mxml"
    creationComplete="onCreationComplete();" >

    <mx:Script>
        <![CDATA[
            import mx.controls.Button;
            import mx.containers.Panel;
            import flash.events.MouseEvent;

            private var myButton:Button;
            private var myPanel:Panel;

            // An event handler for  creationComplete
            private function onCreationComplete():void {

               myPanel=new Panel();
               myPanel.width=200;
               myPanel.height=150;
               myPanel.layout="absolute";
               myPanel.title="Just a Panel";
               addChild(myPanel);

               myButton = new Button();
               myButton.label = "Click me";
               myButton.x=60.5;
               myButton.y=38;
               myPanel.addChild (myButton);
```

```
                // Adding the click event processing
                myButton.addEventListener(MouseEvent.CLICK, buttonClickHandler);
                myPanel.addEventListener(MouseEvent.CLICK, panelClickHandler);
            }

            // The button click handler (the target phase)
            private function buttonClickHandler(event:MouseEvent) :void{
              trace ("click event in the Button");
            }
            // The panel  handler to demo bubbling
            private function panelClickHandler(event:MouseEvent) :void{
              trace ("click event in the Panel");
            }

        ]]>
    </mx:Script>
</mx:Application>
```

Listing 4.40 AS_Bubbling.mxml

Run this application in debug mode and the console screen will look the same as the MXML version of our application:

```
click event in the Button
click event in the Panel
```

The order of these messages is a clear indication that the target event was processed first and the panel responded in the bubbling phase.

Typically, during the capture stage event, listeners on the parent components aren't called, but there's a version of the addEventListener()method that can request calling the listeners during the capture phase. To turn on event handling during the capture phase, you should use the three-arguments version of the addEventListener() function in the panel:

```
myPanel.addEventListener(MouseEvent.CLICK, panelClickHandler, true);
```

When the third argument equals true, it tells the Flash Player that we are registering this particular listener for the capture phase (there's no way to do this in MXML). Now run the application through the debug mode again and you'll see that the panel responds first, then the target button. There's no event processing in the bubbling phase.

```
click event in the Panel
click event in the Button
```

If you'd like to process parent events during both the capture as well as bubbling phase, register two listeners for the panel – one with the three arguments and one with two. These listeners

```
myButton.addEventListener(MouseEvent.CLICK, buttonClickHandler);
 myPanel.addEventListener(MouseEvent.CLICK, panelClickHandler, true);
 myPanel.addEventListener(MouseEvent.CLICK, panelClickHandler);
```

will produce the output proving that the panel has processed the button click event twice: during both the capture and bubbling phases.

```
click event in the Panel
click event in the Button
click event in the Panel
```

Let's make a change in the panel event handler to show how you can prevent the event from being delivered to the target if something bad has occurred (from a business application perspective):

```
private function panelClickHandler(event:MouseEvent) :void{
 var badNews: Boolean = true; // a flag to emulate a bad situation
 if (event.eventPhase == EventPhase.CAPTURING_PHASE){
   trace ("Capturing phase: click event in the Panel");
   if (badNews){
  trace ("Capturing phase: Bad news. Will not propagate click to  But
      ton");
    event.stopPropagation();
   }
 }else {
   trace ("click event in the Panel");
 }
}
```

The stopPropagation() method can be called at any phase of the event flow. The line

```
myPanel.addEventListener(MouseEvent.CLICK, panelClickHandler);
```

means "listen to the click event, and when it'll occur, call the function panelClickHandler."

Handling events was so much easier in MXML...

Why do we even need to know about these addEventListener() function calls? Well, first, there are some classes that don't have equivalents in MXML, hence you don't have a choice. Second, if your program is adding components dynamically, addListener() is your only choice since there's no way to use MXML notation there. And third, you may prefer writing your components only in AS3.

Custom Events

While Flex components come with their pre-defined events, developers can create custom events specific to their applications. Event-driven programming is a very important design concept because it allows an application to react to user interaction without imposing a pre-defined "flow" on the end user. It means that unlike back-end processes that tend to have a "single track of mind" design, front-end applications have to react to what often seems like an unrelated sequence of end-user actions. Fortunately, the event-driven model offers an excellent architecture for such interaction based on loosely coupled components consuming and throwing the events.

This simply means a properly designed component knows how to perform some functionality and notifies the outside world by broadcasting one or more custom events. We need to stress that such a component doesn't send these events to any other component(s). It just broadcasts its "exciting news" to the event dispatcher. If any other component is interested in processing this event, it must register a listener for this event. Unlike direct component-to-component calls via public interfaces, this approach lets you add processing components and set up priorities without affecting the working components.

Before explaining how to create an event-driven component, we'll state how to use them. This is a typical scenario: MyApplication uses Component1 and Component2. The components don't know about each other. Any event-handling component has to define this event inside.

For example, Component1 dispatches this custom event and sends out an instance of the event object, which may or may not carry some additional component-specific data. MyApplication handles this custom event and, if needed, communicates with Component2 with or without feeding it with data based on the results of the first component event.

We'll create a new shopping cart application that will include a main file and two components: the first, a large green button, and the second, a red TextArea field. We'll create two separate directories, "controls" and "cart," respectively, where our components will live.

To create our first MXML component in Flex Builder, select the "controls" directory and click on the menu File | New MXML Component. In the pop-up screen we'll enter LargeGreenButton as a component name and we'll pick Button from a dropdown as a base class for our component.

Flex Builder will generate the following code:

```
<?xml version="1.0" encoding="utf-8"?>
<mx:Button xmlns:mx="http://www.adobe.com/2006/mxml">

</mx:Button>
```

Next, we'll make this button large and green with rounded corners (just to give it a Web 2.0 look). This component will dispatch an event named greenClickEvent. But when? You've got it: when someone clicks on large and green.

Custom events in MXML are annotated within the metadata tag to be visible to MXML. In Listing 4.41 we declared a custom event of the generic flash.events.Event type in the metadata tag. Since the purpose of this component is to notify the sibling objects that someone has clicked the button, we'll define the greenClickEventHandler()event handler to create and dispatch our custom event.

```
<?xml version="1.0" encoding="utf-8"?>
<mx:Button xmlns:mx="http://www.adobe.com/2006/mxml"
  width="104" height="28" cornerRadius="10" fillColors="[#00ff00, #00B000]"
  label="Add Item" fontSize="12" click="greenClickEventHandler()">

  <mx:Metadata>
     [Event(name="addItemEvent", type="flash.events.Event")]
  </mx:Metadata>

  <mx:Script>
     <![CDATA[
        private function greenClickEventHandler():void{
             trace("Ouch! I got clicked! Let me tell this to the world.");
       dispatchEvent(new Event("addItemEvent", true));// bubble to parent
        }
     ]]>
  </mx:Script>
</mx:Button>
```

Listing 4.41 LargeGreenButton.mxml

Please note that the LargeGreenButton component has no idea what will process its addItemEvent. It's none of its business – loose coupling in action!

In dynamic languages the following naming conventions are common practice: to add an "Event" suffix to each of the custom events you declare, and a "Handler" suffix to each of the event-handler functions.

Here's the application that will use the LargeGreenButton component:

```
<?xml version="1.0" encoding="utf-8"?>
<mx:Application xmlns:mx="http://www.adobe.com/2006/mxml"
  xmlns:ctrl="controls.*"   layout="absolute">

  <ctrl:LargeGreenButton greenClickEvent="greenButtonHandler(event)"/>

   <mx:Script>
    <![CDATA[
       private function greenButtonHandler(event:Event):void{
```

```
            trace("Someone clicked on the Large Green Button!");
        }
    ]]>
  </mx:Script>
</mx:Application>
```

Listing 4.42 EventApplication.mxml

We have defined an extra namespace "ctrl" here to make the content of the "controls" directory visible to this application. Run this application in debug mode, and it'll display the window in Figure 4.17. When you click on the green button it will output the following on the console:

Ouch! I got clicked! Let me tell this to the world. Someone clicked on the Large Green Button.

While adding attributes to <ctrl:LargeGreenButton>, please note that code hints work and Flex Builder properly displays the greenClickEvent in the list of available events under the new custom component button.

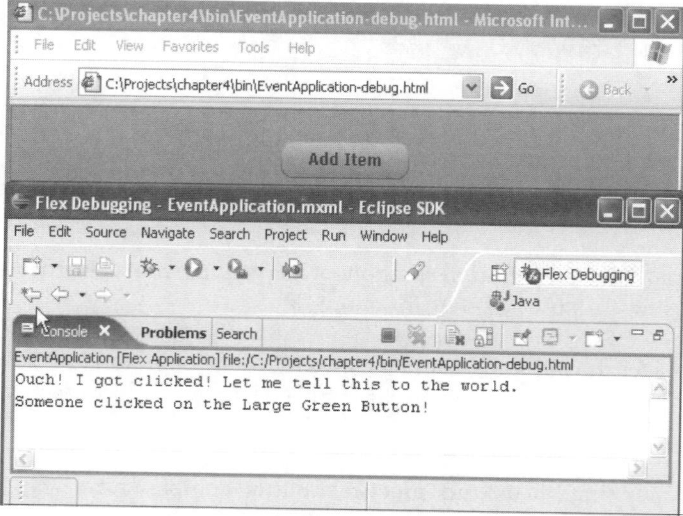

Figure 4.17 The output of GreenApplication.xmxl

Our next component will be called BlindShoppingCart. This time we'll create a component in the "cart" directory based on the TextArea:

```
<?xml version="1.0" encoding="utf-8"?>
<mx:TextArea xmlns:mx="http://www.adobe.com/2006/mxml"
     backgroundColor="#ff0000"  creationComplete="init()">
```

```
  <mx:Script>
    <![CDATA[
        private function init():void{
          parent.addEventListener("addItemEvent",addItemToCartEventHandler);
        }

        private function addItemToCartEventHandler(event:Event){
          this.text+="Yes! Someone has put some item inside me, but I do not know what
it is. \n";
        }
    ]]>
  </mx:Script>
</mx:TextArea>
```

Listing 4.43 BlindShoppingCart.mxml

Note that the BlindShoppingCart component doesn't expose any public properties or methods to the outside world. It's a black box. The only way for other components to add something to the cart is by dispatching the addItemEvent event. The next question is how to map this event to the function that will process it. When someone instantiates the BlindShoppingCart, Flash Player will dispatch the creationComplete event on the component and our code will call the init() private method that adds the addItemEvent event listener mapping to the addItemToCartEventHandler function. This function just appends the text "Yes! Someone has put…" to its red TextArea.

The RedAndGreenApplication application uses the LargeGreenButton and BlindShoppingCart components.

```
<?xml version="1.0" encoding="utf-8"?>
<mx:Application xmlns:mx="http://www.adobe.com/2006/mxml" layout="vertical"
  xmlns:ctrl="controls.*"   xmlns:cart="cart.*">
  <ctrl:LargeGreenButton addItemEvent="greenButtonHandler(event)"/>
  <cart:BlindShoppingCart width="350" height="150" fontSize="14"/>
   <mx:Script>
     <![CDATA[
       private function greenButtonHandler(event:Event):void{
         trace("Someone clicked on the Large Green Button!");
       }
     ]]>
   </mx:Script>
</mx:Application>
```

Listing 4.44 RedAndGreenApplication.mxml

Let's Go Through the Sequence of Events

When the green button is clicked, the greenButtonHandler is called and it creates and dispatches the addItemEvent event back to itself. The event bubbles to the parent container(s), notifying all listening parties of the event. The BlindShoppingCart listens for such an event and responds by adding text. Run this application, click on the button, and the window should look like this:

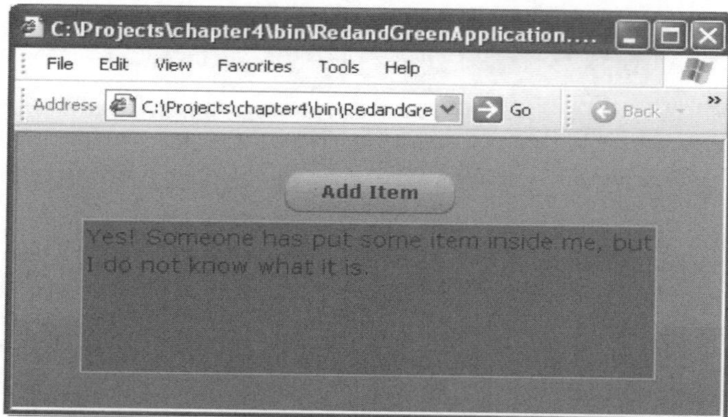

Figure 4.18 The output of RedAndGreenApplication.mxml

Now one more time: the green button component shoots the event to the outside world without knowing anything about it. That is very different from the case when we would write "glue" code like cart.addEventListener("click", applicationResponseMethodDoingSomethingInsideTheCart).

Sending Data Using Custom Events

To make our blind shopping cart more useful, we have to be able not only to fire a custom event, but have this event deliver a description of the item that was passed to shopping cart. To do this, we'll have to create a custom event class with an attribute that will store application-specific data.

This class has to extend flash.events.Event; override its method clone to support event bubbling; and call the constructor of the super-class, passing the type of the event as a parameter. The AS3 class below defines a itemDescription property that will store the application-specific data.

```
package cart {
   import flash.events.Event;

   public class ItemAddedEvent extends Event {
      var itemDescription:String; //an item to be added to the cart
      public static const ITEMADDEDEVENT:String ="ItemAddedEvent";
      public function ItemAddedEvent(description:String )
      {
         super(ITEMADDEDEVENT,true, true); //bubble by default
```

```
            itemDescription=description;
        }

            override public function clone():Event{
            return new ItemAddedEvent(itemDescription);  //  bubbling support inside
            }
    }
}
```

Listing 4.45 The custom event ItemAddedEvent

The new version of the shopping cart component is called ShoppingCart and its event handler extracts the itemDescription from the received event and adds it to the text area.

```
<?xml version="1.0" encoding="utf-8"?>
<mx:TextArea xmlns:mx="http://www.adobe.com/2006/mxml"
     backgroundColor="#ff0000"  creationComplete="init()">

   <mx:Script>
      <![CDATA[
      private function init():void{
        parent.addEventListener(ItemAddedEvent.ITEMADDEDEVENT,addItemToCartEventHandler);
      }

      private function addItemToCartEventHandler(event:ItemAddedEvent){
        text+="Yes! Someone has put " + event.itemDescription + "\n";
      }
      ]]>
   </mx:Script>
</mx:TextArea>
```

Listing 4.46 ShoppingCart.mxml

There's a design pattern called Inversion of Control or Dependency Injection, which means that an object doesn't ask other objects for required values, but assumes that someone will provide the required values from outside. This is also known as the Hollywood principle or "Don't call me, I'll call you." Our ShoppingCart does exactly this – it waits until some unknown object triggers an event it listens to that carries an item description. Our component knows what to do with it, i.e., display in the red text area, validate it against the inventory, send it over to the shipping department, and so on.

Next, we'll completely rework our LargeGreenButton class into a NewItem component to include a label and a text field to enter some item description and the same old green button:

```
<?xml version="1.0" encoding="utf-8"?>
```

```
<mx:HBox    xmlns:mx="http://www.adobe.com/2006/mxml" >

  <mx:Metadata>
    [Event(name="addItemEvent", type="flash.events.Event")]
  </mx:Metadata>
  <mx:Label  text="Item name:"/>
  <mx:TextInput id="enteredItem" width="300"/>
  <mx:Button
    width="104" height="28" cornerRadius="10" fillColors="[#00ff00, #00B000]"
    label="Add Item" fontSize="12" click="greenClickEventHandler()"/>
  <mx:Script>
    <![CDATA[
      import cart.ItemAddedEvent;
       private function greenClickEventHandler():void{
        trace("Ouch! I got clicked! Let me tell this to the world.");
        dispatchEvent(new ItemAddedEvent(enteredItem.text));
       }
    ]]>
  </mx:Script>
</mx:HBox>
```

When we look at our new application with its new ShoppingCart and NewItem components, it's almost indistinguishable from the original one. If we kept the old class names, we could have used the old application.

```
<?xml version="1.0" encoding="utf-8"?>
<mx:Application xmlns:mx="http://www.adobe.com/2006/mxml" layout="vertical"
   xmlns:ctrl="controls.*"   xmlns:cart="cart.*">
   <ctrl:NewItem />
   <cart:ShoppingCart width="350" height="150" fontSize="14"/>
</mx:Application>
```

Listing 4.47 RedAndGreenApplication2.mxml

When the user enters the item description and clicks the green one, the application creates a new instance of the ItemAddedEvent, passing the entered item to its constructor, and the ShoppingCart properly displays the selected "New Item to Add" on the red carpet (see Figure 4.19).

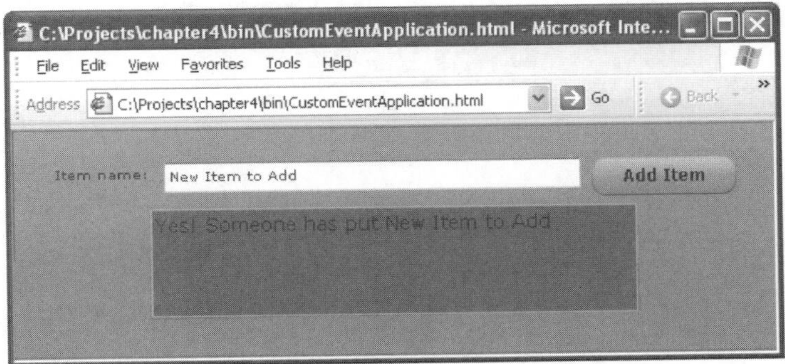

Figure 4.19 The output of RedAndGreenApplication.mxml

Making components loosely bound simplifies development and distribution but comes at a higher cost in testing and maintenance. Depending on the delivery timeline, size, and lifespan of your application, you'd have to make a choice between loosely coupled or strongly typed components.

One last note. The itemDescription in Listing 4.45 doesn't have an access-level qualifier. It's so-called package-level protection. The ShoppingCart can access itemDescription directly, but the classes outside the "cart" package can't.

Summary

This was a large chapter and it just covered the basic concepts of ActionScript programming. As you start building your Flex application, the coding described will become routine. Making a choice of which approach to take will not. We hope that such a high-level overview will help you to make an informed choice about the path to take.

Endnotes

1. To be exact the appropriate Java classloader on each side should be able to find the class in the parental chain of the classloaders.
2. The function object becomes a candidate for garbage collection.

CHAPTER

5

A Complete Application with RPC Communications and JMS

A Complete Application with RPC Communications and JMS

Multi-Tier Application Development with Flex

This chapter describes the process of creating a complete Flex-Java distributed application. Upgrading Flex applications to Java Enterprise Edition applications is done with Flex Data Services. FDS provides transparent access to POJO, EJBs, and JMS and comes with adapters for frameworks like Spring and Hibernate. These powerful capabilities come free for a single-CPU server, otherwise see your local Adobe dealer. Flex can also invoke any SOAP Web Service or send an HTTP request to any URL via Web Services and HTTPService components.

In this chapter we will illustrate Flex controls, HTTPService, RemoteObject, and Consumer via two versions of a stock portfolio application. The first version will show communications between Flash and a plain old Java object (POJO) using Flex remoting. We'll also explain how to use the HTTPService to read the RSS news feed. In the other version we'll add the stock (aka security) price feed using Flex Messaging and the Java Messaging Service (JMS).

While explaining the FDS capabilities, we will also walk you through a typical design with Flex containers.

Designing a Stock Portfolio Application

Our goal is to create a Web application that will receive and display a feed containing security prices and the latest financial news as in Figures 5.1 and 5.2. This section contains a sort of functional specification of such an application.

We'll populate the top portion of the screen with the stocks included in the user's portfolio. For simplicity's sake, we'll store the user's portfolio in the XML file as in Listing 5.1.

```
<portfolio>
  <security>
    <Symbol>MSFT</Symbol>
    <Quantity>10000</Quantity>
    <Price>33.38</Price>
```

```
      <Value>1</Value>
   </security>
   <security>
      <Symbol>IBM</Symbol>
      <Quantity>3000</Quantity>
      <Price>82.15</Price>
      <Value>1</Value>
   </security>
   ...
</portfolio>
```

Listing 5.1 A fragment of a portfolio.xml

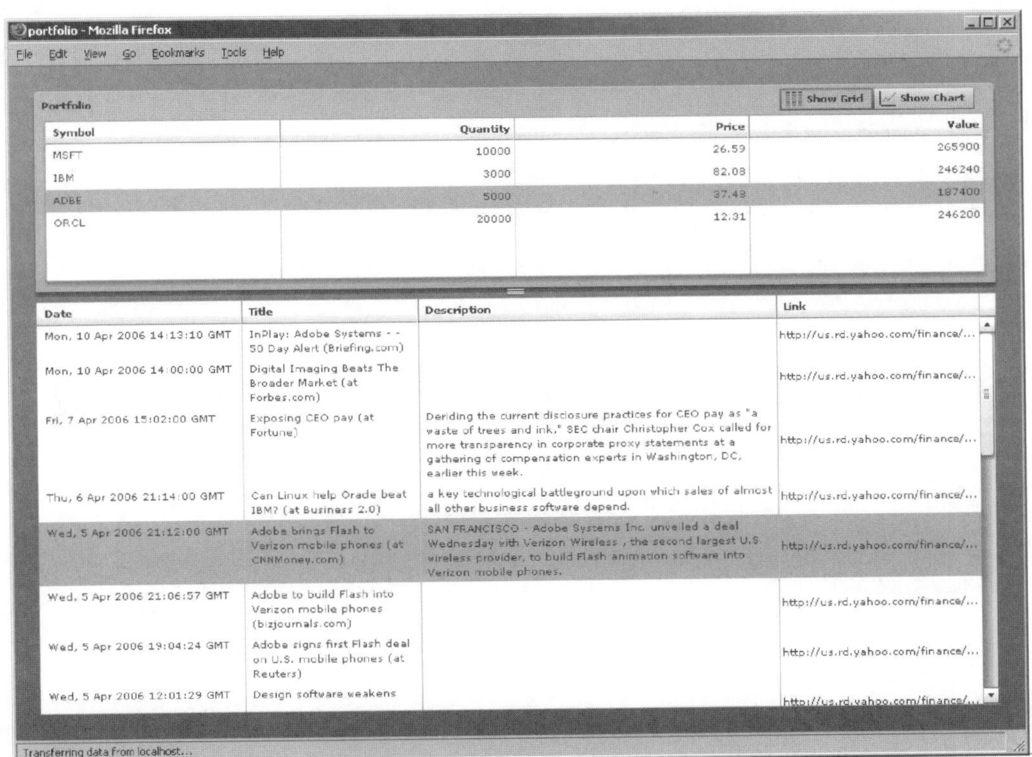

Figure 5.1 Stock portfolio screen - the show grid view

When the user clicks on a row with a particular stock (i.e., ADBE as in Figure 5.1), it will populate the lower data grid with the headlines related to the selected stock. The news should be coming from http://finance.yahoo.com/rss/headline. The column Link will contain the URL of the news, and when the user clicks on the link, a new browser window pops up displaying the selected news article.

The top of the screen contains the toggle buttons Show Grid/Show Chart. When the Show Grid option is selected, the user will see the screen as in Figure 5.1, and when Show Chart is selected, the top data grid will be replaced with the pie chart (see Figure 5.2), preserving the same functionality (clicking on the pie slice repopulates the news headlines according to the selected security). The market data is refreshed on the screen every second or so.

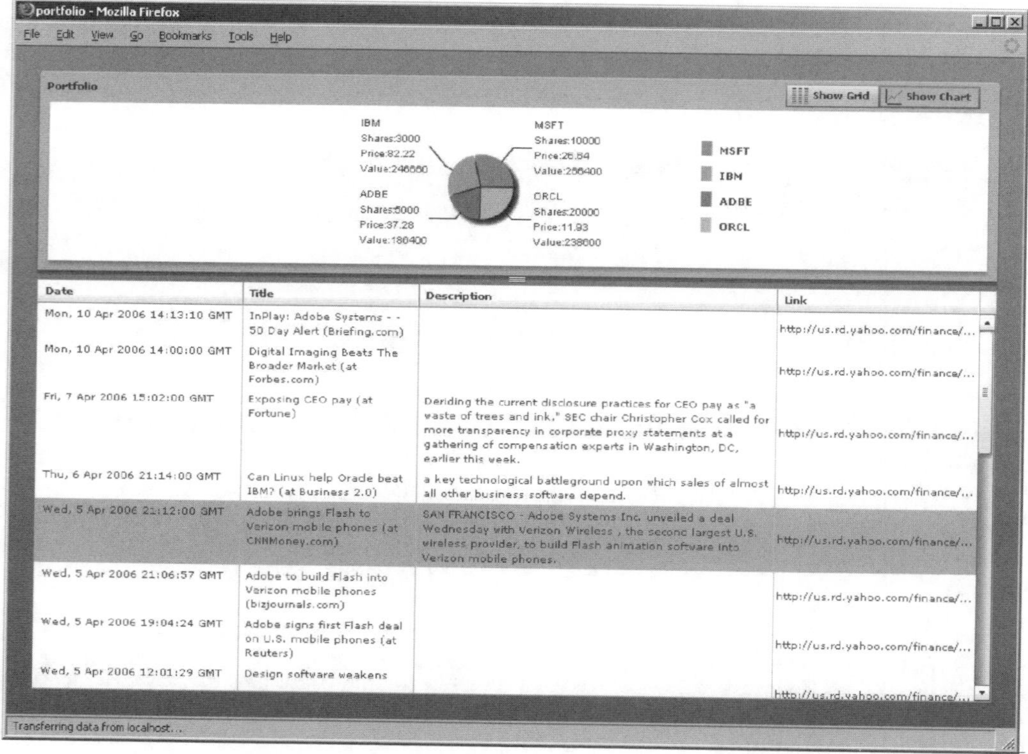

Figure 5.2 Stock portfolio screen – the show chart view

The first version of the application will query the server POJO that generates random numbers. Later in this chapter, we'll subscribe to JMS topic and consume a real-time data feed from an external Java application.

In this application we'll use the basic MXML and ActionScript from the first chapters of this book. We assume that the reader has a basic knowledge of Java syntax. We've included mini-references on the Java Naming and Directory Interface and JMS. So let's roll up our sleeves…

Adding a Data Grid

We'll start by adding the top grid displaying the stock portfolio. The Flex *dataGrid* component is a natural choice for data that can be presented as rows and columns. MXML is a great tool for modularizing development. The name of the new .mxml file automatically becomes the name of a new tag that can be reused in other files. For example, the code in Listing 5.2 assumes that there is an MXML file named PortfolioView1.mxml (in reality it can also be an ActionScript file named PortfolioView1.as or any other file that is assigned to this tag via the component library manifest):

```
<?xml version="1.0" encoding="utf-8"?>
<!--portfolio1.mxml -->
<mx:Application xmlns:mx="http://www.adobe.com/2006/mxml"  xmlns="*" >
  <PortfolioView1 id="pv"/>
</mx:Application>
```

Listing 5.2 The first version – portfolio1.mxml

In case of a default namespace (xmlns="*"), our PortfolioView1.mxml from Listing 5.3 will be co-located in the same directory with the application file portfolio.mxml.

Let's discuss the design of PortfolioView1. It contains DataGrid *portfolioGrid* in a Flex Panel with the title "Portfolio." XML from Listing 5.1 is loaded into the *portfolioModel* e4x object. The list of securities from that file is fed into *portfolioGrid* via a binding expression {portfolioModel.security}. This expression returns an XMLList of all nodes named "security" that are direct children of the root node:

```
<?xml version="1.0" encoding="utf-8"?>
<!-- PortfolioView1.mxml -->
<mx:Panel xmlns:mx="http://www.adobe.com/2006/mxml"
  title="Portfolio" width="100%" height="100%" ...>
  <mx:XML format="e4x" id="portfolioModel" source="portfolio.xml" />
  <mx:DataGrid id="portfolioGrid" width="100%"
   dataProvider="{portfolioModel.security}">
    <mx:columns>
     <mx:DataGridColumn dataField="Symbol"/>
     <mx:DataGridColumn dataField="Quantity" textAlign="right"/>
     <mx:DataGridColumn dataField="Price" textAlign="right"/>
     <mx:DataGridColumn dataField="Value" textAlign="right"/>
  </mx:columns>
  </mx:DataGrid>
   ...
</mx:Panel>
```

Listing 5.3 The first version of PortfolioView.mxml

Even if we won't add any more code, isn't it impressive that it takes only a dozen lines of code to read the XML file, parse it, and display it in a grid shown in Figure 5.3? But this application has a static nature: it does not connect to any price quote feed. In other words you would always see $33.38 as the price for Microsoft, and $82.15 for IBM.

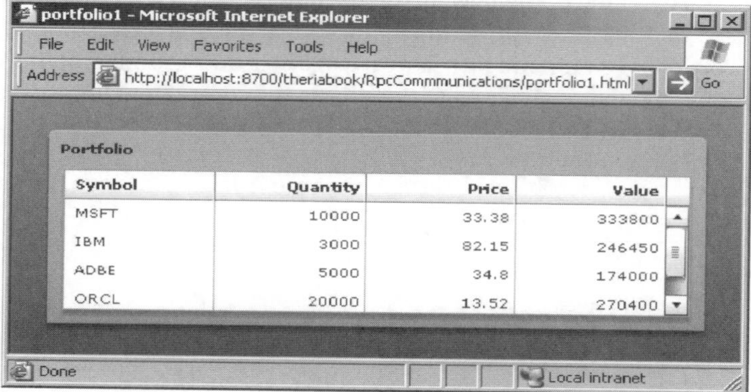

Figure 5.3 A data grid populated from Portfolio.xml

In Listing 5.3, the curly braces surrounding the expression indicate that this expression is being used as a source in data binding. It is crucial for Flex programming to fully understand the strengths and weaknesses of binding. Binding is based on event listeners automatically generated by the Flex compiler as a response to declarative binding annotations. To initiate binding generation, developers use a combination of curly braces, mx:Binding tags, and [Bindable] metadata directives. (Refer to the Adobe Flex manual for more detail.) In Chapter 4, we've given you some examples of data binding, and in this chapter we'll keep emphasizing the convenience of binding for automatic asynchronous code invocation.

Next, we need to periodically connect to the server for new prices and update the Price and Value columns. So let's use a special Flex component called RemoteObject:

```
<mx:RemoteObject id="freshQuotes" destination="Portfolio"…> .
```

The RemoteObject component allows calling methods of a specified remote POJO, which is configured on the server as a destination *Portfolio* in a special XML file. We'd like to emphasize that Flex transparently calls Java from ActionScript. The client needs to know the name of the destination and the method to call, for example, getQuotes(). All the dirty work of data marshaling between ActionScript and Java is done for you by the Flex framework. If, for example, a Java method returns an object of the StockQuoteDTO.java type, Flex de-serializes the Java object and builds its ActionScript peer on the client. However, for performance reasons, it is recommended that you create the peer ActionScript class and register it with the framework. We'll show the StockQuoteDTO.as later in this chapter.

Please note that all RPC communications, including *RemoteObject*, are asynchronous. In other words, we don't exactly *call* a remote method, but rather *send* a message to the server, requesting a call of the specific Java method. Not only is the client's request(s) executed asynchronously, but even sending to the server is done asynchronously. And if you need to do multiple RemoteObject invocations in your script, Flex will batch them together and send in the end of the script execution.

The results of remote invocations are returned via events. RemoteObject provides the *result* event for success or *fault* for failures. You should write the corresponding handler functions. Flex will call these methods, supplying an Event object as a parameter. It's your responsibility to get the information from the event and act accordingly. Friendly advice: you will save yourself hours of time if you supply a fault handler.

In the next code snippet we set *concurrency* to *last*, because if Flex decides to batch the outgoing requests, we do not want to send out more then one request in a batch; if a user clicks on the screen sending more than one request in quick succession, the last request will suppress all previous ones. Similarly, when the results are coming back we are interested only in the one we sent last:

```
<mx:RemoteObject id="freshQuotes" destination="portfolio" fault="onFault(event);">
  <mx:method name="getQuotes" concurrency="last" result="onResult(event);"/>
</mx:RemoteObject>
```

Listing 5.4 RemoteObject Tag

The tag <mx:RemoteObject> allows using result and fault handling on both the object and method levels. The method settings will take precedence over the RemoteObject's ones.

For server-side support, you have to download and install Flex Data Services 2 Express Edition (http://www.adobe.com/products/flex/), and deploy it as a Web application in the J2EE server of your choice, for example, in Tomcat. FDS comes with a set of XML files, which you will use to configure your server-side objects.

To register a POJO class with a Flex client we need to update the configuration file on the server side. This lets you hide details of the service provider (i.e., actual Java class names) by specifying so-called *destinations* where you specify access constraints, etc. The following section has to be added to the remoting-config.xml file.

```
<destination id="Portfolio">
  <properties>
    <source>com.theriabook.ro.Portfolio</source>
  </properties>
</destination>
```

Listing 5.5 Configuring a Flex remoting service

Clients won't know that the actual name of our POJO is com.theriabook.ro.Portfolio, but they'll be able to refer to it by the nickname Portfolio. Flex looks for classes specified in destination mappings on the Web Application classpath including jars inside WEB-INF/lib and classes under WEB-INF/classes. The Java class Portfolio.java (see Listing 5.6) is a simple random number generator simulating market-like real-time price changes for several hard-coded securities.

```
package com.theriabook.ro;
import java.util.Random;
import com.theriabook.jms.dto.StockQuoteDTO;

public class Portfolio {
   static Random random = new Random();
static StockQuoteDTO[] quotes = {
      new StockQuoteDTO("IBM", 82.0),
      new StockQuoteDTO("MSFT", 27.0),
      new StockQuoteDTO("ADBE", 38.0),
      new StockQuoteDTO("ORCL", 13.0)};
double volatility=.05;
public StockQuoteDTO[] getQuotes() {
   for (int i = 0; i < quotes.length;i++){
      quotes[i].last += random.nextGaussian()* volatility;
   }
return quotes;
}
}
```

Listing 5.6 A simple stock quote generator – Portfolio.java

The StockQuoteDTO.Java (see Listing 5.7) contains the last price of a particular stock.

```
package com.theriabook.jms.dto;
import java.io.Serializable;
public class StockQuoteDTO implements Serializable {
  private static final long serialVersionUID = 4672447577075475117L;
  public String symbol;
  public double last;
  public StockQuoteDTO(String sym, double newPrice){
    symbol = sym;
    last = newPrice;
  }
}
```

Listing 5.7 The Java DTO - StockQuoteDTO.java

However, the client can really benefit from knowledge of the structure and the datatypes of the returned DTOs. Listing 5.8 shows the ActionScript's counterpart for the StockQuoteDTO.java object. While Flex does not need this definition in order to deserialize the Java object that includes member variables of standard types (by default it creates a dynamic object and adds the required properties of the Java object that's being deserialized), it does help performance (since the deserialized object is immediately allocated in memory), ensures the output datatypes and enforces the type conversion. The [RemoteClass…] metadata tag above the class definition tells the Flex de-serialization method to use this particular class for de-serialization whenever the server sends com.theriabook.jms.dto.StockQuoteDTO object down.

```
package com.theriabook.jms.dto {
[RemoteClass(alias="com.theriabook.jms.dto.StockQuoteDTO")]
public dynamic class StockQuoteDTO
{
   public var symbol:String;
   public var last:Number;
}
```

Listing 5.8 The ActionScript on the client: StockQuoteDTO.as

When the client successfully gets the quotes, it processes them and asks for new ones:

```
private function onResult(event:ResultEvent):void {
      …
   var quotes:Array = event.result as Array;
   applyQuotes(quotes);
   // Pull the next set of quotes
   pullQuotes();
}

   private function applyQuotes(quotes: Array):void {
      for (var i:int=0; i<quotes.length; i++) {
         var quote:StockQuoteDTO = StockQuoteDTO(quotes[i]);
         var list: XMLList = portfolioModel.security.(Symbol==quote.symbol);
         if (list.length()!=0) {
            var row:XML = XML(list);
            row.Price = Math.round(100*quote.last)/100;
            row.Value = Math.round(row.Price * row.Quantity);
         }
      }
   }
```

Listing 5.9 Processing received quotes

The E4X provides a very elegant solution for navigating an XML object here. The *applyQuotes* function iterates though the quotes from our portfolio and gets the XMLList based on the matching *Symbol* attribute via evaluation of the *portfolioModel.security* expression. (*Symbol==quote.symbol.*) This looks similar to XPath, but it's easier, isn't it? Since there's a chance that the E4X expression above will return an empty XMLList, it's better to check for zero-length to avoid exceptions. We are modifying the same XMLList that has been set as the data provider of our grid. In fact, for data grids Flex maintains an internal XMLListCollection with this XMLList as a source. When the program changes the data in the XMLList, these changes are automatically reflected on the screen.

Error reporting is often done by calling *Alert()*, which brings up a pop-up window. But we suggest a less obtrusive way, whereby as an error condition disappears, the normal display restores without user interaction. Let's put a simple red Label control right above the data grid. Later in this chapter we'll embed it in the Panel's title. An error, if any, will be displayed in this Label control, and to make it a bit fancier, the detailed error description will be displayed as a tooltip whenever the user moves the mouse over this field:

```
<mx:Label color="red" toolTip="{errorTip}" text="{errorText}" width="100%"/>
```

To implement this functionality, in the scripting section we will create two bindable variables:

```
[Bindable]
private var errorText:String;
[Bindable]
private var errorTip:String;
```

When an error occurs, the *onFault* function sets the values of the variables *errorText* and *errorTip*, and their bindable nature will immediately display these values in the <mx:Label>. But most importantly, we will attempt to recover by pulling the new quotes set.

```
private function onFault(event:FaultEvent):void {
    errorText = "Portfolio feed failure...";
    errorTip = "Destination:" + event.currentTarget.destination + "\n" +
          "Fault code:" + event.fault.faultCode + "\n" +
          "Detail:" + event.fault.faultDetail;
      // Try to pull the new quotes
          pullQuotes();
}
```

Listing 5.10 Error processing

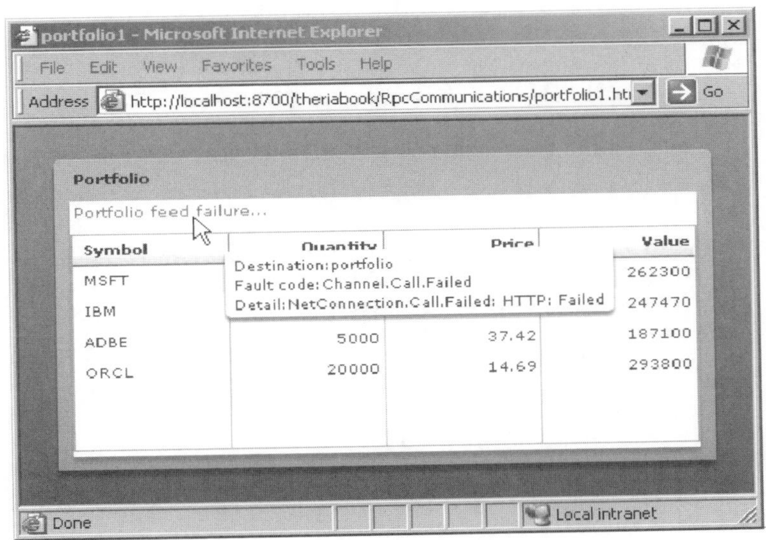

Figure 5.4 Error display

Do not forget to clean the *errorText* and *errorTip* variables in the function *onResul*t, if the next attempt to pull the quotes will be successful.

Let's spend some time discussing the process of initiating the quote request. The function pullQuotes() gets initially invoked upon creation of the Panel:

```
<mx:Panel xmlns:mx="http://www.adobe.com/2006/mxml"  title="Portfolio" . . .
   creationComplete="pullQuotes();">
```

To generate a remote call of some anonymous function every second, we'll use the *setTimeout* mechanism. The anonymous function initiates the call of the Java object proxied by the remoting destination *freshQuotes*:

```
private function pullQuotes():void{
 setTimeout(function ():void {freshQuotes.getQuotes();},1000);
}
```

Listing 5.11 has the complete code of the first version of PortfolioView1.mxml, which contains just a data grid.

```
<?xml version="1.0" encoding="utf-8"?>
<!-- PortfolioView1.mxml -->
<mx:Panel xmlns:mx="http://www.adobe.com/2006/mxml"
   title="Portfolio"
```

```
    width="100%" height="100%"
     creationComplete="pullQuotes();"
  >
    <mx:XML format="e4x" id="portfolioModel" source="portfolio.xml" />
    <mx:Label color="red" toolTip="{errorTip}" text="{errorText}" width="100%"/>
    <mx:DataGrid id="portfolioGrid" width="100%" dataProvider="{portfolioModel.security}"
  >
      <mx:columns><mx:Array>
            <mx:DataGridColumn dataField="Symbol"/>
            <mx:DataGridColumn dataField="Quantity" textAlign="right"/>
            <mx:DataGridColumn dataField="Price" textAlign="right"/>
            <mx:DataGridColumn dataField="Value" textAlign="right"/>
      </mx:Array></mx:columns>
    </mx:DataGrid>
  <mx:RemoteObject id="freshQuotes" destination="portfolio"
     fault="onFault(event);"  >
    <mx:method name="getQuotes" concurrency="last"
     result="onResult(event);"
     />
  </mx:RemoteObject>
   <mx:Script><![CDATA[
     import mx.rpc.events.*;
     import com.theriabook.jms.dto.StockQuoteDTO;

     [Bindable]
     private var errorText:String;
     [Bindable]
     private var errorTip:String;

     private function onResult(event:ResultEvent):void {
      errorText = "";
      errorTip = "";
      var quotes:Array = event.result as Array;
      applyQuotes(quotes);
      // Pull new quotes set
      pullQuotes();
     }

      private function onFault(event:FaultEvent):void {
         errorText = "Portfolio feed failure...";
         errorTip = "Destination:" + event.currentTarget.destination + "\n" +
          "Fault code:" + event.fault.faultCode + "\n" +
          "Detail:" + event.fault.faultDetail;
      // Pull new quotes set
```

```
        pullQuotes();
      }

    private function applyQuotes(quotes: Array):void {
        for (var i:int=0; i<quotes.length; i++) {
              var quote:StockQuoteDTO = StockQuoteDTO(quotes[i]);
              var list: XMLList = portfolioModel.security.(Symbol==quote.symbol);
              if (list.length()!=0) {
                 var row:XML = XML(list);
                 row.Price = Math.round(100*quote.last)/100;
                 row.Value = Math.round(row.Price * row.Quantity);
              }
        }
    }
      private function pullQuotes():void{
         setTimeout(function ():void {freshQuotes.getQuotes();  },1000  );
      }
   ]]></mx:Script>
</mx:Panel>
```

Listing 5.11 PortfolioView1.mxml

Adding the Charting Component

The population of the data grid is complete, and we are ready to work on adding a Flex charting component.

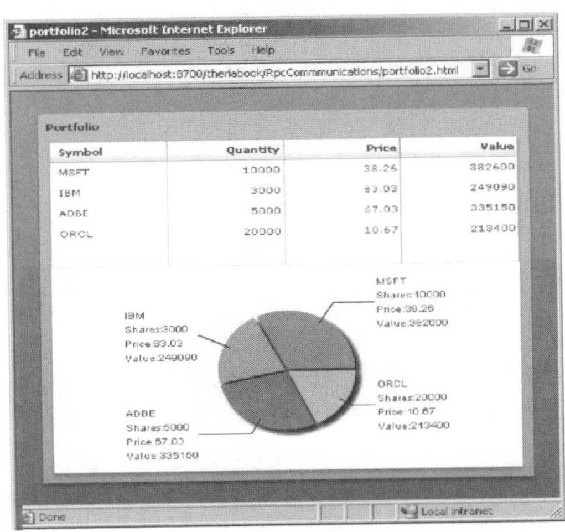

Figure 5.5 Adding a charting component

Let's create a simple application that adds the pie chart below the data grid and gives the grid and the chart 50% of the screen height each:

```
<?xml version="1.0" encoding="utf-8"?>
<!--portfolio2.mxml -->
<mx:Application xmlns:mx="http://www.adobe.com/2006/mxml" xmlns="*" >
  <PortfolioView2 id="pv"/>
</mx:Application>
```

The fragment of the PortfolioView2.mxml is shown below:

```
<?xml version="1.0" encoding="utf-8"?>
<!-- PortfolioView2.mxml -->
<mx:Panel xmlns:mx=http://www.adobe.com/2006/mxml>
   ...
   <mx:DataGrid id="portfolioGrid" width="100%" height="50%"
                dataProvider="{portfolioModel.security}"
   </mx:DataGrid>
    <mx:PieChart id="portfolioPie" dataProvider="{portfolioModel.security}"
   showDataTips="true" width="100%" height="50%">
      <mx:series>
    <mx:Array>
     <mx:PieSeries labelPosition="callout" field="Value"
         labelFunction="showPosition" nameField="Symbol" explodeRadius="2"/>
    </mx:Array>
    </mx:series>
   </mx:PieChart>
  ...
 <mx:Script>
  ...
  private function showPosition(data:Object, field:String, index:Number,
                      percentValue:Number):String {
   return data.Symbol + "\n" + "Shares:" + data.Quantity + "\n" +
          "Price:" + data.Price + "\n" + "Value:" + data.Value ;
  }
 </mx:Script>
</mx:Panel>
```

Listing 5.12 Adding the pie chart to the PortfolioView

Flex Panel containers have a *layout* property (horizontal, vertical, and absolute). Since the vertical layout is the default, our chart is positioned right under the grid. Please note that chart's *dataProvider* is based on the same XMLList *portfolioModel.security* as is the dataProvider of the portfolioGrid. In other words, we have two views of the same data model. The data binding feature results in immediate updates of both controls on each change of the model. Java Swing developers will appreciate the benefits of this feature as opposed to the JavaBean and property listeners hassle.

```
<?xml version="1.0" encoding="utf-8"?>
<!-- PortfolioView2.mxml -->
<mx:Panel xmlns:mx="http://www.adobe.com/2006/mxml"  title="Portfolio"
   width="100%" height="100%"   creationComplete="pullQuotes();" >
   <mx:XML format="e4x" id="portfolioModel" source="portfolio.xml" />
   <mx:Label color="red" toolTip="{errorTip}" text="{errorText}" width="100%"/>
   <mx:DataGrid id="portfolioGrid" width="100%" height="50%"
                 dataProvider="{portfolioModel.security}">
      <mx:columns><mx:Array>
            <mx:DataGridColumn dataField="Symbol"/>
            <mx:DataGridColumn dataField="Quantity" textAlign="right"/>
            <mx:DataGridColumn dataField="Price" textAlign="right"/>
            <mx:DataGridColumn dataField="Value" textAlign="right"/>
      </mx:Array></mx:columns>
   </mx:DataGrid>

  <mx:PieChart id="portfolioPie" dataProvider="{portfolioModel.security}"
 showDataTips="true" width="100%" height="50%">
      <mx:series>
      <mx:Array>
      <mx:PieSeries labelPosition="callout"  field="Value"
        labelFunction="showPosition" nameField="Symbol" explodeRadius="2" />
     </mx:Array>
     </mx:series>
   </mx:PieChart>

 <mx:RemoteObject id="freshQuotes" destination="portfolio"
     fault="onFault(event)">
    <mx:method name="getQuotes" concurrency="last" result="onResult(event)"/>
 </mx:RemoteObject>
  <mx:Script><![CDATA[
     import mx.rpc.events.*;
     import com.theriabook.jms.dto.StockQuoteDTO;

     [Bindable]
     private var errorText:String;
     [Bindable]
     private var errorTip:String;

     private function onResult(event:ResultEvent):void {
       errorText = "";
```

```
        errorTip = "";
        var quotes:Array = event.result as Array;
        applyQuotes(quotes);
        // Pull new quotes set
        pullQuotes();
      }

        private function onFault(event:FaultEvent):void {
          errorText = "Portfolio feed failure...";
          errorTip = "Destination:" + event.currentTarget.destination + "\n" +
           "Fault code:" + event.fault.faultCode + "\n" +
           "Detail:" + event.fault.faultDetail;
        // Pull new quotes set
          pullQuotes();
        }
      private function applyQuotes(quotes: Array):void {
        for (var i:int=0; i<quotes.length; i++) {
            var quote:StockQuoteDTO = StockQuoteDTO(quotes[i]);
            var list: XMLList = portfolioModel.security.(Symbol==quote.symbol);
            if (list.length()!=0) {
              var row:XML = XML(list);
              row.Price = Math.round(100*quote.last)/100;
              row.Value = Math.round(row.Price * row.Quantity);
            }
      }
      }
       private function pullQuotes():void{
          setTimeout(function ():void {  freshQuotes.getQuotes();},1000);
       }

       private function showPosition(data:Object, field:String, index:Number,
                    percentValue:Number):String {

    return data.Symbol + "\n" + "Shares:" + data.Quantity +
       "\n" + "Price:" + data.Price + "\n" + "Value:" + data.Value ;
  }

    ]]></mx:Script>
  </mx:Panel>
```

Listing 5.13 PortfolioView2.mxml

For the pie chart, we've selected a *callout* type of label positioning, specified so the size of the pie is proportional to the attribute Value, and we've added a 3D depth to the chart by setting *explode*

Radius to 0.02. Note how we've assigned the function name *showPosition* to the *labelFunction* attribute of the pie chart. The signature of the *labelFunction* assumes that the first argument brings the element of the dataProvider corresponding to the current wedge in the series.

Chart/DataGrid Toggling

Imagine a deck of playing cards: only the top card is visible. Hide the top card and you'll see the next one. We'll use the deck of two "cards": one card will display the grid, and another one – the chart. To Java Swing developers this should look like the CardLayout. In Flex jargon it's called <mx:ViewStack>. The screen snapshot in Figure 5.6 was made when the portfolioPie was on the top of the portfolioGrid:

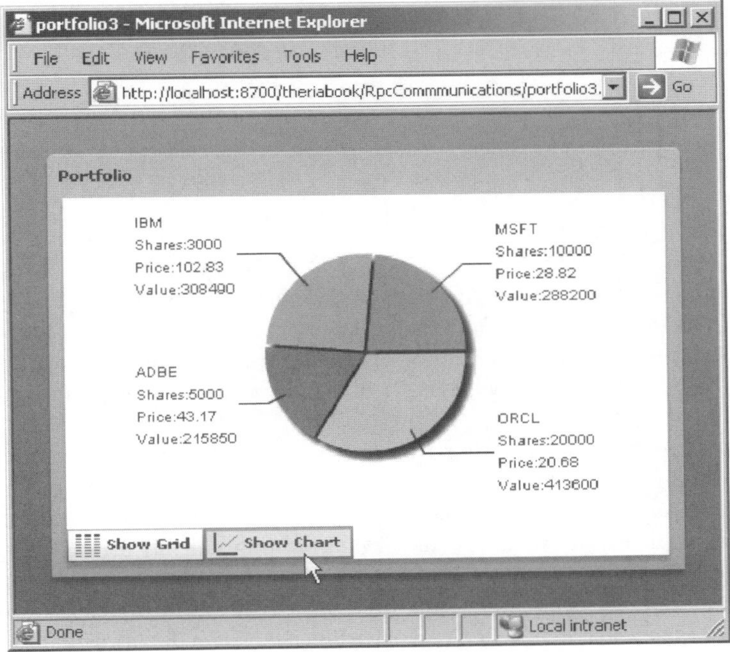

Figure 5.6 Using ViewStack for toggling

A fragment of PortfolioView3.mxml introduces MXML components <mx:ViewStack>, <mx:ToggleButtonBar>, and <mx:Canvas>.

```
<?xml version="1.0" encoding="utf-8"?>
<!-- PortfolioView3.mxml -->
<mx:Panel…>
 <mx:ViewStack id="vs" width="100%" height="100%">
   <mx:Canvas label="Show Grid" icon="{iconGrid}" >
      <mx:DataGrid id="portfolioGrid" …height="100%"/>
```

```
      </mx:Canvas>
      <mx:Canvas label="Show Chart" icon="{iconChart}" >
          <mx:PieChart id="portfolioPie" … height="100%"/>
   </mx:Canvas>
    </mx:ViewStack>
          <mx:ToggleButtonBar dataProvider="{vs}" horizontalGap="5" />
    <mx:RemoteObject id="freshQuotes" …/>
   <mx:Script><![CDATA[
      …
   [Embed(source="images/icon_chart.png")]
   [Bindable]
   public var iconChart : Class;
   [Embed(source="images/icon_grid.png")]
   [Bindable]
   public var iconGrid : Class;
   ]]></mx:Script>
   </mx:Panel>
```

Listing 5.14 Adding a stacked view

The most suitable Flex containers for toggling the views are ViewStack or its direct descendant TabNavigator. The latter uses more screen real estate to paint the tabs. So we'd rather put the view toggling controls on the unused area of the Panel's title bar. The ViewStack component provides programmatic indexed access to the child containers and shows them one at a time.

The simplest Flex container is called Canvas, so we wrap up the DataGrid and the PieChart separately inside it. A Canvas is a descendant of the Container ActionScript class and has the properties *label* and *icon*. There are two "non-programmatic" ways to use these properties. First, certain containers use them implicitly, for instance, TabNavigator automatically arranges its tabs to display labels and show icons from the nested child containers. The second way is to explicitly use the ViewStack as a data provider for the descendants of the NavBar control such as ButtonBar, LinkBar, and, in our case, ToggleButtonBar. When you use a ViewStack as a data provider, the *label* and *icon* properties of the ViewStack container's children are used to populate the navigation items. The ViewStack feeds ToggleButtonbar and ToggleButtonbar controls the ViewStack in return.

```
<?xml version="1.0" encoding="utf-8"?>
<!-- PortfolioView3.mxml -->
<mx:Panel xmlns:mx="http://www.adobe.com/2006/mxml"  title="Portfolio"
   width="100%" height="100%"  creationComplete="pullQuotes();" >
   <mx:XML format="e4x" id="portfolioModel" source="portfolio.xml" />
   <mx:Label color="red" toolTip="{errorTip}" text="{errorText}" width="100%"/>
  <mx:ToggleButtonBar dataProvider="{vs}" horizontalGap="5" />

   <mx:ViewStack id="vs" width="100%" height="100%">
```

```
  <mx:Canvas label="Show Grid" icon="{iconGrid}" >
    <mx:DataGrid id="portfolioGrid" width="100%" height="100%"
     dataProvider="{portfolioModel.security}">
       <mx:columns><mx:Array>
            <mx:DataGridColumn dataField="Symbol"/>
            <mx:DataGridColumn dataField="Quantity" textAlign="right"/>
            <mx:DataGridColumn dataField="Price" textAlign="right"/>
            <mx:DataGridColumn dataField="Value" textAlign="right"/>
       </mx:Array></mx:columns>
    </mx:DataGrid>
  </mx:Canvas>
  <mx:Canvas label="Show Chart" icon="{iconChart}" >
     <mx:PieChart id="portfolioPie" dataProvider="{portfolioModel.security}"
                 showDataTips="true" width="100%" height="100%">
       <mx:series>
        <mx:Array>
         <mx:PieSeries labelPosition="callout"
           field="Value" labelFunction="showPosition"
           nameField="Symbol" explodeRadius="0.02" />
        </mx:Array>
      </mx:series>
     </mx:PieChart>
  </mx:Canvas>
 </mx:ViewStack>

 <mx:RemoteObject id="freshQuotes" destination="portfolio"
    fault="onFault(event)">
   <mx:method name="getQuotes" concurrency="last"
    result="onResult(event)"
    />
</mx:RemoteObject>
 <mx:Script><![CDATA[
   import mx.rpc.events.*;
   import com.theriabook.jms.dto.StockQuoteDTO;

  [Bindable]
   private var errorText:String;
   [Bindable]
   private var errorTip:String;

   private function onResult(event:ResultEvent):void {
      errorText = "";
      errorTip = "";
      var quotes:Array = event.result as Array;
```

```
        applyQuotes(quotes);
        // Pull new quotes set
        pullQuotes();
    }

        private function onFault(event:FaultEvent):void {
          errorText = "Portfolio feed failure...";
          errorTip = "Destination:" + event.currentTarget.destination + "\n" +
           "Fault code:" + event.fault.faultCode + "\n" +
           "Detail:" + event.fault.faultDetail;
        // Pull new quotes set
          pullQuotes();
        }
    private function applyQuotes(quotes: Array):void {
        for (var i:int=0; i<quotes.length; i++) {
             var quote:StockQuoteDTO = StockQuoteDTO(quotes[i]);
             var list: XMLList = portfolioModel.security.(Symbol==quote.symbol);
             if (list.length()!=0) {
                var row:XML = XML(list);
                row.Price = Math.round(100*quote.last)/100;
                row.Value = Math.round(row.Price * row.Quantity);
             }
     }
     }
       private function pullQuotes():void{
         setTimeout(function ():void { freshQuotes.getQuotes(); },1000);
       }

       private function showPosition(data:Object, field:String, index:Number,
                         percentValue:Number):String {
       return data.Symbol + "\n" + "Shares:" + data.Quantity + "\n" +
            "Price:" + data.Price + "\n" + "Value:" + data.Value ;
     }

       [Embed(source="images/icon_chart.png")]
    [Bindable]
       public var iconChart : Class;
    [Embed(source="images/icon_grid.png")]
    [Bindable]
    public var iconGrid : Class;

  ]]></mx:Script>
```

Listing 5.15 PortfolioView3.mxml

The toggle buttons *Show Grid/Show Chart* use images, and it's a good idea to embed these resources right into the SWF file. This way the browser can download the entire client in one HTTP request (but the size of the SWF file becomes larger). For the same reason, the multi-file Java applets are packaged into a single jar.

The next step is to move the toggle buttons up:

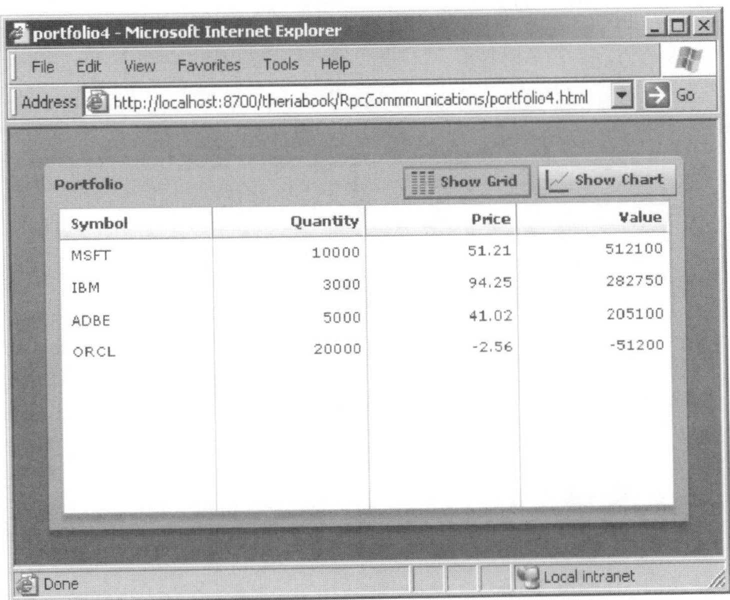

Figure 5.7 Using ViewStack for toggling

In the previous code sample, we use canvases to wrap, but now we're going wrap up the entire Portfolio Panel. Yes, the Panel will become a child of the Canvas. Here is why we need it. The Canvas is the simplest container, and it's also the absolute positioning container. In other words, if you place A and B as children of the Canvas, they overlap unless each of them has specific *x* and *y* coordinate settings. So we're planning on overlapping the ToggleButtonBar and the PortfolioPanel in a single Canvas. As an additional measure, to make the ToggleButtonBar appear on the far right, we put the ToggleButtonBar inside the HBox container. Make sure that the RemoteObject and the XML are moved out to become children of the Canvas; they have to be at the outermost level – this is an MXML requirement.

```
<?xml version="1.0" encoding="utf-8"?>
<!-- PortfolioView4.mxml -->
<mx:Canvas xmlns:mx="http://www.adobe.com/2006/mxml" width="100%" height="100%" >
   <mx:RemoteObject id="freshQuotes" destination="portfolio" fault="onFault(event)">
   <mx:method name="getQuotes" concurrency="last" result="onResult(event)" />
```

```
    </mx:RemoteObject>
    <mx:XML format="e4x" id="portfolioModel" source="portfolio.xml" />

  <mx:Panel title="Portfolio" width="100%" height="100%" creationComplete="pullQuotes();"
  >
    <mx:ViewStack id="vs" width="100%" height="100%">
    <mx:Canvas label="Show Grid" icon="{iconGrid}" >
      <mx:DataGrid id="portfolioGrid" width="100%" height="100%"
       dataProvider="{portfolioModel.security}">
        <mx:columns><mx:Array>
            <mx:DataGridColumn dataField="Symbol"/>
            <mx:DataGridColumn dataField="Quantity" textAlign="right"/>
            <mx:DataGridColumn dataField="Price" textAlign="right"/>
            <mx:DataGridColumn dataField="Value" textAlign="right"/>
        </mx:Array></mx:columns>
      </mx:DataGrid>
    </mx:Canvas>
    <mx:Canvas label="Show Chart" icon="{iconChart}" >
       <mx:PieChart id="portfolioPie" dataProvider="{portfolioModel.security}"
      showDataTips="true" width="100%" height="100%">
        <mx:series>
        <mx:Array>
          <mx:PieSeries labelPosition="callout"
            field="Value" labelFunction="showPosition"
            nameField="Symbol" explodeRadius="0.02" />
        </mx:Array>
      </mx:series>
     </mx:PieChart>
   </mx:Canvas>
  </mx:ViewStack>

  <mx:Script><![CDATA[
    import mx.rpc.events.*;
    import com.theriabook.jms.dto.StockQuoteDTO;

    [Bindable]
    private var errorText:String;
    [Bindable]
    private var errorTip:String;

    private function onResult(event:ResultEvent):void {
      errorText = "";
      errorTip = "";
      var quotes:Array = event.result as Array;
```

```
    applyQuotes(quotes);
    // Pull new quotes set
    pullQuotes();
  }

    private function onFault(event:FaultEvent):void {
       errorText = "Portfolio feed failure...";
       errorTip = "Destination:" + event.currentTarget.destination + "\n" +
        "Fault code:" + event.fault.faultCode + "\n" +
        "Detail:" + event.fault.faultDetail;
    // Pull new quotes set
       pullQuotes();
    }

  private function applyQuotes(quotes: Array):void {
     for (var i:int=0; i<quotes.length; i++) {
          var quote:StockQuoteDTO = StockQuoteDTO(quotes[i]);
          var list: XMLList = portfolioModel.security.(Symbol==quote.symbol);
          if (list.length()!=0) {
             var row:XML = XML(list);
             row.Price = Math.round(100*quote.last)/100;
             row.Value = Math.round(row.Price * row.Quantity);
          }        }
   }
     private function pullQuotes():void{
        setTimeout( function ():void {freshQuotes.getQuotes();  },1000  );
     }

   private function showPosition(data:Object, field:String, index:Number,
                        percentValue:Number):String {
     return data.Symbol + "\n" + "Shares:" + data.Quantity + "\n" +
          "Price:" + data.Price + "\n" + "Value:" + data.Value ;
  }

     [Embed(source="images/icon_chart.png")]
  [Bindable]
     public var iconChart : Class;
  [Embed(source="images/icon_grid.png")]
  [Bindable]
  public var iconGrid : Class;

  ]]></mx:Script>
</mx:Panel>
<mx:HBox horizontalAlign="right" width="100%" paddingRight="5" paddingTop="5">
```

```
    <mx:Label color="red" toolTip="{errorTip}" text="{errorText}" width="150"/>
     <mx:ToggleButtonBar dataProvider="{vs}" horizontalGap="5" />
</mx:HBox>
</mx:Canvas>
```

Listing 5.16 PortfolioView4.mxml

Dealing with Financial News

Let's set up the scene for the financial news first, and then we'll add them to the screen that we've developed so far. The first cut of our financial news screen will look like Figure 5.8. The data you see here are provided by an RSS feed. RSS stands for Real Simple Syndication and is used for presenting such data as news, blogs, or other Web content in a form of XML that contains summaries of the articles as well links to the full version of the content. We use it simply to illustrate the client/server communication via the Flex component called <mx:HTTPService>, which facilitates HTTP POST and GET requests from the Flash player to a remote URL with automatic embedding of the parameters.

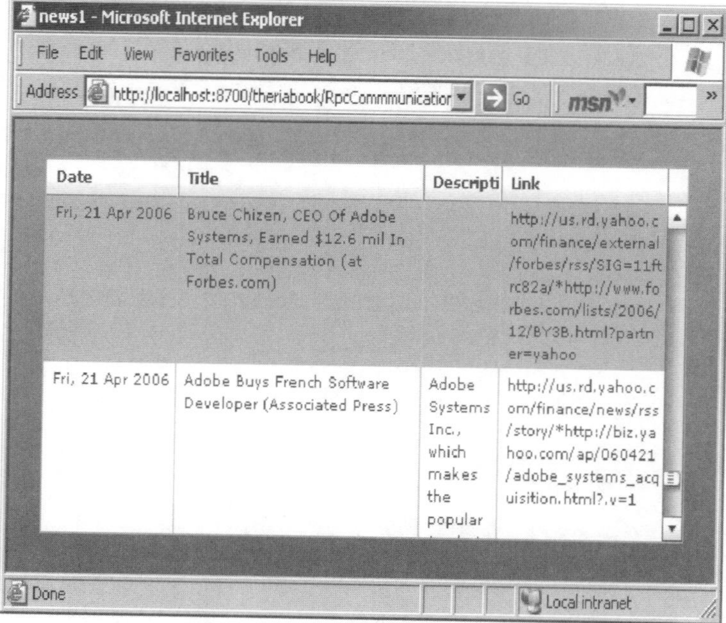

Figure 5.8 Financial news - the first cut

In particular, we'll be using the RSS news generator offered by Yahoo! Finance. Just enter the following URL in your browser: http://biz.yahoo.com/rss.html.

You should see a screen similar to the one depicted in Figure 5.9. This Web site lets you enter a stock symbol, for example, ADBE.

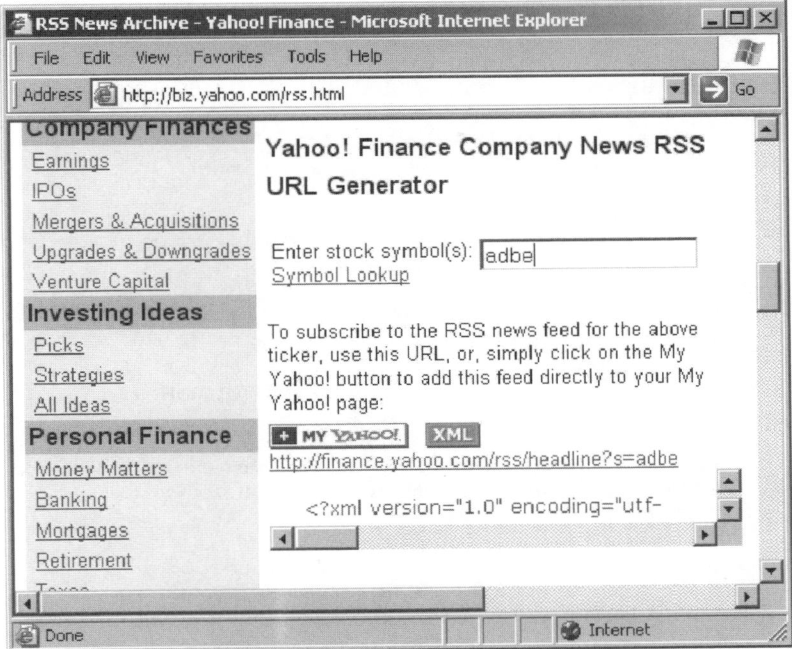

Figure 5.9 RSS news archive from Yahoo! Finance

You'll see a little orange XML button, with a new URL that looks like http://finance.yahoo.com/rss/headline?s=adbe. Just follow this link, which will bring you to the RSS XML feed withthe latest news about the symbol ADBE, as in Figure 5.10.

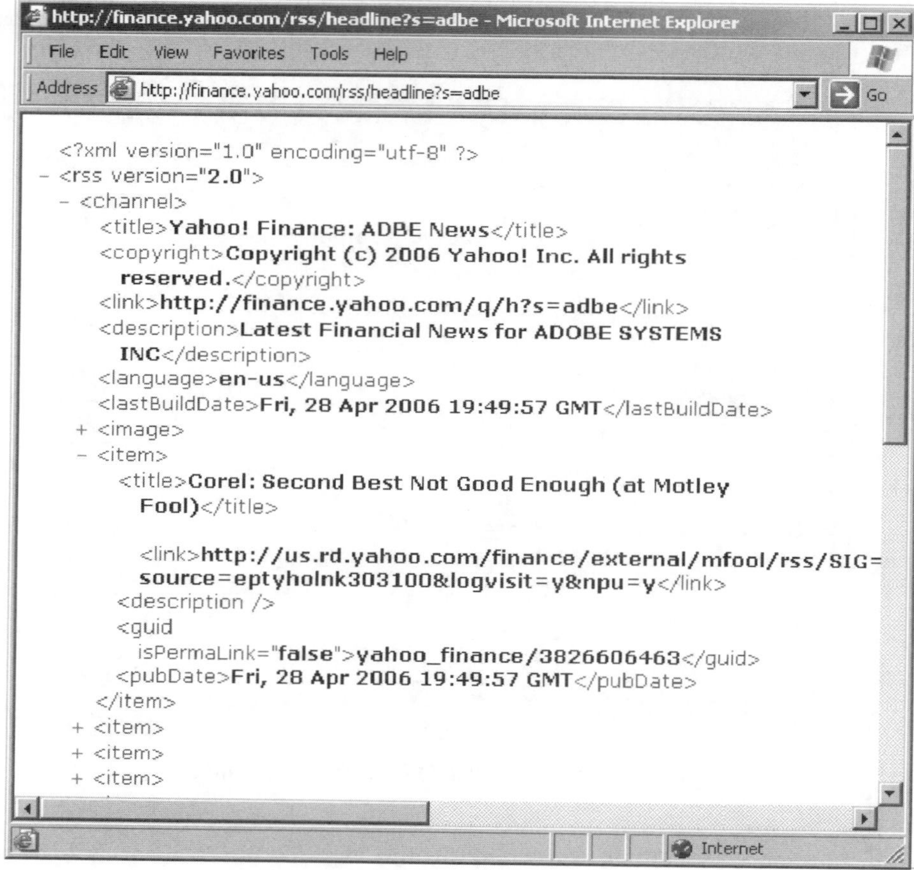

Figure 5.10 A sample RSS feed

By the end of this chapter we'll be done with programming master-detail relationships; our users will click on the row in the portfolio grid (Figure 5.7) and see the news as in Figure 5.9, then click on one of the lines in the column Link, which opens a new Web browser's window with the full news content. Let's implement this chain of actions one step at a time.

Our new MXML application will contain the following HTTPService element:

```
<mx:HTTPService id="newsFeed" useProxy="true" destination="YahooFinancialNews"
    concurrency="last" resultFormat="e4x" >
</mx:HTTPService>
```

Your client application will be loaded from some server, which is expected to have a configured *news* destination named YahooFinancialNews, or whatever name you prefer.

Configuring the Server-Side Destination and Proxy

For security reasons (similar to the Java sandbox concept), Flash clients can only access the domains they come from, unless other servers declare, explicitly or implicitly, trust to SWF files downloaded from our domain by a corresponding record in a *crossdomain.xml* file. But our portfolio SWF wasn't loaded from finance.yahoo.com, and we aren't allowed to install crossdomain.xml on the Yahoo! servers. We'll use another technique called Flex proxy. When the user clicks on the News link in the data grid, the portfolio client will connect to our FDS Web application deployed under Tomcat (JRun, WebLogic), which will proxy our communication with Yahoo!. To configure the Flex proxy service, use the following section of the proxy-config.xml located in the \WEB-INF\flex directory:

```
<destination id="YahooFinancialNews">
  <properties>
    <url>http://finance.yahoo.com/rss/headline</url>
  </properties>
</destination>
```

Listing 5.17 Configuring the proxy to access an external server

Now Flex will contact http://finance.yahoo.com, get the news for the symbol specified, and return it back to the Flash client.

Processing the News Feed

The HTTPService converts the received data according to the value of the *resultFormat* property: *e4x, flashvars, object* (this is default), *text,* or *xml.*

If we knew that the results were coming back as name/value pairs concatenated with an ampersand, we could have picked the *flashvars* format. The *text* format is suitable for any raw text, but it's not easy to parse. The XML format is maintained for compatibility with pre-E4X versions of the ActionScript, so we'll pass on this one as well. Considering the other formats listed above, for our application, we prefer e4X XML. An e4X expression *newsFeed.lastResult.channel.item* is all you need to populate the XMLListCollection with news headlines. This XMLListCollection will be used as the *dataProvider* of the news DataGrid.

As usual, we'll separate the code that merely starts the application from the FinancialNews view in Listing 5.18:

```
<?xml version="1.0" encoding="utf-8"?>
<!--news1.mxml -->
<mx:Application xmlns:mx="http://www.adobe.com/2006/mxml"  xmlns="*" >
  <FinancialNews1 id="fn"/>
</mx:Application>
```

Our *newsFeed* will initiate the following request from the *creationComplete* event:

```
newsFeed.send({s:"ADBE"});
```

As part of the send method, Flex converts the object's property into a GET URL parameter using the object's properties as parameter names. Here s:"ADBE" will be concatenated in the form of "?s=ADBE" to the http://finance.yahoo.com/rss/headline specified by the news destination. Since RSS data can be verbose, we'll set the relevant columns of the grid with *wordWrap="true"* and the height of the Grid row to be flexible: *variableRowHeight="true"*.

```
<?xml version="1.0" encoding="utf-8"?>
<!-- FinancialNews1.mxml -->
<mx:Panel xmlns:mx="http://www.adobe.com/2006/mxml"
   title="News" width="100%" height="100%" creationComplete="onCreationComplete()" >
   <mx:DataGrid id="newsGrid" width="100%" height="100%"
      dataProvider="{newsFeed.lastResult.channel.item}" variableRowHeight="true">
   <mx:columns>
      <mx:Array>
         <mx:DataGridColumn headerText="Date" dataField="pubDate" width="200"/>
         <mx:DataGridColumn headerText="Title" dataField="title" wordWrap="true" />
         <mx:DataGridColumn headerText="Description" dataField="description"
                                 wordWrap="true" />
         <mx:DataGridColumn headerText="Link" width="130" dataField="link"
                                  wordWrap="true" />
      </mx:Array>
   </mx:columns>
   </mx:DataGrid>

   <mx:HTTPService id="newsFeed" useProxy="true" destination="YahooFinancialNews"
   concurrency="last" resultFormat="e4x" fault="onFault(event)" >
   </mx:HTTPService>

   <mx:Script>
      <![CDATA[
         private function onCreationComplete():void {
            newsFeed.send({s:"ADBE"});
         }
         import mx.rpc.events.*;
         private function onFault(event:FaultEvent):void {
            mx.controls.Alert.show(
             "Destination:" + event.currentTarget.destination + "\n" +
             "Fault code:" + event.fault.faultCode + "\n" +
             "Detail:" + event.fault.faultDetail, "News feed failure"
```

```
            );
        }
    ]]>
  </mx:Script>
</mx:Panel>
```

Lising 5.18 FinancialNews1.mxml

Introducing Item Renderers

To make the data grid's column Link open a news story in a separate browser window, we need to customize the way of displaying (rendering) the cells of this column. We will use the so-called *item-Renderer* in the <mx:DataGridColumn> tag (see more samples of using item renderers in Chapters 8 and 9). There are two major kinds of item renderers:

drop-in, which is an ActionScript class that you specify as the value of the itemRenderer of any list-derived control.

inline, where you use an <mx:Component> tag to define a renderer component inside the <mx:itemRenderer> element.

To create an inline renderer, we'd need to change:

```
<mx:DataGridColumn headerText="Link" width="130" dataField="link"
wordWrap="true"/>
```

into the following code:

```
<mx:DataGridColumn headerText="Link" width="130">
 <mx:itemRenderer>
   <mx:Component>
      <mx:LinkButton label="{data.link}" click="navigateToURL(new
                      URLRequest(data.link), '_blank')"/>
   </mx:Component>
 </mx:itemRenderer>
</mx:DataGridColumn>
```

The ActionScript function flash.net.navigateToURL opens or replaces a window in the Flash Player's container application – opens it, in our case, in a blank browser.

While inline renderers excel in readability, drop-in renderers are reusable. If you expect to have links with similar presentation and functionality you may decide to create a class out of it.

Let us introduce the write-only *security* property for the FinancialView2 class. Please note that we provide a setter method to send a *newsFeed* request every time the security (stock symbol) is updated:

```
public function set security(value:String):void {
  newsFeed.send({s:value});
}
```

A bit later in this chapter, the value of the selected security will be passed to the news data grid based on the selected row in the portfolio data grid (see Figure 5.1) or the selected slice of the pie (see Figure 5.2). At this point let's remove the *creationComplete* event handler in FinancialNews and hard-code the stock symbol ADBE as a valve of *security* for the FinancialNews2 tag:

```
<?xml version="1.0" encoding="utf-8"?>
<!--news2.mxml -->
<mx:Application xmlns:mx="http://www.adobe.com/2006/mxml" xmlns="*" >
   <FinancialNews2 id="fn" security="ADBE"/>
</mx:Application>
```

Listing 5.19 An application file news2.mxml

The FinancialNews2 tag is spelled out in Listing 5.20.

```
<?xml version="1.0" encoding="utf-8"?>
<!-- FinancialNews2.mxml -->
<mx:Panel xmlns:mx="http://www.adobe.com/2006/mxml"  title="News" width="100%"
                                 height="100%" >
   <mx:DataGrid id="newsGrid" width="100%" height="100%"
      dataProvider="{newsList}" variableRowHeight="true">
   <mx:columns>
      <mx:Array>
         <mx:DataGridColumn headerText="Date" dataField="pubDate" width="200"/>
         <mx:DataGridColumn headerText="Title" dataField="title" wordWrap="true" />
         <mx:DataGridColumn headerText="Description" dataField="description"
                              wordWrap="true" />
         <mx:DataGridColumn headerText="Link" width="130">
            <mx:itemRenderer>
               <mx:Component>
                  <mx:LinkButton label="{data.link}"
              click="navigateToURL(new URLRequest(data.link), '_blank')"/>
               </mx:Component>
            </mx:itemRenderer>
         </mx:DataGridColumn>
      </mx:Array>
   </mx:columns>
   </mx:DataGrid>
```

```
<mx:XMLListCollection id="newsList" source="{newsFeed.result.channel.item}" />
<mx:HTTPService id="newsFeed" useProxy="true" destination="YahooFinancialNews"
concurrency="last" resultFormat="e4x" fault="onFault(event)" >
</mx:HTTPService>

<mx:Script>
   <![CDATA[
      import mx.rpc.events.*;
      public function set security(value:String):void {
         this.title = "News: " + value;
         newsFeed.send({s:value});
      }

      private function onFault(event:FaultEvent):void {
         mx.controls.Alert.show(
          "Destination:" + event.currentTarget.destination + "\n" +
          "Fault code:" + event.fault.faultCode + "\n" +
          "Detail:" + event.fault.faultDetail, "News feed failure"
         );
      }
   ]]>
</mx:Script>
</mx:Panel>
```

Listing 5.20 FinancialNews2.mxml

Another minor modification in Listing 5.20 is that the XML received with Yahoo! Financial news is now a source property of the <mx:XMLListCollection>. The data grid's *dataProvider* is populated from this collection. You don't have to use a collection as the middleman between the data and the GUI component, but it does become handy for customization. In particular you can apply a sort or set a filter on the collection.

Programming Master-Detail Relationships

It's time to start thinking about connecting the portfolio and news data grids, which represent typical master-detail relationships. The user selects one security in the grid or the pie, and the news data grid has to be repopulated with potentially multiple rows representing the latest financial news on selected security. Or, technically speaking, we are planning to convert the line:

```
<FinancialNews2 id="fn" security="ADBE"/>
```

from Listing 5.19 into a security bound to *portfolioView.selectedSecurity*. So in the scripting section of PorfolioView5.mxml we'll declare a bindable variable *selectedSecurity*:

```
[Bindable]
public var selectedSecurity:String;
```

The metatag [Bindable] provides an elegant two-line solution for our master-detail parameter passing. The tag PortfolioView5 will go by the ID pv, hence a simple {pv.selectedSecurity} represents the value of this bindable property:

```
<?xml version="1.0" encoding="utf-8"?>
<mx:Application xmlns:mx="http://www.adobe.com/2006/mxml"
    "xmlns="*" >
   <mx:VDividedBox width="100%" height="100%">
    <PortfolioView5 id="pv"/>
    <FinancialNews2 id="fn" security="{pv.selectedSecurity}"/>
   </mx:VDividedBox>
</mx:Application>
```

Listing 5.21 A master-details application

To be precise, the curly braces denote *binding* between the *FinancialNews2.security*, the *target* of the binding, and the *Portfolio5.selectedSecurity* as the binding *source*.

Here is the short explanation of how it works. When Flex compiles PortfolioView5.mxml with the bindable *selectedSecurity* (see Listing 5.22), it will produce code that dispatches an event on every change of that property. Then, while compiling our application, Flex will notice that *FinancialNews2.security* depends on the binding expression. But the expression, in turn, depends on the value of *PortfolioView5.selectedSecurity*, doesn't it? Accordingly, Flex will add a listener to the change event associated with *pv.selectedSecurity*. The task of this listener will be to keep the expression recalculated at every change of *PortfolioView5.selectedSecurity*. Following the same logic, Flex will keep *FinancialNews2.security* recalculated on every change of the expression. You can read more about binding in the Flex documentation.

Our application keeps the Portfolio on top of the financial news in a vertical box. To facilitate resizing between the two parts, we've used the *VDividedBox* container instead of the *VBox* because it has a divider between the parts (similar to Java Swing split panes).

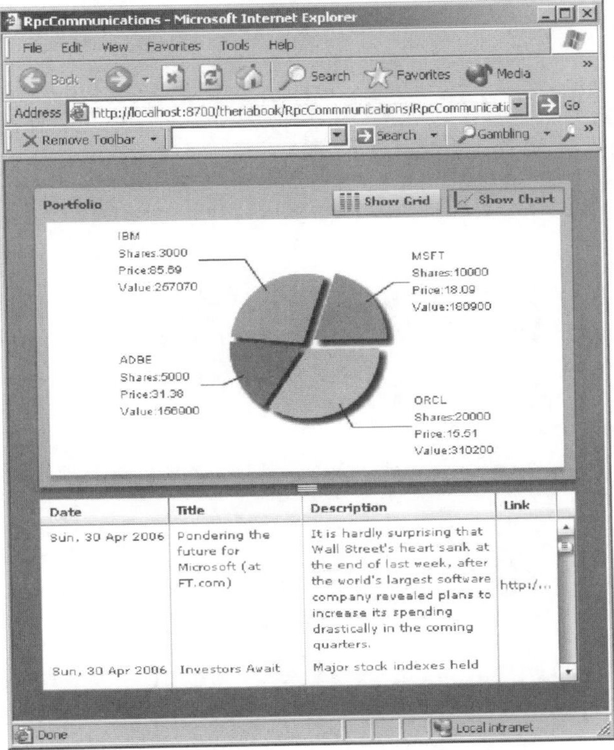

Figure 5.12 Applying the vertical box with divider VDividedBox

Each click on a wedge of the pieChart will generate an *itemClick* event (the sole parameter of this event will be of type CharItemEvent) that will include the attribute *event.hitData.item* corresponding to the selected item (an XML object) in the underlying data provider. That's why, to populate the variable *selectedSecurity* we can write:

```
<mx:PieChart id="portfolioPie" itemClick="selectedSecurity=event.hitData.item.
Symbol …"/>
```

In the case of the DataGrid, we'll be intercepting the *change* event, which is dispatched when the *selectedIndex* or *selectedItem* property changes as a result of the user's actions. Note the selectable="true" Listng 5.22. This is done to enable highlighting of the selected row.

The following fragment from PortfolioView5.mxml shows the changes/additions that we've made to PortfolioView4. A complete listing is included with the source code in the book samples.

```
<mx:Canvas xmlns:mx="http://www.adobe.com/2006/mxml" width="100%" height="100%" >
```

```
…   <mx:DataGrid id="portfolioGrid" dataProvider="{portfolioModel.security}"
    selectable="true" change="selectedSecurity=portfolioGrid.selectedItem.Symbol">
        …
     </mx:DataGrid>
     …
     <mx:PieChart id="portfolioPie" itemClick="portfolioPieOnClick(event)"
    dataProvider="{portfolioModel.security}" showDataTips="true" >
        …
     </mx:PieChart>
  …
 <mx:Script><![CDATA[
    import mx.controls.Alert;
    import mx.rpc.events.FaultEvent;

     [Bindable]
     public var selectedSecurity:String;

     import mx.charts.events.*;
     private function portfolioPieOnClick(event:ChartItemEvent):void {
        selectedSecurity=event.hitData.item.Symbol;
     }
     …
 ]]></mx:Script>
  …
</mx:Canvas>
```

Listing 5.22 Setting up selectedSecurity for binding

Finally, to add a visual effect of the selected security in the pie we will explode the clicked wedge a bit more (see Figure 5.11):

```
private function portfolioPieOnClick(event:ChartItemEvent):void {
 selectedSecurity=event.hitData.item.Symbol;
 var currentWedgeIndex:int = event.hitData.index;
 var perWedgeExplosion:Array = [];
 for (var i:int=0; i<portfolioPie.dataProvider.length; i++) {
   perWedgeExplosion[i] = (i==currentWedgeIndex)?10:2;
 }
 portfolioPie.series[0].perWedgeExplodeRadius = perWedgeExplosion;
}
```

Listing 5.23 Exploding the pie wedge

This concludes our series of Stock Portfolio applications based on Flex remoting.

Adding the JMS Feed to the Stock Portfolio

In the second part of this chapter we will reuse the POJO that we used to remote to – Portfolio.java (Listing 5.6). This time, however, we will invoke it from inside a Java program, which will publish the quotes to a topic available to the Flex application. But first, let's take a look at the Java techniques we will be relying on.

Introduction to the Java Naming and Directory Interface

The Flex applications in the second part of our chapter will be subscribing to the messages published to a certain *destination* by the JMS-based Java program; hence the Flex Data Services have to be able to find the proper destination. In the Java world, the location of the objects is facilitated by JNDI, which exposes and locates objects via their names. JNDI decouples the physical implementation of the naming services from the client API.

JNDI has one or more *contexts*, which comprise a naming tree similar to directories/sub-directories in a PC file system. The "root directory" in JNDI vocabulary is called the *initial context*. The Tomcat server that we will use in our illustration supports it own JNDI tree. So does the ActiveMQ implementation of the JMS that we will use to complement Tomcat. (When this was written ActiveMQ was available under the Apache 2.0 license at http://www.activemq.org/.)

Let's consider an example that shows how to obtain and use the appropriate naming context.

A client program JndiExample (Listing 5.10) creates an instance of the *InitialContext* class passing it hard-coded properties relevant to the specific JNDI provider. In particular, the settings of tcp://localhost:61616 as the value of *PROVIDER_URL* and *ActiveMQInitialContextFactory* as the value of the *INITIAL_CONTEXT_FACTORY* are unique to ActiveMQ. (There is an alternative technique for keeping these settings in the *jndi.properties* on the execution classpath, but it is entirely up to the JNDI provider to make use of this file.):

```
public class JndiExample {
   public static void main(String[] args) {

      Context ctx = null;
      try {
         Hashtable env = new Hashtable();
         env.put(Context.INITIAL_CONTEXT_FACTORY,
            "org.apache.activemq.jndi.ActiveMQInitialContextFactory");
         env.put(Context.PROVIDER_URL, " tcp://localhost:61616");
         env.put(Context.SECURITY_PRINCIPAL, "admin");
         env.put(Context.SECURITY_CREDENTIALS , "admin");

         ctx = new InitialContext(env);
         System.out.println("ActiveMQ initial context is obtained");
```

```
// Now you can lookup for JMS objects, i.e. topic connection factory
// TopicConnectionFactory factory = (TopicConnectionFactory)
//              ctx.lookup("jms/flex/TopicConnectionFactory");

        } catch(Excaption e){…}
    }
}
```

Listing 5.24 A sample JNDI program

In this program we assume that the ActiveMQ creates the JNDI tree and binds *TopicConnectionFactory* some time prior to the name lookup. Your program also can programmatically bind the object to the JNDI tree, provided you have enough access privileges to run the following line of code:

```
ctx.bind(someName, someObject);
```

This concludes our short introduction to JNDI, but you can find a more detailed JNDI tutorial at http://java.sun.com/products/jndi/tutorial.

Introduction to the Java Messaging Service

People are sending messages to each other via e-mail and applications can send messages to each other using Message-Oriented-Middleware (MOM). One of the major advantages of MOM is that it provides asynchronous communication between the applications. It's somewhat similar to e-mail operations – you don't have to be online when someone sends you a message – you can read it later.

JMS is the standard API to work with MOM. JMS does not transport messages. JMS-to-MOM is the same as JDBC-to-a-database management system. Java applications could use the same JMS classes with any MOM vendor.

Two Modes of Message Delivery

A program could either send a message to the queue or publish a message to the topic. The first scenario is called Point-to-Point (P2P) messaging. In this mode a message is deleted from the queue as soon as it is successfully received. The second scenario is called Publish/Subscribe (Pub/Sub) messaging. With Pub/Sub many recipients can get the same message as long as they stay subscribed to it.

In this chapter we'll use the Pub/Sub mode for publishing the stock quotes. Do we need to persist our messages so the subscribers who are not online at the moment can eventually get them? Apparently not, since it does not make sense to store the price of MSFT as of 11:53:59a.m. and show it an hour later when the subscriber decides to go online. So our subscribers (and topics) will be *non-durable*. Do we need to guarantee the successful delivery of each and every quote, given their frequency? Again, the answer is, most likely, no. So our publishing will not be *transacted*.

JMS Classes and Terms

Below are the names and a short description of the relevant JMS classes:

- **TopicPublisher**: An object that publishes messages to topics
- **TopicSubscriber**: An object that receives messages
- **Topic**: An object used to store messages in the Pub/Sub mode
- **TopicPublisher**: An object that publishes messages to a topic
- **Message**: An wrapper object that contains some data; it can be put in a queue or published to a topic

Types of Messages

Every message created by the JMS provider contains a *header*, a *body* (aka payload), and *properties*. The header contains standard message identification such as message ID, destination, etc. Properties and body are optional.

In a typical scenario, properties – name/value pairs – can be used as a "mark" to filter messages by business purpose. Accordingly, body is best suited to deliver the content. JMS offers the following message types:

- **TextMessage**: This could be any Java String (any text, CVS, XML, etc.)
- **ObjectMessage**: This could be any serializable Java object
- **BytesMessage**: An array of bytes
- **StreamMessage**: A stream of Java primitives for sequential reading
- **MapMessage**: Any key/value pair, for example, id=123
- **Message**: A message that contains the header and maybe properties, but no body

When you're configuring Flex messaging destinations specific to JMS, keep in mind that at the time of writting, Flex only supported TextMessage and ObjectMessage types.

How to Publish a Message

Programs publish messages to topics. For a given topic, multiple subscribers can get messages published in a "one-to-many" mode (as opposed to "one-to-someone" mode for a queue).

The snippet of code in Listing 5.25 illustrates the steps that will be included in our *TickerFeed* Java program: look up the topic factory, create the topic connection, session, and publisher and, finally, publish a serialized object:

```
// Lookup factory and create topic connection
TopicConnectionFactory factory = (TopicConnectionFactory) context.lookup("topicConnectio
nFactory");
Topic connection = factory.createTopicConnection();
// Create publisher session
boolean transacted = false;
```

```
pubSession = connection.createTopicSession(transacted, Session.AUTO_ACKNOWLEDGE);
// Lookup topic
Topic topic = (Topic) context.lookup("ticker");
// Create a publisher
publisher = pubSession.createPublisher(topic);

ObjectMessage message = pubSession.createObjectMessage( mySerializableObject);
publisher.publish(message);
```

Listing 5.25 A code fragment of a message publisher

How to Subscribe for a Topic

In our scenario, the Java TickerFeed program will do the publishing and the Flex application, via the mx:Consumer tag, will act as the subscriber. The code in the section, therefore, is purely educational. And yet, you may find it useful, particularly to unit-test your publisher without leaving the confines of the Java side of the wire.

Subscribers can be *durable* and *non-durable.* A durable topic subscriber gets all of the messages sent to a destination, including those sent while the consumer is inactive. A non-durable message consumer gets messages from its chosen destination only if the messages are available while the consumer is active. This mode is similar to the way the chat rooms operate – you must be online to get the messages. Please be aware that you cannot possibly create a durable subscriber on the non-durable transport. In the case of Flex, you'd have to declare your messaging destination (more on that later in this chapter) as durable.

The code snippet in Listing 5.26 creates a non-durable subscriber:

```
TopicConnectionFactory factory = (TopicConnectionFactory) context.lookup("topicConnectionFa
ctory");
TopicSession subSession = connection.createTopicSession(false,
                       Session.AUTO_ACKNOWLEDGE);

Topic topic = (Topic) ctx.lookup("ticker");
TopicSubscriber subscriber = subSession.createSubscriber(topic);
connection.start();
subscriber.setMessageListener(this);

public void onMessage(Message message) {
=  // Work with your message here
   // Cast it to your specific type, etc. ge");
}
```

Listing 5.26 A code snippet of a non-durable subscriber

Now that we've touched on the subject of JMS, let's look at the integration of JMS and native Flex messaging.

Integrating Flex and Java Messaging Services

Flex provides a Messaging Service of its own, which enables messaging between many clients via a Flex server component. Unlike JMS, Flex Messaging Services are not simply an API, but a full implementation as well. Flex Messaging Services in and of itself are completely sufficient to establish messaging between clients in your enterprise application. Flex Messaging integrates with external messaging via an adapter architecture. In particular, Flex provides a specific adapter class for JMS. This adapter acts as a middleman between the two messaging components, translating message flows from the Java destinations to Flex ones and vice versa.

An important point here is that Flex and Java have separate message destinations. The mapping between the Flex destinations and external messaging destinations has to be configured in the XML configuration file (under the default configuration scenario – *WEB-INF/flex/messaging-config.xml*). Figure 5.12 shows an integration between Flex and Java Messaging using a JMS adapter.

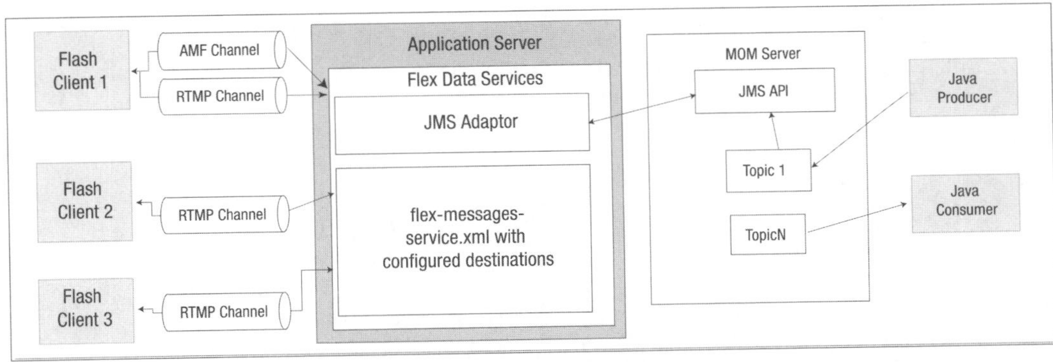

Figure 5.12 A Flex-MOM integration

Flex clients can connect to servers using different transport protocols: the Real-Time Messaging Protocol (RTMP) and the Action Message Format (AMF) that runs over HTTP (you'd need polling in the latter case). When you configure a destination in the messaging-config.xml, you can specify more than one channel and Flex will try to access the destination using the protocols in the order specified. We'd like to emphasize that Flex clients just need to know the names of the FDS destinations. They are decoupled from MOM servers and JMS names. All features of the Flex messaging are described in the Flex manual called the Flex Developer's Guide. Now we'll get back to our stock portfolio application, but this time we'll make it JMS-enabled.

Configuring Flex Messaging Destination

Let's start by configuring the topic on the Flex side. We will modify the file messaging-config.xml in

/WEB-INF/flex, and create the destination for the "ticker-topic-jms" as in Listing 5.27. Please note the difference between the destination ID "ticker-topic-jms," which will be used by the Flex client, and the *jndi-name* "ticker," which the Flex JMS adapter will use for look up in the JNDI tree. The middleman subscriber created by the Flex JMS adapter won't be durable; it's okay to lose the quote if you aren't online.

```
<?xml version="1.0" encoding="UTF-8"?>
<service id="message-service" class="flex.messaging.services.MessageService"
messageTypes="flex.messaging.messages.AsyncMessage">

 <adapters>
  <adapter-definition id="actionscript" class="flex.messaging.services.messaging.adapters.
ActionScriptAdapter" default="true" />
  <adapter-definition id="jms"
     class="flex.messaging.services.messaging.adapters.JMSAdapter"/>
  </adapters>
  <destination id="ticker-topic-jms">
    <properties>
      <server>
        <durable>false</durable>
        <durable-store-manager>flex.messaging.durability.FileStoreManager</durable-store-
        manager>
      </server>
      <jms>
        <destination-type>Topic</destination-type>
        <message-type>javax.jms.ObjectMessage</message-type>
        <connection-factory>topicConnectionFactory</connection-factory>
        <destination-jndi-name>ticker</destination-jndi-name>
        <destination-name>Ticker</destination-name>
        <durable-consumers>false</durable-consumers>
        <delivery-mode>NON_PERSISTENT</delivery-mode>
        <message-priority>DEFAULT_PRIORITY</message-priority>
        <acknowledge-mode>AUTO_ACKNOWLEDGE</acknowledge-mode>
        <transacted-sessions>false</transacted-sessions>
    <initial-context-environment>
       <property>
                    <name>java.naming.factory.initial</name>
                    <value>org.apache.activemq.jndi.ActiveMQInitialContextFactory</
                     value>
               </property>
               <property>
                    <name>java.naming.provider.url</name>
                    <value>tcp://localhost:61616</value>
               </property>
```

```
            </initial-context-environment>
        </jms>
      </properties>

      <channels>
        <channel ref="my-rtmp"/>
        <channel ref="my-polling-amf"/>
      </channels>

      <adapter ref="jms"/>

    </destination>
  </service>
```

Listing 5.27 A fragment of the flex-message-services.xml

Note the channel tags. The RTMP channel is listed first, and the AMF polling is the second option. This means the following: try the push first, but if it doesn't work (because of firewalls), start polling.

Configuring ActiveMQ JMS

There are different ways to start ActiveMQ. For purposes of this chapter it's convenient to start ActiveMQ with the same process that's running the Tomcat when the Web application starts. Accordingly, we use a Web application context listener and start the ActiveMQ broker from the *contextInitialized()* method:

```
public void contextInitialized(ServletContextEvent arg0) {
        try{
             broker.addConnector("tcp://localhost:61616?trace=true");
             broker.start();
        }catch(Exception e){
             e.printStackTrace();
             throw new RuntimeException(e);
        }
   }
```

Naturally, we have to guarantee the availability of the ActiveMQ classes on the Web application class path. To that end we dropped *activemq-4.0-M4.jar* into the *common/lib* folder off the Tomcat root. Here is the full listing of the application listener:

```
package com.theriabook.jms;
import javax.servlet.ServletContextEvent;
import javax.servlet.ServletContextListener;
import org.apache.activemq.broker.BrokerService;
```

```
public class ActiveMQBrokerListener implements ServletContextListener {

    BrokerService broker = new BrokerService();

    public void contextInitialized(ServletContextEvent arg0) {
          try{
             broker.addConnector("tcp://localhost:61616?trace=true");
             broker.start();
          }catch(Exception e){
             e.printStackTrace();
             throw new RuntimeException(e);
          }
    }

    public void contextDestroyed(ServletContextEvent arg0) {
       try{
          broker.stop();
       }catch(Exception e){
          e.printStackTrace();
          throw new RuntimeException(e);
          }
    }
}
```

Listing 5.28 Message Broker for Web application server

To register the listener with the Web application we modify the web.xml file and add the following XML snippet (according to the DTD it should go right after the filter mappings. If your app does not have a filter, the placement is right after the application context parameters):

```
<listener>
     <listener-class>com.theriabook.jms.ActiveMQBrokerListener</listener-class>
</listener>
```

Writing the TickerFeed Java Program

In our data feeding program the quotes will be published to a JMS topic, but we are still going to reuse the class Porfolio.java, which we used to pull quotes via the RemoteObject. When it comes to sending the message, we will be putting the return of the Portofolio *getQuotes()* method into the serializable QuotesHolder:

```
Portfolio port = new Portfolio();
. . . .
  StockQuoteDTO[] quotes = port.getQuotes();
```

```
QuotesHolder holder = new QuotesHolder();
```

The listing for the QuotesHolder class is below:

```
package com.theriabook.jms;
import java.io.Serializable;
import com.theriabook.jms.dto.StockQuoteDTO;

public class QuotesHolder implements Serializable{
   private static final long serialVersionUID = -8823588238987890758L;
   public StockQuoteDTO[] quotes;
}
```

Listing 5.29 The quotes wrapper QuotesHolder.java

To avoid hard-coding the JNDI properties in the TickerFeed program, we will make sure that the file *jndi.properties* as shown in Listing 5.30 belongs to the application classpath:

```
#jndi.properties for TickerFeed program running against ActiveMQ
#
java.naming.factory.initial = org.apache.activemq.jndi.ActiveMQInitialContextFactory

# use the following property to configure the default connector
java.naming.provider.url = tcp://localhost:61616

# use the following property to specify the JNDI name the connection factory
connectionFactoryNames = connectionFactory, queueConnectionFactory, topicConnectionFac-
tory

# register some topics in JNDI using the form
# topic.[jndiName] = [physicalName]
```

Listing 5.30 Content of jndi.properties for the TickerFeed program

Now we're ready to complete our TickerFeed.java program. It continuously publishes the Quotes-Holder objects to the JMS topic called "ticker." On your console you should see output similar to this one:

```
Publishing quotes...
Publishing quotes...
```

The complete code for TickerFeed.java is in Listing 5.31:

```
// TickerFeed.java
```

```
package com.theriabook.jms;

import com.theriabook.ro.Portfolio;
import java.util.*;
import javax.jms.*;
import javax.naming.*;
import com.theriabook.jms.dto.StockQuoteDTO;

public class TickerFeed {

  public static void main(String args[]) {

    TopicSession pubSession;
    TopicPublisher publisher;
    TopicConnection connection;

   try {
      // Obtain JNDI Context
      Context context = new InitialContext();

      // Lookup a JMS connection factory
      TopicConnectionFactory factory = (TopicConnectionFactory) context.lookup("topicCon
        nectionFactory");

      // Create a JMS connection
      connection = factory.createTopicConnection();

      // Create publisher session
      boolean transacted = false;
      pubSession = connection.createTopicSession(transacted, Session.AUTO_ACKNOWLEDGE);

      // or lookup a JMS topic
      Topic topic = (Topic) context.lookup("ticker");

      // Create a publisher and a subscriber
      publisher = pubSession.createPublisher(topic);

    Portfolio port = new Portfolio();
     while (true) {
        StockQuoteDTO[] quotes = port.getQuotes();
        QuotesHolder holder = new QuotesHolder();
        holder.quotes = quotes;
       Thread.sleep(1000); // just to slow down the feed
```

```
          ObjectMessage message = pubSession.createObjectMessage( holder);
          publisher.publish(message);
          System.out.println("Publishing quotes..." );
        }
      } catch (InterruptedException e) {
        e.printStackTrace();
      } catch (NamingException e) {
        e.printStackTrace();
      } catch (JMSException e) {
        e.printStackTrace();
      }
    }
  }
```

Listing 5.31 The marked datafeed – TickerFeed.java

Modifying the Flex Client to Consume Messages

The final part is to make changes to the Flex client. We will use the last version of PortfolioView from the remoting series and make the following modifications.

First, we will replace the <mx:RemoteObject> tag with the following <mx:Consumer> tag:

```
<mx:Consumer id="consumer" destination="ticker-topic-jms" message="applyQuotes(eve
nt.message.body.quotes)" />
```

This is an example of decoupling the application components. If you need to change the MOM provider, or you decide to use message queues instead of topics, no code modification is needed. Just change the destination parameter and you're set.

The second change is to actually start consuming messages. The modified *startQuotes* will look as follows:

```
private function startQuotes():void{
   consumer.subscribe();
}
```

The third and last change is in the *processFault* method, due to the differences in *mx.messaging.events.ChannelFaultEvent* instead of *mx.rpc.events.FaultEvent*:

```
private function processFault(evt:ChannelFaultEvent):void{
     errorText = "Server Error";
     errorTip = evt.faultDetail;
```

```
        startQuotes();
    }
```

In all other respects the JMS code specific to the PortfolioView is the same as in its remoting counterpart:

```
<?xml version="1.0" encoding="utf-8"?>
<!—PortflolioViewJMS.mxml ‡
<mx:Canvas xmlns:mx="http://www.adobe.com/2006/mxml" xmlns="*"
    width="100%" height="100%"  creationComplete="startQuotes();" >
<mx:XML  format="e4x" id="portfolioModel" source="portfolio.xml" />
<mx:Panel width="100%" height="100%" title="Portfolio">
  <mx:ViewStack id="vs" width="100%" height="100%">
  <mx:VBox label="Show Grid"  icon="{iconGrid}" >
  <mx:DataGrid id="portfolioGrid" width="100%" height="100%"
     dataProvider="{portfolioModel.security}"
    change="selectedSecurity = portfolioGrid.selectedItem.Symbol;">
     <mx:columns><mx:Array>
          <mx:DataGridColumn dataField="Symbol"/>
          <mx:DataGridColumn dataField="Quantity" textAlign="right"/>
          <mx:DataGridColumn dataField="Price" textAlign="right"/>
          <mx:DataGridColumn dataField="Value" textAlign="right"/>
     </mx:Array></mx:columns>
  </mx:DataGrid>
  </mx:VBox>
  <mx:HBox label="Show Chart"  icon="{iconChart}"   horizontalAlign="center" 
verticalAlign="middle">
  <mx:PieChart id="portfolioPie" dataProvider="{portfolioModel.security}" 
showDataTips="true"
     itemClick="selectedSecurity=event.hitData.item.Symbol"  height="90%">
     <mx:series><mx:Array>
               <mx:PieSeries labelPosition="callout" field="Value"   labelFunction="showP
osition" nameField="Symbol"
               explodeRadius="2"/>
          </mx:Array>
     </mx:series>
  </mx:PieChart>
  <mx:Legend  verticalAlign="middle" dataProvider="{portfolioPie}" label="{data.Sym-
bol}"/>
  </mx:HBox>
  </mx:ViewStack>
</mx:Panel>
<mx:HBox horizontalAlign="right"  width="98%" >
     <mx:Label color="red" toolTip="{errorTip}" text="{errorText}" width="100"/>
```

```
      <mx:ToggleButtonBar   dataProvider="{vs}" paddingTop="4" />
</mx:HBox>

<mx:Consumer   id="consumer"  destination="ticker-topic-jms" message="applyQuotes(event.
message.body.quotes)"
   channelFault="processFault(event)" />

   <mx:Script><![CDATA[
      import mx.controls.Alert;
         [Bindable] public var selectedSecurity:String;
         private function showPosition(data:Object, field:String, index:Number, percentVal
ue:Number):String    {
            return data.Symbol +  "\n" + "Shares:" + data.Quantity + "\n" + "Price:" +
data.Price + "\n" + "Value:" + data.Value ;
         }
         [Embed(source="./images/icon_chart.png")] [Bindable] public var iconChart :
Class;
         [Embed(source="./images/icon_grid.png")]  [Bindable] public var iconGrid :
Class;
         import com.theriabook.jms.dto.StockQuoteDTO;
         internal var row:XML;
      [Bindable]
      private var errorText:String="";
      [Bindable]
      private var errorTip:String="";
      import mx.messaging.events.ChannelFaultEvent;
      private function processFault(evt:ChannelFaultEvent):void{
         errorText = "Server Error";
         errorTip = evt.faultDetail;
         startQuotes();
      }
         private function applyQuotes(quotes: Array):void {
            errorText = "";
         errorTip = "";
            for (var i:int=0; i<quotes.length; i++) {
           var quote:StockQuoteDTO = StockQuoteDTO(quotes[i]);
           var list: XMLList = portfolioModel.security.(Symbol==quote.symbol);
           if (list.length()!=0) {
              var row:XML = XML(list);
              row.Price = Math.round(100*quote.last)/100;
              row.Value = Math.round(row.Price * row.Quantity);
           }
            }
         }
```

```
        internal var quote:StockQuoteDTO = null;
        private function startQuotes():void{
          consumer.subscribe();
        }
      ]]></mx:Script>
  </mx:Canvas>
```

Listing 5.32 The JMS-based version of PortfolioView

Summary

In this chapter we went through different ways of establishing RPC communications between Flex and Java. In particular, we've been using RemoteObject, HTTPService, and Flex JMS adapters to establish communications.

CHAPTER

6

End-to-End Rapid Application Development with Flex Data Management Services

End-to-End Rapid Application Development with Flex Data Management Services

Flex Data Management Services: Flex Remoting on Steroids

Flex Data Services include Flex Remoting and Flex Data Management Services. We have already illustrated Remoting in Chapter 5. For the purposes of this chapter, dedicated to Data Management Services, we will be referring to them as DS, omitting the "Management" part. Thus herein DS should be treated in a "narrow" context, as the counterpart of Flex Remoting and not as Flex Data Services, which encompass both components.

The simplest way to explain Data Management Services (DS) is to compare them with Remoting. Whereas Flex Remoting enables one-way requests, FDS combines one-way requests with the publish/subscribe mechanism so that besides the original result set DS sends the client live updates produced by other clients of the same destination. And there's one more dimension in which Data Services depart from Flex Remoting – support for hierarchical collections, but we won't be covering that subject in this book.

In other words, DS resolves the task of programming data collaboration: Several users may edit different rows and columns of the "same" DataGrid and see each other's changes automatically pushed by the server. Now, what if they overlap each other's work? In terms of DS that's called a conflict and the DS API provides for flexible conflict resolution, which may require the user's intervention.

A DS destination can be configured for working with the data that is persisted to a data store as well as supporting scenarios that persist the data in the server's memory. To that end, FDS provides Java and ActionScript data adapters that are responsible for reading and updating a persistent data store according to its type. In this chapter we'll focus on use cases involving Java adapters.

Flex Data Services and Automation: Problem Statement and Solution

Robust in enabling collaborative manipulation of data, DS demand a substantial development effort in case of persistent data stores. In particular, you need to build:

- A Java Data Access Object class that implements retrieve, update, delete, and insert of the data
- Java Data Transfer Objects (DTO)

- A matching ActionScript data transfer object class
- A configuration file, which registers identity columns of the result set and, optionally, argument types for every retrieval method and other parameters

We just mentioned four classes/files containing hard-coded names of the fields and there are more. To function properly, these hard-coded values have to be kept in sync, which is an additional maintenance effort whenever the data structures change.

Instead of this complexity, the main idea of this chapter is not to cover every twist of the DS API, but rather automate the development effort that DS takes for granted. We'll start with a "manual," albeit simplified, example of using DataServices. Then we'll introduce you to the methodology of complete code generation based on the pre-written XSL templates and DS-friendly XML metadata, which will be extracted from the annotated Java abstract classes.

This methodology is fully implemented in DAOFlex – an open source utility that's a complementary addition to this book. We'll gradually introduce this tool by leading you through a process of creating the most comprehensive template that generates a complete DataServices Data Access Object (DAO). Finally, we'll show you how to run and customize DAOFlex in your development environment so that writing and synchronizing routine DataServices support classes becomes a task of the Ant building tool and not yours!

A "Manual" FDS Application

Let's handcraft the application presented in Figure 6.1. This application displays a Panel with a scrollable DataGrid that we consciously did not size in the horizontal dimension, so that all columns can be viewed without shrinking. The database result set is ultimately produced by the following SQL query that will use a bound variable in place of the question mark:

```
select * from employee where start_date < ?
```

There are two buttons below the DataGrid: Fill and Commit. As the names imply, these buttons pull the original data from the database table and submit the data changes back to an DS destination. A separate *Parameters* panel permits entering parameters of the back-end method behind the *Fill* button, which, in our case, is the employee start date :

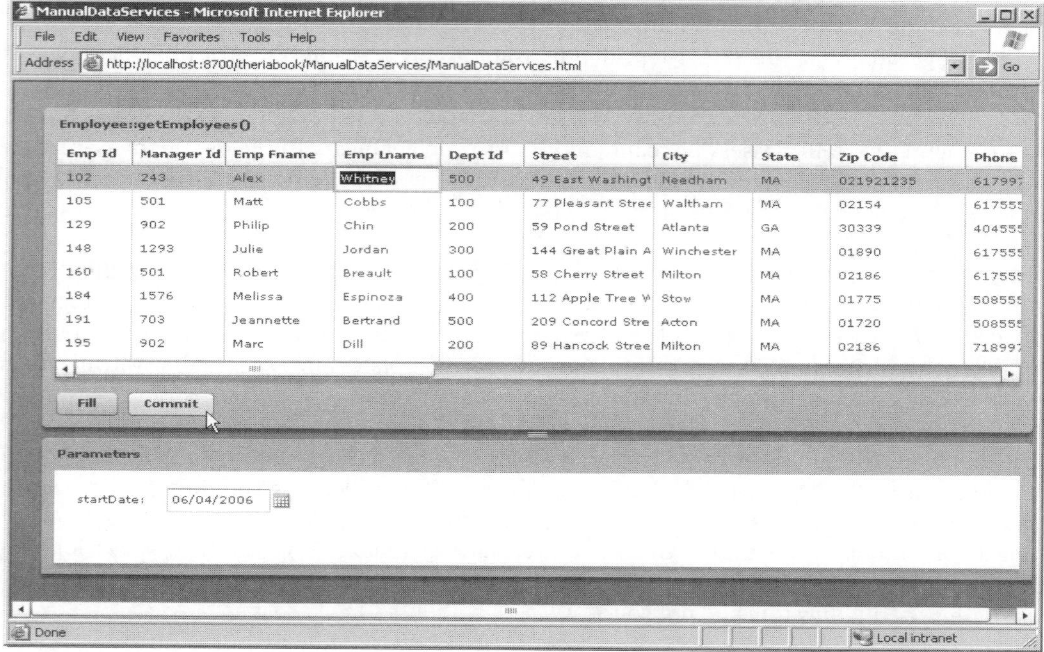

Figure 6.1 Stock portfolio screen – the show grid view

Building the Client Application

Let's build the client application first. The full listing of the application is presented in Listing 6.1. We start with defining the *mx:DataServices* object (aka ds), which points to the destination "Employee." Later, when we get to the server components, we'll discuss mapping this destination to the backing Java class:

```
<mx:DataService id="ds"   destination="Employee" fault="onFault(event)"  />
```

We provide only a rudimentary handler of the *fault* event, that's sufficient to keep us aware of any anomalies that may occur along the way. Dynamic referencing of *fault* and *faultString* properties will spare us from casting to a specific event:

```
private function onFault(evt:Event):void {
   Alert.show(evt["fault"]["faultString"], "Fault");
}
```

Then we define a handler of the application's *onCreationComplete* event, where we instantiate a collection to be eventually associated with our *mx:DataService* object and, most important, set both *autoCommit* and *autoSyncEnabled* of the ds to false:

```
private function onCreationComplete() : void {
    collection = new ArrayCollection();
    ds.autoCommit=false;
    ds.autoSyncEnabled=false;
}
```

By setting *autoCommit* to false we state that all updates have to be batched and explicitly submitted to the server as a single transaction during the ds.commit() call. By setting *autoSyncEnabled* to false we effectively protect our local instance of data from the delivery of messages caused by other clients connected to destination "Employee." Setting autoSyncEnabled to false is entirely optional, and we use it to avoid dealing with application specific conflict resolution. In particular, in the handler of the *Commit* button's click event you might uncomment the first line to support the "optimistic" way of handling the conflicts:

```
private function commit_onClick():void  {
    //ds.conflicts.acceptAllClient();  // Optimistic conflict handling, as oppose
to ds.conflicts.acceptAllServer():
    ds.commit();
}
```

Last, we have to initiate the population of the local collection with the *ds.fill()* method, which we do inside the click event handler of the button *Fill*:

```
private function fill_onClick():void {
    ds.release();
    ds.fill(collection,  param_getEmployees_startDate.selectedDate);
}
```

The scripting portion of the application is completed so let's build the UI. We create a DataGrid with the *dataProvider* bound to our collection in Listing 6.1. For brevity's sake, we didn't list all the columns here: you'll have a chance to scrutinize them in the subsequent section of this chapter. The DataGrid and ControlBar with *Fill* and *Commit* buttons are put inside a Panel, with DataGrid's title bearing the name of the destination and a specific *getEmployees* method of that destination, which will ultimately be invoked during the *ds.fill()* call. The second panel, titled *Parameters*, contains a form with a single item mx:DateField. Both panels are embraced by the VDividedBox.

We've included a linkage variable of the data transfer type to ensure that the corresponding ActionScript class (EmployeeDTO) will be linked into the generated SWF file.

```
<?xml version="1.0" encoding="UTF-8"?>
<mx:Application xmlns:mx="http://www.adobe.com/2006/mxml" backgroundColor="#FFFFFF"
creationComplete="onCreationComplete()">
    <mx:DataService id="ds"  destination="Employee" fault="onFault(event)"  />
    <mx:VDividedBox width="800" height="100%">
```

```
        <mx:Panel title="Employee::getEmployees()" width="800" height="70%">
            <mx:DataGrid id="dg" dataProvider="{collection}" editable="true" height="100%">
                <mx:columns><mx:Array>
                    <mx:DataGridColumn dataField="EMP_ID" headerText="Emp Id"  />
                    <mx:DataGridColumn dataField="MANAGER_ID" headerText="Manager Id"  />
                    <mx:DataGridColumn dataField="EMP_FNAME" headerText="Emp Fname" />
                    . . . .
                </mx:Array></mx:columns>
            </mx:DataGrid>
            <mx:ControlBar>
                <mx:Button label="Fill" click="fill_onClick()"/>
                <mx:Button label="Commit" click="commit_onClick()" enabled="{ds.commitRe
                    quired}"/>
            </mx:ControlBar>
        </mx:Panel>
        <mx:Panel title="Parameters" width="100%" height="30%">
            <mx:HBox height="100%" width="100%">
                <mx:Form label="getEmployees()">
                    <mx:FormItem label="startDate:">
                        <mx:DateField id="param_getEmployees_startDate" selectedDate="{new
                            Date()}"/>
                    </mx:FormItem>
                </mx:Form>
            </mx:HBox>
    </mx:Panel>
</mx:VDividedBox>
<mx:Script>
    <![CDATA[
    import mx.controls.Alert;
    import mx.collections.ArrayCollection;
    import com.theriabook.datasource.dto.EmployeeDTO;
    private var linkage:com.theriabook.datasource.dto.EmployeeDTO = null;
     [Bindable]
    private var collection : ArrayCollection;
    private function fill_onClick():void {
        ds.release();
        ds.fill(collection, param_getEmployees_startDate.selectedDate);
    }
    private function onCreationComplete() : void {
        collection = new ArrayCollection();
        ds.autoCommit=false;
        ds.autoSyncEnabled=false;
    }
    private function commit_onClick():void {
```

```
      ds.conflicts.acceptAllClient();
      ds.commit();
   }
   private function onFault(evt:Event):void {
      Alert.show(evt["fault"]["faultString"], "Fault");
   }

   ]]>
</mx:Script>
</mx:Application>
```

Listing 6.1 The handcrafted DataServices sample application

The application above doesn't cover all use cases of the DS API. We tried to keep it as small as possible for one reason: to enable metadata-based code generation. Ultimately, it will be entirely up to you which code you'd elect to generate by modifying the DAOFlex templates.

Finally, we present the listing of the ActionScript class EmployeeDTO that our collection uses in communicating with the Employee destination:

```
package com.theriabook.datasource.dto
{

   [Managed]
   [RemoteClass(alias="com.theriabook.datasource.dto.EmployeeDTO")]
   public dynamic class EmployeeDTO
   {

      // Properties
      public var EMP_ID : Number;
      public var MANAGER_ID : Number;
      public var EMP_FNAME : String;
      public var EMP_LNAME : String;
      public var DEPT_ID : Number;
      public var STREET : String;
      public var CITY : String;
      public var STATE : String;
      public var ZIP_CODE : String;
      public var PHONE : String;
      public var STATUS : String;
      public var SS_NUMBER : String;
      public var SALARY : Number;
      public var START_DATE : Date;
      public var TERMINATION_DATE : Date;
```

```
        public var BIRTH_DATE : Date;
        public var BENE_HEALTH_INS : String;
        public var BENE_LIFE_INS : String;
        public var BENE_DAY_CARE : String;
        public var SEX : String;

        public function EmployeeDTO() {
        }
    }  //EmployeeDTO
}
```

Listing 6.2 The ActionScript DTO class – EmployeeDTO

Creating Assembler and DTO Classes

The time has come to work on the Java side, which is a rather tedious process, so we'll gradually go top-down.

Our first stop is an Assembler class that the DS *Employee* destination should map to. As the Flex documentation suggests, you can implement the methods on your Assembler class in several ways:

- Extend flex.data.assemblers.AbstractAssembler and override the fill(), getItem(), createItem(), updateItem(), and deleteItem() methods as needed.
- Configure these methods via XML definitions against a class that doesn't extend the AbstractAssembler class.
- Combined approach, where methods defined via XML declarations are used if defined, otherwise the AbstractAssembler methods are invoked.

We'll take an XML approach that lets us declare a so-called sync-method. The XML contract of the destination's sync-method prescribes that it accepts a single parameter: a List of flex.data.ChangeObject elements. We find it convenient to control how we want to process data changes. In particular, we'd like to maintain the following order: all deletes, then all updates, and then all inserts. After all, if the user deletes a record for an employee with EMP_ID= 123 and then inserts a new record with EMP_ID=123, we certainly wouldn't want our sync-method to issue the INSERT, followed by DELETE FROM employee WHERE EMP_ID=123 during the batched DS data modifications.

Let's keep in mind that our ultimate focus is the metadata-based code generation. Should you decide to have your Assemblers as descendants of the AbstractAssembler, you'd have the liberty of modifying the corresponding DAOFlex template.

Listing 6.3 presents the complete XML describing the destination Employee. Under the default configuration scenario, this XML would go inside the <services> node of the flex-data-services.xml file, located in the WEB-INF/lib/flex folder of your Web application.

We set com.theriabook.datasource.EmployeeAssembler as the exact name of the class mapped by our destination, with the methods java.util.List getEmployees_fill(java.util.Date dt) and the List getEmployees_sync(List lst) acting as the fill and sync methods, respectively.

You'd be able to configure more than one fill-method, although all of them should operate with the same type of DTO. In the <metadata> node we specified that the EMP_ID property of the DTO has to be considered as a single key, or identity property of the elements distributed by the destination. You could use a generated Universal Unique Identifier (UUID) instead of the real data-store field in place of the identity, which is arguably more flexible, because DS didn't support updates to the identity fields when this piece was written.

Even though XML doesn't explicitly declare that the fill-method returns a List or that the sync-method takes a List, this is a part of the XML contract for Assembler classes in destinations:

```
<destination id="Employee">
  <adapter ref="java-dao"/>
<properties>
  <source>com.theriabook.datasource.EmployeeAssembler</source>
  <scope>application</scope>
  <metadata>
    <identity property="EMP_ID"/>
  </metadata>
<network>
<session-timeout>0</session-timeout>
<paging enabled="false"/>
<throttle-inbound policy="ERROR" max-frequency="500"/>
<throttle-outbound policy="ERROR" max-frequency="500"/>
</network>
<server>
  <fill-method>
  <name>getEmployees_fill</name>
  <params>java.util.Date</params>
  </fill-method>
  <sync-method>
    <name>getEmployees_sync</name>
  </sync-method>
</server>
</properties>
</destination>
```

Listing 6.3 The destination Employee for flex-data-services.xml

The structure of the EmployeeAssembler Java class is pretty straightforward. This class delegates the actual data retrieval and update of the data store to the EmployeeDataServiceDAO class, which we'll discuss next:

```
package com.theriabook.datasource;
import java.util.*;

public final class EmployeeAssembler
{
   public EmployeeAssembler()
   { }

   public final List getEmployees_fill(Date startDate) {
      return new EmployeeDataServiceDAO().getEmployees(startDate);
   }

   public final List getEmployees_sync(List items) {
      return new EmployeeDataServiceDAO().getEmployees_sync(items);
   }

}
```

Listing 6.4 EmployeeAssembler.java

Finally, here's the EmployeeDTO class that the EmployeeAssembler-based destination will be operating with. It offers a simplistic approach to UUID generation that has to be replaced by a UUID generator of your choice:

```
package com.theriabook.datasource.dto;
import java.io.Serializable;

public class EmployeeDTO implements Serializable
{
   private static final long serialVersionUID = 1L;

   public int EMP_ID;
   public int MANAGER_ID;
   public String EMP_FNAME;
   public String EMP_LNAME;
   public int DEPT_ID;
   public String STREET;
   public String CITY;
   public String STATE;
   public String ZIP_CODE;
```

```
    public String PHONE;
    public String STATUS;
    public String SS_NUMBER;
    public double SALARY;
    public java.util.Date START_DATE;
    public java.util.Date TERMINATION_DATE;
    public java.util.Date BIRTH_DATE;
    public String BENE_HEALTH_INS;
    public String BENE_LIFE_INS;
    public String BENE_DAY_CARE;
    public String SEX;
    public String DEPT_NAME;

    private String _uid;
    private static long _UID = 1L;

    public EmployeeDTO()  {
          _uid = getUUID();
    }


    public String getUid() {
       return _uid;
    }
    public void setUid(String value) {
       _uid = value;
    }
    public static synchronized String getUUID() {
       return "" + _UID++;
    }
}
```

Listing 6.5 Listing of the Java DTO class – EmployeeDTO

Implementing the Fill-Method of the DataServices Data Access Object

Our next stop is the EmployeeDataServicesDAO class, which is responsible for actual data manipulation in the data store. This section will cover its fill-method, and the sync-method will be covered next. We outsource the utility functions of getting a JDBC connection, converting values from java.util.Date to java.sql.Date and vice versa to a handful of classes from the com.theriabook.DAOFlex package, which takes less than 200 lines of source code. For brevity's sake we'll omit the listings of these classes; you can find the complete source code in the DVDD accompanying the book (look for the folder TheRiaBook/tools/DaoFlex/dist/runtime/src).

The code for the fill portion of the EmployeeDataServiceDAO is presented in Listing 6.6. By wrapping any *Throwable* into *com.theriabook.DAOFlex.DAOException*, a descendant of *RuntimeException*, we avoid unnecessary throws in both the DAO and Assembler implementation, since fatal exceptions will bubble up to the Flex framework classes and show up on the client side as a DataServices fault event. Other than that, most of this code is generic, which is precisely why it's an excellent candidate for template-based code-generation:

```
public final List /*EmployeeDTO[]*/ getEmployees(java.util.Date startDate){
   String sql = "select * from employee where start_date < ?";
   ArrayList list = new ArrayList();
   PreparedStatement stmt = null;
   ResultSet rs = null;
   Connection conn = null;
   try{
      conn = JDBCConnection.getConnection("jdbc/theriabook");
      stmt = conn.prepareStatement(sql);
      stmt.setDate(1, DateTimeConversion.toSqlDate(startDate));
      rs   = stmt.executeQuery();
      while( rs.next() )
      {
         EmployeeDTO dto = new EmployeeDTO();
         dto.EMP_ID = (rs.getInt("EMP_ID"));
         dto.MANAGER_ID = (rs.getInt("MANAGER_ID"));
         dto.EMP_FNAME = (rs.getString("EMP_FNAME"));
         dto.BIRTH_DATE = DateTimeConversion.toUtilDate(rs.getDate("BIRTH_DATE"));
         . . . . . . . . .
         list.add(dto);
      }
      return list;

   } catch(Throwable te) {
      te.printStackTrace();
      throw new DAOException(te);
   } finally {
      try {rs.close(); rs = null;} catch (Exception e){//your error logging code goes
         here}
      try {stmt.close(); stmt = null;} catch (Exception e){ //your error logging code
         goes here }
      JDBCConnection.releaseConnection(conn);
   }
}
```

Listing 6.6 Fill-method of the EmployeeDataServiceDao

Implementing the Sync-Method of FDS Data Access Object

By definition, the sync-method gets a List of *flex.data.ChangeObject* elements as an argument. A single ChangeObject can carry the information in an updated original record or, alternatively, a record that is supposed to be deleted or inserted. Since we want to process all changes as a single unit of work, we'll iterate over the List three times: on the first pass we'll pick and execute all deletes, then we'll proceed to all updates, and finally we perform all inserts. This logic is presented in Listing 6.7. Similar to the implementation of the *getEmployees()* above, our *getEmployees_sync()* throws only *RuntimeExceptions*:

```
public final List getEmployees_sync(List items)
{
  Connection conn = null;
    ChangeObject co = null;
  try  {
    conn = JDBCConnection.getConnection("jdbc/theriabook");
    Iterator iterator = items.iterator();
    while (iterator.hasNext() ) {  // Do all deletes first
      co = (ChangeObject)iterator.next();
      if(co.isDelete()) doDelete_getEmployees(conn, co);
    }
    iterator = items.iterator();
    while (iterator.hasNext()) {   // Perform  updates
      co = (ChangeObject)iterator.next();
      if(co.isUpdate()) doUpdate_getEmployees(conn, co);
    }
    iterator = items.iterator();
    while (iterator.hasNext()) {   // Finish with inserts
      co = (ChangeObject)iterator.next();
      if (co.isCreate()) doCreate_getEmployees(conn, co);
    }
  } catch(DataSyncException dse) {
    dse.printStackTrace();
    throw dse;
  } catch(Throwable te) {
    te.printStackTrace();
    throw new DAOException(te.getMessage(), te);
  } finally {
    if( conn!=null ) JDBCConnection.releaseConnection(conn);
  }
  return items;
}
```

Listing 6.7 Sync-method of the EmployeeDataServiceDao

The next topic is the methods *doUpdate…()*, *doDelete…()* and *doInsert…()*.

Implementing Update, Delete and Insert Methods

Let's start with *doUpdate_getEmployees()*. Ultimately, we have to dynamically build a JDBC SQL string for the PreparedStatement. As an example, given a change of salary, phone number, and insurance coverage, we need to build a string UPDATE EMPLOYEE SET SALARY=?, PHONE=?, BENE_HEALTH_INS=? WHERE EMP_ID=?. After that, we have to execute a preparedStatement.setXXX() for all parameters to substitute the question marks.

Conveniently, the creators of DS enabled the ChangedObject to return an array of all property names that underwent modification, which lets us build a SET clause by iterating over the array returned by the co.getChangedPropertyNames():

```
StringBuffer sql = new StringBuffer("UPDATE EMPLOYEE SET ");
String [] names = co.getChangedPropertyNames();
for (int ii=0; ii < names.length; ii++) {
   sql.append((ii!=0?", ":"") + names[ii] +" = ? ");
}
```

Now let's set the values for all the modified fields. Here we'll take advantage of another function of the ChangeObject – *getChangedValues()*. This method returns a map of the new values and based on this map and the array names we can execute relevant setXXX() methods against our prepared statement:

```
Map values = co.getChangedValues();
int ii=0;
for (ii=0; ii < names.length; ii++) {
   stmt.setObject( ii+1,  values.get(names[ii]));
}
ii++;
```

To set the value of the WHERE clause-based parameter EMP_ID, we'll use another ChangeObject's method – getPreviousVersion(), which returns a copy of the old DTO:

```
stmt.setObject(ii++, co.getPreviousValue("EMP_ID"));
```

The complete listing of *doUpdate_getEmployees()* is presented in Listing 6.8:

```
   private void doUpdate_getEmployees(Connection conn, ChangeObject co) throws SQLExcep-
tion{
      PreparedStatement stmt = null;
      try {
         StringBuffer sql = new StringBuffer("UPDATE EMPLOYEE SET ");
         String [] names = co.getChangedPropertyNames();
```

```
        for (int ii=0; ii < names.length; ii++) {
           sql.append((ii!=0?", ":"") + names[ii] +" = ? ");
        }
        sql.append( " WHERE (EMP_ID=?)" );
        stmt = conn.prepareStatement(sql.toString());

        Map values = co.getChangedValues();
        int ii=0;
        for (ii=0; ii < names.length; ii++) {
           stmt.setObject( ii+1,  values.get(names[ii]));
        }
        ii++;

        stmt.setObject(ii++, co.getPreviousValue("EMP_ID"));


        if (stmt.executeUpdate()==0) throw new DataSyncException(co);
     } finally {
        try { if( stmt!=null) stmt.close(); stmt = null;} catch (Exception e){}
     }
  }
```

Listing 6.8 Update section of the sync-method of EmployeeDataServiceDao

The implementation of the *doDelete_getEmployees()* is trivial and is presented in Listing 6.9:

```
   private void doDelete_getEmployees(Connection conn, ChangeObject co) throws SQLExcep-
tion{
      PreparedStatement stmt = null;
      try {
         StringBuffer sql = new StringBuffer("DELETE FROM EMPLOYEE WHERE (EMP_ID=?)");
         stmt = conn.prepareStatement(sql.toString());

         EmployeeDTO item = (EmployeeDTO) co.getPreviousVersion();
         stmt.setInt(1, item.EMP_ID);

         if (stmt.executeUpdate()==0) throw new DataSyncException(co);
      } finally {
         try { if( stmt!=null) stmt.close(); stmt = null;
         } catch (Exception e){// error processing goes here}
      }
   }
```

Listing 6.9 The Delete section of the sync-method of the EmployeeDataServiceDao

Implementation of the *doCreate_getEmployees()*, in turn, is based on the ChangeObject's method getNewVersion(), which returns the copy of the new DTO:

```
EmployeeDTO item = (EmployeeDTO) co.getNewVersion();
```

Please note how we rely on Double.isNaN() to distinguish nulls from non-nulls (the alternative and, arguably, more reliable approach applicable to all nullable types would be to supply explicit null indicators as part of the DTO from ActionScript to Java and vice versa):

```
if (Double.isNaN(item.SALARY))
   stmt.setNull(13,Types.DOUBLE);
else
   stmt.setDouble(13, item.SALARY);
```

The abbreviated listing of *doCreate_getEmployees()* is presented in Listing 6.10:

```
   private ChangeObject doCreate_getEmployees(Connection conn, ChangeObject co) throws
SQLException{
      PreparedStatement stmt = null;
      try {
         String sql = "INSERT INTO EMPLOYEE " +
         "(EMP_ID,MANAGER_ID,EMP_FNAME,EMP_LNAME,DEPT_ID,STREET,CITY,STATE,ZIP_
CODE,PHONE,STATUS,SS_NUMBER,SALARY,START_DATE,TERMINATION_DATE,BIRTH_DATE,BENE_HEALTH_
INS,BENE_LIFE_INS,BENE_DAY_CARE,SEX)"+
         " values (?,?,?,?,?,?,?,?,?,?,?,?,?,?,?,?,?,?,?,?)";

         stmt = conn.prepareStatement(sql);

         EmployeeDTO item = (EmployeeDTO) co.getNewVersion();

         stmt.setInt(1, item.EMP_ID);
         .  .  .  .
         stmt.setString(12, item.SS_NUMBER);
         if (Double.isNaN(item.SALARY))
            stmt.setNull(13,Types.DOUBLE);
         else
            stmt.setDouble(13, item.SALARY);
         stmt.setDate(14, DateTimeConversion.toSqlDate(item.START_DATE));
         .  .  .  .
         if (stmt.executeUpdate()==0) throw new DAOException("Failed inserting.");
         co.setNewVersion(item);
         return co;
      } finally {
         try { if( stmt!=null) stmt.close(); stmt = null;} catch (Exception e){}
```

```
    }
  }
```

Listing 6.10 The "Insert" section of the sync-method of the EmployeeDataServiceDao

And this concludes the handcrafting of our DataServices-based example. Now that we've been through the whole process, let's see how it could have been avoided and automated.

Introducing Metadata

Let's look at the snippet from the XML file generated by the DAOFlex utility – Employee.xml. Please note the name of the Java package – *com.theriabook.datasource*, the name of the Assembler's fill-method – *getEmployees()*, names on the transferring structures on the Java and ActionsScript side, both pointing to the array of *com.theriabook.dto.EmployeeDTO* objects, the name of the connection pool – *jdbc/theriabook*, and the name of the method's parameter – *startDate*:

```
<?xml version="1.0" encoding="UTF-8"?>
<WEBSERVICE NAME="Employee" PACKAGE="com.theriabook.datasource" TYPE="DAOFlex" >
  <SERVER LANGUAGE="Java" MODE="JEE">
    <SQL ACTION="SELECT"
      NAME="getEmployees" POOL="jdbc/theriabook" SCOPE="public"
      ASTYPE="com.theriabook.dto.EmployeeDTO[]" JAVATYPE="com.theriabook.dto.
EmployeeDTO[]"
    >
      <PARAM IN="Y" INDEX="1" JAVATYPE="Date" NAME="startDate"/>
    </SQL>
  </SERVER>
</WEBSERVICE>
```

Starting at this point, we'll be working our way through this XML while building the complete XSL stylesheet from scratch. Once we make this stylesheet, it'll manufacture any DataServiceEmployeeDAO, DataServiceDepartmentDAO, etc. – as long as we have the metadata XMLs like the above one. You're probably wondering at this point: "What's the input of the DAOFlex that lets it generate this XML?"

The input for DAOFlex is an annotated Java class, like the one presented in Listing 6.11:

```
package com.theriabook.datasource;

import java.util.Date;
import java.util.List;

/**
 * @DAOFlex:webservice   pool=jdbc/theriabook
```

```
 */

public abstract class Employee {
      /**
      * @DAOFlex:sql
      *  sql=select * from employee where start_date < :startDate or start_date=:start-
Date
      *  transferType=com.theriabook.dto.EmployeeDTO[]
      *  updateTable=employee
      *  keyColumns=emp_id
      */
      public abstract List getEmployees(Date startDate);
}
```

Listing 6.11 Source of the DAOFlex code-generation process – An annotated Java class

Introducing Templates

Let's put out our first iteration of the SimpleDataServiceDao.xsl stylesheet, which will eventually automatically build DataServiceDao objects for us. We assume that the reader is familiar with XSL basics, but if you haven't had a chance to use XSL yet, here's a good place to start: http://www.w3schools.com/xsl/.

We'll be using XSL transformations to produce not an XML, but a plain text (Java code), so let's start our stylesheet as follows:

```
<?xml version="1.0"?>
<xsl:stylesheet
  version="1.0"
  xmlns:xsl="http://www.w3.org/1999/XSL/Transform"
>
<xsl:output omit-xml-declaration="yes" method="text"/>
….
</xsl:stylesheet>
```

For the topmost element in our metadata (WEBSERVICE) we'll print out the value of the package, required utility imports, declaration of the class, and its constructor (Listing 6.12):

```
<xsl:template match="/WEBSERVICE">
/* Generated by SimpleDataServiceDao.xsl */
package <xsl:value-of select="@PACKAGE"/>;

import java.util.*;
import java.sql.*;
import flex.data.*;
```

```
import com.theriabook.DAOFlex.JDBCConnection;
import com.theriabook.DAOFlex.DAOException;
import com.theriabook.DAOFlex.DateTimeConversion;

public final class <xsl:value-of select="@NAME"/>SimpleDataServiceDAO  extends <xsl:
value-of select="@NAME"/>
{
   public <xsl:value-of select="@NAME"/>SimpleDataServiceDAO()
   {
   }
<xsl:apply-templates select="SERVER[@MODE='JEE']/SQL"/>
} //<xsl:value-of select="@NAME"/>SimpleDataServiceDAO

</xsl:template>
```

Listing 6.12. The first cut of the SimpleDataServiceDao.xsl

We'll discuss the <xsl:apply-templates select="SERVER[MODE='JEE']/SQL"/> a bit later. For now, let's look at the output that we'd get if we applied the stylesheet to the Employee.XML:

```
/* Generated by SimpleDataServiceDao.xsl */
package com.theriabook.datasource;

import java.util.*;
import flex.data.*;
import java.sql.*;
import com.theriabook.DAOFlex.JDBCConnection;
import com.theriabook.DAOFlex.DAOException;
import com.theriabook.DAOFlex.DateTimeConversion;

public final class EmployeeDataServiceDAO  extends Employee
{
   public EmployeeDataServiceDAO()
   {
   }

} //EmployeeDataServiceDAO
```

Listing 6.13 The output of the transformation per the SimpleDataServiceDao.xsl

The tag <xsl:apply-templates .../> from Listing 6.11 effectively delegates the processing of all nodes that can be located relative to the WEBSERVICE via the XPath expression "SERVER[MODE='JEE']/SQL" to a template that matches "SQL." Before adding such a template, let's look a bit deeper at the Employee.xml metadata file.

Metadata for Input Parameters

A closer look at the metadata produced by the DAOFlex utility against the source file Employee.java from Listing 6.10 will reveal two sections with SQL. The first one – WEBSERVICE/SERVICE/SQL/BODY – contains the SQL in its source form, while the other – WEBSERVICE/SERVICE/SQL/BODY/COMPILED – contains the same SQL in a form applicable for the JDBC PreparedStatement. The COMPILED section also contains the result of the matching of the original parameters against the JDBC question mark placeholders:

```
<?xml version="1.0" encoding="UTF-8"?>
<WEBSERVICE NAME="Employee" PACKAGE="com.theriabook.datasource" TYPE="DAOFlex"  VER-
SION="2.0">
   <SERVER LANGUAGE="Java" MODE="JEE">
      <SQL ACTION="SELECT"
         NAME="getEmployees" POOL="jdbc/theriabook" SCOPE="public"
         ASTYPE="com.theriabook.dto.EmployeeDTO[]" JAVATYPE="com.theriabook.dto.Employ-
eeDTO[]"
      >
         <PARAM IN="Y" INDEX="1" JAVATYPE="Date" NAME="startDate"/>
<BODY >
   <![CDATA[ select * from employee where start_date < :startDate or start_date=:start-
Date  ]]>
  </BODY>
<COMPILED>
   <PARAM IN="Y" INDEX="1" JAVATYPE="Date" NAME="startDate" />
    <PARAM IN="Y" INDEX="2" JAVATYPE="Date" NAME="startDate" />
   <BODY>
      <![CDATA[ select * from employee where start_date < ? or start_date=?  ]]>
     </BODY>
 </COMPILED>
      </SQL>
   </SERVER>
</WEBSERVICE>
```

Listing 6.14 A second look at the Employee.xml metadata with input parameters

Templates for Implementing the Fill Method

Let's modify the stylesheet to generate the *fill-method* by adding the template matching the SQL context. The abbreviated form of this template is presented further down in Listing 6.16. First have a look at the code that this template generates:

```
   public final List /*com.theriabook.datasource.dto.EmployeeDTO[]*/ getEmployees(java.
util.Date startDate)
   {
```

```
    String sql = "select * from employee where start_date < ? or start_date=?";
    ArrayList list = new ArrayList();
    PreparedStatement stmt = null;
    ResultSet rs = null;
    Connection conn = null;
    try  {
       conn = JDBCConnection.getConnection("jdbc/theriabook");
       stmt = conn.prepareStatement(sql);
       // ....

       }
       return list;
    } catch(Throwable te) {
       te.printStackTrace();
       throw new DAOException(te);
    } finally
    {
       try {rs.close(); rs = null;} catch (Exception e){// log your errors here}
       try {stmt.close(); stmt = null;} catch (Exception e){ // log your errors here }
       JDBCConnection.releaseConnection(conn);
    }
  }
```

Listing 6.15 The output of the <xsl:template match="SQL"/> against Employee.xml

Listing 6.16 presents a template that generates the code above. Please note that this template in turn delegates the processing of the input parameters to the named template *declareFillParameters* as seen in Listing 6.17. The template is abbreviated and we'll be looking at what's hidden behind the commented ellipses "//..." in the next section of the chapter:

```
<xsl:template match="SQL">
   public final List /*<xsl:value-of select="@JAVATYPE"/>*/ <xsl:value-of select="@NAME"/
>(<xsl:call-template name="declareFillParameters"/>
      String sql = "<xsl:value-of select="COMPILED/BODY"/>";
   public final List /*<xsl:value-of select="@JAVATYPE"/>*/ <xsl:value-of select="@NAME"/
>(<xsl:call-template name="declareFillParameters"/>)
   {
      String sql = "<xsl:value-of select="COMPILED/BODY"/>";
      ArrayList list = new ArrayList();
      PreparedStatement stmt = null;
      ResultSet rs = null;
      Connection conn = null;
      try  {
         conn = JDBCConnection.getConnection("<xsl:value-of select="@POOL"/>");
```

```
            stmt = conn.prepareStatement(sql);
            // . . . .
            return list;
        } catch(Throwable te) {
            te.printStackTrace();
            throw new DAOException(te);
        } finally
        {
            try {rs.close(); rs = null;} catch (Exception e){ // log your errors here }
            try {stmt.close(); stmt = null;} catch (Exception e){ // log your errors here }
            JDBCConnection.releaseConnection(conn);
        }
    }
</xsl:template>
```

Listing 6.16 This template generates the fill method for each SQL context

Here is the auxiliary template that helped us generate a declaration of parameters for the fill-method. It puts a comma after each parameter, except the latest and narrows the definition of the *Date* to *java.util.Date* to avoid ambiguity between java.sql and java.util packages imported at the beginning of the class:

```
<xsl:template name="declareFillParameters">
    <xsl:for-each select="PARAM[@IN='Y']">
        <xsl:if test="position()!=1">, </xsl:if>
        <xsl:choose>
            <xsl:when test="@JAVATYPE='Date'">java.util.Date</xsl:when>
            <xsl:otherwise><xsl:value-of select="@JAVATYPE"/></xsl:otherwise>
        </xsl:choose>
        <xsl:text> </xsl:text>
        <xsl:value-of select="@NAME"/>
    </xsl:for-each>
</xsl:template>
```

Listing 6.17 The template declareFillParameters, used by <xsl:template match="SQL"/>

Completing the Fill Method

Let's upgrade our stylesheet to a state where it can generate a fully functional fill-method. In the case of the *Employee.xml* metadata, we'd like to see our template generate the code presented in Listing 6.18:

```
    public final List /*com.theriabook.datasource.dto.EmployeeDTO[]*/ getEmployees(java.
util.Date startDate)
```

```
{
  String sql = "select * from employee where start_date < ? or start_date=?";
  ArrayList list = new ArrayList();
  PreparedStatement stmt = null;
  ResultSet rs = null;
  Connection conn = null;
  try  {
    conn = JDBCConnection.getConnection("jdbc/theriabook");
    stmt = conn.prepareStatement(sql);


    stmt.setDate(1, DateTimeConversion.toSqlDate(startDate));
    stmt.setDate(2, DateTimeConversion.toSqlDate(startDate));

    rs   = stmt.executeQuery();
    while( rs.next() ) {
      com.theriabook.datasource.dto.EmployeeDTO dto = new com.theriabook.data
                source.dto.EmployeeDTO();
      dto.EMP_ID = (rs.getInt("EMP_ID"));
      dto.MANAGER_ID = (rs.getInt("MANAGER_ID"));
      dto.EMP_FNAME = (rs.getString("EMP_FNAME"));
      dto.EMP_LNAME = (rs.getString("EMP_LNAME"));
      dto.DEPT_ID = (rs.getInt("DEPT_ID"));
      dto.STREET = (rs.getString("STREET"));
      dto.CITY = (rs.getString("CITY"));
      dto.STATE = (rs.getString("STATE"));
      dto.ZIP_CODE = (rs.getString("ZIP_CODE"));
      dto.PHONE = (rs.getString("PHONE"));
      dto.STATUS = (rs.getString("STATUS"));
      dto.SS_NUMBER = (rs.getString("SS_NUMBER"));
      dto.SALARY = (rs.getDouble("SALARY"));
      dto.START_DATE = DateTimeConversion.toUtilDate(rs.getDate("START_DATE"));
      dto.TERMINATION_DATE = DateTimeConversion.toUtilDate(rs.getDate("TERMINATION_
            DATE"));
      dto.BIRTH_DATE = DateTimeConversion.toUtilDate(rs.getDate("BIRTH_DATE"));
      dto.BENE_HEALTH_INS = (rs.getString("BENE_HEALTH_INS"));
      dto.BENE_LIFE_INS = (rs.getString("BENE_LIFE_INS"));
      dto.BENE_DAY_CARE = (rs.getString("BENE_DAY_CARE"));
      dto.SEX = (rs.getString("SEX"));

      list.add(dto);
    }
    return list;
  } catch(Throwable te) {
```

```
            te.printStackTrace();
            throw new DAOException(te);
        } finally {
            try {rs.close(); rs = null;} catch (Exception e){}
            try {stmt.close(); stmt = null;} catch (Exception e){}
            JDBCConnection.releaseConnection(conn);
        }
    }
```

Listing 6.18 Complete fill-method getEmployees() generated by SimpleDataServiceDao.xsl

To "teach" our stylesheet to produce this code, we'll replace the try clause generated by the *<template match="SQL">* currently containing:

```
    try  {
       conn = JDBCConnection.getConnection("<xsl:value-of select="@POOL"/>");
       stmt = conn.prepareStatement(sql);
       // .   .   .   .
       return list;
    }
```

with the following:

```
    try  {
       conn = JDBCConnection.getConnection("<xsl:value-of select="@POOL"/>");
       stmt = conn.prepareStatement(sql);

       <xsl:call-template name="setParameters"/>

       rs   = stmt.executeQuery();
       while( rs.next() ) {
          <xsl:variable name="itemType" select="substring(string(@JAVA
TYPE), 1, string-length(string(@JAVATYPE))-2)"/>            <xsl:value-of
select="$itemType"/> dto = new <xsl:value-of select="$itemType"/>();
          <xsl:call-template name="readRecord"/>
          list.add(dto);
       }
       return list;
    }
```

As you can see, we've delegated the work of calling the setXXX() methods to the named template *setParameters* and reading of the result set – to the named template *readRecord*. Let's walk through these templates one at a time.

Setting JDBC Statement Parameters

While setting the input arguments of the prepared statement, we'll have to convert the Java types of the parameters listed in the COMPILED node into JDBC types. In particular, we have to convert the Date in our use case to *java.sql.Date* to accommodate the following lines:

```
stmt.setDate(1, DateTimeConversion.toSqlDate(startDate));
stmt.setDate(2, DateTimeConversion.toSqlDate(startDate));
```

We've centralized this and similar conversions under the named template *convertJavaArgument-ToJDBC*:

```
<xsl:template name="convertJavaArgumentToJDBC">
  <xsl:choose>
    <xsl:when test="@JAVATYPE='Date'">DateTimeConversion.toSqlDate(<xsl:value-of
select="@NAME"/>)</xsl:when>
    <xsl:when test="@JAVATYPE='Time'">DateTimeConversion.toSqlTime(<xsl:value-of
select="@NAME"/>)</xsl:when>
    <xsl:otherwise>
      <xsl:value-of select="@NAME"/>
    </xsl:otherwise>
  </xsl:choose>
</xsl:template>
```

After taking care of the Java-to-JDBC conversion, the template *setParameters* becomes easy:

```
<xsl:template name="setParameters">
  <xsl:for-each select="COMPILED/PARAM[@IN='Y']">
      stmt.set<xsl:value-of select="@JAVATYPE"/>(<xsl:value-of select="@INDEX"/>,
<xsl:call-template name="convertJavaArgumentToJDBC"/>);</xsl:for-each>
</xsl:template>
```

Reading the Result Set Record

Reading the result set record would require another look at the metadata. For each SQL annotated method, the DAOFlex utility generates a description of the result set. To do that, DAOFlex connects to the target database during the generation of the metadata. Connection credentials are expected in the properties file named exactly as the JNDI data source name, and our file is called *theriabook.properties* and is located in the *jdbc* folder[1]. Here is the snippet of metadata that represents the description of the result set associated with the *getEmployees()* method :

```
<SQL … NAME="getEmployees" . . .>
<DATASET>
  <FIELDS>
  <FIELD key="yes" name="EMP_ID" precision="11" scale="0" tableName="employee"
```

```
type="integer" updatable="yes" />
  <FIELD name="MANAGER_ID" precision="11" scale="0" tableName="employee" type="integer"
updatable="yes" />
  <FIELD name="EMP_FNAME" precision="20" scale="0" tableName="employee" type="char"
updatable="yes" />
  <FIELD name="EMP_LNAME" precision="20" scale="0" tableName="employee" type="char"
updatable="yes" />
  <FIELD name="DEPT_ID" precision="11" scale="0" tableName="employee" type="integer"
updatable="yes" />
  <FIELD name="STREET" precision="40" scale="0" tableName="employee" type="char"
updatable="yes" />
  <FIELD name="CITY" precision="20" scale="0" tableName="employee" type="char"
updatable="yes" />
  <FIELD name="STATE" precision="4" scale="0" tableName="employee" type="char"
updatable="yes" />
  <FIELD name="ZIP_CODE" precision="9" scale="0" tableName="employee" type="char"
updatable="yes" />
  <FIELD name="PHONE" precision="10" scale="0" tableName="employee" type="char"
updatable="yes" />
  <FIELD name="STATUS" precision="1" scale="0" tableName="employee" type="char"
updatable="yes" />
  <FIELD name="SS_NUMBER" precision="11" scale="0" tableName="employee" type="char"
updatable="yes" />
  <FIELD name="SALARY" precision="20" scale="3" tableName="employee" type="decimal"
updatable="yes" />
  <FIELD name="START_DATE" precision="10" scale="0" tableName="employee" type="date"
updatable="yes" />
  <FIELD name="TERMINATION_DATE" precision="10" scale="0" tableName="employee"
type="date" updatable="yes" />
  <FIELD name="BIRTH_DATE" precision="10" scale="0" tableName="employee" type="date"
updatable="yes" />
  <FIELD name="BENE_HEALTH_INS" precision="1" scale="0" tableName="employee" type="char"
updatable="yes" />
  <FIELD name="BENE_LIFE_INS" precision="1" scale="0" tableName="employee" type="char"
updatable="yes" />
  <FIELD name="BENE_DAY_CARE" precision="1" scale="0" tableName="employee" type="char"
updatable="yes" />
  <FIELD name="SEX" precision="1" scale="0" tableName="employee" type="char"
updatable="yes" />
  </FIELDS>
  </DATASET>
</SQL>
```

Listing 6.19 The description of the result set produced by DAOFlex

There is one more point to make before we can look at the implementation of the *readRecord* template. The data types per DATASET/FIELDS/FIELD nodes are database-specific types, not JDBC ones. For example, we have to apply additional mapping to produce *getString()* for the *char* database columns and *getDouble()* for the *decimal* ones. This mapping is provided by the named template *mapDBtoJDBC* (you may need to tweak it a bit for your DBMS):

```
<xsl:template name=" mapDBtoJDBC">
<xsl:choose>
<xsl:when test="@type='boolean'">Boolean</xsl:when>
<xsl:when test="@type ='byte'">Byte</xsl:when>
<xsl:when test="@type ='byte[]'">Bytes</xsl:when>
<xsl:when test="@type ='char'">String</xsl:when>
<xsl:when test="@type='date'">Date</xsl:when>
<xsl:when test="@type='datetime'">Timestamp</xsl:when>
<xsl:when test="@type='decimal'">Double</xsl:when>
<xsl:when test="@type='double'">Double</xsl:when>
<xsl:when test="@type='float'">Float</xsl:when>
<xsl:when test="@type='int'">Int</xsl:when>
<xsl:when test="@type='integer'">Int</xsl:when>
<xsl:when test="@type='lvarchar'">String</xsl:when>
<xsl:when test="@type='money'">Double</xsl:when>
<xsl:when test="@type='nchar'">String</xsl:when>
<xsl:when test="@type='nvarchar'">String</xsl:when>
<xsl:when test="@type='nvarchar2'">String</xsl:when>
<xsl:when test="@type='number' and @scale='0'">Long</xsl:when>
<xsl:when test="@type='number' and @scale!='0'">Double</xsl:when>
<xsl:when test="@type='numeric'">Double</xsl:when>
<xsl:when test="@type='smallint'">Int</xsl:when>
<xsl:when test="@type='smallfloat'">Float</xsl:when>
<xsl:when test="@type='text'">String</xsl:when>
<xsl:when test="@type='time'">Time</xsl:when>
<xsl:when test="@type='timestamp'">Timestamp</xsl:when>
<xsl:when test="@type='varchar'">String</xsl:when>
<xsl:when test="@type='varchar2'">String</xsl:when>
<xsl:otherwise>Object</xsl:otherwise>
</xsl:choose></xsl:template>
```

Listing 6.20 Template mapping database types to JDBC ones

And now, let's look at the readRecord template, which iterates over all the fields of the result set and generates lines like:

```
dto.EMP_ID = (rs.getInt("EMP_ID"));
dto.SALARY = (rs.getDouble("SALARY));
```

In addition, JDBC-related date/time types get converted from java.sql to java.util form:

```
dto.START_DATE = DateTimeConversion.toUtilDate(rs.getDate("START_DATE"));
```

Here is the readRecord template:

```
<xsl:template name="readRecord">
        <xsl:for-each select="DATASET/FIELDS/FIELD">dto.<xsl:value-of
select="@name"/> = <xsl:choose>
  <xsl:when test="string(@type)='date'">DateTimeConversion.toUtilDate</xsl:when>
  <xsl:when test="string(@type)='datetime'">DateTimeConversion.toUtilDate</xsl:
when>
  <xsl:when test="string(@type)='time'">DateTimeConversion.toUtilDate</xsl:when>
  <xsl:when test="string(@type)='timestamp'">DateTimeConversion.toUtilDate</xsl:
when>
  <xsl:otherwise></xsl:otherwise>
</xsl:choose>(rs.get<xsl:call-template name="mapDBtoJDBC"/>("<xsl:value-of
select="@name"/>"));
        </xsl:for-each>
  </xsl:template>
```

This concludes the complete implementation of the fill-method. The *sync-method* templating comes next.

Templates for Implementing Sync-Method

We'll be generating the sync-method using precisely the same metadata that we've extracted from the annotated Java class presented in Listing 6.10. We're particularly interested in the attribute *updateTable=employee* of the @DAOFlex:sql tag that tells us which table from the SELECT statement should be used as an update target (your select statement can have more than one table, but the current version of the DAOFlex can update only one).

Listing 6.21 presents the XML metadata we've been working with in this chapter, but it's the first time that we show the UPDATE node. As expected, the UPDATE node holds the name of the table to update. It also indicates that the WHERE clause of the generated INSERT/DELETE/UPDATE statements should be based on the key fields (as opposed to the other alternatives: modified fields and the combination key-and-modified):

```
<?xml version="1.0" encoding="UTF-8"?>
<WEBSERVICE NAME="Employee" PACKAGE="com.theriabook.datasource" TYPE="DAOFlex" VER-
SION="2.0">
  <SERVER LANGUAGE="Java" MODE="JEE">
    <SQL ACTION="SELECT"
      NAME="getEmployees" POOL="jdbc/theriabook" SCOPE="public"
```

```
        ASTYPE="com.theriabook.dto.EmployeeDTO[]" JAVATYPE="com.theriabook.dto.
           EmployeeDTO[]"
      >
        <PARAM IN="Y" INDEX="1" JAVATYPE="Date" NAME="startDate"/>
        . . . .
      </COMPILED >
        <UPDATE TARGET="EMPLOYEE">
           <TABLE NAME="EMPLOYEE" UPDATEMETHOD="key"/>
        </UPDATE>
        <DATASET><FIELDS>
              <FIELD key="yes" name="EMP_ID" tableName="employee" type="integer"
updatable="yes"/>
              . . . .
        </FIELDS></DATASET>
      </SQL>
   </SERVER>
</WEBSERVICE>
```

Listing 6.21 The DAOFlex metadata with information for the sync-method

Interestingly, the top-level code for the sync-method doesn't really depend on any of this. Indeed, we need to process the entire input List of ChangeObjects. We'll do it in three passes (as we did in a manual mode in Listing 6.7) and execute all DELETEs first, with UPDATEs and INSERTs, but again, the code will be pretty agnostic relative to the underlying SQL. Listing 6.22 presents the template that automatically generates such a sync-method given the content of the <SQL /> metadata node as the context:

```
<xsl:template match="SQL" mode="update">
public final List <xsl:value-of select="@NAME"/>_sync(List items)
   {
      Connection conn = null;
         ChangeObject co = null;
      try  {
         conn = JDBCConnection.getConnection("<xsl:value-of select="@POOL"/>");
         Iterator iterator = items.iterator();
         while (iterator.hasNext() ) {  // Do all deletes first
            co = (ChangeObject)iterator.next();
            if(co.isDelete()) doDelete_<xsl:value-of select="@NAME"/>(conn, co);
         }
         iterator = items.iterator();
         while (iterator.hasNext()) {    // Proceed to all updates next
            co = (ChangeObject)iterator.next();
            if(co.isUpdate()) doUpdate_<xsl:value-of select="@NAME"/>(conn, co);
         }
```

```
            iterator = items.iterator();
            while (iterator.hasNext()) {    // Finish with inserts
               co = (ChangeObject)iterator.next();
               if (co.isCreate()) doCreate_<xsl:value-of select="@NAME"/>(conn, co);
            }
        } catch(DataSyncException dse) {
            dse.printStackTrace();
            throw dse;
        } catch(Throwable te) {
            te.printStackTrace();
            throw new DAOException(te.getMessage(), te);
        } finally {
            if( conn!=null ) JDBCConnection.releaseConnection(conn);
        }
        return items;
</xsl:template>
```

Listing 6.22 The template to generate the"top-level" of the sync-method

Now, to make sure this template accompanies the original *<xsl:template match="SQL">* we'll modify the latter with the *<xsl:apply-templates>* as shown in the following snippet:

```
<xsl:template match="SQL">
   <xsl:variable name="itemType" select="substring(string(@JAVATYPE), 1, string-length(st
ring(@JAVATYPE))-2)"/>

   public final List /*<xsl:value-of select="@JAVATYPE"/>*/ <xsl:value-of select="@NAME"/
>(<xsl:call-template name="declareFillParameters"/>)
   {
      . . . .
   }
   <xsl:if test="@ACTION='SELECT' and boolean(UPDATE)"> <xsl:apply-templates select="."
mode="update"/></xsl:if>

</xsl:template>
```

Since we're transforming our *Employee.xml* metadata with the SimpleDataServiceDao.xsl in its current state, the relevant fragment of the output will look like Listing 6.23:

```
public final List searchEmployees_sync(List items)
   {
      logger.debug("searchEmployees_sync(...)");

      Connection conn = null;
```

```
        ChangeObject co = null;
    try  {
      conn = JDBCConnection.getPooledConnection("jdbc/theriabook");
      Iterator iterator = items.iterator();
      while (iterator.hasNext() ) {  // Do all deletes first
        co = (ChangeObject)iterator.next();
        if(co.isDelete()) doDelete_searchEmployees(conn, co);
      }
      iterator = items.iterator();
      while (iterator.hasNext()) {   // Proceed to all updates next
        co = (ChangeObject)iterator.next();
        if(co.isUpdate()) doUpdate_searchEmployees(conn, co);
      }
      iterator = items.iterator();
      while (iterator.hasNext()) {   // Finish with inserts
        co = (ChangeObject)iterator.next();
        if (co.isCreate()) doCreate_searchEmployees(conn, co);
      }
    } catch(DataSyncException dse) {
      dse.printStackTrace();
      throw dse;
    } catch(Throwable te) {
      te.printStackTrace();
      throw new DAOException(te.getMessage(), te);
    } finally {
      if( conn!=null ) JDBCConnection.releasePooledConnection(conn);
    }
    return items;
  }
```

Listing 6.23 Top-level sync-method code generated by our template

Our next task is to generate *doUpdate()*, *doDelete()*, and *doInsert()* methods.

Completing the Sync Method

We'll delegate the generation process of the *doUpdate()*, *doDelete()*, and *doInsert()* methods to three correspondingly named templates. We'll alter the template presented in Listing 6.22 as shown below:

```
<xsl:template match="SQL" mode="update">
  public final List <xsl:value-of select="@NAME"/>_sync(List items)
  {
    . . . .
```

```
    }
    <xsl:call-template name="doUpdate" />
    <xsl:call-template name="doDelete" />
    <xsl:call-template name="doInsert" />

</xsl:template>
```

Let's start with doUpdate. Remember our exercise with handcrafted DataService-based code? That *doUpdate()* contained a StringBuffer of the UPDATE statement. Given that our XML context is the *<SQL>* node we can generate the required line as

```
   StringBuffer sql = new StringBuffer("UPDATE <xsl:value-of select="UPDATE/
@TARGET"/> SET ");
```

To produce the WHERE clause, which will enumerate all the key columns in the form "key1=?, key2=?" we can do the following:

```
     sql.append( " WHERE (<xsl:for-each select="DATASET/FIELDS/
FIELD[@key='yes']"><xsl:if test="position()!=1"> AND </xsl:if><xsl:value-of
select="@name"/>=?</xsl:for-each>)" );
```

Then, to substitute the "?" symbols with the key values we will employ the similar *<xsl:for-each/>*: combined with what we learned about the ChangedObject's *getPreviousValue()* method:

```
     <xsl:for-each select="DATASET/FIELDS/FIELD[@key='yes']">
     stmt.setObject(ii++, co.getPreviousValue("<xsl:value-of select="@name"/>"));</xsl:
      for-each>
```

Ultimately we'll arrive at the text of the doUpdate template as shown in Listing 6.24:

```
  <xsl:template name="doUpdate" >
     private void doUpdate_<xsl:value-of select="@NAME"/>(Connection conn, ChangeObject co)
  throws SQLException{
        PreparedStatement stmt = null;
        try {
           StringBuffer sql = new StringBuffer("UPDATE <xsl:value-of select="UPDATE/
  @TARGET"/> SET ");
           String [] names = co.getChangedPropertyNames();
           for (int ii=0; ii &lt; names.length; ii++) {
              sql.append((ii!=0?", ":"") + names[ii] +" = ? ");
           }
           sql.append( " WHERE (<xsl:for-each select="DATASET/FIELDS/
  FIELD[@key='yes']"><xsl:if test="position()!=1"> AND </xsl:if><xsl:value-of
  select="@name"/>=?</xsl:for-each>)" );
```

```
        stmt = conn.prepareStatement(sql.toString());

        Map values = co.getChangedValues();
        int ii=0;
        for (ii=0; ii &lt; names.length; ii++) {
           stmt.setObject( ii+1,  values.get(names[ii]));
        }
        ii++;

        <xsl:for-each select="DATASET/FIELDS/FIELD[@key='yes']">
        stmt.setObject(ii++, co.getPreviousValue("<xsl:value-of select="@name"/>"));</
xsl:for-each>

        if (stmt.executeUpdate()==0) throw new DataSyncException(co);
     } finally {
        try { if( stmt!=null) stmt.close(); stmt = null;} catch (Exception e){}
     }
   }
</xsl:template>
```

Listing 6.24 The template of the doUpdate() method

The template implementing the *doDelete* method is very similar, except that, due to the syntax of the DELETE statement it ventures into enumerating the WHERE-hosted keys right off the bat while preparing the StringBuffer:

```
<xsl:template name="doDelete" >
   private void doDelete_<xsl:value-of select="@NAME"/>(Connection conn, ChangeObject co)
throws SQLException{
      PreparedStatement stmt = null;
      try {
         StringBuffer sql = new StringBuffer("DELETE FROM <xsl:value-of select="UPDATE/
@TARGET"/> WHERE (<xsl:for-each select="DATASET/FIELDS/FIELD[@key='yes']"><xsl:if
test="position()!=1"> AND </xsl:if><xsl:value-of select="@name"/>=?</xsl:for-each>)");
         stmt = conn.prepareStatement(sql.toString());

         <xsl:for-each select="DATASET/FIELDS/FIELD[@key='yes']">
              stmt.setObject(<xsl:value-of select="position()"/>, co.getPreviousValue("<x
sl:value-of select="@name"/>"));
         </xsl:for-each>
         if (stmt.executeUpdate()==0) throw new DataSyncException(co);
      } finally {
         try { if( stmt!=null) stmt.close(); stmt = null;} catch (Exception e){}
      }
```

```
    }
</xsl:template>
```

Listing 6.25 The template of the doDelete() method

We did not list the results of the XSL transformation here because they are literally identical to the handcrafted code we modeled our templates after.

We're almost there. The only remaining part of the SimpleDataServiceDao.xsl to discuss is the do-*Create* template, which will be covered next.

The Template for the doCreate() Method

It's time to do another kind of mapping exercise. We've been through such an exercise when reading the ResultSet with the getXXX() functions. Knowing the database type of the result set element we had to determine the proper choice of the *getInt(), getString()*, etc., and on top of that, perform the conversions like converting *java.sql.Date* into *java.util.Date.* On the same note, we have to pick the right *setInt(), setString()*, and the like, based on the database data type and do the proper conversions.

The named template "mapDBtoJDBC" (see Listing 6.20) comes in handy again. Provided the context is a metadata node <FIELD>, we can generate the proper setXXX() call with the line:

```
stmt.set<xsl:call-template name="mapDBtoJDBC"/>(arguments);
```

To perform the type conversion, we'll add another named template, *convertJavaColumnToJDBC.* It expects to use the value of the database column's type and an expression for conversion. For the date/time/timestamp types it converts the Java value of the DTO property into the corresponding value from the java.sql package leaving other expressions intact:

```
<xsl:template name="convertJavaColumnToJDBC">
<xsl:param name="type"/>
<xsl:param name="expression"/>
<xsl:when test="type='date'">DateTimeConversion.toSqlDate(<xsl:value-of
select="$expression"/>)</xsl:when>
<xsl:when test="type='datetime'">DateTimeConversion.toSqlTimestamp(<xsl:value-of
select="$expression"/>)</xsl:when>
<xsl:when test="type='time'">DateTimeConversion.toSqlTime(<xsl:value-of
select="$expression"/>)</xsl:when>
<xsl:when test="type='timestamp'">DateTimeConversion.toSqlTimestamp(<xsl:value-of
select="$expression"/>)</xsl:when>
<xsl:otherwise><xsl:value-of select="$expression"/></xsl:otherwise></xsl:choose></xsl:
template>
```

Listing 6.26 The template of converting date/time targeting values to java.sql.* values

And here is the last component. In the absence of dedicated null indicators traveling along with the DTO, the only way to set NULL values for types like double and float is to have an if statement similar to:

```
if (Double.isNaN(item.SALARY))
  stmt.setNull(4,Types.DOUBLE);
else
  stmt.setDouble(4, item.SALARY);
```

Putting it all together, we arrive at the template *writeRecord*. It starts with converting source expressions like *item.BIRTH_DATE, item.START_DATE*, etc., into a *jdbcValue*. Then, depending on the FIELD type, it generates an if-statement like the one above or outputs a setXXX() statement with the code:

```
  stmt.set<xsl:call-template name="mapDBtoJDBC"/>(<xsl:value-of
select="position()"/>,
                                                          <xsl:value-of
select="$jdbcValue"/>);
```

The full listing of the *writeRecord* template follows:

```
<xsl:template name="writeRecord">
  <xsl:for-each select="DATASET/FIELDS/FIELD">
  <xsl:variable name="jdbcValue">
        <xsl:call-template name="convertJavaColumnToJDBC">
          <xsl:with-param name="type" select="@type"/>
          <xsl:with-param name="exp">item.<xsl:value-of select="@name"/>
          </xsl:with-param>
        </xsl:call-template>
  </xsl:variable>
  <xsl:choose>
        <xsl:when test="@type='double' or @type='decimal' or @type='money' or
(@type='number' and @scale!='0') or @type='numeric'">
        if (Double.isNaN(item.<xsl:value-of select="@name"/>))
          stmt.setNull(<xsl:value-of select="position()"/>,Types.DOUBLE);
        else
          stmt.setDouble(<xsl:value-of select="position()"/>, item.<xsl:value-of
select="@name"/>);</xsl:when>
      <xsl:when test="@type='float' or @type='smallfloat'">
        if (Float.isNaN(item.<xsl:value-of select="@name"/>))
          stmt.setNull(<xsl:value-of select="position()"/>,Types.FLOAT);
        else
          stmt.setFloat(<xsl:value-of select="position()"/>, item.<xsl:value-of
select="@name"/>);</xsl:when>
```

```
    <xsl:otherwise>
      stmt.set<xsl:call-template name="mapDBtoJDBC"/>(<xsl:value-of
select="position()"/>, <xsl:value-of select="$jdbcValue"/>);</xsl:otherwise>
  </xsl:choose>
  </xsl:for-each>
</xsl:template>
```

Listing 6.27 The writeRecord template

If you've made it so far, the XSL template for *doCreate* will look trivial. It builds the SQL INTO clause of the INSERT iterating over the result set fields, and iterates over it again to place an adequate number of comma-separated "?" characters. Then, on calling *conn.prepareStatement()* it invokes the template *writeRecord*. That's it.

```
<xsl:template name="doCreate" >
   <xsl:variable name="itemType" select="substring(string(@JAVATYPE), 1, string-length(st
ring(@JAVATYPE))-2)"/>
   private ChangeObject doCreate_<xsl:value-of select="@NAME"/>(Connection conn, Chan-
geObject co) throws SQLException{he
      PreparedStatement stmt = null;
      try {
         String sql = "INSERT INTO <xsl:value-of select="UPDATE/@TARGET"/> " +
         "(<xsl:for-each select="DATASET/FIELDS/FIELD">
         <xsl:value-of select="@name"/><xsl:if test="not(position()=last())">,</xsl:if>
         </xsl:for-each>)"+
         " values (<xsl:for-each select="DATASET/FIELDS/FIELD">?<xsl:if test="not(positio
n()=last())">,</xsl:if></xsl:for-each>)";

         stmt = conn.prepareStatement(sql);

         <xsl:value-of select="$itemType"/> item = (<xsl:value-of select="$itemType"/>)
co.getNewVersion();
         <xsl:call-template name="writeRecord"/>
         if (stmt.executeUpdate()==0) throw new DAOException("Failed inserting.");
         co.setNewVersion(item);
         return co;
      } finally {
         try { if( stmt!=null) stmt.close(); stmt = null;} catch (Exception e){}
      }
   }
</xsl:template>
```

Listing 6.28 The template of the doCreate() method

Here is the output of the *doCreate()* template against the *Employee.xml* metadata:

```
   private ChangeObject doCreate_getEmployees(Connection conn, ChangeObject co) throws
SQLException{
      PreparedStatement stmt = null;
      try {
         String sql = "INSERT INTO EMPLOYEE " +
         "(EMP_ID,MANAGER_ID,EMP_FNAME,EMP_LNAME,DEPT_ID,STREET,CITY,STATE,ZIP_
CODE,PHONE,STATUS,SS_NUMBER,SALARY,START_DATE,TERMINATION_DATE,BIRTH_DATE,BENE_HEALTH_
INS,BENE_LIFE_INS,BENE_DAY_CARE,SEX)"+
         " values (?,?,?,?,?,?,?,?,?,?,?,?,?,?,?,?,?,?,?,?)";

         stmt = conn.prepareStatement(sql);

         com.theriabook.dto.EmployeeDTO item = (com.theriabook.dto.EmployeeDTO)
co.getNewVersion();

         stmt.setInt(1, item.EMP_ID);
         stmt.setInt(2, item.MANAGER_ID);
         stmt.setString(3, item.EMP_FNAME);
         stmt.setString(4, item.EMP_LNAME);
         stmt.setInt(5, item.DEPT_ID);
         stmt.setString(6, item.STREET);
         stmt.setString(7, item.CITY);
         stmt.setString(8, item.STATE);
         stmt.setString(9, item.ZIP_CODE);
         stmt.setString(10, item.PHONE);
         stmt.setString(11, item.STATUS);
         stmt.setString(12, item.SS_NUMBER);
         if (Double.isNaN(item.SALARY))
            stmt.setNull(13,Types.DOUBLE);
         else
            stmt.setDouble(13, item.SALARY);
         stmt.setDate(14, DateTimeConversion.toSqlDate(item.START_DATE));
         stmt.setDate(15, DateTimeConversion.toSqlDate(item.TERMINATION_DATE));
         stmt.setDate(16, DateTimeConversion.toSqlDate(item.BIRTH_DATE));
         stmt.setString(17, item.BENE_HEALTH_INS);
         stmt.setString(18, item.BENE_LIFE_INS);
         stmt.setString(19, item.BENE_DAY_CARE);
         stmt.setString(20, item.SEX);
         if (stmt.executeUpdate()==0) throw new DAOException("Failed inserting.");
         co.setNewVersion(item);
         return co;
      } finally {
```

```
            try { if( stmt!=null) stmt.close(); stmt = null;} catch (Exception e){}
        }
    }
```

Listing 6.29 The output produced by the doCreate template

This makes out SimpleDataServiceDao.xsl complete.

Who Owns the DAOFlex Templates?

The DAOFlex is an open source utility distributed under the GPL license and you can use and modify it as you see fit as long as you mention Farata Systems as its original creator. The SimpleDataServiceDao.xsl, described here, is a somewhat simplified version of the real one – Dao.xsl – distributed with the DAOFlex.

We need to emphasize why we went to such lengths explaining how these stylesheets work.

As we said earlier the rapid application development tools (RAD) that use automated code generation assume that you feel comfortable with XSL templates. For instance, a JDBC-related template like the one we've been making so far may work slightly differently for a particular JDBC driver. The metadata reported by different JDBC drivers may also be slightly different. For instance we've omitted BLOB and CLOB support from our template. While working with a specific database, you can tune the stylesheet to match your driver and forget the tedious process of handcrafting, debugging, and testing the code doing the routine database processing.

Rapid Application Development with DAOFlex

The rest of the chapter describes the open source version of DAOFlex. (You can outright cut-down these configuration efforts and automate entire Flex/Java development by downloading a commercial DAOFlex Eclipse plugin developed by FarataSystems, LLC. The download URL is http://www.myflex.org.) Since DAOFlex is nothing but a metadata extractor with a bunch of XSL transformations, you already know how to customize it – you have to modify or add the stylesheets. Now let's look at DAOFlex's directory structure shown in Figure 6.2.

DAOFlex Directory Structure and Configuration Files

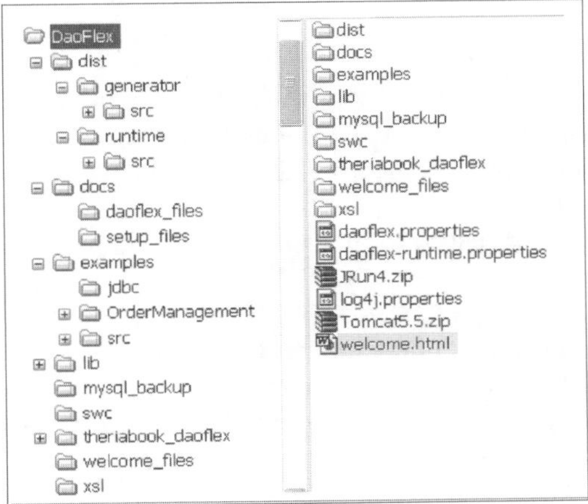

Figure 6.2 The DAOFlex directory structure

Start with the welcome.html file located in the root directory to get a brief intro to DAOFlex, its setup and usage. Other documents – setup.htm and syntax.html – are located in the docs folder.

Please note file JRun4.zip and Tomcat5.5.zip. These files contain "deltas" – everything you need to unzip on top of existing Tomcat or JRun to have DAOFlex up and running, including the database connectivity. You'd also need to install the MySQL test database, applying the backup file test.sql from *mysql_backup* folder. All required steps are described in /docs/setup.htm.

The folder dist contains DAOFlex's Java sources. The Ant *build.xml files*, residing in *dist/generator* and *dist/runtime*, produce relevant *JARS* in the build folder. These Ant files rely on the *JARS* from the lib folder explained below.

The folder *examples* contains sample Java source files annotated with the DAOFlex:sql tag. It also contains a build.xml file to run DAOFlex code generation, with dependencies on the build/daoFlex-generator.jar and other files from the */lib* folder. While setting up your DAOFlex project you'll be copying and modifying this build.xml file. Folder examples also contain the OrderManagement subfolder, with the source files relevant to the transactional application from Chapter 7.

(Please note that due to differences between Java4 and Java5 we supply two distinct versions of build files. These build files correspond to two distinct versions or daoflex-runtime.jar and daoflex-generator.jar from the lib folder. In particular, you'd use Java5 jars and *build.xml* for Tomcat5.5 and Java4 versions for JRun4.)

The folder *lib* contains jars required to build DAOFlex and run code generation by build.xml from inside the *examples* folder or your own DAOFlex-based project. You may need to extend the contents of the lib with your specific JDBC driver. We provided late drivers, as of the time of writing, drivers for Oracle, Sybase, and MySQL. Pre-built daoflex-generator.jar and daoflex-runtime.jar are also stored here.

The *xsl* folder contains XSL stylesheets used by the DAOFlex generator. Since the stylesheets' look-up is done along the classpath of the DAOFlex doclet, you can overload standard templates with your own without physically replacing the originals in the *DAOFlex/xsl* folder.

The root folder of the DAOFlex distribution also contains two properties files: *daoflex.properties* and *daoflex-runtime.properties.*

The file daoflex.properties lists all of the templates that are being applied against the metadata extracted from the annotated Java files. Here you can explicitly tell DAOFlex to go through your own template, instead of the standard one, or add templates that, perhaps, generate Grid descendant controls, etc.

The file DAOFlex-runtime.properties has to be visible to the classloader's chain of your Web application. At present it contains one line with the JNDI prefix of the JDBC namespace and isn't required if your application server is JRun or WebLogic (but you would need it for Tomcat and WebSphere):

```
datasource.jndi.root=java:comp/env
```

If you're planning to use DS under the Apache Tomcat server, you'll have to install and configure Java Open Transaction Manager (JOTM), an implementation of the full distributed transaction support for Java applications. You'll have to drop the JOTM jars into the *<tomcat>/common/lib* or WEB-INF/lib of your Web Application. You also would have to add the following lines to the application configuration file <tomcat>/conf/Catalina/localhost/theriabook.xml:

```
<Context docBase="c:/theriabook/www" privileged="true" antiResourceLocking="false"
antiJARLocking="false">
....
<Transaction factory="org.objectweb.jotm.UserTransactionFactory" jotm.time-
out="60"/>
....
</Context>
```

You can get details on JOTM/Tomcat configuration in the documentation section at http://jotm.objectweb.org/index.html. Again, if you simply unzip Tomcat5.5.zip from the DAOFlex root on top of your Tomcat installation, every configuration step will have been taken care of. You can browse this zip file to study the required changes in detail.

DAOFlex Project Setup

To set up your DAOFlex project, copy and modify the content of the *examples* folder. You'd need to modify the build.xml file, create the *xyz.properties* file(s), where xyz is the name of your dataSource(s), and create the source Java file annotated with the @DAOFlex:sql tag.

Let's start with the configuration properties contained in the *build.xml.* (The up-to-date version of the examples/build.xml file may be different from the one described in this section.)

The first group of properties relates to original and generated text files. They are:

```
source.java.root     - root location of DAOFlex-annotated abstract Java classes;
generated.meta.root - root location of extracted metadata;
generated.web.root   - root location of ActionScript DTO
generated.java.root - root location of Java DTOs, DAOs & Assemblers
generated.test.root - root location of Flex Test Applications
```

Here's how these values are set up in examples/build.xml:

```
  <property name="source.java.root"    value="c:/theriabook/tools/DAOFlex/exam-
ples/src" />
  <property name="generated.meta.root" value="c:/theriabook/tools/DAOFlex/
examples/generated/meta"/>
  <property name="generated.web.root"  value="c:/theriabook/tools/DAOFlex/
examples/generated/web" />
  <property name="generated.java.root" value="c:/theriabook/tools/DAOFlex/
examples/generated/java"/>
  <property name="generated.test.root" value="c:/theriabook/tools/DAOFlex/
examples/generated/web/test"/>
```

You can change these values any way you want, but take into account that it doesn't make a lot of sense to keep generated Java files or compiled classes in the source control system. For that reason, we find it convenient to keep generated Java files in the separate subtree and, for the same reason, build.xml creates two separate JAR files for compiled source classes and compiled generated classes.

The second group of properties relates to the location of the DAOFlex home directory and the deployment location of the application as a whole and output JAR files in particular:

- **DAOFlex.home**: Location of DAOFlex root directory
- **deployment.web.root**: Location of the context root of your Web application
- **original.jar.destination**: Name/location of the JAR with compiled abstract classes
- **generated.jar.destination**: Name/location of the JAR with compiled generated classes

These values are set up in examples/build.xml as follows:

```
   <property name="DAOFlex.home" value="c:/TheRIABook/tools/DAOFlex"/>
   <property name="deployment.web.root" value="C:/fds3jrun/jrun4/servers/default/
theriabook"/>
   <property name="original.jar.destination" value="${deployment.web.root}/WEB-INF/
lib/DAOFlex-examples.jar"/>
   <property name="generated.jar.destination" value="${deployment.web.root}/WEB-
INF/lib/DAOFlex-examples-generated.jar"/>
```

Once you figure out the values of the above configuration properties you can proceed to setting up the dataSource (database connection pool)-related files. These files contain the driver URL, userid, and password to enable the DAOFlex generator to connect to your database and get the SQL metadata. No harm will be done to the database, and the DAOFlex generator will make sure that design-time queries return no data. Just to remind you, the file *theriabook.properties* is inside the *examples/jdbc* folder. It corresponds to the connection pool (dataSource name) jdbc/theriabook per the annotation in *examples/src/com/theriabook/datasource/Employee.java.*

Similar to the stylesheets, connection pool properties files are looked up via the DAOFlex Doclet classpath. According to *examples/build.xm*l, the Doclet classpath includes examples and DAOFlex home, so if you have multiple projects sharing the same connection parameters you can provide JDBC connection files relative to DAOFlex's home directory.

Finally, before running the DAOFlex generator, put the annotated files under the folder pointed to by the property *source.java.root* (see above).

Running the DAOFlex Code Generator

Running DAOFlex is pretty simple: you execute the Ant script on the command prompt provided that the current working directory contains the build.xml file that we described in the previous section. Did we mention you've got to have ANT.EXE on the system PATH?

As a result, you'll see the files generated, the Java code compiled, and JARred split into two separate JARs, and placed as per your settings.

Alternatively, you may use Eclipse. You'd need to go to Java Perspective and create a new Java project from the existing Ant file defaulting to the javac task build-original, as shown in Figure 6.3:

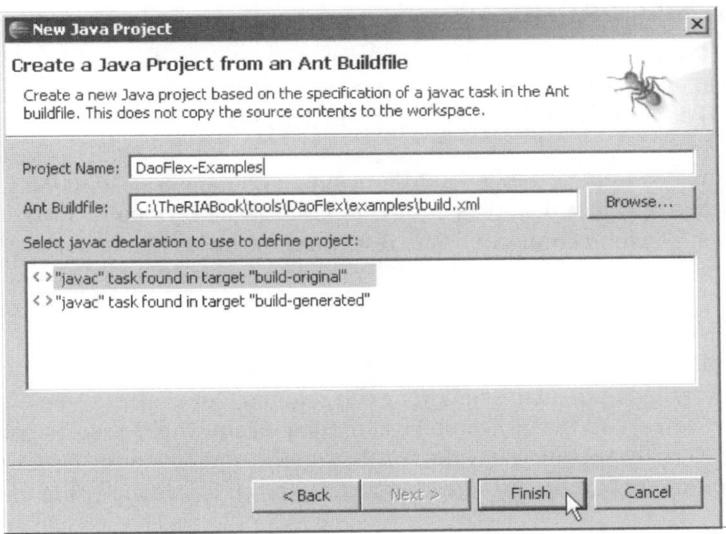

Figure 6.3 Setting the DAOFlex code-generating project in Eclipse

Then you'd be able to run and rerun the code-generation process, compilation, and jarring – everything your build.xml does with the Run Ant right-mouse menu off the highlighted build.xml.

Here's a sample extract from the console output of the DAOFlex code generator:

```
  [javadoc] Processing "com.theriabook.datasource.Employee" class...
  [javadoc] ---->Java DTO
  [javadoc] ---->ActionScript DTO
  [javadoc] Warning[1]: Using already created "com.theriabook.datasource.dto.EmployeeDTO" bean type.
  [javadoc] Warning[2]: Using already created "com.theriabook.datasource.dto.EmployeeDTO" bean type.
  [javadoc] ---->RemotingDao
  [javadoc] ---->DataServiceDao
  [javadoc] ---->Assembler
  [javadoc] ---->TestApplication (Grid/DataService)
  [javadoc] ---->data-management-config.xml
  [javadoc] ---->remoting-config.xml
  [javadoc] ---->TestApplication (Grid/Remoting)
  [javadoc] Done. 0 errors, 2 warnings.
build-original:
    [javac] Compiling 2 source files to C:\theriabook\workspace\DaoFlex-Examples\bin\original
      [jar] Building jar: C:\fds3jrun\jrun4\servers\default\theriabook\WEB-INF\lib\daoflex-examples.jar
build-generated:
    [javac] Compiling 8 source files to C:\theriabook\workspace\DaoFlex-Examples\bin\generated
      [jar] Building jar: C:\fds3jrun\jrun4\servers\default\theriabook\WEB-INF\lib\daoflex-examples-gen
build:
BUILD SUCCESSFUL
Total time: 7 seconds
```

Figure 6.4 Console output of the DAOFlex code generator

Testing and Using DAOFlex Output

Once the DAOFlex generation is complete you can move the ActionScript classes from the folder pointed by generated.web.root of your build.xml. Better yet, you can have generated.web.root point to the final destination of these classes so you don't have to move them.

Next, you can find a complete generated MXML single-grid application in the folder pointed by generated.test.root. Specifically in case of the Employee.java provided in our examples, the Data Services testing application Employee__GridTest.mxml will be located under the folder:

```
examples/generated/web/test/ds/com/theriabook/datasource
```

Let's assume again that you allow DAOFlex to output test MXML files directly inside the Flex project you're working on or, conversely, that you set up a Flex project using the folder with the generated file. If you set up the project to be compiled locally, you'll need one additional step to run Employee__GridTest.mxml – copy the contents to the root of your project. Otherwise, if your project is set up to compile on the server, you can run the Employee__GridTest.mxml from its current location.

Either way Figure 6.5 shows how the application will look. Look familiar? Yep, that's the application we started the chapter with, with one very essential difference: we didn't write a single line of code other than a simple annotated Java class as in Listing 6.10. We just processed this class with DAOFlex.

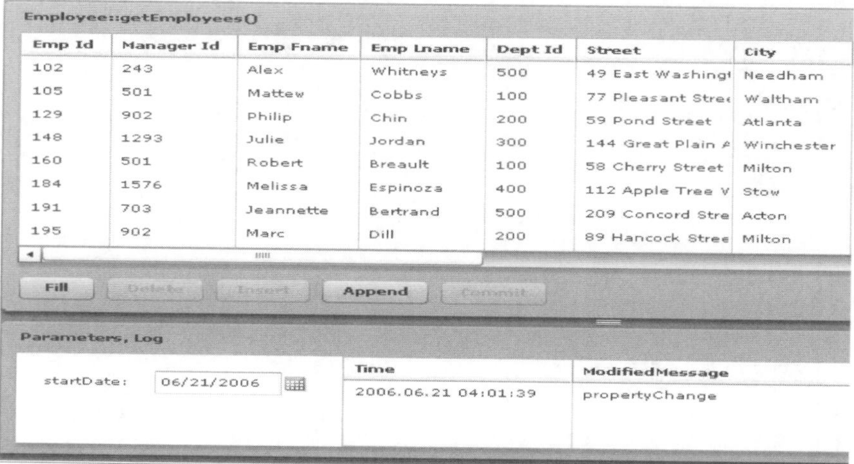

Figure 6.5 Application generated with the DAOFlex code generator

Summary

In this chapter not only have we shown you a tool that can automate tedious programming of the datagrid/database communication, but have also explained how you could create such a tool on your own. In other words, we've both given you a fish and taught you how to fish. We generated Java, MXML, and ActionScript code with Java doclets. With Java5 we could have used Java annotations and the Annotation Processing Tool (APT) that are beyond the scope of this book.

In addition to the open source version of DAOFlex described in this chapter, there is a commercial DaoFlex plugin for Eclipse, developed by FarataSystems, LLC. You can download this and other plugins for Flex at http://www.myflex.org.

Endnote

1. In this case DaoFlex looks for *jdbc/theriabook.properties* in the project folder and then in the DaoFlex home folder.

CHAPTER

7

How to Write Your Own Data Management Services

How to Write Your Own Data Management Services[1]

This chapter is about data management, client/server data synchronization, and transaction processing: the classic topics that represent a large portion of the budget of any enterprise project whether your industry is e-commerce, financial, manufacturing, or healthcare – any application centered around data.

We touched on this subject in the previous chapter, when we discussed Flex Data Services, which are focused on peer-server-peer data replication at the price of server-side caching complexity. At the same time Flex offers an elegant yet powerful mechanism of Flex Remoting, which has zero impact on server architecture and, by virtue of absolving the server from data persistence chores, allows your systems to scale practically without limits.

We'll start by upgrading a regular Flex Collection to what we call a "destination-aware" collection, capable of populating itself from a remote destination. Through a detailed study of the mechanics of Flex Collections and the anatomy of Managed ActionScript objects we will then lead you to the creation of a "change-tracking" and "updatable" Data Collection. This collection accumulates all changes in a controlled manner and, at your command, sends them to the server-side Java *sync()* method packaged exactly as a *DataService* would package them for *commit()*.

Finally, we will teach you how you can batch the execution of any arbitrary remote calls so that, for instance, your ActionScript client can control sophisticated transactions spanning multiple destinations, including calls to sync() methods, calls to stored procedures or, in general, anything that your application may need to incorporate in a transaction executed by the server.

At the end of this chapter, we will illustrate the use of Flex Remoting for data synchronization tasks with a sample OrderEntryDemo application.

Setting the Scene

While Flex Data Management Services is focused on server-side caching and peer-server-peer data replication, Flex Remoting enables a straight Remote Procedure Call (RPC) from an ActionScript client to the server. Reiterating the points brought up in Chapter 5, we should remind our readers that the AMF 3 protocol is by far the fastest Flash Player/Server communication mechanism, and this is why invoking a Java POJO via Flex Remoting can yield an order of magnitude performance gain over XML/Web Services, depending on the data volume.

In this chapter we will be reusing the DAO class com.theriabook.datasource.EmployeeDataServiceDAO that we built in Chapter 6. You might ask, if that is a _DataService_ DAO, how we can use it for remoting? The answer is: we can use it as is without even a tiny change. This is possible because of the thoughtful FDMS API design.

To employ the EmployeeDataServiceDao class for Flex Remoting we will configure WEB-INF/flex/remoting-config.xml to contain the destination "Employee" as shown in Listing 7.1 below:

```
<?xml version="1.0" encoding="UTF-8"?>
<service id="remoting-service"
    class="flex.messaging.services.RemotingService"
    messageTypes="flex.messaging.messages.RemotingMessage">

    <adapters>
        <adapter-definition id="java-object"
          class="flex.messaging.services.remoting.adapters.JavaAdapter" default="true"/>
    </adapters>

    <default-channels>
        <channel ref="my-amf"/>
    </default-channels>

    <destination id="Employee">
        <properties>
           <source>com.theriabook.datasource.EmployeeDataServiceDAO</source>
        </properties>
    </destination>
</service>
```

Listing 7.1 Flex Remoting configuration with EmployeeDataServiceDAO

Now our class is a legitimate remoting destination – we will use it a bit later.

Introducing Destination-Aware Collections

Remember the DataService *fill()* method? To populate an ArrayCollection via a DataService you'd write something like this:

```
var ac:ArrayCollection = new ArrayCollection();
```

```
var ds:DataService = new DataService("Employee");
ds.fill(ac);
```

How about eliminating the middleman – ds? We are talking about a destination-aware collection capable of taking care of filling itself:

```
var ac:DestinationAwareCollection = new DestinationAwareCollection();
ac.destination = "Employee";
ac.method = "getEmployees";
ac.fill();
```

It took us one extra line of ActionScript:

```
ac.method = "getEmployees";
```

Importantly, we brought back to ActionScript what had been hardwired on the server-side by the DataService approach. Let's see how the application code can benefit from any data-awareness of our collection. Listing 7.2 presents an MXML application that we called DestinationAwareCollectionDemo:

```
<?xml version="1.0" encoding="UTF-8"?>
<!-- DestinationAwareCollectionDemo.mxml -->
<mx:Application xmlns:mx="http://www.adobe.com/2006/mxml"
   creationComplete="onCreationComplete()">
   <mx:DataGrid id="dg" dataProvider="{collection}">
      <mx:columns><mx:Array>
         <mx:DataGridColumn dataField="EMP_FNAME" headerText="Emp Fname" />
         <mx:DataGridColumn dataField="EMP_LNAME" headerText="Emp Lname" />
         <mx:DataGridColumn dataField="STREET" headerText="Street" />
         <mx:DataGridColumn dataField="CITY" headerText="City" />
         <mx:DataGridColumn dataField="STATE" headerText="State" />
      </mx:Array></mx:columns>
   </mx:DataGrid>
   <mx:Script>
      <![CDATA[
         import com.theriabook.collections.DataCollection;
         import DestinationAwareCollection;
         [Bindable] private var collection:DestinationAwareCollection;

         private function onCreationComplete():void {
            collection = new DestinationAwareCollection();
            collection.destination = "Employee";
            collection.method = "getEmployees";
            collection.fill(new Date());
```

```
        }
      ]]>
   </mx:Script>
</mx:Application>
```

Listing 7.2 DestinationAwareCollectionDemo application

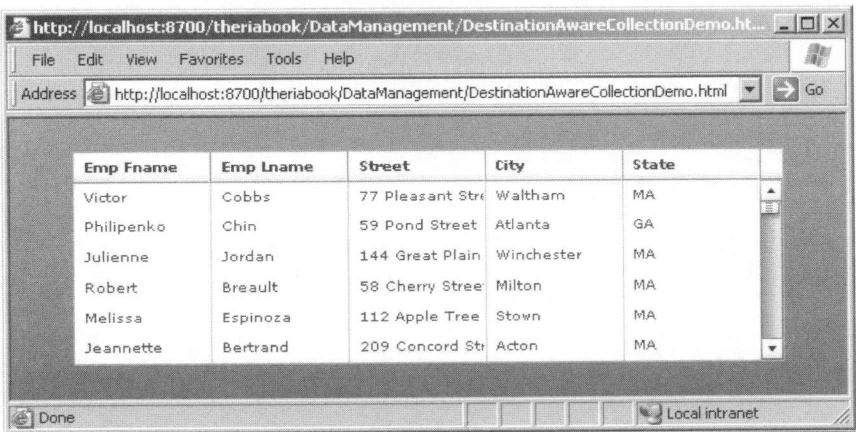

Figure 7.1 A snapshot of DestinationAwareDemo output

This application contains a data grid with a dataProvider bound to an instance of DestinationAwareCollection. There is no RemoteObject in sight, no event handlers for ResultEvent and FaultEvent. The only data-related code contained in our application is the initialization of collection parameters and the invocation of its fill() method:

```
collection = new DestinationAwareCollection();
collection.destination = "Employee";
collection.method = "getEmployees";
collection.fill(new Date());
```

Simple, isn't it? But what's inside this black box called DestinationAwareCollection?

Making a Destination-Aware Collection

The simplicity of DestinationAwareCollection takes its roots in the way it's constructed. To make DestinationAwareCollection, Listing 7.3, we extend an ArrayCollection and add two public variables: *destination* and *method*:

```
public class DestinationAwareCollection extends  ArrayCollection {
   public var destination:String=null;
```

```
    public var method : String = null;
}
```

Then we introduce a public method *fill()*. Since all AMF invocations are asynchronous messages, we design fill() to return an AsyncToken, which is a locally cached object. In your typical scenario, AsyncToken gets accessed twice: you use it to store some data related to the particular request during the send and then, when the response comes, you look up the same data for a just-in-time perusal:

```
public function fill(... args): AsyncToken  {
   var act:AsyncToken = invoke(method, args);
   act.method = "fill";
   return act;
}
```

Now let's get to the implementation details. The only parameter of the *fill()* method is defined as... rest array, which in turn is passed to the invocation of the remoting operation:

```
protected function invoke(method:String, args:Array):AsyncToken {
   if( ro==null ) ro = createRemoteObject();
   ro.showBusyCursor = true;
   var operation:AbstractOperation = ro.getOperation(method);
   operation.arguments = args;
   var act:AsyncToken = operation.send();
   return act;
}
```

The *createRemoteObject()* function ties a dynamically created RemoteObject with its_onResult() and onFault() methods. Please notice that we enforced "last" as ro's *concurrency* setting, which will result in canceling pending outgoing requests, if any[2]:

```
protected function createRemoteObject():RemoteObject {
   var ro:RemoteObject;
   if( destination==null || destination.length==0 )
      throw new Error("No destination specified");

   ro = new RemoteObject();
   ro.destination     = destination;
   ro.concurrency     = "last";
   ro.addEventListener(ResultEvent.RESULT, ro_onResult);
   ro.addEventListener(FaultEvent.FAULT,   ro_onFault);
   return ro;
}
```

In the case of FaultEvent, we just pop up an optional Alert. But in the ResultEvent handler we change the underlying data source of the collection, and that's why we call the ArrayCollection's *refresh()* method updating all the views associated with the collection:

```
protected function ro_onResult(evt:ResultEvent):void {
   CursorManager.removeBusyCursor();
   dispatchEvent(evt);
   source = evt.result.source;
   refresh();
}
```

In both event handlers we re-dispatch the event to the collection itself. You may want to add more logic here, allowing your collection to prevent the default processing. For instance, you may have some new content appended to the collection instead of wiping out the existing rows. The full listing of DestinationAwareCollection is presented in Listing 7.3:

```
// DestinationAwareCollection.as
package {

   import mx.collections.ArrayCollection;
   import mx.controls.Alert;
   import mx.managers.CursorManager;
   import mx.rpc.AbstractOperation;
   import mx.rpc.AsyncToken;
   import mx.rpc.events.FaultEvent;
   import mx.rpc.events.ResultEvent;
   import mx.rpc.remoting.mxml.RemoteObject;

   [Event(name="result", type="mx.rpc.events.ResultEvent")]
   [Event(name="fault", type="mx.rpc.events.FaultEvent")]
   public class DestinationAwareCollection extends  ArrayCollection {
      public var destination:String=null;
      public var method : String = null;
      public var alertOnFault:Boolean=true;
      protected var ro:RemoteObject = null;

      public function DestinationAwareCollection(source:Array=null){
         super(source);
      }

      public function fill(... args): AsyncToken  {
         var act:AsyncToken = invoke(method, args);
         act.method = "fill";
         return act;
      }
```

```
        protected function invoke(method:String, args:Array):AsyncToken {
           if( ro==null ) ro = createRemoteObject();
           ro.showBusyCursor = true;
           var operation:AbstractOperation = ro.getOperation(method);
           operation.arguments = args;
           var act:AsyncToken = operation.send();
           return act;
        }

        protected function createRemoteObject():RemoteObject {
           var ro:RemoteObject;
           if( destination==null || destination.length==0 )
              throw new Error("No destination specified");

           ro = new RemoteObject();
           ro.destination    = destination;
           ro.concurrency    = "last";
           ro.addEventListener(ResultEvent.RESULT, ro_onResult);
           ro.addEventListener(FaultEvent.FAULT,   ro_onFault);
           return ro;
        }

        protected function ro_onResult(evt:ResultEvent):void {
           CursorManager.removeBusyCursor();
           dispatchEvent(evt);
           source = evt.result.source;
           refresh();
           trace("RESULT: " + destination + "::" + method + "() returned " +
                                                    evt.result.source.length + " records");
        }
        protected function ro_onFault(evt:FaultEvent):void {
           CursorManager.removeBusyCursor();
           dispatchEvent(evt);
           if (alertOnFault) {
              Alert.show(evt.fault.faultString + evt.fault.faultDetail, "Error calling
                                                 destination " + evt.message.destination);
           }
        }
    }
}
```

Listing 7.3 DestinationAwareCollection.as

Sensing Collection Changes

Whenever the underlying data of an ArrayCollection changes, it dispatches a CollectionEvent with an *event.kind* property containing the values "add," "remove," "update," "reset," etc. By tapping into the mechanism of the CollectionEvent, we are going to improve our destination-aware collection. Ultimately we will be maintaining a clone of the original record for each record that's been modified as well as keeping an exact roll of all new and deleted records. First, though, let's illustrate the CollectionEvent. Suppose we upgrade our testing application by adding the two buttons *Remove* and *Add* as shown in Figure 7.2:

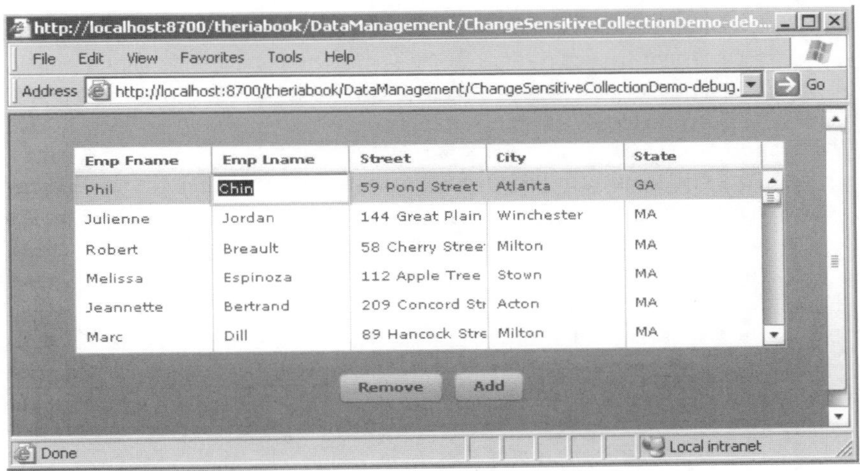

Figure 7.2 Snapshot of ChangeSensitiveCollectionDemo

The code of the new ChangeSensitiveCollectionDemo testing application is presented in Listing 7.4. We've made the data grid editable and changed the collection references from DestinationAwareCollection to *ChangeSensitiveCollection*:

```
<?xml version="1.0" encoding="UTF-8"?>
<!-- ChangeSensitiveCollectionDemo.mxml -->
<mx:Application xmlns:mx="http://www.adobe.com/2006/mxml"
   creationComplete="onCreationComplete()">
   <mx:DataGrid id="dg" dataProvider="{collection}" editable="true">
      <mx:columns><mx:Array>
         <mx:DataGridColumn dataField="EMP_FNAME" headerText="Emp Fname" />
         <mx:DataGridColumn dataField="EMP_LNAME" headerText="Emp Lname" />
         <mx:DataGridColumn dataField="STREET" headerText="Street" />
         <mx:DataGridColumn dataField="CITY" headerText="City" />
         <mx:DataGridColumn dataField="STATE" headerText="State" />
      </mx:Array></mx:columns>
   </mx:DataGrid>
```

```
    <mx:ControlBar>
      <mx:Button label="Remove" click="collection.removeItemAt(dg.selectedIndex)"
        enabled="{dg.selectedIndex != -1}"/>
      <mx:Button label="Add" click="collection.addItemAt(new EmployeeDTO(),
                                           Math.max(0,dg.selectedIndex+1)) "/>
    </mx:ControlBar>

    <mx:Script>
      <![CDATA[
        import ChangeSensitiveCollection;
        import com.theriabook.datasource.dto.EmployeeDTO;
        [Bindable] private var collection:ChangeSensitiveCollection;

        private function onCreationComplete():void {
          collection = new ChangeSensitiveCollection();
          collection.destination = "Employee";
          collection.method = "getEmployees";
          collection.fill(new Date());
        }
      ]]>
    </mx:Script>
  </mx:Application>
```

Listing 7.4 ChangeSensitiveCollectionDemo.mxml

The ChangeSensitiveCollection, a descendant of DestinationAwareCollection, handles the CollectionEvent differently (see Listing 7.5). Here, we just trace removed, added, or modified items. As far as added or removed items go, we get them directly via the *event.items* array. In case of updates, the *event.items* property carries the array of the PropertyChangeEvent elements, and the *currentTarget* property of each PropertyChangeEvent element should be used to access the modified item:

```
// ChangeSensitiveCollection.as
package {
  import mx.events.CollectionEvent;
  import mx.events.PropertyChangeEvent;
  import mx.utils.ObjectUtil;

  public class ChangeSensitiveCollection extends  DestinationAwareCollection {

    override public function set source(s:Array):void {
      super.source = s;
      list.addEventListener( CollectionEvent.COLLECTION_CHANGE, onCollectionEvent);
    }
    private function onCollectionEvent(event:CollectionEvent) :void {
```

```
            switch(event.kind) {
               case "remove":
                  for (var i:int = 0; i < event.items.length; i++) {
                     var item:Object = event.items[i];
                     trace ("REMOVED:" + mx.utils.ObjectUtil.toString(item));
                  }
                  break;
               case "add":
                  for ( i = 0; i < event.items.length; i++) {
                     item = event.items[i];
                     trace ("ADDED:" + mx.utils.ObjectUtil.toString(item) );
                  }
                  break;
               case "update":
                  for (i = 0; i < event.items.length; i++) {
                     item = null;
                     var pce:PropertyChangeEvent = event.items[i] as PropertyChangeEvent;
                     if ( pce != null) {
                        item = pce.currentTarget;
                     }
                     if (item != null) {
                        trace ("MODIFIED: " + mx.utils.ObjectUtil.toString(item));
                  }
                  }
                  break;
            }
         }
      }
}
```

Listing 7.5 ChangeSensitiveCollection.as

If we debug the ChangeSensitiveCollectionDemo and, say, delete one row by clicking "Remove" and type something into another row,[3] we'll see the following trace output:

```
[SWF] /theriabook/DataManagement/ChangeSensitiveCollectionDemo-debug.swf - 871,671
bytes after decompression
RESULT: Employee::getEmployees() returned 73 records
REMOVED:(com.theriabook.datasource.dto::EmployeeDTO)#0
  EMP_FNAME = "Matthew"
  EMP_LNAME = "Cobbs"
   . . . .
MODIFIED: (com.theriabook.datasource.dto::EmployeeDTO)#0
  EMP_FNAME = "Phil"
```

```
EMP_LNAME = "Chin"
. . . .
```

As you can see, the CollectionEvent is pretty talkative and we are going to tap into that pretty soon, building a collection that's capable of managing its state.

Anatomy of Managed ActionScript Objects

We need to clarify one very important point: dispatching the CollectionEvent shouldn't be taken for granted. Earlier we mentioned that the CollectionEvent is dispatched whenever an ArrayCollection "feels" the changes to the underlying data. While this is certainly true, the grim reality is that ArrayCollection on its own is pretty senseless. It doesn't feel anything unless it's told to. We're not talking here about collection methods like *addItem(x)* or *removeItem(x)*. Whenever you use these, the collection will obediently dispatch the CollectionEvent with the *kind* property set to add or remove.

But take a simple assignment like *x.firstName="Joe"* where x is the record in the array that backs a collection. Such an assignment might go completely unnoticed by the collection. Luckily, the collection API offers an *itemUpdated()* method to give the application a way to notify the collection of the data modifications.

Please notice the word "might" above; if an array's elements dispatch the PropertyChangeEvent, collection is notified automatically and the idiosyncratic itemUpdated() is out of a job. Flex collection classes live and breath PropertyChangeEvent so your best bet is to make sure that you "collect" objects that follow the pattern.

Obviously, you can dispatch PropertyChange events explicitly, but this book isn't about how to make you work harder. Flex automates this task for you. One way to automatically dispatch the PropertyChangeEvent is to use a [Bindable] metadata tag. If you place [Bindable] in front of a class declaration, Flex will generate the code to dispatch a PropertyChange event for all public properties; optionally you may annotate individual properties of the class as [Bindable].

An alternative way of ensuring the dispatch of the PropertyChangeEvent is to use managed classes. If you put [*Managed*] in front of the class declaration, Flex generates a wrapper class that turns all your properties [*Bindable*] and implements an IManaged interface comprised of three other interfaces as shown below:

```
public interface IManaged extends IPropertyChangeNotifier, IEventDispatcher, IUID
```

The *IPropertyChangeNotifier* interface, as the name suggests, mandates dispatching the PropertyChangeEvent. Actually, it goes further. Not only are you supposed to dispatch the event to the properties of your class, but you have to do it for the properties of complex data types as well.

An implementation of this interface is expected to construct update events using a special method of the PropertyChangeEvent class called *createUpdateEvent()*.

The second interface – *IEventDispatcher* – is the main interface required to enable the dispatching of any event. The simplest way to implement IEventDispatcher is to extend the flash.events.EventDispatcher class; another solution is to aggregate an instance of the EventDispatcher acting as a wrapper around it.

Finally, implementers of the *IUID* interface have to provide a getter/setter pair implementing a *uid* property.

Loaded with this knowledge, let's look at the implementation of the EmployeeDTO class, Listing 7.6:

```
/* Generated by DAOFLEX Utility (ActionScriptDTO_IManaged.xsl) */
package com.theriabook.datasource.dto
{
   import flash.events.EventDispatcher;
   import mx.data.IManaged;
   import mx.events.PropertyChangeEvent;
   import mx.core.IUID;
   import mx.utils.UIDUtil;

   [RemoteClass(alias="com.theriabook.datasource.dto.EmployeeDTO")]
   [Bindable(event="propertyChange")]
   public dynamic class EmployeeDTO extends EventDispatcher implements IManaged
   {
      // Properties
      private var _EMP_ID : Number;
      private var _EMP_FNAME : String;
      . . . .
      public function get EMP_ID() : Number{
         return _EMP_ID;
      }
      public function set EMP_ID( value : Number):void{
         var oldValue:Object = this._EMP_ID;
         if (oldValue !== value)   {
            this._EMP_ID = value;
            dispatchUpdateEvent("EMP_ID", oldValue, value);
         }
      }

      public function get EMP_FNAME() : String{
         return _EMP_FNAME;
      }
      public function set EMP_FNAME( value : String):void{
```

```
            var oldValue:Object = this._EMP_FNAME;
            if (oldValue !== value)   {
               this._EMP_FNAME = value;
               dispatchUpdateEvent("EMP_FNAME", oldValue, value);
            }
         }
         . . . .

         private var _uid:String;
         public function get uid():String {
            return _uid;
         }
         public function set uid(value:String):void {
            _uid = value;
         }

         public function EmployeeDTO() {
            _uid = UIDUtil.createUID();
         }

         private function dispatchUpdateEvent(
            propertyName:String, oldValue:Object, value:Object):void {
            dispatchEvent(
               PropertyChangeEvent.createUpdateEvent(this, propertyName, oldValue, value)
            );
         }
      }//EmployeeDTO

   }
```

Listing 7.6 An example of the AS class implementing an IManaged interface

The class starts with a [RemoteClass] annotation, stating that this class should be marshaled and re-created as its peer com.theriabook.datasource.dto.EmployeeDTO on the server side. Then we have a [Bindable] class-scope annotation. Notice that we've implemented all the properties as getter/setter pairs: we couldn't just let them stay public variables since we've been contracted to use createUpdateEvent(). In other words, we couldn't let Flex auto-generate the event dispatching code. Besides functional properties like EMP_ID and EMP_FNAME, our class also contains a setter and getter for the *uid* property; this qualifies the class as an IUID implementer. Since our class is extending the EventDispatcher, it already implements inherently IEventDispatcher, and that completes the list of requirements to qualify the class as an implementation of the IManaged interface.

Everything we've done so far can be also achieved by putting a [*Managed*] annotation in front of the class as shown in Listing 7.7. As you might remember, having your classes managed is a must-have requirement with DataServices. That's why [*Managed*] or, alternatively, the explicit implementation of IManaged, becomes an ideal common denominator between DataServices and handmade just-in-time collections notified by underlying objects:

```
/* Generated by DAOFLEX Utility (ActionScriptDTO_Managed.xsl) */
package com.theriabook.datasource.dto
{
   import mx.core.IUID;
   import mx.utils.UIDUtil;

   [RemoteClass(alias="com.theriabook.datasource.dto.EmployeeDTO")]
   [Managed]
   public dynamic class EmployeeDTO
   {
      // Properties
      public var EMP_ID : Number;
      public var EMP_FNAME : String;
      . . . .

      private var _uid:String;
      public function get uid():String {
         return _uid;
      }
      public function set uid(value:String):void {
         _uid = value;
      }

      public function EmployeeDTO() {
         _uid = UIDUtil.createUID();
      }
   }//EmployeeDTO

}
```

Listing 7.7 An example of a class with a "managed"metadata tag

As a reminder, if you use the DAOFlex utility introduced in Chapter 6, you don't have to write ActionScript DTO classes at all. DAOFlex generates them based on the SQL metadata that it, in turn, extracts from SQL query or the stored procedure annotating the signature of the Java method. You can also use the daoFlex Eclipse plugin available at http://www.myflex.org. It has many extra features; in particular, it supports the generation of ActionsScript DTO from existing Java DTO.

The Two Faces of ChangedObject

Remember the two faces of the Roman god Janus? Janus faces the past and the future at the same time. It may be a stretch, but you can spot traces of this divine idea in the Flex Data Services' *Change-Object interface*. Whenever Flex commits accumulated client-side changes, an array of flex.data.ChangeObjects gets sent to the DataService destination on the server. Each ChangeObject carries a pair *(previousVersion, newVersion)* representing the object (DTO) in two incarnations. Obviously, you don't need the previousVersion for inserting and the newVersion for deleting.

Now important things: a DataServiceDAO class from Chapter 6 contains a *sync()* method that takes a single parameter – java.util.List of ChangeObjects. Packaging ChangeObjects and the very invocation of *sync()* have so far been internal FDS affairs. But what stops us from calling sync() methods from ActionScript directly? Nothing. We're going to enable 100% reuse of the DAO classes between FDS and Flex Remoting.

Here's the plan. First, we'll make sure that our change-tracking collection class accumulates the updates, deletes, and inserts done to the collection data. Second, we will teach the collection to pack all the accumulated changes as an array of ActionScript objects, and each of them will contain *newVersion* and *previousVersion* along with the create/delete/update state variant:

```
public var state:int;
public var newVersion:Object = null;
public var previousVersion:Object = null;
```

Last, we'll make sure that these objects get marshaled into Java objects implementing the flex.data.ChangeObject interface. In Listing 7.8 we indicate that each ChangeObject has to be marshaled to its counterpart ChangeObjectImpl in com.theriabook.remoting package[4]:

```
package
{
   // This line gets required only in UpdatableCollection
   [RemoteClass(alias="com.theriabook.remoting.ChangeObjectImpl")]
   public class ChangeObject
   {
      public var state:int;
      public var newVersion:Object = null;
      public var previousVersion:Object = null;
      public var changedPropertyNames:Array= null;

      public static const UPDATE:int=2;
      public static const DELETE:int=3;
      public static const CREATE:int=1;

       public function ChangeObject(state:int=0, newVersion:Object=null,
                                    previousVersion:Object = null) {
```

```
        this.state = state;
        this.newVersion = newVersion;
        this.previousVersion = previousVersion;
      }
      public function isCreate():Boolean {
        return state==ChangeObject.CREATE;
      }
      public function isUpdate():Boolean {
        return state==ChangeObject.UPDATE;
      }
      public function isDelete():Boolean {
        return state==ChangeObject.DELETE;
      }
    }
  }
```

Listing 7.8 ChangeObject.as

So let's implement our plan. As once said, "The goals are clear, tasks are set. To the work, comrades!"

Tracking Collection Changes

The simplest way to make a ChangeTrackingCollection is by extending the DestinationAwareCollection. Let's start with extra properties: an array of *deleted* items and a dictionary of *modified* ones. Whereas the former contains an array of original items, the latter is a dictionary of ChangeObjects containing (newVersion, previousVersion) pairs:

```
public var deleted:Array = new Array();
public var modified:Dictionary = new Dictionary();
```

In addition, we introduce *deletedCount* and *modifiedCount*, implemented as getter/setter pairs:

```
private var _deletedCount : int = 0;
public function get deletedCount():uint {
  return _deletedCount;
}

public function set deletedCount(val:uint):void {
  var oldValue :uint = _deletedCount ;
  _deletedCount = val;
  dispatchEvent(mx.events.PropertyChangeEvent.createUpdateEvent(this,
                                            "deletedCount", oldValue, _deleted-
Count));
```

```
    }

    private var _modifiedCount : int = 0;
    . . . .
```

Accordingly, we need to modify the onCollectionEvent() handler. Take the remove case, for instance. We have to react differently to original and newly inserted items. Deleting the newly inserted items shouldn't get reported to the server. Further, we have to be careful about what we ask the server to delete because an item might have been modified and then deleted. In this event it's the original item that has to be deleted, not the newVersion of it. All along, we maintain the values for *modifiedCount* and *deletedCount*:

```
        case "remove":
          for (var i:int = 0; i < event.items.length; i++) {
            var item:Object = event.items[i];
            var co:ChangeObject = ChangeObject(modified[item]);
            var originalItem:Object=null;
            if (co == null) {    // item has not been modified
              originalItem = item;
            } else if (!co.isCreate()) {  // original item has been modified
              originalItem = co.previousVersion;
              delete modified[item];
              modifiedCount--;
            } else {          // item has been inserted and modified
              delete modified[item];
              modifiedCount--;
            }
            if (originalItem!=null) {
              deleted.push(originalItem);
              deletedCount = deleted.length;
            };
          }
          break;
    . . . .
    }
```

The complete code of ChangeTrackingCollection is in Listing 7.9. Besides maintaining the *deleted* and *modified* info, our collection includes methods to check and modify the state of the item: *isItemNew(), isItemModified(),* and *setItemNotModified()*. Lastly, it includes *resetState()*methods that clear all knowledge about the deleted and modified items and *undoItem()* that reverts the item's properties to their original values:

```
// ChangeTrackingCollection.as
package {
```

```
import flash.utils.Dictionary;
import mx.events.CollectionEvent;
import flash.events.Event;
import mx.events.PropertyChangeEvent;
import mx.utils.ObjectUtil;
import ChangeObject;

[Bindable(event="propertyChange")]
public class ChangeTrackingCollection extends  DestinationAwareCollection {

   public function ChangeTrackingCollection(source:Array=null){
      super(source);
   }

   public var deleted:Array = new Array();
   public var modified:Dictionary = new Dictionary();

   private var _deletedCount : int = 0;
   public function get deletedCount():uint {
      return _deletedCount;
   }

   public function set deletedCount(val:uint):void {
      var oldValue :uint = _deletedCount ;
      _deletedCount = val;
      dispatchEvent(mx.events.PropertyChangeEvent.createUpdateEvent(this,
                              "deletedCount", oldValue, _deletedCount));
   }

   private var _modifiedCount : int = 0;
   public function get modifiedCount():uint {
      return _modifiedCount;
   }

   public function set modifiedCount(val:uint ) : void{
      var oldValue :uint = _modifiedCount ;
      _modifiedCount = val;
      dispatchEvent(mx.events.PropertyChangeEvent.createUpdateEvent(this,
            "modifiedCount", oldValue, _modifiedCount));
   }

   private var trackChanges:Boolean = true;
```

```
override public function set source(s:Array):void {
   super.source = s;
    list.addEventListener( CollectionEvent.COLLECTION_CHANGE, onCollectionEvent);

 }
 private function onCollectionEvent(event:CollectionEvent) :void {
      if (!trackChanges) return;
   switch(event.kind) {
      case "remove":
         for (var i:int = 0; i < event.items.length; i++) {
            var item:Object = event.items[i];
            var co:ChangeObject = ChangeObject(modified[item]);
            var originalItem:Object=null;
            if (co == null) {
               // NotModified
               originalItem = item;
               } else if (!co.isCreate()) {
                  // Modified
               originalItem = co.previousVersion;
               delete modified[item];
               modifiedCount--;
            } else {
               // NewModified
               delete modified[item];
               modifiedCount--;
            }
            if (originalItem!=null) {
               deleted.push(originalItem);
               deletedCount = deleted.length;
            };
         }
         break;
      case "add":
         for ( i = 0; i < event.items.length; i++) {
            item = event.items[i];
            modified[item] = new ChangeObject(ChangeObject.CREATE, item, null);
            modifiedCount++;
         }
         break;
      case "update":

         for (i = 0; i < event.items.length; i++) {
            item = null;
            var pce:PropertyChangeEvent = event.items[i] as PropertyChangeEvent;
```

```
            if ( pce != null) {
               item = pce.currentTarget;
            }
            var previousVersion:Object;
            if (item != null) {
               if(modified[item] == null) {
                  previousVersion = ObjectUtil.copy(item);
                  previousVersion[pce.property] = pce.oldValue;
                  modified[item] = new ChangeObject(ChangeObject.UPDATE, item,
                                                                previousVersion);

                  modifiedCount++;
               }
               co = ChangeObject(modified[item]);
               if (co.changedPropertyNames == null) {
                  co.changedPropertyNames = [];
               }
               co.changedPropertyNames.push(pce.property);  // TODO avoid duplicates
            }
         }
         break;

   }
  }
public function isItemNew(item:Object):Boolean {
   var co:ChangeObject = modified[item] as ChangeObject;
   return (co!=null && co.isCreate());
}
public function isItemModified(item:Object):Boolean {
   var co:ChangeObject = modified[item] as ChangeObject;
   return (co!=null && !co.isCreate());
}
public function setItemNotModified(item:Object):void {
   var co:ChangeObject = modified[item] as ChangeObject;
   if (co!=null) {
      delete modified[item];
         modifiedCount--;
   }
}

public function resetState():void {
   deleted = new Array();
   modified = new Dictionary();
   modifiedCount = 0;
   deletedCount = 0;
```

```
        }

        public function undoItem(item:Object):void {
           var co:ChangeObject = modified[item] as ChangeObject;
           if (co!=null && !co.isCreate()) {
              trackChanges= false;
              for each (var property:String in co.changedPropertyNames) {
                 item[property] = co.previousVersion[property];
              }
              trackChanges = true;
              delete modified[item];
                 modifiedCount--;
           }
        }


     }
  }
```

Listing 7.9 ChangeTrackingCollection.as

Now let's play with this collection. We'll create a ChangeTrackingCollectionDemo demo application with four tabs: "Current," "Deleted," "Updated," and "Created." At any given moment, each of these tabs will reveal the state of the corresponding item set. In addition, the "Current" tab will contain the buttons "Remove," "Add," and "Undo" along with counters for the modified and deleted items:

```
   <mx:TabNavigator id="tab"  change="onChange(event)">
      <mx:Panel label="Current"> .  .  .  .
      <mx:ControlBar>
         <mx:Button label="Remove" click="collection.removeItemAt(dg.selectedIndex)
"

           enabled="{dg.selectedIndex != -1}"/>
         <mx:Button label="Add" click="collection.addItemAt(new EmployeeDTO(), Math.
max(0,dg.selectedIndex+1)) "/>
         <mx:Button label="Undo"
           click="collection.undoItem(dg.selectedItem) "
           enabled="{collection.isItemModified(EmployeeDTO(dg.selectedItem))}"
         />
         <mx:Text text="Modified:{collection.modifiedCount}"/>
         <mx:Text text="Deleted:{collection.deletedCount}"/>
      </mx:ControlBar>
      </mx:Panel>
      <mx:Canvas label="Deleted"> .  .  .  .
      </mx:Canvas>
```

```
    <mx:Canvas label="Updated"> . . . .
    </mx:Canvas>
  </mx:TabNavigator>
```

A snapshot of ChangeTraskingCollectionDemo is illustrated in Figure 7.3. The snapshot was taken after modifying the original value of the "Emp Frame" in the first row from Matthew to Matteus. Notice that the first row is shown in a bold font since the application will declare a Label-based renderer for each column that turns *fontWeight* to bold, if the item is modified:

```
<mx:DataGrid  id="dg" dataProvider="{collection}" editable="true">
  <mx:columns><mx:Array>
    <mx:DataGridColumn dataField="EMP_FNAME" headerText="Emp Fname" >
      <mx:itemRenderer><mx:Component>
        <mx:Label
fontWeight="{outerDocument.collection.isItemModified(data)?'bold':'normal'}"/>
      </mx:Component></mx:itemRenderer>
    </mx:DataGridColumn>
    <mx:DataGridColumn dataField="EMP_LNAME" headerText="Emp Lname" > . . . .
  </mx:Array></mx:columns>
</mx:DataGrid>
```

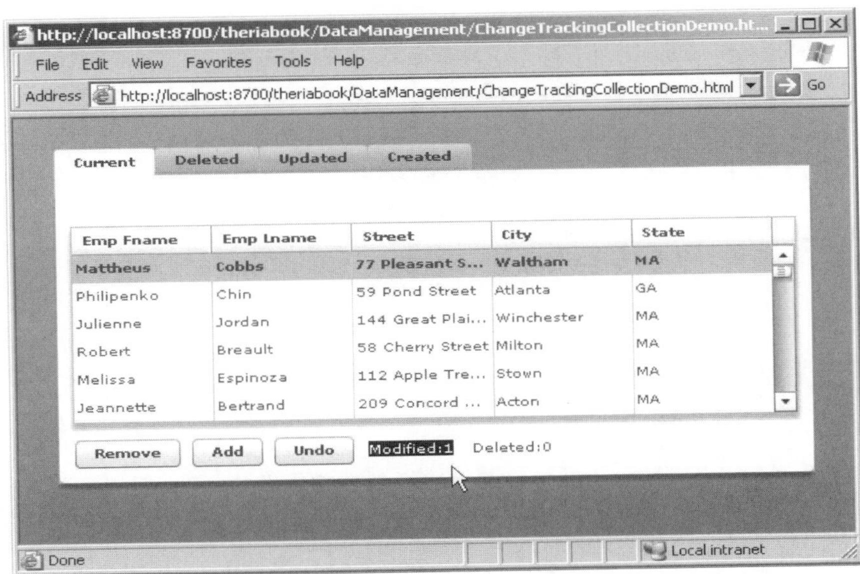

Figure 7.3 A snapshot of ChangeTrackingCollectionDemo (current data)

The next snapshot (see Figure 7.4) was taken when the "Updated" tab was clicked. It shows the original value of the collection item. To be precise, our application will rebuild the dataProviders for the Deleted/Updated/Created data grid when the relevant tab is selected:

```
private function onChange(event:Object):void {
  var co:ChangeObject;
  var item:Object;
  switch (tab.selectedIndex) {
    case 1:
      dg_deleted.dataProvider =
                                          collection.deleted;
      break;
    case 2:
      var updated:Array = [];
      for ( item in collection.modified) {
        co = collection.modified[item];
        if (co.isUpdate()) updated.push(
                                          co.previousVersion);
      }
      dg_updated.dataProvider = updated;
      break;
    case 3:
      var created:Array = [];
      for ( item in collection.modified) {
        co = collection.modified[item];
        if (co.isCreate()) created.push(
                                               co.newVersion);
      }
      dg_created.dataProvider = created;
      break;
  }
}
```

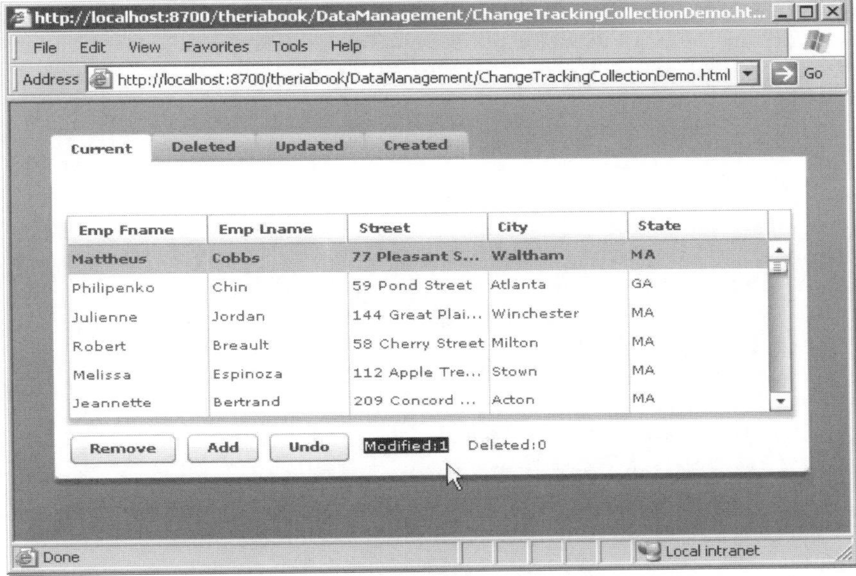

Figure 7.4 A snapshot of the ChangeTrackingCollectionDemo (original data)

Similarly, you can view the "Deleted" and "Created" items going to the corresponding tabs. The complete code for ChangeTrackingCollectionDemo is presented in Listing 7.10:

```
<?xml version="1.0" encoding="UTF-8"?>
<!-- ChangeTrackingCollectionDemo.mxml -->
<mx:Application xmlns:mx="http://www.adobe.com/2006/mxml"
  creationComplete="onCreationComplete()">
  <mx:TabNavigator id="tab"  change="onChange(event)">
    <mx:Panel label="Current">
    <mx:DataGrid  id="dg" dataProvider="{collection}" editable="true">
      <mx:columns><mx:Array>
        <mx:DataGridColumn dataField="EMP_FNAME" headerText="Emp Fname" >
          <mx:itemRenderer><mx:Component>
            <mx:Label
 fontWeight="{outerDocument.collection.isItemModified(data)?'bold':'normal'}"/>
          </mx:Component></mx:itemRenderer>
        </mx:DataGridColumn>
        <mx:DataGridColumn dataField="EMP_LNAME" headerText="Emp Lname" >
          <mx:itemRenderer><mx:Component>
            <mx:Label
fontWeight="{outerDocument.collection.isItemModified(data)?'bold':'normal'}"/>
          </mx:Component></mx:itemRenderer>
```

```
            </mx:DataGridColumn>
                    <mx:DataGridColumn dataField="STREET" headerText="Street" >
              <mx:itemRenderer><mx:Component>
                 <mx:Label
                 fontWeight="{outerDocument.collection.isItemModified(data)?'bold':'normal
'}"/>
              </mx:Component></mx:itemRenderer>
            </mx:DataGridColumn>

            <mx:DataGridColumn dataField="CITY" headerText="City" >
              <mx:itemRenderer><mx:Component>
                 <mx:Label
                 fontWeight="{outerDocument.collection.isItemModified(data)?'bold':'normal
'}"/>
              </mx:Component></mx:itemRenderer>
            </mx:DataGridColumn>

            <mx:DataGridColumn dataField="STATE" headerText="State" >
              <mx:itemRenderer><mx:Component>
                 <mx:Label
                 fontWeight="{outerDocument.collection.isItemModified(data)?'bold':'normal
'}"/>
              </mx:Component></mx:itemRenderer>
            </mx:DataGridColumn>

         </mx:Array></mx:columns>
      </mx:DataGrid>
      <mx:ControlBar>
         <mx:Button label="Remove" click="collection.removeItemAt(dg.selectedIndex)"
            enabled="{dg.selectedIndex != -1}"/>
         <mx:Button label="Add" click="collection.addItemAt(new EmployeeDTO(), Math.
max(0,dg.selectedIndex+1)) "/>
         <mx:Button label="Undo"
            click="collection.undoItem(dg.selectedItem) "
            enabled="{collection.isItemModified(EmployeeDTO(dg.selectedItem))}"
         />
         <mx:Text text="Modified:{collection.modifiedCount}"/>
         <mx:Text text="Deleted:{collection.deletedCount}"/>
      </mx:ControlBar>
      </mx:Panel>
      <mx:Canvas label="Deleted">
         <mx:DataGrid id="dg_deleted" >
            <mx:columns><mx:Array>
               <mx:DataGridColumn dataField="EMP_FNAME" headerText="Emp Fname" />
```

```
            <mx:DataGridColumn dataField="EMP_LNAME" headerText="Emp Lname" />
            <mx:DataGridColumn dataField="STREET" headerText="Street" />
            <mx:DataGridColumn dataField="CITY" headerText="City" />
            <mx:DataGridColumn dataField="STATE" headerText="State" />
         </mx:Array></mx:columns>
      </mx:DataGrid>
   </mx:Canvas>
   <mx:Canvas label="Updated">
      <mx:DataGrid id="dg_updated" >
         <mx:columns><mx:Array>
            <mx:DataGridColumn dataField="EMP_FNAME" headerText="Emp Fname" />
            <mx:DataGridColumn dataField="EMP_LNAME" headerText="Emp Lname" />
            <mx:DataGridColumn dataField="STREET" headerText="Street" />
            <mx:DataGridColumn dataField="CITY" headerText="City" />
            <mx:DataGridColumn dataField="STATE" headerText="State" />
         </mx:Array></mx:columns>
      </mx:DataGrid>
   </mx:Canvas>
   <mx:Canvas label="Created">
      <mx:DataGrid id="dg_created" >
         <mx:columns><mx:Array>
            <mx:DataGridColumn dataField="EMP_FNAME" headerText="Emp Fname" />
            <mx:DataGridColumn dataField="EMP_LNAME" headerText="Emp Lname" />
            <mx:DataGridColumn dataField="STREET" headerText="Street" />
            <mx:DataGridColumn dataField="CITY" headerText="City" />
            <mx:DataGridColumn dataField="STATE" headerText="State" />
         </mx:Array></mx:columns>
      </mx:DataGrid>
   </mx:Canvas>
</mx:TabNavigator>


<mx:Script>
   <![CDATA[
      import mx.collections.ArrayCollection;
      import ChangeTrackingCollection;
      import com.theriabook.datasource.dto.EmployeeDTO;
      [Bindable] public var collection:ChangeTrackingCollection;
      private function onCreationComplete():void {
         collection = new ChangeTrackingCollection();
         collection.destination = "Employee";
         collection.method = "getEmployees";
         collection.fill(new Date());
      }
```

```
        private function onChange(event:Object):void {
          var co:ChangeObject;
          var item:Object;
          switch (tab.selectedIndex) {
            case 1:
              dg_deleted.dataProvider = collection.deleted;
              break;
            case 2:
              var updated:Array = [];
              for ( item in collection.modified) {
                co = collection.modified[item];
                if (co.isUpdate()) updated.push( co.previousVersion);
              }
              dg_updated.dataProvider = updated;
              break;
            case 3:
              var created:Array = [];
              for ( item in collection.modified) {
                co = collection.modified[item];
                if (co.isCreate()) created.push( co.newVersion);
              }
              dg_created.dataProvider = created;
              break;
          }
        }
      ]]>
    </mx:Script>
  </mx:Application>
```

Listing 7.10 ChangeTrackingCollectionDemo.mxml

But wait, what was the real purpose of tracking down the changes in the first place? Were we supposed to send them up to the server? Patience, dear reader, check the next section.

Making Collection Updateable

Once we know how to track and accumulate changes, there's very little left to send these changes to the server. In this section we'll upgrade our collection to UpdatableCollection and illustrate its work with UpdatableCollectionDemo as shown in Figure 7.5:

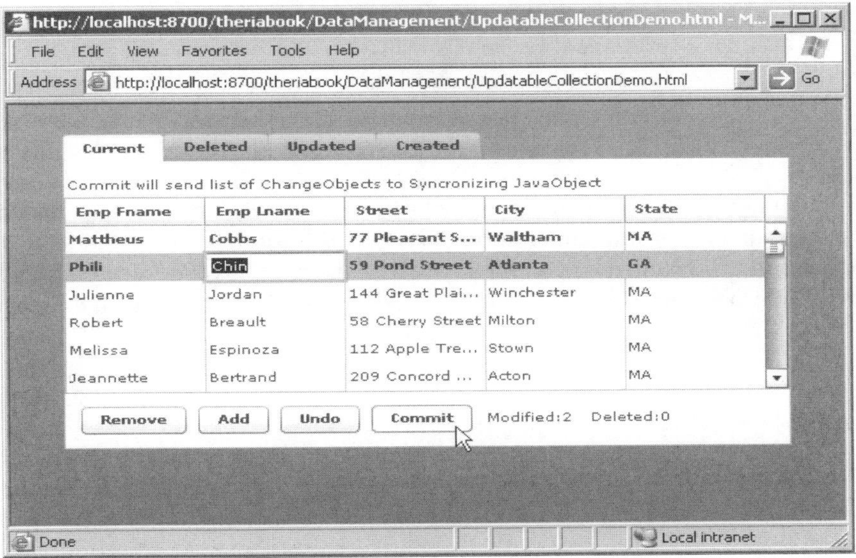

Figure 7.5 A snapshot of UpdateableCollectionDemo

Let's start with the collection class. We'll extend the ChangeTrackingCollection and introduce an additional property – *commitRequired*, which will be implemented as a getter/setter pair so that any modifications to deletedCount and *modifiedCount* also "touches" the property *commitRequired*:

```
public class UpdatableCollection extends  ChangeTrackingCollection {
  private var _commitRequired:Boolean = false;
  public function set commitRequired(val :Boolean) :void {
    if (val!==_commitRequired) {
      _commitRequired = val;                    dispatchEvent(mx.events.Prope
rtyChangeEvent.createUpdateEvent(this,
                 "commitRequired", !_commitRequired, _commitRequired));
    }
  }
  public function get commitRequired() :Boolean {
    return _commitRequired;
  }

  public override function set deletedCount(val:uint):void {
    super.deletedCount = val;
    commitRequired = (modifiedCount>0 || deletedCount>0);
  }
```

```
    public override function set modifiedCount(val:uint ) : void{
      super.modifiedCount = val;
      commitRequired = (modifiedCount>0 || deletedCount>0);
    }
    .   .   .   .
}
```

The most notable feature of the UpdatableCollection is its *sync()* method. It sends an array of changes to the server. Our implementation of *sync()* will assume success and so we'll clear the state information in advance, right on the asynchronous send (invoke). However, to handle any potentially unpleasant surprises, we'll preserve the same state information in the asynchronous token:

```
    public function sync(): void {
      var act:AsyncToken = invoke(method + "_sync", [new
                                   ArrayCollection(changes)]);
      act.method = "sync";
      act.modified = modified;
      act.deleted = deleted;
      act.modifiedCount=modifiedCount;
      resetState();
    }

    public function get changes():Array {
      var args:Array = [];
      for ( var i :int = 0; i < deleted.length; i++) {
        args.push(
          new ChangeObject(
            ChangeObject.DELETE, null, deleted[i]
          )
        );
      }
      for ( var obj:Object in modified) {
        args.push( modified[obj]);
      }
      return args;
    }
```

Now, if things don't work out, we'll restore the status quo in the FAULT event handler:

```
    override protected function ro_onFault(evt:FaultEvent):void {
      CursorManager.removeBusyCursor();
      if (evt.token.method == "sync") {
        modified = evt.token.modified;
```

```
        modifiedCount = evt.token.modifiedCount;
        deleted = evt.token.deleted;
    }
    dispatchEvent(evt);
    if (alertOnFault) {
        Alert.show(evt.fault.faultString, "Error on destination: "
                                    + evt.message.destination);
    }
}
```

We are all set, short of separating a ResultEvent related to sync() from a ResultEvent originating in response to fill():

```
override protected function ro_onResult(evt:ResultEvent):void {
    CursorManager.removeBusyCursor();
  if (evt.token.method == "fill") {
     source = evt.result.source;
     trace(destination + "::" + method + "() fill returned " +
                    evt.result.source.length + " records");
     resetState();
     refresh();
  } else {
     trace( destination + "::" + method + "() completed");          }
  dispatchEvent(evt);
}
```

Believe it or not, but this is all there is to the UpdatableCollection; the complete code is in Listing 7.11:

```
// UpdatableCollection.as
package {
   import mx.collections.ArrayCollection;
   import mx.controls.Alert;
   import mx.events.*;
   import mx.managers.CursorManager;
   import mx.rpc.AsyncToken;
   import mx.rpc.events.*;

   import ChangeObject;

   public class UpdatableCollection extends  ChangeTrackingCollection {

      // We need this to allow marshalling of DataSyncException into
      // DataErrorMessage as part of FaultEvent
```

```
// Otherwise we will get something like
// type Coercion failed: cannot convert ... to mx.messaging.messages.IMessage
import mx.data.messages.DataErrorMessage;
private var linkage:DataErrorMessage;

public function UpdatableCollection(source:Array=null){
   super(source);
}
private var _commitRequired:Boolean = false;
public function set commitRequired(val :Boolean) :void {
   if (val!==_commitRequired) {
      _commitRequired = val;
      dispatchEvent(mx.events.PropertyChangeEvent.createUpdateEvent(this,
                     "commitRequired", !_commitRequired, _commitRequired));
   }
}
public function get commitRequired() :Boolean {
   return _commitRequired;
}

public override function set deletedCount(val:uint):void {
   super.deletedCount = val;
   commitRequired = (modifiedCount>0 || deletedCount>0);
}

public override function set modifiedCount(val:uint ) : void{
   super.modifiedCount = val;
   commitRequired = (modifiedCount>0 || deletedCount>0);
}

public function get changes():Array {
   var args:Array = [];
   for ( var i :int = 0; i < deleted.length; i++) {
      args.push(
         new ChangeObject(
            ChangeObject.DELETE, null, deleted[i]
         )
      );
   }
   for ( var obj:Object in modified) {
      args.push( modified[obj]);
   }
   return args;
}
```

```
    public function sync(): void {
        var act:AsyncToken = invoke(method + "_sync", [new ArrayCollection(changes)]);

        act.method = "sync";
        act.modified = modified;
        act.deleted = deleted;
        act.modifiedCount=modifiedCount;
        resetState();
    }

    override protected function ro_onFault(evt:FaultEvent):void {
         CursorManager.removeBusyCursor();
        if (evt.token.method == "sync") {
            modified = evt.token.modified;
            modifiedCount = evt.token.modifiedCount;
            deleted = evt.token.deleted;
        }
        dispatchEvent(evt);
        if (alertOnFault) {
            Alert.show(evt.fault.faultString, "Error on destination: " +
                                        evt.message.destination);
        }
    }

    override protected function ro_onResult(evt:ResultEvent):void {
         CursorManager.removeBusyCursor();
        if (evt.token.method == "fill") {
            source = evt.result.source;
            trace(destination + "::" + method + "() fill returned " +
                               evt.result.source.length + " records");
            resetState();
            refresh();
        } else {
            trace( destination + "::" + method + "() completed");

        }
        dispatchEvent(evt);
    }

  }
}
```

Listing 7.11 UpdatableCollection.as

Now let's spin our UpdatableCollection. The testing application, UpdatableCollectionDemo, is practically the same as the one we used to test ChangeTrackingCollection; we've just added a "Commit" button and changed the collection references:

```
<?xml version="1.0" encoding="UTF-8"?>
<!-- UpdatableCollectionDemo.mxml -->
<mx:Application xmlns:mx="http://www.adobe.com/2006/mxml"
  creationComplete="onCreationComplete()"
>
  <mx:TabNavigator id="tab"  change="onChange(event)">
    <mx:Panel label="Current">
    .  .  .  .  .
    <mx:ControlBar>
      <mx:Button label="Remove" click="collection.removeItemAt(dg.selectedIndex)"
        enabled="{dg.selectedIndex != -1}"/>
      <mx:Button label="Add" click="collection.addItemAt(new EmployeeDTO(),
                                        Math.max(0,dg.selectedIndex+1)) "/>
      <mx:Button label="Undo"
        click="collection.undoItem(dg.selectedItem) "
        enabled="{collection.isItemModified(EmployeeDTO(dg.selectedItem))}"
      />
      <mx:Button label="Commit"
        click="collection.sync()"
        enabled="{collection.commitRequired}"
      />
      <mx:Text text="Modified:{collection.modifiedCount}"/>
      <mx:Text text="Deleted:{collection.deletedCount}"/>
    </mx:ControlBar>
    </mx:Panel>
    .  .  .  .  .
  </mx:TabNavigator>

  <mx:Script>
    <![CDATA[
      import mx.collections.ArrayCollection;
      import UpdatableCollection;
      import com.theriabook.datasource.dto.EmployeeDTO;
      [Bindable] public var collection:UpdatableCollection;
      private function onCreationComplete():void {
        collection = new UpdatableCollection();
        collection.destination = "Employee";
        collection.method = "getEmployees";
        collection.fill(new Date());
```

```
        }
      ]]>
    </mx:Script>
  </mx:Application>
```

Listing 7.12 UpdatableCollectionDemo.mxml

All in all we 've taken you through the full cycle: we've built a self-sufficient collection that can feed itself with server-side data and that's capable of synchronizing changes with the server[5]. As you probably realize by now, three layers of inheritance – DestinationAware/ChangeTracking/UpdateableCollection – were required purely for didactic purposes. The source code accompanying this book contains the DataCollection in the com.theriabook.collections package that combines all functionality in one class.

Taking Care of Business: Transactions

Now that we've tamed DataCollection, let's think about business applications. More often than not, synchronizing client data with the server can't be confined to one database table or, in general, to one source of data. Take a simple case: customers place orders, each order can have several items with their own prices, quantities. etc.:

```
create table simple_order_item(
order_id char(32) not null,
item_id char(32) not null,
product_name varchar(32) not null,
quantity int(11) default '1' not null)
```

The order, as a whole, has its own attributes, such as the address and order date:

```
create table simple_order(
  order_id char(32) PRIMARY KEY not null,
  customer_first_name varchar(32) not null,
  customer_last_name varchar(32) not null,
  order_date datetime default '0000-00-00 00:00:00' not null,
  address varchar(64) not null)
```

Once the order is placed, the customer can update it. The customer will expect that the order creation as well as the order updates follow the transaction or "unit of work" paradigm: it can be completed only entirely; partial updates won't happen.

How can we implement transactions in RIA? One thing is certain: BEGIN and COMMIT (or ROLLBACK) should happen on the server. If our Java DAO is invoked via a DataServices adapter, the BEGIN has already happened. In a Flex Remoting scenario, we should handle transactions ourselves. Listing 7.13 represents the implementation of the DAO sync() method that would seamlessly work for both DataServices and Remoting:

```
public final List getOrders_sync(List items)
{
   logger.debug("getOrders_sync(...)");
   UserTransaction userTransaction = null;
   boolean localTransaction = false;
   boolean commit=false;
   try  {
      Context ctx = new InitialContext();
      String jndiName = "java:comp/UserTransaction";
      userTransaction = (UserTransaction)ctx.lookup(jndiName);
      if (userTransaction!=null) {
         if (userTransaction.getStatus()==Status.STATUS_NO_TRANSACTION) {
            localTransaction = true;
            userTransaction.begin();
            if (logger.isDebugEnabled()) logger.debug("BEGIN userTransaction");

         } else {
            if (logger.isDebugEnabled()) logger.debug("START PARTICIPATING in external
                                                                  transaction");
      }
         getOrders_deleteItems(items);
         getOrders_updateItems(items);
         getOrders_insertItems(items);
         commit = true;
      } else {
           logger.error("Cannot start/take part in a JTA transaction");
      }
   } catch(DataSyncException dse) {
      dse.printStackTrace();
      throw dse;
   } catch(Throwable te) {
      te.printStackTrace();
      throw new DAOException(te.getMessage(), te);
   } finally {
      if (userTransaction!=null) {
         try {
            if (localTransaction) {
               if (commit) {
                  userTransaction.commit();
                  if (logger.isDebugEnabled()) logger.debug("COMMIT userTransaction");

               } else {
```

```
                    userTransaction.rollback();
                    if (logger.isDebugEnabled()) logger.debug("ROLLBACK
                                                                userTransaction");
                }
            } else {
                if (!commit)
                    userTransaction.setRollbackOnly();
                    if (logger.isDebugEnabled()) logger.debug("Marked ROLLBACKONLY for
                                                         external transaction");
            }
        } catch (Exception e){
            logger.error("Could not rollback/mark transaction for rollback", e);
        }
    }
  }
  return items;
}
```

Listing 7.13 A "universal" Java sync() method for FDS and Remoting

This snippet follows the standard Java Transaction API (JTA) to tentatively begin, commit. or roll back transactions. If a transaction has been started earlier, it marks it for rollback with setRollback-Only(); such a transaction can never be committed; it'll throw an exception if someone attempts to do it. Please notice that we have broken the real sync into three parts, which will be explained a bit later:

```
getOrders_deleteItems(items);
getOrders_updateItems(items);
getOrders_insertItems(items);
```

Java Batch Gateway: Many Remote Calls in One Shot

The transaction handled by the sync() method works fine for only one table. In particular, the code in Listing 7.13 ensures that all deletes, updates, and inserts in the simple_order_item table are atomic. But how about transactions that span two tables: simple_orders and simple_order_items?

When we dealt with one DataCollection everything was simple: we remotely invoked the *syncMethod* and it took care of the transaction. In real life we have to deal with multiple DataCollections at a time. The issue then boils down to:

- Batching changes from multiple collections for a single remote call
- Creating a generic Flex Remoting destination that would process the batches so that all the changes get applied within the boundaries of the external JTA transaction

So let's step back and look at the DataCollection sync method or at any remote method for that matter. They can be completely described by *destination, method,* and *parameter* values. The Java's *BatchMember* class matches this triad:

```
package com.theriabook.remoting;
import java.util.*;

public class BatchMember {
   public String   destinationName;
   public String   methodName;
   public List     parameters;
}
```

Listing 7.14 Java BatchMember class

Setting aside the client's task of packing matching ActionScript BatchMembers into an ActionScript array, let's see how we could organize the sequential execution of the batch:

```
public List executeBatch(List batch) throws Throwable {
   List result = new ArrayList();
   Iterator iterator = batch.iterator();
   while(iterator.hasNext()) {
      BatchMember member = (BatchMember)iterator.next();
      result.add(invoke( member.destinationName, member.methodName,
                                                 member.parameters));
   }
   return result;
}
```

The *invoke()*method also consists of three major parts, which use the Flex Data Services API. First we find the destination by name:

```
MessageBroker mb = MessageBroker.getMessageBroker(null);
RemotingService srv = (RemotingService)mb.getServiceByType(
   "flex.messaging.services.RemotingService"
);
```

```
RemotingDestination remotingDestination = (RemotingDestination)srv.getDestinati
onByName(destinationName);
```

Then we get the object's instance and calculate the method reference:

```
FactoryInstance factoryInstance = remotingDestination.getFactoryInstance();
```

```
Object instance = factoryInstance.lookup();
Class clazz = instance.getClass();
MethodMatcher methodMatcher = remotingDestination.getMethodMatcher();
Method method = methodMatcher.getMethod(clazz, methodName, parameters);
```

Finally, we invoke the method and, in the case of an exception, unwrap the cause of the real exception from within the *InvocationTargetException* so that by the time the mx.rpc.events.FaultEvent comes to the ActionScript, it carries an exception as if it was a non-batched call:

```
try {
  result = method.invoke(instance, parameters.toArray());
} catch ( InvocationTargetException e) {
  logger.error(e, e.getCause());
  throw e.getCause();
}finally {
  factoryInstance.operationComplete(instance);

}
```

The complete code of the BatchGateway class is presented in Listing 7.15:

```
package com.theriabook.remoting;

  import java.lang.reflect.InvocationTargetException;
  import java.lang.reflect.Method;
  import java.util.*;

  import flex.data.DataServiceTransaction;
  import flex.messaging.FactoryInstance;
  import flex.messaging.util.*;
  import flex.messaging.services.remoting.RemotingDestination;
  import flex.messaging.MessageBroker;
  import flex.messaging.services.RemotingService;
  import javax.naming.Context;
  import javax.naming.InitialContext;
  import javax.transaction.*;

  import org.apache.log4j.Logger;
  import com.theriabook.daoflex.JDBCConnection;


  public class BatchGateway  {
    public Object invoke(String destinationName, String methodName, List parameters )
  throws IllegalAccessException, IllegalArgumentException, Throwable  {
```

```
        // This class throws up all exceptions, since this invoke
        // sequentially happens inside the bigger invoke of the JavaAdapter
        // which handles all of them anyway. However, we unwrap Invocation
        // target to avoid double wrapping.
        Object result = null;
        MessageBroker mb = MessageBroker.getMessageBroker(null);
        RemotingService srv = (RemotingService)mb.getServiceByType("flex.messaging.services.
          RemotingService");
        RemotingDestination remotingDestination = (RemotingDestination)srv.getDestinationBy
    Name(destinationName);
          FactoryInstance factoryInstance = remotingDestination.getFactoryInstance();
          Object instance = factoryInstance.lookup();
          Class clazz = instance.getClass();
        MethodMatcher methodMatcher = remotingDestination.getMethodMatcher();
        Method method = methodMatcher.getMethod(clazz, methodName, parameters);
        try {
          result = method.invoke(instance, parameters.toArray());
        } catch ( InvocationTargetException e) {
          logger.error(e, e.getCause());
          throw e.getCause();
        }finally {
          factoryInstance.operationComplete(instance);

        }
        return result;
    }


    public List executeBatch(List batch) throws Throwable {
        List result = new ArrayList();
        Iterator iterator = batch.iterator();
        while(iterator.hasNext()) {
          BatchMember member = (BatchMember)iterator.next();
          result.add(invoke( member.destinationName, member.methodName, member.param-
eters));
        }
        return result;
    }
    public List executeTransactionBatch(List batch) throws Throwable {
        UserTransaction userTransaction = null;
        List result = new ArrayList();
        boolean commit=false;
        try {
          Context ctx = new InitialContext();
```

```
        String jndiName = DataServiceTransaction.USER_TX_JNDI_NAME;//"java:comp/User-
Transaction";
        userTransaction = (UserTransaction)ctx.lookup(jndiName);
        userTransaction.begin();
        if (logger.isDebugEnabled()) logger.debug("BEGIN userTransaction");

        result = executeBatch(batch);
        commit = true;
        return result;
      } finally {
        if (userTransaction!=null) {
          if (commit) {
            userTransaction.commit();
            if (logger.isDebugEnabled()) logger.debug("COMMIT userTransaction");

          } else {
            userTransaction.rollback();
            if (logger.isDebugEnabled()) logger.debug("ROLLBACK userTransaction");

          }
        }
      }
    }
    static Logger logger;
    static
    {
          logger = Logger.getLogger(BatchGateway.class);
    }
  }
```

Listing 7.15 The Java BatchGateway class

We've added *executeTransactionBatch()*, which has the same mission as *executeBatch()*; it's sequentially calling all the listed remote methods and all this is done in a JTA transaction.

So Why bother with a non-transactional batch in the first place? Because a batch comes in very handy for retrieving. For example, if your screen presents the data from several tables, you don't want your application to be in an inconsistent state (half the screen is populated, half is done, half is refreshed, etc).

To be useful, this BatchGateway class has to be declared as a remoting destination:

```
<?xml version="1.0" encoding="UTF-8"?>
<!-- WEB-INF/flex/remoting-config.xml -->
```

```
<service id="remoting-service"
    class="flex.messaging.services.RemotingService"
    messageTypes="flex.messaging.messages.RemotingMessage">
    <adapters>
        <adapter-definition id="java-object" class="flex.messaging.services.remoting.
adapters.JavaAdapter" default="true"/>
    </adapters>

    <default-channels>
        <channel ref="my-amf"/>
    </default-channels>
   . . . .
    <destination id="batchGateway">
        <properties>
           <source>com.theriabook.remoting.BatchGateway</source>
        </properties>
   </destination>
</service>
```

Listing 7.16 Remoting-config.xml with "batchGateway" destination

BatchMember: Order Matters

We have created our own BatchGateway so let's see how to use it. To call *executeTransactionBatch()*, we need to prepare an array of ActionScript classes that will be marshaled into the Java List com. theriabook.remoting.BatchMember objects expected by BatchGateway. Here's the definition of the matching ActionScript class:

```
package com.theriabook.remoting {
      .
   [RemoteClass(alias="com.theriabook.remoting.BatchMember")]
   public class BatchMember {

      public var destinationName:String;
      public var methodName:String;
      public var parameters:Array;

       public function BatchMember(destinationName:String, methodName:String,
                                                           parameters:Array=null) {
        this.destinationName = destinationName;
        this.methodName = methodName;
        this.parameters = parameters;
       }
```

```
        public function toString():String { return "com.theriabook.remoting.BatchMember {
                    "+" destinationName:"+destinationName+" methodName:"+methodName+"
                                                parameters:"+parameters + "}" };
    }
}
```

Listing 7.17 ActionScript BatchMember class

We are almost there: for each collection that needs to join to the batch, we can write something like:

```
var bm:BatchMember;
var batch:Array=[];
bm = new BatchMember(
    orderCollection.destination,
    orderCollection.syncMethod,
    [orderCollection.changes]
);
batch.push(bm);
```

Then we could place a remote call to BatchGateway and process the callbacks. Mission accomplished…or so it seems.

Here's the problem, however. The *simple_orde*r and *simple_order_item* database tables represent a master/detail relationship. In referential integrity terms, simple_order_item could have had a foreign key on the column order_id from *simple_order*. In this scenario you won't be able to insert an item with a non-existent foreign key value; your transaction would succeed only if you inserted orders first.

In the case of a delete operation, a foreign key definition could possibly prescribe a cascade-deletion of all dependent order items, when an order is being deleted. That's something we could live with. But how about this: a foreign key could restrict the deletion of the order until the dependant order items exist. In other words, try to sync your collections in the wrong order and you're doomed!

BatchService

To solve the problem identified above, we'll create a *BatchService* class that once given a collection, adds three BatchMembers to the batch: one with deletes, one with inserts, and one with updates. In the case of more than one collection, our BatchService will consider its priorities and add deletes for all the collections in reverse order of priority, then add inserts and updates for all – in the opposite order.

Earlier we promised to explain why on the Java DAO side we've split the job of sync() into three calls of this sequence:

```
getOrders_deleteItems(items);
getOrders_updateItems(items);
getOrders_insertItems(items);
```

The reason is the need to expose these methods for remoting. As Anton Chekhov used to say[6]: "If in the first act you've hung a pistol on the wall, then in the following one it should be fired."

We'll see how pistols fire from inside our BatchService after introducing a BatchService's API. Suppose we have two collections – *orders* and *orderItems*:

```
orders = new DataCollection();
orders.destination="Order";
orders.method="getOrders";

orderItems = new DataCollection();
orderItems.destination="Order";
orderItems.method="getOrderItems";
```

Once the collections are created, we register them with the BatchService specifying their priorities:

```
batchService = new BatchService();
batchService.addEventListener(FaultEvent.FAULT, onCommitFault);

batchService.registerCollection(orders,0);
batchService.registerCollection(orderItems,1);
```

When it's time to synchronize – perhaps when the user clicks on the Save button – we ask the BatchService to make the batch and send it to the BatchGateway:

```
var batch:Array = batchService.batchRegisteredCollections();
batchService.sendBatch(batch);
```

That's all there is to a BatchService API and we can turn our attention to the implementation, see Listing 7.18. The focal point here is the batchRegisteredCollections() method. This method sends accumulated collection changes three times,[7] which, in case of a getOrdersDAO, translates to a sequential call via the BatchGateway:

```
getOrders_deleteItems(items)
getOrders_updateItems(items)
getOrders_insertItems(items)
```

The other two public methods – registerCollection() and sendBatch() – are rather simple. Please note how we re-dispatch ResultEvent and FaultEvent from the remote object to the instance of the BatchService so that the application can process it accordingly.

```
package com.theriabook.remoting
{
   import com.theriabook.collections.DataCollection;
   import com.theriabook.remoting.BatchMember;
   import mx.rpc.events.*;
   import mx.managers.CursorManager;

   import mx.rpc.*;
   import mx.rpc.remoting.mxml.RemoteObject;
   import flash.events.EventDispatcher;

   [Event(name="result", type="mx.rpc.events.ResultEvent")]
   [Event(name="fault", type="mx.rpc.events.FaultEvent")]
   public class BatchService extends EventDispatcher
   {
      public static const BATCH_GATEWAY_DESTINATION:String="batchGateway";
      protected var ro:RemoteObject = null;
      private var registeredCollections:Array=[];

      public function registerCollection(collection:DataCollection, priority:int=0):void
{
         registeredCollections.push({collection:collection, priority:priority});
      }


      public function batchRegisteredCollections():Array {
         var batch:Array = [];
         registeredCollections.sort(sortOnPriority);
         var collection:DataCollection;
         var member:BatchMember;
         for (var i:int=registeredCollections.length-1; i>=0; i-- ) {
            collection = registeredCollections[i].collection as DataCollection;
            member = new BatchMember(
               collection.destination,
               collection.method + "_deleteItems",
               [collection.changes]
            );
            batch.push(member);
         }
         for (i=0; i< registeredCollections.length; i++ ) {
            collection = registeredCollections[i].collection as DataCollection;
            member = new BatchMember(
               collection.destination,
               collection.method + "_updateItems",
```

```
            [collection.changes]
          );
          batch.push(member);
        }
        for (i=0; i< registeredCollections.length; i++ ) {
          collection = registeredCollections[i].collection as DataCollection;
          member = new BatchMember(
            collection.destination,
            collection.method + "_insertItems",
            [collection.changes]
          );
          batch.push(member);
        }
        return batch;
      }

      public function sendBatch(batch:Array, transaction:Boolean=true): AsyncToken {
        if( ro==null )  ro = createRemoteObject();
        var operation:AbstractOperation =
            ro.getOperation(transaction?"executeTransactionBatch":"executeBatch");
        operation.arguments = [batch];
        var act:AsyncToken = operation.send();
        act.arguments = batch;
        return act;
      }

      private function createRemoteObject():RemoteObject {
        var ro:RemoteObject = new RemoteObject(BATCH_GATEWAY_DESTINATION);
        ro.showBusyCursor = true;
        ro.concurrency    = "last";
        ro.addEventListener(ResultEvent.RESULT, ro_onResult);
        ro.addEventListener(FaultEvent.FAULT,  ro_onFault);
        return ro;
      }

      private function ro_onFault(event:FaultEvent):void {
        CursorManager.removeBusyCursor();
        dispatchEvent(event);
      }

      private function ro_onResult(evt:ResultEvent):void {
        var collection:DataCollection;
        for (var i:int=0; i< registeredCollections.length; i++ ) {
        collection = registeredCollections[i].collection as DataCollection;
```

```
        collection.resetState();
        }
        CursorManager.removeBusyCursor();
        dispatchEvent(evt);
    }

    private function sortOnPriority(a:Object, b:Object):int {
         var pa:int = a.priority;
         var pb:int = b.priority;
        if (pa > pb) {
             return 1;
         } else if (pa < pb) {
             return -1;
         } else  {
           //pa == pb
           return 0;
        }
    }
  }
}
```

Listing 7.18 BatchService.as

A Sample Application – An Order Entry

The following sections describe a sample application – OrderEntryDemo – that allows transactional data entry into the tables *simple_order and simple_order_item*. The application is composed of two panels: OrdersPanel and OrderItemsPanel with controller class – OrderManager as shown in Listing 7.19:

```
<?xml version="1.0" encoding="UTF-8"?>
<!--OrderEntryDemo.mxml -->
<mx:Application
   xmlns:mx="http://www.adobe.com/2006/mxml"
   xmlns="*"
   >
   <OrderManager id="orderManager" />
   <mx:ControlBar>
      <mx:Button label="Fill"  click="orderManager.fillOrders()"  />
      <mx:Button label="Commit"  click="orderManager.commit()" enabled="{orderManager.com
mitRequired}" />
   </mx:ControlBar>
   <mx:VDividedBox  >
      <OrdersPanel id="master" />
```

```
        <OrderItemsPanel id="detail" width="100%"/>
    </mx:VDividedBox>
</mx:Application>
```

Listing 7.19 OrderEntryDemo.mxml

The snapshot of a running OrderEntryDemo is presented in Figure 7.6. A click on the Fill button populates the Orders panel and the selection of a particular order repopulates OrderItems. Whenever the data is modified on either panel, the Commit button gets enabled and you can click on it to save the data changes to simple_order and simple_order_item in one transaction:

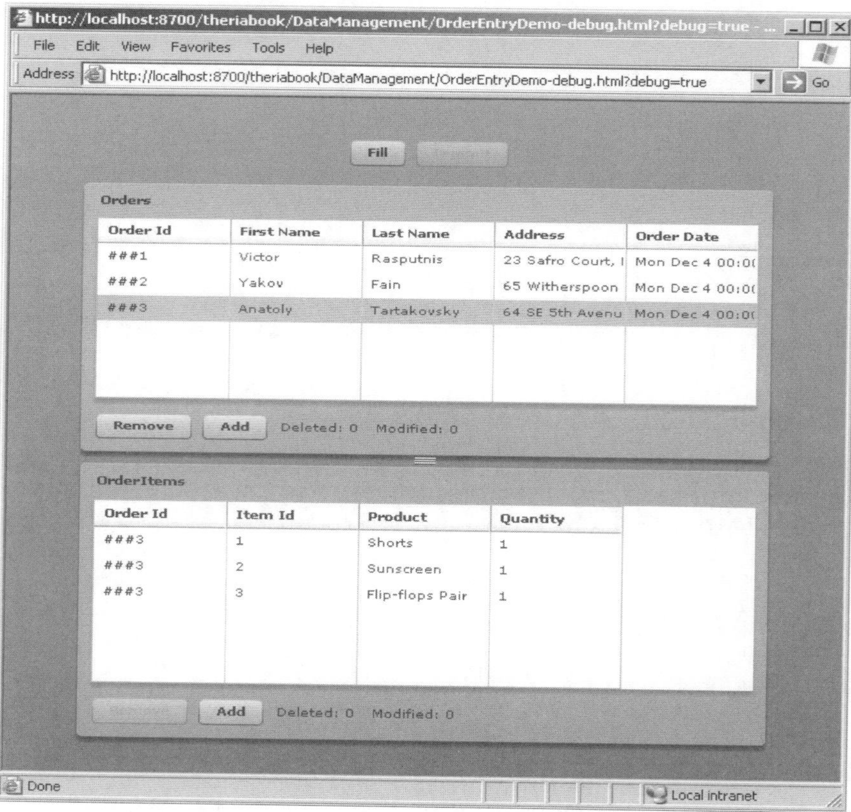

Figure 7.6 A snapshot from the OrderEntryDemo application

OrderEntryDemo Pre-requisites

We're not going to burden the reader again with the details of preparing DAO, Java, and Action-Script DTO, etc. Suffice it to say that to get everything in one shot, we process the source code of the Java class below with a DAOFlex generator:

```
package com.theriabook.datasource;
import java.util.List;

/**
 * @daoflex:webservice
 *   pool=jdbc/theriabook
 */

public abstract class Order {
      /**
      * @daoflex:sql
      *  sql=::
         select order_id, customer_first_name firstName,
         customer_last_name lastName, order_date,  address
        from   simple_order
         ::
      *  transferType=OrderDTO[]
      *  keyColumns=order_id
      *  updateTable=simple_order
      */

      public abstract List getOrders();

      /**
      * @daoflex:sql
      *  sql=select * from simple_order_item WHERE ORDER_ID=:orderId
      *  transferType=OrderItemDTO[]
      *  updateTable=simple_order_item
      *  keyColumns=order_id,item_id,product_name
      */

      public abstract List getOrderItems(String orderId);
}
```

Listing 7.20 The DAOFlex Java source file for an OrderEntryDemo application

As a result, all classes and JARs are properly deployed, and the only remaining thing to take care of is that our remoting-service.xml points to a generated destination-include file Order.xml:

```
<?xml version="1.0" encoding="UTF-8"?>
<service id="remoting-service"
    class="flex.messaging.services.RemotingService"
```

```
    messageTypes="flex.messaging.messages.RemotingMessage">
    <adapters>
        <adapter-definition id="java-object" class="flex.messaging.services.remoting.
adapters.JavaAdapter" default="true"/>
    </adapters>

    <default-channels>
        <channel ref="my-amf"/>
    </default-channels>

    <destination id="batchGateway">
        <properties>
            <source>com.theriabook.remoting.BatchGateway</source>
        </properties>
    </destination>
    <destination-include file-path="daoflex/remoting-config/Order.xml" />

</service>
```

Listing 7.21 Remoting-config.xml with a manually included Order.xml

```
<?xml version="1.0" encoding="UTF-8"?>
<!--Order.xml.
 Generated by DaoFlex via remoting-config.xsl-->
<destination id="Order">
<properties>
<source>com.theriabook.datasource.OrderDAO</source>
</properties>
</destination>
```

Listing 7.22 Generated Order.xml with an Order destination

OrderEntryDemo: OrdersPanel

Now let's look at the details of the application code. The top panel of the application, OrdersPanel, binds its data grid to the collection, a private variable of the component:

```
<mx:DataGrid id="dg" dataProvider="{collection}" .../>
```

Importantly, this variable, upon execution of the onCreationComplete(), carries a reference to a bindable *orders* collection hosted by the OrderManager. In other words, the data grid of *orders* serves as a pure view of the orders collection from the OrderManager:

```
private function onCreationComplete() : void {
   orderManager = Application.application.orderManager;
   collection = orderManager.orders;
}
```

The buttons Add and Remove delegate their work to the orderManager in a clean MVC style:

```
private function onAdd(position:int):void  {
   orderManager.addOrder(position);
   dg.selectedIndex = position;
}
private function onRemove(position:int):void {
   orderManager.removeOrder(position);
}
```

Finally, whenever the user is changing the row selection, we communicate the selected *orderId* to the OrderManager:

```
<mx:DataGrid id="dg" dataProvider="{collection}"
    change="orderManager.orderId=dg.selectedItem.ORDER_ID">
```

The complete code for the OrdersPanel is presented in Listing 7.23:

```
<?xml version="1.0" encoding="UTF-8"?>
<!-- OrdersPanel.mxml -->
<mx:Panel title="Orders"
   xmlns:mx="http://www.adobe.com/2006/mxml"
   creationComplete="onCreationComplete()">

   <mx:DataGrid id="dg" dataProvider="{collection}" editable="true" height="100%"
       change="orderManager.orderId=dg.selectedItem.ORDER_ID">
      <mx:columns>
         <mx:Array>
            <mx:DataGridColumn dataField="ORDER_ID" headerText="Order Id" />
            <mx:DataGridColumn dataField="FIRSTNAME" headerText="First Name" />
            <mx:DataGridColumn dataField="LASTNAME" headerText="Last Name" />
            <mx:DataGridColumn dataField="ADDRESS" headerText="Address"  />
            <mx:DataGridColumn dataField="ORDER_DATE" headerText="Order Date"
itemEditor="mx.controls.DateField" editorDataField="selectedDate"/>
         </mx:Array>
      </mx:columns>
   </mx:DataGrid>
   <mx:ControlBar width="100%">
      <mx:Button label="Remove" click="onRemove(dg.selectedIndex)" enabled="{dg.selectedI
```

```
ndex != -1}"/>
        <mx:Button label="Add" click="onAdd(Math.max(0,dg.selectedIndex+1)); "/>
        <mx:Label text="Deleted: {collection.deletedCount}"/>
        <mx:Label text="Modified: {collection.modifiedCount}"/>
    </mx:ControlBar>
    <mx:Script>
    <![CDATA[
    import mx.core.Application;
    import com.theriabook.collections.DataCollection;

    [Bindable]
    private var collection:DataCollection;
    private var orderManager:OrderManager ;

    private function onCreationComplete() : void {
       orderManager = Application.application.orderManager;
       collection = orderManager.orders;
    }
    private function onAdd(position:int):void {
       orderManager.addOrder(position);
       dg.selectedIndex = position;
    }
    private function onRemove(position:int):void {
       orderManager.removeOrder(position);
    }

    ]]>
    </mx:Script>
</mx:Panel>
```

Listing 7.23 OrdersPanel.mxml

OrderEntryDemo: OrderItemsPanel

The bottom panel of the application, OrderItemsPanel, populates its data grid with data from a bindable *orderItems* collection, hosted by the OrderManager:

```
<mx:DataGrid id="dg" dataProvider="{collection}" editable="true" height="100%"
..../>

  [Bindable]private var collection:DataCollection ;
  [Bindable]private var orderManager:OrderManager ;

  private function onCreationComplete() : void {
```

```
    orderManager = Application.application.orderManager;
    collection = orderManager.orderItems;
  }
```

Similar to the OrdersPanel, the buttons Add and Remove delegate their work to the OrderManager:

```
  private function onAdd(position:int):void  {
    orderManager.addOrderItem(position);
    dg.selectedIndex = position;
  }

  private function onRemove(position:int):void {
    orderManager.removeOrderItem(position);
  }
```

The complete code of the OrderItemsPanel is presented in Listing 7.24:

```
<?xml version="1.0" encoding="utf-8"?>
<!-- OrderItemsPanel.mxml -->
<mx:Panel title="OrderItems"
    xmlns:mx="http://www.adobe.com/2006/mxml"
    creationComplete="onCreationComplete()"
    >
<mx:DataGrid id="dg" dataProvider="{collection}" editable="true" height="100%">
      <mx:columns>
        <mx:Array>
          <mx:DataGridColumn dataField="ORDER_ID" headerText="Order Id" />
          <mx:DataGridColumn dataField="ITEM_ID" headerText="Item Id" />
          <mx:DataGridColumn dataField="PRODUCT_NAME" headerText="Product" />
          <mx:DataGridColumn dataField="QUANTITY" headerText="Quantity" />
        </mx:Array>
      </mx:columns>
    </mx:DataGrid>
    <mx:ControlBar width="100%">
      <mx:Button label="Remove" click="onRemove(dg.selectedIndex);" enabled="{dg.selected
Index != -1}"/>
      <mx:Button label="Add" click="onAdd(Math.max(0,dg.selectedIndex + 1)); "
enabled="{orderManager.orderId!=null}"/>
      <mx:Label text="Deleted: {collection.deletedCount}"/>
      <mx:Label text="Modified: {collection.modifiedCount}"/>
    </mx:ControlBar>
    <mx:Script>
      <![CDATA[
```

```
        import mx.core.Application;
        import com.theriabook.collections.DataCollection;

        [Bindable]private var collection:DataCollection ;
        [Bindable]private var orderManager:OrderManager ;

        private function onCreationComplete() : void {
           orderManager = Application.application.orderManager;
           collection = orderManager.orderItems;
        }
        private function onAdd(position:int):void {
           orderManager.addOrderItem(position);
           dg.selectedIndex = position;
        }
        private function onRemove(position:int):void {
           orderManager.removeOrderItem(position);
        }
     ]]>
     </mx:Script>
  </mx:Panel>
```

Listing 7.24 OrderItemsPanel.mxml

OrderEntryDemo: OrderManager

A class OrderManager is also important. It encapsulates *orders* and *orderItems* collections along with the methods that manipulate these collections.

The most important things here are the methods that populate collections and communicate the changes to the server. Populating is rather trivial; we delegate it to the *fill()* method of the appropriate collection:

```
orders.fill();
orderItems.fill(orderId);
```

To send the changes to the server in one transactional batch, we use the BatchService:

```
batchService = new BatchService();
batchService.addEventListener(FaultEvent.FAULT, onCommitFault);
batchService.registerCollection(orders,0);
batchService.registerCollection(orderItems,1);
  . . . .
var batch:Array = batchService.batchRegisteredCollections();
batchService.sendBatch(batch);
```

How do you determine that changes are pending on a DataCollection? You can use the bindable property *commitRequired*. And what if you have several DataCollections? Please notice the technique we used to determine if anything needs to be saved on at least one of the DataCollections:

```
[Bindable]public var commitRequired:Boolean;

. . .
orders.addEventListener(
  PropertyChangeEvent.PROPERTY_CHANGE, onPropertyChange
);
orderItems.addEventListener(
  PropertyChangeEvent.PROPERTY_CHANGE, onPropertyChange
);
. . .

public function onPropertyChange(event:PropertyChangeEvent):void {
  if (event.property == "commitRequired") {
    commitRequired = (
      orders.commitRequired || orderItems.commitRequired
    );
  }
}
```

We have covered the most interesting details of OrderManager. The complete code for the OrderManager class is in Listing 7.25:

```
// OrderManager.as
package
{
  import flash.events.EventDispatcher;
  import mx.events.PropertyChangeEvent;
  import mx.rpc.events.FaultEvent;
  import mx.controls.Alert;
  import com.theriabook.collections.DataCollection;
  import com.theriabook.datasource.dto.OrderDTO;
  import com.theriabook.datasource.dto.OrderItemDTO;
  import com.theriabook.remoting.BatchService;

  public class OrderManager
  {

    [Bindable]public var orders:DataCollection ;
    [Bindable]public var orderItems:DataCollection ;
```

```
[Bindable]public var commitRequired:Boolean;
private var _orderId:String;

[Bindable]
public function set orderId(newOrderId:String):void {
   _orderId = newOrderId;
   fillOrderItems(newOrderId);
}
public function get orderId():String {
   return _orderId;
}

public var batchService:BatchService;
public function OrderManager(){
   orders = new DataCollection();
   orders.destination="Order";
   orders.method="getOrders";
   orderItems = new DataCollection();
   orderItems.destination="Order";
   orderItems.method="getOrderItems";
   batchService = new BatchService();
   batchService.addEventListener(FaultEvent.FAULT, onCommitFault);
   batchService.registerCollection(orders,0);
   batchService.registerCollection(orderItems,1);
   orders.addEventListener(PropertyChangeEvent.PROPERTY_CHANGE, onPropertyChange);
   orderItems.addEventListener(PropertyChangeEvent.PROPERTY_CHANGE, onProper-
tyChange);
}

public function onPropertyChange(event:PropertyChangeEvent):void {
   if (event.property == "commitRequired") {
      commitRequired = (orders.commitRequired || orderItems.commitRequired);
   }
}
public function fillOrders():void {
   orders.fill();
}

public function fillOrderItems(orderId:String):void {
   orderItems.fill(orderId);
}

public function commit():void {
   var batch:Array = batchService.batchRegisteredCollections();
```

```
        batchService.sendBatch(batch);
    }

    public function onCommitFault(event:Object):void {
        Alert.show(event.fault.faultString , "Error");
    }

    public function addOrder (position:int):OrderDTO {
        var item:OrderDTO = new OrderDTO();
        item.ORDER_DATE = new Date();
        orders.addItemAt(item, position);
        orderItems.removeAll();
        orderItems.resetState(); // We do not want deletes, don't we?
        return item;
    }
    public function removeOrder(position:int):void {
        orderItems.removeAll();
        orders.removeItemAt(position);
        commit();
    }
    public function addOrderItem (position:int):OrderItemDTO {
        var item:OrderItemDTO = new OrderItemDTO();
        item.ORDER_ID = orderId;
        item.QUANTITY = 1;
        orderItems.addItemAt(item, position);
        return item;
    }
    public function removeOrderItem(position:int):void {
        orderItems.removeItemAt(position);
    }

  }
}
```

Listing 7.25 OrderManager.as

Conclusion

Flex Remoting, as this chapter illustrates, can be a simplified alternative to Flex Data Services. We didn't attempt to provide all the functionality offered by FDS. For example, we didn't address the data push and pagination that come free with FDS. And yet, there are distinct advantages to using Flex Remoting:

- Your server's memory isn't burdened with persisting identities for each subscribed collection.
- You don't depend on session replication or, for that matter, any clustering features.

- You have unlimited flexibility in managing your data from the ActionScript side.

Either mechanism, as we have shown in this and previous chapters, requires building a routine set of Java and ActionScript objects, a process that with an open source DAOFlex generator utility can be completly automated.

Endnotes

1. Flex Data Services terminology might look a bit confusing. At the architectural level, Flex Data Services encompass Data Management Services, Remoting Services and Messaging Services. At the API level, DataService object maps to a Data Management Service, which is only a part of the FDS. This chapter discusses data management with remoting, which is also a part of FDS. Please be aware that elsewhere in the chapter, when we refer to Data Services we mean a specific part of the Data Management Service.

2. We mean a request possibly pending for this remote object. Flex accumulates requests in batches; a batch is sent to the Flex MessageBroker servlet after a cycle of script execution and drawing is complete.

3. To be precise, typing alone is not enough: you need to change the focus from the modified cell to activate the lower-level event that, eventually, results in CollectionEvent.

4. We have omittedthe implementation details of com.theriabook.remoting.ChangeObjectImpl for brevity, but you can find the code in the accompanying CD and download.

5. In all honesty, we can't credit UpdatableCollection with being completely self-sufficient. At the end of the day it takes two to tango, and without a server-side DAO class it wouldn't happen.

6. A Russian doctor and short story author who became a world famous playwrite.

7. You may suggest that we don't send the entire list of changes each time. Indeed, the copy of BatchService that comes with the book extracts deletes, updates, and inserts separately and sends only what is required. We omitted these details here for clarity's sake.

CHAPTER

8

Enhancing and Extending Flex Controls

Enhancing and Extending Flex Controls

The Flex framework contains a pretty impressive Flex library of off-the-shelf controls, which can fit the bill for many rich Internet applications needs. Yet, it's just the tip of the iceberg, because Flex lets you create, combine, and extend existing components with a simplicity and elegance hardly ever offered by other GUI development systems.

In this chapter we're going to lead you step-by-step through the process of extending a standard ComboBox component, which is a combination of an edit field, button, and dropdown list. We'll be customizing the API and adding some new functionality, making our ComboBox a bit handier than the standard one. In particular, we'll create a ComboBox with a multi-column dropdown list, then we'll create a "destination-aware" ComboBox populated from the server using an RPC call, and we'll show you how to implement the autocomplete feature for editable controls.

ComboBox Challenges

A typical task, while working with a standard ComboBox, is to programmatically select a specific value. Suppose our ComboBox is populated with an array of states:

```
private var usStates:Array=[
   {label:"New York", data:"NY"},
   {label:"Colorado", data:"CO"},
   {label:"Texas", data:"TX"}
];
.   .   .   .   .   .   .   .
<mx:ComboBox id="cbx_states" dataProvider="{states}"/>
```

To programmatically select Texas (in the visible portion of the ComboBox), you can write the following index-fetching loop, comparing val against the label of each element of the dataProvider:

```
var val:String;
```

```
val = 'Texas' ;
for (var i: int = 0; i < cbx.dataProdider.length; i++) {
  if ( val == cbx_states.dataProvider[i].label) {
   cbx_states.selectedIndex = i;
   break;
  }
}
```

Alternatively, you could look up the data of the dataProvider's elements:

```
var val:String;

val = 'TX'  ;
for (var i: int = 0; i < cbx.dataProdider.length; i++) {
  if ( val == cbx.dataProvider[i].data) {
   cbx_states.selectedIndex = i;
   break;
  }
}
```

Either way these index-fetching loops will clutter the application code instead of the simple *cbx_states.value='Texas.'*

On top of that, index fetching via data is often unapplicable. Consider real-life ComboBox records coming from databases, messages, etc. We can't "mandate" these data sources to contain a data field in the relevant record sets. And while the standard ComboBox provides a *labelField* property, allowing us to draw a label value from an arbitrary property, there's no *dataField* property, which would provide a similar flexibility for data.

So far we've identified what we would like to improve in *setting* the *value*. Now let's look at the opposite operations. The standard ComboBox offers the properties *selectedIndex* and *selectedItem*. When a ComboBox is populated with strings, selectedItem returns the selected string (or null if nothing is selected). If it's populated with objects, selectedItem references the selected object (or contains null):

```
<mx:Application xmlns:mx=http://www.adobe.com/2006/mxml creationComplete="onCreationComp
lete()">

private function onCreationComplete():void {
   mx.control.Alert.show(cbx_states.selectedItem.label); // displays 'New York'
   cbx_states.selectedIndex=-1;         //Removes initial selection
   mx.control.Alert.show(cbx_states.selectedItem); // "displays" null
}
. . . . . . . . . .
```

```
</mx:Application>
```

Listing 8.1 Using selectedItem and selectedIndex properties

But wait, there's also a read-only *value* property: if a selected object has something in the data property, the value refers to data, otherwise *value* refers to the *label*:

```
mx.control.Alert.show(cbx_states.value); // displays 'NY'
```

As you can see *value* does half the job: it gives us "read" access and shields us from *selectedItem/selectedIndex*. What we miss is the other half and in the following sections we'll turn *value* into a read-write property. That will forever absolve us from index-fetching loops to modify the ComboBox selection.

We'll also introduce the *dataField* property to allow any arbitrary property in place of the data, depending on a specific ComboBox use case.

Making the Value Property Writeable

Let's start with upgrading the *value* to a first-class writeable property. The simplest way to do this is by extending the original ComboBox so that the derived class provides a special setter for the value property. The setter attempts to find the item in the dataProvider's collection with either *data* or *label* property matching the new value of *value*. Once a match is found, it modifies the *selectedIndex*, which should cause the ComboBox to select the matching object:

```
<?xml version="1.0" encoding="utf-8"?>
<mx:ComboBox xmlns:mx="http://www.adobe.com/2006/mxml" >
<mx:Script>
<![CDATA[
   public function set value(val:Object)  : void {
      if ( val != null ) {
         for (var i : int = 0; i < dataProvider.length; i++) {
            if ( val == dataProvider[i].data || val == dataProvider[i].label) {
               selectedIndex = i;
               return;
      } } }
      selectedIndex = -1;
   }
]]>
</mx:Script>
</mx:ComboBox>
```

Listing 8.2 Making the value property writeable

If the ComboBox.mxml is located under the *com/theriabook/controls*, it's test application can look like Listing 8.3.

```
<?xml version="1.0" encoding="utf-8"?>
<mx:Application xmlns:mx="http://www.adobe.com/2006/mxml" xmlns="*" xmlns:lib="com.the-
riabook.controls.*">
   <mx:ArrayCollection id="comboData" >
      <mx:Array>
         <mx:Object label="New York" data="NY"/>
         <mx:Object label="Connecticut" data="CT"/>
         <mx:Object label="Illinois" data="IL"/>
      </mx:Array>
   </mx:ArrayCollection>
   <mx:Label text="Current bound value is &quot;{cbx_1.value}&quot;" />
   <lib:ComboBox id="cbx_1" value="IL" width="150" dataProvider="{comboData}"/>
</mx:Application>
```

Listing 8.3 Using our new ComboBox

Run this application and you'll see the ComboBox displaying the value New York when we'd expect Illinois. We forgot about the order in which objects' properties get initialized. The value property in our case is initialized before the *dataProvider*. Then the initialization of *dataProvider* makes the first (default) item selected and the work done by our value setter is wasted. You can prove the point just by trading the places of the *value* and *dataProvider* in the application code above.

Should we rely on the order of the attributes in the MXML components? Apparently not. Especially when Flex offers an excellent mechanism to coordinate the updates to multiple properties of the control – the *commitProperties()* method.

Here's how it works: whenever you need to modify a property, raise some indicator, store the value in the temporary variable, and call *invalidateProperties()* as in the following snippet:

```
private var candidateValue:Object;
private var valueDirty:Boolean = false;

public function set value(val:Object)  : void {
   candidateValue = val;
   valueDirty = true;
   invalidateProperties();
}
```

In response to *invalidateProperties()* Flex will schedule a call of *commitProperties()* for later execution so that all property changes deferred in the above manner can be consolidated in a single place and in a pre-determined order:

```
override protected function commitProperties():void {
   super.commitProperties();

   if (dataProviderDirty) {
      super.dataProvider = candidateDataProvider;
      dataProviderDirty = false;
   }

   if (valueDirty) {
      applyValue(candidateValue);
      valueDirty = false;
   }
   }
```

Aside from co-ordinating updates to different properties, this coding pattern helps to avoid multiple updates to the same property and, in general, allows setter methods to return faster, improving the overall performance of the control. The entire code of our "value-aware" ComboBox is presented in Listing 8.4:

```
<?xml version="1.0" encoding="utf-8"?>
<mx:ComboBox xmlns:mx="http://www.adobe.com/2006/mxml" >
<mx:Script>
   <![CDATA[

   private var candidateValue:Object;
   private var valueDirty:Boolean = false;
   private var candidateDataProvider:Object;
   private var dataProviderDirty:Boolean = false;

   private function applyValue(val:Object):void {
      if ((val != null) && (dataProvider != null)) {

         for (var i : int = 0; i < dataProvider.length; i++) {
            if ( val == dataProvider[i].data || val == dataProvider[i].label) {
               selectedIndex = i;
               return;
      } } }
      selectedIndex = -1;
   }

   public function set value(val:Object)  : void {
      candidateValue = val;
      valueDirty = true;
      invalidateProperties();
```

```
    }
    override public function set dataProvider(value:Object):void {
       candidateDataProvider = value;
       dataProviderDirty = true;
       invalidateProperties();
    }

    override protected function commitProperties():void {
       super.commitProperties();

       if (dataProviderDirty){
          super.dataProvider = candidateDataProvider;
          dataProviderDirty = false;
       }

       if (valueDirty) {
          applyValue(candidateValue);
          valueDirty = false;
       }
    }
    ]]>
  </mx:Script>
  </mx:ComboBox>
```

Listing 8.4 The value-aware ComboBox

Now everything works as expected. The screenshot of the running application is presented in Figure 8.1.

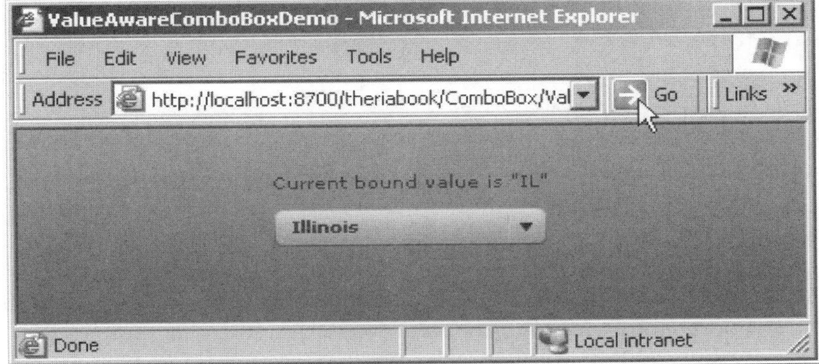

Figure 8.1 The "value-aware ComboBox in action

If you change the ComboBox selection, the top label, which initially contains a current bound value, is "IL" and will change accordingly. No miracles here, a regular Flex data binding, one would say. Indeed, good things are easy to take for granted. Still, we haven't provided any binding declarations or binding code in our ComboBox. So why does it work? It works because the original Flex definition of the value getter ComboBox has already been marked with a metadata tag ["Bindable"], which makes the property bindable (you don't have to have a setter to be bindable):

```
[Bindable("change")]
[Bindable("valueCommitted")]
```

But wait, you may say, these binding definitions indicate that data modifications bound to the value property get triggered in response to change or valueCommitted events. Yet our value setter doesn't contain a single dispatchEvent call. What's the catch? Events are dispatched inside the code that assigns a *selectedIndex*. This assignment results in invoking a selectedIndex *setter*, which ultimately dispatches the events.

Adding a dataField Property

Two important structural elements of an object populating the ComboBox are *label* and *data*. To map the *label* property to a field of such a business object, Flex ComboBox offers a read-write property called *labelField* (there's another mapping mechanism, *labelFunction*, a callback that returns the string to be stored in the object's label). However, Flex ComboBox doesn't give you the same choice in the *data* property. We'll fill this gap by introducing a new *dataField* property. In other words, we'd like to be able to write something like:

```
<mx:Application xmlns:mx=http://www.adobe.com/2006/mxml
xmlns:lib="com.theriabook.controls.*">
. . . . . . . .
  <lib:ComboBox   id="cbx_1" width="150" value="123" labelField="state_name"
dataField="state_code" dataProvider="{comboData}"/>
</mx:Application>
```

To do this, we'll start by adding a public variable *dataField* to our ComboBox that by default will store the same value as in the *data* property:

```
public var dataField:String = "data";
```

Next, we'll modify the *applyValue()* to do the data comparison of the *dataField* and the *labelField*, instead of directly operating on the *data* and *label* properties:

```
private function applyValue(val:Object)  : void {
   if ((val != null) && (dataProvider != null)) {
      for (var i : int = 0; i < dataProvider.length; i++) {
       if (val==dataProvider[i][dataField] ||
```

```
                    val==  dataProvider[i][labelField]) {
              selectedIndex = i;
              return;
              }
                }
         }
         selectedIndex = -1;
   }
```

This time we also have to override the default value getter to recognize the newly introduced dataField similar to the setter:

```
   override public function get value()  : Object {
         var item:Object = selectedItem;
         if (item == null || typeof(item) != "object") return item;
         return item[dataField] ? item[dataField] : item.label;
    }
```

When overriding system properties you should take care of the metadata as well. As long as we were only responsible for the setter, we could have relied on the metadata bindings coming through the standard getter in the ancestor class. Now that we've overridden the getter as well, we're on our own. The following lines should be added in front of either the getter or setter for the value property:

```
   [Bindable("change")]
   [Bindable("valueCommitted")]
   [Inspectable(defaultValue="0", category="General", verbose="1")]
```

The complete listing for the customized ComboBox with the new dataField property is presented in Listing 8.5:

```
   <?xml version="1.0" encoding="utf-8"?>
   <mx:ComboBox xmlns:mx="http://www.adobe.com/2006/mxml" >
   <mx:Script>
      <![CDATA[

      public var dataField:String = "data";

      private var candidateValue:Object;
      private var valueDirty:Boolean = false;
      private var candidateDataProvider:Object;
      private var dataProviderDirty:Boolean = false;

      [Bindable("change")]
      [Bindable("valueCommit")]
```

```
[Inspectable(defaultValue="0", category="General", verbose="1")]
override public function get value()  : Object {
     var item:Object = selectedItem;
     if (item == null || typeof(item) != "object") return item;
     return item[dataField] ? item[dataField] : item.label;
 }

private function applyValue(val:Object):void {
   if ((val != null) && (dataProvider != null)) {

      for (var i : int = 0; i < dataProvider.length; i++) {
         if ( val == dataProvider[i][dataField] || val == dataProvider[i][labelField])
{
            selectedIndex = i;
            return;
   } } }
   selectedIndex = -1;
}

public function set value(val:Object)  : void {
   candidateValue = val;
   valueDirty = true;
   invalidateProperties();
}
override public function set dataProvider(value:Object):void {
   candidateDataProvider = value;
   dataProviderDirty = true;
   invalidateProperties();
}
override protected function commitProperties():void {
   super.commitProperties();

   if (dataProviderDirty){
      super.dataProvider = candidateDataProvider;
      dataProviderDirty = false;
   }

   if (valueDirty) {
      applyValue(candidateValue);
      valueDirty = false;
   }
}

]]>
```

```
</mx:Script>
</mx:ComboBox>
```

Listing 8.5 A ComboBox with the DataField value

The test application code is presented in Listing 8.6. Now you can map any business object's properties (regardless of what their names are) while declaring the new version of the ComboBox, which will give you extra flexibility.

```
<?xml version="1.0" encoding="utf-8"?>
<mx:Application xmlns:mx="http://www.adobe.com/2006/mxml" xmlns:lib="com.theriabook.
controls.*">
   <mx:ArrayCollection id="comboData" >
      <mx:Array>
         <mx:Object state_name="New York" state_code="NY"/>
         <mx:Object state_name="Connecticut" state_code="CT"/>
         <mx:Object state_name="Illinois" state_code="IL"/>
      </mx:Array>
   </mx:ArrayCollection>
   <mx:Label id="lbl_1" text="Current bound value is &quot;{cbx_1.value}&quot;" />
   <lib:ComboBox   id="cbx_1" width="150" value="IL" labelField="state_name"
dataField="state_code" dataProvider="{comboData}"/>
</mx:Application>
```

Listing 8.6 A test application for the ComboBox

ComboBox with a Multi-Column List

Let's make our ComboBox a bit fancier by teaching the dropdown list portion of the ComboBox to carry multiple columns of data. It may please users and does not require any code changes to the ComboBox: the underlying mechanism, known as *item rendering*, is provided by Flex off-the-shelf.

Flex creators envisioned that most of the application-specific richness should come from application developers. In particular, while on the surface the standard ComboBox still resembles its HTML counterpart, an elegant Flex mechanism of custom item renderers lets us turn the boring single-column dropdown into a fancy multi-column one. We have to mention that it can also implement the multi-column ComboBox without resorting to an explicit item renderer. Please see *MultiColumnComboBoxDropDownFactoryDemo.mxml* in the samples that come with the book. This sample is based on the *dropdownFactory* property of the ComboBox:

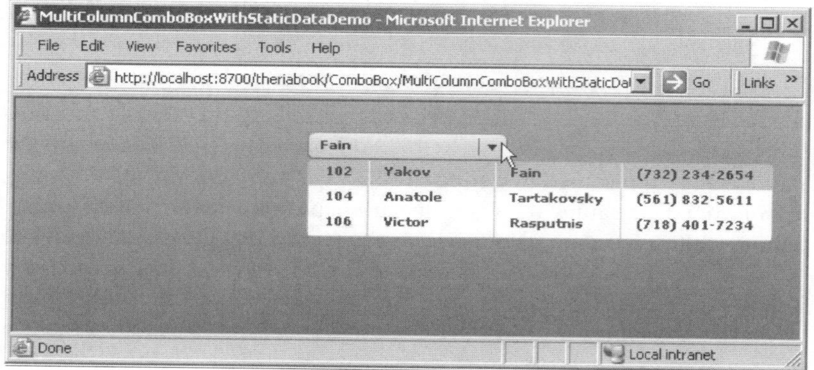

Figure 8.2 A ComboBox with a multi-column dropdown

Flex item renderers go inline with the best traditions of Macintosh, OS/2, and Windows presentation engines, where similar mechanisms were known as an "owner draw" painting. Specifically, item renderer lets us modify the look-and-feel of items in any list-based control, such as DataGrid, List, Tree, etc. The dropdown portion of the ComboBox is nothing but the List. Hence we'e going to build a renderer that will show four columns with controlled widths, separated with vertical lines, as shown in Figure 8.2.

First, though, we'll modify the data used to populate the ComboBox. So far we've been working with a collection of U.S. states, each element of the collection being a name-code value pair. Now we'll change the *comboData* collection into an array of four-field objects containing *emp_id, fname, lname,* and *phone*:

```
<mx:ArrayCollection id="comboData" >
  <mx:Array>
    <mx:Object emp_id="102" fname="Yakov" lname="Fain" phone="7322342654"/>
    <mx:Object emp_id="104" fname="Anatole" lname="Tartakovsky"
                                                  phone="5618325611"/>
   <mx:Object emp_id="106" fname="Victor" lname="Rasputnis"
                                                  phone="7184017234"/>
 </mx:Array>
</mx:ArrayCollection>
```

The data is ready, and we proceed to the renderer. One way of packaging the item renderer is to create a special ActionScript class or MXML component file. Alternatively, Flex provides a way to define a nested MXML component with an <mx:Component> tag. To simplify our example we'll go with such an *inline* renderer; although we were looking for unlimited reusability we'd certainly select the dedicated file, aka *drop-in* renderer.

Below is the definition of our inline renderer. We start with the Component tag, which carries specific scoping arrangements. Most importantly, the property *data* in the scope of the inline renderer references the element of the dataProvider that corresponds to the relevant item of the list. (On par with *data* there's another property – *outerDocument* – that references the same scope that our ComboBox is within).

The inline component includes an HBox containing four Labels, a separating VRule between each column, and a PhoneFormatter to format the phone number with a default phone format. We split the width of the dropdown list between our columns as 10%, 35%, 35%, and 20%. We'll just set the height of the HBox to 20 pixels to accommodate the size of the default font. To avoid individual scrollbars in each cell of the list we turn off both the horizontal and vertical scroll policy styles:

```
<mx:Component
   <mx:HBox horizontalScrollPolicy="off" verticalScrollPolicy="off" height="20">
     <mx:PhoneFormatter id="phoneFormatter"/>
    <mx:Label text="{data.emp_id}" width="10%"/><mx:VRule />
    <mx:Label text="{data.fname}" width="35%"/><mx:VRule />
    <mx:Label text="{data.lname}"   width="35%"/><mx:VRule />
    <mx:Label text="{phoneFormatter.format(data.phone)}" width="20%"/>
   </mx:HBox>
</mx:Component>
```

For a standard ComboBox to actually inline an item renderer we'd have to write:

```
  <mx:ComboBox id="cbx_1" value="102"   width="150" . . .>
    <mx:itemRenderer>
   <mx:Component
   <mx:HBox
.  .  .  .  .  .  .  .
      </mx:HBox>
   </mx:Component>
    </mx:itemRenderer>
  </mx:ComboBox>
```

However, our case is a bit more complicated because we reference the custom ComboBox through a different namespace prefixed with lib. Accordingly, to avoid the compiler error "Could not resolve <mx:itemRenderer> to component implementation," we'll prefix the itemRender with lib as well:

```
  <lib:ComboBox id="cbx_1" value="102" width="150" . . .>
    <lib:itemRenderer>
   <mx:Component
   <mx:HBox
.  .  .  .  .  .  .  .
      </mx:HBox>
   </mx:Component>
```

```
    </lib:itemRenderer>
  </lib:ComboBox>
```

Let's set the *width* of the dropdown list to 350 pixels to accommodate the total width of the four columns:

```
 <lib:ComboBox id="cbx_1" value="102" width="150" dropdownWidth="350"
     dataProvider="{comboData}"   labelField="lname" dataField="emp_id">
```

MXML creators gave us a handy *dropdownWidth* property. There is also the ability to decorate a dropdown list with CSS styles. To avoid gaps between two adjacent vertical VRule lines we set the CSS vertical padding to zero:

```
<mx:Style>
     .noVerticalPadding{padding-top:0;padding-bottom:0}
</mx:Style>
<lib:ComboBox id="cbx_1" value="102"  width="150"
dropdownWidth="350" dropDownStyleName="noVerticalPadding"
     dataProvider="{comboData}"   labelField="lname" dataField="emp_id">
```

The complete code of the sample application is presented in Listing 8.7:

```
  <mx:Application xmlns:mx="http://www.adobe.com/2006/mxml"    xmlns:lib="com.theriabook.
  controls.*">
     <mx:ArrayCollection id="comboData" >
  <mx:Array>
       <mx:Object emp_id="102" fname="Yakov" lname="Fain" phone="7322342654"/>
       <mx:Object emp_id="104" fname="Anatole" lname="Tartakovsky" phone="5618325611"/>
       <mx:Object emp_id="106" fname="Victor" lname="Rasputnis" phone="7184017234"/>
     </mx:Array>
    </mx:ArrayCollection>
  <mx:Style>
       .noVerticalPadding{padding-top:0;padding-bottom:0}
  </mx:Style>

    <lib:ComboBox id="cbx_1" value="102"    width="150"
               dropdownWidth="350" dropDownStyleName="noVerticalPadding"
       dataProvider="{comboData}"   labelField="lname" dataField="emp_id">
      <lib:itemRenderer>
     <mx:Component>
     <mx:HBox height="20" horizontalScrollPolicy="off" verticalScrollPolicy="off" >
        <mx:PhoneFormatter id="phoneFormatter"/>
  <mx:Label text="{data.emp_id}" width="10%"/><mx:VRule />
  <mx:Label text="{data.fname}" width="35%"/><mx:VRule />
```

```
<mx:Label text="{data.lname}"   width="35%"/><mx:VRule />
<mx:Label text="{phoneFormatter.format(data.phone)}" width="20%"/>
       </mx:HBox>
   </mx:Component>
     </lib:itemRenderer>
  </lib:ComboBox>
</mx:Application>
```

Listing 8.7 A sample application with a multi-column dropdown

Populating a ComboBox with Server-Side Data

So far we've been populating our ComboBox controls with the static data. Let's change the pattern and load the ComboBox with data coming from a server-side database. The purpose of such an exercise in the context of this chapter is simply to have all the artifacts handy for the subsequent sections in which we'll improve our custom ComboBox further. And the end of the section, we'll build an application that will look like Figure 8.3.

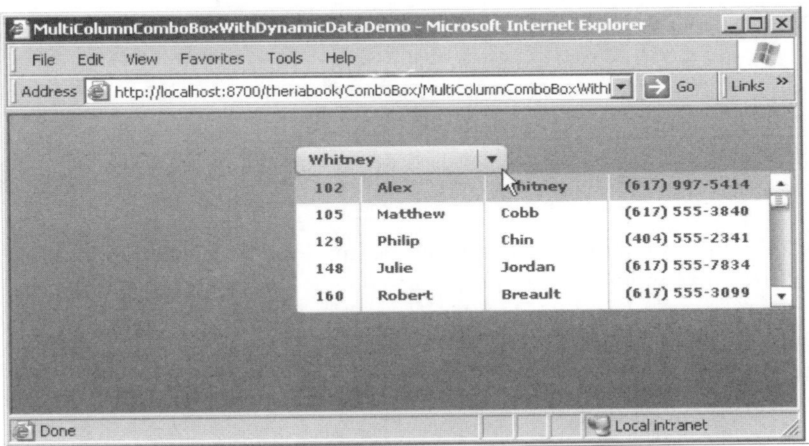

Figure 8.3 A ComboBox populated from the database

We'll be using the RemoteObject tag to communicate with the server-side Java classes (we went through this excersise in the Stock Portfolio example in Chapter 5). The RemoteObject enables asynchronous calls to a Java class as long as this class can be found by the Web application. Here's the snippet of the MXML application where we declare the service: an instance of the RemoteObject. The implementation of the Java method getEmployees is shown in Listing 8.8.

```
<mx:RemoteObject id="service"
          destination="com_theriabook_composition_EmployeeDAO"
  result="onServiceDataReady(event)" showBusyCursor="true"
```

```
    fault="onServiceFault(event)">
        <mx:method name="getEmployees" />
</mx:RemoteObject>
```

The name of the server *destination* looks like the fully qualified Java class name, where the dots are replaced by underscores. Actually, you shouldn't use this naming style in your projects since it discloses the internal structure of your server-side code. We use such a naming convention in this book just to help you understand what Java's counterpart MXML uses.

You don't have to enumerate remote functions via the method MXML tags, although these tags let you reconfigure properties such as *result, fault,* and *showBusyCursor* on a per-method basis. We'll get to these properties a bit later.

A RemoteObject facilitates calls to the Java class mapped through a configurable server-side destination. Assuming the default setup, all remoting destinations should be listed as children of the services node of the *remoting-config.xml,* located inside the WEB-INF/flex folder of our Web application. Here's the relevant fragment of the *remoting-config.xml* that maps our logical destination to the physical Java class:

```
<destination id="com_theriabook_composition_EmployeeDAO">
    <properties>
        <source>com.theriabook.composition.EmployeeDAO</source>
    </properties>
</destination>
```

Listing 8.8 shows the com.theriabook.composition.EmployeeDAO.java, the class that our service remotes to. It uses two utility classes (the source code is available for download): JDBCConnection, which isolates us from connecting to the datasource and the unchecked DAOException. This sample assumes that you've configured the JDBC data source called *jdbc/theriabook* on the Java EE application server.

```
package com.theriabook.composition;

import java.sql.Connection;
import java.sql.PreparedStatement;
import java.sql.ResultSet;
import java.sql.SQLException;
import java.util.ArrayList;

import com.theriabook.composition.to.EmployeeDTO;
import com.theriabook.daoflex.DAOException;
import com.theriabook.daoflex.DateTimeConversion;
import com.theriabook.daoflex.JDBCConnection;
```

```
public final class EmployeeDAO
{
   public EmployeeDAO()
   {
   }
   public final EmployeeDTO[] getEmployees(){
   String sql = "select * from EMPLOYEE";
   EmployeeDTO[] result = null;
   ArrayList list = new ArrayList();
   PreparedStatement stmt = null;
   ResultSet rs = null;
   Connection conn = null;
   try {
      conn = JDBCConnection.getConnection("jdbc/theriabook");
      stmt = conn.prepareStatement(sql);
      rs   = stmt.executeQuery();
      while( rs.next() ){
        EmployeeDTO to = new EmployeeDTO();
        to.EMP_ID = (rs.getInt(1));
        to.EMP_FNAME = (rs.getString(3));
        to.EMP_LNAME = (rs.getString(4));
        //.  .  .  .  .
        to.SEX = (rs.getString(20));
        list.add(to);
      }
      result = new EmployeeDTO[list.size()];
      result = (EmployeeDTO[])list.toArray(result);
      return result;

      }catch (SQLException se){
      throw new DAOException(se);
      } catch(Throwable te){
          throw new DAOException("Internal error", te);
      } finally  {
        try {rs.close(); rs = null;} catch (Exception e){…}
        try {stmt.close(); stmt = null;} catch (Exception e){…}
        JDBCConnection.releaseConnection(conn);
   }
 }
 }
```

Listing 8.8 The server-side class EmployeeDAO.java

Java programmers may not like the fact that we named the non-final variables in capital letters, but this is done to simplify the mapping between these variables and the database column names used later in this book.

The method *getEmployees()* returns an array of Java objects shown in Listing 8.9.

```
package com.theriabook.composition.dto;
public class EmployeeDTO
{
   public int EMP_ID;
   public String EMP_FNAME;
   public String EMP_LNAME;
      //. . . . . . . .
   public String SEX;


   public EmployeeDTO()
   {
   }

}
```

Listing 8.9 A Java class EmployeeDTO

Here's an interesting situation: a RemoteObject can't deliver Java objects to the Flash Player, so Flex will marshall Java EmployeeDTO objects into the matching ActionScript objects. The best practice – both performance- and usability-wise – is to have ActionScript packages and classes match their Java counterparts. Otherwise, the incoming data will be un-marshalled into anonymous Objects. (Flex documentation describes this under the topic Type-to-Type Mapping.)

In our case, we have defined the ActionScript class *com.theriabook.composition.dto.EmployeeDTO* as shown in Listing 8.10.

But declaring the ActionScript class matching its Java counterpart property by property is only half the deal. The second half of successful Java/ActionScript marshalling is to register the class with the marshalling mechanism. The Flex ActionScript compiler facilitates this registration with a RemoteClass metadata directive:

```
package com.theriabook.composition.dto
{
[RemoteClass(alias="com.theriabook.composition.dto.EmployeeDTO")]
   public dynamic class EmployeeDTO
   {
      public var EMP_ID : Number;
```

```
        public var EMP_FNAME : String;
        public var EMP_LNAME : String;
        . . . . . . . . . . .
        public var SEX : String;

    }
    }
```

Listing 8.10 The ActionScript class com.theriabook.composition.dto.EmployeeDTO

Flex does lookup among the registered classes when Java objects come from the server. The class name of the Java object is used as a key to find the registered ActionScript class to deserialize to. Conversely, when data is sent to the server, Flex carries the information of the Java class – alias – to create proper objects on the server side.

In the MXML declaration of the RemoteObject service, we have to provide event handlers for the *result*, which is dispatched when the method returns successfully, and for the fault, which is dispatched when something goes wrong. As a reminder, both events are asynchronous:

```
   <mx:RemoteObject id="service" destination="com_theriabook_composition_Employ-
eeDAO"
        result="onServiceDataReady(event)" showBusyCursor="true"
concurrency="last"
        fault="onServiceFault(event)">
      <mx:method name="getEmployees" />
   </mx:RemoteObject>
```

To process *result* we add the function called *onServiceDataReady*. This function makes use of the C#-style typecasting introduced in ActionsScript 3 – A as B. The ActionScript compiler wouldn't let us get away with the following line because the type on the left isn't compatible with the type on the right:

```
      var employees:Array = event.result; // Compiler error (incompatible types),
```

On the other hand, had we done

```
          var employees:Array = new Array(event.result);
```

or

```
          var employees:Array = Array(event.result);
```

we'd end up converting whatever comes through event.result into an array. The outcome of such a conversion would be a brand new array with one element containing whatever came with the *event.result*. The *as* casting to the rescue![1] Now we request an explicit casting instead of conversion.

```
    public function onServiceDataReady(event:ResultEvent):void {
        // We have to use "as" here, otherwise array conversion
        // will take precedence over casting to array, leaving
        // us with 1-element array wrapped around our result

        var employees:Array = event.result as Array;
      employeeCollection = new ArrayCollection(employees);

 }
```

Listing 8.11 The function onServiceDataReady

Finally, somewhere in our application we have to invoke *getEmployees()*. Let's do it right before the application's screen becomes visible, that's during the processing of the application's *creationComplete* event:

```
<mx:Application xmlns:mx="http://www.adobe.com/2006/mxml  creationComplete="onCrea
tionComplete()">
   <mx:Script>
    <![CDATA[
  public function onCreationComplete():void {
     service.getEmployees();
  }
.   .   .   .   .
```

The complete listing of the client application is represented in Listing 8.12.

```
<?xml version="1.0" encoding="utf-8"?>
<mx:Application xmlns:mx="http://www.adobe.com/2006/mxml" xmlns:lib="com.theriabook.
controls.*"
   creationComplete="onCreationComplete()">
   <mx:Script>
    <![CDATA[
      import mx.collections.ArrayCollection;
      import mx.rpc.events.*;
      import mx.managers.CursorManager;
      import mx.controls.Alert.*;

      [Bindable]
      public var employeeCollection:ArrayCollection;
      public function onCreationComplete():void {
         service.getEmployees();
      }
```

```
      public function onServiceDataReady(event:ResultEvent):void {
         // We have to use "as" cast style to avoid result2array conversion,
      // which would leave us with 1-element array wrapped around the
      // result
         var employees:Array = event.result as Array;
         employeeCollection = new ArrayCollection(employees);
      }


      private function onServiceFault(event:FaultEvent):void {
      // Remove busy cursor or it will spin forever (:
         CursorManager.removeBusyCursor();
         // Error processing ...
         Alert.show("Failed retrieving data: "+event.message, "[ComboBox]" + id);
}
    ]]>
   </mx:Script>
   <mx:Label text="Current bound value is &quot;{cbx_1.value}&quot;" />

   <lib:ComboBox id="cbx_1" value="102"
      width="150" dataProvider="{employeeCollection}"
        labelField="EMP_LNAME" dataField="EMP_ID" dropdownWidth="350"   dropDownStyleName
="noVerticalRadding" >
<lib:itemRenderer>
   <mx:Component  >
       <mx:HBox height="20" horizontalScrollPolicy="off" verticalScrollPolicy="off" >
         <mx:PhoneFormatter id="phoneFormatter"/>
            <mx:Label text="{data.EMP_ID}" width="10%"/><mx:VRule />
            <mx:Label text="{data.EMP_FNAME}" width="35%"/><mx:VRule />
            <mx:Label text="{data.EMP_LNAME}"   width="35%"/><mx:VRule />
              <mx:Label text="{phoneFormatter.format(data.PHONE)}"    width="20%"/>
        </mx:HBox>
   </mx:Component>
</lib:itemRenderer>
</lib:ComboBox>
   <mx:RemoteObject id="service" destination="com.theriabook.composition.EmployeeDAO"
      showBusyCursor="true" concurrency="last"
      result="onServiceDataReady(event)" fault="onServiceFault(event)">
        <mx:method name="getEmployees" />
   </mx:RemoteObject>

</mx:Application>
```

Listing 8.12 The code that populates the Combobox from a database

Hurray! Our application is running. Remote Java classes are sending us data on demand. Don't you feel good? Well, we don't want to ruin the party, but the Java-to-ActionScript marshalling didn't work as expected. Not that the marshalling didn't happen at all, but despite all of our meticulous efforts, EmployeeDTO Java classes were converted into anonymous ActionScript Objects.

Here's what happened.

When we discussed marshaling Java EmployeeDTO into its EmployeeDTO.as counterpart, we made an assumption that class EmployeeDTO.as is available during runtime.[2] The truth is, while compiling and linking our application into the SWF file, Flex had no reason to believe that this class has to be included in the SWF, because there's no direct use of a variable of this class in the entire application, including implementing the ComboBox. We'll cover class loading in more detail later in the book, but for now, let's just fool the Flex compiler by having a variable declaration somewhere in the application:

```
var linkageDummy: com.theriabook.composition.dto.EmployeeDTO;
```

That will do the job and the marshalling will indeed consider the Employee DTO.as class.

Encapsulating a Remote Object Inside the ComboBox

Now that we've populated the ComboBox via the RemoteObject, recall the technique introduced in Chapter 7, where we have made our collections "destination-aware." The rationale there was to eliminate the boring routine of creating RemoteObject and programming standard *onResult() and onFault()* handlers. We achieved our goal by encapsulating this functionality directly into the collection object.

Such collections are self-sufficient, they don't need external controllers and, at the end of the day, this technique allows you to avoid writing and maintaining mundane code that's not needed in the first place.

So is the story with ComboBoxes, because as far as application partitioning goes, there's a compelling argument to encapsulate instantiation and interoperation with the RemoteObject inside the visual component, making it a destination-aware one. In this section we'll demonstrate a technique for embedding the RemoteObject directly into the ComboBox, which will make our "Employees ComboBox" fully autonomous and reusable. The following snippet illustrates the suggested usage pattern of the ComboBox we're going to make.

```
<lib:ComboBox   id="cbx_1"
width="150" dropdownWidth="350"
labelField="EMP_LNAME" dataField="EMP_ID"
  destination="com_theriabook_composition_EmployeeDAO"
  method="getEmployees" creationComplete="cbx_1.fill()"
/>
```

This design approach sets application business logic free from low-level details like mundane remoting.

Now, you might be worried about our adherence to sacred architectural pillars like separation of presentation from data, MVC, etc. Let us assure you, MVC is fully preserved, the only change being that the mix of M, V, and C has been delegated from the application to the component level.

We'll start by adding two more properties to our ComboBox control – *destination* and *method*. We'll declare them public so they can be accessed from the outside, and, in particular, at the MXML level:

```
<?xml version="1.0" encoding="utf-8"?>
<mx:ComboBox xmlns:mx="http://www.adobe.com/2006/mxml"  >
<mx:Script>
<![CDATA[
   .  .  .  .  .  .  .  .  .
   public var destination:String=null;
   public var method:String = null;
]]>
 </mx:Script>
</mx:ComboBox>
```

We'll also embed a reference to a RemoteObject instance – ro – and declare a fill() method that creates (if not created earlier) a real instance of the RemoteObject:

```
<?xml version="1.0" encoding="utf-8"?>
<mx:ComboBox xmlns:mx="http://www.adobe.com/2006/mxml"  >
<mx:Script>
<![CDATA[
   .  .  .  .  .  .  .  .  .
public var destination:String=null;
public var method:String = null;
protected var ro:RemoteObject = null;

   public function fill(... args): void {
      if( ro==null ) {
         ro = new RemoteObject(destination);
         ro.showBusyCursor = true;
      }
      .  .  .  .  .
   }
 ]]>
  </mx:Script>
 </mx:ComboBox>
```

Proceeding with the *fill()* method, we set the *concurrency* of the RemoteObject to last (similar to what we did in Chapter 5, and we'll cover more on this later in this chapter) and associate the event listener functions with the *result* and *fault* events.

```
ro.concurrency    = "last";
ro.addEventListener(ResultEvent.RESULT, ro_onResult);
ro.addEventListener(FaultEvent.FAULT,   ro_onFault);
```

Now, suppose ro has been created. How can we call our dynamic method? In a typical scenario, the following two lines would do the job (the method *apply()* is equivalent to Java reflection's *invoke()*:

```
var functionObject:Function = ro[method];
functionObject.apply(ro, args);
```

However, our ro is an instance of RemoteObject and so it has the method *getOperation()*, which accepts the name of the operation as its argument and returns an instance of *mx.rpc.AbstractOperation*. Conveniently, the AbstractOperation's *send()* method assumes the value of the arguments property as the parameters:

```
var operation:AbstractOperation = ro.getOperation(method);
operation.arguments = args;
operation.send();
```

(Check the Flex MXML and ActionScript Language Reference to get more familiar with mx.rpc. AbstractOperation.)

Hence, our implementation of *fill()* will look like Listing 8.13.

```
public function fill(... args): void {
   if( ro==null ) {
      if( destination==null || destination.length==0 )
         throw new Error("No destination specified");
      if( method==null || method.length==0 )
         throw new Error("No retrieveMethod specified");

      ro = new RemoteObject(destination);
      ro.showBusyCursor = true;
      ro.concurrency    = "last";
      ro.addEventListener(ResultEvent.RESULT, ro_onResult);
      ro.addEventListener(FaultEvent.FAULT,   ro_onFault);
   }
   // In a simple scenario,to dynamically invoke a method on ro:
   //var functionObject:Function = ro[method];
```

```
        //functionObject.apply(ro, args);

        var operation:AbstractOperation = ro.getOperation(method);
        operation.arguments = args;
        operation.send();

    }
```

Listing 8.13 Implementation of the method fill()

Another method called *ro_onResult()* updates the ComboBox's dataProvider with a brand new result set when it's ready:

```
  private function ro_onResult(evt:ResultEvent):void {
    dataProvider = evt.result;
  }
```

And this is the sketchy *ro_onFault()*:

```
  private function ro_onFault(evt:FaultEvent):void {
    CursorManager.removeBusyCursor();
     // Do your own error processing with event.message
  }
```

We must emphasize that we deliberately dropped the MXML-based RemoteObject in favor of a programmatic instantiation of one. We've done it for performance reasons: with MXML, you pay a penalty for creating the RemoteObject upfront, during the creation of the ComboBox. But in some applications programmatic creation of the RemoteObject may be deferred or may not be needed at all.

Having all this code in place, we can further modify the definition of the ComboBox to the following:

```
<lib:ComboBox id="cbx_1" width="150"  dropdownWidth="350"
   labelFunction="fullName" dataField="EMP_ID"
  destination="com_theriabook_composition_EmployeeDAO"
  method="getEmployees" creationComplete="cbx_1.fill()"
>
```

To sanitize the application code, let's remove the references to RemoteObject from our sample application. In Listing 8.14, the data population is simply handled by calling *cbx_1.fill()* from within the ComboBox's event handler *creationComplete*.

```
  <?xml version="1.0" encoding="utf-8"?>
```

```
<mx:Application xmlns:mx="http://www.adobe.com/2006/mxml" xmlns:lib="com.theriabook.
controls.*">
<mx:Style>
      .noVerticalPadding{padding-top:0;padding-bottom:0}
</mx:Style>
<mx:Script>
      import com.theriabook.composition.dto.*;
      private var linkage:EmployeeDTO;
</mx:Script>
<lib:ComboBox   id="cbx_1" width="150" value="1039" labelField="EMP_LNAME"
dataField="EMP_ID"
   destination="com_theriabook_composition_EmployeeDAO"
   method="getEmployees"   creationComplete="cbx_1.fill()"
   dropdownWidth="350" dropDownStyleName="noVerticalPadding"
   >
<lib:itemRenderer>
   <mx:Component  >
       <mx:HBox height="20" horizontalScrollPolicy="off" verticalScrollPolicy="off" >
      <mx:PhoneFormatter id="phoneFormatter"/>
           <mx:Label text="{data.EMP_ID}" width="10%"/><mx:VRule />
           <mx:Label text="{data.EMP_FNAME}" width="35%"/><mx:VRule />
           <mx:Label text="{data.EMP_LNAME}"  width="35%"/><mx:VRule />
         <mx:Label text="{phoneFormatter.format(data.PHONE)}"   width="20%"/>
         </mx:HBox>
   </mx:Component>
</lib:itemRenderer>
</lib:ComboBox>
</mx:Application>
```

Listing 8.14. A sample application using a destination-aware ComboBox

The complete source of our destination-aware ComboBox is presented in Listing 8.15.

```
<?xml version="1.0" encoding="utf-8"?>
<mx:ComboBox xmlns:mx="http://www.adobe.com/2006/mxml"  >
<mx:Script>
   <![CDATA[
   public var dataField:String = "data";

   private var candidateValue:Object;
   private var valueDirty:Boolean = false;
   private var candidateDataProvider:Object;
   private var dataProviderDirty:Boolean = false;
```

```
[Bindable("change")]
[Bindable("valueCommit")]
[Inspectable(defaultValue="0", category="General", verbose="1")]
override public function get value()  : Object {
     var item:Object = selectedItem;
     if (item == null || typeof(item) != "object") return item;
     return item[dataField] ? item[dataField] : item.label;
 }

private function applyValue(val:Object):void {
   if ((val != null) && (dataProvider != null)) {

      for (var i : int = 0; i < dataProvider.length; i++) {
         if ( val == dataProvider[i][dataField] || val == dataProvider[i][labelField])
{
            selectedIndex = i;
            return;
   } } }
   selectedIndex = -1;
}

public function set value(val:Object)  : void {
   candidateValue = val;
   valueDirty = true;
   invalidateProperties();
}
override public function set dataProvider(value:Object):void {
   candidateDataProvider = value;
   dataProviderDirty = true;
   invalidateProperties();
}
override protected function commitProperties():void {
   super.commitProperties();

   if (dataProviderDirty){
      super.dataProvider = candidateDataProvider;
      dataProviderDirty = false;
   }

   if (valueDirty) {
      applyValue(candidateValue);
      valueDirty = false;
   }
 }
```

```
import mx.rpc.remoting.mxml.RemoteObject;
import mx.rpc.AbstractOperation;
import mx.controls.Alert;

import mx.rpc.events.ResultEvent;
import mx.rpc.events.FaultEvent;
import mx.managers.CursorManager;
import mx.collections.ArrayCollection;

public var destination:String=null, method : String = null;
public var autoFill : Boolean = true;
protected var ro:RemoteObject = null;

public function fill(... args): void {
   if( ro==null ) {
      if( destination==null || destination.length==0 )
         throw new Error("No destination specified");
      if( method==null || method.length==0 )
         throw new Error("No retrieveMethod specified");

      ro = new RemoteObject(destination);
      ro.showBusyCursor = true;
      ro.concurrency    = "last";
      ro.addEventListener(ResultEvent.RESULT, ro_onResult);
      ro.addEventListener(FaultEvent.FAULT,   ro_onFault);
   }
   var operation:AbstractOperation = ro.getOperation(method);
   operation.arguments = args;
   operation.send();

}
private function ro_onFault(evt:FaultEvent):void {
     CursorManager.removeBusyCursor();
     Alert.show("Failed retrieving data: "+evt.message, "[DestinationAwareComboBox]"
+ id);
}

private function ro_onResult(evt:ResultEvent):void {
   if (evt.result.length != 0)
      dataProvider = evt.result;
}

]]>
```

```
</mx:Script>

</mx:ComboBox>
```

Listing 8.15 A destination-aware ComboBox

Adding Autocomplete Support to TextInput

Moving on with improving the functionality of the ComboBox, in this section the autocomplete feature is on our radar screen. According to Wikipedia, autocomplete involves the program predicting a word or phrase that the user wants to type in without the user actually typing it in completely. In our case, we're going to offer predictions in response to the user's keystrokes in the editable portion of the ComboBox. Since our ComboBox is now destination-aware, we won't stop short of searching for matches against the remote data stores (during the autocomplete process). In other words, once the user types a character, we'll be retrieving all the matching records and highlighting the predicted part so that the user can type the next character over it. Visually it will look like Figure 8.4.

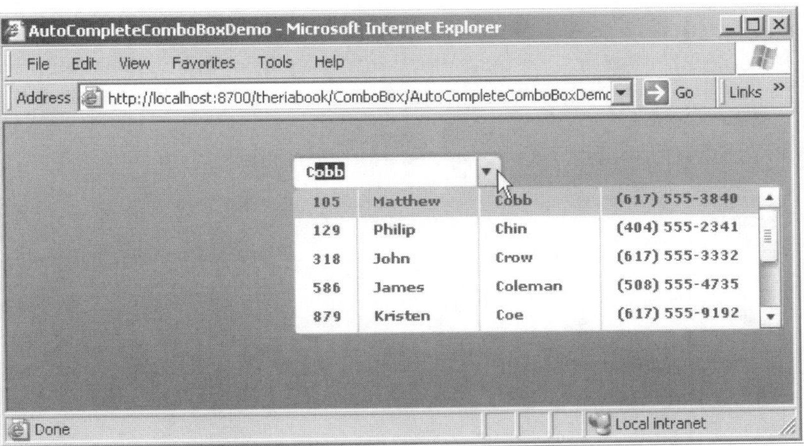

Figure 8.4 A ComboBox with autocomplete support

The autocomplete requirements can be adjusted according to the needs of a particular business application. Take, for instance, a customer account search. You may want to defer a search until at least the first three characters of the account are entered, etc.

Before we venture to improve the ComboBox, or to be more accurate, a TextInput child of the ComboBox, we'll pilot autocompletion functionality on a plain TextInput control. Similarly, before we get to search the remote database records, let's practice searching against some local ArrayCollection.
We're going to create an application containing two controls: TextInput *inp_1* and *List list_1*. We'll use a vertical layout so that our TextInput is positioned above the List:

```
<?xml version="1.0" encoding="utf-8"?>
<mx:Application xmlns:mx="http://www.adobe.com/2006/mxml" layout="vertical">
   <mx:TextInput id="inp_1" />
   <mx:List id="list_1" width="180">
      <mx:dataProvider>
         <mx:Array>
            <mx:String>Apple</mx:String>
            <mx:String>Application</mx:String>
            <mx:String>Sign</mx:String>
            <mx:String>Signature</mx:String>
            <mx:String>Singleton</mx:String>
         </mx:Array>
      </mx:dataProvider>
   </mx:List>
</mx:Application>
```

Listing 8.16 Code for a client with TextInput and List controls

Here's our goal: whenever a user modifies the inp_1 field, a matching value from the list_1, if any, jumps into inp_1. And when this happens, the predicted part of that value should be highlighted. Thereafter the first user keystroke will replace the selection and the whole process starts all over.

Figure 8.5 shows a screenshot of the pilot application we're going to develop.

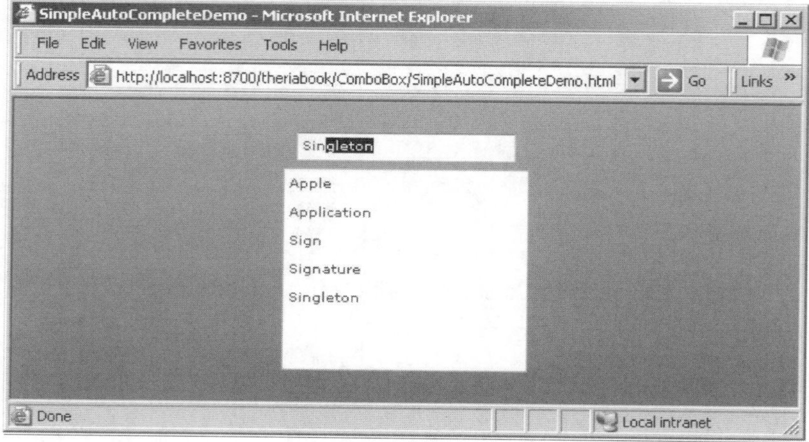

Figure 8.5 Simple AutoComplete with TextInput and List controls

Let's get the ball rolling by intercepting all interactive changes to a TextInput via its change event:

```
<mx:TextInput id="inp_1" change="autocomplete()"/>
```

The autocomplete() function can scan the objects in the dataProvider until it finds a string that starts with the inp_1.text. If so, the TextOnput field inp_1 should be updated with the string and the remaining portion of the string should be highlighted:

```
<?xml version="1.0" encoding="utf-8"?>
<mx:Application xmlns:mx=http://www.adobe.com/2006/mxml . . .>
<mx:Script>
   <![CDATA[
    private function autocomplete():void {
      var typedText:String = inp_1.text.toLowerCase();
      var typedLenth :int = typedText.length;
      for (var i : int = 0; i < list_1.dataProvider.length; i++) {
        if ( typedText == list_1.dataProvider[i].substr(0, typedLenth).toLowerCase()) {
         inp_1.text = list_1.dataProvider[i];
         inp_1.setSelection (typedLenth, inp_1.text.length); // won't work!!!
         break;
        }
      }
  }
  . . . . .
</mx:Application>
```

Listing 8.17 The first (broken) version of the autocomplete implementation

The only drawback to this approach is that, since *autocomplete()* is a handler of *change* event, the selection we apply to inp_1 will get dismissed by default processing on the return from *autocomplete()*. The delayed rendering causes that. One working solution to alleviate this situation is to defer the text selection through the *setTimeout()* function. As a reminder, the first parameter of the *setTimeout()* is a reference to a function object to be called, the second parameter is the timeout when you want the call to happen, while the rest are, well, the rest-style parameters of the function. In our case, the first parameter is the nested function *select():*

```
setTimeout(
 function select(fromChar:int, toChar:int):void {
 inp_1.setSelection(fromChar, toChar);
  }, 50, typedLenth, inp_1.text.length );
```

The function autocomplete() will look the following way:

```
private function autocomplete():void {
var typedText:String = inp_1.text.toLowerCase();
   var typedLenth :int = typedText.length;
   for (var i : int = 0; i < list_1.dataProvider.length; i++) {
     if ( typedText == list_1.dataProvider[i].substr(0, typedLenth).toLowerCase()) {
```

```
      inp_1.text = list_1.dataProvider[i];
                   setTimeout(
  function select(fromChar:int, toChar:int):void {
  inp_1.setSelection(fromChar, toChar);
  },50, typedLenth, inp_1.text.length);
      break;
     }
   }
  }
```

Listing 8.18 The second (fixed) version of the autocomplete function

Finally, we'll take care of the BackSpace button. The user may be annoyed if, after hitting the BackSpace button, the autocomplete restores the value instead of letting her type a different ending. Let's add the processing to the *keyDown* event on *inp_1* so that we'll know if the last key was the BackSpace. The full listing of our example is presented in Listing 8.19.

```
<?xml version="1.0" encoding="utf-8"?>
<!-SimpleAutoCompleteDemo.mxml-->
<mx:Application xmlns:mx="http://www.adobe.com/2006/mxml" xmlns="*"  layout="vertical">
   <mx:Script>
   <![CDATA[
   private var lastText:String = null;
    private var lastKeyBackspace:Boolean = false;

    private function onKeyDown(evt:KeyboardEvent):void {
     if(evt.charCode == flash.ui.Keyboard.BACKSPACE)
      lastKeyBackspace = true;
    }
   private function autocomplete(text:String):void {
     var typedText:String = text.toLowerCase();
          var typedLenth :int = text.length;

      if (lastKeyBackspace) {
        lastKeyBackspace = false;
        return;
      }

     for (var i : int = 0; i < list_1.dataProvider.length; i++) {
     if ( typedText == list_1.dataProvider[i].substr(0, typedLenth).toLowerCase() ) {
      inp_1.text = list_1.dataProvider[i];
      setTimeout(
         function select(fromChar:int, toChar:int):void {
            inp_1.setSelection(fromChar, toChar);
```

```
            },
            50, typedLenth, inp_1.text.length
         );
         break;
         }
      }
      }
      ]]>
      </mx:Script>
      <mx:TextInput id="inp_1"  change="autocomplete(inp_1.text)"  keyDown="onKeyDown(event
)"/>
      <mx:List id="list_1" width="180">
         <mx:dataProvider>
            <mx:Array>
               <mx:String>Apple</mx:String>
               <mx:String>Application</mx:String>
               <mx:String>Sign</mx:String>
               <mx:String>Signature</mx:String>
               <mx:String>Singleton</mx:String>
            </mx:Array>
         </mx:dataProvider>
      </mx:List>
   </mx:Application>
```

Listing 8.19 Complete listing of the SimpleAutoCompleteDemo.mxml

Integrating DataBase Search and ComboBox with Autocomplete

We're getting closer to integrating autocomplete directly into our ComboBox control. One remaining piece is the remote database search. We'll have to make certain changes on the Java side so that the Java class mapped to the destination attribute can fetch the employee database record, based on the provided SQL statement in the format similar to "SELECT … WHERE emp_lname like ?". As soon as the Java side produces the result set, we'll get back to the TextInput child of the ComboBox and modify the processing of the *change* event. That will complete our autocomplete escapade.

Let's start with Java. Earlier in this chapter we implemented the method *getEmployees()* in the EmployeeDAO class (see Listing 8.8). Now we will add one more method *getEmployeesByName()* as shown in Listing 8.20:

```
package com.theriabook.composition;
import  .  .  .

public final class EmployeeDAO
```

```
{
   public EmployeeDAO()
   {
   }
   public final EmployeeDTO[] getEmployees()
   {
      .   .   .   .
   }
    public final EmployeeDTO[] getEmployeesByName(String namePart)
   {
   String sql = "select * from EMPLOYEE where emp_lname like ?";
   EmployeeDTO[] result = null;
   ArrayList list = new ArrayList();
   PreparedStatement stmt = null;
   ResultSet rs = null;
   Connection conn = null;
   try
   {
      conn = JDBCConnection.getConnection("jdbc/theriabook");
      stmt = conn.prepareStatement(sql);
      stmt.setString(1, namePart);
      rs   = stmt.executeQuery();
      while( rs.next() ){
        EmployeeDTO to = new EmployeeDTO();
        to.EMP_ID = (rs.getInt(1));
        to.EMP_FNAME = (rs.getString(3));
        to.EMP_LNAME = (rs.getString(4));
        .   .   .   .   .
        to.SEX = (rs.getString(20));
        list.add(to);
      }
      result = new EmployeeDTO[list.size()];
      result = (EmployeeDTO[])list.toArray(result);
      return result;

      catch (SQLException se){
      throw new DAOException(se);
      } catch(Throwable te){
          throw new DAOException("Internal error", te);
      } finally  {
        try {rs.close(); rs = null;} catch (Exception e){…}
        try {stmt.close(); stmt = null;} catch (Exception e){…}
        JDBCConnection.releaseConnection(conn);
  }
```

```
  }
  }
```

Listing 8.20. Retrieving employees by name in Java

We're done with the Java part. Now, let's find out how the standard ComboBox control is processing *change* events for its TextInput child component and modify this routine.

We'll do something like Sherlock Holmes did at the end of each solved case. He'd explain to Dr. Watson how he solved the mystery.

Flex 2.0 comes with source code and we found the class ComboBox.as and its ancestor – ComboBase.as – inside the folder frameworks\source\mx\controls. The easiest way to find the location of the event-handling code is to search for "addEventListener" in these two files. Here's what we've found in ComboBase.as:

```
    . . . . . . .
    public var textInput:TextInput;
    public var downArrowButton:Button;
    protected function textInput_changeHandler(event:Event):void
    . . . . . .
    override protected function createChildren():void
      {
          super.createChildren();
          // Create the border first, in the back.
              . . . . . . .
          // Next, create the downArrowButton before creating the textInput,
          // because it can be as large as the entire control.
          if (!downArrowButton)    {
              downArrowButton = new Button();
      . . . . . . .
              addChild(downArrowButton);
              downArrowButton.addEventListener(
  FlexEvent.BUTTON_DOWN, downArrowButton_buttonDownHandler
      );
          }
          // Create the textInput on top.
          if (!textInput)
          {
              textInput = new TextInput();
              textInput.editable = _editable;
      . . . . . . .
              addChild(textInput);
              textInput.addEventListener(Event.CHANGE, textInput_changeHandler);
```

```
        . . . . . . .
        }
    }
```

Listing 8.21 A fragment of ComboBase.as

Do you know what real happiness is for a component developer? Are you ready to learn? Okay, we'll share it with you. The pinnacle of happiness for a component developer is finding out that the function he wants to enhance wasn't declared private in the ancestor class. Yes! The *textInput_changeHandler* was declared protected. So in our ComboBox, we could simply override the handler in the following manner:

```
override protected function textInput_changeHandler(event:Event):void
{
   super.textInput_changeHandler(event);
   if (editable && destination != null)
      fill(    text + "%");  // async call, we will call autoComplete
                  // when we get result
   else
      autoComplete(text);
}
```

"Elementary, my dear Watson!" In fact, the line doesn't appear in the Conan Doyle books, only in Sherlock Holmes movies.

Please note that the only argument of *fill()* is the *text* + "%" expression, where *text* is the ComboBox's property that contains, well, the text, as the user typed it in the editable portion of the ComboBox. As per the implementation of *getEmployeesByName(String partName)*, its argument is used to prepare the query *select * from EMPLOYEE where emp_lname like* ?. This query will bring us all the data that start with the specified text, if any.

Note the if-statement in our *textInput_changeHandler()*. If a ComboBox turns out to be uneditable or doesn't have a source of remote data, i.e., a *destination*, we call the *autocomplete()* and use whatever is in the dropdown List child of the ComboBox. If the remote destination was defined, we'll invoke *fill()* but we can't call the *autocomplete()* right away, because the content of the List (aka dataProvider) can be updated only on completion of the RemoteObject call, which in Flex is always asynchronous. Now the fact that the method *ro_onResult()* is in the scope of the ComboBox control becomes very handy. Here's the modified version of *ro_onResult()*:

```
private function ro_onResult(event:ResultEvent):void {
   var txt:String = text;   // Keep the text as in old dataProvider
   if (event.result.length != 0)
      dataProvider = event.result;
```

```
    autoComplete(txt);    // Restore and complete original text
  }
```

Now we can implement the *autocomplete()* similar to our pilot example in the previous section. There's one important distinction though. In our pilot example the dataProvider was a collection of strings. Now that we're dealing with a collection of objects, several scenarios are equally possible:

a. Objects contain *label* property
b. *labelField* is declared on the ComboBox in MXML
c. *labelFunction* is declared on the ComboBox
d. Combinations of the above

How do we get the true label? Or, to put it differently, how do we know what should be considered a label by the ComboBox? Praise the Flex creators again, because there's a convenient public method *itemToLabel()* that covers all the scenarios. Check with the Flex documentation (see Adobe Flex 2 ActionScript and MXML Language Reference) about the exact order of preferences implemented by *itemToLabel()*. Meanwhile we're going to use it for our benefit here:

```
private function autoComplete(txt:String){
   var typeLength:int = txt.length;
   var lText:String = txt.toLowerCase();
for (var i : int = 0; i < dataProvider.length; i++) {
  var label:String = itemToLabel(dataProvider[i]);
     if ( label.substr(0, typeLength).toLowerCase()==lText) {
      textInput.text = label;
      setTimeout(
         function select(fromChar:int, toChar:int) {
            textInput.setSelection(fromChar, toChar);
         },
50, typedLength, textInput.text.length
);
      break;
      }
}
}
```

But wait, the RPC calls that are hitting the database are expensive, aren't they? Suppose a user types really fast. Shouldn't we skip the RPC between two fast keystrokes? One way to minimize the number of RPCs is to wait and issue a call after, say, 300 milliseconds via a *setTimeout()*:

```
   var  timer:uint = 0;
   override public function textInput_changeHandler(event:Event):void
   {
     super.textInput_changeHandler(event);
```

```
    if (editable && destination != null) {
        killTimeout(timer);
        timer = setTimeout(function() { fill( text + "%");}, 300);
    } else
        autoComplete(text);
}
```

But if an RPC is expensive why add an extra 300 milliseconds on top of an already slow operation? Shouldn't we just issue the RPC requests as soon as possible? Quite a dilemma, isn't it? The answer depends on the network configuration and the threading limitation of your servers.

Another important point is in setting the *concurrency* property of the Remote Object method to *last*. Its default value is *multiple*, and it allows as many invocations on the server side as there are incoming requests. But the value *last* asserts that any new RPC request will cancel the ones that are in progress or haven't been started. This is exactly what we need because we don't need to process outdated requests. And since our implementation of *fill()* method is using *last*, it will guarantee that the outdated result set will be disregarded. You may need to tune the timeout based on the network and threading capacity of Java EE server.

Here's the sample application to test our ComboBox. Note that in this application we've turned the ComboBox *editable* property to *true*:

```
<?xml version="1.0" encoding="utf-8"?>
<!AutoCompleteComboBoxDemo.mxml-->
<mx:Application xmlns:mx="http://www.adobe.com/2006/mxml"
   xmlns:lib="com.theriabook.controls.*" >
<mx:Style>
      .noVerticalPadding{padding-top:0;padding-bottom:0}
</mx:Style>
<mx:Script>
      import com.theriabook.composition.dto.*;
      private var linkage:EmployeeDTO;
</mx:Script>
   <lib:ComboBox id="cbx_1"
      width="150"
      labelField="EMP_LNAME" dataField="EMP_ID"
      destination="com_theriabook_composition_EmployeeDAO"
      method="getEmployeesByName"
      editable="true"
      dropdownWidth="350" dropDownStyleName="noVerticalPadding"
   >
<lib:itemRenderer>
   <mx:Component  >
      <mx:HBox height="20" horizontalScrollPolicy="off" verticalScrollPolicy="off" >
```

```
        <mx:PhoneFormatter id="phoneFormatter"/>
          <mx:Label text="{data.EMP_ID}" width="10%"/><mx:VRule />
          <mx:Label text="{data.EMP_FNAME}" width="35%"/><mx:VRule />
          <mx:Label text="{data.EMP_LNAME}"   width="35%"/><mx:VRule />
            <mx:Label text="{phoneFormatter.format(data.PHONE)}"    width="20%"/>
        </mx:HBox>
    </mx:Component>
</lib:itemRenderer>
  </lib:ComboBox>
</mx:Application>
```

Listing 8.22 A sample application to test the destination-aware ComboBox

The complete code of our destination-aware ComboBox with autocomplete and *dataField* support is presented below:

```
<?xml version="1.0" encoding="utf-8"?>
<mx:ComboBox xmlns:mx="http://www.adobe.com/2006/mxml"  >
<mx:Script>
   <![CDATA[

   public var dataField:String = "data";

   private var candidateValue:Object;
   private var valueDirty:Boolean = false;
   private var candidateDataProvider:Object;
   private var dataProviderDirty:Boolean = false;

   [Bindable("change")]
    [Bindable("valueCommit")]
   [Inspectable(defaultValue="0", category="General", verbose="1")]
   override public function get value()  : Object {
        var item:Object = selectedItem;
        if (item == null || typeof(item) != "object") return item;
        return item[dataField] ? item[dataField] : item.label;
    }

   private function applyValue(val:Object):void {
      if ((val != null) && (dataProvider != null)) {

         for (var i : int = 0; i < dataProvider.length; i++) {
            if ( val == dataProvider[i][dataField] || val == dataProvider[i][labelField])
{
               selectedIndex = i;
```

```
                return;
            } } }
            selectedIndex = -1;
        }

        public function set value(val:Object)  : void {
            candidateValue = val;
            valueDirty = true;
            invalidateProperties();
        }
        override public function set dataProvider(value:Object):void {
            candidateDataProvider = value;
            dataProviderDirty = true;
            invalidateProperties();
        }
        override protected function commitProperties():void {
            super.commitProperties();

            if (dataProviderDirty){
                super.dataProvider = candidateDataProvider;
                dataProviderDirty = false;
            }

            if (valueDirty) {
                applyValue(candidateValue);
                valueDirty = false;
            }
        }

        private var lastKeyBackspace:Boolean = false;
        private function textInput_onKeyDown(evt:KeyboardEvent):void {
              if(evt.charCode == flash.ui.Keyboard.BACKSPACE)
               lastKeyBackspace = true;
        }
        private function textInput_onChange(event:Event):void
        {
            if (lastKeyBackspace) {
                    lastKeyBackspace = false;
                    return;
            }

            if (editable && destination != null)
              fill(  text + "%");
            else
```

```
        autoComplete(text);

    }

    override protected function createChildren():void
     {
       super.createChildren();
       textInput.addEventListener("keyDown", textInput_onKeyDown );
     }
    override public function textInput_changeHandler(event:Event):void
    {
       super.textInput_changeHandler(event);

       if (lastKeyBackspace) {
            lastKeyBackspace = false;
            return;
       }

       if (editable && destination != null)
         fill( text + "%");
       else
         autoComplete(text);

    }
    private function autoComplete(txt:String):void{
       var textLength:int = txt.length;
       for (var i : int = 0; i < dataProvider.length; i++) {
          var label:String = itemToLabel(dataProvider[i]);
          if ( label.substr(0, textLength).toLowerCase() == txt.toLowerCase() ) {
             textInput.text = label;
             setTimeout(
                function select(fromChar:int, toChar:int):void {
                   textInput.setSelection(fromChar, toChar);
                },
                50, textLength, textInput.text.length);
             break;
       } }
    }

     import mx.controls.Alert;
     import mx.rpc.remoting.mxml.RemoteObject;
     import mx.rpc.events.ResultEvent;
     import mx.rpc.events.FaultEvent;
```

```
    public var destination:String=null, method : String = null;
    protected var ro:RemoteObject = null;
    public function fill(... args): void {
       if( ro==null ) {
          if( destination==null || destination.length==0 )
             throw new Error("No destination specified");
          if( method==null || method.length==0 )
             throw new Error("No retrieveMethod specified");

          ro = new RemoteObject(destination);
          ro.destination    = destination;
          ro.showBusyCursor = true;
          ro.concurrency    = "last";
          ro.addEventListener(ResultEvent.RESULT, ro_onResult);
          ro.addEventListener(FaultEvent.FAULT,   ro_onFault);
       }

    var operation:AbstractOperation = ro.getOperation(method);
    operation.arguments = args;
    operation.send();
    }
    private function ro_onFault(evt:FaultEvent):void {
       mx.controls.Alert.show("Failed retrieving data: "+evt.message, "[AutoCompleteCombo-
 Box]" + id);
    }

    private function ro_onResult(evt:ResultEvent):void {
       var txt:String = text;
       if (evt.result.length != 0)
          dataProvider = evt.result;

       autoComplete(txt);
    }

    ]]>
 </mx:Script>

 </mx:ComboBox>
```

Listing 8.23 A destination-aware ComboBox

Separating Business Resources from Generic Component Code

So far we've been busy extending the standard ComboBox component and all along our sample applications have contained a single instance of the ComboBox populated with employee records. But how do we avoid the temptation of a cut-and-paste solution from screen-to-screen if we need this component in two different screens? We'll face a similar question when a screen needs two instances of the same component to display different data.

We're going to offer two solutions here. The first solution will be to build a business-specific EmployeeComboBox as an extension of the ComboBox with extra properties containing a remote destination and method. The second solution will be to encapsulate these extra properties in a separate *resource class* and have our generic ComboBox point to resource instances when the design choice is referred to as an "is" versus "has" pattern.

Listing 8.24 is a reprint of the AutoCompleteComboBoxDemo, Listing 8.22, with some lines printed in bold.

```
<?xml version="1.0" encoding="utf-8"?>
<mx:Application xmlns:mx="http://www.adobe.com/2006/mxml"
   xmlns:lib="com.theriabook.controls.*" >
<mx:Style>
      .noVerticalPadding{padding-top:0;padding-bottom:0}
</mx:Style>
<mx:Script>
      import com.theriabook.composition.dto.*;
      private var linkage:EmployeeDTO;
</mx:Script>
   <lib:ComboBox id="cbx_1"
      width="150"
      labelField="EMP_LNAME" dataField="EMP_ID"
      destination="com_theriabook_composition_EmployeeDAO"
      method="getEmployeesByName"
      editable="true"
      dropdownWidth="350" dropDownStyleName="noVerticalPadding"
   >
<lib:itemRenderer>
   <mx:Component  >
      <mx:HBox height="20" horizontalScrollPolicy="off" verticalScrollPolicy="off" >
        <mx:PhoneFormatter id="phoneFormatter"/>
           <mx:Label text="{data.EMP_ID}" width="10%"/><mx:VRule />
           <mx:Label text="{data.EMP_FNAME}" width="35%"/><mx:VRule />
           <mx:Label text="{data.EMP_LNAME}"   width="35%"/><mx:VRule />
             <mx:Label text="{phoneFormatter.format(data.PHONE)}"    width="20%"/>
        </mx:HBox>
   </mx:Component>
```

```
  </lib:itemRenderer>
    </lib:ComboBox>
  </mx:Application>
```

Listing 8.24 A sample application with highlighted tags

To illustrate the first solution we'll encapsulate all the lines, except the bold ones, inside the new ActionScript class EmployeeComboBox. For the second solution, we'll encapsulate these lines inside the EmployeeComboBoxResource and modify our custom ComboBox from Listing 8.24 to recognize such resource classes.

Under the first scenario, our application is going to get simplified to this one:

```
<?xml version="1.0" encoding="utf-8"?>
<mx:Application xmlns:mx="http://www.adobe.com/2006/mxml"
   xmlns:lib="com.theriabook.controls.*" >
<lib:EmployeeComboBox   id="cbx_1" width="150" />
</mx:Application>
```

Alternatively, under the second scenario, our application will look like:

```
<?xml version="1.0" encoding="utf-8"?>
<mx:Application xmlns:mx="http://www.adobe.com/2006/mxml"
   xmlns:lib="com.theriabook.controls.*" >
   <mx:Script>
      import com.theriabook.resources.*;
      private var linkage:EmployeeComboBoxResource;
   </mx:Script>
        <lib:ComboBox   id="cbx_1" width="150"
      resource="com.theriabook.resources.EmployeeComboBoxResource"
        />
</mx:Application>
```

Building a Business-Specific ComboBox

Let's look at the file com.theriabook.controls.EmployeeComboBox.mxml – the component that extends our custom ComboBox. It's got the predefined settings *labelField, dataField, destination*, and *method* – all four tightly integrated with each other:

```
<lib:ComboBox xmlns:mx="http://www.adobe.com/2006/mxml"
     xmlns:lib="com.theriabook.controls.*"
     labelField="EMP_LNAME" dataField="EMP_ID"
     destination="com_theriabook_composition_EmployeeDAO"
     method="getEmployeesByName"
```

```
. . . . .
</lib:ComboBox>
```

The *itemRenderer* of the EmployeeComboBox is the one-to-one copy of the inline implementation we had before:

```
ComboBox xmlns:mx="http://www.adobe.com/2006/mxml"
     xmlns="com.theriabook.controls.*"
     . . . . . .
>
<itemRenderer>
   <mx:Component  >
      <mx:HBox height="20" horizontalScrollPolicy="off" verticalScrollPolicy="off"
>
        <mx:PhoneFormatter id="phoneFormatter"/>
           <mx:Label text="{data.EMP_ID}" width="10%"/><mx:VRule />
           <mx:Label text="{data.EMP_FNAME}" width="35%"/><mx:VRule />
           <mx:Label text="{data.EMP_LNAME}"  width="35%"/><mx:VRule />
            <mx:Label text="{phoneFormatter.format(data.PHONE)}"   width="20%"/>
        </mx:HBox>
   </mx:Component>
</itemRenderer>
. . . . . . .
</ComboBox>
```

The style trick, which helped us create a vertical grid with VRules, has moved inside EmployeeComboBox and so has the declaration of a linkage variable that we used to force EmployeeDTO to be included in the generated SWF:

```
<?xml version="1.0" encoding="utf-8"?>
<ComboBox xmlns:mx="http://www.adobe.com/2006/mxml"
     xmlns="com.theriabook.controls.*"
     . . . .
dropDownStyleName="noVerticalPadding"
>
. . . . . . .
<mx:Style>
     .noVerticalPadding{padding-top:0;padding-bottom:0}
</mx:Style>
<mx:Script>
   <![CDATA[
     import com.theriabook.composition.dto.*;
     private var linkage:EmployeeDTO;
   ]]>
```

```
</mx:Script>
</CompleteComboBox>
```

The full listing of EmployeeComboBox is presented below:

```
<?xml version="1.0" encoding="utf-8"?>
<ComboBox xmlns:mx="http://www.adobe.com/2006/mxml"
      xmlns="com.theriabook.controls.*"
      labelField="EMP_LNAME" dataField="EMP_ID"
      destination="com_theriabook_composition_EmployeeDAO"
      method="getEmployeesByName"
      editable="true"
      dropdownWidth="350" dropDownStyleName="noVerticalPadding"
>
<itemRenderer>
   <mx:Component  >
      <mx:HBox height="20" horizontalScrollPolicy="off" verticalScrollPolicy="off" >
        <mx:PhoneFormatter id="phoneFormatter"/>
          <mx:Label text="{data.EMP_ID}" width="10%"/><mx:VRule />
          <mx:Label text="{data.EMP_FNAME}" width="35%"/><mx:VRule />
          <mx:Label text="{data.EMP_LNAME}"   width="35%"/><mx:VRule />
            <mx:Label text="{phoneFormatter.format(data.PHONE)}"    width="20%"/>
      </mx:HBox>
   </mx:Component>
</itemRenderer>
<mx:Style>
      .noVerticalPadding{padding-top:0;padding-bottom:0}
</mx:Style>
<mx:Script>
   <![CDATA[
      import com.theriabook.composition.dto.*;
      private var linkage:EmployeeDTO;
   ]]>
</mx:Script>
</ComboBox>
```

Listing 8.25 The EmployeeComboBox

This illustrates the resource separation technique based on the control extension ("is"). The second solution ("has"), based on the dedicated resource classes, is covered in a following section.

Building and Using the Resource Classes

The resource-based approach is essential for large projects with a lot of objects that are reused by different modules. It helps isolate developers working on screen prototyping from the implementation details of the database communications. It simplifies solutions that are based on dynamically changing the component's functionality and presentation during the runtime. And it paves the way for building systems that allow on-demand loading of business-driven metadata repositories.

Let's start with the definition of the base class for all the ComboBox resources. This class will be extended by EmployeeComboBoxResource and other ComboBox resource classes alike:

```
package com.theriabook.resources {
   import mx.core;
   public class ComboBoxResource  {
      public var dataField : String = null;
      public var destination:String=null;
      public var dropdownWidth : int = 0;
      public var editable:Boolean = false;
      public var itemRenderer:IFactory = null;
      public var labelFunction : Function = null;
      public var method : String = null;

      public var resourceProps : Array = [
         "dataField","destination","dropdownWidth",
         "editable","itemRenderer","labelFunction","method"

      ];
      //Code to be shared by all instances of the resource
      .  .  .  .  .  .
   }
}
```

Listing 8.26 The first cut of the ComboBoxResource.as

As you can see from Listing 8.26, the EmployeeComboBoxResource relies on the compiler mapping the MXML attributes d*ataField, destination, method, editable,* and *dropdownWidth* to the matching public variables of the underlying class ComboBoxResource:

```
<?xml version="1.0" encoding="utf-8"?><!—EmployeeComboBoxResource.mxml‡
<ComboBoxResource xmlns:mx="http://www.adobe.com/2006/mxml"
   xmlns="com.theriabook.resources.*"
   dataField="EMP_ID"
   destination="com_theriabook_composition_EmployeeDAO"
   method="getEmployeesByName"
   editable="true"
   dropdownWidth="350"
   >
```

```
. . . . . . .
</ComboBoxResource>
```

Similarly, the value of the *itemRenderer* variable in the EmployeeComboBoxResource will be set to the class factory of the inline component based on the HBox:

```
<?xml version="1.0" encoding="utf-8"?><!—EmployeeComboBoxResource.mxml ‡
<ComboBoxResource xmlns:mx="http://www.adobe.com/2006/mxml"
   xmlns="com.theriabook.resources.*"
   . . . . . . .
>
   <itemRenderer>
      <mx:Component>
       <mx:HBox  height="20"
          horizontalScrollPolicy="off" verticalScrollPolicy="off"  >
          <mx:PhoneFormatter id="phoneFormatter"/>
               <mx:Label text="{data.EMP_LNAME}"   width="40%"/><mx:VRule/>
               <mx:Label text="{data.EMP_FNAME}"   width="40%"/><mx:VRule />
               <mx:Label text="{phoneFormatter.format(data.PHONE)}" width="20%"/>
        </mx:HBox>
      </mx:Component>
   </itemRenderer>
</ComboBoxResource>
```

We're going to do some more work with both ComboBoxResource and EmployeeComboBoxResource classes a bit later. For now, let's put the resource classes to work as they are. Let's add a new property – *resource* with setter and getter – to our custom ComboBox. The setter, given the resource class name, creates an instance of this object and copies its properties into this object of the ComboBox. For brevity's sake, we'll show only the part of the ComboBox listing relevant to the *resource*:

```
<?xml version="1.0" encoding="utf-8"?>
<mx:ComboBox xmlns:mx="http://www.adobe.com/2006/mxml"  >
. . . . . . .
   import resources.ComboBoxResource;
   private var _resource:String = null;

   public function set resource(resourceName:String) : void {
      var clazz:Class = flash.utils.getDefinitionByName(resourceName);
      var instance: * = new clazz();
      _resource = resourceName;

      var props:Array = instance.resourceProps;
      for (var i:int = 0; i < props.length;i++){
```

```
        if (instance[props[i]] != null) {
          this[props[i]] = instance[props[i]];
        }
      }

      // The style ".comboBoxResourceDropDownStyle" is getting created on
      // constructor of the ComboBoxResource class, if not created already.
// Here we just apply it
      this.setStyle("dropDownStyleName", "comboBoxResourceDropDownStyle");
   }
   public function get resource():String {
        return _resource;
   }
...
</mx:ComboBox>
```

Now we can run the application using the new *resource* property.

```
<?xml version="1.0" encoding="utf-8"?>
<mx:Application xmlns:mx="http://www.adobe.com/2006/mxml"
   xmlns="com.theriabook.controls.*"  >
   <mx:Script>
      import com.theriabook.resources.*;
      private var linkage:EmployeeComboBoxResource;
</mx:Script>
        <ComboBox   id="cbx_1" width="150"
       resource="com.theriabook.resources.EmployeeComboBoxResource"
        />
</mx:Application>
```

To complete the ComboBoxResource we'll emulate the vertical grid with our VRules by creating and using a style that eliminates vertical padding. In the above code snippet, we've referred to this style as the *comboBoxResourceDropDownStyle*. Although it's possible to declare this style through a document-wide stylesheet or via the default stylesheet used by the compiler, we're going to create and initialize this style in the constructor of the ComboBoxResource. We'll be checking for the existence of the style in the global StyleManager, since the style could have already been created by another call to the same constructor (if not created through the global or default stylesheet):

```
package com.theriabook.resources {
   import mx.core.IFactory;
   import mx.core.UIComponent;
   import mx.styles.CSSStyleDeclaration;
   import mx.styles.StyleManager;
```

```
public class ComboBoxResource  {
   public var dataField : String = null;
   public var destination:String=null;
   public var dropdownWidth : int = 0;
   public var editable:Boolean = false;
   public var itemRenderer:IFactory = null;
   public var labelFunction : Function = null;
   public var method : String = null;

   public var resourceProps : Array = [
      "dataField","destination","dropdownWidth",
      "editable","itemRenderer","labelFunction","method"
   ];

   public function ComboBoxResource() {
     var sd:CSSStyleDeclaration =
StyleManager.getStyleDeclaration(".comboBoxResourceDropDownStyle ");
     if (!sd) {
      sd = new CSSStyleDeclaration();
      StyleManager.setStyleDeclaration(
".comboBoxResourceDropDownStyle ", sd, false
);
      sd.setStyle("paddingBottom", 0);
      sd.setStyle("paddingTop", 0);
     }
   }
  }
}
```

And finally, let's make one more modification to the EmployeeComboBoxResource class. We'll make it carry functions, in particular – the implementation of the labelFunction, which was included in the class on purpose. The full listing of the EmployeeComboBox is presented below:

```
<?xml version="1.0" encoding="utf-8"?>
<ComboBoxResource xmlns:mx="http://www.adobe.com/2006/mxml"
   xmlns="com.theriabook.resources.*"
   dataField="EMP_ID"  labelFunction="fullName"
   destination="com_theriabook_composition_EmployeeDAO"
   method="getEmployeesByName"
   editable="true"
   dropdownWidth="350"
   >
   <itemRenderer>
      <mx:Component>
```

```
        <mx:HBox  height="20"
            horizontalScrollPolicy="off" verticalScrollPolicy="off"  >
            <mx:PhoneFormatter id="phoneFormatter"/>
                <mx:Label text="{data.EMP_LNAME}"   width="40%"/><mx:VRule/>
                <mx:Label text="{data.EMP_FNAME}"   width="40%"/><mx:VRule />
                <mx:Label text="{phoneFormatter.format(data.PHONE)}" width="20%"/>
          </mx:HBox>
        </mx:Component>
    </itemRenderer>
    <mx:Script>
        <![CDATA[
            import com.theriabook.composition.dto.*;
            private var linkage:EmployeeDTO;
            private function fullName(data:Object):String {
                return data.EMP_LNAME + "," + data.EMP_FNAME;
            }
        ]]>
    </mx:Script>
</ComboBoxResource>
```

Listing 8.27 EmployeeComboBox control

This change will affect all the screens using this resource without needing to modify each and every use case. Unlike the direct classes, like EmployeeComboBox, the resources don't need to be linked with the modules that use them, making development by a team of programmers much easier. And it shows that the resources are full-blown classes, letting you mix data, presentation, and script.

This concludes the illustration of the resource-classes technique. Arguably, this is a much cleaner way to separate code from metadata: you modify the resource property on the ComboBox to a CustomerComboBoxResource of your own and – voila! – you can search customers instead of employees using the same code.

In industrial-scale systems spanning a set of Flex projects, it makes sense to maintain the resources as well as the reusable components in shared runtime libraries. We'll cover the topic of creating, loading, and using such libraries in Chapter 10.

Summary

In this chapter we went through several practical examples of customizing a Flex component, namely ComboBox.[3] Such customization has several benefits:

- Your productivity increases as you create components that can be reused in multiple projects.
- Commonly used components can help you divide your application into distinct modules.
- The functionality of Flex controls can be substantially enhanced.

- The new breed of destination-aware components can in some cases literally provide drag-and-drop programming of Web applications. You drop a component on the screen that not only knows on which remote server its data resides, but also arrives on your Web browser pre-populated with data.

The Flex component model lets you extend visual and non-visual components as you see fit.

Endnotes

1. A major difference between the two ways of casting is not highlighted here, but is worth mentioning anyway: if an object you are trying to cast a traditional way is not matching the target type, you will get a runtime exception; under the same scenario *as* casting will return *null*.

2. Strictly speaking Flash Player operates with *class definitions* that get loaded into *application domains*; here we are discussing the presence of the definition of EmployeeDTO.as in the main application domain.

3. Please be aware that as of Chapter 8 we have not made sure that the ComboBox will work well as a renderer in the List-based controls. The complete version would require overriding the setter for the *data* property. The adequate ComboBox code can be found inside /TheRiaBook/code/flex/theriabook folder of the DVD that comes with the book.

CHAPTER

9

Trees with Dynamic Data Population

Trees with Dynamic Data Population

In Chapter 3, we introduced the Flex Tree control in a very simplistic scenario. It's time to switch gears and slowly push the accelerator pedal to the floor.

We will cover the following techniques on the Flex Tree:

- A dynamic on-demand population of tree branches from a remote data source rather than from a static XML or hierarchy of arrays.
- Encapsulation of data-acquisition logic similar to our DataCollection and destination-aware ComboBox from Chapters 7 and 8.
- Custom rendering of the tree so checkboxes can be added to the nodes. During this we'll take a detailed look at drop-in item renderers as opposed to the inline item renderers that we introduced in Chapter 8.

Basics of Tree Control

Tree control is a data-driven control derived from the List control. It lets hierarchical data be presented as a structure of the *branch* and *leaf* nodes, which comes in handy when you have to display a hierarchy of some items that have parent-child relations. A good example of a multi-level hierarchy is a computer file system that can be represented as a tree structure of folders and files. A two-level hierarchy would be the American states and their cities.

What comes to mind when you have to represent a hierarchical data structure, but forgot everything you learned in your college Data Structures class? XML, of course. Let's build a simple tree based on a static XML file of U.S. states and cities.

```
<?xml version="1.0"?>
<!-- PlainXmlTreeDemo.mxml -->
<mx:Application xmlns:mx="http://www.adobe.com/2006/mxml">
    <mx:Tree id="tree1"  labelField="@label" showRoot="false"
width="160">
        <mx:dataProvider>
            <mx:XML format="e4x">
```

```
            <states>
              <state label="California" data="CA" isBranch="true"/>
              <state label="Pennsylvania" data="PA">
                 <city label="Philadelphia" population="1479339" />
              </state>
              <state label="Arizona" data="AZ" isBranch="true"/>
              <state label="Texas" data="TX" />
              <state label="Illinois" data="IL" />
              <state label=»New York» data=»NY» />
            </states>
          </mx:XML>
       </mx:dataProvider>
    </mx:Tree>
</mx:Application>
```

Listing 9.1 PlainXmlTreeDemo.mxml

The Tree control gets its data from a hierarchical data provider. Since the *dataProvider* property of the control is implemented as a setter function, there's a lot of flexibility in what we can assign. In particular, instead of the E4X XML object (above) we could have assigned a string with a valid XML text, XMLList, XMLListCollection, or any object that could be interpreted as a hierarchical data provider according to the rules of the ITreeDataDescriptor interface.

In Listing 9.1, only the Pennsylvania <state> node has a real child – the <city> of Philadelphia. But if you look at Figure 9.1, you'll notice that California and Arizona are also folder nodes. We've achieved this effect by using the node attribute *isBranch="true*." Similarly, if for any reason you don't want to process a particular branch of the tree, explicitly set *isBranch="false*" and the child nodes will be ignored.

Each node in our XML contains an attribute "label" that is supposed to be displayed as a value of the tree node. Had it been an array of objects, each containing a *label* property, Tree controls could readily act on that. However, we're dealing with XML and because of that we have to explicitly specify via the *labelField* property of the Tree control that our labels are stored as attributes:

```
labelField="@label"
```

Why? The attribute "label" and the child node <label> are equally good choices (and that's just for starters because we could have had a child node <name> with the attribute "label", etc.). How on earth does the Tree control know the location of the *label*? It doesn't, until we intervene.

Another specific of XML data sources is that they always have a root node. If you don't want to display the root node, just set the *showRoot* property to false.

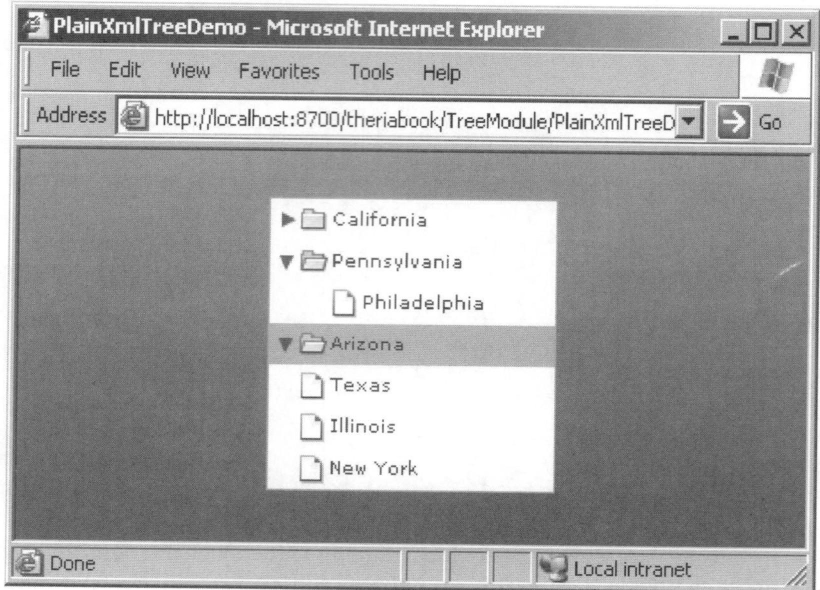

Figure 9.1 A plain XML-based TreeView component

Our next example will use an Array as a data provider. Note that we don't need to set a *showRoot="false"* here. We also don't have to explicitly declare a *labelField= "label"* because the *label* attribute is assumed by default.

In the next example we'll use nested arrays of ActionScript objects to populate the tree. A default implementation of *ITreeDataDescriptor* interface – DefaultDataDescriptor – interprets the children property as a repository of the branch nodes. With MXML we can lay out sub-node arrays with an mx:children tag:

```
<?xml version="1.0"?>
<!-- PlainArrayTreeDemo.mxml -->
<mx:Application xmlns:mx="http://www.adobe.com/2006/mxml">
    <mx:Tree id="tree1"  width="160">
        <mx:dataProvider>
        <mx:Array>
            <mx:Object label="California" data="CA" >
                <mx:children><mx:Array/></mx:children>
            </mx:Object>
            <mx:Object label="Arizona" data="AZ" >
                <mx:children><mx:Array/></mx:children>
             </mx:Object>
             <mx:Object label="Pennsylvania" data="PA">
```

```
                <mx:children>
                  <mx:Object label="Philadelphia" population="1479339" />
                </mx:children>
              </mx:Object>
              <mx:Object label="Texas" data="TX" />
              <mx:Object label="Illinois" data="IL" />
              <mx:Object label=»New York» data=»NY» />
        </mx:Array>
        </mx:dataProvider>
    </mx:Tree>
</mx:Application>
```

Listing 9.2 PlainArrayTreeDemo.mxml

Warning: When you use arrays as data providers, you can't use the property isBranch.

The Role of dataDescriptor

A Tree control delegates all parsing, adding and removing nodes to a specific controller object. This controller object is registered via the dataDescriptor property of the Tree control and, by default, refers to an internally created instance of the DefaultDataDescriptor that is a default implementation of the ITreeDataDescriptor interface. Those relevant to our chapter methods of the ITreeDataDescriptor interface are presented in Table 9.1.

addChildAt(item:Object, child:Object, index:int, model:Object = null):Boolean	Adds a child node to a node at the specified index.
getChildren(item:Object, model:Object = null):ICollection-View	Provides access to a node's children, returning a collection view of the children if they exist.
isBranch(item:Object, model:Object = null):Boolean	Tests a node for termination.
removeChildAt(item:Object, child:Object, index:int, model:Object = null):Boolean	Removes a child node to a node at the specified index.

Table 9.1

While these APIs are definitely fine for shaping your Tree control to any form, they're synchronous methods. As long as data is already on the client side, these methods let you customize the process of assembling the tree. But the ability to act as a retriever for the server data is entirely missing here.

Moving to the Real Asynchronous World

In a standard Flex Tree component a *getChildren()* callback is called synchronously; it waits until this method's code completes. On the other hand, when you request the remote data, be it with the RemoteObject, WebService, DataService, or messaging, your program gets the data asynchronously. This means that ITreeDataDescriptor is helpless when you have to dynamically compose your tree from remote data sources.

Abandoning ITreeDataDescriptor, we'll illustrate the approach to dynamic population of the tree based on using the *itemOpen* event of the Tree control.

Let's create a tree populated by a pseudo-remote data feed. To emulate the asynchronous nature of data retrieval we'll use the setTimeout() function. We'll also use plain vanilla arrays for data and focus on handling the asynchronous data returns.

The itemOpen event is dispatched when a corresponding branch has been expanded. While processing this event, we'll only initiate data retrieval. We can't expect more from an asynchronous call, can we? However, while initiating data retrieval we should also make a provision that lets us identify the response when (and if) it comes back. The program from Listing 9.3 dynamically appends the nodes by reacting to the event itemOpen.

```
<?xml version="1.0" encoding="utf-8"?>
<!--CompositeAsyncLocalDataTreeDemo.mxml-->
<mx:Application
   xmlns:mx="http://www.adobe.com/2006/mxml"
   xmlns=»*»
   xmlns:lib=»com.theriabook.controls.*»
   layout=»vertical»
   creationComplete=»onCreationComplete()»>
   <mx:Script>
      <![CDATA[
            import mx.collections.*;
            import mx.events.*;
         import mx.managers.CursorManager;

         private var bigStates:Array=[
              {label:»California», data:»CA», children:[]},
                {label:»Pennsylvania», data:»PA», children:[]},
                {label:»Arizona», data:»AZ», children:[]},
                {label:»Texas», data:»TX», children:[]},
                {label:»Illinois», data:»IL», children:[]},
                {label:»New York», data:»NY», children:[]},
              ];

         private var stateCities:Object={
```

```
      AZ: [ {label:»Phoenix», population:1388416} ],
      CA: [ {label:»Los Angeles», population:3819951},
            {label:»San Diego», population:1266753} ],
      TX: [ {label:»Dallas», population:1208318},
            {label:»Houston», population:2009690},
            {label:»San Antonio», population:1214725}],
      PA: [ {label:»Philadelphia», population:1479339} ],
      NY: [ {label:»New York», population:8085742} ],
      IL: [ {label:»Chicago», population:2869121} ]
};

public function onCreationComplete():void {
      tree.addEventListener(«itemOpen», tree_onItemOpen);
      //Emulate asynch call to RPC object
   CursorManager.setBusyCursor();
   var RESPONSE_TIME:uint = 2000;
   setTimeout(onRootChildrenReady, RESPONSE_TIME, bigStates);
    }

public function tree_onItemOpen(event:TreeEvent):void {
   var item:Object = event.item;
   if (item.isPopulated == undefined) {
      item.isPopulated = true;
      CursorManager.setBusyCursor();
      tree.dataDescriptor.addChildAt(
         item, {label:»...»}, 0, tree.dataProvider
      );
         //Emulate the asynch call to RPC object
      var RESPONSE_TIME:uint = 2000;
      setTimeout(onChildrenReady, RESPONSE_TIME, item, stateCities[item.data]);
   }
}

public function onChildrenReady(item:Object, children:Array):void {
      var list:IList =
       IList(tree.dataDescriptor.getChildren(item,tree.dataProvider))
   var ellipsisItem:Object = list.getItemAt(0);

   tree.dataDescriptor.removeChildAt(
      item, ellipsisItem, 0, tree.dataProvider
   );

   for (var i:int=0; i<children.length; i++) {
      tree.dataDescriptor.addChildAt(
```

```
                item, children[i], item.children.length, tree.dataProvider
            );
        }
        tree.expandItem(item,false);
        tree.expandItem(item,true,true);
        CursorManager.removeBusyCursor();
    }

    public function onRootChildrenReady(children:Array):void {
            tree.dataProvider = new ArrayCollection(children);
        CursorManager.removeBusyCursor();
    }
  ]]>
 </mx:Script>
 <mx:Tree id=»tree» width=»50%» />
</mx:Application>
```

Listing 9.3 CompositeAsyncLocalDataTreeDemo.mxml

During the application start, the *CompositeAsyncLocalDataTreeDemo* registers a listener to the tree's itemOpen event and then emulates the RPC call to populate the children of the root node:

```
public function onCreationComplete():void {
  tree.addEventListener("itemOpen", tree_onItemOpen);
   //Emulate asynch call to RPC object
  CursorManager.setBusyCursor();
  var RESPONSE_TIME:uint = 2000;
setTimeout(onRootChildrenReady, RESPONSE_TIME, bigStates);
}
```

The code snippet above says, "Two seconds from now please call the function *onRootChildren-Ready()*, passing it the argument array bigStates."

Our function onRootChildrenReady() simply assigns the array of the states to the tree's dataProvider. Since we've started the busy cursor during the *onCreationComplete()*, on the data "return" we need to take it out:

```
public function onRootChildrenReady(children:Array):void
   // Imagine that the data came back from RPC
    tree.dataProvider = new ArrayCollection(children);
   CursorManager.removeBusyCursor();
}
```

Now that we've taken care of the root level, let's look at the children. The expansion of a tree *item* will be intercepted by our event listener – *tree_OnItemOpen* shown below. Please note that "item" is an instance of the Object, i.e., the dynamic class. The property *item.isPopulated* is a dynamic property that's set just once to indicate that the node has been populated.

Prior to sending a request for children we create a visual node that contains the label "…" *(ellipsisItem)* to indicate the progress to the user. It will be removed when the data comes back and the folder is filled.

```
public function tree_onItemOpen(event:TreeEvent):void {
     var item:Object = event.item;
     if (item.isPopulated == undefined) {
        item.isPopulated = true;
        CursorManager.setBusyCursor();
        tree.dataDescriptor.addChildAt(
           item, {label:"..."}, 0, tree.dataProvider
        );
          //Emulate asynch call to RPC object
          var RESPONSE_TIME:uint = 2000;
        setTimeout(onChildrenReady, RESPONSE_TIME, item, stateCities[item.data]);
     }
  }
```

As soon as the first child arrives, we have to remove the ellipsis and repopulate the branch by adding the real children. We cast the children of the item to IList, which gives us an agnostic way of navigating through the collection, be it a collection based on XMLList or Array. Once ellipsisItem is removed, we add all children iteratively. In both item removal and addition, we delegate to the tree's dataDescriptor. To ensure the immediate visual update of the tree branch, we collapse and then expand the item again:

```
public function onChildrenReady(item:Object, children:Array):void {

  var list:IList =
            IList(tree.dataDescriptor.getChildren(item,tree.dataProvider))
  var ellipsisItem:Object = list.getItemAt(0);

  tree.dataDescriptor.removeChildAt(
     item, ellipsisItem, 0, tree.dataProvider
  );

  for (var i:int=0; i<children.length; i++) {
     tree.dataDescriptor.addChildAt(
        item, children[i], item.children.length, tree.dataProvider       );
  }
  tree.expandItem(item,false);
```

```
   tree.expandItem(item,true,true); CursorManager.removeBusyCursor();
}
```

No More Fake Remoting!

In this section we'll start using real remote data. Let's switch to our regular database department/employee sample. The table structure of the database tables is listed in Appendix 3. Our goal is to write the application that's presented in Figure 9.2.

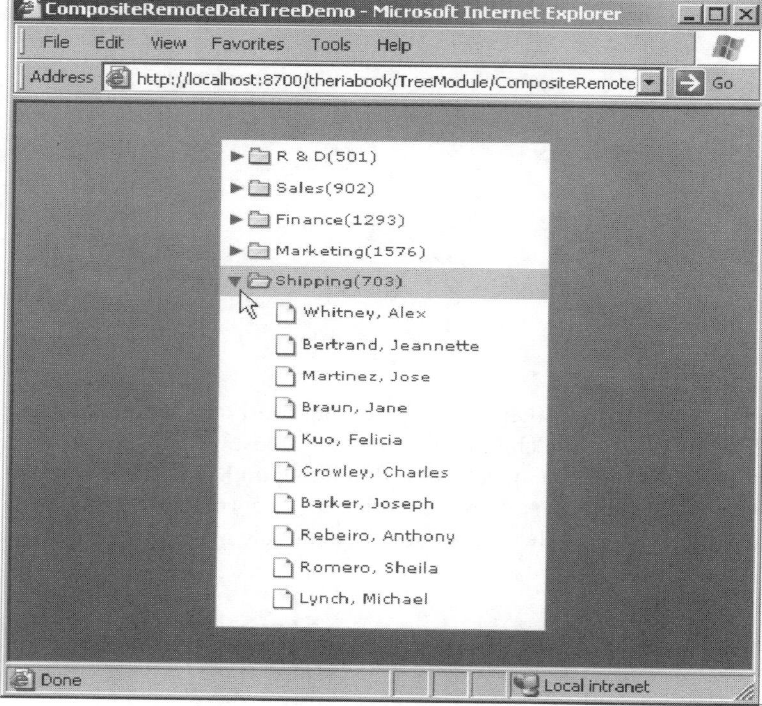

Figure 9.2 Departments and employees

To relate the process to Java EE standard procedures in the following sections, we'll present a handful of patterns used in the book for one and only one purpose: to justify our naming convention.

Design Patterns in Our Life

We've done quite a few code snippets so far. Let's present a snippet of a different sort, one from the play by French author Jean Baptiste Molière, *The Bourgeois Gentlemen*, written more then 300 years ago. Here M. Jourdain wants his philosophy master to write a letter for him. Does he want it in verse or prose? What's prose? Whatever isn't verse:

Philosopher:	Did you want to write…poetry?
M. Jordain:	No, definitely not poetry.
Philosopher:	Right, so a piece of prose then.
M. Jordain:	Ugh, no! Can't stand prose either!
Philosopher:	I'm afraid it will have to be one or the other.
M. Jordain:	Why?
Philosopher:	Because, Monsieur, there are regrettably only two forms in which you may express yourself: poetry and prose.
M. Jordain:	What? Nothing else?
Philosopher:	No, Monsieur. All that is not poetry is prose and all that is not prose, sadly, is po etry.
M. Jordain:	What about the stuff we talk all day? What do you call that?
Philosopher:	Prose.
M. Jordain:	What? You mean to tell me that when I say, "Nicole, bring me my slippers and nightcap," that's prose?
Philosopher:	Yes, Monsieur.
M. Jordain:	Snap me! Here I am speaking prose for over 40 years without ever realizing it! I am very grateful to you for teaching me that!

This joke has obviously been circulating for a long time now. But please note the following: M. Jordain takes pride in his sudden intimacy with prose, but he's not sure whether it's a universal ability or whether he's special.

By now you have probably guessed our take on the subject. Time and again the authors of this book have been pleasantly surprised to find how often we speak… well, use one or the other pattern without realizing it.

Data Transfer Object

Sometimes this design pattern is also called a *Data Transfer Object* or *Value Objec*t. The Data Transfer Object is a wrapper class that holds multiple discrete values that are passed from one application tier to another. In our case, we called the data class describing the department – DepartmentDTO:

```
public class DepartmentDTO  {
   public int DEPT_ID;
   public String DEPT_NAME;
   public int DEPT_HEAD_ID;
}
```

Listing 9.4 DepartmentDTO.java

You can read more on the DTO pattern at http://www.corej2eepatterns.com/Patterns2ndEd/TransferObject.htm.

Data Access Object

The *Data Access Object* (DAO) pattern promotes the separation of the client and physical data source implementation. DAO acts as a middleman between the client and the data source (not necessarily a database). In our scenario, we call the class that takes full responsibility for retrieving from the database DepartmentDAO:

```
public final class DepartmentDAO {
   public final DepartmentDTO[] getDepartments(){
      String sql = "select * from DEPARTMENT";
      DepartmentDTO[] result = null;
      ArrayList list = new ArrayList();
      PreparedStatement stmt = null;
      ResultSet rs = null;
      Connection conn = null;
      try {
         conn = JDBCConnection.getConnection("jdbc/theriabook");
         stmt = conn.prepareStatement(sql);
         rs   = stmt.executeQuery();
         while( rs.next() ) {
            DepartmentDTO to = new DepartmentDTO();
            to.DEPT_ID = (rs.getInt("DEPT_ID"));
            to.DEPT_NAME = (rs.getString("DEPT_NAME"));
            to.DEPT_HEAD_ID = (rs.getInt("DEPT_HEAD_ID"));
            list.add(to);
         }
         result = new DepartmentDTO[list.size()];
         result = (DepartmentDTO[])list.toArray(result);
         return result;

      } catch (SQLException se){...}
      } catch(Throwable te){...}
      } finally {// Close the JDBC objects here}
   }
}
```

Listing 9.5 The code fragment of DepartmentDAO.java

Complete code for DepartmentDAO.java is on the DVD that is included with the book.

You can find the formal description of the DAO design pattern at http://java.sun.com/blueprints/corej2eepatterns/Patterns/DataAccessObject.html.

Asynchronous Completion Token

The *Asynchronous Completion Token* (ACT) design pattern solves identity problems inherent in the processing of callbacks of asynchronous operations. To illustrate the usefulness of the ACT pattern, let's assume the user will click on one node of the Tree control, and then within a split second on another one. If the nodes are populated by asynchronous calls through the RemoteObject and the concurrency mode of the call is set to multiple, the results can come in any order. How then can we tell the results of one request from another? To do this, each asynchronous operation or, to be more specific, HTTP request that carries such an operation is associated with a unique object – Asynchronous Completion Token.

ACT is created before the HTTP request is sent to the server (you remember that all RPC requests go through HTTP, don't you?). Importantly, a "stub" of the ACT travels to the server. Both the client and server continue their processing, and when the server sends a response, bad or good, it includes the ACT "stub" in the response. Then, the client uses the ACT stub to identify the original ACT object and all the properties associated with it react accordingly. For example, Listing 9.7 has the following lines:

```
var token:AsyncToken = remoteObject.getChildren(item);
token.item = item;
```

To understand these lines, think of how people mail a certified letter at the post office. First you get a receipt #12345 (var token) confirming that you've asked for a particular postal service (getChildren). You can scribble any useful information on this receipt, such as a reference to an *item*. The fact that you have a receipt doesn't mean that the letter has been delivered to the recipient. Two days later, confirmation #12345 comes in the mail, so you can make a note that this particular letter has been delivered and do whatever you need with the *item* reference, which has been thoughtfully scribbled on your receipt. Here's an example of how an ACT token can be used at the completion of the operation:

```
private function remoteObject_onResult(event:ResultEvent):void {
        var token:AsyncToken = event.token;
     var item:Object = event.token.item;
     var children:Array = event.result as Array;
     onChildrenReady(item,children);
}
```

For more details on the ACT pattern, please read http://www.cs.wustl.edu/~schmidt/PDF/ACT.pdf.

Assembler Design Pattern

The Classic *Transfer Object Assemble*r constructs a composite Data Transfer Object that represents the data from different data sources. The DTO holds all the data for the model(s) and is delivered to the client in one method call (http://java.sun.com/blueprints/corej2eepatterns/Patterns/TransferObjectAssembler.html).

The *Flex Developer's Guide* in the section "Data Management Service Destinations" says it differently: "An assembler class is a Java class that interacts indirectly or directly with a data resource. A common design pattern is for assembler to call a Data Access Object (DAO) that calls a data resource."

Not that this deviation is accidental – it represents a major paradigm shift toward the assembly of DTOs in the client. Accordingly, the server-side Assembler most of the time (but not necessarily always) acts as a pure *façade*.

Façade Design Pattern

Façade helps to hide the internals of the server-side processing from the client. In our scenario, the client's code doesn't have to know that we have separate DAOs for departments, employees, and whatnot. Our TreeViewAssembler has the overloaded method getChildren(): depending on the class of the parameter this method will return the children for each type of tree node.

This façade will return an array of appropriate DTOs, either departments or employees:

```
public class TreeViewAssembler {

   public DepartmentDTO[] getChildren() {
      return new DepartmentDAO().getDepartments();
   }

   public EmployeeDTO[] getChildren(DepartmentDTO parentNode) {
      return new EmployeeDAO().getEmployeesByDepartment("" +
                                           parentNode.DEPT_ID);
   }
}
```

Listing 9.6 TreeViewAssembler.java

To make this class accessible from the client, we'll add the following destination in the flex-remoting-service.xml:

```
<?xml version="1.0" encoding="UTF-8"?>
<service id="remoting-service"   .  .   .>
 . . . .
    <destination id="treeAssembler">
        <properties>
            <source>com.theriabook.assembler.TreeViewAssembler</source>
        </properties>
    </destination>
</service >
```

For more information on the façade pattern, please visit the Web page http://en.wikipedia.org/wiki/Facade_pattern.

Working with Employees and Departments

In this section we'll present an application shown in Figure 9.4. The client/server communication will utilize DAO, Façade, Assembler, DTO, and ACT patterns.

The code of the application – *CompositeRemoteDataTreeDemo.mxml* – is shown in Listing 9.7. Please note how we make use of the Java overloading of the method getChildren() in our treeAssembler. We populated the top level of the tree by calling the no-argument getChildren() that returns DepartmentDTO[], yet populating the departments within tree_onItemOpen() was done with getChildren(item), which returns the EmployeeDTO[] array.

```
<?xml version="1.0" encoding="utf-8"?>
<!-- CompositeRemoteDataTreeDemo.mxml -->
<mx:Application  xmlns:mx="http://www.adobe.com/2006/mxml"
   layout="vertical"  creationComplete="onCreationComplete()">
   <mx:Script>
      <![CDATA[
         import mx.controls.Alert;
           import mx.collections.*;
           import mx.events.*;
           import mx.rpc.*;
           import mx.rpc.events.*;
         import mx.managers.CursorManager;

            private function onCreationComplete():void {
              tree.addEventListener(«itemOpen», tree_onItemOpen);
              tree.dataProvider=[{label: "..."}];
           var token:AsyncToken = remoteObject.getChildren();
           token.item = null;
            }

          private function tree_onItemOpen(event:TreeEvent):void {
           var item:Object = event.item;
           if (item.isPopulated == undefined) {
              item.isPopulated = true;
              CursorManager.setBusyCursor();
              addEllipsis(item);
                var token:AsyncToken = remoteObject.getChildren(item);
              token.item = item;
           }
         }
```

```
private function remoteObject_onResult(event:ResultEvent):void {
   CursorManager.removeBusyCursor();
   var token:AsyncToken = event.token;
   var item:Object = event.token.item;
   var children:Array = event.result as Array;
   onChildrenReady(item,children);
}

private function onChildrenReady(item:Object, children:Array):void {
   removeEllipsis(item);

   for (var i:int=0; i<children.length; i++) {
      tree.dataDescriptor.addChildAt(
        item, children[i],
      item?item.children.length:tree.dataProvider.length, tree.dataProvider
      );
   }
   tree.expandItem(item,false);
   tree.expandItem(item,true,true);
   CursorManager.removeBusyCursor();
}

private function addEllipsis(item:Object):void {
   tree.dataDescriptor.addChildAt(
      item, {label:"..."}, 0, tree.dataProvider
   );
}
private function removeEllipsis(item:Object):void {

   var list:IList;
   if (item!=null)
      list = IList(tree.dataDescriptor.getChildren(item,tree.dataProvider));
   else
      list = IList(tree.dataProvider);

   var ellipsisItem:Object = list.getItemAt(0);

   tree.dataDescriptor.removeChildAt(
      item, ellipsisItem, 0, tree.dataProvider
   );

}

private function remoteObject_onFault(event:FaultEvent):void {
```

```
            CursorManager.removeBusyCursor();
            var token:AsyncToken = event.token;
            var item:Object = event.token.item;
            removeEllipsis(item);

            // Do your own error processing ...
            Alert.show("Failed retrieving data:  "+event.fault.description,
                                "[ CompositeRemoteDataTreeDemo]" + id);

        }

        // Make sure classes are linked into SWF
        import com.theriabook.composition.dto.*;
        private var linkage:Object={l1:DepartmentDTO, l2:EmployeeDTO};

      ]]>
   </mx:Script>
   <mx:Tree id="tree"    width="50%"  height="100%"/>

   <mx:RemoteObject id="remoteObject" destination="treeAssembler"
      result="remoteObject_onResult(event)" showBusyCursor="true" concurrency="multiple"
      fault="remoteObject_onFault(event)">
      <mx:method name="getChildren" />
   </mx:RemoteObject>
</mx:Application>
```

Listing 9.7 CompositeRemoteDataTreeDemo.mxml

The Destination-Aware Tree

Earlier in the book we introduced destination-aware DataCollection and ComboBox. In this section we'll apply similar techniques to encapsulate the data acquisition logic inside the custom Tree control. The goal is to replace the rather long CompositeRemoteDataTreeDemo.mxml with the simplified application shown in Listing 9.8.

```
<?xml version="1.0" encoding="utf-8"?>
<!-- CompositeDestinationAwareTreeDemo.mxml -->
<mx:Application  xmlns:mx="http://www.adobe.com/2006/mxml"
   xmlns:lib="com.theriabook.controls.*"  layout="vertical"
   initialize="onCreationComplete()">
   <mx:Script>
      <![CDATA[
           public function onCreationComplete():void {
           tree.fill(null);
```

```
        }
        // Force to link all required objects into SWF
        import com.theriabook.composition.dto.*;
        internal var linkage:Object={t1:DepartmentDTO, t2:EmployeeDTO};
      ]]>
    </mx:Script>

    <lib:Tree id="tree" width="50%"  height="100%"
      destination="treeAssembler"    >
    </lib:Tree>
</mx:Application>
```

Listing 9.8 MXML application with the destination-aware Tree

This code looks more elegant than the one in Listing 9.7, doesn't it? This is encapsulation in action.

In particular, we will move the *creationComplete()* code from the application in Listing 9.7 into the custom Tree control's *creationComplete()*. This, in turn, will enable us to keep the onItemOpen() event listener as a private method of our Tree.

Also, similar to the DataCollection and destination-aware ComboBox, we will create a *fill()* method, which executes the remote call against the externally provided destination. To simplify the code, we stick to the name *getChildren()*. (In comparison, in Chapter 8 we showed how to parameterize both destination and method.)

Naturally, we will localize the instantiation of the RemoteObject along with *onResult()* and *onFault()* callbacks. Notice, however, that now we will change the concurrency mode to *multiple*, so that the fast clicking user could expand more than one item at a time. The last remaining move is to encapsulate *onChildrenReady()* and that will complete our job:

```
<?xml version="1.0" encoding="utf-8"?>
<!-- [CompositeDestinationAware]Tree.mxml -->
<mx:Tree xmlns:mx="http://www.adobe.com/2006/mxml" xmlns="*"
    creationComplete="onCreationComplete()">

  <mx:Script>
    <![CDATA[
  import mx.collections.*;
  import mx.controls.Alert;
  import mx.events.TreeEvent;
  import mx.managers.CursorManager;
  import mx.rpc.*;
  import mx.rpc.events.*;
```

```
import mx.rpc.remoting.mxml.RemoteObject;

public function onCreationComplete():void {
  addEventListener(«itemOpen», onItemOpen);
}

private function onItemOpen(event:TreeEvent):void {
      var item:Object = event.item;
      if (item.isPopulated == undefined) {
         item.isPopulated = true;
         CursorManager.setBusyCursor();
         addEllipsis(item);
            fill(item);
      }
}

public var destination:String=null;
protected var ro:RemoteObject = null;

public function fill(item:Object):Object {
   if (dataProvider==null) {
      dataProvider = [{label: «...»}];
   }

   if( ro==null )  ro = createRemoteObject();
   var token:AsyncToken;
   if (item==null)
      // We help Flex RPC gateway with specific -
      // getChildren() - signature for root level
      token = AsyncToken(ro.getChildren());
   else
      token = AsyncToken(ro.getChildren(item));
   token.item = item;
   return token;
}

protected function createRemoteObject():RemoteObject {
   var ro:RemoteObject;
   if( destination==null || destination.length==0 )
      throw new Error(«No destination specified»);

   ro = new RemoteObject(destination);
   ro.concurrency    = «multiple";
   ro.addEventListener(ResultEvent.RESULT, ro_onResult);
```

```
        ro.addEventListener(FaultEvent.FAULT,   ro_onFault);
        return ro;
    }

    private function ro_onResult(event:ResultEvent):void {
        CursorManager.removeBusyCursor();
        var token:AsyncToken = event.token;
        var item:Object = event.token.item;
        var children:Array = event.result as Array;
        onChildrenReady(item,children);
    }
    private function onChildrenReady(item:Object, children:Array):void {
        removeEllipsis(item);

        for (var i:int=0; i<children.length; i++) {
            dataDescriptor.addChildAt(
                  item, children[i],
                  item?item.children.length:dataProvider.length, dataProvider
            );
        }
        expandItem(item,false);
        expandItem(item,true,true);
        CursorManager.removeBusyCursor();
    }

    private function addEllipsis(item:Object):void {
        dataDescriptor.addChildAt(
            item, {label:"..."}, 0, dataProvider
        );
    }

    private function removeEllipsis(item:Object):void {
        var list:IList;
        if (item!=null)
            list = IList(dataDescriptor.getChildren(item,dataProvider));
        else
            list = IList(dataProvider);

        var ellipsisItem:Object = list.getItemAt(0);
        if ((ellipsisItem) && (ellipsisItem.label=="...")) {
dataDescriptor.removeChildAt(
                item, ellipsisItem, 0, dataProvider
            );
        }
```

```
}
private function ro_onFault(event:FaultEvent):void {
        CursorManager.removeBusyCursor();
        var token:AsyncToken = event.token;
        var item:Object = event.token.item;
        removeEllipsis(item);

        // Do your own error processing ...
        Alert.show("Failed retrieving data:  "+event.fault.description,
                                    "[CompositeDestinationAwareTree]" + id);

        }
]]>
</mx:Script>
</mx:Tree>
```

Listing 9.9 CompositeDestinationAwareTree.mxml

You may ask, what's the big deal? The total number of lines of code stays almost the same. There's an important difference though. We've created a reusable Tree component that can be included in any application that needs composite hierarchical data and the code to do this will be almost identical to Listing 9.8. All you need to do to adapt it to different databases/tables is to change the code in the treeAssembler and DAOs behind it. The Tree we created is data-agnostic. The only assumption it makes is that you'll provide a POJO assembler with overloaded *getChildren()* methods that return whatever your business hierarchy is about. This solution supports as many levels of hierarchy as the treeAssembler cares to provide.

Adding Checkboxes to a Tree

Up till now, we'd been building a data-agnostic Tree control that features a dynamic population from a remote data source on the server. The second half of this chapter will be dedicated exclusively to the client. More specifically, we'll gradually build "checkboxed" Tree, i.e., a Tree with checkboxes in each item as shown in Figure 9.5.

As a reminder, List-based controls (Tree, List, DataGrid, et al) delegate the display of individual data items using so-called item renderers. We've touched on this topic in Chapter 5, where we made the DataGrid column appear as a clickable LinkButton and in Chapter 8 where we emulated a "dropdown DataGrid" inside the ComboBox List part. In both cases we've been placing our own item renderers instead of default ones. Similarly, we will be replacing the default item renderer of the Tree control.

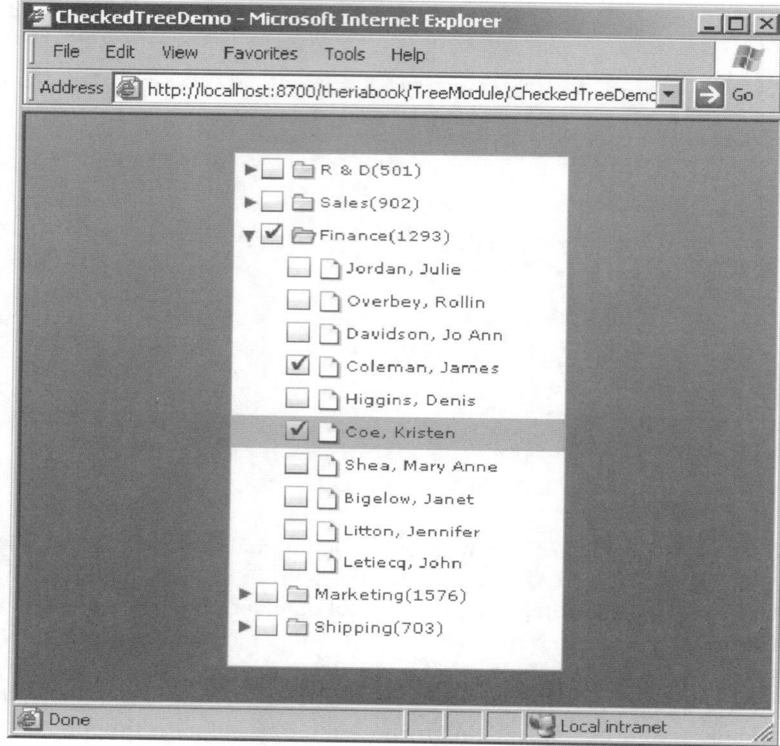

Figure 9.3 Checkboxed Tree

Listing 9.10 contains the MXML code of the application that will make use of our custom item renderer (once we complete it toward the end of the chapter) to produce such a checkboxed tree:

```
<?xml version="1.0" encoding="utf-8"?>
<!-- CheckedTreeDemo.mxml -->
<mx:Application
   xmlns:mx="http://www.adobe.com/2006/mxml"
   xmlns:lib=»com.theriabook.controls.*»
   layout=»vertical»
   initialize=»onCreationComplete()»>
   <mx:Script>
      <![CDATA[
            public function onCreationComplete():void {
            tree.fill();
            }
            // Force Flex to link all required objects into the SWF
```

```
        import com.theriabook.composition.dto.*;
        internal var linkage:Object={t1:DepartmentDTO, t2:EmployeeDTO};

    ]]>
  </mx:Script>

  <lib:Tree id=»tree» width=»50%»  height=»100%» destination=»treeAssembler»
     itemRenderer=»com.theriabook.controls.CheckedTreeItemRenderer»>
   </lib:Tree>
</mx:Application>
```

Listing 9.10 CheckedTreeDemo.mxml

This code is pretty compact for the obvious reason: all functionality is encapsulated in the *CheckedTreeItemRenderer.as*. Now we'll start building this item renderer.

Customizing the TreeItemRenderer

There are two types of item renderers:

- **drop-in** renderer is a class implementing several mandatory interfaces, *IDropInListItemRenderer* in particular. An explicit class of the drop-in renderer can be specified as the value of the *itemRenderer* property of a list-derived control (you can specify a class name or an existing instance of the class). Creating a drop-in renderer may take a bit more time, but it will give you a reusable component

- **Inline** is a render implemented using <mx:Component> and <mx:itemRenderer> tags to define the renderer component inside the MXML of the hosting List control. Inline renderers are good for ad hoc/prototyping purposes, but they clutter code, especially if you have more then one in the same MXML. Also, once you need a correction in your renderer, you'd have to replicate the change in all instances.

The Flex Tree control employs a default drop-in renderer called *TreeItemRenderer*. This renderer draws the text associated with each item in the tree, an optional icon, and – for branch nodes – a default triangle disclosure icon (by default, the triangle) that the user can click on to expand or collapse the branch.

If you peek at the source code of this renderer – *mx.controls.treeClasses.TreeItemRenderer*.as – you'll see all interfaces that it implements:

```
public class TreeItemRenderer extends UIComponent
          implements IDataRenderer, IDropInListItemRenderer, IlistItemRenderer {
  public var disclosure:IFlexDisplayObject;
  public var icon:IFlexDisplayObject;
```

```
   public var label:UITextField;
   ...
}
```

In our case, when we're adding a checkbox to each item of the Tree, extending TreeItemRenderer seems quite natural. Accordingly, we'll be building our custom CheckedTreeItemRenderer as a descendant of TreeItemRenderer.

According to the Flex manual, all children of the custom components must be created in the *createChildren()* method. TreeItemRenderer follows the rules and so will we. In our first version of the custom renderer – *CheckedTreeItemRenderer1* – we'll override the createChildren() method. That will let us create a default set of children by delegating to super.createChildren() and then add an extra CheckBox child. Please note how we follow the Flex component creation practice of passing the component's style definition to its children:

```
package com.theriabook.controls {
   import mx.controls.CheckBox;
   import mx.controls.treeClasses.*;
   public class CheckedTreeItemRenderer1 extends TreeItemRenderer {
      public var checkBox:CheckBox;
      override protected function createChildren():void
      {
         super.createChildren();
         if (!checkBox) {
            checkBox = new CheckBox();
            checkBox.styleName = this;
            addChild(checkBox);
         }
      }
   }
}
```

Listing 9.11 The first version of the CheckedTreeItemRenderer

This first version of the custom renderer produces the screen shown in Figure 9.6. We have omitted the listing of the *CheckedTreeDemo1* application since it is the exact replica of *CheckedTreeDemo with CheckedTreeItemRenderer1* instead of *CheckedTreeItemRenderer*:

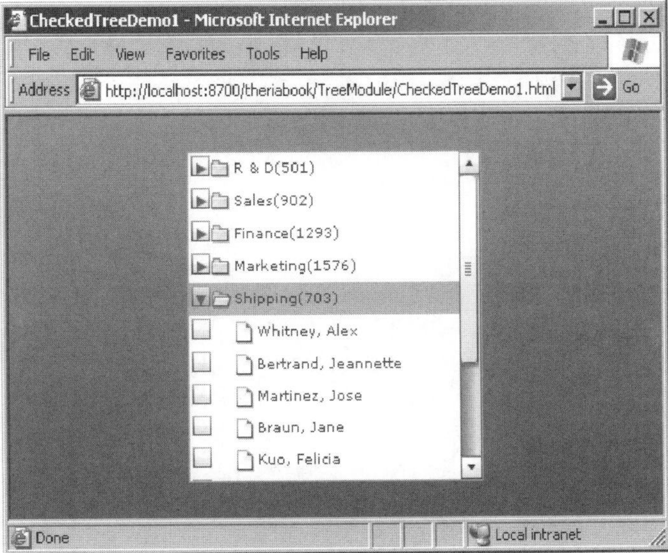

Figure 9.4 The first version of the checkboxed tree

The empty squares on the left side are the empty checkboxes added by the renderer. Clearly the checkboxes aren't participating in the layout and have landed at the leftmost position of each List item.

Following the manual, positioning (as well as sizing) the component children has to be done via the *updateDisplayList()* method, which is called before the Flex component appears on the screen. Flex schedules a call to the updateDisplayList() in response to one or more calls to another method – *invalidateDisplayList()*. At any rate, the very execution of the updateDisplayList() happens during the next rendering event. The implementation of the *addChild()* method also automatically results in invalidateDisplayList() and so causes updateDisplayList().

In other words, we can address positioning issues by overriding updateDisplayList(), which is guaranteed to happen due to our addChild() in particular. The second version of the renderer is shown in Listing 9.12.

```
//CheckedTreeItemRenderer2.as
package com.theriabook.controls {
   import mx.controls.treeClasses.*;
   import mx.controls.*;

   public class CheckedTreeItemRenderer2 extends TreeItemRenderer {
      public var checkBox:CheckBox;
```

```
        override protected function createChildren():void
        {
              super.createChildren();
           if (!checkBox) {
              checkBox = new CheckBox();
              checkBox.styleName = this;
              addChild(checkBox);
           }
        }

     override protected function updateDisplayList(unscaledWidth:Number,
                                 unscaledHeight:Number):void  {

        super.updateDisplayList(unscaledWidth, unscaledHeight);
        if (checkBox) {
           checkBox.x = (icon)?icon.x:label.x;
           checkBox.setActualSize(checkBox.measuredWidth, checkBox.measuredHeight);
           if (icon) {
              icon.x = icon.x + checkBox.measuredWidth - 6;
           }
           label.x = label.x + checkBox.measuredWidth - 6;

        }

     }
     } //CheckedTreeItemRenderer2
  }
```

Listing 9.12 The second version of the CheckTreeItemRenderer

We want to put our checkbox in front of the icon. However, if the tree item chooses not to display the icon, we want the checkbox in front of the label. Let's position the checkbox:

```
checkBox.x = (icon)?icon.x:label.x;
```

Then we'll set the checkbox size to its measured size (every control has one):

```
checkBox.setActualSize(checkBox.measuredWidth, checkBox.measuredHeight);
```

Now let's move the icon and the label to the right for the width of the checkbox:

```
  if (icon) {
     icon.x = icon.x + checkBox.measuredWidth ;
  }
```

```
  label.x = label.x + checkBox.measuredWidth;
```

This second version of CheckedTreeItemRenderer produces the visual in Figure 9.5. The empty boxes have moved aside, but now there's a gap between the checkbox and the icon:

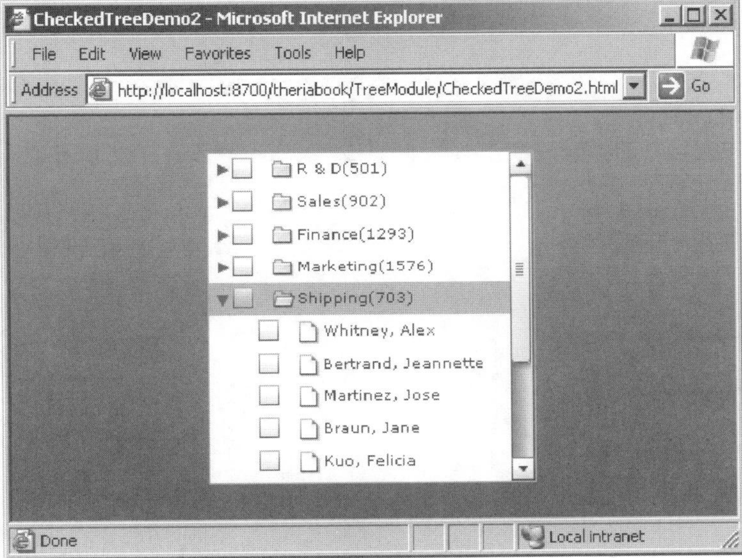

Figure 9.5 The second version of the checkboxed tree with gaps

A minor correction adjusting the width will remove the gaps:

```
override protected function updateDisplayList(unscaledWidth:Number,
                                unscaledHeight:Number):void {

  super.updateDisplayList(unscaledWidth, unscaledHeight);
    if (checkBox) {
      checkBox.x = (icon)?icon.x:label.x;
      checkBox.setActualSize(checkBox.measuredWidth,
                  checkBox.measuredHeight);
      if (icon) {
        icon.x = icon.x + checkBox.measuredWidth - 6;
      }
      label.x = label.x + checkBox.measuredWidth - 6;
    }
}
```

This hard-coded number six doesn't looks too good. But the Flex CheckBox class extends the class

Button and when we wrote this chapter the class *mx.controls.Button*.as had the following:

```
package mx.controls
{
public class Button extends UIComponent
      implements IDataRenderer, IDropInListItemRenderer,
      IFocusable, IlistItemRenderer {
   ...
    override protected function measure():void
    {
   super.measure();
...
    // Pad with additional spacing, but only if we have a label.
        if (label && label.length != 0)
            w += extraSpacing;
        else
            w += 6; //This is our hardcoded value
        measuredMinWidth = measuredWidth = w;
        measuredMinHeight = measuredHeight = h;
    }
  }
}
```

We're sure this will be fixed in the next version of Flex, so we are merely compensating for the w+=6.

The last missing detail is sizing. That's done with the *measure()* method, which sets the component's default size and, optionally, suggests the component's minimum size. This method is called as a result of one or more *invalidateSize()* calls happening before the screen's next refresh. In particular, method addChild() calls *invalidateSize()* and so results in *measure()*.

Our implementation of *measure()* is pretty straightforward; we'll add the width of the checkbox to the total width of the rendered item:

```
override protected function measure():void
{
   super.measure();
   if (checkBox) {
      measuredWidth = measuredWidth +
          checkBox.measuredWidth -6;
   }
}
```

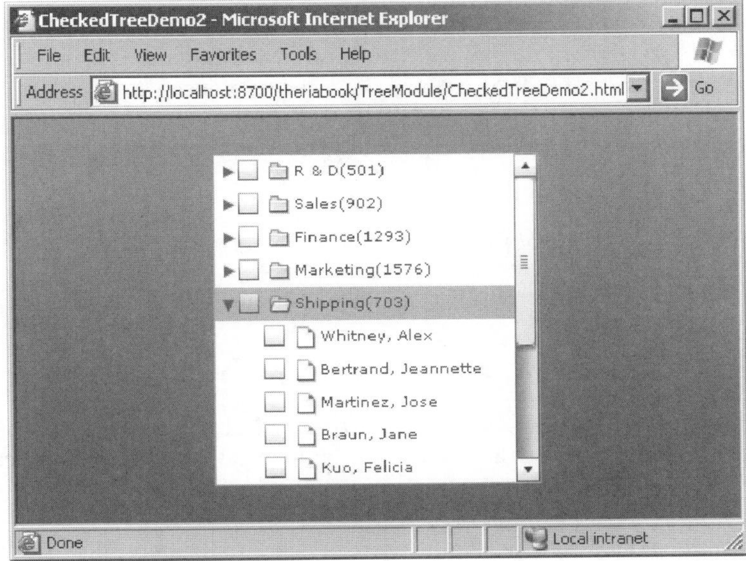

Figure 9.6 The second version of the checkboxed tree

The Data Binding of Checkboxes

Do you want to see a kaleidoscope of checkboxes? Do this: check one checkbox then resize your screen so the tree has a vertical scrollbar and watch how during the scrolling the checked items pop up randomly. The reason is simple: we didn't take care of the proper display of the data model values, and we also forgot about changing the data model values when the user clicks on a checkbox.

Let's take care of the user input first. We'll register the listener to the "click" event immediately after the checkbox is added to the renderer:

```
override protected function createChildren():void {
        super.createChildren();

        if (!checkBox) {
    checkBox = new CheckBox();
    checkBox.styleName = this;
    addChild(checkBox);
    checkBox.addEventListener(MouseEvent.CLICK,
                                                checkBoxClickHandler);

        }
    }
```

The listener – *checkBoxClickHandler()* – has to reflect the changes to the checkbox's *selected* property in the checked property of the appropriate dataProvider's item. How do we get to the item? Good question. An instance of drop-in item renderers has a property *listData.* (A pair of getter and setter methods for listData property is mandated by the IDropInListItemRenderer interface.) In case of Tree item renderers, reference to the dataProvider's item can be found after casting *listData* to *TreeListData*, as shown below:

```
private function checkBoxClickHandler(event:MouseEvent):void{
   var tld:TreeListData = TreeListData(listData);
   var item:Object = tld.item;
   item.checked = checkBox.selected;
}
```

Beware: this technique works only as long as items of the tree's dataProvider have property *checked* or are outright dynamic classes. Otherwise, an assignment to *item.checked* will cause a runtime exception.

With the user input handled, let's look at the proper display of the item state. The natural place to handle it is in the setter of the *listData.* We'll set the *selected* property of the checkBox to true when the underlying *item.checked* is *true.* In the remaining cases – *item.checked* is *false* and *item.checked* is undefined – we set checkBox's *selected* to false:

```
public override function set listData(value:BaseListData):void {
   var checked:Boolean = false;
   if (value!=null) {
      var item:Object = TreeListData(value).item;
      if (item.checked == true) {
         // can be undefined as well
         checked = true;
      }
      if (checkbox) checkBox.selected = checked;
   }
   super.listData = value;
 }
}
```

Here's the complete listing of the custom renderer for the checkboxed tree:

```
package com.theriabook.controls {
   import mx.controls.treeClasses.*;
   import mx.controls.*;
   import flash.events.*;
   import mx.controls.listClasses.*
```

```
public class CheckedTreeItemRenderer extends TreeItemRenderer {
   public var checkBox:CheckBox;

   override protected function createChildren():void
   {
        super.createChildren();

      if (!checkBox) {
         checkBox = new CheckBox();
         checkBox.styleName = this;
         addChild(checkBox);
         checkBox.addEventListener(MouseEvent.CLICK, checkBoxClickHandler);
      }

   }

   override protected function updateDisplayList(unscaledWidth:Number,
                                 unscaledHeight:Number):void {

      super.updateDisplayList(unscaledWidth, unscaledHeight);
      if (checkBox) {
       checkBox.x = (icon)?icon.x:label.x;
       checkBox.setActualSize(checkBox.measuredWidth,
                        checkBox.measuredHeight);
       if (icon) {
          icon.x = icon.x + checkBox.measuredWidth -6;
       }
       label.x = label.x + checkBox.measuredWidth -6;
     }
}
override protected function measure():void
{
   super.measure();
   if (checkBox) {
      measuredWidth = measuredWidth +
          checkBox.measuredWidth -6;
   }
}

private function checkBoxClickHandler(event:MouseEvent):void{
   var tld:TreeListData = TreeListData(listData);
   var item:Object = tld.item;
   item.checked = checkBox.selected;
}
```

```
    public override function set listData(value:BaseListData):void {
      var checked:Boolean = false;
      if (value!=null) {
        var item:Object = TreeListData(value).item;
        if (item.checked == true) {
          // the item can be true, false or undefined
          checked = true;
        }
        if (checkBox) checkBox.selected = checked;
      }
      super.listData = value;
    }
  }
}
```

Listing 9.13 The final version of CheckedTreeItemRenderer

You can test our item renderer with the demo application CheckedTreeDemo presented earlier in Listing 9.10 and Figure 9.3. The kaleidoscope of checkboxes is gone; positioning, sizing, and checkbox values are all taken care of.

Summary

In this chapter we showed you how to asynchronously populate Tree controls from remote sources, where hierarchy of the data is not pre-built, but rather dynamic and, possibly, composite. The custom Tree control that we built can be applied for a use case with any number of levels by changing the server-side *treeAssembler* and DAO classes. We also demonstrated the complete process of extending a standard item renderer for the Flex Tree control. All in all, we showed how standard Flex framework controls can be enhanced to provide developers with simple yet powerful components.

CHAPTER

10

Working with Large Applications

Working with Large Applications

In this chapter we'll cover how to set up large applications intended for Web or, more broadly speaking, distributed deployment. As an example let's consider an enterprise application that consists of hundreds of screens, reports, forms, and dashboards. Accordingly, about a dozen engineers specializing in GUIs, frameworks, data layers, and business domains are working on this application in parallel.

Large monolithic applications, the way Flex builds application SWFs by default, have several problems: they take a lot of time to build on each change, they do not support the isolation of two teams working on two independent "portlets", they do not allow the incremental delivery of patches to the systems, and they do not support the independent delivery of libraries of reusable components without rebuilding the entire application.

We'll show how to accommodate these requirements emphasizing the productivity of team development and deployment flexibility. But first let's review the deployment scenarios from the business point-of-view in detail.

Deployment Scenarios

Throughout this chapter we'll use the term *patches*, which are the fixes made to an application between releases. *Add-ons* are the parts of the application that are typically added over time. Paches as well as add-ons blend seamlessly into the hosting application, both visually and programmatically.

In some cases the application build may not even "know" about specific add-ons since they're different for each user type. For example, an enterprise application can reveal more screens or more functionality within these screens to internal users. In this case we talk about *portlet-style* add-ons.

Plug-ins are independent applications that don't share the look-and-feel of the main application. No intensive interaction between the main application and plug-ins is expected.

Application Domains 101

As much as we don't like to duplicate the work done by the Adobe Flex documentation team, we have to cover the subject of Application Domains since it's essential to this chapter. So, here are the facts.

The Flash Player loads class definitions from SWF files into the instances of the *flash.system.ApplicationDomain* class – *aka application domains*. Application domains are organized in a hierarchy with *system domain* containing all application domains. If a class is already loaded into a parent domain, loading a different definition into the child domain will have no effect. If this sounds familiar, you may have worked with Java ClassLoaders.

Don't mistake application domains for *security domains*. The latter are relevant for issues like subloading an SWF file from a different server and are outside the scope of this chapter.

Let's move on. There are three classes in the Flex library that facilitate SWF loading: *flash.display.Loader, mx.controls.SWFLoader*, and mx.modules.ModuleLoader. With each of them you get two choices of where you want to load the classes: a new (child) domain or an existing application domain. ModuleLoader has an *applicationDomain* property. If you set it to *new ApplicationDomain(ApplicationDomain.currentDomain)*, new classes will be loaded into a child of the *currentDomain* (the domain where the main application runs); to enforce loading in the same domain you should set applicationDomain's value to *ApplicationDomain.currentDomain*. In each case with Loader and SWFLoader, you control the target domain by similarly assigning the object's *loaderContext.applicationDomain*.

We have mentioned the overshadowing of children's class definitions by the parent ones. Accordingly, when you bring existing Flex subsystems (perhaps even written in a different version of Flex) under a common application umbrella, it makes sense to resort to a separate application domain, i.e., a child of the system domain. On the other end of the specter, if you need to dynamically load resources like DataGrid definitions, you will be better off with the same domain where the main application is running.

Runtime Shared Libraries 101

Flex documentation defines Runtime Shared Libraries (RSL) as "a library of components." We would like to start with the clarification that RSL is not a file but a pattern of using an SWF file from within another SWF file.

Specifically, when you compile with RSLs, Flex generates code to preload the relevant SWFs during the application's bootstrap. To be exact, definitions contained in the SWF are loaded directly into the *applicationDomain* of the hosting application.

Now how does the application's bootstrap know which SWF files are to be pre-loaded?

Here is an answer. Let's assume that:

a. You made the file *FlexLibrary.SWC* (running the compc compiler explicitly or just by rebuilding the *Flex Builder's Library Project*).
b. You've created the file *FlexApplication.mxml*, which refers to components from *FlexLibrary.SWC*.
c. While compiling *FlexApplication.mxml* you instructed the mxmlc compiler that *FlexLibrary.SWC* contains an image of an SWF to be pre-loaded during the bootstrap (this will be explained later in this chapter).

Then, the corresponding ActionScript file generated by the *mxmlc* compiler will have the code fragment shown in Listing 10.1. You'll find this and other files in the *generated* folder of your application project once you set the compiler's option to *keep-generated-actionscript=true*:

```
public class _FlexApplication_mx_managers_SystemManager extends mx.managers.SystemManage
r implements IFlexModuleFactory {
  public function _FlexApplication_mx_managers_SystemManager() {
   super();
  }
  override public function info():Object {
   return {
     "currentDomain": ApplicationDomain.currentDomain,
     "layout" : "absolute",
     "mainClassName" : "FlexApplication",
     "mixins" : ["_FlexApplication_FlexInit", ......]
     ,
     "rsls" : [{url: "FlexLibrary.swf", size: -1}]
  };
 }
}
}
```

Listing 10.1 The fragment of the generated SystemManager class for FlexApplication.mxml

Listing 10.1 contains the code of the SystemManager class of the FlexApplication. Flex SystemManager is the first display class created within an application and the parent of all other displayable objects. SystemManager also creates the *mx.preloaders.Preloader* that loads SWF files.

Please note that FlexLibrary.swf in and of itself is not an RSL. As we said above, RSL is a usage pattern rather than a file. What makes FlexLibrary.swf part of this pattern is the intent to pre-load it during the application startup communicated by us to the *mxmlc* compiler.

Also note the line:

```
"currentDomain": ApplicationDomain.currentDomain,
```

This is why class definitions from the FlexLibrary.swf are loaded into the same domain where the definition of the application classes belong. Accordingly we find the RSL technique especially useful for delivering various patches, which should be loaded prior to any other class definitions. RSLs are also the best way to package component libraries and resources.

SWFs and SWCs: What's Under the Hood

How do our SWC files relate to SWFs? An SWC is an archive file, much like ZIP or JAR, and contains *library.swf* and *catalog.xml* files. The latter describes the hierarchy of dependencies found the former; *library.swf* may, but it won't nessesarily become FlexLibrary.swf (depending on the selected *Link Type* described below).

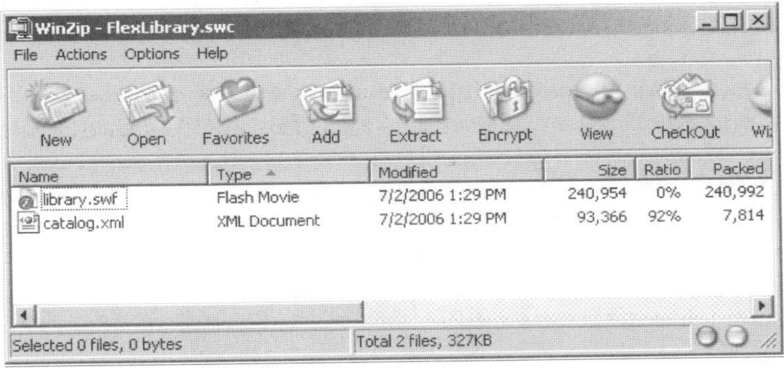

Figure 10.1 The content of the FlexLibrary.SWC file

When we compile *FlexApplication.mxml* containing references to FlexLibrary.SWC in the library search path, there are three link types to choose from:

- **External:** The *catalog.xml* in the *FlexLibrary.swc* will be used to resolve references; however the definitions contained in *library.swf* won't be included in the body of the *FlexApplication.swf*. The External link type assumes that by the time *FlexApplication* needs to create instances of classes from the *library.swf* part the definitions for these classes will be accessible from the currentDomain.

- **RSL:** The *catalog.xml* in the *FlexLibrary.swc* will be used to resolve references; the definitions contained in *library.swf* won't be included in the body of the *FlexApplication.swf*. So far sounds like External, right? Here's the difference: all definitions originally contained in the *library.swf* part will be upfront-loaded into the main applicationDomain during application startup.

- **Merge-in:** Definitions contained in *library.swf* get embedded directly into FlexApplication.swf, but wait ... only those that are explicitly referenced by the application code. This is a default option for statically linked applications and guarantees that the definitions of all referenced classes as well as the classes they depend on are loaded into the main application-Domain.

A Merge-in scenario is often called *static linking*, while External and RSL are cases of *dynamic linking*.

Suppose we went with *dynamic linking* via RSL. As illustrated in Listing 10.1, this means pre-loading the FlexLibrary.swf. Here's the question: where do we get this FlexLibrary.swf from? Under one scenario we can let Flex Builder extract and rename the *library.swf* from the *FlexLibrary.swc*. In Flex Builder (project Properties >Flex Build Path> Library Path) this option is called *Auto extract*. Alternatively, we could have declined auto-extracting and unzipped the SWF from the SWC ourselves. As we'll show later, there's yet another way of explicitly controlling the upfront build of FlexLibrary.swf.

We'll illustrate these cases in the next section.

Making the FlexLibrary.swc

Let's make an SWC in Flex Builder by creating a new Flex Library Project. The only component we're going to add to this SWC is the *CustomPanel* from Listing 10.2. The Customer Panel enumerates the instances of itself and imprints the number of the instance as part of its title, using the variable *instanceNumber* that we've declared *bindable*:

```
<?xml version="1.0" encoding="utf-8"?>
<!-- CustomPanel.mxml -->
<mx:Panel xmlns:mx="http://www.adobe.com/2006/mxml"  title="'Custom' Panel
 #{instanceNumber}" width="300" height="150"  creationComplete="instanceNumber=++count;"
>
   <mx:Script>
      public static var count:int;
        [Bindable]
         private var instanceNumber:int;
    </mx:Script>
</mx:Panel>
```

Listing 10.2 Custom Panel.mxml

To ensure that our CustomPanel is accounted for (in both *library.swf* and *catalog.xml*) we have to verify that it's included in the Flex Library Build Path. Please be aware that every time you add or rename files in your Library Project, the corresponding checkbox in Flex Builder gets cleared.

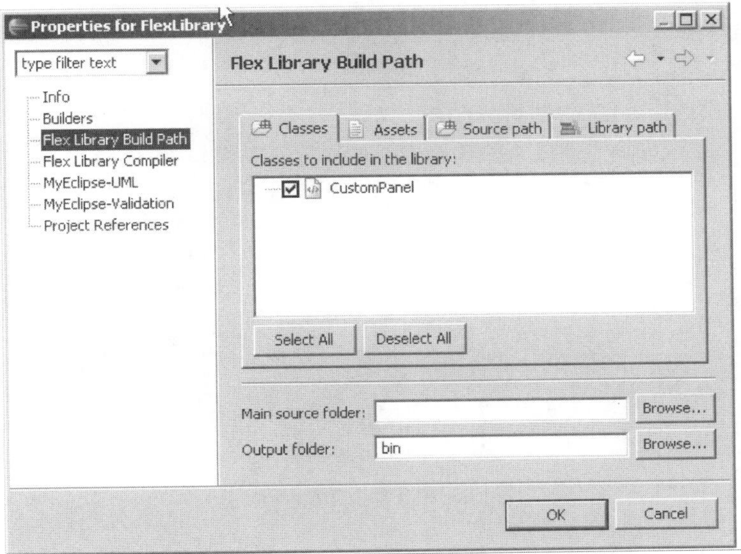

Figure 10.2 Checked state of the CustomPanel in FlexLibrary.swc

After we click OK, Flex Builder will invoke the compc compiler to create the *FlexLibrary.swc* in the output bin folder[1].

Making a FlexApplication Application

Now let's make the application in a separate Flex Builder project. Nothing fancy, we'll just make a static reference to the *CustomPanel*:

```
<?xml version="1.0" encoding="utf-8"?>
<!-- FlexApplication.mxml -->
<mx:Application xmlns:mx="http://www.adobe.com/2006/mxml" layout="absolute" xmlns="*">
   <CustomPanel />
</mx:Application>
```

Listing 10.3 FlexApplication.mxml

Then we'll link our library (see Figure 10.4), compile, and run the application. The output window will look like this:

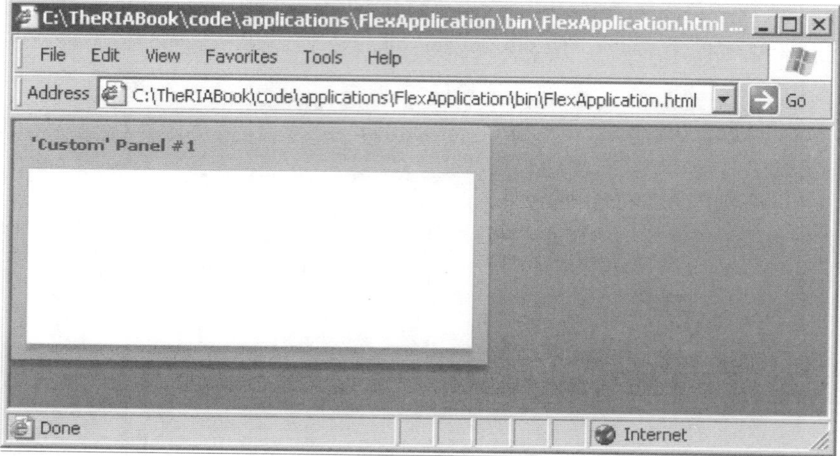

Figure 10.3 A Custom Panel

Figure 10.4 illustrates the details of adding our recently created library *FlexLibrary.swc* to the project's *Library Build Path*. The default link type is to merge-in the SWC's content (to change the link type, if needed, select the Link Type line and press the button Edit on the screen below):

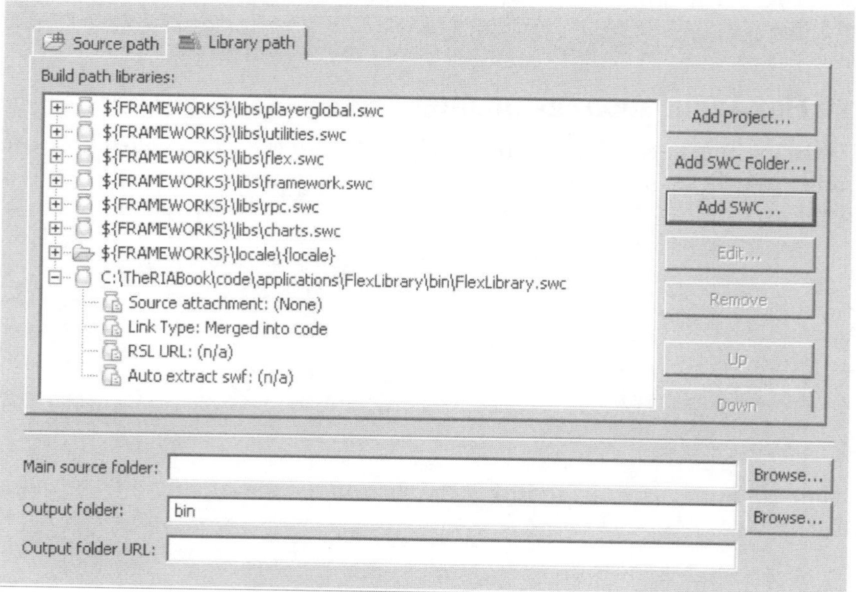

Figure 10.4 Linking FlexLibary.swc to FlexApplication – "Merged into code"

Merging the contents of SWC results in an optimized, non-overlapping size of the monolithic application. As shown in Figure 10.5, the size of such a self-sufficient FlexApplication.swf is 123KB.

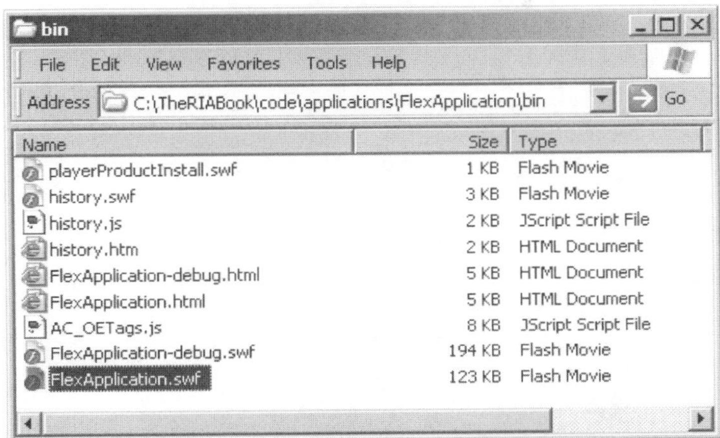

Figure 10.5 The FlexApplication deployment folder after merging-in FlexLibrary.swc

Now let's change the *Link type* to *RSL*. We'll accept the default value of *Auto extract=true*:

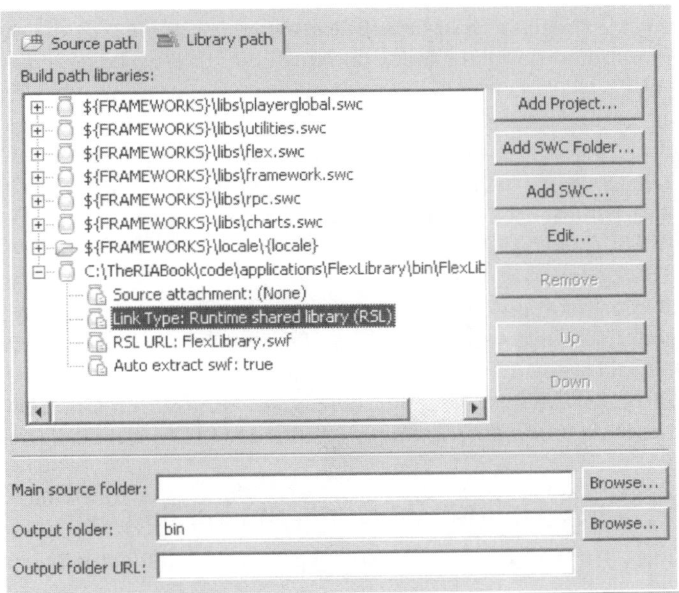

Figure 10.6 Linking FlexLibary.swc to FlexApplication – "RSL"

As a result of the *Auto extract*, the file *FlexLibrary.swf* will appear adjacent to the *FlexApplication.swf*. The size of the *FlexLibrary.swf* will be 236K, nearly as much as the entire *FlexLibrary.swc*, but the size of the *FlexApplication.swf* will decrease to 40K:

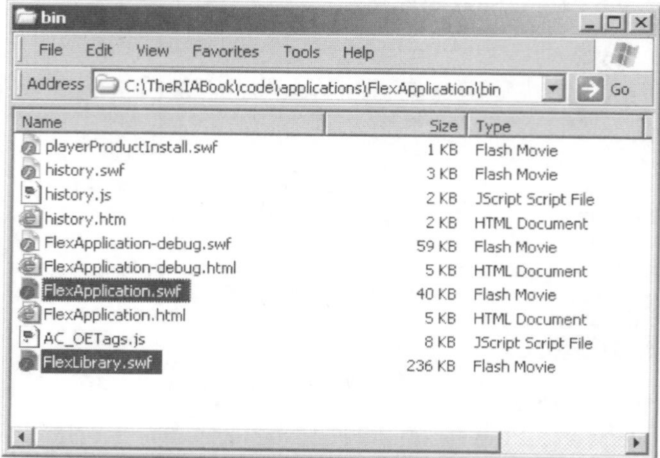

Figure 10.7 The file view of the FlexApplication deployment folder after auto-extracting the FlexLibrary.swf

Now you can see why the default Link Type in Flex is *Merge into code*. This ensures the smallest size of the resulting monolithic SWF that carries only the code that was deemed relevant during the compilation process.

Naturally, the total of 236K + 40K takes two times longer to download then downloading of the statically linked 123K. However, once you have a family of three applications to offer the same user, all approximately the same size and all reusing the same FlexLibrary.swf, it becomes (236 + 3*40) versus 3*123 and you break even.

The size/download considerations are less relevant on the fast connections and, perhaps, are not relevant at all in scenarios where you can count on the browser cache to keep SWF files loaded for the next run of the application. A typical example where the time of the initial download is not an issue would be a corporate environment, but then again, some administrators set policies to wipe out the browser's cache on user logoff.

Static versus Dynamic Linking: Development Perspective

Let's change the subject from download time to a developer's productivity, a factor far more important for enterprise applications.

Let's look at enterprise applications. Driven by user requirements, these applcations tend to change frequently, growing in functionality and, accordingly, size, with phased delivery to the users. As an application gets to tens of megabytes, the time required to *build* the monolithic SWF becomes a noticeable setback to developer productivity. The problem gets magnified in a team development where it translates into many man-hours wasted every day.

And, regardless of size, let's look at the use case of portlet-style add-ons. These are modules that are simply impossible to reference statically in advance. In fact, they are not even supposed to be preloaded at all: unlike RSLs they get loaded on demand (more on that later in the chapter).

All in all, we need to be able break the application into a set of modules that can be built independently and linked dynamically at runtime.

So, You Say Dynamic Linking?

By now the reader may say, "OK, I got the message, I'll go with RSLs to modularize my development with dynamic linking." Not so fast. Like ancient Achilles, these mighty RSLs have a small weak spot: their well-being depends on static linkage from the main application.

Oh, but doesn't that ruin the hope of dynamic linking? The answer is no, and the explanation is just around the corner in the next section.

First, however, let's create an application to expose the problem. We'll build a *FlexApplication2* application. Unlike our previous example, it won't contain static references to CustomPanel. Instead, *FlexApplication2* will create instances of a *CustomPanel* (or any other object for that matter) dynamically, given a name of the class definition as it's done in the function *createComponent()* of Listing 10.4:

```
<?xml version="1.0" encoding="utf-8"?>
<!-- FlexApplication2-->
<mx:Application xmlns:mx="http://www.adobe.com/2006/mxml" layout="absolute" xmlns="*">
   <!--CustomPanel /-->
    <mx:Button label="CreatePanel" click="createComponent('CustomPanel')"/>
   <mx:Script>
      <![CDATA[
         private var displayObject:DisplayObject;
         private function createComponent(componentName:String) : void {
            var clazz : Class = getDefinitionByName(componentName) as Class;
            displayObject = DisplayObject(new clazz() );
            this.addChild(displayObject);
         }
      ]]>
   </mx:Script>
</mx:Application>
```

Listing 10.4 FlexApplication2.mxml

If you run the application and click the "Create Panel" button, the code terminates abnormally as shown in Figure 10.8.

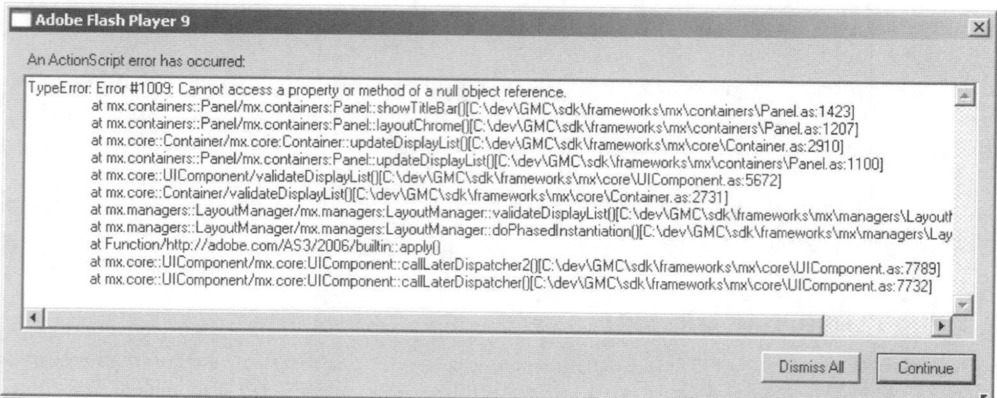

Figure 10.8 An error related to a lack of initializing the library

The reason for this error is that many times *mxmlc* complements classes with additional initialization code at the SystemManager level. But if the relevant classes are completely shielded from *mxmlc* it's absolved from taking care of them. Let's explain this in detail. Please have another look at the generated SystemManager corresponding to *FlexApplication* from Listing 10.3.

```
package {
import mx.managers.SystemManager;
import flash.utils.*;
import flash.system.ApplicationDomain;
import mx.core.IFlexModuleFactory;
public class _FlexApplication_mx_managers_SystemManager extends mx.managers.SystemManage
r implements IFlexModuleFactory {
  public function _FlexApplication_mx_managers_SystemManager() {
      super();
  }
  override public function info():Object {
   return {
   "currentDomain": ApplicationDomain.currentDomain,
   "layout" : "vertical",
   "mainClassName" : "FlexApplication",
   "mixins" : ["_FlexApplication_FlexInit",
         "_activeTabStyleStyle", …
         "_ControlBarStyle", "_PanelStyle", "_CustomPanelWatcherSetupUtil"
   ]
   ,
```

```
    "rsls" : [{url: "FlexLibrary.swf", size: -1}]
    };
  }
} //_FlexApplication_mx_managers_SystemManager
}
```

Listing 10.5 The Generated SystemManager class for FlexApplication.mxml

If we compare this SystemManager with the one generated for our latest example – *FlexApplication2* – we'll see that in the latter case the mixins array is short of the three values: "_ControlBarStyle," "_PanelStyle," and "_CustomPanelWatcherSetupUtil."

The classes referenced in the *mixins* array take part in the initialization sequence of the application upon the initial load. In particular, *CustomPanelWatcherSetupUtil* is the class that facilitates the binding for the variable *instanceNumber* of *CustomPanel*. In the case of *FlexApplication2*, this part of the initialization "gets forgotten."

SystemManager files _<ApplicationName>_mx_managers_System.Manager.as are not the only ones affected. The next interesting set of files to look after are *<ApplicationName>_FlexInit.as*. For example, in Chapter 8 we used to annotate the *EmployeeDTO* class with the metadata keyword *RemoteClass*:

```
[RemoteClass(alias="com.theriabook.composition.dto.EmployeeDTO")]
```

Below is the relevant part from a generated *<ApplicationName>FlexInit* class:

```
package {
[Mixin]
public class _SimpleAutoCompleteWithDynamicDataDemo_FlexInit
{
   . . . .
   public static function init(fbs:IFlexModuleFactory):void
   {
   . . . .
   flash.net.registerClassAlias(
      "com.theriabook.composition.dto.EmployeeDTO",
      com.theriabook.composition.dto.EmployeeDTO
   );
   . . . .
   }
}  // FlexInit
}  // package
```

And again, the registration snippet

```
flash.net.registerClassAlias(
   "com.theriabook.composition.dto.EmployeeDTO",
   com.theriabook.composition.dto.EmployeeDTO
);
```

Now imagine the scenario in which your RSL defines EmployeeDTO and the classes in RSL anticipate using it, but the application does not explicitly mention EmployeeDTO anywhere. What happens? The above initialization code does not get generated at all.

All in all, MXML files as well as metadata-annotated ActionScript classes might not get the expected initialization support if you put them in RSL and don't explicitly reference them in the calling application.

Self-Initializing Libraries – Applications

Enough of the problems, let's get back to positive thinking. Here's a short description of the solution:

We will politely decline a suggestion to "AutoExtract" SWF from SWC. We will be making the right SWF ourselves via an Ant build file that controls *how* we build the SWF. Namely, we will build it as an application to guarantee that, effectively, our library will initialize itself. As far as SWC goes, we will restrict its role to merely supporting the name resolution during the compilation of the main application.

To that end, we'll add the following *FlexLibraryMain.xml* application and *FlexLibraryMain.as* class (Listings 10.6 and 10.7, respectively):

```
<?xml version="1.0" encoding="utf-8"?>
<!-- FlexLibrary.mxml -->
<FlexLibraryMain xmlns="*"/>
```

Listing 10.6 FlexLibrary.mxml

```
// FlexLibraryMain.as
package {
   import mx.core.SimpleApplication;
   public class FlexLibraryMain extends SimpleApplication {
      public function FlexLibraryMain() {
      // Custom library initialization code should go here
         trace("FlexLibrary.swf has been loaded and initialized");
      }
      // Enforce merging-on of required classes by static references here
      private var linkage:Object = {
         r1:CustomPanel
```

```
        };
    }//FlexLibraryMain
}
```

Listing 10.7 FlexLibraryMain.as class

Inheriting your FlexLibraryMain from mx.core.SimpleApplication ensures that the compiler will initialize all the classes referenced by your application, while wrapping it as FlexLibrary.mxml will support the CSS-style-related portion of the initialization.

We've said that we wanted to build the FlexLibrary.swf ourselves. Since we started with Flex Builder's Library Project, the default outcome of the project is only an SWC file. However, nothing stops us from creating the ANT file that will be calling the *mxmlc* compiler against our *FlexLibrary.mxml* "application."[2]

Before we present the listing of the *Ant build.xml* file let's ask ourselves several questions.

There could be references to the Flex framework classes from the *FlexLibrary project*. Do we want to merge-in the contents of the *framework.swc, utilities.swc*, etc., to the *FlexLibrary.swf*? If we want to keep our library tiny, the answer is "no," assuming of course that the required Flex framework classes will somehow be present in the target application domain. That's why in our *build.xml* we'll *extern* the framework swc files with lines like the following:

```
<arg line="-external-library-path='${swclibs}/framework.swc'"/>
```

The next question is where is the deployment destination of *FlexLibrary.swf*? It should go into the same folder that the *FlexApplication* expects it to be. In our scenario, that means:

```
c:/theriabook/code/applications/FlexApplication/bin/FlexLibrary.swf
```

Ultimately we arrive at the following build.xml file:

```
<project name="Lib-App" default="compileMXML" basedir="c:/theriabook/code/applications/
FlexLibrary" >
   <target name="compileMXML">
      <property name="sdkdir" value="C:/Program Files/Adobe/Flex Builder 2 Plug-in/Flex
SDK 2" />
      <property name="swclibs" value="${sdkdir}/frameworks/libs" />
      <property name="fileName" value="FlexLibrary.mxml" />
      <exec executable="${sdkdir}/bin/mxmlc.exe" dir="${basedir}">
            <arg line="-external-library-path='${swclibs}/playerglobal.swc'"/>
            <arg line="-external-library-path='${swclibs}/utilities.swc'"/>
            <arg line="-external-library-path='${swclibs}/framework.swc'"/>
            <arg line="${fileName}"/>
```

```
            <arg line="-output
                  c:/theriabook/code/applications/FlexApplication/bin/FlexLibrary.swf"/>
        </exec>
    </target>
</project>
```

Listing 10.8 The Ant build file to create a self-sufficient FlexLibrary.swf

Please note that the value of the *sdkdir* property will be different if you use *FlexBuilder* instead of *Flex Builder Plugin*:

```
<property name="sdkdir" value="C:/Program Files/Adobe/Flex Builder 2/Flex SDK 2"
/>
```

When you "Run As Ant" the *build.xml* above will generate the customized *FlexLibrary.swf* that will replace the one previously auto-extracted during the build of the *FlexApplication*. Now we need to prevent future unwanted auto-extracts. To that end we need to revisit Flex Build Path and turn off the "Auto Extract swf" option for FlexLibrary.swc.

But wait, who's going to ensure that everything from *framework.swc, utilities.swc,* etc., is going to await our *FlexLibrary.swf* in the runtime? Here's the issue: the default setting for *framework.swc, utilities.swc, flex.swc,* and *rpc.swc* (although the later isn't relevant to our example) was to "merge-in" their contents. This was meant to pick only statically referenced classes. When we denied the *FlexApplication* rights to auto-extract *FlexLibrary.swf* we also absolved it from responsibility for accounting for all the classes that *FlexLibrary.swf* might need from these "merge-ins" (remember *catalog.xml*?).

Eureka! We'll turn *framework.swc, utilities.swc,* and *flex.swc* to "auto-extract" RSLs. All the above *Flex Application* settings are presented on Figure 10.9:

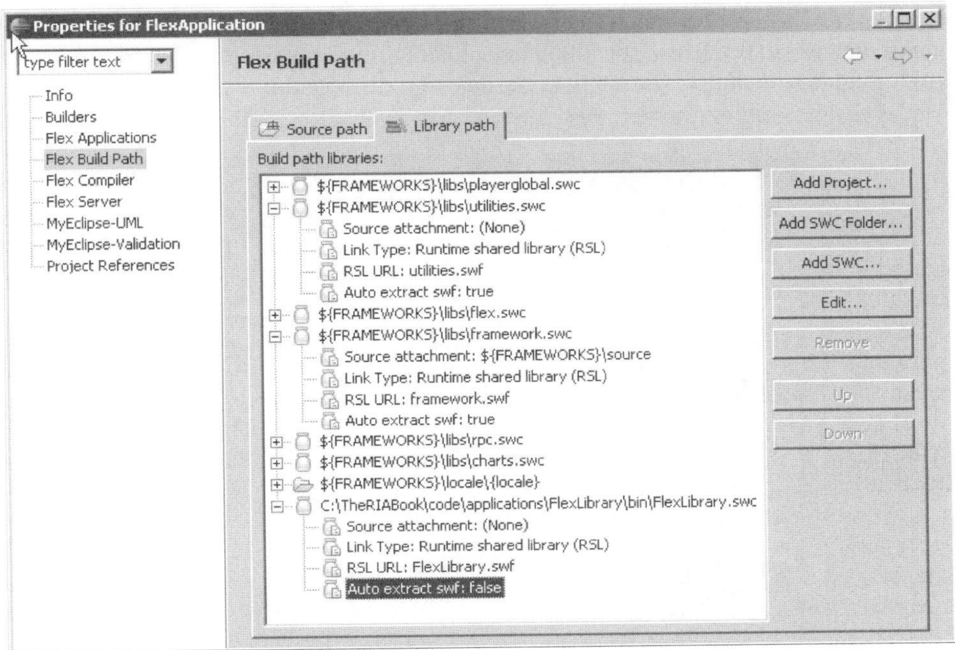

Figure 10.9 The FlexApplication Build path extracts framework libraries and doesn't extract FlexLibrary.swf

After we do a clean build (see Flex Builder's Project menu) and run our application, it functions properly, as shown in Figure 10.10:

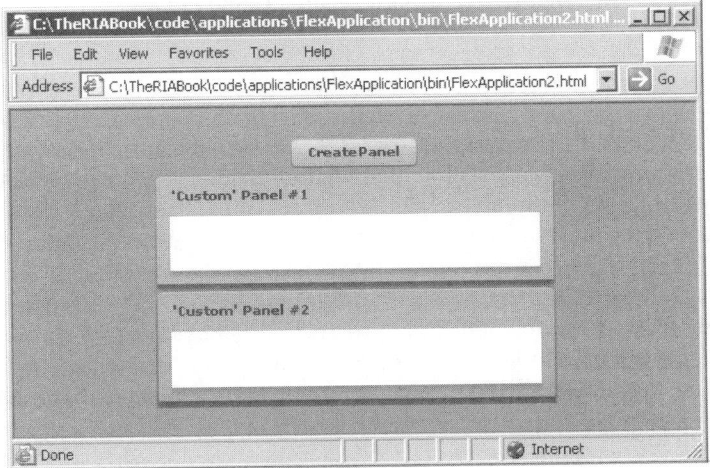

Figure 10.10 FlexApplication2 after two clicks on "Create Panel"

Figure 10.11 shows the deployment directory of the FlexApplication project at this point. You can see a major increase in the size of the initial download because of the 1Mb of framework.swf. This is the price paid for the utmost flexibility in the delivery of the modules and development productivity.

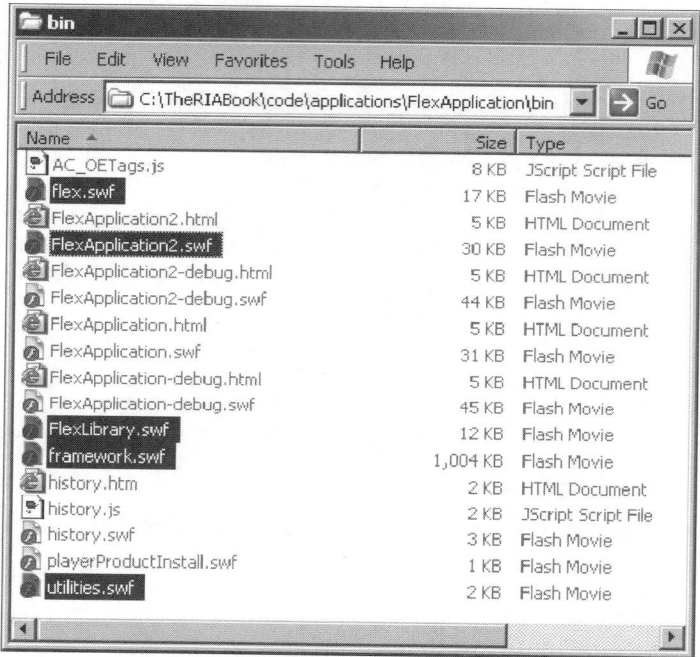

Figure 10.11 Deployment directory of the FlexApplication project again

Recap of the Technique

Let us go back to Chapter 8 and review the final sections where we introduced the idea of separating the resources from the components. The next level of logical progression is to keep classes, which serve as resources in the resourse-only-libraries, separate from the components' and application's SWFs.

To illustrate this, we'll create the application project *ComboBoxCode* that will contain everything from the original project *ComboBox* except the sub-folders *com/theriabook/resources* and *com/theriabook/composition/dto*. We'll also create the library project *Resources* containing precisely these sub-folders as shown in Figure 10.12.

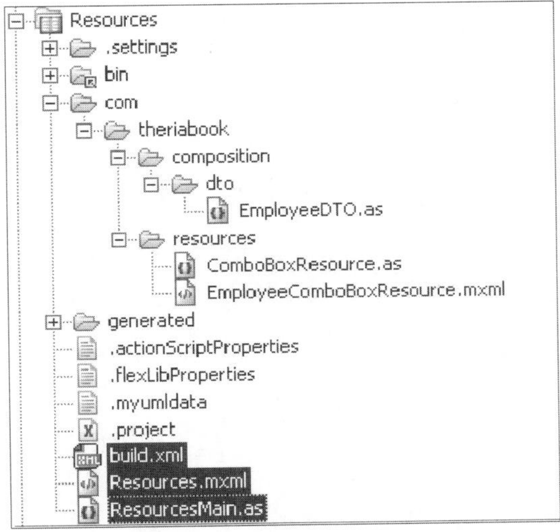

Figure 10.12 Resources project.

Please note that we show the state of the *Resources* project after three extra files *Resources.mxml, ResourcesMain.as,* and *build.xml* have been added to the project. Let's go over them one by one.

Resources.mxml is a clone of FlexLibrary.mxml from Listing 10.6 except that it refers to Resources-Main.as:

```
<?xml version="1.0" encoding="utf-8"?>
<!-- ResourcesMain.mxml -->
<ResourcesMain xmlns="*"/>
```

Listing 10.9 ResourcesMain.mxml.

The file ResourcesMain.as enforces the static linkage of the classes EmployeeComboBoxResources and EmployeeDTO and registers the alias of the EmployeeDTO class:

```
// ResourcesMain.as
package {
   import mx.core.SimpleApplication;

   import com.theriabook.composition.dto.EmployeeDTO;
   import com.theriabook.resources.EmployeeComboBoxResource;
   import flash.net.registerClassAlias;

   public class ResourcesMain extends SimpleApplication {
      public function ResourcesMain() {
```

```
// Custom library initialization code should go here
   registerClassAlias(
      "com.theriabook.composition.dto.EmployeeDTO",
           EmployeeDTO
       );
   trace("Resources.swf has been loaded and initialized");
}
// Static linking of the required classes should go here
private var linkage:Object = {
   t1:EmployeeComboBoxResource
};
}//ResourcesMain
```

Listing 10.10 ResourcesMain.as

The third file – *build.xml* – facilitates building Resources.swf with Ant and mxmlc. Please note that unlike the example in Listing 10.8, where we referenced the Flex SDK SWC files, here we point to *WEB-INF/flex/libs* folder. The reason is that we need fds.swc, which isn't a part of the Flex SDK. Also note that we direct the *Resources.swf* output file straight into the deployment folder of the *ComboBoxCode* application:

```
<project name="Flex 2 Build File" default="compileMXML" basedir="c:/theriabook/code/ap-
plications/Resources" >
   <target name="compileMXML">
      <property name="sdkdir" value="C:/Program Files/Adobe/Flex Builder 2 Plug-in/Flex
SDK 2"  />
   <property name="WEB-INF" value="C:/fds/jrun4/servers/default/theriabook/WEB-INF"/>
      <property name="swclibs" value="${WEB-INF}/flex/libs" />
      <property name="fileName" value="Resources.mxml" />
      <exec executable="${sdkdir}/bin/mxmlc.exe" dir="${basedir}">
            <arg line="-external-library-path='${swclibs}/playerglobal.swc'"/>
            <arg line="-external-library-path='${swclibs}/utilities.swc'"/>
            <arg line="-external-library-path='${swclibs}/framework.swc'"/>
            <arg line="-external-library-path='${swclibs}/rpc.swc'"/>
            <arg line="-external-library-path='${swclibs}/fds.swc'"/>
            <arg line="-keep-generated-actionscript=true "/>
            <arg line="${fileName}"/>
            <arg line="-output
                C:/fds/jrun4/servers/default/theriabook/ComboBoxCode/Resources.swf"/>
      </exec>
   </target>
</project>
```

Listing 10.11 The Ant build.xml file to build Resources.swf library

When we run this build.xml as an Ant task, it produces a Resources.swf file of 20,851 bytes.

At the same time, let's not forget the original purpose of Resources.swc – it should help in resolving all references during the application's build. That's why we check off all the classes the application might need as shown in Figure 10.13. The output folder for the Resources.swc will be *WEB-INF\flex\user_classes*:

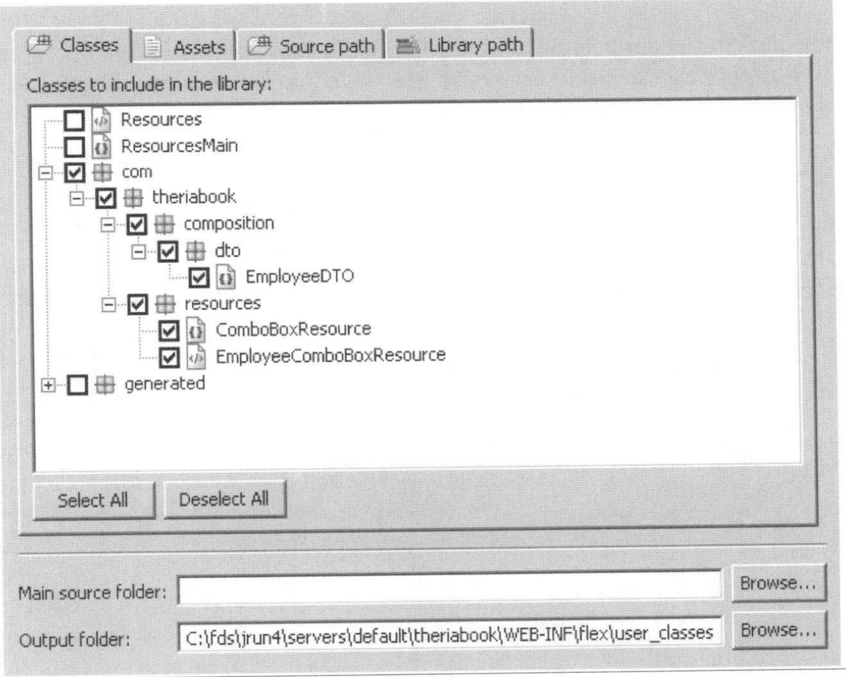

Figure 10.13 Classes for .flexLibProperties for the Resources project

These checkboxes correspond to the following contents of the.flexLibProperties file:

```
<?xml version="1.0" encoding="UTF-8"?>
<flexLibProperties version="1">
  <includeClasses>
    <classEntry path="com.theriabook.composition.dto.EmployeeDTO"/>
    <classEntry path="com.theriabook.resources.ComboBoxResource"/>
    <classEntry path="com.theriabook.resources.EmployeeComboBoxResource"/>
  </includeClasses>
  <includeResources/>
  <namespaceManifests/>
```

```
</flexLibProperties>
```

Listing 10.12 The flexLibPropertiesAnt file of the Resource project

As you can see, out of the three files listed in (DOT) directly in front of *flexLibProperties*, our Resources.as, shown in Listing 10.10, explicitly references EmployeeComboBoxResource and EmployeeDTO. We did not have to register the base class – ComboBoxResource – as this is the compiler's job.

Now let's take care of the application settings. For the ComboBoxCode project we'll set the *Link Type* of all the libraries except Resources.swc to RSL *with* Auto extract, while Resources.swc will be set as RSL *without* Auto extract as in Figure 10.14.

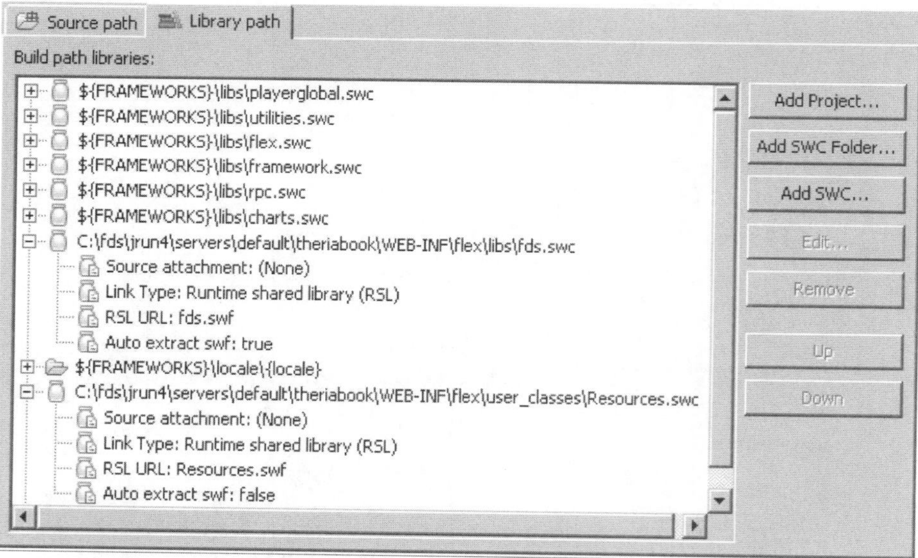

Figure 10.14 The library path for the ComboBoxCode project

Finally, we'll comment out of the linkage variable in the application, since the pre-load of Resources.swf that we have built as a self-initializing library will automatically load the EmployeeComboBoxResource class in the *currentDomain*.

```
<?xml version="1.0" encoding="utf-8"?>
<!-- ResourceComboBoxDemo.mxml -->
<mx:Application xmlns:mx="http://www.adobe.com/2006/mxml"
   xmlns="com.theriabook.controls.*" >
   <mx:Script>
//    import com.theriabook.resources.*;
```

```
//    private var linkage:EmployeeComboBoxResource;
</mx:Script>
<ResourceComboBox   id="cbx_1"
   width="150"
   resource="com.theriabook.resources.EmployeeComboBoxResource"
/>
</mx:Application>
```

Listing 10.13 The code for the ResourceComboBoxDemo from the ComboBoxCode project

The application is ready to run and after a slight delay it will display a familiar picture:

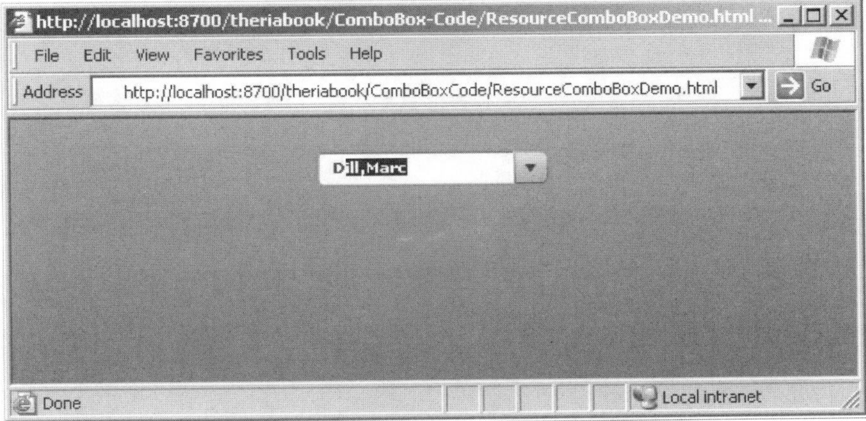

Figure 10.15 The ResourceComboBoxDemo from the ComboBoxCode project

RSL versus Custom Loading of the Dynamic Code

Up till now, we've been building self-initializing libraries and pre-loading them during the application bootstrap in the RSL style. But there are different use cases, such as add-on modules that have to be loaded on demand. These use cases could be related to a portlet-style personalization of the applications and, in general, such add-ons may not even exist at the time of the application build. An extra benefit of explicit on-demand loading (applicable even if you know all your libraries in advance) is that it reduces the initial load time and memory footprint of the application.

Unlike RSLs, on-demand loading leaves open the choice of an *application domain* to load to. Arguably, complete independent subsystems should be loaded into separate domains. On the other hand, when we load a small "flexlet" that contains some extra business function to augment the existing application, we load it into the main application domain to allow seamless interoperability between the new and old classes.

That said, everything we 've done so far to guarantee the self-sufficiency of the libraries is equally relevant to all of them irrespective of the exact loading method: on demand or pre-loaded as in RSL case.

The Custom Loading Example

To illustrate custom loading, we'll create another application – *FlexApplication3* – that will let us load a DataGrid definition from the *FlexLibrary* and show this DataGrid with the help of two buttons "1.Load Library" and "2.Show Library Grid" as shown in Figure 10.16.

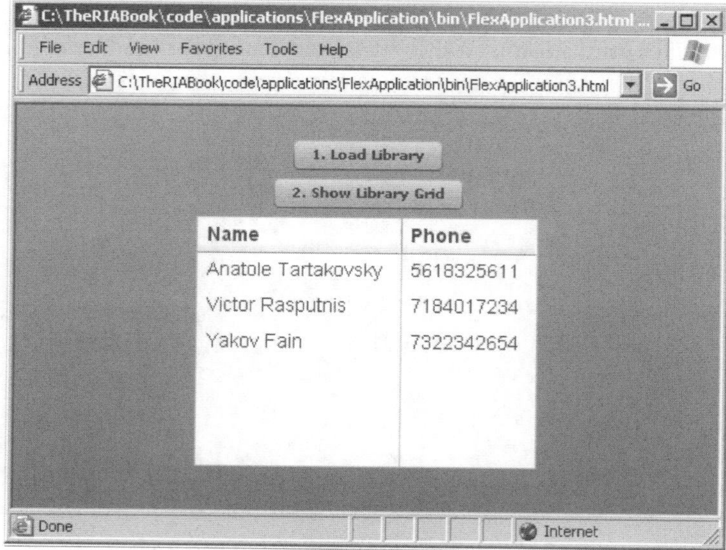

Figure 10.16 FlexApplication3 with DataGrid loaded on demand.

If you click on the "2. Show Library Grid" button, the application will assign an array of data to the DataGrid's *dataProvider* as it would to any ordinary loaded DataGrid:

```
dg.dataProvider = [
   {name:"Anatole Tartakovsky", phone:"5618325611"},
   {name:"Victor Rasputnis", phone:"7184017234"},
   {name:"Yakov Fain",phone:"7322342654"}
];
```

Meanwhile the DataGrid won't contain any data, being a pure "resource" file, as shown in Listing 10.14:

```
<?xml version="1.0" encoding="utf-8"?>
<!-- AuthorsGrid.mxml -->
```

```
<mx:DataGrid xmlns:mx="http://www.adobe.com/2006/mxml">
   <mx:columns>
      <mx:Array>
         <mx:DataGridColumn  dataField="name" headerText="Name" width="150"/>
         <mx:DataGridColumn  dataField="phone" headerText="Phone"/>
      </mx:Array>
   </mx:columns>
</mx:DataGrid>
```

Listing 10.14 AuthorsGrid.mxml from FlexLibrary project

We'll begin working on our application by adding the *AuthorsGrid* to the *FlexLibrary* project and registering it with the FlexLibraryMain.as class:

```
// FlexLibraryMain.as
package {
   import mx.core.SimpleApplication;
   public class FlexLibraryMain extends SimpleApplication {
      public function FlexLibraryMain() {
      // Custom library initialization code should go here
         trace("FlexLibrary.swf has been loaded and initialized");
      }
      // Static linking of the required classes should go here
      private var linkage:Object = {
         t1:CustomPanel,
         t2:AuthorsGrid
      };
   }//FlexLibraryMain
}
}
```

Listing 10.15 The Resources.as file with the static linkage of AuthorsGrid

At this point we can rerun the Ant's *build.xml* file, which will place the updated *FlexLibrary.swf* in the same folder that we expect our *FlexApplication3* to run from.

Let's "prepare" this application by removing the *FlexLibrary.swc* from the FlexApplication project's *Build Path.* Up till now we've been pre-loading the *FlexLibrary.swf* the RSL way, which we don't want it any more. Accordingly, we will comment out the static reference to *CustomPanel* inside the *FlexApplication.mxml,* otherwise the project's build will fail:

```
<?xml version="1.0" encoding="utf-8"?>
<!-- FlexApplication.mxml -->
<mx:Application xmlns:mx="http://www.adobe.com/2006/mxml" layout="absolute"
```

```
    xmlns="*">
    <!-- Comment out to illustrate on demand loading with FlexApplication3-->
    <!--CustomPanel /-->
</mx:Application>
```

Listing 10.16 FlexApplication.mxml with a commented-out CustomPanel

Now we'll code the component that facilitates the loading process – *LibraryLoader*; a partial listing of the component is shown in Listing 10.17. It can be further developed to provide the progress and error handling. We'll inherit this component from the *flash.display.Sprite* class and make it contain a child instance of the *flash.display.Loader*:

```
public class LibraryLoader extends Sprite {
    private var loader:Loader = null;
    public function LibraryLoader() {
        loader = new Loader();
        addChild(loader);
      . . . .
    }

    public function load(url:String):void {
        var request:URLRequest = new URLRequest(url);
        loader.load(request, …);
    }
}
```

Listing 10.17 A partial listing of LibraryLoader.as

Since we prefer seamless programmatic access to classes of dynamically loaded resources, we'll put the loaded classes in the loading application's domain:

```
loaderContext = new LoaderContext();
loaderContext.applicationDomain = ApplicationDomain.currentDomain;
```

We'll also listen to all relevant events on the *loader.contentLoaderInfo* object:

```
dispatcher.addEventListener(Event.COMPLETE, onEvent);
dispatcher.addEventListener(HTTPStatusEvent.HTTP_STATUS, onEvent);
dispatcher.addEventListener(Event.INIT, onEvent);
dispatcher.addEventListener(IOErrorEvent.IO_ERROR, onEvent);
dispatcher.addEventListener(Event.OPEN, onEvent);
dispatcher.addEventListener(ProgressEvent.PROGRESS, onEvent);
dispatcher.addEventListener(Event.UNLOAD, onEvent);
```

The full listing of LibraryLoader is presented below:

```
// LibraryLoader.as
package com.theriabook.util
{
    import flash.display.Sprite;
    import flash.display.Loader;
    import flash.net.URLRequest;
    import flash.events.*;
    import flash.system.LoaderContext;
    import flash.system.ApplicationDomain;

    public class LibraryLoader extends Sprite {
        private var loader:Loader = null;
        private var loaderContext:LoaderContext = null;
        public function LibraryLoader() {
        loader = new Loader();
        addChild(loader);
        configureListeners(loader.contentLoaderInfo);

        loaderContext = new LoaderContext();
        loaderContext.applicationDomain = ApplicationDomain.currentDomain;
        }
        public function load(url:String):void {
            var request:URLRequest = new URLRequest(url);
            loader.load(request, loaderContext);
        }
        private function configureListeners(dispatcher:IEventDispatcher):void {
            dispatcher.addEventListener(Event.COMPLETE, onEvent);
            dispatcher.addEventListener(HTTPStatusEvent.HTTP_STATUS, onEvent);
            dispatcher.addEventListener(Event.INIT, onEvent);
            dispatcher.addEventListener(IOErrorEvent.IO_ERROR, onEvent);
            dispatcher.addEventListener(Event.OPEN, onEvent);
            dispatcher.addEventListener(ProgressEvent.PROGRESS, onEvent);
            dispatcher.addEventListener(Event.UNLOAD, onEvent);
        }
        private function onEvent(event:Event):void {
            trace(event.type + event);
        }
    }
}
```

Listing 10.18 LibraryLoader.as

We're ready to write the application *FlexApplication3.mxml.* To illustrate that fonts bound to the application's SystemManager are proliferated to the loaded classes, we'll purposely throw in a non-standard style definition for the DataGrid fonts (please notice the larger than usual characters in Figure 10.16):

```
   <mx:Style>
DataGrid {
      fontFamily: Arial; fontSize: 14; headerStyleName:"dgHeader";
}
.dgHeader {
      fontFamily: Arial; fontSize: 14pt; fontWeight:bold;
}
   </mx:Style>
```

We'll prepare two functions, individually invoked from the buttons "1. Load Library" and "2. Show Library Grid." The *showGrid()* function instantiates the DataGrid freshly loaded by *loadLibrary()*, given the name *AuthorsGrid*:

```
private function loadLibrary() :void {
   var loader:LibraryLoader = new LibraryLoader();
   loader.load("FlexLibrary.swf");
}
private function showGrid():void {
   var clazz:Class = Class(getDefinitionByName("AuthorsGrid"));
   var dg:DataGrid  = DataGrid(new clazz());
   dg.dataProvider = [
      {name:"Anatole Tartakovsky", phone:"5618325611"},
      {name:"Victor Rasputnis", phone:"7184017234"},
      {name:"Yakov Fain",phone:"7322342654"}
   ];
   addChild(dg);
}
```

The full listing of FlexApplication3.mxml is presented in Listing 10.19:

```
<?xml version="1.0" encoding="utf-8"?>
<!-- FlexApplication3.mxml -->
<mx:Application xmlns:mx="http://www.adobe.com/2006/mxml"
   layout="vertical">
   <mx:Style>
DataGrid {
      fontFamily: Arial; fontSize: 14; headerStyleName:"dgHeader";
}
.dgHeader {
```

```
        fontFamily: Arial; fontSize: 14; fontWeight:bold;
}
   </mx:Style>

   <mx:Button  label="1. Load Library" click="loadLibrary()"/>
   <mx:Button  label="2. Show Library Grid" click="showGrid()"/>
   <mx:Script>
      <![CDATA[
         import mx.controls.DataGrid;
         import com.theriabook.util.LibraryLoader;

         private function loadLibrary() :void {
            var loader:LibraryLoader = new LibraryLoader();
            loader.load("FlexLibrary.swf");
         }
         private function showGrid():void {
            var clazz:Class = Class(getDefinitionByName("AuthorsGrid"));
            var dg:DataGrid  = DataGrid(new clazz());
            dg.dataProvider = [
               {name:"Anatole Tartakovsky", phone:"5618325611"},
               {name:"Victor Rasputnis", phone:"7184017234"},
               {name:"Yakov Fain",phone:"7322342654"}
            ];
            addChild(dg);
         }
      ]]>
   </mx:Script>
</mx:Application>
```

Listing 10.19 FlexApplication3.mxml

Let's run the application in the debug mode to see the debugger's trace messages. This is what you'll see in the console window when the application starts:

```
[SWF] C:\TheRIABook\code\applications\FlexApplication\bin\utilities.swf - 1,827 bytes
after decompression
[SWF] C:\TheRIABook\code\applications\FlexApplication\bin\flex.swf - 49,833 bytes after
decompression
[SWF] C:\TheRIABook\code\applications\FlexApplication\bin\FlexApplication3-debug.swf -
104,664 bytes after decompression
[SWF] C:\TheRIABook\code\applications\FlexApplication\bin\framework.swf - 2,235,667
bytes after decompression
```

Listing 10.20 Console window messages when FlexApplication3 starts

These messages reflect the fact that all of the above libraries are marked as RSLs with "Auto extract." Now let's press the "1. Load Library" button. The following output will go to the console:

```
open[Event type="open" bubbles=false cancelable=false eventPhase=2]
progress[ProgressEvent type="progress" bytesLoaded=0 bytesTotal=16440]
progress[ProgressEvent type="progress" bytesLoaded=8192 bytesTotal=16440]
progress[ProgressEvent type="progress" bytesLoaded=16384 bytesTotal=16440]
progress[ProgressEvent type="progress" bytesLoaded=16440 bytesTotal=16440]
[SWF] C:\TheRIABook\code\applications\FlexApplication\bin\FlexLibrary.swf - 36,126 bytes
after decompression
init[Event type="init" bubbles=false cancelable=false eventPhase=2]
httpStatus[HTTPStatusEvent type="httpStatus" bubbles=false cancelable=false eventPhase=2
status=0]
complete[Event type="complete" bubbles=false cancelable=false eventPhase=2]
Module file://C:\TheRIABook\code\applications\FlexApplication\bin\FlexLibrary.swf com-
plete.
FlexLibrary.swf has been loaded and initialized
```

Listing 10.21 Console messages in response to library loading

At this point we can press the button "2. Show Library Grid." The grid with the data will appear exactly as shown in Figure 10.16.

Congrats! We've just loaded a visual dynamic object AuthorsGrid that can access other objects and be accessed the same way as any other class. In particular, AuthorsGrid adheres to global styles while its properties and methods are directly accessible from the application class.

Embedded Applications and the SWFLoader Object

In this section we'll discuss plug-ins. Fortunately, Flex has a perfect out-of-the-box solution for this type of integration via the SWFLoader control, which lets you embed any SWF file that represents Flex 2.0 application or just any Flash movie. Let's embed one application, InnerApplication.swf, into another application, OuterApplication.swf.

Here is the listing of InnerApplication.mxml, which shows the Panel with two label controls on a light pink background:

```
<?xml version="1.0"?>
<!-- InnerApplication.mxml-->
<mx:Application xmlns:mx="http://www.adobe.com/2006/mxml"  backgroundColor="0xffeeff">
    <mx:Script>
        [Bindable]
        public var value:String = "From InnerApp with love!";
    </mx:Script>
```

```
    <mx:Panel title="This Panel is a part of InnerApplication" >
    <mx:Label id="label_1"  text="This label contains static text" />
      <mx:Label text="This label is bound to 'value', currently - {value}"/>
    </mx:Panel>
</mx:Application>
```

Listing 10.22 InnerApplication.mxml

Before compiling InnerApplication.mxml into InnerApplication.swf, let's figure out the *Link Type* for the Flex framework libraries. If we plan to run the InnerApplication as standalone and offer it to the broad unprepared clientele over the Internet, we need to keep the size minimal, so we would choose to merge the framework libraries. However, this is not our case.

If the purpose of the InnerApplication is to be host to a suite of other applications or portlets, we would choose Auto extract. This is not our case either.

Specifics of our case is that the InnerApplication is being brought to life by the OuterApplication, which has already taken care of the framework libraries. That is why we will mark all the framework libraries as *external*.

But, if we're going to keep the OuterApplication.mxml and InnerApplication.mxml in the same Flex Builder project, they will compete for a single set of Flex Build Path settings. Settings for OuterApplication are not supposed to *extern* framework libraries, rather they should AutoExtract them. To avoid the problem and allow both InnerApplication and OuterApplication to stay in one project, we will leave the Library path to the *OuterApplication* and take care of the InnerApplication with the additional InnerApplication-config.xml file to the project, as in Listing 10.22. Both Flex Builder and a command-line *mxmlc* compiler try to read an *<ApplicationName>-config.xml* file (aka, local configuration guide) before using the project properties (you can read more on the precedence of files and command-line parameters in the Adobe Flex manual in the section "Using Command-line Compilers"). InnerApplication-config.xml, shown below, exclusively externs all the framework libraries for the *InnerApplication*:

```
<flex-config>
    <!--InnerApplication-config.xml-->
   <compiler>
      <external-library-path>
         <path-element>C:/Program Files/Adobe/Flex Builder 2 Plug-in/Flex SDK 2/frame-
works/libs/playerglobal.swc</path-element>
         <path-element>C:/Program Files/Adobe/Flex Builder 2 Plug-in/Flex SDK 2/frame-
works/libs/framework.swc</path-element>
         <path-element>C:/Program Files/Adobe/Flex Builder 2 Plug-in/Flex SDK 2/frame-
works/libs/utilities.swc</path-element>
         <path-element>C:/Program Files/Adobe/Flex Builder 2 Plug-in/Flex SDK 2/frame-
works/libs/flex.swc</path-element>
```

```
      </external-library-path>
    </compiler>
  </flex-config>
```

Listing 10.23 InnerApplication-config.xml

Let's mark the *InnerApplication* as the default one and build the project. This will build an InnerApplication.swf.

Now let's focus on the *OuterApplication*. First and foremost, it will to have an instance of SWFLoader, which loads the *InnerApplication.swf*:

```
<mx:SWFLoader id="swfLoader"  source="InnerApplication.swf"  />
```

Next, it will have a label, whose value gets replaced by the value obtained from the *label_1* of the *InnerApplication* when the "Read inner label" button is clicked:

```
<mx:Label id="label_1" text="This 'outer' label contains static text" />
<mx:Button label="Read Inner Label"  click="readInnerLabel();"/>
```

It will also contain a text field, where we'll type some text, and two buttons to pass this text directly into the InnerApplication's *label_1* and the corresponding *value* variable:

```
<mx:Button label="Modify Inner Label" click="modifyInnerLabel();"/>
<mx:Button label="Change Inner Variable" click="changeInnerVariable();"/>
<mx:TextInput id="new_value" />
```

The default setting of the *loaderContext* of the SWFLoader is to load new definitions into the child domain. Accordingly, to access the *label_1* inside the InnerApplication we may do something like this:

```
var systemManager:SystemManager = SystemManager(swfLoader.content);
var innerApplication:Application = Application(systemManager.application);
trace(innerApplication["label_1"].text);
```

(Flex provides several other ways Outer- and Inner-applications can interoperate, such as SharedObjects, LocalConnection, and ExternalInterface. We discuss the last two in Chapter 15.)

The full listing of the OuterApplication.mxml is presented below:

```
<?xml version="1.0"?>
<!-- OuterApplication.mxml -->
<mx:Application xmlns:mx="http://www.adobe.com/2006/mxml">
    <mx:Script>
```

```
<![CDATA[
    import mx.managers.SystemManager;
    public var innerApplication:Application = null;

    private function getInnerApplication():Application {
      var systemManager:SystemManager = SystemManager(swfLoader.content);
        return Application(systemManager.application);
    }
    public function readInnerLabel():void {
      if (!innerApplication) innerApplication = getInnerApplication();
        label_1.text=innerApplication["label_1"].text;
    }
    public function modifyInnerLabel():void {
      if (!innerApplication) innerApplication = getInnerApplication();
    innerApplication["label_1"].text = new_value.text;
    }
    public function changeInnerVariable():void {
      if (!innerApplication) innerApplication = getInnerApplication();
innerApplication["value"] = new_value.text;
    }
]]>
</mx:Script>

<mx:Label id="label_1" text="This 'outer' label contains static text" />
<mx:SWFLoader id="swfLoader"  source="InnerApplication.swf"  />

<mx:Button label="Read Inner Label"  click="readInnerLabel();"/>
<mx:Button label="Modify Inner Label" click="modifyInnerLabel();"/>
<mx:Button label="Change Inner Variable" click="changeInnerVariable();"/>

<mx:TextInput id="new_value" />

</mx:Application>
```

Listing 10.24 OuterApplication.mxml

When we run the *OuterApplication* it displays the picture shown in Figure 10.17. As you can see, applications are isolated in different application domains and their style settings (backGround color) are different:

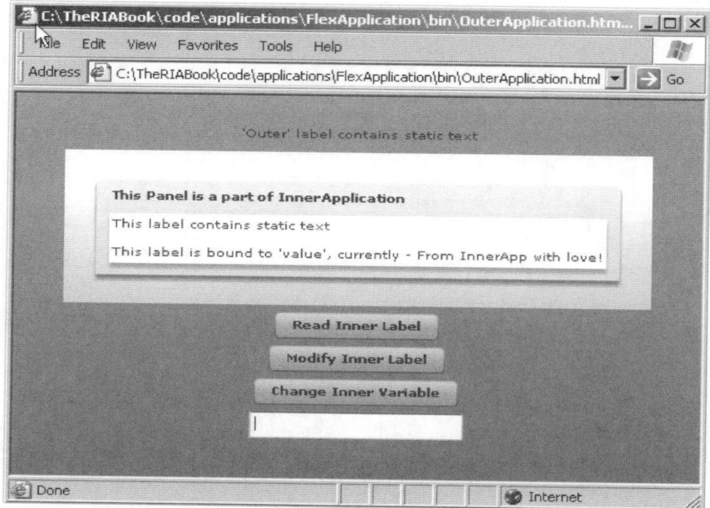

Figure 10.17 The screen showing the OuterApplication at startup

Now let's type "Passed From Outer App" in the text field and click all three buttons in a row. The first button click will read the control's value from the *InnerApplication*, while the clicks on the second and the third buttons will modify the values of the InnerApplication's control and public variable, respectively. The outcome is shown in Figure 10.18.

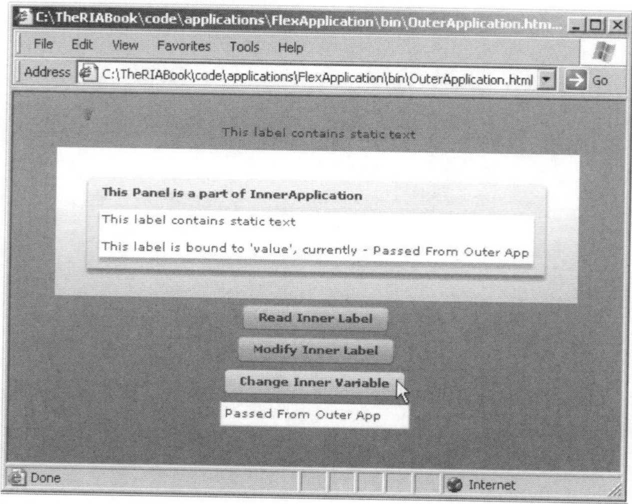

Figure 10.18 The OuterApplication after clicking on "Modify Inner Label" and "Change Inner Variable"

You may say that the communications between the applications is not as seamless as it is with add-ons. This is correct. But let's face it, plug-ins serve a different purpose: they're an easy way to add third-party content to your application. They're complete applications with their own UI, including styling. Their functionality doesn't depend on host applications. In fact, you have to be very careful with references to the objects from the plug-in, since live references will prevent the unloading of plug-in classes.

Modules and ModuleLoaders

Weeks before this book was going to print Adobe released Flex 2.0.1, introducing the mx.modules package with *ModuleLoader* and Module classes, in particular. ModuleLoader behaves very much like SWFLoader with some nuances, for example, ModuleLoader extends VBox while SWFLoader is only a UIComponent.

ModuleLoader facilitates the loading of *modules*. Take a regular Flex application, replace <mx:Application> with <mx:Module>, compile, and you have the module. Not surprisingly, modules are completely self-initialized, much like normal applications.

Programmatically, loading modules looks almost identical to using SWFLoader. To illustrate this point, we have rewritten our OuterApplication/InnerApplication example and created InnerModule and OuterModuleLoader.

All in all, modules seem to be an ideal way of plugging in independent UI widgets, subsystems, or applications, similar to SWFLoader.

Listing 10.23 presents the code for InnerModule. We cloned the code from InnerApplication and added the lines in bold:

```
<?xml version="1.0"?>
<!-- InnerModule.mxml-->
<mx:Module xmlns:mx="http://www.adobe.com/2006/mxml"  implements="IHeyModule"
     backgroundColor="0xffeeff">
    <mx:Script>
        [Bindable]
        public var value:String = "From InnerModule with love!";
        public function getProperty(name:String):* {
         if (name=="value") return value; else return undefined;
        }
        public function setProperty(name:String, newVal:*):void {
         if (name=="value") value=newVal;
        }
    </mx:Script>
    <mx:Panel title="This Panel is a part of InnerModule" >
      <mx:Label id="label_1"  text="This label contains static text" />
```

```
      <mx:Label text="This label is bound to 'value', currently - {value}"/>
    </mx:Panel>
</mx:Module>
```

Listing 10.23 InnerModule.mxml

You'll notice that our module implements the IHeyModule interface, but please don't get the idea that modules have anything to do with interfaces. Likewise, modules and applications loaded by SWFLoader are free to implement any interface, much as OuterApplication and OuterModuleLoader (later in this section) are free to ignore an interface as long as the names of the public properties are known and there is an abundance of double quotes.

We modeled InnerModule-config.xml, Listing 10.24, after InnerApplication-config.xml. Since we externed the Flex framework, the build results in a 12K size of the InnerModule.swf.

```
<flex-config>
   <!--InnerModule-config.xml-->
   <compiler>
      <external-library-path>
         <path-element>C:/Program Files/Adobe/Flex Builder 2 Plug-in/Flex SDK 2/frame-
works/libs/playerglobal.swc</path-element>
         <path-element>C:/Program Files/Adobe/Flex Builder 2 Plug-in/Flex SDK 2/frame-
works/libs/framework.swc</path-element>
         <path-element>C:/Program Files/Adobe/Flex Builder 2 Plug-in/Flex SDK 2/frame-
works/libs/utilities.swc</path-element>
         <path-element>C:/Program Files/Adobe/Flex Builder 2 Plug-in/Flex SDK 2/frame-
works/libs/flex.swc</path-element>
      </external-library-path>
   </compiler>
</flex-config>
```

Listing 10.24 Local config file InnerModule-config.xml

Here is the definition of the IHeyModule interface:

```
// IHeyModule.as
package
{
   public interface IHeyModule
   {

      function getProperty(name:String):*;
      function setProperty(name:String, value:* ):void;
```

```
    }
}
```

Listing 10.25 Interface IHeyModule

Then, we cloned OuterModuleLoader from OuterApplication. The only difference in the code is that while with SWFLoader we had to look at the loaded SWF as an instance of the SystemManager, here we are dealing with an instance of DisplayObject:

```
<?xml version="1.0"?>
<!-- OuterModuleLoader.mxml -->
<mx:Application xmlns:mx="http://www.adobe.com/2006/mxml">
    <mx:Script>
        <![CDATA[
            import mx.managers.SystemManager;
            public var innerDisplayObject:DisplayObject = null;

            private function getInnerDisplayObject():DisplayObject {
                return moduleLoader.child;
            }
            public function readInnerLabel():void {
              if (!innerDisplayObject) innerDisplayObject = getInnerDisplayObject();
                label_1.text=innerDisplayObject["label_1"].text;
            }
            public function modifyInnerLabel():void {
              if (!innerDisplayObject) innerDisplayObject = getInnerDisplayObject();
              innerDisplayObject["label_1"].text = new_value.text;
            }
            public function changeInnerVariable():void {
              if (!innerDisplayObject) innerDisplayObject = getInnerDisplayObject();
            // If you know name of the properties/methods of the InnerModule, you can
            // use them directly:

            // innerDisplayObject["value"] = new_value.text;

            // or, alternatively, if InnerModule "implements" IHeyModule you can use
            // interface to dereference available properties & methods
            IHeyModule(innerDisplayObject).setProperty("value",new_value.text);
             }
        ]]>
    </mx:Script>

    <mx:Label id="label_1" text="This 'outer' label contains static text" />
    <mx:ModuleLoader id="moduleLoader"  url="InnerModule.swf"  creationComplete="module
Loader.loadModule()" />
```

```
    <mx:Button label="Read Inner Label"  click="readInnerLabel();"/>
    <mx:Button label="Modify Inner Label" click="modifyInnerLabel();"/>
    <mx:Button label="Change Inner Variable" click="changeInnerVariable();"/>

    <mx:TextInput id="new_value" />

</mx:Application>
```

Listing 10.26 OuterModuleLoader application

When you run OuterModuleLoader, its look and behavior will be indistinguishable from OuterApplication, Figure 10.18.

Finally, we present samples of using the IHeyModule interface by InnerApplication and OuterApplication, Listings 10.27 and 10.28, respectively.

```
<?xml version="1.0"?>
<!-- InnerApplication.mxml-->
<mx:Application xmlns:mx="http://www.adobe.com/2006/mxml" implements="IHeyModule"
     backgroundColor="0xffeeff" >
    <mx:Script>
        [Bindable]
        public var value:String = "From InnerApp with love!";
        public function getProperty(name:String):* {
        if (name=="value") return value; else return undefined;
        }
        public function setProperty(name:String, newVal:*):void {
        if (name=="value") value=newVal;
        }
    </mx:Script>
    <mx:Panel title="This Panel is a part of InnerApplication">
       <mx:Label id="label_1"  text="This label contains static text" />
      <mx:Label text="This label is bound to 'value', currently - {value}"/>
    </mx:Panel>
</mx:Application>
```

Listing 10.27 Version of InnerApplication that implements the IHeyModule interface

```
<?xml version="1.0"?>
<!-- OuterApplication.mxml -->
<mx:Application xmlns:mx="http://www.adobe.com/2006/mxml">

    <mx:Script>
        <![CDATA[
```

```
        import mx.managers.SystemManager;
        public var innerApplication:Application = null;

        private function getInnerApplication():Application {
          var systemManager:SystemManager = SystemManager(swfLoader.content);
            return Application(systemManager.application);
        }
        public function readInnerLabel():void {
          if (!innerApplication) innerApplication = getInnerApplication();
            label_1.text=innerApplication[«label_1»].text;
        }
        public function modifyInnerLabel():void {
          if (!innerApplication) innerApplication = getInnerApplication();
        innerApplication[«label_1»].text = new_value.text;
        }
        public function changeInnerVariable():void {
          if (!innerApplication) innerApplication = getInnerApplication();
        // If you know name of the properties/methods of the InnerApp, you can
        // use them directly:

        // innerApplication[«value»] = new_value.text;

        // or, alternatively, if InnerApp «implements» IHeyModule you can use
        // interface to dereference available properties & methods
        IHeyModule(innerApplication).setProperty("value",new_value.text);

        }
      ]]>
    </mx:Script>

    <mx:Label id="label_1" text="This 'outer' label contains static text" />
    <mx:SWFLoader id="swfLoader"  source="InnerApplication.swf"  />

    <mx:Button label="Read Inner Label"  click="readInnerLabel();"/>
    <mx:Button label="Modify Inner Label" click="modifyInnerLabel();"/>
    <mx:Button label="Change Inner Variable" click="changeInnerVariable();"/>

    <mx:TextInput id="new_value" />

</mx:Application>
```

Listing 10.28 Version of OuterApplication that makes use of the IHeyModule interface

When Size Matters

Flex compilers support the *-link-report* option. It lets you specify a file to be populated with the linker dependencies found during the build of your SWF. There is a matching *-load-externs* compiler option that lets you specify the classes you don't want to link, but rather prefer to *extern*. Conveniently, *-load-externs* anticipates the input to be in exactly the same XML format as is produced by *-link-report*.

Speaking of modules and applications, just as an example case, this pair of options enables you to *extern* for the module everything that will be loaded by the application. However, if you plan to ever reuse the same module for the different hosting application, this technique is not applicable.

There is an opposite way to use the *-link-report* option. Earlier we explained why you should use self-initialized RSLs for component and resource libraries (as opposed to visual plugins, where modules and applications reign). If you recall, we managed to keep these RSLs extremely tiny by *externing* an entire set of Flex framework SWC files under the assumption that the main application would supply those via AutoExtract. The only downside has been the indiscriminating extract of the entire set of classes (resulting in a large 1Mb framework.swf in particular). But why tolerate a wholesale extract? If you use the compiler's option *–include* you can go back to *merge-in* Link Type and have the application merge in all the classes required by your libraries.

In this scenario, which applies to self-initialized RSLs as well as modules, you run *-link-report* on the module or library and instead of optimizing the module, you optimize the application. No need to rebuild your libraries or modules to satisfy an individual application – they stay 100% reusable. Instead, you tune your applications.4

And, speaking of size, don't forget the *-debug* option. By turning it to f*alse*, you may strip up to 30% of the size taken by the debugging information. By the same token, you may want to recompile framework.swf from the Adobe Flex Framework source files to take its size down in the first place, prior to resorting to *–include*.

Summary

In this chapter we went through a number of techniques of utmost importance when it comes to large application development. We showed you how to:

- Break a monolithic build process into a set of smaller independent builds
- Enable developers to work with isolated libraries of components and resources
- Do "on-demand" loading of functionality that's impossible to forecast and package in advance
- Optimizate the total size of the application's size

Endnotes

1. A word of advice: make a decision where you want to keep your SWC files and stick to it. Avoid the situation where the SWC linked in by your application is not the same one that you're making with the Flex Builder Project.

2. In Flex 2.0.1 you can coordinate running the Ant file with the build of the SWC by adding the extra "builder" to the project.

3. During the lifetime of any resource project or component library project, the corresponding *ResourceMain.as* file will need to be kept in sync with the project contents. One way to achieve this is to include a code-generation target in your Ant script and treat the contents of *.flexLibProperties* as input data. Alternatively, to automate this and all other Flex build-related tasks, you can use the Flex2Ant utility developed by FarataSystems, see http://www.myflex.org for more information.

4. The current release of Flex does not provide automation tools for this optimization, so you may want to create the automation process yourself. Alternatively, you can use Flex2Ant, by FarataSystems, see http://www.myflex.org for more information

CHAPTER

11

Advanced DataGrid

Advanced DataGrid

The subject of DataGrid control, let alone advanced control, has no limits. In any UI framework, the robustness of the DataGrid, or whatever the name might be, depends on formatting and validating utilities as well as a whole suite of data input controls: CheckBoxes, ComboBoxes, RadioButtons, all sorts of Inputs, Masks, and so on. Using theatrical terminology, the role of the king is played by his entourage. Practically speaking, touching up on the DataGrid is touching up on a large part of the Flex framework. Hence this chapter is a ride with fast-changing scenery.

We'll start our DataGrid journey upgrading a standard DataGrid to a "destination-aware" control capable of populating itself. Since we introduced this technique in earlier chapters you should ease right on in. Next, we'll look at formatting DataGrid columns and that would naturally lead us to a hidden treasury of the DataGridColumn, which, once you start treating it like a companion rather than a dull element of MXML syntax, can help you do amazing things.

To set the stage for the DataGrid's satellite controls, we'll lead you through making a reusable Flex library that supports the mapping of your custom tags to the arbitrary hierarchy of implementation classes. We will show you the power of computed expressions in place of styles such as color, and font, making our DataGrid truly data-driven. We will build a suite of effective controls to use as item renderers/editors, as well as standalone. Then we will step up the offense and show you how the entire sets of DataGridColumn definitions, including item editors and renderers, can be dynamically computed based on the data!

Making DataGrid Destination-Aware

In Chapters 7 and 8 we introduced the concept of destination-awareness for collections and controls. It helps to eliminate the tedious effort required to populate your controls with Remoting or DataServices-based data. Here's how an MXML application with a destination-aware DataGrid might like if we apply the familiar remoting destination *com_theriabook_composition_EmployeeDAO*:

```
<!-- DestinationAwareDataGridExDemo.mxml-->
<?xml version="1.0" encoding="utf-8"?>
```

```
<mx:Application xmlns:mx=http://www.adobe.com/2006/mxmllayout="vertical"
           xmlns:fx="com.theriabook.controls.*">
   <fx:DataGridEx id="dg"
        destination="com_theriabook_composition_EmployeeDAO"
        method="getEmployees"
        creationComplete="dg.fill()"
   />
</mx:Application>
```

In the listing below we've subclassed the standard Flex DataGrid. The code in our DataGrid borrows the relevant code from Listing 8.12:

```
// DataGrid.as
package com.theriabook.controls {
   import mx.controls.DataGrid;

   public class DataGrid  extends mx.controls.DataGrid {

   import mx.rpc.remoting.mxml.RemoteObject;
   import mx.rpc.AbstractOperation;
   import mx.rpc.events.*;
   import mx.controls.Alert;
   import mx.managers.CursorManager;

   public var destination:String=null, method : String = null;
   public var autoFill : Boolean = true;
   protected var ro:RemoteObject = null;

   public function fill(... args): void {
      if( ro==null ) {
         if( destination==null || destination.length==0 )
            throw new Error("No destination specified");
         if( method==null || method.length==0 )
            throw new Error("No retrieveMethod specified");

         ro = new RemoteObject(destination);
         ro.showBusyCursor = true;
         ro.concurrency    = "last";
         ro.addEventListener(ResultEvent.RESULT, ro_onResult);
         ro.addEventListener(FaultEvent.FAULT,   ro_onFault);
      }
      var operation:AbstractOperation = ro.getOperation(method);
      operation.arguments = args;
      operation.send();
```

```
    }
    private function ro_onFault(evt:FaultEvent):void {
      CursorManager.removeBusyCursor();
       Alert.show("Failed retrieving data: "+evt.message, "[DestinationAwareDataGrid]" +
id);
    }

    private function ro_onResult(evt:ResultEvent):void {
       CursorManager.removeBusyCursor();
      if (evt.result.length != 0)
         dataProvider = evt.result;
    }
    }
}
```

Listing 11.1 DataGrid.as, the first version with "destination-awareness"

If we run the application, our screen will show the employee records grid in its default formatting:

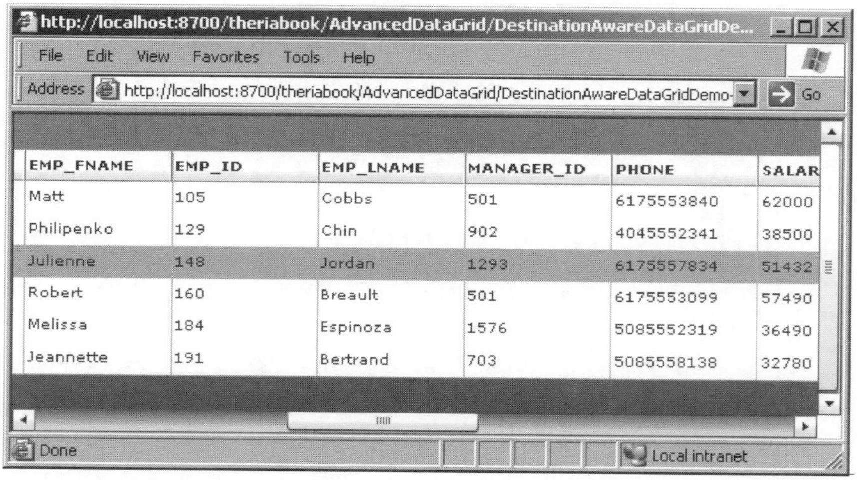

http://localhost:8700/theriabook/AdvancedDataGrid/DestinationAwareDataGridDe...
File Edit View Favorites Tools Help
Address http://localhost:8700/theriabook/AdvancedDataGrid/DestinationAwareDataGridDemo- Go

EMP_FNAME	EMP_ID	EMP_LNAME	MANAGER_ID	PHONE	SALAR
Matt	105	Cobbs	501	6175553840	62000
Philipenko	129	Chin	902	4045552341	38500
Julienne	148	Jordan	1293	6175557834	51432
Robert	160	Breault	501	6175553099	57490
Melissa	184	Espinoza	1576	5085552319	36490
Jeannette	191	Bertrand	703	5085558138	32780

Done Local intranet

Figure 11.1 The "destination-aware" DataGrid demo running

Formatting with labelFunction

We've just looked at the default data formatting provided by DataGrid out-of-the-box. The easiest way to improve column formatting is by supplying a *labelFunction* (introduced in Chapter 4) for each column that requires extra attention:

```
<mx:DataGridColumn    dataField="PHONE"  labelFunction="phoneLabelFunction" />
```

A labelFunction is a callback and being invoked by the DataGrid, it receives the appropriate data item plus information about the column, so that you can technically apply one function to more than one column. As far as the formatting techniques per se, Flex offers plenty of pre-defined formatters that can be used out-of-the-box or be customized to your specific needs. For instance, to format social security numbers (SS_NUMBER) we could have used mx.formatters.SwitchSymbol-Formatter and created the following function:

```
import mx.formatters.SwitchSymbolFormatter;
private var sf:SwitchSymbolFormatter;
private function ssnLabelFunction(item:Object, column:DataGridColumn):String {
     if (!sf) {
       sf = new SwitchSymbolFormatter();
      }
      return sf.formatValue("###-##-####", item["SS_NUMBER"]);
      }
```

Then inside the DataGridColumn we can mention this function name:

```
<mx:DataGridColumn  dataField="SS_NUMBER" labelFunction="ssnLabelFunction"  />
```

Similarly, in Listing 11.2 we can apply the same technique to the PHONE field, setting the format-String to (###)###-####:

```
<?xml version="1.0" encoding="utf-8"?>
<!-- LabelFunctionFormattingDemo.mxml -->
<mx:Application xmlns:mx="http://www.adobe.com/2006/mxml" xmlns="*" layout="vertical"
xmlns:fx="com.theriabook.controls.*">
   <fx:DataGrid  id="dg" creationComplete="dg.fill()"
     destination="com_theriabook_composition_EmployeeDAO" method="getEmployees"


   >
      <fx:columns>
         <mx:Array>
            <mx:DataGridColumn    dataField="EMP_LNAME"   />
            <mx:DataGridColumn    dataField="EMP_FNAME"  />
            <mx:DataGridColumn    dataField="PHONE"  labelFunction="phoneLabelFunction"
/>
            <mx:DataGridColumn    dataField="SS_NUMBER" labelFunction="ssnLabelFunction"
/>
         </mx:Array>
      </fx:columns>
   </fx:DataGridEx>
   <mx:Script>
      <![CDATA[
```

```
            import mx.formatters.SwitchSymbolFormatter;
            private var sf:SwitchSymbolFormatter;
            private function ssnLabelFunction(item:Object, column:DataGridColumn):String {
               if (!sf) {
                  sf = new SwitchSymbolFormatter();
               }
               return sf.formatValue("###-##-####", item["SS_NUMBER"]);
            }
            private function phoneLabelFunction(item:Object, column:DataGridColumn):String {
               if (!sf) {
                  sf = new SwitchSymbolFormatter();
               }
               return sf.formatValue("(###)###-####", item[column.dataField]);
            }
         ]]>
      </mx:Script>
   </mx:Application>
```

Listing 11.2 LabelFunctionFormattingDemo.mxml

Here's how our formatting looks on the screen:

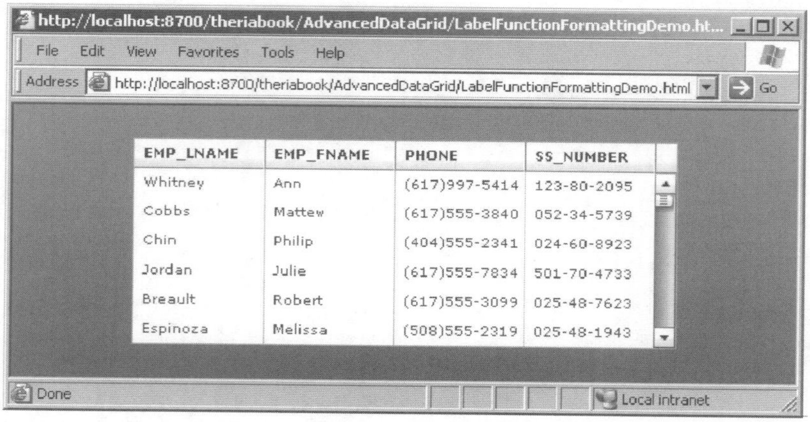

http://localhost:8700/theriabook/AdvancedDataGrid/LabelFunctionFormattingDemo.ht...

File Edit View Favorites Tools Help

Address http://localhost:8700/theriabook/AdvancedDataGrid/LabelFunctionFormattingDemo.html Go

EMP_LNAME	EMP_FNAME	PHONE	SS_NUMBER
Whitney	Ann	(617)997-5414	123-80-2095
Cobbs	Mattew	(617)555-3840	052-34-5739
Chin	Philip	(404)555-2341	024-60-8923
Jordan	Julie	(617)555-7834	501-70-4733
Breault	Robert	(617)555-3099	025-48-7623
Espinoza	Melissa	(508)555-2319	025-48-1943

Done Local intranet

Figure 11.2 Screenshot of the running LabelFunctionFormatting demo

Formatting with Extended DataGridColumn

The labelFunction-based formatting does the job. The price tag is hard-coding labelFunction(s) names in the DataGridColumn definitions. If you packaged a set of label functions in the *mydomain.LabelFunction* class, your column definitions might look like this:

```
<mx:DataGridColumn    dataField="PHONE"  labelFunction="mydomain.LabelFunctions.
phone" />
<mx:DataGridColumn    dataField="SS_NUMBER" labelFunction=" mydomain.LabelFunc-
tions.ssn"  />
```

A more pragmatic approach is to introduce the *formatString* as an extra attribute for DataGridColumn and have it encapsulate the implementation details. We're talking about the following alternative:

```
<fx:DataGridColumn    dataField="PHONE"  formatString="phone" />
<fx:DataGridColumn    dataField="SS_NUMBER" formatString="ssn"  />
```

Implementation of such syntax is within arm's reach. We just need to extend – well, not the arm, but the DataGridColumn, so that instead of mx:DataGridColumn we would use, say, our fx:DataGridColumn. The mx.controls.dataGridClasses.DataGridColumn is just a respository of styles and properties to be used by the DataGrid. In the Flex class hierarchy it merely extends CSSStyleDeclaration. Nothing prevents us from extending it further and adding an extra attribute. In the case of *formatString* we delegate the actual job of assigning the value of labelFunction to a helper class - FormattingManager:

```
public class DataGridColumn  extends mx.controls.dataGridClasses.DataGridColumn {
  public function  set formatString( fs:String ) : void{
    FormattingManager.setFormat(this, fs);
  }
}
```

Wait a minute, where did the FormattingManager come from? Well, we'll get to the implementation of that class a bit later. At this point, we have to eliminate a possible naming collision between our to-be-made DataGridColumn and the standard mx.controls.dataGridClasses.DataGridColumn.

Introducing a Component Manifest File

Up till now we've been keeping folders with classes of our custom components under the application MXML files folder. To reference these components we've been declaring namespaces pointing to some hard-coded albeit relative paths such as xmlns:lib="com.theriabook.controls.*" or xmlns="*". The problem with this approach is that these namespaces point to one folder at a time. As a result, we end up with either multiple custom namespaces or a wild mix of components in one folder.

To break the spell and abstract the namespace from the exact file location, we have to use the *component manifest file*. Component manifest is an XML file that allows mapping component names to the implementing classes. Below is an example of a component manifest that combines our custom DataGrid and DataGridColumn located in different folders:

```
<?xml version="1.0"?>
<componentPackage>
    <component id="DataGrid" class="com.theriabook.controls.DataGrid"/>
    <component id="DataGridColumn"
        class="com.theriabook.controls.dataGridClasses.DataGridColumn"/>
</componentPackage>
```

To benefit from the use of this component manifest you have to compile your components with the *compc* or use the Flex Library project. To be more specific, you have to instruct compc to select the URL that your application can later use in place of the hard-coded folder in the *xmlns* declaration. So we'll create a new FlexLibrary project – *theriabook*, where we will put the *theriabook-manifest.xml* containing the XML above and set the relevant project properties as shown in the Figure 11.3:

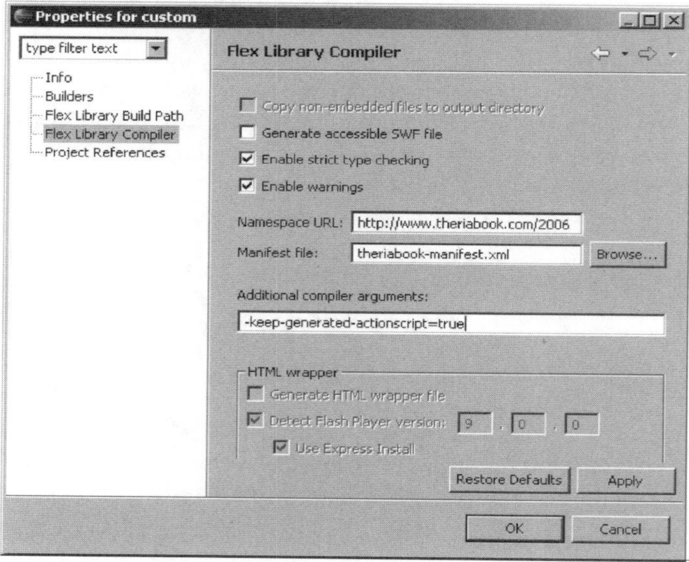

Figure 11.3 The manifest file and namespace definition for the Flex Library Project

We will add theriabook project to the Flex Build Path of our application project as "SWC folder". Now we can move the DataGrid from our application project to *theriabook* and replace *xmlns:fx="com.theriabook.controls"* with *xmlns:fx="http://www.theriabook.com/2006"*, provided that the Flex Build Path of our application project includes a reference to *theriabook.swc*. As a result, our application will reference *fx:DataGrid* and *fx:DataGridColumn*, irrespective of their physical location.

Having done that, let's get back to customizing the DataGridColumn.

More on Customizing the DataGridColumn

We'll put our DataGridColumn in the subfolder *dataGridClasses* as a sign of our respect to the well-thought-out directory structure of the Flex framework:

```
// DataGridColumn.as (first version)
package com.theriabook.controls.dataGridClasses  {
   import mx.controls.dataGridClasses.DataGridColumn;

   public class DataGridColumn  extends mx.controls.dataGridClasses.DataGridColumn {
      public function  set formatString( fs:String ) : void{
         FormattingManager.setFormat (this, fs);
      }
   }
}
```

Listing 11.3 DataGridColumn.as, the first version

As we mentioned, the "dirty" job of locating and assigning the proper label function has been delegated to the helper class FormattingManager. This class, presented in Listing 11.4, should be put into our theriabook project:

```
// FormattingManager.as, first version

package com.theriabook.controls.dataGridClasses
{
   public class FormattingManager
   {
         import mx.controls.dataGridClasses.DataGridColumn;
         import mx.formatters.SwitchSymbolFormatter;
         private static var sf:SwitchSymbolFormatter;

         public static function setFormat(dgc:mx.controls.dataGridClasses.DataGridColumn

 formatString:String):void {
            switch (formatString.toLowerCase()) {
               case "ssn":
                  dgc.labelFunction = ssnLabelFunction;
               case "phone":
                  dgc.labelFunction = phoneLabelFunction;
            }
         }
         private static function ssnLabelFunction(item:Object, column:
                                       mx.controls.dataGridClasses.DataGridColumn):
 String {
```

```
            if (!sf) {
               sf = new SwitchSymbolFormatter();
            }
            return sf.formatValue("###-##-####", item["SS_NUMBER"]);
            }
         private static function phoneLabelFunction(item:Object, column:DataGridColumn):S
tring {
            if (!sf) {
               sf = new SwitchSymbolFormatter();
            }
            return sf.formatValue("(###)###-####", item[column.dataField]);
            }

   }
}
```

Listing 11.4 FormattingManager.as, the first version

Tada! And the winner is… the developer. Once we add *theriabook.swc* (with DataGrid, DataGridColumn, and FormattingManager) to the library path, the application code gets reduced to the following:

```
<?xml version="1.0" encoding="utf-8"?>
<mx:Application xmlns:mx="http://www.adobe.com/2006/mxml"  layout="vertical"
   xmlns:fx="http://www.theriabook.com/2006">
   <fx:DataGrid  id="dg" creationComplete="dg.fill()"
      destination="com_theriabook_composition_EmployeeDAO" method="getEmployees"

   >
      <fx:columns>
         <mx:Array>
            <mx:DataGridColumn    dataField="EMP_LNAME"   />
            <mx:DataGridColumn    dataField="EMP_FNAME"  />
            <fx:DataGridColumn    dataField="PHONE"  formatString="phone" />
            <fx:DataGridColumn    dataField="SS_NUMBER" formatString="ssn"  />
         </mx:Array>
      </fx:columns>
   </fx:DataGridEx>
</mx:Application>
```

Listing 11.5 A Simple application illustrating FormattingManager.as

Improving FormattingManager

In the previous examples we've used the SwitchSymbolFormatter for both *phone* and *ssn* formatting. As soon as we start formating numbers or currency values, it's natural to use NumberFormatter or CurrencyFormatter – descendants of mx.formatters.Formatter. In fact, Flex offers a dedicated formatter even for the phone formatting.

While SwitchSymbolFormatter derives from Object, all the rest of the formatters descend from Formatter. By encapsulating this specific SwitchSymbolFormatter in the custom class MaskFormatter, we'll help ourselves to base the next version of FormattingManager entirely on Formatters:

```
//MaskFormatter.as

package com.theriabook.formatters {
   import mx.formatters.Formatter;
   import mx.formatters.SwitchSymbolFormatter;

   public class MaskFormatter extends  Formatter {
      private var formatString:String;
      private var sf:SwitchSymbolFormatter;
      public function MaskFormatter( fs:String) {
         formatString = fs;
         sf = new SwitchSymbolFormatter();
      }
      public override function format(val:Object):String {
         return sf.formatValue( formatString, val);
      }
   }
}
```

Listing 11.6 MaskFormatter.as

Look how this MaskFormatter[1] simplifies our FormattingManager: we can replace all private methods with an anonymous function, as shown in Listing 11.7. Please note that the reference to the appropriate formatter is preserved with the closure:

```
//com.theriabook.controls.dataGridClasses.FormattingManager.as

package com.theriabook.controls.dataGridClasses
{
   public class FormattingManager
   {
         import mx.controls.dataGridClasses.DataGridColumn;
         import mx.formatters.*;
         import com.theriabook.formatters.MaskFormatter;

         public static function setFormat(
```

```
            dgc:mx.controls.dataGridClasses.DataGridColumn,
            formatString:String):void {
            var  formatter:Formatter = null;
            switch (formatString.toLowerCase()) {
               case "ssn":
                  formatter = new MaskFormatter("###-##-####");
                  break;
               case "money":
                  formatter = new CurrencyFormatter();
                  CurrencyFormatter(formatter).precision=2;
                  break;
               case "phone":
                  formatter = new PhoneFormatter();
                  break;
               case "shortdate":
                  formatter = new DateFormatter();
                  break;
               case "zip":
                  formatter = new ZipCodeFormatter();
                  break;
               }
               if (formatter) {
                  dgc.labelFunction = function (
                     item:Object,
                     dgc:mx.controls.dataGridClasses.DataGridColumn):String
                  {
                     return formatter.format(item[dgc.dataField]);
                  }
               }
         }
      }
   }
```

Listing 11.7 FormattingManager.as

Here is the testing application FormatStringDemo, see Listing 11.8:

```
<?xml version="1.0" encoding="utf-8"?>
<!-- FormatStringDemo.mxml -->
<mx:Application xmlns:mx="http://www.adobe.com/2006/mxml"  layout="vertical"
   xmlns:fx="http://www.theriabook.com/2006">
   <fx:DataGrid  id="dg" creationComplete="dg.fill()"
      destination="com_theriabook_composition_EmployeeDAO" method="getEmployees"
```

```
  >
    <fx:columns>
      <mx:Array>
        <mx:DataGridColumn    dataField="EMP_LNAME"   />
        <mx:DataGridColumn    dataField="EMP_FNAME"  />
        <fx:DataGridColumn    dataField="SALARY" formatString="money" />
        <fx:DataGridColumn    dataField="PHONE" formatString="phone" />
        <fx:DataGridColumn    dataField="SS_NUMBER" formatString="ssn" />
      </mx:Array>
    </fx:columns>
  </fx:DataGrid>
</mx:Application>
```

Listing 11.8 FormatStringDemo.mxml

If you run it, the DataGrid dg will be formatted as shown in Figure 11.4:

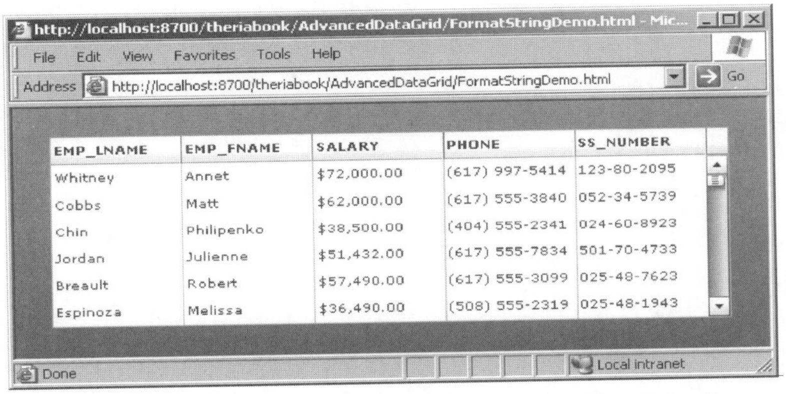

http://localhost:8700/theriabook/AdvancedDataGrid/FormatStringDemo.html - Mic...

File Edit View Favorites Tools Help

Address http://localhost:8700/theriabook/AdvancedDataGrid/FormatStringDemo.html Go

EMP_LNAME	EMP_FNAME	SALARY	PHONE	SS_NUMBER
Whitney	Annet	$72,000.00	(617) 997-5414	123-80-2095
Cobbs	Matt	$62,000.00	(617) 555-3840	052-34-5739
Chin	Philipenko	$38,500.00	(404) 555-2341	024-60-8923
Jordan	Julienne	$51,432.00	(617) 555-7834	501-70-4733
Breault	Robert	$57,490.00	(617) 555-3099	025-48-7623
Espinoza	Melissa	$36,490.00	(508) 555-2319	025-48-1943

Done Local intranet

Figure 11.4 DataGrid formatted with columns' formatString attributes

Let's focus on the hard-coding that we allowed in the case of the money value:

```
case "money":
   formatter = new CurrencyFormatter();
   CurrencyFormatter(formatter).precision=2;                    break;
```

This hard-coding reflects, perhaps, the most "popular" case. But what if we want to have the full advantage of the properties of the corresponding formatter such as precision in the case of the CurrencyFormatter? To address these cases we're going to introduce one more fx:DataGridColumn property – *formatData*. Here's how it will be used in the application MXML:

```
<fx:DataGridColumn    dataField="SALARY" >
```

```
        <fx:formatData>
            <mx:Object formatString="money" precision="0"/>
        </fx:formatData>
    </fx:DataGridColumn>
```

The elegance of MXML lets us implement this extension with just a few lines of extra code in com.theriabook.controls.dataGridClasses.DataGridColumn[2]:

```
public function  set formatData(fd :Object) : void{
   FormattingManager.setFormat(this, fd);
  }
```

Then, to accommodate the change on the FormattingManager side, we'll iterate through all the properties of the *formatData* object and attempt to assign them to the appropriate properties of the *formatter* with an emphasis on the word "appropriate." The MXML compiler isn't going to help us check the properties of the unsealed <mx:Object> against the properties of the *formatter*. So, to protect ourselves from the no-such-property-exceptions, we surround the property assignments with try/catch:

```
public static function setFormat(
     dgc:mx.controls.dataGridClasses.DataGridColumn,
     formatData:Object
):void {
   .  .  .  .  .
   if (!(formatData is String)) {
      for (var property:String in formatData) {                           try {
           formatter[property] = formatData[property];
         } catch (err:Error) {
            // Property does not match formatter type
         }
      }
   }
   .  .  .  .  .
}
```

The complete listing of renewed FormattingManager is presented below[3]. Of course, when maintaining your own framework, you'd transform this class to accommodate your particular requirements:

```
//FormattingManager.as
package com.theriabook.controls.dataGridClasses
{
   public class FormattingManager
   {
      import mx.controls.dataGridClasses.DataGridColumn;
```

```
import mx.formatters.*;
import com.theriabook.formatters.MaskFormatter;

public static function setFormat(
   dgc:mx.controls.dataGridClasses.DataGridColumn,
   formatData:Object):void {

   var  formatter:Formatter = null;
   var  fs:String;
   if (formatData is String)
      fs = formatData as String;
   else
      fs = formatData.formatString;

   switch (fs.toLowerCase()) {
      case "ssn":
         formatter = new MaskFormatter("###-##-####");
         break;
      case "money":
         formatter = new CurrencyFormatter();
         CurrencyFormatter(formatter).precision=2;
break;
      case "phone":
         formatter = new PhoneFormatter();
         break;
      case "shortdate":
         formatter = new DateFormatter();
         break;
      case "zip":
         formatter = new ZipCodeFormatter();
break;
      default:
         if (fs.indexOf("#")!=-1) {
            formatter = new MaskFormatter(fs);
};
   }
   if (!(formatData is String)) {
      for (var property:String in formatData) {
         try {
            formatter[property] = formatData[property];
         } catch (err:Error) {
            // Property does not match formatter type
         }
      }
```

```
            }
            if (formatter) {
               dgc.labelFunction = function (
                  item:Object,
                  dgc:mx.controls.dataGridClasses.DataGridColumn
               ):String {
                  return formatter.format(item[dgc.dataField]);
               }
            }
         }

      }
   }
```

Listing 11.9 FormattingManager.as, the complete listing

Finally, here's the sample application to test our changes, FormatDataDemo:

```
<mx:Application xmlns:mx="http://www.adobe.com/2006/mxml"  layout="vertical"
   xmlns:fx="http://www.theriabook.com/2006">
   <!—FormatDataDemo.mxml -->
   <fx:DataGrid  id="dg" creationComplete="dg.fill()"
      destination="com_theriabook_composition_EmployeeDAO" method="getEmployees"
   >
      <fx:columns>
         <mx:Array>
            <mx:DataGridColumn     dataField="EMP_LNAME"   />
            <mx:DataGridColumn     dataField="EMP_FNAME"  />
            <fx:DataGridColumn     dataField="BIRTH_DATE"  formatString="shortdate"/>
            <fx:DataGridColumn     dataField="SALARY" >
               <fx:formatData>
                  <mx:Object formatString="money" precision="0"/>
               </fx:formatData>
            </fx:DataGridColumn>
            <fx:DataGridColumn  dataField="PHONE">
               <fx:formatData>phone</fx:formatData>
            </fx:DataGridColumn>
            <fx:DataGridColumn  dataField="SS_NUMBER" formatString="ssn" />
         </mx:Array>
      </fx:columns>
   </fx:DataGrid>
</mx:Application>
```

Listing 11.10 FormatDataDemo.mxml

When you run the application it will produce the DataGrid shown in Figure 11.5:

EMP_LNAME	EMP_FNAME	BIRTH_DATE	SALARY	PHONE	SS_NUMBER
Whitney	Ann	06/05/1951	$72,000	(617) 997-5414	123-80-2095
Cobbs	Mattew	12/04/1961	$62,000	(617) 555-3840	052-34-5739
Chin	Philip	10/30/1967	$38,500	(404) 555-2341	024-60-8923
Jordan	Julie	12/13/1952	$51,432	(617) 555-7834	501-70-4733
Breault	Robert	05/13/1948	$57,490	(617) 555-3099	025-48-7623
Espinoza	Melissa	12/14/1940	$36,490	(508) 555-2319	025-48-1943

Figure 11.5 DataGrid formatted with formatString and formatData attributes

We'll continue beefing up our custom DataGridColumn after a short detour into CheckBox and RadioButton controls.

CheckBox as a Drop-In Renderer

As we warned at the beginning of the chapter, DataGrids rarely come alone. In this section we're going to suggest customizing the CheckBox, which will help us illustrate the additional features of custom DataGridColumns.

The state of a CheckBox control is managed by the Boolean property *selected*. At the same time, many business systems use either Y/N or, sometimes, 0/1 flags. As a result, translating business-specific values into *selected* and vice versa burdens the application code. Listing 11.11 presents a custom CheckBox that supports application-specific *on* and *off* values along with the current *value*:

```
//CheckBox.as
package com.theriabook.controls
{
 import mx.controls.CheckBox;

 public class CheckBox extends mx.controls.CheckBox
 {

   public var onValue:Object=true;
   public var offValue:Object=false;
   private var _value:Object;

   public function set value(val:Object) :void {
```

```
        _value = val;
        invalidateProperties();
     }
     public function get value():Object  {
        return selected?onValue:offValue;
     }
     override protected function commitProperties():void {
        selected = (_value == onValue);
        super.commitProperties();
     }
  }
  }
```

Listing 11.11 CheckBox.as, first version

So, using this CheckBox, we could have written

```
<fx:CheckBox value="Y" onValue="Y" offValue="N"  />
```

to have *selected* CheckBox, or

```
<fx:CheckBox value="N" onValue="Y" offValue="N"  />
```

to set *selected* to false.

DataGridColumn as ItemRenderer's Knowledge Base

Now let's get back to the DataGrid world. What if we wanted to use our CheckBox as the DataGrid item renderer? Here's a suggested use case example:

```
<fx:DataGridColumn  dataField="BENE_DAY_CARE"
      itemRenderer="com.theriabook.controls.CheckBox" >
  </fx:DataGridColumn>
```

Obviously, we have to modify the CheckBox some more to take care of the value in the data setter:

```
override public function set data(item:Object):void
{
   super.data = item;
   if( item!=null ) {
      value = item[DataGridListData(listData).dataField];
   }
}
```

But how will we communicate to our CheckBox-turned-itemRenderer the *offValue* and *onValue* properties? Ideally, we'd need something like:

```
<fx:DataGridColumn  dataField="BENE_DAY_CARE"
        itemRenderer="com.theriabook.controls.CheckBox" >
   <fx:extendedProperties>
      <mx:Object onValue="Y" offValue="N" />
   </fx:extendedProperties>
</fx:DataGridColumn>
```

Flex creators thought of this in advance. An object referenced by itemRenderer isn't a CheckBox, but rather an instance of mx.core.ClassFactory wrapped around the CheckBox. The mechanism of mx.core.ClassFactory lets Flex generate multiple instances of another class – com.theriabook.controls.CheckBox, in our case. Importantly, each instance created by the factory is assigned identical properties borrowed from the properties of the factory object. So, all we have to do is pass the value of the *extendedProperties* as *properties* of the itemRenderer.

```
//DataGridColumn.as
package com.theriabook.controls.dataGridClasses{
   import mx.controls.dataGridClasses.DataGridColumn;

   public class DataGridColumn  extends mx.controls.dataGridClasses.DataGridColumn {
      public function set extendedProperties(val:Object) :void {
            this.itemRenderer["properties"] = val;
      }

      public function  set formatString( fs :String ) : void{
         FormattingManager.setFormat(this, fs);
      }

      public function  set formatData( fd :Object ) : void{
         FormattingManager.setFormat(this, fd);
      }
   }
}
```

Listing 11.12 DataGridColumn, third version

Below is the listing of the test application, ExtendedPropertiesDemo. When you run it, it produces the DataGrid shown in Figure 11.6.

```
<?xml version="1.0" encoding="utf-8"?>
<!-- ExtendedPropertiesDemo.mxml -->
<mx:Application xmlns:mx="http://www.adobe.com/2006/mxml"  layout="vertical"
```

```
xmlns:fx="http://www.theriabook.com/2006">
<fx:DataGrid  id="dg" creationComplete="dg.fill()"
   destination="com_theriabook_composition_EmployeeDAO" method="getEmployees"

>
   <fx:columns>
      <mx:Array>
         <mx:DataGridColumn    dataField="EMP_LNAME"   />
         <mx:DataGridColumn    dataField="EMP_FNAME"  />
         <fx:DataGridColumn  dataField="BENE_DAY_CARE" itemRenderer="com.theriabook.
               controls.CheckBox" >
            <fx:extendedProperties>
               <mx:Object onValue="Y" offValue="N" />
            </fx:extendedProperties>
         </fx:DataGridColumn>
         </mx:Array>
   </fx:columns>
</fx:DataGrid>
</mx:Application>
```

Listing 11.13 ExtendedPropertiesDemo.mxml

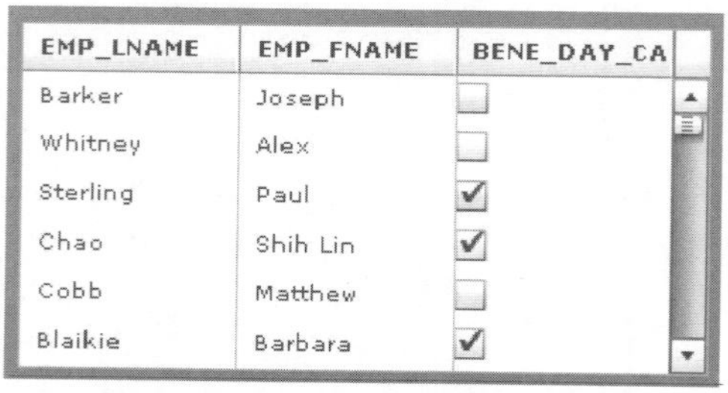

EMP_LNAME	EMP_FNAME	BENE_DAY_CA
Barker	Joseph	☐
Whitney	Alex	☐
Sterling	Paul	☑
Chao	Shih Lin	☑
Cobb	Matthew	☐
Blaikie	Barbara	☑

Figure 11.6 Custom CheckBox used as a drop-in renderer with extended properties

We should have mentioned the alternative run-of-the-mill approach with inline itemRenderer, Listing 11.14:

```
<?xml version="1.0" encoding="utf-8"?>
<mx:Application xmlns:mx="http://www.adobe.com/2006/mxml"  layout="vertical" xmlns:
fx="com.theriabook.controls.*">
   <fx:DataGrid  id="dg"
         destination="com_theriabook_composition_EmployeeDAO"
   method="getEmployees"    creationComplete="dg.fill()" >
      <fx:columns>
```

```
        <mx:Array>
          <mx:DataGridColumn    dataField="EMP_LNAME"   />
          <mx:DataGridColumn    dataField="EMP_FNAME"  />
          <mx:DataGridColumn    dataField="BENE_DAY_CARE">
            <mx:itemRenderer>
              <mx:Component>
                <fx:CheckBox onValue="Y" offValue="N"/>
              </mx:Component>
            </mx:itemRenderer>
          </mx:DataGridColumn>
        </mx:Array>
      </fx:columns>
    </fx:DataGrid>
  </mx:Application>
```

Listing 11.14 Using CheckBox as an inline renderer

Arguably, the *extendedProperties* approach is more efficient, since it absolves MXML of generating an extra nested class (mx:Component) for each column of this kind[4]. We've introduced you to yet another way of customizing a DataGridColumn, and we'll continue building on top of it in the following sections.

Nitpicking CheckBox

There are some additional remarks that we ought to make about our CheckBox implementation at this point.

The first one is related to the horizontal alignment of the CheckBox. Instinct tells us that a label-free checkbox should be centered in the column rather than stuck in the left-most position. At first, you may try applying a *textAlign* style to the DataGridColumn – to no avail. Then you might resort to another run-of-the-mill approach to center the checkbox by putting it inside a container such as an HBox. Here's the performance-based advice endorsed by Flex Framework engineers: avoid containers inside the DataGrid cell at all reasonable cost. In particular, instead of using HBox, why not subclass the CheckBox and override the *updateDisplayList()* method? It gets quite natural, once you've stepped on this path, so we'll add the code shown below to our CheckBox (the complete code for the com.theriabook.controls.CheckBox is presented in Listing 11.15):

```
import mx.core.mx_internal;
use namespace mx_internal;  . . . .
 override protected function updateDisplayList(
   unscaledWidth:Number, unscaledHeight:Number):void
 {
   super.updateDisplayList(unscaledWidth, unscaledHeight);
   if (currentIcon) {
```

```
        var style:String = getStyle("textAlign");
        if ((!label) && (style=="center") ) {
           currentIcon.x = (unscaledWidth - currentIcon.measuredWidth)/2;
        }
    }
}
```

Note the use of namespace *mx_internal*. It's required to reference the *currentIcon* that visualizes the checkbox, since currentIcon – the child of the original CheckBox – is originally scoped as mx_internal.

Now we modify the testing application to include *textAlign="center"*:

```
<fx:DataGridColumn  dataField="BENE_DAY_CARE" textAlign="center"
   itemRenderer="com.theriabook.controls.CheckBox" >
   <fx:extendedProperties>
      <mx:Object onValue="Y" offValue="N" />
   </fx:extendedProperties>
</fx:DataGridColumn>
```

And, when we run it, all checkboxes are in their proper place:

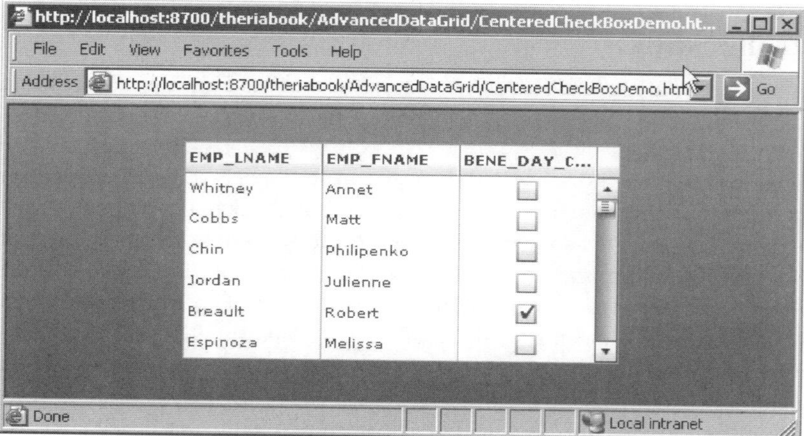

Figure 11.7 CenteredCheckBoxDemo screenshot

The second nitpicking point is related to *undefined* as a possible value of a property. Under our current business scenario, we can assume that some of the employees are not eligible for the daycare benefit, and relevant items in the dataProvider's collection are lacking the BENE_DAY_CARE property, which for dynamic items can be expressed as *item.BENE_DAY_CARE=="undefined."*

Does it make sense to show checkboxes for non-eligible employees? Perhaps, it doesn't. In this case we'd make currentIcon invisible. You can select a different approach and show a fuzzy checkbox image instead, but this is beyond the point[5]. The following modification of *updateDisplayList()* does the job of removing checkBox when the value is undefined:

```
override protected function updateDisplayList(unscaledWidth:Number,

                                unscaledHeight:Number):void
  {

    super.updateDisplayList(unscaledWidth, unscaledHeight);
    if (currentIcon) {
      var style:String = getStyle("textAlign");
      if ((!label) && (style=="center") ) {
        currentIcon.x = (unscaledWidth - currentIcon.measuredWidth)/2;
      }
      currentIcon.visible = (_value!=undefined);
    }
  }
```

To accommodate this change we have to loosen up the class definitions for *value* as shown in Listing 11.15, where we change Object to *undefined*.

The next and probably the most important fix is that our CheckBoxes have been silenced. Try to click on one, scroll the row out of view and scroll it back in. The checkbox doesn't retain your selection and it shouldn't; we've never communicated the change to the underlying data. To remedy the situation we'll add the constructor method, where we'd start listening on the "change" event; once the event is intercepted we'll modify the data item with the CheckBox value. That, in turn, will result in either *onValue* or *offValue*, as per our value getter:

```
  public function CheckBox() {
    super();
    addEventListener(Event.CHANGE,
      function(event:Event):void{
        if (listData && listData is DataGridListData
) {
          data[DataGridListData(listData).dataField] = value;
        }
      }
    );
  }
```

And the last point: Flex collections by themselves do not notice any changes done to the underlying data items; it is the application's responsibility to keep the collections informed, especially if you have more then one view based on the same collection. In our case, change of the data would go totally unnoticed by the collection displayed by DataGrid, until we explicitly notify it with the COLLECTION_CHANGE event. The complete code for the second version of CheckBox is presented in Listing 11.15:

```
//CheckBox.as
package com.theriabook.controls
{
 import flash.events.Event;
 import mx.controls.CheckBox;
 import mx.controls.dataGridClasses.DataGridListData;
 import mx.core.mx_internal;
 use namespace mx_internal;

 public class CheckBox extends mx.controls.CheckBox
 {
   public var onValue:Object=true;
   public var offValue:Object=false;
   private var _value:*;

   public function CheckBox() {
      super();
      addEventListener(Event.CHANGE,
         function(event:Event):void{
            if (listData && listData is DataGridListData) {
               data[DataGridListData(listData).dataField] = value;
               var evt:CollectionEvent = new CollectionEvent(CollectionEvent.COLLECTION_
               CHANGE, false, false, CollectionEventKind.UPDATE, -1, -1, [data]);
               mx.controls.DataGrid(DataGridListData(listData).owner).dataProvider.
               dispatchEvent(evt);
            }
         }
      );
   }
   public function set value(val:*) :void {
      _value = val;
      invalidateProperties();
   }
   public function get value():Object  {
      if (_value==undefined)
        return _value;
      else
        return selected?onValue:offValue;
   }
```

```
    override protected function commitProperties():void {
       if (_value!=undefined)
          selected = (_value == onValue);
       super.commitProperties();
    }

    override public function set data(item:Object):void  {
       super.data = item;
       if( item!=null ) {
          value = item[DataGridListData(listData).dataField];
       }
    }

     override protected function updateDisplayList(unscaledWidth:Number,
                                    unscaledHeight:Number):void
    {

       super.updateDisplayList(unscaledWidth, unscaledHeight);
       if (currentIcon) {
          var style:String = getStyle("textAlign");
          if ((!label) && (style=="center") ) {
             currentIcon.x = (unscaledWidth - currentIcon.measuredWidth)/2;
          }
          currentIcon.visible = (_value!=undefined);
       }
    }
  }
}
```

Listing 11.15 CheckBox.as, the second version

Next comes the test application. We've added the "Revoke day care benefit" button, which turns DAY_CARE_BENE into *undefined* on the currently selected DataGrid item. We also had to notify the collection with the *itemUpdated()* call:

```
<?xml version="1.0" encoding="utf-8"?>
<!-- UndefinedCheckBoxDemo.mxml -->
<mx:Application xmlns:mx="http://www.adobe.com/2006/mxml"  layout="vertical"
   xmlns:fx="http://www.theriabook.com/2006">
   <mx:Button label="Revoke day care benefit"
      click="dg.selectedItem.BENE_DAY_CARE=undefined;
             dg.dataProvider.itemUpdated(dg.selectedItem);" />
   <fx:DataGrid  id="dg" creationComplete="dg.fill();dg.selectedIndex=0;"
      destination="com_theriabook_composition_EmployeeDAO" method="getEmployees"
```

```
    >
      <fx:columns>
        <mx:Array>
          <mx:DataGridColumn    dataField="EMP_LNAME"   />
          <mx:DataGridColumn    dataField="EMP_FNAME"  />
          <fx:DataGridColumn  dataField="BENE_DAY_CARE" textAlign="center"
            itemRenderer="com.theriabook.controls.CheckBox" >
            <fx:extendedProperties>
              <mx:Object onValue="Y" offValue="N" />
            </fx:extendedProperties>
          </fx:DataGridColumn>
          </mx:Array>
      </fx:columns>
    </fx:DataGrid>

  </mx:Application>
```

Listing 11.16 UndefinedCheckBoxDemo.mxml

When you run the above application, you'll see that checkboxes retain the selection after scrolling out and back into view. If you click the "Revoke" button for the first two rows, you're going to see a picture similar to the one below:

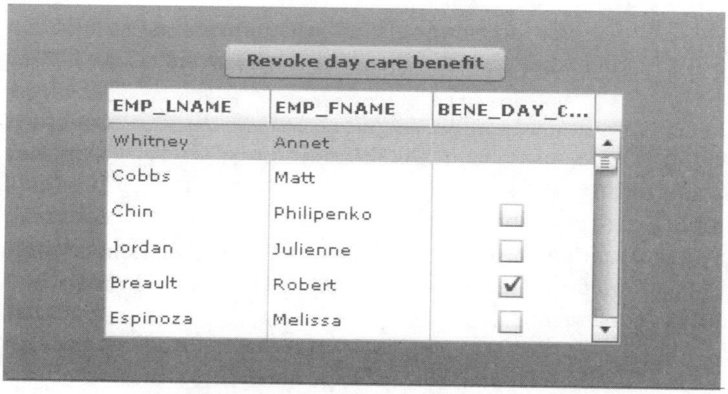

Figure 11.8 UndefinedCheckBoxDemo partial screenshot

The last CheckBox fix will come in handy once you declare the DataGrid editable. Why declare it editable in the first place if we seem to be editing the DataGrid already? Let's not forget that the only field we've been editing so far is the checkbox BENE_DAY_CARE. Should you decide to allow editing of the text fields, you would have to change the definition of the DataGrid as it is shown in bold in the following snippet[6]:

```
<fx:DataGrid  id="dg" creationComplete="dg.fill();dg.selectedIndex=0;"
editable="true"
    destination="com_theriabook_composition_EmployeeDAO" method="getEmployees"

>
```

But once you do that, a click on the beautiful checkbox of ours would turn it into a default editor – TextInput, quite like in a Cinderella story. To make the miracle last, you'd declare that your *renderer* is good to go as an *editor* as well:

```
<fx:DataGridColumn  dataField="BENE_DAY_CARE" textAlign="center"
     itemRenderer="com.theriabook.controls.CheckBox" rendererIsEditor="true">
     . . .
</fx:DataGrid>
```

By default, DataGrid reads the *text* property of the item editor. You can nominate a different property via *editorDataField* (in our case that would be *value*). Alternatively, and that will help us later in the chapter, you can "upgrade" the checkbox to carry the *text* property:

```
public function set text(val:String) :void {
   value = val;
}

public function get text():*  {
   return value;
}
```

We leave it to the reader to try the latest changes in the CheckBox and test the application. Or you can find the solution in the source code that comes with the book. We'll be counting on it later in the chapter.

RadioButtonGroupBox as Drop-In Renderer

We can apply similar techniques to RadioButton controls. Here's the code snippet suggesting how the group of RadioButton controls can be used as a drop-in item renderer (and editor). Instead of an onValue/offValue pair, we're introducing an array of options[7]:

```
<fx:DataGridColumn dataField="STATUS" width="300" headerText="Status"
rendererIsEditor="true"  itemRenderer="com.theriabook.containers.RadioButtonGroupBox">
     <fx:options>
          <mx:Array id="options">
               <mx:Object data="A" label="Active"/>
               <mx:Object data="T" label="Terminated"/>
               <mx:Object data="L" label="On leave"/>
```

```
            </mx:Array>
        </fx:options>
    </fx:DataGridColumn>
```

To support this use case we need to build the renderer class and make the DataGridColumn pass it the array of options. The latter can be done by adding the following options setter to our DataGrid-Column:

```
package com.theriabook.controls.dataGridClasses{
  . . . . .
  public class DataGridColumn  extends mx.controls.dataGridClasses.DataGridColumn
{
      . . . . .
      public function set options(val:Array):void {
         if (itemRenderer) itemRenderer ["properties"] = {options:val};
      }
  }
}
```

Now let's build the renderer. By definition, to be an item renderer, the component has to implement an IListItemRenderer interface. To qualify as *drop-in*, a component also has to implement IDropInListItemRenderer. A standard CheckBox implements both interfaces, so when we were extending CheckBox in the last section, we didn't have to mention a single *implements* and just merrily used *data* and *listData* at our convenience.

This is not the case now. Had RadioButtonGroup been at least a UIComponent, we'd need to implement IDataRenderer and IDropInListItemRenderer interfaces and be done. But RadioButtonGroup isn't even a DisplayObject! So we'll base our renderer on mx.containers.Box with RadioButtonGroup embedded[8]:

```
    private var group:RadioButtonGroup=null ;

    public function RadioButtonGroupBox() {
       super();
       group = new RadioButtonGroup();
    }
```

Having a RadioButtonGroup is just the beginning. Whenever our component gets assigned options, we'll translate them into a set of RadioButton controls. Each RadioButton will be added as a child of the renderer (container):

```
    private var _options:Array=null;
    public function set options(opt:Array):void {
       var i:int;
```

```
    . . . .
    _options=opt;
    for (i= 0; i < opt.length; i++) {
      var rb:RadioButton = new RadioButton();
      rb.label = opt[i].label;
      rb.value = opt[i].data;
      addChild(rb);
    }
  }

  override public function addChild(child:DisplayObject):DisplayObject {
    if (child is RadioButton) {
      (child as RadioButton).group = group;
      group.addInstance(child as RadioButton);
    }
    return super.addChild(child);
  }
}
```

Note how subscribing a RadioButton to the group is delegated to the overridden addChild() method:

```
(child as RadioButton).group = group;
group.addInstance(child as RadioButton);
```

Had we done it directly in the options setter, there would be no need for addChild() at all, so why go the convoluted way? The answer is: to enable the potential use of RadioButtonGroupBox as a regular container, outside the renderer context. In other words, whenever a RadioButton gets added to the component – as part of the options or not – it gets associated with the group.

Next, since we want the component as a drop-in renderer, we need to implement the IDropInListItemRenderer interface, so that the extra information about the hosting List will be at our fingertips:

```
private var _listData:BaseListData=null;
public function get listData():BaseListData  {
  return _listData;
}
public function set listData(value:BaseListData):void  {
  _listData = value;
}
```

And once we have the *listData*, we can offer the following override of the *data* setter of IDataRenderer:

```
override public function set data(item:Object):void {
   super.data = item;
   if( item!=null ) {
      group.selectedValue = item[DataGridListData(listData).dataField];
   }
}
```

Similarly, we consider both use cases of the standalone component and item renderer while implementing the property *value*. In the case of the item renderer, our component updates the underlying *data*:

```
public function get value():Object {
   return group.selectedValue;
}
public function set value(v:Object) : void {
   group.selectedValue = v;
   if (listData && listData is DataGridListData) {
      data[DataGridListData(listData).dataField] = group.selectedValue;
      var event:CollectionEvent = new CollectionEvent(CollectionEvent.COLLEC
      TION_CHANGE, false, false, CollectionEventKind.UPDATE, -1, -1, [data]);
      DataGrid(DataGridListData(listData).owner).dataProvider.
      dispatchEvent(event);
    }
  }
```

Finally, how about capturing the *selection* of a radiobutton? Since we need to listen to the *change* event on the RadioButtonGroup, we'll set up the listener right in the constructor method, handling the Event.CHANGE with the anonymous function:

```
public function RadioButtonGroupBox() {
   . . . .
   group = new RadioButtonGroup();
   group.addEventListener(Event.CHANGE,
      function event:Event):void {
         value = event.target.selectedValue;
      }
   );
}
```

The complete code of the RadioButtonGroupBox is presented in Listing 11.17. See if you can discover the discrepancies between the listing and what we outlined in our snippets. There are really just a few things.

- We've added the *text* property so that in the item editor use case we don't have to specify *editorValue="value"*.

- We've made the properties *text* and *value* bindable by "change" and "valueCommit" events, dispatching events being done by the anonymouos Event.CHANGE handler and *value* setter correspondingly.
- We allowed the dynamic re-assignment of *options* by removing the existing dynamic RadioButtons before building new ones from the options array.

```
// RadioButtonGroupBox.as
package com.theriabook.containers
{
   import flash.display.DisplayObject;
   import flash.events.Event;
   import mx.containers.Box;
   import mx.core.IDataRenderer;
   import mx.controls.dataGridClasses.DataGridListData;
   import mx.controls.listClasses.BaseListData;
   import mx.controls.listClasses.IDropInListItemRenderer;
   import mx.controls.RadioButton;
   import mx.controls.RadioButtonGroup;
   import mx.events.FlexEvent;
   import mx.core.mx_internal;
   use namespace mx_internal;

   public class RadioButtonGroupBox extends Box implements  IDataRenderer,  IDropInLis-
tItemRenderer
   {
      private var group:RadioButtonGroup=null ;

      public function RadioButtonGroupBox() {
         super();
         verticalScrollPolicy = "off";
         horizontalScrollPolicy = "off";

         group = new RadioButtonGroup();
         group.addEventListener(Event.CHANGE,
            function (event:Event):void {
               value = event.target.selectedValue;
               dispatchEvent(event);
            }
         );
      }

      override public function addChild(child:DisplayObject):DisplayObject {
         if (child is RadioButton) {
            (child as RadioButton).group = group;
```

```
            group.addInstance(child as RadioButton);
        }
        return super.addChild(child);
    }

    override public function set data(item:Object):void  {
        super.data = item;
        if( item!=null ) {
            group.selectedValue = item[DataGridListData(listData).dataField];
        }
    }

    [Bindable("valueCommit")]
    [Bindable("change")]
    public function get text():Object {
        return value;
    }

    public function set text(v:Object) : void {
        value = v;
    }

    [Bindable("valueCommit")]
    [Bindable("change")]
    [Inspectable(category="General")]
    public function get value():Object {
        return group.selectedValue;
    }
    public function set value(v:Object) : void {
        group.selectedValue = v;
        if (listData && listData is DataGridListData) {
            data[DataGridListData(listData).dataField] = group.selectedValue;
            var event:CollectionEvent = new CollectionEvent(CollectionEvent.COLLECTION_
            CHANGE, false, false, CollectionEventKind.UPDATE, -1, -1, [data]);
            DataGrid(DataGridListData(listData).owner).dataProvider.dispatchEvent(event);
        }
        dispatchEvent(new FlexEvent(FlexEvent.VALUE_COMMIT));
    }

    private var _listData:BaseListData=null;
    public function get listData():BaseListData  {
        return _listData;
    }
    public function set listData(value:BaseListData):void   {
```

```
            _listData = value;
        }

        private var _options:Array=null;
        public function set options(opt:Array):void {
            var i:int;
            if (_options!=null) {
                for (i=0; i<_options.length; i++) {
                    var child:RadioButton = group.getRadioButtonAt(i);
                    removeChild(child);
                }

            }
            _options=opt;

            for (i= 0; i < opt.length; i++) {
                var rb:RadioButton = new RadioButton();
                rb.label = opt[i].label;
                rb.value = opt[i].data;
                addChild(rb);
            }
        }
    }
}
```

Listing 11.17 RadioButtonGroupBox.as

To take the standalone RadioButtonGroupBox for a spin, we wrote the small application RadioButtonGroupBoxStandAloneDemo presented in Listing 11.18. When you run it, Figure 11.9, you can check that it's still a normal Box container enriched with the ability to dynamically create as many RadioButton controls as there are option values.

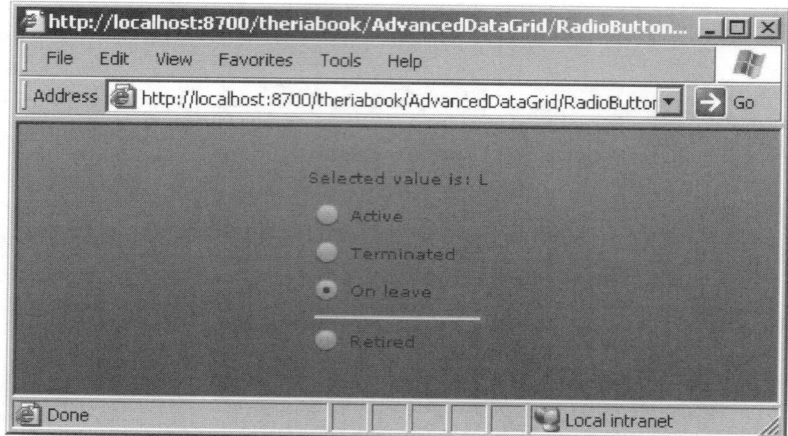

Figure 11.9 A snapshot of the RadioButtonGroupBoxStandaloneDemo

```
<?xml version="1.0" encoding="utf-8"?>
<!-- RadioButtonGroupBoxStandaloneDemo.mxml -->
<mx:Application  xmlns:mx="http://www.adobe.com/2006/mxml"
   xmlns:fx="http://www.theriabook.com/2006"
   layout="vertical">
         <mx:Text text="Selected value is: {rbgb.value}"/>
         <fx:RadioButtonGroupBox id="rbgb" value="L" direction="vertical">
            <fx:options>
               <mx:Array id="options">
                  <mx:Object data="A" label="Active"/>
                  <mx:Object data="T" label="Terminated"/>
                  <mx:Object data="L" label="On leave"/>

               </mx:Array>
            </fx:options>
            <mx:HRule/>
            <mx:RadioButton value="R" label="Retired"/>
         </fx:RadioButtonGroupBox>
</mx:Application>
```

Listing 11.18 UndefinedCheckBoxDemo.mxml

Now let's test the itemRenderer/itemEditor scenario. Not that it's required, but we would prefer to lay out the radiobuttons horizontally. So, we'll create RadioButtonGroupHBox as a simple extension of RadioButtonGroupHBox, taking care of the box's *direction* and adding a couple of padding pixels (the default Box padding is 0):

```
// RadioButtonGroupHBox.as
package com.theriabook.containers
{
   public class RadioButtonGroupHBox extends RadioButtonGroupBox {
      public function RadioButtonGroupHBox() {
         super();
         direction = "horizontal";
         setStyle("paddingLeft", "5");
      }
   }
}
```

Listing 11.19 RadioButtonGroupHBox.as

A screenshot of the test application RadioButtonGroupHBoxDemo is in Figure 11.10. As you may notice in the corresponding Listing 11.20, we've declared the entire DataGrid *editable* and indicated for the "status" column that *rendererIsEditor="true"*:

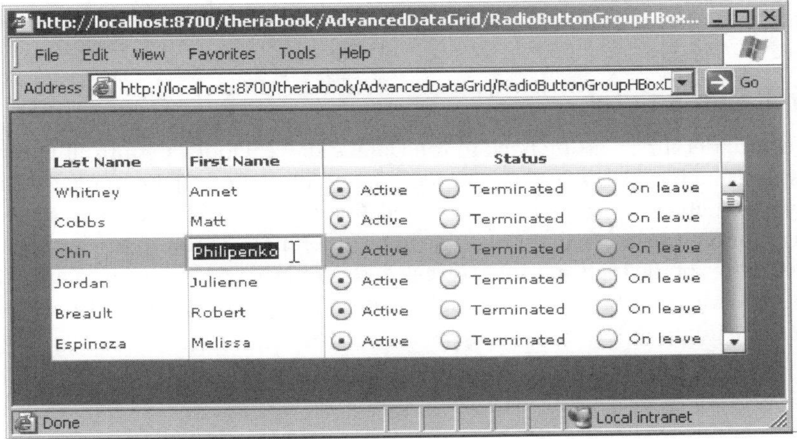

Figure 11.10 A snapshot of the RadioButtonGroupHBoxDemo

```
<?xml version="1.0" encoding="utf-8"?>
<!-- RadioButtonGroupHBoxDemo.mxml -->
<mx:Application  xmlns:mx="http://www.adobe.com/2006/mxml"
   xmlns:fx="http://www.theriabook.com/2006"
   layout="vertical">
   <fx:DataGrid  id="dg" creationComplete="dg.fill();dg.selectedIndex=0;" editable="true"
      destination="com_theriabook_composition_EmployeeDAO" method="getEmployees"


   >
```

```
      <fx:columns>
         <mx:Array>
            <mx:DataGridColumn    dataField="EMP_LNAME" headerText="Last Name"  />
            <mx:DataGridColumn    dataField="EMP_FNAME" headerText="First Name" />
            <fx:DataGridColumn dataField="STATUS" width="270" headerText="Status"
rendererIsEditor="true"  itemRenderer="com.theriabook.containers.RadioButtonGroupHBox">
               <fx:options>
                  <mx:Array id="options">
                     <mx:Object data="A" label="Active"/>
                     <mx:Object data="T" label="Terminated"/>
                     <mx:Object data="L" label="On leave"/>
                  </mx:Array>
               </fx:options>
            </fx:DataGridColumn>
         </mx:Array>
      </fx:columns>
   </fx:DataGrid>
</mx:Application>
```

Listing 11.20 RadioButtonGroupHBoxDemo.as

Computed Column Color

Enough of control detours! Getting back to the DataGrid, we'll look at controlling the style of the DataGridColumn: such as color, backGroundcolor, font, and so on. To be exact, we'll focus on defining the style in such a way that it is re-evaluated along with the data changes. Many times there are business requirements that call for the style to be different from row to row. Suppose we have to highlight the salaries of the high-paid employees in red and show the regular salary value in green. Leaving aside the twilight subject of what "high-paid" is, let's put the threshold at 50k. One solution is to use an in-line itemRenderer:

```
<mx:DataGridColumn    dataField="SALARY" textAlign="right">
      <mx:itemRenderer>
         <mx:Component>
            <mx:Label>
               <mx:Script>
         <![CDATA[
            override protected function updateDisplayList(unscaledWidth:Number,
                           unscaledHeight:Number):void
            {
               super.updateDisplayList(unscaledWidth, unscaledHeight);
               if (data && listData) { // Check that we are in a List and we are
                  "smart"
                  if (data.SALARY > 50000) {
                     setStyle("color", "red");
```

```
                } else {
                  setStyle("color", "green");
                }
              }
            }
            ]]>
              </mx:Script>
            </mx:Label>
          </mx:Component>
        </mx:itemRenderer>
      </mx:DataGridColumn>
```

As you can see, we used Label, an immediate descendant of UIComponent, as a component base. Why? Because *updateDisplayList()*, a UIComponent's method, would be out of reach for a standard DataGridItemRenderer based on the UITextField. Alernatively, we could have achieved the same functionality with a more elegant binding expression syntax:

```
<mx:DataGridColumn    dataField="SALARY" textAlign="right">
  <mx:itemRenderer>
    <mx:Component>
      <mx:Label
           color="{data.SALARY&gt;50000?255*256*256:255*256}"
        >
      </mx:Label>
    </mx:Component>
  </mx:itemRenderer>
</mx:DataGridColumn>
```

Listing 11.21 presents the complete code for the sample application StandardDynamicStyleDemo. Besides the DataGrid, we've thrown in "Increase" and "Decrease" buttons that let us modify the salary values in increments of 10k:

```
<?xml version="1.0" encoding="utf-8"?>
<!-- StandardDynamicStyleDemo.mxml -->
<mx:Application xmlns:mx="http://www.adobe.com/2006/mxml"  layout="vertical"
  xmlns:fx="http://www.theriabook.com/2006">
  <mx:HBox >
    <mx:Button label="Increase"
      click="dg.selectedItem.SALARY+=10000.00;
           dg.dataProvider.itemUpdated(dg.selectedItem);" />
    <mx:Button label="Decrease"
      click="dg.selectedItem.SALARY-=10000.00;
           dg.dataProvider.itemUpdated(dg.selectedItem,'SALARY');" />
```

```
</mx:HBox> <fx:DataGrid  id="dg" creationComplete="dg.fill();dg.selectedIndex=0;"
   destination="com_theriabook_composition_EmployeeDAO" method="getEmployees"

>
   <fx:columns>
      <mx:Array>
         <mx:DataGridColumn    dataField="EMP_LNAME"   />
         <mx:DataGridColumn    dataField="EMP_FNAME"  />
         <mx:DataGridColumn    dataField="SALARY" textAlign="right">
            <mx:itemRenderer>
               <mx:Component>
                  <mx:Label
                     color="{data.SALARY&gt;50000?255*256*256:255*256}"
                  />
               </mx:Component>
            </mx:itemRenderer>
         </mx:DataGridColumn>
      </mx:Array>
   </fx:columns>
</fx:DataGrid>

</mx:Application>
```

Listing 11.21 StandardDynamicStyleDemo.mxml

When you run StandardDynamicStyleDemo, you'll see the picture in Figure 11.11:

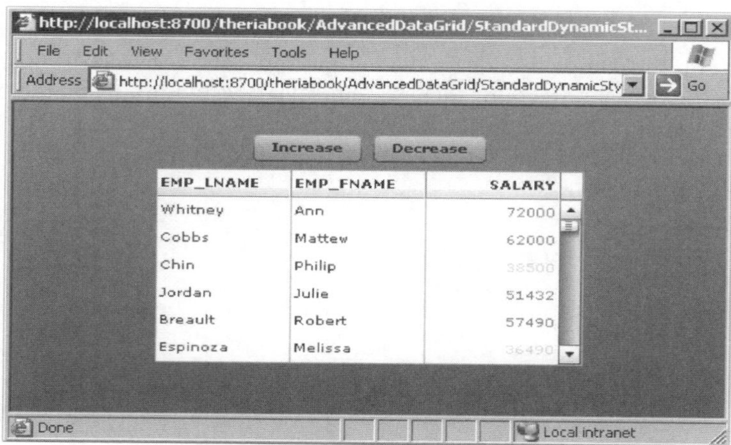

Figure 11.11 A snapshot of the StandardDynamicStyleDemo

Computed Column Background

We can't apply the same technique for background color because Label doesn't support backgroundColor style. We can resort to TextInput, which does have backgroundColor, but missing some backgroundColor doesn't seem a good reason for giving up a lightweight Label in favor of TextInput. After all, the beauty of Flex is that framework controls are open to extension. So, here it is, our custom Label extended with backgroundColor support, Listing 11.22:

```
// Label.as (theriabook.swc)
package com.theriabook.controls
{
   import mx.controls.Label;

   [Style(name="backgroundAlpha", type="Number", inherit="no")]
   [Style(name="backgroundColor", type="uint", format="Color", inherit="no")]

   dynamic public class Label extends mx.controls.Label
   {
      override protected function updateDisplayList(unscaledWidth:Number,
unscaledHeight:Number):void    {
         super.updateDisplayList(unscaledWidth, unscaledHeight);
         if (getStyle("backgroundColor")){
            graphics.clear();
            graphics.beginFill(getStyle("backgroundColor"), getStyle("backgroundAlpha"));
            graphics.drawRect(0, 0, unscaledWidth, unscaledHeight);
            graphics.endFill();
         }
      }

   }
}
```

Listing 11.22 Label.as

As you can see, we've defined not one, but two styles – backgroundAlpha and backgroundColor – and we use both values with *graphics.beginFill()* inside the overridden implementation of *updateDisplayList()*. Once we add Label.as to theriabook.swc and register it in the component manifest XML, the DataGridColumn can be redefined as in the following snippet:

```
<mx:DataGridColumn    dataField="SALARY" textAlign="right">
   <mx:itemRenderer>
      <mx:Component>
         <fx:Label
            backgroundColor="{data.SALARY&gt;50000?255*256*256:255*256}"
         />
```

```
            </mx:Component>
        </mx:itemRenderer>
    </mx:DataGridColumn>
```

The difference between the approach above and the way we defined a similar DataGridColumn in Listing 11.22 is that now we compute backgroundColor instead of the color and use fx:Label instead of the one from mx namespace. If you do the replacement and run the program, you'll see the picture in Figure 11.12.

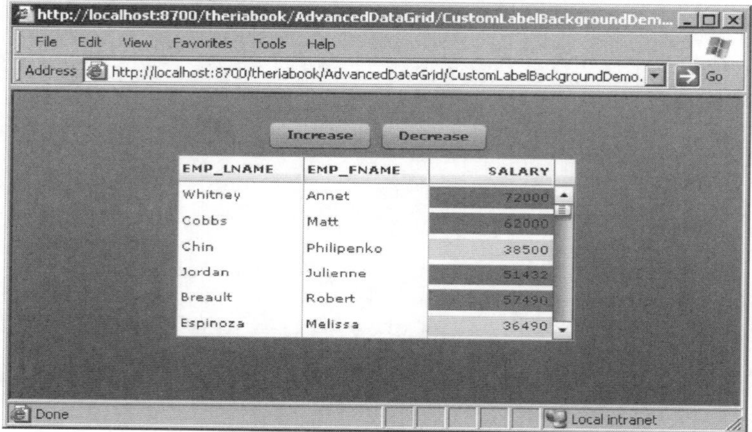

Figure 11.12 Snapshot of the background color computed with binding expression

Despite the seemingly satisfying result, there's something wrong here: using the powerful item renderer mechanism to manage styles seems to be design overkill. Let's speak our minds: we're after dynamic runtime styles, right? So, wouldn't it be nice if we added an extra DataGridColumn attribute, called, say, *runtimeStyles*, where we could list all styles and abstract from the implementation. Below is an example:

```
<fx:DataGridColumn  dataField="SALARY" textAlign="right" formatString="money">
   <fx:runtimeStyles>
        <mx:Object
           backgroundColor="{function(item:Object):String {return (item.SALARY&g
              t;50000)?'red':'green';}}"
                 />
   </fx:runtimeStyles>
</fx:DataGridColumn>
```

This approach would let developers concentrate on the substance rather than on the process. Let's make it happen.

Runtime Column Styles Unleashed

Here's the plan. We'll upgrade the default itemRenderer of the fx:DataGrid from UITextField to our custom fx:Label. We'll extend fx:DataGridColumn with an extra property – *runtimeStyles*. Finally, we'll intercept data changes to an item renderer, whether default or not, to reassign all *runtime Styles* on each.

Here's how the constructor of the standard DataGrid assigns itemRenderer:

```
package mx.controls {
public class DataGrid extends DataGridBase implements IIMESupport
{
  public function DataGrid()
  {
       super();
     itemRenderer = new ClassFactory(DataGridItemRenderer);
     .  .  .  .  .  .
  }
}
}
```

We have to fight the temptation to replace the assignment of the itemRenderer with

```
     itemRenderer = new ClassFactory(com.theriabook.controls.Label);
```

Here is why. A ClassFactory instance is a "factory object," which is used to generate instances of another class (aka a *generator* class), with the newInstance() method. According to our plan we need to intercept data changes to *any* instance of the generator class item renderer. Precisely, we'll have to listen to the FlexEvent.DATA_CHANGE event on every instance of the com.theriabook.controls. Label created by "the factory." Hmm, what could be simpler than adding the needed event listener to the controls? That would be okay if we commit ourselves to fx:Label as the only item renderer and by no means do we propose to take the power of custom item renderers away. To make the *runtimeStyles* control mechanism agnostic to the type of renderer, we'd like to listen to FlexEvent. DATA_CHANGE on the instances of *any* generator class.

It only sounds difficult. After all, a ClassFactory is nothing but an implementation of the IFactory interface with a single property – *properties* and single method – *newInstance()*. That's it. So we can easily wrap a standard ClassFactory inside our custom one to intercept the *newInstance()* call. We'll call our wrapping class factory the UIClassFactory:

```
   function DataGrid() {
     super();
     itemRenderer = new UIClassFactory(ClassFactory(com.theriabook.controls.La-
bel));
   }
```

The constructor of the UIClassFactory would simply store the reference to the instance of the real class factory – *cf*. Meanwhile UIClassFactory's newInstance() would delegate the call to the *cf.newInstance()*. It would also register the listener to the FlexEvent.DATA_CHANGE event as shown below:

```
public class UIFactory implements IFactory
{
   . . . . .
   public function UIClassFactory( cf:ClassFactory ) {
      wrappedClassFactory = cf;
   }

   public function newInstance():* {
      var obj:* = wrappedClassFactory.newInstance();
      obj.addEventListener(FlexEvent.DATA_CHANGE, onDataChange);
      return obj;
   }

   private function onDataChange(event:FlexEvent):void{
      . . . . .
   }
}
```

As a reminder, properties of factory-manufactured objects get assigned by iterating over… fasten your seat belts please…properties of the specific property of the factory object. The name of this aggregating property is *properties*. That way all instances are initialized with the same values. Wrapping the *properties* property is quite simple:

```
public function set properties(v:Object):void{
   wrappedClassFactory.properties = v;
}
public function get properties():* {
   return wrappedClassFactory.properties ;
}
```

The complete code of UIClassFactory is presented in Listing 11.23. The only part of it that remains uncovered is the *onDataChange()* handler.

The implementation of the default DataGridUtemRenderer emits a DATA_CHANGE event from two places: setter of *data* and setter of *listData*. We will ignore changes of *listData* and, for every *data* change, we will reassign all style name *properties* carried by runtimeStyles. The values of these properties may be literal or, alternatively, function references. In the latter case, we apply the *call* operator () before setting the style value with the *setStyle()*:

```
//UIClassFactory.as
package com.theriabook.util
{
   import mx.core.IFactory;
   import mx.core.ClassFactory;
   import mx.events.FlexEvent;
   import mx.controls.dataGridClasses.DataGridColumn;

   public class UIClassFactory implements IFactory
   {
      private var wrappedClassFactory : ClassFactory;

      public function set properties(v:Object):void  {
         wrappedClassFactory.properties = v;
      }
      public function get properties():* {
         return wrappedClassFactory.properties ;
      }
      public function UIClassFactory( cf:ClassFactory ) {
         wrappedClassFactory = cf;
      }

      public function newInstance():* {
         var obj:* = wrappedClassFactory.newInstance();
         obj.addEventListener(FlexEvent.DATA_CHANGE, onDataChange);
         return obj;
      }

      private function onDataChange(event:FlexEvent):void{

         var renderer:Object = event.currentTarget;

// In the default DataGridItemRenderer both data and listData are
//    Bindable("dataChange")]
         // We want to skip assinments to listData
         if (renderer.data is mx.controls.dataGridClasses.DataGridColumn) return;

         // Act only on 'dynamic style' columns
         if (renderer.styleName && renderer.styleName.hasOwnProperty("runtimeStyles")) {
            var runtimeStyles:Object = renderer.styleName["runtimeStyles"];
            for (var style:String in runtimeStyles) {
               if ( runtimeStyles[style] is Function ) {
                  var functionObject : Function = runtimeStyles[style];
                  renderer.setStyle(style, functionObject(renderer.data));
```

```
                }
                else
                    renderer.setStyle(style, runtimeStyles[style]);
            }
            renderer.invalidateDisplayList();
        }

    }
  }
}
```

Listing 11.23 UIClassFactory.as, first version

One chore is remaining. As long as we want to communicate the *runtimeStyles* to any item renderer, including the ones that are individually set on a per-column basis, we need to route them through our UIClassFactory. Accordingly we will modify our DataGridColumn and override the implementation of the DataGridColumn's itemRenderer setter:

```
override public function set itemRenderer( val : IFactory ) : void {
   super.itemRenderer = new UIClassFactory(val as ClassFactory);
}
```

The full listing of our DataGridColumn is shown in Listing 11.24

```
// DataGridColumn.as
package com.theriabook.controls.dataGridClasses{
   import com.theriabook.util.UIClassFactory;
   import mx.controls.dataGridClasses.DataGridColumn;
   import mx.core.ClassFactory;
   import mx.core.IFactory;

   public class DataGridColumn  extends mx.controls.dataGridClasses.DataGridColumn {

      public var runtimeStyles:Object = null;
      public var runtimeProperties:Object = null;
      public function set extendedProperties(val:Object) :void {
         if (itemRenderer)
            itemRenderer["properties"] = val;
      }

      override public function set itemRenderer( val : IFactory ) : void {
         super.itemRenderer = new UIClassFactory(val as ClassFactory);
      }
```

```
      public function  set formatString( fs :String ) : void{
         formatData = fs;
      }

      public function  set formatData( fd :Object ) : void{
         FormattingManager.setFormat(this, fd);
      }
   }
}
```

Listing 11.24 DataGridColumn.as

Here is our test application – RuntimeStyleDemo, Listing 11.25:

```
<?xml version="1.0" encoding="utf-8"?>
<!-- RuntimeStylesDemo.mxml -->
<mx:Application xmlns:mx="http://www.adobe.com/2006/mxml"  layout="vertical"
   xmlns:fx="http://www.theriabook.com/2006">
   <mx:Script>
      <![CDATA[
         import com.theriabook.composition.dto.EmployeeDTO;
         private var linkage:com.theriabook.composition.dto.EmployeeDTO
         private function computedFontWeight(item:Object):String {
            return (item.SALARY>55000)?'bold':'normal';
         }
      ]]>
   </mx:Script>
   <mx:Button label="Increase"
      click="dg.selectedItem.SALARY+=10000.00;
             dg.dataProvider.itemUpdated(dg.selectedItem);" />
   <mx:Button label="Decrease"
      click="dg.selectedItem.SALARY-=10000.00;
             dg.dataProvider.itemUpdated(dg.selectedItem,'SALARY');" />
   <fx:DataGrid  id="dg" creationComplete="dg.fill();dg.selectedIndex=0;"
      destination="com_theriabook_composition_EmployeeDAO" method="getEmployees"

   >
      <fx:columns>
         <mx:Array>
            <mx:DataGridColumn    dataField="EMP_LNAME"   />
            <mx:DataGridColumn    dataField="EMP_FNAME"  />
            <fx:DataGridColumn    dataField="SALARY" textAlign="right"
formatString="money">
               <fx:runtimeStyles>
```

```
                    <mx:Object
                       backgroundColor="{function(item:Object):String {return
                            (item.SALARY&gt;50000)?'red':'green';}}"
                        fontWeight="{computedFontWeight}"
                    />
                </fx:runtimeStyles>
            </fx:DataGridColumn>
        </mx:Array>
    </fx:columns>
</fx:DataGrid>

</mx:Application>
```

Listing 11.25 RuntimeStyleDemo.mxml

Figure 11.13 depicts RuntimeStylesDemo running[9]:

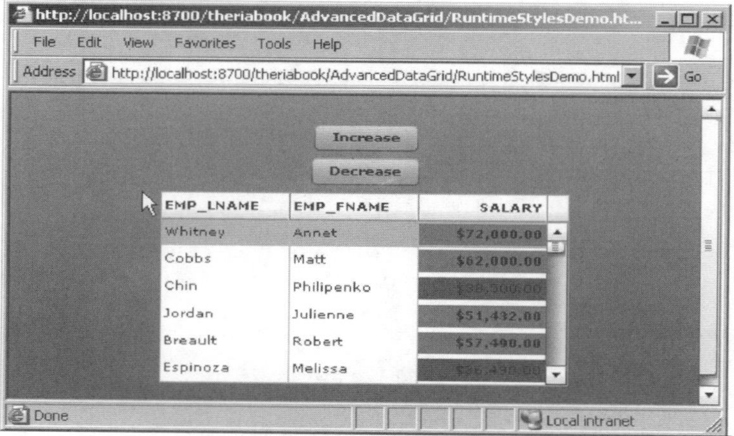

Figure 11.13 A RuntimeStyleDemo application

So far we've shown that it's possible to control runtime styles via anonymous or explicit functions *(backgroundColor* versus *computedFontWeight* in the demo application above). You can take our approach further and completely outsource the dynamic styling to a separate controller object flexibly instantiated via the *getDefinitionByName()* method. Come to think of it, you'd completely shield developers from formatting and styling problems of a particular project!

Let's leave the reader with this thought and turn our attention from formatting to the *editing* side of the DataGrid. Before we go there though, we'd like to take one more detour, introducing a couple of additional controls: *MaskedInput* and *NumericInput.*

Masked Input and Numeric Input

Input masking is akin to crime prevention. The least that input masking does is stop a user from entering non-appropriate characters. Stricter masks can prevent users from entering inomplete numbers, less-than-required text, etc. – details are always implementation-specific. Taken to the extreme, masks can completely obliterate validation programming, albeit at the cost of fixing a specific user experience.

The first control of this section – MaskedInput – was created by Peter Ent from Adobe. We'll be using it only for illustrative purposes and the code walkthrough of MaskedInput is beyond the scope of this chapter. MaskedInput is a lightweight mask where you can indicate the maximum number of positions in the mask and prescribe the type of the characters the user can type. The movement of the insertion point is controlled by the control. For example, if you set a mask for entering a U.S. phone number as (###) ###-#### in response to the end user typing 6175551212, the control will display (617) 555-1212. Alpha keys will be blocked, but the completeness of the phone is up to the user. The control is an extension of the mx.controls.TextInput and its *text* returns the "mask-free" data input, i.e., 6175551212 in our use case. The main controlling property of MaskedInput is the inputMask, which can consist of any characters except:

- #, which stands for a single digit
- C, which capitalizes a letter (no digits allowed)
- C, which forces a letter to lowercase (no digits allowed)
- A or a, which allows any character.

Like all other components in this chapter, we've added a MaskedInput to *theriabook.swc* and registered it in the component manifest file *theriabook-manifest.xml*. The only modifications we've done to the original MaskedInput: changed the original packaging of the MaskedInput to *com.theriabook.controls* and overrode the implementation of the TextInput data setter to accommodate its use in the DataGrid:

```
public override  function set data(data:Object):void {
   super.data = data;
   var dgListData:DataGridListData =  DataGridListData(listData);
   text = data[dgListData.dataField];
}
```

The complete code for com.theriabook.controls.MaskedInput is provided in the accompanying DVD.

The second mask that we present in this section is NumericInput. It doesn't control the insertion point so that typing and pasting isn't restricted. However, it blocks any typing or pasting that contains invalid characters. Here's the first iteration of the NumericInput code:

```
// NumericInput.as
package com.theriabook.controls
```

```
{
   import mx.controls.TextInput;
   import flash.events.Event;

   public class NumericInput extends TextInput
   {
        public function NumericInput() {
        super();
           addEventListener(flash.events.TextEvent.TEXT_INPUT, onTextInput);
        }

   private function onTextInput(event:flash.events.TextEvent):void {
      // TODO Find out number separators from the locale settings
      var re:RegExp =
      new RegExp("[^0-9,.-]", "i");
      var illegalCharacterFound:Boolean = re.test(event.text);
      if (illegalCharacterFound) {
         event.preventDefault();
      }
   }
   }
}
```

Listing 11.26 NumericInput.as, first version

As you can see, we listen to TextEvent.TEXT_INPUT, which corresponds to a character or sequence of characters (paste) entered by the user. Whatever's been entered comes as *event.text* and we test it with a regular expression trying to find illegal characters. The string literal that we used for RegExp reads as "anything but characters in the range 0-9 or comma or dot or minus." If an illegal character is found, we reject the typing or pasting by cancelling the default behavior of the event[10] with:

```
event.preventDefault();
```

That's all it takes to bulletproof your input fields from undesired characters. Two more small patches before we leave the NumericInput, though.

In the course of marshalling the Java data across the wire, chances are your numeric data will come as *Number.NaN*, a direct counterpart of Java *Double.NaN or Float.NaN*. In general, unless you use special DTOs with embedded null indicators, this is the natural way to marshal numeric nulls; no one would appreciate the lettering NaN staring at the user instead of the empty cell. So, following the established pattern, we're going expand our NumericInput with a property *value*, then have it produce the appropriate *text* required for presentation. Hence the following addition to NumericInput code:

```
private var _value:*;
[Bindable("change")]
public function set value(v:*):void {
   _value = v;
   if ((isNaN(v)) || (v==null /*null or undefined*/)) {
      text="";
   } else {
      text = String(v as Number);
   }
}

public function get value():* {
   // Preserve NaN | null | undefined, when nothing has been entered
   if (((_value!=null )&& (String(_value)!="NaN")) || (text!="") ) {
      _value = Number(text.replace(/,/g,"")); // deformat first
   }
   return _value;
}

public override  function set data(item:Object):void {
   if (listData && listData is DataGridListData) {
      var dgListData:DataGridListData = DataGridListData(listData);
      value = item[dgListData.dataField];
   }
   super.data = item;
}
```

In the code fragment above we intervened in the setter for *data* property in case the NumericInput is embedded in the DataGrid as a renderer. There we modify the *value* and let the *value*, in turn, modify the *text*.

In the value getter we return the original content: *null, undefined,* or *Number.NaN* provided the user hasn't entered anything. Otherwise, we use a regular expression to convert the text to Number globally, eliminating the spaces and thousand separators first:

```
_value = Number(text.replace(/,/g,""));
```

Strictly speaking we should have operated with a locale-specific thousands-separator character instead of ",". For reference, U.S. English-specific definitions of String constants decimalSeparator and thousandsSeparator ("." and ",") are located in the file *Flex SDK/ 2/frameworks/locale/en_US/ validator.properties*.

If you're delivering your application to Brasil, you could create a similar or smaller file in the Flex SDK/ 2/frameworks/locale/pr_BR folder, where you'd redefine decimalSeparator as "," and thousandsSeparator as ".". Supposedly you'd keep the original name[11] – *validators.properties*. Then you'd modify compiler options for *theriabook.swc* to specify the pr_BR locale and rebuild NumericInput after adding the following code:

```
    import mx.resources.ResourceBundle;

 public class NumericInput extends TextInput {

    .  .  .  .

    [ResourceBundle("validators")]
    private static var rb:ResourceBundle;

    public static var decimalSeparator:String;
    public static var thousandsSeparator:String;

    // Load resources during class definition loading
    loadResources();

    private static function loadResources():void {
       decimalSeparator =  rb.getString("decimalSeparator");
       thousandsSeparator = rb.getString("thousandsSeparator");
    }
   }
```

Let's move on to the testing application – NumericInputDemo. When you run it, try to type anything but digits, commas, and dots into the "Number" column. You won't be able to. Again, please make no mistake: NumericInput is a lightweight mask and it doesn't replace the need to validate. In particular, if you like regular expressions as much as we do, you may base the validation of the currency field on the mx.vaidators.RegExpValidator, applying the regular expression that's the best match for your use case, for instance, something like:

```
^\$?([1-9]{1}[0-9]{0,2}(\,[0-9]{3})*(\.[0-9]{0,2})?|[1-9]{1}[0-9]{0,}(\.[0-
9]{0,2})?|0(\.[0-9]{0,2})?|(\.[0-9]{1,2})?)
```

We leave it up to the reader to try. Another feature to notice while running the demo app is how *NaN, null,* and *undefined* values are preserved in the absence of a meaningful input in the corresponding cells:

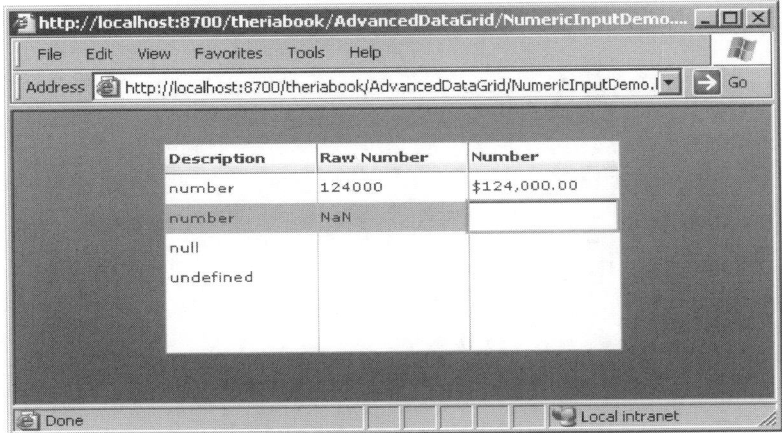

Figure 11.14 NumericInputDemo application

The code of the testing application is shown below. The helper class NumberScope.as is presented in Listing 11.28:

```
When you run it, try to type anything but digits, comma and dot into the
<?xml version="1.0" encoding="utf-8"?>
<!--NumericInputDemo.mxml -->
<mx:Application xmlns:mx="http://www.adobe.com/2006/mxml"
   xmlns:fx="http://www.theriabook.com/2006"
   layout="vertical"
    creationComplete="onCreationComplete();">
    <mx:Script>
      <![CDATA[
         import mx.collections.*;
         [Bindable]
         private var collection:ArrayCollection;
         private function onCreationComplete():void {
            collection = new ArrayCollection ([
               new NumberScope(124000.00),
               new NumberScope(Number.NaN),
               new NumberScope(null),
               new NumberScope(undefined)
            ]);
         }

      ]]>
    </mx:Script>
```

```
    <fx:DataGrid id="dg" dataProvider="{collection}" editable="true" >
        <fx:columns>
        <mx:Array>
            <fx:DataGridColumn dataField="description" headerText="Description"
editable="false"/>
            <mx:DataGridColumn dataField="number" headerText="Raw Number"
editable="false"/>
            <fx:DataGridColumn dataField="number" headerText="Number" editable="true"
editorDataField="value" itemEditor="com.theriabook.controls.NumericInput"
formatString="money"/>
        </mx:Array>
        </fx:columns>
    </fx:DataGrid>
</mx:Application>
```

Listing 11.27 NumericInputDemo.mxml

```
//NumberScope.as, helper class for NumericInputDemo.mxml
package {
    public class NumberScope {
        public var number:*;
        public function get description():String {
            if (number===null) return 'null';
            if (number===undefined) return 'undefined';
            return (typeof number);
        }
        public function NumberScope(n:*) {
            number=n;
        }
    }
}
```

Listing 11.28 NumberScope.as, helper class for NumericInputDemo

Finally, Listing 11.29 depicts the complete code for NumericInput:

```
// NumericInput.as
package com.theriabook.controls
{
    import mx.controls.TextInput;
    import flash.events.Event;
    import mx.controls.List;

    public class NumericInput extends TextInput
```

```
{
    import mx.controls.listClasses.BaseListData;
  import mx.events.FlexEvent;
    import mx.controls.dataGridClasses.DataGridListData;


    public function NumericInput() {
     super();
     addEventListener(flash.events.TextEvent.TEXT_INPUT, onTextInput);
     }

  private var _value:*;
  [Bindable("change")]
  public function set value(v:*):void {
     _value = v;
     if ((String(v)=="NaN") || (v==null /*or undefined*/)) {
        text="";
     } else {
        text = String(v as Number);
     }
  }

  public function get value():* {
     // Preserve NaN - null - undefined, when nothing has been entered
     if (((_value!=null )&& (String(_value)!="NaN")) || (text!="") ) {
        _value = Number(text.replace(/,/g,"")); // deformat first
     }
     return _value;
  }

  public override  function set data(item:Object):void {
     if (listData && listData is DataGridListData) {
        var dgListData:DataGridListData = DataGridListData(listData);
        value = item[dgListData.dataField];
        dispatchEvent(new FlexEvent(FlexEvent.DATA_CHANGE));
        return;
     }
     super.data = item;
  }

  private function onTextInput(event:flash.events.TextEvent):void {
     // TODO Find out number separators from the locale settings
     var re:RegExp =  new RegExp("[^0-9,.-]", "i");
     var illegalCharacterFound:Boolean = re.test(event.text);
```

```
            if (illegalCharacterFound) {
               event.preventDefault();
            }
         }
      }
   }
```

Listing 11.29 NumericInput.as, final version

DataGrid with Automatic Item Editors

Armed with MaskedInput and NumericInput, we can proceed with automating DataGrid editing features. Here's the issue at hand: once you make your DataGrid as editable, you are in charge of manually assigning the appropriate item editors for each column. Compare this to the standard formatting approach, which assumes that for each column, you *manually* assign an item renderer or labelFunction. Do you see the 100% similarity? Make no mistake we're not comparing item editors with label function. It's the "manually" we're after.

As the reader is probably sensing by now, we are about to automate the programming of editors with the same technique we applied for formatting. Namely, we'll take the burden off developers' shoulders and make DataGrid accountable for picking up and initializing proper item editors.

If you recall, mapping label functions, albeit anonymous ones, had been delegated to a separate class, FormattingManager. Quite similarly, we are about to introduce an additional class Editing-Manager, with a single method *setFormat()* so that our custom DataGridColumn will be calling it right after it invokes the similar method of the FormattingManager:

```
// DataGridColumn.as
package com.theriabook.controls.dataGridClasses{
   import com.theriabook.util.UIClassFactory;
   import mx.controls.dataGridClasses.DataGridColumn;
   import mx.core.ClassFactory;
   import mx.core.IFactory;

   public class DataGridColumn  extends mx.controls.dataGridClasses.DataGridColumn {

      public var runtimeStyles:Object = null;
      public var runtimeProperties:Object = null;
      public function set extendedProperties(val:Object) :void {
         if (itemRenderer)
            itemRenderer["properties"] = val;
      }

      override public function set itemRenderer( val : IFactory ) : void {
```

```
            super.itemRenderer = new UIClassFactory(val as ClassFactory);
        }

        public function  set formatString( fs :String ) : void{
            formatData = fs;
        }

        public function  set formatData( fd :Object ) : void{
            FormattingManager.setFormat(this, fd);
            EditingManager.setFormat(this, fd);
        }
    }
}
```

Listing 11.30 DataGridColumn.as, improved with EditingManager

Now let's focus on EditingManager.

Its method *setFormated* has to assign the value of the itemEditor property for the column. The decision of which itemEditor to choose should be based entirely on the formatString. As you can see, the setFormat() method carries all the required information in its signature, and column and formatting information as method parameters. Before we go coding, let's recap that itemEditor is a property of type IFactory. When you set its value in MXML, the compiler automatically creates an instance of ClassFactory, a class that implements the IFactory interface based on your class as "generator." Our approach is different and we'll be creating the ClassFactory[12] explicitly.

Here's an example of creating the ClassFactory for the column with the "shortdate" format. We create the ClassFactory based on the DateField and set its properties with an anonymous object so that, ultimately, each instance of the manufactured DateField will have its *formatString* set to "MM/DD/YY." Not only do we assign the itemEditor to the DataGridColumn, we also specify the *editorDataField* (DataGrid assumes the *text* property otherwise):

```
case "shortdate":
    cf = new ClassFactory(DateField);
    cf.properties = { formatString : "MM/DD/YY"};
    dgc.editorDataField="selectedDate";
    dgc.itemEditor = cf;
    break;
```

Like the "zip," "phone," and "ssn" formats, all of which conform nicely to MaskedInput, we encapsulate the assignment of itemEditor inside the helper function *setMaskedEditor()*:

```
    private static function setMaskedEditor(dgc:DataGridColumn, mask:String):
void{
```

```
      var cf:ClassFactory;
      cf = new ClassFactory(MaskedInput);
      cf.properties = {inputMask : mask};
      dgc.itemEditor = cf;
   }
```

The full code for EditingManager is presented in Listing 11.31. Note that, like FormattingManager, we programmed the default case to handle the non-listed formatString with a "#" character in it as an unknown mask:

```
// EditingManager.as
package com.theriabook.controls.dataGridClasses
{
   import mx.core.ClassFactory;
   import mx.controls.TextInput;
   import com.theriabook.controls.MaskedInput;
   import com.theriabook.controls.NumericInput;
   import mx.controls.DateField;

   public class EditingManager
   {
      import com.theriabook.controls.dataGridClasses.DataGridColumn;
      import mx.formatters.*;
      import com.theriabook.formatters.MaskFormatter;

      private static function setMaskedEditor(dgc:DataGridColumn, mask:String):void{
         var cf:ClassFactory;
         cf = new ClassFactory(MaskedInput);
         cf.properties = {inputMask : mask};
         dgc.itemEditor = cf;
      }

      public static function setFormat(dgc:DataGridColumn, formatData:Object):void{
         var  fs:String;
         var cf:ClassFactory;
         if (formatData is String)
            fs = formatData as String;
         else
            fs = formatData.formatString;
         switch (fs.toLowerCase()) {
            case "ssn":
               setMaskedEditor(dgc, "###-##-####");
               break;
            case "money":
```

```
                cf = new ClassFactory(NumericInput);
                dgc.itemEditor = cf;
                break;
             case "shortdate":
                cf = new ClassFactory(DateField);
                cf.properties = { formatString : "MM/DD/YY"};
                dgc.editorDataField="selectedDate";
                dgc.itemEditor = cf;
                break;
             case "zip":
                setMaskedEditor(dgc, "#####-####");
                break;
             case "phone":
                setMaskedEditor(dgc, "(###) ###-####");
                break;
             default:
                if (fs.indexOf("#")!=-1) {
                   setMaskedEditor(dgc, fs);
                };
          }
       }
    }
}
```

Listing 11.31 EditingManager.as

Finally, Listing 11.32 presents the test application – ComputedEditorDemo:

```
<?xml version="1.0" encoding="utf-8"?>
<!-- ComputedEditorDemo.mxml -->
<mx:Application xmlns:mx="http://www.adobe.com/2006/mxml"  layout="vertical"
   xmlns:fx="http://www.theriabook.com/2006">
   <mx:Script>
      <![CDATA[
         import com.theriabook.composition.dto.EmployeeDTO;
         private var linkage:com.theriabook.composition.dto.EmployeeDTO
      ]]>
   </mx:Script>
   <fx:DataGrid  id="dg" creationComplete="dg.fill()" editable="true"
      destination="com_theriabook_composition_EmployeeDAO" method="getEmployees"


   >
      <fx:columns>
         <mx:Array>
```

```
            <mx:DataGridColumn    dataField="EMP_LNAME"   />
            <mx:DataGridColumn    dataField="EMP_FNAME"  />
            <fx:DataGridColumn    dataField="PHONE"    formatString="phone" />
            <fx:DataGridColumn    dataField="SS_NUMBER"   formatString="ssn"  />
            <fx:DataGridColumn    dataField="START_DATE"    formatString="shortdate"  />
            <fx:DataGridColumn    dataField="SALARY" textAlign="right"
formatString="money"/>
        </mx:Array>
      </fx:columns>
   </fx:DataGrid>
</mx:Application>
```

Listing 11.32 ComputedEditorDemo.as

No application code to populate the DataGrid, no coding to display, no coding to edit. Just indicate the format of the column and off you go. And, keep in mind our quest for DataGrid automation isn't over yet! Meanwhile, if you run the application it will resemble Figure 11.15:

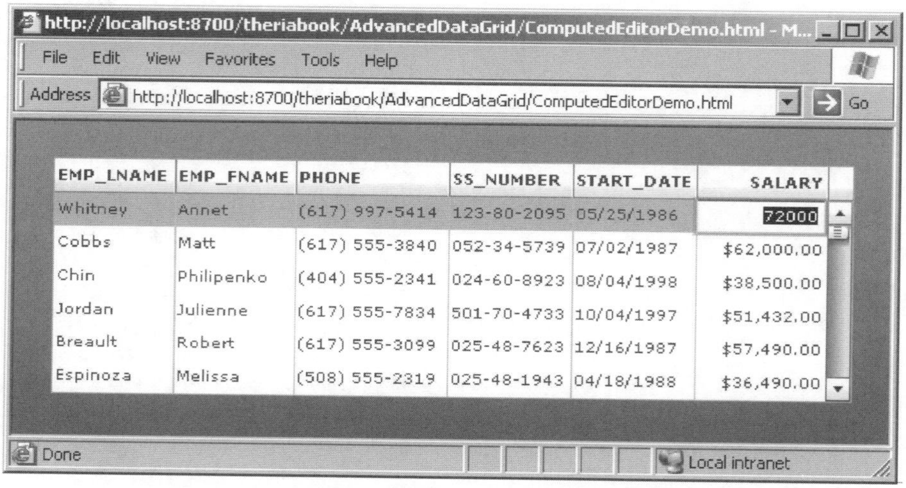

EMP_LNAME	EMP_FNAME	PHONE	SS_NUMBER	START_DATE	SALARY
Whitney	Annet	(617) 997-5414	123-80-2095	05/25/1986	72000
Cobbs	Matt	(617) 555-3840	052-34-5739	07/02/1987	$62,000.00
Chin	Philipenko	(404) 555-2341	024-60-8923	08/04/1998	$38,500.00
Jordan	Julienne	(617) 555-7834	501-70-4733	10/04/1997	$51,432.00
Breault	Robert	(617) 555-3099	025-48-7623	12/16/1987	$57,490.00
Espinoza	Melissa	(508) 555-2319	025-48-1943	04/18/1988	$36,490.00

Figure 11.15 A snapshot of the ComputedEditorDemo application

Data-Driven Programming Unleashed

So far we've been slowly but surely reducing the manual effort of defining DataGrid columns. How about taking it to the extreme and completely *eliminating* the need to define DataGridColumns? The following snippet illustrates the dynamic creation of the columns we have in mind:

```
private function onCreationComplete() :void {
   // Load metadata from external datasource …
```

```
    var columns :Array = new Array();
    for ( var i:int = 0; i < cols.length; i++)  {
      var dgc:DataGridColumn=  new DataGridColumn();
      // Assign column properties from metadata
      .   .   .   .
      columns.push(dgc);
    }
    dg.columns = columns;
  }
      .   .   .   .
  <fx:DataGrid  id="dg" dataProvider="{dp}"  />
```

The properties of each column could be derived from some external respository, for instance – a database. But if we plan to dynamically assign properties like itemRenderer, we need to"train" our UIClassFactory to dynamically create the *generator* object given its class name.

As a reminder, UIClassFactory is a typical wrapper class. The constructor of UIClassFactory accepts an instance of the wrapped ClassFactory:

```
    public function UIClassFactory( cf:ClassFactory ) {
      wrappedClassFactory = cf;
    }
```

Accordingly, our up-to-the-minute implementation of the *newInstance()* delegates real instantiation to the wrappedClassFactory:

```
    public function newInstance():* {
      var obj:* = wrappedClassFactory.newInstance();
      obj.addEventListener(FlexEvent.DATA_CHANGE, onDataChange);
      return obj;
    }
```

Let's modify the constructor to allow String arguments in addition to ClassFactory ones. We will loosen the strict definition of the argument type from ClassFactory to Object. In case of the String, the constructor will attempt to load the correposnding class definition dynamically[13] and then create the matching ClassFactory:

```
  function UIClassFactory( cf: Object ) {
    if ( cf is ClassFactory) {
      wrappedClassFactory = ClassFactory(cf);
    } else if (cf is String) {
      var className:String = String(cf);
      var clazz:Class = getDefinitionByName(className);
      wrappedClassFactory = new  ClassFactory(clazz);
```

```
    } else {
      throw new Error("Invalid argument for UIClassFactory constructor");
    }
  }
```

As soon as you think "definition by name," you have to ask yourself: "Is the class definition accessible?" If the answer is positive, it means you are confident about the way you build and load your SWFs. To force SWF to contain an application-specific class, you can simply declare a variable of the class. We don't find this appropriate for libraries, hence the need for the library initialization sections that we explained in Chapter 9. Following the pattern established in Chapter10, we'll create *theriabook.mxml, theriabook_code*.as and *build.xml* files in the root of the theriabook project. Below is Listing 11.33 of theriabook_code.as. The other two files we will omit for brevity's sake (you can find them on the accompanying DVD):

```
//theriabook_code.as
package {
  import mx.core.SimpleApplication;
  import com.theriabook.containers.*;
  import com.theriabook.controls.*;
  import com.theriabook.controls.dataGridClasses.*;
  import com.theriabook.formatters.*;
  import com.theriabook.util.UIClassFactory;

  public class theriabook_code extends SimpleApplication {
    public function theriabook_code() {
      // Custom library initialization code should go here
      trace("theriabook.swf has been loaded and initialized 2");
    }

  private var linkage:Object = {
      t0:com.theriabook.containers.RadioButtonGroupBox,
      t1:com.theriabook.containers.RadioButtonGroupHBox,
      t2:com.theriabook.controls.CheckBox,
      t3:com.theriabook.controls.DataGrid,
      t4:com.theriabook.controls.DateField,
      t5:com.theriabook.controls.Label,
      t6:com.theriabook.controls.MaskedInput,
      t7:com.theriabook.controls.NumericInput,
      t8:com.theriabook.controls.dataGridClasses.DataGridColumn,
      t9:com.theriabook.controls.dataGridClasses.EditingManager,
      t10:com.theriabook.controls.dataGridClasses.FormattingManager,
      t11:com.theriabook.formatters.MaskFormatter,
      t12:com.theriabook.util.UIClassFactory
    };
```

```
    }
}
```

Listing 11.33 theriabook_code.as

Using build.xml we will run Ant to build the theriabook.swf. As per the DVD version of the code, the Flex application folder for this chapter has been named *AdvancedDataGrid* and build.xml creates theriabook.swf in *C:/fds/jrun4/servers/default/theriabook/*AdvancedDataGrid. Accordingly, in the AdvancedDataGrid project, we will to go to Properties->FlexBuildPath-> LibraryPath and turn the Link Type for all SWC entries to RSL/AutoExtract(YES). Then we will remove the reference to *theriabook* project as "SWC Folder", adding instead a reference to *theriabook.swc* as a file. We will set the Link Type of theriabook.swc to RSL/AutoExtract (NO), since we have already produced the SWF during the Ant step.

Now we are fully prepared to cut the application code, which is presented in Listing 11.34:

```
<?xml version="1.0" encoding="utf-8"?>
<!-- DataGridAutomationDemo.mxml.
     Please make sure to use theriabook.swf as self-initialized library.
-->
<mx:Application xmlns:mx="http://www.adobe.com/2006/mxml" layout="vertical"
   xmlns:fx="http://www.theriabook.com/2006"  creationComplete="onCreationComplete()">
   <mx:Script>
      <![CDATA[
         import com.theriabook.controls.dataGridClasses.DataGridColumn;
         import com.theriabook.util.UIClassFactory;
         [Bindable]
         private var dp:Array = [];
         private var cols:Array = [];

         //import com.theriabook.containers.RadioButtonGroupHBox;
         //private var linkage:Object={a:com.theriabook.containers.RadioButtonGroupHBox};

         private function onCreationComplete() :void {
            cols =[
               {dataField:"firstName", headerText:"First Name"},
               {dataField:"lastName", headerText:"Last Name"},
               {dataField:"phone", headerText:"Phone", formatString:"phone"},
               {dataField:"status",headerText:"First Name",width:280,
                itemRenderer:"com.theriabook.containers.RadioButtonGroupHBox",
                options:[
                  {data:"A",label:"Active"},
                  {data:"T",label:"Terminated"},
```

```
                {data:"L",label:"On leave"}
              ]
            }
          ];
          dp=[
            {firstName:"Anatole",   lastName:"Tartakovsky", phone:"7141237890",
status:"A"},
            {firstName:"Victor", lastName:"Rasputnis", phone:"3053425470", status:"L"},
            {firstName:"Yakov",  lastName:"Fain", phone:"2013335748", status:"A"}
          ];
          var columns :Array = new Array();
          for ( var i:int = 0; i < cols.length; i++)  {
            var dgc:DataGridColumn=  new DataGridColumn();
            for (var prop:String in cols[i]) {
                if (prop=="itemRenderer") {
                  dgc.itemRenderer = new UIClassFactory(cols[i][prop]);
                  dgc.rendererIsEditor=true;
                } else {
                  dgc[prop] = cols[i][prop];
                }
            }
            columns.push(dgc);
          }
          dg.columns = columns;
        }
    ]]>
  </mx:Script>
  <fx:DataGrid  id="dg" dataProvider="{dp}"  editable="true"  height="100%" >
  </fx:DataGrid>
</mx:Application>
```

Listing 11.34 DataGridAutomationDemo.mxml

Please notice two arrays: *cols*, with metadata for DataGrid columns, and *dp*, with the dataProvider-to-be data. Both arrays get hard-coded inside the *onCreationComplete()* method, but you can easily imagine how they get loaded, say, from a database.

Right above the *onCreationComplete()* there are commented-out imports of the RadioButtonGroupHBox and the linkage variable declaration. These lines, if left to compile, could absolve us from turning the theriabook.swc into a self-initialized library. But, how can we know in advance which class definitions are required by the column's metadata if it gets loaded from the database? We can't and, again, we recommend making libraries self-sufficient as a "rule of thumb."

The last comment to the application concerns the way we've assigned DataGridColumn properties: we clearly sided out itemRenderer to make the corresponding UIClassFactory (had we wanted to, a similar route would have been taken for itemEditor):

```
var dgc:DataGridColumn=  new DataGridColumn();
for (var prop:String in cols[i]) {
    if (prop=="itemRenderer") {
      dgc.itemRenderer = new UIClassFactory(cols[i][prop]);
      dgc.rendererIsEditor=true;
    } else {
      dgc[prop] = cols[i][prop];
    }
}
```

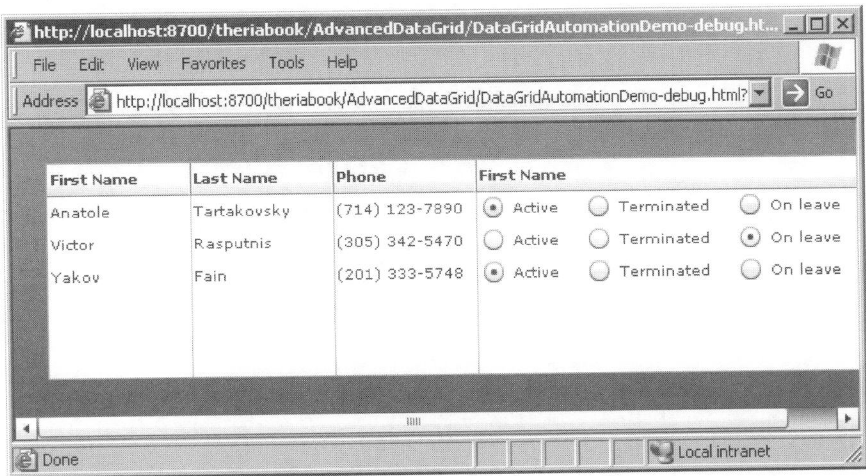

Figure 11.16 A snapshot of the DataGridAutomationDemo application

Figure 11.14 depicts the DataGridAutomation running[14]. We hope it sparks the reader's interest in dynamic applications. What could be next here? Well, the structure of the metadata *cols*, resembles one-to-one the MXML section of the DataGridColumn definitions. So, we could possibly store the MXML in the database and interpret it with ActionScript as E4X. Potentially, we could even allow interactive editing of such MXML, making it a self-modifying program. But this would take us way beyond the boundaries of this chapter[15].

Pivoted DataGrid or Property Bag

To complete our journey into DataGrid automation land we'll show how DataGrid can be applied in a very popular use case: a scrollable property bag. Let's look at Figure 11.15. How many DataGrids do you think are there? The answer is two. The left part of the screen is not a Form but a DataGrid. We took off the vertical grid lines, removed the headers, and had the alternate line colors match the background of the application, but underneath this veneer it's still a good old DataGrid.

```
<fx:DataGrid   id="dg" dataProvider="{dp}"  editable="true" height="100%"
   showHeaders="false"  alternatingItemColors="[#869CA7,#869CA7]"
   verticalGridLines="false"  variableRowHeight="true"  >
   . . .
</fx:DataGrid>
```

Both DataGrids share the dataProvider – the ArrayCollection based on an array of ColumnRecord types:

```
//ColumnRecord.as
package
{
   public class ColumnRecord
   {
      public  var columnLabel:String;
      public  var columnType:String;
      public  var columnValue:*;
      public  var expando:Object;

      public function ColumnRecord(l:String, t:String, v:*, x:Object=null) {
         columnLabel=l;
         columnType=t;
         columnValue=v;
         expando=x;
      }
   }
}
```

Listing 11.35 ColumnRecord.as, used by PropertyBagDemo

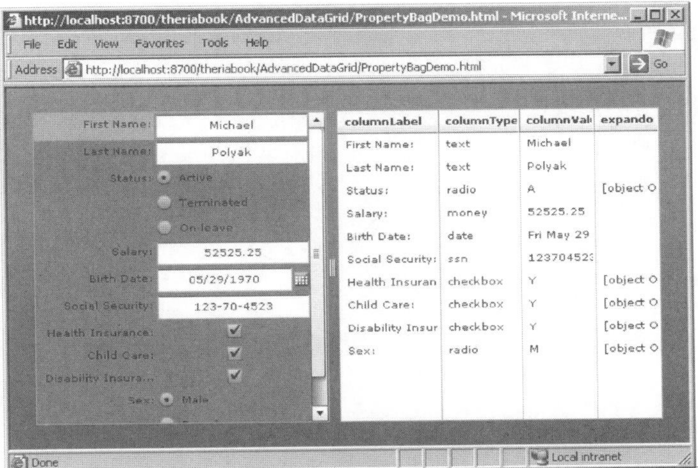

Figure 11.17 The PropertyBagDemo application

The complete code for the application – PropertyBagDemo – is in Listing 11.36:

```
<?xml version="1.0" encoding="utf-8"?>
<!-- PropertyBagDemo.mxml -->
<mx:Application xmlns:mx="http://www.adobe.com/2006/mxml" layout="vertical"
  xmlns:fx="http://www.theriabook.com/2006"  creationComplete="init()">
  <mx:Script>
    <![CDATA[
      import mx.collections.ArrayCollection;
      import mx.controls.dataGridClasses.DataGridColumn;
      import mx.controls.dataGridClasses.DataGridItemRenderer;
      import mx.controls.RadioButton;
      import mx.controls.RadioButtonGroup;
      import mx.controls.TextInput;
      import com.theriabook.controls.NumericInput;
      import com.theriabook.containers.RadioButtonGroupBox;
      import com.theriabook.controls.CheckBox;
      import com.theriabook.controls.DateField;
      import com.theriabook.controls.Label;
      import com.theriabook.controls.MaskedInput;
      import com.theriabook.util.UIClassFactory;

      [Bindable]
      private var dp:ArrayCollection;
      private function init() :void {
        dp= new ArrayCollection ([
```

```
        new ColumnRecord("First Name: ", "text", "Michael" ),
        new ColumnRecord("Last Name: ", "text", "Polyak" ),
        new ColumnRecord("Status: ", "radio", "A", {options:[
          {data:"A", label:"Active"},
          {data:"T", label:"Terminated"},
          {data:"L", label:"On leave"}
        ]} ),
        new ColumnRecord("Salary: ", "money", 52525.25 ),
        new ColumnRecord("Birth Date: ", "date", new Date(1970,4,29) ),
        new ColumnRecord("Social Security: ", "ssn", "123704523" ),
        new ColumnRecord("Health Insurance: ", "checkbox", "Y", {onValue:"Y",
offValue:"N"} ),
        new ColumnRecord("Child Care: ", "checkbox", "Y", {onValue:"Y",
offValue:"N"} ),
        new ColumnRecord("Disability Insurance: ", "checkbox", "Y", {onValue:"Y",
offValue:"N"} ),
        new ColumnRecord("Sex: ", "radio", "M", {options:[
          {data:"M", label:"Male"},
          {data:"F", label:"Female"}
        ]} )
      ]);
    }
    private function controlPicker(data:Object = null) :*{
      if (data == null) return new  Label();
      switch(data.columnType) {
      case "ssn":
         var mi:MaskedInput = new MaskedInput();
         mi.inputMask = "###-##-####";
        return mi;
      case "text":
        return new  TextInput();
      case "radio":
        var rbgb:RadioButtonGroupBox = new  RadioButtonGroupBox();
        rbgb.options = data.expando.options;

        return rbgb;
      case "checkbox":
        var cb:CheckBox = new CheckBox()
        cb.offValue = data.expando.offValue;
        cb.onValue = data.expando.onValue;
        return cb;
      case "money":
        return new NumericInput();
      case "date":
```

```
                var df:DateField = new   DateField();
                df.editable = true;
                return df;
             default:
                return new  DataGridItemRenderer();
             }
          }
       ]]>
    </mx:Script>
    <mx:HDividedBox width="100%" height="100%">
       <fx:DataGrid   id="dg" dataProvider="{dp}"  editable="true" height="100%"
          showHeaders="false"  alternatingItemColors="[#869CA7,#869CA7]"
          verticalGridLines="false"  variableRowHeight="true"  >
          <fx:columns>
             <mx:Array>
                <mx:DataGridColumn width="120"  dataField="columnLabel" headerText="Field"
textAlign="right"   editable="false"/>
                <fx:DataGridColumn width="150"   preventRendererReuse="true"
textAlign="center" dataField="columnValue"   headerText="Value"
                      wordWrap="true"  rendererIsEditor="true"
                      itemRenderer="{new UIClassFactory(function():* {return
controlPicker(dg.rendererData)})}"
                   />
             </mx:Array>
          </fx:columns>
       </fx:DataGrid>
       <mx:DataGrid editable="true" dataProvider="{dp}" height="100%">
       </mx:DataGrid>
    </mx:HDividedBox>
</mx:Application>
```

Listing 11.36 PropertyBagDemo.mxml

The point of interest in the PropertyBagDemo is the definition of the DataGridColumn:

```
<fx:DataGridColumn width="150"   preventRendererReuse="true"
  textAlign="center" dataField="columnValue"   headerText="Value"
         wordWrap="true"  rendererIsEditor="true"
         itemRenderer="{new UIClassFactory(function():* {return
           controlPicker(dg.rendererData)})}"
       />
```

Notice the property *preventRendererReuse*. It's a property that we are going to introduce to toggle certain default functionality of the DataGrid on and off. As mentioned earlier, the DataGrid maintains a pool of reusable renderers per column. This is done for performance reasons to avoid the proliferation of renderers for each row of the dataProviders collection. Since our use case – the property bag – doesn't assume many hundreds of lines, we've turned this functionality off, forcing the DataGrid to dynamically create a renderer for each line anew.

Next, notice how itemRenderer isn't assigned a ClassFactory, or even a String, but rather a *function* that calculates the generator for the UIClassFactory based on the data. At the end of the day we rely on the quite simple application function *controlPicker()*, but the ability to pass Function as an argument to the UIClassFactory is another implementation task for us to accomplish.

Last, we introduced an additional DataGrid property – *rendererData* – that captures the last item the IViewCursor passed through, assigning the data to the renderer.

Now let's look at the implementation details. We'll start with UIClassFactory. In the previous section we made the UIClassFactory constructor accept the String argument. Here we add a private variable f*actoryFunction* and modify the constructor again to take the Function in addition to the ClassFactory and String:

```
private var factoryFunction : Function = null;
. . . .
function UIClassFactory( cf: * ) {
    if ( cf is ClassFactory) {
      wrappedClassFactory = ClassFactory(cf);
   } else if (cf is String) {
      var className:String = String(cf);
      var clazz:Class = getDefinitionByName(className) as Class;
      wrappedClassFactory = new  ClassFactory(clazz);
   } else if (cf is Function) {
      factoryFunction = cf;
   } else {
      throw new Error("Invalid argument for UIClassFactory constructor");
   }
   if (wrappedClassFactory) {
      wrappedClassFactory = new ClassFactory(Object);
   }
}
```

Appropriate provisions have to be made in the *newInstance()* method. Namely, when it's time to manufacture an object via *factoryFunction* we invoke the function with the call operator() and then make sure the newly made object has the same properties as other instances do:

```
public function newInstance():* {
   var obj:*;
   if (factoryFunction!=null)    {
```

```
        obj = factoryFunction();
        // Now we have to do what regular ClassFactory does by itself
        if (properties != null)  {
             for (var p:String in properties) {
                obj[p] = properties[p];
        }
           }
     } else
         obj = wrappedClassFactory.newInstance();
     obj.addEventListener(FlexEvent.DATA_CHANGE, onDataChange);
     return obj;
  }
```

The final code of UIClassFactory is in Listing 11.37:

```
// UIClassFactory.as
package com.theriabook.util
{
   import mx.events.FlexEvent;
   import mx.controls.dataGridClasses.DataGridColumn;
   import mx.core.ClassFactory;
   import mx.core.IFactory;

   public class UIClassFactory implements IFactory
   {
      private var wrappedClassFactory : ClassFactory;
      private var factoryFunction : Function = null;

      public function set properties(v:Object):void {
         wrappedClassFactory.properties = v;
      }
      public function get properties():* {
         return wrappedClassFactory.properties ;
      }

      function UIClassFactory( cf: * ) {
          if ( cf is ClassFactory) {
            wrappedClassFactory = ClassFactory(cf);
         } else if (cf is String) {
            var className:String = String(cf);
            var clazz:Class = getDefinitionByName(className) as Class;
            wrappedClassFactory = new  ClassFactory(clazz);
         } else if (cf is Function) {
            factoryFunction = cf;
```

```
            } else {
               throw new Error("Invalid argument for UIClassFactory constructor");
            }
            if (wrappedClassFactory) {
               wrappedClassFactory = new ClassFactory(Object);
            }
         }

         public function newInstance():* {
            var obj:*;
            if (factoryFunction!=null)    {
               obj = factoryFunction();
               // Now we have to do what internal CF does itself
               if (properties != null)  {
                  for (var p:String in properties) {
                     obj[p] = properties[p];
                  }
                  }
            } else
                obj = wrappedClassFactory.newInstance();
            obj.addEventListener(FlexEvent.DATA_CHANGE, onDataChange);
            return obj;
         }

         private function onDataChange(event:FlexEvent):void{

            var renderer:Object = event.currentTarget;

            // In the default DataGridItemRenderer both data and listData are
[Bindable("dataChange")]
            // We want to skip assinments to listData
            if (renderer.data is mx.controls.dataGridClasses.DataGridColumn) return;

            // Act only on 'dynamic style' columns
            if (renderer.styleName && renderer.styleName.hasOwnProperty("runtimeStyles")) {
               var runtimeStyles:Object = renderer.styleName["runtimeStyles"];
               for (var style:String in runtimeStyles) {
                  if ( runtimeStyles[style] is Function ) {
                     var functionObject : Function = runtimeStyles[style];
                     renderer.setStyle(style, functionObject(renderer.data));
                  }
                  else
                     renderer.setStyle(style, runtimeStyles[style]);
               }
```

```
            renderer.invalidateDisplayList();
        }
      }
    }
  }
```

Listing 11.37 UIClassFactory.as, final version

Now let's look at the finalized code for our custom DataGridColumn, Listing 11.38. Notice the definition of the *preventRendererReuse* variable, which will be used a bit later by the DataGrid class. We also modified the itemRenderer setter slightly. Instead of:

```
super.itemRenderer = new UIClassFactory(val as ClassFactory);
```

we do

```
super.itemRenderer = val is UIClassFactory?val:new UIClassFactory(val);
```

to avoid wrapping on top of wrapping, when the passed value is already an UIClassFactory.

Here's the finalized DataGridColumn:

```
//DataGridColumn.as
package com.theriabook.controls.dataGridClasses{
   import com.theriabook.util.UIClassFactory;
   import mx.controls.dataGridClasses.DataGridColumn;
   import mx.core.ClassFactory;
   import mx.core.IFactory;

   public class DataGridColumn  extends mx.controls.dataGridClasses.DataGridColumn {
      public var runtimeStyles:Object = null;
      public var runtimeProperties:Object = null;
      public var preventRendererReuse :Boolean = false;

      public function set extendedProperties(val:Object) :void {
         if (itemRenderer)
            itemRenderer["properties"] = val;
      }
      public function  set formatString( fs :String ) : void{
         formatData = fs;
      }

      public function  set formatData( fd :Object ) : void{
         FormattingManager.setFormat(this, fd);
```

```
        EditingManager.setFormat(this, fd);
    }

    override public function set itemRenderer( val : IFactory ) : void {
//was       super.itemRenderer = new UIClassFactory(val as ClassFactory);
        super.itemRenderer = val is UIClassFactory?val:new UIClassFactory(val);
    }
  }
}
```

Listing 11.38 DataGridColumn.as, final version

The last class to be modified in this chapter is the DataGrid itself. We'll introduce a new read-only property, *rendererData*, which gives us the latest value that has been scanned over by the *iterator*, a protected member of the mx.controls.listClasses.ListBase:

```
public function get rendererData() : Object {
  var data:Object = null;
  if (iterator) {
    iterator.movePrevious();
    data = iterator.current;
    iterator.moveNext();
  }
  return data;
}
```

As you'll remember, we created a column-level property, *preventRendererReuse*, to help us turn the default renderer pooling on and off. Now, in the DataGrid, we override the *addToFreeItemRenderers()* method of DataGridBase class: we check that the column is our *custom* type and, if so, do not populate the corresponding freeItemRenderersTable (see Listing 11.39), thus leaving it empty at all times. As a reminder, our goal wasn't so much to prevent reuse of renderers as to enforce dynamic re-creation on them on every line, since in our use case every line may need a different control:

```
    override protected function addToFreeItemRenderers(item:IListItemRenderer):void
    {
      if (columnMap[item.name] &&
        columnMap[item.name] is com.theriabook.controls.dataGridClasses.DataGridColumn
&&
        columnMap[item.name].preventRendererReuse) {
          delete rowMap[item.name];

          if (columnMap[item.name]){
            var c:Object = columnMap[item.name];
            //Commented out 3 lines of original addToFreeItemRenderers
```

```
            //if (freeItemRenderersTable[c] == undefined)
            //    freeItemRenderersTable[c] = [];
            //freeItemRenderersTable[c].push(item);
            delete columnMap[item.name];
         }
         item.parent.removeChild(DisplayObject(item));
   } else
         super.addToFreeItemRenderers(item);
}
```

Listing 11.39 Overriding of DataGrid's addToFreeItemRenderers() method

The finalized code of our custom DataGrid is in Listing 11.40:

```
//com.theriabook.controls.DataGrid
package com.theriabook.controls {
   import mx.controls.DataGrid;

   public class DataGrid  extends mx.controls.DataGrid {

   import com.theriabook.controls.dataGridClasses.DataGridColumn;
   import com.theriabook.controls.Label;
   import com.theriabook.util.UIClassFactory;
   import flash.display.DisplayObject;
   import mx.controls.Alert;
   import mx.controls.listClasses.IListItemRenderer;
   import mx.core.ClassFactory;
   import mx.managers.CursorManager;
   import mx.rpc.AbstractOperation;
   import mx.rpc.events.*;
   import mx.rpc.remoting.mxml.RemoteObject;

   function DataGrid() {
      super();
      itemRenderer = new UIClassFactory(new ClassFactory(Label));
   }

   public function get rendererData() : Object {
      var data:Object = null;
      if (iterator) {
         iterator.movePrevious();
         data = iterator.current;
         iterator.moveNext();
      }
```

```
    return data;
  }

  override protected function addToFreeItemRenderers(item:IListItemRenderer):void
  {
    if (columnMap[item.name] &&
     columnMap[item.name] is com.theriabook.controls.dataGridClasses.DataGridColumn &&
       columnMap[item.name].preventRendererReuse) {
         delete rowMap[item.name];

         if (columnMap[item.name]){
           var c:Object = columnMap[item.name];
           delete columnMap[item.name];
         }
         item.parent.removeChild(DisplayObject(item));
    } else
         super.addToFreeItemRenderers(item);

  }

  public var destination:String=null, method : String = null;
  public var autoFill : Boolean = true;
  protected var ro:RemoteObject = null;

  public function fill(... args): void {
    if( ro==null ) {
      if( destination==null || destination.length==0 )
        throw new Error("No destination specified");
      if( method==null || method.length==0 )
        throw new Error("No retrieveMethod specified");

      ro = new RemoteObject(destination);
      ro.showBusyCursor = true;
      ro.concurrency    = "last";
      ro.addEventListener(ResultEvent.RESULT, ro_onResult);
      ro.addEventListener(FaultEvent.FAULT,   ro_onFault);
    }
    var operation:AbstractOperation = ro.getOperation(method);
    operation.arguments = args;
    operation.send();

  }
  private function ro_onFault(evt:FaultEvent):void {
      CursorManager.removeBusyCursor();
```

```
        Alert.show("Failed retrieving data: "+evt.message, "[DestinationAwareDataGrid]" +
id);
    }

    private function ro_onResult(evt:ResultEvent):void {
        CursorManager.removeBusyCursor();
        if (evt.result.length != 0)
            dataProvider = evt.result;
      }
    }
}
```

Listing 11.40 DataGrid.as, the final version

Summary

This chapter concentrates on the automation of DataGrid programming through what we call the data-driven approach. Along these lines we've extended the concept of destination-aware controls to the DataGrid, customized controls like CheckBox, created new ones like RadioButtonBox and NumericMask, and introduced computed styles and computed editors. The turnpoint techniques introduced in this chapter have been the custom DataGridColumn and UIClassFactory.

If you've made it this far, you'll probably change the way you've dealt with DataGrid. Most importantly, your work with DataGrid will become more productive and enjoyable.

Endnotes

1. As a reminder, all custom controls we hereafter add to theriabook.swc, extending the manifest and checking the appropriate checkboxes under project properties/Flex Library Build Path-/Classes.

2. We omitted replicating the DataGridColumn code here, but please count this as the second version.

3. The content of FormattingManager may be modified on a per-project basis. Alternatively, you can come up with a strategy that allows dynamic selection and loading the proper FormattingManager.

4. In fact, a quick peek in the generated folder can reveal that inline components references cause generation of three files.

5. The bigger underlying topic is the role of undefined in the data collection edited via the DataGrid. As a use case let's consider the DataGrid exposing combined data from two different arrays, which share all but a few attribites. The DataGrid will show missing attributes – undefined – as empty cells. Once you click on such a cell and leave it, DataGrid will attempt to dynamically create the property on the underlying ActionScript object – that alone would fail on the sealed object – and then assign null to it. That might

not be a desired behavior.

6. Theoretically, you could go as far as to start assigning item renderers even to the text fields. In that case there would be no need to declare DataGrid editable as long as your item renderers take care of changes in the underlying data collection.

7. We could have gone further and upgraded <fx:options> to <fx:dataProvider> like the ButtonBar and LinkBar controls.

8. You may want to compare this situation with the HBox use merely for centering the CheckBox, which we advocated against in the previous section. Back there, using an extra container was a luxury, expensive as luxury items often are. Here we face the alternative of reusing the container versus developing a new implementation for the whole set of interfaces: IFlexDisplayObject, ILayoutManagerClient, ISimpleStyleClient, IUIComponent.

9. We can hear the inquisitive reader wondering about the performance implications of this solution, since we've replaced the ultra-light UITextField with a heavier UIComponent-Label. The answer is that given that the DataGrid recycles item renderers – by maintaining a pool of them to cover the visible portion of the column – possible damage is limited by the number of visible rows. You may conduct your own stress tests, although ours haven't shown any noticeable difference.

10. As a reminder, to cancel the default event behavior with preventDefault() the event should be cancelable in the first place. You can check the latter via cancelable property of the event object.

11. That would be a good decision after all, since mx.validators.NumberValidator also looks for this file.

12. Again, all object instances manufactured by a ClassFactory share the same initial values of their properties: the ClassFactory method newInstance() doesn't take parameters and all future values of the properties are preset upfront as attributes of the dedicated properties object on the ClassFactory itself.

13. The method getDefinitionByName() will throw a ReferenceError in case the class image isn't found in the application or RSL SWFs.

14. When it comes to dynamically loaded libraries, during development we recommend Debug as…versus Run as…to avoid Alerts, one per loaded RSL that come during the application startup. Please be assured that these Alerts come only on developers' machines that have a debugging version of the Flash Player installed; your users are not going to see them.

15. This is exactly what is happening behind the scenes of FlexBI, a reporting/Business Intelligence product and solution created by FarataSystems. FlexBI allows business users to modify layout, sorting, grouping and formulas of their reports on the fly and persists these settings in the database; see http://www.myflex.org for more information.

CHAPTER

12

Logging and Debugging Flex and Java Applications

Logging and Debugging Flex and Java Applications

No, this chapter is not about how to use the Flex Builder debugger. In this chapter we'll discuss the techniques of logging and debugging mixed Flex/Java projects with or without Flex Builder.

Flex comes with a set of logging facilities and some prebuilt loggers. It also includes a blueprint of client logging and implementation utilizing tracing, which is built into the debug version of the Flash Player. We'll start by covering the standard Flex logging facilities and use cases.

Logging

Typically, you use logging to solve the cases that can not be solved using the debugger. For example, if you try to validate the code that implements drag-and-drop, the Flex debugger will keep interrupting the program event flow and make debugging impossible.

Another use case for logging would be the need to test code on the communication protocol level, i.e., you'd like to know what's happening under the hood during RPC and FDS calls. In the case of errors, developers often don't even have error handling code and can not easily identify the problem.

Also, there may be issues on the server, and they are not necessarily reported in full to the client.

Flex supports both client- and server-side logging, and it allows you to trace client/server messages both on the client and the server. Let's take closer look.

Configuring Web Application (Server) Logging

On the server side, you need logging in the following cases:

- You might want to log the methods being called as well as the data exchange between the client and server.
- You're using the server-side Flex compiler and need to log errors for the developers or support personnel.

Applications that use Flex Data Services can utilize an extensive set of prebuilt logging features in the communication and execution packages. You can trace the inner workings of the system classes by using a detailed hierarchy of loggers. It's a bit different from Java logging where you create loggers based on the package/class hierarchy. Adobe uses a logical hierarchy of the loggers that's not directly related to the package structure, but you can select the layer with a pattern or particular end node that will help in logging the types of operations you are interested in. The logical categories for logging are listed below:

```
Configuration,
DataService.[* |General | Hibernate | Transaction],
Endpoint.[* | AMF | HTTP | RTMP | Deserialization |General],
Message.*, Message.Command.[* | subscribe | unsubscribe | poll | poll_interval |
client_sync | server_ping | client_ping | cluster_request | login | logout],
Message.General
Message.Data.[* | create | fill get | update | delete | batched | multi_batch |
transacted | page | count | get_or_create | create_and_sequence | get_sequence_id
| association_add | association_remove | fillids | refresh_fill | update_collec-
tion],
Message.RPC , MessageSelector ,
Resource ,
Security
Service.[*  | Cluster | HTTP | Message Message.JMS | Remoting]
```

Brackets represent a choice of a pattern; for example, you can specify the logging category DataService.General. The code snippet below has some samples of using these patterns in the section filters.

You can log into a system console (Java's System.out.println) or use regular logging configured within the Web application servlet context (context.log) by specifying the *class* attribute of the target file in the configuration. Below are some typical settings in /WEB-INF/flex/services-config.xml:

```
<logging>
    <!-- You may also use class="flex.messaging.log.ServletLogTarget" -->
    <target class="flex.messaging.log.ConsoleTarget" level="Error">
        <properties>
            <prefix>[Flex] </prefix>
            <includeDate>false</includeDate>
            <includeTime>true</includeTime>
            <includeLevel>false</includeLevel>
            <includeCategory>true</includeCategory>
        </properties>
        <filters>
            <pattern>Endpoint.*</pattern>
            <pattern>Service.*</pattern>
```

```
                <pattern>Configuration</pattern>
            </filters>
        </target>
    </logging>
```

The logging-level attribute can have one of the following values: all, debug, info, warn, error, or none.

You can also control the output of the server-side MXML compiler. You can log messages sent to the Web application server's logging mechanism by using the log-compiler-errors property in the /WEB-INF/flex/flex-webtier-config.xml file. The Web application logger does not log runtime messages, but only logs server-side compiler messages.

To log compiler errors to a file or console, you must set the value of the tag <production-mode> to false and <log-compiler-errors> to true.

```
<production-mode>false</production-mode>
...
<debugging>
    <log-compiler-errors>true</log-compiler-errors>
</debugging>
```

```
The location,  number of backups and log file sizes are  specified in the logging
block of the flex-webtier-config.xml file.
```

```
 <logging>
    <level>info</level>
    <console><enable>true</enable></console>
    <file>
        <enable>true</enable><file-name>/WEB-INF/flex/logs/flex.log</file-name>
        <maximum-size>200KB</maximum-size>
        <maximum-backups>3</maximum-backups>
    </file>
</logging>
```

When switching to production mode, always switch the logging level to *info* or *errors* as logging tends to be expensive since it accesses the file system and performs data serialization. Don't forget that verification of the logging levels in the code is target-oriented versus a typical Java package/class granularity, and this presents additional performance challenges. The same applies to the logging organization on the client. We will illustrate this in detail in the next section.

Client-Side Logging

There are two commonly used techniques for logging the Flex programs. First, the debugging version of the player provides a built-in global function *trace()*. Its output goes to the file flashlog.txt that's located in the same folder as mm.cfg file. Please refer to the product documentation to find the name of the folder in your OS (see http://livedocs.macromedia.com/flex/2/docs/wwhelp/wwhimpl/common/html/wwhelp.htm?context=LiveDocs_Parts&file=00001528.html). If you don't file mm.cfg in this directory, create one with the following content:

ErrorReportingEnable=1
TraceOutputFileEnable=1
TraceOutputFileName=c:\flexLog.txt
MaxWarnings=50.

In mm.cfg, you must set TraceOutputFileEnable to 1, and you can set a custom value for TraceOutputFileName. More important, trace() automatically goes to the console panel of the Flex Builder. It's a good way to start tracing, similar to System.out.println in Java. The only difference is that the latter works in both debug and runtime modes, while the function trace() works only in the debug mode.

The second approach is to use the Logging API, which allows developers to control logging based on two parameters – levels and categories – in a more convenient way. It also allows developers to create and designate *targets* – classes responsible for writing the logging messages to some output media, which can be local resources, server logs/messaging, or even a remote workstation used for debugging/support.

Let's take a more detailed look at the Flex logging API.

Using the Logging API

To start logging messages you need two objects: a logger and a log target. The class mx.logging.Log out of the box provides basic logging functionality with a pre-built implementation of the logger interface ILogger with error(), info(), warn(), and debug() methods. Application developers just need to define the logger and call the messaging methods on its behalf:

```
<?xml version="1.0" encoding="utf-8"?>
<mx:Application xmlns:mx="http://www.adobe.com/2006/mxml" layout="vertical">
<mx:Script>
import mx.logging.Log;
import mx.logging.ILogger;
private static var logger:ILogger=Log.getLogger("MyCategory.subcotegory.morede-
tails");
</mx:Script>
<mx:Button label="LogDebug" click="logger.debug(' Debug Message Submitted')"/>
</mx:Application>
```

In the code snippet above, MyCategory is just a logical name that is not linked to any real class name. This code is quite generic and does not specify where to output messages. Flex includes two standard targets: TraceTarget and MiniDebugTarget. TraceTarget uses trace to write out the messages and requires you to use a debugging version of the player and to do the trace setup described earlier. MiniDebugTarget uses LocalConnection to transfer messages to other Flash/Flex applications. Here is a sample of setting TraceTarget with some formatting to include time and level along with the message:

```
<?xml version="1.0" encoding="utf-8"?>
<mx:Application xmlns:mx="http://www.adobe.com/2006/mxml" layout="vertical"
 creationComplete="setTarget()" >
<mx:Script>
   import mx.logging.targets.TraceTarget;
   import mx.logging.Log;
   import mx.logging.ILogger;
   private static var logger:ILogger = Log.getLogger("MyCategory");
   private function setTarget() : void {
      var target : TraceTarget  = new  TraceTarget();
      target.includeTime = target.includeLevel = true;
      Log.addTarget( target );
   };
</mx:Script>
<mx:Button label="LogDebug" click="logger.debug('Debug Message Submitted')"/>
</mx:Application>
```

While TraceTarget is good for some cases, it's important that a developer has the option to output to other services such as a server log, remote workstations, or OS consoles. Let's create other targets.

Server Log Target

Here we'll create a simple target to output messages to the server using Log4J, a popular Java tool. The Java portion implementing logging is very small:

```
package com.theriabook.logging;
import org.apache.log4j.Logger;
import org.apache.log4j.Level;

public class ServerFlexLogger{
static public void log(String levelStr, String message) {
      logger.log(Level.toLevel(levelStr), message);
   }

   static Logger logger;
   static  {
            logger = Logger.getLogger("FlexLogger");
      logger.setLevel(Level.ALL);
   }
}
```

Listing 12.1 ServerFlexLogger.java

Once compiled, deployed, and registered with Flex Remoting, the server-side Java class ServerFlexLogger is ready to be called from the client-side ActionScript class ServerTarget:

```
package com.theriabook.util.logging {
    import mx.logging.LogEvent;
   import mx.rpc.remoting.RemoteObject;
   import mx.rpc.events.FaultEvent;
   import mx.logging.AbstractTarget;
   import mx.logging.LogEventLevel;

   // Outputs logs to the web server.
   public class ServerTarget extends AbstractTarget  {
      private var _destination: String;
      private  var ro: RemoteObject;

      public function ServerTarget(destination: String) {
         super();
         this.destination=destination;
      }
      override public function logEvent(event:LogEvent):void
      {
         var message:String = event.message;
         var  category:String = ILogger(event.target).category;
         var level:int= event.level;
         if ((category == "mx.messaging.Producer" ||
             category == "mx.messaging.Channel" ||
             category.substr(0,7) == "mx.rpc." ) && level <  LogEventLevel.ERROR)
                return;
               ro.log(LogEvent.getLevelString(level),message);
      }

         public function get destination(): String {
         return _destination;
         }

         public function set destination(val: String): void {
      _destination=val;
      ro = new RemoteObject();
      ro.destination=_destination;
      ro.addEventListener(FaultEvent.FAULT,ro_onFault);
         }

         protected function ro_onFault(evt:FaultEvent):void {
```

```
            trace(evt.fault.faultString+" --- "+evt.message.destination);
        }
    }
}
```

Listing 12.2 ServerTarget.as

We had to limit the logging of the messages from the mx.messaging and mx.rpc packages to avoid getting into an endless loop. The reason is that mx.messaging and mx.rpc packages contain their own logging messages about internal communication processes that allow application developers to debug the flow of server communications, and these messages can pile up pretty fast.

Finally, let's create a Flex application that registers the ServerTarget:

```
<?xml version="1.0" encoding="utf-8"?>
<mx:Application xmlns:mx="http://www.adobe.com/2006/mxml" layout="vertical"
 creationComplete="setTarget()"  >
<mx:Script>
   import mx.logging.Log;
   import mx.logging.ILogger;
   private static var logger:ILogger = Log.getLogger("MyCategory");
   private function setTarget() : void {
      var target : ServerTarget  = new  ServerTarget("logging");
      Log.addTarget( target );
   };
</mx:Script>
<mx:Button label="LogDebug" click="logger.debug('Debug Message Submitted')"/>
</mx:Application>
```

Listing 12.3 A Sample Flex Application with Logging

Server Log Target Using Plain HTTP

Listing 12.4 will use a raw socket communication on the client and a servlet on the server to remove the trap of falling into the cyclic logging of mx.rpc and mx.messaging.

```
package {
   import mx.logging.AbstractTarget;
   import flash.net.URLRequest;
   import flash.net.sendToURL;
   import mx.logging.LogEvent;
   import mx.logging.ILogger;
   import flash.net.URLVariables;

   public class SocketTarget extends AbstractTarget  {
```

```
    public function SocketTarget(destination: String) {
       super();
       this.destination=destination;
    }

    private var _destination: String;
    private var req: URLRequest;

    override public function logEvent(event:LogEvent):void {
       var msg : URLVariables = new URLVariables();
       msg.level=LogEvent.getLevelString(event.level);
       msg.message=event.message;
       msg.category = ILogger (event.target).category;
           req.data= msg;
           sendToURL( req);
    }
     public function get destination(): String {
       return _destination;
       }
     public function set destination(val: String): void {
       _destination=val;
       req = new  URLRequest(val);
       req.method = «POST»;
    }
  }
}
```

Listing 12.4 SocketTarget.as

In the application object we need to instantiate SocketTarget with the URL "logging".

```
<?xml version="1.0" encoding="utf-8"?>
<mx:Application xmlns:mx="http://www.adobe.com/2006/mxml" layout="vertical"
 creationComplete="setTarget()"   >
<mx:Script>
   import mx.logging.Log;
   import mx.logging.ILogger;
   private static var logger:ILogger = Log.getLogger("MyCategory");
   private function setTarget() : void {
      var target : SocketTarget  = new  SocketTarget("logging");
      Log.addTarget( target );
   };
</mx:Script>
<mx:Button label="LogDebug" click="logger.debug('Debug Message Submitted')"/>
```

```
</mx:Application>
```

Listing 12.5 Logging with SocketTarget

We will also need to convert the Java class from Listing 12.1 into a servlet:

```
package com.theriabook.logging;
import org.apache.log4j.Logger;
import org.apache.log4j.Level;

import javax.servlet.http.HttpServlet;
import javax.servlet.http.HttpServletRequest;
import javax.servlet.http.HttpServletResponse;

public class FlexLoggerServlet extends HttpServlet {
   protected void doPost(final HttpServletRequest request, final HttpServletResponse re-
sponse)  {
      final String levelStr = request.getParameter("level");
      final String message = request.getParameter("message");
      logger.log(Level.toLevel(levelStr), message);
   }

   static Logger logger;
   static
   {
         logger = Logger.getLogger("MyFlexLogger");
      logger.setLevel(Level.ALL);
   }
}
```

Listing 12.6 FlexLoggerServlet.java

You might want to include the client's IP address and the user information in the log in order to distinguish the output from multiple clients.

The Client-Side Target

Finally, we'll create a target to communicate log messages to a standalone Flash application using the class LocalConnection. Listing 12.7 provides the implementation of the LocalConnectionTarget class:

```
package {
   import mx.logging.LogEvent;
   import mx.logging.AbstractTarget;
```

```
import mx.logging.Log;
import flash.events.StatusEvent;
import flash.net.LocalConnection;
import mx.controls.Alert;
import mx.logging.LogEventLevel;
   import mx.logging.ILogger;

public class LocalConnectionTarget extends AbstractTarget  {
   private var _destination: String;
   private var preventSubsequentErrors: Boolean = false;
   private var conn:LocalConnection;
   public function LocalConnectionTarget (destination: String) {
      super();
      this.destination=destination;
   }

   override public function logEvent(event:LogEvent):void {
      var level:String = LogEvent.getLevelString(event.level);
      var message:String = event.message;
      var category : String= ILogger (event.target).category;
      conn.send(destination, «lcHandler», message,category,level,new Date());
   }

         private function onStatus(event:StatusEvent):void {
            switch (event.level) {
                 case «error»:
                   if (!preventSubsequentErrors){
                       Alert.show(«LocalConnection.send() failed\n»+
                                                  «destination: «+destination);

                   }
               preventSubsequentErrors =true;
             }
      }
      public function get destination(): String {
      return _destination;
      }

      public function set destination(val: String): void {
      _destination=val;
      preventSubsequentErrors=false;
    conn = new LocalConnection();
    conn.addEventListener(StatusEvent.STATUS, onStatus);
      }
```

```
        public function releaseOutput ():void {

        }
    }
}
```

Listing 12.7 LocalConnectionTarget.as

The class LocalConnectionTarget can be used to deliver logging messages to any client application that either embeds a Flash component or implements LocalConnection with a native implementation using low-level programming languages. The code that comes with the book includes a free native implementation for the Windows platform of a console application that allows you to output the log to the display monitor, the files, and the Windows native debugging log (see http://www.microsoft.com/technet/sysinternals/Miscellaneous/DebugView.mspx).

Creating a Tracing Console for LocalConnection

To output the logging messages, we'll need some display panels. We've created a simple DataGrid-based component LogsPanel that will display new log messages upon their arrival (see Figure 12.1).

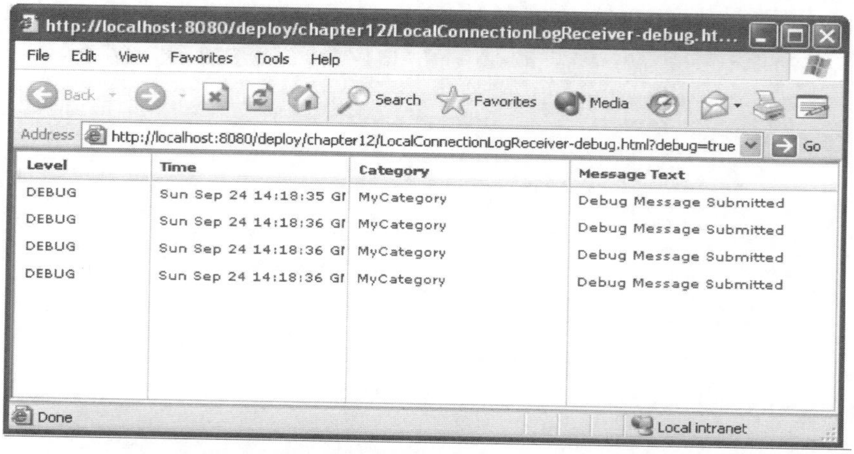

Figure 12.1 Displaying local log messages using logspanel

Listing 12.8 provides sample code to direct the log messages to our panel:

```
<?xml version="1.0" encoding="utf-8"?>
<mx:Application xmlns:mx="http://www.adobe.com/2006/mxml" layout="vertical"
  applicationComplete="onCreationComplete()" xmlns:fx=" *" >
```

```
<mx:Script>
<![CDATA[
  import flash.net.LocalConnection;
  import mx.controls.Alert;

  private var conn:LocalConnection  ;

  public function onCreationComplete(): void {
          conn = new LocalConnection();
          conn.client = this;
          conn.allowDomain('*');
     try {
       // _LocalPanelLog is the connection name used by both the calling program
       //  and connection console
       conn.connect("_LocalPanelLog");

        conn.addEventListener(AsyncErrorEvent.ASYNC_ERROR, showError);
     } catch (error:ArgumentError) {
Alert.show("Can't connect. The connection name is already being used by another SWF"  +
error.message);
          }
  }

  private function showError(evt: AsyncErrorEvent):void {Alert.show(evt.text )};
  public function lcHandler(message:String, category:String, level:String,
                                                    time:Date):void {

    log.addLog(message,category,level,time);
  }
]]>
</mx:Script>
<fx:LoggingGrid id="log" width="100%" height="100%"/>
</mx:Application>
```

Listing 12.8 A Sample Application that Logs to LogsPanel

The LoggingGrid component (see Listing 12.8) is inherited from the DataGrid:

```
<?xml version="1.0" encoding="utf-8"?>
<mx:DataGrid xmlns="*" xmlns:mx="http://www.adobe.com/2006/mxml"  dataProvid-
er="{[]}" >
  <mx:columns>
    <mx:DataGridColumn id="levelColumn" dataField="level" headerText="Level" />
    <mx:DataGridColumn dataField="date" headerText="Time" />
    <mx:DataGridColumn dataField="category" headerText="Category" />
```

```
      <mx:DataGridColumn dataField="message" headerText="Message Text" />
   </mx:columns>
   <mx:Script>
      <![CDATA[
       public function addLog(message:String, category:String, level:String,
date:Date):void {
        this.dataProvider.addItem({message:message,  category:category, level:level,
               date:date});
        }
      ]]>
   </mx:Script>
</mx:DataGrid>
```

The RIA Aspect of Flex Logging

The developer might want to change the settings of the logging while debugging the application. During the lifespan of the application, you may need to be able to redirect the log messages to a different target(s). Such functionality can be implemented by developing a LoggingManager, which is a UI component that allows interactive control levels, categories, and targets.

A logging manager should support the following functionality on the client side:

- Automatically discover and list logging categories, and allow change in the logging level for each category or package.
- List registered targets/destinations, and set a default logging level and other common parameters.
- Provide the client-side persistence of logging settings.

Figure 12.2 shows a sample logger panel that meets all of the above requirements.

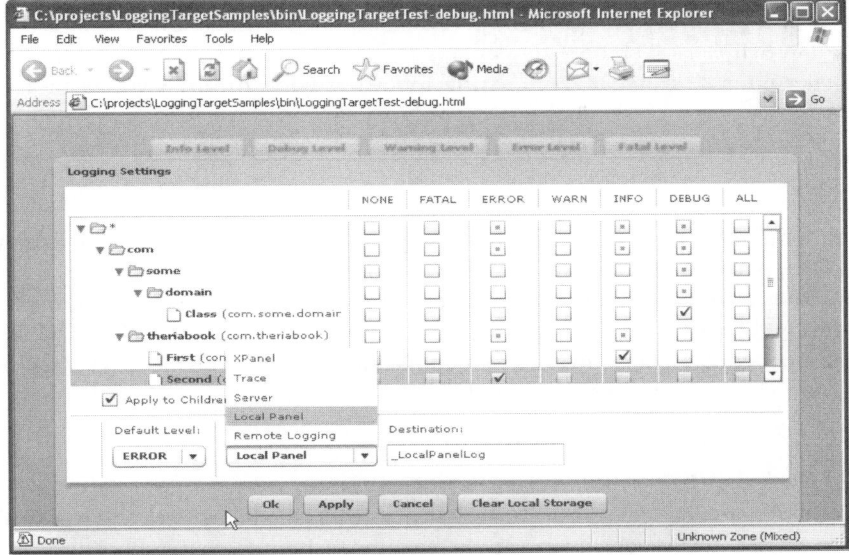

Figure 12.2 A sample logging manager

Figure 12.3 shows an extension to our LoggingGrid component that provides client-side filtering, searching, and other custom logging functions.

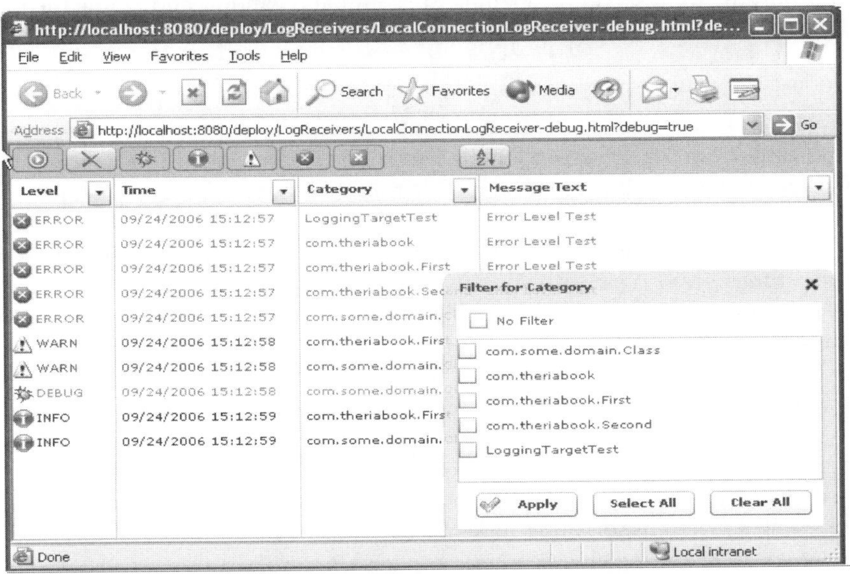

Figure 12.3 A sample extension of a LoggingGrid component

There are a number of freeware and commercial components that allow you to direct and show logging data in Eclipse, a Web browser, and a standalone application. You can find a free open source tracing console called XPanel at the following URL: http://www.faratasystems.com/?page_id=45.

Debugging

In this section we'll go through some scenarios of debugging Java server-side code deployed in one of the Java EE application servers. We'll discuss two modes:

- **Remote Debugging:** When you can connect to a running application server through a dedicated port and debug your Java application
- **Internal Debugging:** When you start your application server inside the Eclipse IDE and then debug the code according to set breakpoints

Remote Debugging

We'll illustrate remote debugging, assuming that you've installed Flex Data Services with the integrated JRun server, even though you can apply the same techniques with other Java EE application servers. The plan is to engage the Java Platform Debugger Architecture (JPDA), which allows you to debug applications (JRun in our case) running in a JVM. Besides running the server, JVM will also listen to a particular port, and the Flex application that we'd like to debug will attach to this port for debugging the server-side Java code.

Usually, you start the JRun server by opening the command window and typing the following (it's the Windows version):

```
C:\fds2\jrun4\bin>jrun -start default
```

JRun uses settings from the configuration file jvm.config located in the bin directory of JRun. Our goal is to start JRun in the debug mode, and to do this we'll modify the file jvm.config.

To load a reference implementation of JPDA, its manual (http://java.sun.com/j2se/1.5.0/docs/guide/jpda/conninv.html) suggests using the JVM option agentlib:jdwp for Java 5.0, and with the pre-5.0 JVM you should use –Xdebug to enable debugging and –Xrunjdwp. For example, the java.args line may look as follows:

```
java.args=-Xms32m -Xmx384m -Dsun.io.useCanonCaches=false  -Xdebug -Xrunjdwp:
transport=dt_socket,address=8000,server=y,suspend=n
```

In the line above, -Xrunjdwp:transport=dt_socket,address=8000,server=y,suspend=n instructs the JVM to use a socket as a transport and listen for a connection on port 8000. The server doesn't need to be suspended while waiting for a debugger application to connect.

After your JRun instance is started in the debug mode, you need to create the Eclipse debug configuration for this remote Java application. Select the menus Run | Debug and right-click the option Remote Java Application (see Figure 12.4).

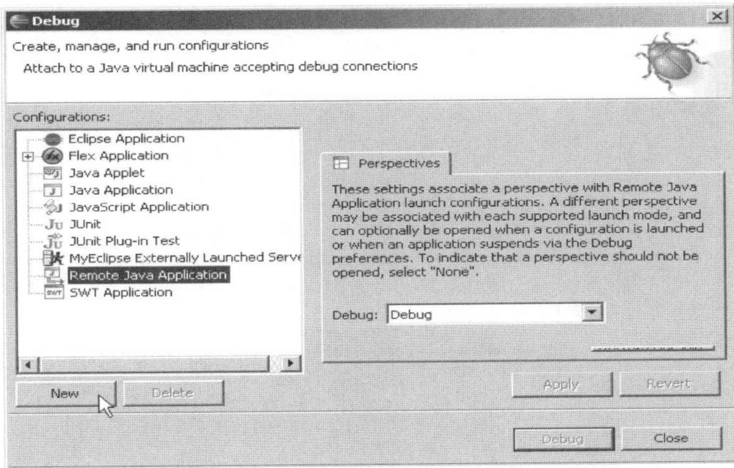

Figure 12.4 Creating the new debug configuration

In the popup window enter the name of the Eclipse Java project you'd like to debug that contains code deployed under JRun, as in Figure 12.5. Please note that the port number should match the one specified in JRun's file jvm.config. As an example, we are using the Java Order Entry application from Chapter 7.

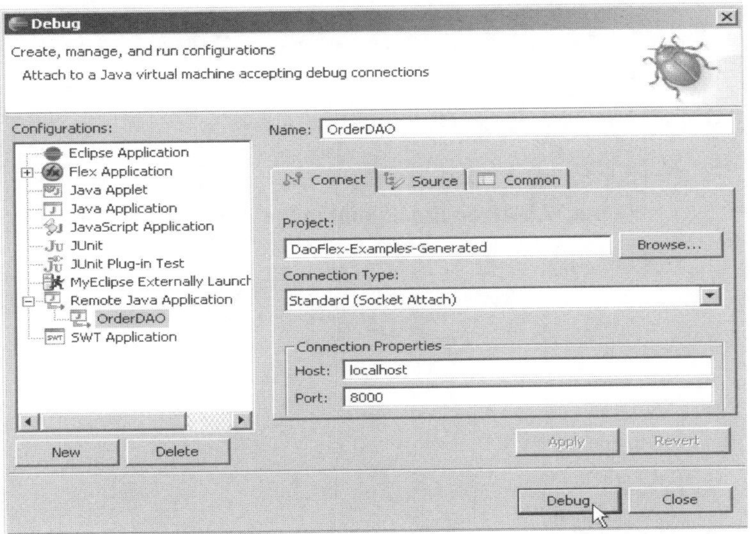

Figure 12.5 Mapping the Eclipse Java project to JVM's JPDA port

This is pretty much it. Now you can set your breakpoints in the Java source code, which has to correspond to the code deployed in JRun.

Figures 12.6 and 12.7 show the snapshots of the Eclipse debugger perspective, illustrating breakpoints in both ActionScript and Java source code.

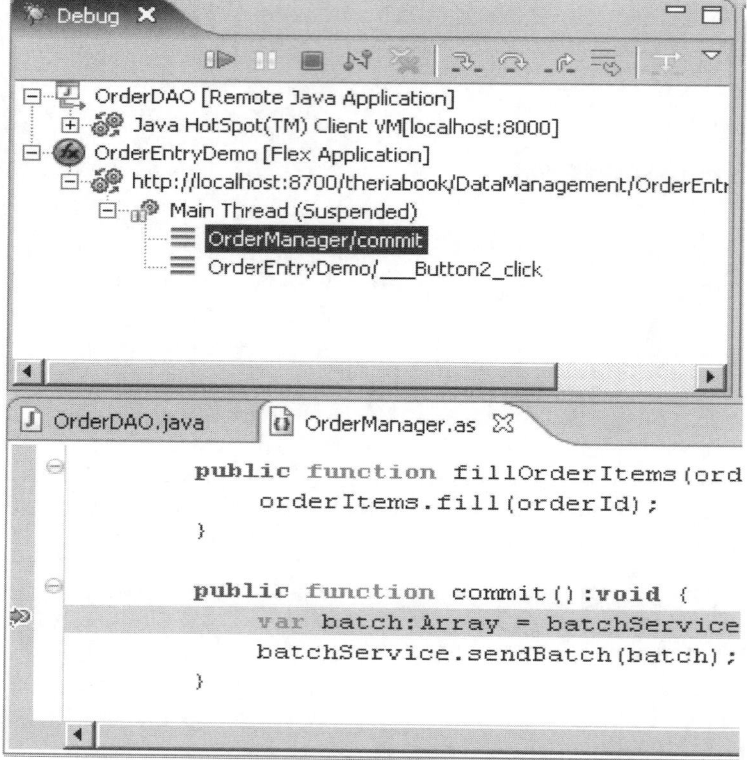

Figure 12.6 At the breakpoint in the ActionScript code

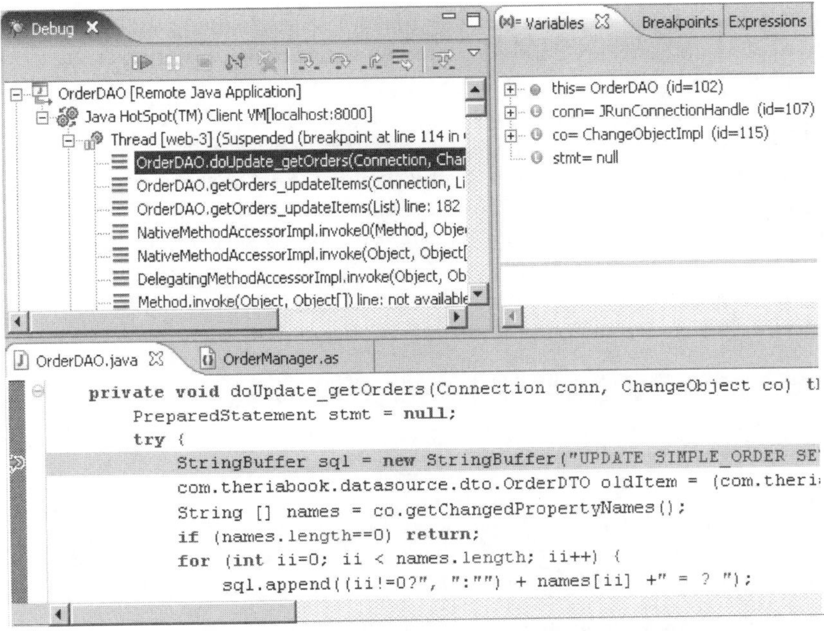

Figure 12.7 At the breakpoint in the Java code

Using Eclipse WTP for Debugging Java EE Servers

Our next goal is to learn how to start your Java EE application server inside Eclipse. This time we'll use Apache Tomcat 5.5, which is available for download at http://tomcat.apache.org/download-55.cgi.

If we are able to start the server inside Eclipse, the rest is easy: just set your breakpoints in the server-side Java code and off you go.

There could be different ways of doing this – in some cases it's just a matter of configuring your server's startup runtime in Eclipse. An alternative way is to find and install the Eclipse plugin for your Java EE server.

A more generic way is to use an open source Eclipse project called the Web Tools Platform (WTP), available from the Eclipse Foundation at the following Web site: http://www.eclipse.org/webtools/.

While Eclipse WTP adds various useful tools for the development of Java EE and Web applications, we'll just explore how it can help us debug Java code deployed in application servers.

The easiest way to get WTP is to download its all-in-one zip file from http://download.eclipse.org/webtools/downloads/. It contains the Eclipse IDE with all required plugins. At the time of this writing, WTP 1.5.x is meant for Eclipse 3.2 and WTP 1.0.x works with Eclipse 3.1.

To install this version of Eclipse with preconfigured WTP, simply unzip the contents of this file on your disk drive. Reinstall the Flex Builder plugin and start Eclipse, pointing at the workspace with your Flex projects.

Configuring Tomcat

After installing WTP, you'll find a new perspective called J2EE. Open it, go to the menu Windows | Preferences, and you'll find some new items there – one of which is called Server. Let's add Tomcat as our default server by selecting Installed Runtimes under the Server item. After pressing the button Add you'll see a popup window listing a number of Java EE servers such as WebLogic or JBoss. If you don't see the one you're looking for (i.e., IBM's WebSphere), click on the "Don't see your server listed? Click Here" link shown in Figure 12.8.

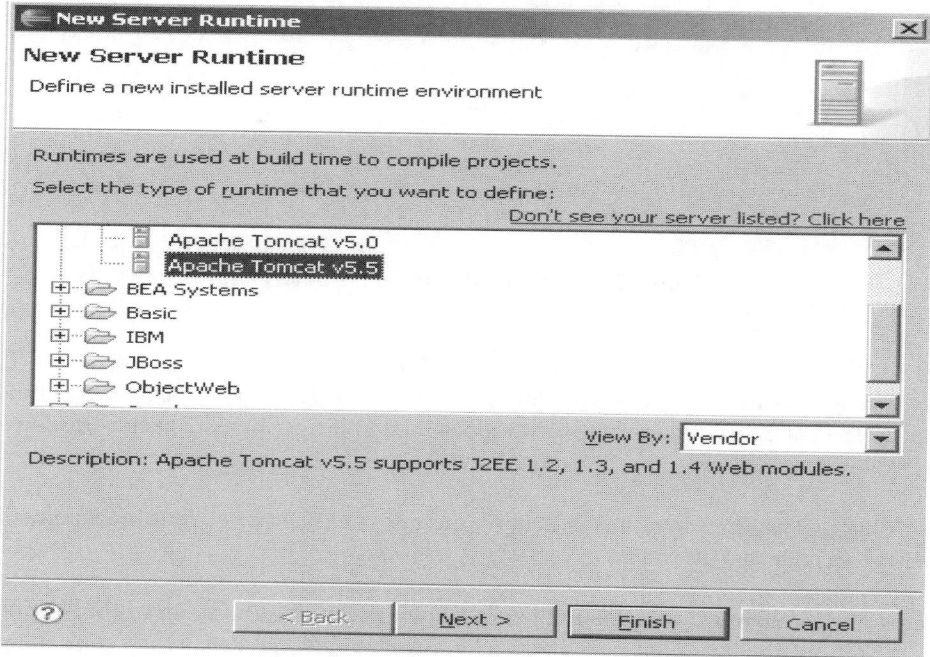

Figure 12.8 Adding a new server Eclipse

Select Apache Tomcat 5.5, and specify its installation directory as in Figure 12.9.

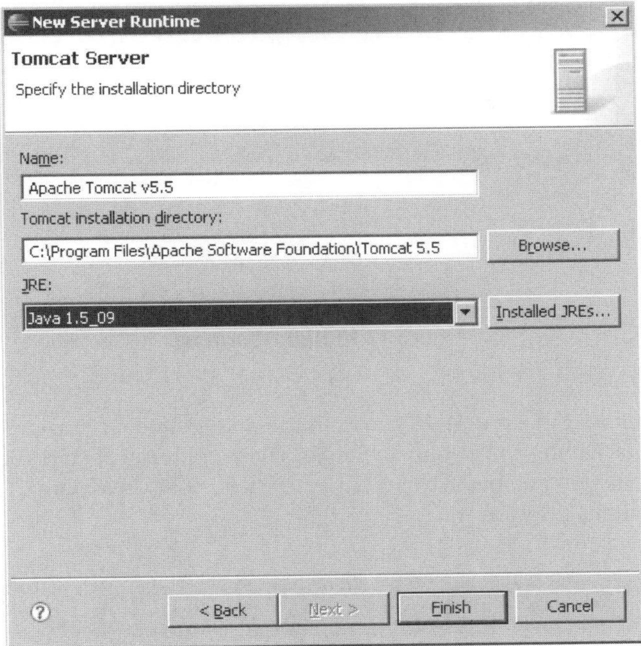

Figure 12.9 Configuring Tomcat as a default server

Create a new Dynamic Web project called Portfolio_Java, where Tomcat is a target (menus File | New Project | Web | Dynamic Web project).

We'll ask WTP to create a JavaServer Page file HelloWorld.jsp to pay respect to Hello World and ensure that we can debug any Java Web application. Just imagine that we are not debugging HelloWorld, but the Order Entry from Chapter 7, or TickerFeed.java from Chapter 5.

Open J2EE perspective and right-click on the WebContent under Portfolio_Java project. Select the menus New | JSP, enter the name HelloWorld, and the boilerplate JSP code will be created in a second.

We'll just add one line <% out.print("Hello World!!"); %> between the HTML <body> and </body> tags and set a breakpoint on this line (see Figure 12.10).

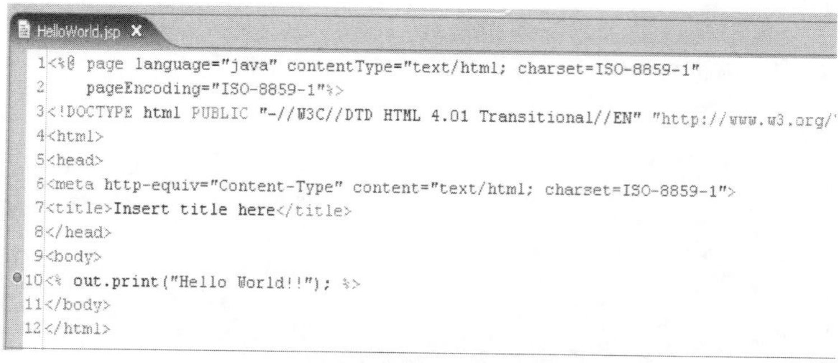

HelloWorld.jsp

```
<%@ page language="java" contentType="text/html; charset=ISO-8859-1"
    pageEncoding="ISO-8859-1"%>
<!DOCTYPE html PUBLIC "-//W3C//DTD HTML 4.01 Transitional//EN" "http://www.w3.org/'
<html>
<head>
<meta http-equiv="Content-Type" content="text/html; charset=ISO-8859-1">
<title>Insert title here</title>
</head>
<body>
<% out.print("Hello World!!"); %>
</body>
</html>
```

Figure 12.10 HelloWorld.jsp

Finally, let's start HelloWorld.jsp under Tomcat in the debug mode: right-click on HelloWorld.jsp and select the options Debug As | Debug on Server. These actions will start Tomcat inside Eclipse, and it'll open the debugger perspective as soon as it reaches our breakpoint. The screenshot from Figure 12.11 looks familiar, doesn't it?

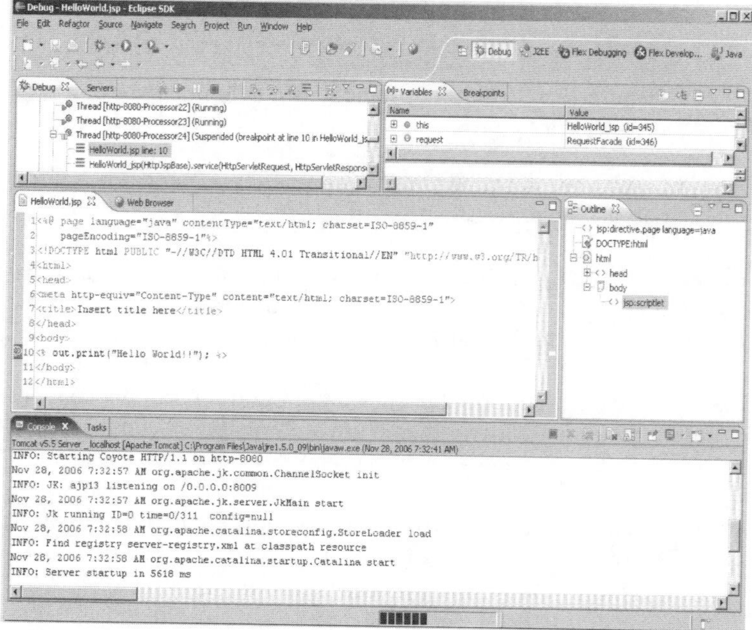

Figure 12.11 Debugging HelloWorld.jsp under the Tomcat server

If you just want to start the server without running any Web application, open the server's view in the J2EE perspective, right-click on the server, and press the Start button.

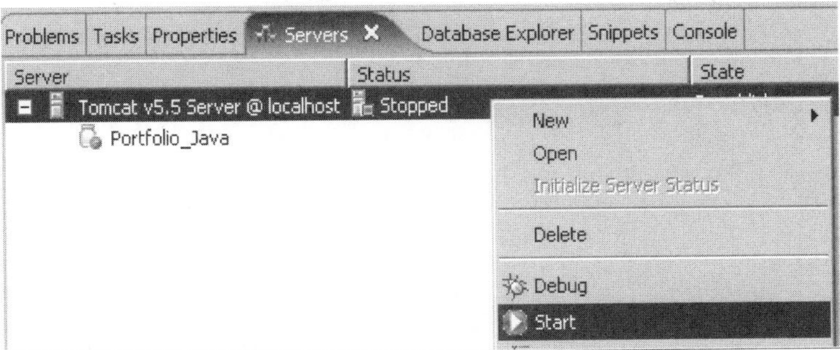

Figure 12.12 Starting the Java EE Server in Eclipse WTP

In this section we've been using Apache Tomcat, but the same debugging techniques work for other Java EE servers as well.

Deploying a Web Application Locally

Your choice of debugging techniques depends on the development environment your team works in. A typical project consists of Flex and Java portions, and the Web application is being built and deployed using a common build script (i.e., Ant build.xml). This build may produce just one .war file that is deployed in a Java EE application server. What if you are experiencing errors in your Flex portion that did not surface prior to the final Flex-Java Ant build?

In this case, install and run the Java application server on your development machine, unzip the .war file into a separate directory, and deploy it in the exploded form from this directory. Make sure that the Flex Builder compiler's options of your project include the option *services* pointing at the services-config.xml.

Note: This solution will work if your Flex Builder project type is Flex Data Services.

Summary

It's hard to overestimate the importance of debugging and logging in distributed Web applications.

In this chapter we've shown different tools and techniques that can help you to prevent or localize and fix development and production problems in Flex/Java applications.

CHAPTER
13

Building a SlideShow Application

By Ben Stucki

Building a SlideShow Application

In this chapter we'll be building a narrated slideshow application in Flex 2 that will use the popular Flickr (www.flickr.com) Web Services to retrieve the photos. Users will also be able to input a custom URL as the photo or audio location and have a few extra settings and image effects that can be applied at runtime. When users are done creating slideshows, the application will provide them with a URL that others can use to view the result.

This application may be handy for Flickr users who want to share their personal photos with friends and family in a slideshow format, but it could be used for a number of business purposes as well. For example, a realty company may want to display photos of a property narrated by the local realtor, or a car dealership may want to do the same for its cars. Some businesses may even use the application to give presentations similar to those Microsoft PowerPoint would provide.

No matter what the end result is, we want users to experience RIAs at their best. We'll make the application so that users spend no more time creating a slideshow than they would spend watching it. Hopefully, with correct planning, you'll spend no more time developing it than you would spend reading this chapter. Fortunately, Flex 2 makes both of these goals possible. Let's take a look at what we'll be building.

Application Overview

The application will have two primary states: *design* and *preview*. We'll start by developing a few components of the *preview* portion of the application. It will contain all the functionality needed to view and navigate a slideshow, including the timing control, audio playback, image effects processing, and a thumbnail preview of each image for navigation. The *design* state will let users explore photos from flickr.com, add and remove photos from the slideshow, include audio, and set the timing and effects for each photo (see Figure 13.1).

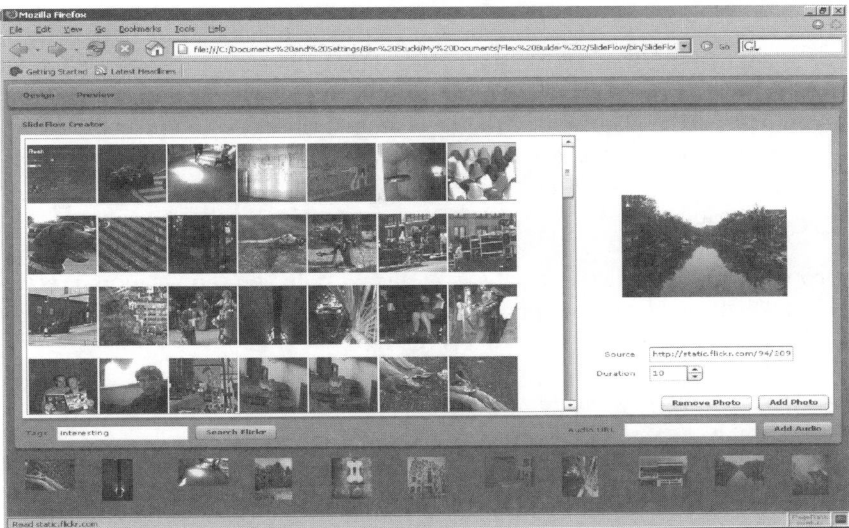

Figure 13.1 The application's design state

Like most RIAs, this application is going to include a number of custom components that are used together to create a unique experience. These components include the thumbnail scroller shown in Figure 13.1 as well as the SlideShow component that we'll be developing in a moment. We're also going to cover timer events, working with the HTTPService control and creating rich user interfaces with ActionScript 3. We've got a lot to go over, so let's get started by designing the SlideShow component.

Developing the SlideShow Component

The slideshow component encapsulates all the functionality needed to play and navigate a slideshow. Start by creating a new file named *SlideShow.mxml* in your component directory of choice. In this book we're keeping user interface components at the relative path com/theriabook/controls, so the relative path from the application to this MXML file would be com/theriabook/controls/SlideShow.mxml for me. In its simplest form the SlideShow component is just an Image inside a Canvas as shown in Listing 13.1.

```
<?xml version="1.0" encoding="utf-8"?>
<mx:Canvas xmlns:mx="http://www.adobe.com/2006/mxml"
horizontalScrollPolicy="off" verticalScrollPolicy="off" verticalCenter="0" background-
Color="#000000" borderColor="#ffffff" borderStyle="solid"
                                                        borderThickness="5">
   <mx:Image id="image" horizontalCenter="0" verticalCenter="0"/>
</mx:Canvas>
```

Listing 13.1 The first version of the SlideShow MXML component

Notice that I've set the horizontalScrollPolicy and verticalScrollPolicy attributes to *off* on the Canvas and have given the Image an ID of *image*. We're going to be adding some ActionScript to this component later, so it's important that we can modify the image through code without creating unnecessary scrollbars. I've also included some styling attributes with this component to make it look a little more SlideShow-like. These attributes are available because they are part of the Canvas component, which SlideShow is inheriting, but they can be overridden when the component is included in an application.

To test our component we'll have to create an application. In your application directory, create a new file named *SlideShowPlayer1.mxml*. Simply declare your component's namespace and use the filename as the MXML element as shown in Listing 13.2.

```
<?xml version="1.0" encoding="utf-8"?>
<mx:Application xmlns:mx="http://www.adobe.com/2006/mxml"
                    xmlns:lib="com.theriabook.controls.*" layout="absolute">
     <lib:SlideShow width="100%" height="100%" horizontalCenter="0" />
</mx:Application>
```

Listing 13.2 Including an MXML component in an application

Compile and run your application and you should see a large blank Canvas (see Figure 13.2) with the styling attributes you've set in the component.

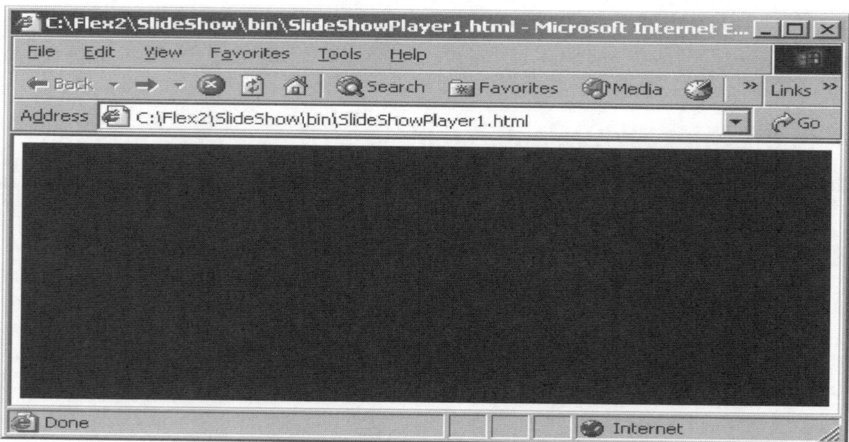

Figure 13.2 Running the SlideShow1.mxml

We're going to add some ActionScript to the application and SlideShow component in a while to get our images working, but first we need to take a look at how slideshow data is represented.

Loading SlideShow Data

For this application a slideshow is represented by any XML file with a root node of *slideshow* in which images are represented by a *photo* node and sound files by an *audio* node. Any child nodes of the root should include a *source* attribute (in which a URL with images and audio files is provided), and *photo* nodes should include a *duration* attribute (in which a time duration measured in seconds is provided). Images must be JPEG, PNG, GIF, or SWF files, and audio must be an MP3 file. Create a new XML file named *test.xml* in your application root and populate it with slideshow data such as the XML shown in Listing 13.3.

```
<?xml version="1.0" encoding="utf-8" ?>
<slideshow>
   <audio source="http://www.theriabook.com/narration.mp3" />
   <photo duration="10" source="http://www.theriabook.com/mary.jpg" />
   <photo duration="20" source="http://www.theriabook.com/lou.jpg" />
   <photo duration="20" source="http://www.theriabook.com/mom.jpg" />
</slideshow>
```

Listing 13.3 SlideShow XML data

In this chapter we're only displaying a single image at a time and using a single audio track to synch with the images, so the above XML format is all the data we need. However, this format could be expanded to create a more advanced application.

Now that we've got some slideshow data, let's pull it into the application using an HTTPService object in MXML and feed the result into our SlideShow component as shown in Listing 13.4.

```
<?xml version="1.0" encoding="utf-8"?>
<mx:Application xmlns:mx="http://www.adobe.com/2006/mxml" xmlns:lib="com.theriabook.
controls.*" layout="absolute" initialize="init();">
   <mx:Script>
      <![CDATA[
         import mx.rpc.events.ResultEvent;
         private function init():void {
            service.send();
         }
      ]]>
   </mx:Script>
   <mx:HTTPService id="service" url="test.xml" resultFormat="e4x" result="show.loadShow(
XML(event.result) );" />
   <lib:SlideShow id="show" width="100%" height="100%" horizontalCenter="0" />
</mx:Application>
```

Listing 13.4 SlideShowPlayer application

When our application starts, it will now make a request for *test.xml* and pass the result to the Slide-Show's *loadShow* method. However, the Slideshow component from Listing 13.1 doesn't have a *load-Show* method yet. We'll need to add this method by creating the public function in the component file. There, we can also add the preloading functionality required. We'll need to include a ProgressBar MXML component and some variables to hold the loaded content as shown in Listing 13.5.

```
<?xml version="1.0" encoding="utf-8"?>
<mx:Canvas xmlns:mx="http://www.adobe.com/2006/mxml"
      xmlns:lib="com.theriabook.controls.*" horizontalScrollPolicy="off"
                                                  verticalScrollPolicy="off">
   <mx:Script>
      <![CDATA[

   import mx.collections.ArrayCollection;
   import flash.display.Loader;

   [Bindable]
   private var _xml:XML;
   private var photos:ArrayCollection = new ArrayCollection();
   private var sound:Sound;
   private var iLoaded:uint = 1;
   private var isLoaded:Boolean = false;

   public function loadShow( xml:XML ):void {
      _xml = xml;
photos = new ArrayCollection();
   iLoaded = 1;
   isLoaded = false;
   photoIndex = 0;
   nextPhotoTime = 1;
   progress.visible = true;
      play.visible = false;
      for each(var photoNode:XML in _xml.photo) {
         var photo:Loader = new Loader();
         photo.load(new URLRequest(photoNode.@source));
         photo.contentLoaderInfo.addEventListener(ProgressEvent.PROGRESS,
                                                            onProgress);
         photo.contentLoaderInfo.addEventListener(Event.COMPLETE,
                                                            onComplete);
         photos.addItem(photo);
      }
      progress.label="Loading Image " + iLoaded +" of " + photos.length + ".";
      }
```

```
    private function onProgress( event:ProgressEvent ):void {
      var loaded:Number = 0;
      var total:Number = 0;
      if(iLoaded<photos.length) {
        for each(var item:Loader in photos) {
          loaded += item.contentLoaderInfo.bytesLoaded;
          total += item.contentLoaderInfo.bytesTotal;
        }
      } else {
        loaded = event.bytesLoaded;
        total = event.bytesTotal;
      }
        progress.setProgress(loaded,total);
    }

    private function onComplete( event:Event ):void {
      if(iLoaded<photos.length) {
        iLoaded++;
        progress.label="Loading Image " + iLoaded + "of" +
                                                  photos.length;
      } else if (sound==null && _xml.audio[0].@source!="") {
        sound = new Sound();
        sound.addEventListener(ProgressEvent.PROGRESS, onProgress);
        sound.addEventListener(Event.COMPLETE, onComplete);
        sound.load(new URLRequest(_xml.audio[0].@source));
        progress.label="Loading Audio";
      } else {
        progress.visible = false;
        play.visible = true;
        isLoaded = true;
      }
    }
    ]]>
  </mx:Script>
  <mx:LinkButton id="play" label="Play" horizontalCenter="0" verticalCenter="0"
visible="false" color="0xFFFFFF" />
  <mx:ProgressBar id="progress" mode="manual" width="60%" horizontalCenter="0" vertical-
Center="0" color="0xFFFFFF" />
  <mx:Image id="image" horizontalCenter="0" verticalCenter="0" />
```

Listing 13.5 The second version of the SlideShow component: SlideShow2.mxml

In the code above we've used ActionScript to create a Loader object for each image and store it in an ArrayCollection. *The loadShow* event kicks things off by loading the value of the *source* attribute for each *photo* node (represented by the variable *photoNode*) into a new *Loader* object and attaching event listeners for the *Progress* and *Complete* events. The *Progress* event will be broadcast each time a substantial chunk of data has been downloaded from the file. This lets us update the ProgressBar MXML component programmatically to display the download progress (provided by the Loader object) to the user. When the images are done loading, the *Complete* event triggers the *onComplete* method, which loads the audio file in the same manner. Preloading makes audio and image syncing much simpler.

Since we know the audio and images will begin playing at the same time and that new images will display immediately when requested, we can simply represent syncing by assigning a time duration to each photo. When all the audio and images are loaded, we display a LinkButton Play to the user. The play functionality isn't implemented yet, but you can compile and run this application to test the loading and progress bar functionality (see Figure 13.3).

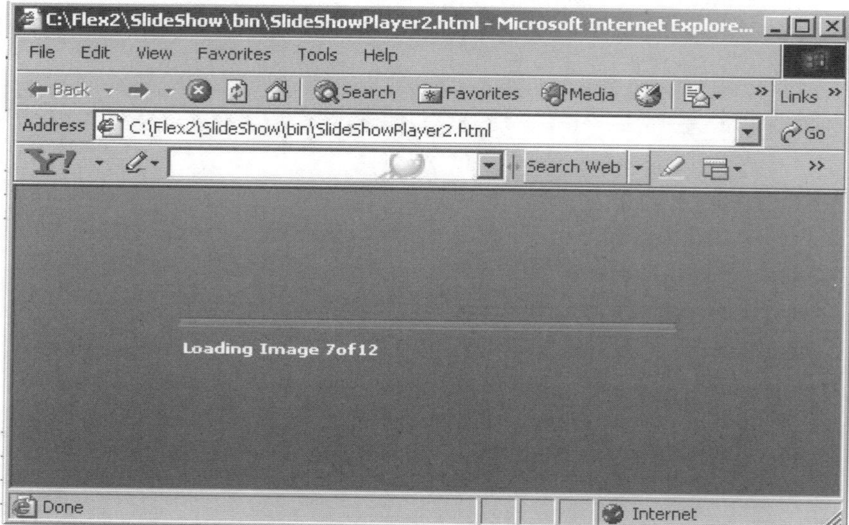

Figure 13.3 Running SlideShow2: loading images and the progress bar

Animating the SlideShow

To get our slideshow running, we need to create a Timer object that coordinates the images and has logic in its *Timer* event to change the image source at the specified time intervals. Let's create a method called *playShow* to initialize and start the timer and set the *play* button's click event to invoke this method.

```
private var timer:Timer = new Timer(1000,0);
private var photoIndex:int = 0;
private var nextPhotoTime:int = 1;
```

```
public function playShow():void {
   if(isLoaded) {
      play.visible = false;
      timer = new Timer(1000,0);
      timer.addEventListener( TimerEvent.TIMER, onTime );
      timer.start();
      if(sound!=null) {sound.play();}
   } else { loadShow( _xml ); }
}

private function onTime( event:TimerEvent ):void {
   if( event.currentTarget.currentCount == nextPhotoTime ) {
      if( photos.length > photoIndex ) {
         image.load(Loader(photos[photoIndex]).content);
                    // using e4x to access the photo duration attribute
         nextPhotoTime += int(_xml.photo[photoIndex].@duration);
         photoIndex++;
      } else {
         stopShow();
      }
   }
}

public function stopShow():void {
   timer.stop();
   timer.reset();
   image.source="";
   SoundMixer.stopAll();
   photoIndex = 0;
   nextPhotoTime = 1;
   play.visible = true;
}
```

Listing 13.6 SlideShow3: the timer and play functionality

We've also included a function to stop the slideshow and display the play button again once the slideshow has finished. This will let users replay the slideshow after their first viewing, but there's still no way to navigate from slide to slide while you're watching.

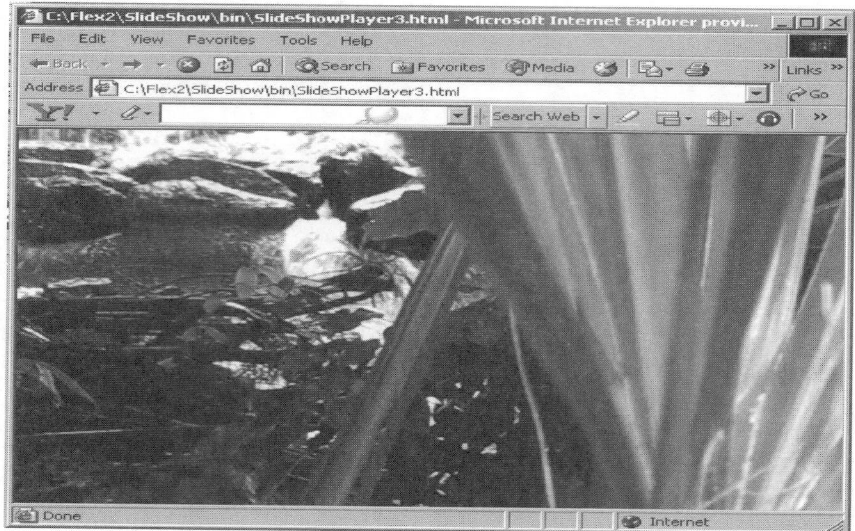

Figure 13.4 Running the SlideShowPlayer3.mxml

After adding the code from Listing 13.6 to the SlideShow component, we need to add the call to the playShow() method in the SlideShowPlayer.mxml. For example:

```
   <mx:HTTPService id="service" url="test.xml" resultFormat="e4x" result="show.
loadShow( XML(event.result) ); show.playShow();" />
```

Adding Interactive Thumbnail Navigation

So far we've encapsulated all the logic needed to preload and play a slideshow. Our component even displays graphical progress indicators and syncs images with audio, but users still can't view image thumbnails or skip ahead to the slide that interests them most. This is an especially important feature if this component is to be used for business. Let's create another MXML component in the com/theriabook/controls directory and put the code from Figure 13.7 inside. Alternately, you could download the Scroller component from the Flex 2 Exchange at http://www.adobe.com/exchange/.

```
<?xml version="1.0" encoding="utf-8"?>
<mx:Canvas xmlns:mx="http://www.adobe.com/2006/mxml"
                         horizontalScrollPolicy="off" initialize="init()">
   <mx:Metadata>
      [Event("change")]
   </mx:Metadata>
   <mx:Script>
      <![CDATA[
```

```
private const SENSITIVITY:Number = 15;
private const FRICTION:Number = 1.1;
private var momentum:Number = 0;
private var _dataProvider:Object = null;

public function set dataProvider(value:Object):void {
   _dataProvider = value;
   this.contents.removeAllChildren();
   for each (var obj:Object in _dataProvider) {
      var child:* = itemRenderer.newInstance();
      child.data = obj;
      child.addEventListener(MouseEvent.CLICK, onChange);
      this.contents.addChild(child);
   }
   if(this.contents.numChildren>0) {
      this.selectedItem = this.contents.getChildAt(0);
      this.selectedIndex = 0;
   }
}

public var itemRenderer:IFactory = null;
public var selectedItem:Object = null;
public var selectedIndex:int = -1;

private function init():void {
   this.addEventListener(Event.ENTER_FRAME, onEnterFrame);
}

private function onEnterFrame( e:Event ):void {
   if (this.mouseX >= 0 && this.mouseX <= this.width && this.mouseY >= 0 &&
                                                this.mouseY <= this.height) {
      momentum = ((this.mouseX - this.width/2)/SENSITIVITY)*-1;
   } else {
      momentum = momentum/FRICTION;
   }
   if((this.contents.x + momentum >= 0 && momentum > 0) ||
                                       this.contents.width < this.width ) {
      this.contents.x = 0;
      this.momentum = 0;
   }
   else if(this.contents.x + momentum <= this.width - this.contents.width &&
                                                momentum < 0) {
      this.contents.x = this.width - this.contents.width;
      this.momentum = 0;
```

```
        }
        else {
            this.contents.x += momentum;
        }
        this.filters = new Array(new BlurFilter(Math.abs(momentum)/2-3, 0));
    }

    private function onChange( event:MouseEvent ):void {
        this.selectedItem = event.currentTarget.data;
        this.selectedIndex =
                contents.getChildIndex(DisplayObject(event.currentTarget));
        this.dispatchEvent( new Event( "change", true ) );
    }

        ]]>
    </mx:Script>
    <mx:HBox id="contents" clipContent="true" width="100%" height="100%"
verticalAlign="middle" />
</mx:Canvas>
```

Listing 13.7 Scroller component code

In this code the display objects are kept in a single container named *contents* so that they can be moved in unison. The set method for the dataProvider is used to clear any existing children in the *contents* object and create a new instance of the *itemRenderer* for each item in the *dataProvider*. This way, the component provides similar functionality to Flex's TileList component, but it has a significantly different user interface. The Scroller tiles each generates an item in a horizontal row and provides automatic scrolling based on mouse position. This rich interactive behavior is defined inside the *onEnterFrame* method (which is a listener for the *ENTER_FRAME* event). It moves the contents' position based on the position of the mouse relative to the center (width/2) of the component. The constants *SENSITIVITY* and *FRICTION* can be used to adjust the component's mouse sensitivity and speed degradation, respectively. It's ideal for our thumbnail display since space is limited. We're going to add it to the SlideShow component and bind it to the data we already have by adding some MXML to our SlideShow component as shown in the code snippet in Listing 13.8 (see the complete code of the SlideShow in Listing 13.11).

```
<lib:Scroller dataProvider="{_xml.photo}"
 itemRenderer="com.theriabook.controls.SlideThumb"
 width="100%" height="85" bottom="0" />
```

Listing 13.8 Adding the Scroller component in MXML

Notice that in Listing 13.8 we've referenced *com.theriabook.controls.SlideThumb* as the item renderer. The SlideThumb component simply displays an Image inside a Canvas control. When the Scroller generates this component it will assign each instance the correct xml node using the *data* property. We just need to bind the Image's *source* attribute (see Listing 13.3) to *data.@source* as in Listing 13.9 and our custom itemRenderer will load the image as expected.

```
<?xml version="1.0"?>
<mx:Canvas xmlns:mx="http://www.adobe.com/2006/mxml" width="75" height="75"
buttonMode="true" horizontalScrollPolicy="off" verticalScrollPolicy="off" horizontalCen-
ter="0" verticalCenter="0" >
   <mx:Image id="image" source="{data.@source}" width="75" height="75" horizontalCen-
ter="0" verticalCenter="0" />
</mx:Canvas>
```

Listing 13.9 SlideThumb component

We can also include rich interactive behavior by adding code to the SlideThumb's enterFrame event, which measures the distance from this image to the mouse position and uses the value to set the image's width, height, and alpha transparency between a hard-coded maximum and minimum value. Insert the code from Listing 13.10 in the SlideThumb component and use the initialized event to invoke the init function. This will give each thumbnail fluid resizing behavior based on mouse position.

```
<mx:Script>
   <![CDATA[
   private function init():void {
      this.addEventListener(Event.ENTER_FRAME, onEnterFrame);
   }

   private function onEnterFrame( event:Event ):void {
     if (this.mouseY >= 0 && this.mouseY <= this.height) {
         this.image.width += (75 -
          Math.min(50,Math.abs(this.mouseX+this.width/2)/20) - this.image.width)/3;
         this.image.height += (75 -
         Math.min(50,Math.abs(this.mouseX+this.width/2)/20) - this.image.height)/3;
         this.alpha = (75 -
                          Math.min(50,Math.abs(this.mouseX+this.width/2)/20))/85;
    } else if(this.image.width > 51 || this.image.width < 49) {
         this.image.width += (50 - this.image.width)/3;
         this.image.height += (50 - this.image.height)/3;
    }
   }
   ]]>
</mx:Script>
```

Listing 13.10 Thumb component behavior code

All of the components for the SlideShowPlayer have been created, but we still need to add code that will navigate to any given slide based on the user's thumbnail selection.

Let's create a gotoSlide method in SlideShow.xml and use the Scroller's change event to pass it the correct slide index. The method will need to loop through each node in the XML and sum the duration where the slide at the given index begins. It will then reset the sound to play, starting at the correct time, and set the current photoIndex and nextPhotoTime to display the selected photo immediately. The full code for the SlideShow component is given in Listing 13.11.

```
<?xml version="1.0" encoding="utf-8"?>
<mx:Canvas xmlns:mx="http://www.adobe.com/2006/mxml" xmlns:lib="com.theriabook.
controls.*" horizontalScrollPolicy="off" verticalScrollPolicy="off" backgroundCol-
or="#000000" borderColor="#ffffff" borderStyle="solid" borderThickness="5">
    <mx:Script>
      <![CDATA[
        import mx.collections.ArrayCollection;
        import flash.display.Loader;

        [Bindable]
        private var _xml:XML;
        private var photos:ArrayCollection = new ArrayCollection();
        private var sound:Sound;
        private var iLoaded:uint = 1;
        private var isLoaded:Boolean = false;
        private var timer:Timer = new Timer(1000,0);
        private var photoIndex:int = 0;
        private var nextPhotoTime:int = 1;


        public function loadShow( xml:XML ):void {
          _xml = xml;
        photos = new ArrayCollection();
        iLoaded = 1;
        isLoaded = false;
        photoIndex = 0;
        nextPhotoTime = 1;
        progress.visible = true;
          play.visible = false;
          for each(var photoNode:XML in _xml.photo) {
            var photo:Loader = new Loader();
            photo.load(new URLRequest(photoNode.@source));
            photo.contentLoaderInfo.addEventListener(ProgressEvent.PROGRESS, on-
```

```
Progress);
            photo.contentLoaderInfo.addEventListener(Event.COMPLETE, onComplete);
            photos.addItem(photo);
         }
         progress.label="Loading Image "+iLoaded+" of "+photos.length+".";
      }

      public function playShow():void {
         if(isLoaded) {
            play.visible = false;
            timer = new Timer(1000,0);
            timer.addEventListener( TimerEvent.TIMER, onTime );
            timer.start();
            if(sound!=null) {sound.play();}
         } else { loadShow( _xml ); }
      }

      private function onProgress( event:ProgressEvent ):void {
         var loaded:Number = 0;
         var total:Number = 0;
         if(iLoaded<photos.length) {
            for each(var item:Loader in photos) {
               loaded += item.contentLoaderInfo.bytesLoaded;
               total += item.contentLoaderInfo.bytesTotal;
            }
         } else {
            loaded = event.bytesLoaded;
            total = event.bytesTotal;
         }
         progress.setProgress(loaded,total);
      }

      private function onComplete( event:Event ):void {
         if(iLoaded<photos.length) {
            iLoaded++;
            progress.label="Loading Image "+
                                 iLoaded+ " of " +photos.length;
         } else if (sound==null && _xml.audio[0].@source!="") {
            sound = new Sound();
            sound.addEventListener(ProgressEvent.PROGRESS,
                                                            onProgress);
            sound.addEventListener(Event.COMPLETE, onComplete);
            sound.load(new URLRequest(_xml.audio[0].@source));
            progress.label="Loading Audio";
```

```
            } else {
                progress.visible = false;
                play.visible = true;
                isLoaded = true;
            }
        }

        private function onTime( event:TimerEvent ):void {
            if( event.currentTarget.currentCount == nextPhotoTime ) {
              if( photos.length > photoIndex ) {
                            image.load(Loader(photos[photoIndex]).content);
                nextPhotoTime += int(_xml.photo[photoIndex].@duration);
                  photoIndex++;
              } else {
                  stopShow();
              }
            }
        }

        public function gotoSlide( index:int ):void {
            var gotoTime:uint = 0;
            for(var i:uint=0;i<=index;i++) {
                gotoTime += int(_xml.photo[i].@duration);
            }
            nextPhotoTime = timer.currentCount+1;
            photoIndex = index;
            SoundMixer.stopAll();
            if(sound!=null) { sound.play(gotoTime); }
            if(!timer.running) { timer.start(); }
        }

        public function stopShow():void {
            timer.stop();
            timer.reset();
            image.source="";
            SoundMixer.stopAll();
            photoIndex = 0;
            nextPhotoTime = 1;
            play.visible = true;
        }

    ]]>
</mx:Script>
```

```
    <mx:LinkButton id="play" label="Play" click="playShow();" horizontalCenter="0" verti-
calCenter="0" visible="false" color="0xFFFFFF" />

    <mx:ProgressBar id="progress" mode="manual" width="60%" horizontalCenter="0" vertical-
Center="0" color="0xFFFFFF" />

    <mx:Image id="image" horizontalCenter="0" verticalCenter="0" />

    <lib:Scroller id="scroller" dataProvider="{_xml.photo}" change="gotoSlide( event.
currentTarget.selectedIndex );" itemRenderer="com.theriabook.controls.SlideThumb"
width="100%" height="85" bottom="0" />
</mx:Canvas>
```

Listing 13.11 Slideshow component source code

Developing the SlideShow Player Application

To finish the SlideShowPlayer we started earlier, let's modify the code to accept a QueryString parameter named slideshow and pass its value to the HTTPService. To do this we'll reference the *Application.application.parameters* object, which contains any query string name-value pairs from the URL used to reference the SWF file (note that this may not be the URL used to reference the current Web page). Parameters can be specified directly in the URL as key-value pairs right after the question mark (http://myserver.com/myApp.swf?slideshow="someURLofYourShow") or embedded in the HTML wrapper using flashvars parameters.

In this example the query string parameter we're looking for is named *slideshow.* To specify your own slideshow, simply set *slideshow* equal to a URL that points to a valid slideshow XML file. The full code for the SlideshowPlayer is given in Listing 13.12, and the resulting SWF is shown in Figure 13.5.

```
<?xml version="1.0" encoding="utf-8"?>
<mx:Application xmlns:mx="http://www.adobe.com/2006/mxml" xmlns:lib="com.theriabook.
controls.*" layout="absolute" initialize="init();">
   <mx:Script>
      <![CDATA[
         import mx.rpc.events.ResultEvent;
         private function init():void {
            service.send();
         }
      ]]>
   </mx:Script>

   <mx:HTTPService id="service"
         url="{Application.application.parameters.slideshow}"
            resultFormat="e4x" result="show.loadShow( XML(event.result) );" />
```

```
    <lib:SlideShow id="show" width="100%" height="100%" horizontalCenter="0"
        verticalCenter="0" backgroundColor="#000000" borderColor="#ffffff"
                                    borderStyle="solid" borderThickness="5"/>
</mx:Application>
```

Listing 13.12 SlideshowPlayer application source

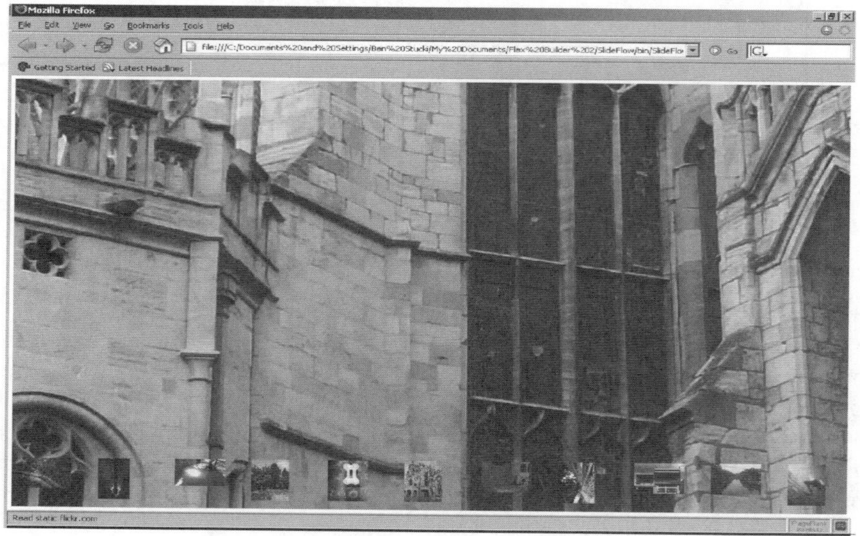

Figure 13.5 SlideshowPlayer application

Developing the SlideShow Creator

We've already got a great slideshow player, but we still have to create an application that lets users make their own slideshow. To get started, let's create a new MXML file named SlideShowCreator.mxml:

```
<?xml version="1.0" encoding="utf-8"?>
<mx:Application xmlns:mx="http://www.adobe.com/2006/mxml" xmlns:lib="com.theriabook.
controls.*" layout="absolute" >
    <mx:Panel layout="absolute" title="Slideshow Creator" id="creator" left="10"
                                        right="10" bottom="100" top="50">
        <mx:TileList id="gallery" right="310" bottom="5" top="5" left="5"/>
        <mx:ControlBar horizontalAlign="left" verticalAlign="middle">
            <mx:Label text="Tags"/>
            <mx:TextInput id="tags"/>
            <mx:Button label="Search Flickr" id="search"
                                            click="service.send();" />
```

```
    </mx:ControlBar>
  </mx:Panel>
</mx:Application>
```

Listing 13.13 A fragment of the SlideShowCreator.mxml

In Listing 13.13, we've created a Panel area to search and select images based on a given tag. It includes a TileList to hold the images and a ControlBar with text input for search terms. Now we need a method for retrieving images based on the user input given. The variable service (see Listing 13.14) represents a Web Service of the popular Web portal flickr.com that lets people store and share their photos.

Integrating with Flickr Web Services

Flickr provides documentation on how to connect to its services, and many third-party products use them (see http://www.flickr.com/services/). There's an API at http://www.flickr.com/services/api and its manual says that we can use query strings to pass our search text to a specific URL. It will then return an XML response containing the data we need to reference a given image. It will also let us know that we can use the images in Flex because flickr.com has put a cross-domain XML file in the appropriate domain. This file is required to allow any Flash-based application to access images outside the Web domain in which it runs. Based on that documentation, we can define and use an HTTPService control that includes the dynamic user input from the TextInput control in its URL as shown in Listing 13.14

```
<mx:HTTPService id="service" url="http://www.flickr.com/services/rest/?method=flickr.pho-
tos.search&amp;api_key=
                                        your_api_key&amp;text={tags.text}" />
```

Listing 13.14 Defining flickr HTTPService with a text parameter

Note that you'll need to replace the term *your_api_key* with your own API key obtained from Flickr. You can request one from the Flickr API site I mentioned earlier.

When a request with this URL is sent to Flickr, we can expect an XML file in return. A sample response is shown in Listing 13.15.

```
<?xml version="1.0" encoding="utf-8" ?>
<rsp stat="ok">
<photos page="1" pages="1483" perpage="100" total="148239">
   <photo id="209424451" owner="83276940@N00" secret="0193620991" server="62"
title="Eastern Pondhawk" ispublic="1" isfriend="0" isfamily="0" />
   <photo id="209413116" owner="35237092727@N01" secret="0e09c465f9" server="81"
title="Inspiration: Refresh Jacksonville" ispublic="1" isfriend="0" isfamily="0" />
   <photo id="209406820" owner="12915821@N00" secret="515b9f22c1" server="63" title="HMS
```

```
Belfast  - Engine Room" ispublic="1" isfriend="0" isfamily="0" />
   <photo id="209395531" owner="64362703@N00" secret="cd71e12304" server="70"
title="Jenson Button" ispublic="1" isfriend="0" isfamily="0" />
</photos>
</rsp>
```

Listing 13.15 Flickr Web Service response

We'll need to create an itemRenderer for the TileList that uses the XML data received from Flickr to retrieve and display images. Let's create a new MXML component named FlickrThumb:

```
<?xml version="1.0" encoding="utf-8"?>
<mx:VBox xmlns:mx="http://www.adobe.com/2006/mxml" width="75" height="75"
buttonMode="true" horizontalScrollPolicy="off" verticalScrollPolicy="off" horizontalCen-
ter="0" verticalCenter="0">
   <mx:Image
      id="image"
      width="75" height="75"
      source="http://static.flickr.com/{data.server}/{data.id}_{data.secret}_s.jpg"
      toolTip="{data.title}"
      verticalCenter="0"
      completeEffect="Fade"
   />
</mx:VBox>
```

Listing 13.16 FlickrThumb.mxml

The string concatenation used is based on Flickr's documentation at http://www.flickr.com/services/api/misc.urls.html. It shows that we can expect to load an image that is 75 pixels in width and 75 pixels in height using the constructed URL. You can find the attributes server, ID, and secret in Listing 13.15.

Now that all the necessary components are in place we can bind the appropriate HTTPService result to the TileList in our SlideShowCreator application by setting its dataProvider property to "{service.lastResult.rsp.photos.photo}".

The "rsp.photos.photo" portion of this code is referencing the actual XML response from Flickr. Let's also set the itemRenderer as FlickrThumb and the search button's click event to invoke the HTTPService object's send method. Run the SlideSlowCreator application to test our Flickr integration and search through images to your heart's content. The progam will output the screen (without photos) as in Figure 13.6.

Editing SlideShow Data

We've finally got lots of Flickr images to look at, but users still can't do anything with them. We need to create an XML object to hold our slideshow data as we manipulate it and a second one to hold the currently selected photo data. Then we can create methods to select, add, and remove slides based on their URL as shown in Listing 13.17:

```
<mx:Script>
      <![CDATA[
         [Bindable]
         public var xml:XML = <slideshow><audio source="" /></slideshow>;
         [Bindable]
         public var selected:XML = <slideshow><photo duration="" source=""/>
               </slideshow>;

         private function selectSlide( source:String, duration:uint ):void {
            var slide:XML = <slideshow><photo duration="" source=""/>
                     </slideshow>;
            slide.photo.@source = source;
            slide.photo.@duration = duration;
            selected = slide;
            imgDuration.value = duration;
         }

         private function addSelectedSlide():void {
            selected.photo.@source = image.source;
            selected.photo.@duration = imgDuration.value
            xml.appendChild( selected.photo );
         }

         private function removeSelectedSlide():void {
            xml.photo = xml.photo.(@source!=selected.photo.@source);
         }

      ]]>
   </mx:Script>
```

Listing 13.17 Manipulating XML data in ActionScript

Once again, we've used E4X in this code to store and manipulate XML data. If this was a larger or more complex application it might have been necessary to create business objects instead, but since the slideshow data is ultimately represented as XML, this may be a better option.

Now we've got all the methods needed to create a slideshow. We just need to fill in some of the user interface required. Inside the Panel we'll create a VBox containing an Image control and a Form with input for the photo source and duration. This should include a TextInput control called *imgSource* and a NumericStepper control named *imgDuration*. We can bind the Image control to "selected.photo.@source" to be sure it always shows the selected image. We've already referenced the NumericStepper *imgDuration* (just a text field with up and down arrows) in the code above so that it updates correctly. We'll also need to invoke the selectSlide method inside of the TileList's change event and the addSelectedSlide and removeSelectedSlide methods inside of button click events as shown in Listing 13.18.

```
<mx:Panel layout="absolute" title="SlideShow Creator" id="creator" left="10" right="10"
bottom="100" top="50">
      <mx:TileList id="gallery" change="selectSlide('http://static.flickr.com/' + event.
currentTarget.selectedItem.server + '/' + event.currentTarget.selectedItem.id + '_' +
event.currentTarget.selectedItem.secret + '_m.jpg', 10);" dataProvider="{service.las-
tResult.rsp.photos.photo}" itemRenderer="FlickrThumb"  right="310" bottom="5" top="5"
left="5"/>
      <mx:VBox top="5" width="300" bottom="5" horizontalAlign="center"
                                        verticalAlign="bottom" right="5">
         <mx:Image id="image" source="{selected.photo.@source}" width="200"
                                                      height="200"/>
         <mx:Form width="100%">
            <mx:FormItem label="Source" horizontalAlign="left">
               <mx:TextInput id="imgSource"
                        text="{selected.photo.@source}" width="175"/>
            </mx:FormItem>
            <mx:FormItem label="Duration">
               <mx:NumericStepper id="imgDuration" value="10"
                                        minimum="1" maximum="300" />
            </mx:FormItem>
         </mx:Form>
         <mx:HBox width="100%" horizontalAlign="right">
            <mx:Button label="Remove Photo"
                                        click="removeSelectedSlide();" />
            <mx:Button label="Add Photo" click="addSelectedSlide();" />
         </mx:HBox>
      </mx:VBox>
      <mx:ControlBar horizontalAlign="left" verticalAlign="middle">
         <mx:Label text="Tags"/>
         <mx:TextInput id="tags"/>
         <mx:Button label="Search" id="search" click="service.send();" />
      </mx:ControlBar>
   </mx:Panel>
```

Listing 13.18 Panel with Image selection and control

Now that we've got some of the interface in place, users can add and remove photos to and from the slideshow XML object, but there's still no feedback to show users the current list of slides. Fortunately, we've already created a Scroller component and Thumb component that can be reused and bound to the slideshow XML. Simply add the Scroller component we created earlier underneath the Panel and bind it to the XML object as shown in Listing 13.19.

```
<lib:Scroller id="scroller" dataProvider="{xml.photo}" change="selectSlide( event.curren
tTarget.selectedItem.@source );" itemRenderer="Thumb" bottom="10" left="10" right="10"
height="85"/>
```

Listing 13.19 Adding the Scroller component

Notice that we've also set the Scroller's *change* event to invoke the *selectSlide* method. This is the only interactivity we need to define. Flex's rich data binding will take care of updating the list when items are added or removed. Run your application and be sure that everything is in working order. You should be able to browse photos from Flickr, select photos to preview, adjust settings, and add photos to the slideshow list. You should also be able to select photos from the slideshow list and remove them. The last thing we need to include is the capability to add audio from a URL. Insert the code from Listing 13.20 into the ControlBar component already in the application.

```
<mx:HBox width="100%" horizontalAlign="right" verticalAlign="middle">
   <mx:Label text="Audio"/>
   <mx:TextInput id="soundURL"/>
   <mx:Button label="Add Sound" click="xml.audio.@source = soundURL.text;" />
</mx:HBox>
```

Listing 13.20 HTTPService

In Listing 13.20 we've provided a TextInput control for the user to enter a URL and a button whose click event sets the appropriate value in our slideshow XML. Also note that we have surrounded these input fields with a VBox container that has a horizontalAlign value of *right.* This is provided so that the controls align themselves on the opposite side of the Flickr search controls.

For example, enter New York in the Tags text field and press the button Search Flickr. The SlideShowCreator will display the thumbs with the images of the photos of New York. Select the image that you'd like to include in your slideshow, and you'll see the URL of the source file. Enter required duration. Press the button Add Photo and repeat this procedure for other photos.

Now that we've developed a way for users to create a slideshow, let's include a way for them to preview it in the SlideShowCreator application.

Figure 13.6 The SlideShowCreator window: Design mode

Developing the SlideShow Preview

To preview slideshows, we can simply reuse our SlideShow component. We'll need to create a new view state and include a way for users to navigate between both view states in the application. To create a new view state we can use the MXML State control as shown in Listing 13.21.

```
<mx:states>
   <mx:State name="preview" enterState="preview.loadShow( xml );"
                                                  exitState="preview.stopShow();">
      <mx:SetProperty target="{creator}" name="visible" value="false"/>
      <mx:SetProperty target="{scroller}" name="visible" value="false"/>
      <mx:AddChild>
         <lib:SlideShow id="preview" bottom="10" left="10" right="10" top="50" />
      </mx:AddChild>
   </mx:State>
</mx:states>
```

Listing 13.21 State control

In this section of the code we've defined a new state named preview. In the *preview* state we're setting the Panel and Scroller controls to be hidden and creating a new SlideShow component on stage. We've also set the enterState and exitState events to play and stop the slideshow, respectively. Now all we need to do is provide the user with a way to navigate to the appropriate application state. We've left some room at the top of our application for an ApplicationControlBar and we're going to use it to provide links to our two application states as shown in Listing 13.22.

```
<mx:ApplicationControlBar top="5" left="5" right="5">
   <mx:LinkButton label="Design" click="currentState='';" />
   <mx:LinkButton label="Preview" click="currentState='preview';" />
</mx:ApplicationControlBar>
```

Listing 13.22 State control

In the click event of the LinkButton for our Design view we've set the application view state back to the default view by assigning currentState equal to a blank string. Run the application to create a new slideshow and preview it using our SlideShow component. If you have any trouble running your application, reference the full SlideShowCreator.mxml source shown in Listing 13.23.

```
<?xml version="1.0" encoding="utf-8"?>
<mx:Application xmlns:mx="http://www.adobe.com/2006/mxml" xmlns:lib="com.theriabook.
controls.*" xmlns="*" layout="absolute" >
   <mx:states>
      <mx:State name="preview" enterState="preview.loadShow( xml );"
                                               exitState="preview.stopShow();">
         <mx:SetProperty target="{creator}" name="visible" value="false"/>
         <mx:SetProperty target="{scroller}" name="visible" value="false"/>
         <mx:AddChild>
            <SlideShow id="preview" bottom="10" left="10" right="10" top="50" />
         </mx:AddChild>
      </mx:State>
   </mx:states>
   <mx:Script>
      <![CDATA[
         [Bindable]
         public var xml:XML = <slideshow><audio source="" /></slideshow>;
         [Bindable]
         public var selected:XML = <slideshow><photo duration="" source=""/>
               </slideshow>;

         private function selectSlide( source:String, duration:uint ):void {
            var slide:XML = <slideshow><photo duration="" source="" />
                     </slideshow>;
            slide.photo.@source = source;
            slide.photo.@duration = duration;
            selected = slide;
            imgDuration.value = duration;
         }
```

```
        private function addSelectedSlide():void {
           selected.photo.@source = image.source;
           selected.photo.@duration = imgDuration.value
           xml.appendChild( selected.photo );
        }

        private function removeSelectedSlide():void {
           xml.photo = xml.photo.(@source!=selected.photo.@source);
        }

     ]]>
  </mx:Script>
  <mx:HTTPService id="service" url="http://www.flickr.com/services/rest/?method=flickr.
photos.search&amp;api_key=fa5d101b8564317c248aa429302468ee&amp;text={tags.text}" />
  <mx:ApplicationControlBar top="5" left="5" right="5">
     <mx:LinkButton label="Design" click="currentState='';" />
     <mx:LinkButton label="Preview" click="currentState='preview';" />
  </mx:ApplicationControlBar>
  <mx:Panel layout="absolute" title="SlideShow Creator" id="creator" left="10"
                                     right="10" bottom="100" top="50">
     <mx:TileList id="gallery" change="selectSlide('http://static.flickr.com/' + event.
currentTarget.selectedItem.server + '/' + event.currentTarget.selectedItem.id + '_' +
event.currentTarget.selectedItem.secret + '_o.jpg', 10);" dataProvider="{service.las-
tResult.rsp.photos.photo}" itemRenderer="FlickrThumb"  right="310" bottom="5" top="5"
left="5"/>
     <mx:VBox top="5" width="300" bottom="5" horizontalAlign="center"
                                     verticalAlign="bottom" right="5">
        <mx:Image id="image" source="{selected.photo.@source}" width="200"
                                                          height="200" />
        <mx:Form width="100%">
           <mx:FormItem label="Source" horizontalAlign="left">
              <mx:TextInput id="imgSource"
                               text="{selected.photo.@source}" width="175"/>
           </mx:FormItem>
           <mx:FormItem label="Duration">
              <mx:NumericStepper id="imgDuration" value="10"
                                          minimum="1" maximum="300" />
           </mx:FormItem>
        </mx:Form>
        <mx:HBox width="100%" horizontalAlign="right">
           <mx:Button label="Remove Photo"
                                    click="removeSelectedSlide();" />
           <mx:Button label="Add Photo" click="addSelectedSlide();" />
        </mx:HBox>
```

```
    </mx:VBox>
    <mx:ControlBar horizontalAlign="left" verticalAlign="middle">
      <mx:Label text="Tags"/>
      <mx:TextInput id="tags"/>
      <mx:Button label="Search Flickr" id="search"
                                              click="service.send();" />
      <mx:HBox width="100%" horizontalAlign="right"
                                                 verticalAlign="middle">
       <mx:Label text="Audio URL"/>
       <mx:TextInput id="soundURL"/>
       <mx:Button label="Add Audio" click="xml.audio.@source =
                                                      soundURL.text;" />
      </mx:HBox>
    </mx:ControlBar>
  </mx:Panel>
  <lib:Scroller id="scroller" dataProvider="{xml.photo}" change="selectSlide( event.
currentTarget.selectedItem.@source, event.currentTarget.selectedItem.@duration );"
itemRenderer=" com.theriabook.controls.SlideThumb "  bottom="10" left="10" right="10"
height="85"/>
</mx:Application>
```

Listing 13.23 SlideShowCreator.mxml

When our application is running in preview mode, the SlideShow component should automatically load and let users interact with it just as they would in the SlideShowPlayer application. See Figure 13.7.

When all slides are selected and an MP3 audio file is ready, click on preview and enjoy the show!

Figure 13.7 SlideShowCreator Preview state

Summary

In this chapter we've developed an application that can be used to create and preview custom slideshows using the Flickr API. Hopefully we've gotten you well on your way to creating a very rich and useful application in Flex with relatively little effort. We've also had another chance to review several important Flex 2 topics including:

- Developing components for reuse
- Animating with ActionScript 3
- Using Timer events
- Integrating with Web Services
- Using E4X with databinding
- Managing view states

Flex 2 makes desktop-like applications a reality for the Web. We hope you can expand on the ideas presented in this chapter and create your own media applications targeted for the Web.

CHAPTER

14

Developing Custom Charts

Developing Custom Charts

In Chapter 5 we used a <mx:PieChart> component in a sample portfolio application. Flex Charting lets you not only offer better visualization of your data, but also create interactive dashboard-type applications in which the charts can respond to a user's actions. For example, the user's click on a pie slice in the portfolio application would repopulate the data grid with the news about selected stock.

Check out the Google Finance application at http://finance.google.com/finance. Just enter a stock symbol (e.g., ADBE) and enjoy working with a highly interactive line chart representing the stock performance over a selected period of time.

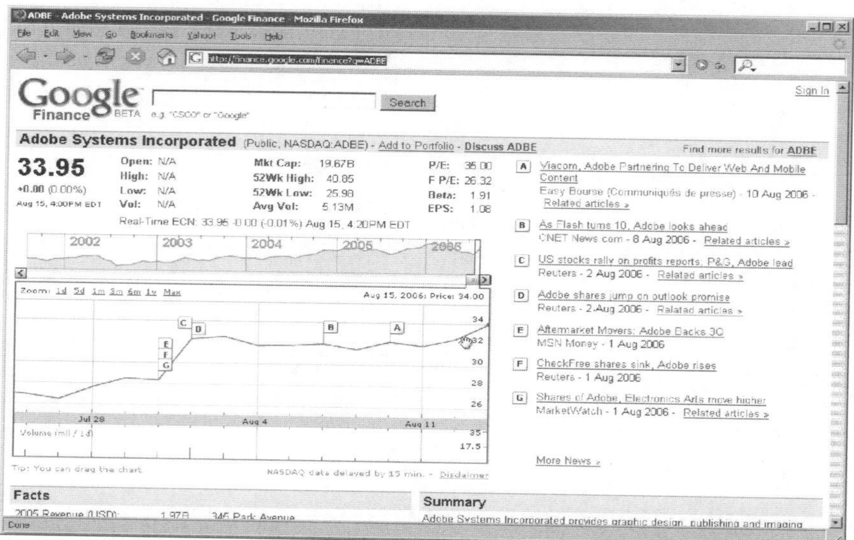

Figure 14.1 Google Finance with interactive charting

This line chart is rendered by the Flash Player and it reacts to your mouse movements, displaying the date and time under the mouse cursor; it has a zoom feature; and you can change the time period by dragging the timeline above the chart. This Flash chart is smart enough to interact with the rest of the non-Flash Web page components. Click on one of these little flags and the corresponding news item is highlighted on the right. Interactive charts will give your end users a lot more control than static ones, and will make them happy.

In this chapter, we'll show you how you can program similarly interactive charts by creating your own and extending standard Flex Charting components. We assume the reader is familiar with the basics of Flex Charting. To get a feeling for what Flex Charting is about, check out the following URL that demos various samples of charts in action and shows the MXML source code for each: http://flexapps.macromedia.com/flex15/chartexplorer/explorer.mxml?versionCheck ed=true.

To simplify digesting this material, we'll build the following five applications adding, complexity as we go:

- A program that draws a rectangular area right within the line chart component
- A line chart with a hundred data points
- A line chart with two data series and a movable vertical line
- The line chart described above with a tool tip displaying data point values from two series
- All of the above plus a chart zooming feature

While these applications won't have all the functionality Google Finance offers, it'll definitely give you a little push in the right direction.

How to Develop a Chart from Scratch

Flex provides a large number of pre-built charts and flexible ways to customize them, in some cases you might find that developing your own charts has its benefits. It gives you the flexibility to implement the functionality, ranging from simply highlighting areas of the chart to providing superior interactivity and presentation.

In our first example, we'll try to override the standard painting of a chart component. Let's start with a simple example that will only use ActionScript. Suppose you want to implement limits – each limit representing some rectangular region on the chart filled with some color. This can be useful in highlighting some business-specific range of values. For example, if a stock price drops below some resistance value, the line chart should be displayed in a red area. We'll create two AS3 classes:

- A CartesianLimit that's the data model of the limit
- An ExtendedCartesianChart that's responsible for the line chart and the limit-area painting

Please note that in this example, we're painting this area right on the same graphic object. Later in this chapter we'll use a different technique (programmatic skins) and create additional objects to be put on the chart.

To begin with, let's create a CartesianLimit class that will hold all the values required to paint the limits area:

```
Package com.theriabooks.limits {
    import mx.graphics.IFill;
    import mx.graphics.SolidColor;
    import mx.graphics.IStroke;
    import mx.charts.chartClasses.CartesianChart;
    import flash.geom.Point;
    import flash.geom.Rectangle;

  public class CartesianLimit {
      public var minX: Object;
      public var maxX: Object;
      public var minY: Object;
      public var maxY: Object;
      public var fillStyle:IFill = new SolidColor(0xFF0000);
      public var lineStyle:IStroke;

    public function paint(chart: CartesianChart): void {
      var pt0 : Point = chart.dataToLocal(minX,minY);
      var pt1 : Point = chart.dataToLocal(maxX,maxY);

      var x: Number = Math.min(pt0.x,pt1.x);
      var y: Number = Math.min(pt0.y,pt1.y);

      var width: Number = Math.abs(pt0.x-pt1.x);
      var height: Number = Math.abs(pt0.y-pt1.y);

      if(lineStyle != null)
        lineStyle.apply(chart.graphics);
      else
        chart.graphics.lineStyle();

      if(fillStyle != null)
        fillStyle.begin(chart.graphics, new Rectangle(x,y,width,height));

      chart.graphics.drawRect(x,y,width,height);

      if(fillStyle != null)
        fillStyle.end(chart.graphics);
```

```
    }
  }
}
```

Listing 14.1 The ActionScript class CartesianLimit.as

This class lets you store the information about the region coordinates, fill, and the line style used to render this region. The method paint() here computes the coordinates of the rectangle based on the provided minimum and maximum values and paints the area according to the fill and line style. This is not a callback as Java programmers might assume; we'll call it from the class Extended-CartesianChart. This method has one argument of the CartesianChart type, which is a base Flex class of all standard two-dimensional rectangular charts.

The user-defined ActionScript classes can be used as MXML tags as in Listing 14.4.

Object-oriented purists may not like the fact that we didn't define the properties (minX, maxX, et al) of the private CartesianLimit class with public getters and setters. If we went that route, we'd have to clutter our code with a bunch of the following statements (one per each private property):

```
[Inspectable]
private var _minX: Object;

public function get minX() : Object {
   return _minX;
}
public function set minX(value:Object) : void {
   _minX=value;
}
```

Listing 14.2 Private properties with getters and setters

But if these getters and setters don't include any additional processing, but are just passing the data from the outside world to private variables and back, we can get away without getters and setters. You don't have to abide by the JavaBean specification to make your code visible to tools like Flex Builder.

To help Flex Builder provide code hints, you can mark the private properties of the ActionScript class with a metatag [Inspectable]. For public properties this wouldn't be required. Flex Builder's MXML editor can offer you code hints as shown below:

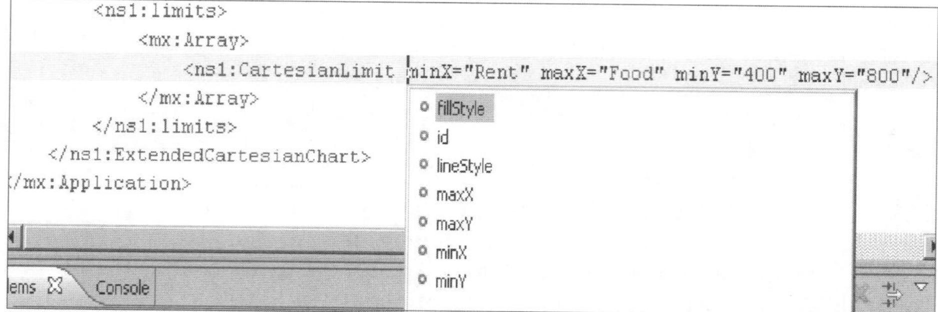

Figure 14.2 Flex Builder code hinting for the user-defined properties

To create our custom chart, we need to extend the CartesianChart class (a base class for all rectangular 2D charts), and override its callback method updateDisplayList. Flex calls the updateDisplayList() method when the component is added to a container using the addChild() method, and when the component's invalidate DisplayList() method is called. Don't miss the fact that the method updateList() first calls its peer from the superclass to provide the default drawing of the chart, and then paints the limits area on top of it.

We've also added a new public property limits to this class:

```
package com.theriabook.limits {
import mx.charts.chartClasses.CartesianChart;

  public class ExtendedCartesianChart extends CartesianChart  {
   [Inspectable(category="Data",arrayType="com.theriabook.limits.CartesianLimit")]
   public var limits: Array;

   protected override function updateDisplayList(unscaledWidth:Number,
             unscaledHeight:Number):void {
      super.updateDisplayList(unscaledWidth, unscaledHeight);
      if(limits != null)
         for(var i:int =0;i<limits.length;i++)
            limits[i].paint(this);
   }
  }
}
```

Listing 14.3 The ActionScript class ExtendedCartesianChart

Finally, let's create an MXML application to test our chart:

```
<mx:Application xmlns:mx="http://www.adobe.com/2006/mxml" layout="absolute" xmlns:
```

```
ns1="com.theriabooks.limits.*">

<mx:Script>
     [Bindable]
      public var results:Object = [
        {Expense: "Taxes", Amount: 2000},
        {Expense: "Rent", Amount: 1500},
        {Expense: "Bills", Amount: 100},
        {Expense: "Car", Amount: 450},
        {Expense: "Gas", Amount: 100},
        {Expense: "Food", Amount: 200}
    ];
</mx:Script>

   <ns1:ExtendedCartesianChart x="82" y="182" id="linechart1"
           dataProvider="{results}" showDataTips="true" width="300" height="200">
   <ns1:fill>
      <mx:SolidColor color="0xffffff"/>
   </ns1:fill>
       <ns1:horizontalAxis>
            <mx:CategoryAxis  padding="0" dataProvider="{results}"
                                                categoryField="Expense"/>

        </ns1:horizontalAxis>

        <ns1:series>
            <mx:Array>
                <mx:LineSeries form="curve" yField="Amount" name="Apple" >

                </mx:LineSeries>
            </mx:Array>
        </ns1:series>
        <ns1:limits>
          <mx:Array>
         <ns1:CartesianLimit minX="Rent" maxX="Food" minY="400" maxY="800"/>
          </mx:Array>
        </ns1:limits>
    </ns1:ExtendedCartesianChart>
 </mx:Application>
```

Listing 14.4 The mxml application Limits.mxml

We put the tag <mx:Array> inside the <ns1:limits> just to make the code more generic as the application may need more than one <ns1:CartesianLimit> area.

Run the application and it'll display the chart with a red rectangle:

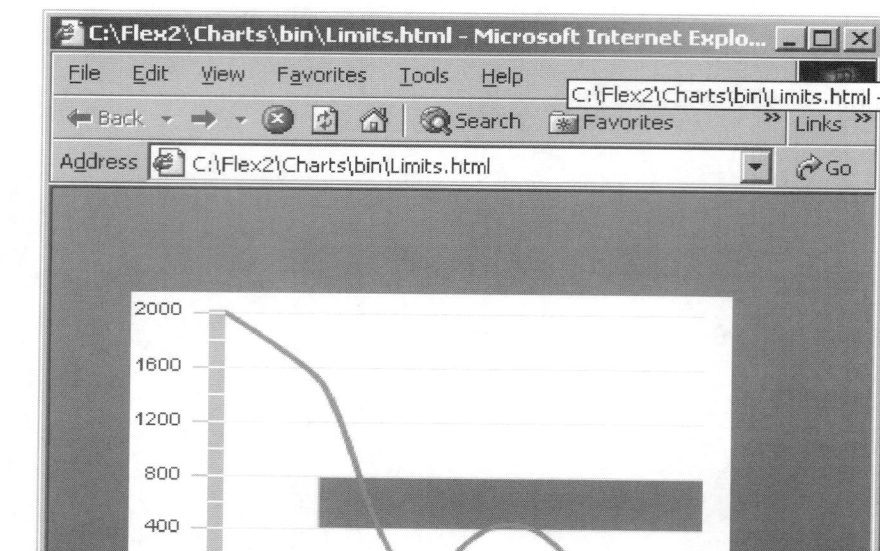

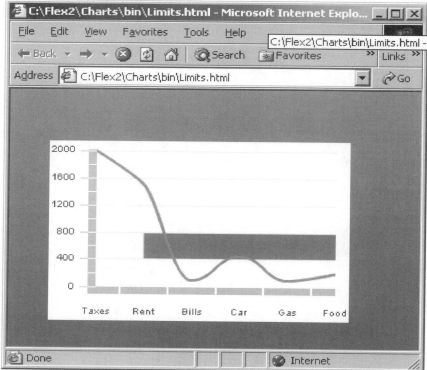

Figure 14.3 Adding a rectangle with specified limits to the chart

Working with Larger Data Sets

It often happens that you need to display a relatively large data set inside a chart. Let's try to plot 100 data points as a line chart. This time we'll use MXML. The data values for each point will be generated randomly for a hundred days starting January 1, 2006. All these data will be put in the array that will be used as a data provider for our line chart.

```
<?xml version="1.0" encoding="utf-8"?>
<mx:Application xmlns:mx="http://www.adobe.com/2006/mxml"
            layout="absolute" backgroundColor="0xFFFFFF">

<mx:Script>
   <![CDATA[
      private function createData(count:uint) : Array {
       var date: Date = new Date(2006,0); // starting from the new year day
```

```
        var day : uint = 1000*60*60*24;  //msec in one day

        var retval: Array = new Array();
        for(var i:int = 0; i< count;i++,
             // Add one day
             date.setMilliseconds(date.getMilliseconds()+day))
             // Set the random data for the current day
            retval[i] = { Date: date.toDateString(), Value: Math.random()*100} ;
            return retval;
       }

       private function parseDate(date: String) : Date {
          return new Date(date);
       }

       [Bindable]
       private var dataSet:Array = createData(100);
    ]]>
</mx:Script>

<mx:LineChart x="127" y="72" width="400" height="300" id="linechart1"
                              dataProvider="{dataSet}" showDataTips="true">
   <mx:seriesFilters><mx:Array/></mx:seriesFilters>
   <mx:horizontalAxis>
      <mx:DateTimeAxis   dataUnits="days" parseFunction="parseDate"/>
   </mx:horizontalAxis>
   <mx:series>
      <mx:LineSeries displayName="Series 1" xField="Date" yField="Value">
       <mx:lineStroke>
         <mx:Stroke weight="1" color="0xff0000"  />
          </mx:lineStroke>
      </mx:LineSeries>
   </mx:series>
</mx:LineChart>

</mx:Application>
```

Listing 14.5 The line chart with 100 data points: LineChart100.mxml

This code will produce a line chart that may look like this:

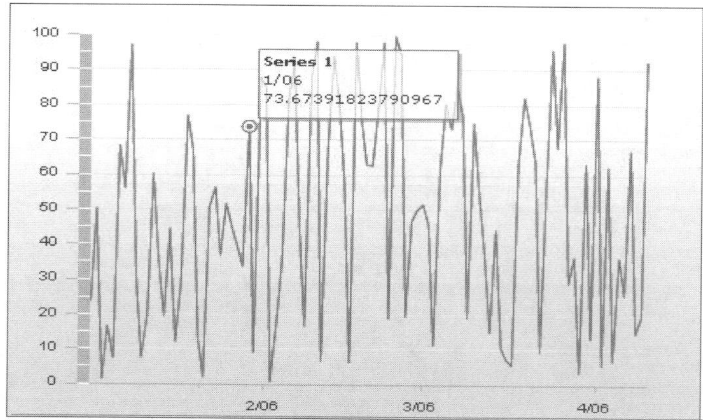

Figure 14.4 The line chart with 100 data points

Unfortunately, as we start moving the cursor over the chart, we recognize that there's an issue – the tool tip is shown only when we put our cursor over the actual data point (shown as a little circle). Even with 100 points it makes extracting the data from the chart difficult. And what if we want to plot multiple series and compare values at the same date?

Adding a Vertical Line

Ideally we'd like to show the vertical line moving horizontally over the chart, following your current mouse position. We'd also like to add data tips showing the data for multiple stocks (assuming that each line represents some stock prices) at the selected point in time.

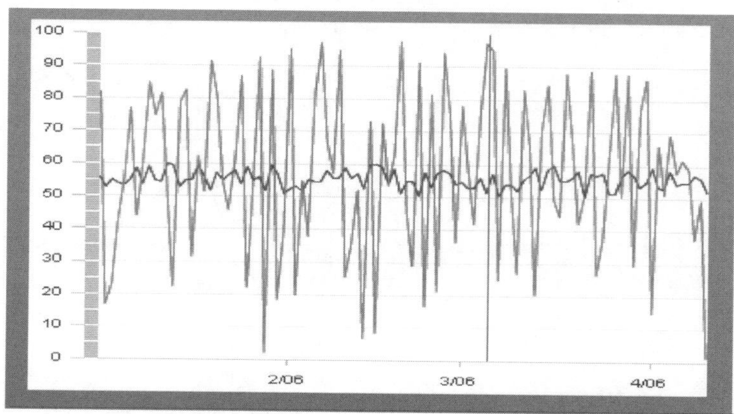

Figure 14.5 A two-stock chart with a vertical line

Let's subclass our chart and implement this functionality.
We'll split the implementation into multiple classes for demonstration purposes. The first version of our program will display a line chart with two data series emulating the data on two stocks. We'll also display the vertical line in the chart as shown in Figure 14.5.

At this point, we are going to create two ActionScript classes:

- **ExtendedLineChart**: This class extends the LineChart and is responsible for drawing the line chart

- **VLineLayer**: This class extends the ProgrammaticSkin class and its purpose is to draw the vertical line on top of the ExtendableLine Chart.

Non-Typical Use of Skinning

Skinning in Flex can be implemented by rendering graphics (a jpg file). But skins can also be rendered programmatically as an ActionScript class.

Originally, Flex skinning was created to change the look-and-feel of the visual parts of the same component easily (for example, a popular media player WinAmp offers hundreds of skins). But this time we'll use the skinning capabilities of Flex just to draw the line on top of the chart. We aren't planning to change the skin of the thin vertical line, but rather use this technique to put an object on top of the chart and control it (we're going to move this line along the horizontal axis).

Drawing a line is a fairly simple task – we'll use a new VlineLayer class inherited from the ProgrammaticSkin class. This class will draw the line (it'll play the role of a skin) and add it as a child to our chart.

```
package com.theriabook.charts.line1{

 import mx.skins.ProgrammaticSkin;
 import flash.geom.Rectangle;

 public class VLineLayer extends  ProgrammaticSkin {

   protected override function updateDisplayList(
                 unscaledWidth:Number, unscaledHeight:Number):void {

     super.updateDisplayList(unscaledWidth, unscaledHeight);

     var rect: Rectangle = (parent as ExtendedLineChart).viewBounds;

     graphics.clear();
```

```
        if(rect.x<=parent.mouseX && (rect.x+rect.width)>=parent.mouseX &&
               rect.y<=parent.mouseY && (rect.y+rect.height)>=parent.mouseY) {
          graphics.lineStyle(1,0x808080);
          graphics.moveTo(parent.mouseX, rect.y);
          graphics.lineTo(parent.mouseX, rect.y+rect.height);
       }
     }
  }
}
```

Listing 14.6 The VlineLayer class that draws a line

Flex designers declared the CartesianChart's property dataRegion that defines the coordinates of the actual data rectangle as protected. Since we need this information to be accessible from the outside of this inheritance hierarchy, we've defined in our subclass a viewBounds public property that will return the value of the dataRegion to any class that may need it:

```
public function get viewBounds() : Rectangle {
   return super.dataRegion;
}
```

And the complete code for the ExtendedLineChart will look like:

```
package com.theriabook.charts.line1{
   import mx.charts.LineChart;
   import flash.events.MouseEvent;
   import flash.geom.Rectangle;

 public class ExtendedLineChart extends LineChart {
   private var skin: VLineLayer;

   public function ExtendedLineChart() {
      addEventListener(MouseEvent.MOUSE_MOVE, onMouseMove);
   }

   protected override function updateDisplayList(
            unscaledWidth:Number, unscaledHeight:Number):void {
      super.updateDisplayList(unscaledWidth, unscaledHeight);
      skin.width = width;
      skin.height = height;
   }

   protected override function createChildren()  : void {
      super.createChildren();
```

```
      if(skin == null)
         addChild(skin = new VLineLayer());
   }

   public function get viewBounds() :  Rectangle {
      return super.dataRegion;
   }
   private function onMouseMove(event: MouseEvent) : void {
      skin.invalidateDisplayList();
   }
  }
}
```

Listing 14.7 The ActionScript class ExtendedLineChart

Let's modify our MXML application from Listing 14.5 to support a two-line series:

```
<?xml version="1.0" encoding="utf-8"?>
<mx:Application xmlns:mx="http://www.adobe.com/2006/mxml"
   layout="absolute"  xmlns:ns1="com.theriabook.charts.line1.*">
<mx:Script>
   <![CDATA[
      private function createData(count:uint) : Array {
         var date: Date = new Date(2006,0);
         var day : uint = 1000*60*60*24;

         var retval: Array = new Array();
         for(var i:int = 0; i< count;i++,
                  date.setMilliseconds(date.getMilliseconds()+day))
            retval[i] = { Date: date.toDateString(),
                              ABCD: 50+Math.random()*10, XYZT:Math.random()*100} ;
         return retval;
      }

      private function parseDate(date: String) : Date {
         return new Date(date);
      }

      [Bindable]
      private var dataSet:Array = createData(100);
   ]]>
</mx:Script>
<ns1:ExtendedLineChart x="127" y="72" width="400" height="300" id="linechart1"
dataProvider="{dataSet}" showDataTips="false">
```

```
<ns1:seriesFilters>
        <mx:Array/>
    </ns1:seriesFilters>
<ns1:horizontalAxis>
   <mx:DateTimeAxis   dataUnits="days" parseFunction="parseDate"/>
</ns1:horizontalAxis>
   <ns1:series>
   <mx:LineSeries displayName="ABCD" xField="Date" yField="ABCD">
   <mx:lineStroke>
      <mx:Stroke weight="1" color="0x00ff"  />
   </mx:lineStroke>
   </mx:LineSeries>
   <mx:LineSeries displayName="XYZT" xField="Date" yField="XYZT">
   <mx:lineStroke>
      <mx:Stroke weight="1" color="0xff0000"  />
   </mx:lineStroke>
   </mx:LineSeries>
</ns1:series>
<ns1:fill>
   <mx:SolidColor color="0xFFFFFF" />
</ns1:fill>
</ns1:ExtendedLineChart>

</mx:Application>
```

Listing 14.8 LineChartVLine1.mxml

Run this program and you'll see a chart that looks like Figure 14.5.

This class draws a movable vertical line, but we also need a tool tip that can show the data of multiple series based on the position of the vertical line. The standard tool tip window can only show the information about one series, so we'll create a new class to implement it (we'll omit some properties declarations to make the code more readable):

```
public class ToolTip extends  UIComponent {

  private var _borderWidth : uint = 1;
   private var _borderColor : uint = 0xff;
   private var _backColor : uint = 0xffff00;
   private var _backAlpha: Number = 0.5;

   private var textField : TextField = new TextField();

   protected override function createChildren():void {
```

```
      textField.background = false;
      textField.x=2;
      textField.y=2;
      textField.selectable = false;
      addChild(textField);
   }

   protected override function measure():void {
      super.measure();
        // add eight pixels around the text field  in the tool tip to
        // just to look prettier
      measuredWidth = measuredMinWidth = textField.textWidth +2;
      measuredHeight= measuredMinHeight= textField.textHeight+2;
   }

   protected override function updateDisplayList(
unscaledWidth:Number, unscaledHeight:Number):void {
      textField.width=unscaledWidth-4;
      textField.height=unscaledHeight-4;
      graphics.clear();
      graphics.lineStyle(_borderWidth, _borderColor);
      graphics.beginFill(_backColor, _backAlpha);
      graphics.drawRect(0,0,unscaledWidth, unscaledHeight);
   }

   public function get text() :String {
      return textField.text;
   }

   public function set text(text:String) : void {
      textField.text = text;
      invalidateSize();
      validateNow();
   }
}
```

Listing 14.9 The ActionScript class ToolTip

We'll display the text in the tool tip using a text contol. To do this, we override the createChildren method of the UIComponent, which sets no background, margins, makes it non-editable, and adds the text as a child component.

In the measure callback we'll add a couple of pixels margin around the text.

The next step is to implement a function that can take an *x*-coordinate and return the information about the nearest data point for each series. FlexCharts support two functions for converting data points into the actual screen coordinates and vice versa – localToData and dataToLocal. But localToData requires both *x* and *y* coordinates, and we don't know the *y* coordinate of the point at the current *x* since all we know is the *x* coordinate of the vertical line. The solution is to create a list of all actual coordinates for all the data points and then use it to determine the closest data points at a given *x* coordinate. Our assumptions are:

- All values are provided in ascending order (sorted by date) .
- Each data series has the same number of data points and the *x* coordinate of each data series is the same for a given date.

Now we can implement a simple PointCache class to "remember" the closest data points at each *x* coordinate. The method getPointIndexByX will return the index of the data point inside the data series.

```
public class PointCache {
   private var points : Array ;
   private var chart  : ExtendedLineChart;

   public function PointCache(chart: ExtendedLineChart) {
      this.chart = chart;
   }

   public function reset() : void {
      points = null;
   }

   public function getPointIndexByX(x: int, index:int=0) : int {
      if(points == null)
         init();
      if(!chart.viewBounds.contains(chart.mouseX,chart.mouseY))
         return -1;

      var row: Array = points[index] as Array;

      for(var i:int = 0;i< row.length;i++) {
         if(row[i].x > x) {
            if(i == 0) return 0;
                     // deltas are distances btwn the line and the closest ponts
                     // on the left and on the right
            var delta0 : Number = x-row[i-1];
            var delta1: Number = row[i]-x;
            return delta0<delta1 ? i-1 : i;         }
```

```
      }
      return row.length-1;
   }

   private function init():void {
      points = new Array(chart.series.length);
      if(points.length == 0) return ;
      var xField: String = chart.series[0].xField, yField: String;

      for(var j:int = 0;j<chart.series.length;j++) {
         yField = chart.series[j].yField;
         var dp: ICollectionView  = chart.series[j].dataProvider
as ICollectionView;
         var elem: Array = new Array(dp.length);
         for(var i:int = 0;i<dp.length;i++)
            elem[i] = chart.dataToLocal(dp[i][xField],
dp[i][yField]);
         points[j] = elem;
      }
   }
}
```

Listing 14.10 The ActionScript class PointCache

It's relatively easy to modify this class to support an arbitrary order of points by sorting the points based on the *x* coordinate.

Finally, we can put together a new ExtendedLineChart class. Since we want to show in the tool tip window the date, the name, and the value for the element on this date (the *x* coordinate) for all series, we'll have to implement a custom tool tip getToolTipText formating function that can extract the information from all the series and present it nicely:

```
public class ExtendedLineChart extends LineChart {
   private var _cache: PointCache ;
   private var _layer: VLineLayer ;
   private var _dataTip: ToolTip = new ToolTip();
   private var tipDateFormatter: DateFormatter;
   private var tipNumberFormatter: NumberFormatter;

   public function ExtendedLineChart() {
      _cache = new PointCache(this);
      _layer = new VLineLayer():
      addEventListener(MouseEvent.MOUSE_MOVE, onMouseMove);
```

```
        tipDateFormatter = new DateFormatter();
        tipDateFormatter.formatString = "MMM DD, YYYY";

        tipNumberFormatter = new NumberFormatter();
        tipNumberFormatter.precision = 2;
    }

    public function get viewBounds() : Rectangle {
        return super.dataRegion;
    }

    // calculate and update position of the  tool tip
    protected override function updateDisplayList(unscaledWidth:Number,
unscaledHeight:Number):void {
        super.updateDisplayList(unscaledWidth, unscaledHeight);
        _layer.width = width;
        _layer.height = height;

        var index: int = _cache.getPointIndexByX(mouseX);

        if(index>=0) {
            _dataTip.visible = true;
            _dataTip.text = getToolTipText(index);
            _dataTip.width = _dataTip.measuredWidth;
            _dataTip.height= _dataTip.measuredHeight;

                    // move the text box two pixels to the right
                    // and one box hight up, so the mouse pointer
                    // is below the tool tip box
    _dataTip.x = mouseX+2;
            _dataTip.y = mouseY-_dataTip.height;
        }
        else
            _dataTip.visible = false;
    }

    private function getToolTipText(index: int): String {
        var sb:String ="" ;
        for(var i:int=0;i<series.length;i++) {
          if(i==0)
            sb +=
    tipDateFormatter.format(series[0].dataProvider[index][series[0].xField])+"\n";
            var elem: LineSeries = this.series[i];
```

```
            var dp: ICollectionView  = elem.dataProvider as ICollectionView;

            var pt:Object = dp[index];
            sb += elem.displayName + ": ";
            sb += tipNumberFormatter.format(pt[elem.yField]);
            sb += "\n";
            }
        return sb;
    }

    protected override function createChildren()  : void {
        super.createChildren();
        if(!contains(_dataTip))
            addChild(_dataTip);
        if(!contains(_layer))
            addChild(_layer);
    }

    private function onMouseMove(event: MouseEvent) : void {
        invalidateDisplayList();
    }

    public override function invalidateProperties():void {
        if(_cache!=null)
            _cache.reset();

        super.invalidateProperties();
    }

    public override function invalidateSize():void {
        if(_cache!=null)
            _cache.reset();

        super.invalidateSize();
    }
}
```

Listing 14.11 A new version of the ExtendedLineChart

Once you run the application, you can see the chart shown in Figure 14.6 with the tool tip containing the information on two data points that represent the line series for ABCD and XYZT, located close to the vertical line. It doesn't really matter now if your mouse pointer is located by the data point: the vertical line (aka skin) position guarantees that the proper data will be displayed.

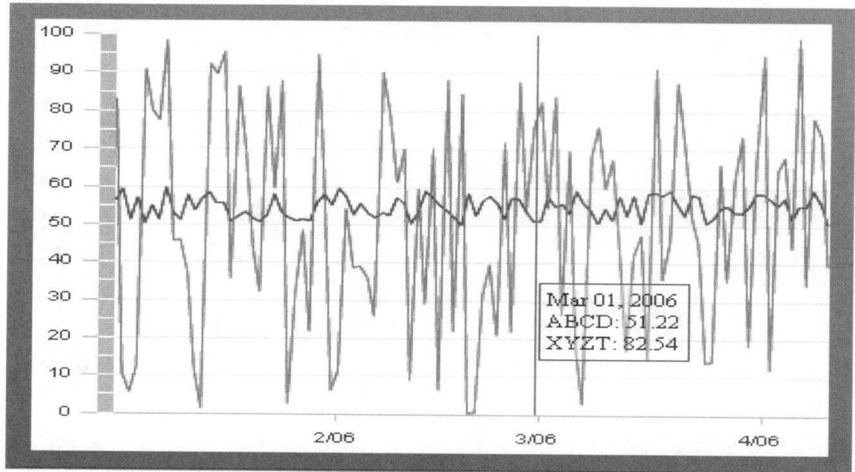

Figure 14.6 A tool tip with the data about two series: ABCD and XYZT

Adding Scrolling and Zooming

It's often desirable to let the user zoom in on the data and scroll zoomed charts. With Flex Charts this can be done easily by adjusting the minimum and maximum values of the *x* axis (the date range in our case).

First, we'll implement a very simple zoom function in the ExtendedLineChart class, which will increase or decrease the range of the *x* axis by some predefined value. Note that when we change the axis's range, we also have to reset the point cache.

```
public function zoom(delta: int ) : void {
   var axis: DateTimeAxis = DateTimeAxis(horizontalAxis);
   var newmin : Date= maxDate(axisMin,addDays(axis.minimum,  -delta));
   var newmax : Date= minDate(axisMax,addDays(axis.maximum,   delta));
   if(diffDays(newmax,newmin) >= MIN_RANGE) {
      axis.minimum = newmin;
      axis.maximum = newmax;
      _cache.reset();
      this.invalidateDisplayList();
   }
}

private function get axisMin() : Date {
   return DateTimeAxis(horizontalAxis).
         parseFunction(series[0].dataProvider[0][series[0].xField]);
}
```

```
private function get axisMax() : Date {
   var dp: ICollectionView = series[0].dataProvider;
   return DateTimeAxis(horizontalAxis).
         parseFunction(dp[dp.length-1][series[0].xField]);
}

// utility functions to work with dates
private static function addDays(date: Date, days:int): Date {
      return new Date(date.getTime()+days*MSEC_IN_DAY);
}

private static function minDate(date1: Date, date2: Date):Date {
      return date1.getTime()<date2.getTime() ? date1 : date2;
}

private static function maxDate(date1: Date, date2: Date):Date {
      return date1.getTime()>date2.getTime() ? date1 : date2;
}
private static function diffDays(date1 : Date, date2: Date): Number {
   return (getDate(date1).getTime()-getDate(date2).getTime())/MSEC_IN_DAY;
}
```

Listing 14.12 Zooming and date processing

The function zoom() ensures that the axis range won't go outside the underlying data values and will always be at least MIN_RANGE days.

Now we can simply add two buttons to our MXML file to zoom the chart in and out. Usually you'd provide a more sophisticated mechanism for zooming the chart, but we'll keep this example simple for demonstration purposes.

```
<?xml version="1.0" encoding="utf-8"?>
<mx:Application xmlns:mx="http://www.adobe.com/2006/mxml"
 xmlns:ns1="com.theriabook.charts.zoom.*" layout="absolute">
 <mx:Script>
  <![CDATA[
   private function createData(count:uint) : Array {
    var date: Date = new Date(2006,0);
    var day : uint = 1000*60*60*24;

    var retval: Array = new Array();
    for(var i:int = 0; i< count;i++, date.setMilliseconds(date.getMilliseconds()+day))
     retval[i] = { Date: date.toDateString(), ABCD: 50+Math.random()*10,
```

```
                                                    XYZT: 75+Math.random()*50} ;
    retval[0].ABCD = 0;
    retval[retval.length-1].ABCD=0;
    return retval;
   }

   private function parseDate(date: String) : Date {
    return new Date(date);
   }

   [Bindable]
   private var dataSet:Array = createData(100);
  ]]>
 </mx:Script>
  <mx:VBox x="33" y="24" height="445" width="606">
    <ns1:ExtendedLineChart width="600" height="400" id="myChart"
                              dataProvider="{dataSet}" showDataTips="false" >
      <ns1:seriesFilters>
            <mx:Array/>
        </ns1:seriesFilters>
     <ns1:horizontalAxis>
      <mx:DateTimeAxis dataUnits="days" parseFunction="parseDate"/>
     </ns1:horizontalAxis>

     <ns1:series>
      <mx:LineSeries displayName="ABCD" xField="Date" yField="ABCD">
      <mx:lineStroke>
       <mx:Stroke weight="1" color="0x00ff"  />
      </mx:lineStroke>
      </mx:LineSeries>
      <mx:LineSeries displayName="XYZT" xField="Date" yField="XYZT">
      <mx:lineStroke>
       <mx:Stroke weight="1" color="0xff0000"  />
      </mx:lineStroke>
      </mx:LineSeries>
     </ns1:series>
     <ns1:fill>
      <mx:SolidColor color="0xFFFFFF" />
     </ns1:fill>
    </ns1:ExtendedLineChart>
    <mx:HBox width="100%">
    <mx:Button label="Zoom In" id="zoomIn" fontWeight="bold" click="myChart.zoom(-2)"/>
    <mx:Button label="Zoom Out" id="zoomOut" fontWeight="bold" click="myChart.zoom(2)"/>
    </mx:HBox>
```

```
  </mx:VBox>
</mx:Application>
```

Listing 14.13 The final application LineChartVLineZoom.mxml

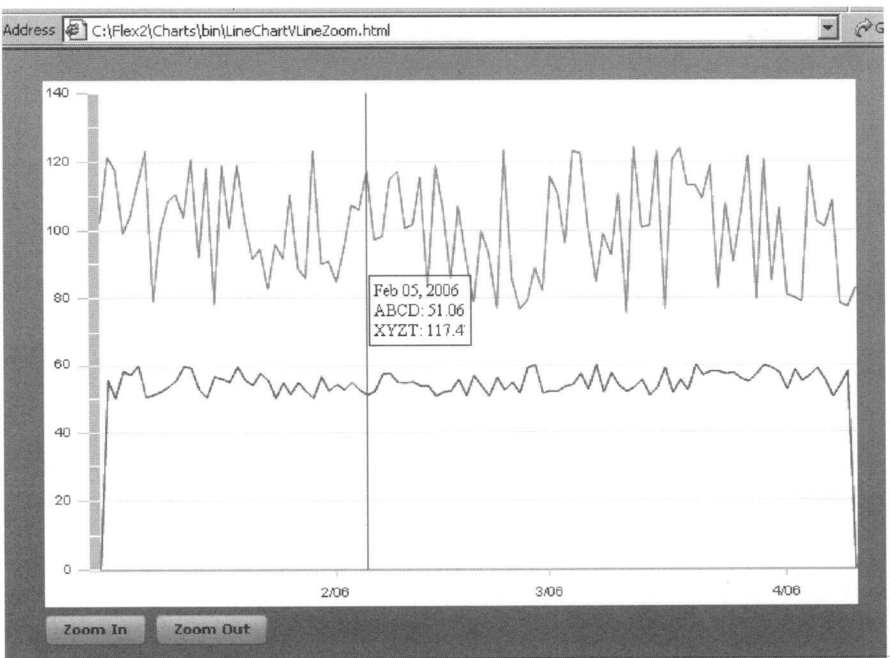

Figure 14.7 Running LineChartVLineZoom.mxml before zooming in

Press the Zoom In button several times, and the Line chart will change as shown below. The zooming ration is controlled by the value you're passing to the zoom() function under the zoom buttons.

```
<mx:Button label="Zoom In" id="zoomIn" fontWeight="bold" click="myChart.zoom(-2)"/>
    <mx:Button label="Zoom Out" id="zoomOut" fontWeight="bold"
                                             click="myChart.zoom(2)"/>
```

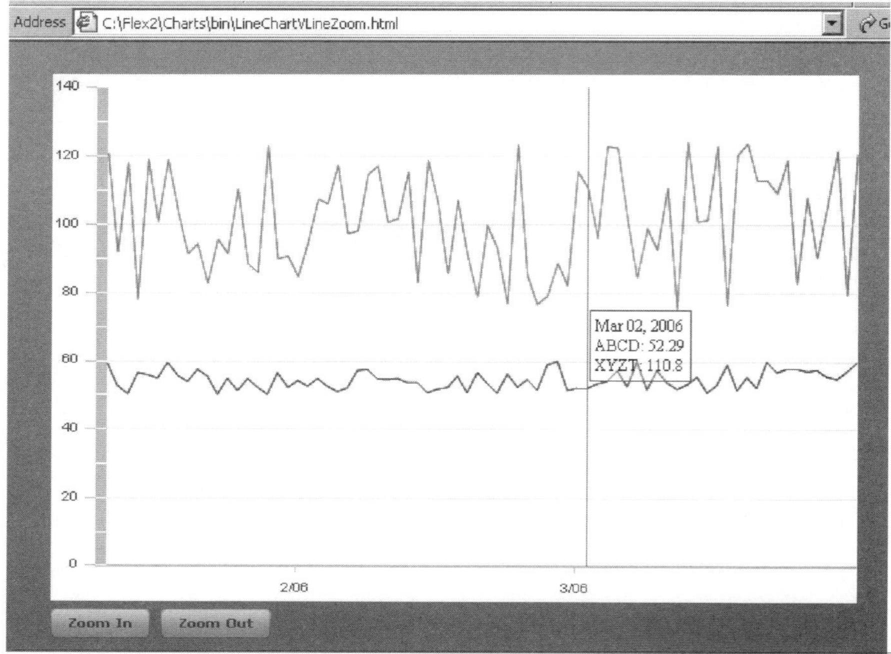

Figure 14.8 Running LineChartVLineZoom.mxml after zooming in

After you zoom in to the chart, you can't see the entire time interval. For example, you don't see the January data on Figure 14.8. Hence, we need to implement horizontal scrolling so the user can drag the mouse to the left or right.

For this scrolling we'll introduce the member variables _ancorX and _ancorY in the ExtendedLineChart class that will store the last mouse position and define the mouse down and mouse up event handlers that will toggle the isDragging flag.

Our new onMouseMove event handler will compute the required change based on the new and old mouse location and adjust the axis's minimum and maximum accordingly. The final version of the ExtendedLineChart class is shown in Listing 14.14.

```
public class ExtendedLineChart extends LineChart {
   private static const MIN_RANGE: int= 7;
   private static const MSEC_IN_DAY:int = 24*60*60*1000;
   private var isDragging : Boolean = false;
   private var _ancorX: int;
   private var _ancorY: int;
   private var _cache: PointCache ;
   private var _layer: VLineLayer ;
```

```
    private var _dataTip: ToolTip = new ToolTip();
    private var tipDateFormatter: DateFormatter;
    private var tipNumberFormatter: NumberFormatter;

    public function ExtendedLineChart() {
        _cache = new PointCache(this);
        _layer = new VLineLayer();
        addEventListener(MouseEvent.MOUSE_MOVE, onMouseMove);

        tipDateFormatter = new DateFormatter();
        tipDateFormatter.formatString = "MMM DD, YYYY";

        tipNumberFormatter = new NumberFormatter();
        tipNumberFormatter.precision = 2;

        addEventListener(MouseEvent.MOUSE_DOWN, onMouseDown);
        addEventListener(MouseEvent.MOUSE_UP, onMouseUp);
        addEventListener(MouseEvent.MOUSE_MOVE,onMouseMove);
}

    private function onMouseDown(evt: MouseEvent) :void {
    isDragging = true;
        _ancorX = mouseX;
        _ancorY = mouseY;
        invalidateDisplayList() ;
    }

    private function onMouseUp(evt:MouseEvent) :void {
        isDragging = false;
        invalidateDisplayList() ;
    }

    private function onMouseMove(event: MouseEvent) : void {
    if(!isDragging) {
            invalidateDisplayList();
            return;
        }

        var axis: DateTimeAxis = DateTimeAxis(horizontalAxis);
        var min : Date = axisMin;
        var max : Date = axisMax;
        var vWidth : int = dataToLocal(axis.maximum).x -dataToLocal(axis.minimum).x;
    var change: int = (axis.maximum.getTime()-axis.minimum.getTime())*-(mouseX-
                                                                    _ancorX)/vWidth;
```

```
        var newmin: Date = new Date(axis.minimum.getTime()+change);
      var newmax: Date = new Date(axis.maximum.getTime()+change);

        if(newmin.getTime()<min.getTime()) {
          newmax.setTime(newmax.getTime()+min.getTime()-newmin.getTime());
          newmin = min;
        } else
        if(newmax.getTime()>max.getTime()) {
          newmin.setTime(newmin.getTime()+max.getTime()-newmax.getTime());
          newmax = max;
        }

        _ancorX = mouseX;
        _ancorY = mouseY;
        axis.minimum = newmin;
        axis.maximum = newmax;
        _cache.reset();
        this.invalidateDisplayList();
      }

      public function zoom(delta: int ) : void {
        var axis: DateTimeAxis = DateTimeAxis(horizontalAxis);
        var newmin : Date= maxDate(axisMin,addDays(axis.minimum,  -delta));
        var newmax : Date= minDate(axisMax,addDays(axis.maximum,   delta));
        if(diffDays(newmax,newmin) >= MIN_RANGE) {
          axis.minimum = newmin;
          axis.maximum = newmax;
          _cache.reset();
          this.invalidateDisplayList();
        }
      }

      private function get axisMin() : Date {
        return DateTimeAxis(horizontalAxis).parseFunction(series[0].dataProvider[0][seri
es[0].xField]);
      }

      private function get axisMax() : Date {
        var dp: ICollectionView = series[0].dataProvider;
        return DateTimeAxis(horizontalAxis).parseFunction(dp[dp.length-
                                                    1][series[0].xField]);
      }

      private static function addDays(date: Date, days:int): Date {
```

```
        return new Date(date.getTime()+days*MSEC_IN_DAY);
    }

    private static function minDate(date1: Date, date2: Date):Date {
        return date1.getTime()<date2.getTime() ? date1 : date2;
    }

    private static function maxDate(date1: Date, date2: Date):Date {
        return date1.getTime()>date2.getTime() ? date1 : date2;
    }

    private static function diffDays(date1 : Date, date2: Date): Number {
        return (getDate(date1).getTime()-getDate(date2).getTime())/MSEC_IN_DAY;
}

    private static function getDate(date : Date) : Date {
        return new Date(date.getFullYear(), date.getMonth(), date.getDate());
    }

    private static function toDateString(date:Date) : String {
        var d: DateFormatter = new DateFormatter();
        d.formatString = "MM/DD/YY JJ:NN:SS";
        return d.format(date);
    }

    public function get viewBounds() : Rectangle {
        return super.dataRegion;
    }

    protected override function updateDisplayList(unscaledWidth:Number,
                                                  unscaledHeight:Number):void {
        super.updateDisplayList(unscaledWidth, unscaledHeight);

        _layer.width = width;
        _layer.height = height;
        var index: int = _cache.getPointIndexByX(mouseX);
        _dataTip.visible = index>=0 ;

        if(_dataTip.visible) {
            _dataTip.text = getToolTipText(index);
            _dataTip.width = _dataTip.measuredWidth;
            _dataTip.height= _dataTip.measuredHeight;
            _dataTip.x = mouseX+2;
            _dataTip.y = mouseY-_dataTip.height;
```

```
        }
    }

    private function getToolTipText(index: int): String {
        var sb:String ="" ;
        for(var i:int=0;i<series.length;i++) {
                if(i==0)
                    sb +=
         tipDateFormatter.format(series[0].dataProvider[index][series[0].xField])+"\n";
                var elem: LineSeries = this.series[i];
                var dp: ICollectionView  = elem.dataProvider as ICollectionView;
            var pt:Object = dp[index];
                sb += elem.displayName + ": ";
                sb += tipNumberFormatter.format(pt[elem.yField]);
                sb += "\n";
            }
        return sb;
    }

    protected override function createChildren()  : void {
        super.createChildren();
        if(!contains(_dataTip))
            addChild(_dataTip);
        if(!contains(_layer))
            addChild(_layer);
    }

    public override function invalidateProperties():void {
        if(_cache!=null)
            _cache.reset();
        super.invalidateProperties();
    }

    public override function invalidateSize():void {
        if(_cache!=null)
            _cache.reset();
        super.invalidateDisplayList();
    }
}
```

Listing 14.14 The final version of the class ExtendedLineChart

Summary

In this chapter we gradually built an application that should give you a good start in developing your own application that can look as good or even better than Google Finance. We've hard-coded the symbols of imaginary stocks ABCD and XYZT in our MXML application to keep the reader focused on the charting aspects of Flex, but if you've read this far, it shouldn't be too difficult to add some external data feed that will serve as the provider for this chart, as shown in Chapter 5. We'd like to thank the folks at GreenPoint, Inc., (http://gpoint.com/) for their valuable input to this chapter.

CHAPTER

15

Integration with External Applications

CHAPTER 15

Integration with External Applications

This subject of this chapter assumes a broad use of technologies besides the ones provided by Adobe, let alone Adobe Flex. Whenever you integrate two systems you need intimate familiarity with both. Obviously we had to pick one external application that the reader will be familiar with so that, besides the educational value, our solutions would have immediate practical use. We picked Microsoft Excel.

Hence the composition of our chapter includes references to LocalConnection and External API intervened with JavaScript, VBA, and XSLT to name just a few. The ride might feel hard, but it is worth it: by the end of the chapter we'll have presented a series of generic solutions that you can use off-the-shelf.

All examples are thoroughly commented, although we permitted ourselves less detail on the Microsoft subjects.

Using Excel as a counter-party example, we'll address the needs of Flex applications to communicate with the standalone native applications running on a user's computer. We'll also show the integration of Flex and a spreadsheet in a single HTML page. The Flex-to-Flex communications, irrespective of the mode the Flex applications are running in (embedded inside an ActiveX container or run by a standalone Flash Player), will get on our radar as well.

Overview of Flash External Interfacing Methods

Historically, releases of Flash have been consistently introducing more and more methods of interfacing with external applications.

First, developers got access to a bunch of methods like FSCommand, CallFrame, CallLabel, and SetVariable. These methods, exposed by a Flash ActiveX plug-in, allow one-way control of the Flash from a hosting container.

Macromedia Flash 6.0 added SharedObject to a set of available ActionScript classes. The Shared

Object class is used to read and store limited amounts of data on a user's computer. Besides its primary function, SharedObject allows a data exchange between two Flash movies running on the same computer (a second type of communication).

Flash 6.0 also provides a LocalConnection class. LocalConnection objects can communicate only among SWF files that are running on the same client computer, but they can be running in different applications – again, we're talking about Flash-to-Flash communication. Note that the LocalConnection API and security model underwent several significant changes with further releases.

Finally, release 8.0 adds ExternalInterface to the developers' arsenal. The External API enables straightforward two-way communication between ActionScript and the host application, i.e., you can call ActionScript functions from the Flash Player container and invoke container functions from ActionScript as well.

In this chapter we'll discuss only communications using ExternalInterface and LocalConnection. Even though the FSCommand & Co. methods are fully supported by the current Flash Player (9.0 when this was written), it's recommended to avoid them for integrating applications. The External API is more straightforward, flexible, and generally applicable.

Using External API

We start with the simplest External API example possible – communications between Flex SWF embedded in HTML and JavaScript running inside the Web page.

Calling an external JavaScript function is trivial:

```
import flash.external.ExternalInterface;
...
var retVal:Object = ExternalInterface.call( "javaScriptFunction", arg1, arg2, ...,
argN );
```

This will call a JavaScript function named "javaScriptFunction" declared somewhere on the HTML page with arguments supplied as the rest of the parameters and will get the result of the function execution as a *retVal* variable. You can use a wide range of types for arguments and the return value: strings, numbers, Boolean values, instances of Date class, Object, Array, and any combination thereof like Array of Objects or Object with Array properties. User-defined types are not supported.

If you're just starting Flex application development, everything should look so natural to you that it doesn't even deserve further explanation. However, if you're a seasoned Flash developer, you may notice a number of improvements. Unlike *FSCommand* that accepts one and only one argument of the String type, you can use any number of parameters with an *ExternalInterface.call*. Another improvement over the "old approach" is that dealing with return values is absolutely transparent: you just get the value returned by JavaScript function as a result of its operation. In dark ancient days you'd have to cope with dynamic properties and either *Object.watch* or *onEnterFrame* events.

The code snippet above has a serious problem: if you accidentally run your SWF in a hosting application that has no External API support (like a standalone Flash Player), you'll get an error message. When you have to develop a Flex application that works in different containers and not all of them support the External API, you definitely need a way to detect the availability of the External API. To do this, it's necessary to check a static property *available* to the *ExternalInterface* class:

```
import flash.external.ExternalInterface;
...
if ( ExternalInterface.available )
  ExternalInterface.call( "javaScriptFunctionName", arg1, arg2, ..., argN );
```

To declare an ActionScript function as callable from JavaScript you have to perform two steps. First, you have to declare a callback function in your ActionScript class:

```
private function myCallback(arg1:type1, arg2:type2, ..., argN:typeN):Type {
  ...
  return something;
}
```

Second, you have to register your function using *ExternalInterface.addCallback*:

```
import flash.external.ExternalInterface;
...
if ( ExternalInterface.available )
  ExternalInterface.addCallback( "myFunction", myCallback );
```

The first parameter to *ExternalInterface.addCallback* is the name of the function as it will be visible to JavaScript. The second parameter is the function closure to invoke. Notice that you may expose your ActionScript function to JavaScript under a different name, but for the sake of clarity, using the same name is recommended.

ExternalInterface.addCallback supports different kinds of functions as a second parameter: a method closure referencing an instance method, a static class method, even an in-line anonymous function as in the example below:

```
import flash.external.ExternalInterface;
import mx.controls.Alert;
...
if ( ExternalInterface.available )
  ExternalInterface.addCallback( "myFunction", function():void{ Alert.
show("Called fromJavaScript"); } );
```

When you pass an instance method closure as an argument, the callback is directed at the method of a particular object instance, so you can access other instance methods or properties of this object. The set of supported arguments' types is exactly the same as for arguments passed with *ExternalInterface.call.*

Typically, callback functions are registered when an application is created, i.e., in the *creationComplete* event handler's chain. However, you can register a callback at any time during the application lifecycle, or even replace one callback with another if necessary. However, there's no method to remove a callback completely. As a workaround, replace already registered callbacks with a function that doesn't do anything.

Believe it or not, this is all you have to know about the External API to start using it. The only important point left uncovered is the security aspect. When you're accessing a Flex function from JavaScript running on an HTML page, or when you call a JavaScript function from Flex, stringent security restrictions are applied. According to the default security policy both HTML and SWF files must originate from the same domain. In most cases this requirement is quite easy to follow.

If you want to relax the restrictions associated with the *ExternalInterface.call* method, then you have to tweak the *allowScriptAccess* parameter of the HTML <OBJECT> tag or the attribute with same name in the HTML <EMBED> tag. Changing this setting from the *sameDomain* default value to liberate *always* lets you execute JavaScript functions regardless of whether the JavaScript source is in the same domain as Flex swf. If you set the aforementioned property to *never*, you effectively cause any *ExternalInterface.call* invocation to fail with a security error.

To relax the security policy that's applied to JavaScript calling a Flex function, you must use one of the ActionScript methods, S*ecurity.allowDomain* or *Security.allowInsecureDomain*. Supply the list of domain names you want to grant access to as parameters:

```
Security.allowDomain("www.host-a.com", "www.host-b.net");
```

Or use the wildcard "*" to grant access to the JavaScript code loaded from any host:

```
Security.allowDomain("*");
```

The latest option is to edit your global Flash Player Security Settings and add certain domains to trusted sites. You must do this if you run this chapter's examples from your local file system. To do this visit the Global Security Settings panel at http://www.macromedia.com/support/documentation/en/flashplayer/help/settings_manager04.html and add directory with examples to the list of trusted sites.

We're done with the theory so let's proceed with a small working example. What we need is just a simple Flex application and a small HTML page.

Here's the code for Flex MXML:

```
<?xml version="1.0" encoding="utf-8"?>
```

```
<!-- File ./FxJavaScript.mxml                  -->
<!-- Flex / JavaScript communications example -->
<mx:Application xmlns:mx="http://www.adobe.com/2006/mxml" layout="absolute" creationCo
mplete="onCreationComplete()">
   <mx:Script>
   <![CDATA[
      import mx.controls.Alert;
      import flash.external.ExternalInterface;
      private var counter:int = 0;

      private function onCreationComplete():void {
         if (!ExternalInterface.available)
            Alert.show( "No ExternalInterface available for container" );
         else
            ExternalInterface.addCallback( "asFunction", callActionScript );
      }

      private function callActionScript(newMessage:String):void {
         input.text = newMessage;
      }

      private function callJavaScript():void {
         if (!ExternalInterface.available) return;

         counter++;
         var retVal:Object = ExternalInterface.call("jsFunction",
            input.text, counter, new Date(), counter % 2 == 0);

         var newMessage:String = retVal as String;
         if (newMessage != null) input.text = newMessage;
      }
   ]]>
   </mx:Script>
   <mx:VBox width="100%" paddingLeft="10" paddingRight="10" paddingTop="10" padding-
Bottom="10">
      <mx:TextInput id="input" width="100%"/>
      <mx:Button id="button" width="100%" label="Call JavaScript" click="callJavaScrip
t()"/>
   </mx:VBox>
</mx:Application>
```

Listing 15.1 An External API sample

We start with an *onCreationComplete* event handler. Here we first check whether the External API is available and, if so, register an *callActionScript* instance method closure under the name "asFunction" so JavaScript code can invoke this method like:

```
flexObject.asFunction("String argument");
```

Now take a look at the *callActionScript* method itself. As long as we use an instance method closure, we can refer to other instance variables or methods. In the example above we just assign the given text to the TextInput control.

The second method is used to invoke a *jsFunction* JavaScript function from a Flex application in response to the button click. Again, we start with an External API availability check. You may choose a different strategy for your application and just disable the button after the initial check. We're passing several parameters of different types to the JavaScript function: the number of invocations as Number, user-entered text as String, current timestamp as Date, and even/odd invocation flag as Boolean. Finally, the method handlers return a value from the JavaScript function. If it returns a String then we update the text of TextInput control.

Next, we have to create an HTML file that embeds the Flex SWF:

```
<html lang="en">
<!-- File ./html-template/FxJavaScript.template.html -->
<!-- Flex / JavaScript communications example       -->
<head>
  <meta http-equiv="Content-Type" content="text/html; charset=utf-8" />
  <title>Basic External API Example</title>
  <style type="text/css">
    #fxJavaScript { width: 15em; height: 80px; }
    #html_controls {
      width: 15em; margin-top: 1em; padding: 1em;
      color: white; border: solid 1px white;
      font-family: Arial
    }
    body>#html_controls {
      width: 13em;
    }
    body {
      background-color: #869CA7;
    }
  </style>
  <script language="JavaScript">
    function jsFunction(string, number, date, boolean) {
        alert(
```

```
            ["String  = ", string,  ", ", typeof string,  "\n",
             "Number  = ", number,  ", ", typeof number,  "\n",
             "Date    = ", date,    ", ", typeof date,    "\n",
             "Boolean = ", boolean, ", ", typeof boolean, "\n"
            ].join("")
        );
        return string ? string.toUpperCase() : string;
      }

      function callActionScript () {
        var fxControl = document.fxJavaScript || window.fxJavaScript;
        var value = document.getElementById("txtMessage").value;
        fxControl.asFunction( value );
      }
    </script>
  </head>
  <body scroll="no">
    <object classid="clsid:D27CDB6E-AE6D-11cf-96B8-444553540000"
      id="fxJavaScript"
      codebase="http://fpdownload.macromedia.com/get/flashplayer/current/swflash.cab">
      <param name="movie" value="FxJavaScript.swf" />
      <param name="quality" value="high" />
      <param name="bgcolor" value="#869CA7" />
      <param name="allowScriptAccess" value="sameDomain" />
      <embed src="FxJavaScript.swf"
        name="fxJavaScript"
        id="fxJavaScript"
        align="middle"
        bgcolor="#869CA7"
        quality="high"
        play="true"
        loop="false"
        quality="high"
        allowScriptAccess="sameDomain"
        type="application/x-shockwave-flash"
        pluginspage="http://www.adobe.com/go/getflashplayer">
      </embed>
    </object>
    <div id="html_controls">
      Send message to Flex<br/>
      <input type="text" id="txtMessage" /><button
      onclick="callActionScript ()">Send</button>
    </div>
  </body>
```

```
</html>
```

Listing 15.2 The HTML page for the sample External API application

To save the book space, we've removed the boilerplate code generated by Flex Builder that handles automatic Flash plug-in installation, disabled JavaScript, and browser history navigation. So to run this example you must have Flash Player 9 installed and JavaScript enabled.

The HTML file embeds the Flex application via both the <OBJECT> and <EMBED> tags to support a wide range of browsers and provide a minimal set of controls to invoke an ActionScript function from JavaScript. The most interesting part is a pair of JavaScript functions defined in the <SCRIPT> tag.

The first one is a *jsFunction* that's invoked from our Flex application. This function just dumps supplied parameters using the built-in *window.alert* method and returns the string parameter to ActionScript transformed into upper case. While executing this example, you may see that the JavaScript function receives parameters of the same type (String, Number, Date, Boolean) as on the ActionScript side.

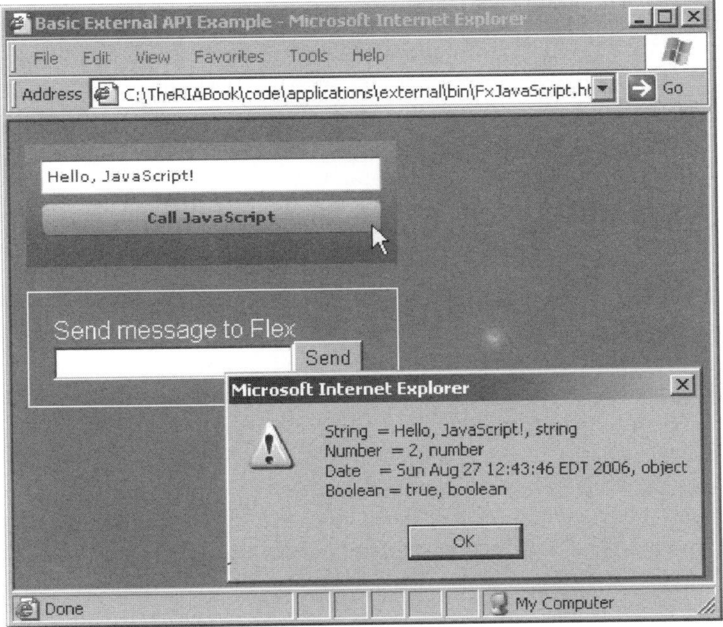

Figure 15.1 External API notification received by JavaScript

Note that the name of this function must exactly match the first parameter of the *ExternalInterface.call* (Listing 15.1) and must be defined in the *global* scope[1]. If you mistype the name either in the Flex application or in the HTML, the External API silently returns an *undefined* value to

ActionScript without any errors! If you supply more parameters to the *ExternalInterface.call*, then the JavaScript function expects the rest of them will be ignored. If the argument list is shorter than expected, the remaining ones will have *undefined* values.

The second function – *callActionScript* – shows how easy it is to invoke an ActionScript function exposed via the External API:

```
fxControl.asFunction( value );
```

The only tricky part here is to get a reference to fxControl (Flex ActiveX or a plug-in). We used common JavaScript "or" shorthand to get this reference either from the *window* object (Internet Explorer) or from the *document* (Gecko-based browsers or Safari):

```
var fxControl = document.fxJavaScript || window.fxJavaScript;
```

When we invoke *asFunction* the content of the TextInput control inside the Flex application is updated accordingly.

Unlike JavaScript, ActionScript has optional strong typing. In fact, the Flex Builder compiler uses strong typing by default. So unless the function closure passed to *ExternalInterface.addCallback* allows a variable number of arguments, supplying more or less arguments than expected will result in an error. To test this, you can modify the *fxControl.asFunction(...)* from Listing 15.2 to pass either no arguments at all or, say, two arguments – either scenario will cause an error. Supplying arguments of a non-expected type forces the implicit type conversion on the ActionScript side. If the type conversion fails, you'll see an error again. But wait, if it succeeds, it's even worse: there's a good chance of falling into the trap of hard-to-find bugs.

For example, consider an ActionScript callback that defines Number and String parameters. However, JavaScript code passes them in the wrong order: first String, then Number. This call will succeed with the first parameter containing the result of String-to-Number conversion (zero, if the String contains non-numeric characters) and the second parameter presenting Number as String *(Number.toString())*, but the final result will hardly be correct.

Interesting enough, all built-in JavaScript global functions as well as methods of the window object are also available to the ExternalInterface. In other words, you can use methods like *alert, confirm, navigate, open,* and many others directly from Flex applications. For example:

```
private function openAboutWindow():void {
    if ( !ExternalInterface.available) return;

    var confirmed:Boolean = ExternalInterface.call("confirm",
  "This will open \"About\" page in new browser window.\nPress \"OK\" to con-
tinue."
    );
```

```
      if ( !confirmed ) return;
      ExternalInterface.call("open",
       "http://myhost/about.html", "_blank" );
  };
```

```
This remains true for JavaScript global functions like eval:
```

```
  private function applyHtmlStyle():void {
     if ( !ExternalInterface.available) return;
     ExternalInterface.call("eval",
        'document.getElementById("' + ExternalInterface.objectID + '").style.border
=  "solid 3px red";'
     );
  }
```

Bear in mind, however, that many JavaScript programmers say eval is B.A.D. – Broken As Designed. The ratio of flexibility versus readability of code using *eval* is also disputable; the performance lost is proven by practice: JavaScript will have to switch back to interpreter mode when executing a statement passed to *eval*.

Two-Way Flex – OWC Spreadsheet Integration

In the last section we discussed the basics: what ExternalInterface is and how it enables bidirectional communications between JavaScript inside the HTML page and the embedded Flex application.

Now we'll consider a more complex example of integration with external applications. The solution involves two ActiveX objects embedded in an HTML page with instant as well as on-demand data synchronization between the objects.

One of these ActiveX objects is the Flash Player control, executing a Flex application. The second ActiveX is a spreadsheet from Microsoft Office Web Components (OWC). You may think of the spreadsheet as a miniature Microsoft Excel application running inside the HTML page. We hope you find our choice of the external application quite natural; data entry or analytical applications with no Excel integration are hard to find. Be it saving data in native Excel format or CSV, accepting data entered in Excel, or dynamically creating Excel charts based on the database queries – we see it everywhere.

Later in this chapter we'll show the integration of Flex with a real Microsoft Office Excel application, but for now Spreadsheet ActiveX will do just fine, given the large set of common functionality between Excel and the OWC Spreadsheet.

Before diving into coding, let's briefly outline the design of the complete solution.

First, we need a Flex application to play with. We'll build a simple Master/Detail screen with DataGrid and Form exposing the basic set of data entry operations: Create-Read-Update-Delete, commonly referred to as CRUD. Every operation will be notifying the hosting environment about the data changes using the *ExternalInterface.call* method.

Second, we need a Spreadsheet ActiveX control embedded in the same HTML page. As with any third-party ActiveX component we can script it using methods of a Dispatch interface also known as an automation interface. Thankfully, Spreadsheet's objects have a rich API with all the necessary methods to read/write data and change tracking events.

Finally, we need some mediator that orchestrates communications between both parties. This task is carried out by a set of JavaScript functions/event handlers inside the HTML page.

As far as ActiveX components are used, the example can run only under Internet Explorer on the Microsoft Windows platform (any modern version like Windows 2000 or Windows XP). See Figure 15.2 to get an impression of what the final result looks like.

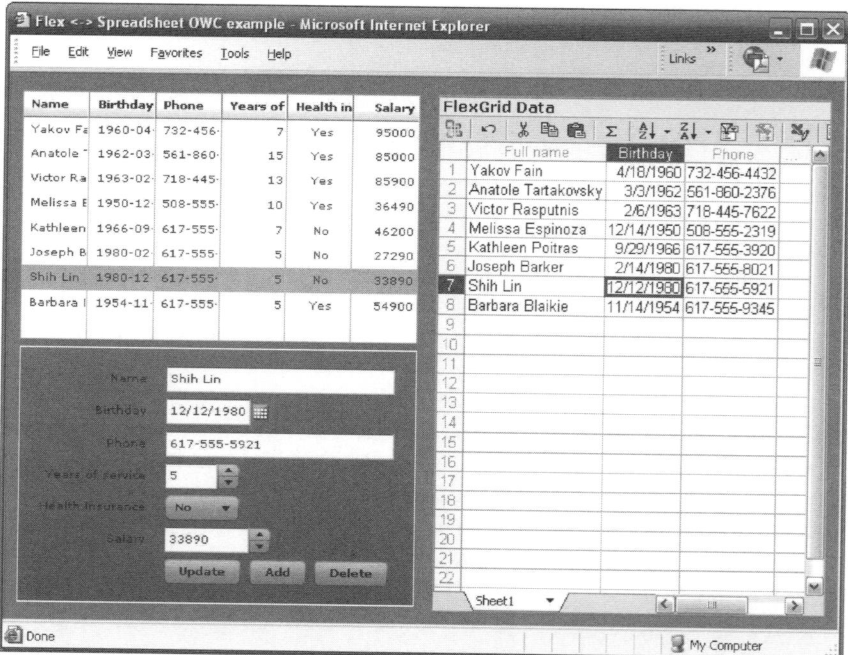

Figure 15.2 Flex + Spreadsheet OWC example running

After the page is loaded and the initial data for the Flex application is available, the user can edit the records using either the Flex application or a Spreadsheet OWC control. Any changes like altering the cell value in the Spreadsheet or inserting/deleting records in the Flex application are immediately synchronized between two controls. Moreover, the "undo" functionality is fully supported: if the user modifies a record in the Flex application, it can revert changes in the Spreadsheet OWC and both controls will be updated accordingly.

Flex Application for OWC Spreadsheet Integration

Okay, we start with a Flex application. After all, Flex serves the data in our scenario so it has an upper hand, besides the fact that we already know everything to start on the Flex part immediately:

```
<?xml version="1.0" encoding="utf-8"?>
<!-- File ./FxSpreadsheet.mxml                    -->
<!-- Flex / Spreadsheet OWC communications example -->
<mx:Application xmlns:mx="http://www.adobe.com/2006/mxml"
      layout="absolute" creationComplete=" onCreationComplete()">
      <mx:Script>
      <![CDATA[
      import mx.collections.ArrayCollection;

      [Bindable]
      private var employees:ArrayCollection = new ArrayCollection();
      [Bindable]
      public var bhiOptions:Array = [{label: "No", data:false}, {label:"Yes", data:
true}];

      private var notify:Boolean;

      private function onCreationComplete():void {
         notify = ExternalInterface.available;
         if (notify) {
            ExternalInterface.addCallback("xlImportRows", xlImportRows);
            ExternalInterface.addCallback("xlResend",     xlResend);
            fxMetadata();
         }
         loadData();
      }

      public function xlResend():void {
         fxMetadata()();
         fxRowsUpdated(0, employees.toArray(), true);
      }

      public function xlImportRows(offset:int, cells:Array, reset:Boolean):void {
         if (reset) {
            if (employees) employees.removeAll();
```

```
            else employees = new ArrayCollection();
            cells.forEach( function(el:Object,idx:int,array:Array):void {
               var employee:Object = {};
               for (var name:String in el) employee[name] = el[name];
               employees.addItem(employee);
            });
            if (employees.length)
            dataGrid.selectedIndex = 0;
         }
         else
            cells.forEach( function(el:Object,idx:int,array:Array):void {
               var pos:int = idx + offset;
               var employee:Object = employees.getItemAt(pos);
               for (var name:String in el)
                  employee[name] = el[name];
               employees.setItemAt(employee, pos);
            });
      }

      private function addRow():void {
         if (frmName.text != "") {
            var item:Object = employee(
            frmName.text,  frmBirthday.selectedDate, frmPhone.text,
            frmYos.value, frmHealthInsurance.selectedItem.data,  frmSalary.value
            );
            var idx:int = dataGrid.selectedIndex;
            var nextIdx:int = idx >= 0 ? idx + 1 : 0;
            employees.addItemAt( item, nextIdx );
            dataGrid.selectedIndex = nextIdx;
            fxRowsInserted(idx, [item]);
         }
         }

      private function updateRow():void {
         var idx:int = dataGrid.selectedIndex;
         if (idx >= 0) {
            var item:Object = employee(
               frmName.text, frmBirthday.selectedDate, frmPhone.text,
               frmYos.value, frmHealthInsurance.selectedItem.data, frmSalary.value
            );
            employees.setItemAt(item, idx);
            employees.itemUpdated( item );
            fxRowsUpdated(idx, [item], false);
         }
```

```
    }
    private function deleteRow():void {
       var idx:int = dataGrid.selectedIndex;
       if (idx >= 0) {
          employees.removeItemAt(idx);
          if ( !employees.length ) {
             frmName.text = frmPhone.text = "";
             frmBirthday.selectedDate = new Date;
             frmYos.value = 1; frmSalary.value = 0;
          }
          else
             dataGrid.selectedItem = employees.getItemAt(Math.min(idx, employees.length
- 1));
          fxRowsRemoved(idx, 1);
       }
    }

    private function applyResult(data:Array):void {
       employees = new ArrayCollection(data);
       fxRowsUpdated(0, data, true);
    }

    private function fxRowsInserted(offset:int, content:Array):void {
       if ( notify ) ExternalInterface.call("fxRowsInserted", offset, content);
    }

    private function fxRowsUpdated(offset:int, content:Array, reset:Boolean):void {
       if ( notify) ExternalInterface.call("fxRowsUpdated", offset, content, reset);
    }

    private function fxRowsRemoved(offset:int, size:int):void {
       if ( notify ) ExternalInterface.call("fxRowsRemoved", offset, size);
       }

    private function fxMetadata():void {
       if ( notify )  ExternalInterface.call("fxMetadata", [
          {name:"name",             title:"Full name",        type:"string"},
          {name:"birthday",         title:"Birthday",         type:"date"},
          {name:"phone",            title:"Phone",            type:"string"},
          {name:"yos",              title:"Years of srv.",    type:"number"},
          {name:"healthInsurance", title:"Health insurance", type:"boolean"},

          {name:"salary",           title:"Salary",           type:"number"}
       ]);
```

```
    }
    private function loadData():void {
       applyResult([
          employee("Yakov Fain",          d("1960/04/18"), "732-456-4432",
yos("1999/05/20"), true,  95000.0),
          employee("Anatole Tartakovsky", d("1962/03/03"), "561-860-2376",
yos("1991/03/01"), true,  85000.0),
          employee("Victor Rasputnis",    d("1963/02/06"), "718-445-7622",
yos("1993/07/02"), true,  85900.0),
          employee("Melissa Espinoza",    d("1950/12/14"), "508-555-2319",
yos("1996/04/18"), true,  36490.0),
          employee("Kathleen Poitras",    d("1966/09/29"), "617-555-3920",
yos("1999/05/29"), false, 46200.0),
          employee("Joseph Barker",       d("1980/02/14"), "617-555-8021",
yos("2001/09/10"), false, 27290.0),
          employee("Shih Lin",            d("1980/12/12"), "617-555-5921",
yos("2001/11/11"), false, 33890.0),
          employee("Barbara Blaikie",     d("1954/11/14"), "617-555-9345",
yos("2001/11/20"), true,  54900.0)
       ]);
    }

    private static function employee(name:String, birthday:Date, phone:String,
       yos:int, healthInsurance:Boolean, salary:Number):Object {
       return {
          name:name, birthday:birthday, phone:phone,
          yos:yos, healthInsurance: healthInsurance, salary:salary
       };
    }

    private static function d(s:String):Date {return new Date( Date.parse(s) );}
    private static const THIS_YEAR:int = new Date().getFullYear();
    private static function yos(startDate:String):int {return THIS_YEAR - d(startDate).
getFullYear();}

    private static function formatDate(itm:Object, col:Object):String {
       var d:Date = itm.birthday;
       return d ? [d.getFullYear(), pad(d.getMonth() + 1), pad(d.getDate())].join("-")
: "";
    }

    private function formatHealthInsurance(itm:Object, col:Object):String {
       return bhiOptions[itm.healthInsurance * 1].label;
    }
```

```
private static function pad(v:int):String {  return (v < 10 ? "0" : "") + v; }
]]>
</mx:Script>
<mx:VBox width="100%" height="100%">
   <mx:DataGrid id="dataGrid" width="100%" height="100%" dataProvider="{employees}"
      editable="false" sortableColumns="false">
      <mx:columns>
      <mx:Array>
         <mx:DataGridColumn dataField="name" headerText="Name"/>
         <mx:DataGridColumn labelFunction="formatDate" headerText="Birthday"/>

         <mx:DataGridColumn dataField="phone" headerText="Phone"/>

         <mx:DataGridColumn dataField="yos" headerText="Years of Srv." textAlign="
            right"/>
         <mx:DataGridColumn labelFunction="formatHealthInsurance"
            headerText="Health insurance" textAlign="center"/>
         <mx:DataGridColumn dataField="salary" headerText="Salary" textAlign="right
            "/>
      </mx:Array>
      </mx:columns>
   </mx:DataGrid>


   <mx:Form width="100%" height="100%" borderStyle="solid" borderColor="#ffffff">
      <mx:FormItem label="Name">
         <mx:TextInput id="frmName" width="200" text="{dataGrid.selectedItem.
            name}"/>
      </mx:FormItem>
      <mx:FormItem label="Birthday">
         <mx:DateField id="frmBirthday" selectedDate="{dataGrid.selectedItem.
            birthday}"/>
      </mx:FormItem>
      <mx:FormItem label="Phone">
         <mx:TextInput id="frmPhone" width="200" text="{dataGrid.selectedItem.
            phone}"/>
      </mx:FormItem>
      <mx:FormItem label="Years of service">
         <mx:NumericStepper id="frmYos" value="{dataGrid.selectedItem.yos}"
         maxChars="3" minimum="1" maximum="99"/>
      </mx:FormItem>
      <mx:FormItem label="Health insurance">
         <mx:ComboBox id="frmHealthInsurance"
            selectedIndex="{dataGrid.selectedItem.healthInsurance}"
```

```
                dataProvider="{bhiOptions}"/>
        </mx:FormItem>
        <mx:FormItem label="Salary">
            <mx:NumericStepper id="frmSalary" value="{dataGrid.selectedItem.salary}"
                maxChars="10" minimum="0" maximum="999999"/>
        </mx:FormItem>
        <mx:FormItem>
            <mx:HBox>
                <mx:Button label="Update" click="updateRow()"/>
                <mx:Button label="Add" click="addRow()"/>
                <mx:Button label="Delete" click="deleteRow()"/>
                </mx:HBox>
        </mx:FormItem>
    </mx:Form>
  </mx:VBox>
</mx:Application>
```

Listing 15.3 Flex application for OWC integration sample

Rather than going through a compete code walkthrough, let's just focus on the particular key methods. The first one, *fxMetadata*, notifies the hosting container about the metadata used. As long as we strive to keep the JavaScript on the HTML page as generic as possible, neither hard-coded nor "well-known" names are valid options. *fxMetadata* notification enables the JavaScript code to be used with a wide range of Flex applications. The metadata format used in our example is sufficient to describe the order of fields, user-friendly field names, and types of fields. The last feature is very important. Both Microsoft Excel and Microsoft Spreadsheet OWC support type-specific formating options, and we plan to exploit this functionality.

Next comes the trio of methods *fxRowsInserted*, *fxRowsUpdated*, and *fxRowsRemoved*. As their names suggest, these are data change notifications to the hosting container. Note that the notification for the complete data (re)load is *fxRowsUpdated* with the Boolean flag *reset* equals *true*. All data notifications use the *offset* parameter to define the positions where changes take place.

In this example we match the records in the Flex application and the rows in the Spreadsheet OWC by position, i.e., a record in the Flex application corresponds to a row in the Spreadsheet if they both have the same index. Other types of "equality" are possible as well, for example, matching a data record and the Spreadsheet row by key attributes. However, anything more complex than a simple index would require lengthy code examples that won't fit in a book chapter.

Finally, we have a pair of *xlImportRows* and *xlResend* methods as ActionScript callbacks exposed via the *ExternalInterface.addCallback*. The purpose of the first is fairly obvious: this is data change notification in the opposite direction from the Spreadsheet OWC to the Flex application. The second method deals with possible timing issues related to loading the SWF file by the Flash Player control. If HTML JavaScript was unable to get the pair of initial fxMetadata/fxRowsUpdated notifications, it can query the Flex application to resend them.

HTML Template Embedding Our ActiveX Components

It's time to write an HTML page that will carry our Flex application and the OWC Spreadsheet. Here's our first draft. It doesn't contain the OWC Spreadsheet, only the FxSpreadsheet.swf is embedded so far:

```
<html lang="en">
<!-- File ./html-template/FxSpreadsheet.template.html  -->
<!-- Flex / Spreadsheet OWC communications example     -->
<head>
<meta http-equiv="Content-Type" content="text/html; charset=utf-8" />
<title>Flex &lt;-&gt; Spreadsheet OWC example</title>
<style type="text/css">
   body { overflow: hidden; background: #869CA7 }
   #fxGrid { float:left; width: 50%; height: 100%; margin-right: 1em; }
   #xlBox { width: 99%; height: 100% }
   #xlOWC { width: 100%; height: 100%; border: 1px solid rgb(183,186,188) }
   * { font-family: Verdana, Arial; font-size: 10pt; color: white }
</style>
<script language="JavaScript" type="text/javascript">
   /* CODE TO DETECT CURRENT BROWSER / VERSION */
   var fxMetadata, fxRowsUpdated, fxRowsInserted, fxRowsRemoved;
   fxMetadata =  fxRowsUpdated = fxRowsInserted = fxRowsRemoved = function() {};
   /* MAIN JAVASCRIPT CODE */
</script>
</head>
<body scroll="no">
   <object classid="clsid:D27CDB6E-AE6D-11cf-96B8-444553540000"
      id="fxGrid" width="100%" height="100%"
      codebase="http://download.macromedia.com/pub/shockwave/cabs/flash/swflash.cab">
      <param name="movie" value="FxSpreadsheet.swf" />
      <param name="quality" value="high" />
      <param name="bgcolor" value="#869ca7" />
      <param name="allowScriptAccess" value="sameDomain" />
      <embed src="FxSpreadsheet.swf" name="fxGrid" quality="high" bgcolor="#869ca7"
         width="100%" height="100%" align="middle"
         play="true"
         loop="false"
         quality="high"
         allowScriptAccess="sameDomain"
         type="application/x-shockwave-flash"
```

```
            pluginspage="http://www.macromedia.com/go/getflashplayer">
        </embed>
</object>
<div id="xlBox">
    <!-- CODE TO WRITE SPREADSHEET ACTIVEX -->
</div>
</body>
</html>
```

Listing 15.4 The draft of an HTML page for OWC integration sample

Now we have to include the Spreadsheet OWC control in the HTML page. This control is available only as Microsoft Windows ActiveX, which leaves users of other platforms and browsers out in the cold. In any event, we feel obligated to relieve these users of JavaScript errors or browser crashes. Concrete fallback strategies may vary, but in the simplest form we have it here, it's just a message about the unsupported environment. More complex JavaScript may first analyze the browser and OS and then suggest more specific steps.

Here's the first block of JavaScript code that detects the version of the browser and OS. It's based on a conditional compilation, manifested by an @cc_on statement, an IE-specific feature. As long as the logic based on @cc_on is nested inside the /**/ comments, all other browsers simply treat it as a comment, nothing more:

```
<script language="JavaScript" type="text/javascript">
var ie_win32 = 0;
/* MS-only conditional compilation for JScript     */
/* Besides the fact that this is the most simple   */
/* guaranted way to detect IE, it provides OS info */
/*@cc_on @*/
/*@if (@_win32)
ie_win32 = 1;
/*@end @*/
</script>
```

Listing 15.5 The browser-detection script

As a net result, the variable ie_win32 gets sets to 1 if and only if the script is running under Microsoft Internet Explorer 5+ on Windows 95/NT 4.0 or higher. Browsers other than Microsoft Internet Explorer 5+ see the assignment as commented-out code. If the browser isn't IE our page will display the "complaint" and do nothing (see Listing 15.6 below):

```
if (!ie_win32) {document.write(wrong_env); return;}
```

Once IE is confirmed, our JavaScript must be robust enough to detect the availability of the Microsoft Office Web Components and to select the most recent version[2]. Currently, there are four versions of Microsoft Office Web Components: Office 2000, XP, XP SP3, and 2003 as shown, along with the corresponding CLSID in Table 15.1.

Microsoft OWC Version (Build)	Microsoft Office Version	CLSID of Spreadsheet OWC
09	Microsoft Office 2000	0002E510-0000-0000-C000-000000000046
10 (prior 4109)	Microsoft Office XP	0002E551-0000-0000-C000-000000000046
10 (4109 and above)	Microsoft Office XP SP3	0002E541-0000-0000-C000-000000000046
11	Microsoft Office 2003	0002E559-0000-0000-C000-000000000046

Table 15.1 A summary of OWC versions

And whether you're surprised with this abundance of versions or not, you have to understand and accept it to make your code run on all OWC-enabled systems.

The first version of Office Web Components released to the public was OWC 9. To say that it was released along with Microsoft Office 2000 would be an understatement because ordering the Office 2000 CD was the only way to get it. Aside from this questionable distribution model, the OWC9 API has been anything but practical. For example, a Spreadsheet component from that release lacks content change notification events, so essentially when used with OWC9 our example will be a one-way road from Flex to OWC.

The second big release was OWC coming with Microsoft Office XP (2002). The API was seriously reworked to match the object hierarchy and functionality of the corresponding Office applications. With this single release Microsoft contrived to make several important changes:

- It changed the CLSID of all Office Web Components after the release of Service Pack 3, see Table 15.1.
- It enhanced OWC licensing. Originally, to use OWC 10 Components in editable mode (as with version 9), you needed a Microsoft Office product or license file installed on your PC. The new licensing model introduced the notion of a "shared license" for business entities that have a special agreement with Microsoft. This opened the door for using OWC Components in an interactive mode within organizations' intranets even when a specific client computer has no Microsoft Office product or license file installed. For a full description refer to Microsoft's Knowledge Base article #555094 (http://support.microsoft.com/?scid=kb;en-us;555094&spid=2488&sid=714).
- The recent version 11 of Office Web Components has no dramatic changes comparable to previous versions. However, the API has been extended according to the enhancements in Microsoft Office 2003 (mostly XML-related stuff) and the set of CLSIDs used was changed again.

Now that we've completed this version-hell walkthrough, we're ready to write the JavaScript code that attempts to embed the most recent version of the Spreadsheet OWC Component or, alternatively, degrades the HTML page when no OWC is available, the IE security settings prohibit running ActiveX, or a combination of the browser/OS isn't supported:

```
<script language="JavaScript" type="text/javascript">
   (function(){
   var wrong_env =
   "<p>This sample requires Microsoft Internet Explorer " +
   "browser, running on Windows platform.Also you need "  +
   "Microsoft Office Web Components (OWC) installed.</p>"

   if (!ie_win32) {document.write(wrong_env); return;}

/* The very first entry in versions is     */
/* version-independend ProgID (vi-ProgID) */
/* However, it seems to always cause       *
/* errors, so we try versions from         */
/* higher to lower and lastly vi-ProgID    */
var versions = ['',9,10,11];
var version_clsids = {
      "09.0.0.0000": "0002E510",
      "10.0.0.0000": "0002E551", /*PRE-SP3*/
      "10.0.0.4109": "0002E541", /*SP3 and above, probably need to check 6619 build*/
      "11.0.0.0000": "0002E559"
  };
  var version_ids = [];
  for (var key in version_clsids) version_ids.push(key);
  version_ids.sort();

var clsidPrefix;
var versionInfo = "&lt;unknown&gt;";
LOOP_VERSIONS:
for (var i = versions.length - 1; i >=0; i--) {
      var owc = null;
      var ver = versions[i];
      var progid = "OWC" + ver + ".Spreadsheet" + (ver ? "." + ver : "");
      try { owc = new ActiveXObject(progid) } catch(e) {}
      if (owc) {
         versionInfo = (owc.majorVersion < 10 ? "0" : "") + owc.version;
         if (!ver) ver = parseInt(versionInfo);
         for (var i = version_ids.length - 1; i >= 0; i--) {
            var lastVersion = version_ids [i];
            var guess = version_clsids[lastVersion];
            if ( versionInfo >= lastVersion ) {
```

```
                clsidPrefix = guess;
                break LOOP_VERSIONS;
            }
        }
    }
}
if ( clsidPrefix )
    document.write(
      '<object id="xlOWC" classid="CLSID:' + clsidPrefix + '-0000-0000-C000-
000000000046" ' +
      'title="Microsoft Office Web Component / Excel Spreadsheet v' + versionInfo +
'">' +
      wrong_env + '</object>'
    );
else
    document.write(
      "<p>Unable to resolve Spreadsheet component CLSID for " +
      "Microsoft Office Web Components (OWC) version " + versionInfo + "</p>"
    );
})();
</script><noscript>
<p>Unable to detect OWC version: JavaScipt disabled.<br/>
This sample requires Microsoft Internet Explorer browser, running on Windows platform.
Also you need Microsoft Office Web Components (OWC) installed.</p></noscript>
```

Listing 15.6 Inserting the Spreadsheet ActiveX

The code traverses a list of available versions in reverse order (from tale to head, from higher version to lower) trying to instantiate a Spreadsheet component via the JScript-specific global function *ActiveXObject*. If object is created, we get its exact version and check it against the registry of CLSID prefixes (suffixes are the same for all versions). If a match is found, we write the <OBJECT> tag in place. If we fail for any reason (the wrong environment, no OWC installed), the problem description is provided.

Note that the complete scripting part of Listing 15.6 is enveloped in a single anonymous function call:

```
(function(){
   /* CODE HERE */
})();
```

Here's how you can read this: an expression that returns an anonymous function and immediately executes it. Quite simple but a powerful technique. First, all variables declared in the function are, naturally, encapsulated in the scope of the function. Therefore global scope isn't polluted; there's no chance to override global variables accidentally with the same names. Second, we may exit from the function early with a *return* statement – in traditional "global" script we'd rather use nested *if/else* statements.

Once we complete embedding the OWC SpreadSheet and the Flex application shown in the previous section, we get a page that results in this:

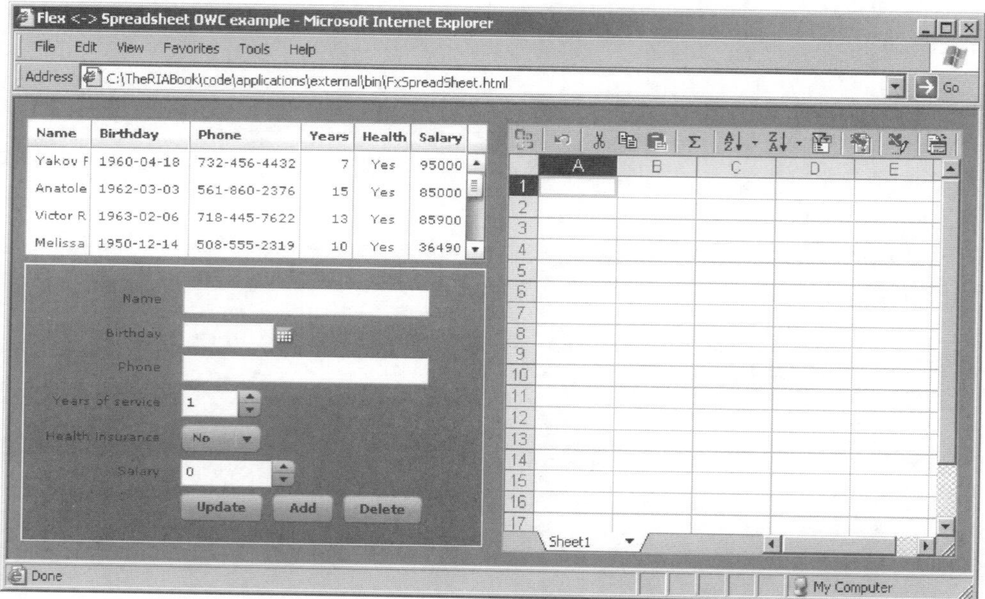

Figure 15.3 Flex and Spreadsheet OWC embedded

Making Flex and Spreadsheet Talk

We've got a pair of ActiveX controls separated by a 10-pixels spacer. We have to add a substantial dose of JavaScript glue to make them "talk" to each other. A truncated version of HTML with the "glue" added is presented in Listing 15.7. For purposes of clarity, we skipped the content covered earlier and separated the initialization procedure into several blocks. We're going to discuss these blocks one by one.

```
<html lang="en">
<!-- File ./html-template/FxSpreadsheet.template.html  -->
<!-- Flex / Spreadsheet OWC communications example     -->
<head>
<meta http-equiv="Content-Type" content="text/html; charset=utf-8" />
<title>Flex &lt;-&gt; Spreadsheet OWC example</title>
<style type="text/css">
```

```
    <!-- STYLES AS IN EXAMPLE ABOVE -->
  </style>
  <script language="JavaScript" type="text/javascript">
    var ie_win32 = 0;
    /*@cc_on @*/
    /*@if (@_win32)
    ie_win32 = 1;
    /*@end @*/

    var missedNotification = false; // Changed to true if Flex loads data quicker then
page initialized
    /* JavaScript callbacks invoked from Flex */
    var fxMetadata, fxRowsUpdated, fxRowsInserted, fxRowsRemoved;
    /* JavaScript callbacks invoked from Excel */
    var xlOWCEvents;
    (function(){
      var MISSED = function(){missedNotification = true; };
      fxMetadata     = MISSED; /* function(meta) {}                         */
      fxRowsUpdated  = MISSED; /* function(offset, content, reset) {} */
      fxRowsInserted = MISSED; /* function(offset, content) {};        */
      fxRowsRemoved  = MISSED; /* function(offset, count) {};          */

      var NOP = function(){};
      xlOWCEvents = { sheetChange: NOP,  beforeContextMenu: NOP, commandBeforeExecute:
NOP };
    })();

    window.onload = function() {
      var xlOWC = document.getElementById("xlOWC")
      if (!xlOWC) return; // No OWC component available

      var fxGrid  = window["fxGrid"];
      if (!fxGrid) return; // No Flex component available

      var COLUMNS_XL = [];
      var COLUMNS_FX = {};
      var COLUMNS_COUNT = COLUMNS_XL.length;
      var ROW_COUNT;

      var xlVersion = parseInt(xlOWC.version);
      var XLConstants = xlOWC.Constants;

      var xlSheet = xlVersion >= 10 ? xlOWC.activeSheet : xlOWC;
```

```
        if ( xlVersion >= 10) {
           /* Some small UI tweaks */
           var titleBar = xlOWC.titleBar;
           with (titleBar) { visible = true; caption = "FlexGrid Data"; interior.color =
"#F0F0F0"; }
           with (titleBar.font) { color = "#000000"; size  = 10; bold  = true;   name  =
"Verdana"; }
           xlOWC.activeWindow.enableResize = false;
        }

        function setupFxMetadata()          {  /* CODE WILL BE DISCUSSED BELOW */  }
        function setupFxDataNotifications() {  /* CODE WILL BE DISCUSSED BELOW */  }
        function setupXlDataNotifications() {  /* CODE WILL BE DISCUSSED BELOW */  }
        function setupXlContextMenu()       {  /* CODE WILL BE DISCUSSED BELOW */  }

        setupFxMetadata();
        setupFxDataNotifications();
        setupXlDataNotifications();
        setupXlContextMenu();

        /* If Flex application did not send data yet, then returns */
        /* Otherwise query for current data                        */
        if  (missedNotification)  fxGrid.xlResend();
     };
  </script>
  <script language='JavaScript' for='xlOWC' event='sheetChange(sheet,range)'>
     xlOWCEvents.sheetChange(sheet,range);
  </script>
  <script language='JavaScript' for='xlOWC' event='beforeContextMenu(x, y,
menu,cancel)'>
     xlOWCEvents.beforeContextMenu(x, y, menu, cancel);
  </script>
  <script language='JavaScript' for='xlOWC' event='commandBeforeExecute(cmd,cancel)'>
     xlOWCEvents.commandBeforeExecute(cmd,cancel);
  </script>
  </head>
  <body scroll="no">
     <!-- FLASH OBJECT/EMBED -->
     <!-- DIV WITH SCRIPT TO INSERT SPREADSHEET -->
  </body>
  </html>
```

Listing 15.7 The final HTML page for the OWC integration sample

The page is being initialized in two phases: when HTML starts loading and after the complete page content is available (see the *window.onload* event handler in Listing 15.7). During the first phase we provide a fallback implementation for both Flex notifications and Spreadhsheet OWC event handlers (packaged as *xlOWCEvents* object methods). You may be surprised to see that both groups of methods contain no real functionality. Let's assure the reader that the content of these methods is going to be dynamically reassigned later. For now, we keep them at bay so that no harm is done if they are invoked in the unsupported browser or at the wrong time.

To understand the kind of problems we're trying to avoid, imagine that our HTML page with an OWC example is opened in Firefox. The Spreadsheet control is unavailable in this environment, but the Flex application can run successfully (as long as the Flash plug-in is installed). The very first notification from Flex would cause a JavaScript error if the corresponding handler attempted to access a non-existing control. Sure, it's possible to add the necessary check to every notification handler. However, this is code duplication.

The second sort of problem we solve with "empty" notification handlers are timing-related. The SWF file is loaded asynchronously with the rest of the page and the fxMetadata notification is fired immediately from the *onCreationComplete* event handler (see Listing 15.3). Hence, the HTML page may get this notification earlier when the Spreadsheet ActiveX control is inserted and/or fully initialized. That's why notification handlers in this phase contain no functionality to update the Spreadsheet OWC; they all set the flag *missedNotification* to requery notifications from Flex when initialization is complete.

The second phase of the page initialization is executed when the *window.onload* event happens. It starts by looking for the *xlOWC* HTML element that we attempted to dynamically instantiate in Listing 15.6. If no object is returned for this ID, there's no sense in taking further action – HTML is running in the unsupported environment. Otherwise initialization continues and the reference to the second ActiveX control, Flash Player running the Flex application, is stored as well.

Next, the *window.onload* handler declares several metadata-related variables. Briefly, these variables describe the structure of the records coming from the Flex application and the associated rules to convert field values back and forth between Flex and the Spreadsheet (we'll make full use of these variables in the *fxMetadata* notification handler a bit later). As long as we need a bidirectional communication channel, two mapping structures are required:

- The number-indexed *COLUMNS_XL* array defines the mapping between the Spreadsheet column numbers and ActionScript field names. The position in this array corresponds to the index of the column.
- The associative *COLUMNS_FX* array defines the mapping between the ActionScript field name and the column index. The key in this array is the name of field.

The variables *COLUMN_COUNT* and *ROW_COUNT* hold the number of available fields (columns) and records (rows) correspondingly. Strictly speaking, *ROW_COUNT* relates to the data rather than to metadata.

To discuss the next variable – *xlSheet* – we at least need a recap of the Microsoft Excel/Spreadsheet OWC object model, which we're going to provide right here in a "Shakespeare on the eggshell" format.

The root of the object hierarchy is the *Application* object. For Spreadsheet OWC it's the control itself. Every *Application* contains a collection of *Workbooks*, every *Workbook*, in turn, holds a collection of *Worksheets*. Many objects in the hierarchy have a notion of "active" sub-elements. Active means "currently visible to the user and ready to accept the user's input." So an *Application* has an *ActiveWorkbook*, and a *Workbook* has an *ActiveSheet*. Transitively, *Application* has an *ActiveSheet* property as well.

When a Spreadsheet control is initialized, it pre-creates one active *Workbook* with three *Worksheets*; the first Worksheet is active. It's the reference to this very worksheet that's stored as an *xlSheet* variable during the initialization time.

Remember, there are a number of differences between existing OWC versions. To keep track of the currently used OWC version we defined the variable *xlVersion*. The version differences come into play immediately. In fact, everything we've said about the object model is true for the Microsoft Excel application and Spreadsheet OWC of versions 10/11, but doesn't stand for Spreadsheet version 9, which uses a completely different API. There are no such things like *Workbook*, *Worksheet*, and the collections thereof in OWC9. The Spreadsheet is a mix of Application with a sole active *Workbook* that has one and only one (active) Worksheet. However, the combination of the Microsoft COM late-binding mechanism, the JavaScript "duck typing," and the similarities between *Spreadsheet* and *Worksheet* APIs let us treat Spreadsheet as a Worksheet in certain cases: at least OWC9 functionality is enough to implement Flex-to-Spreadsheet communications fully; when it comes to anything beside this, our script degrades gracefully.

XLConstants provides a shortcut to all constants used in the Spreadsheet OWC methods. In scripting languages like JScript or VBScript there's no way to refer the constants declared in ActiveX-type libraries by name. Hence, every OWC control exposes a set of constants as its own complex property.

Just before returning from the *window.onload* event handler, when all setup and preparation is done, a check for lost notifications from the Flex application is done. If there are any, the Flex application is asked to resend notifications for both metadata and available data entries (see *fxGrid.xlResend()* invocation).

Handling Flex Metadata Notification

As a reminder, one of our primary design goals is to make the JavaScript code generic and reusable while fully using Excel formating capabilities. To that extent we externalize the metadata. This part of the code, which also fulfils our promise of overwriting the Flex metadata notification function, is presented in Listing 15.8:

```
   function setupFxMetadata() {
      function AS_IS(v) { return v; }
      function variantDate2jsDate (v) { return null == v ? null : new Date(v);  }
      XL_FORMATTERS = {
         date: variantDate2jsDate,  time: variantDate2jsDate,  dateTime:
variantDate2jsDate,
         boolean: function(v)  { return v == null ? null : !!v; },
         string: AS_IS, number: AS_IS
      };

      function fmtDate(v) { return [v.getFullYear(), v.getMonth() + 1, v.getDate()].
join("-"); }
      function fmtTime(v) { return [v.getHours(), v.getMinutes(), v.getSeconds()].
join(":"); }
      FX_FORMATTERS = {
         date: fmtDate, time: fmtTime, dateTime: function(v) { return fmtDate(v) + " " +
fmtTime(v); },
         boolean: AS_IS, string: AS_IS, number: AS_IS
      };

         fxMetadata = function(meta) {
         meta = meta || [];
         ROW_COUNT = 0;
         fxRowsUpdated(0, [], true);

         COLUMNS_FX = {};
         COLUMNS_COUNT = meta.length;
         COLUMNS_XL = new Array(COLUMNS_COUNT);
         var xlHeadings;
         if (xlVersion >= 10) {
            var xlWnd = xlOWC.activeWindow;
            xlWnd.resetHeadings();
            xlHeadings = xlWnd.columnHeadings;
         }
         else {
            var FAKE_HEADING = {};
            xlHeadings = function(idx) { return FAKE_HEADING; }
         }

         for (var i = 0; i < COLUMNS_COUNT; i++) {
            var field = meta[i];
            COLUMNS_XL[i] = field.name;
            field.idx = i + 1;
            field.xl = XL_FORMATTERS[field.type];
```

```
            field.fx = FX_FORMATTERS[field.type];
            COLUMNS_FX[field.name] = field;
            xlHeadings(i + 1).caption = field.title;
        }
    }
}
```

Listing 15.8 Initializing metadata functions

When our JavaScript is notified of metadata changes (the function *fxMetadata*), it must do several things. First, it's necessary to reset all existing variables that are related to the metadata. We also need to drop the existing content. Otherwise the user will be confused to see a logical mismatch between column headings and cell content. Afterwards, the handler re-creates JavaScript metadata variables according to parameters from ActionScript.

We use the active *Window* instance to overwrite a default text of column headings with user-friendly field titles (compare the Spreadsheet column heading texts in Figures 15.2 and 15.3). Note that though the *Window* object is present in both Excel and Spreadsheet OWC 10/11, the column/row headings functionality is unique to the Spreadsheet component. As you can see from the workaround applied, Spreadsheet OWC 9 has no such functionality.

The remaining part of the code in Listing 15.8 deals with type formats. Excel is smart enough to auto-format a cell based on the values entered. So if we transform the original value to the Excel-friendly form, the necessary formatting will be applied automatically.

Be aware that the primary scripting language of Microsoft Office Applications is Visual Basic. It could either be VBA inside Office applications or VBScript for Office Web Components. In fact, the very first Visual Basic customer was the Microsoft Excel team!

Many Visual Basic features may look strange from the JavaScript perspective. One of them, for example, is that indexing in Visual Basic starts from 1 (one) whereas in JavaScript or ActionScript it starts from 0 (zero). So be prepared to see "row + 1" statements here and there in example code.

The second issue is that the presentation of certain types differs between Visual Basic and JScript. The most problematic one is Date. Visual Basic accepts a date as a variant of the VT_DATE type. Under the hood, it's a floating-point value, counting days since midnight December 30, 1899. Hours and minutes are represented as fractional days. In the ECMAScript family of languages like JavaScript, ActionScript, or JScript, a date is represented as an object of the Date type and its internal representation is the number of milliseconds since January 1, 1970. There's enough differences to get upset!

That said, Excel is smart enough to parse the date from a string in several formats[3], for example, "2006-06-04 14:30:30" is recognizable as a date/time value. The set of FX_FORMATTERS for date/time types uses this feature. The values of other JavaScript types can be safely passed to Excel as is.

While moving the data in the opposite direction, we need to convert VT_DATE to JavaScript. Thankfully, it's just a Date constructor call with VT_DATE as an argument (see the *variantDate2jsDate* function in Listing 15.8), a neat undocumented feature of JScript. For fields defined as Boolean we need to ensure that the value entered in the Spreadsheet is indeed Boolean. To that end we apply the good old JavaScript "negation of negation" idiom to convert the value entered to the Boolean type:

```
var numberF = 0,    numberT = 255;
var stringF = "",   stringT = "ABC";
var objectF = null, objectT = new Date();

var isNumberF = !!numberF; // false;
var isNumberT = !!numberT; // true;
var isStringF = !!stringF; // false;
var isStringT = !!stringT; // true;
var isObjectF = !!objectF; // false;
var isObjectT = !!objectT; // true;
```

You may have noticed that we are updating the metadata *field* objects that come from ActionScript. Such updates don't affect original objects in ActionScript due to the marshaling used by the External API protocol (we'll discuss this later).

Synchronizing Spreadsheet OWC with Flex Data Changes

To discuss the part of the code that handles data change notifications coming from the Flex application, we have to digress a level deeper in the Microsoft Excel/Spreadsheet OWC objects tree. The code operates on the content of the *Worksheet*, which is made up of cells. There's no *Cell* object in the tree per se, but there's a *Range* object. *Range* is a lightweight object that provides access to any number of cells depending on the range bounds. So you can think of a cell as just a *Range* with the top-left corner equal to the bottom-right one. Similarly, a column is a *Range* with the left bound equal to the right bound, the top bound is equal to one, and the bottom bound is equal to the maximum number of rows allowed (in recent Excel versions it's 2^16). By the same analogy, a row is a *Range* with the top bound equal to the bottom bound, the left equal to one and the right equal to the maximum number of columns allowed (up to 2^8).

The number of methods to get the Range object in the Excel/Spreadsheet OWC far outweighs the number of ways to skin a cat. Depending on your needs, it's possible to construct a *Range* from a *Worksheet* supplying the pair of top/left and bottom/right cells; it's possible to get a *Range* by the name of the cells (for example, "A1:B2"); there's a notion of an active cell and current selection; the result of the intersection/union operations on ranges is, obviously, *Range* as well. For a complete list see the Excel VBA documentation available with the Office Web Components.

A *Range* is a very efficient abstraction when it comes to data operations or formatting. If you read a value from the *Range*, the value returned is taken from the top-level cell. When you assign an individual value to the *Range* or modify its visual property like *FillStyle* it affects all cells in the *Range*.

The code we're going to present in Listing 15.9 reacts to data changes on the Flex side and modifies the Spreadsheet accordingly. In essence, it sequentially assigns values to individual cells. This approach has a serious associated performance penalty. The cost of multiple assignments and in general the cost of multiple calls across COM object boundaries is inherently high. To make things worse, with JScript and VBScript we're limited to the COM IDispatch interface.

We'll address the performance improvements later, when instead of individual value assignments we'll use another feature of *Range* – the support of tabular data assignments such as pasting HTML content from the clipboard or copying values from *ADODB.Recordset*. In these cases *Range* forces data to be split up into individual values, one per cell.

```
function setupFxDataNotifications() {
      function xlCopyCells(offset, content) {
         for (var i = content.length - 1; i >= 0; i--) {
            var obj = content[i];
            var row = i + 1 + offset;
            for (var name in COLUMNS_FX) {
               var col = COLUMNS_FX[name];
               xlSheet.cells(row, col.idx).value = col.fx(obj[name]);
                  }
         }
         }


            function xlTransaction(fn) {
         xlOWC.enableEvents = false;
         xlOWC.beginUndo();
         try { fn(); }
         finally {
            xlOWC.endUndo();
            xlOWC.enableEvents = true;
         }
      }

      fxRowsUpdated = function(offset, content, reset) {
         xlTransaction(function() {
            var cells = xlSheet.cells;
            if (reset) { cells.clear(); offset = 0; }
            xlCopyCells(offset, content);

            var count = content.length;
            if (reset)  ROW_COUNT = count;
```

```
        if ( !count ) return;

        var range = xlSheet.range(
          xlSheet.cells(offset + 1, 1),
          xlSheet.cells(offset + count, COLUMNS_COUNT)
        );
        range.select();
        if (reset && xlVersion >= 10) range.columns.autoFit();
      });
    };

    fxRowsInserted = function(offset, content) {
      var count = content.length;
      if (!count) return;
      xlTransaction(function(){
        var row = offset + 2;
        while (count--) xlSheet.rows(row).insert();
        xlCopyCells(offset + 1, content);
        var range = xlSheet.range(
          xlSheet.cells(row, 1),
          xlSheet.cells(row + content.length - 1, COLUMNS_COUNT)
        );
        range.select();
      });
    };

    fxRowsRemoved = function(offset, count) {
      if (!count) return;
      xlTransaction(function(){
        var row = offset + 1;
        while (count--) xlSheet.rows(row)["delete"]();
        var range = xlSheet.range(
          xlSheet.cells(row, 1),
          xlSheet.cells(row, COLUMNS_COUNT)
        );
        range.select();
      });
    };
  }
```

Listing 15.9 Handling data changes in a Flex application

Methods *xlCopyCells* and *xlTransaction* are used by Flex data change notification handlers. The rationale behind *xlCopyCells* is clear. Given a zero-based offset and content as an array of objects, the method assigns a value of every property to corresponding cells. This is where the *FX_COLUMNS* associative array comes in handy. It provides a way to both order properties and get correct formatting function to convert values as necessary.

The *xlTransaction* method is a pure function decorator. First of all, it disables notification events from Spreadsheet OWC when we're modifying cells. Otherwise, there's a risk of either getting into infinite recursion or issuing an unnecessary update to the Flex application. Second, it lets us enlist a set of operations for a single undo "command," or otherwise users might be surprised with the number of clicks needed to undo the changes on the Spreadsheet side of a single atomic record insertion/modification/deletion done on the side of the Flex application.

On a side note, *beginUndo/endUndo* functionality isn't unique to Spreadsheet OWC. Similar functionality exists in Excel. But it's implemented in a different way as the *Application.OnUndo("MenuText," "ProcedureName")* method.

The Flex notification handlers fxRowsUpdated, fxRowsInserted, and fxRowsRemoved are quite easy to follow. All of them pass processing blocks as function closures to *xlTransaction*. For the insertion/deletion of rows we first get the complete row from an existing Range via the *xlSheet.rows(idx)* call. Both *insert* and *delete* methods have optional parameters that define how to shift the remaining cells. However, if Range is a complete column/row we can safely skip this parameter. Note how we use "key notation" inside fxRowsRemoved to avoid using dot notation against the *delete*, which is a JavaScript keyword.

So far we've enabled the Spreadsheet population with data from the Flex application. Users can edit data in Flex and changes are automatically propagated to Spreadsheet.

In the next section we'll look at Spreadsheet-to-Flex data updates.

Synchronizing Flex with Spreadsheet Data Changes

The code that will send data changed in Spreadsheet back to Flex is presented in Listing 15.10:[4]

```
function setupXlDataNotifications() {
  xlOWCEvents.sheetChange = function(sheet, range) {
    if (!ROW_COUNT || (xlSheet != sheet)) return;
    xlOWC.enableEvents = false;
    try {
      var r1 = range.row;
      var c1 = range.column;
      var rc = range.rows.count;
      var cc = range.columns.count;
      if (r1 > ROW_COUNT || c1 > COLUMNS_COUNT)  return;

      var rows = Math.min(rc, ROW_COUNT - r1 + 1);
```

```
        var cols = Math.min(cc, COLUMNS_COUNT - c1 + 1);
        var content = new Array(rows);
        for (var i = 0; i < rows ; i++) {
          var row = content[i] = {}
          for (var j = 0, col = c1 - 1; j < cols; j++, col++) {
            var prop  = COLUMNS_XL[col];
            row[prop] = COLUMNS_FX[prop].xl( range.cells(i+1, j+1).value );
          }
        }
        fxGrid.xlImportRows(r1 - 1, content, false)
      }
      finally {  xlOWC.enableEvents = true;  }
    };
  }
```

Listing 15.10 Handling data changes in Spreadsheet OWC

The *xlOWCEvents.sheetChange* method gets two parameters from the corresponding event: the reference to the Worksheet where the event occurred and the range of affected cells. Potentially, this range can be large enough to freeze the program forever. Imagine a use case where a user selects several columns and presses the Delete key. The Range parameter for such an event contains 2^16 rows. Clearly, processing all of them would take an unacceptable amount of time. So the first thing the event handler above does is restrict the processing area to some reasonable region. In our case it's an intersection of the parameter *range* with (1,1) : (*ROW_COUNT, COLUMN_COUNT*) area. After getting correct boundaries the only thing left is to construct the payload for the Flex *xlImportRows* method.

Let's stress that the above method supports fine-grained change notifications. If the user updates a value only in one cell, then exactly one property of a single object will be updated. If the user selects a range of cells and updates them at once (as a rule via copying clipboard data or deleting values), then the update package will contain only the rows affected with every row containing only affected properties. The *xlImportRows* method on the Flex side knows about this feature and behaves accordingly.

The definition of the xlOWCEvents.sheetChange method on its own, however, isn't sufficient. This is where the following strange script block comes into play:

```
<script language="JavaScript" for="xlOWC" event="sheetChange(sheet,range)">
xlOWCEvents.sheetChange(sheet,range);
</script>
```

This is an MSIE-specific way to attach event handlers. A script block must contain a *FOR* attribute that specifies an ID of the source HTML element and *EVENT* attribute that describes an event signature. Variable names used inside an event signature may be used in a script block to access event parameters. If the browser can't find an HTML control with the ID provided, or a control doesn't expose the event with the name specified in the signature, then the script block is simply ignored. So a Spreadsheet OWC 9 that has no *SheetChange* event will be safely taken out of the game with no additional coding.

It's worth mentioning that certain browsers have no clue what *FOR* and *EVENT* attributes are for (no pun indeed). But once they see a script block, they just execute it. Do you recall that initially (see Listing 15.7) we created *xlOWCEvents* with "empty" methods? Now you know what we did it for – to prevent users of non-Microsoft browsers from JavaScript errors during page loading.

Another important thing: a separate FOR/EVENT script block is the only valid way to assign an event handler to an ActiveX control. If you try to do the same thing via a DOM Level 0 event-handling mechanism like ay of those below:

```
xlOWC.SheetChange = function() {...};
xlOWC.sheetChange = function() {...};
xlOWC.sheetchange = function() {...};
xlOWC.onsheetchange = function() {...};
xlOWC.onSheetChange = function() {...};
```

you end up with a new property of the *Function* type in an OBJECT HTML element (a so-called "expando" property) instead of an event handler. If you try an MSIE variation of the DOM Level 2 mechanism:

```
xlOWC.attachEvent( "SheetChange",  function() { ... } )
```

you can attach an event handler, but it will cause *Spreadsheet* OWC/Internet Explorer to crash sooner or later. Try to attach an empty event handler to the *SheetChange* event this way and edit 8-15 cells. You'll be forwarded to Microsoft's support center by a gentle quality feedback agent. It's hard to say for sure, but a*ttachEvent* seems to have issues with certain ActiveX threading models.

The remaining block enhances our example with a custom Spreadsheet menu, the ability to save Spreadsheet content to the local file system, and several other miscellaneous functions:

```
function setupXlContextMenu() {
  function copy_vb_array(variant) {
    var vba = new VBArray(variant);
    var low = vba.lbound(1), high = vba.ubound(1);
    var res = new Array(high - low + 1);
    for (var i = low, idx = 0; i <= high; i++) {
      var itm = vba.getItem(i);
      res[idx++] = typeof itm == 'unknown' ? copy_vb_array(itm) : itm ;
    }
    return res;
```

```
    }

    function clone_array(src) {
       var size = src.length;
       var copy = new Array(size);
       for (var i = 0; i < size; i++) {
          var itm = src[i];
          copy[i] = itm && itm.prototype == Array ? clone_array(itm) : itm;
       }
       return copy;
    }

    var xlFileTypes = {};
    xlFileTypes[XLConstants.ssExportXMLSpreadsheet]="Excel";
    xlFileTypes[XLConstants.ssExportHTML]="HTML";
    function saveFile(format) {
       var fileName = window.prompt("Enter complete path for " + xlFileTypes[format] + "
file", "");
       if (!fileName) return;
       /* Saving may cause exceptions due to browser   */
       /* security or if operation canceled by user            */
       try { xlOWC["export"]( fileName, XLConstants.ssExportActionNone, format); }
catch(e) {}
    }

    var customCommands = {
       cmdSaveXls: function(){saveFile(XLConstants.ssExportXMLSpreadsheet)},
       cmdSaveHtml: function(){saveFile(XLConstants.ssExportHTML )},
       cmdSendData: function() {
          var region = xlSheet.cells(1, 1).currentRegion;
          if (!region) return;
          var size  = region.row - 1 + region.rows.count;
          var items = new Array(size);
          for (var i = 0; i < size; i++) {
             var row = i + 1; var item = {};
             for (var j = 0; j < COLUMNS_COUNT; j++) {
                var col  = j + 1;
                var prop = COLUMNS_XL[j];
                item[prop] = COLUMNS_FX[prop].xl( xlSheet.cells(row,col).value );
             }
             items[i] = item;
          }
          fxGrid.xlImportRows(0, items, true);
          ROW_COUNT = items.length;
```

```
    },
    cmdClearFormats: function(){xlOWC.selection.clearFormats()},
    cmdClearValues: function(){xlOWC.selection.clearContents()},
    cmdClear: function() {
       xlOWC.beginUndo();
       try {
          var r = xlOWC.selection;
          r.clearFormats();
          r.clearContents();
       }
       finally { xlOWC.endUndo(); }
    }
};

xlOWCEvents.beforeContextMenu = function(x, y, menu, cancel) {
   // Check for menu roll-outs from toolbar buttons.
   // Try to remove it and see what happens with
   // sorting (A-Z / Z-A) commands.
   if ( y < 40 ) return;

   // First copy original menu from
   // OLE VARIANT array to JS array
   var ctxMenu = copy_vb_array(menu.value);

   var cmClearSubMenu = [
      ["&All", "cmdClear"], ["&Formats", "cmdClearFormats"], ["&Values",
         "cmdClearValues"]
   ];
   // Place "Clear" within other edit commands
   ctxMenu.splice(5, 0, ["Clea&r", cmClearSubMenu]);
   // At the very end of menu add Save / Send to Flex
   ctxMenu.push(
      null /* separator */, ["Save...", "cmdSaveXls"], ["Save as HTML...",
         "cmdSaveHtml"],
      null /* separator */, ["Send data to FlexGrid", "cmdSendData"]
   );

   // Menu and Cancel arguments are ByRef in VB
   // In script (both JS and VBS) it is object
   // with single property "value"
   menu.value = xlVersion >= 11 ? ctxMenu : clone_array(ctxMenu);
};

xlOWCEvents.commandBeforeExecute = function(cmd, cancel) {
```

```
        var handler = customCommands[cmd];
        if ( !handler ) return;
        /* Disable default processing of command */
        cancel.value = true;
        handler();
    };
}
```

Listing 15.11 A custom context menu for Spreadsheet OWC

To add our own context menu commands we need to handle at least two events: *BeforeContext-Menu* and *CommandBeforeExecute*. *BeforeContextMenu* alters or replaces the default menu supplied by a parameter, while *CommandBeforeExecute* will help us perform a concrete action when the user selects the menu item.

Note that the menu parameter of BeforeContextMenu comes as a special *ByRef* type introduced by Spreadsheet OWC to support in/out parameters (unlike Visual Basic neither the JScript nor VB-Script support parameter is passed by reference). Variables of *ByRef* type have a single property – *value*.

Altering the context menu is really a tricky part. When you read the menu's value you get a Visual Basic Array (VT_ARRAY). Every item of this array is either a [*Text, CommandIdentifier*] pair or a [*Text, Submenu*] pair to accommodate the arbitrary nesting of submenus. In a sense you are getting an array of arrays. Before you can do anything else you have to convert the original menu to the JavaScript Array – see the recursive *copy_vb_array* function that does the trick. Handling recursion here is quite easy given that the JavaScript *typeof* fairly reports "unknown" (and undocumented, one might add) for VT_ARRAY.

Next we can extend the menu with its own items using convenient JavaScript Array methods like *splice* and *push*. There are two options for command identifiers: integer codes and strings. Integer codes are reserved by the Spreadsheet OWC so you can only use the ones defined in *XLConstants* to override the behavior of the existing commands or add existing commands if they're not available by default. String identifiers are at your disposal to implement custom commands. To insert separator, use *null* as the menu item.

Remember we converted *menu's* value from the VB array to the JavaScript array for modifications? Funny enough, there's no need to convert the modified array back to a VB array before assigning it to a menu.value. There's another "subtle" problem specific to OWC 10. If a corresponding JavaScript array length has been changed after creation (as a result of assigning an element with the index higher then or equal to the length, invoking push or splice on an array, etc.), the menu is reported as "invalid!" The only workaround is to deep clone the already-built array, supplying the exact length to the constructor at every step.

The functionality of the *xlOWCEvents.commandBeforeExecute* is simple enough. It attempts a lookup via the registry of custom commands and executes one, if found. In this case we have to cancel the default menu processing.

There are three commands of particular interest (see object *customCommands* in Listing 15.11). Two of them – *cmdSaveXls* and *cmdSaveHtml* – save the content of the Spreadsheet OWC Component in a corresponding Excel XML and HTML format. Saving a file to the local file system is subject to security restrictions. So be prepared. These functions may or may not work on a particular client computer depending on its security settings.

The third command, *cmdSendData*, sends a complete data set back to the Flex application. In the current implementation this is the only way to add rows directly in the Spreadsheet while the *xlOWCEvents.sheetChange* event handler ignores any sheet content beyond ROW_COUNT. The *xlSheet.cells(1, 1).currentRegion* lets us get a continuous region from the first cell to anything bounded by an empty row and empty column. Values from this region are packed as parameters to *fxGrid.xlImportRows()* the same way it was done in *xlOWCEvent.sheetChange()* (see Listing 15.10).

Note that we don't disable Spreadsheet events when executing "Clear" commands unlike the *xlTransaction* for Flex data notifications (see Listing 15.9). Now when a *SheetChange* event is fired as a result of a "Clear" command execution, the Flex application content will be cleared as well.

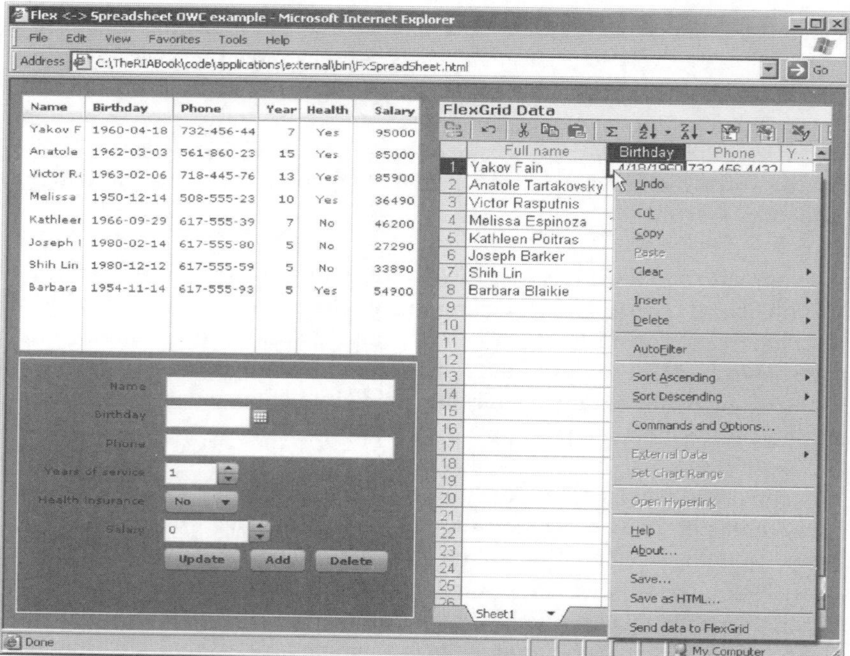

Figure 15.4 The custom context menu for Spreadsheet OWC

We're done. Looking back at Listings 15.3 and 15.7 through 15.11, you may have the feeling that this was all rather complex. However, the complexity is entirely associated with the enormous Spreadsheet OWC API, VB/JScript type conversions, plain OWC bugs, and undocumented JScript features. On the bright side, all the code related to the Flex External API was straightforward and easy to follow.

While being complex, OWC Spreadsheet/Flex integration presents a nice option for hybrid HTML/Flex solutions. On this note we'd like to mention another OWC control – PivotTable, which offers functionality unmatched in Flex. Integration with PivotTable, however, is beyond the scope of this chapter.

One-Way Flex-Excel Integration via the System Clipboard

So far we haven't mentioned the system clipboard – a solution that lets Flex exchange data with native applications. Flex lets you put text data on the system clipboard via the *System.setClipboard()* method. (Unlike typical native clipboard APIs Flex supports only one clipboard format – text. Another limitation, due to security considerations, is that you can't get the clipboard contents.)

Listing 15.12 presents a slightly modified version of the Flex application used in our previous example. We removed code related to *External* notifications and, for simplicity, dropped the fxMetadata() function in favor of a static constant array or metadata. What we've added here is a "Copy to clipboard" button with the action handler:

```
<?xml version="1.0" encoding="utf-8"?>
<!-- File ./FxClipboard.mxml                                    -->
<!-- Flex / Native application data exchange via system clipboard -->
<mx:Application xmlns:mx="http://www.adobe.com/2006/mxml" layout="absolute"
   creationComplete="init()">
      <mx:Script>
      <![CDATA[
      import mx.controls.Alert;
      import mx.collections.IViewCursor;
      import mx.collections.ArrayCollection;

      [Bindable]
      private var employees:ArrayCollection = new ArrayCollection();
      [Bindable]
      public var bhiOptions:Array = [{label: "No", data:false}, {label:"Yes", data:
true}];

      private function init():void { loadData(); }

      private function copyToClipboard():void {
         var nsExcel:Namespace = new Namespace("urn:schemas-microsoft-com:office:excel");
```

```
var html:XML =
   <html
      xmlns:x="urn:schemas-microsoft-com:office:excel"
      xmlns:o="urn:schemas-microsoft-com:office:office">
      <body><table></table></body>
   </html>;
var table:XML = html.body[0].table[0];
for (var cursor:IViewCursor = employees.createCursor(); !cursor.afterLast;
         cursor.moveNext() ) {
   var el:Object = cursor.current;
   var row:XML = <tr/>;
   for (var idx:int = 0, cnt:int = META.length; idx < cnt; idx++) {
      var prop:Object = META[idx];
      var name:String = prop.name;

      var value:Object = el[name];
      var cell:XML = <td nowrap="nowrap"/>;
      switch (prop.type) {
         case "string":
         case "number": break;
         case "boolean":
            cell.@nsExcel::bool = value;
            break;
         case "date":
            var d:Date = value as Date;
            value = d != null ?
              [d.getFullYear(), pad(d.getMonth() + 1), pad(d.getDate())].join("-
                  ") : "";
            break;
         default:
            value = "";
      }
      cell.appendChild( value );
      row.appendChild( cell );
   }
   table.appendChild( row );
};

System.setClipboard( html );
if (ExternalInterface.available) {
   var retVal:Object = ExternalInterface.call( "fxCopyContent" );
   if (retVal) Alert.show(retVal.message + ": " + retVal.rows + "x" + retVal.
      cols);
}
```

```
}

private function addRow():void {
   if (frmName.text != "") {
      var item:Object = employee(
         frmName.text, frmBirthday.selectedDate, frmPhone.text,
      frmYos.value, frmHealthInsurance.selectedItem.data, frmSalary.value);
      var idx:int = dataGrid.selectedIndex;
      var nextIdx:int = idx >= 0 ? idx + 1 : 0;
      employees.addItemAt( item, nextIdx );
      dataGrid.selectedIndex = nextIdx;
   }
   }

private function updateRow():void {
   var idx:int = dataGrid.selectedIndex;
   if (idx >= 0) {
      var item:Object = employee(
         frmName.text, frmBirthday.selectedDate, frmPhone.text,
         frmYos.value, frmHealthInsurance.selectedItem.data, frmSalary.value);
      employees.setItemAt(item, idx);
      employees.itemUpdated( item );
   }
}

private function deleteRow():void {
   var idx:int = dataGrid.selectedIndex;
   if (idx >= 0) {
      employees.removeItemAt(idx);
      if ( !employees.length ) {
         frmName.text = frmPhone.text = ""; frmBirthday.selectedDate = new Date;
         frmYos.value = 1; frmSalary.value = 0;
      }
      else
         dataGrid.selectedItem = employees.getItemAt(Math.min(idx, employees.length
- 1));
   }
}

private static const META:Array = [
   {name:"name",          title:"Full name",        type:"string"},
   {name:"birthday",      title:"Birthday",         type:"date"},
   {name:"phone",         title:"Phone",            type:"string"},
   {name:"yos",           title:"Years of srv.",    type:"number"},
```

```
        {name:"healthInsurance", title:"Health insurance", type:"boolean"},

        {name:"salary",          title:"Salary",           type:"number"}
    ];

    private function applyResult(data:Array):void {  employees = new
ArrayCollection(data); }

    private function loadData():void {
      applyResult([
        employee("Yakov Fain",           d("1960/04/18"), "732-456-4432",
yos("1999/05/20"), true,  95000.0),
        employee("Anatole Tartakovsky", d("1962/03/03"), "561-860-2376",
yos("1991/03/01"), true,  85000.0),
        employee("Victor Rasputnis",    d("1963/02/06"), "718-445-7622",
yos("1993/07/02"), true,  85900.0),
        employee("Melissa Espinoza",    d("1950/12/14"), "508-555-2319",
yos("1996/04/18"), true,  36490.0),
        employee("Kathleen Poitras",    d("1966/09/29"), "617-555-3920",
yos("1999/05/29"), false, 46200.0),
        employee("Joseph Barker",       d("1980/02/14"), "617-555-8021",
yos("2001/09/10"), false, 27290.0),
        employee("Shih Lin",            d("1980/12/12"), "617-555-5921",
yos("2001/11/11"), false, 33890.0),
        employee("Barbara Blaikie",     d("1954/11/14"), "617-555-9345",
yos("2001/11/20"), true,  54900.0)
      ]);
    }

    private static function employee(name:String, birthday:Date, phone:String,
                                     yos:int, healthInsurance:Boolean,
salary:Number):Object {
        return { name:name, birthday:birthday, phone:phone,
        yos:yos, healthInsurance: healthInsurance, salary:salary  };
    }

    private static function d(s:String):Date {return new Date( Date.parse(s) );}
    private static const THIS_YEAR:int = new Date().getFullYear();
    private static function yos(startDate:String):int {return THIS_YEAR - d(startDate).
getFullYear();}

    private static function formatDate(itm:Object, col:Object):String {
       var d:Date = itm.birthday;
       return d ? [d.getFullYear(), pad(d.getMonth() + 1), pad(d.getDate())].join("-")
```

```
: "";
    }

    private function formatHealthInsurance(itm:Object, col:Object):String {
      return bhiOptions[itm.healthInsurance * 1].label;
    }

    private static function pad(v:int):String { return (v < 10 ? "0" : "") + v; }
    ]]>
    </mx:Script>
    <mx:VBox width="100%" height="100%">

      <mx:DataGrid id="dataGrid" width="100%" height="100%" dataProvider="{employees}"
        editable="false" sortableColumns="false">
        <mx:columns>
        <mx:Array>
          <mx:DataGridColumn dataField="name" headerText="Name"/>
          <mx:DataGridColumn labelFunction="formatDate" headerText="Birthday"/>

          <mx:DataGridColumn dataField="phone" headerText="Phone"/>

          <mx:DataGridColumn dataField="yos" headerText="Years of Srv." textAlign="r
            ight"/>
          <mx:DataGridColumn labelFunction="formatHealthInsurance"
            headerText="Health insurance" textAlign="center"/>
          <mx:DataGridColumn dataField="salary" headerText="Salary" textAlign="right
            "/>
        </mx:Array>
        </mx:columns>
      </mx:DataGrid>

      <mx:Form width="100%" height="100%" borderStyle="solid" borderColor="#ffffff">
        <mx:FormItem label="Name">
          <mx:TextInput id="frmName" width="200" text="{dataGrid.selectedItem.
            name}"/>
        </mx:FormItem>
        <mx:FormItem label="Birthday">
          <mx:DateField id="frmBirthday" selectedDate="{dataGrid.selectedItem.
            birthday}"/>
        </mx:FormItem>
        <mx:FormItem label="Phone">
          <mx:TextInput id="frmPhone" width="200" text="{dataGrid.selectedItem.
            phone}"/>
        </mx:FormItem>
```

```
          <mx:FormItem label="Years of service">
             <mx:NumericStepper id="frmYos" value="{dataGrid.selectedItem.yos}"
                maxChars="3" minimum="1" maximum="99"/>
          </mx:FormItem>
          <mx:FormItem label="Health insurance">
          <mx:ComboBox id="frmHealthInsurance" selectedIndex="{dataGrid.selectedItem.
                healthInsurance}"
             dataProvider="{bhiOptions}"/>
          </mx:FormItem>
          <mx:FormItem label="Salary">
             <mx:NumericStepper id="frmSalary" value="{dataGrid.selectedItem.salary}"
             maxChars="10" minimum="0" maximum="999999"/>
          </mx:FormItem>
          <mx:FormItem>
             <mx:HBox>
                <mx:Button label="Update" click="updateRow()"/>
                <mx:Button label="Add" click="addRow()"/>
                <mx:Button label="Delete" click="deleteRow()"/>
                <mx:VRule height="20"/>
                <mx:Button label="Copy to clipboard" click="copyToClipboard()"/>
             </mx:HBox>
          </mx:FormItem>
       </mx:Form>
    </mx:VBox>
</mx:Application>
```

Listing 15.12 A Flex application exporting data to the clipboard

The Flex application above puts HTML with employee data on the clipboard. Run the application, invoke "Copy to clipboard," open any text editor, and "paste." You'll see formatted HTML source, generated by our Flex application, as shown in Figure 15.5.

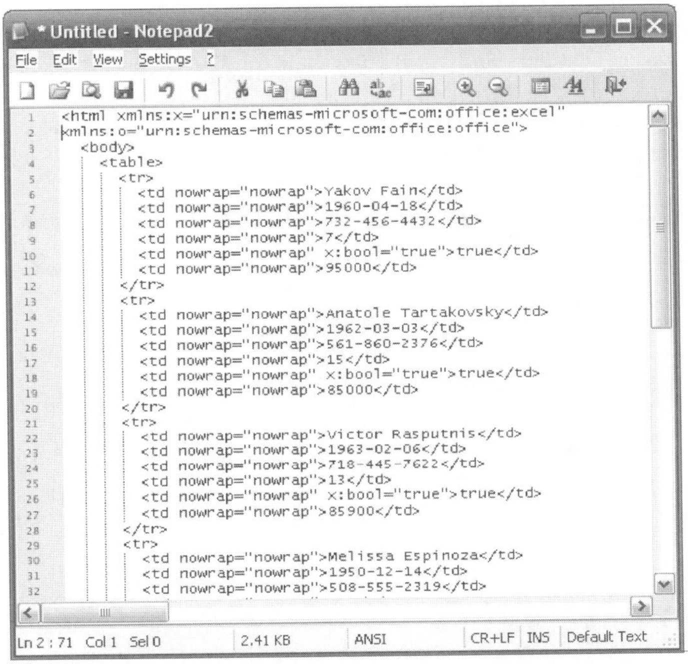

```
<html xmlns:x="urn:schemas-microsoft-com:office:excel"
xmlns:o="urn:schemas-microsoft-com:office:office">
  <body>
    <table>
      <tr>
        <td nowrap="nowrap">Yakov Fain</td>
        <td nowrap="nowrap">1960-04-18</td>
        <td nowrap="nowrap">732-456-4432</td>
        <td nowrap="nowrap">7</td>
        <td nowrap="nowrap" x:bool="true">true</td>
        <td nowrap="nowrap">95000</td>
      </tr>
      <tr>
        <td nowrap="nowrap">Anatole Tartakovsky</td>
        <td nowrap="nowrap">1962-03-03</td>
        <td nowrap="nowrap">561-860-2376</td>
        <td nowrap="nowrap">15</td>
        <td nowrap="nowrap" x:bool="true">true</td>
        <td nowrap="nowrap">85000</td>
      </tr>
      <tr>
        <td nowrap="nowrap">Victor Rasputnis</td>
        <td nowrap="nowrap">1963-02-06</td>
        <td nowrap="nowrap">718-445-7622</td>
        <td nowrap="nowrap">13</td>
        <td nowrap="nowrap" x:bool="true">true</td>
        <td nowrap="nowrap">85900</td>
      </tr>
      <tr>
        <td nowrap="nowrap">Melissa Espinoza</td>
        <td nowrap="nowrap">1950-12-14</td>
        <td nowrap="nowrap">508-555-2319</td>
```

Figure 15.5 HTML source put on the clipboard

Of all the options, such as fixed width, CSV, and tab separated, we've resorted to HTML for a reason. You may notice that we generated a bit of unusual HTML. Some HTML elements and attributes mention an Office Excel namespace. If you recall our Spreadsheet OWC integration example, you can draw parallels with the handling of certain data types. To prove your guess you should open Excel and paste the clipboard content there. Bingo! The cells are populated from the HTML table. Note that this feature is unique to Excel. Neither Word nor Frontpage does the same. Excel is liberal enough with the type of clipboard data: even when the type is plain text, Excel tries to figure out whether the content is HTML.

To take advantage of type-specific Excel formating, we repeated the trick with date type. To force True/False formating of Boolean values, however, we had to explicitly define Excel-specific attributes on the TD element.

Flex Embedded in Microsoft Excel

Although the solution is quite workable, it requires a manual Paste by the user. Could we somehow automate the Paste? Well, to automate an application it has to support automation. Traditional Microsoft mechanisms like DDE (Dynamic Data Exchange) or OLE are out of our reach when we're talking about Flex-Excel integration. However, if we embed Flash ActiveX into an Excel worksheet, then we can get by with VBA language.

Figure 15.6 presents the embedding results. The same Flex application FxClipboard is running as ActiveX inside the Excel worksheet FxClipboard.xls. Whenever you modify the data in a Flex application, the updates are instantly propagated to the cells of the worksheet. This intimacy between an embedded Flex application and Excel will come in handy later when we establish Flex-to-Flex talk via LocalConnection. For now, there's work ahead. We need to build communication accommodating FxClipboard.xls.

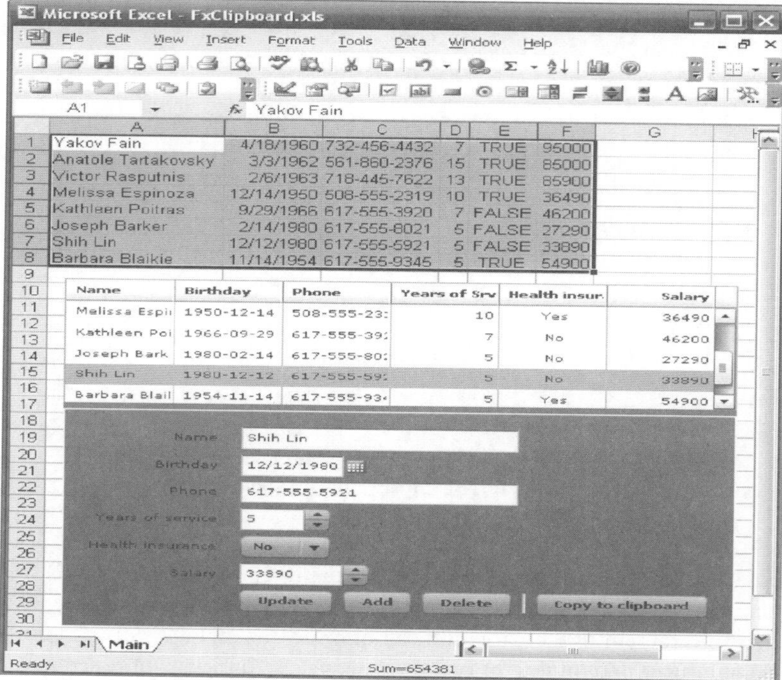

Figure 15.6 FxClipboard running as ActiveX inside an Excel spreadsheet

Straight ahead. Although it's possible to activate the "View/Toolbars/Control Toolbox" toolbar in Excel and then insert "Shockwave Flash Object" from the set of additional ActiveX controls, we choose the more challenging option of embedding a Flash Player ActiveX control dynamically. Obviously, we need a bit of VBA code here.

The code in Listing 15.13 opts to VBA early binding, i.e., uses variables of concrete types from the ActiveX type library rather than a generic Object type. Accordingly, it's necessary to add the type library reference to all used libraries. We need to add just an explicit reference to "Shockwave Flash Object" while references to Office and Excel libraries always add automatically on the first use of a VBA editor for a given Workbook.

Microsoft users learned the danger of VBA macros loaded from untrustworthy sources the hard way. So, by default Excel has a very pessimistic security policy: "Don't execute macros at all." This is way too restrictive for our example though, so to execute it you'd have to lower the security settings to at least medium, see Figure 15.7. (Medium requires confirmation of the macros every time the document is opened.)

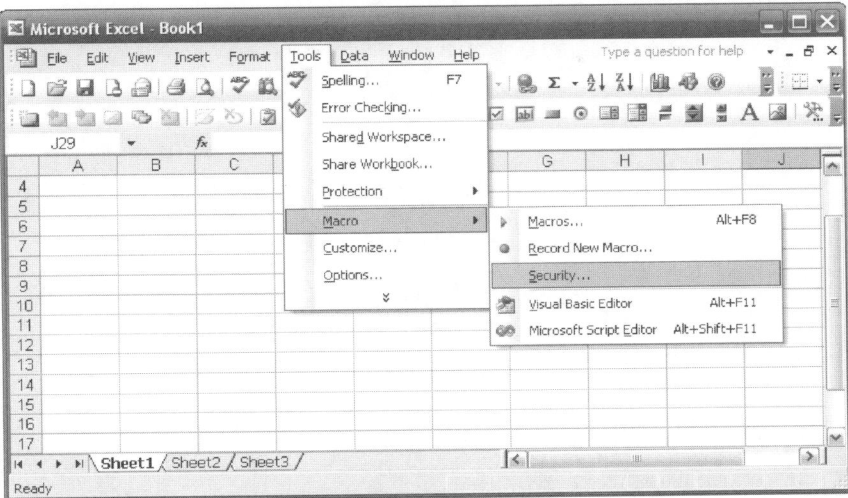

Figure 15.7 Activating an Excel security setting dialog

When all prerequisites are met, go to the VBA editor (F11) and add the following to the Workbook module:

```
' File ./FxClipboard.xls
' Object module ThisWorkbook
Private fxProxy As FlexProxy
Private Sub Workbook_Open()
    Set fxProxy = New FlexProxy
    fxProxy.Initialize 1, "fxObject"
End Sub
```

Listing 15.13 FxClipboard workbook module

We've just declared an event handler for a workbook *Open* event. The event handler instantiates a helper FlexProxy class that does all the work. Now use the Insert/Class module to add a class module, rename it FlexProxy, and add the following from Listing 15.14:

```
' File ./FxClipboard.xls
' Class module FlexProxy
Option Explicit
Private WithEvents pSheet As Excel.Worksheet
```

```
Private WithEvents pFlexObject As ShockwaveFlashObjects.ShockwaveFlash
Private pOleControl As Excel.oleObject

Public Sub Initialize(ByVal sheetID As Variant, ByVal controlID As String)
    Set pSheet = Worksheets(sheetID)

    Dim oleObject As Excel.oleObject
    Dim found As Boolean
    found = False
    For Each oleObject In pSheet.OLEObjects
        If oleObject.Name = controlID Then
            found = True
            Exit For
        End If
    Next oleObject

    If Not found Then
        Set oleObject = pSheet.OLEObjects.Add( _
          ClassType:="ShockwaveFlash.ShockwaveFlash.9", _
          Width:=365, Height:=270, Left:=10, Top:=10 _
        )
        oleObject.Name = controlID
    End If

    With oleObject
        Call .BringToFront
        Call .Activate
    End With

    Set pOleControl = oleObject
    Set pFlexObject = oleObject.Object

    With pFlexObject
        .Loop = False
        .Menu = True
        .Playing = False
        .EmbedMovie = False
        .AllowNetworking = "all"
        .AllowScriptAccess = "always"
        If Not found Then
            .LoadMovie 0, "../bin/FxClipboard.swf"
        End If
    End With
    Call PositionOleControl
```

```
End Sub

Private Sub pFlexObject_FlashCall(ByVal request As String)
    If Not Application.EnableEvents Then Exit Sub
    Application.EnableEvents = False

    If InStr(1, request, "<invoke name=""fxCopyContent""") = 1 Then
        Call UpdateRows

        Dim content As Range
        Set content = pSheet.UsedRange
        Dim rows As Integer, cols As Integer

        If content Is Nothing Then
            rows = 0
            cols = 0
        Else
            rows = content.rows.count
            cols = content.Columns.count
        End If

        pFlexObject.SetReturnValue _
            "<object>" & _
                "<property id='message'><string>" & "Data copied to Excel" & "</
string></property>" & _
                "<property id='rows'><number>" & rows & "</number></property>" & _
                "<property id='cols'><number>" & cols & "</number></property>" & _
            "</object>"
    Else
    End If
ExitSub:
    Application.EnableEvents = True
End Sub

Private Sub UpdateRows()
    Dim Target As Excel.Range
    Set Target = pSheet.Cells(1, 1)

    Call pSheet.Cells.Clear
    '------------------------------
    Target.PasteSpecial xlPasteAll
    '------------------------------
    Call pSheet.Activate
    Dim newSelection As Range
```

```
    Set newSelection = pSheet.UsedRange

    Call newSelection.CurrentRegion.Columns.AutoFit
    Call newSelection.Select
    Call PositionOleControl

    Set newSelection = Nothing
End Sub

Private Sub PositionOleControl()
    'Move Flash ActiveX away from used worksheet region
    Dim allCells As Range
    Set allCells = pSheet.Cells(1, 1).CurrentRegion

    pOleControl.Left = 10
    If allCells Is Nothing Then
        pOleControl.Top = 10
    Else
        pOleControl.Top = allCells.Top + allCells.Height + 10
    End If

    Set allCells = Nothing
End Sub
```

Listing 15.14 FlexProxy class module

The public *Initialize* method is the main initialization routine for FlexProxy. In VBA it's impossible to use a parameterized constructor, so we've moved all the setup code here. We check the availability of a Flash Player control by iterating over the *OLEObjects* collection that holds every ActiveX object available on the worksheet. If a control isn't found, we create and add this object to the collection using the *OLEObjects.Add* method. Visual Basic supports both named and positional parameters. A lot of *OLEObjects.Add* arguments are irrelevant in our use case. The only important one is the *ClassType* that defines the ProgID of the ActiveX object to embed; all the rest define the control position. Accordingly, we resort to named parameters as the simplest option.

When reopening the workbook with the embedded Flash Player, a corresponding SWF movie (compiled from FxClipboard.mxml, see Listing 15.2) starts playing automatically, so it's necessary to call *LoadMovie* explicitly in case we just added the Flash Player control. The path to FxClipboard.swf is relative to the Excel document. Adjust it as necessary (see Listing 15.14, method *Initialize*).

The next method, *pFlexObject_FlashCall*, is of particular interest. It deals with handling notifications of the External API, but this time in a desktop application.

The *FlexProxy* class module defines an instance variable *pFlexObject* type of ShockwaveFlashObjects.Shockwave.Flash. The variable is declared using a "With Events" statement that enables attaching event handlers to the object. The event handler must be a procedure with the name *VariableName_EventName*. This procedure's signature must match the order and types of event parameters. In the case of the Flex External API there's only the *Request* parameter of the String type. But, in fact, it's a serialized form of a complex XML document. The format of this document deserves a close look and we dedicate the following section to it.

XML Format of External API

Although the External API-based communications in the Flex-ActiveX container and Flex-Web browser are similar, there's one important difference. When Flex ActionScript communicates with a browser's JavaScript, the functions are called directly; the formatting details of the function call requests and responses are encapsulated behind the ExternalInterface.call(). However, when the External API is facilitating communication with an ActiveX container application, we have to understand the specific XML messages sent by the Flash Player in place of function calls and return values. Importantly, Flash Player expects the container application to send its function calls (*flashObject.CallFunction*) and return values (*flashObject.SetReturnValue*) in the same XML format.

There are two parts to the XML format used by the External API: the first part is used to represent function calls and the second one defines the formatting of individual values. The second part is used to marshal function parameters and return values.

The following XML fragment shows an example of an XML-formatted function call:

```
<invoke name="functionName" returntype="xml">
    <arguments>
        ... (individual argument values)
    </arguments>
</invoke>
```

The root node is the *<invoke>* node. It has two attributes: *name*, containing the name of the function to call, and *returntype*, which has to be the XML for the ActiveX container other than the HTML page[5]. If the function call has parameters, the *<invoke>* node contains the *<arguments>* child node with individual parameter values formatted, as we'll explain a bit later. Our trivial non-parameter notification Request looks like this:

```
<invoke name="fxCopyContent" returntype="xml"><arguments/></invoke>
```

Now you can see the naïve approach used to check the method name in the *pFlexObject_FlashCall* from Listing 15.14:

```
    If InStr(1, request, "<invoke name=""fxCopyContent""") = 1 Then
        Call UpdateRows
    . . . .
```

If the request prologue looks like a *fxCopyContent* notification, the event handler delegates the processing to the UpdateRows method that just pastes the content of the clipboard into the worksheet starting with the cell (1,1).

To set a return value from an ActiveX container you must use the *SetReturnValue* method on a Flash object. This method can be invoked only in the *CallFunction* event handler. If an invocation of the *SetReturnValue* is omitted, ActionScript receives undefined as a return value from the *ExteranlInterface.call*. Otherwise the ActionScript object parsed from the XML is returned. For example, we reply with a message about the successful operation and the number of rows/columns copied. The encoded XML form of the return value is the following:

```
<object>
     <property id="message"><string>Data copied to Excel</string></property>
     <property id="rows"><number>8</number></property>
     <property id="cols"><number>6</number></property>
"</object>"
```

On the ActionScript side this is transformed to an Object with the fields message, rows, and cols.

To illustrate support for all Action Script classes both as *<arguments>* in the *CallFunction* method/ *FlashCall* event and as a result returned with the *SetReturnValue*, the complete formating scheme, shown in Table 15.2, includes data type information in addition to the actual values:

ActionScript class/value	XML Format	Comments
Null	<null/>	
Boolean true	<true/>	
Boolean false	<false/>	
Number, int, uint	<number>3.14</number> <number>-255</number>	
String	<string>Hello, Flex!</string>	
Date	<date>1151614800000</date>	The encoded value is the number of milliseconds since January 1, 1970, the same result as Date.getTime() or Date.valueOf()
Array	<array> <property id="0"> <string>"ABC"</string> </property> <property id="1"> <string>"XYZ"</string> </property> <property id="2"> <number>128</number> </property> ... </array>	Elements can be any supported type; mixed types are supported and arbitrary nesting is allowed. The <property> node defines individual elements, and the ID attribute is the numeric, zero-based index.
Object	<object> <property id="name"> <string>Alex Whitney</ string> </property> <property id="salary"> <number>72000</number> </property> ... </object>	Individual properties are defined in the <property> element; the ID attribute is the property name (a string).
Custom object	<null> or <object></object>	Either a null or empty object. Any properties of the custom objects are lost.

Table 15.2 External API formatting scheme

The set of supported types is rich enough to serialize the structure of almost any complexity and nesting except with two limitations. The first one is the lack of support for custom objects. The second serious restriction of the External API is that it doesn't handle recursive structures correctly, or strictly speaking, it doesn't track visited objects during marshaling at all:

```
var x:Object = {a:"The First"};
```

```
var y:Object = {a:"The Second"};
x.b = y; y.b = x;
  var retVal:Object = ExternalInterface.call( "someFunction", x );
```

When the following ActionScript snippet is invoked, the External API XML serializer falls into infinite recursion that ends up with a StackOverflow exception.

Be aware that serialization to/from XML has its own associated cost in non-linear dependency so passing large objects via the External API can seriously slow your application down. As a general rule, always analyze what exactly is necessary on either side of the ExternalInterface invocation and avoid sending a complete graph of the objects if only a subset of the data is sufficient.

LiveLink: Standalone Flex - Excel

In the following sections of the chapter we'll integrate a standalone Flex application with a standalone Excel document. The LocalConnection class will play a main role in this effort, which enables one-way Flex-to-Flex communications (to be exact, we should say Flash-to-Flash communication). Ultimately, our communication scheme will look like "Flex Application-Flex Agent-Excel" where the FlexAgent, embedded inside the Excel spreadsheet, talks to Excel via the External API. Meanwhile, the FlexApplication-Flex Agent communication link will be based on the LocalConnection.

LocalConnection 101

LocalConnection has been available since Flash 6.0. There's a saying that it takes two to lie: one to lie and one to listen. The same rule applies to LocalConnection: you need one SWF file that sends notifications and another one that listens to the notifications.

The first SWF file is commonly called the *sending* SWF file; it's the application that invokes the method on the other application. The sending SWF file must create a LocalConnection object and call the *send()* method. The second SWF file is called the *receiving* SWF file; it's the application whose method gets invoked. The receiving SWF must create another LocalConnection object and call the *connect()* method.

In its simplest form, a sending application uses LocalConnection as follows:

```
var LocalConnection sendingLC = new LocalConnection();
sendingLC.addEventListener(StatusEvent.STATUS, statusHandler );
sendingLC.addEventListener(SecurityErrorEvent.SECURITY_ERROR, securityErrorHandler
);

sendingLC.send( "MyConnection", "remoteFunction", arg1, arg2, ...., argN);
...

private function securityErrorHandler(ev:SecurityErrorEvent):void {  /* Handle
```

```
security errors */ }

private function statusHandler(ev:StatusEvent):void { /*Handle status errors like
failed calls to send */ }
```

A corresponding receiving application in its connect() call matches the name used in the send()above and provides the implementation for the *remoteFunction* and any other functions invoked by sending applications:

```
var LocalConnection receivingLC = new LocalConnection();

receivingLC.client = this;
receivingLC.connect( "MyConnection" );
...

private function remoteFunction(arg1:type1, arg2: type2, ..., argN:typeN):void {
    /* Function implementation */
}
```

Importantly, only one serving application is allowed per connection. In other words, only one application may successfully call *LocalConnection.connect()* with the given connection name at a time. If you attempt to connect() with the same name from the second LocalConnection, an *ArgumentError* will be thrown.

The core driver of LocalConnection is defined via the *client* property. This property should reference the object that implements methods remotely called via *send()*, so in the code above we set it to *this* reference, pointing to receiving the application itself. If the receiving application doesn't implement the "sent for" method (the method isn't present, the function name is misspelled, the number or types of method parameters doesn't match expectations of the send()), a runtime AsyncError will be thrown. Note that it's the receiving application that will be getting the exception. Don't attempt to catch the AsyncError with a regular try/catch block; since the remote function is invoked asynchronously, you may only assign a listener for the AsyncErrorEvent and follow up with the custom error-handling strategy.

The remote function in the code snippet above is declared void. This is not accidental; in fact, it's a major limitation of LocalConnection: all communications are one-way; you may not get a reply from a receiving application like you would with the External API.

You may have noticed that we supplied listeners for *Status* and *SecurityError* events for the sending LocalConnection. Both events are fired as a result of the *send()* method. *Status* reports carries well the status of LocalConnection for every invocation of the *send()* – either *status* or *error* – see the property level of the event. For instance, you may get an error event when no listening application is running. A *SecurityError* event is raised when *send()* attempts to cross the security sandbox boundaries.

LocalConnection is subject to certain security restrictions. By default, a connection is allowed only between SWF files from the same domain. Otherwise, the receiving application must enable the sending domain. Interestingly, these rules are intervened with the names you use with methods *send()* and *connect()* – plain as in the earlier example, qualified with a domain prefix, or global that starts with the underscore character.

In the simplest case when both applications originate from the same domain, LocalConnection communications are enabled with no additional effort. This happens, in particular, when you use just the name of the application without specifying a domain name.

The more complex case is when applications are loaded from different domains. Assuming both sending and receiving applications know the names in advance, the following must be done for LocalConnection communication:

1. A receiving application must enable the sending domain with an explicit *receivingLC.allowDomain("sender.domain.com"*) or an indiscriminate *receivingLC.allowDomain(*)*. Make no mistake, *allowDomain* is called on the LocalConnection object, not to be confused with *Security.allowDomain("domain")*!
2. A receiving application must connect() using a "plain" connection name: *receivingLC.connect("MyConnection")*;
3. A sending application must use a connection name qualified with the domain prefix: *sendingLC.send("sender.domain.com:MyConnection", "remoteFunction", args)*.

Instead of typing the full domain name prefix, you can use a connection name that starts with an underscore like "_MyConnection" on both sides. Either way, the receiving application must allow a domain with an *allowDomain()* call.

If you don't specify an explicit domain prefix, or if you use a name beginning with "_", LocalConnection adds the default prefix of the SWF origin domain to the name of the connection for both the *send()* and *connect()*.This enables strict, yet flexibly configurable security and helps avoid name clashes between SWF files coming from different vendors (and, hence, from different domains). You may think of a qualified connection name as a name defined in a certain namespace. Note that you can't define the explicit domain prefix with the *connect()* method of the receiving connection. To understand how security and the namespacing mechanism work together, let's consider examples of the three security options above.

In the simplest case, assume that both the sending and receiving SWF files are loaded from the www.theriabook.com site. The actual name of the connection in both cases is the "theriabook.com: MyConnection" and hence the matching receiving connection for LocalConnection.send will be found once the unqualified connection name is converted to the qualified one.

Now, imagine that the sending application is loaded from www.other-domain.com. In this case a default qualified name of the sending connection is "other-domain.com:MyConnection" and there's no matching receiving connection. However, once you do *receivingLC.allowDomain("other-*

domain.com") the LocalConnection API creates some internal matcher that connects the "theriabook.com:MyConnection" name and "other-domain.com:MyConnectionName," allowing other-domain.com.

Finally, if a connection name starts with an underscore, no domain prefixes are added on either side. So the matching connection can be found by default. However, the receiving security manager prevents incoming calls originating from other domains. So, again it's necessary to explicitly allow the sender's domain or, subject to your discretion, allow all with *receivingConnection.allowDomains("*")*.

There's another LocalConnection API limitation that's worth mentioning. The amount of data you can pass with *LocalConnection.send* is limited to 40KB in serialized form. If you exceed this limit, you'll get an *ArgumentError* exception. The only way to overcome this limitation is to send chunks of data. Sadly, the serialization format isn't documented, so it's hard to imagine another algorithm to calculate the size of the chunk except by trial and error.

Typically, the receiving LocalConnection is automatically destroyed when its reference variable is garbage-collected. If the receiving LocalConnection is declared an application variable, the connection is destroyed when the SWF file is unloaded. You can also programmatically close the connection using an explicit *close()* call. Once the connection is closed, you may reconnect with the same connection name from any Flex application, including the original one.

Table 15.3 summarizes the functionality available for LocalConnection running in both sending and receiving modes:

Sending LocalConnection	Receiving LocalConnection
sendingLC = new LocalConnection();	receivingLC = new LocalConnection();
sendingLC.addEventListener(StatusEvent.STATUS, statusHandler);	receivingLC.addEventListener(AsyncErrorEvent.ASYNC_ERROR, asyncErrorHandler);
sendingLC.addEventListener(SecurityErrorEvent.SECURITY_ERROR securityErrorHandler);	receivingLC.allowDomain("domain.com"); receivingLC.allowInsecureDomain("domain.com");
	receivingLC.client = implObject;
	receivingLC.connect("ConnectionName");
sendingLC.send("domain.com:ConnectionName", "function", arg1, arg2, ..., argN);	
	receivingLC.close();

Table 15.3 LocalConnection API

Flex Excel Agent Application

Now that we've looked at LocalConnection we can move closer to integrating Flex applications with the native Microsoft Excel.

As previously discussed, we need a Flex agent to interface with Excel via the External API. The code for the corresponding application – FxExcelAgent – is presented in Listing 15.15.

According to our plan, FxExcelAgent and a regular Flex application communicate with each other using the LocalConnection API. Actually, since LocalConnection provides only one-way communication, we need two connections to enable data exchange in both directions: outConnection, dedicated to forwarding External API calls to a Flex application, and inConnection, promoting received notifications to Excel.

The initialization of the agent starts with an External API availability check. The existence of the External API is mandatory for FlexAgent; if it's unavailable the agent is useless and no further initialization is done.

The core function of the agent is in forwarding External API calls to the data application via *outConnection*, and promoting notifications received by inConnection to Excel with the External API. The only External API call that has no corresponding LocalConnection invocation is the *fxQueryChannel()* method. The method is used by FxAgent to construct the names of outbound/inbound LocalConnections. To keep the agent generic, we avoided hard-coded names. Instead, the agent queries the hosting Excel document to return the channel ID – the unique name of the bidirectional communication link composed by two LocalConnection objects. To compose names of outbound and inbound connections we add _Agent2App and _App2Agent suffixes to this ID correspondingly. If a channel ID starts with an underscore, then "global" connection names are created. In this case the *outConnection* object is modified to allow connections from any domain.

This approach is generic and configurable. You can switch which Flex application the Excel workbook connects to by altering just one workbook property. Further, you can compose other Excel documents using the workbook created in this example as a template: simply use the Excel command "New from existing workbook…" instead of "New blank workbook." Again, the only configuration effort for the "derived" workbook is to modify the channel ID.

After setting up connections, the agent forces the Flex application to resubmit both metadata and data. This resolves the race condition case when a Flex application has been started before an Excel document with embedded Flex agent is opened. It's similar to the *xlResend* callback in the Spreadsheet OWC example.

Each and every step is logged into the List control. This helps to understand the order of events and what's going on "under the hood." Figure 15.8 shows a FxExcelAgent running inside an Excel spreadsheet:

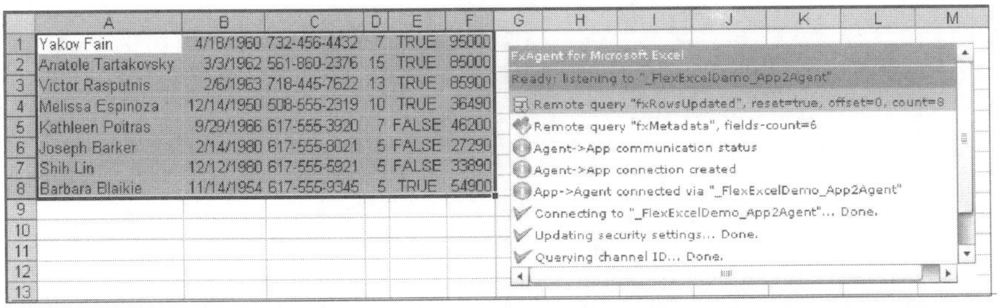

Figure 15.8 Excel spreadsheet with an embedded FxExcelAgent application

Here is the code for the FxExcelAgent:

```
<?xml version="1.0" encoding="utf-8"?>
<!-- File ./FxExcelAgent.mxml                  -->
<!-- Flex Agent running within Microsoft Excel -->
<mx:Application xmlns:mx="http://www.adobe.com/2006/mxml" layout="absolute"
      creationComplete="onCreationComplete()">
      <mx:Script>
      <![CDATA[
         import mx.collections.ArrayCollection;

         [Bindable]
         private var messages:ArrayCollection = new ArrayCollection;
         private var inConnection:LocalConnection;
         private var outConnection:LocalConnection;
         private var outConnectionName:String;

         private function onCreationComplete():void {
            message(INFO, "Application loaded");
            if (!ExternalInterface.available) {
               message(ERROR, "Flex container does not support external interface");
               txtStatus.text = "Disabled: no external interface";
               return;
            }
            // Code here is executed only if there is ExternalInterface available
            var channel:String = queryChannel();
            var isOk:Boolean = !!channel;
            if (isOk) outConnectionName = channel + "_Agent2App";
            isOk = isOk && openReceivingConnection(channel + "_App2Agent");
            isOk = isOk && openSendingConnection();
            if (isOk) {
               xlResend();
               ExternalInterface.addCallback("xlResend", xlResend);
```

```
        ExternalInterface.addCallback("xlImportRows", xlImportRows);

      }
    }

    private function queryChannel():String {
      var channel:String;
      try {
        phase("Querying channel ID...");
        channel = ExternalInterface.call("fxQueryChannel");
        if ( !channel ) message(ERROR, "Hosting application fails to return chan
          nel id");                   else ok();
      } catch(ex:Error) {
        message(ERROR, ex.errorID + ":" + ex.message );
      }

      if (!channel) txtStatus.text = "Disabled: channel id unavailable";

      return channel;
    }

    private function openReceivingConnection(connectionName:String):Boolean {
      inConnection = new LocalConnection();
      inConnection.addEventListener(AsyncErrorEvent.ASYNC_ERROR,
        asyncErrorHandler);
      inConnection.client = this;

      var isConnected:Boolean = false;
      try {
        if ( connectionName.indexOf("_") == 0 ) {
          phase("Updating security settings...");
          inConnection.allowDomain("*");
          inConnection.allowInsecureDomain("*");
          ok();                                   }
        phase("Connecting to \"" + connectionName + "\"...");
        inConnection.connect( connectionName );
        isConnected = true;
        ok();

        message(INFO, "App->Agent connected via \"" + connectionName + "\"");
        txtStatus.text = "Ready: listening to \"" + connectionName + "\"";
      } catch (ex:ArgumentError) {
        message(ERROR, ex.message);
      } catch (ex:SecurityError) {
```

```
        message(ERROR, ex.message);
    }
    if (!isConnected)  txtStatus.text = "Disabled: fail to establish local
        connection";
    return isConnected;
}

private function openSendingConnection():Boolean {
    try {
        outConnection = new LocalConnection();
        outConnection.addEventListener(StatusEvent.STATUS, statusHandler);
        outConnection.addEventListener(SecurityErrorEvent.SECURITY_ERROR,
            securityErrorHandler);
    }  catch (ex:Error) {
        message(ERROR, "Error creating Agent->App connection");
        return false;
    }
    message(INFO, "Agent->App connection created");
    return true;
}

public function xlResend():void {
    outConnection.send(outConnectionName, "lcResend");
}

public function xlImportRows(offset:int, cells:Array, reset:Boolean):void {

    outConnection.send(outConnectionName, "lcImportRows", offset, cells, reset) ;
}

public function fxMetadata(metadata:Array):void {
    if ( !checkConnected("fxMetadata") ) return;
    message( META,
        ["Remote query \"fxMetadata\", ",
         "fields-count=", metadata.length].join('')  );

    ExternalInterface.call("fxMetadata", metadata);
}

public function fxRowsInserted(offset:int, content:Array):void {
    if ( !checkConnected("fxRowsInserted") ) return;
    message( INSERT,
        ["Remote query \"fxRowsInserted\", ",
         "offset=", offset, ", count=", content.length].join('')  );
```

```
            ExternalInterface.call("fxRowsInserted", offset, content);
        }

        public function fxRowsUpdated(offset:int, content:Array, reset:Boolean):void {
            if ( !checkConnected("fxRowsUpdated") ) return;
            message( reset ? RELOAD : UPDATE,
                ["Remote query \"fxRowsUpdated\", ",
                 "reset=", reset,  ", ",
                 "offset=", offset, ", count=", content.length].join('')  );
        ExternalInterface.call("fxRowsUpdated", offset, content, reset);
        }

        public function fxRowsRemoved(offset:int, count:int):void {
            if ( !checkConnected("fxRowsRemoved") ) return;
            message( REMOVE,
                ["Remote query \"fxRowsRemoved\", ",
                 "offset=", offset, ", count=", count].join('')  );
            ExternalInterface.call("fxRowsRemoved", offset, count);
        }

        private function securityErrorHandler(ev:SecurityErrorEvent):void {
message(ERROR, "Security error: " + ev.text );  }
            private function asyncErrorHandler(ev:AsyncErrorEvent):void {  message( ER-
ROR, "Async error: " + ev.text );  }
        private function statusHandler(ev:StatusEvent):void {
            var severity:Number = {error:ERROR, status: INFO, warnin:WARN}[ev.level];
            if (!severity) severity = INFO;
            message(severity, "Agent->App communication " + ev.level +  (ev.code ? ",
code = " + ev.code : "")  );
        }

        private function checkConnected(query:String):Boolean {
              if ( inConnection) return true;
            message(WARN, "Agent not connected, remote query \"" + query + "\"
                skipped.");
            return false;
        }

        private function phase(title:String):void { message(WAIT, title); }

        private function ok():void {
            var item:Object = messages.getItemAt(0);
            item.icon = ICONS[OK];
            item.label = item.label + " Done.";
```

```
    messages.itemUpdated(item);
    lstMessages.selectedIndex = 0;
}

private function message(status:int, message:String):void {
    messages.addItemAt({label:message,icon:ICONS[status]}, 0);
    lstMessages.selectedIndex = 0;
}

/* Image resources */
[Embed(source="assets/icons/wait.png")]
private static const icoWait:String;
[Embed(source="assets/icons/ok.png")]
private static const icoOK:String;
[Embed(source="assets/icons/info.png")]
private static const icoInfo:String;
[Embed(source="assets/icons/warn.png")]
private static const icoWarn:String;
[Embed(source="assets/icons/error.png")]
private static const icoError:String;
[Embed(source="assets/icons/metadata.png")]
private static const icoMeta:String;
[Embed(source="assets/icons/insert.png")]
private static const icoInsert:String;
[Embed(source="assets/icons/update.png")]
private static const icoUpdate:String;
[Embed(source="assets/icons/reload.png")]
private static const icoReload:String;
[Embed(source="assets/icons/remove.png")]
private static const icoRemove:String;

private static const ICONS:Array = [
    icoWait, icoOK, icoInfo, icoWarn, icoError,
    icoMeta, icoInsert, icoUpdate, icoReload, icoRemove
];

private static const WAIT:int  = 0;
private static const OK:int    = 1;
private static const INFO:int  = 2;
private static const WARN:int  = 3;
private static const ERROR:int = 4;

private static const META:int   = 5;
private static const INSERT:int = 6;
```

```
            private static const UPDATE:int = 7;
            private static const RELOAD:int = 8;
            private static const REMOVE:int = 9;
        ]]>
        </mx:Script>
        <mx:VBox width="100%" height="100%" verticalGap="0">
            <mx:Text id="txtTitle" color="#FFFF80"
                text="FxAgent for Microsoft Excel" width="100%" />
            <mx:HRule width="100%" strokeWidth="1" strokeColor="#FFFF80"/>
            <mx:Text id="txtStatus" text="Starting..." width="100%"></mx:Text>
            <mx:List id="lstMessages" dataProvider="{messages}" editable="false"
width="100%" rowHeight="18" liveScrolling="true"
                rowCount="10"></mx:List>
        </mx:VBox>
    </mx:Application>
```

Listing 15.15 FxExcelAgent application

Remember that FxExcelAgent is designed to run embedded inside Excel. We'll be looking at what needs to be done for that once we're through with the Flex-to-Flex LocalConnection discussion.

Flex Standalone Application

Let's build the sample standalone Flex application. Actually, we're going to use the same application that was used in the Spreadsheet OWC integration example. The only change we had to make was to replace the notification mechanism based on the External API with one based on a LocalConnection. The complete application code is in Listing 15.16.

```
<?xml version="1.0" encoding="utf-8"?>
<!-- File ./FxExcelSample.mxml                          -->
<!-- Flex Application providing data to Microsoft Excel -->
<mx:Application xmlns:mx="http://www.adobe.com/2006/mxml" layout="absolute"
      creationComplete="onCreationComplete()">
      <mx:Script>
      <![CDATA[
      import mx.controls.Alert;
      import mx.collections.ArrayCollection;

      [Bindable]
      private var employees:ArrayCollection = new ArrayCollection();
      [Bindable]
      public var bhiOptions:Array = [{label: "No", data:false}, {label:"Yes", data:
         true}];
```

```
private static const LISTEN_AGENT:String = "_FlexExcelDemo_Agent2App";
private static const UPDATE_AGENT:String = "_FlexExcelDemo_App2Agent";

private var outConnection:LocalConnection;
private var inConnection:LocalConnection;

private function onCreationComplete():void {
   outConnection = new LocalConnection;
   outConnection.addEventListener(StatusEvent.STATUS, statusHandler);
   outConnection.addEventListener(SecurityErrorEvent.SECURITY_ERROR,
      securityErrorHandler);

   inConnection = new LocalConnection;
   inConnection.client = this;
   try {
      if (LISTEN_AGENT.indexOf("_") === 0) {
         inConnection.allowDomain("*");
         inConnection.allowInsecureDomain("*");
   }
      inConnection.connect(LISTEN_AGENT);
   }  catch(ex:ArgumentError) {
      Alert.show(ex.message, "Connection error", Alert.OK);
   } catch(ex:SecurityError) {
      Alert.show(ex.message, "Security error", Alert.OK);
   }
   fxMetadata();
   loadData();
}

public function lcResend():void {
   fxMetadata();
   fxRowsUpdated(0, employees.toArray(), true);
}


public function IcImportRows(offset:int, cells:Array, reset:Boolean):void {
   if (reset) {
      if (employees) employees.removeAll();
      else employees = new ArrayCollection();
      cells.forEach( function(el:Object,idx:int,array:Array):void {
         var employee:Object = {};
         for (var name:String in el) employee[name] = el[name];
         employees.addItem(employee);
      });
```

```
        if (employees.length)
        dataGrid.selectedIndex = 0;
      }
      else
        cells.forEach( function(el:Object,idx:int,array:Array):void {
          var pos:int = idx + offset;
          var employee:Object = employees.getItemAt(pos);
          for (var name:String in el)
            employee[name] = el[name];
          employees.setItemAt(employee, pos);
        });
    }

    private function addRow():void {
      if (frmName.text != "") {
        var item:Object = employee(
        frmName.text,  frmBirthday.selectedDate, frmPhone.text,
        frmYos.value, frmHealthInsurance.selectedItem.data,  frmSalary.value
        );
        var idx:int = dataGrid.selectedIndex;
        var nextIdx:int = idx >= 0 ? idx + 1 : 0;
        employees.addItemAt( item, nextIdx );
        dataGrid.selectedIndex = nextIdx;
        fxRowsInserted(idx, [item]);
      }
      }

    private function updateRow():void {
      var idx:int = dataGrid.selectedIndex;
      if (idx >= 0) {
        var item:Object = employee(
          frmName.text, frmBirthday.selectedDate, frmPhone.text,
          frmYos.value, frmHealthInsurance.selectedItem.data, frmSalary.value
        );
        employees.setItemAt(item, idx);
        employees.itemUpdated( item );
        fxRowsUpdated(idx, [item], false);
      }
    }

    private function deleteRow():void {
      var idx:int = dataGrid.selectedIndex;
      if (idx >= 0) {
        employees.removeItemAt(idx);
```

```
      if ( !employees.length ) {
         frmName.text = frmPhone.text = "";
         frmBirthday.selectedDate = new Date;
         frmYos.value = 1; frmSalary.value = 0;
      }
      else
         dataGrid.selectedItem = employees.getItemAt(Math.min(idx, employees.
            length - 1));
      fxRowsRemoved(idx, 1);
   }
}

private function applyResult(data:Array):void {
   employees = new ArrayCollection(data);
   fxRowsUpdated(0, data, true);
}

private function fxRowsInserted(offset:int, content:Array):void {
   outConnection.send(UPDATE_AGENT, "fxRowsInserted", offset, content);
}

private function fxRowsUpdated(offset:int, content:Array, reset:Boolean):void {
   outConnection.send(UPDATE_AGENT, "fxRowsUpdated", offset, content, reset);
}

private function fxRowsRemoved(offset:int, size:int):void {
   outConnection.send(UPDATE_AGENT, "fxRowsRemoved", offset, size);
}

private function fxMetadata():void {
   outConnection.send(UPDATE_AGENT, "fxMetadata", [
      {name:"name",            title:"Full name",        type:"string"},
      {name:"birthday",        title:"Birthday",         type:"date"},
      {name:"phone",           title:"Phone",            type:"string"},
      {name:"yos",             title:"Years of srv.",    type:"number"},
      {name:"healthInsurance", title:"Health insurance", type:"boolean"},

      {name:"salary",          title:"Salary",           type:"number"}
   ]);
}

private function loadData():void {
   applyResult([
      employee("Yakov Fain",         d("1960/04/18"), "732-456-4432",
```

```
yos("1999/05/20"), true,  95000.0),
            employee("Anatole Tartakovsky", d("1962/03/03"), "561-860-2376",
yos("1991/03/01"), true,  85000.0),
            employee("Victor Rasputnis",    d("1963/02/06"), "718-445-7622",
yos("1993/07/02"), true,  85900.0),
            employee("Melissa Espinoza",    d("1950/12/14"), "508-555-2319",
yos("1996/04/18"), true,  36490.0),
            employee("Kathleen Poitras",    d("1966/09/29"), "617-555-3920",
yos("1999/05/29"), false, 46200.0),
            employee("Joseph Barker",       d("1980/02/14"), "617-555-8021",
yos("2001/09/10"), false, 27290.0),
            employee("Shih Lin",            d("1980/12/12"), "617-555-5921",
yos("2001/11/11"), false, 33890.0),
            employee("Barbara Blaikie",     d("1954/11/14"), "617-555-9345",
yos("2001/11/20"), true,  54900.0)
         ]);
         }

      private static function employee(name:String, birthday:Date, phone:String,
         yos:int, healthInsurance:Boolean, salary:Number):Object {
         return {
            name:name, birthday:birthday, phone:phone,
            yos:yos, healthInsurance: healthInsurance, salary:salary
         };
      }

      private static function d(s:String):Date {return new Date( Date.parse(s) );}
      private static const THIS_YEAR:int = new Date().getFullYear();
      private static function yos(startDate:String):int {return THIS_YEAR - d(startDate).
            getFullYear();}

      private static function formatDate(itm:Object, col:Object):String {
         var d:Date = itm.birthday;
         return d ? [d.getFullYear(), pad(d.getMonth() + 1), pad(d.getDate())].join("-")
: "";
      }

      private function formatHealthInsurance(itm:Object, col:Object):String {
         return bhiOptions[itm.healthInsurance * 1].label;
      }

      private static function pad(v:int):String {  return (v < 10 ? "0" : "") + v; }

      private function securityErrorHandler(event:SecurityErrorEvent):void { Alert.
```

```
show(event.text, "Security error", Alert.OK); }
        private function statusHandler(event:StatusEvent):void {}

    ]]>
    </mx:Script>
    <mx:VBox width="100%" height="100%">
      <mx:DataGrid id="dataGrid" width="100%" height="100%" dataProvider="{employees}"
        editable="false" sortableColumns="false">
        <mx:columns>
        <mx:Array>
          <mx:DataGridColumn dataField="name" headerText="Name"/>
          <mx:DataGridColumn labelFunction="formatDate" headerText="Birthday"/>

          <mx:DataGridColumn dataField="phone" headerText="Phone"/>

          <mx:DataGridColumn dataField="yos" headerText="Years of Srv." textAlign="r
            ight"/>
          <mx:DataGridColumn labelFunction="formatHealthInsurance"
            headerText="Health insurance" textAlign="center"/>
          <mx:DataGridColumn dataField="salary" headerText="Salary" textAlign="right
            "/>
        </mx:Array>
        </mx:columns>
      </mx:DataGrid>

      <mx:Form width="100%" height="100%" borderStyle="solid" borderColor="#ffffff">
        <mx:FormItem label="Name">
          <mx:TextInput id="frmName" width="200" text="{dataGrid.selectedItem.
            name}"/>
        </mx:FormItem>
        <mx:FormItem label="Birthday">
          <mx:DateField id="frmBirthday" selectedDate="{dataGrid.selectedItem.birth
            day}"/>
        </mx:FormItem>
        <mx:FormItem label="Phone">
          <mx:TextInput id="frmPhone" width="200" text="{dataGrid.selectedItem.
            phone}"/>
        </mx:FormItem>
        <mx:FormItem label="Years of service">
          <mx:NumericStepper id="frmYos" value="{dataGrid.selectedItem.yos}"
          maxChars="3" minimum="1" maximum="99"/>
        </mx:FormItem>
        <mx:FormItem label="Health insurance">
          <mx:ComboBox id="frmHealthInsurance"
```

```
                selectedIndex="{dataGrid.selectedItem.healthInsurance}"
                dataProvider="{bhiOptions}"/>
            </mx:FormItem>
            <mx:FormItem label="Salary">
              <mx:NumericStepper id="frmSalary" value="{dataGrid.selectedItem.salary}"
                maxChars="10" minimum="0" maximum="999999"/>
            </mx:FormItem>
            <mx:FormItem>
              <mx:HBox>
                <mx:Button label="Update" click="updateRow()"/>
                <mx:Button label="Add" click="addRow()"/>
                <mx:Button label="Delete" click="deleteRow()"/>
                </mx:HBox>
            </mx:FormItem>
          </mx:Form>
        </mx:VBox>
</mx:Application>
```

Listing 15.16 The Flex data source application

Excel Worksheet – The Flex Agent Host

Finally, we must create a Microsoft Excel document that embeds a Flex agent application (to be precise, it embeds a Flash Player ActiveX set to play the FxExcelAgent.swf) and provides the VBA modules needed to handle External API notifications. We'll base our code on the previous Excel example.

To start over, create a new Excel document. The VBA code uses early binding, so it's necessary to add references to the required type libraries. Besides the standard Excel libraries added by default, you need to add references to Shockwave Flash, Microsoft ActiveX Data Objects (ADO), and Microsoft XML 3.0 or higher. As you will soon see, handling the Flex External API in an ActiveX container is all about XML processing.

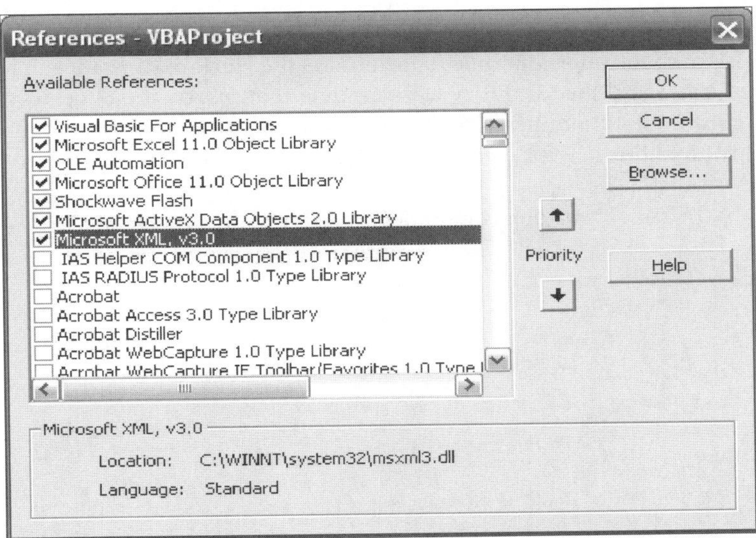

Figure 15.9 Adding required typelib references for Excel VBA code

Next, define the workbook's custom property FxChannel: select menu File/Properties to open the Properties dialog, switch to tab Custom, and add the property FxChannel of type *String*. Set it to _FlexExcelDemo. This property defines the ID of the channel that must be returned in response to the fxQueryChannel notification sent from the Flex agent. The Flex application from Listing 15.16 hard-codes names for listening and sending connections; these names assume the channel with ID _FlexExcelDemo. If you deviate from _FlexExcelDemo, then adjust *LISTEN_AGENT* and *UPDATE_AGENT* in FxExcelSample.mxml. As a convenience, you can get to the workbook properties by right-clicking menu on the workbook file:

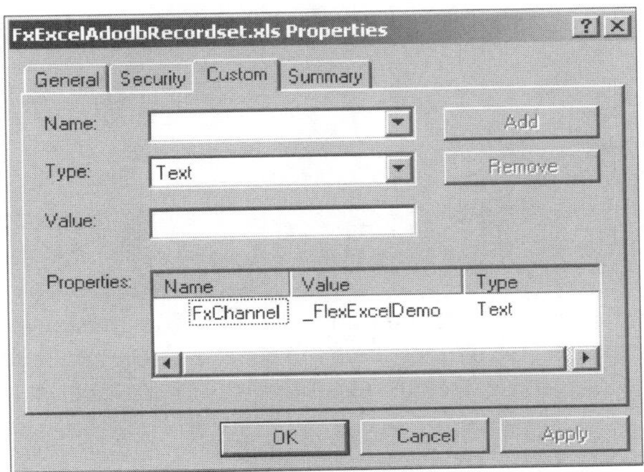

Figure 15.10 Adding custom Workbook properties

Now we're ready to add the necessary Excel VBA modules. Two of them are already familiar to you; we need the ThisWorkbook object module to instantiate the FlexProxy instance in response to the Workbook_Open event and the FlexProxy class module that inserts the Shockwave Flash object and handles the External API notifications. The latest one is a new XmlUtils module that exposes convenient utility functions to work with XML/XSLT.

Let's start with the *ThisWorkbook* object module:

```
' File ./FxExcelAdodbRecordset.xls
' Object module ThisWorkbook
Private fxProxy As FlexProxy
Private Sub Workbook_Open()
      Dim Property As Object
      Dim fxChannel As String
      For Each Property In CustomDocumentProperties
         If Property.Name = "FxChannel" Then
            fxChannel = Property.Value
         End If
      Next Property

      If IsEmpty(fxChannel) Or Len(fxChannel) = 0 Then
         Dim CRLF As String
         CRLF = Chr(13) & Chr(10)
         MsgBox "Flex channel property ""FxChannel"" not found." & CRLF & CRLF & _
         "Please open workbook properties and define " & CRLF & _
         "custom property ""FxChannel"" of type ""string""." & CRLF & _
         "Re-open workbook afterwards.", _
         vbCritical + vbOKOnly, "WorkBook Configuration Error"
         Exit Sub
      End If

      Set fxProxy = New FlexProxy
      fxProxy.Initialize 1, "fxObject", fxChannel
End Sub
```

Listing 15.17 The FxExcelAdodbRecordset workbook module

As you can see, the Workbook_Open event handler checks for the presence of the custom *FxChannel* document property that we just added. Once the check is successfully passed, it creates a FlexProxy instance and delegates all the work to this object – as in the Excel example.

```
' File ./FxExcelAdodbRecordset.xls
' Class module FlexProxy
Option Explicit
```

```
Private WithEvents pSheet As Excel.Worksheet
Private WithEvents pFlexObject As ShockwaveFlashObjects.ShockwaveFlash
Private pOleControl As Excel.oleObject
Private pXmlLayout As MSXML2.IXMLDOMElement
Private pFieldsCount As Integer
Private pChannelID As String
Private pTotalRows As Integer
Public Sub Initialize(ByVal sheetID As Variant, ByVal controlID As String, ByVal chan-
nelID As String)
      Set pSheet = Worksheets(sheetID)
      pChannelID = channelID

      Dim oleObject As Excel.oleObject
      Dim found As Boolean
      found = False
      For Each oleObject In pSheet.OLEObjects
      If oleObject.Name = controlID Then
         found = True
         Exit For
      End If
      Next oleObject

      If Not found Then
         Set oleObject = pSheet.OLEObjects.Add( _
         ClassType:="ShockwaveFlash.ShockwaveFlash.9", _
         Width:=300, Height:=165, Left:=10, Top:=10 _
         )
         oleObject.Name = controlID
      End If

      With oleObject
         Call .BringToFront
         Call .Activate
      End With

      Set pOleControl = oleObject
      Set pFlexObject = oleObject.Object

      With pFlexObject
         .Loop = False
         .Menu = True
         .Playing = False
         .EmbedMovie = False
         .AllowNetworking = "all"
```

```
        .AllowScriptAccess = "always"
        If Not found Then
          .LoadMovie 0, "../bin/FxExcelAgent.swf"
        End If
    End With
    Call PositionOleControl
End Sub

Private Sub pFlexObject_FlashCall(ByVal request As String)
    If Not Application.EnableEvents Then Exit Sub
    Application.EnableEvents = False

    Dim xmlRequest As MSXML2.FreeThreadedDOMDocument, method As String
    Set xmlRequest = CreateXmlDocument(request)

    method = xmlRequest.selectSingleNode("/invoke/@name").Text
    If pXmlLayout Is Nothing And method <> "fxMetadata" And method <> "fxQueryChannel"
Then
        MsgBox "Protocol exception: call to method """ & method & """ before metadata
available", _
        vbCritical + vbOKOnly, "Fx Protocol Error"
        GoTo ExitSub
    End If
    Select Case method
      Case "fxQueryChannel":
        pFlexObject.SetReturnValue "<string>" + pChannelID + "</string>"
      Case "fxMetadata":
        InitMetadata xmlRequest
        pFlexObject.SetReturnValue "<null/>"
      Case "fxRowsInserted":
        UpdateRows xmlRequest, True
        pFlexObject.SetReturnValue "<null/>"
      Case "fxRowsUpdated":
        UpdateRows xmlRequest, False
        pFlexObject.SetReturnValue "<null/>"
      Case "fxRowsRemoved":
        RemoveRows xmlRequest
        pFlexObject.SetReturnValue "<null/>"
    End Select

ExitSub:
    Set xmlRequest = Nothing
    Application.EnableEvents = True
End Sub
```

```
Private Sub InitMetadata(ByVal xmlRequest)
      Dim xmlLayoutDoc As MSXML2.FreeThreadedDOMDocument
      Set xmlLayoutDoc = CreateXmlDocument(TransformFlexMetadata(xmlRequest))
      Set pXmlLayout = xmlLayoutDoc.documentElement
      pFieldsCount = pXmlLayout.selectNodes("/layout/field").Length

      Set xmlLayoutDoc = Nothing
End Sub

Private Sub UpdateRows(ByVal xmlRequest As MSXML2.FreeThreadedDOMDocument, ByVal isIn-
sert As Boolean)
      Dim row As Integer, count As Integer, reset As Boolean
      row = CInt(xmlRequest.selectSingleNode("/invoke/arguments/number[0]").Text) + 1
      count = xmlRequest.selectNodes("/invoke/arguments/array/property").Length

      Dim newContent As String
      newContent = TransformFlexContent(xmlRequest, pXmlLayout)

      Dim Target As Excel.range

      If isInsert Then
         row = row + 1
         Dim rows As range
         Set rows = pSheet.rows(row)
         Dim i As Integer
         For i = 1 To count
            Call rows.Insert
         Next i
         Set Target = pSheet.Cells(row, 1)
         pTotalRows = pTotalRows + count
      Else
         If Not xmlRequest.selectSingleNode("/invoke/arguments/true") Is Nothing Then
            reset = True
            pTotalRows = count
            Call pSheet.Cells.Clear
         End If
         Set Target = pSheet.Cells(row, 1)
      End If
      PopulateRange Target, newContent

      Call pSheet.Activate
      Dim newSelection As range
      If reset Then
         Set newSelection = pSheet.UsedRange
```

```
        Else
           Set newSelection = pSheet.range(Target, pSheet.Cells(row + count - 1,
              pFieldsCount))
        End If
        Set Target = Nothing

        Call newSelection.CurrentRegion.Columns.AutoFit
        Call newSelection.Select
        Call PositionOleControl

        Set newSelection = Nothing
End Sub

Private Sub RemoveRows(ByVal xmlRequest As MSXML2.FreeThreadedDOMDocument)
        Dim row As Integer, count As Integer
        row = CInt(xmlRequest.selectSingleNode("/invoke/arguments/number[0]").Text) + 1
        count = CInt(xmlRequest.selectSingleNode("/invoke/arguments/number[1]").Text)
        pTotalRows = pTotalRows - count

        While count > 0
           Call pSheet.rows(row).Delete
           count = count - 1
        Wend

        Call pSheet.Activate
        If Not pSheet.UsedRange Is Nothing Then
           Dim newSelection As range
           Set newSelection = pSheet.range(pSheet.Cells(row, 1), pSheet.Cells(row,
                pFieldsCount))
           Call newSelection.Select
        End If

        Call PositionOleControl
End Sub

Private Sub PositionOleControl()
        Dim allCells As range
        Set allCells = pSheet.Cells(1, 1).CurrentRegion

        pOleControl.Top = 10
        If allCells Is Nothing Then
           pOleControl.Left = 10
        Else
           pOleControl.Left = allCells.Left + allCells.Width + 10
```

```
        End If

        Set allCells = Nothing
    End Sub

    Private Sub PopulateRange(ByVal Target As range, ByVal newContent As String)
        Dim rsContent As ADODB.Recordset
        Set rsContent = CreateObject("ADODB.Recordset")
        rsContent.Open CreateXmlDocument(newContent)

        Target.CopyFromRecordset rsContent

        Call rsContent.Close
        Set rsContent = Nothing
    End Sub
```

Listing 15.18 The FlexProxy class module

The Module FlexProxy should look familiar to you. It's an extended version of the module we used for passing data to Excel via the clipboard (see Listing 15.14).

The *Initialize()* method is almost the same. The only difference is the name of the swf plus an additional *channelID* parameter that's saved to the instance variable.

The *pFlexObject_FlashCall* method got more complex: it handles several events now. Using a helper function, which we'll discuss shortly, it parses an XML request to determine the name of the invoked method. Then, depending on the method name, processing is dispatched to the appropriate function.

Processing the *fxQueryChannel* request is trivial: code just returns a value previously saved as a *pChannelID* instance variable.

Processing *fxMetadata, fxUpdateRows,* and *fxInsertRows* requests deserve extra clarification. As you remember, we're using an Array of Objects to describe the field order, ID, titles, and types. This structure has quite a complex internal XML representation. The same is true for data records passed with *fxUpdateRows* and *fxInsertRows*. A naïve approach would be to use the DOM API: traverse the request DOM document, extract the necessary values, and assign them cell-by-cell.

Fortunately, we know better than that. Recall that in the Spreadsheet OWC example we mentioned more efficient ways to copy tabular data into a range of cells. The first option possible with Excel is to put content on the Windows Clipboard and then apply it with the *Range.PasteSpecial()* method. Although it would be a logical continuation of our example with *System.setClipboard(text)*, it has serious drawbacks in an automated scenario. Come to think of it, we're hijacking the system clipboard: whatever the user puts on the clipboard gets wiped out by our automation code. Is there anything to replace the clipboard?

Well, instead of populating the Excel range from the clipboard we can use the Microsoft ADODB. Recordset paired with the *Range.CopyFromRecordset(adodbRecordset)* method. The wonderful thing about ADODB.Recordset is its ability to load and save records in XML format. We'll take this route.

In sum, we have a classic task for XSL transformation: get an XML DOM document as input (the *request* parameter of the *FlashCall* event) and produce an XML DOM document as output (the content of ADODB.Recordset). The only issue here is that there are two input XML documents: metadata and the data change notification. To overcome this problem we'll add a metadata document element as a child to the root of the data change request document.

After performing the XSL transformation, we pass the generated content to the *PopulateRange()* method. This method creates the ADODB.Recordset with the generated content and then calls *Range.CopyFromRecordset()* to populate the range.

The last method of the FlexProxy module – fxRemoveRows() – doesn't deserve much attention here since it closely resembles the corresponding method from the Spreadsheet OWC example.

Now it's time to look at the custom XmlUtils module (Listing 15.19). It exposes three public functions:

- **CreateXmlDocument**: Creates the instance of the XML DOM document object by the string source provided
- **TransformFlexMetadata**: Transforms the content of the metadata notification to the XML format used by the FlexProxy class
- **TransformFlexContent**: Turns the content of the data change notification into the ADODB. Recordset format

```
' File ./ FxExcelAdodbRecordset.xls
' Module XmlUtils
Option Explicit
Private xslDataTemplate As MSXML2.xslTemplate
Private xslMetaTemplate As MSXML2.xslTemplate

Private Sub InitXmlUtils()
      Dim xlHelperSheet As Worksheet
      Set xlHelperSheet = Worksheets(2)

      'Create HTML template
      Set xslDataTemplate = CreateObject("MSXML2.XSLTemplate")
      Set xslDataTemplate.stylesheet = CreateXmlDocument(xlHelperSheet.Cells(1, 1).Value)
```

```
        'Create META template
        Set xslMetaTemplate = CreateObject("MSXML2.XSLTemplate")
        Set xslMetaTemplate.stylesheet = CreateXmlDocument(xlHelperSheet.Cells(1, 2).Value)
        Set xlHelperSheet = Nothing
End Sub

Private Function ExecuteTransformation(ByVal xmlSource As MSXML2.FreeThreadedDOMDocument
, ByVal xslTemplate As MSXML2.xslTemplate)
        Dim xslProcessor As MSXML2.IXSLProcessor
        Set xslProcessor = xslTemplate.createProcessor
        xslProcessor.input = xmlSource
        xslProcessor.transform
        ExecuteTransformation = xslProcessor.output

        Set xslProcessor = Nothing
End Function

Public Function CreateXmlDocument(ByVal source As String) As MSXML2.FreeThreadedDOMDocum
ent
        Dim xmlDoc As MSXML2.FreeThreadedDOMDocument
        Set xmlDoc = CreateObject("MSXML2.FreeThreadedDOMDocument")
        xmlDoc.async = False
        xmlDoc.loadXML source
        Set CreateXmlDocument = xmlDoc
End Function

Public Function TransformFlexMetadata(ByVal fxRequest As MSXML2.FreeThreadedDOMDocument)
As String
        If xslMetaTemplate Is Nothing Then
            Call InitXmlUtils
        End If
        TransformFlexMetadata = ExecuteTransformation(fxRequest, xslMetaTemplate)
End Function

Public Function TransformFlexContent(ByVal fxRequest As MSXML2.FreeThreadedDOMDocument,
ByVal layout As MSXML2.IXMLDOMElement) As String
        If xslDataTemplate Is Nothing Then
            Call InitXmlUtils
        End If
        fxRequest.documentElement.appendChild layout.CloneNode(True)6
        TransformFlexContent = ExecuteTransformation(fxRequest, xslDataTemplate)
End Function
```

Listing 15.19 The XmlUtils module

Note that *TransformFlexMetadata()* and *TransformFlexContent()* use XSL templates. The XSL template allows the reuse of the Data Transformation Model (DTM) instead of creating and loading it every time a transformation is performed. Importantly, to use the template the source document has to be created as a FreeThreadedDOMDocument. The initialization of the XSL templates is done on-demand in the *InitXmlUtils()* procedure.

The XSL stylesheets that the templates are based on are stored in the cells on the second worksheet (we renamed it "Helper," see Figure 15.11): cell "A1" contains the XSL source for transforming data content, cell "B1" is used to hold the metadata XSL template. If you're using different names or indexes, adjust the *InitXmlUtils()* procedure correspondingly.

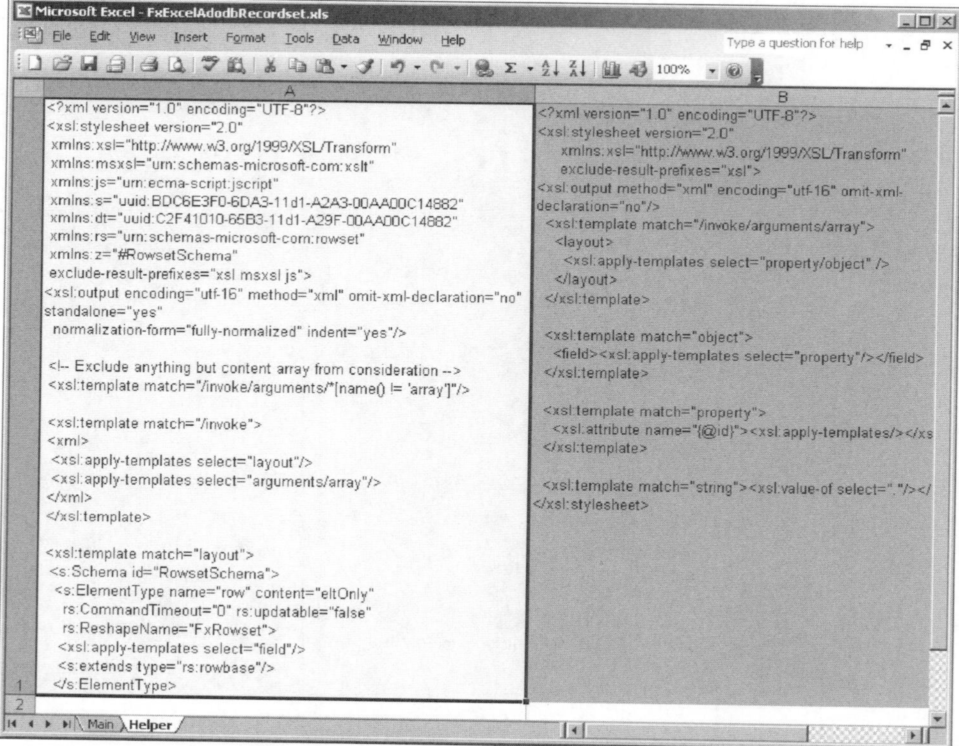

Figure 15.11 The "Helper" worksheet with XSL template sources

The XSL template for transforming metadata is relatively simple. Here we strip out unnecessary elements from the original Flex External API XML format and produce the document that has the root *<layout>* element with nested *<field>* definitions.

```
<?xml version="1.0" encoding="UTF-8"?>
<xsl:stylesheet version="2.0"
```

```
    xmlns:xsl="http://www.w3.org/1999/XSL/Transform"
    exclude-result-prefixes="xsl">
    <xsl:output method="xml" encoding="utf-16" omit-xml-declaration="no"/>

    <xsl:template match="/invoke/arguments/array">
      <layout><xsl:apply-templates select="property/object" /></layout>
    </xsl:template>

    <xsl:template match="object">
      <field><xsl:apply-templates select="property"/></field>
    </xsl:template>

    <xsl:template match="property">
      <xsl:attribute name="{@id}"><xsl:apply-templates/></xsl:attribute>
    </xsl:template>

    <xsl:template match="string"><xsl:value-of select="."/></xsl:template>
</xsl:stylesheet>
```

Listing 15.20 XSL template for metadata

As an illustration, consider the *xMetadata* request coming from the FxExcelSample application:

```
<invoke name="fxMetadata" returntype="xml">
    <arguments>
      <array>
        <property id="0">
          <object>
            <property id="type"><string>string</string></property>
            <property id="name"><string>name</string></property>
            <property id="title"><string>Full name</string></property>
          </object>
        </property>
        <property id="1">
          <object>
            <property id="type"><string>date</string></property>
            <property id="name"><string>birthday</string></property>
            <property id="title"><string>Birthday</string></property>
          ...
          <object>
            <property id="type"><string>number</string></property>
            <property id="name"><string>salary</string></property>
            <property id="title"><string>Salary</string></property>
          </object>
```

```
        </property>
      </array>
    </arguments>
</invoke>
```

The transformation of this document with the above XSL results in the following XML:

```
<?xml version="1.0" encoding="UTF-16"?>
<layout>
  <field title="Full name" type="string" name="name"></field>
  <field title="Birthday" type="date" name="birthday"></field>
  ...
  <field title="Salary" type="number" name="salary"></field>
</layout>
```

By the way, it's this very document that is used by the *InitMetadata()* method of *FlexProxy*. In particular, we've used *selectNodes("/layout/field").Length* to determine the number of fields (columns).

As mentioned earlier, we modify *fxRowsUpdated()* and *fxRowsInserted()* requests, adding *<layout>* as a child node of the document element. This lets us easily apply metadata in the second XSL template that transforms the content of the data change nodification from the External API to the ADODB.Recordset format:

```
<?xml version="1.0" encoding="UTF-8"?>
<xsl:stylesheet version="2.0"
    xmlns:xsl="http://www.w3.org/1999/XSL/Transform"
    xmlns:msxsl="urn:schemas-microsoft-com:xslt"
    xmlns:js="urn:ecma-script:jscript"
    xmlns:s="uuid:BDC6E3F0-6DA3-11d1-A2A3-00AA00C14882"
    xmlns:dt="uuid:C2F41010-65B3-11d1-A29F-00AA00C14882"
    xmlns:rs="urn:schemas-microsoft-com:rowset"
    xmlns:z="#RowsetSchema"
    exclude-result-prefixes="xsl msxsl js">
    <xsl:output encoding="utf-16" method="xml" omit-xml-declaration="no"
standalone="yes"
      normalization-form="fully-normalized" indent="yes"/>

    <!-- Exclude anything but content array from consideration -->
    <xsl:template match="/invoke/arguments/*[name() != 'array']"/>

    <xsl:template match="/invoke">
      <xml>
        <xsl:apply-templates select="layout"/>
        <xsl:apply-templates select="arguments/array"/>
```

```
      </xml>
    </xsl:template>

    <xsl:template match="layout">
      <s:Schema id="RowsetSchema">
        <s:ElementType name="row" content="eltOnly" rs:CommandTimeout="0" rs:
updatable="false"
            rs:ReshapeName="FxRowset">
            <xsl:apply-templates select="field"/>
            <s:extends type="rs:rowbase"/>
        </s:ElementType>
      </s:Schema>
    </xsl:template>

    <xsl:template match="field">
      <s:AttributeType name="{@name}"  rs:number="{position()}"  rs:
writeunknown="true"
          rs:basecatalog="FxRowsetCatalog"
          rs:basetable="FxRowsetTable" rs:basecolumn="{@name}">
          <s:datatype dt:type="{@type}" rs:maxLength="255" rs:long="false" rs:
maybenull="true"/>
      </s:AttributeType>
    </xsl:template>

    <xsl:template match="array">
      <rs:data><xsl:apply-templates select="property/object"/></rs:data>
    </xsl:template>

    <xsl:template match="object">
      <xsl:variable name="row">
        <z:row><xsl:apply-templates select="property"/></z:row>
      </xsl:variable>
      <xsl:copy-of select="$row"/>
    </xsl:template>

    <xsl:template match="property">
      <xsl:attribute name="{@id}"><xsl:apply-templates/></xsl:attribute>
    </xsl:template>

    <xsl:template match="string | number"><xsl:value-of select="."/></xsl:template>
      <xsl:template match="date">
      <xsl:variable name="prop" select="parent::node()/@id"/>
      <xsl:variable name="typeOf" select="/invoke/layout/field[@name=$prop]/@type"/>
      <xsl:choose>
```

```
            <xsl:when test="$typeOf='date'"><xsl:value-of select="js:date( number(.)
              )"/></xsl:when>
            <xsl:when test="$typeOf='time'"><xsl:value-of select="js:time( number(.)
              )"/></xsl:when>
            <xsl:otherwise><xsl:value-of select="js:dateTime( number(.) )"/></xsl:
              otherwise>
          </xsl:choose>
        </xsl:template>

        <xsl:template match="true">true</xsl:template>
        <xsl:template match="false">false</xsl:template>

        <msxsl:script language="JScript" implements-prefix="js">
        <![CDATA[
          function dateTime(v) {
            var dt = new Date( v );
            return [dt.getFullYear(), __(dt.getMonth()+1), __(dt.getDate())].join('-')
+
            " " + [__(dt.getHours()), __(dt.getMinutes()), __(dt.getSeconds())].
join(':');
          }
          function time(v) {
            var dt = new Date( v );
            return [__(dt.getHours()), __(dt.getMinutes()), __(dt.getSeconds())].
join(':');
          }
          function date(v) {
            var dt = new Date( v );
            return [dt.getFullYear(), __(dt.getMonth()+1), __(dt.getDate())].join('-
');
          }
          function __(v) { return v < 10 ? "0" + v : v; }
        ]]>
        </msxsl:script>
      </xsl:stylesheet>
```

Listing 15.21 The XSL template for data

The ADODB.Recordset format requires recordset schema meta-information. Having rich metadata available as a <layout> element is a trifling task – we merely transform the *<field>* elements of the original document into the *<rs:AttributeType>* of the rowset schema.

To transform data entries the template first finds the */invoke/arguments/array* node and produces *<rs:Data>*. From there the template cascades to generate rows for every array element.

Next, for every object property the XSL template creates a corresponding attribute in the *<z:row/>* element, applying the necessary type formatting. XSLT is a functional language, and here its nature simply shines: we just declare rules for processing special types and leave it up to the transformation to automatically pick up a rule depending on the property type!

You can draw parallels with the examples already seen: strings and numbers go as is, Boolean type requires extra effort to convert a node name to node text, and any Date-based type is a problem! Through all the examples we have used several sub-types of date: date-only, time, and timestamp (or full date). However, in ActionScript all we have is Date, and in the External API it's encoded as a *<date>* element with the number of milliseconds since "epoch." To format the date values, we resort to an excellent feature of XSLT 2.0 – the extension functions mechanism. You have to declare your own namespace (urn:ecma-script:jscript) and implement functions in this namespace in a vendor-specific way. The Microsoft-specific way is an attractive one: you declare a script block in JScript and specify that global functions in this block implement an extension function in a certain namespace. Simple and elegant. Conveniently, we just reuse the formatting functions from the Spreadsheet OWC example.

You may notice that the transformation doesn't add a *z:row* element directly to the result XML tree, but does create a variable first and then outputs the variable. This trick is necessary to create an empty XML element, i.e., *<z:row/>* instead of an element with no content *<z:row></z:row>*. Otherwise ADODB.Recordset fails to read anything except the very first row[7].

We're done preparing. Let's party! To run the example you have to have the FxExcelSample application running and the FxExcelAdodbRecordset.xls workbook open – in any order. Figure 15.12 shows the Flex application partially overlapping the workbook. You can modify the Flex data and the Excel workbook will be updated instantly. As you can tell, we purposely let the FxExcelAgent hang in the visible portion of the workbook for purposes of illustration.

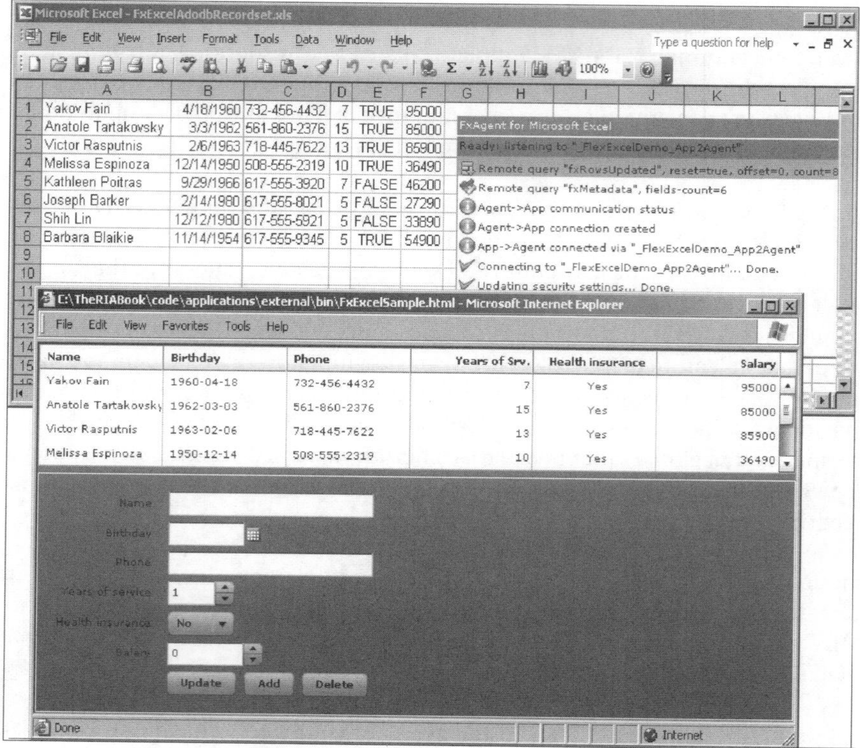

Figure 15.12 The Flex/Excel application running

Congratulations, everyone! We've got something to write home about.

Getting in the Nitpicking Mood

As you probably noticed, the communication between Flex and Excel applications in our latest example are one-way – the changes in an Excel spreadsheet aren't propagated back to the Flex data source application. The reason is an unfortunate bug that shows when Shockwave Flash ActiveX is embedded in Excel and manifests in a call to the ShockwaveFlash.CallFunction, failing with a cryptic COM exception.

We sincerely hope that Adobe will have this bug fixed by the time you read these lines. In Listing 15.22 you can find the code necessary for the *Worksheet_Change* event handler that traverses modified cells and constructs the request XML in the External API format. In fact, the code in Listing 15.22 closely resembles the corresponding event handler in the Spreadsheet OWC example; the only difference is that XML elements are created instead of JavaScript objects. The code should be added to the FlexProxy class module.

```
Private Sub pSheet_Change(ByVal Target As Range)
    Application.EnableEvents = False

    If pXmlLayout Is Nothing Or pTotalRows < 1 Then
        GoTo ExitSub
    End If

    Dim fields As MSXML2.IXMLDOMNodeList
    Set fields = pXmlLayout.selectNodes("/layout/field")

    If Target.row > pTotalRows Or Target.Column > fields.Length Then
        GoTo ExitSub
    End If

    Dim rowCount As Integer, colCount As Integer
    rowCount = Min(Target.rows.count, pTotalRows - Target.row + 1)
    colCount = Min(Target.Columns.count, fields.Length - Target.Column + 1)

    Dim xmlRequest As MSXML2.DOMDocument
    Set xmlRequest = CreateXmlDocument( _
      "<invoke name=""importRows"" returntype=""xml"">" & _
      "<arguments><number/><array/><false/></arguments></invoke>" _
    )

    'Offset parameter
    Dim paramOffset As MSXML2.IXMLDOMElement
    Set paramOffset = xmlRequest.selectSingleNode("/invoke/arguments/number")
    paramOffset.appendChild xmlRequest.createTextNode(Target.row - 1)

    Dim asArray As MSXML2.IXMLDOMElement
    Set asArray = xmlRequest.selectSingleNode("/invoke/arguments/array")

    Dim row As Integer, col As Integer

    For row = 1 To rowCount
        Dim asIdx As MSXML2.IXMLDOMElement
        Set asIdx = xmlRequest.createElement("property")
        asIdx.setAttribute "id", row - 1

        Dim asObj As MSXML2.IXMLDOMElement
        Set asObj = xmlRequest.createElement("object")

        For col = 1 To colCount
            Dim fldProps As MSXML2.IXMLDOMNamedNodeMap
```

```
        Set fldProps = fields(col + Target.Column - 2).Attributes

        Dim asProp As MSXML2.IXMLDOMElement
        Set asProp = xmlRequest.createElement("property")
        asProp.setAttribute "id", fldProps.getNamedItem("name").Text

        Dim value As MSXML2.IXMLDOMElement
        Dim formula As String
        formula = Target.Cells(row, col).formula
        If Len(formula) = 0 Then
            Set value = xmlRequest.createElement("null")
        Else
            Dim xlValue As Variant
            xlValue = Target.Cells(row, col).value
            Select Case fldProps.getNamedItem("type").Text
                Case "boolean":
                    If xlValue = False Or xlValue = True Then
                        Set value = xmlRequest.createElement( _
                            IIf(CBool(xlValue), "true", "false") _
                        )
                    End If
                Case "number":
                    Set value = xmlRequest.createElement("number")
                    If IsNumeric(xlValue) Then
                        value.appendChild xmlRequest.createTextNode(formula)
                    End If
                Case "string":
                    Set value = xmlRequest.createElement("string")
                    value.appendChild xmlRequest.createTextNode(xlValue)
                Case Else
                    Set value = xmlRequest.createElement("date")
                    If IsDate(xlValue) Then
                        value.appendChild xmlRequest.createTextNode( _
                            DateDiff("s", #1/1/1970#, xlValue) * 1000 _
                        )
                    End If
            End Select
        End If

        asProp.appendChild value
        asObj.appendChild asProp
    Next col

    asIdx.appendChild asObj
```

```
            asArray.appendChild asIdx
        Next row

        'MsgBox xmlRequest.XML
        pFlexObject.CallFunction xmlRequest.XML
    ExitSub:
      Application.EnableEvents = True
End Sub
```

Listing 15.22 The Worksheet_Change event handler

What if the bug still persists and you need bidirectional communications? Well, one option is to replace the asynchronous call to CallFunction with polling. Briefly, it could be implemented as described below:

- The *Worksheet_Change* event handler should be modified to create an object that describes the modification in the External API format (refer to Table 15.2 for details). Instead of <invocation> you must create <object> as a root element and then add both *asArray* and *offset* as <property> sub-nodes; assign the result to a new FlexProxy instance field, for example, pLastChange of type MSXML2.DOMDocument. Obviously, the *CallFunction* invocation must be removed from the code.

- The *pFlexObject_FlashCall* method (see Listing 15.18) should be modified to handle additional notification, say, fxQueryChanges. In response to this notification, XML content previously saved to the *pLastChange* field must be returned with the *ShockwaveFlash.SetReturnValue*; field cleared afterwards.

- FxExcelAgent (see Listing 15.15) should set up an instance of a *flash.utils.Timer* to periodically invoke *ExternalInterface.call("fxQueryChanges")*. If the result of the External API call isn't empty, then offset and content must be extracted from the returned object and passed to the *xlImportRows* method of FxExcelAgent.

Another issue you might find annoying is that when closing the spreadsheet, the user is prompted to save the workbook even when a single cell hasn't been altered. The cause is the automation code that updates cells immediately after opening the workbook (if the Flex data source application is running). Actually, there's no single recipe here: every possible option should be validated against the particular use case. For some applications you can invoke the *Workbook.Save* method to persist changes automatically; for others it's possible to set the *Workbook.Saved* property to True and skip confirmations along with saving; for the rest the only valid option is to leave the behavior as is.

Summary

This chapter took you through the jungles of Flash technologies such as the External API and LocalConnection as well as through the maze of Microsoft old-timers like ADODB and OWC. We've been coding in VBA, JavaScript, XSLT, not to mention ActionScript.

Frankly, it's only the length of this chapter that prevents us from diving into C++ DLLs or showing you integrating with Excel Pivot tables.

Tough? Well, you didn't think system integrators earn their money for nothing, did you? But let's look at the end result. We presented you with a set of generic, parameterized, reusable solutions:

- Two-way integration of Flex and the Office Windows Component (OWC) Spreadsheet embedded in the same HTML page. As a reminder, we only left out Pivot Table integration because of space limitations.

- The interactive export of Flex content to an Excel application via the clipboard.

- A live-link between a standalone Flex application and an Excel worksheet (the latter has to be templated by our sample one).

If you find that we've paid too much attention to our code, our response is – guilty as charged. But we've transferred every line of our solution to you, so that you can take them to users with no black holes.

Endnotes

1. Experiments show that this is not the only option with the current *ExternalInterface* implementation. You can invoke a method of the JavaScript object from ActionScript in the form of *ExternalInterface.call("jsObjectA.jsObjectB.methodOfB", arg1, arg2, ..., argN)*. Apparently *ExternalInterface* invokes JavaScript code via the *eval* function rather than via *Function.apply*. However, this is an undocumented feature and its behavior may be changed in future releases.

2. It's technically possible to have several versions of Microsoft Office Web Components side by side. A typical cause of this is upgrading Microsoft Office.

3. Spreadsheet OWC would be simply genius if it had explicit support for the JavaScript Date type. The current version converts Date to a UTC string before the assignment and applies string formating to the cell afterwards.

4. As noted, the Spreadsheet OWC 9 API is very limited. Most important, there are no events to track content changes. So the rest of the code is applicable to Spreadsheet OWC 10/11 only.

5. "JavaScript" is used internally by *CallFunction* for the HTML container return type. This forces the result to be a JSON-formated string that's applicable to the *eval* call.

6. Frequently, Microsoft is a standard on its own. W3C defines the *importNode* method on the *Document* interface that must be called to get a copy of the XML node from the other document before adding it.

7. W3C's XML Specification Edition 3 clarifies this issue: if an element is declared in DTD as EMPTY, then the <tag/> form SHOULD be used (see http://www.w3.org/TR/REC-xml/#dt-empty). So the behavior of the ADODB.Recordset XML parser is partly correct. To be absolutely correct it's necessary to report that the XML document doesn't pass DTD/Schema validation rather than return partly parsed content.

INDEX

B

C

D

E

F

G

L

M

N

O

P

T

U

V

W

X

Y

Z